# Women's

# Studies Index

## 1990

G.K. HALL &CO.
*Boston, Massachusetts*

This publication is printed on permanent/durable acid-free paper.

© 1992 by G. K. Hall & Co.
ISBN 0-8161-0511-1
ISSN 1058 8369

# Advisory Board

**Joan Ariel**
Women's Studies Librarian
University Library
University of California at Irvine
Irvine, California

**Barbara Haber**
Curator of Printed Books
Arthur & Elizabeth Schlesinger Library on the
  History of Women in America
Radcliffe College
Cambridge, Massachusetts

**Karen Offen**
Institute for Research on Women and Gender
Stanford University
Stanford, California

**Susan Searing**
Acting Deputy Director
General Library System
University of Wisconsin
Madison, Wisconsin

iii

# Preface

The rapid growth of women's studies in recent years has resulted in a proliferation of both popular and scholarly journals focusing on issues of concern to women. Clearly, there is a need for a single resource that gathers and organizes this wealth of material to provide the scholar, student, and general interest researcher with easy access to it. The *Women's Studies Index* offers this access. Including articles from a total of 86 periodicals, predominantly but not exclusively American, the 1990 volume indexes a wide range of publications, from professional to artistic, academic to popular. The multitude of topics, issues, and disciplines covered illustrates the diversity of pursuits and perspectives alive within the area of women's studies. G. K. Hall is pleased to make a contribution to this dynamic field of endeavor.

Suggestions for additional titles are welcome; these should be directed to Women's Studies Index, G. K. Hall & Co., 70 Lincoln St., Boston, MA 02111.

# Notes on Using the Index

**ARRANGEMENT:** In this index, authors, subjects, and cross-references are interfiled into a single alphabetical arrangement. Headings are alphabetized in a strict letter-by-letter sequence. For example, the heading "Newcastle" appears before the heading "New York," but "New Brunswick" appears before "Newcastle."

**INDEXING CRITERIA:** All periodicals are indexed comprehensively, with the exception of popular journals, which are indexed selectively. Articles from popular journals are indexed only if they are at least one page in length and cover substantive material.

**SUBJECT POLICY:** In general, the authority for subject headings in this index is Library of Congress Subject Headings. It should be noted, however, that these subject headings have been reviewed in conjunction with, and in some cases modified by, terms appearing in *A Women's Thesaurus* by Mary Ellen S. Capek. Owing to the specialized scope of this index the subject "Women" and subjects starting with the word "Women" are used infrequently. Instead, users of the index should refer to appropriate subject headings relating to the specific discipline of issue about which information is sought, such as "Politics" or "Mother-Daughter Relationships."

**PERSONAL NAMES:** The term "(About)" following a personal name means that the name is being used as a subject heading. The term is used only for articles that contain substantive information about the individual, and not for incidental or indirect references.

**GEOGRAPHIC HEADINGS:** Whenever it is possible in choosing headings, specific countries are preferred to broader regions. Headings for specific countries, in turn, are often subdivided by topic: "Great Britain – History."

**CREATIVE WORKS:** These are indexed under the author's name. In addition, the headings "Poems" "Short Stories," and "Fiction" are used for works in those categories.

**REVIEWS:** These are indexed under the name of the author whose work is being reviewed, under the name of the reviewer, and under any appropriate subject headings. The following special headings are also used:

> Book Reviews
> Film Reviews
> Music Reviews
> Play Reviews
> Video Reviews

**CITATION FORMAT:** Each citation in the *Women's Studies Index* contains the article's title and author(s), unless there is no author; the journal title, volume and page numbers; and the month and year of publication. When clarification is needed, additional information, such as "Book review" or "Editorial," is also included. Citations listed in the review sections of the index (e.g., under "Book Reviews" or "Film Reviews") provide the title of the work and the name of the author, director, or composer (where available) together with a cross-reference to the main entry where a full citation appears.

**SAMPLE SUBJECT ENTRY:**

**Art – Images of Women**
**a)** Between Dream and Shadow: William Holman Hunt's Lady of Shalott. **b)** Sharyn R. Udall. **c)** *Woman's Art Journal* **d)** 11, **e)** No. 1 **f)** (Spring-Summer 1990): **g)** 34-38

a) title of article
b) author(s)
c) journal title
d) journal volume number
e) issue number
f) year of publication
g) page numbers

# List of Periodicals Indexed

Adolescence
Affilia: Journal of Women and Social Work
Atlantis
Austrialian Feminist Studies
Belles Lettres
Bridges: A Journal for Jewish Feminists and Our Friends
Camera Obscura
Canadian Women's Studies/Les Cahiers de la Femme
Connexions: An International Women's Quarterly
Differences: A Journal of Feminist Cultural Studies
Essence
Executive Female
Family Circle
Feminist Collections: A Quarterly of Women's Studies Resources
Feminist Issues
Feminist Review
Feminist Studies
Feminist Teacher
Frontiers: A Journal of Women's Studies
Gender and Education
Gender and History
Gender & Society
Genders
Glamour

Good Housekeeping
Harper's Bazaar
Healthright
Healthsharing: A Canadian Women's Health Quarterly
Health Care for Women International
Hecate: A Women's Interdisciplinary Journal
Heresies: A Feminist Publication on Arts and Politics
Hot Wire: Journal of Women's Music and Culture
Hypatia: A Journal of Feminist Philosophy
Iris: A Journal about Women
Isis International/Women in Action
ISIS-WICCE (Women's International Cross-Cultural
    Exchange/Women's World)
Journal of Family History
Journal of Family Welfare
Journal of Feminist Studies in Religion
Journal of Marriage and the Family
Journal of Social Work and Human Sexuality*
Journal of Women & Aging
Journal of Women and Religion*
Journal of Women's History
Ladies' Home Journal
Lear's
Lesbian Ethics
Lilith
Mademoiselle
McCall's
Manushi: A Journal of Women and Society
Media Report to Women
Minerva: Quarterly Report on Women and the Military
Ms.
National Women's Studies Association Journal
New Directions for Women
NWSAction
off our backs
On the Issues: The Journal of Substance for Progressive Women
Out/Look: National Lesbian and Gay Quarterly
Psychology of Women Quarterly

Redbook
Resources for Feminist Research/Documentation sur la Recherche
    Feministe
Sage: A Scholarly Journal on Black Women
Savvy
Signs: A Journal of Women in Culture and Society
Sinister Wisdom: A Journal for the Lesbian Imagination in the Arts
    and Politics
Spare Rib
Trivia: A Journal of Ideas
Tulsa Studies in Women's Literature
Vogue
Woman of Power
Woman's Art Journal
Women & Environments
Women & Health
Women & Language
Women & Performance: A Journal of Feminist Theory
Women & Politics
Women & Therapy
Women Library Workers Journal (WLW)
Women's Review of Books
Women's Rights Law Reporter
Women's Sports & Fitness
Women's Studies International Forum
Women's Studies in Communication
Women's Studies Quarterly
Working Mother
Working Woman

*No 1990 issues were available in time for inclusion in the 1990 index.

# Addresses of Periodicals Indexed

Adolescence
Libra Publishers, Inc.
3089C Clairmont Drive, Suite 383
San Diego, CA 92117

Affilia: Journal of Women &
  Social Work
Sage Publications, Inc.
2111 West Hillcrest Drive
Newbury Park, CA 91320

Atlantis
Mount St. Vincent
  University
166 Bedford Highway
Halifax, Nova Scotia
  B3M 26J
Canada

Australian Feminist Studies
Research Centre for
  Women's Studies
University of Adelaide
G.P.O. Box 498
Adelaide, South Australia
  5001
Australia

Belles Lettres
c/o Janet Mullaney,
  Editor & Publisher
11151 Captain's Walk Court
Gaithersburg, MD 20878

Bridges: A Journal for
  Jewish Feminists and Our
  Friends
P.O. Box 18437
Seattle, WA 98118

Camera Obscura
The Johns Hopkins University Press
Journals Publishing Division
701 West 40th Street,
  Suite 275
Baltimore, MD 21211

Canadian Women's Studies/
  Cahiers de la femme
York University
212 Founders College
4700 Keele Street
Downsview, Ontario
  M3J 1P3
Canada

Connexions:
  An International Women's
  Quarterly
Peoples Translation Service
4228 Telegraph Avenue
Oakland, CA 94609

Differences:
  A Journal of Feminist
  Cultural Studies
Indiana University Press
Journals Manager
10th & Morton Streets
Bloomington, IN 47405

Essence
P.O. Box 53400
Boulder, CO 80322-3400

Executive Female
NAFE (National Association
  for Female Executives,
  Inc.)
127 W. 24th St. 4th Floor
New York, NY 10011

Family Circle
P.O. Box 10599
Des Moines, IA 50947-0599

Feminist Collections
Women's Studies Librarian
The University of Wisconsin
  System
112A Memorial Library
728 State Street
Madison, WI 53706

Feminist Issues
Transaction Periodicals
  Consortium
Rutgers University
New Brunswick, NJ 08903

Feminist Review
Routledge, Chapman and
  Hall, Ltd.
Department J
North Way, Andover
Hampshire SP10 5BE
England

Feminist Studies
c/o Women's Studies
  Program
University of Maryland
College Park, MD 20742

Feminist Teacher
442 Ballantine Hall
Indiana University
Bloomington, IN 47405

Frontiers: A Journal of
  Women's Studies
University Press of Colorado
P.O. Box 849
Niwot, CO 80544

Gender and Education
Carfax Publishing
85 Ash Street
Hopkinton, MA 01748

Gender and History
Journal Subscriptions
  Department
Marston Book Services
P.O. Box 87
Oxford OX2 ODT
England

Genders
University of Texas Press
P.O. Box 7819
Austin, TX 78713

Gender & Society
Sage Publications, Inc.
2455 Teller Road
Newbury Park, CA 91320

Glamour
P.O. Box 53700
Boulder, CO 80322-3700

Good Housekeeping
P.O. Box 10056
Des Moines, IA 50340-0056

Harper's Bazaar
P.O. Box 10093
Des Moines, IA 50340

Health Care for Women,
  International
Hemisphere Publishing
  Corp.
79 Madison Avenue
New York, NY 10016

Healthrites
Family Planning Association
NSW Education Unit
328-336 Liverpool Road
Ashfield 2131
Australia

Healthsharing: A Canadian
  Women's Health Quarterly
14 Skey Lane
Toronto, Ontario M6J 3C4
Canada

Hecate: A Women's
Interdisciplinary Journal
Hecate Press
c/o English Department
University of Queensland
St. Lucia, Queensland 4067
Australia

Heresies: A Feminist Publication on
Art & Politics
Heresies Collective, Inc.
P.O. Box 1306
Canal Street Station
New York, NY 10013

Hot Wire: Journal of Women's
Music & Culture
Empty Closet Enterprises
5210 N. Wayne
Chicago, IL 60640

Hypatia: A Journal of
  Feminist Philosophy
Indiana University Press
Journals Manager
10th & Morton Streets
Bloomington, IN 47405

Iris: A Journal About
  Women
Women's Center
Box 323, HSC
University of Virginia
Charlottesville, VA 22903

ISIS-WICCE:
  Women's International
  Cross-Cultural Exchange/
  Women's World
3 Chemin des Campanules
CH-1219 Aire (Geneva)
Switzerland

Isis International/
  Women in Action
#85-A East Maya Street
Philamlife Homes
Quezon City
Philippines

Journal of Family History
JAI Press, Inc.
Subscription Department
P.O. Box 1678
55 Old Post Rd., No. 2
Greenwich, CT 06836

Journal of Family Welfare
Family Planning Association
  of India
Bajaj Bhavan
Nariman Point
Bombay 400021
India

Journal of Feminist Studies
  in Religion
Scholars Press
Box 15288
Atlanta, GA 30333

Journal of Marriage and the
  Family
National Council on Family
  Relations
3989 Central Avenue N.E., Suite
550
Columbia Heights, MN
  55421

Journal of Social Work and Human
Sexuality
The Haworth Press, Inc.
10 Alice Street
Binghamton, NY 13904

Journal of Women and
  Aging
The Haworth Press, Inc.
10 Alice Street
Binghamton, NY 13904

Journal of Women and
  Religion
The Center for Women and
  Religion
2400 Ridge Road
Berkeley, CA 94709

Journal of Women's History
Indiana University Press
Journals Manager
10th & Morton Streets
Bloomington, IN 47405

Ladies' Home Journal
1716 Locust Street
Des Moines, IA 50336

Lear's
P.O. Box 53201
Boulder, CO 80321-3201

Lesbian Ethics
LE Publications
P.O. Box 4723
Albuquerque, NM 87196

Lilith
Lilith Publications, Inc.
250 W. 57th Street,
  Suite 2432
New York, NY 10017

Mademoiselle
P.O. Box 54332
Boulder, CO 54332

Manushi
Manushi Trust
C-1/202 Lajpat Nagar-1
New Delhi 110 024
India

McCall's
P.O. Box 10739
Des Moines, IA 50340-0739

Media Report to Women
Communication Research
  Associates, Inc.
10606 Mantz Road
Silver Spring, MD 20903-
  1228

Minerva:
  Quarterly Report on Women and
the Military
1101 South Arlington
  Ridge Road, #110
Arlington, VA 22202

Ms. Magazine
P.O. Box 57132
Boulder, CO 80322-7132

National Women's Studies
  Association Journal
c/o Barbara Bernstein
Ablex Publishing
  Corporation
355 Chestnut Street
Norwood, NJ 07648

NWSAction
National Women's Studies
  Association
University of Maryland
College Park, MD 20742-1325

New Directions for Women
New Directions for Women,
  Inc.
108 West Palisade Avenue
Englewood, NJ 07631

Off Our Backs
off our backs, inc.
2423 18th Street NW,
  2d Floor
Washington, DC 20009

On the Issues: The Journal
  of Substance for Progressive
Women
97-77 Queens Boulevard
Forest Hills, NY 11374

Out/Look: National Lesbian
  and Gay Quarterly
2940 16th Street, Suite 319
San Francisco, CA 94103

Psychology of Women
  Quarterly
Cambridge University Press
Cambridge Journals
110 Midland Avenue
Port Chester, NY 10573

Redbook
250 West 55th Street
New York, NY 10019

Resources for Feminist
  Research/ Documentation
  sur la Recherche Feministe
Ontario Institute for Studies
  in Education (OISE)
252 Bloor Street West
Toronto, Ontario M5S 1V6
Canada

Sage: A Scholarly Journal on
  Black Women
Sage Women's Educational
  Press, Inc.
P.O. Box 42741
Atlanta, GA 30311-0741

Savvy
P.O. Box 359045
Palm Coast, FL 32035-9045

Signs: A Journal of Women
  in Culture & Society
The University of Chicago
  Press
Journals Division
P.O. Box 37005
Chicago, IL 60637

Sinister Wisdom: A Journal
  for the Lesbian Imagination in the
Arts and Politics
P.O. Box 3252
Berkeley, CA 94703

Spare Rib
27 Clerkenwell Close
London EC1R 0AT
ENGLAND

Trivia: A Journal of Ideas
P.O. Box 606
N. Amherst, MA 01059

Tulsa Studies in Women's
  Literature
University of Tulsa
600 South College Avenue
Tulsa, OK 74104

Vogue Magazine
P.O. Box 55964
Boulder, CO 80322-5964

Woman of Power
P.O. Box 827
Cambridge, MA 02238

Woman's Art Journal
1711 Harris Road
Laverock, PA 19118

Women and Environments
The Weed Foundation
736 Bathurst Street
Toronto, Ontario M5S 2R4
Canada

Women & Health
The Haworth Press, Inc.
10 Alice Street
Binghamton, NY 13904

Women & Language
c/o Anita Taylor
Communication Department
George Mason University
Fairfax, VA 22030

Women Library Workers
 Journal (WLW)
c/o Women's Resource
 Center
Building T-9, Room 116
University of California/
 Berkeley
Berkeley, CA 94720

Women & Performance: A
 Journal of Feminist Theory
NYU/TSOA, 721 Broadway,
 6th Floor
New York, NY 10003

Women & Politics
The Haworth Press, Inc.
10 Alice Street
Binghamton, NY 13904

Women & Therapy
The Haworth Press, Inc.
10 Alice Street
Binghamton, NY 13904

Women's Review of Books
Wellesley College
Center for Research on
 Women
Wellesley, MA 02181

Women's Rights Law
 Reporter
15 Washington Street
Newark, NJ 07102

Women's Sports & Fitness
P.O. Box 472
Mount Morris, IL 61054

Women's Studies in
 Communication
c/o Barbara Gayle
Institutional Subscriber
 Coordinator
Department of
 Communication Studies
University of Portland
5000 N. Willamette Boulevard
Portland, OR 97203

Women's Studies
 International Forum
Pergamon Press, Inc.
Journals Division
Maxwell House/
 Fairview Park
Elmsford, NY 10523

Women's Studies Quarterly
The Feminist Press
 at the City University of
 New York
311 East 94th Street
New York, NY 10128

Working Mother
P.O. Box 53832
Boulder, CO 80322

Working Woman
P.O. Box 10131
Des Moines, IA 50340-0131

# A

**Aamiry, Arwa**

Jordan: The Gulf Refugees. *Ms.* 1, No. 3 (November/December 1990):13

**Abad-Sarmiento, La-Rainne**

A Profile in Documentation Work: In the Service of Women's Movement. *Women's World* 23 (April 1990):25-22

**Abandoned Children – History**

The Foundlings of Milan: Abandoned Children and Their Parents from the Seventeenth to the Nineteenth Centuries. By Volker Hunecke. Reviewed by Edith Saurer. *Gender & History* 2, No. 3 (Autumn 1990):356-358

Mothers of Misery, Child Abandonment in Russia. By David L. Ransel. Reviewed by Judith Pallot. *Gender & History* 2, No. 3 (Autumn 1990):358-359

**Abarbanel, Stephanie**

Toxic Nightmare on Main Street. *Family Circle* 103, No. 11 (August 14, 1990):77-80+

Women Who Make a Difference: Reaching Out to Refugees. *Family Circle* 103, No. 9 (June 26, 1990):15-20

**Abbey, Susannah**

Act Up Zaps US Immigration. *Spare Rib* No. 216 (September 1990):49

**Abdullah, Tahrunnesa** and Zeidenstein, Sondra (editors)

Village Women of Bangladesh: Prospects for Change. Reviewed by Kalpana Bardhan. *Journal of Women's History* 2, No. 1 (Spring 1990):200-219

**Abel, Elizabeth**

Virginia Woolf and the Fictions of Psychoanalysis. Reviewed by Peggy Phelan. *The Women's Review of Books* 7, No. 6 (March 1990):16-17

**Abel, Emily** (joint author). *See* Sofaer, Shoshanna

**Abernathy, Ralph D.** (about)

Back Talk: Friendship and Betrayal. Armstrong Williams. *Essence* 20, No. 9 (January 1990):110

**Abner, Allison**

Mysteries of Melanin. Bibliography. *Essence* 21, No. 7 (November 1990):30-31

**Abod, Jennifer**

A Radio Profile of Audre Lorde. Reviewed by Jacqui Alexander. *NWSA Journal* 2, No. 1 (Winter 1990):129-131

**Aboriginals.** *See also* Australia – Aboriginals; Indians of North America

**Aboriginals – Conferences**

International Indigenous Women's Conference. Jackie Huggins. *Australian Feminist Studies* No. 11 (Autumn 1990):113-114

**Aborn, Shana**

Family Portrait: Three-Million-Dollar Quints. *Ladies' Home Journal* 107, No. 2 (February 1990):74-78

**Aborn, Shana** and Wait, Marianne

Everybody Loves a Baby. *Ladies' Home Journal* 107, No. 3 (March 1990):141-146

**Abortion.** *See also* Contraception

Abortion, Class, and Empowerment. Carol Anne Douglas. *off our backs* 20, No. 2 (February 1990):5

Abortion: Empty Womb. Felicia R. Lee. *Essence* 21, No. 1 (May 1990):51-52

Abortion: Is There a Doctor in the Clinic? Gayle Kirshenbaum. *Ms.* 1, No. 2 (September/October 1990):86-87

Abortion: The Clash of Absolutes. By Laurence H. Tribe. Reviewed by Diana Blackwell. *The Women's Review of Books* 7, No. 12 (September 1990):8-9

Another American Tragedy: The Death of Becky Bell. Mary Lou Greenberg. *On the Issues* 17 (Winter 1990):10-13+

Canada: Woman Dies from Self-Induced Abortion. *Spare Rib* 218 (November 1990):45-56

The Children I Almost Had. David Mills. *Essence* 20, No. 10 (February 1990):36

Compassion Comes for the Archbishop. Paula Kamen. *Ms.* 1, No. 1 (July/August 1990):85-86

A $5 Declaration of Independence. Gayle Kirshenbaum. *Ms.* 1, No. 1 (July/August 1990):87

Decoding Abortion Rhetoric: Communicating Social Change. By Celeste Michelle Condit. Reviewed by Diana Blackwell. *The Women's Review of Books* 7, No. 12 (September 1990):8-9

Emotional Response to Abortion: A Critical Review of the Literature. Susan C. Turell, Mary W. Armsworth, and John P. Gaa. *Women and Therapy* 9, No. 4 (1990):49-68

Post-Abortion Psychological Sequelae. M. S. Bhatia and others. *Journal of Family Welfare* 36, No. 4 (December 1990):67-74

In a Semantic Fog: How to Confront the Accusation That Abortion Equals Killing. Susanne V. Paczensky. *Women's Studies International Forum* 13, No. 3 (1990):177-184

The Unknown Women's Memorial. Toni Carabillo. *Woman of Power* 18 (Fall 1990):50-52

Video Crusade: "Shattering Young Women's Lives." Video review. *Ms.* 1, No. 2 (September/October 1990):90

**Abortion – Clinics**

Fake Abortion Clinics: The Threat to Reproductive Self-Determination. Julie A. Mertus. *Women and Health* 16, No. 1 (1990):95-113

**Abortion – Media Portrayal**

The Decontextualization of Abortion: An Analysis of "The Silent Scream." Bonnie A. Haaland. *Women's Studies in Communication* 12, No. 2 (Fall 1989):57-76

News Coverage of Abortion Gives More Exposure to Pro-Choicers, Study Says. *Media Report to Women* 18, No. 1 (January/February 1990)1

**Abortion – Opposition**

AT&T, the Bishops and Other Bad Connections. Ann F. Lewis. *Ms.* 1, No. 1 (July/August 1990):88

Fighting Fire with Fire: Civil RICO and Anti-Abortion Activists. Geri J. Yonover. *Women's Rights Law Reporter* 12, No. 3 (Fall 1990): 153-175

**Abortion – Sex Selection**

Sex-Selective Abortions in India: Parental Choice or Sexist Discrimination? Manju Parikh. *Feminist Issues* 10, No. 2 (Fall 1990):19-32

Sex Selective Fertility Control. R. K. Sachar and others. *Journal of Family Welfare* 36, No. 2 (June 1990):30-35

**Abortion Laws**

Abortion: Is There a Doctor in the Clinic? Gayle Kirshenbaum. *Ms.* 1, No. 2 (September/October 1990):86-87

Abortion Bans Mostly Foiled. Carol Anne Douglas. *off our backs* 20, No. 5 (May 1990):5

Abortion on Request – One Step Closer. Anne Kane. *Spare Rib* No. 212 (May 1990):44

Medical Termination of Pregnancy and Concurrent Contraceptive Acceptance. Armin Jamshedji and Narayan Kokate. *Journal of Family Welfare* 36, No. 3 (September 1990):39-53

Regrouping for Choice. Mary Hickmore. *Healthsharing* 11, No. 2 (March 1990):8

States Act on Abortion. Carol Anne Douglas. *off our backs* 20, No. 3 (March 1990):12; 20, No. 4 (April 1990):7

Struggle for Choice on Vancouver Island. Kim Goldberg. *Healthsharing* 11, No. 2 (March 1990):6

Webster – One Year and Many Battles Later. Mary Suh. *Ms.* 1, No. 1 (July/August 1990):87

What We Know as Women: A New Look at *Roe v. Wade.* Judith A. Baer. *NWSA Journal* 2, No. 4 (Autumn 1990):558-582

Which Way After Webster? Irene Davall. *On the Issues* 17 (Winter 1990):8-9+

Women Lose Freedom of Choice. B. Lee. *Healthsharing* 11, No. 3 (June 1990):10-11

**Abortion Rights.** *See also* Pregnancy; Reproductive Choice

Abortion: Ambiguous Criteria and Confusing Policies. Josefina Figueira-McDonough. *AFFILIA* 5, No. 4 (Winter 1990):27-54

Abortion: Election Turnaround? Anne Summers. *Ms.* 1, No. 2 (September/October 1990):93-94

On the Bias. Edited by Carol Meyer and Alma Young. *AFFILIA* 5, No. 1 (Spring 1990):97-102

Editorial: Promoting Reproductive Rights in 1990. Betty Sancier. *AFFILIA* 5, No. 1 (Spring 1990):5

**Abrahms, Sally** (joint author). *See* Fisher, Martin

**Abramovitz, Mimi**

Dependency and Poverty: Old Problems in a New World. Book Review. *Journal of Women and Aging* 2, No. 4 (1990):111-113

Low-Income Women's Activism. *off our backs* 20, No. 10 (November 1990):15

**Abramowitz, Benjamin L**

Anna Ella Carroll: Invisible Member of Lincoln's Cabinet. *Minerva* 8, No. 4 (Winter 1990):30-40

**Abrams, Maxine**

Breast Cancer: New Hope in the '90s. *Good Housekeeping* 211, No. 4 (October 1990):77-80

**Abramson, Pamela**

Flour Power. *Ladies' Home Journal* 107, No. 9 (September 1990):52-56

**Abramson, Zelda**

Don't Ask Your Gynecologist If You Need a Hysterectomy . . . *Healthsharing* 11, No. 3 (June 1990):12-17

Lupron – New Wonder Drug? *Healthsharing* 11, No. 4 (December 1990):7

**Abrash, Barbara** and Sandlin, Martha (producers)

Indians, Outlaws, and Angie Debo. Reviewed by Theda Perdue. *NWSA Journal* 2, No. 4 (Autumn 1990):646-649

**Abray, L. J.**

The Woman Question: Society and Literature in Britain and America, 1837-1883. Book Review. *Resources for Feminist Research* 19, No. 1 (March 1990):38-39

**Abu-Lughod, Lila**

Can There Be A Feminist Ethnography? *Women and Performance: A Journal of Feminist Theory* 5, No. 1, Issue #9 (1990): 7-27

**Aburdene, Patricia**

How to Think Like a CEO for the 90's. *Working Woman* (September 1990):134-137

**Aburdene, Patricia** (about)

Lunch. Interview. Frances Lear. *Lear's* (October 1990):21-22

**Abused Children.** *See* Child Abuse

**Abused Wives.** *See also* Violence Against Women

Feminist Perspectives on Wife Abuse. Edited by K. Yllö and M. Bograd. Reviewed by Lorraine M. Gutiérrez. *AFFILIA* 5, No. 1 (Spring 1990):119-120

No Place to Hide. Ellen Hopkins. *Essence* 21, No. 4 (August 1990):66-68+

**Abused Wives – Self-Defense**

Justifiable Homicide: Battered Women, Self-Defense and the Law. By Cynthia K. Gillespie. Reviewed by Pamela A. Brown. *AFFILIA* 5, No. 2 (Summer 1990):106-109

When Battered Women Kill. By Angela Browne. Reviewed by Pamela A. Brown. *AFFILIA* 5, No. 2 (Summer 1990):106-109

**Abzug, Bella**

"Martin, What Should I Do Now?" *Ms.* 1, No. 1 (July/August 1990):94-96

**Abzug, Martin** (about)

"Martin, What Should I Do Now?" Bella Abzug. *Ms.* 1, No. 1 (July/August 1990):94-96

**Academic Achievement**

Family, School and Society. Edited by Martin Woodhead and Andrea McGrath. Reviewed by C. R. Miller. *Gender and Education* 2, No. 1 (1990):100-102

Family Size and Academic Achievement of Children. Varghese I. Cherian. *Journal of Family Welfare* 36, No. 4 (December 1990):56-60

Parent-Adolescent Communication, Family Functioning, and School Performance. Venus S. Masselam, Robert F. Marcus, and Clayton L. Stunkard. *Adolescence* 25, No. 99 (Fall 1990):737

Parental Separation and the Academic Self-Concepts of Adolescents: An Effort to Solve the Puzzle of Separation Effects. Thomas Ewin Smith. *Journal of Marriage and the Family* 52, No. 1 (February 1990):107-118

Parenting: Taking Back Our Schools. Valerie Wilson Wesley. *Essence* 20, No. 10 (February 1990):102 +

**Accad, Evelyne**

Maternal Thinking: Towards a Politics of Peace. Book Review. *Women's Studies International Forum* 13, No. 5 (1990):526-527

**Accessories.** *See* Dress Accessories

**Accidents.** *See* Children – Accidents; Winter – Accidents

**Accidents – Prevention.** *See* Home Accidents – Prevention

**Achievement.** *See also* Academic Achievement; Success

Bicoastal Career. Mary Alice Kellogg. *Harper's Bazaar* (October 1990):176-177 +

In From the Cold. Jane Howard. *Lear's* (October 1990):146-150

Double Play. *Harper's Bazaar* (June 1990):106-109+

The Effect of Husband's Occupational Attainment on Wife's Achievement. William W. Philliber and

Dana Vannoy-Hiller. *Journal of Marriage and the Family* 52, No. 2 (May 1990):323-329

Face of the '90s. Alison Lurie. *Lear's* (January 1990):61-69

200 Words: Lear's Women Caught in the Act. I. E. Franklin. *Lear's* (February 1990):94-97

World Class. Jon Etra. *Harper's Bazaar* (May 1990):33-40

**Achievement Motivation**

Parental Loss and Achievement. By Marvin Eisenstadt, André Haynal, Pierre Rentchnick, and Pierre De Senarclens. Book Review. *Adolescence* 25, No. 98 (Summer 1990):499-500

**Achievement Need**

Are You Too Good? Kathryn Stechert Black. *Glamour* (March 1990):164-167

Personal Journal. *Ladies' Home Journal* 107, No. 11 (November 1990):110-114

**Acker, Joan**

Doing Comparable Worth: Gender, Class and Pay Equity. Reviewed by Peggy Kahn. *The Women's Review of Books* 7, No. 12 (September 1990):21-23

Hierarchies, Jobs, Bodies: A Theory of Gendered Organizations. *Gender and Society* 4, No. 2 (June 1990):139-158

Wage Justice: Comparable Worth and the Paradox of Technocratic Reform. Book Review. *NWSA Journal* 2, No. 2 (Spring 1990):305-306

**Acker, Sandra**

Teachers, Gender and Careers. Reviewed by Jenny Shaw. *Gender and Education* 2, No. 2 (1990):242-243

Women Teaching for Change: Gender, Class and Power. Book Review. *Gender and Education* 2, No. 1 (1990):105-107

**Ackerly, Leone** (about). *See also* Leadership

**Ackerman, Rosalie J.**

Career Developments and Transitions of Middled-Aged Women. *Psychology of Women Quarterly* 14, No. 4 (December 1990):513-530

**Acland, Charles**

The "Space" Behind the Dialogue: The Gender-Coding of Space on *Cheers*. Notes. *Women & Language* 13, No. 1 (Fall 1990):38-40

**Acosta-Belén, Edna** and Bose, Christine E.

From Structural Subordination to Empowerment: Women and Development in Third World Contexts. *Gender and Society* 4, No. 3 (September 1990):299-320

**Acquired Immune Deficiency Syndrome.** *See also* Health Care Workers – Acquired Immune Deficiency Syndrome; Sexually Transmitted Diseases – Prevention

AIDS 1990: What We Can Do. Anna Wintour. *Vogue* (November 1990):366

AIDS and its Metaphors. By Susan Sontag. Reviewed by Catherine Mason. *Healthright* 9, No. 4 (August 1990):40

AIDS in the Workplace. Lloyd Gite. *Glamour* (November 1990):116

Attitudes: The Sexual Revolution. Karen Grigsby Bates. *Essence* 21, No. 1 (May 1990):54-56

Beyond Condom-Bound Solutions. Sara Scott. *Connexions* 33 (1990):21-23

Beyond Pity. Duncan Stalker. *Vogue* (November 1990):372-373+

Big Night Out. By David Greig. Reviewed by Dave Burrows. *Healthright* 9, No. 4 (August 1990):47

Confidentiality and Blackmail. *Connexions* 33 (1990):25

Desire Cannot Be Fragmented. Sabine Marx. *Connexions* 33 (1990):6-9

Dispatches: The AIDS Catch. By Joan Shenton. Reviewed by Judi Wilson. *Spare Rib* No. 215 (August 1990):32-33

Healthworkers and AIDS. Kendra Sundquist. *Healthright* 9, No. 2 (February 1990):10-12

HIV-Positive. *Connexions* 33 (1990):14-15

"I Don't Want My Son to Be Forgotten." Ann Marie Cunningham. *Ladies' Home Journal* 107, No. 8 (August 1990):102-103+

Imported AIDS. Sarah Sexton, Chantawipa Apisuk, and Anchana Suwannond. *Connexions* 33 (1990):16-18

Is It Genocide? Karen Grigsby Bates. *Essence* 21, No. 5 (September 1990):76-78+

I Tested HIV-Positive. Marlene Cimons. *Essence* 20, No. 12 (April 1990):72-75

Kenji, My Friend. Teresa Cronin. *Essence* 20, No. 11 (March 1990):40+

Lessons From My Mother's Life. Aphra Frank. *Glamour* (May 1990):300+

Let's Fight it Together. *Connexions* 33 (1990):5

Memoir of an AIDS Volunteer. Sara Nelson. *Lilith* 15, No. 1 (Winter 1990):13-14

Moving Forward Together. *Connexions* 33 (1990):13

A New Intimacy. *Connexions* 33 (1990):26

NGOs Against AIDS. Sarah Sexton. *Connexions* 33 (1990):19

Parenting. Bibliography. *Essence* 21, No. 3 (July 1990):96

"Pass the Clingfilm, dear!" *Connexions* 33 (1990):28

Ruth Brinker's Meals Feed Body and Soul. Julie Lew. *McCall's* 117, No. 7 (April 1990):23

Sanitary Policing. Debi Brock. *Connexions* 33 (1990):

Testing Positive. Darien Taylor. *Healthsharing* 11, No. 2 (March 1990):9-13

Transfusions. *Connexions* 33 (1990):24

Ways of Caring. Margaretta Northrop. *Vogue* (November 1990):368-369

We Have No Sex: Soviet Gays and AIDS in the Era of Glasnost. Masha Gessen. *Out/Look* No. 9 (Summer 1990):42-54

"When Penis Equals Sexuality." *Connexions* 33 (1990):11-12

Women Who Make a Difference. Randi Henderson. *Family Circle* 103, No. 12 (September 4, 1990):19+

**Acquired Immune Deficiency Syndrome – ACT-UP**

Act Up Zaps US Immigration. Susannah Abbey. *Spare Rib* No. 216 (September 1990):49

Art Acts Up: A Graphic Response to AIDS. Excerpt. Douglas Crimp. *Out/Look* No. 9 (Summer 1990):22-30

**Acquired Immune Deficiency Syndrome – Africa.** *See also* Uganda – Acquired Immune Deficiency Syndrome

Women and AIDS. Ntiense Ben Edemikpong. *Women and Therapy* 10, No. 3 (1990):25-34

**Acquired Immune Deficiency Syndrome – Children**

Breastfeeding Encouraged. *Connexions* 33 (1990):10

Caring for Children with HIV and AIDS. Kendra Sundquist. *Healthright* 9, No. 2 (February 1990):35

One Couple's Crusade for Children. Jean Liebman Block. *Good Housekeeping* 211, No. 5 (November 1990):90+

A State of Shock: Recollections of Romania. Darrell L. Paster. *On the Issues* 16 (Fall 1990):19-21

**Acquired Immune Deficiency Syndrome – Conferences**

Montreal AIDS Conference. Mary Louise Adams. *Healthsharing* 11, No. 1 (December 1989):6

Sixth International AIDS Conference: Good News, Bad News and Protests. *Spare Rib* No. 216 (September 1990):48-49

## Acquired Immune Deficiency Syndrome – Education

AIDS: How to Answer the Hard Questions. Jo Calluy and Helen Jones. *Healthright* 9, No. 3 (May 1990):14-16

AIDS: Late Adolescents' Knowledge and Its Influence on Sexual Behavior. Bruce Roscoe and Tammy L. Kruger. *Adolescence* 25, No. 97 (Spring 1990):39-48

The AIDS Challenge: Prevention Education for Young People. Edited by Marcia Quackenbush, Mary Nelson, and Kay Clark. Reviewed by Sue Kaiser. *Healthsharing* 11, No. 2 (March 1990):33

AIDS Education in the Yukon. Lorene Benoit. *Healthsharing* 11, No. 1 (December 1989):6

Changing People's Behavior. *Connexions* 33 (1990):30-31

Get That Condom on Your Loogboub. Debra Chasnoff. *Out/Look* No. 7 (Winter 1990):62-64

Managing Risk and Experiencing Danger: Tensions Between Government AIDS Education Policy and Young Women's Sexuality. Janet Holland, Caroline Ramazanoglu and Sue Scott. *Gender and Education* 2, No. 2 (1990):125-146

## Acquired Immune Deficiency Syndrome – Gender Issues

AIDS in Uganda as a Gender Issue. Mere Nakateregga Kisekka. *Women and Therapy* 10, No. 3 (1990):35-53

## Acquired Immune Deficiency Syndrome – Lesbians

Mapping: Lesbians, AIDS and Sexuality. Sue O'Sullivan and Cindy Patton. *Feminist Review* No. 34 (Spring 1990):120-133

## Acquired Immune Deficiency Syndrome – Personal Narratives

Sam's Secret. Denise Jefferson. *Essence* 21, No. 6 (October 1990):86-88+

## Acquired Immune Deficiency Syndrome – Prostitutes

AIDS: A Double-Edged Sword. *Women's World*, No. 24 (Winter 1990/91): 53-55

Dutch Recommendation on AIDS Policies. *Women's World*, No. 24 (Winter 1990/91): 57-58

Green Cards in Thailand. *Women's World*, No. 24 (Winter 1990/91): 55

A Positive Verdict. Shaila Shah. *Spare Rib* No. 216 (September 1990):36-37

"Prostitutes as Pariah in the Age of AIDS": A Content Analysis of Coverage of Women Prostitutes in *The New York Times* and the *Washington Post* September 1985-April 1988. Donna King. *Women and Health* 16, Nos. 3/4 (1990):155-176

## Acquired Immune Deficiency Syndrome – Women

AIDS: The Women. Edited by Ines Reider and Patricia Ruppelt. Reviewed by Christine Pierce. *NWSA Journal* 2, No. 1 (Winter 1990):134-139

AIDS and Sexual Assault. Megan Williams. *Healthsharing* 11, No. 3 (June 1990):11

AIDS and Women: An International Perspective. Suzy H. Fletcher. *Health Care for Women International* 11, No. 1 (1990):33-42

Alison Gertz: Champagne, Roses . . . and AIDS. Lisa DePaulo. *Mademoiselle* (December 1990):176-179+

The Real Truth about Women and AIDS: How to Eliminate the Risks without Giving Up Love and Sex. By Helen Singer Kaplan. Reviewed by Kathryn Quina. *Psychology of Women Quarterly* 14, No. 2 (June 1990):296-298

Triple Jeopardy: Women and AIDS. *Spare Rib* 219 (December 1990-January 1991):58-61

Women, HIV and AIDS. *Spare Rib* No. 211 (April 1990):58

Women and AIDS: A Nurse's Perspective. Deborah L. Bowers. *Iris* 23 (Spring-Summer 1990):58-61

Women and AIDS: A Practical Guide for Those Who Help Others. By Bonnie Lester. Reviewed by Kathryn Quina. *Psychology of Women Quarterly* 14, No. 2 (June 1990):296-298

Women and AIDS. By Diane Richardson. Reviewed by Kathryn Quina. *Psychology of Women Quarterly* 14, No. 2 (June 1990):296-298

Women and AIDS: Reexamining the Risk. Leanne Kleinmann. *Glamour* (May 1990):88-92

Women at Risk. Peggy Orenstein. *Vogue* (November 1990):370-371+

Women HIV and AIDS: Speaking Out in the UK. By Hummingbird Films. Reviewed by Judi Wilson. *Spare Rib* 219 (December 1990-January 1991):34-35

Women Negotiating Heterosex: Implications for AIDS Prevention. Susan Kippax, June Crawford, Cathy Waldby, and Pam Benton. *Women's Studies International Forum* 13, No. 6 (1990):533-542

## Acquired Immune Deficiency Syndrome and Homophobia

Gay Lib vs. AIDS: Averting Civil War in the 1990s. Eric E. Rofes. *Out/Look* No. 8 (Spring 1990):8-17

**Activism.** *See also* Celebrities – Activism; Hollywood Women's Political Committee; Political Activists; Protest Actions; Support Systems

An Outbreak of Peace. By Sarah Pirtle. Reviewed by Mitzi Myers. *NWSA Journal* 2, No. 2 (Spring 1990):273-281

Back Talk: The Struggle Is Ours. Joan L. Morgan. *Essence* 21, No. 1 (May 1990):216

Laugh with Father. Ellen Byron. *Redbook* 175, No. 2 (June 1990):59-63

Melanie Mellows Out. Bonnie Siegler. *Ladies' Home Journal* 107, No. 10 (October 1990):154-155+

Move Over, Rambo: There's a New Sly in Town. Laura Morice. *Mademoiselle* (February 1990):176-177+

Prime-Time Affairs. Yona Zeldis McDonough. *Harper's Bazaar* (August 1990):50

Three Men and a Little Lady's Home Journal. Jeff Rovin. *Ladies' Home Journal* 107, No. 12 (December 1990):46-53

Thrill Out. *Harper's Bazaar* (July 1990):80-83

Word On . . . *Glamour* (July 1990):113

Word On Entertainment. *Glamour* (February 1990):121-122; (June 1990):183

Working Whirl. Jess Bravin. *Harper's Bazaar* (November 1990):170-171

**Actors – Autobiography.** *See* Garbo, Greta (about); Gardner, Ava

**Actors – Interviews.** *See also* Baxter-Birney, Meredith (about); Garr, Teri (about); Gibson, Mel (about); Goldberg, Whoopi (about); Schwarzenegger, Arnold (about); Stallone, Sylvester (about); Stapleton, Jean (about)

Candid Candice. Interview. Linda Ellerbee. *Ladies' Home Journal* 107, No. 6 (June 1990):126-130+

Lunch. Interview. Frances Lear. *Lear's* (November 1990):23-24

Word On Entertainment. *Glamour* (January 1990):84-85

**Actors – Photographs**

Great Faces. Lois Joy Johnson. *Ladies' Home Journal* 107, No. 11 (November 1990):224-228

Marilyn Monroe: The Lost Photographs. Bob La Brasca. *Redbook* 175, No. 6 (October 1990):118-121

**Actors – Wages**

Why Meryl Streep Earns So Much Less than Sylvester Stalone. Charla Krupp. *Glamour* (July 1990):114-115

**ACT-UP.** *See* Acquired Immune Deficiency Syndrome – ACT-UP

**Adair, Christy**

Egg Dances. *Spare Rib* No. 211 (April 1990):28

**Adam, Margie**

Greta Garbo's "Mysterious" Private Life. *Out/Look* No. 10 (Fall 1990):25

**Adam, Peter**

Eileen Gray: Architect/Designer. Reviewed by Pamela H. Simpson. *Woman's Art Journal* 11, No. 2 (Fall 1990-Winter 1991):44-48

**Adams, Aileen** (about)

Lunch. Interview. Frances Lear. *Lear's* (May 1990):17-18

**Adams, Alice**

After You've Gone. Reviewed by Rosalind A. Warren. *The Women's Review of Books* 7, No. 8 (May 1990):8-9

**Adams, Alison K.**

Mapping the Moral Domain. Book Review. *AFFILIA* 5, No. 3 (Fall 1990):111-113

**Adams, Brooks**

Art on the Edge. *Vogue* (July 1990):94-99

Cascade of Color. *Harper's Bazaar* (July 1990):30

Shock of the Mundane. *Vogue* (March 1990):344-350

**Adams, Carole Elizabeth**

Counter Cultures: Saleswomen, Managers and Customers in American Department Stores, 1890-1940. Book Review. *Gender & History* 2, No. 3 (Autumn 1990):343-348

Ladies and Gentlemen of the Civil Service: Middle Class Workers in Victorian America. Book Review. *Gender & History* 2, No. 3 (Autumn 1990):343-348

The White Blouse Revolution: Female Office Workers Since 1870. Book Review. *Gender & History* 2, No. 3 (Autumn 1990):343-348

**Adams, Carol J.**

The Sexual Politics of Meat: A Feminist-Vegetarian Critical Theory. Reviewed by Bettyann Kevles. *The Women's Review of Books* 7, No. 8 (May 1990):11-12

The Sexual Politics of Meat: A Feminist-Vegetarian Critical Theory. Reviewed by Kore Archer. *New Directions for Women* 19, No. 4 (July-August 1990):19

**Adams, Cindy**

Barbara Bush: First Lady, First Class. *Ladies' Home Journal* 107, No. 11 (November 1990):196+

Donald and Ivana Trump: What Went Wrong? *Good Housekeeping* 210, No. 5 (May 1990):62-67

Leona's Lament. *Ladies' Home Journal* 107, No. 5 (May 1990):80-85+

**Adams, Gail**, Miles, Martha, and Yoder, Linda

The Sourcebook for Women Who Create. Reviewed by Elaine Hedges. *NWSA Journal* 2, No. 2 (Spring 1990):282-287

**Adams, Gerald R.** (joint editor). *See* Montemayor, Raymond

**Adams, Henry** (about)

Private Connives. Patricia O'Toole. *Lear's* (August 1990):98-101

**Adams, Jane**

My Daughter and Me: Déjà Vu All Over Again. *Lear's* (May 1990):72-74

**Adams, Jane** (joint author). *See* Calabrese, Raymond L.

**Adams, Margaret E.** (joint author). *See* Prince, Joyce

**Adams, Margaret O.**

Electronic Records at the National Archives: Resources for Women's Studies. *NWSA Journal* 2, No. 2 (Spring 1990):269-272

**Adams, Mary Louise**

Family Fortunes: Men and Women of the English Middle Class, 1780-1850. Book Review. *Resources for Feminist Research* 19, No. 1 (March 1990):10-11

Montreal AIDS Conference. *Healthsharing* 11, No. 1 (December 1989):6

**Adams, Maud** (about)

Figure Study. *Harper's Bazaar* (August 1990):32 +

**Adams, Michael**

The House that Brenda Built: A Transvestite Response to AIDS in Brazil. *Out/Look* No. 8 (Spring 1990):22-26

**Adams, Oleta**

Circle of One. Reviewed by Elorine Grant. *Spare Rib* No. 216 (September 1990):26

**Adams-Ender, Clara** (about). *See* Dent, David

**Adams Family**

The Adams Women: Abigail and Louisa Adams, Their Sisters and Daughters. By Paul C. Ng. Reviewed by Elaine Forman Crane. *NWSA Journal* 2, No. 4 (Autumn 1990):661-664

**Adamson, Nancy**; Briskin, Linda; and McPhail, Margaret

Feminist Organizing for Change: The Contemporary Women's Movement in Canada. Reviewed by Linda Christiansen-Ruffman. *Women's Studies International Forum* 13, Nos. 1-2 (1990):163-165

**Addiction.** *See also* Eating Disorders; Substance Abuse

Adolescent Substance Abuse: Practice Implications. John S. Wodarski. *Adolescence* 25, No. 99 (Fall 1990):667-688

Child Star, Child Addict. Joanne Kaufman. *Ladies' Home Journal* 107, No. 3 (March 1990):116-124

How Not to Get the D.T.'s When Happy. *Lear's* (September 1990):81-82

If This Isn't Love, It Could Be a Fix. John Bradshaw. *Lear's* (September 1990):79-80

The Making of an Addict Takes Training. John Bradshaw. *Lear's* (November 1990):84

Shopping Until You Can't Stop. John Bradshaw. *Lear's* (October 1990):75

**Addiction–Food.** *See* Eating Disorders

**Addiction–Newborns**

I Gave Birth to an Addicted Baby. Mary Ann Grand and Denise Fortino. *Good Housekeeping* 210, No. 4 (April 1990):130-131, 172-178

**Addiction–Treatment**

The Twelve-Step Controversy. Charlotte Davis Kasl. *Ms.* 1, No. 3 (November/December 1990):30-31

Twelve Step Programs: A Lesbian Feminist Critique. Bette S. Tallen. *NWSA Journal* 2, No. 3 (Summer 1990):390-407

**Addison (Texas)–Mayors.** *See* Texas–Mayors

**Adegbalola, Gaye** Lewis, Earlene, and Rabson, Ann

Saffire: The Uppity Blues Women. Reviewed by Lynn Wenzel. *New Directions for Women* 19, No. 3 (May/June 1990):8

**Adelmann, Pamela K.**, Antonucci, Toni C., Crohan, Susan E., and Coleman, Lerita M.

A Causal Analysis of Employment and Health in Midlife Women. *Women and Health* 16, No. 1 (1990):5-20

**Adeyanju, Matthew**

Adolescent Health Status, Behaviors and Cardiovascular Disease. *Adolescence* 25, No. 97 (Spring 1990):155-169

**Adisa, Opal Palmer**

Bake-Face and Other Guava Stories. Reviewed by Suzanne Scafe. *Spare Rib* No. 209 (February 1990):31

**Adlaka, R.** (joint author). *See* Sachar, R. K.

**Adler, Fran**

Begot. Poem. *Bridges* 1, No. 1 (Spring 1990): 31

Switchback. Poem. *Bridges* 1, No. 1 (Spring 1990): 31

**Adler, Jo** (joint author). *See* Levinger, Leah

**Adlon, Percy**

Rosalie Goes Shopping. Reviewed by Katy Watson. *Spare Rib* No. 209 (February 1990):35

Rosalie Goes Shopping. Reviewed by Ron Rosenbaum. *Mademoiselle* (May 1990):112-114

**Adolescents.** *See also* Employment, Part-Time

Adolescents' Chores: The Differences Between Dual- and Single-Earner Families. Mary Holland Benin and Debra A. Edwards. *Journal of Marriage and the Family* 52, No. 2 (May 1990):361-373

Families and Adolescents: A Review of the 1980s. Viktor Gecas and Monica A. Seff. *Journal of Marriage and the Family* 52, No. 4 (November 1990):941-598

Tweens. Hilary Cosell. *Working Mother* (November 1990):132-134; (December 1990):74

**Adolescents – Attitudes**

Adolescents' Attitudes Toward Women in Politics: A Follow-up Study. Diane Gillespie and Cassie Spohn. *Women & Politics* 10, No. 1 (1990):1-16

Adolescents' Orientation to the Future: Development of Interests and Plans, and Related Attributions and Affects, in the Life-Span Context. By Jari-Erik Nurmi. Book Review. *Adolescence* 25, No. 99 (Fall 1990):755

Causal Attributions for Losing as Perceived by Adolescents. Shirley A. Wisniewski and Eugene L. Gaier. *Adolescence* 25, No. 97 (Spring 1990):239-247

Coming of Age in Buffalo: Youth and Authority in the Postwar Era. By William Graebner. Book Review. *Adolescence* 25, No. 99 (Fall 1990):753

**Adolescents – Communication**

Communication Assessment and Intervention Strategies for Adolescents. By Vicki Lord Larson and Nancy L. McKinley. Book Review. *Adolescence* 25, No. 98 (Summer 1990):501-502

**Adolescents – Counseling**. *See also* Cognitive Therapy – Adolescents; Group Therapy – Adolescents

Clinical Interviews with Children and Adolescents. By Philip Barker. Book Review. *Adolescence* 25, No. 97 (Spring 1990):249

School-Based Social Work and Family Therapy. Thomas L. Millard. *Adolescence* 25, No. 98 (Summer 1990):401-408

School Counselors' Knowledge of Eating Disorders. Joy A. Price, Sharon M. Desmond, James H. Price, and Amy Mossing. *Adolescence* 25, No. 100 (Winter 1990):945-947

Talking to Teenagers. Gillian Checkley. *Healthright* 9, No. 4 (August 1990):25-27

**Adolescents – Delinquency**

Alienation: A Cause of Juvenile Delinquency. Raymond L. Calabrese and Jane Adams. *Adolescence* 25, No. 98 (Summer 1990):435-440

Delinquency in Adolescence. By Scott W. Henggeler. Book Review. *Adolescence* 25, No. 97 (Spring 1990):250

Juvenile Recidivism: A Comparison of Three Prediction Instruments. José B. Ashford and Craig Winston LeCroy. *Adolescence* 25, No. 98 (Summer 1990):442-450

Neutralization and Delinquency: A Comparison by Sex and Ethnicity. Jim Mitchell, Richard A. Dodder, and Terry D. Norris. *Adolescence* 25, No. 98 (Summer 1990):487-497

**Adolescents – Family Relationships**

Adolescent Separation-Individuation and Family Transitions. Jill A. Daniels. *Adolescence* 25, No. 97 (Spring 1990):105-116

Evaluations of Family by Youth: Do They Vary as a Function of Family Structure, Gender, and Birth Order? Thomas S. Parish. *Adolescence* 25, No. 98 (Summer 1990):353-356

Family Factors Related to Adolescent Autonomy. Jean A. Pardeck and John T. Pardeck. *Adolescence* 25, No. 98 (Summer 1990):311-319

Growing Up with Violence. Kathy Dobie. *Vogue* (December 1990):310-315+

The Impact of Parental Loss on Adolescents' Psychosocial Characteristics. Beverley Raphael, Jeff Cubis, Michael Dunne, Terry Lewin, and Brian Kelly. *Adolescence* 25, No. 99 (Fall 1990):689-700

**Adolescents – Health Care**

Adolescent Health Status, Behaviors and Cardiovascular Disease. Matthew Adeyanju. *Adolescence* 25, No. 97 (Spring 1990):155-169

Preventive Health Services for Adolescents. By John S. Wodarski. Book Review. *Adolescence* 25, No. 97 (Spring 1990):252

**Adolescents – Homosexuality**

The Psychoanalytic Perspective of Adolescent Homosexuality: A Review. Jon K. Mills. *Adolescence* 25, No. 100 (Winter 1990):913-922

Who Speaks for Lesbian/Gay Adolescents: Voices to Be Silenced, Voices to Be Heard. Dean Pierce. *Women & Language* 13, No. 2 (Winter 1990):37-41

**Adolescents – Learning Disabilities**

Transition Goals for Adolescents with Learning Disabilities. By Catherine Trapani. Book Review. *Adolescence* 25, No. 99 (Fall 1990):755

**Adolescents, Minority**

Black Adolescents. Edited by Reginald L. Jones. Book Review. *Adolescence* 25, No. 99 (Fall 1990):753

Children of Color: Psychological Interventions with Minority Youth. By Jewelle Taylor Gibbs, Larke Nahme Huang, and associates. Book Review. *Adolescence* 25, No. 97 (Spring 1990):250

Coming-of-Age among Contemporary American Indians as Portrayed in Adolescent Fiction. Carol Markstrom-Adams. *Adolescence* 25, No. 97 (Spring 1990):225-237

Reclaiming Youth at Risk: Our Hope for the Future. By Larry K. Brendtro, Martin Brokenleg, and Steve Van Bockern. Book Review. *Adolescence* 25, No. 100 (Winter 1990):997

**Adolescents, Minority – Sexual Behavior**

Sexual Decision Making in Young Black Adolescent Females. Joanette M. Pete and Lydia DeSantis. *Adolescence* 25, No. 97 (Spring 1990):145-154

## Adolescents – Political Activism

Is Political Activism Still a "Masculine" Endeavor? Gender Comparisons among High School Political Activists. Nancy Romer. *Psychology of Women Quarterly* 14, No. 2 (June 1990):229-243

## Adolescents – Pregnancy

The Girl Nobody Loved: Psychological Explanations for White Single Pregnancy in the Pre-*Roe v. Wade* Era, 1945-1965. Rickie Solinger. *Frontiers* 11, Nos. 2-3 (1990):45-54

Hush-a-Bye Baby. By Margo Harkin. Reviewed by Margaret Gillan. *Spare Rib* 219 (December 1990-January 1991):34

On the Issues. Merle Hoffman. *On the Issues* 14 (1990):2-3+

Trying It on for Size: Mutual Support in Role Transition for Pregnant Teens and Student Nurses. Judith Wuest. *Health Care for Women International* 11, No. 4 (1990):383-392

## Adolescents – Psychiatric Care

Motivating Adolescents to Reduce Their Fines in a Token Economy. Robert P. Miller, Jean M. Cosgrove, and Larry Doke. *Adolescence* 25, No. 97 (Spring 1990):97-104

Notes on the History of Adolescent Inpatient and Residential Treatment. D. Patrick Zimmerman. *Adolescence* 25, No. 97 (Spring 1990):9-38

Prediction of Length of Hospitalization of Adolescent Psychiatric Inpatients Utilizing the Pd Scale of the MMPI and Demographic Data. Wanda C. Faurie. *Adolescence* 25, No. 98 (Summer 1990):305-310

The "Rest" Program: A New Treatment System for the Oppositional Defiant Adolescent. David B. Stein and Edward D. Smith. *Adolescence* 25, No. 100 (Winter 1990):891-904

Restraint and Seclusion with Institutionalized Adolescents. Tony D. Crespi. *Adolescence* 25, No. 100 (Winter 1990):825-829

A Theoretical Model for the Practice of Residential Treatment. R.W. Miskimins. *Adolescence* 25, No. 100 (Winter 1990):867-890

## Adolescents – Psychology. *See also* Family Life – Problems; Million Adolescent Personality Inventory (MAPI)

Adolescent Rebellion . . . Or Sheer Defiance? Lee Salk. *McCall's* 117, No. 10 (July 1990):56

After-School Jobs: Are They Good for Kids? Lee Salk. *McCall's* 118, No. 1 (October 1990):102-106

Cultural-Developmental Tasks and Adolescent Development: Theoretical and Methodological Considerations. Paul A. Klaczynski. *Adolescence* 25, No. 100 (Winter 1990):811-823

Dear Mom, I Lost My Retainers. Gayle Lea Brown. *McCall's* 118, No. 3 (December 1990):14-21

Decision-Making Processes of Youth. J. William Moore, Brian Jensen, and William E. Hauck. *Adolescence* 25, No. 99 (Fall 1990):583-592

"Don't Put Me Away, Mom, Please!" Patti Jones. *Redbook* 175, No. 6 (October 1990):140-147

Early Adolescent Age and Gender Differences in Patterns of Emotional Self-Disclosure to Parents and Friends. Dennis R. Papini, Frank F. Farmer, Steven M. Clark, Jill C. Micka, and Jawanda K. Barnett. *Adolescence* 25, No. 100 (Winter 1990):959-976

Effects of Rational Emotive Education on the Rationality, Neuroticism and Defense Mechanisms of Adolescents. Daniel J. Kachman and Gilbert E. Mazer. *Adolescence* 25, No. 97 (Spring 1990):131-144

Getting Through. Trish Vradenburg. *Ladies' Home Journal* 107, No. 11 (November 1990):140

Handbook of Clinical Assessment of Children and Adolescents. Edited by Clarice J. Kestenbaum and Daniel T. Williams. Book Review. *Adolescence* 25, No. 99 (Fall 1990):754

The Importance of Being Eleven. Lindsy Van Gelder. *Ms.* 1, No. 1 (July/August 1990):77-79

Loneliness, Coping Strategies and Cognitive Styles of the Gifted Rural Adolescent. *Adolescence* 25, No. 100 (Winter 1990):977-988

Medical Checkups for Teenagers. Martin Fisher and Sally Abrahms. *Good Housekeeping* 211, No. 3 (September 1990):158-160

"Mom, Please Get Me Out!" Katherine Barrett and Richard Greene. *Ladies' Home Journal* 107, No. 5 (May 1990):98-107

Parenting: Learning to Let Go. Valerie Wilson Wesley. *Essence* 21, No. 1 (May 1990):188

The Prevalence of Depression in High School Students. Marion F. Ehrenberg, David N. Cox, and Raymond F. Koopman. *Adolescence* 25, No. 100 (Winter 1990):905-912

Relationships: Happy One Day, Sad the Next. Stephen P. Herman. *Family Circle* 103, No. 16 (November 27, 1990):53-55

Seat Belt Use and Stress in Adolescents. Aric Schichor, Arne Beck, Bruce Bernstein, and Ben Crabtree. *Adolescence* 25, No. 100 (Winter 1990):773-779

Social Adjustment and Symptomatology in Two Types of Homeless Adolescents: Runaways and Throwaways. Sally J. Hier, Paula J. Korboot, and Robert D. Schweitzer. *Adolescence* 25, No. 100 (Winter 1990):761-771

The Teen Years: Secrets. Sandra Forsyth Enos. *Family Circle* 103, No. 13 (September 25, 1990):49-52

## Adolescents, Runaway

Patterns of Runaway Behavior within a Larger Systems Context: The Road to Empowerment. A. Therese Miller, Colleen Eggertson-Tacon, and Brian Quigg. *Adolescence* 25, No. 98 (Summer 1990):271-289

## Adolescents – Self-Concept

Body Image Satisfaction in Turkish Adolescents. Figen Çok. *Adolescence* 25, No. 98 (Summer 1990):409-413

Clothing Interests, Body Satisfaction, and Eating Behavior of Adolescent Females: Related or Independent Dimensions? Mary Ann Littrell, Mary Lynn Damhorst, and John M. Littrell. *Adolescence* 25, No. 97 (Spring 1990):77-95

Parental Separation and the Academic Self-Concepts of Adolescents: An Effort to Solve the Puzzle of Separation Effects. Thomas Ewin Smith. *Journal of Marriage and the Family* 52, No. 1 (February 1990):107-118

Self-Concept as a Factor in the Quality of Diets of Adolescent Girls. G. Kathleen Newell, Cynthia L. Hammig, Anthony P. Jurich, and Dallas E. Johnson. *Adolescence* 25, No. 97 (Spring 1990):117-130

Singapore Youth: The Impact of Social Status on Perceptions of Adolescent Problems. Richard E. Isralowitz and Ong Teck Hong. *Adolescence* 25, No. 98 (Summer 1990):357-362

The Teenage World: Adolescents' Self-Image in Ten Countries. By Daniel Offer, Eric Ostrov, Kenneth I. Howard, and Robert Atkinson. Book Review. *Adolescence* 25, No. 100 (Winter 1990):999

## Adolescents – Self-Esteem

Adolescent Stress and Self-Esteem. George A. Youngs, Jr., Richard Rathge, Ron Mullis, and Ann Mullis. *Adolescence* 25, No. 98 (Summer 1990):333-341

The Contribution of Significant Others to Adolescents' Self-Esteem. Katica Lackovic2-Grgin and Maja Dekovic2. *Adolescence* 25, No. 100 (Winter 1990):839-846

The Relationship of Career Goal And Self-Esteem among Adolescents. Lian-Hwang Chiu. *Adolescence* 25, No. 99 (Fall 1990):593-597

## Adolescents – Services

Hub Holds Out Hope to Teens. Eleanor J. Rader. *New Directions for Women* 19, No. 1 (January/February 1990):metrö+

## Adolescents – Sexual Development

Menarche: Responses of Early Adolescent Females. Arlene McGrory. *Adolescence* 25, No. 98 (Summer 1990):265-270

The Relationship between Early Development and Psychosexual Behaviors in Adolescent Females. Virginia G. Phinney, Larry Cyril Jensen, Joseph A. Olsen, and Bert Cundick. *Adolescence* 25, No. 98 (Summer 1990):321-332

## Adolescents – Sexuality

Adolescent Sexual Behavior, Pregnancy, and Parenting: Research Through the 1980s. Brent C. Miller and Kristin A. Moore. *Journal of Marriage and the Family* 52, No. 4 (November 1990):1025-1044

Adolescent Sexuality. By Jules H. Masserman and Victor M. Uribe. Book Review. *Adolescence* 25, No. 99 (Fall 1990):754

Adolescent Sexuality and Gynecology. By Donald E. Greydanus and Robert B. Shearin. Book Review. *Adolescence* 25, No. 99 (Fall 1990):753

AIDS: Late Adolescents' Knowledge and Its Influence on Sexual Behavior. Bruce Roscoe and Tammy L. Kruger. *Adolescence* 25, No. 97 (Spring 1990):39-48

Alcohol Use as a Situational Influence on Young Women's Pregnancy Risk-Taking Behaviors. Beverly Flanigan, Ann McLean, Chris Hall, and Veronica Propp. *Adolescence* 25, No. 97 (Spring 1990):205-214

Choosing Lovers. Patterns of Romance: How You Select Partners in Intimacy. By Martin Blinder and Carmen Lynch. Book Review. *Adolescence* 25, No. 98 (Summer 1990):499

Comparisons of Female and Male Early Adolescent Sex Role Attitude and Behavior Development. Christine Nelson and Joanne Keith. *Adolescence* 25, No. 97 (Spring 1990):183-204

The Development of Intimate Relationships in Late Adolescence. Elizabeth L. Paul and Kathleen M. White. *Adolescence* 25, No. 98 (Summer 1990):375-400

Early Onset of Adolescent Sexual Behavior and Drug Involvement. Emily Rosenbaum and Denise B. Kandel. *Journal of Marriage and the Family* 52, No. 3 (August 1990):783-798

Managing Risk and Experiencing Danger: Tensions Between Government AIDS Education Policy and Young Women's Sexuality. Janet Holland, Caroline Ramazanoglu and Sue Scott. *Gender and Education* 2, No. 2 (1990):125-146

Reproductive Health: The Knowledge and Attitudes and Needs of Adolescents. By S. Wright, Margaret Ryan, and Roger Golds. Reviewed by Isla Tooth. *Healthright* 9, No. 4 (August 1990):40-41

Sexual Behavior of Colombian High School Students. Bernardo Useche, Magdalena Villegas, and Heli Alzate. *Adolescence* 25, No. 98 (Summer 1990):291-304

## Adolescents – Social Networks

Analysis of a Double-Layered Support System. Rachel Seginer. *Adolescence* 25, No. 99 (Fall 1990):739-752

## Adolescents – Substance Abuse

Adolescent Substance Abuse: Practice Implications. John S. Wodarski. *Adolescence* 25, No. 99 (Fall 1990):667-688

Divorce, Remarriage, and Adolescent Substance Use: A Prospective Longitudinal Study. Richard H. Needle, S. Susan Su, and William J. Doherty. *Journal of Marriage and the Family* 52, No. 1 (February 1990):157-169

Family Structure as a Predictor of Initial Substance Use and Sexual Intercourse in Early Adolescence. Robert L. Flewelling and Karl E. Bauman. *Journal of Marriage and the Family* 52, No. 1 (February 1990):171-181

MMPI Profiles of Adolescent Substance Abusers in Treatment. Steven Walfish, Renelle Massey, and Anton Krone. *Adolescence* 25, No. 99 (Fall 1990):567-572

State-by-State Report: Laws to Stop Kids from Smoking. *Good Housekeeping* 211, No. 4 (October 1990):245-246

## Adolescents – Suicide

Crisis Intervention and Suicide Prevention: Working with Children and Adolescents. By Gary A. Crow and Letha I. Crow. Book Review. *Adolescence* 25, No. 98 (Summer 1990):499

Development of a Tool to Assess Suicide Risk Factors in Urban Adolescents. George L. White, Jr., Richard T. Murdock, Glenn E. Richardson, Gary D. Ellis, and L.J. Schmidt. *Adolescence* 25, No. 99 (Fall 1990):655-666

Ecological Correlates of Adolescent Attempted Suicide. David Lester. *Adolescence* 25, No. 98 (Summer 1990):483-485

San Diego Suicide Study: The Adolescents. Charles L. Rich, Miriam Sherman, and Richard C. Fowler. *Adolescence* 25, No. 100 (Winter 1990):855-865

Social Skills and Depression in Adolescent Suicide Attempters. Anthony Spirito, Kathleen hart, James Overholser, and Jayna Halverson. *Adolescence* 25, No. 99 (Fall 1990):543-552

A Suicidal Adolescent's Sleeping Beauty Syndrome: Cessation Orientations toward Dying, Sleep, and Drugs. Irving Babow and Robin Rowe. *Adolescence* 25, No. 100 (Winter 1990):791-798

Suicidal Tendencies and Ego Identity in Adolescence. Hanna Bar-Joseph and David Tzuriel. *Adolescence* 25, No. 97 (Spring 1990):215-223

Teenage Suicide in Zimbabwe. David Lester and C. Wilson. *Adolescence* 25, No. 100 (Winter 1990):807-809

## Adolescents as Parents

Absent Does Not Equal Uninvolved: Predictors of Fathering in Teen Mother Families. Sandra K. Danziger and Norma Radin. *Journal of Marriage and the Family* 52, No. 3 (August 1990):636-642

Adjustment of Children Born to Teenage Mothers: The Contribution of Risk and Protective Factors. Eric F. Dubow and Tom Luster. *Journal of Marriage and the Family* 52, No. 2 (May 1990):393-404

Adolescent Mothers in Later Life. By Frank F. Furstenberg, Jr., J. Brooks-Gunn, and S. Philip Morgan. Book Review. *Adolescence* 25, No. 97 (Spring 1990):250

Enhancing the Adolescent Reproductive Process: Efforts to Implement a Program for Black Adolescent Fathers. Barbara A. Sachs, Marilyn L. Poland, and Paul T. Giblin. *Health Care for Women International* 11, No. 4 (1990):447-460

Initial Parenting Attitudes of Pregnant Adolescents and a Comparison with the Decision about Adoption. Richard A. Hanson. *Adolescence* 25, No. 99 (Fall 1990):629-643

Parental Responsibility of African-American Unwed Adolescent Fathers. Kenneth Christmon. *Adolescence* 25, No. 99 (Fall 1990):645-653

Parenting Attitudes of Adolescent and Older Mothers. Marc D. Baranowski, Gary L. Schilmoeller, and Barbara S. Higgins. *Adolescence* 25, No. 100 (Winter 1990):781-790

Social Support and Gender Role Attitude among Teenage Mothers. Kris Kissman. *Adolescence* 25, No. 99 (Fall 1990):709-716

## Adolescents in Literature

Images of Adolescence in English Literature: The Middle Ages to the Modern Period. Claudio Violato and Arthur J. Wiley. *Adolescence* 25, No. 98 (Summer 1990):253-264

**Adoption.** *See also* Foster Care; Mentally Handicapped Children – Adoption; Parents of Disabled Children

Birth Bond: Reunions Between Birthparents and Adoptees: What Happens After. By Judith S. Gediman and Linda P. Brown. Reviewed by Datha Clapper Brack. *New Directions for Women* 19, No. 6 (November-December 1990):25

Boundless Love. Eileen McHenry. *Ladies' Home Journal* 107, No. 12 (December 1990):132-136+

Children of Open Adoption. By Kathleen Silber and Patricia Martinez Dorner. Reviewed by Datha Clapper Brack. *New Directions for Women* 19, No. 6 (November-December 1990):25

Family Portrait:"There's Always Room for One More." Sylvia Whitman. *Ladies' Home Journal* 107, No. 3 (March 1990):126-131

Feminist Considerations of Intercountry Adoptions. Susan E. Barrett and Carol M. Aubin. *Women and Therapy* 10, Nos. 1/2 (1990):127-138

Giving Up a Baby. Amy Engeler. *Glamour* (June 1990):252-255+

The Little Boy Nobody Wanted. Patrick T. Murphy. *Good Housekeeping* 211, No. 4 (October 1990):135+

Motherhood, Ideology, and the Power to Technology: In Vitro Fertilization Use by Adoptive Mothers. Linda S. Williams. *Women's Studies International Forum* 13, No. 6 (1990):543-552

Parenting: An Advocate for Adoption. Bibliography. Joy Duckett Cain. *Essence* 21, No. 7 (November 1990):110

Rescued by Love. Barbara Raymond. *Redbook* 176, No. 2 (December 1990):116-118+

A Tale of Two Mothers. Deborah Beroset Diamond. *Ladies' Home Journal* 107, No. 7 (July 1990):83-85+

"We are So Lucky to Have Him." Catherine Breslin. *Ladies' Home Journal* 107, No. 12 (December 1990):136+

**Adoption – Personal Narratives**

After 20 Years, I Met the Daughter I Thought Was Dead. Joan Gage. *Good Housekeeping* 210, No. 4 (April 1990):102-109

**Adult Children**

How to Have a More Loving Relationship with Your Mom. Victoria Secunda. *Redbook* 175, No. 1 (May 1990):138-139+

Private Lives: You and Your Mom. Kathleen McCoy. *Family Circle* 103, No. 17 (December 18, 1990):74-81

**Adult Children of Alcoholics**

Recovering from Recovery. Mary McNamara. *Glamour* (November 1990):176

**Adult Children of Dysfunctional Families**

Dilemmas and Demands: Working with Adult Survivors of Sexual Abuse. Ferol E. Mennen. *AFFILIA* 5, No. 4 (Winter 1990):72-86

**Adult Development**

New Signs of Adulthood. *Glamour* (November 1990):163-164

**Adult Education.** *See also* Illiteracy

Nigerian Women's Quest for Role Fulfillment. Judith D.C. Osuala. *Women and Therapy* 10, No. 3 (1990):89-98

**Adultery.** *See* Extramarital Affairs

**Adult Students**

Surviving the Cut. Ellen Wulfhorst. *Savvy Woman* (September 1990):33-37

**Adventurers**

Pleasure Plus: The New Way to Travel. Gary Belsky. *Working Woman* (June 1990):44-46

On Riding the Edges. Ralph Blum. *Lear's* (March 1990):138-143

**Advertising.** *See also* McNamee, Louise (about); Moore, Mary (about); Radio Broadcasting – Commercials

Calling a Shade a Shade. Amy Engeler. *Savvy Woman* (November 1990):44

Catch of the Season. Alison Simko. *Savvy Woman* (November 1990):56

The People Picker. Erik Hedegaard. *Savvy Woman* (November 1990):14

Satisfaction Guaranteed: The Making of the American Mass Market. By Susan Strasser. Reviewed by Lois R. Helmbold. *The Women's Review of Books* 7, No. 8 (May 1990):12-13

Women in Advertising. Bibliography. Nanine Alexander. *Essence* 20, No. 9 (January 1990):35-40

The Yellow Pages Pitch. Jeffrey P. Davidson. *Executive Female* 13, No. 6 (November-December 1990):18

**Advertising, Direct-Mail**

Circle This. Margaret Jaworski. *Family Circle* 103, No. 14 (October 16, 1990):11-14

**Advertising – Images of Women**

An Analysis of the Mythical Function of Reproductive Advertisements. Dawn Eden, Joe Ayres, and Tim Hopf. *Women's Studies in Communication* 12, No. 2 (Fall 1989):77-90

Are They Selling Her Lips: Advertising and Identity. By Carol Moog. Reviewed by Noreen Ash Mackay. *On the Issues* 17 (Winter 1990):

Images of Women in Ads Improve Little between 1973 and 1986. *Media Report to Women* 18, No. 2 (March/April 1990):5

Never Underestimate the Power of a Woman. Myrna Blyth. *Ladies' Home Journal* 107, No. 11 (November 1990):16-25

Undeniably Billy. Elsie B. Washington. *Essence* 20, No. 12 (April 1990):14-15

**Advertising, Personal**

Mate Selection Patterns of Men and Women in Personal Advertisements: New Bottle, Old Wine. Aysan Sev'er. *Atlantis* 15, No. 2 (Spring 1990):70-76

**Advertising – Psychological Aspects**

The Secret Life of the Female Consumer. Bernice Kanner. *Working Woman* (December 1990):68-71

**Advertising – Sexism**

Steinem to Detail *Ms.* Advertiser Pressure in Re-Launch Issue in June. *Media Report to Women* 18, No. 3 (May/June 1990):1

**Advertising – Sexual Content**

No End to Use of Sex in Ads as Long as Products Sell. *Media Report to Women* 18, No. 2 (March/April 1990):5-6

Surge in Complaints about Sex in Ads. *Spare Rib* 217 (October 1990):48

**Advertising Agencies**

The World's Hippest Office. Julia Claiborne Johnson. *Mademoiselle* (May 1990):210-213, 232

**Advertising Industry**

Selling the Mechanized Household: 70 Years of Ads in *Ladies Home Journal*. Bonnie J. Fox. *Gender and Society* 4, No. 1 (March 1990):25-40

Women Changing Ad Business, Says UNC Advertising. *Media Report to Women* 18, No. 1 (January/February 1990):8

**Advertising Industry – Gender Discrimination**

British Survey Shows Advertising Women Not in Top Jobs. *Media Report to Women* 18, No. 2 (March/April 1990):6-7

Sex, Lies and Advertising. Globia Steinem. *Ms.* 1, No. 1 (July/August 1990):18-28

**Advice Columns**

Mr. Manners. Stephen Rae. *Harper's Bazaar* (February 1990):76

**Aebi, Tania**

Go Away, Little Girl. *Mademoiselle* (April 1990):227, 262

**Aerobic Exercise**

Getting in Step. Len Kravitz. *Women's Sports and Fitness* 12, No. 3 (April 1990):18

Health & Fitness. Stephanie Young. *Glamour* (June 1990):47-48+

A Legend's Views and New Tapes to Use. Jacki Sorenson. *Women's Sports and Fitness* 12, No. 2 (March 1990):20-21

Living Well. *Women's Sports & Fitness* 12, No. 6 (September 1990):12-14

Pack a Punch. Therese Iknoian. *Women's Sports and Fitness* 12, No. 7 (October 1990):18

Tunes to Tone By. Diane French. *Women's Sports and Fitness* 12, No. 7 (October 1990):16

**Aesthetics.** *See also* Art

Aestheticism, Feminism, and the Dynamics of Reversal. Amy Newman. *Hypatia* 5, No. 2 (Summer 1990):20-32

Beyond Feminist Aesthetics: Feminist Literature and Social Change. By Rita Felski. Reviewed by Jane Kneller. *Hypatia* 5, No. 3 (Fall 1990):165-168

Feminine Perspectives and Narrative Points of View. Ismay Barwell. *Hypatia* 5, No. 2 (Summer 1990):63-75

Feminist Film Aesthetics: A Contextual Approach. Laurie Shrage. *Hypatia* 5, No. 2 (Summer 1990):137-148

Gender and Genius: Towards a Feminist Aesthetic. By Christine Battersby. Reviewed by Margaret Beetham. *Gender and Education* 2, No. 2 (1990):259-261

A Gynecentric Aesthetic. Renée Cox. *Hypatia* 5, No. 2 (Summer 1990):43-62

Introduction. Hilde Hein and Carolyn Korsmeyer. *Hypatia* 5, No. 2 (Summer 1990):1-6

Is There a Feminist Aesthetic? Marilyn French. *Hypatia* 5, No. 2 (Summer 1990):33-42

Re-enfranchising Art: Feminist Interventions in the Theory of Art. Estella Lauter. *Hypatia* 5, No. 2 (Summer 1990):91-106

Towards a Lesbian Aesthetic. Jorjet Harper. *Hot Wire* 6, No. 1 (January 1990):14-15+

**Afek, Dina**

Sarah and the Women's Movement: The Experience of Infertility. *Women and Therapy* 10, Nos. 1/2 (1990):195-203

**Affairs.** *See* Extramarital Affairs

**AFFILIA – Conferences**

On the Lookout: A Model Project in Support of AFFILIA. Audrey Faulkner. *AFFILIA* 5, No. 3 (Fall 1990):101-104

**Affirmative Action**

Affirmative Action in Perspective. By F.A. Blanchard and F.J. Crosby. Reviewed by Arnold S. Kahn. *Psychology of Women Quarterly* 14, No. 1 (March 1990):145-147

Working: What Have They Done for Us Lately? Linda Villarosa. *Essence* 21, No. 1 (May 1990):66-71

**Affonso, Dyanne D.** and Mayberry, Linda J.

Common Stressors Reported by a Group of Childbearing American Women. *Health Care for Women International* 11, No. 3 (1990):331-345

**Afkhami, Mahnaz**

Iran: Exiles in Their Own Land. *Ms.* 1, No. 2 (September/October 1990):10

**Africa**

Africa on My Mind: Gender, Counter Discourse and African-American Nationalism. E. Frances White. *Journal of Women's History* 2, No. 1 (Spring 1990):73-97

Elizabeth of Toro: The Odyssey of an African Princess. By Elizabeth Nyabongo. Reviewed by Carole Boyce Davies. *Belles Lettres* 5, No. 3 (Spring 1990):13

Maasai Days. By Cheryl Bentsen. Reviewed by Jill Fritz-Piggott. *The Women's Review of Books* 7, No. 4 (January 1990):17

In the Shadow of the Sacred Grove. By Carol Spindel. Reviewed by Jill Fritz-Piggott. *The*

*Women's Review of Books* 7, No. 4 (January 1990):17

Whose Goddesses Are They? Christina Springer. *New Directions for Women* 19, No. 4 (July-August 1990):4

**Africa – Art**

A Window on Walls. Photo essay. Margaret Courtney-Clarke. *Ms.* 1, No. 3 (November/December 1990):46-51

**Africa – Bibliographies**

*Journal of Women's History* 2, No. 2 (Fall 1990):185-190

**Africa – Craft Arts.** *See* Craft Arts – Africa

**Africa – Culture**

Contemporary Living: Afrocentricity. *Essence* 21, No. 8 (December 1990):83

Iron Pots and Wooden Spoons. Excerpt. Jessica Harris. *Essence* 21, No. 6 (October 1990):101-104

Parenting: The Harvest of Kwanzaa. Dee Watts-Jones. *Essence* 21, No. 8 (December 1990):114

The Power of Culture: A Review of the Idea of Africa's Influence on Family Structure in Antebellum America. Antonio McDaniel. *Journal of Family History* 15, No. 2 (April 1990):225-238

Reclaiming Our Culture. Rosemary Bray. *Essence* 21, No. 8 (December 1990):84-86+

**Africa – Economic Assistance**

Back Talk: Lobby for Aid to Africa. Frank Dexter Brown. *Essence* 21, No. 5 (September 1990):142

**Africa – Family Life**

Changing Family Life in East Africa: Women and Children at Risk. By Philip Leroy Kilbride and Janet Capriotti Kilbride. Reviewed by Agnes Riedmann. *Journal of Marriage and the Family* 52, No. 4 (November 1990):1155

**Africa – Feminism**

African Feminism(s) and the Question of Marital and Non-Marital Loneliness and Intimacy. E. Imafedia Okhamafe. *Sage* 6, No. 1 (Summer 1989):33-39

**Africa – History**

African-American Women Missionaries and European Imperialism in Southern Africa, 1880-1920. Sylvia M. Jacobs. *Women's Studies International Forum* 13, No. 4 (1990):381-394

Domesticity and Colonialism in Belgian Africa: Usumbura's *Foyer Social*, 1946-1960. Notes. Nancy Rose Hunt. *Signs* 15, No. 3 (Spring 1990):447-474

"Single Ladies on the Congo": Protestant Missionary Tensions and Voices. Nancy Rose Hunt. *Women's Studies International Forum* 13, No. 4 (1990):395-403

**Africa – Housing**

Women and Housing in Sub-Saharan Africa. Diana Lee-Smith. *Canadian Women's Studies* 11, No. 2 (Fall 1990):68-70

**Africa – Mental Health**

Gender and Mental Health in Africa. Mere Kakateregga Kisekka. *Women and Therapy* 10, No. 3 (1990):1-13

Mental Health Aspects of Zar for Women in Sudan. Edith H. Grotberg. *Women and Therapy* 10, No. 3 (1990):15-24

**Africa – Status of Women**

Demographic Surveys and Nigerian Women. Notes. Barbara Entwisle and Catherine M. Coles. *Signs* 15, No. 2 (Winter 1990):259-284

Women and the State in Africa. Edited by Jane L. Parpart and Kathleen A. Staudt. Reviewed by Barbara Lewis. *Women & Politics* 10, No. 1 (1990):82-84

Women's Research and Documentation Project. *Women's World* 23 (April 1990):38

**Africa – Travel.** *See also* Senegal – Description and Travel

**African-American Families**

Black Family Studies in the *Journal of Marriage and the Family* and the Issue of Distortion: A Trend Analysis. Vasilikie Demos. *Journal of Marriage and the Family* 52, No. 3 (August 1990):603-612

Black Women and Feminism. Clyde Wilcox. *Women & Politics* 10, No. 3 (1990):65-84

Captain of the Ship. James Clayton. *Essence* 21, No. 2 (June 1990):36

Contemporary Living: Families. Bibliography. *Essence* 21, No. 4 (August 1990):75-84

Developments in Research on Black Families: A Decade Review. Robert Joseph Taylor, Linda M. Chatters, M. Belinda Tucker, and Edith Lewis. *Journal of Marriage and the Family* 52, No. 4 (November 1990):993-1014

Interiors: Mama's Legacy. Billie Jean Young. *Essence* 21, No. 8 (December 1990):28

Need for Support and Family Involvement Among Black Americans. Robert Joseph Taylor. *Journal of Marriage and the Family* 52, No. 3 (August 1990):584-590

A Very Special Gift. Marilyn Milloy. *Essence* 21, No. 8 (December 1990):62-64+

What Has Gone Before: The Legacy of Racism and Sexism in the Lives of Black Mothers and Daughters. Beverly A. Greene. *Women and Therapy* 9, Nos. 1-2 (1990):207-230

**African-American Families – Parenting**

Sturdy Bridges: The Role of African-American Mothers in the Socialization of African-American

Children. Beverly Greene. *Women and Therapy* 10, Nos. 1/2 (1990):205-225

**African-American History.** *See* African-American Women – History; Black History

**African-American Literature**

Inspiriting Influences: Tradition, Revision, and Afro-American Women's Novels. By Michael Awkward. Reviewed by Claudia Tate. *Tulsa Studies in Women's Literature* 9, No. 2 (Fall 1990):317-321

**African-American Literature – Study and Teaching**

A Meeting of Minds and Cultures: Teaching Black Women's Literature in the Canary Islands. Justine Tally and others. *Sage* 6, No. 1 (Summer 1989):63-65

Strategies for Teaching Black Women's Literature in a White Cultural Context. Valerie Lee. *Sage* 6, No. 1 (Summer 1989):74-76

**African-American Men**

Black Men: Single, Obsolete, and Dangerous? By Haki Madhubuti. Reviewed by Maceo Crenshaw Dailey, Jr. *Sage* 6, No. 2 (Fall 1989):66-67

**African-Americans – Homosexuality**

Talking about It: Homophobia in the Black Community. Jewelle Gomez and Barbara Smith. *Feminist Review* No. 34 (Spring 1990):46-55

**African-Americans – Self-Concept**

Family Ties, Friendships, and Subjective Well-being Among Black Americans. Christopher, G. Ellison. *Journal of Marriage and the Family* 52, No. 2 (May 1990):298-310

**African-American Students**

On Being an American Black Student. Clarissa Sligh. *Heresies* 25 (1990):29-33

**African-American Women.** *See also* Black Women's Studies; Women of Color

. . . But Some of Us Are (Still) Brave. Yolanda Moses. *The Women's Review of Books* 7, No. 5 (February 1990):31-32

A Black Woman in Rural Japan. Viki Radden. *Sage* 6, No. 1 (Summer 1989):52-53

Black Women and Inventions. Patricia Carter Sluby. *Sage* 6, No. 2 (Fall 1989):33-35

Black Women as Do-ers: The Social Responsibility of Black Women. Joyce A. Ladner. *Sage* 6, No. 1 (Summer 1989):87-88

Forum: "What if We Made Racism a Woman's Issue..." Johnnetta B. Cole. *McCall's* 118, No. 1 (October 1990):39-40

"I Dream a World." Eleanor J. Bader and Brian Lanker. *On the Issues* 14 (1990):16-20

In Our Own Words. Ruby Sales. *The Women's Review of Books* 7, No. 5 (February 1990):24-25

And Still We Rise: African American Women and the U.S. Labor Market. Monica L. Jackson. *Feminist Issues* 10, No. 2 (Fall 1990):55-64

**African-American Women – Career Opportunities**

Black Women Engineers and Technologists. Valerie Thomas. *Sage* 6, No. 2 (Fall 1989):24-32

Black Women in Science and Technology: A Selected Bibliography. Ronald Mickens. *Sage* 6, No. 2 (Fall 1989):54

Black Women in the Biological Sciences. Rosalyn Patterson. *Sage* 6, No. 2 (Fall 1989):8-14

Black Women Mathematicians: In Short Supply. Sylvia Bozeman. *Sage* 6, No. 2 (Fall 1989):18-23

Increasing the Participation of Black Women in Science and Technology. Shirley Malcom. *Sage* 6, No. 2 (Fall 1989):15-17

**African-American Women – Economic Status**

Poverty Among Black Elderly Women. Vanessa Wilson-Ford. *Journal of Women and Aging* 2, No. 4 (1990):5-20

**African-American Women – Education**

Black Women's Literary Scholarship: Reclaiming an Intellectual Tradition. Nellie Y. McKay. *Sage* 6, No. 1 (Summer 1989):89-91

Cross-Cultural Perspectives on Women in Higher Education. Beverly Lindsay. *Sage* 6, No. 1 (Summer 1989):92-96

**African-American Women – Feminism**

Audre Lorde: Vignettes and Mental Conversations. Gail Lewis. *Feminist Review* No. 34 (Spring 1990):100-114

Black Women and Feminism. Clyde Wilcox. *Women & Politics* 10, No. 3 (1990):65-84

The Combahee River Collective Statement: Black Feminist Organizing in the Seventies and Eighties. By the Combahee River Collective. Reviewed by Jacqueline E. Wade. *NWSA Journal* 2, No. 2 (Spring 1990):315-319

I Am Your Sister: Black Women Organizing across Sexualities. By Audre Lorde. Reviewed by Jacqueline E. Wade. *NWSA Journal* 2, No. 2 (Spring 1990):315-319

Talking Back: Thinking Feminist, Thinking Black. By Bell Hooks. Reviewed by Nancie E. Caraway. *Sage* 6, No. 2 (Fall 1989):58-59

**African-American Women – Health Care**

Back Talk: Donor Organs: A Crisis. Sharon Jefferson. *Essence* 21, No. 6 (October 1990):146

The Black Women's Health Book. Edited by Evelyn C. White. Reviewed by Beverly Guy-Sheftall. *Ms.* 1, No. 1 (July/August 1990):68-69

The Black Women's Health Book: Speaking for Ourselves. Edited by Evelyn C. White. Reviewed by

C. J. Walker. *New Directions for Women* 19, No. 6 (November-December 1990):20

The Black Women's Health Book: Speaking for Ourselves. Edited by Evelyn C. White. Reviewed by Evelynn Hammonds. *The Women's Review of Books* 7, No. 9 (June 1990):1-4

Breathing Life into Ourselves: The Evolution of the National Black Women's Health Project. Byllye Y. Avery. *Woman of Power* 18 (Fall 1990):22-25

The Heart of the Matter. Susan Festa. *Essence* 21, No. 6 (October 1990):25-28

I Know I Am Important, Because I Feel It. M. Stephanie Ricks. *Belles Lettres* 5, No. 4 (Summer 1990):27-28

Sick and Tired of Being Sick and Tired: The Politics of Black Women's Health. Angela Y. Davis. *Woman of Power* 18 (Fall 1990):26-29

**African-American Women – History**

Afro-American Women of the South and the Advancement of the Race, 1895-1925. By Cynthia Neverdon-Morton. Reviewed by Wilma Peebles-Wilkins. *AFFILIA* 5, No. 1 (Spring 1990):108-110

American Autobiographies. Nancy Grey Osterud. *Gender & History* 2, No. 1 (Spring 1990):83-87

Exploding the Myth of African-American Progress. Notes. James A. Geschwender and Rita Carroll-Seguin. *Signs* 15, No. 2 (Winter 1990):285-299

For the Good of Family and Race: Gender, Work, and Domestic Roles in the Black Community, 1880-1930. Notes. Sharon Harley. *Signs* 15, No. 2 (Winter 1990):336-349

Invented Lives: Narratives of Black Women 1860-1960. By Mary Helen Washington. Reviewed by Ann Phoenix. *Gender and Education* 2, No. 2 (1990):252-254

Property-Owning Free African-American Women in the South, 1800-70. Loren Schweninger. *Journal of Women's History* 1, No. 3 (Winter 1990):13-44

Roger Arliner Young. Kenneth Manning. *Sage* 6, No. 2 (Fall 1989):3-7

Sojourner Truth in Life and Memory: Writing the Biography of an American Exotic. Nell Irvin Painter. *Gender & History* 2, No. 1 (Spring 1990):3-16

From Three-Fifths to Zero: Implications of the Constitution for African-American Women, 1787-1870. Mamie E. Locke. *Women & Politics* 10, No. 2 (1990):33-46

Two Outstanding Women in Social Welfare History: Mary Church Terrell and Ida B. Wells-Barnett. Wilma Peebles-Wilkins and E. Aracelis Francis. *AFFILIA* 5, No. 4 (Winter 1990):87-100

"Us Colored Women Had to Go Through A Plenty": Sexual Exploitation of African-American Slave Women. Thelma Jennings. *Journal of Women's History* 1, No. 3 (Winter 1990):45-74

**African-American Women – History – Sources**

Women of Color and the Core Curriculum: Tools for Transforming the Liberal Arts, Part 3. Susan E. Searing. *Feminist Collections* 11, No. 4 (Summer 1990):11-16

**African-American Women – Leadership.** *See also* Jordon, June (about); Leadership

Legends in Our Time: Clap Your Hands. Alexis De Veaux, Marilyn Milloy and Michael Erik Ross. *Essence* 21, No. 1 (May 1990):101-122

**African-American Women – Lesbianism**

Racism: Lesbian Artists Have Their Say. *Out/Look* No. 8 (Spring 1990):38-43

Taking the Home Out of Homophobia: Black Lesbians Look in Their Own Backyards. Jewelle L. Gomez and Barbara Smith. *Out/Look* No. 8 (Spring 1990):32-37

What It Means to Be Colored Me. Jackie Goldsby. *Out/Look* No. 9 (Summer 1990):8-17

**African-American Women – Media Portrayal**

TV Portrayal of the Childless Black Female: Superficial, Unskilled, Dependent. *Media Report to Women* 18, No. 2 (March/April 1990):4

**African-American Women – Military**

Black, Female and in Uniform: An African-American Woman in the United States Army, 1973-1979. Brenda L. Moore. *Minerva* 8, No. 2 (Summer 1990):62-66

The Southern Side of "Glory": Mississippi African-American Women During the Civil War. Noralee Frankel. *Minerva* 8, No. 3 (Fall 1990):28-36

**African-American Women – Photographs**

"Tempered in the Fire of Experience." *New Directions for Women* 19, No. 1 (January/February 1990):14-15

**African-American Women – Psychology**

Back Talk: The Struggle Is Ours. Joan L. Morgan. *Essence* 21, No. 1 (May 1990):216

"I Made the Ink": (Literary) Production and Reproduction in *Dessa Rose* and *Beloved*. Anne E. Goldman. *Feminist Studies* 16, No. 2 (Summer 1990):313-330

Teaching and Learning about Black Women: The Anatomy of a Course. Barbara J. Haile and Audreye E. Johnson. *Sage* 6, No. 1 (Summer 1989):69-72

Toward a Stress Scale for African-American Women. Danielle Watts-Jones. *Psychology of Women Quarterly* 14, No. 2 (June 1990):271-275

**African-American Women – Religion**

White Women's Christ and Black Women's Jesus: Feminist Christology and Womanist Response. By Jacquelyn Grant. Reviewed by Paula Giddings. *Essence* 21, No. 6 (October 1990):52

## African-American Writers

Afro-American Women Writers, 1746-1933: An Anthology and Critical Guide. Edited by Ann Allen Shockley. Reviewed by Claudia Tate. *Tulsa Studies in Women's Literature* 9, No. 2 (Fall 1990):317-321

Their Place on the Stage: Black Women Playwrights in America. By Elizabeth Brown-Guillory. Reviewed by Leslie Sanders. *Canadian Women's Studies* 11, No. 1 (Spring 1990):108-109

## African-American Writers – Literary Tradition

Black Women's Literary Scholarship: Reclaiming an Intellectual Tradition. Nellie Y. McKay. *Sage* 6, No. 1 (Summer 1989):89-91

Mother of Mind. Elsa Barkley Brown. *Sage* 6, No. 1 (Summer 1989):4-10

**African Diaspora.** *See* Pan-Africanism

## Africans – Great Britain

The Family. By Buchi Emecheta. Reviewed by Elsie B. Washington. *Essence* 21, No. 4 (August 1990):50

**Afrocentricity.** *See* Africa – Culture

**After-School Jobs.** *See* Child Labor

## After-School Programs

The Early Years: After-School Orphans. T. Berry Brazelton. *Family Circle* 103, No. 14 (October 16, 1990):52-56

## Age and Employment

A Causal Analysis of Employment and Health in Midlife Women. Pamela K. Adelmann, Toni C. Antonucci, Susan E. Crohan, and Lerita M. Coleman. *Women and Health* 16, No. 1 (1990):5-20

**Ageism.** *See* Older Adults – Discrimination

## Agent Orange

Dioxin Levels in Adipose Tissues of Hospitalized Women Living in the South of Vietnam in 1984-89 with a Brief Review of Their Clinical Histories. Nguyen Thi Ngoc Phuong, Bui Sy Hung, Arnold Schecter, and Dan Quoc Vu. *Women and Health* 16, No. 1 (1990):79-93

## Aggleton, Peggy

Homosexuality and Education. Book Review. *Gender and Education* 2, No. 2 (1990):247-249

## Aggression – Adolescents

A Cognitive/Affective Empathy Training Program as a Function of Ego Development in Aggressive Adolescent Females. Edward V. Pecukonis. *Adolescence* 25, No. 97 (Spring 1990):59-76

**Aghadashloo, Shoreh.** *See* Azadeh, "Iranian Women Filmmakers"

**Aging.** *See also* Older Adults

Breaking the Age Barrier: It's Within Your Power. Sharon Begley. *Family Circle* 103, No. 14 (October 16, 1990):112+

Breaking the Age Barrier: The Lifestyle Connection. *Family Circle* 103, No. 14 (October 16, 1990):115-117

Contraception for Women Over 35. John Guillebaud. *Healthright* 9, No. 4 (August 1990):17-21

Eat Well. Carol Ann Rinzler. *Family Circle* 103, No. 8 (June 5, 1990):40+

Life Trek: The Odyssey of Adult Development. By Robert Stockmyer and Robert Williams. Reviewed by Violet Franks. *Journal of Women and Aging* 2 No. 3 (1990):117-118

Making Better Bodies. Cheryl Solimini. *Family Circle* 103, No. 14 (October 16, 1990):113-114

A Multidisciplinary Facts on Women's Aging Quiz to Enhance Awareness. Helen Rippier Wheeler. *Journal of Women and Aging* 2, No. 4 (1990):91-107

Passages: Aging Lesbians Meet. Carol Anne Douglas. *off our backs* 20, No. 5 (May 1990):8

Playing with Time. Rita Baron-Faust. *Harper's Bazaar* (August 1990):46+

Self-Assessment and Change in One's Profession: Notes on the Phenomenology of Aging Among Mid-Life Women. Virginia Olesen. *Journal of Women and Aging* 2, No. 4 (1990):69-79

The Wisdom of Menopause. Janine O'Leary Cobb. *Healthsharing* 11, No. 4 (December 1990):8-12

Women and Elderly Parents: Moral Controversy in an Aging Society. Stephen G. Post. *Hypatia* 5, No. 1 (Spring 1990):83-89

You Can Reverse Aging: How Anti-Aging Clinics Turn Back the Clock. Anne Cassidy. *Family Circle* 103, No. 14 (October 16, 1990):118-122

## Aging – Periodicals

Journal of Women and Aging. Reviewed by Zella Luria. *Psychology of Women Quarterly* 14, No. 4 (December 1990):617

## Aging – Personal Narratives

Beauty & Fashion Journal. *Ladies' Home Journal* 107, No. 6 (June 1990):31-36

Being Old: Seven Women, Seven Views. Noreen Hale. *Journal of Women and Aging* 2, No. 2 (1990):7-17

The Crisis of Legacy: Life Review Interviews with Elderly Women Religious. Mary Alice Wolf. *Journal of Women and Aging* 2 No. 3 (1990):67-79

Editorial: Roots of Heaven. Frances Lear. *Lear's* (August 1990):136

Love and Work After 60: An Integration of Personal and Professional Growth Within a Long-Term Marriage. Rachel Josefowitz Siegel. *Journal of Women and Aging* 2, No. 2 (1990):69-79

Reflections of Midlife Lesbians on Their Adolescence. Barbara E. Sang. *Journal of Women and Aging* 2, No. 2 (1990):111-117

**Aging – Psychological Aspects.** *See also* Beauty Standards; Health Education

About Face: Beyond Cosmetic Surgery. Elena Oumano. *Lear's* (July 1990):35-36

Body Management: Your Future Face: A Four-Decade Forecast. Ann Goldberg. *Working Woman* (May 1990):111-114

Forty Fine. Alexis DeVeaux. *Essence* 20, No. 9 (January 1990):50-52 +

Guessing Your Age. Tracy Young. *Vogue* (July 1990):224

Our Families, Ourselves. John Bradshaw. *Lear's* (April 1990):55-56

Surgery Stars. Lorraine Daigneault. *Harper's Bazaar* (August 1990):128-129+

Visiting Space: Autumnal Face. Margaret Morganroth Gullette. *Lear's* (January 1990):136+

Women As They Age: Challenge, Opportunity, and Triumph. Edited by J. Dianne Garner and Susan O. Mercer. Reviewed by Judith G. Gonyea. *AFFILIA* 5, No. 4 (Winter 1990):116-117

Youth – Or Consequences? The Truth About the New Aging Antidotes. Laura Flynn McCarthy. *Working Woman* (May 1990):116-118

**Agins, Teri**

Beauty: Business Scents. *Essence* 20, No. 11 (March 1990):20-23

**Agnelli, Gianni** (about). *See also* Sexual Attraction, "200 Words"

**Agoraphobia**

Prisoners at Home. John E. Frook. *Family Circle* 103, No. 2 (February 1, 1990):60-62

**Agosín, Marjorie**

Chile: Since the Plebiscite. *Ms.* 1, No. 3 (November/December 1990):12

Poems. *Lilith* 15, No. 3 (Summer 1990):13-14

Teresa Wilms Montt: A Forgotten Legend. *Women's Studies International Forum* 13, No. 3 (1990):195-199

Zones of Pain/Las Zonas del Dolor. Reviewed by Zoë Anglesey. *Belles Lettres* 5, No. 2 (Winter 1990):17

**Agosín, Marjorie** (about)

Marjorie Agosin: A Woman, a Jew and a Chilean. Susan Schnur. *Lilith* 15, No. 3 (Summer 1990):12

**Agosín, Marjorie** (editor)

Landscapes of a New Land: Short Fiction by Latin American Women. Reviewed by Bessy Reyna. *New Directions for Women* 19, No. 5 (September-October 1990):15

**Agrawal, Abha** (joint author). *See* Singh, Padam

**Agriculture**

Agriculture, Women and Land: The African Experience. Edited by Jean Davison. Reviewed by E. A. Cebotarev. *Resources for Feminist Research* 19, No. 1 (March 1990):3-4

The Myth of the Miracle Seeds. Vandana Shiva. *Women in Action* 1-2 (1990):11-12

**Agriculture and Fertility**

Agricultural Modernization, Its Associated Factors and Fertility Behaviour. P. V. Murthy. *Journal of Family Welfare* 36, No. 4 (December 1990):61-66

**Aharoni, Ada** and Wolf, Thea

Night of the Staircase. *Lilith* 15, No. 4 (Fall 1990):7-9

**Ahern, Maureen** (editor)

A Rosario Castellanos Reader: An Anthology of Her Poetry, Short Fiction, Essays, and Drama. Reviewed by Mercedes Tasende-Grabowski. *Frontiers* 11, No. 1 (1990):88-89

**Ahmad, Rukhsana**

Benazir Bhutto Defeated at the Polls. *Spare Rib* 218 (November 1990):45

to Do Something Beautiful: Interview with Rohini Hensman. *Spare Rib* 213 (June 1990):6-8

The Handmaid's Tale. Film Review. *Spare Rib* 218 (November 1990):19

Pakistan: A Constitutional Coup. *Spare Rib* No. 216 (September 1990):20-23

Song for a Sanctuary. Play. Reviewed by Daljit Kaur. *Spare Rib* No. 209 (February 1990):33

Stolen. Television Series Review. *Spare Rib* No. 209 (February 1990):34

**Ahmed, Bashir**

Determinants of Desired Family Size in Rural Bangladesh: A Two-Stage Analysis. *Journal of Family Welfare* 36, No. 1 (March 1990):22-31

**Ahmedabad Women's Action Group.** *See* India – Violence Against Women

**Ahna, Barbara**

Soviet Sisters. *The Women's Review of Books* 7, Nos. 10-11 (July 1990):33-34

A Week Like Any Other. Book Review. *The Women's Review of Books* 7, Nos. 10-11 (July 1990):33-34

**Ahrens, Lynn** and Flaherty, Stephen

Vogue Arts: Once On This Island. Reviewed by Alex Witchel. *Vogue* (September 1990):428-434

**Ahrentzen, Sherry** (joint editor). *See* Franck, Karen A.

**Ahsan, Ekramul** (joint author). *See* Wallace, Ben J.

**Ahsan, Rosie Mujid** (joint author). *See* Wallace, Ben J.

**AIDS.** *See* Acquired Immune Deficiency Syndrome

**AIDS Coalition to Unleash Power.** *See* Acquired Immune Deficiency Syndrome – ACT-UP

**Aid to Africa.** *See* Africa – Economic Assistance

**Aid to Families with Dependent Children**

Welfare and Out-of-Wedlock Childbearing: Evidence from the 1980s. Robert D. Plotnick. *Journal of Marriage and the Family* 52, No. 3 (August 1990):735-746

**Aiken, Susan Hardy**

Changing Our Minds: Feminist Transformations of Knowledge. Reviewed by Elizabeth Higginbotham. *NWSA Journal* 2, No. 1 (Winter 1990):105-111

Half Savage and Hardy and Free: Women and Rural Radicalism in the Nineteenth-Century Novel. Book Review. *Signs* 16, No. 1 (Autumn 1990):188-192

In Other Worlds: Essays in Cultural Politics. Book Review. *NWSA Journal* 2, No. 1 (Winter 1990):145-147

Uneven Developments: The Ideological Work of Gender in Mid-Victorian England. Book Review. *Signs* 16, No. 1 (Autumn 1990):188-192

Woman to Woman: Female Friendship in Victorian Fiction. Book Review. *Signs* 16, No. 1 (Autumn 1990):188-192

**Aiken, Susan Hardy** and others (editors)

Changing Our Minds: Feminist Transformations of Knowledge. Reviewed by Margot I. Duley. *Signs* 15, No. 3 (Spring 1990):648-650

**Ailes, Roger** and Kraushar, Jon

Public-Speaking Survival Strategies: How to Make an Audience Love You. *Working Woman* (November 1990):118-119+

**Airlines – Food Service.** *See* Air Travel

**Air Pollution – Indoors**

Is Your Office Making You Sick? Charles Piller and Michael Castleman. *Redbook* 174, No. 6 (April 1990):114-115+

Is Your Office Making You Sick? Patricia Canole. *Executive Female* (May/June 1990):32-33+

My Healthy Home. Carolyn B. Noyes. *Ladies' Home Journal* 107, No. 1 (January 1990):110-118

**Air Travel**

Now, Now, Voyager: A Traveler's Lament. Peter Feibleman. *Lear's* (June 1990):24-26

Secret of the Airlines. Edward Jay Epstein. *Lear's* (February 1990):26-30

**Air Travel – Frequent Flyer Program**

Of Limos and Lonely Dinners. Suzanne Weber. *Executive Female* (May/June 1990):38-39

**Air Travel – Health Aspects**

Image: The Business Traveler's Beauty Advisory. Nina Malkin. *Working Woman* (March 1990):122-124

Radiation Alert: Will Flying Give You Cancer? *Glamour* (May 1990):196

**Aisenberg, Nadya** and Harrington, Mona

Women of Academe: Outsiders in the Sacred Grove. Reviewed by Joan C. Chrisler. *Feminist Teacher* 5, No. 2 (Fall 1990):37

Women of Academe: Outsiders in the Sacred Grove. Reviewed by Linda McKie. *Gender and Education* 2, No. 2 (1990):257-258

Women of Academe: Outsiders in the Sacred Grove. Reviewed by Therese L. Baker. *Gender and Society* 4, No. 2 (June 1990):277-281

**Akers, Karen** (about)

Encore! David Hinckley. *Lear's* (August 1990):70-71+

**Akers, Regina T.**

Female Naval Reservists During World War II: A Historiographical Essay. *Minerva* 8, No. 2 (Summer 1990):55-61

**Akiwumi, Viki**

Ancient Rite. Poem. *Essence* 20, No. 11 (March 1990):125

**Alai, Susan**

Ask the Dentist: Smart Helps to a Healthy Smile. *Family Circle* 103, No. 16 (November 27, 1990):144

Serious Headaches. *Family Circle* 103, No. 15 (November 6, 1990):63-67

**Alami, Samar**

Palestine: Remembering Sabra and Shatila. *Spare Rib* 217 (October 1990):51

On the Third Anniversary of the Intifada. *Spare Rib* 219 (December 1990-January 1991):52-53

**Alarcón, Norma**, Castillo, Ana, and Moraga, Cherrié (editors)

The Sexuality of Latinas. Reviewed by Marisol Gonzalez. *NWSA Journal* 2, No. 2 (Spring 1990):298-301

**Albany (New York) – WAMC Public Radio**

McCallmanack: Tuning In to Women's Issues. Elizabeth Kolbert. *McCall's* 117, No. 11 (August 1990):62

**Albera, Dionigi** (joint author). *See* Viazzo, Pier Paolo

**Albert, Peter J.** (joint author). *See* Hoffman, Ronald

**Alberti, Johanna**

Inside Out: Elizabeth Haldane as a Women's Suffrage Survivor in the 1920s and 1930s. *Women's Studies International Forum* 13, Nos. 1-2 (1990):117-125

**Alberts, Michelle M.**

Osteoporosis: A Health Issue for Women. *Health Care for Women International* 11, No. 1 (1990):11-19

**Albright, Mia**

Feminism: Freedom from Wifism. Reviewed by Margaret Maxwell. *On the Issues* 15 (Summer 1990):29-30

**Alcock, Beverley** and Robson, Jocelyn

Cagney and Lacey Revisited. *Feminist Review* No. 35 (Summer 1990):42-53

**Alcohol**

Alcohol and the Family. Edited by R. Lorraine Collins, Kenneth E. Leonard, and John S. Searles. Reviewed by Joan F. Robertson. *Journal of Marriage and the Family* 52, No. 4 (November 1990):1154-1155

Alcohol and Women's Health: Cause for Concern? Alex Wodack. *Healthright* 9, No. 3 (May 1990):17-22

Cheers? The Sobering News About Women and Alcohol. Dava Sobel. *Mademoiselle* (May 1990):138

Health Department. Dava Sobel. *Lear's* (March 1990):70

**Alcohol Abuse**

Alcohol Use as a Situational Influence on Young Women's Pregnancy Risk-Taking Behaviors. Beverly Flanigan, Ann McLean, Chris Hall, and Veronica Propp. *Adolescence* 25, No. 97 (Spring 1990):205-214

Women and Alcohol: Menace or Medicine? Anne Cassidy. *Family Circle* 103, No. 17 (December 18, 1990):63-65

Writers and Booze. Geoffrey Wolff. *Lear's* (March 1990):126-131+

**Alcoholic Beverages**

Eating In: How to Stock This Year's Bar. *Glamour* (December 1990):242

**Alcoholics Anonymous**. *See also* Self-Help Techniques

**Alcoholism**. *See also* Children of Alcoholic Parents; Mothers Against Drunk Driving

Alcoholism in Lesbians: Developmental, Symbolic Interactionist, and Critical Perspectives. Joanne M. Hall. *Health Care for Women International* 11, No. 1 (1990):89-107

Predisposed and Stuck With It. John Steinbeck IV. *Lear's* (December 1990):56-57

Recovering from Recovery. Mary McNamara. *Glamour* (November 1990):176

**Alcoholism – Personal Narratives**

Could You Stop Drinking for a Month? Susan Jacoby. *Glamour* (April 1990):288-289+

**Alcoholism – Treatment**

The Twelve-Step Controversy. Charlotte Davis Kasl. *Ms.* 1, No. 3 (November/December 1990):30-31

Twelve Step Programs: A Lesbian Feminist Critique. Bette S. Tallen. *NWSA Journal* 2, No. 3 (Summer 1990):390-407

**Alcott, Louisa May – Parodies**

Louisa May Incest, a One-Act Play. Carolyn Gage. *Trivia* 16/17 (Fall 1990):137-156

**Alcott, Louisa May** (about)

The Borders of Ethical, Erotic, and Artistic Possibilities in *Little Women*. Notes. Ann B. Murphy. *Signs* 15, No. 3 (Spring 1990):562-585

**Alda, Alan** (about). *See also* Writers – Personal Narratives

**Aldous, Joan**

Family Development and the Life Course: Two Perspective on Family Change. *Journal of Marriage and the Family* 52, No. 3 (August 1990):517-583

**Aldous, Joan** and Dumon, Wilfried

Family Policy in the 1980s: Controversy and Consensus. *Journal of Marriage and the Family* 52, No. 4 (November 1990):1136-1151

**Aldrich, Nelson W., Jr.**

No Nonsense. *Lear's* (November 1990):104-107

Simpatico. *Lear's* (August 1990):90-97

**Alegría, Claribel**

Family Album: Stories from a Catholic Girlhood. Reviewed by Marta Rodriguez. *Spare Rib* 217 (October 1990):35

Woman of the River. Reviewed by Judith Vollmer. *The Women's Review of Books* 7, No. 6 (March 1990):12-13

**Alexander, Anne** (joint author). *See* Urquhart, Rachel

**Alexander, Estella Conwill**

Cosmic Iconography. Poem. *Essence* 20, No. 11 (March 1990):129

**Alexander, Jacqui**

The History of Mary Prince: A West Indian Slave, Related by Herself. Book Review. *Women's Studies International Forum* 13, Nos. 1-2 (1990):159

A Radio Profile of Audre Lorde. Book Review. *NWSA Journal* 2, No. 1 (Winter 1990):129-131

**Alexander, Jan**

Your Money. *Family Circle* 103, No. 8 (June 5, 1990):25-27

**Alexander, Joan**

Voices and Echoes: Tales from Colonial Women. Reviewed by Dorothy O. Helly. *Women's Studies International Forum* 13, No. 4 (1990):405-407

**Alexander, Meena**

South of the Nilgiris. Poem. *Manushi* 58 (May-June 1990):21

**Alexander, Nanine**

Women in Advertising. Bibliography. *Essence* 20, No. 9 (January 1990):35-40

**Alexander, Sally** (editor)

Women's Fabian Tracts. Reviewed by Linda Walker. *Gender & History* 2, No. 2 (Summer 1990):244-246

**Alexander, Ziggi**

Let it Lie Upon the Table: The Status of Black Women's Biography in the UK. *Gender & History* 2, No. 1 (Spring 1990):22-33

**Alexis, Kim** (about)

Fresh Dressed. *Redbook* 174, No. 5 (March 1990):124-129

Kim Alexis – First-Rate Mom and Beauty. Beth Weinhouse. *Redbook* 175, No. 1 (May 1990):12-14

**Algeria – History**

Gender and Politics in Algeria: Unraveling the Religious Paradigm. Notes. Marnia Lazreg. *Signs* 15, No. 4 (Summer 1990):755-780

**Algeria – Status of Women**

The Colonial Harem. By Malek Alloula. Reviewed by Írvin Cemil Schick. *Feminist Studies* 16, No. 2 (Summer 1990):345-380

The Colonial Harem. By Malek Alloula. Reviewed by Wendy Kozol. *Gender & History* 2, No. 1 (Spring 1990):110-113

**Ali, Shahrazad**

The Blackman's Guide to Understanding the Blackwoman. Reviewed by Iyanla Vanzant. *Essence* 21, No. 5 (September 1990):55

**Alienation (Social Psychology) – Adolescents**

Alienation: A Cause of Juvenile Delinquency. Raymond L. Calabrese and Jane Adams. *Adolescence* 25, No. 98 (Summer 1990):435-440

**Al-Khalifa, Elisabeth**

Changing Perspectives on Gender. Book Review. *Gender and Education* 2, No. 2 (1990):241-242

**All-China Women's Federation**

Incorporation vs. Separation: An Assessment of Gender and Politics in the People's Republic of China. Cheryl L. Brown. *Women & Politics* 10, No. 1 (1990):59-69

**Allegretto, Michael**

The Watching Shadows. Short Story. *Good Housekeeping* 210, No. 4 (April 1990):231-249, 259-273

**Alleman, Richard**

Reds: The New Red Revolution. *Vogue* (September 1990):552-573

Travel: Last Minute Summer. *Vogue* (July 1990):124-128

Travel News. *Vogue* (January 1990):140; (September 1990):476; (December 1990):228

Vogue Arts: Oh, Kay! Theater review. *Vogue* (December 1990):188-189

**Alleman, Richard** (joint author). *See* Urquhart, Rachel

**Allen, Barbara**

By Design: Incorporating Feminist Ideas into the Political Theory Curriculum. *Feminist Teacher* 5, No. 1 (Spring 1990):15-18

**Allen, Bonnie**

Gulag, U.S.A. *Ms.* 1, No. 1 (July/August 1990):76

Tracey Untamed. *Ms.* 1, No. 1 (July/August 1990):76

**Allen, Carolyn** (joint author). *See* Howard, Judith A.

**Allen, Debbie** (about)

It's a Hectic World for Debbie Allen. Pamela Johnson. *Essence* 21, No. 2 (June 1990):64-66

**Allen, Ellen Vera**

New Households, New Housing. Book Review. *Canadian Women's Studies* 11, No. 2 (Fall 1990):85

**Allen, Eugenie**

Are You Too Good to Be Promoted? *Glamour* (October 1990):118

**Allen, Jeanne**

Counter Cultures: Saleswomen, Managers, and Customers in American Department Stores, 1890-1940. Book Review. *Camera Obscura* No. 22 (January 1990):150-158

**Allen, Jeffner** (editor)

Lesbian Philosophies and Cultures. Reviewed by Carol Anne Douglas. *off our backs* 20, No. 9 (October 1990):18-19

Lesbian Philosophies and Cultures. Reviewed by Elizabeth Wood. *New Directions for Women* 19, No. 6 (November-December 1990):17

**Allen, Katherine R.**

Single Women/Family Ties: Life Histories of Older Women. Reviewed by Sally A. Lloyd. *Journal of Marriage and the Family* 52, No. 1 (February 1990):281

**Allen, Margaret**, Hutchinson, Mary, and Mackinnon, Alison (editors)

Fresh Evidence, New Witnesses: Finding Women's History. Reviewed by Marilyn Lake. *Australian Feminist Studies* No. 12 (Summer 1990):121-122

**Allen, Mariette Pathy**

Tranformations: Crossdressers and Those Who Love Them. Reviewed by Margaret McCarthy. *New Directions for Women* 19, No. 4 (July-August 1990):20

**Allen, Martha Leslie**

Women's Media: The Way to Revolution. *off our backs* 20, No. 2 (February 1990):14 +

**Allen, Myria Watkins**, Seibert, Joy Hart, and Rush, Ramona R.

Gender Differences in Perceptions of Work: Limited Access to Decision-Making Power and Supervisory Support. *Women's Studies in Communication* 13, No. 2 (Fall 1990):1-20

**Allen, Paula Gunn**

Skins and Bones. Reviewed by Laura B. Kennelly. *Belles Lettres* 5, No. 2 (Winter 1990):10

Voice of First Mother. *Ms.* 1, No. 2 (September/October 1990):25-26

The Woman I Love Is a Planet; the Planet I Love Is a Tree. *Woman of Power* 18 (Fall 1990):5-7

**Allen, Paula Gunn** (about)

Interview with Paula Gunn Allen. Jane Caputi. *Trivia* 16/17 (Fall 1990):50-67

**Allen, Paula Gunn** (editor)

Spider Woman's Granddaughters: Traditional Tales and Contemporary Writing by Native American Women. Reviewed by Charlotte Tsoi Goodluck. *Belles Lettres* 5, No. 4 (Summer 1990):40 +

**Allen, Robert C.**

"The Leg Business": Transgression and Containment in American Burlesque. *Camera Obscura* , No. 23 (May 1990): 42-69

**Allen, Sheila** and Wolkowitz, Carol

Homeworking: Myths and Realities. Reviewed by Mary Margaret Fonow. *NWSA Journal* 2, No. 3 (Summer 1990):502-505

Homeworking: Myths and Realities. Reviewed by Robin Leidner. *Gender and Society* 4, No. 2 (June 1990):262-265

**Allergies**. *See* Allergy

**Allergy**. *See also* Air Pollution – Indoors; Asthma; Children – Allergies

Allergies: Latest Finds, Best Treatments. Bibliography. Dava Sobel. *Good Housekeeping* 211, No. 3 (September 1990):226-227 +

Health Department. Leigh Silverman. *Lear's* (May 1990):62

Health Dept. *Lear's* (November 1990):82

Health & Fitness. Bibliography. Stephanie Young. *Glamour* (July 1990):31-39

Prevention: A Season for Sneezin'. Susan Festa. *Essence* 20, No. 11 (March 1990):24-28

**Allfrey, Phyllis Shand**

The Orchid House. Reviewed by Erika Smilowitz. *Belles Lettres* 5, No. 2 (Winter 1990):18

**Allgood, Scot M.** (joint author). *See* Crane, D. Russell

**Allione, Tsultrim**

Sky Dancer. *Woman of Power* 15 (Fall-Winter 1990):30-31

**Allison, Marla Ruth**

Suing Dad: Bat Mitzvah in the Divorce Crossfire. *Lilith* 15, No. 2 (Spring 1990):23-24

**Allman, Kevin**

Talking Fashion: Mimi. *Vogue* (August 1990):378-380

**Alloula, Malek**

The Colonial Harem. Reviewed by Írvin Cemil Schick. *Feminist Studies* 16, No. 2 (Summer 1990):345-380

The Colonial Harem. Reviewed by Wendy Kozol. *Gender & History* 2, No. 1 (Spring 1990):110-113

**Allred, Gloria** (about)

Gloria Allred. Aaron Latham. *Lear's* (June 1990):78-83

**Almodovar, Pedro**

Tie Me Up! Tie Me Down! Reviewed by Sylvia Velasquez. *Spare Rib* No. 216 (September 1990):32

**Aloff, Mindy**

Jazz Cleopatra: Josephine Baker in Her Time. Book Review. *The Women's Review of Books* 7, No. 4 (January 1990):1 +

Private Dancer. *The Women's Review of Books* 7, No. 4 (January 1990):1 +

**Alonso, Harriet Hyman**

The Women's Peace Union and the Outlawry of War, 1921-1941. Reviewed by Cynthia L. Giddle. *New Directions for Women* 19, No. 5 (September-October 1990):18

**Alper, Nancy**

Your Body: Confessions of a Food Addict. *Family Circle* 103, No. 16 (November 27, 1990):26-29

**Alsop, Marin** (about). *See also* Musicians

**Alter, JoAnne**

On the Job. *Family Circle* 103, No. 5 (April 3, 1990):22 +

**Alther, Lisa**

Bedrock. Reviewed by Barbara Rich. *The Women's Review of Books* 7, Nos. 10-11 (July 1990):25-26

**Altman, Dennis**

My America – and Yours: A Letter to US Lesbian and Gay Activists. *Out/Look* No. 8 (Spring 1990):62-65

**Altman, Dennis** and others

Homosexuality, Which Homosexuality?: Essays from the International Scientific Conference on Lesbian and Gay Studies. Reviewed by Alison Oram. *Feminist Review* No. 35 (Summer 1990):121-122

**Altman, Meryl**

A Few Words in the Mother Tongue: Poems Selected and New (1971-1990). Book Review. *The Women's Review of Books* 8, No. 1 (October 1990):16-18

Giacometti's Dog. Book Review. *The Women's Review of Books* 8, No. 1 (October 1990):16-18

History and Geography. Book Review. *The Women's Review of Books* 8, No. 1 (October 1990):16-18

Uneasy Understandings. *The Women's Review of Books* 8, No. 1 (October 1990):16-18

Upstairs in the Garden: Poems Selected and New (1968-1988). Book Review. *The Women's Review of Books* 8, No. 1 (October 1990):16-18

**Altruism**

Why We're Really Good at Heart. *Glamour* (September 1990):302-303 +

**Alvarez, A.**

Romance. *Lear's* (November 1990):98-99 +

**Alvarez, D-L**

A Boy's Guide to Feeling Pretty. *Out/Look* No. 8 (Spring 1990):19-20

**Alvarez, Sonia E.**

Women's Participation in the Brazilian "People's Church": A Critical Appraisal. *Feminist Studies* 16, No. 2 (Summer 1990):381-408

**Alwin, Duane F.**

Cohort Replacement and Changes in Parental Socialization Values. *Journal of Marriage and the Family* 52, No. 2 (May 1990):347-360

**Alworth, Sandra** (about). *See* Business – Ownership

**Alzate, Heli** (joint author). *See* Useche, Bernardo

**Alzheimer's Disease**

Circle This. Margaret Jaworski. *Family Circle* 103, No. 15 (November 6, 1990):9-10

Five Elderly Dementia Patients Who Played with Dolls. Makoto J. Kawai, Mari Miyamoto, and Kimio Miyamoto. *Journal of Women and Aging* 2, No. 1 (1990):99-107

A Guide to Understanding Alzheimer's Disease and Related Disorders. By A. F. Jorm. Reviewed by

Stefania Siedlecky. *Healthright* 9, No. 4 (August 1990):46

Talking with Shelley Fabares: "I'd Do Anything to Help My Mother." Interview. Ellen Byron. *Redbook* 176, No. 2 (December 1990):38-41

**Alzheimer's Disease – Caregiving**

The Caregiving Roles of Asian American Women. Catherine Chase Goodman. *Journal of Women and Aging* 2, No. 1 (1990):109-120

**Amadiume, Ifi**

Women of Africa. Record Review.SR No. 210 (March 1990):41

**Amana, Rue**

Becoming a "Real" Dyke: Employment and Housing. *Canadian Women's Studies* 11, No. 2 (Fall 1990):43-45

**Amatenstein, Sherry**

Tactics That Get Him to Help Out. *Family Circle* 103, No. 5 (April 3, 1990):89-91

**Amato, Paul R.**

Dimensions of the Family Environment as Perceived by Children: A Multidimensional Scaling Analysis. *Journal of Marriage and the Family* 52, No. 3 (August 1990):613-620

**Amaya, Alba**

Romero. Film Review. *Spare Rib* No. 210 (March 1990):38

**Ambassadors**. *See* Black, Shirley Temple (about); Bloch, Julia Chang (about)

**Ambrose, Jamie**

Willa Cather: Writing at the Frontier. Reviewed by Lady Falls Brown. *Tulsa Studies in Women's Literature* 9, No. 2 (Fall 1990):334-337

**American Ballet Theatre**

Grande Dame of Dance. Yona Zeldis McDonough. *Harper's Bazaar* (January 1990):55

**American Broadcasting Company**

ABC Has Poorest Network Showing of On-Air Women Correspondents. *Media Report to Women* 18, No. 4 (July-August 1990):1

**American Red Cross**. *See* Disaster Relief

**American Sign Language**

ASL Interpreting for Concerts: What Producers Should Know. Sara. *Hot Wire* 6, No. 3 (September 1990):18-19 +

**American Silverplate**. *See* Antiques and Collectibles

**American Society of Newspaper Editors**

ASNE Undertaking Survey of Anti-Gay Attitudes in U.S. Newsrooms. *Media Report to Women* 18, No. 1 (January/February 1990):7-8

**American Telephone and Telegraph – Political Activities**

AT&T, the Bishops and Other Bad Connections. Ann F. Lewis. *Ms.* 1, No. 1 (July/August 1990):88

**American Woman's Economic Development Corporation.** *See* Entrepreneurs

**Amin, Amina** (joint author). *See* Pathak, Ila

**Amis, Martin** (about). *See* Matousek, Mark, "English Accents"

**Ammiano, Tom** and Strobel, Jeanine

List This! *Out/Look* No. 10 (Fall 1990):63

**Amniocentesis.** *See* Fetal Monitoring; Pregnancy – Amniocentesis

**Amon, Kamernebti Mer**

Unraveling. Poem. *Essence* 21, No. 6 (October 1990):124

**Amos, Emma**

Beating the Odds. Poem. *Heresies* 25 (1990):74

**Amott, Teresa** and Matthaei, Julie

Before the "Trail of Tears." *Ms.* 1, No. 3 (November/December 1990):82-83

**Amram, Helena** (about)

The Meet Market. Peter Wilkinson. *Savvy Woman* (July/August 1990):52-55 +

**Amrouche, Fadhma**

My Life Story: The Autobiography of a Berber Woman. Reviewed by Suha Sabbagh. *The Women's Review of Books* 7, Nos. 10-11 (July 1990):42-43

**Amsel, Eric** (joint author). *See* Kuhn, Deanna

**Amsel, Rhonda** (joint author). *See* Brown-Rowat, Beverly

**Amusement Parks**

Temptations of Pleasure: Nickelodeons, Amusement Parks, and the Sights of Female Sexuality. Lauren Rabinovitz. *Camera Obscura* , No. 23 (May 1990): 70-89

**Anand, Tinnu**

Main Azad Hoon: The Politics of Myth and Reality. Reviewed by Harsh Sethi. *Manushi* 56 (January-February 1990):43-44

**Anarchists.** *See* Goldman, Emma (about)

**Anastos, Ernie**

Polling America: Church vs. State. *Family Circle* 103, No. 16 (November 27, 1990):20

Polling America. *Family Circle* 103, No. 12 (September 4, 1990):37-39

Polling America: Where's a Woman's Place? *Family Circle* 103, No. 14 (October 16, 1990):74-77

**Anchors, Television.** *See* Television Journalists

**Anders, Shirley**

Waving from Shore. Book Review. *Iris* 24 (Fall-Winter 1990):66-67

**Andersen, Christopher**

Jaclyn Smith: "I'm Still the Marrying Kind." *Ladies' Home Journal* 107, No. 8 (August 1990):62-66

Viva Sophia! *Ladies' Home Journal* 107, No. 4 (April 1990):58-62

**Andersen, Marguerite**

An Interview with Freda Guttman, Montreal Artist and Activist. *Resources for Feminist Research* 19, No. 1 (March 1990):48-50

Frauen Lexikon. Book Review. *Resources for Feminist Research* 19, No. 1 (March 1990):16

**Anderson, Bonnie S.** and Zinsser, Judith P.

A History of Their Own: Women in Europe, from Pre-History to the Present. Reviewed by Janaki Nair. *Gender and Society* 4, No. 4 (December 1990):563-565

A History of Their Own: Women in Europe from Prehistory to the Present. Reviewed by Margaret Saunders. *Iris* 24 (Fall-Winter 1990):60-65

A History of Their Own: Women in Europe from Prehistory to the Present. Reviewed by Mary Beth Emmerichs. *Feminist Collections* 11, No. 2 (Winter 1990):3-4

A History of Their Own: Women in Europe from Pre-history to the Present, Volume 2. Reviewed by Nancy Erber-Cadet. *New Directions for Women* 19, No. 3 (May/June 1990):18

**Anderson, Candy**

Too Many Faces of Me. Poem. *New Directions for Women* 19, No. 3 (May/June 1990):5

**Anderson, Carol M.** (joint editor). *See* McGoldrick, Monica

**Anderson, Gregory** (editor)

The White Blouse Revolution: Female Office Workers Since 1870. Reviewed by Carole Elizabeth Adams. *Gender & History* 2, No. 3 (Autumn 1990):343-348

**Anderson, Jamie**

Closer to Home. Reviewed by Lynn Wenzel. *New Directions for Women* 19, No. 3 (May/June 1990):8

Humor in Women's Music. *Hot Wire* 6, No. 1 (January 1990):46-47 +

**Anderson, Jean**

Giving Thanks. *Family Circle* 103, No. 16 (November 27, 1990):74-77

**Anderson, Julie** (about). *See* Success

**Anderson, June** (about). *See* Achievement

**Anderson, Kamili**

Report from the Zora Neale Hurston Society Conference. *Belles Lettres* 6, No. 1 (Fall 1990):63

Sans Souci and Other Stories. Book Review. *New Directions for Women* 19, No. 4 (July-August 1990):19

Stories of the Dispossed. *New Directions for Women* 19, No. 4 (July-August 1990):19

**Anderson, Karen** (joint editor). *See* Aiken, Susan Hardy

**Anderson, Laurie** (about)

Performance: Multi-Mediator. John Leland. *Vogue* (January 1990):90-91

**Anderson, Owen**

Getting Faster, Faster. *Women's Sports & Fitness* 12, No. 6 (September 1990):30-32

**Anderson, Shelley**

Falling Borders, Rising Hopes: Europe in 1992. *Out/Look* No. 10 (Fall 1990):30-35

**Andolsen, Barbara Hilkert**

Good Work at the Video Display Terminal: A Feminist Ethical Analysis of Changes in Clerical Work. Reviewed by Susan Klitzman. *Women and Health* 16, Nos. 3/4 (1990):205-206

**Andreae, Janice**

Conversation Fragments: Colette Whiten. *Canadian Women's Studies* 11, No. 1 (Spring 1990):91

Conversation Fragments: Winsom. *Canadian Women's Studies* 11, No. 1 (Spring 1990):90

**Andreae, Janice** (joint author). *See* Burgess, Marilyn

**Andreasen, Nancy C.**

Brave New Brain. *Vogue* (January 1990):196-199+

**Andrew, Caroline**

Sexes et militantisme. Book Review. *Resources for Feminist Research* 19, No. 2 (June 1990):45-46

**Andrew, Elizabeth**

Preparing for Birth. Book Review. *Healthright* 9, No. 2 (February 1990):36

**Andrews, Bernice** and Brewin, Chris R.

Attributions of Blame for Marital Violence: A Study of Antecedents and Consequences. *Journal of Marriage and the Family* 52, No. 3 (August 1990):757-767

**Andrews, Cathy**

Doing the Festivals: Or, How I Spent My Summer. *Hot Wire* 6, No. 3 (September 1990):43+

**Andrews, Jane**

Don't Pass Us By: Keeping Lesbian and Gay Issues on the Agenda. *Gender and Education* 2, No. 3 (1990):351-355

**Andrews, Janice L.**

Female Social Workers in the Second Generation. *AFFILIA* 5, No. 2 (Summer 1990):46-59

**Andrews, Lori**

Between Stangers: Surrogate Mothers, Expectant Fathers, and Brave New Babies. Reviewed by Mary

Gibson. *Women and Health* 16, No. 2 (1990):134-137

The Gene Prophets. *Vogue* (January 1990):198-199+

**Andrus, Pat**

The Gold-Taloned Mirrors. *Women and Therapy* 10, Nos. 1/2 (1990):11

I Was in Hawaii. Poem. *Women and Therapy* 10, Nos. 1/2 (1990):9-10

**Anesthesia**

Anesthesia: The Essence of It All. Claudia M. Caruana. *Lear's* (May 1990):53-54

**Angela, Angie** and Iazzetto, Demetria

Commari: Excerpt of a Dialogue. *Sinister Wisdom* 41 (Summer-Fall 1990):82-88

**Angelou, Maya**

Our Grandmothers. Poem. *Ms.* 1, No. 3 (November/December 1990):22-23

**Angelou, Maya** (about). *See* De Veaux, Alexis, Milloy, Marilyn, and Ross, Michael Erik

**Anger.** *See also* Conflict Resolution; Emotions; Fighting (Psychology)

Prevention: The Angry Heart. Linda Villarosa. *Essence* 20, No. 12 (April 1990):26-28

The Shameful Shock Waves of Rage. John Bradshaw. *Lear's* (June 1990):63

**Angier, Natalie**

Moody News: Can a Pill Called Prozac End Depression? *Mademoiselle* (April 1990):229, 261-263

**Anglesey, Zoë**

Alfonsina Storni: Selected Poems. Book Review. *Belles Lettres* 5, No. 2 (Winter 1990):17

Southern Cone. *Belles Lettres* 5, No. 2 (Winter 1990):17

Zones of Pain/Las Zonas del Dolor. Book Review. *Belles Lettres* 5, No. 2 (Winter 1990):17

**Anglin, Mary K.**

Kinship to Kinship: Gender Hierarchy and State Formation in the Tongan Islands. Book review. *Signs* 15, No. 3 (Spring 1990):642-645

**Animal Behavior**

Never Cry Bull Moose: Of Mooses and Men: The Case of the Scheming Gene. Susan Kray. *Women & Language* 13, No. 1 (Fall 1990):31-37

**Animal Reproduction.** *See* Reproduction

**Animal Rights**

Animal Rights and Feminist Theory. Notes. Josephine Donovan. *Signs* 15, No. 2 (Winter 1990):350-375

The Dreaded Comparison: Human and Animal Slavery. By Marjorie Spiegel. Reviewed by Kore

Archer. *New Directions for Women* 19, No. 1
(January/February 1990):19

Editorial: *People's* Rights Above Animal Rights.
*Glamour* (June 1990):92

The Fur Furor: Which Side Are You On? Stacey
Okun. *Savvy Woman* (October 1990):48-51+

Innocent Casualties in the War on Drugs. Betsy
Swart. *On the Issues* 17 (Winter 1990):27-28+

On the Issues. Merle Hoffman. *On the Issues* 16
(Fall 1990):2-3+

Rape of the Wild: Man's Violence Against Animals
and the Earth. By Joyce Contrucci. Reviewed by
Linda Vance. *NWSA Journal* 2, No. 3 (Summer
1990):485-489

Take Back Your Mink! *Glamour* (January 1990):83

Whose Life Is More Important: An Animal's or a
Child's? Alice Steinbach. *Glamour* (January
1990):1440-141+

**Animals**

With a Fly's Eye, Whale's Wit, and Woman's Heart.
Edited by Theresa Corrigan and Stephanie Hoppe.
Reviewed by Patricia Roth Schwartz. *Belles Lettres*
5, No. 2 (Winter 1990):12

With a Fly's Eye, Whale's Wit and Woman's Heart:
Animals and Women. Edited by Theresa Corrigan
and Stephanie Hoppe. Reviewed by Nancy Lloyd.
*On the Issues* 16 (Fall 1990):32

**Animal Stories**

Through Other Eyes: Animal Stories by Women.
Edited by Irene Zahave. Reviewed by Kore Archer.
*New Directions for Women* 19, No. 1
(January/February 1990):19

**Animal Welfare – Moral and Ethical Aspects.** *See*
Animal Rights

**Ann Arbor (Michigan) – Reproductive Freedom**

A $5 Declaration of Independence. Gayle
Kirshenbaum. *Ms.* 1, No. 1 (July/August 1990):87

**Anne, Sheila**

Dykes-Loving-Dykes. Book Review. *off our backs*
20, No. 11 (December 1990):15

**Anniversaries**

Honor Thy Marriage (and Anniversary). Judith
Viorst. *Redbook* 175, No. 2 (June 1990):48-51

**Annuities**

The Year of Living Cautiously. Nancy Dunnan. *Lear's*
(June 1990):38-40

**Anorexia Nervosa.** *See also* Eating Disorders

Fasting Girls: The Emergence of Anorexia as a
Nervous Disease. By Joan Jacobs Brumberg.
Reviewed by Anne Digby. *Gender & History* 2, No.
3 (Autumn 1990):370-371

**Anryon, Julien** (about). *See also* Carter, Charla,
"European Designers to Watch."

**Ansa, Tina McElroy**

Baby of the Family. Reviewed by Paula Giddings.
*Essence* 20, No. 11 (March 1990):44

**Ansfield, Alice** (interview)

A Vision of Radiance. Joan Price. *Woman of Power*
18 (Fall 1990):62-63

**Anthologies**

Women of Color and the Core Curriculum: Tools
for Transforming the Liberal Arts, Part 4. Susan E.
Searing. *Feminist Collections* 12, No. 1 (Fall
1990):21-24

**Anthony, Evelyn**

The Scarlet Thread. Short Story. *Good
Housekeeping* 211, No. 1 (July 1990):163-180, 192-
198, 205-206

**Anthony, Joseph**

Code B, for Bothered and Bewildered. *Lear's*
(November 1990):42-44

**Anthropology**

The Language of the Goddess. By Marija Gimbutas.
Reviewed by Ruby Rohrlich. *The Women's Review
of Books* 7, No. 9 (June 1990):14-16

**Anthropology – Feminist Perspectives.** *See also*
Feminism – Ethnography

Feminism and Anthropology. By Henrietta L.
Moore. Reviewed by Gillian Cowlishaw. *Australian
Feminist Studies* No. 11 (Autumn 1990):121-122

On Vicky Kirby versus Marilyn Strathern Vers(us).
Gillian Cowlishaw and Teresa Lea. *Australian
Feminist Studies* No. 11 (Autumn 1990):87-89

**Anthropology – Study and Teaching**

Transforming Introductory Anthropology: The
American Anthropological Association Project on
Gender and the Curriculum. Sandra Morgen and
Mary Moran. *Women's Studies Quarterly* 18, Nos.
1-2 (Spring-Summer 1990):95-103

**Anthropology – Theoretical Perspectives**

Deceptive Dichotomies: Private/Public, and
Nature/Culture: Gender Relations in Tonga in the
Early Contact Period. Caroline Ralston. *Australian
Feminist Studies* No. 12 (Summer 1990):65-82

**Antigena**

Suitable Weapons . . . *Connexions* 32 (1990):29-31

**Antill, John K.** (joint author). *See* Cotton, Sandra

**Antinova, Eleanora**

Before the Revolution. Ballet. *Women and
Performance: A Journal of Feminist Theory* 5, No. 1,
Issue #9 (1990): 93-119

**Antinuclear Movement**

Listen to the Tangata Whenua. *Spare Rib* 217
(October 1990):50

## Antiques and Collectibles

Boxes for Our Treasures. Pat Ross. *McCall's* 117, No. 10 (July 1990):93-96

Silver Plate Grabs the Spotlight. Sally Clark. *McCall's* 117, No. 9 (June 1990):55

## Anti-Semitism. *See also* Poland – Anti-Semitism; Soviet Union – Anti-Semitism

The Anti-Choice Movement: Bad News for Jews. Susan Weidman Schneider. *Lilith* 15, No. 3 (Summer 1990):8-11

Anti-Semitism in the Women's Movement: A Jewish Lesbian Speaks. Bonnie Morris. *off our backs* 20, No. 11 (December 1990):12-13

T.V. Men: Wimps or What? Maria Stieglitz. *Lilith* 15, No. 3 (Summer 1990):28-29

## Antivivisection Movement. *See* Animal Rights

## Antler, Joyce (editor)

America and I: Short Stories by American Jewish Women Writers. Reviewed by Ruth Knafo Setton. *Lilith* 15, No. 4 (Fall 1990):33

America and I: Short Stories by American Jewish Women Writers. Reviewed by Ruth Magder. *Belles Lettres* 6, No. 1 (Fall 1990):13

## Antonucci, Toni C. (joint author). *See* Adelmann, Pamela K.

## Anu

Rihaee. Film review. *Manushi* 57 (March-April 1990):43-44

## Anxiety. *See also* Panic Disorders; Stress

Mind Health: Panic. Peter Jaret. *Vogue* (September 1990):462-467

## Anyi, Wang

Baotown. Reviewed by Judy Yung. *Belles Lettres* 6, No. 1 (Fall 1990):30-31

## Anzaldúa, Gloria (editor)

Making Face, Making Soul/Haciendo Caras: Creative and Critical Perspectives by Women of Color. Reviewed by Sharon Davenport. *Sinister Wisdom* 42 (Winter 1990-1991):114-117

Making Face, Making Soul/Haciendo Caras: Creative and Critical Perspectives by Women of Color. Reviewed by Valerie Matsumoto. *The Women's Review of Books* 8, No. 2 (November 1990):1+

## Aotani, Dawn

Bone by Bone: How and Why to Research the Work of Asian-American Women Artists. *Heresies* 25 (1990):50-52

## Apartheid. *See* South Africa – Apartheid

No Reforming Apartheid. Nolthando Mandla. *Spare Rib* 219 (December 1990-January 1991):20-23

## Aphorisms and Apothegms

Line Drawings: Aphorisms. Tonie Doe and Paul Degen. *Lear's* (February 1990):88-93

## Apisuk, Chantawipa (joint author). *See* Sexton, Sarah

## Aponovich, James and Weller, Sheila

Young Father's Story: A Portrait of My Daughter. *Redbook* 175, No. 2 (June 1990):36-40

## Appalachia

Industrialization and Household and Family Life Course Characteristics: Appalachian Kentucky Young Adults in 1880 and 1910. Thomas A. Arcury. *Journal of Family History* 15, No. 3 (July 1990):285-312

## Appearance. *See* Beauty Standards; Makeup

## Appelo, Tim

Eye of the Storm. *Savvy Woman* (January 1990):60-62, 94

She's Got the Look. *Savvy Woman* (January 1990):48-51, 88-91

Straight Up with a Twist. *Savvy Woman* (September 1990):56-59+

The World According to Garr. *Savvy Woman* (March 1990):49-52

## Apple

Apples! *Family Circle* 103, No. 13 (September 25, 1990):84-85+

## Apple, Robin F. (joint author). *See* Morell, Marie A.

## Appleman-Jurman, Alicia (about). *See* Holocaust (1939-1945) – Survivors

## Apter, Emily S.

The Story of I: Luce Irigaray's Theoretical Masochism. *NWSA Journal* 2, No. 2 (Spring 1990):186-198

## Aptheker, Bettina

Imagining Our Lives: The Novelist as Historian. *Woman of Power* 16 (Spring 1990):32-35

Promissory Notes: Women in the Transition to Socialism. Book Review. *New Directions for Women* 19, No. 5 (September-October 1990):19

Socialism Examined. *New Directions for Women* 19, No. 5 (September-October 1990):19

Tapestries of Life: Women's Work, Women's Consciousness, and the Meaning of Daily Existence. Reviewed by Hester Eisenstein. *New Directions for Women* 19, No. 3 (May/June 1990):17

Tapestries of Life: Women's Work, Women's Consciousness, and the Meaning of Daily Experience. Reviewed by Susan S. Arpad. *NWSA Journal* 2, No. 2 (Spring 1990):311-314

Tapestries of Life: Women's Work, Women's Consciousness, and the Meaning of Daily

Experience. Reviewed by Toni Flores. *Frontiers* 11, Nos. 2-3 (1990):121-122

Tapestries of Life: Women's Work, Women's Consciousness, and the Meaning of Daily Life. Reviewed by Elizabeth Dane. *AFFILIA* 5, No. 4 (Winter 1990):110-111

Tapestries of Life: Women's Work, Women's Consciousness, and the Meaning of Daily Life. Reviewed by Linda Roman. *On the Issues* 15 (Summer 1990):28-29

**Aquarium Fishes**

Pet Life. Michael W. Fox. *McCall's* 118, No. 2 (November 1990):156

**Aquatic Sports – Safety**

Kids in the Water. Barbara Hey. *McCall's* 117, No. 10 (July 1990):85-90

**Aquilino, William S.**

The Likelihood of Parent-Adult Child Coresidence: Effects of Family Structure and Parental Characteristics. *Journal of Marriage and the Family* 52, No. 2 (May 1990):405-419

**Arabs.** *See also* Middle Eastern Women; Palestinian Arabs; Persian Gulf War

**Arab Women's Solidarity Association**

In Conversation with Nawal El Saadawi. Marcel Farry. *Spare Rib* 217 (October 1990):22-26

**Araji, Sharon K.**

Males at Risk. Book Review. *Journal of Marriage and the Family* 52, No. 3 (August 1990):801

**Arauz, Rita** (interview)

Moving Forward Together. *Connexions* 33 (1990):13

**Arbour, Rose-Marie**

L'histoire de l'art au féminin. *Canadian Women's Studies* 11, No. 1 (Spring 1990):86-89

**Arcana, Judith**

Return. Poem. *Bridges* 1, No. 2 (Fall 1990): 23

**Archaeology**

Archaeomythology: An Interview with Marija Gimbutas. Joan Marler. *Woman of Power* 15 (Fall-Winter 1990):6-13

Women in Australian Prehistory. Wendy Beck and Lesley Head. *Australian Feminist Studies* No. 11 (Autumn 1990):29-48

**Archer, Anne** (about)

Star Quality. Deborah Sroloff. *Harper's Bazaar* (February 1990):148-149

**Archer, Kore**

The Dreaded Comparison: Human and Animal Slavery. Book Review. *New Directions for Women* 19, No. 1 (January/February 1990):19

The Other Sappho. Book Review. *off our backs* 20, No. 7 (July 1990):14

The Other Sappho. Book Review. *Sinister Wisdom* 40 (Spring 1990):130-131

The Sexual Politics of Meat: A Feminist-Vegetarian Critical Theory. Book Review. *New Directions for Women* 19, No. 4 (July-August 1990):19

Through Other Eyes: Animal Stories by Women. Book Review. *New Directions for Women* 19, No. 1 (January/February 1990):19

Vegetarians Boycott Patriarchy. *New Directions for Women* 19, No. 4 (July-August 1990):19

Violence Increases After Earthquake. *off our backs* 20, No. 3 (March 1990):15

**Archer, Melanie**

The Entrepreneurial Family Economy: Family Strategies and Self-Employment in Detroit, 1880. *Journal of Family History* 15, No. 3 (July 1990):261-283

**Archer, Nuala**

The Spaces Between the Words. *The Women's Review of Books* 8, No. 3 (December 1990):21-24

**Archer, Robyn**

Mama Said There'd Be Days Like This – My Life in the Jazz World. Book Review. *Feminist Review* No. 35 (Summer 1990):123-124

**Architects**

The Lady Architects, Lois Lilley Howe, Fleanor Manning and Mary Almy, 1913-1937. By Doris Cole and Karen Taylor. Reviewed by Pamela H. Simpson. *Woman's Art Journal* 11, No. 2 (Fall 1990-Winter 1991):48

**Architecture.** *See also* House Design; Landscape Architecture

Architecture: A Place for Women. Edited by Ellen Perry Berkeley and Matilda McQuaid. Reviewed by Judith A. Moldenhauer. *The Women's Review of Books* 7, No. 6 (March 1990):29-30

Architecture: A Place for Women. Edited by Ellen Perry Berkeley and Matilda McQuaid. Reviewed by Pamela H. Simpson. *Woman's Art Journal* 11, No. 2 (Fall 1990-Winter 1991):44-48

Art: Modernism. Herbert Muschamp. *Vogue* (January 1990):118-120

Family Togetherness in Style. *Redbook* 175, No. 1 (May 1990):134-137

The House That Jack Built. Shelley Hornstein-Rabinovitch. *Canadian Women's Studies* 11, No. 1 (Spring 1990):65-67

Master Builders. Karen Stein. *Harper's Bazaar* (August 1990):1668-171+

**Architecture – Bibliography**

Architecture and Women: A Bibliography. By Lamia Doumato. Reviewed by Pamela H. Simpson. *Woman's Art Journal* 11, No. 2 (Fall 1990-Winter 1991):44-48

**Architecture – Conservation and Restoration**

Historic Colors. *Redbook* 175, No. 4 (August 1990):80-85

The House of Our Dreams. Lauren Payne. *Ladies' Home Journal* 107, No. 10 (October 1990):162-165

Inside the Governors' Mansions. Lauren Payne. *Ladies' Home Journal* 107, No. 7 (July 1990):98-104

A New England Christmas. Lauren Payne. *Ladies' Home Journal* 107, No. 12 (December 1990):138-143

**Arcury, Thomas A.**

Industrialization and Household and Family Life Course Characteristics: Appalachian Kentucky Young Adults in 1880 and 1910. *Journal of Family History* 15, No. 3 (July 1990):285-312

**Ardant, Fanny** (about)

Passion Player. Anne-Elisabeth Moutet. *Harper's Bazaar* (August 1990):134-137 +

**Ardill, Susan** and O'Sullivan, Sue

Butch/Femme Obsessions. *Feminist Review* No. 34 (Spring 1990):79-85

**Arenal, Electa** and Schlau, Stacey

Stratagems of the Strong, Stratagems of the Weak: Autobiographical Prose of the Seventeenth-Century Hispanic Convent. *Tulsa Studies in Women's Literature* 9, No. 1 (Spring 1990):25-42

**Arenal, Electa** and Zingo, Martha T.

Singing Softly/Cantando Bajito. Book Review. *New Directions for Women* 19, No. 3 (May/June 1990):24

**Arend, Sylvie**

La conservatisme politique féminin en Suisse: Mythe ou réalité. Book Review. *Canadian Women's Studies* 11, No. 2 (Fall 1990):93

**Argentina – Family Life**

A History of Schooling and Family Life on Southern Argentine Sheep Ranches. Sara Mansfield Taber. *Journal of Family History* 15, No. 3 (July 1990):335-356

**Argentina – Fifth Latin American and Caribbean Feminist Meeting**

Documentation Centers Workshop: Our Collective Memory. *Women in Action* 3 & 4 (1990):15

Domestic and Sexual Violence Network Workshop. *Women in Action* 3 & 4 (1990):14

Fifth Latin American and Caribbean Feminist Meeting. Carmen Gloria Dunnage. *Women in Action* 3 & 4 (1990):3-8

Interview with an Organizer: "We Must Coordinate for the Next Meeting." Interview. Carmen Gloria Dunnage. *Women in Action* 3 & 4 (1990):9-10

Women in Communications Workshop: Birds of a Feather. Regina Rodriguez. *Women in Action* 3 & 4 (1990):11-13

**Argentina – Health Care – History**

Public Health, Gender, and Private Morality: Paid Labor and the Formation of the Body Politic in Buenos Aires. Donna J. Guy. *Gender & History* 2, No. 3 (Autumn 1990):297-317

**Argentina – Terrorism**

Mothers of the Disappeared. By Jo. Fisher. Reviewed by Marta Rodriguez. *Spare Rib* No. 212 (May 1990):25

**Argentina – the Disappeared**

Mothers of the Disappeared. By Jo Fisher. Reviewed by Patricia Hilliard. *New Directions for Women* 19, No. 5 (September-October 1990):15

**Arguedas, Cristina** (about)

The Best Defense. Karen Cook. *Savvy Woman* (February 1990):67-70, 96-97

**Arico, Santo L.**

Donna: Women in Italian Culture. Book Review. *Canadian Women's Studies* 11, No. 2 (Fall 1990):91

**Arkansas Governor's Mansion.** *See* Governors – United States – Mansions

**Arkin, Marian** and Shollar, Barbara (editors)

The Longman Anthology of World Literature by Women, 1875-1975. Reviewed by Shirley Goek-Lin Lim. *The Women's Review of Books* 7, Nos. 10-11 (July 1990):15-16

**Armani, Georgio** (about). *See also* Fashion Designers, "Battle-Weary Designers"

**Armani, Giorgio** (about)

Bravo Armani! *Harper's Bazaar* (February 1990):136-139

**Armatrading, Joan**

Hearts and Flowers. Reviewed by Elorine Grant. *Spare Rib* No. 214 (July 1990):24

**Armed Forces.** *See also* Military Service

**Armin, Ann**

Women Composers: A Lost Tradition Found. Book Review. *Canadian Women's Studies* 11, No. 1 (Spring 1990):109

**Armstrong, Louise**

A Fearful Freedom: Women's Flight from Equality. Book Review. *The Women's Review of Books* 8, No. 2 (November 1990):9-10

Ideal Freedoms, Real Fears. *The Women's Review of Books* 8, No. 2 (November 1990):9-10

The Personal Is Apolitical. *The Women's Review of Books* 7, No. 6 (March 1990):1 +

Solomon Says: A Speakout on Foster Care. Reviewed by Eleanor J. Bader. *On the Issues* 16 (Fall 1990):33-34

Solomon Says: A Speakout on Foster Care. Reviewed by Nancy D. Polikoff. *The Women's Review of Books* 7, No. 9 (June 1990):23-24

Solomon Says: A Speakout on Foster Care. Reviewed by Stephanie Stein. *New Directions for Women* 19, No. 3 (May/June 1990):19-20

**Armstrong, Nancy**

Desire and Domestic Fiction: A Political History of the Novel. Reviewed by Katharine M. Rogers. *Signs* 15, No. 4 (Summer 1990):878-882

The Occidental Alice. *Differences* 2, No. 2 (Summer 1990):3-40

**Armstrong, Terese** (about). *See* Art–Exhibitions, "Racism"

**Armstrong, Toni, Jr.**

Education as Entertainment: Lesbian Sexpert JoAnn Loulan. *Hot Wire* 6, No. 1 (January 1990):3-5+

Holly Near. *Hot Wire* 6, No. 3 (September 1990):2-5+

How Melissa Etheridge Did Not Get Her Start in Women's Music. *Hot Wire* 6, No. 1 (January 1990):24-25

A Taste of the Canadian Prairies: Heather Bishop. *Hot Wire* 6, No. 2 (May 1990):2-4+

**Armsworth, Mary W.** (joint author). *See* Turell, Susan C.

**Arnaz, Lucie** (about)

Lucie Arnaz: The Gift of Laughter. Vicki Jo Radovsky. *Ladies' Home Journal* 107, No. 10 (October 1990):48-54

**Arnold, David**

Women Who Make a Difference. *Family Circle* 103, No. 7 (May 15, 1990):15-19

**Arnold, Georgiana**

Fat War. *Essence* 21, No. 3 (July 1990):52-53+

**Arnold, June**

Sister Gin. Reviewed by Suzanne Scott. *Belles Lettres* 5, No. 3 (Spring 1990):22

**Aron, Cindy**

Ladies and Gentlemen of the Civil Service: Middle Class Workers in Victorian America. Reviewed by Carole Elizabeth Adams. *Gender & History* 2, No. 3 (Autumn 1990):343-348

**Aronie, Nancy Slonim**

Driven to Question: What Is a Car, Anyway? *Lear's* (April 1990):52

Looking for Her Field of Dreams. *Lear's* (July 1990):40

**Arora, Uma** and Desai, Amprapali

Sex Determination Tests in Surat–A Survey Report. *Manushi* 60 (September-October 1990):37-38

**Arpad, Susan S.**

Taking Our Time: Feminist Perspectives on Temporality. Book Review. *NWSA Journal* 2, No. 2 (Spring 1990):311-314

Tapestries of Life: Women's Work, Women's Consciousness, and the Meaning of Daily Experience. Book Review. *NWSA Journal* 2, No. 2 (Spring 1990):311-314

**Arquette, Kerry** (joint author). *See* Collins, Sue

**Arrarte, Anne**

Sweet Victory. *Ladies' Home Journal* 107, No. 7 (July 1990):44-47

**Arriaga, Isabel** (about)

Mamacita Mía: Her Three Lives. María de la Luz Reyes. *Frontiers* 11, No. 1 (1990):53-59

**Arru, Angiolina**

The Distinguishing Features of Domestic Service in Italy. *Journal of Family History* 15, No. 4 (October 1990):547-566

**Arruda, Angela**

"I Don't Know What It Is to Have a Child." *Connexions* 32 (1990):20

**Arruda, Eloita Neves** (joint author). *See* Meleis, Afaf I.

**Art.** *See also* Aesthetics; Africa–Art; Discrimination in Art; *particular artists and countries*

The Arlington Arts Center: Saving a Space Within the Sprawl. Elisa Barsoum. *Iris* 23 (Spring-Summer 1990):10-12

Art à la Russe. Rosamund Bernier. *Vogue* (May 1990):182-190

Art Makes Political Waves. Phyllis Rosser. *New Directions for Women* 19, No. 4 (July-August 1990):8

Congress Disapproves the Dinner Party. Lorraine Sorrel. *off our backs* 20, No. 9 (October 1990):21

Culture Shock. Jed Perl. *Vogue* (October 1990):377-378

Gold Rush. Jed Perl. *Vogue* (February 1990):216, 225

Medusa Faced. Helen Klebesadel. *Woman of Power* 15 (Fall-Winter 1990):58

The Narrative Paintings of India's Jitwarpuri Women. Jagdish J. Chavda. *Woman's Art Journal* 11, No. 1 (Spring-Summer 1990):26-28

The NEA Is the Least of It. Barbara Smith. *Ms.* 1, No. 3 (November/December 1990):65-67

Nobody's Coming to Dinner Party. Paula Kassel. *New Directions for Women* 19, No. 6 (November-December 1990):12

The Nude: A New Perspective. By Gil Saunders. Reviewed by Sylvia Moore. *New Directions for Women* 19, No. 6 (November-December 1990):24

NWSA Workshop: Old Women in Art. Farar Elliott. *off our backs* 20, No. 8 (August/September 1990):18

Shock of the Mundane. Brooks Adams. *Vogue* (March 1990):344-350

"The World Wall: A Vision of the Future Without Fear": An Interview with Judith F. Baca. Frances K. Pohl. *Frontiers* 11, No. 1 (1990):33-43

Vogue Arts: In Brief. *Vogue* (December 1990):212

Waiting for the Angel. *Spare Rib* 218 (November 1990):30-31

Women, Art, and Power and Other Essays. By Linda Nochlin. Reviewed by Whitney Chadwick. *Woman's Art Journal* 11, No. 2 (Fall 1990-Winter 1991):37-38

### Art – Bibliographies

Annotated Bibliography on Feminist Aesthetics in the Visual Arts. Linda Krumholz and Estella Lauter. *Hypatia* 5, No. 2 (Summer 1990):158-172

**Art – Censorship.** *See also* National Endowment for the Arts

Of Torture and Tangents: Consequences of the Robert Mapplethorpe Exhibition. Stuart Edelson. *Out/Look* No. 7 (Winter 1990):52-53

### Art – Curatorial Practice

Feminism and Art Curatorial Practice. Renee Baert. *Canadian Women's Studies* 11, No. 1 (Spring 1990):9

### Art, Erotic

Patterns of Desire. By Joyce Kozloff. Reviewed by Elizabeth Hess. *The Women's Review of Books* 7, No. 12 (September 1990):10

**Art – Exhibitions.** *See also* New York (City) – Metropolitan Museum of Art – Exhibitions

Altar Ego: A Titian Renaissance at the National Gallery. Thomas Connors. *Harper's Bazaar* (November 1990):168-169

The Other Story: Afro-Asian Artists in post-war Britain. Rita Keegan. *Spare Rib* No. 209 (February 1990):36

Racism: Lesbian Artists Have Their Say. *Out/Look* No. 8 (Spring 1990):38-43

### Art, Feminist

Goddesses Unite: The Making of a Mural. Judy Springer. *Canadian Women's Studies* 11, No. 1 (Spring 1990):97-98

Guess Who's Not Coming to Dinner. Mary Suh. *Ms.* 1, No. 2 (September/October 1990):87

Suffrage Art and Feminism. Alice Sheppard. *Hypatia* 5, No. 2 (Summer 1990):122-136

The Toiled Garden. Lupe Rodriguez. *Canadian Women's Studies* 11, No. 1 (Spring 1990):99

### Art – Feminist Perspectives

Crossing Over: Feminism and Art of Social Concern. By Arlene Raven. Reviewed by Pamela Gerrish Nunn. *Woman's Art Journal* 11, No. 2 (Fall 1990-Winter 1991):42-44

Feminism, Family and Photography. Susan McEachern. *Canadian Women's Studies* 11, No. 1 (Spring 1990):14-15

Feminism in Fine Arts Education. Lynn Hughes, Kathryn Lipke, Barbara MacKay, Cathy Mullen, Elizabeth Sacca, and others. *Canadian Women's Studies* 11, No. 1 (Spring 1990):43-45

Feminist Art Criticism, An Anthology. Edited by Arlene Raven, Cassandra L. Langer, and Joanna Frueh. Reviewed by Pamela Gerrish Nunn. *Woman's Art Journal* 11, No. 2 (Fall 1990-Winter 1991):42-44

Introduction. Marilyn Burgess and Janice Andreae. *Canadian Women's Studies* 11, No. 1 (Spring 1990):5-6

La théorie, un dimanche. By Louky Bersianik, Nicole Brossard, Louise Cotnoir, Louise Dupré, Gail Scott, and others. Reviewed by Dominique Bourque. *Canadian Women's Studies* 11, No. 1 (Spring 1990):107-108

L'autre oeil: Le nu féminin dans l'art masculin. By Marie-Jeanne Musiol. Reviewed by Susanne de Lothinie4re-Harwood. *Canadian Women's Studies* 11, No. 1 (Spring 1990):106

L'histoire de l'art au féminin. Rose-Marie Arbour. *Canadian Women's Studies* 11, No. 1 (Spring 1990):86-89

Male Artists Upstairs, Females in the Basement. Norah Phillips. *Canadian Women's Studies* 11, No. 1 (Spring 1990):103

Towards a Feminist Visual Practice. Alice Mansell. *Canadian Women's Studies* 11, No. 1 (Spring 1990):29-30

### Art – Images of Women

Between Dream and Shadow: William Holman Hunt's Lady of Shalott. Sharyn R. Udall. *Woman's Art Journal* 11, No. 1 (Spring-Summer 1990):34-38

Depoliticizing Women: Female Agency, the French Revolution, and the Art of Boucher and David. Erica Rand. *Genders* 7 (Spring 1990):47-68

Engendering Imaginary Modernism: Henri Matisse's *Bonheur de vivre*. Margaret Werth. *Genders* 9 (Fall 1990):49-74

"Milk White Angels of Art": Images of Women in Turn-of-the-Century America. Bailey Van Hook. *Woman's Art Journal* 11, No. 2 (Fall 1990-Winter 1991):23-29

*The Order of Release* and *Peace Concluded*: Millais's Reversal of a Victorian Formula. Elaine Shefer. *Woman's Art Journal* 11, No. 2 (Fall 1990-Winter 1991):30-33

Women, Pleasure, and Painting (e.g., Boucher). Eunice Lipton. *Genders* 7 (Spring 1990):69-86

## Art, Video

Screens of Resistance: Feminism and Video Art. Dot Tuer. *Canadian Women's Studies* 11, No. 1 (Spring 1990):73-74

## Art Activism

The Guerrilla Girls. *Ms.* 1, No. 2 (September/October 1990):60-63

Painting for Peace: Break the Silence Mural Project. Miranda Bergman, Susan Greene, Dina Redman, and Marlene Tobias. *Bridges* 1, No. 2 (Fall 1990): 39-57

SisterSerpents Strike Abortion Foes. Suzanne Messing. *New Directions for Women* 19, No. 1 (January/February 1990):11

Wee Papa Girls Rap Against the Tax. *Spare Rib* No. 211 (April 1990):12-14

## Art and Politics

Women and the State. Jamelie Hassan. *Canadian Women's Studies* 11, No. 1 (Spring 1990):25-26

## Art Criticism

Koons Crazy. Dodie Kazanjian. *Vogue* (August 1990):338-343+

Oil and Water. Herbert Muschamp. *Vogue* (July 1990):200-205+

Vogue Arts: Charmed Lives. Jed Perl. *Vogue* (August 1990):224-232

## Art Deco

Grand Designs. John McLaughlin. *Harper's Bazaar* (July 1990):84-85+

## Art Education

On Failure and Anonymity. Mira Schor. *Heresies* 25 (1990):7-9

Learning the Arts at University. Raquel Rivera. *Canadian Women's Studies* 11, No. 1 (Spring 1990):46-47

Rap Sheet. Pamela Shoemaker. *Heresies* 25 (1990):61

Toward a Synthetic Art Education. Sheila Pinkel. *Heresies* 25 (1990):66-67

## Artemis Capital Group, Incorporated

Women Watch: Women-Run Companies Create a New Corporate Culture. Patti Watts. *Executive Female* (May/June 1990):10-11

**Art History.** See also Germany – Art History; Modernism (Art)

Art on the Edge. Brooks Adams. *Vogue* (July 1990):94-99

Cascade of Color. Brooks Adams. *Harper's Bazaar* (July 1990):30

Collage Barrage. Thomas Connors. *Harper's Bazaar* (December 1990):50

Deconstructive Criticism. Hunter Drohojowsky. *Harper's Bazaar* (March 1990):46

Drawing the Lines. Kristine McKenna. *Harper's Bazaar* (April 1990):196-197+

The Looks of Light. Allan Schwartzman. *Harper's Bazaar* (January 1990):118-119+

Moroccan Idyll. Jo Ann Lewis. *Harper's Bazaar* (February 1990):166-167+

Out of the Ordinary. Robin Cembalest. *Harper's Bazaar* (October 1990):146-150

Prints of Darkness. Jo Ann Lewis. *Harper's Bazaar* (May 1990):56+

Reflections on Making. Jane Buyers and Susan Shantz. *Canadian Women's Studies* 11, No. 1 (Spring 1990):27-28

The Starker Image. Suzanne Muchnic. *Harper's Bazaar* (April 1990):132

Vogue Arts: Art. Douglas Blau. *Vogue* (September 1990):424-428

## Art History – Feminist Perspectives

Mythology and Misogyny: The Social Discourse of Nineteenth-Century British Classical-Subject Painting. By Joseph A. Kestner. Reviewed by Marcia Pointon. *Gender & History* 2, No. 2 (Summer 1990):238-239

Vision and Difference: Feminism, Femininity and the History of Art. By Griselda Pollock. Reviewed by Eunice Lipton. *Gender & History* 2, No. 1 (Spring 1990):91-97

## Art History – Images of Women

The Female Nude: Pornography, Art, and Sexuality. Notes. Lynda Nead. *Signs* 15, No. 2 (Winter 1990):323-335

## Arthritis

Relationships Among Hardiness, Social Support, Severity of Illness, and Psychological Well-Being in Women with Rheumatoid Arthritis. Vickie A. Lambert, Clinton E. Lambert, Gary L. Klipple, and Elizabeth A. Mewshaw. *Health Care for Women International* 11, No. 2 (1990):159-173

**Arthur, Bea** (about). *See* Sherman, Eric, "Gabbing with the Golden Girls"

## Artificial Fur

Circle This. Margaret Jaworski. *Family Circle* 103, No. 16 (November 27, 1990):11-12

Faking It. *Vogue* (September 1990):620-627

Fantastic Faux: Artful Deception. *Harper's Bazaar* (November 1990):68-72

Great Pretenders. *Harper's Bazaar* (November 1990):176-179

## Artificial Intelligence

Office Tech: The Thinking Machines. Laurel Touby. *Working Woman* (November 1990):87-98

**Artist Books**

Making Artists' Books. Barbara Harman. *Belles Lettres* 5, No. 4 (Summer 1990):4-5

**Artiste, Cindy**

Meridian. Play Adapted from Alice Walker's Novel. Reviewed by Elorine Grant. *Spare Rib* No. 210 (March 1990):36

**Artists**

Artist's Work Reclaims the Female Body. Phyllis Rosser. *New Directions for Women* 19, No. 1 (January/February 1990):10+

Bone by Bone: How and Why to Research the Work of Asian-American Women Artists. Dawn Aotani. *Heresies* 25 (1990):50-52

A Gallery of Women Artists. *Belles Lettres* 5, No. 4 (Summer 1990):7-8

Japanese Women Artists: 1600-1900. By Patricia Fister. Reviewed by Janis Hoogstraten. *Resources for Feminist Research* 19, No. 1 (March 1990):21-22

Making Their Mark: Women Artists Move into the Mainstream, 1970-85. By Randy Rosen, Ellen G. Landau, Calvin Tomkins, Judith E. Stein, Ann-Sargeant Wooster, and others. Reviewed by Thalia Gouma-Peterson. *Woman's Art Journal* 11, No. 2 (Fall 1990-Winter 1991):38-41

Portfolio. Gene Wesley Elder. *Out/Look* No. 7 (Winter 1990):42-43

Six from Un/Common Ground: Virginia Artists 1990. *Iris* 24 (Fall-Winter 1990):30-33

A Studio of One's Own. Scarlet Cheng. *Belles Lettres* 5, No. 4 (Summer 1990):5-6

Toying with Art. Rachel Urquhart. *Vogue* (April 1990):382-388, 420

Women Artists in the United States: A Selective Bibliography and Resource Guide on the Fine and Decorative Arts, 1750-1986. By Paula Chiarmonte. Review. *Feminist Collections* 11, No. 3 (Spring 1990):14

Women in the Arts. Bibliography. Evette Porter. *Essence* 21, No. 1 (May 1990):80-86

**Artists, African-American**

When I Breathe There Is a Space: An Interview with Buseje Bailey. Susan Douglas. *Canadian Women's Studies* 11, No. 1 (Spring 1990):40-42

**Artists, Asian**

In Focus. Prasanna Probyn. *Spare Rib* No. 210 (March 1990):43

**Artists – Personal Narratives.** *See also* Gilot, Franc2oise

**Arts and Crafts.** *See* Craft Arts

**Arts Organizations – Politics**

Squeeze Play at the Kennedy Center. Alison Cook. *Lear's* (November 1990):88-92+

**Asceticism.** *See also* Sexual Repression

The Body and Society: Men, Women and Sexual Renunciation in Early Christianity. By Peter Brown. Reviewed by Elizabeth A. Clark. *Gender & History* 2, No. 1 (Spring 1990):106-109

**Asch, Adrienne** (joint editor). *See* Fine, Michelle

**Ascher, Carol**

Affliction. Book Review. *The Women's Review of Books* 7, No. 7 (April 1990):21

The Roots of Rage. *The Women's Review of Books* 7, No. 7 (April 1990):21

**Ashby, Neal**

Redbook's Home Accident-Prevention Guide for Parents. *Redbook* 176, No. 2 (December 1990):83-88

**Ashe, Arthur** (about)

Smashing! Jon Etra. *Harper's Bazaar* (February 1990):146-147+

**Ashe, Kaye**

Mary's Pence: Refurbishing an Old Tradition. *Woman of Power* 16 (Spring 1990):52-55

**Ashford, José B.** and Le Croy, Craig Winston

Juvenile Recidivism: A Comparison of Three Prediction Instruments. *Adolescence* 25, No. 98 (Summer 1990):442-450

**Ashworth, Georgina** (joint author). *See* Paredes, Ursula

**Asia.** *See also* Family Planning – Asia

Women's Asia. By Matsui Yayori. Reviewed by Yukiko Hanawa. *The Women's Review of Books* 8, No. 2 (November 1990):25-26

**Asia – Bibliographies**

*Journal of Women's History* 2, No. 2 (Fall 1990):190-202

**Asian-American Women.** *See also* Artists

An Analysis of Domestic Violence in Asian American Communities: A Multicultural Approach to Counseling. Christine K. Ho. *Women and Therapy* 9, Nos. 1-2 (1990):129-150

Between Worlds: Women Writers of Chinese Ancestry. By Amy Ling. Reviewed by Scarlet Cheng. *Belles Lettres* 6, No. 1 (Fall 1990):21-22

The Caregiving Roles of Asian American Women. Catherine Chase Goodman. *Journal of Women and Aging* 2, No. 1 (1990):109-120

NWSA Workshop: Asian Immigrant Women. Carol Anne Douglas. *off our backs* 20, No. 8 (August/September 1990):18-19

Power, Patriarchy, and Gender Conflict in the Vietnamese Immigrant Community. Nazli Kibria. *Gender and Society* 4, No. 1 (March 1990):9-24

A Reviews of the Health Status of Southeast Asian Refugee Women. Judith C. Kulig. *Health Care for Women International* 11, No. 1 (1990):49-63

## Asian-American Women – Anthologies

The Forbidden Stitch: An Asian American Women's Anthology. Edited by Shirley Goek-Lin Lim and Mayumi Tsutakawa. Reviewed by Marina Heung. *The Women's Review of Books* 7, No. 4 (January 1990):8-10

Making Waves: An Anthology of Writings By and About Asian American Women. By Asian Women United of California. Reviewed by Dorothy Rony. *Belles Lettres* 5, No. 2 (Winter 1990):12

Making Waves: An Anthology of Writings by and about Asian American Women. Edited by Asian Women United of California. Reviewed by Marina Heung. *The Women's Review of Books* 7, No. 4 (January 1990):8-10

Without Ceremony. By Asian Women United of New York. Reviewed by Dorothy Rony. *Belles Lettres* 5, No. 2 (Winter 1990):12

## Asian-American Women – Employment

With Silk Wings: Asian American Women at Work. Produced by Asian Women United. Reviewed by Keiko Yamanaka. *NWSA Journal* 2, No. 1 (Winter 1990):120-124

## Asian-American Women – Gender Roles

Gender-Role Perceptions: An Intergenerational Study on Asian-American Women. Chi-Kwan Ho. *NWSA Journal* 2, No. 4 (Autumn 1990):679-681

## Asian Art

Europe's Myths of Orient. By Rana Kabbani. Reviewed by Írvin Cemil Schick. *Feminist Studies* 16, No. 2 (Summer 1990):345-380

## Asian Literature

Europe's Myths of Orient. By Rana Kabbani. Reviewed by Írvin Cemil Schick. *Feminist Studies* 16, No. 2 (Summer 1990):345-380

## Asian Studies Association of Australia – Conferences

Asian Studies Association of Australia 8th Biennial Conference. Louise Edwards. *Australian Feminist Studies* No. 12 (Summer 1990):113-114

Asian Studies Association of Australia 8th Biennial Conference, Women's Caucus Day. Tamara Jacka. *Australian Feminist Studies* No. 12 (Summer 1990):109-111

## Asian Studies Curricula

The Politics and Pedagogy of Asian Literatures in American Universities. Rey Chow. *Differences* 2, No. 3 (Fall 1990):29-51

## Asian Women

Asian Women Workers: Organising, Educating and Solidarity. *Women in Action* 1-2 (1990):7-8

Being a Woman in South Asia. *Journal of Women's History* 2, No. 1 (Spring 1990):200-219

The Endless Day: Some Case Material on Asian Rural Women. Book Review. *Journal of Women's History* 2, No. 1 (Spring 1990):200-219

The Endless Day: Some Case Material on Asian Rural Women. Edited by Scarlett T. Epstein and Rosemary A. Watts. Reviewed by Kalpana Bardhan. *Journal of Women's History* 2, No. 1 (Spring 1990):200-219

The Far East Comes Near: Autobiographical Accounts of Southeast Asian Students in America. Edited by Lucy Nguyen-Hong-Nhiem and Joel Martin Halpern. Reviewed by Miriam Ching Louie. *Belles Lettres* 6, No. 1 (Fall 1990):27-28

The Many Sins of "Miss Saigon." Mary Suh. *Ms.* 1, No. 3 (November/December 1990):63

Rural Women at Work: Strategies for Development in South Asia. Book Review. *Journal of Women's History* 2, No. 1 (Spring 1990):200-219

Rural Women at Work: Strategies for Development in South Asia. By Ruth Dixon. Reviewed by Kalpana Bardhan. *Journal of Women's History* 2, No. 1 (Spring 1990):200-219

They Changed Their Worlds: Nine Women of Asia. Book Review. *Journal of Women's History* 2, No. 1 (Spring 1990):200-219

They Changed Their Worlds: Nine Women of Asia. Edited by Mae Handy Esterline. Reviewed by Kalpana Bardhan. *Journal of Women's History* 2, No. 1 (Spring 1990):200-219

## Asian Women – Status

Centre for Women's Research. *Women's World* 23 (April 1990):42

## Asian Women United of California (editors)

Making Waves: An Anthology of Writings By and About Asian American Women. Reviewed by Dorothy Rony. *Belles Lettres* 5, No. 2 (Winter 1990):12

Making Waves: An Anthology of Writings by and about Asian American Women. Reviewed by Marina Heung. *The Women's Review of Books* 7, No. 4 (January 1990):8-10

## Asian Women United of New York

Without Ceremony. Reviewed by Dorothy Rony. *Belles Lettres* 5, No. 2 (Winter 1990):12

## Asian Women United (producer)

With Silk Wings: Asian American Women at Work. Reviewed by Keiko Yamanaka. *NWSA Journal* 2, No. 1 (Winter 1990):120-124

## Asiyo, Phoebe Muga (about)

Daughter of Warriors Aids World's Women. Charlotte Innes. *New Directions for Women* 19, No. 1 (January/February 1990):3

## Asnes, Marion

Economies. Bibliography. *Lear's* (September 1990):42

Economies. *Lear's* (October 1990):44; (November 1990):50; (December 1990):44

Lear's Bulletin. Bibliography. *Lear's* (January 1990):38; (February 1990):36

Lear's Bulletin. *Lear's* (March 1990):44; (April 1990):36; (May 1990):48; (June 1990):44; (July 1990):32; (August 1990):32

## Aspen, CO

Little Nell's: Colorado Cuisine. Dena Kaye. *Harper's Bazaar* (February 1990):186

Rocky Mountain High. Diane Tegmeyer. *Harper's Bazaar* (February 1990):185+

The Ski-and-be-Seen Scene. *Harper's Bazaar* (February 1990):26-38

Stars in Aspen. Susan Price. *Ladies' Home Journal* 107, No. 12 (December 1990):54-59

**Aspen, Kristan** (joint author). *See* MacAuslan, Janna

## Assertive Behavior

Executive Agenda. *Working Woman* (September 1990):130-131

On Your Own. Judith Stone. *Glamour* (June 1990):146

## Association of American Colleges – Project on the Status and Education of Women

Conflict in Academia: Why Was Bunny Sandler Sacked? Peggy Simpson. *Ms.* 1, No. 3 (November/December 1990):86-87

## Association of University Teachers (Scotland)

The Situation of Women Members in Scottish Universities: A Questionnaire Study. Reviewed by Linda McKie. *Gender and Education* 2, No. 2 (1990):257-258

## Association of Women's Music and Culture

The 1990 AWMAC Conference. Jorjet Harper. *Hot Wire* 6, No. 2 (May 1990):34-35+

## Asthma. *See also* Allergy

Could the Problem Be Hidden Asthma? Bruce A. Berlow. *Working Mother* 13, No. 5 (May 1990):72-74

Snooze News. *Essence* 20, No. 12 (April 1990):32

## Astrology

The Great Astrology Test. *Ladies' Home Journal* 107, No. 1 (January 1990):58-65

In the Stars: The Goddess as the Great Astrological Wheel of Life. Geraldine Thorsten. *Woman of Power* 15 (Fall-Winter 1990):70-72

## Asungi

The Face of Mama Is the Blackfaced One. *Woman of Power* 15 (Fall-Winter 1990):36-37

## Atattimur, Sara Deniz (about)

Community Mourns Loss: Sara Deniz Atattimur. Caroline Foty. *off our backs* 20, No. 3 (March 1990):29

## Atcheson, Richard

Back to the Potsdamer Platz. *Lear's* (April 1990):92-97

Ready to Wear: A Clothes Encounter. *Lear's* (October 1990):62-64

**Athavale, Parvati** (about). *See* India – Status of Women

## Atheism

Devotions of a Feminist Atheist. Leah Fritz. *Ms.* 1, No. 2 (September/October 1990):18-19

**Athletes.** *See also* Evert, Chris (about); Garrison, Zina (about); Jennings, Lynn (about); Navratilova, Martina; Spitz, Mark

The Competitive Edge. *Harper's Bazaar* (June 1990):49-54

Good Sports: Mind Games. Joanne Mattera. *Glamour* (December 1990):76

Sporting News. *Women's Sports & Fitness* 12, No. 6 (September 1990):54-57

## Athletics. *See also* Sports

Feminist Issues in Sport. Elizabeth H. Jarratt. *Women's Studies International Forum* 13, No. 5 (1990):491-499

Good Sports. Joanne Mattera. *Glamour* (April 1990):82

Ruling Women Out. Allison Heisch. *The Women's Review of Books* 7, No. 5 (February 1990):23-24

## Athletics – Career Opportunities

It's Not Just a Job, It's a Sport. Kathryn Reith. *Women's Sports & Fitness* 12, No. 6 (September 1990):58-59

## Athletics – Sex Discrimination

Sidelined. Frances Munnings. *Women's Sports & Fitness* 12, No. 6 (September 1990):40-43

## Athletic Shoes. *See* Running Shoes

## Atkin, Sharon

Labour: Auditioning for the General Election. *Spare Rib* 218 (November 1990):43

Labour's New Policies. *Spare Rib* 213 (June 1990):24-25

"The Men in Grey Suits" say Bye Bye Maggie. *Spare Rib* 219 (December 1990-January 1991):62-64

## Atkins, Andrea

The Take-Charge Patient. Bibliography. *Ladies' Home Journal* 107, No. 11 (November 1990):163-174

**Atkins, Andrea** (joint author). *See* Solorzano, Lucia

**Atkinson, Clarissa W.** and others (editors)

Shaping New Vision: Gender and Values in American Culture. Reviewed by Naomi R. Goldenberg. *Signs* 15, No. 4 (Summer 1990):874-878

**Atkinson, Diane**

Votes for Women. Reviewed by Fiona Terry. *Gender & History* 2, No. 3 (Autumn 1990):371-373

**Atkinson, Robert** (joint author). *See* Offer, Daniel

**Atlanta Feminist Women's Chorus**

This Longest Concert: Therese Edell's 40th Birthday Bash. Charlene Ball. *Hot Wire* 6, No. 3 (September 1990):28-29+

**Atlantic Records**

Rap-Sody & Blues. Andrea Davis. *Executive Female* (May/June 1990):44-46

**Attebury, Mary Ann**

Women and Their Wartime Roles. *Minerva* 8, No. 1 (Spring 1990):11-28

**Attention Deficit Disorders**

Managing Attention Disorders in Children: A Guide for Practioners. By Sam Goldstein and Michael Goldstein. Book Review. *Adolescence* 25, No. 100 (Winter 1990):998

**Attention Deficit Hyperactivity Disorder**

Is Your Child Hyperactive? Stephen W. Garber, Marianne Daniels Garber, and Robyn Freedman Spizman. *Redbook* 175, No. 6 (October 1990):32-35

"School was a Nightmare for Tracey." Bonnie Gold and Ellen Byron. *Redbook* 174, No. 5 (March 1990):46-49

**Attorneys.** *See* Lawyers

**Atungaye, Monifa**

Callers. Poem. *Essence* 20, No. 12 (April 1990):109

Ghost Dancing. Poem. *Essence* 20, No. 11 (March 1990):129

**Atwater, Lynn**

Adultery: An Analysis of Love and Betrayal. Book Review. *Journal of Marriage and the Family* 52, No. 2 (May 1990):564

**Atwood, Margaret**

The Age of Lead. Short story. *Lear's* (September 1990):114-119+

Cat's Eye. Reviewed by B. A. St. Andrews. *Belles Lettres* 5, No. 3 (Spring 1990):9

Three Chronicles. Fiction. *Ms.* 1, No. 2 (September/October 1990):80-83

Weight. Short story. *Vogue* (August 1990):328-331+

**Atwood, Margaret – Criticism and Interpretation**

"Basic Victim Positions" and the Women in Margaret Atwood's The Handmaid's Tale. Michael Foley. *Atlantis* 15, No. 2 (Spring 1990):50-58

**Atwood, Margaret – Film Adaptations**

The Handmaid's Tale. Directed by Volker Schlondorff. Reviewed by Laura Flanders. *New Directions for Women* 19, No. 3 (May/June 1990):7

**Aubin, Carol M.** (joint author). *See* Barrett, Susan E.

**Aubin, Jacinthe** (joint author). *See* Paquin, Ghislaine

**Auburn, Sandy**

Caring for the Disabled Elderly: Who Will Pay? Book Review. *Journal of Women and Aging* 2 No. 3 (1990):113-114

**Audiarayana, N.** and Senthilnayaki, M.

Socio-Economic Characteristics Influencing Age at Marriage in a Tamil Nadu Village. *Journal of Family Welfare* 36, No. 1 (March 1990):48-55

**Auel, Jean**

The Plains of Passage. Excerpt. Short story. *Ladies' Home Journal* 107, No. 11 (November 1990):184-193

**Auerbach, Nina**

Ellen Terry: Player in Her Time. Reviewed by Robin Sheets. *Tulsa Studies in Women's Literature* 9, No. 1 (Spring 1990):163-165

**Auletta, Gale Schroeder** (joint author). *See* Paige-Pointer, Barbara

**Aurientis, Dominique** (about)

View: Dominique Aurientis. Charla Carter. *Vogue* (December 1990):120-124

**Auschwitz (Poland) – Carmelite Convent**

When Will We Come to Understand the Jews as They Do Themselves? Sister Rose Thering. *Lilith* 15, No. 2 (Spring 1990):19

**Austin, Barbara** (joint author). *See* Roemer, Joan

**Austin, Mary** (about)

Mary Austin: Song of a Maverick. By Esther Lanigan Stineman. Reviewed by Mary Titus. *Belles Lettres* 6, No. 1 (Fall 1990):40-42

Mary Austin: Songs of a Maverick. By Esther Lanigan Stineman. Reviewed by Lois Rudnick. *The Women's Review of Books* 7, No. 7 (April 1990):22

**Austin, Nancy K.**

"Just Do It": The New Job Strategy. *Working Woman* (April 1990):78-80+

Management: The Death of Hierarchy. *Working Woman* (July 1990):22-25

Managing: How to Get Your Staff Psyched. *Working Woman* (September 1990):68-73

Managing: Race Against Time – and Win. *Working Woman* (November 1990):48-54

**Australasian Political Studies**
**Association – Conferences**

1989 Australasian Political Studies Association
Conference. Lesley Caust. *Australian Feminist
Studies* No. 11 (Autumn 1990):115-116

**Australia – Aboriginals**

Aboriginal Ancestors Journey Home. Rizu Hamid.
*Spare Rib* No. 215 (August 1990):22-25

Women in Australian Prehistory. Wendy Beck and
Lesley Head. *Australian Feminist Studies* No. 11
(Autumn 1990):29-48

**Australia – Aboriginals – Oral Histories**

Life (H)istory Writing: The Relationship between
Talk and Text. Margaret Somerville. *Australian
Feminist Studies* No. 12 (Summer 1990):29-42

**Australia – Education**

Demanding Skill: Women and Technical Education
in Australia. Edited by Barbara Pocock. Reviewed
by Autumn Stanley. *NWSA Journal* 2, No. 4
(Autumn 1990):640-645

Gender Issues and Education. Lesley Johnson.
*Australian Feminist Studies* No. 11 (Autumn
1990):17-27

**Australia – Families**

The Impact of Parental Loss on Adolescents'
Psychosocial Characteristics. Beverley Raphael, Jeff
Cubis, Michael Dunne, Terry Lewin, and Brian
Kelly. *Adolescence* 25, No. 99 (Fall 1990):689-700

**Australia – Feminism**

Bureaucrats, Technocrats, Femocrats: Essays on
the Contemporary Australian State. By Anna
Yeatman. Reviewed by Lois Bryson. *Australian
Feminist Studies* No. 12 (Summer 1990):133-136

Crossing Boundaries: Feminism and the Critique of
Knowledge. By Elizabeth A. Grosz and Marie de
Lepervanch. Reviewed by Elizabeth Higginbotham.
*NWSA Journal* 2, No. 1 (Winter 1990):105-111

Playing the State: Australian Feminist Interventions.
Edited by Sophie Watson. Reviewed by Lois
Bryson. *Australian Feminist Studies* No. 12
(Summer 1990):133-136

Sisters in Suits. By Marian Sawer. Reviewed by Lois
Bryson. *Australian Feminist Studies* No. 12
(Summer 1990):133-136

Staking a Claim: Feminism, Bureaucracy and the
State. By Suzanne Franzway, Dianne Court, and R.
W. Connell. Reviewed by Lois Bryson. *Australian
Feminist Studies* No. 12 (Summer 1990):133-136

**Australia – Film and Filmmakers**

Tale of a Twisted Sister. Jonathan Van Meter.
*Harper's Bazaar* (February 1990):63

**Australia – History**

The Market for Marriage in Colonial Queensland.
Katie Spearritt. *Hecate* 16, Nos. 1-2 (1990):23-42

Seduction and Punishment. Lyn Finch. *Hecate* 16,
Nos. 1-2 (1990):8-22

**Australia – Homosexuality**

Australia: Lesbian Discrimination Fought. Deborah
Singerman. *off our backs* 20, No. 7 (July 1990):9

**Australia – Immigration**

My America – and Yours: A Letter to US Lesbian
and Gay Activists. Dennis Altman. *Out/Look* No. 8
(Spring 1990):62-65

The Politics of Nostalgia: Community and
Difference in Migrant Writing. Efi Hatzimanolis.
*Hecate* 16, Nos. 1-2 (1990):120-127

**Australia – Industrial Relations**

Blue, White and Pink Collar Workers in Australia:
Technicians, Bank Employees and Flight
Attendants. By Claire Williams. Reviewed by
Colleen Chesterman. *Australian Feminist Studies*
No. 11 (Autumn 1990):123-126

Getting Equal: Labour Market Regulation and
Women's Work. By Carol O'Donnell and Philippa
Hall. Reviewed by Cora Vellekoop Baldock.
*Australian Feminist Studies* No. 12 (Summer
1990):43-49

Job Evaluation and Broadbanding in the Western
Australian Public Service. By Diane Loxton and
Patricia Harris. *Australian Feminist Studies* No. 12
(Summer 1990):43-49

Managing Gender: The State, the New Middle
Class and Women Workers, 1830-1930. By Desley
Deacon. Reviewed by Colleen Chesterman.
*Australian Feminist Studies* No. 11 (Autumn
1990):123-126

New Brooms, Restructuring and Training Issues for
Women in the Service Sector. By Women's
Research and Employment Initiatives Program.
Reviewed by Cora Vellekoop Baldock. *Australian
Feminist Studies* No. 12 (Summer 1990):43-49

Patriarchy in the Diamond Mines: Women's Work,
Research and Affirmative Action. By Joan Eveline.
Reviewed by Cora Vellekoop Baldock. *Australian
Feminist Studies* No. 12 (Summer 1990):43-49

Tools of Change: New Technology and the
Democratisation of Work. By John Mathews.
Reviewed by Cora Vellekoop Baldock. *Australian
Feminist Studies* No. 12 (Summer 1990):43-49

**Australia – Inner Cities**

Inner Cities: Australian Women's Memory of Place.
Edited by Drusilla Modjeska. Reviewed by Susan
Sheridan. *Australian Feminist Studies* No. 11
(Autumn 1990):133-135

**Australia – Prostitution**

Decriminalisation in Australia. *Women's World* ,
No. 24 (Winter 1990/91): 44

**Australia – Women's Studies**

Recent Women's Studies Scholarship, 1: History.
Kay Saunders. *Hecate* 16, Nos. 1-2 (1990):171-183

**Austria – Gender Identity**

The Vienna Project on Autobiographies and Gender Identities in Austria. Monika Bernold and Christa Ha1mmerle. *Gender & History* 2, No. 1 (Spring 1990):82-83

**Austria – Prostitution**

Austrian Association of Prostitutes. *Women's World* , No. 24 (Winter 1990/91): 49

Austria's Case. *Women's World* , No. 24 (Winter 1990/91): 43

**Austria – Violence Against Women**

Little Red Riding Hood. *Connexions* 34 (1990):24-25

**Austrian, Sonia G.**

Embryos, Ethics and Women's Rights. Book Review. *AFFILIA* 5, No. 3 (Fall 1990):113-114

**Authority**

Resisting Authority. Carole Ferrier. *Hecate* 16, Nos. 1-2 (1990):134-139

When Yielding Is Not Consenting: Material and Psychic Determinants of Women's Dominated Consciousness and Some of Their Interpretations in Ethnology, Part 2. Nicole-Claude Mathieu. *Feminist Issues* 10, No. 1 (Spring 1990):51-90

On Your Own: Young and In Charge. Judith Stone. *Glamour* (September 1990):178

**Autistic Children**

Establishing the First Stages of Early Reciprocal Interactions between Mothers and Their Autistic Children. Dorothy Gartner and Nancy M. Schultz. *Women and Therapy* 10, Nos. 1/2 (1990):159-167

**Autobiography** The Private Self: Theory and Practice of Women's Autobiographical Writings.. *See also* Biography; Epistolary Literature

American Autobiographies. Nancy Grey Osterud. *Gender & History* 2, No. 1 (Spring 1990):83-87

Autobiographical Voices: Race, Gender, Self-Portraiture. By Françoise Lionnet. Reviewed by Elizabeth R. Baer. *Belles Lettres* 5, No. 2 (Winter 1990):4-6+

Autobiographical Voices: Race, Gender, Self-Portraiture. By Francoise Lionnet. Reviewed by Laura Weiss Zlogar. *Feminist Collections* 11, No. 3 (Spring 1990):7-8

Autobiographical Writings: Women in English Social History, 1800-1914. A Guide to Research, Volume III. Barbara Kanner. *Gender & History* 2, No. 1 (Spring 1990):89-90

Ava: My Story. Excerpt. Ava Gardner. *Good Housekeeping* 211, No. 4 (October 1990):118-120+

Black Texas Women: Literary Self-Portraits. Ruthe Winegarten. *Woman of Power* 16 (Spring 1990):29-31

Double-dealing Fictions. Sarah Schuyler. *Genders* 9 (Fall 1990):75-92

Edith Wharton's Mothers and Daughters. Susan Goodman. *Tulsa Studies in Women's Literature* 9, No. 1 (Spring 1990):127-131

The Female Autobiograph: Theory and Practice of Autobiography from the Tenth to the Twentieth Centuries. Edited by Donna Stanton. Reviewed by Elizabeth R. Baer. *Belles Lettres* 5, No. 2 (Winter 1990):4-6+

The Female Autograph: Theory and Practice of Autobiography from the Tenth to the Twentieth Century. Edited by Domna C. Stanton. Reviewed by Barbara Green. *Tulsa Studies in Women's Literature* 9, No. 1 (Spring 1990):135-139

Hanging up on Mum or Questions of Everyday Life in the Writing of History. Julia Swindells. *Gender & History* 2, No. 1 (Spring 1990):68-78

H.D.'s Auto*heterography*. Dianne Chisholm. *Tulsa Studies in Women's Literature* 9, No. 1 (Spring 1990):79-106

I'll Tell You No Lies: Mary McCarthy's *Memories of a Catholic Girlhood* and the Fictions of Authority. Barbara Rose. *Tulsa Studies in Women's Literature* 9, No. 1 (Spring 1990):107-126

Interpreting Women's Lives: Feminist Theory and Personal Narratives. Edited by Personal Narratives Group. Reviewed by Elizabeth R. Baer. *Belles Lettres* 5, No. 2 (Winter 1990):1 6 i

"Inventing the Self": Oral History as Autobiography. Paula Hamilton. *Hecate* 16, Nos. 1-2 (1990):128-133

Life/Lines: Theorizing Women's Autobiography. Edited by Bella Brodzki and Celeste Schenck. Reviewed by Elizabeth R. Baer. *Belles Lettres* 5, No. 2 (Winter 1990):4-6+

Life/Lines: Theorizing Women's Autobiography. Edited by Bella Brodzki and Celeste Schenck. Reviewed by Patricia Madoo-Lengermann and Jill Niebrugge-Brantley. *Tulsa Studies in Women's Literature* 9, No. 1 (Spring 1990):133-135

The Lund Project on Women's Autobiographies and Diaries in Sweden. Christina Sjöblad. *Gender & History* 2, No. 1 (Spring 1990):87-88

Modern English Auto/Biography and Gender: Introduction. Tinne Vammen. *Gender & History* 2, No. 1 (Spring 1990):17-21

A Poetics of Women's Autobiography: Marginality and the Fictions of Self-Representation. By Sidonie Smith. Reviewed by Elizabeth R. Baer. *Belles Lettres* 5, No. 2 (Winter 1990):4-6+

A Poetics of Women's Autobiography: Marginality and the Fictions of Self-Representation. By Sidonie Smith. Reviewed by Linda Wagner-Martin. *Tulsa Studies in Women's Literature* 9, No. 1 (Spring 1990):139-142

The Private Self: Theory and Practice of Women's Autobiographical Writings. Edited by Shari Benstock. Reviewed by Elizabeth R. Baer. *Belles Lettres* 5, No. 2 (Winter 1990):4-6+

Self, Subject, and Resistance: Marginalities and Twentieth-Century Autobiographical Practice. Sidonie Smith. *Tulsa Studies in Women's Literature* 9, No. 1 (Spring 1990):11-24

"The synthesis of my being": Autobiography and the Reproduction of Identity in Virginia Woolf. *Tulsa Studies in Women's Literature* 9, No. 1 (Spring 1990):59-78

Writing a Woman's Life. By Carolyn Heilbrun. Reviewed by Elizabeth R. Baer. *Belles Lettres* 5, No. 2 (Winter 1990):4-6+

## Autobiography, African-American

Black Women Writing Autobiography: A Tradition Within a Tradition. By Joanne Braxton. Reviewed by Elizabeth R. Baer. *Belles Lettres* 5, No. 2 (Winter 1990):4-6+

## Autobiography and Gender

Biography, Autobiography and Gender in Japan. Noriyo Hayakawa. *Gender & History* 2, No. 1 (Spring 1990):79-82

Masculinity, Autobiography and History. David Morgan. *Gender & History* 2, No. 1 (Spring 1990):34-39

The Vienna Project on Autobiographies and Gender Identities in Austria. Monika Bernold and Christa Ha1mmerle. *Gender & History* 2, No. 1 (Spring 1990):82-83

Auto Mechanics. *See* Automobile Mechanics

## Automobile Driving

In the Driver's Seat. Paul A. Eisenstein. *Family Circle* 103, No. 4 (March l3, 1990):67-69

Tips for Safe Winter Driving. *Good Housekeeping* 211, No. 5 (November 1990):60+

## Automobile Engineers

Sue Cischke: Driving Smart. Celia Slom. *McCall's* 118, No. 1 (October 1990):60-62

## Automobile Mechanics

A Woman for Lear's: Overhaul. Jane Howard. *Lear's* (July 1990):120-123

## Automobiles – Design and Construction

Driving. Cynthia Heimel. *Vogue* (September 1990):480-484

Fast Lane: Capital Style. Lesley Hazleton. *Lear's* (February 1990):32-35

Fast Lane. Lesley Hazleton. *Lear's* (January 1990):36

The Queen of Cars. Lesley Hazleton. *Lear's* (December 1990):40-42

Room on the Road Most Taken. Lesley Hazleton. *Lear's* (October 1990):41-42

Spotlight on a User-Friendly Car. Lesley Hazleton. *Lear's* (November 1990):48

A Zippy Hatchback in Apple Green. Lesley Hazleton. *Lear's* (September 1990):36-37

## Automobiles – Driver Education

Spins, Skids, Curves and Clutches. Leanne Kleinmann. *Savvy Woman* (March 1990):30-32

Turn the Radio Down. Joy Horseman. *Lear's* (March 1990):68

## Automobiles – Equipment and Supplies

Cruise in the Fast Lane. George L. Beiswinger. *Executive Female* (May/June 1990):30-31+

## Automobiles – Maintenance and Repair

Cars: 10 Expert Auto-Body Tips. Alan Wellikoff. *Essence* 20, No. 11 (March 1990):100

On the Road: Car Care for the Couldn't-Care-Less. Denise McCluggage. *Glamour* (June 1990):110

## Automobiles – Purchasing

Anatomy of the Year's Best-Seller. Lesley Hazleton. *Lear's* (July 1990):28-29

Driven to Question: What Is a Car, Anyway? Nancy Slonim Aronie. *Lear's* (April 1990):52

In the Driver's Seat: Families Pick the Winners. Celeste Mitchell. *Family Circle* 103, No. 15 (November 6, 1990):156

In the Driver's Seat. Maxine Lipner. *Executive Female* 13, No. 1 (January-February 1990):26-28

Fantasy or Function: Getting the Car You Want. Don Chaikin. *Essence* 21, No. 7 (November 1990):96-102

Fast Lane: A Gallant Import. Lesley Hazleton. *Lear's* (March 1990):40-42

Fast Lane: Care in the Spirit of Summer. Lesley Hazleton. *Lear's* (August 1990):24-25

Fast Lane: The Van Is Back in Town. Lesley Hazleton. *Lear's* (April 1990):34

Lexus and Infiniti: Luxury for Less. Lesley Hazleton. *Lear's* (May 1990):42-44

The New Family Car. Don Chaikin. *Essence* 21, No. 4 (August 1990):100

On the Road Again. Peter McAlevey. *Savvy Woman* (July/August 1990):25-26

Shopping Smart. Joan Hamburg. *Family Circle* 103, No. 9 (June 26, 1990):26-28

A Tale of Two Mercedes-Benzes. Lesley Hazleton. *Lear's* (June 1990):42-43

Women and Cars: On a Roll. Joanne Mattera. *Glamour* (May 1990):254-259

## Automobiles – Renting

A Wayfarer's Guide to the Dollar. Bibliography. Nancy Dunnan. *Lear's* (July 1990):26-27

**Automobiles – Safety – Child Restraint Systems**

Medinews. Bibliography. Sally Squires. *Ladies' Home Journal* 107, No. 1 (January 1990):84

**Automobiles – Safety – Seat Belts**

Seat Belt Use and Stress in Adolescents. Aric Schichor, Arne Beck, Bruce Bernstein, and Ben Crabtree. *Adolescence* 25, No. 100 (Winter 1990):773-779

**Automobiles – Touring**

Are We There Yet? A Guide to Enjoying Car Travel With Your Kids. Marjorie Cohen. *Family Circle* 103, No. 9 (June 26, 1990):117

Driving. Tad Friend. *Vogue* (August 1990):258-260

Travel. Bibliography. *Glamour* (October 1990):173-176

Travel USA: Trips by Car. *Glamour* (April 1990):173-176

**Automobile Travel.** *See* Automobiles – Touring

**Autonomy (Psychology)**

Family Factors Related to Adolescent Autonomy. Jean A. Pardeck and John T. Pardeck. *Adolescence* 25, No. 98 (Summer 1990):311-319

**Autumn Leaves.** *See* Fall Foliage

**Avdela, Effie** and Psarra, Angelika (editors)

Feminism in Greece Between the Wars: An Anthology. Reviewed by Mary Voyatis. *Gender & History* 2, No. 1 (Spring 1990):122-123

**Aveling, Marian – Criticism and Interpretation**

Postmodernism and History: A Reply to Marian Aveling. Kay Schaffer. *Australian Feminist Studies* No. 11 (Autumn 1990):91-94

**Avery, Byllye Y.**

Breathing Life into Ourselves: The Evolution of the National Black Women's Health Project. *Woman of Power* 18 (Fall 1990):22-25

**Avery, Byllye Y.** (about)

Health Care for the Whole Woman. Liza Nelson. *McCall's* 118, No. 3 (December 1990):35

**Avi-ram, Amitai F.**

The Unreadable Black Body: "Conventional" Poetic Form in the Harlem Renaissance. *Genders* 7 (Spring 1990):32-46

**Awards.** *See* Performance Awards

**Awiakta, Marilou**

The Grandmothers are Coming Back. *Woman of Power* 15 (Fall-Winter 1990):41-42

**Awkward, Michael**

Inspiriting Influences: Tradition, Revision, and Afro-American Women's Novels. Reviewed by Claudia Tate. *Tulsa Studies in Women's Literature* 9, No. 2 (Fall 1990):317-321

**Axelbank, Jeff**

Anxiety 101: Leading the Passover Seder. *Lilith* 15, No. 2 (Spring 1990):13-15

**Axelrod, Toby**

Finding Homes for Jewish Babies. *Lilith* 15, No. 3 (Summer 1990):4-5

**Axinn, June**

Hard-Hatted Women. Book Review. *AFFILIA* 5, No. 2 (Summer 1990):111-112

**Axinn, June** and Stern, Mark

Dependency and Poverty: Old Problems in a New World. Reviewed by Mimi Abramovitz. *Journal of Women and Aging* 2, No. 4 (1990):111-113

**Ayer, M. Jane**

Women and a New Academy: Gender and Cultural Contexts. Book Review. *Feminist Collections* 11, No. 3 (Spring 1990):3-4

Women in Academe: Progress and Prospects. Book Review. *Feminist Collections* 11, No. 3 (Spring 1990):3-4

**Ayre-Jaschke, Leslie**

A Natural Resource. *Healthsharing* 11, No. 2 (March 1990):29-31

**Azadeh**

Iranian Women Filmmakers: A Conference on Contemporary Iranian Cinema. *Spare Rib* No. 210 (March 1990):39

**Azar, Suzanne S.** (about). *See* Texas – Mayors

**Azmon, Yael**

Women and Politics: The Case of Israel. *Women & Politics* 10, No. 1 (1990):43-57

**Azpadu, Dodici**

Omertà. Poem. *Sinister Wisdom* 41 (Summer-Fall 1990):71

# B

**Bâ, Mariama – Criticism and Interpretation**

Mariama Bâ: Parallels, Convergence, and Interior Space. Obioma Nnaemeka. *Feminist Issues* 10, No. 1 (Spring 1990):13-35

**Babow, Irving** and Rowe, Robin

A Suicidal Adolescent's Sleeping Beauty Syndrome: Cessation Orientations toward Dying, Sleep, and Drugs. *Adolescence* 25, No. 100 (Winter 1990):791-798

**Baby Boomers.** *See* Baby Boom Generation

**Baby Boom Generation**

All Grown Up. Lois Joy Johnson. *Ladies' Home Journal* 107, No. 1 (January 1990):102-108

Baby Boomer Odyssey. *Lear's* (May 1990):124-125

Having It All. Frances Lear. *Lear's* (February 1990):136

**Baby Boom Generation – Career Planning**

The Brash Pack. Katherine Ann Samon. *Working Woman* (August 1990):66-69

**Baby Boom Generation – Demographic Measurements**

Beyond Thirtysomething. Debra Kent. *Working Woman* (September 1990):150-153+

**Baby Boom Generation – Financial Planning**

Saving Grace: Leave It to Boomer? Patricia O'Toole. *Lear's* (July 1990):22-23

**Baby Foods**

A Feed-Your-Baby Quiz. Michelle Patrick. *Essence* 20, No. 11 (March 1990):104+

**Baby M.** *See* Whitehead, Mary Beth

**Baby Sitters** . *See* Child Care

**Baca, Judith F.** (interview)

"The World Wall: A Vision of the Future Without Fear": An Interview with Judith F. Baca. Frances K. Pohl. *Frontiers* 11, No. 1 (1990):33-43

**Bacci, Massimo Livi** and Breschi, Marco

Italian Fertility: An Historical Account. *Journal of Family History* 15, No. 4 (October 1990):385-408

**Bachmann, Ingeborg**

Three Paths to the Lake. Reviewed by Nancy Derr. *Belles Lettres* 5, No. 4 (Summer 1990):10

**Bachrach, Judy**

Casanova Slept Here . . . and You Had to Make the Bed. *Savvy Woman* (June 1990):58-59

How Can Cupid Be So Stupid? *Savvy Woman* (February 1990):56-58, 92

Puce Becomes You . . . And Other Secrets of European Style. *Savvy Woman* (November 1990):68-71+

**Back – Diseases.** *See* Backache

**Back – Exercise**

Weight Training Back in Action. Marjorie McCloy and Sophie Taggart. *Women's Sports & Fitness* 12, No. 6 (September 1990):18

**Back, Rachel Tzvia**

A Second Sara. Poem. *Bridges* 1, No. 2 (Fall 1990): 59

From the Watertower. Poem. *Bridges* 1, No. 2 (Fall 1990): 93-94

**Backache**

Compact Disks, Pelvic Twists. William Harrel. *Lear's* (December 1990):45-46

Safe Sex for Bad Backs. Jane Shiyen Chou. *McCall's* 117, No. 10 (July 1990):60

**Back Pain.** *See* Backache

**Backstrom, Kirsten**

Rogue. *Trivia* 16/17 (Fall 1990):3-17

**Bad Breath.** *See* Breath, Offensive

**Bádéjo4dot, Diedre L.**

The Goddess O4dotsdotun as a Paradigm for African Feminist Criticism. *Sage* 6, No. 1 (Summer 1989):27-32

**Bader, Eleanor J.**

Bird of Paradise. Book Review. *New Directions for Women* 19, No. 5 (September-October 1990):20

The Blue Nature. Book Review. *Belles Lettres* 5, No. 2 (Winter 1990):21

A Common Voice That Refutes Terrorism. *Belles Lettres* 5, No. 3 (Spring 1990):2-3

Damage to the Newborns. *New Directions for Women* 19, No. 2 (March/April 1990):8

Dredging in the Depths of Dysfunction. *Belles Lettres* 5, No. 3 (Spring 1990):6

Emma Goldman in Exile: From the Russian Revolution to the Spanish Civil War. Book review. *Lilith* 15, No. 1 (Winter 1990):7

Environmental Action: Time Is Running Out. *On the Issues* 17 (Winter 1990):24-26+

Falling Angels. Book Review. *Belles Lettres* 5, No. 3 (Spring 1990):8

Fourth International Book Fare, June 1990. *Belles Lettres* 6, No. 1 (Fall 1990):59-61

Friends: Who We Like, Why We Like Them and What We Do with Them. Book review. *Lilith* 15, No. 3 (Summer 1990):6-7

Holding the Line: Women in the Great Arizona Mine Strike of 1983. Book Review. *Belles Lettres* 5, No. 4 (Summer 1990):16

I Am of Ireland: Women of the North Speak Out. Book Review. *Belles Lettres* 5, No. 3 (Spring 1990):2-3

Mary Heaton Vorse: The Life of an American Insurgent. Book Review. *Belles Lettres* 5, No. 2 (Winter 1990):13

NOW Confronts Racism. *New Directions for Women* 19, No. 6 (November-December 1990):3+

NOW Seeks Racial Diversity. *New Directions for Women* 19, No. 6 (November-December 1990):11

Political Prisoner's Trials. *New Directions for Women* 19, No. 3 (May/June 1990):metrö

Pregnant Drug Users Face Jail. *New Directions for Women* 19, No. 2 (March/April 1990):1+

Solomon Says: A Speakout on Foster Care. Book Review. *On the Issues* 16 (Fall 1990):33-34

From Stones to Statehood: The Palestinian Uprising. Book Review. *On the Issues* 15 (Summer 1990):16-17+

They Would Not Be Moved. *Belles Lettres* 5, No. 4 (Summer 1990):16

Topsy Dingo Wild Dog. Book Review. *New Directions for Women* 19, No. 2 (March/April 1990):21

Toward a Feminist Theory of the State. Book Review. *On the Issues* 14 (1990):26-28

White Girls. Book Review. *Belles Lettres* 5, No. 3 (Spring 1990):8

The Woman Who Was Not All There. Book Review. *Belles Lettres* 5, No. 2 (Winter 1990):13

Women in Ireland. Book Review. *Belles Lettres* 5, No. 3 (Spring 1990):2-3

**Bader, Eleanor J.** and Lanker, Brian

"I Dream a World." *On the Issues* 14 (1990):16-20

**Badgley, Mark** (about). *See also* Popular Culture

**Badinter, Elisabeth**

The Unopposite Sex: The End of the Gender Battle. Reviewed by Marianne LaFrance. *Psychology of Women Quarterly* 14, No. 3 (September 1990):441-443

**Badminton**

Badminton Is No Picnic. Elliot Tannenbaum. *Women's Sports and Fitness* 12, No. 7 (October 1990):57-58

**Badran, Margot** and Cooke, Miriam (editors)

Opening the Gates: A Century of Arab Feminist Writing. Reviewed by Lina Mansour. *Spare Rib* No. 214 (July 1990):36-41

**Baer, Elizabeth R.**

Autobiographical Voices: Race, Gender, Self-Portraiture. Book Review. *Belles Lettres* 5, No. 2 (Winter 1990):4-6+

Black Women Writing Autobiography: A Tradition Within a Tradition. Book Review. *Belles Lettres* 5, No. 2 (Winter 1990):4-6+

The Female Autobiograph: Theory and Practice of Autobiography from the Tenth to the Twentieth Centuries. Book Review. *Belles Lettres* 5, No. 2 (Winter 1990):4-6+

Interpreting Women's Lives: Feminist Theory and Personal Narratives. Book Review. *Belles Lettres* 5, No. 2 (Winter 1990):4-6+

Life/Lines: Theorizing Women's Autobiography. Book Review. *Belles Lettres* 5, No. 2 (Winter 1990):4-6+

A Poetics of Women's Autobiography: Marginality and the Fictions of Self-Representation. Book Review. *Belles Lettres* 5, No. 2 (Winter 1990):4-6+

The Private Self: Theory and Practice of Women's Autobiographical Writings. Book Review. *Belles Lettres* 5, No. 2 (Winter 1990):4-6+

The Texts of Self. *Belles Lettres* 5, No. 2 (Winter 1990):4-6+

Writing a Woman's Life. Book Review. *Belles Lettres* 5, No. 2 (Winter 1990):4-6+

**Baer, Judith A.**

What We Know as Women: A New Look at *Roe v. Wade*. *NWSA Journal* 2, No. 4 (Autumn 1990):558-582

**Baert, Renee**

Feminism and Art Curatorial Practice. *Canadian Women's Studies* 11, No. 1 (Spring 1990):9

**Bagby, Rachel**

Poem. *Woman of Power* 15 (Fall-Winter 1990):19

**Bailey, Buseje** (interview)

When I Breathe There Is a Space: An Interview with Buseje Bailey. Susan Douglas. *Canadian Women's Studies* 11, No. 1 (Spring 1990):40-42

**Bailey, Esther**

All Hail Queen Latifah. Music Review. *Spare Rib* 217 (October 1990):27

Down to Earth. *Spare Rib* 218 (November 1990):38-39

Driving Miss Daisy. Film Review. *Spare Rib* No. 211 (April 1990):31

Limit Up. Film Review. *Spare Rib* No. 214 (July 1990):32

Mo' Better Blues. Film Review. *Spare Rib* 217 (October 1990):29

Roger and Me. Film Review. *Spare Rib* No. 212 (May 1990):28

Romuald & Juliet. Film Review. *Spare Rib* No. 216 (September 1990):32-33

She Rockers Live at the Fridge. *Spare Rib* No. 209 (February 1990):32

**Bailey, Janet**

Stunning Success. *Harper's Bazaar* (October 1990):174-175+

**Bailey, Peter**

Parasexuality and Glamour: The Victorian Barmaid as Cultural Prototype. *Gender & History* 2, No. 2 (Summer 1990):148-172

**Bair, Deirdre**

Simone de Beauvoir: A Biography. Reviewed by Carol Anne Douglas. *off our backs* 20, No. 7 (July 1990):20

Simone de Beauvoir: A Biography. Reviewed by Germaine Brée. *The Women's Review of Books* 8, No. 1 (October 1990):1+

Simone de Beauvoir: A Biography. Reviewed by Isabel Hill Fucigna. *Belles Lettres* 6, No. 1 (Fall 1990):45-46

**Baird, Barbara**

Feminist History Conference. *Australian Feminist Studies* No. 12 (Summer 1990):117-119

**Bajaj, Rupan** (about)

How Elite Is Elite?: Women in the Civil Services. *Manushi* 56 (January-February 1990):18-21

**Baker, Anita**

Compositions. Reviewed by Elorine Grant. *Spare Rib* No. 215 (August 1990):30

**Baker, Anita** (about). *See* Musicians, Popular, "Repeat Performance"

**Baker, Ann**

Spiritual Warfare: The Politics of the Christian Right. Book Review. *New Directions for Women* 19, No. 1 (January/February 1990):25

**Baker, Ava J.** (about). *See also* Lawyers

**Baker, Deborah** (joint editor). *See* Skevington, Suzanne

**Baker, Donna**

O My Cordelia. Romantic Novel. *Good Housekeeping* 211, No. 5 (November 1990):235-238+

**Baker, Ella** (about). *See also* Black History

Fundi: The Story of Ella Baker. Directed by Joanne Grant. Reviewed by C. Alejandra Elenes. *Feminist Collections* 11, No. 3 (Spring 1990):10-11

**Baker, Josephine** (about)

Jazz Cleopatra: Josephine Baker in Her Time. By Phyllis Rose. Reviewed by Mindy Aloff. *The Women's Review of Books* 7, No. 4 (January 1990):1+

Jazz Cleopatra: Josephine Baker in Her Time. By Phyllis Rose. Reviewed by Perdita Schaffner. *New Directions for Women* 19, No. 3 (May/June 1990):25

Vocal Heroes. David Thigpen. *Harper's Bazaar* (November 1990):172-175

**Baker, Kristin** (about). *See* Title, Stacy

Queen of the Beasts. James Gordon Bennett. *Vogue* (June 1990):238-241, 281

**Baker, Lynn S.**

Haunted by Intellect, Hobbled by Wisdom. *Lear's* (September 1990):60-64

**Baker, Nicholson**

Room Temperature. Reviewed by Anne Lamott. *Mademoiselle* (April 1990):130

**Baker, Russell**

My Best Cellar. *Lear's* (August 1990):66-69

**Baker, Sandy** (about). *See* Fashion Designers, "Top Women Designers"

**Baker, Sharlene**

Finding Signs. Reviewed by Jane Smiley. *Vogue* (April 1990):278-281

**Baker, Therese L.**

Women in Academe: Progress and Prospects. Book Review. *Gender and Society* 4, No. 2 (June 1990):277-281

Women of Academe: Outsiders in the Sacred Grove. Book Review. *Gender and Society* 4, No. 2 (June 1990):277-281

**Bakerman, Jane**

The Criminal Element. *Belles Lettres* 5, No. 2 (Winter 1990):19; 5, No. 3 (Spring 1990):21; 5, No. 4 (Summer 1990):36-37; 6, No. 1 (Fall 1990):51-52

**Bakers and Bakeries**

Bake-Shop Secrets. *Ladies' Home Journal* 107, No. 4 (April 1990):192-197

**Baking**

As American as Apple Pie. Excerpt. Phillip Stephen Schulz. *Ladies' Home Journal* 107, No. 4 (April 1990):205-208

Best Baking Guide. *Family Circle* 103, No. 16 (November 27, 1990):102-119

Big-Deal Desserts. Maida Heather. *Ladies' Home Journal* 107, No. 9 (September 1990):190-191+

Homemade Bread! *Good Housekeeping* 211, No. 4 (October 1990):172-176

The Most-Common Cooking Mistakes. *Ladies' Home Journal* 107, No. 4 (April 1990):210-214

**Bakker, Tammy Faye** (about)

Tammy at Twilight. Cliff Jahr. *Ladies' Home Journal* 107, No. 7 (July 1990):88-96

**Bakos, Susan Crain**

Endless Desire. *Harper's Bazaar* (August 1990):36

**Bal, Mieke**

Death and Dissymmetry: The Politics of Coherence in the Book of Judges. Reviewed by Kelly Oliver. *Hypatia* 5, No. 3 (Fall 1990):169-171

**Bal, Vidya** (interview)

Fighting Wife Abuse in India. Alice Henry. *off our backs* 20, No. 3 (March 1990):21

**Balaban, Nancy**

How to Give a Great Birthday Party. *Good Housekeeping* 211, No. 3 (September 1990):116-118

"That Drives Me Crazy." *Working Mother* (December 1990):76-81

Toddlers Need Understanding. *Working Mother* 13, No. 10 (October 1990):86-88

**Balahoutis, Linda** (about). *See* Partnerships

**Balancing Work and Family Life.** *See also* Career-Family Conflict; Lasker, Joan (about); Marriage – Counseling; Mothers Working Outside the Home; Priorities; Stoppi, Isa (about); Tynan, Kathleen (about)

Attention Working Women: Rate Your Stress Life. *Redbook* 175, No. 2 (June 1990):83-90

Backtalk: Worked Up. Barbara Ehrenreich. *Lear's* (January 1990):125-131

The Busy Life: The Career, the Husband, the Kids and Everything. Margaret Shakespeare. *Working Woman* (December 1990):94-98

Can This Marriage Be Saved? "He's There for Everyone Except Me." Margery D. Rosen. *Ladies' Home Journal* 107, No. 3 (March 1990):10-21

Can This Marriage Be Saved? "We Can't Stop Fighting." Margery D. Rosen. *Ladies' Home Journal* 107, No. 2 (February 1990):14-20

Claiming the Future. Mary Catherine Bateson. *Lear's* (February 1990):84-87

A Delicate Balance: "The Trick Is Not to Panic." Robin Sanders. *Ladies' Home Journal* 107, No. 3 (March 1990):163-166

Few Choices: Women, Work and Family. By Ann Duffy, Nancy Mandell, and Norene Pupo. Reviewed by Peta Tancred. *Resources for Feminist Research* 19, No. 1 (March 1990):15

The Good News about Women and Work and the 90's. Betty Friedan. *Glamour* (March 1990):260-265+

Having It All. Frances Lear. *Lear's* (February 1990):136

On Her Own: Growing Up in the Shadow of the American Dream. By Ruth Sidel. Reviewed by Carolyn Keith. *AFFILIA* 5, No. 4 (Winter 1990):117-118

How Is Your Work Affecting Your Health, Your Family, Your Life? *McCall's* 117, No. 9 (June 1990):29-34

How to *Really* Enjoy Your Kids. Pamela Redmond Satran. *Ladies' Home Journal* 107, No. 11 (November 1990):146-151

Instant Chic: Busy Moms' Timesaving Tips. *Ladies' Home Journal* 107, No. 9 (September 1990):34-38

Living Beautifully: Make Time to Do It Now! Alexandra Stoddard. *McCall's* 118, No. 1 (October 1990):164

Long Time Love. Pearl Lewis and Peter Lewis. *Essence* 21, No. 1 (May 1990):139-142+

Lunch. Interview. Frances Lear. *Lear's* (May 1990):17-18

Make Room for Daddy. David Laskin. *Redbook* 174, No. 5 (March 1990):122-123+

Managing School-Day Mornings. Bibliography. *McCall's* 118, No. 2 (November 1990):159-166

Opinion Makers: Working Mothers Should . . . *Redbook* 174, No. 6 (April 1990):70

Out Box: Chung's Choice. Gail Collins. *Working Woman* (December 1990):110

Parenthood: A Special Report on Families Today. *Ladies' Home Journal* 107, No. 6 (June 1990):71-75

PB & J: One Mother's Story. Anne Sheffield. *Ladies' Home Journal* 107, No. 8 (August 1990):72

Precious Moments. Jennet Conant. *Harper's Bazaar* (March 1990):21-22

Private Lives: Too Close for Comfort? Sharon Johnson. *Family Circle* 103, No. 13 (September 25, 1990):30-34

Quality Mommy Time. Alice Fleming. *Redbook* 174, No. 6 (April 1990):92-95

Tapestries of Life: Women's Work, Women's Consciousness, and the Meaning of Daily Life. By Bettina Aptheker. Reviewed by Elizabeth Dane. *AFFILIA* 5, No. 4 (Winter 1990):110-111

Time for Love. Joy Duckett Cain and Pamela Toussaint. *Essence* 20, No. 10 (February 1990):90-92

Viewpoint: The Tyranny of Having It All. Ce Ce Iandoli. *Executive Female* (March/April 1990):29-30

Voices of the Decade. Kathryn Casey. *Ladies' Home Journal* 107, No. 1 (January 1990):66-72

What's the Most Stressful Job in the World? Deborah Shaw Lewis and Gregg Lewis. *Redbook* 175, No. 6 (October 1990):102-103+

A Woman for Lear's: Strong Medicine. Jane Howard. *Lear's* (September 1990):156-159

Work Daze. Anita Diamant. *Harper's Bazaar* (October 1990):166-169+

On Your Own: Option Overload. Judith Stone. *Glamour* (April 1990):154

**Balaskas, Janet**

New Active Birth: A Concise Guide to Natural Childbirth. Reviewed by Julia Sundin. *Healthright* 9, No. 3 (May 1990):40

**Baldessari, John** (about)

Deconstructive Criticism. Hunter Drohojowsky. *Harper's Bazaar* (March 1990):46

**Baldock, Cora Vellekoop**

Getting Equal: Labour Market Regulation and Women's Work. Book Review. *Australian Feminist Studies* No. 12 (Summer 1990):43-49

Job Evaluation and Broadbanding in the Western Australian Public Service. Book Review. *Australian Feminist Studies* No. 12 (Summer 1990):43-49

New Brooms, Restructuring and Training Issues for Women in the Service Sector. Book Review. *Australian Feminist Studies* No. 12 (Summer 1990):43-49

Patriarchy in the Diamond Mines: Women's Work, Research and Affirmative Action. Book Review. *Australian Feminist Studies* No. 12 (Summer 1990):43-49

Tools of Change: New Technology and the Democratisation of Work. Book Review. *Australian Feminist Studies* No. 12 (Summer 1990):43-49

**Baldwin, Alec** (about)

Alec Baldwin: A Movie Star for the Discriminating Woman. Charla Krupp. *Glamour* (April 1990):190

**Baldwin, Beverly A.**

Nursing a Loved One at Home: A Care Giver's Guide. Book Review. *Journal of Women and Aging* 2, No. 1 (1990):121-123

**Baldwin, S. Elizabeth** and Baranoski, Madelon Visintainer

Family Interactions and Sex Education in the Home. *Adolescence* 25, No. 99 (Fall 1990):573-582

**Bali – Travel**

Fantasy Island. *Ladies' Home Journal* 107, No. 7 (July 1990):106-111

**Balides, Constance**

Feminism and Foucault: Reflections on Resistance. Book Review. *Camera Obscura* No. 22 (January 1990):138-149

A Question of Silence. Film review. *Feminist Collections* 12, No. 1 (Fall 1990):14-18

**Balk, Leah**

"I Couldn't Cope with Motherhood." *Working Mother* (November 1990):38-43

**Balka, Christie**

On the Picket Lines: Defending Abortion Rights. Excerpt. *Lilith* 15, No. 1 (Winter 1990):4

**Balka, Christie** and Rose, Andy (editors)

Twice Blessed: On Being Lesbian, Gay, and Jewish. Reviewed by Chaia Lehrer. *New Directions for Women* 19, No. 4 (July-August 1990):15

Twice Blessed: On Being Lesbian, Gay, and Jewish. Reviewed by Joan Joffe Hall. *Lilith* 15, No. 3 (Summer 1990):7 +

Twice Blessed: On Being Lesbian, Gay *and* Jewish. Reviewed by Joan Nestle. *Bridges* 1, No. 1 (Spring 1990): 102-104

Twice Blessed: On Being Lesbian, Gay and Jewish. Reviewed by Rebecca Gordon. *The Women's Review of Books* 7, No. 9 (June 1990):7-8

**Ball, Aimee Lee**

The Cradle Will Fall: The Tragedy of Peggy Ann Barsness. *Mademoiselle* (November 1990):184-187 +

Goodbye Paycheck! Hello Apron! *Mademoiselle* (January 1990):1363-137 +

Health: Herbal Tonics. *Vogue* (September 1990):454-458

Single Girls, Married Guys. *Mademoiselle* (July 1990):96-97, 148-151

**Ball, Anna Caroline** (about). *See also* Family Owned Business

**Ball, Charlene**

This Longest Concert: Therese Edell's 40th Birthday Bash. *Hot Wire* 6, No. 3 (September 1990):28-29 +

**Ball, Lucille** (about). *See* Arnaz, Lucie (about); Lamanna, Dean and Leigh, Pamela

**Ballantine, Jeanne** and Lemkau, Jeanne

The Search for Acceptance: Consumerism, Sexuality, and Self among American Women. Book Review. *Psychology of Women Quarterly* 14, No. 3 (September 1990):443-444

**Ballard, Martha** (about)

A Midwife's Tale: The Life of Martha Ballard, Based on Her Diary, 1785-1812. By Laurel Thatcher Ulrich. Reviewed by Lynn Z. Bloom. *Belles Lettres* 6, No. 1 (Fall 1990):48-49

**Ballet.** *See also* American Ballet Theatre; Bolshoi Ballet; Dance

Dance. David Daniel. *Vogue* (July 1990):100-106

**Ballmer-Cao, Thanh-Huyen**

La conservatisme politique féminin en Suisse: Mythe ou réalité. Reviewed by Sylvie Arend. *Canadian Women's Studies* 11, No. 2 (Fall 1990):93

**Ballou, Mary B.**

Approaching a Feminist-Principled Paradigm in the Construction of Personality Theory. *Women and Therapy* 9, Nos. 1-2 (1990):23-40

**Balsamo, Anne**

Reading the Body in Contemporary Culture: An Annotated Bibliography. *Women & Language* 13, No. 1 (Fall 1990):64-85

**Balsamo, Anne** and Treichler, Paula A.

Feminist Cultural Studies: Questions for the 1990s. *Women & Language* 13, No. 1 (Fall 1990):3-6

**Balser, Diane**

Sisterhood and Solidarity: Feminism and Labor in Modern Times. Reviewed by Jane DeHart. *Signs* 15, No. 2 (Winter 1990):405-408

**Balter, Lawrence**

How to Boost Your Child's Self-Esteem. *Ladies' Home Journal* 107, No. 11 (November 1990):106-109

Understanding Kids. *Ladies' Home Journal* 107, No. 3 (March 1990):92; 107, No. 8 (August 1990):74; 107, No. 10 (October 1990):76; 107, No. 12 (December 1990):64

**Bamber, Linda**

Class Struggle. *The Women's Review of Books* 7, No. 5 (February 1990):20-21

**Bamboo Productions**

There's Something About a Convent Girl . . . Reviewed by Irene Coffey. *Spare Rib* 219 (December 1990-January 1991):35

**Banashek, Mary-Ellen**

Beauty: Put Your Best Face Forward. *Essence* 20, No. 10 (February 1990):12-13+

Dark Victory. *Lear's* (October 1990):110-113

Sensitive Skin. *Essence* 20, No. 9 (January 1990):68-70+

**Bancroft, Anne** (about)

Lunch. Interview. Frances Lear. *Lear's* (November 1990):23-24

**Bandini, Angela** (about)

Fitness. Vicki Woods. *Vogue* (April 1990):228-230

**Bandler, Michael J.**

Danny De Vito: Reaching New Heights. *Ladies' Home Journal* 107, No. 1 (January 1990):76-80

Faith Ford: F. Y. I. *Ladies' Home Journal* 107, No. 6 (June 1990):130

Lee Remick's Quiet Fight. *Ladies' Home Journal* 107, No. 5 (May 1990):62-65

Mary Steenburgen: Ahead to the Future. *Ladies' Home Journal* 107, No. 7 (July 1990):38-40

**Banerjee, Sumanta**

Having the Last Laugh: Women in Nineteenth Century Bengali Farces. *Manushi* No. 59 (July-August 1990):15-20

**Bangladesh – Family Planning**

Determinants of Desired Family Size in Rural Bangladesh: A Two-Stage Analysis. Bashir Ahmed. *Journal of Family Welfare* 36, No. 1 (March 1990):22-31

**Bangladesh – Prostitution**

A Suburban Brothel in Bangladesh. *Women's World* , No. 24 (Winter 1990/91): 14

**Bangladesh – Status of Women**

The Invisible Resource: Women and Work in Rural Bangladesh. By Ben J. Wallace, Rosie Mujid Ahsan, Shahnaz Huq Hussain, and Ekramul Ahsan. Reviewed by Sue Ellen Charlton. *Signs* 15, No. 4 (Summer 1990):860-864

Village Women of Bangladesh: Prospects for Change. Edited by Tahrunnesa Abdullah and Sondra Zeidenstein. Reviewed by Kalpana Bardhan. *Journal of Women's History* 2, No. 1 (Spring 1990):200-219

Woes of Tribal Garment Girls: Bangladesh. Rosaline Costa. *Women in Action* 1-2 (1990):20

**Bank Accounts.** *See* Banks and Banking – Checking Accounts

**Bankaitis-Davis, Bunki** (about)

Spinning Their Wheels. Michele Kort. *Ms.* 1, No. 1 (July/August 1990):84-85

**Bankruptcy.** *See also* Business Failures

All Tapped Out, No Place to Go. Debra Wishik Englander. *Savvy Woman* (November 1990):26

**Banks, Ann**

First Person Singular: Out of Joint. *Savvy Woman* (July/August 1990):90+

**Banks, Bill**

Your Brilliant New Career. *Savvy* (December-January 1991):37-38

**Banks, Carolyn**

Viña Delmar. *Belles Lettres* 5, No. 3 (Spring 1990):14

The Virgin of Polish Hill. Short Story. *Belles Lettres* 5, No. 4 (Summer 1990):11-14

**Banks, Olive**

Knowledgeable Women: Structuralism and the Reproduction of Elites. Book Review. *Gender and Education* 2, No. 1 (1990):97-98

**Banks, Russell**

Affliction. Reviewed by Carol Ascher. *The Women's Review of Books* 7, No. 7 (April 1990):21

**Banks and Banking.** *See also* Saving and Investment

**Banks and Banking – Checking Accounts**

First Person Singular: Out of Joint. Ann Banks. *Savvy Woman* (July/August 1990):90+

**Banneker, Revon Kyle**

Marlon Riggs Untied. Interview. *Out/Look* No. 10 (Fall 1990):14-18

**Bannister, Shelley** (joint author). *See* Evans, Lee

**Banta, Martha**

Imaging American Women: Idea and Ideals in Cultural History. Reviewed by Barbara Green. *Tulsa Studies in Women's Literature* 9, No. 1 (Spring 1990):135-139

**Bao, Jiemin**

Sino-Thai Women in Bangkok: Social Change and Marriage Patterns. *NWSA Journal* 2, No. 4 (Autumn 1990):699-700

**Baraban, Regina**

Get Organized. *Working Woman* (January 1990):116-119

**Barad, Elizabeth**

Madame la Présidente. *Ms.* 1, No. 1 (July/August 1990):13

**Barad, Jill** (about). *See also* Success in Business, "Talent at Work"

It's How You Play the Game. Kim Masters. *Working Woman* (May 1990):88-91

**Baranoski, Madelon Visintainer** (joint author). *See* Baldwin, S. Elizabeth

**Baranowski, Marc D.,** Schilmoeller, Gary L., and Higgins, Barbara S.

Parenting Attitudes of Adolescent and Older Mothers. *Adolescence* 25, No. 100 (Winter 1990):781-790

**Baranskaya, Natalya**

A Week Like Any Other. Reviewed by Barbara Ahna. *The Women's Review of Books* 7, Nos. 10-11 (July 1990):33-34

**Barash, Carol**

Reprint Rights, Reprint Wrongs. *The Women's Review of Books* 7, No. 5 (February 1990):11-12

**Barbagli, Marzio** and Kertzer, David

An Introduction to the History of Italian Family Life. *Journal of Family History* 15, No. 4 (October 1990):369-383

**Barbecue Cookery**

Dinner ASAP: Grill Power. Jean Galton. *Working Woman* (September 1990):207

Fired Up, or Fear of Flugging. Peter Feibleman. *Lear's* (July 1990):47-48

Great American Barbecue. *Ladies' Home Journal* 107, No. 7 (July 1990):120-125

Step-by-Step: Barbecued Pork on a Bun. *Good Housekeeping* 211, No. 4 (October 1990):30

Summer Barbecue Cookbook. *McCall's* 117, No. 10 (July 1990):103-107 +

**Barbee-Wootin, Daphne** (about). *See also* Lawyers

**Barber, Phyllis**

Belly Dancers' Reunion. Short Story. *Frontiers* 11, Nos. 2-3 (1990):75-79

The School of Love. Reviewed by Jill Fritz-Piggott. *The Women's Review of Books* 7, No. 12 (September 1990):24-26

**Barden, Carol Isaak**

The Spa Differential. *Lear's* (March 1990):64-67

Surgical Shaping. *Harper's Bazaar* (August 1990):45 +

**Bardhan, Kalpana**

Being a Woman in South Asia. *Journal of Women's History* 2, No. 1 (Spring 1990):200-219

Dangerous Wives and Sacred Sisters: Social and Symbolic Roles of High-Caste Women in Nepal. Book Review. *Journal of Women's History* 2, No. 1 (Spring 1990):200-219

The Endless Day: Some Case Material on Asian Rural Women. Book Review. *Journal of Women's History* 2, No. 1 (Spring 1990):200-219

Indian Women and Patriarchy: Conflicts and Dilemmas of Students and Working Women. Book Review. *Journal of Women's History* 2, No. 1 (Spring 1990):200-219

Invisible Hands: Women in Home-Based Production. Book Review. *Journal of Women's History* 2, No. 1 (Spring 1990):200-219

Pakistani Women: Socioeconomic and Demographic Profile. Book Review. *Journal of Women's History* 2, No. 1 (Spring 1990):200-219

Profiles in Female Poverty: A Study of Five Poor Working Women in Kerala. Book Review. *Journal of Women's History* 2, No. 1 (Spring 1990):200-219

Rural Women at Work: Strategies for Development in South Asia. Book Review. *Journal of Women's History* 2, No. 1 (Spring 1990):200-219

They Changed Their Worlds: Nine Women of Asia. Book Review. *Journal of Women's History* 2, No. 1 (Spring 1990):200-219

Village Women of Bangladesh: Prospects for Change. Book Review. *Journal of Women's History* 2, No. 1 (Spring 1990):200-219

We Will Smash this Prison! Indian Women in Struggle. Book Review. *Journal of Women's History* 2, No. 1 (Spring 1990):200-219

Women, Work and Property in North-West India. Book Review. *Journal of Women's History* 2, No. 1 (Spring 1990):200-219

Women and Family in Rural Taiwan. Book Review. *Journal of Women's History* 2, No. 1 (Spring 1990):200-219

**Bardwell, Leland**

Different Kinds of Love. Reviewed by Patricia Roth Schwartz. *Belles Lettres* 5, No. 3 (Spring 1990):3

**Barfoot, Joan**

Family News. Reviewed by Natasha Moar. *Spare Rib* No. 215 (August 1990):29

**Baril, Joan**

The Centre of the Backlash – Montreal. *off our backs* 20, No. 4 (April 1990):13-15

**Bariteau, Corinne Adria**

Home at Last! Poem. *Good Housekeeping* 211, No. 4 (October 1990):220

Love and Romance. Poem. *Good Housekeeping* 211, No. 3 (September 1990):304

**Bar-Joseph, Hanna** and Tzuriel, David

Suicidal Tendencies and Ego Identity in Adolescence. *Adolescence* 25, No. 97 (Spring 1990):215-223

**Barker, Judy** (about). *See* Davis, Andrea R., "Power Players"

**Barker, Philip**

Clinical Interviews with Children and Adolescents. Book Review. *Adolescence* 25, No. 97 (Spring 1990):249

**Barkin, Ellen** (about). *See* Sexual Attraction

**Barnard, Melanie** and Dojny, Brooke

12 Great Meals for Small Families. *Redbook* 174, No. 5 (March 1990):141-152

**Barnett, Jawanda K.** (joint author). *See* Papini, Dennis R.

**Barnett, Marguerite Ross** (about)

Marguerite Ross Barnett: University President. David Thigpen. *Essence* 21, No. 6 (October 1990):50

**Barnett, Rosalind C.**

Women over Forty: Visions and Realities. Book Review. *Psychology of Women Quarterly* 14, No. 4 (December 1990):618-619

**Barolini, Helen**

Cosima. Book Review. *Belles Lettres* 5, No. 3 (Spring 1990):7

The Dream Book: An Anthology of Writings by Italian-American Women. Reviewed by Mary DeLorenzo Pelc. *Sinister Wisdom* 41 (Summer Fall 1990):79-81

A House in the Shadows. Book Review. *Belles Lettres* 5, No. 3 (Spring 1990):7

Maria Zef. Book Review. *Belles Lettres* 5, No. 3 (Spring 1990):7

A Walk in the Shadows. *Belles Lettres* 5, No. 3 (Spring 1990):5

**Baron-Faust, Rita**

Health News: Dangerous Doctors and Phony Cures. *Redbook* 175, No. 6 (October 1990):54-59

Playing with Time. *Harper's Bazaar* (August 1990):46+

**Barr, Amy Biber**

Breast-Feeding Can Work for Working Mothers. *Working Mother* 13, No. 7 (July 1990):62-66

**Barr, Marleen S.**

Alien to Femininity: Speculative Fiction and Feminist Theory. Reviewed by Hoda M. Zaki. *Women's Studies International Forum* 13, No. 3 (1990):277-279

**Barr, Roseanne**

My Life as a Woman. *Woman of Power* 17 (Summer 1990):24-29

**Barreca, Regina**

The Leader of the Band. Book Review. *Belles Lettres* 5, No. 2 (Winter 1990):14

**Barrett, Carol**

Fear of Feathers. Poem. *The Women's Review of Books* 7, No. 5 (February 1990):14

The Robbery of Rosalind Franklin. Poem. *The Women's Review of Books* 7, No. 5 (February 1990):14

**Barrett, Carolann**

Be Bold and Be Bad. *Woman of Power* 17 (Summer 1990):60-63

A Network of Disabled Women. *Woman of Power* 18 (Fall 1990):31-34

Spiderwoman Theater. *Woman of Power* 17 (Summer 1990):34-37

**Barrett, Icelene**

Voices from Prison. *New Directions for Women* 19, No. 3 (May/June 1990):5

**Barrett, Katherine** and Greene, Richard

"Mom, Please Get Me Out!" *Ladies' Home Journal* 107, No. 5 (May 1990):98-107

Video: The New Family Fix. *Ladies' Home Journal* 107, No. 2 (February 1990):118-120+

**Barrett, Lois**

Style to Go. *Essence* 21, No. 5 (September 1990):22-24

**Barrett, Mary Ellin**

Irving Berlin. *Lear's* (June 1990):84-92+

**Barrett, Mary Ellin** (joint author). *See* Lerner, Steve

**Barrett, Susan E.**

Paths Toward Diversity: An Intrapsychic Perspective. *Women and Therapy* 9, Nos. 1-2 (1990):41-52

**Barrett, Susan E.** and Aubin, Carol M.

Feminist Considerations of Intercountry Adoptions. *Women and Therapy* 10, Nos. 1/2 (1990):127-138

**Barrington, Judith**

Feminist Formalist. *The Women's Review of Books* 7, Nos. 10-11 (July 1990):28

Going Back to the River. Book Review. *The Women's Review of Books* 7, Nos. 10-11 (July 1990):28

History and Geography. Reviewed by Meryl Altman. *The Women's Review of Books* 8, No. 1 (October 1990):16-18

**Barrows, Anita**

Movements toward form. Poem. *Bridges* 1, No. 2 (Fall 1990): 95-99

**Barry, Dave** (about)

Barry Funny. Michael Kiefer. *Ladies' Home Journal* 107, No. 10 (October 1990):78-85

**Barry, Kathleen**

The New Historical Synthesis: Women's Biography. *Journal of Women's History* 1, No. 3 (Winter 1990):75-105

**Barry, Kathleen L.** and Leidholdt, Dorchen

Coalition Against Trafficking in Women. *Woman of Power* 18 (Fall 1990):46-49

**Barry, Ursula**

Women and the Military System. Book Review. *Women's Studies International Forum* 13, No. 3 (1990):281

**Barrymore, Drew** (about)

Child Star, Child Addict. Joanne Kaufman. *Ladies' Home Journal* 107, No. 3 (March 1990):116-124

**Barsky, June**

The Wives Take the Heat: Ethel Rosenberg and Anne Pollard. *Lilith* 15, No. 1 (Winter 1990):28-29

**Barsness, Peggy Ann** (about)

The Cradle Will Fall: The Tragedy of Peggy Ann Barsness. Aimee Lee Ball. *Mademoiselle* (November 1990):184-187+

**Barsoum, Elisa**

The Arlington Arts Center: Saving a Space Within the Sprawl. *Iris* 23 (Spring-Summer 1990):10-12

**Bart, Pauline B.**

Pornography and Civil Rights: A New Day for Women's Equality. Book Review. *NWSA Journal* 2, No. 3 (Summer 1990):516-518

**Bartering**

My Kingdom for a Horse. Paul Neimark. *Executive Female* 13, No. 4 (July-August 1990):32-34

**Barth, Richard P.**

Reducing the Risk: Building Skills to Prevent Pregnancy. Reviewed by Peggy Brick. *New Directions for Women* 19, No. 3 (May/June 1990):21

**Barthel, Diane**

Charismatic Capitalism: Direct Selling Organizations in America. Book Review. *Gender and Society* 4, No. 2 (June 1990):266-267

**Barthel, Joan**

Clooney! *Lear's* (February 1990):102-107+

Sidney Poitier. *Lear's* (November 1990):100-103+

**Barthes, Roland – Criticism and Interpretation**

Wilde, Barthes, and the Orgasmics of Truth. Kevin Kopelson. *Genders* 7 (Spring 1990):22-31

**Bartlett, Harriett M.** (about)

Female Social Workers in the Second Generation. Janice L. Andrews. *AFFILIA* 5, No. 2 (Summer 1990):46-59

**Bartocci, Barbara**

Best Friends. *Good Housekeeping* 211, No. 4 (October 1990):144-145+

Leap into the Light. *Good Housekeeping* 210, No. 6 (June 1990):52-56

**Barton, Clara** (about)

Clara Barton: Champion of Equal Pay. Allen D. Spiegel. *Executive Female* 13, No. 6 (November-December 1990):38+

Clara Barton: Professional Angel. By Elizabeth Brown Pryor. Reviewed by Nancy L. Noel. *Signs* 15, No. 3 (Spring 1990):640-642

**Barton, Rae Lynn**

A Date with Mom. *McCall's* 118, No. 1 (October 1990):14

**Baruch, Elaine Hoffman** and others (editors)

Embryos, Ethics and Women's Rights. Reviewed by Sonia G. Austrian. *AFFILIA* 5, No. 3 (Fall 1990):113-114

**Baruch, Elaine Hoffman** and Serrano, Lucienne J. (editors)

Women Analyze Women in France, England, and the United States. Reviewed by Elaine Marks. *NWSA Journal* 2, No. 1 (Winter 1990):131-134

**Barwell, Ismay**

Feminine Perspectives and Narrative Points of View. *Hypatia* 5, No. 2 (Summer 1990):63-75

**Barzilai, Shuli**

Reading "Snow White": The Mother's Story. Notes. *Signs* 15, No. 3 (Spring 1990):515-534

**Bashore, Juliet**

Kamikaze Hearts. Reviewed by Sarah Payton. *Spare Rib* No. 215 (August 1990):35

**Basia** (about)

Basia – Coming to America. Karen Schoemer. *Mademoiselle* (September 1990):160

**Basinger, Kim** (about). *See also* Sexual Attraction

**Basketball**

The Pick-Up Game. Michele Kort. *Women's Sports and Fitness* 12, No. 4 (May-June 1990):68-71

**Basnayake, Sriani**

The Virginity Test: A Bridal Nightmare. *Journal of Family Welfare* 36, No. 2 (June 1990):50-59

**Basow, Susan A.** and Campanile, Florence

Attitudes toward Prostitution as a Function of Attitudes toward Feminism in College Students. *Psychology of Women Quarterly* 14, No. 1 (March 1990):135-141

**Bass, Emily**

A Community at War. *The Women's Review of Books* 7, No. 7 (April 1990):9-10

Holding the Line: Women in the Great Arizona Mine Strike of 1983. Book Review. *The Women's Review of Books* 7, No. 7 (April 1990):9-10

**Bass, Ruth** and Cummins, Marsha

Aesthetic Questions. *Heresies* 25 (1990).53-54

**Bassi, Laurie J.**

Confessions of a Feminist Economist: Why I Haven't Yet Taught an Economics Course on Women's Issues. *Women's Studies Quarterly* 18, Nos. 3-4 (Fall-Winter 1990):42-45

**Bastion, Hilda**

The Tentative Pregnancy – Prenatal Diagnosis and the Future of Motherhood. Book Review. *Healthright* 9, No. 4 (August 1990):42-43

**Basu, Alaka**

The North-South Difference: Contrasting Cultural Traditions of Two Migrant Groups in Delhi. *Manushi* 57 (March-April 1990):16-21

**Basu, Rajshekhar**

By the Grace of Shasthi. Short story. *Manushi* 58 (May-June 1990):39-42

**Bataille, Gretchen M.** and Sands, Kathleen Mullen

American Indian Women: Telling Their Lives. Reviewed by Manuel G. Gonzales. *Tulsa Studies in Women's Literature* 9, No. 1 (Spring 1990):152-156

**Bates, Barbara** (about). *See* Fashion Designers, "Top Women Designers"

**Bates, Carolyn** and Brodsky, Annette

Sex In the Therapy Hour. A Case of Professional Incest. Reviewed by Julia A. Sherman. *Psychology of Women Quarterly* 14, No. 2 (June 1990):289-290

**Bates, Karen Grigsby**

Attitudes: The Sexual Revolution. *Essence* 21, No. 1 (May 1990):54-56

Is It Genocide? *Essence* 21, No. 5 (September 1990):76-78+

Never Can Say Goodbye. *Essence* 20, No. 10 (February 1990):61-62

**Bates, Marian**

The Girl of His Dreams. Short Story. *Good Housekeeping* 211, No. 5 (November 1990):168-169

**Bateson, Mary Catherine**

Claiming the Future. *Lear's* (February 1990):84-87

Composing a Life. Reviewed by Deborah Solomon. *The Women's Review of Books* 7, No. 12 (September 1990):26-27

Holidays Are about the Future More than the Past. *McCall's* 118, No. 2 (November 1990):35-37

**Bateson, Mary Catherine** (about)

Finding the Guts to Go. Interview. Michele Morris. *Working Woman* (May 1990):86+

**Bathing Customs**

The Body Shop: Baths for Shower People, Showers for Bath People. *Mademoiselle* (February 1990):24-26

**Bathing Suits.** *See* Clothing and Dress – Swimwear

**Bathrooms**

Ladies in Waiting. Maggie Malone. *Savvy* (December-January 1991):14

**Baths.** *See also* Bathing Customs

Aquatic. Melissa Dunst. *Lear's* (September 1990):128-133

**Baton Rouge – Description and Travel**

A Taste for Southern Comfort. Moira Crone. *Savvy Woman* (September 1990):54-55 +

**Batorska, Danuta**

The Fabric of Memory, Ewa Kuryluk: Cloth Works, 1978-1987. Book Review. *Woman's Art Journal* 11, No. 2 (Fall 1990-Winter 1991):34-35

**Battaglia, Debbora**

Cultural Alternatives and a Feminist Anthropology: An Analysis of Culturally Constructed Gender Interests in Papua New Guinea. Book review. *Signs* 15, No. 4 (Summer 1990):869-872

**Battagliola, Françoise**

La fin du mariage? jeunes couples des annees' 80. Reviewed by Denise Veillette. *Resources for Feminist Research* 19, No. 1 (March 1990):15-16

**Battered Women.** *See* Domestic Violence; Spouse Abuse; Violence Against Women; Women's Shelters

**Battersby, Christine**

Gender and Genius: Towards a Feminist Aesthetic. Reviewed by Margaret Beetham. *Gender and Education* 2, No. 2 (1990):259-261

**Bauer, Sandra**

The Violent Family. Book Review. *AFFILIA* 5, No. 1 (Spring 1990):114-115

**Baughman, Linda**

A Psychoanalytic Reading of a Female Comic Book Hero: *Electra: Assassin.* Notes. *Women & Language* 13, No. 1 (Fall 1990):27-30

**Bauman, Karl E.** (joint author). *See* Flewelling, Robert L.

**Bauman, Mark** (joint author). *See* Chittum, Samme

**Bauman, Raquel Portillo**

Comment on Suleiman's "On Maternal Splitting." *Signs* 15, No. 3 (Spring 1990):653-655

**Bauman, Raquel Portillo** (about)

Reply to Bauman. Susan Rubin Suleiman. *Signs* 15, No. 3 (Spring 1990):656-659

**Bavaria, Joan** (about). *See also* Activism

**Bawdy Songs.** *See* Rugby Football – Bawdy Songs

**Baxter-Birney, Meredith** (about)

Talking with Meredith Baxter-Birney: "Being Single Again Is Scary – and Glorious." Interview. Vicki Jo Radovsky. *Redbook* 175, No. 3 (July 1990):42-44

**Bay Area Women's Philharmonic (BAWP)**

Yes, Mendelssohn Was a Woman. Lynn Wenzel. *New Directions for Women* 19, No. 1 (January/February 1990):9

**Baye, Betty Winston**

Father Love. *Essence* 21, No. 2 (June 1990):34+

**Bayes, Jane**

Women in the World: 1975-1985, The Women's Decade. Book Review. *Women & Politics* 10, No. 3 (1990):125-127

**Baynton, Barbara – Criticism and Interpretation**

The Enigma of Woman: Barbara Baynton's *Human Toll*. Rosemary Moore. *Australian Feminist Studies* No. 12 (Summer 1990):83-93

**Bayrakal, Sadi** and Kope, Teresa M.

Dysfunction in the Single-Parent and Only-Child Family. *Adolescence* 25, No. 97 (Spring 1990):1-7

**Beaches**

Beach Beauty. *Harper's Bazaar* (June 1990):28-35

Beaches I Have Known and Loved. Rosanne Keller. *Lear's* (July 1990):38-39

**Beacon Black Women Writers Series**

Speaking in Pieces: A Review of the Beacon Black Women Writers Series. Cheryl A. Wall. *Iris* 23 (Spring-Summer 1990):31-34

**Beale, Jennifer**

Women in Ireland. Reviewed by Eleanor J. Bader. *Belles Lettres* 5, No. 3 (Spring 1990):2-3

**Beaman, Libby** (about)

Libby, the Alaskan Diaries and Letters of Libby Beaman, 1879-1880. By Betty John. Reviewed by Lynn Wenzel. *New Directions for Women* 19, No. 2 (March/April 1990):14

**Beamon, Eric** (about)

Be Jeweled. Elsie B. Washington. *Essence* 21, No. 5 (September 1990):68-69

**Bean, Thom**

A Matter of Personal Pride: A Conversation about Black and White Men Together. *Out/Look* No. 9 (Summer 1990):70-71

**Beard, Lillian McLean** and Satow, Susan

Is Your Child Overweight? *Good Housekeeping* 211, No. 3 (September 1990):164+

**Beard, Patricia**

Country Charm. *Harper's Bazaar* (October 1990):236

Dinner at Eight. *Harper's Bazaar* (August 1990):173+

Tray Chic. *Harper's Bazaar* (June 1990):138

**Beat Generation**

Off the Road: My Years with Cassady, Kerouac, and Ginsberg. By Carolyn Cassady. Reviewed by Francine Prose. *The Women's Review of Books* 8, No. 2 (November 1990):10-11

**Beaton, Janet I.**

Dimensions of Nurse and Patient Roles in Labor. *Health Care for Women International* 11, No. 4 (1990):393-408

**Beattie, Ann**

Books: Picturing Will. Reviewed by Gene Lyons. *Vogue* (January 1990):106-110

**Beatty, Patricia** (interview)

Earth Is Our Root: An Interview with Patricia Beatty. Karen Lavut and Frances Beer. *Canadian Women's Studies* 11, No. 1 (Spring 1990):

**Beauchamp, Rachelle Sender** (joint author). *See* Helene Cummins

**Beauticians.** *See* Beauty Culture

**Beauty, Personal.** *See also* Aging – Personal Narratives; Beauty Standards; Fashion Models; Images of Women; Miss America, 1990

America's 10 Most Beautiful Women. *Harper's Bazaar* (September 1990):256-281

Beauty: Our Luscious Lips. *Essence* 21, No. 1 (May 1990):29

Beauty: The Beauty of Black. *Essence* 21, No. 1 (May 1990):30

Beauty Bazaar: 10 Most Beautiful Women. *Harper's Bazaar* (September 1990):54-80+

Beauty & Health Report: Bad Breath. Andrea Pomerantz Lynn. *Glamour* (February 1990):41

Beauty Heritage. *Harper's Bazaar* (August 1990):116-121+

Beauty's New Nature. Shirley Lord. *Vogue* (October 1990):394-398

Express Yourself. *Family Circle* 103, No. 2 (February 1, 1990):54-59

Face of the '90s. Alison Lurie. *Lear's* (January 1990):61-69

Find Your Own Beauty Style. *Glamour* (October 1990):240-242

Great Faces. Lois Joy Johnson. *Ladies' Home Journal* 107, No. 11 (November 1990):224-228

Michelle Reeves: A True Winner. *Essence* 21, No. 3 (July 1990):12

Say Cheese. Marshall Blonsky. *Lear's* (January 1990):70-75

Prime Time Beauty. *Essence* 20, No. 11 (March 1990):14-15

Queen for a Day: The Royal Treatment. *Family Circle* 103, No. 9 (June 26, 1990):55

Red Hot. *Ladies' Home Journal* 107, No. 8 (August 1990):108-111

Rich Girl Beauty, Real Girl Price. *Mademoiselle* (January 1990):110-115

The Seductive Face. Shirley Lord. *Vogue* (September 1990):594-599

Simply Beautiful. *Lear's* (March 1990):132-137

Spa Luxury to Go. *Lear's* (May 1990):24

10 Hot Holiday Maneuvers You'll Want to Try Right Now. *Essence* 21, No. 8 (December 1990):8-13

Ten Office Emergencies. *Mademoiselle* (June 1990):46

10 Super Fine-Alists. *Essence* 21, No. 3 (July 1990):10-11

Trade Secrets. Bibliography. Nina Malkin. *Harper's Bazaar* (September 1990):82

Visiting Space: Autumnal Face. Margaret Morganroth Gullette. *Lear's* (January 1990):136+

What a Body! *Glamour* (June 1990):210-215

**Beauty Culture – History**

Images: History of the Hairdresser. Jody Shields. *Vogue* (July 1990):77-83

**Beauty Queens**

The Making of a Beauty Queen. Jeannie Ralston. *Glamour* (October 1990):276-279+

**Beauty Shops**

By the Dawn's Early Light. Bibliography. *Mademoiselle* (November 1990):60

**Beauty Standards.** *See also* Aging – Psychological Aspects; Beauty, Personal; Body Image; Business Travel; Celebrities; Dentistry – Aesthetics; Fat Acceptance; Liposuction; Obesity; Physical Fitness; Skin Color

Are You a Beauty Addict? *Mademoiselle* (September 1990):266-267+

Beauty & Fashion Journal. *Ladies' Home Journal* 107, No. 6 (June 1990):31-36

Beauty & Health Report: Five Steps to a Flat, Strong Stomach. Andrea Pomerantz Lynn. *Glamour* (April 1990):58

The Beauty Report. *Ladies' Home Journal* 107, No. 3 (March 1990):174-180

Beauty Secrets: Women and the Politics of Appearance. By Wendy Chapkis. Reviewed by Ruth P. Rubinstein. *Gender and Society* 4, No. 1 (March 1990):110-111

Big Girls Don't Cry. *Mademoiselle* (February 1990):148-153

Brainy, Beautiful & Blond. Judith Viorst. *Redbook* 175, No. 6 (October 1990):122-126

Dark Victory. Mary-Ellen Banashek. *Lear's* (October 1990):110-113

Does Your Image Need Fine-Tuning? Colleen Sullivan. *Working Woman* (November 1990):142-144

Dos and Don'ts. *Glamour* (June 1990):296

Exploding the Beauty Myth. Naomi Wolfe. *Spare Rib* 218 (November 1990):6-10

Fashion: Teeny Bikinis (For Not-So-Tiny Bodies. *Mademoiselle* (June 1990):52-54

Fashion Dos and Don'ts. *Glamour* (April 1990):342

Forty Fine. Alexis DeVeaux. *Essence* 20, No. 9 (January 1990):50-52+

14 Slimming Looks. *Redbook* 175, No. 3 (July 1990):88-93

Good Show: How to Look Your Best When You Feel Your Worst. Andrea Messina. *Working Woman* (October 1990):130-132

Hers: The Nose Job. Kathleen Rockwell Lawrence. *Glamour* (September 1990):338+

Images: American Style. Joan Juliet Buck. *Vogue* (September 1990):311-316

Kiss Health Terrorism Goodbye. *Glamour* (April 1990):122

Natural Beauties. Janet Siroto. *Harper's Bazaar* (January 1990):78-85

The New Sexy. Peter Mehlman. *Harper's Bazaar* (February 1990):120-127+

The One-Inch Solution. Rowann Gilman. *Working Woman* (September 1990):190-192

Rethinking Pink. *Mademoiselle* (February 1990):170-173

Role Models. Lois Joy Johnson. *Ladies' Home Journal* 107, No. 10 (October 1990):172-180

Saving Face. Carolyn J. Cline. *Lear's* (January 1990):96-99

'90s Forecast: Best in Beauty. *Harper's Bazaar* (January 1990):15-28+

The 10 Best Swimsuits. *Redbook* 175, No. 1 (May 1990):103-111

200 Words: Beauty and the Man. *Lear's* (January 1990):76-79

On Wearing Skirts. Kim Klausner. *Out/Look* No. 8 (Spring 1990):18+

What Suits You? *Redbook* 175, No. 2 (June 1990):122-127

What Went Wrong Here: The New Year's Eve Style Crisis. *Mademoiselle* (January 1990):39

Why I Hate Hunks. Skip Hollandsworth. *Mademoiselle* (October 1990):86-91

**Beauvoir, Simone de**

She Came to Stay. Reviewed by Joanne Schmidt. *Belles Lettres* 6, No. 1 (Fall 1990):46

**Beauvoir, Simone de** (about)

Simone de Beauvoir: A Biography. By Deirdre Bair. Reviewed by Carol Anne Douglas. *off our backs* 20, No. 7 (July 1990):20

Simone de Beauvoir: A Biography. By Deirdre Bair. Reviewed by Germaine Brée. *The Women's Review of Books* 8, No. 1 (October 1990):1+

Simone de Beauvoir: A Biography. By Deirdre Bair. Reviewed by Isabel Hill Fucigna. *Belles Lettres* 6, No. 1 (Fall 1990):45-46

Simone de Beauvoir and the Demystification of Motherhood. By Yolanda Astarita Patterson. Reviewed by Sonia Jaffe Robbins. *New Directions for Women* 19, No. 3 (May/June 1990):20

**Bechdel, Alison** (interview)

Alison Bechdel and Kris Kovick. *Hot Wire* 6, No. 3 (September 1990):12-14+

**Beck, Arne** (joint author). *See* Schichor, Aric

**Beck, Cornelia**, Shultz, Cathleen, Walton, Chris Gorman, and Walls, Robert

Predictors of Loneliness in Older Women and Men. *Journal of Women and Aging* 2, No. 1 (1990):3-31

**Beck, Evelyn Torton**

Dreams of an Insomniac: Jewish Feminist Essays, Speeches and Diatribes. Book Review. *Belles Lettres* 6, No. 1 (Fall 1990):2-5

From Nightmare to Vision: An Introduction to the Essays of Irena Klepfisz. *Belles Lettres* 6, No. 1 (Fall 1990):2-5

**Beck, Evelyn Torton**, Greer, Sandra C., Jackson, Diana R., and Schmitz, Betty

The Feminist Transformation of a University: A Case Study. *Women's Studies Quarterly* 18, Nos. 1-2 (Spring-Summer 1990):174-188

**Beck, Evelyn Torton** (editor)

Nice Jewish Girls: A Lesbian Anthology. Reviewed by Felice Kornbluh. *off our backs* 20, No. 9 (October 1990):15-16

Nice Jewish Girls: A Lesbian Anthology. Reviewed by Joan Nestle. *Bridges* 1, No. 1 (Spring 1990): 98-101

Nice Jewish Girls: A Lesbian Anthology. Reviewed by Rebecca Gordon. *The Women's Review of Books* 7, No. 9 (June 1990):7-8

**Beck, Wendy** and Head, Lesley

Women in Australian Prehistory. *Australian Feminist Studies* No. 11 (Autumn 1990):29-48

**Becker, Jody**

Ann Richards: Plain-Speaking Texan. *McCall's* 117, No. 9 (June 1990):70

Becoming Skilled, Getting Ahead. *McCall's* 118, No. 2 (November 1990):38-40

Career Makeover: "I Needed to Define My Life." *McCall's* 118, No. 1 (October 1990):31-32

Dianne Feinstein: Charismatic Centrist. *McCall's* 117, No. 9 (June 1990):70-74

Kay Orr: Mrs. Middle America. *McCall's* 117, No. 9 (June 1990):74

**Becker, Robin**

Giacometti's Dog. Reviewed by Meryl Altman. *The Women's Review of Books* 8, No. 1 (October 1990):16-18

**Becket, Marta** (about)

Desert Dream. Scott LaFee. *Lear's* (April 1990):50

**Beckett, Mary**

A Belfast Woman. Reviewed by Maureen Murphy. *Feminist Collections* 11, No. 2 (Winter 1990):5-6

Give Them Stones. Reviewed by Susan Swartzlander. *Belles Lettres* 5, No. 3 (Spring 1990):5

**Beckett-Young, Kathleen**

The Busy Life: Design for Living. *Working Woman* (October 1990):140-144

Scentiment. *Lear's* (November 1990):136-139

Timeless Objects. *Savvy Woman* (October 1990):38-40

**Beckman, Amy** (joint author). *See* Meleis, Afaf I.

**Bedard, Marcia**

Domestic Tyranny: The Making of American Social Policy Against Family Violence from Colonial Times to the Present. Book Review. *NWSA Journal* 2, No. 3 (Summer 1990):464-475

Feminist Perspectives on Wife Abuse. Book Review. *NWSA Journal* 2, No. 3 (Summer 1990):464-475

Heroes of Their Own Lives: The Politics and History of Family Violence. Book Review. *NWSA Journal* 2, No. 3 (Summer 1990):464-475

Terrifying Love: Why Battered Women Kill and How Society Responds. Book Review. *NWSA Journal* 2, No. 3 (Summer 1990):464-475

Women, Policing, and Male Violence: International Perspectives. Book Review. *NWSA Journal* 2, No. 3 (Summer 1990):364-375

**Bedelia, Bonnie** (about)

What's Hot: Summer Stars. Kathryn Casey and Bonnie Siegler. *Ladies' Home Journal* 107, No. 8 (August 1990):52-60

**Bedolis, Melissa**

Born to Sing. *Mademoiselle* (November 1990):150-153

**Bedrooms – Remodeling.** *See also*
Children – Rooms; Interior Design

A Little Night Style. *Glamour* (November 1990):252-255

A Magical Nursery. *Good Housekeeping* 211, No. 3 (September 1990):120

**Beds**

Beds I Have Known. Alexa LaFortune. *Lear's* (April 1990):48-49

**Beechey, Veronica** and Perkins, Tessa

A Matter of Hours: Women, Part-time Work and the Labour Market. Reviewed by Judith Wittner. *Gender and Society* 4, No. 2 (June 1990):258-262

**Beef.** *See* Cookery (Meat)

**Beene, Geoffrey** (about). *See* Fashion Designers, "Gentlemen's Choice"

**Beer, Frances**

Conversation Fragments: Betty White. *Canadian Women's Studies* 11, No. 1 (Spring 1990):93

**Beer, Frances** (joint author). *See* Lavut, Karen

**Beer, William R.**

Strangers in the House. Reviewed by Lawrence H. Ganong. *Journal of Marriage and the Family* 52, No. 1 (February 1990):281-282

**Beers, David**

The Gene Screen. *Vogue* (June 1990):236-237, 278-279

**Beetham, Margaret**

Gender and Genius: Towards a Feminist Aesthetic. Book Review. *Gender and Education* 2, No. 2 (1990):259-261

**Begley, Ed, Jr.** (about). *See also*
Celebrities – Activism

**Begley, Sharon**

Breaking the Age Barrier: It's Within Your Power. *Family Circle* 103, No. 14 (October 16, 1990):112 +

Life in 2010. *Family Circle* 103, No. 2 (February 1, 1990):76-77

Your Environment: The Good, the Bad, the Biodegradable. *Family Circle* 103, No. 14 (October 16, 1990):71-72

**Begole, Christine**

Office Technology: Five Successful Alternatives to In-Person Meetings. *Working Woman* (October 1990):70-76

**Behar, Ruth**

Rage and Redemption: Reading the Life Story of a Mexican Marketing Woman. *Feminist Studies* 16, No. 2 (Summer 1990):223-258

**Behavior Change**

You *Can* Change Your Life. Marlin S. Potash. *Good Housekeeping* 211, No. 4 (October 1990):94-96

**Behavior Disorders**

Obsessed. Nancy Shulins. *Family Circle* 103, No. 8 (June 5, 1990):57-59

**Behnke, Karen** (about). *See* Entrepreneurs

**Behnke, Karen** and Calvacca, Lorraine

Performance Review: Fitting In Fitness. *Working Woman* (September 1990):199

Performance Review: Going Places, Staying Healthy. *Working Woman* (October 1990):139

**Behuniak-Long, Susan**

Radical Conceptions: Reproductive Technologies and Feminist Theories. *Women & Politics* 10, No. 3 (1990):39-64

**Bei, Ai**

Red Ivy, Green Earth Mother. Reviewed by Helen Zia. *Ms.* 1, No. 3 (November/December 1990):56

**Beig, Maria**

Lost Weddings. Reviewed by Nancy Derr. *Belles Lettres* 5, No. 4 (Summer 1990):9-10

**Beirut – Hostages.** *See* Lebanon – Hostages

**Beiswinger, George L.**

Cruise in the Fast Lane. *Executive Female* (May/June 1990):30-31 +

**Belafonte, Julie** (about)

Julie Rejoicing. *Lear's* (October 1990):106-109

**Belfiore, Tasha**

I Capelli Moltissimi. *Sinister Wisdom* 41 (Summer-Fall 1990):111-113

**Belgian Congo – Colonization.** *See* Zaire – History

**Bell, Alison**

The Grateful Head. *Women's Sports and Fitness* 12, No. 4 (May-June 1990):26

**Bell, Becky** (about)

Another American Tragedy: The Death of Becky Bell. Mary Lou Greenberg. *On the Issues* 17 (Winter 1990):10-13 +

**Bell, Derrick** (about)

Derrick Bell: Harvard's Conscience. Benilde Little. *Essence* 21, No. 7 (November 1990):44

A Man Who Wouldn't Speak for Women. *Ms.* 1, No. 1 (July/August 1990):59

**Bell, Ellen**

Women Abusing Women. *Connexions* 34 (1990):28-30

**Bell, Friedl Elaine**

Full Circle: The Wall. *Family Circle* 103, No. 9 (June 26, 1990):154

**Bell, Linda**

Feminist Theory and the Philosophies of Man. Book Review. *Hypatia* 5, No. 1 (Spring 1990):127-132

**Bell, Nancy J.** (joint editor). *See* Bell, Robert W.

**Bell, Robert W.** and Bell, Nancy J. (editors)

Sociobiology and the Social Sciences. Reviewed by Jetse Sprey. *Journal of Marriage and the Family* 52, No. 4 (November 1990):1152-1153

**Bell, Susan Groag**

Women Create Gardens in Male Landscapes: A Revisionist Approach to Eighteenth-Century English Garden History. *Feminist Studies* 16, No. 3 (Fall 1990):471-491

**Belle, Regina** (about). *See* Musicians, Popular, "Repeat Performance"

Regina Belle: Showing Us the Way. Carol Cooper. *Essence* 20, No. 11 (March 1990):44

**Bell-Scott, Patricia** (joint author). *See* Davis, Hilda A.

**Belsky, Gary**

Pleasure Plus: The New Way to Travel. *Working Woman* (June 1990):44-46

**Belsky, Jay**

Parental and Nonparental Child Care and Children's Socioemotional Development: A Decade in Review. *Journal of Marriage and the Family* 52, No. 1 (November 1990):884-903

**Belsky, Jay** and Rovine, Michael

Patterns of Marital Change across the Transition to Parenthood: Pregnancy to Three Years Postpartum. *Journal of Marriage and the Family* 52, No. 1 (February 1990):5-19

**Belton, Robert J.**

Unexpected Journeys: The Art and Life of Remedios Varos. Book Review. *Woman's Art Journal* 11, No. 2 (Fall 1990-Winter 1991):35-36

**Belzer, Ellen J.**

The Negotiating Art: You *Can* Always Get What You Want. *Working Woman* (April 1990):98-99+

**Benamou, Catherine** (joint author). *See* Burns, Judy

**Benara, S. K.** and Chaturvedi, S. K.

Impact of Training on the Performance of Traditional Birth Attendants. *Journal of Family Welfare* 36, No. 4 (December 1990):32-35

**Benatar, Giselle**

Talking Fashion. *Vogue* (July 1990):219

**Benavides, Marta**

Cristi, Compañera: Memorial for a Friend. *Woman of Power* 16 (Spring 1990):48-51

**Ben-Barak, Shalvia**

Fertility Patterns Among Soviet Immigrants to Israel: The Role of Cultural Variables. *Journal of Family History* 15, No. 1 (January 1990):87-100

**Bend, Jill**

Refugee from El Salvador. *off our backs* 20, No. 5 (May 1990):1-2

**Benda, Brent B.** and Dattalo, Patrick

Homeless Women and Men: Their Problems and Use of Services. *AFFILIA* 5, No. 3 (Fall 1990):50-82

**Benderly, Jill**

Among East European Women: A Reporter's Notebook. *On the Issues* 16 (Fall 1990):16-17+

Balancing Acts: Contemporary Stories by Russian Women. Book Review. *The Women's Review of Books* 7, Nos. 10-11 (July 1990):19

Classic Conflicts. *The Women's Review of Books* 7, Nos. 10-11 (July 1990):19

Czechoslovak Women Back into Feminism. *New Directions for Women* 19, No. 5 (September-October 1990):1+

Does Corporate Giant Fill Health Care Needs Like Feminist Clinics? *New Directions for Women* 19, No. 1 (January/February 1990):13

Drum Drama. Music Review. *On the Issues* 14 (1990):28

Feminist Clinics Lose Out to Profit-Making Clones. *New Directions for Women* 19, No. 1 (January/February 1990):3+

Freedom to Love. Music Review. *On the Issues* 14 (1990):29

The Image of Women in Contemporary Soviet Fiction: Selected Short Stories from the USSR. Book Review. *The Women's Review of Books* 7, Nos. 10-11 (July 1990):19

Margaret Sanger: An Alternate View. *On the Issues* 14 (1990):13

Sky Dances. Music Review. *On the Issues* 14 (1990):28-29

Two Nice Girls. Music Review. *On the Issues* 14 (1990):29

What Price Unity? *New Directions for Women* 19, No. 3 (May/June 1990):1+

Yugoslavian Women Pull Together. *New Directions for Women* 19, No. 5 (September-October 1990):3

**Benedict, Elizabeth**

Separate Vacations. *Glamour* (July 1990):188+

**Benedict, Helen**

A World Like This. Reviewed by Rosellen Brown. *The Women's Review of Books* 7, Nos. 10-11 (July 1990):33

**Benhabib, Seyla** and Cornell, Drucilla (editors)

Feminism as Critique: On the Politics of Gender. Reviewed by Mary Janell Metzger. *Hypatia* 5, No. 3 (Fall 1990):118-124

**Benham, Barbara**

Breakthrough. Book Review. *Belles Lettres* 5, No. 2 (Winter 1990):18

Cerebral, Real, and Classic Tales. *Belles Lettres* 5, No. 2 (Winter 1990):18

Enclosed Garden. Book Review. *Belles Lettres* 5, No. 2 (Winter 1990):18

The Gold Mine. Book Review. *Belles Lettres* 5, No. 2 (Winter 1990):18

**Benhassine-Miller, Amel** (about)

The Dance of Amel Benhassine-Miller. Lina Mansour. *Spare Rib* 213 (June 1990):30-31

**Benin, Mary Holland** and Edwards, Debra A.

Adolescents' Chores: The Differences Between Dual- and Single-Earner Families. *Journal of Marriage and the Family* 52, No. 2 (May 1990):361-373

**Benjamin, Walter — Criticism and Interpretation**

Body and Image Space: Problems and Representability of a Female Dialectic of Enlightenment. Sigrid Weigel. *Australian Feminist Studies* No. 11 (Autumn 1990):1-15

**Bennett, James Gordon**

Queen of the Beasts. *Vogue* (June 1990):238-241, 281

**Bennett, Lynn**

Dangerous Wives and Sacred Sisters: Social and Symbolic Roles of High-Caste Women in Nepal. Reviewed by Kalpana Bardhan. *Journal of Women's History* 2, No. 1 (Spring 1990):200-219

**Bennett, Pat** (about)

Decision Changes Support Laws. Junior Bridge. *New Directions for Women* 19, No. 5 (September-October 1990):5

**Bennett, Robin**

Sex Can Be Spiritual. *New Directions for Women* 19, No. 4 (July-August 1990):7

**Bennett, William** (about)

The Great American Drug Muddle. Pete Hamill and Mark A. R. Kleiman. *Lear's* (March 1990):156-157+

**Bennetts, Leslie**

The Fast-Paced Days of Blair Brown. *McCall's* 117, No. 11 (August 1990):31-32

Reel Stylishness. *Lear's* (July 1990):64-67+

Tandy. *Lear's* (April 1990):80-83+

Tyne Daly: Riding the Second Wave of Success. *McCall's* 117, No. 7 (April 1990):84-88

**Bennis, Phyllis** and Cassidy, Neal

From Stones to Statehood: The Palestinian Uprising. Reviewed by Eleanor J. Bader. *On the Issues* 15 (Summer 1990):16-17+

**Bennis, Warren**

How to Be the Leader They'll Follow. *Working Woman* (March 1990):75-78

**Benoit, Lorene**

AIDS Education in the Yukon. *Healthsharing* 11, No. 1 (December 1989):6

Yukon Vaccination Update. *Healthsharing* 11, No. 2 (March 1990):7

**Ben-Shalom, Miriam** (joint author). *See* Phelps, Johnnie

**Benson, Bjorn**, Hampsten, Elizabeth, and Sweney, Kathryn (editors)

Day In, Day Out: Women's Lives in North Dakota. Reviewed by Jane M. Pederson. *NWSA Journal* 2, No. 3 (Summer 1990):519-520

**Benson, Miriam**

Israeli Women Press for Change. *Lilith* 15, No. 4 (Fall 1990):12-13

**Benson, Morton**

A Note on the Elimination of Sexism in Dictionaries. *Women & Language* 13, No. 1 (Fall 1990):51

**Benson, Paul**

Feminist Second Thoughts About Free Agency. *Hypatia* 5, No. 3 (Fall 1990):47-64

**Benson, Susan Porter**

Counter Cultures: Saleswomen, Managers, and Customers in American Department Stores, 1890-1940. Reviewed by Jeanne Allen. *Camera Obscura* No. 22 (January 1990):150-158

Counter Cultures: Saleswomen, Managers and Customers in American Department Stores, 1890-1940. Reviewed by Carole Elizabeth Adams. *Gender & History* 2, No. 3 (Autumn 1990):343-348

**Benstock, Shari**

Women of the Left Bank: Paris, 1900-1940. Reviewed by Megan Roughley. *Gender & History* 2, No. 1 (Spring 1990):118-120

**Benstock, Shari** (editor)

The Private Self: Theory and Practice of Women's Autobiographical Writings. Reviewed by Elizabeth R. Baer. *Belles Lettres* 5, No. 2 (Winter 1990):4-6+

The Private Self: Theory and Practice of Women's Autobiographical Writings. Reviewed by Linda Wagner-Martin. *Tulsa Studies in Women's Literature* 9, No. 1 (Spring 1990):139-142

**Bentley, Elisabeth**

In Defence of Their Livelihood: Hirabehn Parmar and Waste Pickers of Ahmedabad. *Manushi* 60 (September-October 1990):16-21

"How We Poor Women Work Together": Profile of Karimabibi Shaikh. *Manushi* No. 59 (July-August 1990):2-10

**Bentley, Toni** (joint author). *See* Farrell, Suzanne

**Benton, Pam** (joint author). *See* Kippax, Susan

**Bentsen, Cheryl**

Maasai Days. Reviewed by Jill Fritz-Piggott. *The Women's Review of Books* 7, No. 4 (January 1990):17

**Benzodiazepines**

A Natural Therapies Approach to Minor Tranquilliser Withdrawal. Ginny Codd. *Healthright* 9, No. 2 (February 1990):16-20

Withdrawing from Benzodiazepines. Sheila Knowlden. *Healthright* 9, No. 2 (February 1990):13-15

**Berardo, Donna Hodgkins**

Women, Work, and Divorce. Book Review. *Journal of Marriage and the Family* 52, No. 4 (November 1990):1153

**Berardo, Felix M.**

Trends and Directions in Family Research in the 1980s. *Journal of Marriage and the Family* 52, No. 4 (November 1990):809-817

**Bercu, Michaela** (about). *See also* Fashion Models

**Bereavement**

Bereavement and Stress in Career Women. Wilhelmina Kalu. *Women and Therapy* 10, No. 3 (1990):75-87

Brothers: I Want to Cry. G. Modele Clarke. *Essence* 21, No. 7 (November 1990):38-39

Facilitating Productive Bereavement of Widows: An Overview of the Efficacy of Widow's Support Groups. Cheryl H. Kinderknecht and Laree Hodges. *Journal of Women and Aging* 2, No. 4 (1990):39-54

Family Bereavement and Health in Adult Life Course Perspective. H. Wesley Perkins and Lynne B. Harris. *Journal of Marriage and the Family* 52, No. 1 (February 1990):233-241

The Other Side of Sorrow. Excerpt. Candy Lightner and Nancy Hathaway. *Ladies' Home Journal* 107, No. 9 (September 1990):158-159+

**Berenstein, Rhona**

Remembering History: Films by Women at the 1989 Toronto Film Festival. *Camera Obscura* No. 22 (January 1990):159-166

**Beresford, Bruce**

Driving Miss Daisy. Reviewed by Esther Bailey. *Spare Rib* No. 211 (April 1990):31

**Berg, Mary G.**

New Twist on an Old Tale. *Belles Lettres* 5, No. 2 (Winter 1990):16

The Ship of Fools. Book Review. *Belles Lettres* 5, No. 2 (Winter 1990):16

**Bergen, Candice** (about)

Candid Candice. Interview. Linda Ellerbee. *Ladies' Home Journal* 107, No. 6 (June 1990):126-130+

**Berger, Iris**

Gender, Race, and Political Empowerment: South African Canning Workers, 1940-1960. *Gender and Society* 4, No. 3 (September 1990):398-420

**Berger, Iris** and others

Restoring Women to History: Teaching Packets for Integrating Women's History into Courses on Africa, Asia, Latin America, the Caribbean, and the Middle East. Reviewed by Jjanet J. Ewald. *Gender & History* 2, No. 3 (Autumn 1990):349-351

**Berger, Lori**

Fire and Spice. *Harper's Bazaar* (August 1990):138-139+

**Berger, Pamela M.**

Soups that Make a Meal. *McCall's* 118, No. 2 (November 1990):134

**Berger, Ronald J.**, Searles, Patricia, and Cottle, Charles E.

Ideological Contours of the Contemporary Pornography Debate: Divisions and Alliances. *Frontiers* 11, Nos. 2-3 (1990):30-38

**Bergland, Martha**

The Birds Not Only Be But Mean. Poem. *Iris* 23 (Spring-Summer 1990):37

**Bergman, Marilyn** (about). *See also* Hollywood Women's Political Committee

**Bergman, Marilyn** (about)

Marilyn Bergman, the Way She Is. David Rieff. *Lear's* (December 1990):82-83+

**Bergman, Miranda**, Greene, Susan, Redman, Dina, and Tobias, Marlene

Painting for Peace: Break the Silence Mural Project. *Bridges* 1, No. 2 (Fall 1990): 39-57

**Bergmann, Barbara R.**

Feminism and Economics. *Women's Studies Quarterly* 18, Nos. 3-4 (Fall-Winter 1990):68-73

Reading Lists on Women's Studies in Economics. *Women's Studies Quarterly* 18, Nos. 3-4 (Fall-Winter 1990):75-86

Women's Roles in the Economy: Teaching the Issues. *Women's Studies Quarterly* 18, Nos. 3-4 (Fall-Winter 1990):6-22

**Berk, Bernice** and Owen, Patricia

Are You an Overprotective Parent? *Good Housekeeping* 211, No. 3 (September 1990):100+

**Berkeley, Ellen Perry** and McQuaid, Matilda (editors)

Architecture: A Place for Women. Reviewed by Judith A. Moldenhauer. *The Women's Review of Books* 7, No. 6 (March 1990):29-30

Architecture: A Place for Women. Reviewed by Pamela H. Simpson. *Woman's Art Journal* 11, No. 2 (Fall 1990-Winter 1991):44-48

**Berkman, Meredith**

How to Know it's Over. *Glamour* (November 1990):239

Taking Her Cue. *Savvy Woman* (September 1990):16

**Berko, Jacqueline** (joint author). *See* Frodi, Ann

**Berkowitz, Gila**

And the Sages Say . . . *Lilith* 15, No. 1 (Winter 1990):24-25

**Berkshire Conference on the History of Women**

Two American Conferences. Patricia Grimshaw and Marilyn Lake. *Australian Feminist Studies* No. 12 (Summer 1990):115-116

**Berlin – Description and Travel**

Back to the Potsdamer Platz. Richard Atcheson. *Lear's* (April 1990):92-97

**Berlin, Irving** (about). *See also* Children of Entertainers

**Berlin Wall, 1961-1989**

Full Circle: The Wall. Friedl Elaine Bell. *Family Circle* 103, No. 9 (June 26, 1990):154

Report from Berlin. Elaine Wallace. *Spare Rib* No. 215 (August 1990):26-27

**Berlow, Bruce A.**

Could the Problem Be Hidden Asthma? *Working Mother* 13, No. 5 (May 1990):72-74

**Berman, Barbara**

Another Year in Africa. Book Review. *Belles Lettres* 5, No. 3 (Spring 1990):13

**Berman, Claire**

How to Make Yourself a Stronger Person. *Ladies' Home Journal* 107, No. 11 (November 1990):96-104

**Berman, Donna**

Can Women Change Judaism? *New Directions for Women* 19, No. 4 (July-August 1990):18

Exile in the Promised Land. Book Review. *New Directions for Women* 19, No. 6 (November-December 1990):18

A Handbook for Jewish Women on the Israeli/Palestinian Conflict. Book Review. *New Directions for Women* 19, No. 6 (November-December 1990):18

A Personal Look at Israeli Politics. *New Directions for Women* 19, No. 6 (November-December 1990):18

Standing Again at Sinai: Judaism from a Feminist Perspective. Book Review. *New Directions for Women* 19, No. 4 (July-August 1990):18

**Berman, Eleanor**

Get Control of Clutter. *Working Mother* 13, No. 8 (August 1990):50-51

Kids and Their Grownup Friends. *Working Mother* (November 1990):66-69

Making the Most of Two Paychecks. *Working Mother* 13, No. 4 (April 1990):71-81

Meet Carol Miller: Reader of the Year. *Working Mother* 13, No. 5 (May 1990):18-22

The Tough and Tricky Stages of Childhood. *Working Mother* 13, No. 1 (January 1990):43-54

**Bermuda – History – Feminist Perspectives**

The Socioeconomics of a Female Majority in Eighteenth-Century Bermuda. Notes. Elaine Forman Crane. *Signs* 15, No. 2 (Winter 1990):231-258

**Bernard, L Diane.** *See also* Meyer, Carol and Young, Alma (editors), "On the Bias."

The Social Construction of Lesbianism. Book Review. *AFFILIA* 5, No. 2 (Summer 1990):100-102

**Bernard, L Diane** and Dinerman, Miriam (editors)

On the Lookout. *AFFILIA* 5, No. 1 (Spring 1990):94-96

**Berne, Suzanne**

Friend of My Youth. Book Review. *Belles Lettres* 5, No. 4 (Summer 1990):21-22

The Lonely Life. *Belles Lettres* 5, No. 3 (Spring 1990):6

Splash of Cold Water. *Belles Lettres* 5, No. 4 (Summer 1990):21-22

The Writing Life. Book Review. *Belles Lettres* 5, No. 3 (Spring 1990):6

**Bernhard, Sandra** (about)

Word On . . . Sandra Bernhard. Interview. David Denicolo. *Glamour* (March 1990):192

**Bernheimer, Charles**

Figures of Ill Repute: Representing Prostitution in Nineteenth-Century France. Reviewed by Frances Gouda. *The Women's Review of Books* 7, No. 12 (September 1990):13-14

**Bernier, Rosamund**

Art à la Russe. *Vogue* (May 1990):182-190

Malevich. *Vogue* (September 1990):588-593+

**Bernikow, Louise**

The Devil & Susan Seidelman. *Lear's* (January 1990):108-111

Spunky and Punky, Lauren Hutton Says Her Piece. *Lear's* (October 1990):90-93+

**Bernold, Monika** and Ha1mmerle, Christa

The Vienna Project on Autobiographies and Gender Identities in Austria. *Gender & History* 2, No. 1 (Spring 1990):82-83

**Bernstein, Albert J.** and Rozen, Sydney Craft

Preventing Turf Wars. *Executive Female* 13, No. 1 (January-February 1990):22-24

**Bernstein, Bruce** (joint author). *See* Schichor, Aric

**Berry, Christine M.** (about)

Legal-Eagle Affairs. Flora Skelly. *Mademoiselle* (October 1990):154-155+

**Berry, Eileen**

A Home Divided: Women and Income in the Third World. Book Review. *Women's Studies International Forum* 13, No. 6 (1990):614-617

**Berry, Halle** (about)

Prime Time Beauty. *Essence* 20, No. 11 (March 1990):14-15

**Berry, Mary Frances**

Mary Frances Berry on the Ideology of Child Care. *Ms.* 1, No. 3 (November/December 1990):88

**Berry, Philippa**

Of Chastity and Power: Elizabethan Literature and the Unmarried Queen. Reviewed by Shannon Hengen. *Resources for Feminist Research* 19, No. 2 (June 1990):44-45

**Bersch, Suzanne**

Retro '60s. *Lear's* (December 1990):108-111

**Bersianik, Louky,** Brossard, Nicole, Cotnoir, Louise, Dupré, Louise, Scott, Gail, and others

La théorie, un dimanche. Reviewed by Dominique Bourque. *Canadian Women's Studies* 11, No. 1 (Spring 1990):107-108

**Berta, Renée**

The Power in Young Girls. Poem. *Frontiers* 11, Nos. 2-3 (1990):80-81

**Bertinelli, Valerie** (about)

Talking with Valerie Bertinelli: Still Struggling to Save Her Marriage. Interview. Claudia Dreifus. *Redbook* 174, No. 6 (April 1990):38-42

**Bertolucci, Bernardo**

The Sheltering Sky. Reviewed by Linda King. *Spare Rib* 219 (December 1990-January 1991):28

**Bertolucci, Bernardo** (about)

Dreams and Dust: Under a Sheltering Sky. Brian Case. *Lear's* (May 1990):90-97

**Besant, Annie** (criticism)

Feminism Under the Raj: Complicity and Resistance in the Writings of Flora Annie Steel and Annie Besant. Nancy L. Paxton. *Women's Studies International Forum* 13, No. 4 (1990):333-346

**Beta-carotene**

Can Beta-carotene Affect Cervical Abnormalities? – Interview with Dorothy Mackerras. Jo Calluy. *Healthright* 9, No. 2 (February 1990):31-33

**Beth, Karen**

The Accordion: Out of the Closet and into Your Hands! *Hot Wire* 6, No. 2 (May 1990):40-41+

**Bethlehem (Pennsylvania) – Social Life and Customs**

The Way I Want to Live. Barbara Flanagan. *Lear's* (October 1990):80-85

**Betsko, Kathleen** and Koenig, Rachel (editors)

Interviews with Contemporary Women Playwrights. Reviewed by Jill Dolan. *Signs* 15, No. 4 (Summer 1990):864-869

**Better, Nancy Marx**

Résumé Liars. *Savvy* (December-January 1991):26-31

**Betteridge, Anne** and Monk, Janice

Teaching Women's Studies from an International Perspective. *Women's Studies Quarterly* 18, Nos. 1-2 (Spring-Summer 1990):78-85

**Bewley, Sheila** (joint author). *See* Sheffield, Margaret

**Beyette, Beverly**

The Accident. *Family Circle* 103, No. 12 (September 4, 1990):80-82

**Bhachu, Parminder** (joint editor). *See* Westwood, Sallie

**Bhargava, Mahesh** and Khajuria, Sunita

A Comparative Study of Health Distress and Sex Behavioural Attitude of Family Planning Adopters and Non-Adopters. *Journal of Family Welfare* 36, No. 2 (June 1990):23-29

**Bhasin, Sanjiv Kumar** (joint author). *See* Singh, Saudan

**Bhatia, M. S.** and others

Post-Abortion Psychological Sequelae. *Journal of Family Welfare* 36, No. 4 (December 1990):67-74

**Bhattacharya, M.** (joint author). *See* Joshi, P. L.

**Bhraonain, Maire Ni** (interview)

The Singing and the Crack – the Heart of the People. Julie McNamara. *Spare Rib* 219 (December 1990-January 1991):24-26

**Bhullar, Renu**

Massacre at Dome of the Rock. *Spare Rib* 218 (November 1990):15-16

**Bhutto, Benazir** (about)

Benazir Bhutto: Her Rise, Fall – and Rise? Shazia Rafi. *Ms.* 1, No. 3 (November/December 1990):16-20

Benazir Bhutto Defeated at the Polls. Rukhsana Ahmad. *Spare Rib* 218 (November 1990):45

Pakistan: A Constitutional Coup. Rukhsana Ahmad. *Spare Rib* No. 216 (September 1990):20-23

**Biagiotti, Laura** (about)

Italian Nights. Mark Ganem. *Harper's Bazaar* (April 1990):209-211+

**Bialeschki, M. Deborah** and Henderson, Karla A.

More to Women's Lives Than Work?: A Model for a Course Addressing Women and Leisure. *Feminist Teacher* 5, No. 2 (Fall 1990):25-31

**Bialkowski, Carol**

Tech Talk: How to Build a Better Meeting – The On-Line Advantage. *Working Woman* (July 1990):40-42

**Bibb, Elizabeth**

Meet the Real Working Girls. *Mademoiselle* (March 1990):214-215, 244-247

**Bibby, Patricia**

Clown about Town. *Harper's Bazaar* (February 1990):72

**Bible – N. T.**

Women Partners in the New Testament. Mary Rose D'Angelo. *Journal of Feminist Studies in Religion* 6, No. 1 (Spring 1990):65-86

**Bible, O.T. – Versions**

What Dinah Thought. Excerpt. Short story. Deena Metzger. *Lilith* 15, No. 2 (Spring 1990):8-12

**Bible – Scholarship**

Death and Dissymmetry: The Politics of Coherence in the Book of Judges. By Mieke Bal. Reviewed by Kelly Oliver. *Hypatia* 5, No. 3 (Fall 1990):169-171

**Bible – Study**

The Book of J. Translated by David Rosenberg. Reviewed by Deborah Ann Light. *Ms.* 1, No. 2 (September/October 1990):27

**Bible – Translation**

*Les belles infide4les*/Fidelity or Feminism? The Meaning of Feminist Biblical Translation. Elizabeth A. Castelli. *Journal of Feminist Studies in Religion* 6, No. 2 (Fall 1990):25-39

Womanist Interpretation of the New Testament: The Quest for Holistic and Inclusive Translation and Interpretation. Clarice J. Martin, Joanna Dewey, Peggy Hutaff, and Jane Schaberg. *Journal of Feminist Studies in Religion* 6, No. 2 (Fall 1990):41-85

**Bicycle Racing**

Innerviews. Diane French. *Women's Sports and Fitness* 12, No. 7 (October 1990):56

Spinning Their Wheels. Michele Kort. *Ms.* 1, No. 1 (July/August 1990):84-85

Sporting News. *Women's Sports & Fitness* 12, No. 6 (September 1990):54-57

Tour de Tater. Leslee Schenk. *Women's Sports and Fitness* 12, No. 7 (October 1990):29-31

**Bicycle Racing – Tour de France Feminin**

Dropped from the Pack. Erik Schmidt. *Women's Sports and Fitness* 12, No. 3 (April 1990):44-55

**Bicycles**

Calendar. *Women's Sports & Fitness* 12, No. 6 (September 1990):15

**Bicycling**

Annual Guide to Women's Bikes. *Women's Sports and Fitness* 12, No. 3 (April 1990):32-41

Beauty: The Biker Body. *Mademoiselle* (September 1990):62-67

Double Your Pleasure. James Raia and Marjorie McCloy. *Women's Sports & Fitness* 12, No. 6 (September 1990):20

The Grateful Head. Alison Bell. *Women's Sports and Fitness* 12, No. 4 (May-June 1990):26

Health & Fitness. Stephanie Young. *Glamour* (August 1990):55-56+

Living in the Fast Lane. Casey Patterson. *Women's Sports and Fitness* 12, No. 2 (March 1990):14-15

**Bicycling – Touring**

Doing Burgundy by Bicycle for Fun. Marcia Seligson. *Lear's* (September 1990):56-59

**Biederman, Carole A.**

Transforming Body Image. *Woman of Power* 18 (Fall 1990):76-80

**Biernat, Monica** (joint author). *See* Tiedje, Linda Beth

**Big Brothers/Big Sisters.** *See* Dutka, Elaine

**Biggart, Nicole Woolsey**

Charismatic Capitalism: Direct Selling Organizations in America. Reviewed by Diane Barthel. *Gender and Society* 4, No. 2 (June 1990):266-267

**Biggerstaff, Marilyn**

Gender Bias in Scholarship: The Pervasive Prejudice. Book Review. *AFFILIA* 5, No. 1 (Spring 1990):121-123

Gender Issues in Field Research. Book Review. *AFFILIA* 5, No. 1 (Spring 1990):121-123

**Bildungsroman**

The Female *Bildungsroman*: Calling It into Question. Carol Lazzaro-Weis. *NWSA Journal* 2, No. 1 (Winter 1990):16-34

**Bill Collectors.** *See* Collection Agencies

**Billiards**

Taking Her Cue. Meredith Berkman. *Savvy Woman* (September 1990):16

**Billingsley, Janice**

Private Lives. *Family Circle* 103, No. 11 (August 14, 1990):64+

**Bingham, Mindy,** Stryker, Sandy, and Edmonson, Judy

Changes: A Woman's Journal for Self-Awareness and Personal Planning. Reviewed by Cheryl H. Kinderknecht. *Journal of Women and Aging* 2, No. 1 (1990):127

**Binion, Loraine** (about). *See* Watts, Patti (editor), "Free Advice."

**Biodegradation**

Your Environment: The Good, the Bad, the Biodegradable. Sharon Begley. *Family Circle* 103, No. 14 (October 16, 1990):71-72

**Bioethics.** *See also* Medical Ethics; Medical Research; Surrogate Mothers

**Biography.** *See also* Autobiography

Composing a Life. By Mary Catherine Bateson. Reviewed by Deborah Solomon. *The Women's Review of Books* 7, No. 12 (September 1990):26-27

"How Could She?" Unpalatable Facts and Feminists' Heroines. Dea Birkett and Julie Wheelwright. *Gender & History* 2, No. 1 (Spring 1990):49-57

Jane Ellen Harrison: The Mask and the Self. By Sandra J. Peacock. Reviewed by Sandra J. Peacock. *Gender & History* 2, No. 1 (Spring 1990):103-104

Let it Lie Upon the Table: The Status of Black Women's Biography in the UK. Ziggi Alexander. *Gender & History* 2, No. 1 (Spring 1990):22-33

Moments of Writing: Is there a Feminist Auto/Biography? Notes. Liz Stanley. *Gender & History* 2, No. 1 (Spring 1990):50-67

The New Historical Synthesis: Women's Biography. Kathleen Barry. *Journal of Women's History* 1, No. 3 (Winter 1990):75-105

Past and Promise: Lives of New Jersey Women. Edited by The Women's Project, Inc. Reviewed by Phyllis Ehrenfeld. *New Directions for Women* 19, No. 5 (September-October 1990):20

Private Connives. Patricia O'Toole. *Lear's* (August 1990):98-101

True Stories: Biographies of Women for Young Readers. Christine Jenkins. *Feminist Collections* 12, No. 1 (Fall 1990):6-9

Women of the Left Bank: Paris, 1900-1940. By Shari Benstock. Reviewed by Megan Roughley. *Gender & History* 2, No. 1 (Spring 1990):118-120

Writing for Their Lives. By Gillian Hanscombe and Virginia L. Smyers. Reviewed by Megan Roughley. *Gender & History* 2, No. 1 (Spring 1990):118-120

**Biological Clock.** *See* Childless Couples

**Biological Rhythms**

When the Clock Strikes 98.6 – Relax! Carol Orlock. *Lear's* (September 1990):51-55

**Biological Sciences**

Black Women in the Biological Sciences. Rosalyn Patterson. *Sage* 6, No. 2 (Fall 1989):8-14

**Biopolitics**

The Politics of Women's Biology. By Ruth Hubbard. Reviewed by Sheila Tobias. *The Women's Review of Books* 8, No. 2 (November 1990):15

**Biorhythms.** *See* Biological Rhythms

**Biosphere II.** *See also* Oracle (Arizona) – Biosphere II

**Biotechnology**

The Medical Construction of Gender: Case Management of Intersexed Infants. Suzanne J. Kessler. *Signs* 16, No. 1 (Autumn 1990):3-26

Voorplanting Als Bio-Industrie. Edited by Annemiek Ostenk and Linda Wilkens. Reviewed by Rosi Braidotti. *Women's Studies International Forum* 13, No. 5 (1990):529

**Biraciality**

Mothering the Biracial Child: Bridging the Gaps between African-American and White Parenting Styles. Robin L. Miller and Barbara Miller. *Women and Therapy* 10, Nos. 1/2 (1990):169-179

Resolving "Other" Status: Identity Development of Biracial Individuals. Maria P. P. Root. *Women and Therapy* 9, Nos. 1-2 (1990):185-205

**Birds, Ornamental**

Pet News. Nina Keilin. *Ladies' Home Journal* 107, No. 2 (February 1990):80

**Biren, Joan E.**

Chosen Images: A Decade of Jewish Feminism. Photographs. *Bridges* 1, No. 1 (Spring 1990): 57-66

**Birken, Lawrence**

Consuming Desire: Sexual Science and the Emergence of a Culture of Abundance, 1871-1914. Reviewed by Chris Waters. *Gender & History* 2, No. 2 (Summer 1990):218-222

**Birkett, Dea**

Spinsters Abroad: Victorian Lady Explorers. Reviewed by Helen Callaway. *Women's Studies International Forum* 13, No. 4 (1990):405

Spinsters Abroad: Victorian Lady Explorers. Reviewed by Patricia Lamb. *The Women's Review of Books* 7, No. 5 (February 1990):15

Spinsters Abroad: Victorian Lady Explorers. Reviewed by Sarah Graham-Brown. *Gender & History* 2, No. 3 (Autumn 1990):373-375

**Birkett, Dea** and Wheelwright, Julie

"How Could She?" Unpalatable Facts and Feminists' Heroines. *Gender & History* 2, No. 1 (Spring 1990):49-57

**Birnbaum, Stephen**

Best Family Resorts for the Holidays. *Good Housekeeping* 211, No. 6 (December 1990):40+

The Grand Canyon. *Good Housekeeping* 211, No. 5 (November 1990):150+

Mother Nature's Fall Spectacular. Bibliography. *Good Housekeeping* 211, No. 4 (October 1990):106-108

Yes, You Can Afford to Go to Europe! Bibliography. *Good Housekeeping* 211, No. 3 (September 1990):76-81

**Birns, Beverly** (joint author). *See* Yanay, Niza

**Birth Control.** *See* Contraception

**Birth Control Pills.** *See* Contraception

**Birthday Parties.** *See* Birthdays

**Birthdays**

A Gift from Elvis. Melle Starsen. *Ladies' Home Journal* 107, No. 8 (August 1990):18-22

How to Give a Great Birthday Party. Nancy Balaban. *Good Housekeeping* 211, No. 3 (September 1990):116-118

**Birth Defects**

Finding Homes for Jewish Babies. Toby Axelrod. *Lilith* 15, No. 3 (Summer 1990):4-5

McBride: Behind the Myth. By Bill Nicol. Reviewed by Charles Kerr. *Healthright* 9, No. 4 (August 1990):45

**Birth Defects – Prevention**

Postponing Motherhood. Margie Patlak. *Glamour* (March 1990):68-70

**Birthing Centers**

Free-Standing Birth Centers and Medical Control: A Case Study. Kathleen Doherty Turkel. *NWSA Journal* 2, No. 1 (Winter 1990):52-67

**Birth Rates.** *See* Family Planning; Family Size; Population Policy

**Bischoff, Anne**

Children's Corner. *Belles Lettres* 5, No. 4 (Summer 1990):14

**Bishop, Heather** (interview)

A Taste of the Canadian Prairies: Heather Bishop. *Hot Wire* 6, No. 2 (May 1990):2-4+

**Bitter, Adriana Scalamandré** (about)

A Fortune in Silk. Gwen Kinkead. *Savvy Woman* (January 1990):44-46

**Bittle, Camilla R.**

The Day the World Changed. *Good Housekeeping* 211, No. 6 (December 1990):22-27

**Black, Kathryn Stechert**

Are You Too Good? *Glamour* (March 1990):164-167

Can Getting Mad Get the Job Done? *Working Woman* (March 1990):86-90

Easy Ways to Help Him Be a Sexier Lover. *Redbook* 175, No. 6 (October 1990):112-113+

On the Job. *Family Circle* 103, No. 7 (May 15, 1990):42+

The New Professional Temporaries. *Working Mother* (November 1990):58-65

**Black, Kent**

A Few Good Men. Theater review. *Harper's Bazaar* (February 1990):50

The Remains of the Day. Book Review. *Harper's Bazaar* (February 1990):50

A Singular Country. Book Review. *Harper's Bazaar* (May 1990):80+

The Wendy Chronicles. *Harper's Bazaar* (March 1990):154-162

**Black, Naomi** (joint author). *See* Prentice, Alison

**Black, Shirley Temple** (about)

Return to Prague. Vivian Cadden. *McCall's* 117, No. 7 (April 1990):60-66

**Black Entertainment Television**

Robert Johnson: The Eyes Behind BET. Benilde Little. *Essence* 21, No. 7 (November 1990):48

**Blackford, Karen**

A Different Parent. *Healthsharing* 11, No. 3 (June 1990):20-24

**Black History.** *See also* African-American Women – Leadership; Culture and History; Davis, Angela Y. (about)

Back Talk: With Respect to Malcolm. Ron Daniels. *Essence* 20, No. 10 (February 1990):126

Book Marks. Bibliography. Paula Giddings. *Essence* 21, No. 2 (June 1990):44; 21, No. 4 (August 1990):50; 21, No. 7 (November 1990):50

In Celebration of Our Twentieth Anniversary. Edward Lewis. *Essence* 21, No. 1 (May 1990):20-25

Don't We Style! Elsie B. Washington. *Essence* 21, No. 1 (May 1990):125-129

Everything to Live For. K. Maurice Jones. *Essence* 21, No. 1 (May 1990):76

On the Front Lines. *Essence* 20, No. 10 (February 1990):45-50

Graceful Passages. Interviews. *Essence* 21, No. 1 (May 1990):130-136

Graffiti. *Essence* 20, No. 9 (January 1990):103-105; 20, No. 10 (February 1990):120; 20, No. 11 (March 1990):140; 20, No. 12 (April 1990):118; 21, No. 1 (May 1990):208-211

Oakland: Back to the Future. Julianne Malveaux. *Essence* 21, No. 1 (May 1990):157-159

In the Spirit: Give Thanks. Susan L. Taylor. *Essence* 21, No. 5 (September 1990):57

1910. Reviewed by Louise A. Tilly. *Gender and Society* 4, No. 2 (June 1990):269-272

**Blier, Bernard**

Trop Belle Pour Toi (Too Beautiful for You). Reviewed by Sue Murphy. *Spare Rib* No. 211 (April 1990):30

**Blind – Books and Reading**

Bold Types. Barbara Findlen. *Ms.* 1, No. 2 (September/October 1990):29

**Blind – Services for**

No More the Pause that Perplexes. J. R. Moehringer. *McCall's* 117, No. 11 (August 1990):64

**Blind Dates**

His: Blind Dates. David Seeley. *Mademoiselle* (June 1990):83

Scruples: Make a Match, Play With Fire? Ellen Welty. *Mademoiselle* (September 1990):204

**Blinder, Martin** and Lynch, Carmen

Choosing Lovers. Patterns of Romance: How You Select Partners in Intimacy. Book Review. *Adolescence* 25, No. 98 (Summer 1990):499

**Bloch, Gordon Bakoulis**

Slow Down, You Move Too Fast. *Women's Sports and Fitness* 12, No. 3 (April 1990):24

Trail Mix. *Women's Sports and Fitness* 12, No. 4 (May-June 1990):28

**Bloch, Julia Chang** (about)

Witness to Freedom. Grace Lichtenstein. *Savvy Woman* (July/August 1990):56-59+

**Block, Adam**

An Interview with Edmund White. Interview. *Out/Look* No. 10 (Fall 1990):56-62

**Block, Jean Liebman**

One Couple's Crusade for Children. *Good Housekeeping* 211, No. 5 (November 1990):90+

**Block, Joyce**

What's Behind the Mommy Wars? *Working Mother* 13, No. 10 (October 1990):74-79

**Block, Peter**

How to Be the New Kind of Manager. *Working Woman* (July 1990):51-54

**Blodgett, Harriet**

Centuries of Female Days: Englishwomen's Private Diaries. Reviewed by Lillian S. Robinson. *Tulsa Studies in Women's Literature* 9, No. 1 (Spring 1990):144-146

Cicely Hamilton, Independent Feminist. *Frontiers* 11, Nos. 2-3 (1990):99-104

**Blom, Ida**

Changing Gender Identities in an Industrializing Society: The Case of Norway, 1870-1914. *Gender & History* 2, No. 2 (Summer 1990):131-147

**Blonde Hair.** *See* Hair – Dyeing and Bleaching

**Blonsky, Marshall**

Say Cheese. *Lear's* (January 1990):70-75

**Blood – Circulation, Disorders of**

Cardiovascular Stress Reactivity and Mood during the Menstrual Cycle. Gerdi Weidner and Linda Helmig. *Women and Health* 16, Nos. 3/4 (1990):5-21

**Blood Transfusions**

Transfusions. *Connexions* 33 (1990):24

**Bloom, Craig**

A Voice in the Crowd. *Lear's* (October 1990):100-103

**Bloom, Edward A.** and Bloom, Lillian D. (editors)

The Piozzi Letters, Correspondence of Hester Lynch Piozzi, 1784-1821 (Formerly Mrs. Thrale), Volume 1, 1784-1791. Reviewed by Betty Rizzo. *Tulsa Studies in Women's Literature* 9, No. 1 (Spring 1990):147-149

**Bloom, Lillian D.** (joint editor). *See* Bloom Edward A.

**Bloom, Lynn Z.**

Midwife, Mortician, Physician, Pharmacist. *Belles Lettres* 6, No. 1 (Fall 1990):48-49

A Midwife's Tale: The Life of Martha Ballard, Based on Her Diary, 1785-1812. Book Review. *Belles Lettres* 6, No. 1 (Fall 1990):48-49

**Bloom, Marc**

Cold Sweat. *Women's Sports and Fitness* 12, No. 7 (October 1990):26

**Blue Jeans.** *See* Clothing and Dress – Jeans

**Bluestone, Natalie Harris**

Women and the Ideal Society: Plato's Republic and Modern Myths of Gender. Reviewed by Mary Dietz. *Women & Politics* 10, No. 1 (1990):80-82

**Blum, Ralph**

On Riding the Edges. *Lear's* (March 1990):138-143

**Blumenthal, Sidney**

A Capital Proposal. *Lear's* (August 1990):86-89

Subsidizing the Rich. *Lear's* (September 1990):110-113

**Blyth, Eric** (joint author). *See* Milner, Judith

**Blyth, Myrna**

Never Underestimate the Power of a Woman. *Ladies' Home Journal* 107, No. 11 (November 1990):16-25

**Bobb, June**

Annie John. Book Review. *Sage* 6, No. 2 (Fall 1989):55-56

**Bocce**

Bone up on Bocce. Therese Iknoian. *Women's Sports and Fitness* 12, No. 7 (October 1990):58

**Bock, E. Wilbur** (joint author). *See* Shehan, Constance L.

**Bock, Laura**

FAT LIP Readers Theatre. *Woman of Power* 17 (Summer 1990):32-33

**Bodett, Tom**

The Bare Truth. Short story. *Redbook* 175, No. 5 (September 1990):64-66+

**Bodybuilding**

What Price Glory? An Insider's Look at the Sport of Women's Bodybuilding. Laura Dayton. *Women's Sports and Fitness* 12, No. 2 (March 1990):52-55

**Body Image.** *See also* Aging–Psychological Aspects; Beauty, Personal; Beauty Standards; Fat Acceptance; Images of Women; Mastectomy; Obesity; Sexual Attraction

Big Girls Don't Cry. *Mademoiselle* (February 1990):148-153

Body Image. Mary Kay Blakely. *Lear's* (January 1990):52-53

Body Love. Bebe Moore Campbell. *Essence* 20, No. 9 (January 1990):44-49

Bodylove. By Rita Freedman. Reviewed by Patricia A. Connor-Greene. *Women and Health* 16, Nos. 3/4 (1990):211-221

Images: New Cellulite Remedies. Jeannie Ralston. *Vogue* (August 1990):170-179

Kiss Health Terrorism Goodbye. *Glamour* (April 1990):122

9 Show-it-Off Swimsuits. *Glamour* (May 1990):286-293

"Perfect" Bodies to Die for. Bibliography. Judith Warner-Berley. *McCall's* 117, No. 8 (May 1990):64-65

Phallos Politikos: Representing the Body Politic in Athens. John J. Winkler. *Differences* 2, No. 1 (Spring 1990):29-45

Private Time Private Space. *Family Circle* 103, No. 1 (January 9, 1990):46-51

Talking with Victoria Principal: "I'm in Great Shape." Interview. Alan W. Petrucelli. *Redbook* 175, No. 6 (October 1990):72-74

The Truth about Breasts: A Beauty & Health Guide. *Mademoiselle* (October 1990):164-165

What a Body! *Glamour* (June 1990):210-215

Your Body. Susan Jacoby. *Family Circle* 103, No. 2 (February 1, 1990):41-46

**Body Image in Literature–Bibliographies**

Reading the Body in Contemporary Culture: An Annotated Bibliography. Anne Balsamo. *Women & Language* 13, No. 1 (Fall 1990):64-85

**Body Makeup.** *See* Body-Marking

**Body-Marking**

Body Images. *Harper's Bazaar* (November 1990):164-167

**Body Shop International.** *See also* Roddick, Anita (about)

**Boehlert, Bart**

Blue Notes. *Harper's Bazaar* (October 1990):208-213+

**Boethel, Martha**

On Her Own: Growing Up in the Shadow of the American Dream. Book Review. *New Directions for Women* 19, No. 6 (November-December 1990):20

Sing Soft, Sing Loud. Book Review. *New Directions for Women* 19, No. 2 (March/April 1990):18

Unrealistic Visions. *New Directions for Women* 19, No. 6 (November-December 1990):20

**Boetig, Donna E.**

A Leap of Faith. *Family Circle* 103, No. 17 (December 18, 1990):116-120

**Bogolub, Ellen B.**

Feminism, Children, and the New Families. Book Review. *AFFILIA* 5, No. 3 (Fall 1990):116-118

The Invisible Web: Gender Patterns in Family Relationships. Book Review. *AFFILIA* 5, No. 3 (Fall 1990):116-118

**Bograd, Michele** (joint editor). *See* Yllo, Kersti; Yllö, Kersti

**Bogus, Diane**

Her Son. *Sinister Wisdom* 42 (Winter 1990-1991):86-90

**Bohachevsky-Chomiak, Martha**

Feminists Despite Themselves: Women in Ukranian Community Life, 1884-1939. Reviewed by Frances Swyripa. *Resources for Feminist Research* 19, No. 1 (March 1990):13

**Bohan, Janis S.**

Contextual History: A Framework for Re-Placing Women in the History of Psychology. *Psychology of Women Quarterly* 14, No. 2 (June 1990):213-227

**Bohra, Neena** (joint author). *See* Bhatia, M. S.

**Boitano, Brian** (about). *See also* Entertainers

**Boivin, Marie** (joint author). *See* Paquin, Ghislaine

**Bojarska, Anna** (interview)

No Sacred Cows. Halina Filipowicz. *The Women's Review of Books* 7, Nos. 10-11 (July 1990):4-6

**Bolger, Niall** (joint author). *See* Moen, Phyllis

**Bolshoi Ballet.** *See also* Semizorova, Nina (about)

Bolshoi Bravo! Matthew Gurewitsch. *Harper's Bazaar* (July 1990):27

**Bolton, Frank,** Morris, Larry, and McEachron, Ann E.

Males at Risk. Reviewed by Sharon K. Araji. *Journal of Marriage and the Family* 52, No. 3 (August 1990):801

**Bonds.** *See also* Junk Bonds; Municipal Bonds

Awaiting a Nine-Percent Solution. Susan Scherreik. *Lear's* (November 1990):36-38

**Bone Marrow – Transplantation**

One Mother's Fight for Life. Clarita Fonville Buie. *Family Circle* 103, No. 9 (June 26, 1990):70-74

**Boneparth, Ellen** and Stoper, Emily (editors)

Women, Power and Policy: Toward the Year 2000. Reviewed by Joan Hulse Thompson. *Women & Politics* 10, No. 3 (1990):133-134

**Bonet, Lisa** (about)

Let Love Rule. Carol Cooper. *Essence* 20, No. 10 (February 1990):54-55+

**Bonetti, Kay**

Belles Lettres Interview: Marilynne Robinson. *Belles Lettres* 6, No. 1 (Fall 1990):36-39

**Bonfanti, Cheryl**

Voices from Prison. *New Directions for Women* 19, No. 3 (May/June 1990):6

**Bonilla-Santiago, Gloria** (about). *See also* Watts, Patti (editor), "Free Advice."

**Bonner, Marita**

Frye Street and Environs: The Collected Works of Marita Bonner. Edited by Joyce Flynn and Joyce Occomy Stricklin. Reviewed by Phillipa Kafka. *Sage* 6, No. 2 (Fall 1989):60

**Bonnicksen, Andrea L.**

In Vitro Fertilization: Building Policy from Laboratories to Legislatures. Reviewed by Helen Bequaert Holmes. *The Women's Review of Books* 7, No. 4 (January 1990):20-21

In Vitro Fertilization: Building Policy from Laboratories to Legislatures. Reviewed by Leigh Anne Chavez. *NWSA Journal* 2, No. 4 (Autumn 1990):652-656

**Bonophool**

A Woman's Tale. *Manushi* 61 (November-December 1990):32

**Bonuses.** *See* Employee Benefits

**Book Lists.** *See also* Literary Criticism – Feminist Perspectives; Young Adult Literature

Book Bazaar. Bibliography. Brenda Cullerton. *Harper's Bazaar* (November 1990):118

Book Bazaar: Tale Spinners. Brenda Cullerton. *Harper's Bazaar* (December 1990):98

Book Marks. Bibliography. Paula Giddings. *Essence* 21, No. 2 (June 1990):44; 21, No. 4 (August 1990):50; 21, No. 5 (September 1990):52; 21, No. 6 (October 1990):52; 21, No. 7 (November 1990):50; 21, No. 8 (December 1990):38

Book Marks. Paula Giddings. *Essence* 20, No. 11 (March 1990):44

Book Marks: Taking the Stage. Paula Giddings. *Essence* 20, No. 10 (February 1990):42

Books Currently Received. *Feminist Collections* 11, No. 4 (Summer 1990):22-24

Books Recently Received. *Feminist Collections* 11, No. 2 (Winter 1990):30-32; 12, No. 1 (Fall 1990):38-39

The Business Person's Essential Library. Bibliography. Joe Queenan. *Working Woman* (November 1990):101-106

Eating Out: Glamour Rates the Guidebooks. Bibliography. *Glamour* (August 1990):246

Four-Star Ratings. Barbara Kafka. *Family Circle* 103, No. 17 (December 18, 1990):162

Hot Summer Reading. *Ladies' Home Journal* 107, No. 6 (June 1990):112

July. *Glamour* (July 1990):143

Kitties Rule. Bibliography. Anne Lamott. *Mademoiselle* (October 1990):102-104

New Picturebooks: Redbook Picks 10 Winners. Carol Weston. *Redbook* 176, No. 2 (December 1990):26-28

People Are Talking About . . . *Vogue* (July 1990):89

Resources. Charles L. Martin. *Executive Female* (May/June 1990):48

Season's Readings. Bibliography. Anne Lamott. *Mademoiselle* (December 1990):80-82

These Cookbooks Have Legs. Bibliography. Meredith Brody. *Mademoiselle* (November 1990):78

Tsena-Rena. Bibliography. *Lilith* 15, No. 1 (Winter 1990):30; 15, No. 2 (Spring 1990):30-31; 15, No. 3 (Summer 1990):30-31; 15, No. 4 (Fall 1990):43

Vogue Arts: Christmas Gift Books. John Heilpern. *Vogue* (December 1990):208-210

Women Right Now. Bibliography. *Glamour* (October 1990):103-110

Word On Books. Bibliography. Laura Mathews. *Glamour* (April 1990):196

Word on Books. Bibliography. Laura Mathews. *Glamour* (March 1990):196; (May 1990):210; (August 1990):160; (September 1990):222; (November 1990):174; (December 1990):162

Word On Books. Laura Mathews. *Glamour* (January 1990):86; (February 1990):132; (June 1990):188

Word on Books. Laura Mathews. *Glamour* (October 1990):200

**Bookman, Ann** and Morgen, Sandra (editors)

Women and the Politics of Empowerment. Reviewed by Sue Tolleson Rinehart. *Women & Politics* 10, No. 3 (1990):131-132

## Book Reviews

Abandoned Women and Poetic Tradition. *See* Lipking, Lawrence

Abortion: The Clash of Absolutes. *See* Tribe, Laurence H.

Abortion in Northern Ireland: Report of an International Tribunal. *See* Northern Ireland Abortion Law Reform Association

About Men. *See* Chesler, Phyllis

The Acoustic Mirror: The Female Voice in Psychoanalysis and Cinema. *See* Silverman, Kaja

Adam, Eve, and the Serpent. *See* Pagels, Elaine

Adam, Eve and the Serpent. *See* Pagels, Elaine

The Adams Women: Abigail and Louisa Adams, Their Sisters and Daughters. *See* Nagel, Paul C.

Adolescent Mothers in Later Life. *See* Furstenberg, Frank F. (Jr.)

Adolescent Sexuality. *See* Masserman, Jules H.

Adolescent Sexuality and Gynecology. *See* Greydanus, Donald E.

Adolescents' Orientation to the Future: Development of Interests and Plans, and Related Attributions and Affects, in the Life-Span Context. *See* Nurmi, Jari-Erik

Adultery: An Analysis of Love and Betrayal. *See* Lawson, Annette

Adults and Children in the Roman Empire. *See* Wiedemann, Thomas

Affirmative Action in Perspective. *See* Blanchard, F. A.

Affliction. *See* Banks, Russell

Afro-American Women of the South and the Advancement of the Race, 1895-1925. *See* Neverdon-Morton, Cynthia

After Delores. *See* Schulman, Sarah

After Egypt. *See* Dillon, Millicent

After the Fire. *See* Rule, Jane

After the Stroke. *See* Sarton, May

After You've Gone. *See* Adams, Alice

Aging Parents and Adult Children. *See* Mancini, Jay A.

The Aging Population in the Twenty-First Century: Statistics for Health Policy. *See* Gilford, Dorothy M.

Agriculture, Women and Land: The African Experience. *See* Davison, Jean

AIDS: The Women. *See* Reider, Ines

AIDS and its Metaphors. *See* Sontag, Susan

AIDS and Other Sexually Transmitted Diseases. *See* Richmond, Robyn

The AIDS Challenge: Prevention Education for Young People. *See* Quackenbush, Marcia

The Alchemy of Survival: One Woman's Journey. *See* Mack, John E.

Alcohol and the Family. *See* Collins, R. Lorraine

Alfonsina Storni: Selected Poems. *See* Freeman, Marion

Alice to the Lighthouse: Children's Books and Radical Experiments in Art. *See* Dusinberre, Juliet

Alien to Femininity: Speculative Fiction and Feminist Theory. *See* Barr, Marleen S.

All New People. *See* Lamott, Anne

All Work and No Play? The Sociology of Women and Leisure. *See* Deem, Rosemary

Always a Sister: The Feminism of Lillian D. Wald. *See* Daniels, Doris Groshen

Amazons and Military Maids: Women Who Dressed as Men in Pursuit of Life, Liberty and Happiness. *See* Wheelwright, Julie

Amazons and Military Maids: Women Who Dressed as Men in the Pursuit of Life, Liberty and the Pursuit of Happiness. *See* Wheelwright, Julie

America and I: Short Stories by American Jewish Women Writers. *See* Antler, Joyce; Antler, Joyce (editor)

American Cassandra: The Life of Dorothy Thompson. *See* Kurth, Peter

American Indian Women: Telling Their Lives. *See* Bataille, Gretchen M. and Sands, Kathleen Mullen

The Americanization of Sex. *See* Schur, Edwin M.

American Ritual Dramas: Social Rules and Cultural Meanings. *See* Deegan, Mary Jo

The American Women, 1990-1991: A Status Report. *See* Rix, Sara E.

American Women in Poverty. *See* Zopf, Paul E., Jr.

American Women Writers on Vietnam: Unheard Voices: A Selected Annotated Bibliography. *See* Butler, Deborah A.

"Am I That Name?" Feminism and the Category of 'Women' in History. *See* Riley, Denise

Among Schoolchildren. *See* Kidder, Tracy

Among Sisters: Short Stories by Women Writers. *See* Cahill, Susan

An Abyss of Light. *See* O'Neal, Kathleen M.

An American Childhood. *See* Dillard, Annie

Black Women's Literary Scholarship: Reclaiming an Intellectual Tradition. *See* McKay, Nellie Y.

Black Women Writing Autobiography: A Tradition Within a Tradition. *See* Braxton, Joanne

Blood and Water. *See* Dhuibhne, Eilís Ní

Blood at the Root: Motherhood, Sexuality and Male Dominance. *See* Ferguson, Ann

Blood Magic: The Anthropology of Menstruation. *See* Buckley, Thomas

Blue, White and Pink Collar Workers in Australia: Technicians, Bank Employees and Flight Attendants. *See* Williams, Claire

The Blue Nature. *See* Free, Suzanne Hamilton

Bodies at Sea. *See* McGraw, Erin

Bodies of Water. *See* Cliff, Michelle

Bodmin, 1349: An Epic Novel of Christians and Jews in the Plague Years. *See* Kalechofsky, Roberta

The Body and Society: Men, Women, and Sexual Renunciation in Early Christianity. *See* Brown, Peter

The Body and Society: Men, Women and Sexual Renunciation in Early Christianity. *See* Brown, Peter

The Body and the French Revolution: Sex, Class and Political Culture. *See* Outram, Dorinda

Bodylove. *See* Freedman, Rita

Body/Politics: Women and the Discourses of Science. *See* Jacobus, Mary and others (editors)

The Book of J. *See* Rosenberg, David

Books: Coyote Waits. *See* Hillerman, Tony

Books: Picturing Will. *See* Beattie, Ann

Books for Today's Young Readers: An Annotated Bibliography of Recommended Fiction for Ages 10-14. *See* Bracken, Jeanne

Boomer: Railroad Memoirs. *See* Niemann, Linda

Born for Liberty: A History of Women in America. *See* Evans, Sara; Evans, Sara M.

Born for Liberty: A History of Women in America. By Sara M. Evans. Reviewed by Dana D. Nelson Salvino. *Belles Lettres* 5, No. 3 (Spring 1990):28

Both Left and Right Handed: Arab Women Talk About Their Lives. *See* Shaaban, Bouthaina

Boy-Sandwich. *See* Gilroy, Beryl

Brave New Families: Stories of Democratic Upheaval in Late Twentieth-Century America. *See* Stacey, Judith

Breaking Boundaries: Latina Writings and Critical Readings. *See* Horno-Delgado, Asunción

Breaking the Sequence: Women's Experimental Fiction. *See* Friedman, Ellen G.

Breakthrough. *See* Valdivieso, Mercedes

Breast Disease for Gynecologists. *See* Hindle, William H.

British Women Writers: An Anthology. *See* Spender, Dale

The Broken Web: The Educational Experience of Hispanic American Women. *See* McKenna, Teresa

The Burden of Proof. *See* Turow, Scott

Bureaucrats, Technocrats, Femocrats: Essays on the Contemporary Australian State. *See* Yeatman, Anna

A Burst of Light. *See* Lorde, Audre

Buster Midnight's Cafe. *See* Dallas, Sandra

Called to Account. *See* Switzer, M'Liss and Hale, Katherine

Calling Homes: Working-Class Women's Writings. *See* Zandy, Janet

Camille Claudel. *See* Nuytten Bruno

Canadian Women: A History. *See* Prentice, Alison

Canoe Country and Snowshoe Country. *See* Jaques, Florence Page

Can Psychotherapists Hurt You?. *See* Striano, Judy

Cantando Bajito/Singing Softly. *See* De Monteflores, Carmen

Captivity. *See* Derricotte, Toi

Caring: A Feminine Approach to Ethics and Moral Education. *See* Noddings, Nel

Caring by the Hour: Women, Work, and Organizing at Duke Medical Center. *See* Sacks, Karen

Caring for the Disabled Elderly: Who Will Pay?. *See* Rivlin, Alice M.

Carnal Knowing: Female Nakedness and Religious Meaning in the Christian West. *See* Miles, Margaret

Carrington: A Life. *See* Gerzina, Gretchen Holbrook

Cartographies. *See* Sonenberg, Maya

Cat's Eye. *See* Atwood, Margaret

The Cavalry Maid: The Memoirs of a Woman Soldier of 1812. *See* Durova, Nadezhda

Centuries of Female Days: Englishwomen's Private Diaries. *See* Blodgett, Harriet

A Century of Childhood. *See* Humphries, Steve

The Chalice and the Blade. *See* Eisler, Riane

The Chalice and the Blade: Our History, Our Future. *See* Eisler, Riane

Changelings. *See* Murray, Melissa

Changes: A Woman's Journal for Self-Awareness and Personal Planning. *See* Bingham, Mindy

The Endless Day: Some Case Material on Asian Rural Women. *See* Epstein, Scarlett T.

The End of Summer. *See* Setouchi, Harumi

Engels Revisited: New Feminist Essays. *See* Sayers, Janet and others (editors)

English Children and Their Magazines, 1751-1945. *See* Drotner, Kirsten

Enter Password: Recovery. *See* Bulkin, Elly

Enterprising Women. *See* Westwood, Sallie

Equality and Sex Discrimination Law. *See* O'Donovan, K.

Equal Opportunities in the New ERA. *See* NUT Educational Review

Equal or Different: Women's Politics, 1800-1914. *See* Rendall, Jane (editor)

Equal Partners: Successful Women in Marriage. *See* Vannoy-Hiller, Dana

Equity and Gender: The Comparable Worth Debate. *See* Paul, Ellen Frankel

Equity in Education. *See* Secade, Walter G.

Ernestine L. Rose, Women's Rights Pioneer, 2nd edition. *See* Suhl, Yuri

Erotica: An Anthology of Women's Writing. *See* Reynolds, Margaret

Erotic Wars: What Happened to the Sexual Revolution?. *See* Rubin, Lillian

Europe's Myths of Orient. *See* Kabbani, Rana

Eva Gore-Booth and Esther Roper: A Biography. *See* Lewis, Gifford

Eva's War: A True Story of Survival. *See* Krutein, Eva

Even Mississippi. *See* Neilson, Melany

The Everyday World as Problematic. *See* Smith, Dorothy; Smith, Dorothy E.

The Everyday World as Problematic: A Feminist Sociology. *See* Smith, Dorothy

Exchanges: Poems by Women in Wales. *See* Brigley, Jude

Exile in the Promised Land. *See* Freedman, Marcia

Exile in the Promised Land: A Memoir. *See* Freedman, Marcia

The Exploitation of a Desire: Women's Experiences with In Vitro Fertilisation – An Exploratory Survey. *See* Klein, Renate K.

Exposing Nuclear Phallacies. *See* Russell, Diana E. H.

Eye of the Hurricane. *See* Robson, Ruthann

Eyes of Time: Photojournalism in America. *See* Fulton, Marianne

The Fabric of Memory, Ewa Kuryluk: Cloth Works, 1978-1987. By Jan Kott, Edmund White, Elzbieta Grabska, and Ewa Kuryluk. *See* Kott, Jan

From "Fair Sex" to Feminism: Sport and the Socialization of Women in the Industrial and Post-Industrial Eras. *See* Mangan, J. A.

Falling Angels. *See* Gordy, Barbara

The Family. *See* Emecheta, Buchi

Family, School and Society. *See* Woodhead, Martin

Family Album: Stories from a Catholic Girlhood. *See* Alegria, Claribel

The Family and the English Revolution. *See* Durston, Christopher

Family Fortunes: Men and Women of the English Middle Class, 1780-1850. *See* Davidoff, Leonore

The Family Interpreted: Feminist Theory in Clinical Practice. *See* Luepnitz, Deborah Anna

Family News. *See* Barfoot, Joan

Family Pictures. *See* Miller, Sue

Family Planning Handbook for Doctors. *See* Kleinman, Ronald L.

Family Violence in Cross-cultural Perspective. *See* Levinson, David

Fantastic Women: Sex, Gender and Transvestism. *See* Woodhouse, Annie

The Far East Comes Near: Autobiographical Accounts of Southeast Asian Students in America. *See* Nguyen-Hong-Nhiem, Lucy

Far from Home: Families of the Westward Journey. *See* Schlissel, Lillian

Fasting Girls: The Emergence of Anorexia as a Nervous Disease. *See* Brumberg, Joan Jacobs

Fate Cries Enough. *See* Matheson, Clare

Fat Oppression and Psychotherapy: A Feminist Perspective. *See* Brown, Laura S.

A Fearful Freedom: Women's Flight from Equality. *See* Kaminer, Wendy

The Female Autobiograph: Theory and Practice of Autobiography from the Tenth to the Twentieth Centuries. *See* Stanton, Donna

The Female Body and the Law. *See* Eisenstein, Zillah R.

The Female Fear. *See* Gordon, Margaret T. and Riger, Stephanie

The Female Gaze: Women as Viewers of Popular Culture. *See* Gamman, Lorraine and Marshment, Margaret (editors)

The Female Malady: Women, Madness and English Culture, 1830-1980. *See* Showalter, Elaine

Female Spectators: Looking at Film and Television. See Pribram, E. Deidre

Feminine Focus: The New Women Playwrights. See Brater, Enoch

Feminism, Children, and the New Families. See Dornbusch, Sanford M. and Strober, Myra H. (editors)

Feminism: Freedom from Wifism. See Albright, Mia

Feminism and Anthropology. See Moore, Henrietta L.

Feminism and Foucault: Reflections on Resistance. See Diamond, Irene

Feminism and Methodology: Social Science Issues. See Harding, Sandra (editor)

Feminism and Psychoanalysis. See Feldstein, Richard

Feminism and Psychoanalytic Theory. See Chodorow, Nancy J.

Feminism and Science. See Tuana, Nancy (editor)

Feminism and Science Fiction. See Lefanu, Sarah

Feminism and Theatre. See Case, Sue-Ellen

Feminism and the Power of Law. See Smart, Carol

Feminism as Critique: On the Politics of Gender. See Benhabib, Seyla

Feminism in Greece Between the Wars: An Anthology. See Avdela, Effie and Psarra, Angelika (editors)

Feminism Unmodified: Discourses on Life and Law. See MacKinnon, Catharine A.

Feminism within the Science and Health Care Professions: Overcoming Resistance. See Rosser, Sue V.

Feminist Art Criticism, An Anthology. See Raven, Arlene

Feminist Counselling in Action. See Chaplin, Jocelyn

A Feminist Ethic for Social Science Research. See Nebraska Sociological Feminist Collective

Feminist Fables. See Namjoshi, Suniti

Feminist Literary History. See Todd, Janet

Feminist Mothers. See Gordon, Tuula

Feminist Organizing for Change: The Contemporary Women's Movement in Canada. See Adamson, Nancy

Feminist Perspectives on Peace and Education. See Utne, Birgit Brock

Feminist Perspectives on Wife Abuse. See Yllö, K. and Bograd, M. (editors); Yllo, Kersti

Feminist Practice and Poststructuralist Theory. See Weedon, Chris

Feminist Scholarship: Kindling in the Groves of America. See DuBois, Ellen Carol

Feminists Despite Themselves: Women in Ukranian Community Life, 1884-1939. See Bohachevsky-Chomiak, Martha

Feminist Sociology. See Saltzman, Janet

Feminist Theory and the Philosophies of Man. See Nye, Andrea

Feminist Theory in Practice and Process. See Malson, Micheline R. and others (editors)

Feminist Thought: A Comprehensive Introduction. See Tong, Rosemarie

Feminist Utopias. See Bartkowski, Frances

Femmes, culture et révolution. See Harten, Elke

Femmes et prison. See Hamelin, Monique

Femmes sans toit ni voix: La problematique des femmes dites sans-abri ou itinerantes. See Ouellette, Françoise-Romaine

Ferris Beach. See McCorkle, Jill

Few Choices: Women, Work and Family. See Duffy, Ann

A Few Words in the Mother Tongue: Poems Selected and New (1971-1990). See Kelpfisz, Irena

Fifth Chinese Daughter. See Wong, Jade Snow

Figures of Ill Repute: Representing Prostitution in Nineteenth-Century France. See Bernheimer, Charles

Finding Signs. See Baker, Sharlene

Finding the Lesbians: Personal Accounts from Around the World. See Penelope, Julia

Fire and Grace: The Life of Rose Pastor Stokes. See Zipser, Arthur

Fire in the Rain . . . Singer in the Storm: An Autobiography of Holly Near. See Near, Holly

First Births in America: Changes in the Timing of Parenthood. See Rindfuss, Ronald R.

Flight to Objectivity: Essays on Cartesianism and Culture. See Bordo, Susan R.

Floating in My Mother's Palm. See Hegi, Ursula

The Floating World. See Kadohata, Cynthia

Flowers in Salt: The Beginnings of Feminist Consciousness in Modern Japan. See Sievers, Sharon L.

With a Fly's Eye, Whale's Wit and Woman's Heart: Animals and Women. See Corrigan, Theresa

The Forbidden Stitch: An Asian American Women's Anthology. See Lim, Shirley Goek-Lin

The Fortunes of Mary Fortune. See Sussex, Lucy

Making a Spectacle: Feminist Essays on Contemporary Women's Theatre. *See* Hart, Lynda

Making Face, Making Soul/Haciendo Caras: Creative and Critical Perspectives by Women of Color. *See* Anzaldu2a, Gloria

Making Peace with Food. *See* Kano, Susan

Making Their Mark: Women Artists Move into the Mainstream, 1970-85. *See* Rosen, Randy

Making Waves: An Anthology of Writings by and about Asian American Women. *See* Asian Women United of California

Males at Risk. *See* Bolton, Frank

Mama Day. *See* Naylor, Gloria

Mama Said There'd Be Days Like This – My Life in the Jazz World. *See* Wilmer, Val

The Management of Children with Emotional and Behavioral Difficulties. *See* Varma, Ved P.

Managing Attention Disorders in Children: A Guide for Practioners. *See* Goldstein, Sam

Managing Gender: The State, the New Middle Class and Women Workers, 1830-1930. *See* Deacon, Desley

Managing Lives: Corporate Women and Social Change. *See* Freeman, Sue J. M.

Manhood and Politics: A Feminist Reading in Political Theory. *See* Brown, Wendy

Man-Made Women: How New Reproductive Technologies Affect Women. *See* Corea, Gena and others

Mapping the Moral Domain. *See* Gilligan, Carol and others (editors)

From Margin to Mainstream: American Women and Politics Since 1960. *See* Hartmann, Susan M.

Maria Zef. *See* Drigo, Paola

Married Women's Separate Property in England, 1660-1833. *See* Staves, Susan

Mary Austin: Songs of a Maverick. *See* Stineman, Esther Lanigan

Mary Heaton Vorse: The Life of an American Insurgent. *See* Garrison, Dee

Mary Reilly. *See* Martin, Valerie

Mary Shelley: Her Life, Her Fiction, Her Monsters. *See* Mellor, Anne K.

Masculinity and Power. *See* Brittan, Arthur

Maternal Thinking: Towards a Politics of Peace. *See* Ruddick, Sara

Matilda's Mistake. *See* Oakley, Ann

A Matter of Hours: Women, Part-time Work and the Labour Market. *See* Beechey, Veronica

May Sarton Revisited. *See* Evans, Elizabeth

May You Be the Mother of a Hundred Sons: A Journey Among the Women of India. *See* Bumiller, Elisabeth

McBride: Behind the Myth. *See* Nicol, Bill

Meatless Days. *See* Suleri, Sara

Media Matter: TV Use in Childhood and Adolescence. *See* Rosengren, Karl Erik

Medieval Prostitution. *See* Rossiaud, Jacques

Memories and Visions: Women's Fantasy and Science Fiction. *See* Sturgis, Susanna J.

Men, Women, and Work: Class, Gender and Protest in the New England Shoe Industry, 1780-1910. *See* Blewett, Mary A.

Men and Women: Dressing the Part. *See* Kidwell, Claudia Brush

Menopause Without Medicine. *See* Ojeda, Linda

Mercy. *See* Dworkin, Andrea

Mercy, Pity, Peace and Love. *See* Godden, Rumer

The Meridian Anthology of Early Women Writers: British Literary Women from Aphra Behn to Maria Edgeworth 1660-1800. *See* Rogers, Katherine M.

The Message to the Planet. *See* Murdoch, Iris

A Midwife's Tale: The Life of Martha Ballard, Based on Her Diary, 1785-1812. *See* Ulrich, Laurel Thatcher

The Military: More Than Just a Job?. *See* Moskos, Charles C.

The Mind Has No Sex? Women in the Origins of Modern Science. *See* Schiebinger, Londa

Miss You: The World War II Letters of Barbara Wooddall Taylor and Charles E. Taylor. *See* Litoff, Judy Barrett

Mixed Blood: Intermarriage and Ethnic Identity in Twentieth Century America. *See* Spickard, Paul R.

Models of Achievement: Reflections of Eminent Women in Psychology, Volume 2. *See* O'Connell, Agnes N.

Modern Secrets. *See* Lim, Shirley Goek-lin

Moments of Desire: Sex and Sensuality by Australian Feminist Writers. *See* Hawthorne, Susan

Momentum: Women in American Politics Now. *See* Romney, Ronna and Harrison, Beppie

Monstrous Regiment: The Lady Knight in Sixteenth-Century Epic. *See* Robinson, Lillian S.

The Moonbane Magic. *See* Marks, Laurie J.

Moral Vision and Professional Decisions: The Changing Values of Women and Men Lawyers. *See* Rand, Jack

For Reasons of Poverty: A Critical Analysis of the Public Child Welfare System in the United States. *See* Pelton, Leroy H.

Recasting Women: Essays in Colonial History. *See* Sangari, KumKum

Reclaiming Youth at Risk: Our Hope for the Future. *See* Brendtro, Larry K.

Reconstructing Babylon: Essays on Women and Technology. *See* Hynes, H. Patricia

Reconstructing the Academy: Women's Education and Women's Studies. *See* Minnich, E.

Recovering from the War. *See* Mason, Patience

Recreating Motherhood: Ideology and Technology in a Patriarchal Society. *See* Rothman, Barbara Katz

The Recurring Silent Spring. *See* Hynes, H. Patricia; Hynes, Patricia

Red Ivy, Green Earth Mother. *See* Bei, Ai

In the Red Kitchen. *See* Roberts, Michele

Reducing the Risk: Building Skills to Prevent Pregnancy. *See* Barth, Richard P.

Refiguring the Father: New Feminist Readings of Patriarchy. *See* Yaeger, Patricia

Reflections in a Jaundiced Eye. *See* King, Florence

Reflections on the Way to the Gallows: Rebel Women in Prewar Japan. *See* Hane, Mikiso

The Reform of Girls' Secondary and Higher Education in Victorian England. *See* Pedersen, Joyce Senders

The Regulation of Desire: Sexuality in Canada. *See* Kinsman, Gary

Relations of Rescue: The Search for Female Authority in the American West, 1874-1939. *See* Pascoe, Peggy

Reliable Light. *See* Steinbach, Meredith

Religion, Social Change and Fertility Behaviour. *See* Jayasree, R.

The Remains of the Day. *See* Ishiguro, Kazuo

Remember Who You Are: Stories about Being Jewish. *See* Hautzig, Esther

Reproducing the World: Essays in Feminist Theory. *See* O'Brien, Mary

Reproductive Health: The Knowledge and Attitudes and Needs of Adolescents. *See* Wright, S.

Reproductive Laws for the 1990s. *See* Cohen, Sherrill

Reproductive Rights and Wrongs: The Global Politics of Population Control and Contraceptive Choice. *See* Hartmann, Betsy

Reproductive Technologies: Gender, Motherhood and Medicine. *See* Stanworth, Michelle (editor)

Responding to Violence on Campus. *See* Sherill, Jan M.

Restoring Women to History: Teaching Packets for Integrating Women's History into Courses on Africa, Asia, Latin America, the Caribbean, and the Middle East. *See* Berger, Iris and others

Revelations: Essays on Striptease and Sexuality. *See* Dragu, Margaret

Revenge. *See* Saunders, Kate

Reweaving the World: The Emergence of Ecofeminism. *See* Diamond, Irene

Riding in Cars With Boys: Confessions of a Bad Girl Who Makes Good. *See* Donofrio, Beverly

The River with No Bridge. *See* Sumii, Sue

The Road from Coorain. *See* Conway, Jill Ker

A Road Well Traveled: Three Generations of Cuban American Women. *See* Doran, Terry

Rocking the Ship of State: Toward a Feminist Peace Politics. *See* Harris, Adrienne E.

Romance and the Erotics of Property: Mass-Market Fiction for Women. *See* Cohn, Jan

Room Temperature. *See* Baker, Nicholson

A Rosario Castellanos Reader: An Anthology of Her Poetry, Short Fiction, Essays, and Drama. *See* Ahern, Maureen

Rural Women and State Policy: Feminist Perspectives on Latin American Agricultural Development. *See* Deere, Carmen Diana (editor)

Rural Women at Work: Strategies for Development in South Asia. *See* Dixon, Ruth

Russian Women's Studies: Essays on Sexism in Soviet Culture. *See* Mamonova, Tatyana

Sacred Cows. *See* Weldon, Fay

The Safe Sea of Women: Lesbian Fiction 1969-1989. *See* Zimmerman, Bonnie

Samba. *See* Guillermoprieto, Alma

The Same Sea as Every Summer. *See* Tusquets, Esther

Sans Souci and Other Stories. *See* Brand, Dionne

Sarah Orne Jewett: An American Persephone. *See* Sherman, Sarah Way

Sarah's Daughters Sing: A Sampler of Poems by Jewish Women. *See* Wenkart, Henny (editor)

Satisfaction Guaranteed: The Making of the American Mass Market. *See* Strasser, Susan

The Scented Garden: Choosing, Growing and Using the Plants that Bring Fragrance to Your Life, Home and Table. *See* Verey, Rosemary

The School of Love. *See* Barber, Phyllis

Women with Disabilities: Essays in Psychology, Culture and Politics. *See* Fine, Michelle

The Women Writers' Handbook. *See* Robson

Words of Farewell: Stories by Korean Women Writers. *See* Sok-kyong, Kang

Work, Unemployment and Leisure. *See* Deem, Rosemary

Working. *See* French, Dolores

From Working Daughters to Working Mothers: Immigrant Women in a New England Industrial Community. *See* Lamphere, Louise

Working Parents: Transformation in Gender Roles and Public Policies in Sweden. *See* Moen, Phyllis

Working with Children of Alcoholics: The Practitioner's Handbook. *See* Robinson, Bryan E.

A World Like This. *See* Benedict, Helen

The World of Our Mothers: The Lives of Jewish Immigrant Women. *See* Weinberg, Sydney Stahl

Worlds Within Women: Myth and Mythmaking in Fantastic Literature by Women. *See* Shinn, Thelma J.

The Wreath Ribbon Quilt. *See* Moose, Ruth

Writing a Woman's Life. *See* Heilbrun, Carolyn

Writing for Their Lives. *See* Hanscombe, Gillian and Smyers, Virginia L.

Writing in the Feminine: Feminism and Experimental Writing in Quebec. *See* Gould, Karen

A Writing Life. *See* Guiffré, Guilia

The Writing Life. *See* Dillard, Annie

The Writing or the Sex? Or Why You Don't Have to Read Women's Writing to Know It's No Good. *See* Spender, Dale

Writing Red: An Anthology of American Women Writers, 1930-1940. *See* Rabinowitz, Paula

Writing the Female Voice: Essays on Epistolary Literature. *See* Goldsmith, Elizabeth S.

The WRNS: A History of the Women's Royal Naval Service. *See* Fletcher, Marjorie H.

You Can't Kill the Spirit: Stories of Women and Nonviolent Action. *See* McAllister, Pam

You Just Don't Understand: Women and Men in Conversation. *See* Tannen, Deborah

You're Standing In My Light and Other Stories. *See* Devine, Eleanore

The Youth Ministry Resource Book. *See* Roehlkepartain, Eugene C.

Zabat: Poetics of a Family Tree. Poems 1986-1989. *Spare Rib*. *See* Sulter, Maud

Zones of Pain/Las Zonas del Dolor. *See* Agosin, Marjorie

## Booksellers and Bookselling

Woman's Word Bookstore. Kim Dahlstrom. *Feminist Collections* 11, No. 4 (Summer 1990):16-17

## Booksellers and Bookselling – Collectives

Italian Collective Inspiration for Booklovers Everywhere. Ruby Rohrlich. *New Directions for Women* 19, No. 1 (January/February 1990):16

### Borden, Lizzie (director)

Working Girls. Reviewed by Patricia A. Gozemba. *NWSA Journal* 2, No. 2 (Spring 1990):291-295

### Borders, Andrew

My Child Forever. Short story. *Redbook* 175, No. 4 (August 1990):60-68

### Bordo, Susan R.

Flight to Objectivity: Essays on Cartesianism and Culture. Reviewed by Jacquelyn N. Zita. *Signs* 15, No. 3 (Spring 1990):645-648

### Boris, Eileen and Daniels, Cynthia R. (editors)

Homework: Historical and Contemporary Perspectives on Paid Labor at Home. Reviewed by Mary Margaret Fonow. *NWSA Journal* 2, No. 3 (Summer 1990):502-505

Borrowing. *See* Loans

### Borsa, Joan

Towards a Politics of Location: Rethinking Marginality. *Canadian Women's Studies* 11, No. 1 (Spring 1990):36-39

### Boscagli, Maurizia

Unaccompanied Ladies: Feminist, Italian, and in the Academy. *Differences* 2, No. 3 (Fall 1990):122-135

### Bose, Ashish and Desai, P. B. (editors)

Population Planning in India: Policy Issues and Research Priorities. Reviewed by K. Sivaswamy Srikantan. *Journal of Family Welfare* 36, No. 3 (September 1990):107-110

### Bose, Christine E. and Spitze, Glenna (editors)

Ingredients for Women's Employment Policy. Reviewed by Rita Mae Kelly. *Gender and Society* 4, No. 3 (September 1990):429-432

### Bose, Christine E. (joint author). *See* Acosta-Belén, Edna

### Bosetti-Piché, Shelley

As Wise as Serpents: Five Women and an Organization that Changed British Columbia, 1883-1939. Book Review. *Resources for Feminist Research* 19, No. 1 (March 1990):4-5

### Bosher, J. F.

The French Revolution. Reviewed by Susan P. Conner. *Journal of Women's History* 1, No. 3 (Winter 1990):244-260

**Bostick, Barbara A.** (about). *See also* Lawyers

**Boston, Anne** (editor)

Wave Me Goodbye: Stories of the Second World War. Reviewed by Mary Anne Schofield. *Belles Lettres* 5, No. 4 (Summer 1990):38-39

**Boston – Women's History**

Boston Teenagers Debate the Woman Question, 1837-1838. Notes. Margaret McFadden. *Signs* 15, No. 4 (Summer 1990):832-847

**Boston Women's Health Book Collective**

Breast Implants: Deadly News. *Ms.* 1, No. 3 (November/December 1990):25

Incontinence, Implants, and the NIH. *Ms.* 1, No. 3 (November/December 1990):24

Is Health Equity on the Way? *Ms.* 1, No. 3 (November/December 1990):25

Smoking vs. Women. *Ms.* 1, No. 1 (July/August 1990):54-55

Trial by Genetics. *Ms.* 1, No. 2 (September/October 1990):30

The Twentieth Anniversary Celebration of *Our Bodies, Ourselves. Woman of Power* 18 (Fall 1990):8

**Bosveld, Jane**

Into the Nightmare. *Mademoiselle* (November 1990):114

Planet Under Glass. *Lear's* (December 1990):84-89+

**Boswell, John**

Concepts, Experience, and Sexuality. *Differences* 2, No. 1 (Spring 1990):67-87

**Botaish, Janet** (about). *See also* Success in Business, "Talent at Work"

**Bottigheimer, Ruth B.**

Grimms' Bad Girls and Bold Boys: The Moral and Social Vision of the Tales. Reviewed by Marcia Jacobson. *Signs* 15, No. 3 (Spring 1990):633-635

**Bottled Water.** *See* Drinking Water, Bottled

**Bottoms, Talula Gilbert** (about)

Legacy: The Story of Talula Gilbert Bottoms and Her Quilts. By Nancilu B. Burdick. Reviewed by Elaine Hedges. *NWSA Journal* 2, No. 2 (Spring 1990):282-287

**Botulism**

The Case of the Deadly Dinner Party. Jonathan A. Edlow. *Ladies' Home Journal* 107, No. 5 (May 1990):162-166

**Botwin, Carol**

Why Women Cheat. *Ladies' Home Journal* 107, No. 10 (October 1990):98-102

**Boucher, François** (about)

Depoliticizing Women: Female Agency, the French Revolution, and the Art of Boucher and David. Erica Rand. *Genders* 7 (Spring 1990):47-68

Women, Pleasure, and Painting (e.g., Boucher). Eunice Lipton. *Genders* 7 (Spring 1990):69-86

**Boulanger, Nadia** (about)

The Boulanger Sisters. Janna MacAuslan and Kristan Aspen. *Hot Wire* 6, No. 1 (January 1990):12-13+

**Bouquet, Carole** (about)

Easy French Style. *Glamour* (March 1990):278-281

**Bourdillon, Hilary**

Women as Healers: A History of Women and Medicine. Reviewed by Fiona Terry. *Gender & History* 2, No. 3 (Autumn 1990):371-373

**Bourgon, Miche4le** (joint author). *See* Guberman, Nancy

**Bourne, Paula** (joint author). *See* Prentice, Alison

**Bourque, Dominique**

La théorie, un dimanche. Book Review. *Canadian Women's Studies* 11, No. 1 (Spring 1990):107-108

**Bourque, Linda Brookover**

Defining Rape. Reviewed by Gloria Cowan. *Psychology of Women Quarterly* 14, No. 2 (June 1990):294-296

**Bourque, Susan C.** (joint editor). *See* Conway, Jill K.

**Boutelle, Sarah Holmes**

Julia Morgan, Architect. Reviewed by Pamela H. Simpson. *Woman's Art Journal* 11, No. 2 (Fall 1990-Winter 1991):44-48

**Bowen, Gary L.** and Orthner, Dennis K. (editors)

The Organization Family: Work and Family Linkages in the U.S. Military. Reviewed by Patricia Yancey Martin. *Journal of Marriage and the Family* 52, No. 2 (May 1990):565-566

**Bowers, Deborah L.**

Women and AIDS: A Nurse's Perspective. *Iris* 23 (Spring-Summer 1990):58-61

**Bowers, Susan R.**

Medusa and the Female Gaze. *NWSA Journal* 2, No. 2 (Spring 1990):217-235

**Bowlby, Rachel**

Uneven Developments: The Ideological Work of Gender in Mid-Victorian England. Book Review. *Tulsa Studies in Women's Literature* 9, No. 2 (Fall 1990):314-317

**Bowles, Gloria**

Educating the Majority: Women Challenge Tradition in Higher Education. Book Review. *NWSA Journal* 2, No. 2 (Spring 1990):288-290

Teaching Women: Feminism and English Studies. Book Review. *NWSA Journal* 2, No. 2 (Spring 1990):288-290

Women and a New Academy: Gender and Cultural Contexts. Book Review. *NWSA Journal* 2, No. 2 (Spring 1990):288-290

**Bowles, Paul** (about). *See also* Bertolucci, Bernardo (about)

Tangier Dream. Bruce Weber. *Vogue* (January 1990):160-185

**Bowman, Marilyn L.**

Coping Efforts and Marital Satisfaction: Measuring Marital Coping and Its Correlates. *Journal of Marriage and the Family* 52, No. 2 (May 1990):463-474

**Boxer, Barbara** (about). *See also* Leadership

**Boxes, Ornamental**

Boxes for Our Treasures. Pat Ross. *McCall's* 117, No. 10 (July 1990):93-96

**Boycotts**

Nestle Boycott Speeds Up. *Spare Rib* No. 216 (September 1990):46

The Salvador Beanfield War. *Ms.* 1, No. 1 (July/August 1990):15

**Boyd, Blanche McCary**

The Viking Riviera. *Vogue* (November 1990):327 +

**Boyd, Mona Sue**

Nutrition Now: 7 Vitamins & Minerals Women Need Most. *Redbook* 175, No. 4 (August 1990):124-130

**Boyd, Shylah**

Thinking West. Short story. *McCall's* 117, No. 11 (August 1990):75-77

**Boyde, Julia A.**

Ethnic and Cultural Diversity: Keys to Power. *Women and Therapy* 9, Nos. 1-2 (1990):151-167

**Boyer, Jeannine Ross** and Nelson, James Lindemann

A Comment on Fry's "The Role of Caring in a Theory of Nursing Ethics." *Hypatia* 5, No. 3 (Fall 1990):153-158

**Boylan, Anne M.**

Sunday School: The Formation of an American Institution, 1790-1880. Reviewed by Lee Chambers-Schiller. Book Review. *Gender & History* 2, No. 2 (Summer 1990):235-236

**Boyle, Alicia** (about)

The "Daemon Fantasy" in Alicia Boyle's Paintings. Hilary Pyle. *Woman's Art Journal* 11, No. 1 (Spring-Summer 1990):21-25

**Boyle, Lara Flynn** (about)

Innocent Until Proven Otherwise. Jennifer Houlton. *Mademoiselle* (June 1990):88

**Boynton, Lisa Passey**

The Mothers' Page: A House Full of Kids. *McCall's* 117, No. 9 (June 1990):6-8

**Bozeman, Sylvia**

Black Women Mathematicians: In Short Supply. *Sage* 6, No. 2 (Fall 1989):18-23

**Braaten, Jane**

Towards a Feminist Reassessment of Intellectual Virtue. *Hypatia* 5, No. 3 (Fall 1990):1-14

**Brack, Ben** (joint author). *See* Brack, Pat

**Brack, Datha Clapper**

Birth Bond: Reunions Between Birthparents and Adoptees: What Happens After. Book Review. *New Directions for Women* 19, No. 6 (November-December 1990):25

Changes Needed in Adoption. *New Directions for Women* 19, No. 6 (November-December 1990):25

Children of Open Adoption. Book Review. *New Directions for Women* 19, No. 6 (November-December 1990):25

Motherhood: What It Does to Your Mind. Book Review. *New Directions for Women* 19, No. 2 (March/April 1990):24

**Brack, Pat** and Brack, Ben

Moms Don't Get Sick. *Ladies' Home Journal* 107, No. 8 (August 1990):76-82

**Bracken, Jeanne** and Wigutoff, Sharon

Books for Today's Young Readers: An Annotated Bibliography of Recommended Fiction for Ages 10-14. Reviewed by Mitzi Myers. *NWSA Journal* 2, No. 2 (Spring 1990):273-281

**Braden, Kathleen**

Feeding Right From the Start. *Family Circle* 103, No. 1 (January 9, 1990):78 +

**Bradford, Barbara Taylor**

Theodora. Excerpt. Short story. *Ladies' Home Journal* 107, No. 8 (August 1990):90-97

**Bradford, Martina Lewis** (about). *See* Davis, Andrea R., "Power Players"

**Bradford, Michael**

The Legend of Nelson Mandela. Poem. *Essence* 20, No. 11 (March 1990):133

**Bradish, Paula** and Herrmann, Marille

Debating Reproductive Technologies. *Connexions* 32 (1990):26-28

**Bradshaw, Carla K.**

A Japanese View of Dependency: What Can Amae Psychology Contribute to Feminist Theory and Therapy. *Women and Therapy* 9, Nos. 1-2 (1990):67-86

**Bradshaw, John**

The Futility of Magical Thinking. *Lear's* (July 1990):52

How Resentment Can Wreck Divorce. *Lear's* (August 1990):57

If This Isn't Love, It Could Be a Fix. *Lear's* (September 1990):79-80

The Making of an Addict Takes Training. *Lear's* (November 1990):84

Our Families, Ourselves: Addiction of the Narcissistically Deprived. *Lear's* (January 1990):40-41

Our Families, Ourselves. *Lear's* (March 1990):85-86; (April 1990):55-56

Our Families, Ourselves: Living Life While We've Got It. *Lear's* (February 1990):56-57

The Shameful Shock Waves of Rage. *Lear's* (June 1990):63

Shopping Until You Can't Stop. *Lear's* (October 1990):75

Some Greenery for Holiday Blues. *Lear's* (December 1990):60

Thoughts on Caretaking: Shuck Off the Yoke. *Lear's* (May 1990):67

**Brady, Judy**
Why I (Still) Want a Wife. *Ms.* 1, No. 1 (July/August 1990):17

**Brady, Kathleen**
Baby-Sitting Nights, Preteen Days. *McCall's* 118, No. 2 (November 1990):57-58

Namesakes! *McCall's* 117, No. 8 (May 1990):51-52

**Brady, Lois Smith**
A Big Deal Babe. *Mademoiselle* (October 1990):152-154+

Nothing in Common. *Mademoiselle* (March 1990):208-209, 247-248

The Rage to Engage. *Mademoiselle* (March 1990):174-175, 240

**Brady, Sarah**
Full Circle: Ready, Aim, Fire! *Family Circle* 103, No. 13 (September 25, 1990):142

**Brady, Sarah** (about). *See* Leadership, "1990 Women of the Year"

**Braeman, Elizabeth** and Cox, Carol
Andrea Dworkin: From a War Zone. *off our backs* 20, No. 1 (January 1990):8-9+

**Braestrup, Kate**
The Marrying Kind. Short Story. *Mademoiselle* (March 1990):160-167, 234

**Braidotti, Rosi**
Voorplanting Als Bio-Industrie. Book Review. *Women's Studies International Forum* 13, No. 5 (1990):529

**Braidotti, Rosi** and Franken, Christien
United States of Europe or United Colors of Benetton? Some Feminist Thought on the New Common European Community. *Differences* 2, No. 3 (Fall 1990):109-121

**Brailey, L. Joan**
Stress Experienced by Mothers of Young Children. *Health Care for Women International* 11, No. 3 (1990):347-358

**Brain.** *See also* Cerebral Dominance
Brave New Brain. Nancy C. Andreasen. *Vogue* (January 1990):196-199+

**Branagh, Kenneth**
Henry V. Reviewed by Ron Rosenbaum. *Mademoiselle* (April 1990):139-142

**Branagh, Kenneth** (about)
The Hit List: Much Ado About Something. Robert Turnbull. *Harper's Bazaar* (February 1990):47+

**Branch, Shelly**
Unwinding on the Long and Winding Road. *Executive Female* (May/June 1990):42-43

**Brand, Dionne**
Sans Souci and Other Stories. Reviewed by Kamili Anderson. *New Directions for Women* 19, No. 4 (July-August 1990):19

Sans Souci and Other Stories. Reviewed by Rhonda Cobham. *The Women's Review of Books* 7, Nos. 10-11 (July 1990):29-31

**Brandi, Diana**
Muchachas No More: Household Workers in Latin America and the Caribbean. Book Review. *Women's Studies International Forum* 13, No. 5 (1990):520

**Brandon, Barbara** (about)
Barbara Brandon: A Comic Strip about Us. Amy Linden. *Essence* 20, No. 11 (March 1990):46

**Brandon, Ruth**
The New Women and the Old Men: Love, Sex, and the Woman Question. Reviewed by Deborah Epstein Nord. *The Women's Review of Books* 8, No. 3 (December 1990):5-7

**Brandt, Anthony**
Sex and the Married Man. *Lear's* (November 1990):156+

Turning Points. *Family Circle* 103, No. 4 (March 13, 1990):43+

**Brandt, Gail Cuthbert** (joint author). *See* Prentice, Alison

**Brandt, Laurie**
Women Who Make a Difference. *Family Circle* 103, No. 5 (April 3, 1990):15+

**Brandwein, Ruth A..** See also Meyer, Carol and Young, Alma (editors), "On the Bias."

**Brannon, Rebecca**

I Got This Way From Kissing Girlz. Hot Wire 6, No. 2 (May 1990):36-38

**Brant, Beth**

Grandmothers of a New World. Woman of Power 16 (Spring 1990):40-47

**Brater, Enoch (editor)**

Feminine Focus: The New Women Playwrights. Reviewed by Kendall. The Women's Review of Books 7, No. 4 (January 1990):15-16

**Braverman, Kate**

Squandering the Blue. Short story. Lear's (March 1990):122-125+

**Braverman, Lois.** See also Meyer, Carol and Young, Alma (editors), "On the Bias."

The Second Shift: Working Parents and the Revolution at Home. Book Review. AFFILIA 5, No. 4 (Winter 1990):111-113

**Braverman, Lois (editor)**

Women, Feminism and Family Therapy. Reviewed by Karen A. Holmes. AFFILIA 5, No. 1 (Spring 1990):104-106

**Bravin, Jess**

Working Whirl. Harper's Bazaar (November 1990):170-171

**Bravmann, Scott**

Telling (Hi)stories: Rethinking the Lesbian and Gay Historical Imagination. Out/Look No. 8 (Spring 1990):68-74

**Braxton, Joanne**

Black Women Writing Autobiography: A Tradition Within a Tradition. Reviewed by Elizabeth R. Baer. Belles Lettres 5, No. 2 (Winter 1990):4-6+

**Braxton, Joanne and McLaughlin, Andrée Nicola (editors)**

Wild Women in the Whirlwind. Reviewed by Adrienne Rich. Bridges 1, No. 2 (Fall 1990): 111-120

**Braxton, Joanne M. and McLaughlin, Andrée Nicola (editors)**

Wild Women in the Whirlwind: Afra-American Culture and the Contemporary Literary Renaissance. Reviewed by doris davenport. The Women's Review of Books 7, Nos. 10-11 (July 1990):36-37

Wild Women in the Whirlwind: Afra-American Culture and the Contemporary Literary Renaissance. Reviewed by Linda King. Spare Rib No. 214 (July 1990):22-23

**Bray, Diane Carlisle (about)**

When a Widow Takes the Helm in a Male-Dominated Industry. Patti Watts. Executive Female 13, No. 4 (July-August 1990):18-21

**Bray, Rosemary L.**

A Dialogue on Race. Glamour (August 1990):220-221+

Hers: It's Ten O'Clock, and I Worry About Where My Husband Is. Glamour (April 1990):302

Reclaiming Our Culture. Essence 21, No. 8 (December 1990):84-86+

**Braz, Lynn**

Patrick's Rainbow. Executive Female 13, No. 6 (November-December 1990):50+

**Brazelton, T. Berry**

The Early Years: After-School Orphans. Family Circle 103, No. 14 (October 16, 1990):52-56

The Early Years. Family Circle 103, No. 2 (February 1, 1990):37-39; 103, No. 5 (April 3, 1990):42+; 103, No. 10 (July 24, 1990):42; 103, No. 11 (August 14, 1990):41-42+; 103, No. 15 (November 6, 1990):49-54; 103, No. 17 (December 18, 1990):84-87

The Early Years: Mom Loves You More. Family Circle 103, No. 9 (June 26, 1990):41-43

Giant Steps. Family Circle 103, No. 1 (January 9, 1990):72-74

**Brazil – Acquired Immune Deficiency Syndrome**

A Guerrilla Grapples with AIDS. Herbert Daniel. Out/Look No. 8 (Spring 1990):27-30

**Brazil – AIDS**

The House that Brenda Built: A Transvestite Response to AIDS in Brazil. Michael Adams. Out/Look No. 8 (Spring 1990):22-26

**Brazil – Black Movement**

Recomposing the Samba: A Look at the Contemporary Black Movement in Post-Abolition Brazil. Bobbie Hodges-Betts. Sage 6, No. 1 (Summer 1989):49-51

**Brazil – Debts, Public**

I.O.U. $115 Billion. Geri Smith. Savvy Woman (October 1990):58-61+

**Brazil – Lesbianism**

Brazil. Nana Mendonc3a. Feminist Review No. 34 (Spring 1990):8-11

Letter from Sa5 Paulo. Marlene Rodrigues. Feminist Review No. 34 (Spring 1990):11-13

**Brazil – Prostitution**

The Brazilian Prostitute Movement. Women's World , No. 24 (Winter 1990/91): 50

**Brazil – Racism**

Fighting Racism in Brazil. Kali Tal. New Directions for Women 19, No. 6 (November-December 1990):12

**Brazil – Religion**

Women's Participation in the Brazilian "People's Church": A Critical Appraisal. Sonia E. Alvarez. *Feminist Studies* 16, No. 2 (Summer 1990):381-408

**Brazil – Status of Women**

Maternal Role of Women in Clerical Jobs in Southern Brazil: Stress and Satisfaction. Afaf I. Meleis, Judith C. Kulig, Eloita Neves Arruda, and Amy Beckman. *Health Care for Women International* 11, No. 4 (1990):369-382

**Brazile, Donna L.** (about). *See* De Veaux, Alexis, Milloy, Marilyn, and Ross, Michael Erik

**Bread**

Homemade Bread! *Good Housekeeping* 211, No. 4 (October 1990):172-176

**Breakfasts and Brunches**

Breakfast: Don't Leave Home Without It. Valerie Vaz. *Essence* 21, No. 5 (September 1990):87-88

Breakfasts: Quick, Quicker, Quickest. Jonell Nash. *Essence* 21, No. 5 (September 1990):90-93 +

Come Over for Brunch. *Glamour* (January 1990):150-155

Food Advisory. Lori Longbotham. *Working Woman* (October 1990):147

Good Breakfasts on the Go. *McCall's* 117, No. 7 (April 1990):127

Nutrition Now: Wake Up and Smile. *Redbook* 174, No. 5 (March 1990):164-171

Wake Kids Up to Breakfast. *Good Housekeeping* 211, No. 3 (September 1990):123-126

Willard Scott's Breakfast Book. Willard Scott. *Ladies' Home Journal* 107, No. 3 (March 1990):201-216

**Breakthrough Awards**

Women, Men and Media Announces New Breakthrough Awards. *Media Report to Women* 18, No. 4 (July-August 1990):5

**Breast Cancer**

Breast Cancer: New Hope in the '90s. Maxine Abrams. *Good Housekeeping* 211, No. 4 (October 1990):77-80

Breast Cancer and Nutrition: The Hidden Link. Bibliography. Andy Dappen. *Ladies' Home Journal* 107, No. 7 (July 1990):60-68

Breast Cancer Prevention. Susan Ince. *Vogue* (October 1990):278+

The Effect of Type of Relationship on Perceived Psychological Distress in Women with Breast Cancer. B. Jo Hailey, Karen M. Lalor, Kimeron M. Hardin, and Heather A. Byrne. *Health Care for Women International* 11, No. 3 (1990):359-366

8 Dangerous Breast Cancer Myths. Richard Dowden and Joan Houger. *Redbook* 175, No. 1 (May 1990):114-115

Facing Fears about Mammograms. Ronni Sandroff. *McCall's* 117, No. 12 (September 1990):25-29

Fashion Statement. Stephanie Mansfield. *Lear's* (February 1990):52-53

Health and Fitness Notes. *Vogue* (August 1990):242

Healthy Breasts: What's Normal, What's Not. Peggy Eastman. *Family Circle* 103, No. 9 (June 26, 1990):101-104

Her Soul Beneath the Bone: Women's Poetry on Breast Cancer. Edited by Leatrice H. Lifshitz. Reviewed by Alison Townsend. *The Women's Review of Books* 7, No. 8 (May 1990):16

Lifesaving Breast News. *Glamour* (March 1990):248-251

Medical Report: The Mammogram Problem. Laura Fraser. *Glamour* (December 1990):66-72

Medinews. Joan Lippert. *Ladies' Home Journal* 107, No. 7 (July 1990):58

Medinews. *Ladies' Home Journal* 107, No. 6 (June 1990):94

October. Bibliography. *Glamour* (October 1990):230-231

Prevention: Breast Intentions. Annette M. Brown. *Essence* 20, No. 9 (January 1990):21-22

Treating Herself with Kindness. Linda Elovitz Marshall. *Lear's* (August 1990):40-42

What Doctors Aren't Saying. *Glamour* (May 1990):94

**Breast Cancer – Personal Narratives**

I Had a Baby After Breast Cancer. Linda Fine. *Family Circle* 103, No. 16 (November 27, 1990):94-98

Moms Don't Get Sick. Pat Brack and Ben Brack. *Ladies' Home Journal* 107, No. 8 (August 1990):76-82

My Lumpectomy. Gail Mosley. *Good Housekeeping* 210, No. 4 (April 1990):78-82

My Sister's Legacy. Nancy Brinker. *Ladies' Home Journal* 107, No. 10 (October 1990):156-160+

**Breast Disease**

Breast Disease for Gynecologists. Edited by William H. Hindle. Reviewed by Jeanette Sasmore. *Health Care for Women International* 11, No. 2 (1990):233-234

**Breast Examination.** *See* Mammography

**Breast Feeding.** *See also* Wet Nursing

Breast-Feeding Can Work for Working Mothers. Amy Biber Barr. *Working Mother* 13, No. 7 (July 1990):62-66

"Euch, Those Are for Your Husband!": Examination of Cultural Values and Assumptions Associated with Breast-Feeding. Janice M. Morse. *Health Care for Women International* 11, No. 2 (1990):223-232

A Natural Resource. Leslie Ayre-Jaschke. *Healthsharing* 11, No. 2 (March 1990):29-31

PCBs in Inuit Breastmilk. Jo-Ann Lowell. *Healthsharing* 11, No. 1 (December 1989):5

Your Pregnancy. Stephanie Young. *Glamour* (September 1990):100

**Breast Feeding and Acquired Immune Deficiency Syndrome**

Breastfeeding Encouraged. *Connexions* 33 (1990):10

**Breast Feeding and Fertility**

Breastfeeding and Conception Interval – An Emperical Study. K. Krishnakumari. *Journal of Family Welfare* 36, No. 4 (December 1990):46-55

Interrelationship Between Breastfeeding and Lactational Amenorrhoea in a Rural Community of Haryana. M. S. Bhatia and others. *Journal of Family Welfare* 36, No. 4 (December 1990):75-77

**Breasts**

The Big Issue: Safety, Not Size. Gil Schwartz. *Mademoiselle* (October 1990):166-167 +

Dr. Susan Love's Breast Book. By Susan M. Love. Reviewed by Alida Brill. *Ms.* 1, No. 1 (July/August 1990):70

The Truth about Breasts: A Beauty & Health Guide. *Mademoiselle* (October 1990):164-165

**Breasts – Implants**

Breast Implants: Deadly News. Boston Women's Health Book Collective. *Ms.* 1, No. 3 (November/December 1990):25

**Breasts – Prostheses**

Living with Loss, Dreaming of Lace. Mimi Schwartz. *Lear's* (October 1990):54-56

**Breath, Offensive**

Ask the Dentist: Smart Helps to a Healthy Smile. Susan Alai. *Family Circle* 103, No. 16 (November 27, 1990):144

Beauty & Health Report: Bad Breath. Andrea Pomerantz Lynn. *Glamour* (February 1990):41

What Causes Bad Breath? Laura Clark. *Good Housekeeping* 211, No. 4 (October 1990):248

**Breathing Exercises**

Breathing Lessons. *Glamour* (August 1990):212-213

**Brée, Germaine**

Passionate Philosopher. *The Women's Review of Books* 8, No. 1 (October 1990):1 +

Simone de Beauvoir: A Biography. Book Review. *The Women's Review of Books* 8, No. 1 (October 1990):1 +

**Breeze, Jean "Binta"**

Let the Pan's Voice Be Heard. *Spare Rib* No. 216 (September 1990):16-17

Natural High. Poem. *Spare Rib* No. 212 (May 1990):57

**Breeze, Jean "Binta"** (interview)

Hallelujah Anyhow. Claudette Williams. *Spare Rib* 219 (December 1990-January 1991):8-12

**Breitbart, Myrna Margulies**

Quality Housing for Women and Children. *Canadian Women's Studies* 11, No. 2 (Fall 1990):19-24

**Breithaupt, Ellen** (about). *See also* College Students – Leadership

**Brendtro, Larry K.**, Brokenleg, Martin, and Van Bockern, Steve

Reclaiming Youth at Risk: Our Hope for the Future. Book Review. *Adolescence* 25, No. 100 (Winter 1990):997

**Brenna, Susan**

Family Traditions: The Power of Knowing Who You Are. *McCall's* 117, No. 7 (April 1990):76-82

**Brennan, Lisa**

Emerging from Prostitution. *New Directions for Women* 19, No. 3 (May/June 1990):4

**Brennan, Teresa** (editor)

Between Feminism and Psychoanalysis. Reviewed by Denise O'Connor. *Feminist Review* No. 34 (Spring 1990):171-175

Between Feminism and Psychoanalysis. Reviewed by Joonok Huh. *NWSA Journal* 2, No. 3 (Summer 1990):511-514

**Brennan, William** (about)

With Brennan Gone . . . Saving the Bill of Rights. Rhonda Copelon and Kathryn Kolbert. *Ms.* 1, No. 2 (September/October 1990):89

**Brenner, Barbara**

Discipline in Day Care. *Working Mother* 13, No. 5 (May 1990):76-81

**Brenner, Lynn**

Fast Cash: Five Ways to Get It. *Working Woman* (August 1990):38-40

**Breschi, Marco** (joint author). *See* Bacci, Massimo Livi

**Bresheet, Haim**

A State of Danger. Reviewed by Marcia Freedman. *On the Issues* 15 (Summer 1990):30-31

**Breslin, Catherine**

"We Are So Lucky to Have Him." *Ladies' Home Journal* 107, No. 12 (December 1990):136 +

Women and Drugs: The Untold Story. *Ladies' Home Journal* 107, No. 1 (January 1990):89-91 +

**Breslow, Ellen**

Lavish Lengths. *Harper's Bazaar* (October 1990):53-58+

**Bretécher, Claire**

The First Tampon. Comic strip. *Ms.* 1, No. 3 (November/December 1990):26-29

**Breton, Margot** (joint author). *See* Bunston, Terry

**Brett, Jo Ann**

Budget-Smart Family Fare. *Family Circle* 103, No. 16 (November 27, 1990):122-128

**Brettschneider, Cathie**

Confessions of Love. Book Review. *Belles Lettres* 5, No. 3 (Spring 1990):20

The End of Summer. Book Review. *Belles Lettres* 5, No. 3 (Spring 1990):20

Picture Bride. Book Review. *Belles Lettres* 5, No. 3 (Spring 1990):20

Steel Chrysanthemums. *Belles Lettres* 5, No. 3 (Spring 1990):20

**Brewin, Chris R.** (joint author). *See* Andrews, Bernice

**Brick, Peggy**

Reducing the Risk: Building Skills to Prevent Pregnancy. Book Review. *New Directions for Women* 19, No. 3 (May/June 1990):21

The Sexuality Decision-Making Series for Teens. Book Review. *New Directions for Women* 19, No. 3 (May/June 1990):21

**Brickman, Paul**

Men Don't Leave. Reviewed by Sue Murphy. *Spare Rib* No. 216 (September 1990):32

**Brico, Antonia** (about)

Maestra Brico Remembered. Kay Gardner. *Hot Wire* 6, No. 1 (January 1990):52-53+

**Bridal Gowns.** *See* Wedding Costume

**Bridge, Junior**

Decision Changes Support Laws. *New Directions for Women* 19, No. 5 (September-October 1990):5

New Stories By Southern Women. Book Review. *On the Issues* 15 (Summer 1990):27-28

**Bridgeport (Connecticut)—Mayors.** *See* Moran, Mary C. (about)

**Bridges, Beau** (about). *See* Celebrities—Activism

**Bridges, Jeff** (about). *See* Celebrities—Activism

**Bridges, Lisa** (joint author). *See* Frodi, Ann

**Briere, John**

Therapy for Adults Molested as Children: Beyond Survival. Reviewed by Hannah Lerman. *Psychology of Women Quarterly* 14, No. 2 (June 1990):192-194

Therapy for Adults Molested as Children: Beyond Survival. Reviewed by Maria P. P. Root. *Women and Therapy* 9, No. 4 (1990):123-125

**Brightman, Joan**

Getting the Most from Frequent-Flyer Programs. *Executive Female* 13, No. 5 (September-October 1990):24-25

**Brigley, Jude** (editor)

Exchanges: Poems by Women in Wales. Reviewed by Penny Simpson. *Spare Rib* No. 216 (September 1990):25

**Brill, Alida**

Dr. Susan Love's Breast Book. Book Review. *Ms.* 1, No. 1 (July/August 1990):70

Gender Politics and MTV: Voicing the Difference. Book Review. *Ms.* 1, No. 1 (July/August 1990):70

Speaking Freely: Unlearning the Lies of the Fathers' Tongues. Book Review. *Ms.* 1, No. 1 (July/August 1990):70

**Brimstone, Lyndie**

Pat Parker: A Tribute. *Feminist Review* No. 34 (Spring 1990):4-7

**Brines, Julie**

The Second Shift: Working Parents and the Revolution at Home. Book Review. *Journal of Marriage and the Family* 52, No. 1 (February 1990):278-279

**Brinker, Nancy**

My Sister's Legacy. *Ladies' Home Journal* 107, No. 10 (October 1990):156-160+

**Brinker, Ruth** (about)

Ruth Brinker's Meals Feed Body and Soul. Julie Lew. *McCall's* 117, No. 7 (April 1990):23

**Brinson, Susan L.**

TV Rape: Television's Communication of Cultural Attitudes toward Rape. *Women's Studies in Communication* 12, No. 2 (Fall 1989):23-36

**Briskin, Linda**

Identity Politics and the Hierarchy of Oppression: A Comment. *Feminist Review* No. 35 (Summer 1990):102-108

**Briskin, Linda** (joint author). *See* Adamson, Nancy

**Bristol-Howard, Susan**

Boulder Mayor—All in a Day's Work. *Ms.* 1, No. 2 (September/October 1990):90

**Bristow, Joseph**

Nation, Class, and Gender: Tennyson's *Maud* and War. *Genders* 9 (Fall 1990):93-111

**British National Party**

Tower Hamlets: BNP Put Forward Candidates in Local Elections. Joyoti Grech. *Spare Rib* No. 212 (May 1990):46

Tower Hamlets Fascists Pop up Again. Joyoti Grech. *Spare Rib* No. 216 (September 1990):46

**Britt, Julie** (about). *See also* Fashion Merchandising

**Brittan, Arthur**

Masculinity and Power. Reviewed by Jeff Hearn. *Gender & History* 2, No. 3 (Autumn 1990):351-353

**Broadcasting.** *See* Media and Communications; Radio Broadcasting

**Broadous, Lillian II**

Oakland Highlights. *Essence* 21, No. 1 (May 1990):166-170

**Broadwell, Laura**

Girls Just Wanna Work Out. *Women's Sports & Fitness* 12, No. 6 (September 1990):44-48

**Brock, Debi**

Sanitary Policing. *Connexions* 33 (1990):

**Brock, Rita Nakashima**, Cooey, Paula M., Davaney, Sheila Greeve, Gross, Rita M., Klein, Anne C., and others

The Questions That Won't Go Away: A Dialogue about Women in Buddhism and Christianity. *Journal of Feminist Studies in Religion* 6, No. 2 (Fall 1990):87-120

**Brockman, Elin Schoen** and Hales, Dianne

Women Who Make a Difference. *Family Circle* 103, No. 8 (June 5, 1990):I5-I7

**Brodber, Erna**

Myal. Reviewed by Rhonda Cobham. *The Women's Review of Books* 7, Nos. 10-11 (July 1990):29-31

**Brodeur, Paul**

Radiation Update: Danger in the Schoolyard. *Family Circle* 103, No. 13 (September 25, 1990):61-67

**Brodsky, Annette** (joint author). *See* Bates, Carolyn

**Brodsky, Michelle**, Loury, MyKela, Markowitz, Abby, Torres, Eden E., and Wilson, Lauren

Journeys in Our Lives: Learning Feminism. *NWSA Journal* 2, No. 1 (Winter 1990):79-100

**Brody, Claire M.**

Women in a Nursing Home: Living with Hope and Meaning. *Psychology of Women Quarterly* 14, No. 4 (December 1990):579-592

**Brody, Jane E.**

Your Protein Profile. *Family Circle* 103, No. 11 (August 14, 1990):57+

**Brody, Meredith**

Taste: Refriger-Dating. *Mademoiselle* (June 1990):74

Taste: Turning Up the Heat. *Mademoiselle* (September 1990):142

These Cookbooks Have Legs. Bibliography. *Mademoiselle* (November 1990):78

**Brody, Meredith** and Wright, Christine Logan

Can He Bake a Cherry Pie? *Mademoiselle* (September 1990):248-249+

**Brody, Robert**

The Reluctant Go-Between. *Glamour* (October 1990):288+

**Brodzki, Bella** and Schenck, Celeste (editors)

Life/Lines: Theorizing Women's Autobiography. Reviewed by Elizabeth R. Baer. *Belles Lettres* 5, No. 2 (Winter 1990):4-6+

Life/Lines: Theorizing Women's Autobiography. Reviewed by Patricia Madoo-Lengermann and Jill Niebrugge-Brantley. *Tulsa Studies in Women's Literature* 9, No. 1 (Spring 1990):133-135

**Broe, Mary Lynn** and Ingram, Angela (editors)

Women's Writing in Exile. Reviewed by Doris Davenport. *The Women's Review of Books* 7, Nos. 10-11 (July 1990):36-37

Women's Writing in Exile. Reviewed by Mary Anne Schofield. *Belles Lettres* 5, No. 4 (Summer 1990):43-44

**Brogan, Donna** (joint author). *See* Kutner, Nancy G.

**Brokenleg, Martin** (joint author). *See* Brendtro, Larry K.

**Bromley, Anne**

Politics, Perseverance, and Passion from Hollywood. *Iris* 23 (Spring-Summer 1990):56-57

**Bronx (New York)—Art**

Art: Bronx Revival. Paul Taylor. *Vogue* (January 1990):114-117

**Brooches**

Vogue's Last Look. Edited by Candy Pratts Price. *Vogue* (December 1990):344

**Brook, Barbara**

Nettie Palmer. Book Review. *Women's Studies International Forum* 13, No. 3 (1990):275-276

**Brookes, Christine**

The Third Aspect: An Investigation of U.K. Business Networks. *Women's Studies International Forum* 13, No. 6 (1990):577-585

**Brooks, Charlotte K.**

Homespun Images: An Anthology of Black Memphis Writers and Artists. Book Review. *Sage* 6, No. 2 (Fall 1989):61-62

**Brooks, Gwendolyn** (about)

A Life of Gwendolyn Brooks. By George E. Kent. Reviewed by Jacquelyn Y. McLendon. *The Women's Review of Books* 7, Nos. 10-11 (July 1990):26

**Brooks, Paul**

Sales or Service? *Executive Female* 13, No. 5 (September-October 1990):53-54

**Brooks, Philip** (joint author). *See* Powell, Ivor

**Brooks, Richard** (about)

Lunch. Interview. Frances Lear. *Lear's* (February 1990):19-22

**Brooks-Gunn, J.** (joint author). *See* Furstenberg, Frank F.

**Broomfield, Nick** and Sissel, Sandy (directors)

Chicken Ranch. Reviewed by Patricia A. Gozemba. *NWSA Journal* 2, No. 2 (Spring 1990):291-295

**Brophy, Beth**

High Marks. *Ladies' Home Journal* 107, No. 12 (December 1990):122-127+

**Brossard, Nicole** (joint author). *See* Bersianik, Louky

**Brosseau, Jim** (joint author). *See* Spencer, T. M.

**Brotherhood of Sleeping Car Porters (BSCP)**

Marching Together: Women of the Brotherhood of Sleeping Car Porters. Melinda Chateauvert. *NWSA Journal* 2, No. 4 (Autumn 1990):687-689

**Brothers, Joyce**

Answers to Your Questions. *Good Housekeeping* 211, No. 3 (September 1990):214-217; 211, No. 4 (October 1990):111-112

**Brothers, Joyce** (about)

Widowed. Excerpted. Vernon Scott. *Good Housekeeping* 211, No. 5 (November 1990):163+

**Broumas, Olga**

The Choir. Poem. *Ms.* 1, No. 2 (September/October 1990):front cover

Perpetua. Reviewed by Catherine Houser. *The Women's Review of Books* 7, No. 4 (January 1990):19-20

Perpetua. Reviewed by Lee Upton. *Belles Lettres* 5. No. 3 (Spring 1990):24-25

**Brous, Elizabeth**

Images: Spas for Solo Vacations. *Vogue* (December 1990):170-176

**Brown, Aimee** (about). *See* Business – Ownership

**Brown, Alan**

Di's Double. Short story. *Redbook* 174, No. 6 (April 1990):44-53+

**Brown, Alanna**

Coyote Stories. Book Review. *The Women's Review of Books* 8, No. 2 (November 1990):19-20

Mourning Dove, A Salishan Autobiography. Book Review. *The Women's Review of Books* 8, No. 2 (November 1990):19-20

A Voice from the Past. *The Women's Review of Books* 8, No. 2 (November 1990):19-20

**Brown, Amy Belding**

When First He Kissed Me. Short story. *Good Housekeeping* 211, No. 4 (October 1990):70-72

**Brown, Annette M.**

Prevention: Breast Intentions. *Essence* 20, No. 9 (January 1990):21-22

**Brown, Blair** (about)

The Fast-Paced Days of Blair Brown. Leslie Bennetts. *McCall's* 117, No. 11 (August 1990):31-32

**Brown, Cheryl L.**

Incorporation vs. Separation: An Assessment of Gender and Politics in the People's Republic of China. *Women & Politics* 10, No. 1 (1990):59-69

**Brown, Elsa Barkley**

Mothers of Mind. *Sage* 6, No. 1 (Summer 1989):4-10

**Brown, Frank Dexter**

Back Talk: Lobby for Aid to Africa. *Essence* 21, No. 5 (September 1990):142

**Brown, Gayle Lea**

Dear Mom, I Lost My Retainers. *McCall's* 118, No. 3 (December 1990):14-21

**Brown, Georgia**

Mother Inferior. *Lear's* (July 1990):88-89

**Brown, Helen Evans** (about). *See also* Hazard, Jan Turner, "Women Chefs"

**Brown, Jan**

Sex, Lies, and Penetration. *Out/Look* No. 7 (Winter 1990):30-34

**Brown, Kaaren Strauch** and Ziefert, Marjorie

A Feminist Approach to Working with Homeless Women. *AFFILIA* 5, No. 1 (Spring 1990):6-20

**Brown, Karen** and Kohn, Jennifer

Report from Two Campuses. Essay. *Bridges* 1, No. 2 (Fall 1990): 100-108

**Brown, Kathleen** (about). *See also* Leadership

Family Politics. Ellie McGrath. *Savvy Woman* (October 1990):16

**Brown, Lady Falls**

Willa Cather: Writing at the Frontier. Book Review. *Tulsa Studies in Women's Literature* 9, No. 2 (Fall 1990):334-337

Willa Cather and the Fair Tale. Book Review. *Tulsa Studies in Women's Literature* 9, No. 2 (Fall 1990):334-337

**Brown, Laura S.**

Fat-Oppressive Attitude and the Feminist Therapist: Fat Oppression. *Woman of Power* 18 (Fall 1990):64-68

The Meaning of a Multicultural Perspective for Theory-Building in Feminist Therapy. *Women and Therapy* 9, Nos. 1-2 (1990):1-21

**Brown, Laura S.** and Rothblum, Esther D.

Fat Oppression and Psychotherapy: A Feminist Perspective. Reviewed by Carol L. Hill. *Atlantis* 15, No. 2 (Spring 1990):114-115

**Brown, Linda P.** (joint author). *See* Gediman, Judith S.

**Brown, Marie D.** (joint editor). *See* Greene, Cheryll Y.

**Brown, Marla Kell** (about). *See also* Leadership

**Brown, Miche4le** and O'Connor, Ann

The Best of Women's Wit and Humor. *Woman of Power* 17 (Summer 1990):14

**Brown, Oral** (about). *See* Leadership

**Brown, Pamela A.**

Justifiable Homicide: Battered Women, Self-Defense and the Law. Book Review. *AFFILIA* 5, No. 2 (Summer 1990):106-109

When Battered Women Kill. Book Review. *AFFILIA* 5, No. 2 (Summer 1990):106-109

**Brown, Peggy**

How to Read Your Baby's Mind. *Working Mother* 13, No. 4 (April 1990):46-49

**Brown, Peter**

The Body and Society: Men, Women, and Sexual Renunciation in Early Christianity. Reviewed by Michael B. Schwarz. *Out/Look* No. 7 (Winter 1990):76-81

The Body and Society: Men, Women and Sexual Renunciation in Early Christianity. Reviewed by Elizabeth A. Clark. *Gender & History* 2, No. 1 (Spring 1990):106-109

**Brown, Rebecca** (about)

Oregon's Rancher-Politician. Shannon Jackson. *Ms.* 1, No. 2 (September/October 1990):92

**Brown, Rosellen**

Fertile Imagination. *The Women's Review of Books* 7, No. 12 (September 1990):9-10

Getting-Out Story. *The Women's Review of Books* 7, Nos. 10-11 (July 1990):33

Sexing the Cherry. Book Review. *The Women's Review of Books* 7, No. 12 (September 1990):9-10

A World Like This. Book Review. *The Women's Review of Books* 7, Nos. 10-11 (July 1990):33

**Brown, Victoria Bissell**

The Fear of Feminization: Los Angeles High Schools in the Progressive Era. *Feminist Studies* 16, No. 3 (Fall 1990):493-518

**Brown, Wendy**

Manhood and Politics: A Feminist Reading in Political Theory. Reviewed by Judith Wagner DeCew. *Women's Studies International Forum* 13, No. 3 (1990):279-280

Manhood and Politics: A Feminist Reading in Political Theory. Reviewed by Mary Lyndon Shanley. *Signs* 16, No. 1 (Autumn 1990):183-187

Manhood and Politics: A Feminist Reading in Political Theory. Reviewed by Sherri Paris. *Hypatia* 5, No. 3 (Fall 1990):175-180

**Brown, Wendy R.** (about). *See* Lawyers

**Browne, Angela**

Our Turn. *Healthsharing* 11, No. 3 (June 1990):8

Resisting Psychiatry. *Healthsharing* 11, No. 2 (March 1990):17-21

When Battered Women Kill. Reviewed by Pamela A. Brown. *AFFILIA* 5, No. 2 (Summer 1990):106-109

**Brown-Guillory, Elizabeth**

Their Place on the Stage: Black Women Playwrights in America. Reviewed by Leslie Sanders. *Canadian Women's Studies* 11, No. 1 (Spring 1990):108-109

**Browning, Elizabeth Barrett** (about). *See also* David, Deirdre

**Browning, Elizabeth Barrett** (about)

Elizabeth Barrett Browning, Woman and Artist. By Helen Cooper. Reviewed by Joyce Zonana. *Tulsa Studies in Women's Literature* 9, No. 1 (Spring 1990):160-163

**Browning, Genia K.**

Women and Politics in the USSR: Consciousness Raising and Soviet Women's Groups. Reviewed by Elizabeth Waters. *Australian Feminist Studies* No. 11 (Autumn 1990):117-120

**Brown-Rowat, Beverly,** Amsel, Rhonda, and Jeans, Mary Ellen

Professional and Executive Women: Health and Lifestyle Characteristics. *Health Care for Women International* 11, No. 2 (1990):133-149

**Brownstein, Ronald**

Lights, Camera, Activism. *Lear's* (December 1990):78-81 +

**Broyles-González, Yolanda**

The Living Legacy of Chicana Performers: Preserving History Through Oral Testimony. *Frontiers* 11, No. 1 (1990):46-52

**Brubaker, Timothy H.**

Families in Later Life: A Burgeoning Research Area. *Journal of Marriage and the Family* 52, No. 4 (November 1990):959-981

**Bruce, Judith** (joint editor). *See* Dwyer, Daisy

**Bruce, Liza** (about)

View. Page Hill Starzinger. *Vogue* (June 1990):66-68

**Bruckheimer, Jerry** (about). *See* Partnerships

**Bruining, Anne Mi Ok**

Stones in Somerville. Poem. *Sinister Wisdom* 40 (Spring 1990):91-93

**Brumberg, Joan Jacobs**

Fasting Girls: The Emergence of Anorexia as a Nervous Disease. Reviewed by Anne Digby. *Gender & History* 2, No. 3 (Autumn 1990):370-371

**Brunches.** *See* Breakfasts and Brunches

**Brundage, James A.**

Law, Sex, and Christian Society in Medieval Europe. Reviewed by Michael B. Schwarz. *Out/Look* No. 7 (Winter 1990):76-81

**Brunson, Dorothy** (about). *See* De Veaux, Alexis, Milloy, Marilyn, and Ross, Michael Erik

**Brush, Lisa D.**

Violent Acts and Injurious Outcomes in Married Couples: Methodological Issues in the National Survey of Families and Households. *Gender and Society* 4, No. 1 (March 1990):56-67

**Bryson, John**

Katharine Hepburn at Home. *Good Housekeeping* 211, No. 4 (October 1990):136-139

**Bryson, Lois**

Bureaucrats, Technocrats, Femocrats: Essays on the Contemporary Australian State. Book Review. *Australian Feminist Studies* No. 12 (Summer 1990):133-136

Playing the State: Australian Feminist Interventions. Book Review. *Australian Feminist Studies* No. 12 (Summer 1990):133-136

Sisters in Suits. Book Review. *Australian Feminist Studies* No. 12 (Summer 1990):133-136

Staking a Claim: Feminism, Bureaucracy and the State. Book Review. *Australian Feminist Studies* No. 12 (Summer 1990):133-136

**Bübül** (about)

Turkish Nightingale. *Woman of Power* 17 (Summer 1990):50-51

**Buchanan, Constance H.** (joint editor). *See* Atkinson, Clarissa W.

**Buchanan, Lisa K.**

The Mother Who Never Was. Short story. *Mademoiselle* (June 1990):136-138+

**Buchsbaum, Susan**

Enterprise: How to Find a Market and Make It Yours. *Working Woman* (May 1990):39-44

**Buck, Jerry**

Talking with Delta Burke: "Nothing Matters but Our Love." Interview. *Redbook* 174, No. 6 (April 1990):34-36

**Buck, Joan Juliet**

Images: American Style. *Vogue* (September 1990):311-316

**Buckberrough, Sherry**

Sonia Delaunay: Art into Fashion. Book Review. *Woman's Art Journal* 11, No. 1 (Spring-Summer 1990):39-41

Sonia Delaunay. Book Review. *Woman's Art Journal* 11, No. 1 (Spring-Summer 1990):39-41

**Buckley, Bill** (director)

Never Turn Back: The Life of Fanny Lou Hamer. Reviewed by C. Alejandra Elenes. *Feminist Collections* 11, No. 3 (Spring 1990):10

**Buckley, Mary**

Women and Ideology in the Soviet Union. Reviewed by Rochelle Ruthchild. *The Women's Review of Books* 7, No. 6 (March 1990):15

**Buckley, Thomas** and Gottlieb, Alma (editors)

Blood Magic: The Anthropology of Menstruation. Reviewed by Anna Meigs. *Signs* 16, No. 1 (Autumn 1990):180-182

**Budapest**

City Woman. *Mademoiselle* (September 1990):234-241

**Budapest, Zsuzsanna E.**

The Grandmother of Time: A Woman's Book of Celebrations, Spells, and Sacred Objects for Every Month of the Year. Reviewed by Darlene Dowling. *On the Issues* 16 (Fall 1990):32-33

**Buddhism – Status of Women**

The Questions That Won't Go Away: A Dialogue about Women in Buddhism and Christianity. Rita Nakashima Brock, Paula J. Cooey, Sheila Greeve Davaney, Rita M. Gross, Anne C. Klein, and others. *Journal of Feminist Studies in Religion* 6, No. 2 (Fall 1990):87-120

**Budhos, Marina**

Punjab Politics and the Life Within. *Belles Lettres* 6, No. 1 (Fall 1990):24-25

Storm in Chandigarh. Book Review. *Belles Lettres* 6, No. 1 (Fall 1990):24-25

**Budish, Armond D.**

Justice For All. *Family Circle* 103, No. 3 (February 20, 1990):41-43

Justice for All. *Family Circle* 103, No. 10 (July 24, 1990):44+

**Buenos Aires – Fourth International Women's Film Festival, 1990**

Women and Cinema. *Women in Action* 3 & 4 (1990):61

**Buermeyer, Nancy**

Out of the Closet and Into the Fray: Should Gay Politicians and Celebrities Be Forced to "Come Out"? *On the Issues* 16 (Fall 1990):39-40

**Bueso, Rosa Amelia** (about). *See also* Organization for Women's Business Development

**Buffets (Cookery)**

Food for Family Gatherings. Valerie Vaz. *Essence* 21, No. 4 (August 1990):86-87

A Summer Buffet. Jonell Nash. *Essence* 21, No. 4 (August 1990):88-92+

**Buffett, Jimmy**

Boomerang Love. Excerpt. Short story. *Ladies' Home Journal* 107, No. 4 (April 1990):72-77+

**Bufkin, Regina**

The Reluctant Feminist. Poem. *Feminist Review* No. 35 (Summer 1990):109-110

**Buhle, Mari Jo**

Postmodernism and/or Feminism. *The Women's Review of Books* 7, No. 7 (April 1990):23-24

Thinking Fragments: Psychoanalysis, Feminism, and Postmodernism in the Contemporary West. Book Review. *The Women's Review of Books* 7, No. 7 (April 1990):23-24

**Buie, Clarita Fonville**

One Mother's Fight for Life. *Family Circle* 103, No. 9 (June 26, 1990):70-74

**Bulbeck, Chilla**

One World Women's Movement. Reviewed by Mamie E. Locke. *Women & Politics* 10, No. 4 (1990):135-136

One World Women's Movement. Reviewed by Shahnaz Khan. *Resources for Feminist Research* 19, No. 1 (March 1990):26

**Bulkin, Elly**

Enter Password: Recovery. Reviewed by Rebecca Ripley. *Sinister Wisdom* 42 (Winter 1990-1991):124-126

Enter Password: Recovery. Reviewed by Susanna Sturgis. *off our backs* 20, No. 7 (July 1990):12

**Bullet-Proof Vests.** *See* Protective Clothing

**Bullfighters.** *See* Spain – Culture and Society

**Bumiller, Elisabeth**

Images: Japanese Style. *Vogue* (December 1990):147-156

May You Be the Mother of a Hundred Sons: A Journey Among the Women of India. Reviewed by Nina Mehta. *The Women's Review of Books* 8, No. 3 (December 1990):19-20

**Bumpass, Larry,** Sweet, James, and Martin, Teresa Castro

Changing Patterns of Marriage. *Journal of Marriage and the Family* 52, No. 3 (August 1990):747-756

**Bunch, Charlotte**

The Politics of Violence. *On the Issues* 16 (Fall 1990):25

**Bundles, A'Lelia**

Mid-Course Correction. *Essence* 20, No. 9 (January 1990):28+

**Bunkle, Phillida**

Second Opinion: The Politics of Women's Health in New Zealand. Reviewed by Hilary Haines. *The Women's Review of Books* 7, No. 8 (May 1990):20-21

**Bunkle, Phillida** (joint author). *See* Keynes, Milton

**Bunnen, Lucinda** (about). *See* Success, "Achieving Personal Best"

**Bunshaft, Gordon** (about). *See* Muschamp, Herbert

**Bunster, Ximena** and Chaney, Elsa M.

Sellers and Servants: Working Women in Lima, Peru. Reviewed by Doris P. Slesinger. *Gender and Society* 4, No. 3 (September 1990):421-423

**Bunston, Terry** and Breton, Margot

The Eating Patterns and Problems of Homeless Women. _Women and Health| 16, No. 1 (1990):43-62

**Buoniconti, Nick** and Marsa, Linda

Young Father's Story: "Parents Should Be Warned." *Redbook* 175, No. 5 (September 1990):48-50

**Burchell, Helen**

Sex Equity in Education: Readings and Strategies. Book Review. *Gender and Education* 2, No. 3 (1990):375-377

**Burchell, Helen** and Millman, Val (editors)

Changing Perspectives on Gender. Reviewed by Elisabeth Al-Khalifa. *Gender and Education* 2, No. 2 (1990):241-242

**Burd, Jennifer**

Keep. Poem. *Iris* 24 (Fall-Winter 1990):55

**Burdick, Nancilu B.**

Legacy: The Story of Talula Gilbert Bottoms and Her Quilts. Reviewed by Elaine Hedges. *NWSA Journal* 2, No. 2 (Spring 1990):282-287

**Bureaucracy.** *See also* Civil Service Workers; Public Administration

**Bureaucracy – Management Styles**

Gender and Style in Bureaucracy. Georgia Duerst-Lahti and Cathy Marie Johnson. *Women & Politics* 10, No. 4 (1990):67-120

**Buresh, Deborah** (about). *See* Business – Ownership

**Burfoot, Annette**

Pleasure, Power and Technology. Book Review. *Resources for Feminist Research* 19, No. 1 (March 1990):29

**Burford, Barbara**

Gwendolyn. add. *Spare Rib* No. 209 (February 1990):30-31

**Burgess, Averil**

Co-education – the Disadvantages for Schoolgirls. *Gender and Education* 2, No. 1 (1990):91-95

**Burgess, Marilyn** and Andreae, Janice

Introduction. *Canadian Women's Studies* 11, No. 1 (Spring 1990):5-6

**Burgess, Robert**

Symbolizing Society: Stories, Rites and Structure in a Catholic High School. Book Review. *Gender and Education* 2, No. 2 (1990):256-257

**Burgoon, Michael (joint author).** *See* Pfau, Michael

**Burgower, Barbara** (joint author). *See* Weinhouse, Beth

**Burgwyn, Diana**

Sounds of Music. Bibliography. *Harper's Bazaar* (November 1990):74+

**Burke, Anne**

Postcards. Poem. *Canadian Women's Studies* 11, No. 2 (Fall 1990):82

**Burke, Carolyn**

Brief Life. *The Women's Review of Books* 7, No. 5 (February 1990):6-8

Carrington: A Life. Book Review. *The Women's Review of Books* 7, No. 5 (February 1990):6-8

**Burke, Colleen**

The Edge of It. Poem. *Hecate* 16, Nos. 1-2 (1990):63

**Burke, Delta** (about). *See also* Television Programs

Talking with Delta Burke: "Nothing Matters but Our Love." Interview. Jerry Buck. *Redbook* 174, No. 6 (April 1990):34-36

**Burke, Delta** (interview)

Delta Burke: "Learning to Be Happy the Way I Am." Vernon Scott. *Good Housekeeping* 210, No. 5 (May 1990):165, 245-246

**Burke, Ronald J.**

Gender, Bureaucracy and Democracy: Careers and Equal Opportunity in the Public Sector. Book Review. *Atlantis* 15, No. 2 (Spring 1990):116-117

**Burkitt's Lymphoma**

The Baseball Kid Who Beat the Odds. Carolyn Tiner. *Redbook* 175, No. 4 (August 1990):36-38

**Burlesque**

"The Leg Business": Transgression and Containment in American Burlesque. Robert C. Allen. *Camera Obscura* , No. 23 (May 1990): 42-69

**Burley, Diane P.**

Corporate Secrets. *Executive Female* 13, No. 6 (November-December 1990):23

**Burne, Janet**

Express-Lane Cook: One-Skillet Sensation. *Working Woman* (April 1990):124

**Burnett, Carol** (about)

Carol Burnett. Richard Meryman. *Lear's* (August 1990):60-63+

Carol Burnett Comes Home. Eric Sherman. *Ladies' Home Journal* 107, No. 9 (September 1990):92-94

**Burney, Fanny – Criticism and Interpretation**

Writing Innocence: Fanny Burney's *Evelina*. Joanne Cutting-Gray. *Tulsa Studies in Women's Literature* 9, No. 1 (Spring 1990):43-57

**Burnham, Margaret** (about). *See* De Veaux, Alexis, Milloy, Marilyn, and Ross, Michael Erik

**Burnham, Sophy**

Encounters with Angels. *McCall's* 118, No. 3 (December 1990):76-77

**Burnout.** *See also* Activists – Burnout; Occupational Stress

**Burns, Bertha**

"Our Most Precious Gift." *Ladies' Home Journal* 107, No. 12 (December 1990):22-25

**Burns, Eric**

On Screen. *Family Circle* 103, No. 3 (February 20, 1990):101+; 103, No. 12 (September 4, 1990):153-154

On Screen: Lights! Camera! Action! *Family Circle* 103, No. 17 (December 18, 1990):152

On Screen: The New Videos. *Family Circle* 103, No. 16 (November 27, 1990):121

**Burns, Judith**

Dance, Sex and Gender: Signs of Identity, Dominance, Defiance and Desire. Book Review. *NWSA Journal* 2, No. 1 (Winter 1990):147-149

**Burns, Judy** (Editor)

An Interview With Gayatri Spivak. *Women and Performance: A Journal of Feminist Theory* 5, No. 1, Issue #9 (1990): 80-92

**Burns, Khephra**

Head for the Hills. Bibliography. *Essence* 21, No. 8 (December 1990):108-112

**Burns, Monique**

The Baby Bust. *Essence* 21, No. 6 (October 1990):34-35

Gray Matters. Bibliography. *Essence* 20, No. 12 (April 1990):77-79

On the Road Again. Bibliography. *Essence* 21, No. 2 (June 1990):29-30

Sex Drive: A User's Guide. *Essence* 21, No. 4 (August 1990):29

Ten Steps to Self-Esteem. *Essence* 21, No. 4 (August 1990):57-58

**Burns, Robin** (about)

A Nose for Business. John McLaughlin. *Harper's Bazaar* (January 1990):32

**Burrell, Barbara**

The Presence of Women Candidates and the Role of Gender in Campaigns for the State Legislature in an Urban Setting: The Case of Massachusetts. *Women & Politics* 10, No. 3 (1990):85-102

**Burrell, Barbara** (about). *See* Alexander, Nanine

**Burrell-Wells, Natalie** (about)

Heart Like a Wheel. Erik Hedegaard. *Savvy Woman* (June 1990):47-49, 80

**Burrington, Debra D.** (joint author). *See* Schwartz-Shea, Peregrine

**Burroughs, Catherine**

Feminism and Theatre. Book Review. *Tulsa Studies in Women's Literature* 9, No. 2 (Fall 1990):326-329

The Immediate Classroom: Feminist Pedagogy and Peter Brook's *The Empty Space. Feminist Teacher* 5, No. 2 (Fall 1990):10-14

Making a Spectacle: Feminist Essays on Contemporary Women's Theatre. Book Review. *Tulsa Studies in Women's Literature* 9, No. 2 (Fall 1990):326-329

**Burrows, Dave**

Big Night Out. Book Review. *Healthright* 9, No. 4 (August 1990):47

**Burstein, Karen J.**

The Reception: On Learning and Criticism. *Heresies* 25 (1990):68-72

**Burston, Maggie**

Patient's Rights: An Agenda for the Nineties. *Healthsharing* 11, No. 3 (June 1990):25-26

**Burstow, Bonnie** and Weitz, Don (editors)

Shrink Resistant: The Struggle Against Psychiatry in Canada. Reviewed by Dianne Patychuk. *Healthsharing* 11, No. 2 (March 1990):32

**Burton, Antoinette M.**

The White Woman's Burden: British Feminists and the Indian Woman, 1865-1915. *Women's Studies International Forum* 13, No. 4 (1990):295-308

**Burton, Betsy** (about)

Entrepreneurial Edge. Mark Stevens. *Working Woman* (December 1990):45-48

**Bus Driving–Accidents**. *See* School Buses–Accidents

**Bush, Armond D.**

Justice for All. *Family Circle* 103, No. 7 (May 15, 1990):33-35

**Bush, Barbara**

Slave Women in Caribbean Society, 1650-1838. Reviewed by Rosalyn Terborg-Penn. *The Women's Review of Books* 8, No. 1 (October 1990):8-9

**Bush, Barbara** (presidential spouse)

Millie's Book: The First Dog Dictates Her Memoirs to Barbara Bush. *Good Housekeeping* 211, No. 2 (August 1990):95-97, 192-195

**Bush, Barbara** (presidential spouse)(about)

Barbara Bush: First Lady, First Class. Cindy Adams. *Ladies' Home Journal* 107, No. 11 (November 1990):196+

At Home with Barbara Bush. Alison Cook. *Ladies' Home Journal* 107, No. 3 (March 1990):157-159+

**Bush, George**

Christmas 1990: A Message from the President. *Ladies' Home Journal* 107, No. 12 (December 1990):129-131

Forces for Nature. *Harper's Bazaar* (January 1990):72-73+

**Bush, George** (about)

Subsidizing the Rich. Sidney Blumenthal. *Lear's* (September 1990):110-113

**Bush, George and Barbara** (about)

Secrets of a Happy Marriage. Trude B. Feldman. *Family Circle* 103, No. 1 (January 9, 1990):55+

**Bushnell, Candace**

Is He Mr. Right? Or Mr. Right-for-Now? *Mademoiselle* (February 1990):186-187

Tales of Almost Living Together. *Mademoiselle* (May 1990):200-201, 237-239

**Bushy, Angeline**

The Myth of the Cowboy and Its Meaning for Rodeo Families. *Health Care for Women International* 11, No. 1 (1990):75-88

Rural U.S. Women: Traditions and Transitions Affecting Health Care. *Health Care for Women International* 11, No. 4 (1990):503-513

**Business**. *See also* Competitive Behavior; Creative Ability in Business; Dressing for Success; Entrepreneurs; Executives; Retail Trade Industry; Stock Market; Wholesale Trade Industry

Humor as a Professional Tool. Barbara L. Mackoff. *Executive Female* 13, No. 6 (November-December 1990):56-57

Taking Humor Seriously. Theresa Fassihi. *Executive Female* 13, No. 6 (November-December 1990):13-14

When Divorce Rocks a Company. Karen Springen. *Savvy Woman* (March 1990):34-38

You're in the Office Now: The Rules and Regulations of the Work World. Lorraine Dusky. *Mademoiselle* (July 1990):130-131, 153-154

**Business–Bibliography**

The Business Person's Essential Library. Bibliography. Joe Queenan. *Working Woman* (November 1990):101-106

## Business – Drug Testing

Narc in a Can. *Executive Female* 13, No. 6 (November-December 1990):24

## Business – Financial Management

Avoid a Cash Crunch. Doreen Mangan. *Executive Female* 13, No. 5 (September-October 1990):70-71

Building a Bank Alliance. Doreen Mangan. *Executive Female* 13, No. 4 (July-August 1990):74

What Is Your Company Worth? Doreen Mangan. *Executive Female* 13, No. 6 (November-December 1990):74

**Business – Financial Rewards**. *See also* Chief Executive Officers – Financial Rewards

The Perk Report. Anita Gates. *Working Woman* (August 1990):62-64

Six Perks That Make Your Salary Worth More. Pamela Kruger. *Working Woman* (January 1990):108-109

## Business, International

Go Global. Anita Hussey. *Executive Female* 13, No. 5 (September-October 1990):35-38

## Business – Internships

Pioneer Intern Program Teaches Basic Work Skills. Janette Scandura. *Working Woman* (January 1990):76

**Business – Management**. *See also* Management Techniques

Disappointment on the Job. Diane Cole. *Working Mother* 13, No. 8 (August 1990):22-26

The Epi-Scandal. Michele Kort. *Savvy* (December-January 1991):32-34

The Exchange Rate. Kent R. Davies. *Executive Female* 13, No. 6 (November-December 1990):28-31

Managers' Shoptalk. *Working Woman* (February 1990):24-26

Managing Lives: Corporate Women and Social Change. By Sue J. M. Freeman. Reviewed by Felicia Kornbluh. *The Women's Review of Books* 7, No. 8 (May 1990):9-10

The Power of Support Groups. Susan Merrit. *Working Mother* 13, No. 5 (May 1990):24-26

Preventing Turf Wars. Albert J. Bernstein and Sydney Craft Rozen. *Executive Female* 13, No. 1 (January-February 1990):22-24

Rent-a-Veep. Anita Hussey. *Executive Female* (May/June 1990):14-16

Will You Find Management Fulfilling? Eugene Raudsepp. *Executive Female* 13, No. 4 (July-August 1990):57-59

## Business – Mergers and Acquisitions

Entrepreneurial Edge: Grow, Baby, Grow! Ellie Winninghoff. *Working Woman* (September 1990):101-104

A Faucet Firm Lands in Hot Water. Joan Delaney. *Executive Female* 13, No. 6 (November-December 1990):70-71

What's the Big Idea? Sara Nelson. *Working Woman* (July 1990):96-98+

## Business – Personnel

Among the Bogóbo. Ellen E. Schultz. *Savvy* (December-January 1991):90

The Attack of the Headhunters. Isobel McIntyre. *Executive Female* 13, No. 6 (November-December 1990):16-18

People Leasing. Doreen Mangan. *Executive Female* 13, No. 6 (November-December 1990):72-73

Résumé Liars. Nancy Marx Better. *Savvy* (December-January 1991):26-31

**Business – Public Relations**. *See* Public Relations – Business

## Business – Social Policies

The Eco-Executive. Maggie McComas. *Savvy Woman* (October 1990):33-37

The Green Grocer. Kathryn Devereaux. *Women's Sports & Fitness* 12, No. 6 (September 1990):24-25

How Do You Build a $44 Million Company? Patricia O'Toole. *Working Woman* (April 1990):88-92

How to Find Companies Where Women Succeed. Lorraine Dusky. *Working Woman* (January 1990):81-88

How to Manage Office Friction. Andrew S. Grove. *Working Woman* (August 1990):24-26

Is Your Office an Erogenous Zone? Véronique Vienne. *Savvy* (December-January 1991):60-63

On the Lookout. *AFFILIA* 5, No. 4 (Winter 1990):101-104

Managers' Shoptalk. *Working Woman* (August 1990):18-22

Out Box: Office-Party Perverts. Gail Collins. *Working Woman* (November 1990):176

Silk Purse Chronicles. Patricia O'Toole. *Lear's* (March 1990):32-34

Tell Us What You Think: Should Employers Be Required to Provide Family Leave? *Glamour* (September 1990):196

What's Wrong with the Competitive Edge? Michael D'Antonio. *Working Woman* (June 1990):62-63+

You've Fallen Out of Favor. Can You Win It Back? Adele Scheele. *Working Woman* (August 1990):28-30

**Business Cards**

How to Order Typography. *Executive Female* 13, No. 6 (November-December 1990):48-49

It's in the Cards. Ingrid Eisenstadter. *Executive Female* 13, No. 6 (November-December 1990):44-47

**Business Conferences.** *See* Meetings

**Business Dinners.** *See* Business Entertaining

**Business Education.** *See also* Executives – Training of; March, Olivia (about)

**Business Enterprises.** *See also* Entrepreneurs; Financial Planning; Market Research; Small Business; Success in Business; Wholesale Trade Industry

Business Bulletins. *Executive Female* (March/April 1990):75

First Steps. *Executive Female* (March/April 1990):78

Making a List and Checking It Twice. Patricia O'Toole. *Lear's* (December 1990):29-30

Mary Poppins to the Rescue. *Executive Female* (May/June 1990):72

**Business Enterprises – Establishing**

Incubators Help Hatch Businesses. Doreen Mangan. *Executive Female* (May/June 1990):68-69

**Business Enterprises – Franchises**

Check It Out. Doreen Mangan. *Executive Female* 13, No. 4 (July-August 1990):72-73

Is It Time to Clone Your Company? Doreen Mangan. *Executive Female* 13, No. 5 (September-October 1990):68-69

**Business Enterprises – Mail Order**

She's Got the Look. Tim Appelo. *Savvy Woman* (January 1990):48-51, 88-91

**Business Enterprises – Ownership.** *See also* Celebrities – Business Ownership; Family Owned Business; Partnership

Business Is Better the Second Time Around. Joan Delaney. *Executive Female* (May/June 1990):66-67

Career Control: An Owner's Manual. Hope Lampert. *Working Woman* (September 1990):109-110

Job Strategies. Marilyn Moats Kennedy. *Glamour* (August 1990):99-100

Minding Your Own Business. Lorraine Richardson. *Essence* 21, No. 5 (September 1990):39+

The Savvy 60: America's Leading Women Business Owners. Edited by Sarah Stiansen. *Savvy Woman* (November 1990):47-52

A Woman for Lear's: Taking the Cake. Jane Howard. *Lear's* (February 1990):130-132

**Business Enterprises – Planning**

Business Pitches that Score. Doreen Mangan. *Executive Female* (March/April 1990):72-73

Risk-Less: Advice for Entrepreneurs. Ken Sgro. *Executive Female* (May/June 1990):73

What It Takes: Getting Unstuck. Wendy Reid Crisp. *Executive Female* (May/June 1990):76

**Business Entertaining**

Evening Agenda. *Working Woman* (December 1990):80-87

How to Host a Business Bash that's Not a Bore. Will Nixon. *Working Woman* (November 1990):122-125

A Tasty Guide to Business Dining. Karen Heller. *Working Woman* (September 1990):148-149+

This Working Life: Sex, Lies and the Business Dinner. Maureen Dowd. *Working Woman* (June 1990):110

Weekends: Designing the Perfect Party. Leah Rosch. *Working Woman* (March 1990):133-137

**Business Ethics.** *See also* Business – Social Policies; Crime – White Collar

Back Talk: Corporate Sisters. C. R. Saltpaw. *Essence* 21, No. 3 (July 1990):114

Business Ethics: What Are Your Personal Standards? *Working Woman* (February 1990):61-62

Career Strategies: Your Boss Just Stole Your Idea. Can You Get It Back? Adele M. Scheele. *Working Woman* (April 1990):30-32

How Ethical Is American Business? Ronni Sandroff. *Working Woman* (September 1990):113-116

The Lady Is a Thief. Lorraine Dusky. *Mademoiselle* (February 1990):168-169+

Leona's Lament. Cindy Adams. *Ladies' Home Journal* 107, No. 5 (May 1990):80-85+

Management: What's the Right Thing? Everyday Ethical Dilemmas. Andrew S. Grove. *Working Woman* (June 1990):16-20

Office Politics: Five-Fingered Perks. Dennis Rodkin. *Savvy Woman* (October 1990):84+

Tech Talk: The Crackdown on Corporate Pirates. Stephen Davis. *Working Woman* (March 1990):50

The Troubles I've Seen. *Working Woman* (September 1990):129

**Business Etiquette.** *See also* Business Entertaining; Business Travel

Executive Agenda. *Working Woman* (November 1990):109-110

Gift Rap. Robert McGarvey. *Executive Female* 13, No. 6 (November-December 1990):33-34

"Hi! I'm Calling from the Car Phone!" . . . And Other Breaches of High-Tech Etiquette. Gil

Schwartz. *Working Woman* (December 1990):66-67

How to Be Rude Without Really Trying. Peter Feibleman. *Lear's* (May 1990):49-51

How to Bounce Back from a Mega-Embarrassment. Marilyn Moats Kennedy. *Glamour* (November 1990):115

Memos on the Office Environment. *Working Woman* (April 1990):73-74; (May 1990):77-78

Mind Over Manners. Joni Miller. *Savvy Woman* (July/August 1990):36-38

Your Brilliant Career: Must a Business Lunch Be All Business? Rebecca Sharp. *Mademoiselle* (February 1990):99

**Business Failures**

Greed Is Good . . . and Other Management Lessons from Drexel. Margaret Laws. *Working Woman* (August 1990):70-72

Men and Failure. John Katz. *Glamour* (June 1990):244-245+

The War of the Bosses. Ellen Rapp. *Working Woman* (June 1990):57-59

**Business Forecasting**

Are You Ready for the '90s? Lorraine Dusky. *Working Woman* (January 1990):55

Trends: No Frills Dining. Annette Foglino. *Working Woman* (August 1990):42

Why It Won't Be Business as Usual. Ronni Sandroff. *Working Woman* (January 1990):58-62

**Business Leaders.** *See also* Entrepreneurs

The Beauty Queens. Vicki Woods. *Vogue* (January 1990):190-194+

Lear's Bulletin. Marion Asnes. *Lear's* (May 1990):48

National Radio Talk Show Launched on Women and Business. *Media Report to Women* 18, No. 1 (January/February 1990):5

A Nose for Business. John McLaughlin. *Harper's Bazaar* (January 1990):32

Perfect Isle of Calm. Laurie Tarkan. *Lear's* (May 1990):82-89

Power Players. Andrea R. Davis. *Essence* 20, No. 11 (March 1990):71-84

Women Right Now. *Glamour* (August 1990):89-94

**Business Leaders - Social Policies**

The End of the Big Bad Boss. Anne M. Russell. *Working Woman* (March 1990):79

The New Breed of Leaders: Taking Charge in a Different Way. Michele Morris. *Working Woman* (March 1990):73-75

**Business Loans.** *See* Loans

**Business Meetings.** *See* Meetings

**Business Partners.** *See* Partnership

**Business Planning.** *See* Corporate Planning

**Business Presentations**

Business Pitches that Score. Doreen Mangan. *Executive Female* (March/April 1990):72-73

**Business Publications**

Resources. Charles L. Martin. *Executive Female* (May/June 1990):48

**Business Records.** *See* Business – Management; Financial Resources

**Business Services**

Business Services Balance the Books. *Executive Female* 13, No. 4 (July-August 1990):76

**Business Travel**

The Business-Pleasure Trip. Sandy Sheehy. *Working Woman* (June 1990):89-95

A Corporate Wife after the Ball. Kathleen Walker Lawrence. *Lear's* (October 1990):58-60

Finances of the Frequent Flyer. Maria Lenhart. *Executive Female* (May/June 1990):40-41

Foreign Intrigue. Anne R. Field. *Savvy Woman* (November 1990):29-32

Image: The Business Traveler's Beauty Advisory. Nina Malkin. *Working Woman* (March 1990):122-124

Of Limos and Lonely Dinners. Suzanne Weber. *Executive Female* (May/June 1990):38-39

On the Road Again. Bibliography. Monique Burns. *Essence* 21, No. 2 (June 1990):29-30

Unwinding on the Long and Winding Road. Shelly Branch. *Executive Female* (May/June 1990):42-43

**Business Travel - Health Aspects**

Performance Review: Going Places, Staying Healthy. Karen Behnke and Lorraine Calvacca. *Working Woman* (October 1990):139

**Business Writing.** *See* Writing – Business Purposes

**Busselle, Rebecca**

Thoughts on Skimming the Waters. *Lear's* (October 1990):50-52

**Butala, Sharon**

Luna. Reviewed by Eleanor Dudar. *Canadian Women's Studies* 11, No. 1 (Spring 1990):109-110

**Butler, Deborah A.**

American Women Writers on Vietnam: Unheard Voices: A Selected Annotated Bibliography. Review. *Feminist Collections* 11, No. 3 (Spring 1990):14

**Butler, Elizabeth Thompson** (about)

Elizabeth Thompson Butler: A Case of Tokenism. Paul Usherwood. *Woman's Art Journal* 11, No. 2 (Fall 1990-Winter 1991):14-18

**Butler, Judith**

The Force of Fantasy: Feminism, Mapplethorpe, and Discursive Excess. *Differences* 2, No. 2 (Summer 1990):105-125

Gender Trouble: Feminism and the Subversion of Identity. Reviewed by Margaret Nash. *Hypatia* 5, No. 3 (Fall 1990):171-175

Lana's "Imitation": Melodramatic Repetition and the Gender Performative. *Genders* 9 (Fall 1990):1-18

**Butler, Octavia E.** (about). *See* Writers – Interviews, "Graceful Passages"

**Butler, Sandra**

Called to Account. Book Review. *AFFILIA* 5, No. 1 (Spring 1990):110-112

My Father's House. Book Review. *AFFILIA* 5, No. 1 (Spring 1990):110-112

My Jewish Face and Other Stories. Book Review. *Sinister Wisdom* 42 (Winter 1990-1991):122-124

**Buttocks – Weight Loss**

Butt Seriously. *Glamour* (March 1990):272-275

**Buyers, Jane** and Shantz, Susan

Reflections on Making. *Canadian Women's Studies* 11, No. 1 (Spring 1990):27-28

**Byard, Carole** (about). *See also* Artists

**Byatt, A. S.**

Possession. Reviewed by Joyce Carol Oates. *Vogue* (November 1990):274+

**Byerly, Victoria**

Hard Times Cotton Mill Girls: Personal Histories of Womanhood and Poverty in the South. Reviewed by Patricia Hill Collins. *Gender and Society* 4, No. 3 (September 1990):427-429

**Bynum, Caroline Walker** and others (editors)

Gender and Religion: On the Complexity of Symbols. Reviewed by Naomi R. Goldenberg. *Signs* 15, No. 4 (Summer 1990):874-878

**Byrne, Heather A.** (joint author). *See* Hailey, B. Jo

**Byron, Ellen**

Bob Saget's Funniest Family Stories. Interview. *Redbook* 175, No. 5 (September 1990):80-82

Laugh with Father. *Redbook* 175, No. 2 (June 1990):59-63

Talking with Shelley Fabares: "I'd Do Anything to Help My Mother." Interview. *Redbook* 176, No. 2 (December 1990):38-41

Wonderful Family Traditions. *Redbook* 176, No. 2 (December 1990):98-99+

**Byron, Ellen** (joint author). *See* Gold, Bonnie

# C

**Caballé, Montserrat** (about). *See* Spain – Culture and Society

**Cable Television.** *See* Johnson, Robert (about); Television – Cable Programming

**Cable Television Programs**

The Thinking Woman's Cable. Michele Kort. *Savvy Woman* (November 1990):34-36

**Cabral e Sa, Mario**

The Evolution of a Community: *Devdasis* of Goa. *Manushi* 56 (January-February 1990):25-27

**Cadden, Vivian**

Inside Moscow's Grocery Stores. *McCall's* 117, No. 10 (July 1990):78-82

Return to Prague. *McCall's* 117, No. 7 (April 1990):60-66

**Cadden, Vivian** and Kamerman, Sheila

Where in the World Is Child Care Better? *Working Mother* 13, No. 9 (September 1990):62-68

**Caddulo, Mariolina** (about). *See also* Fashion, "Suprema Donnas"

**Cadillac Allanté.** *See* Automobiles – Design and Construction

**Cadoria, Sherian Grace** (about). *See* Dent, David

**Caesar, Shirley** (about). *See* Leadership, "1990 Essence Awards"

**Caffeine**

Eat Well. *Family Circle* 103, No. 7 (May 15, 1990):156

Good (or Bad) to the Last Drop? A Caffeine Update. Cynthia Hacinli. *Mademoiselle* (November 1990):116

**Cage, Maggie** (interview)

Women's Bodies: Sacred Essence in Physical Form. Rebecca Wells Windinwood. *Woman of Power* 18 (Fall 1990):54-56

**Cagney and Lacey**

Cagney and Lacey Revisited. Beverley Alcock and Jocelyn Robson. *Feminist Review* No. 35 (Summer 1990):42-53

**Cahill, Susan** (editor)

Among Sisters: Short Stories by Women Writers. Reviewed by Lynne M. Constantine. *Belles Lettres* 5, No. 3 (Spring 1990):6

**Cahn, Susan**

Industry of Devotion: The Transformation of Women's Work in England, 1500-1660. Reviewed by Diane Willen. *Gender and Society* 4, No. 2 (June 1990):267-269

**Cailan, Hao**

Population Policy of China and Its Impact on Family Size and Structure. *Journal of Family Welfare* 36, No. 1 (March 1990):7-21

**Cain, Joy Duckett**

Head Turner. *Essence* 20, No. 9 (January 1990):54-55

Parenting: An Advocate for Adoption. Bibliography. *Essence* 21, No. 7 (November 1990):110

Parenting: The Wonder Years. *Essence* 21, No. 1 (May 1990):184

The Soul of Whitney. *Essence* 21, No. 8 (December 1990):54-56

Toys that Teach. *Essence* 21, No. 4 (August 1990):102-104

**Cain, Joy Duckett** and Toussaint, Pamela

Time for Love. *Essence* 20, No. 10 (February 1990):90-92

**Cain, Stanley** (joint author). *See* Roberts, Gregory

**Caine, Michael** (about)

Movies: Stairway to Hell. Ron Rosenbaum. *Mademoiselle* (June 1990):104-106

**Caine, Shulamith Wechter**

She Thinks of the Word *Stay*. Poem. *Women's Studies Quarterly* 18, Nos. 3-4 (Fall-Winter 1990):89

Unlearning the Syntax. Poem. *Women's Studies Quarterly* 18, Nos. 3-4 (Fall-Winter 1990):89

**Cake**

A Slice of Heaven. *McCall's* 117, No. 12 (September 1990):122-124

**Cake Decorating**

Cake Master. Jennet Conant. *Harper's Bazaar* (June 1990):140

**Calabrese, Raymond L.** and Adams, Jane

Alienation: A Cause of Juvenile Delinquency. *Adolescence* 25, No. 98 (Summer 1990):435-440

**Calano, Jimmy** and Salzman, Jeff

Had Any Good Ideas Lately? *Working Mother* 13, No. 1 (January 1990):36-40

**Caldwell, Martha**

Irish Women Artists: From the 18th Century to the Present Day. Book Review. *Woman's Art Journal* 11, No. 1 (Spring-Summer 1990):47-49

**Calendars**

February Is a Great Month to . . . Bibliography. *Glamour* (February 1990):149

**Calhoun, Emily M.**

Toward a Feminist Theory of the State. Book Review. *Frontiers* 11, Nos. 2-3 (1990):120-121

**Calhoun, Kitty** (about)

High Aspirations. Jon Krakauer. *Women's Sports and Fitness* 12, No. 7 (October 1990):32+

**California – Fashion**

California Girls. Lois Joy Johnson. *Ladies' Home Journal* 107, No. 4 (April 1990):172-180

**California – History**

Gender, Race, and Culture: Spanish-Mexican Women in the Historiography of Frontier California. Antonia I. Castañeda. *Frontiers* 11, No. 1 (1990):8-20

**California – State Government**

Maxine Waters: Woman of the House. Julianne Malveaux. *Essence* 21, No. 7 (November 1990):55-56+

**Calio, Jim**

What's Hot on TV: At Ease with Gerald McRaney. *Ladies' Home Journal* 107, No. 5 (May 1990):56-58

**Call, Vaughan R. A.** (joint author). *See* Otto, Luther B.

**Callaghan, Maureen**

Housing Rights . . . For Adults Only? *Canadian Women's Studies* 11, No. 2 (Fall 1990):61-62

**Callahan, Nancy**

The Freedom Quilting Bee. Reviewed by Elaine Hedges. *NWSA Journal* 2, No. 2 (Spring 1990):282-287

**Callander, Marilyn Berg**

Willa Cather and the Fair Tale. Reviewed by Lady Falls Brown. *Tulsa Studies in Women's Literature* 9, No. 2 (Fall 1990):334-337

**Callanetics.** *See* Exercise

**Callaway, C. Wayne** and Whitney, Catherine

Diet News. *Redbook* 175, No. 1 (May 1990):20

**Callaway, Helen**

Spinsters Abroad: Victorian Lady Explorers. Book Review. *Women's Studies International Forum* 13, No. 4 (1990):405

A Voyage Out: The Life of Mary Kingsley. Book Review. *Women's Studies International Forum* 13, No. 4 (1990):405

**Calluy, Jo**

Can Beta-carotene Affect Cervical Abnormalities? – Interview with Dorothy Mackerras. *Healthright* 9, No. 2 (February 1990):31-33

Fertility Control in the 90s – An Interview with Malcolm Potts. *Healthright* 9, No. 2 (February 1990):21-24

**Calluy, Jo** and Jones, Helen

AIDS: How to Answer the Hard Questions. *Healthright* 9, No. 3 (May 1990):14-16

Calories. See Food – Caloric Content

Calvacca, Lorraine

Helping Immigrants Adapt Stabilizes a Work Force. Working Woman (January 1990):84

Screening the New Sunscreens. Working Woman (May 1990):120-123

Calvacca, Lorraine (joint author). See Behnke, Karen

Cambodia

A Wish for Cambodia. Esty Dinur. On the Issues 15 (Summer 1990):22-23+

Cambridge, Ada

Sisters. Reviewed by Judith MacBean. Australian Feminist Studies No. 12 (Summer 1990):123-125

Cameras

The Beholder. Daniel Grotta. Lear's (December 1990):68-75

Cameron, Kirk (about). See Dutka, Elaine

Caminiti, Susan

The Natural. Working Woman (September 1990):138-141+

Camino, Rafael (about). See Spain – Culture and Society

Cammisa, Laurie (about)

School for Scandal. Margaret Carlson. Mademoiselle (October 1990):154+

Campanelli, Pauline

Wheel of the Year: Living the Magical Life. Reviewed by D. S. Oliver. The Women's Review of Books 8, No. 2 (November 1990):23-24

Campanile, Florence (joint author). See Basow, Susan A.

Campbell, Bebe Moore

Body Love. Essence 20, No. 9 (January 1990):44-49

Darlene Hayes: Producer Plus. Essence 21, No. 5 (September 1990):50

1990 Essence Awards. Essence 21, No. 6 (October 1990):55-68

Holy Music. Short story. Essence 21, No. 8 (December 1990):58-59+

A Portrait of Angel. Essence 21, No. 7 (November 1990):63-64+

What He's Gotta Have It. Essence 21, No. 8 (December 1990):60-61+

Campbell, Bebe Moore (about). See Writers – Interviews, "Graceful Passages"

Campbell, Bebe Moore (joint author). See Weston, Beverly

Campbell, Heather

Virtue of Necessity: English Women's Writing, 1649-1688. Book Review. Resources for Feminist Research 19, No. 2 (June 1990):47

Campbell, Jane

Bearing the Triple Burden. Belles Lettres 5, No. 4 (Summer 1990):32

How I Wrote Jubilee and Other Essays on Life and Literature. Book Review. Belles Lettres 5, No. 4 (Summer 1990):32

Humid Pitch: Narrative Poetry. Book Review. Belles Lettres 6, No. 1 (Fall 1990):53

Campbell, Katie

What He Really Wants Is a Dog. Short Stories. Reviewed by Sue Murphy. Spare Rib No. 210 (March 1990):34-35

Campbell, Mary Schmidt (about). See De Veaux, Alexis, Milloy, Marilyn, and Ross, Michael Erik

Campbell, Naomi (about). See Fashion Models, "Singular Sensations"

Campeau Corporation – Bankruptcy

More Money: How One Small Supplier Grappled with the Campeau Giant. Doreen Mangan. Executive Female (March/April 1990):18-19

Campion, Jane

An Angel at My Table. Reviewed by Natasha Moar. Spare Rib 218 (November 1990):19

Campion, Jane (about)

Tale of a Twisted Sister. Jonathan Van Meter. Harper's Bazaar (February 1990):63

Canabal, Maria E.

An Economic Approach to Marital Dissolution in Puerto Rico. Journal of Marriage and the Family 52, No. 2 (May 1990):515-530

Canada – Abortion

Canada: Woman Dies from Self-Induced Abortion. Spare Rib 218 (November 1990):45-56

Canada – Abortion Laws

Regrouping for Choice. Mary Hickmore. Healthsharing 11, No. 2 (March 1990):8

Struggle for Choice on Vancouver Island. Kim Goldberg. Healthsharing 11, No. 2 (March 1990):6

Women Lose Freedom of Choice. B. Lee. Healthsharing 11, No. 3 (June 1990):10-11

Canada – Acquired Immune Deficiency Syndrome

Confidentiality and Blackmail. Connexions 33 (1990):25

Sanitary Policing. Debi Brock. Connexions 33 (1990):

Canada – Disabled

The History of the Disabled Women's Movement in Canada. Meryn Stuart and Glynis Ellerington. Women and Environments 12, No. 2 (Spring 1990): 19

Unequal Access: Disabled Women's Exclusion from the Mainstream Women's Movement. Meryn

Stuart and Glynis Ellerington. *Women and Environments* 12, No. 2 (Spring 1990): 16-18

**Canada – Education**

Beyond Plumbing and Prevention: Feminist Approaches to Sex Education. Helen Lenskyj. *Gender and Education* 2, No. 2 (1990):217-230

**Canada – Feminist Movement**

Dreams of Equality: Women on the Canadian Left, 1920-1950. By Joan Sangster. Reviewed by Clare Collins. *Resources for Feminist Research* 19, No. 1 (March 1990):8

Feminist Organizing for Change: The Contemporary Women's Movement in Canada. By Nancy Adamson, Linda Briskin, and Margaret McPhail. Reviewed by Linda Christiansen-Ruffman. *Women's Studies International Forum* 13, Nos. 1-2 (1990):163-165

**Canada – Health Care**

Quebec Nurses' Strike. *Healthsharing* 11, No. 1 (December 1989):9

**Canada – History**. *See also* Temperance Movement

Canadian Women: A History. By Alison Prentice, Paula Bourne, Gail Cuthbert Brandt, Beth Light, Wendy Mitchinson, and others. Reviewed by Magda A. Gere Lewis. *Women's Studies International Forum* 13, Nos. 1-2 (1990).162

Quebec Women: A History. By the Clio Collective. Reviewed by Cath McNaughton. *Women's Studies International Forum* 13, Nos. 1-2 (1990):162-163

**Canada – Homosexuality**

Legalized Invisibility: The Effect of Bill 7 on Lesbian Teachers. Didi Khayatt. *Women's Studies International Forum* 13, No. 3 (1990):185-193

**Canada – Housing Policy**

Gimme Shelter: Toward Housing as a Right, Not a Commodity. Karen Wheeler. *Canadian Women's Studies* 11, No. 2 (Fall 1990):63-66

Mutual Aid and Social Networks: A Feminist-Inspired Housing Co-op in Montreal. Gisele Yasmeen. *Canadian Women's Studies* 11, No. 2 (Fall 1990):25-28

Not Seen, Not Heard: Women and Housing Policy. Sylvia Novac. *Canadian Women's Studies* 11, No. 2 (Fall 1990):53-57

**Canada – Media and Communications**

Public Policy Seen Improving Gender Balance of Canadian TV Anchors. *Media Report to Women* 18, No. 3 (May/June 1990):7

Women Invisible in Canadian Newspapers, MediaWatch Says. *Media Report to Women* 18, No. 6 (November-December 1990):5-6

**Canada – Older Adults**

Caregiving and Care-Receiving: A Double Bind for Women in Canada's Aging Society. Joan Kaden and

Susan A. McDaniel. *Journal of Women and Aging* 2 No. 3 (1990):3-26

**Canada – Race Relations**

In Canada: The Dialogue Continues. Terrie Hamazaki. *Spare Rib* No. 216 (September 1990):38-39

**Canada – Reproductive Technology**

Our Voices Must Be Heard by Royal Commission. *Healthsharing* 11, No. 1 (December 1989):8

**Canada – Sexuality**

The Regulation of Desire: Sexuality in Canada. By Gary Kinsman. Reviewed by Chris Waters. *Gender & History* 2, No. 2 (Summer 1990):218-222

**Canada – Violence Against Women**

Insignificant Violence? *Connexions* 34 (1990):8-10

**Canadian Research Institute for the Advancement of Women (CRIAW)**

Networking at CRIAW. Joann Lowell. *Healthsharing* 11, No. 2 (March 1990):8

**Canan, Janine** (editor)

She Rises Life the Sun: Invocations of the Goddess by Contemporary American Women Poets. Reviewed by Enid Dame. *Belles Lettres* 5, No. 3 (Spring 1990):9

She Rises Like the Sun: Invocations of the Goddess by Contemporary American Women Poets. Reviewed by Annie Finch. *The Women's Review of Books* 7, No. 6 (March 1990):25-26

**Canary Islands – Education**

A Meeting of Minds and Cultures: Teaching Black Women's Literature in the Canary Islands. Justine Tally and others. *Sage* 6, No. 1 (Summer 1989):63-65

**Cancer**. *See also* Breast Cancer; Health Care; Health Education; Leukemia in Children; Nuclear Power – Environmental and Health Aspects; Ovarian Cancer; Skin Cancer

Conquering Cancer. *Harper's Bazaar* (August 1990):46+

Lee Remick's Quiet Fight. Michael J. Bandler. *Ladies' Home Journal* 107, No. 5 (May 1990):62-65

Medinews. Joan Lippert. *Ladies' Home Journal* 107, No. 9 (September 1990):138

Medinews. Sally Squires. *Ladies' Home Journal* 107, No. 3 (March 1990):114; 107, No. 12 (December 1990):72

New Gains in Cancer Therapy. Irene Nyborg-Andersen. *Ladies' Home Journal* 107, No. 5 (May 1990):66

**Cancer – Organizations**

Cancer Organizers Push Feminist Agenda. Mary Jo Foley. *New Directions for Women* 19, No. 3 (May/June 1990):1+

**Cancer – Personal Narratives.** *See also* Leukemia in Children

Treating Herself with Kindness. Linda Elovitz Marshall. *Lear's* (August 1990):40-42

**Candelaria, Cordelia (Chávez)**

Chicana Creativity and Criticism: Charting New Frontiers in American Literature. Book Review. *Frontiers* 11, No. 1 (1990):85-86

**Cannon, Lynn Weber**

Fostering Positive Race, Class, and Gender Dynamics in the Classroom. *Women's Studies Quarterly* 18, Nos. 1-2 (Spring-Summer 1990):126-134

**Cannon, Maureen**

To Kathy, Reading. Poem. *Good Housekeeping* 211, No. 2 (August 1990):172

New Daughter. Poem. *Good Housekeeping* 211, No. 2 (August 1990):172

**Canole, Patricia**

Is Your Office Making You Sick? *Executive Female* (May/June 1990):32-33 +

**Canovas, Isabel** (about)

Night Visions. Christopher Petkanas. *Harper's Bazaar* (October 1990):233 +

**Cantor, Carla**

What a Baby Does to a Marriage. *Working Mother* 13, No. 7 (July 1990):25-31

**Cantrell, Carol H.**

Analogy as Destiny: Cartesian Man and the Woman Reader. *Hypatia* 5, No. 2 (Summer 1990):7-19

**Capek, Mary Ellen**

Charity Begins at Home: Generosity and Self-Interest Among the Philanthropic Elite. Book Review. *The Women's Review of Books* 8, No. 3 (December 1990):12-13

In the Gift Horse's Mouth. *The Women's Review of Books* 8, No. 3 (December 1990):12-13

The Nonsexist Word Finder: A Dictionary of Gender-Free Usage. Book Review. *NWSA Journal* 2, No. 3 (Summer 1990):476-484

Webster's First New Intergalactic Wickedary of the English Language. Book Review. *NWSA Journal* 2, No. 3 (Summer 1990):476-484

Womansword: What Japanese Words Say about Women. Book Review. *NWSA Journal* 2, No. 3 (Summer 1990):476-484

Women in LC's Terms: A Thesaurus of Library of Congress Subject Headings Related to Women. Book Review. *NWSA Journal* 2, No. 3 (Summer 1990):476-484

**Capen, Amy**

New York: Reclaiming Choice Territory. *Ms.* 1, No. 2 (September/October 1990):92

**Capital.** *See also* Loans

Seed Capital. Doreen Mangan. *Executive Female* (May/June 1990):70

**Capitalism – Alternatives**

Development Crises and Alternative Visions. Ursula Paredes and Georgina Ashworth. *Spare Rib* No. 210 (March 1990):23-25

**Caplan, Betty**

Almost Persuaded. *Spare Rib* No. 212 (May 1990):26

Celia. Film Review. *Spare Rib* No. 212 (May 1990):29

Monstrous Regiment: 15 Years. *Spare Rib* No. 210 (March 1990):37

**Caplan, Paula J.**

Don't Blame Mother: Mending the Mother-Daughter Relationship. Reviewed by Barbara G. Collins. *AFFILIA* 5, No. 3 (Fall 1990):122-124

Don't Blame Mother: Mending the Mother-Daughter Relationship. Reviewed by Denise Miller Garman. *Iris* 24 (Fall-Winter 1990):67-68

Don't Blame Mother: Mending the Mother-Daughter Relationship. Reviewed by Michele Clark. *Women and Therapy* 9, No. 4 (1990):112-114

Don't Blame Mother: Mending the Mother-Daughter Relationship. Reviewed by Rachel Hare-Mustin. *Psychology of Women Quarterly* 14, No. 1 (March 1990):143-145

Making Mother-Blaming Visible: The Emperor's New Clothes. *Women and Therapy* 10, Nos. 1/2 (1990):61-70

**Capone, Janet**

In Answer to Their Questions. Poem. *Sinister Wisdom* 41 (Summer-Fall 1990):122-127

Italy. Short Story. *Sinister Wisdom* 41 (Summer-Fall 1990):47-53

**Capra, Joan**

The Italian Jewish Connection, or, The History of America. *Sinister Wisdom* 41 (Summer-Fall 1990):101-104

**Caputi, Jane**

Changing the Channel. *The Women's Review of Books* 8, No. 3 (December 1990):27

Gender Politics and MTV: Voicing the Difference. Book Review. *The Women's Review of Books* 8, No. 3 (December 1990):27

Interview with Paula Gunn Allen. *Trivia* 16/17 (Fall 1990):50-67

The Once and Future Goddess: A Symbol for Our Time. Book Review. *The Women's Review of Books* 7, No. 8 (May 1990):14-15

In Search of Earthly Powers. *The Women's Review of Books* 7, No. 8 (May 1990):14-15

**Caputi, Jane** and Russell, Diana E. H.

"Femicide": Speaking the Unspeakable. *Ms.* 1, No. 2 (September/October 1990):34-37

**Caputi, Jane** (joint author). *See* Daly, Mary; Russell, Diana E. H.

**Carabillo, Toni**

The Unknown Women's Memorial. *Woman of Power* 18 (Fall 1990):50-52

**Caraway, Nancie E.**

Talking Back: Thinking Feminist, Thinking Black. Book Review. *Sage* 6, No. 2 (Fall 1989):58-59

**Carbine, Mary**

"The Finest Outside the Loop": Motion Picture Exhibition in Chicago's Black Metropolis, 1905-1928. *Camera Obscura* , No. 23 (May 1990): 9-41

**Carby, Hazel V.**

The Politics of Difference. *Ms.* 1, No. 2 (September/October 1990):84-85

**Card, Claudia**

Caring: A Feminine Approach to Ethics and Moral Education. Book Review. *Hypatia* 5, No. 1 (Spring 1990):101-108

Caring and Evil. *Hypatia* 5, No. 1 (Spring 1990):101-108

Homophobia: A Weapon of Sexism. Book Review. *Hypatia* 5, No. 3 (Fall 1990):110-117

Why Homophobia? *Hypatia* 5, No. 3 (Fall 1990):110-117

**Cardea, Caryatis** (joint author). *See* Dykewomon, Elana

**Carder, Joan H.**

Older Women: Surviving and Thriving: A Manual for Group Leaders. Book Review. *Journal of Women and Aging* 2, No. 1 (1990):125-126

**Cardinal-Schubert, Joane**

Surviving as a Native Woman Artist. *Canadian Women's Studies* 11, No. 1 (Spring 1990):50-51

**Cardosa de Mello, Zélia** (about)

I.O.U. $115 Billion. Geri Smith. *Savvy Woman* (October 1990):58-61+

**Card Players**

Deal Her In. Mark Stewart Gill. *Savvy Woman* (June 1990):19-20

**Career Change**

Becoming Skilled, Getting Ahead. Jody Becker. *McCall's* 118, No. 2 (November 1990):38-40

Career Control: An Owner's Manual. Hope Lampert. *Working Woman* (September 1990):109-110

Career Management: Are You Flexible Enough to Succeed? Eugene Raudsepp. *Working Woman* (October 1990):106-107

How to Come In from the Cold. Anita Gates. *Working Woman* (July 1990):75-78

Is it Time to Shift Careers? Excerpt. Emily Koltnow and Lynne S. Dumas. *McCall's* 117, No. 12 (September 1990):120-121+

On the Job. Kathryn Stechert Black. *Family Circle* 103, No. 7 (May 15, 1990):42+

Just Do It! Anne B. Fisher. *Savvy Woman* (October 1990):54-57+

The Philadelphia Experiment. Carol Saline. *Lear's* (March 1990):94-101

Switching Careers and Getting a Good Reception. Leah Rosch. *Working Woman* (February 1990):92-93+

A Woman for Lear's: Lessons. Jane Howard. *Lear's* (March 1990):164-167

Workshop: When Change Is In the Air. Judith Gerberg. *Executive Female* (March/April 1990):61-63

**Career Choice**. *See also* Balancing Work and Family Life

Moving Towards a Fair Start: Equal Gender Opportunities and Careers Service. Bob Coles and Mary Maynard. *Gender and Education* 2, No. 3 (1990):297-308

The New Diversity. Marianne Howatson. *Executive Female* (May/June 1990):18

Polling America: Where's a Woman's Place? Ernie Anastos. *Family Circle* 103, No. 14 (October 16, 1990):74-77

Viewpoint: Missing Money. Amy Shapiro. *Glamour* (June 1990):162

On Your Own: Option Overload. Judith Stone. *Glamour* (April 1990):154

**Career Counseling**. *See* Career Change; Counseling

**Career-Family Conflict**. *See also* Balancing Work and Family Life; Career Choice

Backtalk: Worked Over. Susan Foy Spratling. *Lear's* (January 1990):124-128

Drama as a Consciousness-Raising Strategy for the Self-Empowerment of Working Women. Elizabeth Torre. *AFFILIA* 5, No. 1 (Spring 1990):49-65

Free Advice. Edited by Patti Watts. *Executive Female* (May/June 1990):23-26

Sexual Ethics. Carol Lynn Mithers. *Glamour* (June 1990):274

Tell Us What You Think: Connie Chung: Has She Made Life Tougher or Easier for Working Mothers? *Glamour* (November 1990):150

This Is What You Thought: Family Leave: Should It Be Mandated? *Glamour* (November 1990):149

Viewpoint: Questions from the Wellesley Fuss. Rosalie J. Wolf. *Glamour* (August 1990):132

Viewpoint: The Tyranny of Having It All. Ce Ce Iandoli. *Executive Female* (March/April 1990):29-30

**Career Ladders**

Career Management: How to Be the One They Promote. Anita Gates. *Working Woman* (October 1990):100-105

Stretch: The No-Fail Guide to Big Career Jumps. Jill Neimark. *Working Woman* (November 1990):116-117

**Career Management.** *See also* Dressing for Success; Empowerment; Social Skills

Are You Too Good to Be Promoted? Eugenie Allen. *Glamour* (October 1990):118

Boredom on the Job. Marilyn Moats Kennedy. *Glamour* (October 1990):117

Career Developments and Transitions of Middle-Aged Women. Rosalie J. Ackerman. *Psychology of Women Quarterly* 14, No. 4 (December 1990):513-530

Competitive Edge. *Executive Female* (May/June 1990):6-8

Job Strategies: How Promotable Are You? Marilyn Moats Kennedy. *Glamour* (May 1990):143

Job Strategies. Marilyn Moats Kennedy. *Glamour* (August 1990):99-100; (December 1990):109

Lear's Bulletin. Bibliography. Marion Asnes. *Lear's* (February 1990):36

Making a List and Checking It Twice. Patricia O'Toole. *Lear's* (December 1990):29-30

Men and Women Lawyers in In-House Legal Departments: Recruitment and Career Patterns. Sharyn L. Roach. *Gender and Society* 4, No. 2 (June 1990):207-219

Strategic Quitting: Pack Your Bags for Greener Pastures. Robert McGarvey. *Executive Female* (March/April 1990):34-36+

Suite Dreams. Barbara McGarry Peters. *Executive Female* (March/April 1990):46-48+

Surprise! Your New Job Isn't the One You Accepted. Marilyn Moats Kennedy. *Glamour* (November 1990):115-116

When to Take Charge, When to Pass Your Boss the Buck. Marilyn Moats Kennedy. *Glamour* (July 1990):75

Women Right Now. *Glamour* (July 1990):63-64

**Career Planning.** *See also* Baby Boom Generation – Career Planning; Conflict Resolution; Entrepreneurs; Executives – Training of; Leadership; Management Techniques; Office Politics; Performance Appraisal; Science – Study and Teaching; Self-Presentation; Social Skills; Time Management

The Attack of the Headhunters. Isobel McIntyre. *Executive Female* 13, No. 6 (November-December 1990):16-18

Breaking and Entering: How Girls Like You Get Dream Jobs. Irene Daria. *Mademoiselle* (September 1990):272-275+

Career Advice: Dear Betty Harragan. Betty Lehan Harragan. *Working Woman* (January 1990):32-35; (February 1990):38-43

Career Makeover: "I Needed to Define My Life." Jody Becker. *McCall's* 118, No. 1 (October 1990):31-32

Career Management: Are You Flexible Enough to Succeed? Eugene Raudsepp. *Working Woman* (October 1990):106-107

Career Strategies: Burned Out. Can You Get Fired Up Again? Adele Scheele. *Working Woman* (October 1990):46-48

Career Strategies: Male Bonding: Can You Beat It? Adele Scheele. *Working Woman* (December 1990):30-32

Career Strategies: Promises, Promises. Can You Make Your Boss Deliver? Adele Scheele. *Working Woman* (July 1990):26-28

Career Strategies: Same Job, New Boss. Can You Make It Work? Adele Scheele. *Working Woman* (June 1990):22-24

Career Strategies: Should You Push Hard for a Promotion? Adele M. Scheele. *Working Woman* (May 1990):34-37

Career Strategies: Your Boss Just Stole Your Idea. Can You Get It Back? Adele M. Scheele. *Working Woman* (April 1990):30-32

Do You Need (or Want) a Master's Degree? Denise Harrison. *Glamour* (July 1990):76

Enterprise: What I Learned from My Mistakes. Susan Peterson. *Working Woman* (June 1990):29-34

Executive Agenda. *Working Woman* (December 1990):53-54

Financial Workshop: Picking the Risks that Pay Off Big. Mary Rowland. *Working Woman* (March 1990):57-60

Finding the Guts to Go. Interview. Michele Morris. *Working Woman* (May 1990):86+

Good for Business: A Manager's Hot Line. *Working Woman* (September 1990):62-66; (November 1990):41-46; (December 1990):18-23

Healing Professions. Bibliography. Felicia E. Halpert. *Essence* 21, No. 4 (August 1990):32-34

Here *Today* Gone Tomorrow: When Jane Pauley *Should* Have Quit. Claire McIntosh. *Working Woman* (May 1990):82-83

The 25 Hottest Careers. *Working Woman* (July 1990):73-83

How Did Taking Time Out from Your Career Work to Your Benefit? Patti Watts and Shelley Garcia. *Executive Female* 13, No. 6 (November-December 1990):20-22

"How I Did It": Selling Your Idea to Management. Sarah M. Nolan. *Working Woman* (September 1990):83-85

"How I Did It": When Your Image Is Frozen in Time. Carol Kirby. *Working Woman* (October 1990):53-56

How Should You Criticize Your Boss? Carefully. Hendrie Weisinger. *Working Woman* (February 1990):90-91+

Is This a Dead-End Assignment? Kent L. Straat. *Working Woman* (March 1990):84-85+

It's Not Just a Job, It's a Sport. Kathryn Reith. *Women's Sports & Fitness* 12, No. 6 (September 1990).58-59

Job Strategies: Can You Ask for a Raise Right Now? Marilyn Moats Kennedy. *Glamour* (February 1990):85-86

Job Strategies. *Glamour* (January 1990):54-56

Job Strategies. Marilyn Moats Kennedy. *Glamour* (April 1990):125-130

Job Strategies: Surviving a No-Win Situation. Marilyn Moats Kennedy. *Glamour* (June 1990):121-122

"Just Do It": The New Job Strategy. Nancy K. Austin. *Working Woman* (April 1990):78-80+

Lear's Bulletin. Marion Asnes. *Lear's* (May 1990):48; (June 1990):44

Management Secrets They'll Never Teach You at Business School. Jolie Solomon. *Working Woman* (June 1990):53-54+

Managers' Shoptalk. *Working Woman* (May 1990):23-26; (June 1990):10-14; (July 1990):13-21

The Negotiating Art: You *Can* Always Get What You Want. Ellen J. Belzer. *Working Woman* (April 1990):98-99+

The New Corporate Survival Guide: Can You Thrive in Your Company? Thomas L. Quick. *Working Woman* (July 1990):45-48

Push-Button Resumes. Robbie Miller Kaplan. *Executive Female* 13, No. 4 (July-August 1990):35+

Smile, Though Your Heart Is Racing. Jeannie Ralston. *Mademoiselle* (November 1990):182-183+

When Your Career's Hot but You're Not. Anita Gates. *Working Woman* (July 1990):80

Where the Scares Are: 8 Risky Businesses. Shirley Chan, Maryclare Flynn, and Michelle Klingenberg. *Working Woman* (February 1990):81

Working: Red-Hot Jobs. Felicia E. Halpert. *Essence* 20, No. 11 (March 1990):34-37+

The 10 Worst Careers. Anne M. Russell. *Working Woman* (July 1990):82-84

You Like Your Job. But Should You Leave It? Ronni Sandroff. *Working Woman* (May 1990):81-85

Your Brilliant Career: Back to Graduate School? Rebecca Sharp. *Mademoiselle* (October 1990):114

Your Brilliant Career: It's New, It's Improved, It's You! Rebecca Sharp. *Mademoiselle* (November 1990):109

Your Brilliant Career: Must a Business Lunch Be All Business? Rebecca Sharp. *Mademoiselle* (February 1990):99

Your Brilliant Career: Pet Peeves. Rebecca Sharp. *Mademoiselle* (September 1990):180

Your Brilliant Career. Rebecca Sharp. *Mademoiselle* (June 1990):113

Your Brilliant Career: The Friendship Trap. Rebecca Sharp. *Mademoiselle* (December 1990):100

Your Brilliant New Career. Bill Banks. *Savvy* (December-January 1991):37-38

You've Fallen Out of Favor. Can You Win It Back? Adele Scheele. *Working Woman* (August 1990):28-30

**Caregiving.** *See also* Older Adults – Care; Parenting

Caregiving and Care-Receiving: A Double Bind for Women in Canada's Aging Society. Joan Kaden and Susan A. McDaniel. *Journal of Women and Aging* 2 No. 3 (1990):3-26

A Critical Look at Family Care. Paul L. Dressel and Ann Clark. *Journal of Marriage and the Family* 52, No. 3 (August 1990):769-782

Daughters of the Elderly: Building Partnerships in Caregiving. Edited by Jane Norris. Reviewed by Shirley L. Patterson. *Journal of Women and Aging* 2, No. 1 (1990):123-124

The Daughter Track. *Glamour* (May 1990):94

Extended Care-Giving: The Experience of Surviving Spouses. Sandra L. Quinn-Musgrove. *Journal of Women and Aging* 2, No. 2 (1990):93-107

Gender Differences in Spouse Caregiver Strain: Socialization and Role Explanations. Baila Miller. *Journal of Marriage and the Family* 52, No. 2 (May 1990):311-321

Give Your Best. Bibliography. Janet Margolies. *Ladies' Home Journal* 107, No. 12 (December 1990):108-121

The Healers. *Ladies' Home Journal* 107, No. 11 (November 1990):155-160

The Home as Workshop: Women as Amateur Nurses and Medical Care Providers. Nona Y. Glazer. *Gender and Society* 4, No. 4 (December 1990):479-499

Is He Your Boyfriend or Your Baby? Warren Leight. *Mademoiselle* (January 1990):62

The Liberation of Caring: A Different Voice for Gilligan's "Different Voice." Bill Puka. *Hypatia* 5, No. 1 (Spring 1990):58-82

For Love and Money: Women as Foster Mothers. Brenda Smith and Tina Smith. *AFFILIA* 5, No. 1 (Spring 1990):66-80

Nursing a Loved One at Home: A Care Giver's Guide. By Susan Golden. Reviewed by Beverly A. Baldwin. *Journal of Women and Aging* 2, No. 1 (1990):121-123

The Oppression of Caring: Women Caregivers of Relatives with Mental Illness. Anna Scheyetl. *AFFILIA* 5, No. 1 (Spring 1990):32-48

Our Parents Growing Older. Jane Ciabattari. *McCall's* 118, No. 2 (November 1990):81-88+

Pacifism and Care. Victoria Davion. *Hypatia* 5, No. 1 (Spring 1990):90-100

Prime of Life: Sixtysomething. . .*Family Circle* 103, No. 14 (October 16, 1990):46-48

Thoughts on Caretaking: Shuck Off the Yoke. John Bradshaw. *Lear's* (May 1990):67

Two Needs, One Day-Care Center. Celia Slom. *McCall's* 117, No. 10 (July 1990):56

**Carelli, Anne O'Brien** (editor)

Sex Equity in Education: Readings and Strategies. Reviewed by Helen Burchell. *Gender and Education* 2, No. 3 (1990):375-377

**Caretaking.** *See* Caregiving

**Caribbean – Description and Travel.** *See also* Nassau – Description and Travel

Seven Black-Owned Island Guest Houses. Allyson Reid-Dove. *Essence* 20, No. 12 (April 1990):89-92

**Caribbean – Travel**

Travel: How to Get $1,000 Worth of Vacation for $600. Bibliography. *Glamour* (May 1990):193-200

Travel: The Best of the Caribbean. Bibliography. *Glamour* (November 1990):153-154

**Caribbean Writers**

Report on the First International Conference of Women Writers of the English-Speaking Caribbean. Terri Cotton and Selwyn R. Cudjoe. *Sage* 6, No. 1 (Summer 1989):83

**Caris, Jane**

Snow Change. Poem. *Iris* 24 (Fall-Winter 1990):54

**Carleton, Susan**

Good News About the Blues. *Working Mother* 13, No. 4 (April 1990):16-22

**Carlin, Barbara**

Starring Moms. *Family Circle* 103, No. 7 (May 15, 1990):80-85

**Carlin, Lisa**

The Significance of Stones. Poem. *Sinister Wisdom* 42 (Winter 1990-1991):47-48

**Carlisle, Carla**

City Fare. *Harper's Bazaar* (November 1990):204

**Carlisle, Kim**

Checkpoints for the Crawl. *Women's Sports and Fitness* 12, No. 3 (April 1990):22-23

Turning Back the Clock. *Women's Sports and Fitness* 12, No. 4 (May-June 1990):22

**Carlson, Margaret**

Love Among the Ruins. *Savvy Woman* (November 1990):60-63+

School for Scandal. *Mademoiselle* (October 1990):154+

Then and Now: From Epiphany to Excess. *Lear's* (February 1990):72-77

**Carlson, Ron**

A Kind of Flying. Short story. *McCall's* 117, No. 11 (August 1990):69-74

**Carnegie Hall**

Centennial Cheer. Stanley Mieses. *Harper's Bazaar* (September 1990):208

**Carnes, Patty** (about)

A Woman Today: A Home for Patty. Diane Stacy and Cheryl Coggins Frink. *Ladies' Home Journal* 107, No. 5 (May 1990):20-26

**Caron, Ann F.**

Trust Me, Trust Me. *Good Housekeeping* 211, No. 5 (November 1990):87-88

**Carpenter, Betsy**

The State of the Earth. *Ladies' Home Journal* 107, No. 4 (April 1990):162-164+

**Car Phones.** *See* Cellular Telephones

**Car Pools**

Carpooling Incentives Aim at Americans Who Solo (Or: Baby, You Can Drive My Car). Celia Slom. *McCall's* 117, No. 8 (May 1990):63

**Carr, Camilla**

Topsy Dingo Wild Dog. Reviewed by Eleanor J. Bader. *New Directions for Women* 19, No. 2 (March/April 1990):21

**Carr, Carole A.** (joint editor). *See* Larson, Anne E.

**Carr, Emily** (about)

The Art of Emily Carr. By Doris Shadbolt. Reviewed by Merlin Homer. *Canadian Women's Studies* 11, No. 1 (Spring 1990):106-107

The Life of Emily Carr. By Paula Blanchard. Reviewed by Merlin Homer. *Canadian Women's Studies* 11, No. 1 (Spring 1990):106-107

**Carr, Helen** (editor)

From My Guy to Sci-Fi: Genre and Women's Writing in the Postmodern World. Reviewed by Maureen Reddy. *The Women's Review of Books* 7, No. 7 (April 1990):25-26

From My Guy to Sci-Fi: Genre and Women's Writing in the Postmodern World. Reviewed by Shannon Hengen. *Resources for Feminist Research* 19, No. 1 (March 1990):17

**Carr, Irene Campos**

Women's Voices Grow Stronger: Politics and Feminism in Latin America. *NWSA Journal* 2, No. 3 (Summer 1990):450-463

**Car Repair.** *See* Automobiles – Maintenance and Repair

**Carrington** (about)

Carrington: A Life. By Gretchen Holbrook Gerzina. Reviewed by Carolyn Burke. *The Women's Review of Books* 7, No. 5 (February 1990):6-8

**Carroll, Anna Ella** (about)

Anna Ella Carroll: Invisible Member of Lincoln's Cabinet. Benjamin L. Abramowitz. *Minerva* 8, No. 4 (Winter 1990):30-40

**Carroll, Berenice A.**

The Politics of "Originality": Women and the Class System of the Intellect. *Journal of Women's History* 2, No. 2 (Fall 1990):136-163

**Carroll, Diahann** (about). *See* De Veaux, Alexis, Milloy, Marilyn, and Ross, Michael Erik; Leadership, "1990 Essence Awards"

**Carroll-Seguin, Rita** (joint author). *See* Geschwender, James A.

**Carruthers, Elspeth** (joint author). *See* Hanlon, Gregory

**Carson, Johnny** (about)

Retire Early! Miss Nothing! James Kaplan. *Mademoiselle* (October 1990):110

**Carson, Mina**

Settlement Folk: Social Thought and the American Settlement Movement, 1885-1930. Reviewed by Gwendolyn Mink. *The Women's Review of Books* 7, No. 12 (September 1990):23-24

**Carson, Rachel** (about). *See* Environmental Movement

**Carter, Charla**

European Designers to Watch. *Vogue* (August 1990):124-150

Living. *Vogue* (September 1990):501-507

Paris Charm. *Harper's Bazaar* (February 1990):140-143+

View: Dominique Aurientis. *Vogue* (December 1990):120-124

**Carter, Cynthia**

The Female Gaze: Women as Viewers of Popular Culture. Book Review. *Resources for Feminist Research* 19, No. 2 (June 1990):41-42

Female Spectators: Looking at Film and Television. Book Review. *Resources for Feminist Research* 19, No. 2 (June 1990):41-42

**Carter, Dixie** (about). *See* Television Programs

**Carter, Graydon**

Holy Terror: Andy Warhol Close Up. Book Review. *Vogue* (September 1990):448-452

Movies: The Bonfire of the Vanities. Film review. *Vogue* (December 1990):190-194

**Carter, Kathryn** and Spitzack, Carol

Transformation and Empowerment in Gender and Communication Courses. *Women's Studies in Communication* 13, No. 1 (Spring 1990): 92-110

**Carter, Nanette** (about). *See* Artists

**Carter, Ruth** and Kirkup, Gill

Women in Professional Engineering: The Interaction of Gendered Structures and Values. *Feminist Review* No. 35 (Summer 1990):92-101

**Carter, Steven** and Sokol, Julia

Lovetalk: The Quickest Way to Better Sex. *Redbook* 174, No. 6 (April 1990):108-109+

What Smart Women Know. Reviewed by Anne Lamott. *Mademoiselle* (November 1990):96-99

**Carter, Susanne**

Recovering from the War. Book Review. *Minerva* 8, No. 3 (Fall 1990):73-77

Vietnam Wives. Book Review. *Minerva* 8, No. 3 (Fall 1990):73-77

**Cartier, Marie**

A Manual for Survival. Poem. *Heresies* 25 (1990):17

**Cartoons.** *See* Comic Books, Strips, etc.; Illustration

**Car Trips.** *See* Automobiles – Touring

**Carty, Linda**

Women and Environment in the Third World: Alliance for the Future. Book Review. *Resources for Feminist Research* 19, No. 1 (March 1990):40-41

**Caruana, Claudia M.**

Anesthesia: The Essence of It All. *Lear's* (May 1990):53-54

**Case, Brian**

Dreams and Dust: Under a Sheltering Sky. *Lear's* (May 1990):90-97

**Case, Sue-Ellen**

Feminism and Theatre. Reviewed by Catherine Burroughs. *Tulsa Studies in Women's Literature* 9, No. 2 (Fall 1990):326-329

Feminism and Theatre. Reviewed by Chezia Thompson-Cager. *NWSA Journal* 2, No. 4 (Autumn 1990):650-651

Feminism and Theatre. Reviewed by Jill Dolan. *Signs* 15, No. 4 (Summer 1990):864-869

**Casey, Kathryn**

An American Harem. *Ladies' Home Journal* 107, No. 2 (February 1990):116-117+

Lassoing Power. *Savvy Woman* (November 1990):13-14

The New Gold Rush. *Ladies' Home Journal* 107, No. 9 (September 1990):160-164+

Voices of the Decade. *Ladies' Home Journal* 107, No. 1 (January 1990):66-72

**Casey, Kathryn** and Siegler, Bonnie

What's Hot: Summer Stars. *Ladies' Home Journal* 107, No. 8 (August 1990):52-60

**Casey, Kathryn** (joint author). *See* Estefan, Gloria

**Casey, Maude**

Hijacked Spirituality and Buried Herstories. *Spare Rib* No. 215 (August 1990):8-11

**Cashdan, Linda**

Special Interests. Short Story. *Good Housekeeping* 210, No. 6 (June 1990):219-245, 262-267

**Cashmere**

Soft Wear. *Lear's* (July 1990):110-115

View: Cashmere. *Vogue* (December 1990):134-138

**Casinos**

What Goes on Behind the Boardwalk. Janet Gardner. *Savvy Woman* (January 1990):34-36

**Cassady, Carolyn**

Off the Road: My Years with Cassady, Kerouac, and Ginsberg. Reviewed by Francine Prose. *The Women's Review of Books* 8, No. 2 (November 1990):10-11

**Cassatt, Mary** (about)

After Egypt. By Millicent Dillon. Reviewed by Scarlet Cheng. *Belles Lettres* 6, No. 1 (Fall 1990):50

**Casseroles**. *See* Cookery (Casseroles)

**Cassidy, Anne**

Are You Spoiling Your Child? *Working Mother* 13, No. 5 (May 1990):34-46

Don't Let Your Good Baby Turn into a Terrible Toddler! *Working Mother* (November 1990):90-97

Dreams Can Come True. *Family Circle* 103, No. 1 (January 9, 1990):10-13

Ready, Set, Crawl! *Working Mother* 13, No. 10 (October 1990):81-85

Women and Alcohol: Menace or Medicine? *Family Circle* 103, No. 17 (December 18, 1990):63-65

You Can Reverse Aging: How Anti-Aging Clinics Turn Back the Clock. *Family Circle* 103, No. 14 (October 16, 1990):118-122

**Cassidy, Anne** (joint author). *See* Widome, Mark

**Cassidy, Neal** (joint author). *See* Bennis, Phyllis

**Cassini, Oleg** (about). *See* Fashion Designers, "Battle-Weary Designers"

**Castañeda, Antonia I.**

Gender, Race, and Culture: Spanish-Mexican Women in the Historiography of Frontier California. *Frontiers* 11, No. 1 (1990):8-20

**Castellano, Andrea and Michel** (about). *See* Conant, Jennet, "Model Gourmets"

**Castellano, Olivia**

Canto, Locura y Poesia. *The Women's Review of Books* 7, No. 5 (February 1990):18-20

**Castellanos, Rosario**

A Rosario Castellanos Reader: An Anthology of Her Poetry, Short Fiction, Essays, and Drama. Edited by Maureen Ahern. Reviewed by Mercedes Tasende-Grabowski. *Frontiers* 11, No. 1 (1990):88-89

**Castelli, Elizabeth**

*Les belles infide4les*/Fidelity or Feminism? The Meaning of Feminist Biblical Translation. *Journal of Feminist Studies in Religion* 6, No. 2 (Fall 1990):25-39

**Casteras, Susan P.**

Images of Victorian Womanhood in English Art. Reviewed by Debra N. Mancoff. *Woman's Art Journal* 11, No. 1 (Spring-Summer 1990):42-45

**Castillo, Ana** (joint editor). *See* Alarcón, Norma

**Castillo-Speed, Lillian**

Chicana Studies: A Selected List of Materials Since 1980. *Frontiers* 11, No. 1 (1990):66-84

**Castleman, Michael**

Good Health: Lethal Mosquitos. *Redbook* 174, No. 6 (April 1990):22-24

Medical Report: The Common Cold Quiz. *Glamour* (January 1990):30-35

Watch Out for Strep Throat. *Redbook* 176, No. 1 (November 1990):102-103+

**Castleman, Michael** (joint author). *See* Piller, Charles

**Castonguay, Kay** (interview)

Feminists for Life: An Interview with Kay Castonguay. Kristen Staby Rembold. *Iris* 23 (Spring-Summer 1990):49-52

**Castro, Mary Garcia** (joint editor). *See* Chaney, Elsa M.

**Cataldo, Darci**

Two Kinds of People in the World. *Sinister Wisdom* 41 (Summer-Fall 1990):116-117

**Catalogs.** *See* Mail Order Business

**Caterers and Catering.** *See also* Social Entertaining

Food: Catered to Our Style. Jonell Nash. *Essence* 21, No. 8 (December 1990):94-98

Sowing the Free Sample. Ingrid Eisenstadter. *Executive Female* 13, No. 4 (July-August 1990):11-12

Tray Chic. Patricia Beard. *Harper's Bazaar* (June 1990):138

**Cather, Willa – Criticism and Interpretation**

Willa Cather: Writing at the Frontier. By Jamie Ambrose. Reviewed by Lady Falls Brown. *Tulsa Studies in Women's Literature* 9, No. 2 (Fall 1990):334-337

Willa Cather and France: In Search of the Lost Language. By Robert J. Nelson. Reviewed by Patrick W. Shaw. *Tulsa Studies in Women's Literature* 9, No. 2 (Fall 1990):337-339

Willa Cather and the Fair Tale. By Marilyn Berg Callander. Reviewed by Lady Falls Brown. *Tulsa Studies in Women's Literature* 9, No. 2 (Fall 1990):334-337

**Cather, Willa** (about)

Willa Cather: Double Lives. By Hermione Lee. Reviewed by Susan A. Hallgarth. *The Women's Review of Books* 8, No. 1 (October 1990):23-24

**Catholics – Relations with Jews**

When Will We Come to Understand the Jews as They Do Themselves? Sister Rose Thering. *Lilith* 15, No. 2 (Spring 1990):19

**Cats.** *See also* Pets

Oscar, the People Cat. James Herriot. *Good Housekeeping* 211, No. 6 (December 1990):88

Pet Life. Michael W. Fox. *McCall's* 117, No. 9 (June 1990):124; 118, No. 3 (December 1990):145

Pet News. *Ladies' Home Journal* 107, No. 11 (November 1990):134

**Cats in Literature**

Kitties Rule. Bibliography. Anne Lamott. *Mademoiselle* (October 1990):102-104

**Caust, Lesley**

1989 Australasian Political Studies Association Conference. *Australian Feminist Studies* No. 11 (Autumn 1990):115-116

**Cauwels, Janice M.**

Bitter Fame: A Life of Sylvia Plath. Book Review. *New Directions for Women* 19, No. 1 (January/February 1990):20

**Cavandish, Margaret Lucas**

The Reception: On Learning and Criticism. Karen J. Burstein. *Heresies* 25 (1990):68-72

**Cavin, Susan**

Two Decades and Counting. *off our backs* 20, No. 2 (February 1990):19

**Cayleff, Susan E.**

Wash and Be Healed: The Water-Cure Movement and Women's Health. Reviewed by Sue Zschoche. *Signs* 15, No. 2 (Winter 1990):414-416

**Cebotarev, E. A.**

Agriculture, Women and Land: The African Experience. Book Review. *Resources for Feminist Research* 19, No. 1 (March 1990):3-4

**Cederstrom, Lorelei**

The Psychology of the Female Body. Book Review. *Resources for Feminist Research* 19, No. 1 (March 1990):30-31

**Cejka, Susan** (about). *See also* Customer Service

**Cela, Camilo José** (about). *See* Spain – Culture and Society

**Celebrations.** *See also* Anniversaries

Couple Time. *Glamour* (February 1990):104

**Celebrities.** *See also* Aspen, CO; Fashion; Film and Filmmakers; Los Angeles – Celebrities

Backyards of the Rich and Famous. Lauren Payne. *Ladies' Home Journal* 107, No. 8 (August 1990):118-122

Charmed Wives. Rona Jaffe. *Harper's Bazaar* (September 1990):306-307+

Every Face has a Secret. Laura Rosetree. *Redbook* 174, No. 6 (April 1990):54-56

Namesakes! Kathleen Brady. *McCall's* 117, No. 8 (May 1990):51-52

Postcards from the Edge of Mediocrity. Ron Rosenbaum. *Mademoiselle* (November 1990):90-93

Talking Fashion. Gabé Doppelt. *Vogue* (January 1990):229-231+

Talking Parties. Edited by Gabé Doppelt. *Vogue* (December 1990):329-331

Talking Parties. Gabé Doppelt. *Vogue* (January 1990):232-235+

Word On. . .*Glamour* (September 1990):215

**Celebrities – Activism**

Cause Celeb. Bibliography. Elaine Dutka. *McCall's* 118, No. 2 (November 1990):70-72

Cause Celeb. Elaine Dutka. *McCall's* 117, No. 12 (September 1990):112-113

Cause Celeb. Linden Gross. *McCall's* 118, No. 3 (December 1990):56-58

Goodfellas. *Harper's Bazaar* (December 1990):154-155

Lights, Camera, Activism. Ronald Brownstein. *Lear's* (December 1990):78-81+

The New Sexy Men: The Politicos. Charla Krupp. *Glamour* (March 1990):190

Stars Who Care. JoBeth McDaniel. *Ladies' Home Journal* 107, No. 11 (November 1990):74-80

Stars Who Take Care of the Earth. Linden Gross. *Redbook* 176, No. 1 (November 1990):28-32

Women Who Make a Difference: Reaching Out to Refugees. Stephanie Abarbanel. *Family Circle* 103, No. 9 (June 26, 1990):15-20

**Celebrities – Advertising**

A Voice in the Crowd. Craig Bloom. *Lear's* (October 1990):100-103

**Celebrities – Beauty, Personal**

Beauty & Fashion Journal. *Ladies' Home Journal* 107, No. 1 (January 1990):23-35

Who Cuts Who. *Harper's Bazaar* (May 1990):71-74+

**Celebrities – Business Ownership**

Broadway Debut. Jane Freiman. *Harper's Bazaar* (May 1990):157

Vineyard Haven. Mark Ganem. *Harper's Bazaar* (May 1990):160

**Celebrities – Cookery**

Contemporary Living: Can They Cook! Valerie Vaz. *Essence* 21, No. 7 (November 1990):87-90

**Celebrities – Family Life**

Danny De Vito: Reaching New Heights. Michael J. Bandler. *Ladies' Home Journal* 107, No. 1 (January 1990):76-80

Happiness Is Goldie's Secret. Melinda Lawrence. *Redbook* 175, No. 3 (July 1990):22-27

Talking with Arnold Schwarzenegger: Tough Man, Tender Heart. Interview. Sally Ogle Davis. *Redbook* 175, No. 5 (September 1990):84-86

Talking with Mel Gibson: "My Six Kids Come First." Interview. Carson Jones. *Redbook* 175, No. 4 (August 1990):40-42

Where I Grew Up. Linda Konner. *Glamour* (March 1990):174

**Celebrities – Fashion**

Dress Harder: Hollywood's Best and Worst Threads. Janet Charlton. *Mademoiselle* (December 1990):156-157+

**Celebrities – Homosexuality**

Tell Us What You Think: Gay Celebrities and Privacy. *Glamour* (August 1990):140

This Is What You Thought: Gay Celebrities: Should Private Lives Be Made Public? *Glamour* (October 1990):159

**Celebrities – Quotations**

Love's Labours Quoted. Willie Mae Kneupper. *Lear's* (February 1990):49-50

**Celebrities – Spouses**

In the Limelight. Arthur J. Robinson, Jr. *Essence* 21, No. 3 (July 1990):34

**Celebrities – Weight Loss**

Eat Light: How Judith Got Light. Kathleen Mackay. *Redbook* 175, No. 5 (September 1990):26

**Celeste, Dagmar** (about)

Celestial Reasoning – Ohio's First Lady Talks about Love and Feminism. Janyce Katz. *Ms.* 1, No. 2 (September/October 1990):88

First Feminist of Ohio Opens NWSA '90. *NWSAction* 3, No. 3 (Fall 1990): 1-3

**Celibacy**

Chaste Liberation: Celibacy and Female Cultural Status. By Sally L. Kitch. Reviewed by Rickie Solinger. *Women and Health* 16, No. 2 (1990):132-134

My Year Without Sex. Jani Scandura. *Mademoiselle* (July 1990):85-87

**Cellular Telephones**

"Hi! I'm Calling from the Car Phone!."..And Other Breaches of High-Tech Etiquette. Gil Schwartz. *Working Woman* (December 1990):66-67

Tech Talk. *Working Woman* (August 1990):46-48

Where's the Beep? Peter Feibleman. *Lear's* (March 1990):48-52

**Cellulite**

Images: New Cellulite Remedies. Jeannie Ralston. *Vogue* (August 1990):170-179

**Cembalest, Robin**

Candid Camera. *Harper's Bazaar* (November 1990):88-92

Fierce Expressions. *Harper's Bazaar* (September 1990):244-245+

Out of the Ordinary. *Harper's Bazaar* (October 1990):146-150

**Censorship**. *See also* Pornography

Censorship: NEA Denies Grants to Lesbians and Gays. Robin Sawyer. *off our backs* 20, No. 8 (August/September 1990):5

Censorship – Who's Calling the Shots. Marcel Farry. *Spare Rib* 219 (December 1990-January 1991):31-32

Lewd Music. Barbara Grizzuti Harrison. *Mademoiselle* (October 1990):116

Tell Us What You Think: Should There be Limits on Free Speech? *Glamour* (October 1990):160

This Is What You Thought: Should There Be Limits on Free Speech? *Glamour* (December 1990):135

2 Live Crew Lyrics Raise Problem of Censorship vs. Obscenity. *Media Report to Women* 18, No. 4 (July-August 1990):1-2

Who Watches the Watchwomen?: Feminists Against Censorship. Gillian Rodgerson and Linda Semple. *Feminist Review* No. 36 (Autumn 1990):19-28

X Rated: When Hardcore Hits Home. Nancy Shulins. *Family Circle* 103, No. 16 (November 27, 1990):63-69

**Census**

Sabotaging Their Statistics. Marilyn Waring. *Ms.* 1, No. 1 (July/August 1990):82-83

**Center for Media and Public Affairs**

News Coverage of Abortion Gives More Exposure to Pro-Choicers, Study Says. *Media Report to Women* 18, No. 1 (January/February 1990):1

**Center for Women Policy Studies**

The SAT Gender Gap. Excerpt. Leslie R. Wolfe and Phyllis Rosser. *Women & Language* 13, No. 2 (Winter 1990):2-10

**Central Park Jogger** *See* Central Park (New York, N.Y.) – Crime

**Central Park (New York, N.Y.) – Crime**

The Long Road Back. Ellie Grossman. *Ladies' Home Journal* 107, No. 4 (April 1990):160-161+

**Centro de Investigacion para la Accion Femenina**

The Experience of CIPAF in Documentation. Teresa Peralta. *Women's World* 23 (April 1990):21-22

**Cerebral Dominance**

Are You a Right-or Left-Brained Lover? Priscilla Donovan. *Redbook* 175, No. 3 (July 1990):84-87

**Cervantes, Lorna Dee**

The Levee: Letter to No One. Poem. *Frontiers* 11, No. 1 (1990):21

Pleiades from the Cables of Genocide. Poem. *Frontiers* 11, No. 1 (1990):22-23

**Cervical Cancer**

Can Beta-carotene Affect Cervical Abnormalities? – Interview with Dorothy Mackerras. Jo Calluy. *Healthright* 9, No. 2 (February 1990):31-33

Cervical Cancer and Smoking. Alison Dickie. *Healthsharing* 11, No. 3 (June 1990):9

Pap Tests: Can You Trust Them? Peter Jaret. *Glamour* (November 1990):68-75

**Cervical Caps.** *See* Contraception

**Chabrol, Claude** (director)

A Story of Women. Reviewed by Marina Heung. *New Directions for Women* 19, No. 3 (May/June 1990):7

**Chace, James**

The New Concert of Europe. *Lear's* (February 1990):99-101

**Chace, Susan**

Woman of Ideas: Hazel Henderson. *Lear's* (June 1990):98-101+

**Chadwick, Whitney**

Women, Art, and Power and Other Essays. Book Review. *Woman's Art Journal* 11, No. 2 (Fall 1990-Winter 1991):37-38

Women, Art, and Society. Reviewed by Scarlet Cheng. *Belles Lettres* 5, No. 4 (Summer 1990):5-6

**Chaikin, Don**

Fantasy or Function: Getting the Car You Want. *Essence* 21, No. 7 (November 1990):96-102

The New Family Car. *Essence* 21, No. 4 (August 1990):100

**Chaillot, Nicole** and Chevaillier, Dominique

L'épouse de LEUR pe4re: Marâtres mode d'emploi. Reviewed by Francine Descarries. *Resources for Feminist Research* 19, No. 2 (June 1990):41

**Chalmer, Judith**

Judith Uncovers Susanna. Poem. *Bridges* 1, No. 2 (Fall 1990): 24

Stone Bubbles. Poem. *Atlantis* 15, No. 2 (Spring 1990):80

**Chamberlain, Mariam K.** (editor)

Women in Academe: Progress and Prospects. Reviewed by M. Jane Ayer. *Feminist Collections* 11, No. 3 (Spring 1990):3-4

Women in Academe: Progress and Prospects. Reviewed by Therese L. Baker. *Gender and Society* 4, No. 2 (June 1990):277-281

**Chamberlayne, Prue**

The Mothers' Manifesto and Disputes over 'Mütterlichkeit.' *Feminist Review* No. 35 (Summer 1990):9-23

**Chambers, Veronica** (about). *See* College Students – Leadership

**Chambers-Shiller, Lee**

Sunday School: The Formation of an American Institution, 1790-1880. Book Review. *Gender & History* 2, No. 2 (Summer 1990):235-236

**Chambre, Susan Maizel**

All Work and No Play? The Sociology of Women and Leisure. Book Review. *Gender and Society* 4, No. 2 (June 1990):281-283

**Chamorro, Violeta** (about)

Flowers for Violeta. Dennis Covington. *Vogue* (August 1990):318-323+

Sweet Victory. Anne Arrarte. *Ladies' Home Journal* 107, No. 7 (July 1990):44-47

**Chamratrithirong, A.** (joint author). *See* Phillips, James F.

**Chan, Shirley**

How Pay Equity May Narrow the Salary Gap. *Working Woman* (January 1990):107

How to Rid Your Company of VDT Health Hazards. *Working Woman* (March 1990):52

**Chan, Shirley** and others

Where the Scares Are: 8 Risky Businesses. *Working Woman* (February 1990):81

**Chandler, Marilyn**

Lives of Quiet Desperation. *The Women's Review of Books* 7, Nos. 10-11 (July 1990):27

Words of Farewell: Stories by Korean Women Writers. Book Review. *The Women's Review of Books* 7, Nos. 10-11 (July 1990):27

**Chandrasekar, R.** (joint author). *See* Khan, M. E.

**Chanel, Coco** (about). *See also* Fashion Designers; Lagerfeld, Karl (about)

**Chaney, Elsa** and Lundhoff, Catherine

Latinas of the Americas: A Source Book. Book Review. *Journal of Women's History* 2, No. 1 (Spring 1990):220-226

Latin Women of the Americas. *Journal of Women's History* 2, No. 1 (Spring 1990):220-226

**Chaney, Elsa M.** and Castro, Mary Garcia (editors)

Muchachas No More: Household Workers in Latin America and the Caribbean. Reviewed by Diana Brandi. *Women's Studies International Forum* 13, No. 5 (1990):520

Muchachas No More: Household Workers in Latin America and the Caribbean. Reviewed by Diana Decker. *off our backs* 20, No. 5 (May 1990):23

**Chaney, Elsa M.** and Castro, Mary Gracia (editors)

Muchachas No More: Household Workers in Latin America and the Caribbean. Reviewed by Judith Rollins. *Gender and Society* 4, No. 3 (September 1990):423-425

**Chaney, Elsa M.** (joint author). *See* Bunster, Ximena

**Chang, Diana**

In Two. Poem. *Ms.* 1, No. 1 (July/August 1990):83

**Chang, Kyung-Sup**

Socialist Institutions and Wealth Flow Reversal: An Assessment of Post-Revolutionary Chinese Rural Fertility. *Journal of Family History* 15, No. 2 (April 1990):179-200

**Chanteuses**. *See* Singers

**Chapkis, Wendy**

Beauty Secrets: Women and the Politics of Appearance. Reviewed by Ruth P. Rubinstein. *Gender and Society* 4, No. 1 (March 1990):110-111

Boomer: Railroad Memoirs. Book Review. *The Women's Review of Books* 7, No. 7 (April 1990):6-7

Staying on Track. *The Women's Review of Books* 7, No. 7 (April 1990):6-7

**Chaplin, Jocelyn**

Feminist Counselling in Action. Reviewed by Karen A. Holmes. *AFFILIA* 5, No. 1 (Spring 1990):104-106

Feminist Counselling in Action. Reviewed by Nancy Guberman and Miche4le Bourgon. *Resources for Feminist Research* 19, No. 1 (March 1990):12

**Chapman, Tracy** (about). *See* Musicians, Popular, "Repeat Performance"

**Charities**

Burden of the Nouveaux Riches. Lewis H. Lapham. *Lear's* (May 1990):76-81+

People Who Make a Difference: Christmas Angels. *Family Circle* 103, No. 17 (December 18, 1990):17-20

**Charity Balls**. *See also* Society Balls

Causes and Effects. *Harper's Bazaar* (February 1990):191-193

Christmas Stars. *Harper's Bazaar* (December 1990):173+

Cool Million. *Harper's Bazaar* (July 1990):118

Film Fanciers. *Harper's Bazaar* (May 1990):166

Foreign Affair. *Harper's Bazaar* (September 1990):320

Garden Gala. *Harper's Bazaar* (March 1990):244

Greener Pastures. *Harper's Bazaar* (October 1990):239

Pavarotti Plus. *Harper's Bazaar* (June 1990):142

Talking Parties. Edited by Gabé Doppelt. *Vogue* (December 1990):329-331

**Charleston – Hurricane Hugo, 1989**

Charleston: Coming Through the Hurricane. Sandra Rhodes. *Ladies' Home Journal* 107, No. 1 (January 1990):16-20

**Charlton, Janet**

Dress Harder: Hollywood's Best and Worst Threads. *Mademoiselle* (December 1990):156-157+

**Charlton, Sue Ellen**

The Elusive Promise: The Struggle of Women Development Workers in Rural North India. Book review. *Signs* 15, No. 4 (Summer 1990):860-864

The Invisible Resource: Women and Work in Rural Bangladesh. Book review. *Signs* 15, No. 4 (Summer 1990):860-864

Rural Women and State Policy: Feminist Perspectives on Latin American Agricultural Development. Book review. *Signs* 15, No. 4 (Summer 1990):860-864

**Charm**

What Makes a Woman Charming? Judith Viorst. *Redbook* 176, No. 1 (November 1990):84-87

**Charnes, Ximena** and Weinstein, Soledad

Health Networking Programme. *Women's World* 23 (April 1990):27-28

**Chartier, Roger** (editor)

A History of Private Life, Vol. III: Passions of the Renaissance. Reviewed by Elizabeth C. Goldsmith. *The Women's Review of Books* 7, No. 9 (June 1990):24-25

**Chase, Naomi Feigelson**

Susana: The Myth of the "Saved" Child. *On the Issues* 16 (Fall 1990):10-15 +

**Chase Manhattan Bank – Discrimination**

Chase Accused of Harassment, and Racism. Andrea Mitchell. *New Directions for Women* 19, No. 1 (January/February 1990):metro4

**Chasnoff, Debra**

Editorial: Let's Get National. *Out/Look* No. 10 (Fall 1990):3-5

Get That Condom on Your Loogboub. *Out/Look* No. 7 (Winter 1990):62-64

**Chasnoff, Debra** (editor)

Coming Out: Out/Look Readers Tell Their Tales. *Out/Look* No. 10 (Fall 1990):19-24

**Chateauvert, Melinda**

Marching Together: Women of the Brotherhood of Sleeping Car Porters. *NWSA Journal* 2, No. 4 (Autumn 1990):687-689

**Chatiliez, Etienne**

Tatie Danielle. Reviewed by Carrie Tarr. *Spare Rib* 219 (December 1990-January 1991):28-29

**Chatterjee, Debjani** and Islam, Rashida (editors)

Barbed Lines. Reviewed by Tanika Gupta. *Spare Rib* 218 (November 1990):26

**Chatterjee, Indrani**

Refracted Reality: The 1935 Calcutta Police Survey of Prostitutes. Notes. Bibliography. *Manushi* 57 (March-April 1990):26-36

**Chatterji, P. C.**

Women in Indian Broadcasting. *Manushi* 61 (November-December 1990):33-36

**Chatters, Linda M.** (joint author). *See* Taylor, Robert Joseph

**Chaturvedi, S. K.** (joint author). *See* Benara, S. K.

**Chaudhuri, Nupur** and Strobel, Margaret

Western Women and Imperialism: Introduction. *Women's Studies International Forum* 13, No. 4 (1990):289-293

**Chavda, Jagdish J.**

The Narrative Paintings of India's Jitwarpuri Women. *Woman's Art Journal* 11, No. 1 (Spring-Summer 1990):26-28

**Chavez, Leigh Anne**

Beyond Conception: The New Politics of Reproduction. Book Review. *NWSA Journal* 2, No. 4 (Autumn 1990):652-656

Birth Power: The Case for Surrogacy. Book Review. *NWSA Journal* 2, No. 4 (Autumn 1990):652-656

In Vitro Fertilization: Building Policy from Laboratories to Legislatures. Book Review. *NWSA Journal* 2, No. 4 (Autumn 1990):652-656

**Cheatham, Nonna**

1989 DACOWITS Meetings. *Minerva* 8, No. 1 (Spring 1990):1-9

**Checkley, Gillian**

Talking to Teenagers. *Healthright* 9, No. 4 (August 1990):25-27

**Cheese**

Food and Health Bulletin: Good News for Cheese Lovers. *Glamour* (April 1990):314

Food Notes. *Vogue* (January 1990):126

Say "Cheese" for Great Eating. Holly Sheppard. *McCall's* 117, No. 9 (June 1990):119

**Chefs**

City Fare. Carla Carlisle. *Harper's Bazaar* (November 1990):204

Contemporary Living: Can They Cook! Valerie Vaz. *Essence* 21, No. 7 (November 1990):87-90

Cook Like a Pro: Hail to the Chef. *Family Circle* 103, No. 14 (October 16, 1990):66-68

Flour Power. Pamela Abramson. *Ladies' Home Journal* 107, No. 9 (September 1990):52-56

Upper Crusts. Christopher Petkanas. *Harper's Bazaar* (July 1990):113 +

Women Chefs' Hall of Fame. Jan Turner Hazard. *Ladies' Home Journal* 107, No. 11 (November 1990):246-254

**Chemical Industry.** *See also* Morrisonville (Louisiana) – Dow Chemical Company

**Chen, Joan** (about)

Chensation. *Harper's Bazaar* (December 1990):156-157 +

Twin Peaks' Joan Chen: Success Came American-Style. Bonnie Siegler. *McCall's* 118, No. 1 (October 1990):34

View: Joan Chen. Julia Reed. *Vogue* (September 1990):214-218

**Cheney, Ednah Dow Littlehale** (about). *See* Suffrage Movements

**Cheney, Jim**

"The Waters of Separation": Myth and Ritual in Annie Dillard's *Pilgrim at Tinker Creek*. *Journal of Feminist Studies in Religion* 6, No. 1 (Spring 1990):41-63

**Cheng, Scarlet**

After Egypt. Book Review. *Belles Lettres* 6, No. 1 (Fall 1990):50

The Asian Presence. *Belles Lettres* 6, No. 1 (Fall 1990):21-22

Between Worlds: Women Writers of Chinese Ancestry. Book Review. *Belles Lettres* 6, No. 1 (Fall 1990):21-22

Biography as Literary Exercise. *Belles Lettres* 6, No. 1 (Fall 1990):50

Fifth Chinese Daughter. Book Review. *Belles Lettres* 6, No. 1 (Fall 1990):21-22

Gene3t: A Biography of Janet Flanner. Book Review. *Belles Lettres* 5, No. 3 (Spring 1990):8

Living a Life Apart. *Belles Lettres* 5, No. 3 (Spring 1990):6

Morning Breeze. Book Review. *Belles Lettres* 5, No. 2 (Winter 1990):9

The Other Side. Book Review. *Belles Lettres* 5, No. 3 (Spring 1990):5

Reflections in a Jaundiced Eye. Book Review. *Belles Lettres* 5, No. 2 (Winter 1990):9

The Road from Coorain. Book Review. *Belles Lettres* 5, No. 2 (Winter 1990):2

A Studio of One's Own. *Belles Lettres* 5, No. 4 (Summer 1990):5-6

The Weight of That Enormous Sky: Coming of Age in Australia. *Belles Lettres* 5, No. 2 (Winter 1990):2

Women, Art, and Society. Book Review. *Belles Lettres* 5, No. 4 (Summer 1990):5-6

**Cher** (about)

Cher Madness. Paul Rudnick. *Vogue* (December 1990):282-289

Cher the Unstoppable. Cliff Jahr. *Ladies' Home Journal* 107, No. 11 (November 1990):197+

**Cherian, Varghese I.**

Family Size and Academic Achievement of Children. *Journal of Family Welfare* 36, No. 4 (December 1990):56-60

**Chernesky, Roslyn H.**. *See also* Meyer, Carol and Young, Alma (editors), "On the Bias."

**Chernin, Kim** and Stendhal, Renate

Sex and Other Sacred Games: Love, Desire, Power and Possession. Reviewed by Shana Penn. *The Women's Review of Books* 7, No. 6 (March 1990):28-29

**Cherry, Kelly**

The Language of Bees. Short story. *McCall's* 117, No. 12 (September 1990):132-135+

**Cherry, Kittredge**

Womansword: What Japanese Words Say about Women. Reviewed by Mary Ellen S. Capek. *NWSA Journal* 2, No. 3 (Summer 1990):476-484

**Chesanow, Neil**

Men & Romance. *Glamour* (February 1990):166-167+

**Chesler, Phyllis**

About Men. Reviewed by Beverly Lowy. *On the Issues* 14 (1990):25

Mother-Hatred and Mother-Blaming: What Electra Did to Clytemnestra. *Women and Therapy* 10, Nos. 1/2 (1990):71-81

Sacred Bond. *Spare Rib* No. 210 (March 1990):56-58

Women and Madness. Reviewed by Beverly Lowy. *On the Issues* 14 (1990):25

**Chesler, Phyllis** and Roth, Joan

A Song So Brave. *On the Issues* 15 (Summer 1990):19

**Chester, Laverne** (about). *See* Dent, David

**Chesterman, Colleen**

Blue, White and Pink Collar Workers in Australia: Technicians, Bank Employees and Flight Attendants. Book Review. *Australian Feminist Studies* No. 11 (Autumn 1990):123-126

Managing Gender: The State, the New Middle Class and Women Workers, 1830-1930. Book Review. *Australian Feminist Studies* No. 11 (Autumn 1990):123-126

Pleasure, Power and Technology: Some Tales of Gender, Engineering and the Cooperative Workplace. Book Review. *Australian Feminist Studies* No. 11 (Autumn 1990):123-126

Secretaries Talk Sexuality, Power and Work. Book Review. *Australian Feminist Studies* No. 11 (Autumn 1990):123-126

**Chevaillier, Dominique** (joint author). *See* Chaillot, Nicole

**Chevat, Richard**

The Flip Side: Looking for a Few Good Men. *Family Circle* 103, No. 9 (June 26, 1990):12

Child Sexual Abuse: Let the Children Speak. Liz Kelly and Maureen O'Hara. *Spare Rib* 217 (October 1990):44-45

Coping with Child Sexual Abuse: A Guide for Teachers. By Judith Milner and Eric Blyth. Reviewed by Liz Kelly. *Gender and Education* 2, No. 1 (1990):98-100

The Cradle Will Fall: The Tragedy of Peggy Ann Barsness. Aimee Lee Ball. *Mademoiselle* (November 1990):184-187+

Defining Child Maltreatment: Ratings of Parental Behaviors. Bruce Roscoe. *Adolescence* 25, No. 99 (Fall 1990):517-528

Domestic Violence and Sexual Abuse of Children: A Review of Research in the Eighties. Richard J. Gelles and Jon R. Conte. *Journal of Marriage and the Family* 52, No. 4 (November 1990):1045-1058

Every Mother's Nightmare. Bibliography. Elaine F. Whiteley. *Ladies' Home Journal* 107, No. 10 (October 1990):151-153+

Failure to Protect = Murder? Cecile Latham. *off our backs* 20, No. 4 (April 1990):10

The Little Boy from Tacoma. Andrea Gross. *Ladies' Home Journal* 107, No. 5 (May 1990):160+

The Little Boy Nobody Wanted. Patrick T. Murphy. *Good Housekeeping* 211, No. 4 (October 1990):135+

Lost Custody Dooms Child. Mary Lou Greenberg. *New Directions for Women* 19, No. 1 (January/February 1990):18

Males at Risk. By Frank Bolton, Larry Morris, and Ann E. McEachron. Reviewed by Sharon K. Araji. *Journal of Marriage and the Family* 52, No. 3 (August 1990):801

McMartin Preschool Case: Learning from Experience. Jennie Ruby. *off our backs* 20, No. 4 (April 1990):10-11

My Father's House. By Sylvia Fraser. Reviewed by Sandra Butler. *AFFILIA* 5, No. 1 (Spring 1990):110-112

Nobody's Child. Jane Marks. *Family Circle* 103, No. 15 (November 6, 1990):90-94

Presumed Guilty. T. M. Spencer and Jim Brosseau. *Savvy Woman* (October 1990):62-65+

The Seductive Mother. Lily Richards. *Lear's* (October 1990):86-89+

Supermom or Child Abuser? Treatment of the Munchhausen Mother. Elaine Leeder. *Women and Therapy* 9, No. 4 (1990):69-88

What Lisa Knew, The Truths and Lies of the Steinberg Case. By Joyce Johnson. Reviewed by Marjorie Lipsyte. *New Directions for Women* 19, No. 5 (September-October 1990):10+

Women Who Make a Difference. Alice Rindler Shapin. *Family Circle* 103, No. 13 (September 25, 1990):19-23

Women Who Make a Difference. Rosalind Wright. *Family Circle* 103, No. 6 (April 24, 1990):13-14+

**Child Abuse – History**

The Neglect of Female Children and Childhood Sex Ratios in Nineteenth-Century America: A Review of the Evidence. David T. Courtwright. *Journal of Family History* 15, No. 3 (July 1990):313-323

**Child Abuse – Law and Legislation**

Margaret Thatcher Delays Changes in Child Abuse Law. *Spare Rib* No. 216 (September 1990):45

**Child Abuse – Treatment**

Therapy for Adults Molested as Children: Beyond Survival. By John Briere. Reviewed by Hannah Lerman. *Psychology of Women Quarterly* 14, No. 2 (June 1990):192-194

**Childbearing Age.** *See* Middle-Aged Women – Childbirth

**Childbirth.** *See also* Birth Defects – Prevention; Middle-Aged Women – Childbirth

A Causal Model Describing the Relationship of Women's Postpartum Health to Social Support, Length of Leave, and Complications of Childbirth. Dwenda K. Gjerdingen, Debra G. Froberg, and Patricia Fontaine. *Women and Health* 16, No. 2 (1990):71-87

Childbearing after Remarriage. Howard Wineberg. *Journal of Marriage and the Family* 52, No. 1 (February 1990):31-38

Dimensions of Nurse and Patient Roles in Labor. Janet I. Beaton. *Health Care for Women International* 11, No. 4 (1990):393-408

Episiotomy Power for Nurses. Wendy Haaf. *Healthsharing* 11, No. 1 (December 1989):8

"I Couldn't Cope with Motherhood." Leah Balk. *Working Mother* (November 1990):38-43

"I Don't Know What It Is to Have a Child." *Connexions* 32 (1990):20

Instructions for the Birthing Team. Sheila Stanger. *Lilith* 15, No. 1 (Winter 1990):21-23

The Mother Myth: A Feminist Analysis of Post Partum Depression. Debbie Field. *Healthsharing* 11, No. 1 (December 1989):17-21

Out of Wedlock Childbearing in an Ante-Bellum Southern County. Susan Newcomer. *Journal of Family History* 15, No. 3 (July 1990):357-368

Preparing for Birth. By Andrea Robertson. Reviewed by Elizabeth Andrew. *Healthright* 9, No. 2 (February 1990):36

The Psychology of Childbirth. By Joyce Prince and Margaret E. Adams. Reviewed by Andrea Robertson. *Healthright* 9, No. 2 (February 1990):39

Rupture of the Membranes in Labour. *Spare Rib* No. 211 (April 1990):57

Tales from the Delivery Room. Judith Viorst. *Redbook* 174, No. 6 (April 1990):58-62

Welfare and Out-of-Wedlock Childbearing: Evidence from the 1980s. Robert D. Plotnick. *Journal of Marriage and the Family* 52, No. 3 (August 1990):735-746

The Whole Birth Catalog. Ann Ferrar. *Ladies' Home Journal* 107, No. 8 (August 1990):46-50

Women's Choice of Childbirth Setting. Marlene C. Mackey. *Health Care for Women International* 11, No. 2 (1990):175-189

**Childbirth – History**

Private Matters: American Attitudes toward Childbearing and Infant Nurture in the Urban North, 1800-1860. By Sylvia D. Hoffert. Reviewed by Rickie Solinger. *Women and Health* 16, No. 2 (1990):131-134

**Childbirth – Home Birth**

Home Birth. Pam Human. *Spare Rib* No. 209 (February 1990):57

**Childbirth, Natural**

New Active Birth: A Concise Guide to Natural Childbirth. By Janet Balaskas. Reviewed by Julia Sundin. *Healthright* 9, No. 3 (May 1990).40

**Childbirth – Postpartum Care**

A Causal Model Describing the Relationship of Women's Postpartum Health to Social Support, Length of Leave, and Complications of Childbirth. Dwenda K. Gjerdingen, Debra G. Froberg, and Patricia Fontaine. *Women and Health* 16, No. 2 (1990):71-87

**Childbirth – Postpartum Emotions**

Identification of Predictor Variables of a Postpartum Emotional Reaction. Andréa Maria Laizner and Mary Ellen Jeans. *Health Care for Women International* 11, No. 2 (1990):191-207

**Child Care.** *See also* After-School Programs; Balancing Work and Family Life; Day Care Centers; Economic Value of Women's Work; Fathers

The Best Infant Care. Harriet Webster. *Working Mother* 13, No. 7 (July 1990):68-70

Child Care – Who Cares? Does Congress Care? Lorraine Sorrel. *off our backs* 20, No. 2 (February 1990):13+

Child Care – Who Cares? Do Feminists Care? Alice Henry. *off our backs* 20, No. 2 (February 1990):12-13

Children's Cornucopia. Marge Loch-Wouters. *WLW Journal* 14, No. 1 (Fall 1990):15

Discipline in Day Care. Barbara Brenner. *Working Mother* 13, No. 5 (May 1990):76-81

The Flip Side. Bette-Jane Raphael. *Family Circle* 103, No. 2 (February 1, 1990):17

A Giant Step for Day Care at Stride Rite. Patti Watts. *Executive Female* 13, No. 4 (July-August 1990):9+

Managing School-Day Mornings. Bibliography. *McCall's* 118, No. 2 (November 1990):159-166

Mary Frances Berry on the Ideology of Child Care. *Ms.* 1, No. 3 (November/December 1990):88

The Mothers' Page: A House Full of Kids. Lisa Passey Boynton. *McCall's* 117, No. 9 (June 1990):6-8

Parental and Nonparental Child Care and Children's Socioemotional Development: A Decade in Review. Jay Belsky. *Journal of Marriage and the Family* 52, No. 4 (November 1990):884-903

"That Drives Me Crazy." Nancy Balaban. *Working Mother* (December 1990):76-81

Two to Four from 9 to 5: The Adventures of a Day Care Provider. By Joan Roemer and Barbara Austin. Reviewed by Virginia Will Sacchi. *Iris* 24 (Fall-Winter 1990):65-66

Where in the World Is Child Care Better? Vivian Cadden and Sheila Kamerman. *Working Mother* 13, No. 9 (September 1990):62-68

**Child Care – Costs**

Sharing Child Care Costs. Ellen Klavan. *Working Mother* (November 1990):52-56

**Child Care – Employer Provision**

How Employers are Helping Working Moms. James A. Levine. *Good Housekeeping* 211, No. 3 (September 1990):150+

**Child Care – Infants**

Between Friends. *Family Circle* 103, No. 7 (May 15, 1990):176-177

**Child Care – Psychological Effects**

Relations between Early Childhood Care Arrangements and College Students' Psychosocial Development and Academic Performance. Jean M. Ispa, Kathy R. Thornburg, and Mary M. Gray. *Adolescence* 25, No. 99 (Fall 1990):529-542

**Child Care – Public Policy**

Abolition of Tax on Workplace Nurseries. Veronica Fuller. *Spare Rib* No. 211 (April 1990):57

**Child Care Workers**

Mothering Others' Children: The Experiences of Family Day-Care Providers. Notes. Margaret K. Nelson. *Signs* 15, No. 3 (Spring 1990):586-605

**Child Custody.** *See also* Divorce – Custody; Lesbian Mothers

Giving Up a Baby. Amy Engeler. *Glamour* (June 1990):252-255+

The New Babysnatchers. Roberta Grant. *Redbook* 175, No. 1 (May 1990):151-154

Nobody's Child. Jane Marks. *Family Circle* 103, No. 15 (November 6, 1990):90-94

**Child Development.** *See also*
Adolescents – Psychology; Child Psychology; Infant
Development; Infants – Nutrition

Are Kids Growing Up Too Fast? Sally Wendkos
Olds and Diane E. Papalia. *Redbook* 174, No. 5
(March 1990):91-92 +

Are Your Kids Ready for Kindergarten? Kathy
Henderson. *Ladies' Home Journal* 107, No. 9
(September 1990):70-72

Developmental Psychology: Childhood and
Adolescence (2nd ed.). By David R. Shaffer. Book
Review. *Adolescence* 25, No. 100 (Winter
1990):1001

Giant Steps. T. Berry Brazelton. *Family Circle* 103,
No. 1 (January 9, 1990):72-74

How Children Learn. Leah Levinger and Jo Adler.
*Good Housekeeping* 211, No. 3 (September
1990):134 +

Kids' TV: A Report Card. Ron Givens. *Ladies' Home
Journal* 107, No. 10 (October 1990):72-74

Mother & Child. *Good Housekeeping* 211, No. 4
(October 1990):82-84

The Mothers' Page: What Do You Mean My Child's
Not Perfect? *McCall's* 117, No. 10 (July 1990):16-18

Parenting: The Middle Passage. Stephanie Stokes
Oliver. *Essence* 21, No. 1 (May 1990):186

Parenting: The Wonder Years. Joy Duckett Cain.
*Essence* 21, No. 1 (May 1990):184

Parenting: Toilet Training Without Trauma. *Essence*
20, No. 12 (April 1990):100

Parents' Journal. Mary Mohler and Margery D.
Rosen. *Ladies' Home Journal* 107, No. 5 (May
1990):138-144

The Shocking Statistics. Katherine Greene and
Richard Greene. *Redbook* 174, No. 5 (March
1990):93 +

The Tough and Tricky Stages of Childhood. Eleanor
Berman. *Working Mother* 13, No. 1 (January
1990):43-54

What's Happening to Recess? Joanne Oppenheim.
*Good Housekeeping* 211, No. 3 (September
1990):162

Why a Good Mother May Be Better than Perfect.
Anne Mollegen Smith. *McCall's* 117, No. 8 (May
1990):77

**Childfree Marriage.** *See* Childless Couples

**Child Labor**

After-School Jobs: Are They Good for Kids? Lee
Salk. *McCall's* 118, No. 1 (October 1990):102-106

Babe in Toyland. Stacey Okun. *Savvy Woman*
(October 1990):14

Child Labor Laws: What Every Parent Needs to
Know. Julia Kagan and Christina Ferrari. *McCall's*
118, No. 1 (October 1990):106

**Childless Couples.** *See also* Infertility

The Childless Executive: By Choice or By Default?
Stephani Cook. *Working Woman* (November
1990):126-129 +

Interiors: No Bundles of Joy. Jennifer Jordon.
*Essence* 21, No. 6 (October 1990):42

No Accident: The Voices of Voluntarily Childless
Women – An Essay on the Social Construction of
Fertility Choices. Anita Landa. *Women and Therapy*
10, Nos. 1/2 (1990):139-158

Pregnancy, Miscarriage and Hope. Diane Cole.
*Glamour* (January 1990):156

Sperm Story. Larry Wallberg. *Lear's* (September
1990):100-101

**Child Marriage.** *See* Marriage Age

**Child Psychology.** *See also*
Adolescents – Psychology; Child Development;
Children – Self-Esteem; Family Therapy; Learning
Motivation; Parenting; Sex Education

Are Horror Movies Too Horrible for Kids? Barbara
Smalley. *Redbook* 175, No. 6 (October 1990):36-38

Are You an Overprotective Parent? Bernice Berk
and Patricia Owen. *Good Housekeeping* 211, No. 3
(September 1990):100 +

Boost Your Child's Self-Confidence. Benjamin
Spock. *Redbook* 174, No. 6 (April 1990):32

Does Your Child Feel Second-Rate? Benjamin
Spock. *Redbook* 175, No. 1 (May 1990):38

The Early Years. T. Berry Brazelton. *Family Circle*
103, No. 15 (November 6, 1990):49-54

Father Knows Best??? Mom Knows Better. Teryl
Zarnow. *Redbook* 175, No. 2 (June 1990):112-
113 +

Fear of Fat: How Young Can It Start? Lee Salk.
*McCall's* 117, No. 11 (August 1990):65

Homework: Should Parents Help? Lee Salk.
*McCall's* 118, No. 2 (November 1990):56

How to Be a Better Parent – Set Limits! E. Kent
Hayes. *Redbook* 175, No. 4 (August 1990):78-79 +

Is Your Child Hyperactive? Stephen W. Garber,
Marianne Daniels Garber, and Robyn Freedman
Spizman. *Redbook* 175, No. 6 (October 1990):32-
35

The Management of Children with Emotional and
Behavioral Difficulties. Edited by Ved P. Varma.
Book Review. *Adolescence* 25, No. 99 (Fall
1990):755

Parenting: The Taming of the Twos. Michelle
Patrick. *Essence* 21, No. 5 (September 1990):106-
108

Parents' Journal. Mary Mohler and Margery D.
Rosen. *Ladies' Home Journal* 107, No. 2 (February
1990):52; 107, No. 4 (April 1990):82-87; 107, No.

7 (July 1990):78-80; 107, No. 8 (August 1990):70; 107, No. 9 (September 1990):86

Parents' Journal: Peace at Last! Mary Mohler and Margery D. Rosen. *Ladies' Home Journal* 107, No. 11 (November 1990):138

Pediatric Healthline. *Ladies' Home Journal* 107, No. 9 (September 1990):90

Raising Boys, Raising Girls. Lee Salk. *McCall's* 118, No. 3 (December 1990):84-86

A Survival Handbook for Moms. Paddy Yost. *Good Housekeeping* 211, No. 3 (September 1990):130+

To Tell the Truth. Maryrose Hightower-Coyle. *McCall's* 118, No. 2 (November 1990):74

Understanding Kids. Lawrence Balter. *Ladies' Home Journal* 107, No. 3 (March 1990):92; 107, No. 8 (August 1990):74; 107, No. 10 (October 1990):76; 107, No. 12 (December 1990):64

The Way We Are. Lois Wyse. *Good Housekeeping* 211, No. 3 (September 1990):314

What's the Best Advice You Can Give New Moms? Judith Viorst. *Redbook* 175, No. 1 (May 1990):40-43

What to Do When . . . Bruce J. McIntosh and Dava Sobel. *Good Housekeeping* 211, No. 3 (September 1990):132+

What to Do When a Child Won't Read. Lee Salk. *McCall's* 117, No. 7 (April 1990):31

When a Parent Plays Favorites. Lee Salk. *McCall's* 117, No. 12 (September 1990):68

Who Are the Psychological Parents? Philip S. Gutis. *McCall's* 117, No. 12 (September 1990):66-68

Who Do Our Kids Most Admire? *Good Housekeeping* 211, No. 3 (September 1990):174

**Child-Rearing Practices**. *See* Parenting

**Children**

A Break for City Kids. Sandy MacDonald. *Family Circle* 103, No. 4 (March 13, 1990):19-22

Dreams Can Come True. Anne Cassidy. *Family Circle* 103, No. 1 (January 9, 1990):10-13

Elementary Years. Dianne Hales. *Working Mother* (November 1990):130; (December 1990):72

Found: A Home for Left-Behind Kids. John E. Frook. *Family Circle* 103, No. 3 (February 20, 1990):84-88

Great Kid Pleasers. Cheri Fuller *Family Circle* 103, No. 10 (July 24, 1990):72-75

Kids and Their Grownup Friends. Eleanor Berman. *Working Mother* (November 1990):66-69

Little Grownups. Don Fleming and Sarah Wernick. *Working Mother* 13, No. 10 (October 1990):24-29

Toddlers Need Understanding. Nancy Balaban. *Working Mother* 13, No. 10 (October 1990):86-88

What Kids Say (When They Think You're Not Listening). Judith Viorst. *Redbook* 174, No. 5 (March 1990):42-45

Why Kids Need to Help. Kathy Henderson. *Working Mother* 13, No. 7 (July 1990):42-47

**Children – Accidents**

The Boy Who Beat the Odds. Edward J. Sylvester. *Ladies' Home Journal* 107, No. 1 (January 1990):94-95+

"Mommy, Please Come Get Me!" Karen Reese. *Ladies' Home Journal* 107, No. 6 (June 1990):20-22+

"Our Most Precious Gift." Bertha Burns. *Ladies' Home Journal* 107, No. 12 (December 1990):22-25

**Children – Accidents – Prevention**

Patty's Legacy. Bibliography. Karolyn Nunnalee. *Ladies' Home Journal* 107, No. 4 (April 1990):28-36

Redbook's Home Accident-Prevention Guide for Parents. Neal Ashby. *Redbook* 176, No. 2 (December 1990):83-88

**Children – Allergies**

When Children Have Allergies. Thomas J. Fischer and Marilyn Mercer. *Good Housekeeping* 211, No. 3 (September 1990):142-146

**Children – Christmas**

Christmas Presence. *Harper's Bazaar* (December 1990):126-129

**Children – Conferences**

World Summit for Children – Report from New York. Barbara Day. *Spare Rib* 218 (November 1990):46

**Children – Diseases**. *See also* Burkitt's Lymphoma; Fever; Sudden Infant Death Syndrome

Beware the New Measles Epidemic. Nancy Gagliardi. *Redbook* 175, No. 3 (July 1990):34-37

A Leap of Faith. Donna E. Boetig. *Family Circle* 103, No. 17 (December 18, 1990):116-120

Radiation Update: Danger in the Schoolyard. Paul Brodeur. *Family Circle* 103, No. 13 (September 25, 1990):61-67

A Second Chance for Seth. Laura Shapiro Kramer. *Family Circle* 103, No. 4 (March 13, 1990):114-116+

What Happened to Christopher. Laura Claverie. *Family Circle* 103, No. 7 (May 15, 1990):105-108

Young Father's Story: A Portrait of My Daughter. James Aponovich and Sheila Weller. *Redbook* 175, No. 2 (June 1990):36-40

**Children – Sports.** *See* Exercise for Children; Sports for Children

Reading, Running and Arithmetic. Kathryn M. Reith. *Women's Sports and Fitness* 12, No. 7 (October 1990):60

**Children – Television.** *See* Television Programs for Children

**Children – Videos.** *See* Videos for Children

**Children – Writings**

The Write Stuff. Susan Gordon. *Ladies' Home Journal* 107, No. 2 (February 1990):54

**Children and Pets**

My Pet Theory. Benjamin Spock. *Redbook* 175, No. 5 (September 1990):46

**Children as Actors.** *See* Barrymore, Drew (about); Gold, Tracey (about)

**Children of Alcoholic Parents.** *See also* Genetic Determinants

Father Love. Betty Winston Baye. *Essence* 21, No. 2 (June 1990):34 +

**Children of Alcoholic Parents – Treatment**

Working with Children of Alcoholics: The Practitioner's Handbook. By Bryan E. Robinson. Book Review. *Adolescence* 25, No. 100 (Winter 1990):1000

**Children of Entertainers.** *See also* Fisher, Carrie (about)

Close Connections. *Harper's Bazaar* (April 1990):61-75

Irving Berlin. Mary Ellin Barrett. *Lear's* (June 1990):84-92 +

Lucie Arnaz: The Gift of Laughter. Vicki Jo Radovsky. *Ladies' Home Journal* 107, No. 10 (October 1990):48-54

**Children of Prisoners**

Jailed Mothers Risk Losing Their Kids. Linda Roman. *New Directions for Women* 19, No. 2 (March/April 1990):3

**Children's Accidents – Prevention**

Young Father's Story: "Parents Should Be Warned." Nick Buoniconti and Linda Marsa. *Redbook* 175, No. 5 (September 1990):48-50

**Children's Films.** *See* Films for Children

**Children's Literature**

Alice to the Lighthouse: Children's Books and Radical Experiments in Art. By Juliet Dusinberre. Reviewed by Marcia Jacobson. *Signs* 15, No. 3 (Spring 1990):633-635

Children's Corner. Anne Bischoff. *Belles Lettres* 5, No. 4 (Summer 1990):14

Children's Corner. Joanne Jimason. *Belles Lettres* 5, No. 3 (Spring 1990):15

Embers: Stories for a Changing World. Edited by Ruth S. Meyers. Reviewed by Mitzi Myers. *NWSA Journal* 2, No. 2 (Spring 1990):273-281

Eve Reconceived: Religious Perspectives in Feminist Children's Literature in France. Lenore Loft. *Women's Studies International Forum* 13, No. 3 (1990):221-228

Exclusive Christmas Story Starring the Teenage Mutant Ninja Turtles. *Ladies' Home Journal* 107, No. 12 (December 1990):67-70

Gender Stereotypes in Children's Books: Their Prevalence and Influence on Cognitive and Affective Development. Sharyl Bender Peterson and Mary Alyce Lach. *Gender and Education* 2, No. 2 (1990):185-197

Green March Moons. By Mary Tallmountain. Reviewed by Mitzi Myers. *NWSA Journal* 2, No. 2 (Spring 1990):273-281

Grimms' Bad Girls and Bold Boys: The Moral and Social Vision of the Tales. By Ruth B. Bottigheimer. Reviewed by Marcia Jacobson. *Signs* 15, No. 3 (Spring 1990):633-635

New Picturebooks: Redbook Picks 10 Winners. Carol Weston. *Redbook* 176, No. 2 (December 1990):26-28

The Scaredy Cats. Short story. Meredith Graham. *Ladies' Home Journal* 107, No. 2 (February 1990):112-114

True Stories: Biographies of Women for Young Readers. Christine Jenkins. *Feminist Collections* 12, No. 1 (Fall 1990):6-9

**Children's Literature – Bibliographies**

Books for Today's Young Readers: An Annotated Bibliography of Recommended Fiction for Ages 10-14. By Jeanne Bracken and Sharon Wigutoff. Reviewed by Mitzi Myers. *NWSA Journal* 2, No. 2 (Spring 1990):273-281

**Children's Literature – Gender Roles**

Frogs and Snails and Feminist Tales: Preschool Children and Gender. By Bronwyn Davies. Reviewed by Sandra Taylor. *Australian Feminist Studies* No. 12 (Summer 1990):127-128

**Childress, James F.**

Maternal-Fetal Conflicts: When Is Intervention Justified? *Iris* 23 (Spring-Summer 1990):53-55

**Child Support**

Decision Changes Support Laws. Junior Bridge. *New Directions for Women* 19, No. 5 (September-October 1990):5

"Let's Not Forget the Children" Bibliography. Susan Speir. *Ladies' Home Journal* 107, No. 7 (July 1990):22-27

Let Them Eat Cake: Tories Pronounce on Single Parents. *Spare Rib* No. 214 (July 1990):12-13

The Regular Receipt of Child Support: A Multistep Process. James L. Peterson and Christine Winquist Nord. *Journal of Marriage and the Family* 52, No. 2 (May 1990):539-551

Socioeconomic Resources of Parents and Award of Child Support in the United States: Some Exploratory Models. Jay D. Teachman. *Journal of Marriage and the Family* 52, No. 3 (August 1990):689-699

## Chile

Teresa Wilms Montt: A Forgotten Legend. Marjorie Agosin. *Women's Studies International Forum* 13, No. 3 (1990):195-199

## Chile – Censorship

Eye of the Storm. Tim Appelo. *Savvy Woman* (January 1990):60-62, 94

## Chile – Folk Art

Killing Our Sorrows. Bibliography. Susan Schnur. *Lilith* 15, No. 3 (Summer 1990):15

## Chile – Jews – Traditions

A Precious Moment in Chile. Hilary Marcus. *Lilith* 15, No. 4 (Fall 1990):36

## Chile – Politics and Government

Elections in Chile: A Facade of Democracy. *Spare Rib* No. 209 (February 1990):22-23

Marjorie Agosin: A Woman, a Jew and a Chilean. Susan Schnur. *Lilith* 15, No. 3 (Summer 1990):12

## Chile – Prostitution

Pilot Experiences in Chile. *Women's World* , No. 24 (Winter 1990/91):27-28

## Chile – Status of Women

Chile: Since the Plebiscite. Marjorie Agosín. *Ms.* 1, No. 3 (November/December 1990):12

## China. *See also* Literature – China

## China – Actors

Chensation. *Harper's Bazaar* (December 1990):156-157+

## China – Cultural Revolution

Morning Breeze: A True Story of China's Cultural Revolution. By Fulang Lo. Reviewed by Mitzi Myers. *NWSA Journal* 2, No. 2 (Spring 1990):273-281

Morning Breeze. Reviewed by Scarlet Cheng. By Fulang Lo. *Belles Lettres* 5, No. 2 (Winter 1990):9

## China – Family Relations

Gender and Changes in Support of Parents in China: Implications of the One-Child Policy. Lucy C. Yu, Yanju Yu, and Phyllis Kernoff Mansfield. *Gender and Society* 4, No. 1 (March 1990):83-89

Love Matches and Arranged Marriages: A Chinese Replication. Xu Xiaohe and Martin King Whyte. *Journal of Marriage and the Family* 52, No. 3 (August 1990):709-722

## China – Feminism

Women's History and Feminism in China: An Update. Mary Beth Norton. *Journal of Women's History* 2, No. 2 (Fall 1990):166-167

## China – Health Care

Women's Health Care in China: American Travelers' Views. Janice Templeton Gay, Juanzetta Shew Flowers, and Kuei-Shen Tu. *Health Care for Women International* 11, No. 1 (1990):65-74

## China – History

American Women's Open Door to Chinese Women: Which Way Does It Open? Marjorie King. *Women's Studies International Forum* 13, No. 4 (1990):369-379

Opportunities for Women: The Development of Professional Women's Medicine in Canton, China, 1879-1901. Sara W. Tucker. *Women's Studies International Forum* 13, No. 4 (1990):357-368

Socialist Institutions and Wealth Flow Reversal: An Assessment of Post-Revolutionary Chinese Rural Fertility. Kyung-Sup Chang. *Journal of Family History* 15, No. 2 (April 1990):179-200

## China – Language

Nu Shu: An Ancient, Secret, Women's Language. Carolyn Lau. *Belles Lettres* 6, No. 1 (Fall 1990):32-35

Sexism in the Chinese Language. Sexist Language – China. *NWSA Journal* 2, No. 4 (Autumn 1990):635-639

## China – Personal Narratives

"Our Family Fled China." Marsha L. Wagner. *Working Mother* 13, No. 7 (July 1990):32-39

## China – Political Protest. *See also* Tibet – Political Protest

Chai Ling Talks with Robin Morgan. Robin Morgan. *Ms.* 1, No. 2 (September/October 1990):12-16

China: A Year after the Uprising. *Spare Rib* No. 212 (May 1990):40-41

## China – Political Sciences – Study and Teaching

Incorporation vs. Separation: An Assessment of Gender and Politics in the People's Republic of China. Cheryl L. Brown. *Women & Politics* 10, No. 1 (1990):59-69

## China – Population Policy

Population Policy of China and Its Impact on Family Size and Structure. Hao Cailan. *Journal of Family Welfare* 36, No. 1 (March 1990):7-21

## China – Religion

The Persistence of Female Deities in Patriarchal China. Jordon Paper. *Journal of Feminist Studies in Religion* 6, No. 1 (Spring 1990):25-40

## China – Status of Women

Chinese Women Face Increased Discrimination. Mary Erbaugh. *off our backs* 20, No. 3 (March 1990):9+

**China – Women's Studies**

NWSA Workshop: Women's Studies in China. Carol Anne Douglas. *off our backs* 20, No. 8 (August/September 1990):

**Chinchilla, Norma Stoltz**

Revolutionary Popular Feminism in Nicaragua: Articulating Class, Gender, and National Sovereignty. *Gender and Society* 4, No. 3 (September 1990):370-397

**Chinese-Americans**

Twin Peaks' Joan Chen: Success Came American-Style. Bonnie Siegler. *McCall's* 118, No. 1 (October 1990):34

**Chinese-Americans – Humor**

Asian Valley Boy: A Monologue. Patrick Lee. *Out/Look* No. 9 (Summer 1990):18-19

**Chinese Women's Federation.** *See* All-China Women's Federation

**Chinn, Peggy L.**

Man-Made Women: How New Reproductive Technologies Affect Women. Book review. *Signs* 15, No. 2 (Winter 1990):400-405

Reproductive Rights and Wrongs: The Global Politics of Population Control and Contraceptive Choice. Book review. *Signs* 15, No. 2 (Winter 1990):400-405

Reproductive Technologies: Gender, Motherhood and Medicine. Book review. *Signs* 15, No. 2 (Winter 1990):400-405

**Chinoy, Helen Krich** and Jenkins, Linda Walsh (editors)

Women in American Theatre. Reviewed by Jill Dolan. *Signs* 15, No. 4 (Summer 1990):864-869

**Chisholm, Dianne**

H.D.'s Auto*heter*ography. *Tulsa Studies in Women's Literature* 9, No. 1 (Spring 1990):79-106

**Chisholm, Shirley** (about). *See* De Veaux, Alexis, Milloy, Marilyn, and Ross, Michael Erik

**Chitgopekar, Nilima M.**

The Bitch. Poem. *Manushi* 58 (May-June 1990):36

**Chittum, Samme** and others

No Way Out. Bibliography. *Ladies' Home Journal* 107, No. 4 (April 1990):126-134

**Chiu, Lian-Hwang**

The Relationship of Career Goal And Self-Esteem among Adolescents. *Adolescence* 25, No. 99 (Fall 1990):593-597

**Chi-won, Kim** (joint author). *See* Sok-kyong, Kang

**Chiyo, Uno**

Confessions of Love. Reviewed by Cathie Brettschneider. *Belles Lettres* 5, No. 3 (Spring 1990):20

**Chlamydia.** *See* Sexually Transmitted Diseases

**Chocolate.** *See also* Cookery (Chocolate)

For the Love of Chocolate. Valerie Vaz. *Essence* 20, No. 10 (February 1990):83-; 84

Sweet Nothings. Elaine Gonzales. *Ladies' Home Journal* 107, No. 2 (February 1990):158-160

**Chodorow, Nancy J.**

Feminism and Psychoanalytic Theory. Reviewed by Deborah Anna Luepnitz. *The Women's Review of Books* 7, No. 8 (May 1990):17-18

Feminism and Psychoanalytic Theory. Reviewed by Teresa Iles. *Women's Studies International Forum* 13, No. 6 (1990):611-612

**Cholesterol.** *See also* Food – Cholesterol Content

Cholesterol. Mary Roach. *Vogue* (May 1990):300-301, 323

**Chomiak, Dora** (about). *See also* College Students – Leadership

**Chong-hui, O** (joint author). *See* Sok-kyong, Kang

**Chopra, A.** (joint author). *See* Sachar, R. K.

**Chopra, Deepak**

Perfect Health. *Mademoiselle* (August 1990):193-195

**Chorionic Villus Sampling.** *See* Fetal Monitoring

**Chou, Jane Shiyen**

Fat Right, Be Healthier, Live Longer. *McCall's* 117, No. 8 (May 1990):32

Go Ahead and Eat Cake. *McCall's* 117, No. 10 (July 1990):28-34

Nutrition/Fitness: Exercise: How Much Is Too Much? *McCall's* 117, No. 7 (April 1990):14

Safe Sex for Bad Backs. *McCall's* 117, No. 10 (July 1990):60

**Chou, Jane Shiyen** and Murphy, Wendy

The Estrogen Debate. *McCall's* 118, No. 1 (October 1990):157-158

**Chow, Rey**

The Politics and Pedagogy of Asian Literatures in American Universities. *Differences* 2, No. 3 (Fall 1990):29-51

**Chow, Tina** (about). *See* Success in Business, "Talent at Work"

**Chowdhury, Maya** (joint author). *See* Seneviratne, Seni

**Chrisler, Joan C.**

Women of Academe: Outsiders in the Sacred Grove. Book Review. *Feminist Teacher* 5, No. 2 (Fall 1990):37

**Chrisler, Joan C.** and Levy, Karen B.

The Media Construct a Menstrual Monster: A Content Analysis of PMS Articles in the Popular Press. *Women and Health* 16, No. 2 (1990):89-104

**Chrisman, Catherine (Bell)**

My War: WWII – As Experienced by One Woman
Soldier. Reviewed by Eleanor Stoddard. *Minerva* 8,
No. 4 (Winter 1990):48-53

**Christensen, Caren** (about). *See* Entrepreneurs

**Christensen, H.** (joint author). *See* Nygaard, E.

**Christensen, Kathleen E.** (editor)

The New Era of Home-Based Work. Reviewed by
Robin Leidner. *Gender and Society* 4, No. 2 (June
1990):262-265

**Christian, Barbara,** DuCille, Ann, Marcus, Sharon,
Marks, Elaine, Miller, Nancy K., and others

Conference Call. *Differences* 2, No. 3 (Fall
1990):52-108

**Christian Fundamentalism**

Spiritual Warfare: The Politics of the Christian
Right. By Sara Diamond. Reviewed by Ann Baker.
*New Directions for Women* 19, No. 1
(January/February 1990):25

**Christian Fundamentalism in Literature**

Unnatural Passions. *Spare Rib* No. 209 (February
1990):26-29

**Christianity – Feminist Perspectives**

Keeping the Faith: Questions and Answers for the
Abused Woman. By Marie M. Fortune. Reviewed
by Deborah L. Humphreys. *AFFILIA* 5, No. 2
(Summer 1990):109-111

**Christianity – History**

Adam, Eve, and the Serpent. By Elaine Pagels.
Reviewed by Michael B. Schwarz. *Out/Look* No. 7
(Winter 1990):76-81

Adam, Eve and the Serpent. By Elaine Pagels.
Reviewed by Elizabeth A. Clark. *Gender & History*
2, No. 1 (Spring 1990):106-109

The Body and Society: Men, Women, and Sexual
Renunciation in Early Christianity. By Peter Brown.
Reviewed by Michael B. Schwarz. *Out/Look* No. 7
(Winter 1990):76-81

The Body and Society: Men, Women and Sexual
Renunciation in Early Christianity. By Peter Brown.
Reviewed by Elizabeth A. Clark. *Gender & History*
2, No. 1 (Spring 1990):106-109

Law, Sex, and Christian Society in Medieval Europe.
By James A. Brundage. Reviewed by Michael B.
Schwarz. *Out/Look* No. 7 (Winter 1990):76-81

Patrons, Not Priests: Gender and Power in Late
Ancient Christianity. Elizabeth A. Clark. *Gender &
History* 2, No. 3 (Autumn 1990):253-273

Women Partners in the New Testament. Mary Rose
D'Angelo. *Journal of Feminist Studies in Religion* 6,
No. 1 (Spring 1990):65-86

**Christianity – Status of Women**

Jessica Hahn's Strange Odyssey from PTL to
Playboy. Mary Zeiss Stange. *Journal of Feminist
Studies in Religion* 6, No. 1 (Spring 1990):105-116

The Questions That Won't Go Away: A Dialogue
about Women in Buddhism and Christianity. Rita
Nakashima Brock, Paula J. Cooey, Sheila Greeve
Davaney, Rita M. Gross, Anne C. Klein, and others.
*Journal of Feminist Studies in Religion* 6, No. 2 (Fall
1990)87-120

**Christian Names.** *See* Names, Personal

**Christiansen-Ruffman, Linda**

Feminist Organizing for Change: The
Contemporary Women's Movement in Canada.
Book Review. *Women's Studies International Forum*
13, Nos. 1-2 (1990):163-165

Women and Counter-Power. Book Review.
*Resources for Feminist Research* 19, No. 1 (March
1990):39-40

**Christie, Tom**

Woman of Character. *Vogue* (April 1990):394-398,
421

**Christmas**

A Child Is Born. Michael L. Lindvall. *Good
Housekeeping* 211, No. 6 (December 1990):116-
118

Christmas 1990: A Message from the President.
George Bush. *Ladies' Home Journal* 107, No. 12
(December 1990):129-131

The Christmas Conspiracy. Vera Current Thummel.
*Good Housekeeping* 211, No. 6 (December
1990):75 +

The Christmas Eve Caper. Nancy Dillon. *Good
Housekeeping* 211, No. 6 (December 1990):70-
71 +

A Country Christmas. *Redbook* 176, No. 2
(December 1990):121-126 +

The Day the World Changed. Camilla R. Bittle.
*Good Housekeeping* 211, No. 6 (December
1990):22-27

Holiday Tables. *Good Housekeeping* 211, No. 6
(December 1990):148-151

One Magic Christmas. *Family Circle* 103, No. 17
(December 18, 1990):94-103

People Who Make a Difference: Christmas Angels.
*Family Circle* 103, No. 17 (December 18, 1990):17-
20

A Royal Christmas. Andrew Morton. *Good
Housekeeping* 211, No. 6 (December 1990):140 +

Wonderful Family Traditions. Ellen Byron. *Redbook*
176, No. 2 (December 1990):98-99 +

**Christmas – Parties**

Hot Shots. Lois Joy Johnson. *Ladies' Home Journal*
107, No. 12 (December 1990):152-156

Nutrinews. *Ladies' Home Journal* 107, No. 12
(December 1990):198

**Christmas – Personal Narratives**

A Very Special Gift. Marilyn Milloy. *Essence* 21, No. 8 (December 1990):62-64+

**Christmas Cookery**

Christmas Means Cookies. Jan Turner Hazard. *Ladies' Home Journal* 107, No. 12 (December 1990):162+

Classic Holiday Cookies. *Redbook* 176, No. 2 (December 1990):131-140

Fine Art Cookies. Sarah Reynolds. *McCall's* 118, No. 3 (December 1990):98-100+

Food Forecast. Jean Hewitt. *Family Circle* 103, No. 17 (December 18, 1990):83

Gifts Sweet & Sour. Barbara Kafka. *Family Circle* 103, No. 17 (December 18, 1990):199-200

Holiday Parties Cookbook. Marianne Langan. *McCall's* 118, No. 3 (December 1990):103-124

Home for the Holidays. *Ladies' Home Journal* 107, No. 12 (December 1990):184-197

Santa's Favorites. *Family Circle* 103, No. 16 (November 27, 1990):90-91

**Christmas Decorations.** *See also* New England States – Christmas Decorations

Fun for All. *Redbook* 176, No. 2 (December 1990):100-101

Holiday Love. *Harper's Bazaar* (December 1990):120-123+

Home for the Holidays. *Glamour* (December 1990):235-241

Living: Christmas in the Country. Edited by Laurie Schechter. *Vogue* (December 1990):241-245

Make It Merry! *Redbook* 176, No. 2 (December 1990):92-97

Make Yours a Holiday Home. *Family Circle* 103, No. 16 (November 27, 1990):84-89

Natural Wonders. *Redbook* 176, No. 2 (December 1990):114-115

Small Treasures. *Redbook* 176, No. 2 (December 1990):108-109

Star Light, Star Bright. *Family Circle* 103, No. 17 (December 18, 1990):110-115

Storybook Christmas Houses. Marianne Langan. *McCall's* 118, No. 3 (December 1990):90-93

Treasure Chests. Colette Peters. *Ladies' Home Journal* 107, No. 12 (December 1990):160+

**Christmas Gifts.** *See also* Children's Literature; Holidays – Etiquette; Perfumes

Afrocentric Gifts. Kimberly Knight. *Essence* 21, No. 8 (December 1990):90

Ardent Spouse in Search of the Perfect Gift. . .Hugh O'Neill. *McCall's* 118, No. 3 (December 1990):46-48

Beauty Clips. Shirley Lord. *Vogue* (December 1990):146

Beauty & Fashion Journal. *Ladies' Home Journal* 107, No. 12 (December 1990):29-32

Best for Kids: Gifts Galore that Kids will Adore. Burt Hochberg. *Redbook* 176, No. 2 (December 1990):22-24

Boyfriends and Gifts: Present Tense. Ellen Welty. *Mademoiselle* (December 1990):116

Couple Time. *Glamour* (December 1990):126

The Early Years. T. Berry Brazelton. *Family Circle* 103, No. 17 (December 18, 1990):84-87

Easy-Do Gifts. *Family Circle* 103, No. 16 (November 27, 1990):92-93

Eat Light: Fabulous Mail-Order Finds. *Redbook* 176, No. 2 (December 1990):150

The Flip Side: Some Assembly Required. John Leo. *Family Circle* 103, No. 17 (December 18, 1990):43-47

Food: The Best of Everything. Jeffrey Steingarten. *Vogue* (December 1990):230-238

Glamour Guide. *Glamour* (December 1990):85-92

Holiday Gift Guide. Bibliography. *Mademoiselle* (December 1990):62-66

Last Minute Gifts, Decorations, Food. *Family Circle* 103, No. 17 (December 18, 1990):104-108

More for Your Money. Barbara Gilder Quint. *Glamour* (December 1990):118-121

Objects of Desire. *Harper's Bazaar* (December 1990):59-78

Our Annual 55 Great Gifts to Make. *Family Circle* 103, No. 15 (November 6, 1990):70-77

Parents' Journal: 10 Great Gifts for Under $10! Bibliography. Mary Mohler and Margery D. Rosen. *Ladies' Home Journal* 107, No. 12 (December 1990):60-64

75 Great Ways to Sail Through the Season. *Family Circle* 103, No. 17 (December 18, 1990):145-149

Shopping Smart: Bargain Gifts by Mail. Joan Hamburg. *Family Circle* 103, No. 15 (November 6, 1990):40-43

This Year I Want. . .*Glamour* (December 1990):202-207

The True Spirit of Christmas. Pamela Redmond Satran. *Glamour* (December 1990):228-231+

20 Delicious Gifts from Your Kitchen. *Redbook* 176, No. 1 (November 1990):139-154

25 Gifts Under $25. *Family Circle* 103, No. 17 (December 18, 1990):141-142

Vogue Arts: Christmas Gift Books. John Heilpern. *Vogue* (December 1990):208-210

Waste Not! *Redbook* 176, No. 1 (November 1990):34-36

Wrap it Up! *Family Circle* 103, No. 17 (December 18, 1990):156-160

**Christmas Letters**

Christmas Presence. *Harper's Bazaar* (December 1990):126-129

Full Circle: God Bless Us Everyone! Anna Quindlen. *Family Circle* 103, No. 17 (December 18, 1990):208

"Give from the Heart": A Letter from Bill Cosby. Bill Cosby. *Redbook* 176, No. 2 (December 1990):91

Not Home for the Holidays. *Family Circle* 103, No. 17 (December 18, 1990):88-90

**Christmas Parties**

Maestros of Mood. *Harper's Bazaar* (December 1990):176+

**Christmas Trees**

Traditions: O Christmas Tree. Mary Ann Johanson. *McCall's* 118, No. 3 (December 1990):31

**Christmon, Kenneth**

Parental Responsibility of African-American Unwed Adolescent Fathers.

*Adolescence* 25, No. 99 (Fall 1990):645-653

**Christopher, Frank** (director)

The Lemon Grove Incident. Reviewed by C. Alejandra Elenes. *Feminist Collections* 11, No. 3 (Spring 1990):9-10

**Christy, Carol A.**

Sex Differences in Political Participation: Processes of Change in Fourteen Nations. Reviewed by Sue Thomas. *Women & Politics* 10, No. 1 (1990):76-78

**Chronnell, Angela**

Working Towards Equal Opportunity – A Learning Experience. *Gender and Education* 2, No. 3 (1990):345-349

**Chronobiology**

When the Clock Strikes 98.6 – Relax! Carol Orlock. *Lear's* (September 1990):51-55

**Chrystos**

Savage Eloquence. Poem. *Woman of Power* 16 (Spring 1990):inside back cover

**Chudamani, R.**

Bunch of Keys. Short Story. *Manushi* 60 (September-October 1990):39-43

**Chung, Connie** (about). *See also* Television Journalists – Networking

Out Box: Chung's Choice. Gail Collins. *Working Woman* (December 1990):110

Tell Us What You Think: Connie Chung: Has She Made Life Tougher or Easier for Working Mothers? *Glamour* (November 1990):150

**Church, Beverly Reese** (about)

That's Entertainment! Diane Sustendal. *Harper's Bazaar* (January 1990):133+

**Church, Norris** (about)

Art and Leisure: Good Talk. John McLaughlin. *Harper's Bazaar* (February 1990):144-145+

**Church and State**

Polling America: Church vs. State. Ernie Anastos. *Family Circle* 103, No. 16 (November 27, 1990):20

**Chutkow, Paul**

Deciphering Depardieu. *Vogue* (December 1990):294-299+

**Ciabattari, Jane**

Nancy Kassebaum: Heartland Independent. *McCall's* 117, No. 9 (June 1990):68

Our Parents Growing Older. *McCall's* 118, No. 2 (November 1990):81-88+

**Cigarettes.** *See* Smoking

**Cihak, Beatrice**

No-Cook Summer Suppers. *Family Circle* 103, No. 9 (June 26, 1990):145-150

Super-Quick Family Meals. *Family Circle* 103, No. 14 (October 16, 1990):145-150

**Cimons, Marlene**

I Tested HIV-Positive. *Essence* 20, No. 12 (April 1990):72-75

Surviving Sniffle Season. *Working Mother* (December 1990):64-66

**Cinader, Emily** (about). *See* Title, Stacy

She's Got the Look. Tim Appelo. *Savvy Woman* (January 1990):48-51, 88-91

**Cipriani, Giovana** (about)

Stunning Success. Janet Bailey. *Harper's Bazaar* (October 1990):174-175+

**Cisneros, Sandra**

Only Daughter. *Glamour* (November 1990):256+

**Citizenship**

Citizenship in a Woman-Friendly Polity. Notes. Kathleen B. Jones. *Signs* 15, No. 4 (Summer 1990):781-812

City and Town Life. *See* Urban Living

Civil Defense. *See* Disaster Relief

Civil RICO. *See* Abortion–Opposition

Civil Rights. *See also* Allred, Gloria (about); Davis, Angela Y. (about)

Do Not Let the Bailiffs in! *Spare Rib* 217 (October 1990):46

Remaking the Tools: Re-Visioning Rights. Debbie Ratterman. *off our backs* 20, No. 9 (October 1990):12-13

### Civil Rights–History

The Significance of the Nineteenth Amendment: A New Look at Civil Rights, Social Welfare, and Woman Suffrage Alignments in the Progressive Era. Eileen Lorenzi McDonagh. *Women & Politics* 10, No. 2 (1990):59-94

### Civil Rights Movement

Even Mississippi. By Melany Neilson. Reviewed by Shelley Crisp. *Belles Lettres* 5, No. 2 (Winter 1990):3

Lion in the Lobby: Clarence Mitchell, Jr.'s Struggle for the Passage of Civil Rights Laws. By Denton Watson. Reviewed by Paula Giddings. *Essence* 21, No. 7 (November 1990):50

A Tribute to Rosa Parks–Mother of the Civil Rights Movement. Storme Webber. *Spare Rib* 219 (December 1990 January 1991):68

### Civil Service Workers. *See also*

Bureaucracy–Management Styles; Public Administration

Gender, Bureaucracy and Democracy: Careers and Equal Opportunity in the Public Sector. Edited by Mary M. Hale and Rita Mae Kelly. Reviewed by Ronald J. Burke. *Atlantis* 15, No. 2 (Spring 1990):116-117

How Elite Is Elite?: Women in the Civil Services. *Manushi* 56 (January-February 1990):18-21

Ladies and Gentlemen of the Civil Service: Middle Class Workers in Victorian America. By Cindy Aron. Reviewed by Carole Elizabeth Adams. *Gender & History* 2, No. 3 (Autumn 1990):343-348

Civil War. *See* United States–History–Civil War, 1861-1865

Heaviness in the Air. Susan Koppelman. *Belles Lettres* 5, No. 4 (Summer 1990):41

### Clare, Elizabeth

Friends, Lovers and Passion. *Sinister Wisdom* 40 (Spring 1990):96-98

Clark, Ann (joint author). *See* Dressel, Paul L.

### Clark, Carol A. M.

A Course on Women in the Economy. *Women's Studies Quarterly* 18, Nos. 3-4 (Fall-Winter 1990):33-41

### Clark, Elizabeth A.

Adam, Eve and the Serpent. Book Review. *Gender & History* 2, No. 1 (Spring 1990):106-109

The Body and Society: Men, Women and Sexual Renunciation in Early Christianity. Book Review. *Gender & History* 2, No. 1 (Spring 1990):106-109

Patrons, Not Priests: Gender and Power in Late Ancient Christianity. *Gender & History* 2, No. 3 (Autumn 1990):253-273

Clark, Kay (joint editor). *See* Quackenbush, Marcia

### Clark, Laura

What Causes Bad Breath? *Good Housekeeping* 211, No. 4 (October 1990):248

### Clark, Michele

Don't Blame Mother: Mending the Mother-Daughter Relationship. Book Review. *Women and Therapy* 9, No. 4 (1990):112-114

Homeland and Other Stories. Book Review. *The Women's Review of Books* 7, No. 4 (January 1990):13

No Shuttle to Central Vermont. Short Story. *Bridges* 1, No. 2 (Fall 1990): 15-21

In the World of Love and Ritual. *The Women's Review of Books* 7, No. 4 (January 1990):13

### Clark, Sally

Silver Plate Grabs the Spotlight. *McCall's* 117, No. 9 (June 1990):55

A Timesaver Kitchen. *McCall's* 117, No. 9 (June 1990):103-111

Clark, Septima (about). *See also* Black History

### Clark, Shauna and Nelson, Sara

Young Mother's Story: "My Boss Ordered Me to Sleep with Him." *Redbook* 174, No. 6 (April 1990):64-67

Clark, Steven M. (joint author). *See* Papini, Dennis R.

### Clark, Suzanne

A Woman's Place and the Rural School in the United States. *Genders* 8 (Summer 1990):78-90

### Clarke, Cheryl

Humid Pitch: Narrative Poetry. Reviewed by Jane Campbell. *Belles Lettres* 6, No. 1 (Fall 1990):53

### Clarke, D. A.

The Handmaid's Tale. Film Review. *off our backs* 20, No. 6 (June 1990):12-13

### Clarke, G. Modele

Brothers: I Want to Cry. *Essence* 21, No. 7 (November 1990):38-39

### Clarke, Juanne N.

Reproducing the World: Essays in Feminist Theory. Book Review. *Atlantis* 15, No. 2 (Spring 1990):118

**Clark-Jones, Melissa** and Coyne, Patricia

Through the Back Door. *Atlantis* 15, No. 2 (Spring 1990):40-49

**Clarricoates, Katherine M.**

Within School Walls: The Role of Discipline, Sexuality and the Curriculum. Book Review. *Gender and Education* 2, No. 1 (1990):109-110

**Clary, Mike**

A Ranch Where Miracles Happen. *McCall's* 117, No. 8 (May 1990):154-160

**Classic Comics.** *See* Literature – Comic Books, Strips, etc.

**Classification Systems**

Classification Systems: Need, Rationale and Basis. Lakshmi Menon. *Women's World* 23 (April 1990):18-20

**Class Structure**

Ending Difference/Different Endings: Class, Closure, and Collectivity in Women's Proletarian Fiction. Paula Rabinowitz. *Genders* 8 (Summer 1990):62-77

Irreconcilable Differences: Women Defining Class After Divorce and Downward Mobility. Christine E. Grella. *Gender and Society* 4, No. 1 (March 1990):41-55

**Claudel, Camille** (about)

Camille Claudel. Directed by Bruno Nuytten. Reviewed by Judy Simmons. *Ms.* 1, No. 1 (July/August 1990):74-75

**Clausen, Jan**

Captivity. Book Review. *The Women's Review of Books* 7, Nos. 10-11 (July 1990):12-13

Crime Against Nature. Book Review. *The Women's Review of Books* 7, Nos. 10-11 (July 1990):12-13

A Girl in Every Port? *The Women's Review of Books* 8, No. 2 (November 1990):7-8

Grace Notes. Book Review. *The Women's Review of Books* 7, Nos. 10-11 (July 1990):12-13

My Interesting Condition. *Out/Look* No. 7 (Winter 1990):10-21

The Safe Sea of Women: Lesbian Fiction 1969-1989. Book Review. *The Women's Review of Books* 8, No. 2 (November 1990):7-8

Still Inventing History. *The Women's Review of Books* 7, Nos. 10-11 (July 1990):12-13

**Claverie, Laura**

Hurricane! *Family Circle* 103, No. 13 (September 25, 1990):78-82

What Happened to Christopher. *Family Circle* 103, No. 7 (May 15, 1990):105-108

**Clayton, James**

Captain of the Ship. *Essence* 21, No. 2 (June 1990):36

**Cleage, Pearl**

Is Your Life Making You Sick? *Essence* 21, No. 2 (June 1990):55-58+

Let the Church Say Amen! *Essence* 20, No. 12 (April 1990):69-70+

**Cleanliness.** *See also* Personal Hygiene

The Body Shop: Baths for Shower People, Showers for Bath People. *Mademoiselle* (February 1990):24-26

Clean Is Sexy: Skin Care Goes Back to Nature. *Mademoiselle* (February 1990):188-191

**Clear, Caitriona**

Nuns in Nineteenth Century Ireland. Reviewed by Margaret MacCurtain. *Gender & History* 2, No. 3 (Autumn 1990):365-368

**Clegg, Johnny** (about)

Word On. . .*Glamour* (November 1990):167

**Clehane, Diane**

Beauty Care Hits the Road. *Lear's* (December 1990):53

Trading in the New Gold Standard. *Lear's* (December 1990):54

**Clement, Catherine**

Opera, or the Undoing of Women. Reviewed by Pat Hurshell. *NWSA Journal* 2, No. 1 (Winter 1990):141-142

**Clément, Catherine**

Opéra, or the Undoing of Women. Reviewed by Helen Hacker. *Gender and Society* 4, No. 4 (December 1990):561-563

**Clements, Corinne**

Can This Marriage Be Saved? "After Sixteen Years of Marriage, I'm Still a Virgin." *Ladies' Home Journal* 107, No. 9 (September 1990):18-22

**Clements, Linda**

Nicaragua After the Elections. *off our backs* 20, No. 4 (April 1990):1+

**Cleopatra** (about)

Cleopatra: Histories, Dreams and Distortions. By Lucy Hughes-Hallett. Reviewed by Marilyn French. *The Women's Review of Books* 8, No. 2 (November 1990):16-17

**Clergy – Images in Literature**

The Reverend Idol and Other Parsonage Secrets: Women Write Romances about Ministers, 1880-1950. Ann-Janine Morey. *Journal of Feminist Studies in Religion* 6, No. 1 (Spring 1990):87-103

**Clerical Occupations**

Good Work at the Video Display Terminal: A Feminist Ethical Analysis of Changes in Clerical Work. By Barbara Hilkert Andolsen. Reviewed by Susan Klitzman. *Women and Health* 16, Nos. 3/4 (1990):205-206

The White Blouse Revolution: Female Office Workers Since 1870. Edited by Gregory Anderson. Reviewed by Carole Elizabeth Adams. *Gender & History* 2, No. 3 (Autumn 1990):343-348

**Cliburn, Van** (about)

Vogue Arts: Music. David Daniel. *Vogue* (October 1990):264+

**Cliff, Michelle**

Bodies of Water. Reviewed by Judy Scales-Trent. *The Women's Review of Books* 7, No. 12 (September 1990):15

**Clift, Elayne**

Advocate Battles for Safety in Mines and Poultry Plants. *New Directions for Women* 19, No. 3 (May/June 1990):3

Cheers for Mavis Williams. *New Directions for Women* 19, No. 3 (May/June 1990):3

**Clifton, Lucille**

Female. Poem. *Essence* 21, No. 5 (September 1990):132

**Clifton, Lucille** (about). *See* Writers – Interviews, "Graceful Passages"

**Cline, Carolyn J.**

Saving Face. *Lear's* (January 1990):96-99

**Clinton, Kate** (interview)

Be Bold and Be Bad. Carolann Barrett. *Woman of Power* 17 (Summer 1990):60-63

**Clinton, Linda Hamilton** (joint author). *See* Holcomb, Betty

**Clio Collective**

Quebec Women: A History. Reviewed by Cath McNaughton. *Women's Studies International Forum* 13, Nos. 1-2 (1990):162-163

**Clocks and Watches**

Timeless Objects. Kathleen Beckett-Young. *Savvy Woman* (October 1990):38-40

**Clooney, Rosemary** (about)

Clooney! Joan Barthel. *Lear's* (February 1990):102-107+

**Closets**. *See* Clothes Closets

**Clothes Closets**. *See also* Storage in the Home

2 People, 2 Wardrobes, Too Much! *Glamour* (April 1990):298-300

**Clothing and Dress**. *See also* Coats; Dress Accessories; Dressing for Success; Fur Garments; Hats; Homosexuality – Clothing and Dress; Lingerie; Parties; Shoes; Shopping; Sport Clothes; Suits; Sweaters; Textile Fabrics

Add Lib. *Lear's* (March 1990):144-147

For After Hours. *Mademoiselle* (June 1990):198-203

All Day Seersucker. *Mademoiselle* (June 1990):174-181

Beauty and Fashion Hotline: Warming Trends. *Family Circle* 103, No. 15 (November 6, 1990):46

Birds of Paradise. *Mademoiselle* (November 1990):140-147

Breezy. *Lear's* (April 1990):98-105

Career Clothes: The New Ease. *Working Woman* (March 1990):95-121

Clothes Make the Woman . . . Paula Kassall. *New Directions for Women* 19, No. 5 (September-October 1990):6

Confidential for February. *Mademoiselle* (February 1990):137-147

Confidential for January 1990: Bright on the Money. *Mademoiselle* (January 1990):79-85

Confidential for June. *Mademoiselle* (June 1990):141

Cool Summer Whites. *McCall's* 117, No. 9 (June 1990):77-79

Country Classics. *McCall's* 117, No. 12 (September 1990):115-118

Cutting a Dash: The Dress of Radclyffe Hall and Una Troubridge. Katrina Rolley. *Feminist Review* No. 35 (Summer 1990):54-66

For Day: Great White Ways. *Mademoiselle* (December 1990):136 141

Desiging Woman. Joan Delaney. *Executive Female* 13, No. 5 (September-October 1990):66-67

Dress for Less: The Velvet Revolution. *Vogue* (July 1990):210-217

Dressing Down Dressing Up – The Philosophic Fear of Fashion. Karen Hanson. *Hypatia* 5, No. 2 (Summer 1990):107-121

East Meets West: Confidential for September. *Mademoiselle* (September 1990):219-229

Ebony and Ivory. *Lear's* (May 1990):114-123

Fall Fashion Focus. Patrice McLeod. *Essence* 21, No. 5 (September 1990):20

Fashion: Midseason Refreshers. *Working Woman* (January 1990):122-125

Fashion: On the Beach. *Mademoiselle* (June 1990):56-64

Fashion: Sensuous. *Redbook* 175, No. 1 (May 1990):122-127

Fashion: Smooth Transitions. *Working Woman* (May 1990):98-103

Fashion: Something Personal. *Working Woman* (April 1990):100-105

Fashion Clips. Page Hill Starzinger. *Vogue* (January 1990):34

Fashion Fax. *Glamour* (June 1990):206

Fashion Firsts. *Good Housekeeping* 211, No. 3 (September 1990):106-108

Fashion Questions. *Glamour* (June 1990):201

Fashion Workshop. *Glamour* (January 1990):91-95; (April 1990):201-204

Flash! Stripes and Flowers. *Glamour* (April 1990):264-269

Great Updates. Lois Joy Johnson. *Ladies' Home Journal* 107, No. 9 (September 1990):166-174

The Great White Way for Day. *Lear's* (June 1990):112-119

Head of the Classics. *Mademoiselle* (February 1990):180-185

Intense! *Mademoiselle* (December 1990):180-185

It's Clearly a Matter of See-Through. *Lear's* (April 1990):106-111

Keep It Short. *Mademoiselle* (February 1990):192-195

Let's Talk Fashion. *Mademoiselle* (February 1990):58-66

Lipstick Etc. Ruth Wallsgrove. *off our backs* 20, No. 10 (November 1990):13

Look Sharp. *Glamour* (June 1990):216-221

The Many Lives of a Catsuit. *Mademoiselle* (November 1990):64-69

Men and Women: Dressing the Part. Edited by Claudia Brush Kidwell and Valerie Steele. Reviewed by Holly Hall. *Belles Lettres* 5, No. 2 (Winter 1990):13

The New Clan Spirit. *Glamour* (January 1990):134-139

The New Lineup. *Vogue* (January 1990):222-227

Off-Whites are On Again. *Mademoiselle* (January 1990):98-103

Paris Fashion: A Cultural History. By Valerie Steele. Reviewed by Ruth P. Rubinstein. *Woman's Art Journal* 11, No. 1 (Spring-Summer 1990):49-50

Perfect Whites. *Glamour* (July 1990):170-175

The Power of Color. *Ladies' Home Journal* 107, No. 11 (November 1990):64-70

Print It. *Vogue* (July 1990):162-167

Radiant Wraps. *Harper's Bazaar* (November 1990):144-149

Ready-to-Go. *Redbook* 174, No. 5 (March 1990):103-107

Ready to Wear: A Clothes Encounter. Richard Atcheson. *Lear's* (October 1990):62-64

Refinement Redux. *Glamour* (June 1990):256-261

Sexy Marks the Spot. *Mademoiselle* (November 1990):72-76

The Shorts Circuit. *Harper's Bazaar* (January 1990):86-89

Simple Pleasures. *Harper's Bazaar* (January 1990):128-131

Sinning for Silk: Dress-for-Success Fashions of the New Orleans Storyville Prostitute. Gerilyn G. Tandberg. *Women's Studies International Forum* 13, No. 3 (1990):229-248

Softwear. *Essence* 21, No. 5 (September 1990):58-65

The Spice Is Right. *Mademoiselle* (February 1990):160-165

Spring's New Soft Jackets. *McCall's* 117, No. 7 (April 1990):69-75

A Stitch in Time. Melanie Reynolds Jones. *Executive Female* 13, No. 6 (November-December 1990):26

Strapless. *Vogue* (August 1990):360-365

Style: The L.A. Law. *Mademoiselle* (October 1990):192-201

Style Statements for 1990. *Glamour* (January 1990):120-127

Talking Fashion. Giselle Benatar. *Vogue* (July 1990):219

A Touch of Velvet. *McCall's* 118, No. 2 (November 1990):90-98

On the Town. *Savvy Woman* (November 1990):72-77

The Uncolors: Strong Pastels at Very Quiet Prices. *Mademoiselle* (January 1990):86-91

Vogue: Point of View. *Vogue* (July 1990):137

Wall to Wall Denim. *Mademoiselle* (September 1990):276-281

Weekend R & R. *Lear's* (June 1990):120-125

What's Hot: Ice Colors. *Mademoiselle* (October 1990):72-74

What's Hot? *Redbook* 175, No. 2 (June 1990):93-103

What They're Wearing. *Glamour* (April 1990):216; (June 1990):204

What to Wear to a Romance. *Glamour* (February 1990):150-157

Why Not Suede? *Glamour* (October 1990):258-263

**Clothing and Dress – Adolescents**

Clothing Interests, Body Satisfaction, and Eating Behavior of Adolescent Females: Related or Independent Dimensions? Mary Ann Littrell, Mary Lynn Damhorst, and John M. Littrell. *Adolescence* 25, No. 97 (Spring 1990):77-95

**Clothing and Dress – Feminist Aspects**

Deviant Dress. Elizabeth Wilson. *Feminist Review* No. 35 (Summer 1990):67-74

**Clothing and Dress – Jeans**

Injeanious! *Harper's Bazaar* (June 1990):124-127

**Clothing and Dress – Leather**

Gimmie Some Skin! Elsie B. Washington. *Essence* 21, No. 6 (October 1990):72-79

**Clothing and Dress – Swimwear**

The 10 Best Swimsuits. *Redbook* 175, No. 1 (May 1990):103-111

Caught In the Act. *Mademoiselle* (June 1990):226

A Day at the Beach. *McCall's* 117, No. 9 (June 1990):81-92

Fashion: Teeny Bikinis (For Not-So-Tiny Bodies). *Mademoiselle* (June 1990):52-54

Fashion Faux. *Glamour* (July 1990):140

Fashion Questions. *Glamour* (July 1990):136

9 Show-it-Off Swimsuits. *Glamour* (May 1990):286-293

Our Annual Swimsuit Ratings. *Glamour* (June 1990):238-243

In Pursuit of Excellence. Emily Walzer. *Women's Sports and Fitness* 12, No. 4 (May-June 1990):45-49

Retroactive. *Harper's Bazaar* (July 1990):74-77

See Worthy. *Harper's Bazaar* (May 1990):54

Shore Thing! *Essence* 21, No. 2 (June 1990):68-73

Suits You! *Ladies' Home Journal* 107, No. 6 (June 1990):138-142

What Suits You? *Redbook* 175, No. 2 (June 1990):122-127

Your Poolside Style File. *Glamour* (July 1990):144-149

**Clough, Barbara** (about)

A Woman for Lear's: Word for Word. Jane Howard. *Lear's* (August 1990):132-135

**Clower, John**

Bitter Milk: Women and Teaching. Book Review. *Feminist Teacher* 5, No. 2 (Fall 1990):34-36

Review Essay: Pedagogy and Synthesis in Madeleine Grumet's *Bitter Milk*. *Feminist Teacher* 5, No. 2 (Fall 1990):34-36

**Coaching (Athletics)**

Sidelined. Frances Munnings. *Women's Sports & Fitness* 12, No. 6 (September 1990):40-43

**Coal Industry**

Where the Sun Never Shines: A History of America's Bloody Coal Industry. By Priscilla Long.

Reviewed by Barbara Kingsolver. *The Women's Review of Books* 7, No. 9 (June 1990):21-22

**Coates, Rosemary**

Women and Love: A Cultural Revolution in Progress. Book Review. *Healthright* 9, No. 2 (February 1990):37

**Coats**

Baby, It's Getting Colder Outside! *Redbook* 176, No. 1 (November 1990):89-93

Coats Take Chicago by Storm. *Mademoiselle* (October 1990):168-175

Color Coated. *Harper's Bazaar* (December 1990):130-135

The Cover Up. *Lear's* (October 1990):126-131

The 50 Hottest Winter Coats. *Good Housekeeping* 211, No. 3 (September 1990):228-233

The Quest for the Perfect Winter Coat. Debra Wise. *Glamour* (October 1990):214

The Right Winter Coat for Work. *Glamour* (November 1990):120-122

Save It for a Rainy Day. *Ladies' Home Journal* 107, No. 4 (April 1990):39

Top Coats! *McCall's* 117, No. 12 (September 1990):97-102

Weather or Not. *Harper's Bazaar* (April 1990):190-195

**Cobb, Janine O'Leary**

Menopause Resources. *Healthsharing* 11, No. 4 (December 1990):26-27

The Wisdom of Menopause. *Healthsharing* 11, No. 4 (December 1990):8-12

**Cobb, Jewel Plummer**

A Life in Science: Research and Service. *Sage* 6, No. 2 (Fall 1989):39-43

**Cobb, Paul** (about). *See* Leadership

**Cobble, Dorothy Sue**

Rethinking Troubled Relations between Women and Unions: Craft Unionism and Female Activism. *Feminist Studies* 16, No. 3 (Fall 1990):519-548

**Cobham, Rhonda**

Angel. Book Review. *The Women's Review of Books* 7, Nos. 10-11 (July 1990):29-31

Boy-Sandwich. Book Review. *The Women's Review of Books* 7, Nos. 10-11 (July 1990):29-31

Growing Up With Miss Milly. Book Review. *The Women's Review of Books* 7, Nos. 10-11 (July 1990):29-31

Harriet's Daughter. Book Review. *The Women's Review of Books* 7, Nos. 10-11 (July 1990):29-31

Myal. Book Review. *The Women's Review of Books* 7, Nos. 10-11 (July 1990):29-31

Sans Souci and Other Stories. Book Review. *The Women's Review of Books* 7, Nos. 10-11 (July 1990):29-31

Women of the Islands. *The Women's Review of Books* 7, Nos. 10-11 (July 1990):29-31

**Cobson, Corinne** (about). *See* Carter, Charla, "European Designers to Watch"

**Cocaine Abuse**

Back from Crack. Jill Nelson. *Essence* 20, No. 9 (January 1990):57-58+

Terry Williams Takes Drugs Seriously. Paula Giddings. *Essence* 20, No. 10 (February 1990):42

**Cock, Jacklyn**

Maids and Madams: Domestic Workers Under Apartheid. Reviewed by Stanlie M. James. *Feminist Collections* 12, No. 1 (Fall 1990):3-6

**Cockrell, Lila** (about). *See also* Texas – Mayors

**Cocks, Joan Elizabeth**

The Oppositional Imagination: Feminism, Critique and Political Theory. Reviewed by Judith Grant. *The Women's Review of Books* 7, No. 4 (January 1990):21-22

**Codd, Ginny**

A Natural Therapies Approach to Minor Tranquilliser Withdrawal. *Healthright* 9, No. 2 (February 1990):16-20

**Codependency**. *See also* Adult Children of Alcoholics; Substance Abuse

**Coeducation**

Maintaining the Spirit and Tone of Robust Manliness: The Battle Against Coeducation at Southern Colleges and Universities, 1890-1940. Amy Thompson McCandless. *NWSA Journal* 2, No. 2 (Spring 1990):199-216

The Private Eye: Better Dead than Coed. Barbara Grizzuti Harrison. *Mademoiselle* (September 1990):182

**Coen, Ethan** (joint director). *See* Coen, Joel

**Coen, Joel** and Coen, Ethan

Miller's Crossing. Reviewed by Ron Rosenbaum. *Mademoiselle* (October 1990):98-101

**Cofer, Judith Ortiz**

The Line of the Sun. Reviewed by Denise M. Marshall. *Belles Lettres* 5, No. 2 (Winter 1990):16

Silent Dancing: A Partial Remembrance of a Puerto Rican Childhood. Reviewed by Aurora Levins Morales. *The Women's Review of Books* 8, No. 3 (December 1990):9-10

**Coffee.** *See* Caffeine

**Coffer, Helen Lewis**

Along Came Love. Short Story. *Good Housekeeping* 211, No. 5 (November 1990):138-141

**Coffey, Irene**

Lesbian Sleuths. *Spare Rib* 217 (October 1990):34-35

There's Something About a Convent Girl . . . Video Review. *Spare Rib* 219 (December 1990-January 1991):35

Who's That Girl? *Spare Rib* 219 (December 1990-January 1991):27

**Coffey, Marilyn**

Great Plains Patchwork: A Memoir. Reviewed by Barbara Horn. *Belles Lettres* 5, No. 3 (Spring 1990):23

**Coffey, Nora W.**

The Hysterectomy Epidemic. *Woman of Power* 18 (Fall 1990):58-60

**Coffman, Sandra J.**

Developing a Feminist Model for Clinical Consultation: Combining Diversity and Commonality. *Women and Therapy* 9, No. 3 (1990):255-273

**Cognitive Therapy – Adolescents**

A Cognitive/Affective Empathy Training Program as a Function of Ego Development in Aggressive Adolescent Females. Edward V. Pecukonis. *Adolescence* 25, No. 97 (Spring 1990):59-76

**Cohabitation.** *See also* Fawcett, Farrah (about)

Living Together: The Truth and the Consequences. Debra Kent. *Mademoiselle* (May 1990):201, 236

Money: Premarital "Insurance." Julianne Malveaux. *Essence* 20, No. 10 (February 1990):32+

**Cohen, Arthur A.**

Sonia Delaunay. Reviewed by Sherry Buckberrough. *Woman's Art Journal* 11, No. 1 (Spring-Summer 1990):39-41

**Cohen, Jeffrey**

Home-Office Wonders. *Savvy Woman* (October 1990):28-31

The Long-Distance Lowdown. *Savvy Woman* (February 1990):32-36

**Cohen, Joyce**

Great Looks: Hold It! *Redbook* 175, No. 4 (August 1990):14-18

**Cohen, Marcia**

A Real-Life "Norma Rae." *Good Housekeeping* 211, No. 1 (July 1990):98-101

**Cohen, Marjorie**

Are We There Yet? A Guide to Enjoying Car Travel With Your Kids. *Family Circle* 103, No. 9 (June 26, 1990):117

**Cohen, Patricia Cline**

The Helen Jewett Murder: Violence, Gender, and Sexual Licentiousness in Antebellum America. *NWSA Journal* 2, No. 3 (Summer 1990):374-389

**Cohen, Sharleen Cooper**

Dark Deceiver. Short story. *Good Housekeeping* 211, No. 4 (October 1990):209-230+

**Cohen, Sherrill** and Taub, Nadine (editors)

Reproductive Laws for the 1990s. Reviewed by Regina H. Kenen. *Women and Health* 16, Nos. 3/4 (1990):193-196

**Cohen, Sherry Suib**

What Makes a Woman Sexy? *Ladies' Home Journal* 107, No. 11 (November 1990):116-123

**Cohen, Toby**

Just Saying No, No, No to the Sizzle. *Lear's* (October 1990):76

**Cohen, Yolande** (editor)

Women and Counter-Power. Reviewed by Linda Christiansen-Ruffman. *Resources for Feminist Research* 19, No. 1 (March 1990):39-40

**Cohn, Jan**

Romance and the Erotics of Property: Mass-Market Fiction for Women. Reviewed by Katharine M. Rogers. *Signs* 15, No. 4 (Summer 1990):878-882

**Çok, Figen**

Body Image Satisfaction in Turkish Adolescents. *Adolescence* 25, No. 98 (Summer 1990):409-413

**Cokkinades, Vilma E.**, Macera, C. A., and Pate, R. R.

Menstrual Dysfunction among Habitual Runners. *Women and Health* 16, No. 2 (1990):59-69

**Colacello, Bob**

Holy Terror: Andy Warhol Close Up. Reviewed by Graydon Carter. *Vogue* (September 1990):448-452

**Colapinto, John**

By Love Obsessed: The Shocking Story of a Real-Life Fatal Attraction. *Mademoiselle* (August 1990):188-191, 230-232

Men and the "M" Word. *Mademoiselle* (December 1990):142-145

**Colby, Clara B.** (about)

State Historical Society of Wisconsin Welcomes Suffragist's Papers. Cindy Knight. *Feminist Collections* 12, No. 1 (Fall 1990):18-20

**Cold (Disease)**

Medical Report: The Common Cold Quiz. Michael Castleman. *Glamour* (January 1990):30-35

**Cold (Disease) – Prevention**

Winter Wellness Guide: The Best Defense: Understanding Your Immune System. Hal Straus. *Ladies' Home Journal* 107, No. 1 (January 1990):39-43

**Cole, Diane**

Disappointment on the Job. *Working Mother* 13, No. 8 (August 1990):22-26

The Overtime Bind. *Working Mother* 13, No. 4 (April 1990):34-38

Pregnancy, Miscarriage and Hope. *Glamour* (January 1990):156

Staying Cool When the Stakes are High. *Working Woman* (February 1990):80

Stop Procrastinating. *Working Mother* (December 1990):26-28

Take It Standing Up. *Executive Female* 13, No. 4 (July-August 1990):16-17

**Cole, Doris** and Taylor, Karen

The Lady Architects, Lois Lilley Howe, Eleanor Manning and Mary Almy, 1913-1937. Reviewed by Pamela H. Simpson. *Woman's Art Journal* 11, No. 2 (Fall 1990-Winter 1991):48

**Cole, Ellen** and Rothblum, Esther

Commentary on "Sexuality and the Midlife Woman." *Psychology of Women Quarterly* 14, No. 4 (December 1990):509-512

**Cole, Johnnetta B.**

*Another Day Will Find Us Brave*: Inaugural Address, November 6, 1988. *Sage* 6, No. 1 (Summer 1989):85-86

Forum: "What if We Made Racism a Woman's Issue. . ." *McCall's* 118, No. 1 (October 1990):39-40

**Cole, K. C.**

Inertia. *Lear's* (May 1990):112-113+

Spaced Out: Into New Dimensions. *Lear's* (March 1990):110-111

**Cole, Natalie** (about)

Naturally Natalie. Elsie B. Washington. *Essence* 21, No. 6 (October 1990):14-17

**Cole, Wendy**

A Peach Farmer's Harvest: Book Royalties. *McCall's* 118, No. 2 (November 1990):49

**Coleman, Lerita M.** (joint author). See Adelmann, Pamela K.

**Coleman, Liza**

Beauty from the Sea. *Savvy Woman* (July/August 1990):40-42

What's In a Name? *Savvy Woman* (November 1990):42-43

**Coleman, Marilyn** and Ganong, Lawrence H.

Remarriage and Stepfamily Research in the 1980s: Increased Interest in an Old Family Form. *Journal of Marriage and the Family* 52, No. 4 (November 1990):925-940

**Coleman, Marilyn** (joint author). *See* Ganong, Lawrence H.

**Coleman, Nick**

Vogue Arts: The Lady's Got Soul. *Vogue* (August 1990):210-214

**Coleman, Nick** (about). *See also* Carter, Charla, "European Designers to Watch."; Great Britain – Environmental Movement

**Coleman, Pat**

The Education of Harriet Hatfield. add. *Spare Rib* No. 210 (March 1990):34

Out on Tuesday. *Spare Rib* No. 210 (March 1990):40

**Coleman, Wanda** and Leedom-Ackerman, Joanne (editors)

Women for All Seasons: Poetry and Prose about Transitions in Women's Lives. Reviewed by Terri Lynn Jewell. *New Directions for Women* 19, No. 1 (January/February 1990):25

**Colemon, Johnnie** (about). *See* De Veaux, Alexis, Milloy, Marilyn, and Ross, Michael Erik

**Coles, Bob** and Maynard, Mary

Moving Towards a Fair Start: Equal Gender Opportunities and Careers Service. *Gender and Education* 2, No. 3 (1990):297-308

**Coles, Catherine M.** (joint author). *See* Entwisle, Barbara

**Colet, Louise** (criticism)

Rediscovery: Louise Colet. Barbara Meister. *Belles Lettres* 5, No. 4 (Summer 1990):18-20

**Collectibles.** *See* Antiques and Collectibles; Collectors and Collecting

**Collection Agencies – Law and Legislation**

Bill Collectors: How Much Can They Harass You? Barbara Gilder Quint. *Glamour* (February 1990):95-96

**Collectives**

Extending Shelter. Angela Johnson. *off our backs* 20, No. 10 (November 1990):14

Working Collectively. Ruth Wallsgrove. *off our backs* 20, No. 2 (February 1990):20-21

**Collectors and Collecting**

50 Cookie Jars. Louise Messina. *Good Housekeeping* 211, No. 4 (October 1990):146-149+

It's Easy to Collect: Country Pottery. Ralph Kovel and Terry Kovel. *Redbook* 176, No. 1 (November 1990):196

**College Presidents**

Marguerite Ross Barnett: University President. David Thigpen. *Essence* 21, No. 6 (October 1990):50

**College Students.** *See also* Sexual Harassment – College Students

Balancing Personal and Professional Lives: The Unique Concerns of Graduate Students. Judy L. Ellickson and Janet R. Latona. *Women and Therapy* 9, No. 4 (1990):37-47

**College Students – Attitudes**

Attitudes toward Prostitution as a Function of Attitudes toward Feminism in College Students. Susan A. Basow and Florence Campanile. *Psychology of Women Quarterly* 14, No. 1 (March 1990):135-141

Perceptions of Wife Abuse: Effects of Gender, Attitudes toward Women, and Just-World Beliefs among College Students. Connie M. Kristiansen and Rita Giulietti. *Psychology of Women Quarterly* 14, No. 2 (June 1990):177-189

Report from Two Campuses. Karen Brown and Jennifer Kohn. *Bridges* 1, No. 2 (Fall 1990): 100-108

**College Students – Community Service**

Community Service among College and University Students: Individual and Institutional Relationships. Robert C. Serow and Julia I. Dreyden. *Adolescence* 25, No. 99 (Fall 1990):553-566

**College Students – Financial Support**

Student Loans – Banks Withdraw as Thatcher "Fizzes with Fury." *Spare Rib* No. 209 (February 1990):46

**College Students – Leadership**

Glamour's Top Ten College Women, 1990. *Glamour* (October 1990):254-257

**College Students – Nutrition**

Potential Nutrition Messages in Magazines Read by College Students. Ann A. Hertzler and Ingolf Gru1n. *Adolescence* 25, No. 99 (Fall 1990):717-724

**College Students – Rape**

The Glamour Report: Campus Rape. Le Anne Schreiber. *Glamour* (September 1990):292-295+

**College Students – Sexuality**

Gender Comparisons of College Students' Attitudes toward Sexual Behavior. Stephan M. Wilson and Nilufer P. Medora. *Adolescence* 25, No. 99 (Fall 1990):615-627

**College Students – Travel.** *See* Study Abroad

**Collette, Christine**

For Labor and For Women: The Women's Labour League, 1906-18. Reviewed by Linda Walker. *Gender & History* 2, No. 2 (Summer 1990):244-246

**Collier, Elizabeth**

Eye Contact. *Vogue* (August 1990):344

Images: Beauty Answers. *Vogue* (December 1990):166

Images: Hair Answers. *Vogue* (September 1990):362; (December 1990):162

**Collier, June** (about)

A Stitch in Time. Melanie Reynolds Jones. *Executive Female* 13, No. 6 (November-December 1990):26

**Collier, Lee** and Devaney, Kim

Lifeblood: A New Image for Menstruation. Book Review. *Healthright* 9, No. 2 (February 1990):39

**Collins, Barbara G.**

The Dance of Intimacy. Book Review. *AFFILIA* 5, No. 3 (Fall 1990):122-124

Don't Blame Mother: Mending the Mother-Daughter Relationship. Book Review. *AFFILIA* 5, No. 3 (Fall 1990):122-124

Pornography and Social Policy: Three Feminist Approaches. *AFFILIA* 5, No. 4 (Winter 1990):8-26

**Collins, Clare**

Dreams of Equality: Women on the Canadian Left, 1920-1950. Book Review. *Resources for Feminist Research* 19, No. 1 (March 1990):8

Eva Gore-Booth and Esther Roper: A Biography. Book Review. *Gender & History* 2, No. 1 (Spring 1990):116-118

A Singular Marriage: A Labour Love Story in Letters and Diaries. Book Review. *Gender & History* 2, No. 1 (Spring 1990):116-118

**Collins, Eliza**

Why Employees Act the Way They Do: A Manager's Guide to Human Behavior. *Working Woman* (December 1990):58-61

**Collins, Gail**

Jane Pauley's Prime Time. *Savvy* (December-January 1991):52-54+

Out Box: A Job of One's Own. *Working Woman* (September 1990):226

Out Box: Chung's Choice. *Working Woman* (December 1990):110

Out Box: Office-Party Perverts. *Working Woman* (November 1990):176

Out Box: The "Pretty Woman" Problem. *Working Woman* (October 1990):160

Sex and the Savvy Woman. *Savvy Woman* (July/August 1990):66-69

This Working Life: The World According to P.R. *Working Woman* (August 1990):98

**Collins, Jacqueline**

Health Care of Women in the Workplace. *Health Care for Women International* 11, No. 1 (1990):21-32

**Collins, Martha**

Girls. Poem. *The Women's Review of Books* 7, No. 9 (June 1990):24

Party. Poem. *The Women's Review of Books* 7, No. 9 (June 1990):24

**Collins, Merle**

Angel. Reviewed by Rhonda Cobham. *The Women's Review of Books* 7, Nos. 10-11 (July 1990):29-31

Gemini. *Spare Rib* No. 216 (September 1990):40-43

**Collins, Patricia Hill**

Hard Times Cotton Mill Girls: Personal Histories of Womanhood and Poverty in the South. Book Review. *Gender and Society* 4, No. 3 (September 1990):427-429

**Collins, R. Lorraine**, Leonard, Kenneth E., and Searles, John S. (editors)

Alcohol and the Family. Reviewed by Joan F. Robertson. *Journal of Marriage and the Family* 52, No. 4 (November 1990):1154-1155

**Collins, Sue** and Arquette, Kerry

"I Wouldn't Let Them Cheat." *Working Mother* 13, No. 9 (September 1990):36-39

**Colman, Penny**

The Good Mother. *Ladies' Home Journal* 107, No. 1 (January 1990):36

One Mother's Story: Why Didn't I? *Ladies' Home Journal* 107, No. 3 (March 1990):90

**Colombia – Drug Traffic**

"I Fought the Drug Lords." Monica De Greiff and Guy Gugliotta. *Ladies' Home Journal* 107, No. 2 (February 1990):22-27

**Colombia – Journalism**

Colombia's Drug Busting Journalist. María Jimena Duzán *Ms.* 1, No. 1 (July/August 1990):12

**Colombia – Politics and Government**

Vest-Dressed Women. Lynda Gorov. *Savvy Woman* (September 1990):14

**Colombia – Sexual Behavior**

Sexual Behavior of Colombian High School Students. Bernardo Useche, Magdalena Villegas, and Heli Alzate. *Adolescence* 25, No. 98 (Summer 1990):291-304

**Colombia – Status of Women**

Demographic Transition and Life Course Change in Colombia. C. Elisa Florez and Dennis P. Hogan. *Journal of Family History* 15, No. 1 (January 1990):1-21

Women in Colombian Organizations, 1900-1940: A Study in Changing Gender Roles. René De La Pedraja Tomán. *Journal of Women's History* 2, No. 1 (Spring 1990):98-119

**Colonialism**

Gendering Colonialism on Colonising Gender? Recent Women's Studies Approaches to White Women and the History of British Colonialism. Jane Haggis. *Women's Studies International Forum* 13, Nos. 1-2 (1990):105-115

Recasting Women: Essays in Colonial History. Edited by KumKum Sangari and Sudesh Vaid. Reviewed by Chandra T. Mohanty and Satya P. Mohanty. *The Women's Review of Books* 7, No. 6 (March 1990):19-21

Slavery and the French Revolutionists (1788-1805). By Anna Julia Cooper. Reviewed by Leonore Loft. *Women's Studies International Forum* 13, Nos. 1-2 (1990):160

From Structural Subordination to Empowerment: Women and Development in Third World Contexts. Edna Acosta-Belén and Christine E. Bose. *Gender and Society* 4, No. 3 (September 1990):299-320

Voices and Echoes: Tales from Colonial Women. By Joan Alexander. Reviewed by Dorothy O. Helly. *Women's Studies International Forum* 13, No. 4 (1990):405-407

Western Women and Imperialism: Introduction. Nupur Chaudhuri and Margaret Strobel. *Women's Studies International Forum* 13, No. 4 (1990):289-293

### Color in Design

Black Is Out . . . Or Is It? Vicki Woods. *Vogue* (July 1990):220-223

Blue Notes. Bart Boehlert. *Harper's Bazaar* (October 1990):208-213+

Bright Ideas. *Harper's Bazaar* (March 1990):108-112

Brilliant! *Glamour* (June 1990):230-233

Couture Report: Brilliant! *Harper's Bazaar* (October 1990):182-191

Elements. Edited by Candy Pratts Price. *Vogue* (September 1990):290

Glorious Color. *Redbook* 176, No. 2 (December 1990):110-115

The Great White Way. *Ladies' Home Journal* 107, No. 2 (February 1990):130-135

Historic Colors. *Redbook* 175, No. 4 (August 1990):80-85

Living Color. *Harper's Bazaar* (March 1990):91-94

The News Is Color. *Vogue* (September 1990):515-531

A Red Awakening. *Glamour* (February 1990):168-173

The Return of Glamour. Laurie Tarkan. *Lear's* (September 1990):66

Sheer Blues. *Harper's Bazaar* (April 1990):180-183

Talent at Work. *Harper's Bazaar* (March 1990):180-191+

Tropical Punch. *Harper's Bazaar* (December 1990):166-171

Vogue Point of View: Global Fashion. *Vogue* (September 1990):513

**Color of Man.** *See* Melanism

### Columbia University – Protest Actions

Sappho Zaps Plato at Columbia. *New Directions for Women* 19, No. 1 (January/February 1990):5

### Colvin, Lucy

Washington Jails Nikki Craft for Ripping Up *Esquire. off our backs* 20, No. 7 (July 1990):1+

### Colvin, Shawn (about)

The Ode and the New. David Keeps. *Harper's Bazaar* (February 1990):58

### Colwin, Laurie

Becoming Somebody's Mother. Short story. *Redbook* 175, No. 3 (July 1990):46-54

Bringing It All Back Home Again. Short story. *McCall's* 117, No. 8 (May 1990):110-112+

Goodbye without Leaving. Reviewed by Carey Kaplan. *The Women's Review of Books* 8, No. 1 (October 1990):12-13

### Coma – Personal Narratives

"Your Wife May Never Wake Up." Marianne Jacobbi. *Good Housekeeping* 210, No. 6 (June 1990):161, 214-217

### Combahee River Collective

The Combahee River Collective Statement: Black Feminist Organizing in the Seventies and Eighties. Reviewed by Jacqueline E. Wade. *NWSA Journal* 2, No. 2 (Spring 1990):315-319

**Combat Soldiers.** *See* Military Combat; Military Service

### Comedians

Clown about Town. Patricia Bibby. *Harper's Bazaar* (February 1990):72

### Comedians – Interviews

Word On . . . Sandra Bernhard. Interview. David Denicolo. *Glamour* (March 1990):192

**Comediennes.** *See* Comedians

### Comedy

Having the Last Laugh: Women in Nineteenth Century Bengali Farces. Sumanta Banerjee. *Manushi* No. 59 (July-August 1990):15-20

Laughing Loudest. *Spare Rib* 217 (October 1990):18-21

### Comedy, Standup

Take My Broom – Please! Early Steps Along the Path of A Stand-Up Priestess. Marion Weinstein. *Woman of Power* 17 (Summer 1990):48-49

### Comer, Suzanne (editor)

Common Bonds: Stories By and About Modern Texas Women. Reviewed by Elizabeth Hand. *Belles Lettres* 5, No. 4 (Summer 1990):42-43

Comet, Catherine (about). *See* Musicians

**Comic Books, Strips, etc.**

Barbara Brandon: A Comic Strip about Us. Amy Linden. *Essence* 20, No. 11 (March 1990):46

Classics Illustrated Redux. Rick Schindler. *McCall's* 117, No. 8 (May 1990):62

The Comic Mirror: Domestic Surveillance in Mary Worth. Jennifer Fisher. *Canadian Women's Studies* 11, No. 1 (Spring 1990):60-61

Exclusive Christmas Story Starring the Teenage Mutant Ninja Turtles. *Ladies' Home Journal* 107, No. 12 (December 1990):67-70

The First Tampon. Claire Bretécher. *Ms.* 1, No. 3 (November/December 1990):26-29

Japan: "Rapeman" Comics. Natsuko Yamaguchi. *Ms.* 1, No. 3 (November/December 1990):13

Make Way! A Few Portraits of American Women in Cartoons. Monika Franzen and Nancy Ethiel. *Woman of Power* 17 (Summer 1990):68-73

A Psychoanalytic Reading of a Female Comic Book Hero: *Electra: Assassin*. Notes. Linda Baughman. *Women & Language* 13, No. 1 (Fall 1990):27-30

**Comic Books, Strips, etc. – Literary Classics**

Classics Illustrated Redux. Rick Schindler. *McCall's* 117, No. 8 (May 1990):62

**Comings, David E.**

Tourette Syndrome and Human Behavior. Book Review. *Adolescence* 25, No. 100 (Winter 1990):997

**Commitment**. *See also* Marriage – Counseling; Personal Relationships

**Commoner, Barry** (about). *See* D'Amico, Marie and Jubak, Jim

**Communication**

Back Talk: Eat Those Dirty Words! Julianne Malveaux. *Essence* 20, No. 11 (March 1990):146

Career Strategies: The Power of Small Talk: How to Schmooze Successfully. Adele Scheele. *Working Woman* (November 1990):67-68

Documentation and Communication: Strategies for Networking and Change. *Women's World* 23 (April 1990):8-12

Job Strategies. Marilyn Moats Kennedy. *Glamour* (December 1990):109

Office Technology: Five Successful Alternatives to In-Person Meetings. Christine Begole. *Working Woman* (October 1990):70-76

**Communication – Cross-Cultural Studies**

Abstracts from the Thirteenth Annual Conference of the Organization for the Study of Communication, Language and Gender at the University of Nevada at Reno, October 1990. *Women & Language* 13, No. 2 (Winter 1990):50-55

Women's International Cross-Cultural Exchange. Carmen Gloria Dunnage. *Women in Action* 3 & 4 (1990):24-29

**Communication – Gender Differences**

Difficult Dialogues: Report on the 1990 Conference on Research in Gender and Communication. Marsha Houston. *Women & Language* 13, No. 2 (Winter 1990):30-32

Image Metaphors of Women and Men in Personal Relationships. William Foster Owen. *Women's Studies in Communication* 12, No. 2 (Fall 1989):37-57

The Influence of Gender on Reported Disclosure, Interrogation, and Nonverbal Immediacy in Same-Sex Dyads: An Empirical Study of Uncertainty Reduction Theory. Judith A. Sanders, Richard L. Wiseman, and S. Irene Matz. *Women's Studies in Communication* 13, No. 2 (Fall 1990):85-108

Mutual Evaluations of Communication Competence in Superior-Subordinate Relationships: Sex Role Incongruency and Pro-Male Bias. Kevin G. Lamude and Tom D. Daniels. *Women's Studies in Communication* 13, No. 2 (Fall 1990):39-56

Perceptions of Sex Differences in Classroom Communication. Lawrence B. Nadler and Marjorie Keeshan Nadler. *Women's Studies in Communication* 13, No. 1 (Spring 1990): 46-65

Power Talk. Lee A. Lusardi. *Working Woman* (July 1990):92-94

The Relationship between Communication and Marital Uncertainty: Is "Her" Marriage Different from "His" Marriage? Lynn H. Turner. *Women's Studies in Communication* 13, No. 2 (Fall 1990):57-83

Transformation and Empowerment in Gender and Communication Courses. Kathryn Carter and Carol Spitzack. *Women's Studies in Communication* 13, No. 1 (Spring 1990): 92-110

You Just Don't Understand: Women and Men in Conversation. By Deborah Tannen. Reviewed by Anita Taylor. *Women & Language* 13, No. 2 (Winter 1990):44

**Communication – Humor**

The Prattle of the Sexes. John Leo. *McCall's* 117, No. 7 (April 1990):98-99

**Communication in Organizations**

Mutual Evaluations of Communication Competence in Superior-Subordinate Relationships: Sex Role Incongruency and Pro-Male Bias. Kevin G. Lamude and Tom D. Daniels. *Women's Studies in Communication* 13, No. 2 (Fall 1990):39-56

**Communication in the Family**

Family Interactions and Sex Education in the Home. S. Elizabeth Baldwin and Madelon Visintainer Baranoski. *Adolescence* 25, No. 99 (Fall 1990):573-582

Parent-Adolescent Communication, Family Functioning, and School Performance. Venus S. Masselam, Robert F. Marcus, and Clayton L. Stunkard. *Adolescence* 25, No. 99 (Fall 1990):737

Parent-Child Sexual Discussion: Perceived Communicator Style and Subsequent Behavior. Kay E. Mueller and William G. Powers. *Adolescence* 25, No. 98 (Summer 1990):469-482

The Relationship between Communication and Marital Uncertainty: Is "Her" Marriage Different from "His" Marriage? Lynn H. Turner. *Women's Studies in Communication* 13, No. 2 (Fall 1990):57-83

**Communications**

Public-Speaking Survival Strategies: How to Make an Audience Love You. Roger Ailes and Jon Kraushar. *Working Woman* (November 1990):118-119+

**Communities**

The Ten Best Small Cities for Women. G. Scott Thomas. *Savvy Woman* (September 1990):47-49

**Community Life.** *See also* African-American Families

Connectedness. Frances Lear. *Lear's* (March 1990):168

Giving in to the Good Life. Lorrie Moore. *Savvy Woman* (September 1990):50-51+

Rousseau's Political Defense of the Sex-roled Family. Penny Weiss and Anne Harper. *Hypatia* 5, No. 3 (Fall 1990):90-109

Towards a Feminist Reassessment of Intellectual Virtue. Jane Braaten. *Hypatia* 5, No. 3 (Fall 1990):1-14

**Community Organizers**

A Cross Section of Community and Individual Action. Bibliography. Christine Doudna. *McCall's* 117, No. 8 (May 1990):164-167

**Community Service.** *See* College Students – Community Service

**Comparable Worth.** *See also* Economic Value of Women's Work; Foster Care; Wage Equity

Equity and Gender: The Comparable Worth Debate. By Ellen Frankel Paul. Reviewed by Faye Crosby. *Psychology of Women Quarterly* 14, No. 1 (March 1990):147-148

Wage Justice: Comparable Worth and the Paradox of Technocratic Reform. By Sara M. Evans and Barbara J. Nelson. Reviewed by Joan Acker. *NWSA Journal* 2, No. 2 (Spring 1990):303-306

What Women Are Worth. Lorraine Sorrel. *off our backs* 20, No. 2 (February 1990):4+

**Compensation Packages.** *See also* Employee Benefits; Labor Contracts; Wage Equity

The Bonus Bonanza. Debra Wishik Englander. *Savvy Woman* (October 1990):23-24

Four Strategies for Salary Negotiation. Laurel Touby. *Working Woman* (January 1990):110-112

**Competition.** *See* Competitive Behavior

**Competitive Behavior**

"Anything They Can Do, We Can Do Better": Couples in Competition. Sam Johnson. *Mademoiselle* (June 1990):186-187+

The Cat Is Back: The Dirty Little Secret of Women's Competition. Elizabeth Kay. *Mademoiselle* (February 1990):120-127

What's Wrong with the Competitive Edge? Michael D'Antonio. *Working Woman* (June 1990):62-63+

**Composers**

The Boulanger Sisters. Janna MacAuslan and Kristan Aspen. *Hot Wire* 6, No. 1 (January 1990):12-13+

Quincy. Alan Ebert. *Lear's* (August 1990):64-65

Who's On in Classical Music. *Glamour* (July 1990):68

Women Composers: A Lost Tradition Found. By Diane Peacock Jezic. Reviewed by Ann Armin. *Canadian Women's Studies* 11, No. 1 (Spring 1990):109

Women Composers: The Lost Tradition Found. By Diane Peacock Jezic. Reviewed by Priscilla Little. *Iris* 23 (Spring-Summer 1990):74-75

Women Composers and Their Music. Vols. 1 and 2. By Leonarda Productions. Reviewed by Priscilla Little. *Iris* 23 (Spring-Summer 1990):74-75

**Compulsive Behavior**

Your Body: Confessions of a Food Addict. Nancy Alper. *Family Circle* 103, No. 16 (November 27, 1990):26-29

**Computer-Assisted Instruction**

Tech Talk: What Kind of Manager are You? Jon Pepper. *Working Woman* (May 1990):46-52

**Computer Conferences.** *See* Computer Networks

**Computer Crimes**

Tech Talk: The Crackdown on Corporate Pirates. Stephen Davis. *Working Woman* (March 1990):50

**Computer Literacy**

The Army and the Microworld: Computers and the Politics and Gender Identity. Paul N. Edwards. *Signs* 16, No. 1 (Autumn 1990):102-127

Girls and Computers: General Issues and Case Studies of Logo in the Mathematics Classroom. Edited by Celia Hoyles. Reviewed by Lorraine Cully. *Gender and Education* 2, No. 1 (1990):110-111

Mismeasuring Women: A Critique of Research on Computer Ability and Avoidance. Pamela E. Kramer and Sheila Lehman. *Signs* 16, No. 1 (Autumn 1990):158-172

The Smart Office: Can You Tech It? Roxanne Farmanfarmaian. *Working Woman* (April 1990):58-68

Tech Talk. *Working Woman* (September 1990):94-96

Women and Computers: An Introduction. Ruth Perry and Lisa Greber. *Signs* 16, No. 1 (Autumn 1990):74-101

**Computer Networks**

Tech Talk: How to Build a Better Meeting – The On-Line Advantage. Carol Bialkowski. *Working Woman* (July 1990):40-42

**Computers.** *See also* Electromagnetic Waves

Epistemological Pluralism: Styles and Voices within the Computer Culture. Sherry Turkle and Seymour Papert. *Signs* 16, No. 1 (Autumn 1990):128-157

The Latest PC Power: All Plugged In. Barbara E. McMullen and John F. McMullen. *Lear's* (December 1990):36-37

Telecommuting. Victoria Geibel. *Lear's* (December 1990):102-107

**Computer Software.** *See also* Computer-Assisted Instruction

Your Brilliant New Career. Bill Banks. *Savvy* (December-January 1991):37-38

**Computer Technology**

Ambassador of Technology. Suzanne Weber and D. M. Pusateri. *Executive Female* 13, No. 4 (July-August 1990):47-48

Dial 911: Computers Shrink Emergency Response Times. Celia Slom. *McCall's* 117, No. 8 (May 1990):56

Mathematical Formalism as a Means of Occupational Closure in Computing – Why "Hard" Computing Tends to Exclude Women. Karen Mahony and Brett Van Toen. *Gender and Education* 2, No. 3 (1990):319-331

New Information Technologies. *Women's World* 23 (April 1990):14

Office Tech: More Power to Them. *Working Woman* (October 1990):63-68

Office Tech: The Thinking Machines. Laurel Touby. *Working Woman* (November 1990):87-98

The Smart Office: All Systems Go: How to Manage Technological Change. Sharon Efroymson First. *Working Woman* (April 1990):47-54

Technology: How a Knowledge Detective Can Help You Find Success. Georgene Muller. *Working Woman* (February 1990):44-49

Tech Talk. *Working Woman* (June 1990):38-40; (August 1990):46-48; (December 1990):42

**Conant, Jennet**

Broadcast Networking. *Working Woman* (August 1990):58-61

Cake Master. *Harper's Bazaar* (June 1990):140

Model Gourmets. *Harper's Bazaar* (July 1990):94-95+

Natural Balance. *Harper's Bazaar* (October 1990):200-203+

Precious Moments. *Harper's Bazaar* (March 1990):21-22

Quality Time. *Harper's Bazaar* (March 1990):30-38

Skin Care. *Harper's Bazaar* (February 1990):160-165+

**Condit, Celeste Michelle**

Decoding Abortion Rhetoric: Communicating Social Change. Reviewed by Diana Blackwell. *The Women's Review of Books* 7, No. 12 (September 1990):8-9

**Condominiums**

On the Waterfront. Lauren Payne and Karen J. Reisler. *Ladies' Home Journal* 107, No. 4 (April 1990):166-170

**Condoms.** *See* Contraception

**Conduct Disorders in Adolescence**

The MMPI and Jesness Inventory as Measures of Effectiveness on an Inpatient Conduct Disorders Treatment Unit. Gregory Roberts, Kenneth Schmitz, John Pinto, and Stanley Cain. *Adolescence* 25, No. 100 (Winter 1990):989-996

**Conduct of Life**

Living Beautifully: Acts of Caring. Alexandra Stoddard. *McCall's* 117, No. 7 (April 1990):136

**Coney, Sandra**

The Unfortunate Experiment. Reviewed by Hilary Haines. *The Women's Review of Books* 7, No. 8 (May 1990):20-21

**Conferences.** *See also* Teleconferencing

Networking: Playing to Win: A Conference Preview. Leslie Smith. *Executive Female* (May/June 1990):50

**Confidentiality.** *See* Privacy Rights

**Conflict Resolution.** *See also* Feminist Organizations – Division of Labor; Negotiation (in Business); Office Politics

Can Getting Mad Get the Job Done? Kathryn Stechert Black. *Working Woman* (March 1990):86-90

Recipes, Cooking, and Conflict: A Response to Heldke's *Recipes for Theory*. Donald Koch. *Hypatia* 5, No. 1 (Spring 1990):156-164

A Response to Donald Koch's "Recipes, Cooking, and Conflict." Lisa M. Heldke. *Hypatia* 5, No. 1 (Spring 1990):165-170

Trouble at the Top? How to Stay Out of It. Ellen Rapp. *Working Woman* (June 1990):60

Contraception for Men. *Good Housekeeping* 211, No. 3 (September 1990):295

Contraception for Women Over 35. John Guillebaud. *Healthright* 9, No. 4 (August 1990):17-21

Contraceptive Choice, Shift and Use Continuation: A Prospective Study in Gujarat. M. M. Gandotra and N. P. Das. *Journal of Family Welfare* 36, No. 3 (September 1990):54-69

Contraceptive Use Dynamics of Couples Availing of Services from Government Family Planning Clinics: A Case Study of Orissa. M. E. Khan, Bella C. Patel, and R. Chandrasekar. *Journal of Family Welfare* 36, No. 3 (September 1990):18-38

The Correlates of Continuity in Contraceptive Use. James F. Phillips, A. Mundigo, and A. Chamratrithirong. *Journal of Family Welfare* 36, No. 3 (September 1990):3-17

Fertile Ground. Lori Miller Kase. *Savvy Woman* (September 1990):80-82

Fertility Control in the 90s – An Interview with Malcolm Potts. Jo Calluy. *Healthright* 9, No. 2 (February 1990):21-24

Health: Birth Control. Cynthia Marks. *Mademoiselle* (September 1990):188-198

Health: The Etiquette of Birth Control. K. L. France. *Mademoiselle* (September 1990):187

Health & Fitness. Bibliography. Stephanie Young. *Glamour* (May 1990):63-74

Health Notes. *Vogue* (September 1990):468

Improved Abortion Pill on Hold. *Ms.* 1, No. 1 (July/August 1990):54-55

The Influence of a Community-Based Distribution Programme on Contraceptive Choice. K. Seshagiri Rao. *Journal of Family Welfare* 36, No. 3 (September 1990):86-106

The Joy of (Protected) Sex. Marjorie Ingall. *McCall's* 117, No. 12 (September 1990):76-78

Making Love, Making Choices. Michele Kort. *Essence* 20, No. 11 (March 1990):57-58

Oops . . . Did You Take Your Pill Today? Cynthia Hacinli. *Mademoiselle* (September 1990):198

The Origin of the Attitudes. Malcolm Potts. *Healthright* 9, No. 3 (May 1990):29-33

Our Bodies, Our Birth Control. *Ms.* 1, No. 1 (July/August 1990):55

The Pill: How It Changed Our Lives. Ann Marie Cunningham. *Ladies' Home Journal* 107, No. 6 (June 1990):121-123+

The Pill Protection Plan. By Gillian Martlew and Shelley Silver. Reviewed by Kate Griew. *Healthright* 9, No. 3 (May 1990):38-39

The Politics of Birth Control. Peggy Orenstein. *Glamour* (October 1990):264-267+

Reproductive Slights: What's Happened to Contraceptive Research? Boyd Zenner. *Iris* 24 (Fall-Winter 1990):20-24

A Study of MTP Acceptors and Their Subsequent Contraceptive Use. M. E. Khan, Bella C. Patel, and R. Chandrasekar. *Journal of Family Welfare* 36, No. 3 (September 1990):70-85

Thirty Years of the Pill. Patricia Hynes and Patricia Spallone. *Spare Rib* No. 214 (July 1990):48-49

Use of Contraceptives by Women of Upper Socioeconomic Status. Dona J. Lethbridge. *Health Care for Women International* 11, No. 3 (1990):305-318

Women's Health News. *Redbook* 175, No. 5 (September 1990):32-36

### Contraception – Cervical Caps

Caps and Condoms. *Ms.* 1, No. 2 (September/October 1990):31

### Contraception – Condoms

Falling in Love with Condoms. Lyn Stoker. *Healthright* 9, No. 4 (August 1990):35-37

Readability of Commercial Versus Generic Health Instructions for Condoms. Carol Ledbetter, Susan Hall, Janice M. Swanson, and Katherine Forrest. *Health Care for Women International* 11, No. 3 (1990):295-304

### Contraception – Dalkon Shield

Shielding Women from the Truth: The Story of the Dalkon Shield. Marlene Winfield. *Spare Rib* No. 216 (September 1990):58

### Contraception – History

Margaret Sanger: Militant, Pragmatist, Visionary. Lawrence Lader. *On the Issues* 14 (1990):11-12+

"To Create a Race of Thoroughbreds": Margaret Sanger and *The Birth Control Review*. John M. Murphy. *Women's Studies in Communication* 13, No. 1 (Spring 1990): 23-45

### Contraception – RU 486

Ethics and RU 486: Refuting Pro-Choice Arguments. Tracy Johnson. *Iris* 24 (Fall-Winter 1990):25-27

The FDA, Contraception and RU-486. Valerie K. Cotler. *Women's Rights Law Reporter* 12, No. 2 (Summer 1990): 123-136

RU 486: Another Look. Linda Roman. *New Directions for Women* 19, No. 6 (November-December 1990):4

RU 486: The "Abortion Pill." Laura Fraser. *Glamour* (September 1990):316-317+

### Contraception – Tubal Sterilization

Socio-Demographic Profile of Tubectomy Acceptors: An Army Experience. P. K. Dutta, L. S.

Vaz, and Harinder Singh. *Journal of Family Welfare* 36, No. 1 (March 1990):56-60

**Contrucci, Joyce**

Rape of the Wild: Man's Violence Against Animals and the Earth. Reviewed by Linda Vance. *NWSA Journal* 2, No. 3 (Summer 1990):485-489

**Conversation.** *See* Communication

**Conway, Jill Ker**

Daddy, We Hardly Knew You. Book Review. *The Women's Review of Books* 7, No. 9 (June 1990):11

From Daddy to Durga. *The Women's Review of Books* 7, No. 9 (June 1990):11

The Road from Coorain. Reviewed by Scarlet Cheng. *Belles Lettres* 5, No. 2 (Winter 1990):2

**Conway, Jill Ker**, Bourque, Susan C., and Scott, Joan W. (editors)

Learning About Women: Gender, Politics, and Power. Reviewed by Elizabeth Higginbotham. *NWSA Journal* 2, No. 1 (Winter 1990):105-111

**Cooey, Paula M.**

Emptiness, Otherness, and Identity: A Feminist Perspective. *Journal of Feminist Studies in Religion* 6, No. 2 (Fall 1990):7-23

**Cooey, Paula M.** (joint author). *See* Brock, Rita Nakashima

**Cook, Alison**

At Home with Barbara Bush. *Ladies' Home Journal* 107, No. 3 (March 1990):157-159+

Squeeze Play at the Kennedy Center. *Lear's* (November 1990):88-92+

**Cook, Beverly B.**, Goldstein, Leslie F., O'Connor, Karen, and Talarico, Susette M.

Women in the Judicial Process. Reviewed by Joan C. Tronto. *NWSA Journal* 2, No. 3 (Summer 1990):492-495

**Cook, Karen**

The Best Defense. *Savvy Woman* (February 1990):67-70, 96-97

**Cook, Stephani**

The Childless Executive: By Choice or By Default? *Working Woman* (November 1990):126-129+

**Cookbooks.** *See also* Christmas Cookery; Cookery, International; Cookery (Seafood); Thanksgiving Day – Cookery

As American as Apple Pie. Excerpt. Phillip Stephen Schulz. *Ladies' Home Journal* 107, No. 4 (April 1990):205-208

Four-Star Ratings. Barbara Kafka. *Family Circle* 103, No. 17 (December 18, 1990):162

Microwave Cookbook. *Good Housekeeping* 211, No. 3 (September 1990):257-258

These Cookbooks Have Legs. Bibliography. Meredith Brody. *Mademoiselle* (November 1990):78

The Ultimate Low-Fat Cookbook. *Ladies' Home Journal* 107, No. 11 (November 1990):259-272

**Cooke, Miriam**

War's Other Voices: Women Writers on the Lebanese Civil War. Reviewed by Judith Hicks Stiehm. *Women's Studies International Forum* 13, No. 3 (1990):280-281

**Cooke, Miriam** (joint editor). *See* Badran, Margot

**Cooke, Nellie** (about). *See* De Veaux, Alexis, Milloy, Marilyn, and Ross, Michael Erik

**Cookery.** *See also* Baking; Barbecue Cookery; Breakfasts and Brunches; Buffets (Cookery); Chefs; Christmas Gifts; Desserts; Food; Holidays – Cookery; Low Fat Diet; Lunchbox Cookery; Nutrition; Outdoor Cookery; *particular holidays*

Back Home Basics. Jonell Nash. *Essence* 21, No. 1 (May 1990):173-179+

Bake-Shop Secrets. *Ladies' Home Journal* 107, No. 4 (April 1990):192-197

Beat-the-Clock Dinners. Jan Turner Hazard. *Ladies' Home Journal* 107, No. 9 (September 1990):186-188+

Best Baking Guide. *Family Circle* 103, No. 16 (November 27, 1990):102-119

Best 15-Minute Skillet Dinners. *Redbook* 174, No. 6 (April 1990):116-119

Better-than-Sex Desserts. *Ladies' Home Journal* 107, No. 3 (March 1990):218-222

Breakfasts: Quick, Quicker, Quickest. Jonell Nash. *Essence* 21, No. 5 (September 1990):90-93+

Budget-Smart Family Fare. Jo Ann Brett. *Family Circle* 103, No. 16 (November 27, 1990):122-128

Cheap Eats. *Ladies' Home Journal* 107, No. 9 (September 1990):196

Cleansing Diet Recipes. Jonell Nash. *Essence* 20, No. 9 (January 1990):80-83+

Come for the Weekend. Marie Simmons. *Working Woman* (June 1990):79-82+

Contemporary Living: 20 Minute Meals. Jonell Nash. *Essence* 20, No. 11 (March 1990):87-95+

Cooking in the Fast Lane. *Ladies' Home Journal* 107, No. 3 (March 1990):224-227

Cook Like a Pro: The Slim Chef's Dummer Party Tips. *Family Circle* 103, No. 9 (June 26, 1990):48-50

Crescent City Cuisine: Dining Out in New Orleans. Marc Frazier. *Harper's Bazaar* (January 1990):134+

Dinner on a Bed. *Glamour* (April 1990):304-305

30-Minute Menu. *Good Housekeeping* 211, No. 3 (September 1990):82

12 Great Meals for Small Families. Melanie Barnard and Brooke Dojny. *Redbook* 174, No. 5 (March 1990):141-152

20 Minute Cookbook. *McCall's* 117, No. 8 (May 1990):127-140

Warm Desserts for Cold Winter Days. *Ladies' Home Journal* 107, No. 1 (January 1990):144-148

Willard Scott's Breakfast Book. Willard Scott. *Ladies' Home Journal* 107, No. 3 (March 1990):201-216

Women Chefs' Hall of Fame. Jan Turner Hazard. *Ladies' Home Journal* 107, No. 11 (November 1990):246-254

**Cookery, African**

Dishes from Africa and the Diaspora. Jonell Nash. *Essence* 21, No. 6 (October 1990):107-108+

Festive Food. Dee Dee Dailey. *Essence* 21, No. 8 (December 1990):102-106+

Food: Catered to Our Style. Jonell Nash. *Essence* 21, No. 8 (December 1990):94-98

Iron Pots and Wooden Spoons. Excerpt. Jessica Harris. *Essence* 21, No. 6 (October 1990):101-104

**Cookery – Equipment and Supplies**

At Home In the Kitchen. Celia Slom. *McCall's* 117, No. 9 (June 1990):113-117

Kitchens for People Who Love to Cook. Lauren Payne and Jan Turner Hazard. *Ladies' Home Journal* 107, No. 3 (March 1990):184-198

**Cookery, International**

Five-Language Cookbook. *Good Housekeeping* 211, No. 3 (September 1990):236-250+

**Cookery, Italian**

Cuisine of the Sun. Jan Turner Hazard. *Ladies' Home Journal* 107, No. 8 (August 1990):126-137

Express-Lane Cook: An Italian Feast Without Any Fuss. Laurie Goldrich. *Working Woman* (February 1990):112

Southern Exposure. Colette Rossant. *Harper's Bazaar* (April 1990):212

**Cookery – United States**

America's Best One-Dish Meals from Across the Country. *Family Circle* 103, No. 15 (November 6, 1990):78-82

**Cookery (Baby Foods).** *See also* Baby Foods

**Cookery (Beans)**

Diet News: Feel Fuller Longer. *Redbook* 174, No. 5 (March 1990):28

**Cookery (Bread)**

Homemade Bread! *Good Housekeeping* 211, No. 4 (October 1990):172-176

Primal Bread. Jeffrey Steingarten. *Vogue* (November 1990):304-310

Step-by-Step: Italian Onion Bread. *Good Housekeeping* 211, No. 3 (September 1990):74

**Cookery (Cake)**

Country-Style Buttermilk Crumb Cake. *Redbook* 174, No. 5 (March 1990):154

**Cookery (Casseroles)**

This Is *Not* Your Mother's Casserole. *Ladies' Home Journal* 107, No. 2 (February 1990):150-156

**Cookery (Cheese)**

Food and Health Bulletin: Good News for Cheese Lovers. *Glamour* (April 1990):314

Food Notes. *Vogue* (January 1990):126

Say "Cheese" for Great Eating. Holly Sheppard. *McCall's* 117, No. 9 (June 1990):119

**Cookery (Chicken)**

Have a Great Fourth of July Chicken Cookout. *Redbook* 175, No. 3 (July 1990):69-74

**Cookery (Chocolate)**

Decadent Desserts. Jonell Nash. *Essence* 20, No. 10 (February 1990):85-88+

For the Love of Chocolate. Valerie Vaz. *Essence* 20, No. 10 (February 1990):83-; 84

**Cookery (Eggs)**

Eggs, Savory-Style. Karen Sethre White. *McCall's* 117, No. 12 (September 1990):150

Party Quiche! *Redbook* 176, No. 2 (December 1990):148

**Cookery (Fajitas)**

Low-Fat Cooking: Fast, Fabulous Fajitas. *Family Circle* 103, No. 15 (November 6, 1990):58

**Cookery (Frozen Foods).** *See* Frozen Foods

**Cookery (Fruit)**

Apples! *Family Circle* 103, No. 13 (September 25, 1990):84-85+

Pick a Perfect Pear. *Family Circle* 103, No. 14 (October 16, 1990):104-105

**Cookery (Meats)**

All-New Chicken Cookbook. *McCall's* 117, No. 7 (April 1990):101-121

Beef Is Back. *Ladies' Home Journal* 107, No. 9 (September 1990):194+

The Buzz on Beef. Ellen Kunes. *Mademoiselle* (December 1990):186

Family-Favorite Grilled Chicken. Holly Sheppard. *McCall's* 117, No. 11 (August 1990):119

Hot Diggity! *Redbook* 175, No. 4 (August 1990):96-97+

Light & Easy: Veal with Fresh Spinach. *Good Housekeeping* 211, No. 3 (September 1990):218

Nutrition Now: Bone Up on Beef. Lawrence Lindner. *Redbook* 174, No. 5 (March 1990):157-162

Saturday Night Supper: Pork Chops with Cider. *Glamour* (February 1990):214

Skillet Spareribs. *Redbook* 175, No. 5 (September 1990):194

Slim Pork. *Redbook* 175, No. 1 (May 1990):140-148

Step-by-Step: Barbecued Pork on a Bun. *Good Housekeeping* 211, No. 4 (October 1990):30

World Class Chicken. Jan T. Hazard. *Ladies' Home Journal* 107, No. 5 (May 1990):196-202

**Cookery (Pasta)**

Contemporary Living: Pasta. Valerie Vaz. *Essence* 20, No. 12 (April 1990):81-82

Herbal Pasta. Sarah Reynolds. *McCall's* 118, No. 2 (November 1990):131-132

New Wave Pasta Dishes. Jonell Nash. *Essence* 20, No. 12 (April 1990):84-87 +

Pasta Cookbook. Marianne Langan. *McCall's* 117, No. 12 (September 1990):137-148

The Wise Woman's Diet: Pasta Takes Off Pounds! Johanna Dwyer. *Redbook* 175, No. 4 (August 1990):111-120

**Cookery (Pastry)**

Cook Like a Pro: Hail to the Chef. *Family Circle* 103, No. 14 (October 16, 1990):66-68

**Cookery (Pickles, Relish, etc.)**

Flavor to Relish All Year Long. Donna Meadow. *McCall's* 117, No. 11 (August 1990):116

**Cookery (Pizza)**

Easy as Pie. *Ladies' Home Journal* 107, No. 1 (January 1990):122-126

**Cookery (Salads)**

Cool Salads for Hot Summer Days. Lynne Giviskos. *McCall's* 117, No. 9 (June 1990):120

The Sensible Salad. Marie Simmons. *Working Woman* (May 1990):130

**Cookery (Sandwiches)**

Sensational Sandwiches that Make a Meal. *McCall's* 117, No. 8 (May 1990):145

Soup and Sandwich Cookbook. Marianne Langan. *McCall's* 118, No. 1 (October 1990):123-138

**Cookery (Seafood)**

Eating Out: Get a Great Fish Dinner. *Glamour* (April 1990):306

Fish for Life. Valerie Vaz. *Essence* 21, No. 2 (June 1990):75-78

Fish Stories. *Ladies' Home Journal* 107, No. 4 (April 1990):199-203

The Microwave Cookbook. *Good Housekeeping* 211, No. 4 (October 1990):199-200

Sea Fare. Jonell Nash. *Essence* 21, No. 2 (June 1990):80-82

Ultimate Shrimp Rolls. Holly Sheppard. *McCall's* 118, No. 1 (October 1990):108-110

**Cookery (Soup)**

Soup and Sandwich Cookbook. Marianne Langan. *McCall's* 118, No. 1 (October 1990):123-138

Soups that Make a Meal. Pamela M. Berger. *McCall's* 118, No. 2 (November 1990):134

Super Soups, Hot or Cold. *McCall's* 117, No. 7 (April 1990):123

**Cookery (Vegetables)**

Fresh from the Garden Vegetables. *McCall's* 117, No. 11 (August 1990):103-115

Frozen Vegetables Served with a Flourish. *McCall's* 117, No. 8 (May 1990):143

Hot Potatoes! Jan Turner Hazard. *Ladies' Home Journal* 107, No. 2 (February 1990):139-149

Nutrition Now: The Perfect Salad. *Redbook* 175, No. 3 (July 1990):116-121

Pumpkin Treats. *Good Housekeeping* 211, No. 4 (October 1990):180-183

Savor the Flavor of Fall. *Family Circle* 103, No. 14 (October 16, 1990):106-108

**Cookie Jars**

50 Cookie Jars. Louise Messina. *Good Housekeeping* 211, No. 4 (October 1990):146-149 +

**Cookies.** *See also* Cookie Jars

Christmas Means Cookies. Jan Turner Hazard. *Ladies' Home Journal* 107, No. 12 (December 1990):162 +

Classic Holiday Cookies. *Redbook* 176, No. 2 (December 1990):131-140

Cookie Superstars. *Ladies' Home Journal* 107, No. 10 (October 1990):196-201

Fine Art Cookies. Sarah Reynolds. *McCall's* 118, No. 3 (December 1990):98-100 +

Santa's Favorites. *Family Circle* 103, No. 16 (November 27, 1990):90-91

**Cool, Lisa Collier**

Money: Getting Debt-Free in '90. *Essence* 20, No. 11 (March 1990):38

**Cooney, Teresa M.** and Uhlenberg, Peter

The Role of Divorce in Men's Relations with Their Adult Children after Mid-life. *Journal of Marriage and the Family* 52, No. 3 (August 1990):677-688

**Coontz, Stephanie**

The Social Origins of Private Life: A History of American Families, 1600-1900. Reviewed by Patricia Crawford. *Australian Feminist Studies* No. 12 (Summer 1990):131-132

The Social Origins of Private Life: A History of American Families 1600-1900. Reviewed by Joan Entmacher. *Women's Studies International Forum* 13, No. 5 (1990):521-522

**Cooper, Anna Julia**

Slavery and the French Revolutionists (1788-1805). Reviewed by Leonore Loft. *Women's Studies International Forum* 13, Nos. 1-2 (1990):160

**Cooper, Bob**

Everywhere to Run. *Women's Sports & Fitness* 12, No. 6 (September 1990):33

Running Circles Around the Boys. *Women's Sports and Fitness* 12, No. 3 (April 1990):62-65

Sallying Forth. *Women's Sports and Fitness* 12, No. 7 (October 1990):15

**Cooper, Candy J.**

Oakland Exposé: A Hunch Pays Off. Kathleen Tripp. *Ms.* 1, No. 3 (November/December 1990):90

**Cooper, Carol**

Angela Winbush Takes Care of Business. *Essence* 20, No. 10 (February 1990):39

Let Love Rule. *Essence* 20, No. 10 (February 1990):54-55+

Regina Belle: Showing Us the Way. *Essence* 20, No. 11 (March 1990):44

Repeat Performance. *Essence* 21, No. 1 (May 1990):144-148

**Cooper, Carolyn S.**, Dunst, Carl J., and Vance, Sherra D.

The Effect of Social Support on Adolescent Mothers' Styles of Parent-Child Interaction as Measured on Three Separate Occasions. *Adolescence* 25, No. 97 (Spring 1990):49-57

**Cooper, Helen**

Elizabeth Barrett Browning, Woman and Artist. Reviewed by Joyce Zonana. *Tulsa Studies in Women's Literature* 9, No. 1 (Spring 1990):160-163

**Cooper, Helen M.**, Munich, Adrienne Auslander, and Squier, Susan Merrill (editors)

Arms and the Woman: War, Gender, and Literary Representation. Reviewed by Mary Anne Schofield. *Belles Lettres* 5, No. 4 (Summer 1990):38-39

Arms and the Woman: War, Gender, and Literary Representation. Reviewed by Sonya Michel. *The Women's Review of Books* 7, No. 6 (March 1990):26-27

**Cooper, J. California**

Such Good Friends. Short story. *Essence* 21, No. 1 (May 1990):150-154+

**Cooper, Margaret** (joint author). *See* Groce, Stephen B.

**Cooper, Patricia A.**

Once a Cigar Maker: Men, Women and Work Culture in American Cigar Factories, 1900-1919. Reviewed by Elizabeth Faue. *Signs* 15, No. 2 (Winter 1990):391-394

**Cooper, Penelope** (about)

The Best Defense. Karen Cook. *Savvy Woman* (February 1990):67-70, 96-97

**Copelon, Rhonda** and Kolbert, Kathryn

With Brennan Gone . . . Saving the Bill of Rights. *Ms.* 1, No. 2 (September/October 1990):89

**Coping Strategies.** *See also* Management Techniques; Stress Relaxation

**Coppola, Eleanor**

The Godfather Diary. *Vogue* (December 1990):304-309+

**Coppola, Francis Ford** (about). *See* Film and Filmmakers

**Coppola, Sofia** (about)

All in the Family. Joanne Kaufman. *Ladies' Home Journal* 107, No. 12 (December 1990):106

**Coppola, Sophia** (about)

Sophia Coppola. Stephanie Mansfield. *Vogue* (April 1990):126-130

**Cop Rock.** *See* Television Programs

**Copyrighting–Music**

Anonymous in My Own Time. Paula Walowitz. *Hot Wire* 6, No. 2 (May 1990):14-15+

Copyrighting Music. Lori Weiner. *Hot Wire* 6, No. 2 (May 1990):15

**Coqueran, Angie** (about)

Get the Picture. Erik Hedegaard. *Savvy Woman* (January 1990):72-75, 92-93

**Corbel, Eve**

Demolition. *Canadian Women's Studies* 11, No. 2 (Fall 1990):51-52

**Corberó, Xavier** (about). *See* Spain–Culture and Society

**Corbin, Alain**

Women for Hire: Prostitution and Sexuality in France after 1850. Reviewed by Frances Gouda. *The Women's Review of Books* 7, No. 12 (September 1990):13-14

**Corbitt, Helen** (about). *See also* Hazard, Jan Turner, "Women Chefs"

**Corcoran, Clodagh**

Men Against Pornography. *Spare Rib* 217 (October 1990):47

**Corder, Billie F.** and Whiteside, Reid

Structured Role Assignment and Other Techniques for Facilitating Process in Adolescent Psychotherapy Groups. *Adolescence* 25, No. 98 (Summer 1990):343-351

**Cordova, Jeanne**

Kicking the Habit: A Lesbian Nun Story. Reviewed by Carol Anne Douglas. *off our backs* 20, No. 11 (December 1990):19

**Corea, Gena** and others

Man-Made Women: How New Reproductive Technologies Affect Women. Reviewed by Peggy L. Chinn. *Signs* 15, No. 2 (Winter 1990):400-405

**Corey, Anne**

Plain Geometry. Poem. *Sinister Wisdom* 40 (Spring 1990):99-100

**Corey, Deborah Joy**

Doll Baby. Short story. *Mademoiselle* (October 1990):134-136+

**Corinne, Tee A.**

Bodies: A Collage. *Woman of Power* 18 (Fall 1990):70-72

**Corinne, Tee A.** (about). *See also* Art – Exhibitions, "Racism"

**Corinne, Tee A.** (editor)

Intricate Passions. Reviewed by Ruth Mountaingrove. *off our backs* 20, No. 11 (December 1990):13

**Cork, Holly** (about). *See* Title, Stacy

**Cornelia, Marie**

Monstrous Regiment: The Lady Knight in Sixteenth-Century Epic. Book Review. *Tulsa Studies in Women's Literature* 9, No. 1 (Spring 1990):156-158

**Cornelisen, Ann**

Where It All Began: Italy 1954. Reviewed by Mary Taylor Simeti. *The Women's Review of Books* 8, No. 1 (October 1990):13-14

**Cornell, Drucilla** (joint editor). *See* Benhabib, Seyla

**Cornell, Laurel L.**

Peasant Women and Divorce in Preindustrial Japan. Notes. *Signs* 15, No. 4 (Summer 1990):710-732

**Cornwall, Marie** (joint author). *See* Thomas, Darwin L.

**Corporate Liability.** *See also* Hazardous Wastes

Silk Purse Chronicles. Patricia O'Toole. *Lear's* (March 1990):32-34

**Corporations.** *See also* Business Enterprises

**Corporations – Spouses of Employees**

A Corporate Wife after the Ball. Kathleen Walker Lawrence. *Lear's* (October 1990):58-60

**Corpus Christi – Mayors.** *See* Texas – Mayors

**Corrigan, Sheila A.** (joint author). *See* Johnson, Cheryl A.

**Corrigan, Theresa** and Hoppe, Stephanie (editors)

With a Fly's Eye, Whale's Wit, and Woman's Heart. Reviewed by Patricia Roth Schwartz. *Belles Lettres* 5, No. 2 (Winter 1990):12

With a Fly's Eye, Whale's Wit and Woman's Heart: Animals and Women. Reviewed by Nancy Lloyd. *On the Issues* 16 (Fall 1990):32

**Corrothers, Helen** (about). *See* Etra, Jon, "World Class"

**Cortez, Jayne**

If the Drum Is a Woman. Poem. *Essence* 21, No. 5 (September 1990):118

Push Back the Catastropes. Poem. *Essence* 21, No. 1 (May 1990):205

**Cosby, Bill**

"Give from the Heart": A Letter from Bill Cosby. *Redbook* 176, No. 2 (December 1990):91

**Cosby, Bill** (about)

Bill Cosby – Living with Heartbreak. Bill Cosby. *Redbook* 175, No. 2 (June 1990):52-54+

TV's Bill Cosby in Ghost Dad, the Movie. Benilde Little. *Essence* 21, No. 2 (June 1990):38

**Cosell, Hilary**

Tweens. *Working Mother* (November 1990):132-134; (December 1990):74

**Cosgrove, Jean M.** (joint author). *See* Miller, Robert P.

**Cosmetic Dentistry.** *See* Dentistry – Aesthetics

**Cosmetics Industry.** *See also* Krok, Lauren (about); Weinstein, Joan (about)

The Beauty Queens. Vicki Woods. *Vogue* (January 1990):190-194+

The Cowboy as Cosmetician. Karen Stabiner. *Lear's* (January 1990):46-50

Images: Counter Intelligence. Jeannie Ralston. *Vogue* (September 1990):324-340

Natural Balance. Jennet Conant. *Harper's Bazaar* (October 1990):200-203+

**Cosmetic Surgery.** *See also* Plastic Surgery

Cosmetics after Surgery. Lou Ann Walker. *Lear's* (January 1990):99

The Cosmetic Surgery Hoax. Laura Fraser. *Glamour* (February 1990):184-185+

Saving Face. Carolyn J. Cline. *Lear's* (January 1990):96-99

Your Body. Carla Rohlfing. *Family Circle* 103, No. 10 (July 24, 1990): 53-54+

**Coss, Clare** (editor)

Lillian D. Wald: Progressive Activist. Reviewed by Katherine A. Kendall. *AFFILIA* 5, No. 4 (Winter 1990):113-114

**Cosslett, Tess**

Woman to Woman: Female Friendship in Victorian Fiction. Reviewed by Susan Hardy Aiken. *Signs* 16, No. 1 (Autumn 1990):188-192

**Costa, Rosaline**

Woes of Tribal Garment Girls: Bangladesh. *Women in Action* 1-2 (1990):20

**Costa Rica – Feminist Movement**

Feminism in the Barrios of Costa Rica. Carol Anne Douglas. *off our backs* 20, No. 3 (March 1990):1-3+

**Costigan, Kelly**

Stressed Out? Who Isn't. *Savvy Woman* (February 1990):88-89

The Ultimate Birth Control. *Savvy Woman* (January 1990):84-85

**Cost of Living.** *See* Urban Areas – Cost of Living

**Costume Design.** *See also* Sylbert, Anthea (about)

The Dress Circle. John McLaughlin. *Harper's Bazaar* (April 1990):94-103

Grand Designs. John McLaughlin. *Harper's Bazaar* (July 1990):84-85+

Vogue Arts: Design. André Leon Talley. *Vogue* (December 1990):200-202

Word On. . .*Glamour* (November 1990):167

**Costume Jewelry**

Elements: Joseff. Jody Shields. *Vogue* (December 1990):142-144

Fantastic Faux: Artful Deception. *Harper's Bazaar* (November 1990):68-72

Getting Stoned. *Vogue* (August 1990):300-309

Great Pretenders. *Harper's Bazaar* (November 1990):176-179

Talking Fashion. Julia Reed. *Vogue* (December 1990):332-334

Vogue's Last Look. Edited by Candy Pratts Price. *Vogue* (August 1990):392

**Cotler, Valerie K.**

The FDA, Contraception and RU-486. *Women's Rights Law Reporter* 12, No. 2 (Summer 1990): 123-136

**Cotnoir, Louise** (joint author). *See* Bersianik, Louky

**Cottle, Charles E.** (joint author). *See* Berger, Ronald J.

**Cotton, Sandra**, Antill, John K., and Cunningham, John D.

The Work Attachment of Mothers with Preschool Children. *Psychology of Women Quarterly* 14, No. 2 (June 1990):255-270

**Cotton, Terri** and Cudjoe, Selwyn R.

Report on the First International Conference of Women Writers of the English-Speaking Caribbean. *Sage* 6, No. 1 (Summer 1989):83

**Cougar, Jesse**

The Selfish Sperm Theory. *Lesbian Ethics* 4, No. 1 (Spring 1990): 28-43

**Coulter, Sara** (joint author). *See* Hedges, Elaine

**Coultrap-McQuin, Susan**

Doing Literary Business: American Women Writers in the Nineteenth Century. Reviewed by Emily Toth. *The Women's Review of Books* 8, No. 3 (December 1990):15-16

**Council for the Development of Economic and Social Research in Africa**

Documentation and Information Activities of CODICE. Wambui Wagacha. *Women's World* 23 (April 1990):23-24

**Council of Fashion Designers of America**

7th On Sale. *Vogue* (September 1990):514

**Counseling.** *See also* Employee-Employer Relations; Family Therapy; Grandparents; Health Education; Management Techniques; Marriage Counseling; Obsessive-Compulsive Disorders; Parenting; Personal Relationships; Psychotherapy; Self-Help Techniques; Sexual Relationships; Stress – Coping Strategies; Support Systems

The Answer Couple. Bob Reiss and Ann Hood. *Glamour* (June 1990):164-165

Answers to Your Questions. Joyce Brothers. *Good Housekeeping* 211, No. 3 (September 1990):214-217; 211, No. 4 (October 1990):111-112

Between Us. Bibliography. Gwendolyn Goldsby Grant. *Essence* 21, No. 2 (June 1990):26-27; 21, No. 3 (July 1990):26-27; 21, No. 4 (August 1990):30; 21, No. 5 (September 1990):32-33; 21, No. 6 (October 1990):30-32; 21, No. 7 (November 1990):24; 21, No. 8 (December 1990):27

Between Us. Gwendolyn Goldsby Grant. *Essence* 20, No. 10 (February 1990):30-; 20, No. 11 (March 1990):30-31; 20, No. 12 (April 1990):30-31; 31

Breaking Out of the Ex-Wife Trap. Sandra Kahn. *Lear's* (December 1990):48-49

Couple Time. *Glamour* (August 1990):126; (September 1990):174; (October 1990):148

Doctor, Doctor. Maj-Britt Rosenbaum. *Mademoiselle* (December 1990):114

Doctor, Doctor. Maj-Britt Rosenbaum and Judith Sills. *Mademoiselle* (September 1990):202; (October 1990):130

Editorial: 27 Mini-Gripes That Can Split Any Couple's Seams. *Glamour* (February 1990):72

Etiquette: Doing It Right. Charlotte Ford. *McCall's* 117, No. 9 (June 1990):56-57

The Five Biggest Mistakes Most Parents Make. Ellen Galinsky. *Ladies' Home Journal* 107, No. 6 (June 1990):80-87

Glamour Guide. *Glamour* (April 1990):103-107

Health & Mind. Pamela Erens. *Glamour* (June 1990):52; (August 1990):60; (October 1990):60; (December 1990):58

Healthy Love. Lesley Dormen. *Glamour* (October 1990):270-271+

His: Trial by Dial – Should You Call Him First? Warren Leight. *Mademoiselle* (February 1990):93

How Resentment Can Wreck Divorce. John Bradshaw. *Lear's* (August 1990):57

How to Make Yourself a Stronger Person. Claire Berman. *Ladies' Home Journal* 107, No. 11 (November 1990):96-104

The Intelligent Woman's Guide to Sex: Please Skip the Intimate Details! Dalma Heyn. *Mademoiselle* (January 1990):67

The Intelligent Woman's Guide to Sex: 8 Ways to Survive Heartbreak Hell. Dalma Heyn. *Mademoiselle* (February 1990):96

Is He Mr. Right? Or Mr. Right-for-Now? Candace Bushnell. *Mademoiselle* (February 1990):186-187

Jake: A Man's Opinion. *Glamour* (April 1990):148-150

Just Between Us. Gwendolyn Goldsby Grant. *Essence* 20, No. 9 (January 1990):26-27+

Love's Power Plays. Sara Nelson. *Glamour* (January 1990):148-149+

Loving a Man who Is "Different." Carol Lynn Mithers. *Glamour* (March 1990):296

Never Can Say Goodbye. Karen Grigsby Bates. *Essence* 20, No. 10 (February 1990):61-62

The Passion Paradox. Dean C. Delis and Cassandra Phillips. *Glamour* (August 1990):214-215+

6 Rules for Summer Lovers. Pamela Redmond Satran. *Glamour* (May 1990):248-249+

Sex Drive: A User's Guide. Monique Burns. *Essence* 21, No. 4 (August 1990):29

Sex & Health. Shirley Zussman. *Glamour* (January 1990):163; (February 1990):219; (March 1990):298; (April 1990):318; (May 1990):320; (June 1990):276; (August 1990):250

Sex & Health. Shirlley Zussman. *Glamour* (September 1990):86

Sexual Ethics: Men from Our Embarrassing Past. Betsy Israel. *Glamour* (August 1990):248

Single Again. Lesley Dormen. *Glamour* (September 1990):190-193

Smile, Though Your Heart Is Racing. Jeannie Ralston. *Mademoiselle* (November 1990):182-183+

Ten Steps to Self-Esteem. Monique Burns. *Essence* 21, No. 4 (August 1990):57-58

They've Got to Have It: The Twentysomethings Take Over. Jill Neimark. *Mademoiselle* (December 1990):158-160

Who, Me, Ambivalent? Dalma Heyn. *Mademoiselle* (December 1990):71-72

You *Can* Change Your Life. Marlin S. Potash. *Good Housekeeping* 211, No. 4 (October 1990):94-96

On Your Own: Don't Wait for the Last Straw. Judith Stone. *Glamour* (March 1990):122

On Your Own: Feeling Fifteen Again. Judith Stone. *Glamour* (February 1990):107

### Counseling – Feminist Perspectives

Feminist Counselling in Action. By Jocelyn Chaplin. Reviewed by Karen A. Holmes. *AFFILIA* 5, No. 1 (Spring 1990):104-106

Women, Feminism and Family Therapy. Edited by Lois Braverman. Reviewed by Karen A. Holmes. *AFFILIA* 5, No. 1 (Spring 1990):104-106

Women in Families: A Framework for Family Therapy. Edited by Monica McGoldrick, Carol M. Anderson, and Froma Walsh. Reviewed by Ruth Farber. *AFFILIA* 5, No. 1 (Spring 1990):107-108

**Country Inns.** *See* Resorts

**Country Music.** *See* Music, Popular – Country and Western

**Couples.** *See also* Balancing Work and Family Life; Domestic Relations; Female-Male Relationships

Couples: 10 Reasons to Pair Off. Ellen Welty. *Mademoiselle* (September 1990):242-247

Couple Time. *Glamour* (January 1990):64; (July 1990):90

Joint Venture. Judith Stone. *Glamour* (October 1990):154

The Myth of the Perfect Couple. Dalma Heyn. *Mademoiselle* (November 1990):80-82

**Court, Dianne** (joint author). *See* Franzway, Suzanne

**Courtesans.** *See* Prostitution

**Courtney, Carol-Ann**

Morphine and Dolly Mixtures. Reviewed by Penny Simpson. *Spare Rib* No. 209 (February 1990):30

**Courtney-Clarke, Margaret**

A Window on Walls. Photo essay. *Ms.* 1, No. 3 (November/December 1990):46-51

**Courtship**

6 Rules for Summer Lovers. Pamela Redmond Satran. *Glamour* (May 1990):248-249+

**Courtship Customs.** *See also* Dating Customs

Jake: A Man's Opinion. *Glamour* (December 1990):132

**Courtwright, David T.**

The Neglect of Female Children and Childhood Sex Ratios in Nineteenth-Century America: A Review of the Evidence. *Journal of Family History* 15, No. 3 (July 1990):313-323

**Cousins, Norman**

How to Cope with Disaster. *McCall's* 118, No. 1 (October 1990):73-82

**Couturiers.** *See* Fashion Designers

**Cover Letters**

Signed, Sealed, Delivered. Suzanne Weber. *Executive Female* (March/April 1990):36-37

**Covernton, Jane**

Thinking Through Infertility. *Healthsharing* 11, No. 1 (December 1989):29-33

**Covington, Dennis**

Flowers for Violeta. *Vogue* (August 1990):318-323+

**Covington, Vicki**

Bird of Paradise. Reviewed by Eleanor J. Bader. *New Directions for Women* 19, No. 5 (September-October 1990):20

**Cowan, Barbara**

A Safe World for Us All. *Women and Environments* 12, No. 1 (Fall 1989/Winter 1990): 9

**Cowan, Gloria**

Defining Rape. Book Review. *Psychology of Women Quarterly* 14, No. 2 (June 1990):294-296

**Cowan, Tom** (joint author). *See* Ferguson, J. Barry

**Cowasjee, Dosebai** (about). *See also* India – Status of Women

**Cowboys – Myth**

The Myth of the Cowboy and Its Meaning for Rodeo Families. Angeline Bushy. *Health Care for Women International* 11, No. 1 (1990):75-88

**Cowell, Susan** (about)

Susan Cowell Champions the Union Label. Laura Mansnerus. *McCall's* 117, No. 8 (May 1990):51

**Cowlishaw, Gillian**

Feminism and Anthropology. Book Review. *Australian Feminist Studies* No. 11 (Autumn 1990):121-122

The Gender of the Gift: Problems with Women and Problems with Society in Melanesia. Book Review. *Australian Feminist Studies* No. 11 (Autumn 1990):121-122

**Cowlishaw, Gillian** and Lea, Teresa

On Vicky Kirby versus Marilyn Strathern Vers(us). *Australian Feminist Studies* No. 11 (Autumn 1990):87-89

**Cox, Carol** (joint author). *See* Braeman, Elizabeth

**Cox, David N.** (joint author). *See* Ehrenberg, Marion F.

**Cox, Elizabeth Shrader**

Women Force a Government Response. *Connexions* 34 (1990):4-5

**Cox, Jane** (editor)

A Singular Marriage: A Labour Love Story in Letters and Diaries. Reviewed by Clare Collins. *Gender & History* 2, No. 1 (Spring 1990):116-118

**Cox, Kathryn** and Subak-Sharpe, Genell

Women's Health: "I Want a Second Opinion." *Redbook* 175, No. 1 (May 1990):22-28

**Cox, Renée**

A Gynecentric Aesthetic. *Hypatia* 5, No. 2 (Summer 1990):43-62

**Coyne, Patricia** (joint author). *See* Clark-Jones, Melissa

**Crabtree, Ben** (joint author). *See* Schichor, Aric

**Crack (Drug).** *See also* Cocaine Abuse

**Craft, Nikki** (about)

From Expert Witness to Jail Inmate. Diana E. H. Russell. *off our backs* 20, No. 10 (November 1990):4

Washington Jails Nikki Craft for Ripping Up *Esquire.* Lucy Colvin. *off our backs* 20, No. 7 (July 1990):1+

**Craft, Sheila**

The General Was a Lady. Poem. *Minerva* 8, No. 4 (Winter 1990):54-55

**Craft Arts.** *See also* Costume Design; Fashion; Indians of North America – Craft Arts; Pottery; Quilting; Wearable Art

Cabin Fever! *Family Circle* 103, No. 15 (November 6, 1990):84-89

Colored, Cut, or Crystal Clear. Kathryn Lineberger. *Lear's* (November 1990):122-124

Country Cottage. *Family Circle* 103, No. 14 (October 16, 1990):88-93

Country Western. *Redbook* 175, No. 5 (September 1990):144-149

Easter Joys. *Redbook* 174, No. 6 (April 1990):30

Easy-Do Gifts. *Family Circle* 103, No. 16 (November 27, 1990):92-93

Entertaining: Special Settings. Zacki Murphy. *Family Circle* 103, No. 16 (November 27, 1990):59-60

Fields of Dreams. *Family Circle* 103, No. 13 (September 25, 1990):76-77

Help! Vicki Lansky. *Family Circle* 103, No. 17 (December 18, 1990):125-126

Home Decorating: Robert Redford's Rocky Mountain Crafts. *Redbook* 175, No. 6 (October 1990):70

How to: Bright Idea. *Family Circle* 103, No. 9 (June 26, 1990):128-132

Just Folks. *Redbook* 175, No. 3 (July 1990):108-111

Killing Our Sorrows. Bibliography. Susan Schnur. *Lilith* 15, No. 3 (Summer 1990):15

Knocking on Wood. Kathryn Lineberger. *Lear's* (October 1990):138

Last Minute Gifts, Decorations, Food. *Family Circle* 103, No. 17 (December 18, 1990):104-108

Make It Merry! *Redbook* 176, No. 2 (December 1990):92-97

Make Yours a Holiday Home. *Family Circle* 103, No. 16 (November 27, 1990):84-89

Mary Emmerling's American Country. Mary Emmerling. *Good Housekeeping* 211, No. 3 (September 1990):221-225

Natural Wonders. *Redbook* 176, No. 2 (December 1990):114-115

New Country Decorating. *Ladies' Home Journal* 107, No. 9 (September 1990):180-182

Our Annual 55 Great Gifts to Make. *Family Circle* 103, No. 15 (November 6, 1990):70-77

Quick Craft: Trick or Treat? *Family Circle* 103, No. 14 (October 16, 1990):152-158

The Quilt Complex. *Mademoiselle* (September 1990):94 +

Sew and Go! *Family Circle* 103, No. 17 (December 18, 1990):164-166

Small Treasures. *Redbook* 176, No. 2 (December 1990):108-109

The Sourcebook for Women Who Create. By Gail Adams, Martha Miles, and Linda Yoder. *NWSA Journal* 2, No. 2 (Spring 1990):282-287

Tote-All Picnic Set. *Family Circle* 103, No. 9 (June 26, 1990):108-111

Weekend Afghan. *Family Circle* 103, No. 8 (June 5, 1990):85-88

Women in the Arts. Bibliography. Evette Porter. *Essence* 21, No. 1 (May 1990):80-86

Wrap it Up! *Family Circle* 103, No. 17 (December 18, 1990):156-160

**Craft Arts – Africa**

Afrocentric Gifts. Kimberly Knight. *Essence* 21, No. 8 (December 1990):90

**Craig, Sue**

Infertility Counselling: Should Surrogacy Be an Option? *Healthright* 9, No. 2 (February 1990):25-29

Tying the Tubes. Book Review. *Healthright* 9, No. 4 (August 1990):46-47

**Crandall, Prudence** (about)

A Whole-Souled Woman: Prudence Crandall and the Education of Black Women. By Susan Strane. Reviewed by Suzanna Sloat. *Belles Lettres* 6, No. 1 (Fall 1990):47

**Crane, Elaine Forman**

The Adams Women: Abigail and Louisa Adams, Their Sisters and Daughters. Book Review. *NWSA Journal* 2, No. 4 (Autumn 1990):661-664

The Socioeconomics of a Female Majority in Eighteenth-Century Bermuda. Notes. *Signs* 15, No. 2 (Winter 1990):231-258

Women in the Age of the American Revolution. Book Review. *NWSA Journal* 2, No. 4 (Autumn 1990):661-664

**Craniosacral Therapy**

Cranial Therapy: Relief at Last. Susan Danese. *Healthsharing* 11, No. 2 (March 1990):27-28

**Craven-Griffiths, Jennifer**

Equality and Sex Discrimination Law. Book Review. *Gender and Education* 2, No. 3 (1990):373-374

Getting Equal. Book Review. *Gender and Education* 2, No. 3 (1990):373-374

**Crawford, Cindy** (about). *See also* Fashion Models, "Singular Sensations"

Supermodel Cindy Crawford: In the Hot Look of Summer. Lois Joy Johnson. *Ladies' Home Journal* 107, No. 6 (June 1990):132-137

**Crawford, June** (joint author). *See* Kippax, Susan

**Crawford, Patricia**

Eighteenth Century Women: An Anthology. Book Review. *Australian Feminist Studies* No. 12 (Summer 1990):131-132

The Social Origins of Private Life: A History of American Families, 1600-1900. Book Review. *Australian Feminist Studies* No. 12 (Summer 1990):131-132

Society and Culture in Early Modern France: Eight Essays. Book Review. *Australian Feminist Studies* No. 12 (Summer 1990):131-132

The Tradition of Female Transvestism in Early Modern Europe. Book Review. *Australian Feminist Studies* No. 12 (Summer 1990):131-132

**Crawford, Randy** (about)

Randy Crawford: Jazzy Rhythm 'n Blues. Benilde Little. *Essence* 21, No. 4 (August 1990):48

**Crawley, Donna** and Ecker, Martha

Integrating Issues of Gender, Race, and Ethnicity into Experimental Psychology and Other Social-Science Methodology Courses. *Women's Studies Quarterly* 18, Nos. 1-2 (Spring-Summer 1990):105-116

**Crean, Susan**

In the Name of the Fathers: The Story Behind Child Custody. Reviewed by Nancy D. Polikoff. *The Women's Review of Books* 7, No. 9 (June 1990):23-24

**Creative Ability.** *See also* Inspiration

**Creative Ability in Business**

Get Crazy: How to Have a Breakthrough Idea. Magaly Olivero. *Working Woman* (September 1990):144-147+

How Do You Keep the Creative Fires Burning? Patti Watts and Shelley Garcia. *Executive Female* 13, No. 4 (July-August 1990):22-27

"How I Did It": Homing In on the Hottest Trends. *Working Woman* (December 1990):35-36

"How I Did It". Selling Your Idea to Management. Sarah M. Nolan. *Working Woman* (September 1990):83-85

**Creativity.** *See also* Creative Ability in Business

Determinants and Consequences of Creativity in a Cohort of Gifted Women. George E. Vaillant and Caroline O. Vaillant. *Psychology of Women Quarterly* 14, No. 4 (December 1990):607-616

Had Any Good Ideas Lately? Jimmy Calano and Jeff Salzman. *Working Mother* 13, No. 1 (January 1990):36-40

Haunted by Intellect, Hobbled by Wisdom. Lynn S. Baker. *Lear's* (September 1990):60-64

**Credit.** *See also* Debt; Spending

More for Your Money. Barbara Gilder Quint. *Glamour* (April 1990):132-137; (June 1990):132-135

Your Money. *Working Woman* (November 1990):81-84

**Credit Cards**

Credit Card Capital. Doreen Mangan. *Executive Female* (March/April 1990):74

How to get Credit-Card Savvy. Carol Milano. *Essence* 21, No. 2 (June 1990):32

More for Your Money. Barbara Gilder Quint. *Glamour* (September 1990):158-165

Your Money: Stay Out of the Red This Christmas. Barbara Gilder Quint. *Family Circle* 103, No. 16 (November 27, 1990):45-48

**Creech, Kay**

The Michigan Festival Concert Band. *Hot Wire* 6, No. 1 (January 1990):32-33+

**Creet, Julia**

Taking Our Time: Feminist Perspectives on Temporality. Book Review. *Resources for Feminist Research* 19, No. 1 (March 1990):33

**Crespi, Tony D.**

Restraint and Seclusion with Institutionalized Adolescents. *Adolescence* 25, No. 100 (Winter 1990):825-829

**Crime**

Capital Offense. Frederick Eberstadt. *Harper's Bazaar* (October 1990):220-221+

Tell Us What You Think: Violent Crime on the Rise. *Glamour* (December 1990):136

The Trade in Sticky Fingers. Susan Schneider. *Lear's* (September 1990):38-40

Women and Crime: Not Much Is Known. Pat Redmond. *New Directions for Women* 19, No. 3 (May/June 1990):6

**Crime–Hate.** *See also* Rape

Canadian Massacre: It Was Political. Diana E. H. Russell and Jane Caputi. *New Directions for Women* 19, No. 2 (March/April 1990):17

A New Way of Looking at Violence Against Women. Lisa Heinzerling. *Glamour* (October 1990):112

**Crime–White Collar.** *See also* Bakker, Tammy Faye (about); Money Laundering

Bond Girl: The (Surprising) Rise & (Spectacular) Fall of Lisa Ann Jones. Jennie Nash. *Mademoiselle* (February 1990):166-168+

The Lady Is a Thief. Lorraine Dusky. *Mademoiselle* (February 1990):168-169+

The Meet Market. Peter Wilkinson. *Savvy Woman* (July/August 1990):52-55+

Office Politics: Five-Fingered Perks. Dennis Rodkin. *Savvy Woman* (October 1990):84+

**Crime and Criminals, Juvenile.** *See* Adolescents–Delinquency

**Crime Fiction**

The Beverly Malibu. By Katherine V. Forrest. Reviewed by Barbara Findlen. *Ms.* 1, No. 1 (July/August 1990):69

The Criminal Element. Jane Bakerman. *Belles Lettres* 5, No. 2 (Winter 1990):19; 5, No. 3 (Spring 1990):21; 5, No. 4 (Summer 1990):36-37; 6, No. 1 (Fall 1990):51-52

The Dog Collar Murders. By Barbara Wilson. Reviewed by Linda Semple. *Feminist Review* No. 35 (Summer 1990):119-121

Lesbian Sleuths. Irene Coffey. *Spare Rib* 217 (October 1990):34-35

**Crime Prevention**

Glamour Guides. Bibliography. *Glamour* (September 1990):115-122

**Crimes Against Women.** *See* Violence Against Women

**Crime Solving.** *See* Criminal Investigation

**Crime Victims.** *See also* Violence Against Women

Angela. Shirley Steshinsky. *Glamour* (March 1990):268-271+

Hers: It's Ten O'Clock, and I Worry About Where My Husband Is. Rosemary L. Bray. *Glamour* (April 1990):302

The Long Road Back. Ellie Grossman. *Ladies' Home Journal* 107, No. 4 (April 1990):160-161+

No Place to Hide. Ellen Hopkins. *Essence* 21, No. 4 (August 1990):66-68+

This Is What You Think: Rape: Should Victims' Names Be Published? *Glamour* (July 1990):100

Young Mother's Story: "My Boss Ordered Me to Sleep with Him." Shauna Clark and Sara Nelson. *Redbook* 174, No. 6 (April 1990):64-67

**Criminal Investigation**

Can These Mysteries Be Solved? Andrea Gross. *Ladies' Home Journal* 107, No. 8 (August 1990):104-106+

**Crimp, Douglas**

Art Acts Up: A Graphic Response to AIDS. Excerpt. *Out/Look* No. 9 (Summer 1990):22-30

**Crischke, Sue** (about)

Sue Cischke: Driving Smart. Celia Slom. *McCall's* 118, No. 1 (October 1990):60-62

**Crises, Life**

Outrageous Fortune. By Susan Kelly and Prasuna Reddy. Reviewed by Beverley Raphael. *Healthright* 9, No. 4 (August 1990):41

**Crisp, Quentin**

Idle Chatter. *Lear's* (June 1990):72-73

**Crisp, Shelley**

Even Mississippi. Book Review. *Belles Lettres* 5, No. 2 (Winter 1990):3

Motherwit: An Alabama Midwife's Story. Book Review. *Belles Lettres* 5, No. 2 (Winter 1990):3

Remembrances of Things South. *Belles Lettres* 5, No. 2 (Winter 1990):3

Telling Memories Among Southern Women: Domestic Workers and Their Employers in the Segregated South. Book Review. *Belles Lettres* 5, No. 2 (Winter 1990):3

**Crisp, Wendy**

Food for Thought. *Executive Female* (March/April 1990):80

Wake Me When It's Over. *Executive Female* 13, No. 4 (July-August 1990):80

**Crisp, Wendy Reid**

What It Takes: Getting Unstuck. *Executive Female* (May/June 1990):76

**Critically Ill – Family Relationships**

Will Daddy Get Better? Margaret Jaworski. *Family Circle* 103, No. 14 (October 16, 1990):100-102

**Crittenden, Danielle – Criticism and Interpretation**

Women's Magazines Regressing to 'Submissive Domesticity,' Writer Says. *Media Report to Women* 18, No. 1 (January/February 1990):7

**Crohan, Susan E.** (joint author). *See* Adelmann, Pamela K.

**Croll, Dona** (interview)

Hallelujah Anyhow. Claudette Williams. *Spare Rib* 219 (December 1990-January 1991):8-12

**Crone, Dana** (about). *See* Casey, Kathryn, "Voices of the Decade"

**Crone, Moira**

A Taste for Southern Comfort. *Savvy Woman* (September 1990):54-55+

**Cronin, Teresa**

Kenji, My Friend. *Essence* 20, No. 11 (March 1990):40+

**Crosby, F. J.** (joint author). *See* Blanchard, F. A.

**Crosby, Faye**

Equity and Gender: The Comparable Worth Debate. Book Review. *Psychology of Women Quarterly* 14, No. 1 (March 1990):147-148

**Cross, Amy Willard**

So Fellas, Can We Talk? *Savvy Woman* (March 1990):33-34

We Need a Manners Makeover. *Glamour* (April 1990):146

**Cross, Zora** (about)

A Writer's Friends and Associates: Notes from the Correspondence in the Zora Cross Papers. Julia Saunders. *Hecate* 16, Nos. 1-2 (1990):90-96

Zora Cross's Entry into Australian Literature. Michael Sharkey. *Hecate* 16, Nos. 1-2 (1990):65-89

**Cross-Cultural Studies**

Cross-Cultural Perspectives on Women in Higher Education. Beverly Lindsay. *Sage* 6, No. 1 (Summer 1989):92-96

Third Annual Cross-Cultural Black Women's Studies Summer Institute: Harare, Zimbabwe. Andreé Nocila McLaughlin. *Sage* 6, No. 1 (Summer 1989):80

Third Annual Cross-Cultural Black Women's Studies Summer Institute: Harare, Zimbabwe. *Sage* 6, No. 1 (Summer 1989):80

**Cross-Dressing.** *See* Transvestites

**Crossen, Cynthia**

Psst! The New Way to Network Is . . . Softly. *Working Woman* (September 1990):154-156

**Crow, Gary A.** and Crow, Letha I.

Crisis Intervention and Suicide Prevention: Working with Children and Adolescents. Book Review. *Adolescence* 25, No. 98 (Summer 1990):499

**Crow, Letha I.** (joint author). *See* Crow, Gary A.

**Crowley, Mart** (about). *See* Theater

**Croy, Jason** (about). *See also* Beauty Culture, "Who Cuts Who"

**Crozier, Gill**

Education for All: A Landmark in Pluralism. Book Review. *Gender and Education* 2, No. 3 (1990):368-369

**Crozier, Mary** (about)

In-House Mentors Keep Training Costs Down. Claire McIntosh. *Working Woman* (January 1990):68

**Cruise Ships.** *See also* Travel

A Sea Change: His Ship Came In. Peter Feibleman. *Lear's* (November 1990):70-72

Tips on Trips. Caterina Muccia. *Family Circle* 103, No. 14 (October 16, 1990):174

Total Recoil: Babes at Sea. Peter Feibleman. *Lear's* (January 1990):27-29

**Cruzan, Nancy** (about)

Private Agony, Public Cause. Deborah Beroset Diamond. *Ladies' Home Journal* 107, No. 6 (June 1990):124-125+

**Cryer, Jon** (about)

Jon Cryer, Your Big Break Is Calling. Roy Sekoff. *Mademoiselle* (January 1990):44

**Cubas, Juana Herrera** (joint author). *See* Tally, Justine

**Cubis, Jeff** (joint author). *See* Raphael, Beverley

**Cudjoe, Selwyn R.** (joint author). *See* Cotton, Terri

**Cuevas, Maria**

The National Women's History Project. *Woman of Power* 16 (Spring 1990):10-14

**Cullers, Marian** (about). *See* Alexander, Nanine

**Cullerton, Brenda**

Book Bazaar. Bibliography. *Harper's Bazaar* (November 1990):118

Book Bazaar: Tale Spinners. *Harper's Bazaar* (December 1990):98

**Cully, Lorraine**

Girls and Computers: General Issues and Case Studies of Logo in the Mathematics Classroom. Book Review. *Gender and Education* 2, No. 1 (1990):110-111

**Culp, Stephanie**

Beat the Clock. *Family Circle* 103, No. 1 (January 9, 1990):119-121

**Cults**

Love, Death, & Terri Hoffman. Rosalind Wright. *Good Housekeeping* 211, No. 4 (October 1990):62-69

**Cultural Anthropology.** *See also* Papua New Guinea – Anthropology

Discipline and Vanish: Feminism, the Resistance to Theory, and the Politics of Cultural Studies. Ellen Rooney. *Differences* 2, No. 3 (Fall 1990):14-28

At the Receiving End: Reading "Third" World Texts in a "First" World Context. Anuradha Dingwaney Needham. *Women's Studies Quarterly* 18, Nos. 3-4 (Fall-Winter 1990):91-99

Writing Cultures: An Interdisciplinary Approach to Developing Cross-Cultural Courses. Kathleen Mullen Sands. *Women's Studies Quarterly* 18, Nos. 3-4 (Fall-Winter 1990):100-118

**Cultural Identity.** *See also* Kwanzaa

Contemporary Living: Afrocentricity. *Essence* 21, No. 0 (December 1990):83

Reclaiming Our Culture. Rosemary Bray. *Essence* 21, No. 8 (December 1990):84-86+

**Cultural Pluralism**

At the Crossroads of Culture. Peggy Pascoe. *The Women's Review of Books* 7, No. 5 (February 1990):22-23

Passionate Differences: A Working Model for Cross-Cultural Communication. Kristen Metz. *Journal of Feminist Studies in Religion* 6, No. 1 (Spring 1990):131-151

**Cultural Politics**

Abstracts: Gender and the Construction of Culture and Knowledge. *Resources for Feminist Research* 19, No. 1 (March 1990):51-66

The Cultural Politics of Perversion: Augustine, Shakespeare, Freud, Foucault. Jonathan Dollimore. *Genders* 8 (Summer 1990):1-16

*Demon Lover Diary*: Deconstructing Sex, Class, and Cultural Power in Documentary. Patricia R. Zimmermann. *Genders* 8 (Summer 1990):91-109

In Other Worlds: Essays in Cultural Politics. By Gayatri Chakravorty Spivak. Reviewed by Susan Hardy Aiken. *NWSA Journal* 2, No. 1 (Winter 1990):145-147

**Culture, Popular.** *See also* Film and Filmmakers; Music, Popular; Television Programs

**Culture and History.** *See also* Feminism – Theory; Great Britain – History; United States – History

Feminist Cultural Studies: Questions for the 1990s. Anne Balsamo and Paula A. Treichler. *Women & Language* 13, No. 1 (Fall 1990):3-6

Oakland Highlights. Lillian Broadous II. *Essence* 21, No. 1 (May 1990):166-170

**Culture Shock**

Cultural Dislocation Syndrome. Francesca Vivenza. *Canadian Women's Studies* 11, No. 1 (Spring 1990):63-64

**Cumming, Patricia**

Snow Blind. Poem. *The Women's Review of Books* 7, No. 8 (May 1990):18

Song. Poem. *The Women's Review of Books* 7, No. 8 (May 1990):18

**Cummings, Angela** (about)

Country Charm. Patricia Beard. *Harper's Bazaar* (October 1990):236

**Cummings, Katherine**

A Spurious Set (Up): "Fetching Females" and "Seductive" Theories in *Phaedrus*, "Plato's Pharmacy," and *Spurs*. *Genders* 8 (Summer 1990):38-61

**Cummins, Helene,** McDaniel, Susan A., and Beauchamp, Rachelle Sender

Becoming Inventors: Women Who Aspire to Invent. *Atlantis* 15, No. 2 (Spring 1990):90-93

**Cummins, Marsha** (joint author). *See* Bass, Ruth

**Cundick, Bert** (joint author). *See* Phinney, Virginia G.

**Cunningham, Ann Marie**

"I Don't Want My Son to Be Forgotten." *Ladies' Home Journal* 107, No. 8 (August 1990):102-103 +

The Pill: How It Changed Our Lives. *Ladies' Home Journal* 107, No. 6 (June 1990):121-123 +

**Cunningham, Hugh**

Discourse on Popular Culture: Class, Gender and History in Cultural Analysis, 1730 to the Present. Book Review. *Gender & History* 2, No. 1 (Spring 1990):110-113

**Cunningham, John D.** (joint author). *See* Cotton, Sandra

**Cunningham, Laura**

One, Please. Short Story. *Mademoiselle* (August 1990):148, 232-235

Sleeping Arrangements. Reviewed by Susan P. Willens. *Belles Lettres* 5, No. 2 (Winter 1990):7

**Cunningham, Margery**

The Flip Side. *Family Circle* 103, No. 8 (June 5, 1990):30-31

**Cunningham, Peter J.**

Medical Care Use and Expenditures for Children across Stages of the Family Life Cycle. *Journal of Marriage and the Family* 52, No. 1 (February 1990):197-207

**Cunnison, Sheila** and Gurevitch, Christine

Implementing a Whole School Equal Opportunities Policy: A Primary School in Humberside. *Gender and Education* 2, No. 3 (1990):283-295

**Cuomo, Chris**

The Wax Problem. Poem. *Sinister Wisdom* 41 (Summer-Fall 1990):114-115

**Curb, Rosemary**

Lesbian Conference Sets Bold Agenda. *New Directions for Women* 19, No. 1 (January/February 1990):6

Spinning on to Atlanta. *off our backs* 20, No. 7 (July 1990):7

**Curie, Marie** (about)

Grand Obsession: Madame Curie and Her World. By Rosalynd Pflaum. Reviewed by Margaret N. Rogers. *The Women's Review of Books* 7, No. 12 (September 1990):27-28

**Curiosity in Children**

Daydreaming and Curiosity: Stability and Change in Gifted Children and Adolescents. Steven R. Gold and Bruce B. Henderson. *Adolescence* 25, No. 99 (Fall 1990):701-708

**Currie, Ellen**

Anaïs Redux. *Lear's* (February 1990):46-48

**Curry, Landon** (joint author). *See* Sheilds, Patricia M.

**Curtin, Jane** (about)

Jane Curtin: Allie Moves On. Eric Sherman. *Ladies' Home Journal* 107, No. 10 (October 1990):56-59

**Curtis, Jamie Lee** (about)

Jamie Lee Curtis: Anything but Perfect. Eric Sherman. *Ladies' Home Journal* 107, No. 4 (April 1990):66-71

Jamie Lee Curtis. Bonnie Siegler. *McCall's* 117, No. 9 (June 1990):23

**Cushing's Syndrome.** *See* Policoff, Stephen Phillip, "Diseases Your Doctor May Miss"

**Customer Service**

Enterprise: How Customer Service Built a Business. Mark Stevens. *Working Woman* (July 1990):31-38

**Cutschall, Colleen** (interview)

Voice in the Blood. Agnes Grant. *Canadian Women's Studies* 11, No. 1 (Spring 1990):11-14

**Cutting-Gray, Joanne**

Writing Innocence: Fanny Burney's *Evelina*. *Tulsa Studies in Women's Literature* 9, No. 1 (Spring 1990):43-57

Cycling. *See* Bicycling

**Cypess, Sandra Messinger** and others

Women Authors of Hispanic South America: A Bibliography of Literary Criticism and Interpretation. Review. *Feminist Collections* 11, No. 3 (Spring 1990):15

**Cyr, Heather**

Leapole Lester. Short Story. *Good Housekeeping* 210, No. 6 (June 1990):145-146

**Cystitis.** *See* Urinary Tract Infections

**Czechoslovakia**

Czechoslovak Women Back into Feminism. Jill Benderly. *New Directions for Women* 19, No. 5 (September-October 1990):1+

**Czechoslovakia – Art**

Prague's Spring. Eleanor Heartney. *Harper's Bazaar* (March 1990):72-85

**Czechoslovakia – Politics and Government**

Return to Prague. Vivian Cadden. *McCall's* 117, No. 7 (April 1990):60-66

# D

**DACOWITS.** *See* Defense Advisory Committee on Women in the Services

**D'Adamo, Amadeo F., Jr.** (joint editor). *See* Baruch, Elaine Hoffman

**Daedalus Productions**

Film Makers on Hot Topics. Penny Perkins. *New Directions for Women* 19, No. 2 (March/April 1990).metrö

Through the Wire. Reviewed by Penny Perkins. *On the Issues* 15 (Summer 1990):31

**Dafoe, Willem** (about). *See* Actors

**Dagenais, Francine**

Portraits en regard. *Canadian Women's Studies* 11, No. 1 (Spring 1990):18-21

**Dagg, Anne Innis**

The Writing or the Sex? or Why You Don't Have to Read Women's Writing to Know It's no Good. Book Review. *Atlantis* 15, No. 2 (Spring 1990):95-96

**Dahlin, Michael** (joint author). *See* Shammas, Carole

**Dahlstrom, Kim**

Woman's Word Bookstore. *Feminist Collections* 11, No. 4 (Summer 1990):16-17

**Dahl-Wolfe, Louise** (about)

Painting with Light. Kristine McKenna. *Harper's Bazaar* (March 1990):208-209+

**Daigneault, Lorraine**

Surgery Stars. *Harper's Bazaar* (August 1990):128-129+

**Dailey, Dee Dee**

Festive Food. *Essence* 21, No. 8 (December 1990):102-106+

**Dailey, Maceo Crenshaw, Jr.**

Black Men: Single, Obsolete, and Dangerous? Book Review. *Sage* 6, No. 2 (Fall 1989):66-67

**Dailey, Maceo Crenshaw (Jr.)** and Hill, Freddye

Where Do We Stand: African Women of the Diaspora in Kwame Nkrumah's Ghana, 1960. *Sage* 6, No. 1 (Summer 1989):77-79

**Dais.** *See* Midwives – Training

**Dais, Calvin**

Brothers: A Father's Joy, A Father's Pain. *Essence* 21, No. 8 (December 1990):30

**Dall, Caroline Wells Healey** (about). *See* Suffrage Movements

**Dall, Christie** (joint producer). *See* Van Falkenburg, Carole

**Dallas – Mayors.** *See* Texas – Mayors

**Dallas, Sandra**

Buster Midnight's Cafe. Reviewed by Jane Smiley. *Vogue* (April 1990):278-281

**Dallas-Forth Worth – Media and Communications**

Dallas Women Reporting Top Stories Less than One-Third of the Time. *Media Report to Women* 18, No. 1 (January/February 1990):3

**Dalton, Anne B.**

Fidetic Images. Poem. *Sinister Wisdom* 42 (Winter 1990-1991):85

**Dalton, Katherine**

Power of Attorney. Bibliography. *Harper's Bazaar* (June 1990):38-44

**Daly, Christopher B.** (joint author). *See* Hall, Jacquelyn Dowd

**Daly, Mary**

The Haggard Sense of Humor. *Woman of Power* 17 (Summer 1990):7-12

Spiraling into the Nineties: An Invitation to Outercourse. *Woman of Power* 17 (Summer 1990):6-12

**Daly, Mary** and Caputi, Jane

Webster's First New Intergalactic Wickedary of the English Language. Reviewed by Mary Ellen S. Capek. *NWSA Journal* 2, No. 3 (Summer 1990):476-484

**Daly, Tyne** (about)

Tyne Daly: Riding the Second Wave of Success. Leslie Bennetts. *McCall's* 117, No. 7 (April 1990):84-88

**Daly, Victoria Zimet**

Medical Report: Family Medical History. *Glamour* (February 1990):61-62

**D'Amboise, Charlotte and Christopher** (about).
*See also* Children of Entertainers

**Dambroff, Susan**

For Kimi. Poem. *Sinister Wisdom* 40 (Spring
1990):89-90

**Dame, Enid**

A Book for Believers. *Belles Lettres* 5, No. 3 (Spring
1990):9

No Mercy. Book Review. *Belles Lettres* 5, No. 4
(Summer 1990):17

She Rises Life the Sun: Invocations of the Goddess
by Contemporary American Women Poets. Book
Review. *Belles Lettres* 5, No. 3 (Spring 1990):9

**Damhorst, Mary Lynn** (joint author). *See* Littrell,
Mary Ann

**D'Amico, Francine**

Women at Arms: The Combat Controversy.
*Minerva* 8, No. 2 (Summer 1990):1-19

**D'Amico, Marie** and Jubak, Jim

5 Plans to Solve the Garbage Mess. *McCall's* 117,
No. 11 (August 1990):52-60

**D'Amico, Marie** (joint author). *See* Jubak, Jim

**Da Molin, Giovanna**

Family Forms and Domestic Service in Southern
Italy from the Seventeenth to the Nineteenth
Centuries. *Journal of Family History* 15, No. 4
(October 1990):503-527

**Dan, Alice J.**, Wilbur, JoEllen, Hedricks, Cynthia,
O'Connor, Eileen, and Holm, Karyn

Lifelong Physical Activity in Midlife and Older
Women. *Psychology of Women Quarterly* 14, No. 4
(December 1990):531-542

**Danbrot, Margaret** (joint author). *See* Haberman,
Frederic

**Dance.** *See also* Ballet; Burlesque

Before the Revolution. Ballet. Eleanora Antinova.
*Women and Performance: A Journal of Feminist
Theory* 5, No. 1, Issue #9 (1990): 93-119

Bolshoi Bravo! Matthew Gurewitsch. *Harper's
Bazaar* (July 1990):27

Dance. David Daniel. *Vogue* (July 1990):100-106

The Dance of Amel Benhassine-Miller. Lina
Mansour. *Spare Rib* 213 (June 1990):30-31

Educating the Body. Rachel Vigier. *Heresies* 25
(1990):78-79

Lambada: The Sexy Way to Shape Up.
*Mademoiselle* (June 1990):42-44

Sandra Dupiton Loves to Dance. Martha Southgate.
*Essence* 20, No. 10 (February 1990):40

Shall We Dance? *Mademoiselle* (October
1990):180-183

Stepping Up. Julia Szabo. *Harper's Bazaar* (February
1990):72

Vogue Arts: Dance. David Daniel. *Vogue*
(November 1990):284+

**Dance, Afro-Caribbean**

Feeling Irie. Veronica Hill. *Spare Rib* No. 210
(March 1990):16-18

**Dance – Choreography.** *See also* De Mille, Agnes
(about)

Earth Is Our Root: An Interview with Patricia Beatty.
Karen Lavut and Frances Beer. *Canadian Women's
Studies* 11, No. 1 (Spring 1990):

**Dance – Cross-Cultural Studies**

Dance, Sex and Gender: Signs of Identity,
Dominance, Defiance and Desire. By Judith Lynne
Hanna. Reviewed by Judith Burns. *NWSA Journal* 2,
No. 1 (Winter 1990):147-149

**Dance – Samba**

Samba. By Alma Guillermoprieto. Reviewed by
Sally Sommer. *The Women's Review of Books* 7, No.
9 (June 1990):9

**Dandridge, Rita B.**

Ann Allen Shockley: An Annotated Primary and
Secondary Bibliography. Reviewed by Barbara
Williams Jenkins. *Sage* 6, No. 2 (Fall 1989):63-64

**Dane, Elizabeth**

Tapestries of Life: Women's Work, Women's
Consciousness, and the Meaning of Daily Life.
Book Review. *AFFILIA* 5, No. 4 (Winter 1990):110-
111

**Danese, Susan**

Cranial Therapy: Relief at Last. *Healthsharing* 11,
No. 2 (March 1990):27-28

**Daneshvar, Simin**

Daneshvar's Playhouse. Reviewed by Marcia Tager.
*New Directions for Women* 19, No. 1
(January/February 1990):22

**Dangarembga, Tsitsi**

The Learning Crop. Fiction. *Ms.* 1, No. 1
(July/August 1990):61-65

Nervous Conditions. Reviewed by Angela Johnson.
*off our backs* 20, No. 9 (October 1990):17

Nervous Conditions. Reviewed by Elizabeth Ferber.
*New Directions for Women* 19, No. 1
(January/February 1990):22

**D'Angelo, Mary Rose**

Women Partners in the New Testament. *Journal of
Feminist Studies in Religion* 6, No. 1 (Spring
1990):65-86

**Daniel, David**

Dance. *Vogue* (July 1990):100-106

Vogue Arts: Dance. *Vogue* (November 1990):284+

Vogue Arts: Music. *Vogue* (September 1990):436-438; (October 1990):164+; (December 1990):204-208

**Daniel, Herbert**

A Guerrilla Grapples with AIDS. *Out/Look* No. 8 (Spring 1990):27-30

**Daniel, Jere**

Warning: When Exercise Is Hazardous to Your Health. *Family Circle* 103, No. 14 (October 16, 1990):125-127

**Daniels, Arlene Kaplan**

Brave New Families: Stories of Democratic Upheaval in Late Twentieth-Century America. Book Review. *The Women's Review of Books* 8, No. 3 (December 1990):14-15

Feminist Scholarship: Kindling in the Groves of Academe. Book Review. *Gender and Society* 4, No. 1 (March 1990):96-99

The Impact of Feminist Research in the Academy. Book Review. *Gender and Society* 4, No. 1 (March 1990):96-99

Invisible Careers: Women Civic Leaders from the Volunteer World. Reviewed by Beth B. Hess. *Gender and Society* 4, No. 2 (June 1990):283-284

Network News. *The Women's Review of Books* 8, No. 3 (December 1990):14-15

**Daniels, Cynthia R.** (joint editor). *See* Boris, Eileen

**Daniels, Doris Groshen**

Always a Sister: The Feminism of Lillian D. Wald. Reviewed by Katherine A. Kendall. *AFFILIA* 5, No. 4 (Winter 1990):113-114

**Daniels, Jill A.**

Adolescent Separation-Individuation and Family Transitions. *Adolescence* 25, No. 97 (Spring 1990):105-116

**Daniels, Ron**

Back Talk: With Respect to Malcolm. *Essence* 20, No. 10 (February 1990):126

**Daniels, Tom D.** (joint author). *See* Lamude, Kevin G.

**Dankelman, Irene** and Davidson, Joan

Women and Environment in the Third World: Alliance for the Future. Reviewed by Linda Carty. *Resources for Feminist Research* 19, No. 1 (March 1990):40-41

**Danson, Ted** (about). *See also* Celebrities – Activism; Film Criticism

**Dante, Vic**

Happy Exercise for Healthy Kids. *McCall's* 117, No. 12 (September 1990):38+

Nutrition/Fitness: Stretch to Beat Stress. *McCall's* 117, No. 9 (June 1990):20

**D'Antonio, Michael**

What's Wrong with the Competitive Edge? *Working Woman* (June 1990):62-63+

**Danziger, Sandra K.** and Radin, Norma

Absent Does Not Equal Uninvolved: Predictors of Fathering in Teen Mother Families. *Journal of Marriage and the Family* 52, No. 3 (August 1990):636-642

**Dappen, Andy**

Breast Cancer and Nutrition: The Hidden Link. Bibliography. *Ladies' Home Journal* 107, No. 7 (July 1990):60-68

**D'Arcy, Kathleen** (joint editor). *See* DeSalvo, Louise

**Daria, Irene**

Breaking and Entering: How Girls Like You Get Dream Jobs. *Mademoiselle* (September 1990):272-275+

**Das, N. K.** (joint author). *See* Ghosh, A. K.

**Das, N. P.**

The Effect of Birth Spacing on Current Fertility. *Journal of Family Welfare* 36, No. 4 (December 1990):36-45

**Das, N. P.** (joint author). *See* Gandotra, M. M.

**Dascher, Helge**

Mémoire, reconnaissance. *Canadian Women's Studies* 11, No. 1 (Spring 1990):75-77

**Date Rape.** *See* Rape – Acquaintance

**Dating Customs.** *See also* Blind Dates; Single Parents

The Great American Date. *Glamour* (February 1990):176-179

Health & Mind. Pamela Erens. *Glamour* (December 1990):58

Sexual Ethics. Brook Hersey. *Glamour* (September 1990):348

Sexual Ethics: The Image Game. Betsy Israel. *Glamour* (December 1990):244

Where the Boys Are. *Essence* 21, No. 3 (July 1990):62-64+

White Boys. Edited by Diane Weathers. *Essence* 20, No. 12 (April 1990):64-66+

**Dattalo, Patrick** (joint author). *See* Benda, Brent B.

**Daufin, E. K.**

Living Large, Getting Fit. *Essence* 21, No. 4 (August 1990):20-25

Prevention: Fighting Chance. *Essence* 20, No. 10 (February 1990):27-29

**Davall, Irene**

To Pee or Not to Pee . . . Celebrating Women's History. *On the Issues* 15 (Summer 1990):20-21

Which Way After Webster? *On the Issues* 17 (Winter 1990):8-9+

**Davaney, Sheila Greeve** (joint author). *See* Brock, Rita Nakashima

**Davenport, Doris**

The Critic in Exile. *The Women's Review of Books* 7, Nos. 10-11 (July 1990):36-37

Wild Women in the Whirlwind: Afra-American Culture and the Contemporary Literary Renaissance. Book Review. *The Women's Review of Books* 7, Nos. 10-11 (July 1990):36-37

Women's Writing in Exile. Book Review. *The Women's Review of Books* 7, Nos. 10-11 (July 1990):36-37

**Davenport, Sharon**

Making Face, Making Soul/Haciendo Caras: Creative and Critical Perspectives by Women of Color. Book Review. *Sinister Wisdom* 42 (Winter 1990-1991):114-117

**David, Deirdre**

Intellectual Women and Victorian Patriarchy: Harriet Martineau, Elizabeth Barrett Browning, George Eliot. Reviewed by Katharine M. Rogers. *Signs* 15, No. 4 (Summer 1990):878-882

**David, Lester**

Rose Kennedy at 100. *McCall's* 117, No. 8 (May 1990):83-88

**David, Renee** (interview)

Talking Feminist. Letty Cottin Pogrebin. *On the Issues* 14 (1990):15+

**Davidoff, Leonore** and Hall, Catherine

Family Fortunes: Men and Women of the English Middle Class, 1780-1850. Reviewed by Ellen Jordan. *Signs* 15, No. 3 (Spring 1990):650-652

Family Fortunes: Men and Women of the English Middle Class, 1780-1850. Reviewed by Mary Louise Adams. *Resources for Feminist Research* 19, No. 1 (March 1990):10-11

**Davidson, Jeffrey P.**

The Yellow Pages Pitch. *Executive Female* 13, No. 6 (November-December 1990):18

**Davidson, Joan** (joint author). *See* Dankelman, Irene

**Davidson, Louise K.**

Women in East Germany Today. *off our backs* 20, No. 7 (July 1990):8

**Davies, Bronwyn**

Democracy in the Kitchen: Regulating Mothers and Socialising Daughters. Book Review. *Gender and Education* 2, No. 1 (1990):113-115

Frogs and Snails and Feminist Tales: Preschool Children and Gender. Reviewed by Sandra Taylor. *Australian Feminist Studies* No. 12 (Summer 1990):127-128

**Davies, Carole Boyce**

Elizabeth of Toro: The Odyssey of an African Princess. Book Review. *Belles Lettres* 5, No. 3 (Spring 1990):13

The Family. Book Review. *Belles Lettres* 6, No. 1 (Fall 1990):20-21

You Big 'Oman Nuh, June-June. *Belles Lettres* 6, No. 1 (Fall 1990):20-21

**Davies, Gloria Evans**

Welsh Country Diary. Poem. *Feminist Review* No. 36 (Autumn 1990):89-91

**Davies, Kent R.**

The Exchange Rate. *Executive Female* 13, No. 6 (November-December 1990):28-31

**Davies, Stevie**

Primavera. Reviewed by Natasha Moar. *Spare Rib* 213 (June 1990):28

**Davin, Anna**

In Our Foremothers' Footsteps. *The Women's Review of Books* 8, No. 1 (October 1990):11-12

Our Sisters' London: Feminist Walking Tours. Book Review. *The Women's Review of Books* 8, No. 1 (October 1990):11-12

**Davion, Victoria**

Pacifism and Care. *Hypatia* 5, No. 1 (Spring 1990):90-100

**Davis, Allison**

"How Do I Explain Racism to My Son?" *Working Mother* 13, No. 4 (April 1990):30-33

**Davis, Andrea**

Rap-Sody & Blues. *Executive Female* (May/June 1990):44-46

**Davis, Andrea R.**

Parenting: Fat Facts. *Essence* 21, No. 2 (June 1990):95

Power Players. *Essence* 20, No. 11 (March 1990):71-84

**Davis, Angela Y.**

Sick and Tired of Being Sick and Tired: The Politics of Black Women's Health. *Woman of Power* 18 (Fall 1990):26-29

Violence Against Women and the Ongoing Challenge to Racism. Reviewed by Jacqueline E. Wade. *NWSA Journal* 2, No. 2 (Spring 1990):315-319

**Davis, Angela Y.** (about)

Woman Talk. Interviews. Edited by Cheryll Y. Greene and Marie D. Brown. *Essence* 21, No. 1 (May 1990):92-96+

**Davis, Cookie**

Making Jews Visible to Academic Feminists. *Lilith* 15, No. 4 (Fall 1990):6

**Davis, Hilda A.** and Bell-Scott, Patricia

The Association of Deans of Women and Advisers to Girls in Negro Schools, 1929-1954: A Brief Oral History. *Sage* 6, No. 1 (Summer 1989):40-44

**Davis, Natalie**

Society and Culture in Early Modern France: Eight Essays. Reviewed by Patricia Crawford. *Australian Feminist Studies* No. 12 (Summer 1990):131-132

**Davis, Rebecca**

Young Women Fight Movement Racism. *New Directions for Women* 19, No. 1 (January/February 1990):5

**Davis, Sally Ogle**

Talking with Arnold Schwarzenegger: Tough Man, Tender Heart. Interview. *Redbook* 175, No. 5 (September 1990):84-86

**Davis, Stephen**

Tech Talk: The Crackdown on Corporate Pirates. *Working Woman* (March 1990):50

**Davis, Susan E.**

The American Women, 1990-1991: A Status Report. Book Review. *New Directions for Women* 19, No. 6 (November-December 1990):18

Coma Catalyst for Life Change. *New Directions for Women* 19, No. 6 (November-December 1990):7

Daring to Be Bad: Radical Feminism in America 1967-1975. Book Review. *New Directions for Women* 19, No. 5 (September-October 1990):14

Radical Roots. *New Directions for Women* 19, No. 5 (September-October 1990):14

Three for Reference. *New Directions for Women* 19, No. 6 (November-December 1990):18

Unequal Sisters: A Multicultural Reader in U.S. Women's History. Book Review. *New Directions for Women* 19, No. 6 (November-December 1990):18

Unreliable Sources: A Guide to Detecting Bias in News Media. Book Review. *New Directions for Women* 19, No. 6 (November-December 1990):18

**Davis, Susan Schaefer**

Doing Daily Battle: Interviews with Moroccan Women. Book Review. *Belles Lettres* 5, No. 3 (Spring 1990):12

**Davison, Jean** (editor)

Agriculture, Women and Land: The African Experience. Reviewed by E. A. Cebotarev. *Resources for Feminist Research* 19, No. 1 (March 1990):3-4

**Dawber, Pam** (about). *See* Dutka, Elaine

**Dawidowicz, Lucy S.**

From That Time and Place, A Memoir 1938-1947. Reviewed by Miriyam Glazer. *Belles Lettres* 5, No. 2 (Winter 1990):7

**Dawson, Karen**

The Latest Overnight Sensation. *Lear's* (November 1990):76

Saving Face with a Hot New Treatment. *Lear's* (October 1990):66

**Dawson, Karen Gooby**

Color to Dye For. *Savvy Woman* (October 1990):42-44

**Dawson, Katharine**

Women's Collective Action in the Gallup, New Mexico Coalfields during the 1930s. *NWSA Journal* 2, No. 4 (Autumn 1990):690-692

**Dawson, Marie**

Why Women Get Addicted to Food. Bibliography. *Ladies' Home Journal* 107, No. 9 (September 1990):132-136

**Day, Barbara**

Black Women in White: Racial Conflict and Cooperation in the Nursing Profession, 1890-1950. Book Review. *On the Issues* 15 (Summer 1990):25-26

World Summit for Children – Report from New York. *Spare Rib* 218 (November 1990):46

**Day, Doris**

A Cancer Answer: The New Melanoma Vaccine. *Mademoiselle* (January 1990):70

**Day, Lorraine** (about)

Dr. Lorraine Day: Crusader or Cassandra? Susan Edmiston. *Glamour* (July 1990):66

**Day, Phyllis J.**

A New History of Social Welfare. Reviewed by Charles Frost. *AFFILIA* 5, No. 3 (Fall 1990):120

**Dayan, Yael** (about)

Yael Dayan. Interview. Susan Weldman Schneider. *Lilith* 15, No. 4 (Fall 1990):10-15

**Day Care.** *See* Child Care

**Day Care Centers.** *See also* Child Care; Child Care Workers; Fabiano, Sandra (about)

Every Mother's Nightmare. Bibliography. Elaine F. Whiteley. *Ladies' Home Journal* 107, No. 10 (October 1990):151-153+

Two Needs, One Day-Care Center. Celia Slom. *McCall's* 117, No. 10 (July 1990):56

**Daydreams**

Do You Think About Sex Too Much? Eric Klinger. *Glamour* (September 1990):322-323+

**Dayne, Taylor** (about). *See* Entertainers

**Dayton, Laura**

What Price Glory? An Insider's Look at the Sport of Women's Bodybuilding. *Women's Sports and Fitness* 12, No. 2 (March 1990):52-55

**Deacon, Desley**

Managing Gender: The State, the New Middle Class and Women Workers, 1830-1930. Reviewed by Colleen Chesterman. *Australian Feminist Studies* No. 11 (Autumn 1990):123-126

**Deadwood (South Dakota) – Gambling**

The New Gold Rush. Kathryn Casey. *Ladies' Home Journal* 107, No. 9 (September 1990):160-164+

**Deafness.** *See* Hearing Impairments

**Dean, Deborah Gore** (about)

She Stoops to Conquer. Peter Hellman. *Savvy Woman* (March 1990):63-65, 80-83

**Dean, Margie M.** (joint author). *See* Gifford, Vernon D.

**De Angelis, Barbara**

Don't Be His Mother. Excerpt. *Redbook* 174, No. 5 (March 1990):130-131+

Men: Solving the Puzzle. *Ladies' Home Journal* 107, No. 5 (May 1990):116-118+

Private Lives: Are You Too Tired for Sex? *Family Circle* 103, No. 14 (October 16, 1990):32-37

**Dearing, Judy** (about)

Tailor's Daughter. *Essence* 20, No. 9 (January 1990):17

**Dearmond, Rita Victoria Gomez**

Amazons and Military Maids: Women Who Dressed as Men in the Pursuit of Life, Liberty and the Pursuit of Happiness. Book Review. *Gender & History* 2, No. 2 (Summer 1990):229-232

The Cavalry Maid: The Memoirs of a Woman Soldier of 1812. Book Review. *Gender & History* 2, No. 2 (Summer 1990):229-232

The Tradition of Female Transvestism in Early Modern Europe. Book Review. *Gender & History* 2, No. 2 (Summer 1990):229-232

**Death and Dying.** *See also* Bereavement; Illness; Leukemia in Children; Mother-Daughter Relationships

Encounters with Angels. Sophy Burnham. *McCall's* 118, No. 3 (December 1990):76-77

How It All Turned Out. Jane O'Reilly. *Lear's* (March 1990):75-81

Kenji, My Friend. Teresa Cronin. *Essence* 20, No. 11 (March 1990):40+

Motherhood Lost: Cultural Dimensions of Miscarriage and Stillbirth in America. Linda L. Layne. *Women and Health* 16, Nos. 3/4 (1990):69-98

**Death and Dying in Film**

Love Reincarnate. Ron Rosenbaum. *Mademoiselle* (December 1990):84-86

**Death Valley – Theater**

Desert Dream. Scott LaFee. *Lear's* (April 1990):50

**Debo, Angie** (about)

Indians, Outlaws, and Angie Debo. Produced by Barbara Abrash and Martha Sandlin. *NWSA Journal* 2, No. 4 (Autumn 1990):646-649

**Debrovner, Diane**

Exercise Builds Strong Bones. *McCall's* 118, No. 2 (November 1990):28-32

**Debt.** *See also* Bankruptcy; Brazil – Debts, Public

Bill Collectors: How Much Can They Harass You? Barbara Gilder Quint. *Glamour* (February 1990):95-96

Money: Getting Debt-Free in '90. Lisa Collier Cool. *Essence* 20, No. 11 (March 1990):38

**Debutantes**

Pretty in White. *Harper's Bazaar* (December 1990):174+

**DeCew, Judith Wagner**

Manhood and Politics: A Feminist Reading in Political Theory. Book Review. *Women's Studies International Forum* 13, No. 3 (1990):279-280

**Decision-Making**

Decision-Making Processes of Youth. J. William Moore, Brian Jensen, and William E. Hauck. *Adolescence* 25, No. 99 (Fall 1990):583-592

Living with Loose Ends. Judith Stone. *Glamour* (May 1990):184

**Decker, Diana**

Muchachas No More: Household Workers in Latin America and the Caribbean. Book Review. *off our backs* 20, No. 5 (May 1990):23

**Decoration.** *See* Interior Design

**Decorative Arts**

It's the Mix that Refreshes: Formal Country. Pat Ross. *McCall's* 117, No. 7 (April 1990):91-96

**deCordova, Richard**

Ethnography and Exhibition: The Child Audience, the Hays Office and Saturday Matinees. *Camera Obscura*, No. 23 (May 1990):90-107

**De Costa, Caroline**

Tying the Tubes. Reviewed by Sue Craig. *Healthright* 9, No. 4 (August 1990):46-47

**DeCosta-Willis, Miriam**, Delk, Fannie, and Dotson, Philip (editors)

Homespun Images: An Anthology of Black Memphis Writers and Artists. Reviewed by Charlotte K. Brooks. *Sage* 6, No. 2 (Fall 1989):61-62

**Decoury, Lynne H.**

Like Any Woman: Yearning for Time. Poem. *Iris* 23 (Spring-Summer 1990):36

**De Danaan, Llyn**

Center to Margin: Dynamics in a Global Classroom. *Women's Studies Quarterly* 18, Nos. 1-2 (Spring-Summer 1990):135-144

**Deee-Lite** (about)

One Nation Under a Groove. Christian Wright. *Mademoiselle* (December 1990):95

**Deegan, Mary Jo**

American Ritual Dramas: Social Rules and Cultural Meanings. Reviewed by Marlene G. Fine. *Women's Studies International Forum* 13, No. 5 (1990):522-523

**Deem, Rosemary**

All Work and No Play? The Sociology of Women and Leisure. Reviewed by Susan Maizel Chambre. *Gender and Society* 4, No. 2 (June 1990):281-283

Work, Unemployment and Leisure. Reviewed by Claire Wallace. *Gender and Education* 2, No. 1 (1990):118-119

**Deepwell, Katy**

Themata: New Drawings by Deanna Petherbridge. *Spare Rib* No. 210 (March 1990):42

**Deere, Carmen Diana** and León, Magdalena (editors)

Rural Women and State Policy: Feminist Perspectives on Latin American Agricultural Development. Reviewed by Sue Ellen Charlton. *Signs* 15, No. 4 (Summer 1990):860-864

**Defeis, Elizabeth F.** (joint author). *See* Halberstam, Malvina

**Defense Advisory Committee on Women in the Services**

1989 DACOWITS Meetings. Nonna Cheatham. *Minerva* 8, No. 1 (Spring 1990):1-9

**Defense Mechanisms (Psychology)**

Defense Mechanisms: Their Classification, Correlates, and Measurement with the Defense Mechanisms Inventory. By David Ihilevich and Goldine C. Gleser. Book Review. *Adolescence* 25, No. 97 (Spring 1990):251

**Degen, Paul** (joint author). *See* Doe, Tonie

**Degener, Theresia**

Genetic Exploitation: Interview with an Eco-Feminist. *Connexions* 32 (1990):14-15

**De Greiff, Monica** and Gugliotta, Guy

"I Fought the Drug Lords." *Ladies' Home Journal* 107, No. 2 (February 1990):22-27

**DeGroat, Judith**

Spinners and Weavers of Auffay: Rural Industry and the Sexual Division of Labor in a French Village, 1750-1850. Book Review. *Gender and Society* 4, No. 2 (June 1990):272-274

**DeHart, Jane**

Sisterhood and Solidarity: Feminism and Labor in Modern Times. Book review. *Signs* 15, No. 2 (Winter 1990):405-408

Women of the New Right. Book review. *Signs* 15, No. 2 (Winter 1990):405-408

**Deitch, Mark**

Burns, Bites and Rashes. *Working Mother* 13, No. 7 (July 1990):80-83

**Dekker, Rudolf M.** and Van de Pol, Lotte C.

The Tradition of Female Transvestism in Early Modern Europe. Reviewed by Rita Victoria Gomez Dearmond. *Gender & History* 2, No. 2 (Summer 1990):229-232

**Dekker, Rudolf M.** and van de Pol, Lotte C.

The Tradition of Female Transvestism in Early Modern Europe. Reviewed by Patricia Crawford. *Australian Feminist Studies* No. 12 (Summer 1990):131-132

**Dekovic, Maja** (joint author). *See* Lackovic-Grgin, Katica

**De la Claridad, Juana Maria** (about). *See also* Art – Exhibitions, "Racism"

**De la Cruz, Graciela**

Everyday Violence. *Connexions* 34 (1990):26

**De la Cuesta, Barbara**

The Gold Mine. Reviewed by Barbara Benham. *Belles Lettres* 5, No. 2 (Winter 1990):18

**De la Falaise, Loulou** (about). *See* Paris – Social Life and Customs

**Delamont, Sara**

Knowledgeable Women: Structuralism and the Reproduction of Elites. Reviewed by Olive Banks. *Gender and Education* 2, No. 1 (1990):97-98

Reconstructing the Academy: Women's Education and Women's Studies. Book Review. *Gender and Education* 2, No. 2 (1990):245-246

**Delaney, Joan**

Business Is Better the Second Time Around. *Executive Female* (May/June 1990):66-67

Designing Woman. *Executive Female* 13, No. 5 (September-October 1990):66-67

A Faucet Firm Lands in Hot Water. *Executive Female* 13, No. 6 (November-December 1990):70-71

Where There's a Will, There's a Way. *Executive Female* (March/April 1990):70-71

Windshield Wipers Clean Up. *Executive Female* 13, No. 4 (July-August 1990):70-71

**Delany, Dana** (about)

China Beach's Dana Delany. Interview. Fred Robbins. *McCall's* 117, No. 8 (May 1990):42

**De la Peña, Terri**

Palabras. *Sinister Wisdom* 40 (Spring 1990):38-39

Tres Mujeres. Short Story. *Frontiers* 11, No. 1 (1990):60-64

**De La Renta, Oscar** (about). *See* Fashion Designers; Talley, André Leon

**Delaunay, Sonia** (about)

Sonia Delaunay: Art into Fashion. By Elizabeth Morano. Reviewed by Sherry Buckberrough. *Woman's Art Journal* 11, No. 1 (Spring-Summer 1990):39-41

Sonia Delaunay. By Arthur A. Cohen. Reviewed by Sherry Buckberrough. *Woman's Art Journal* 11, No. 1 (Spring-Summer 1990):39-41

**DeLaurentis, Louise Budde**

Janus Days: Fortieth Anniversary Reflection. Poem. *Frontiers* 11, Nos. 2-3 (1990):26-29

**De Lauretis, Teresa** (about)

Feminist Theory as Practice: Italian Feminism and the Work of Teresa de Lauretis and Dacia Maraini. Itala T. C. Rutter. *Women's Studies International Forum* 13, No. 6 (1990):565-575

**Delayed Parenthood.** *See* Life Styles; Parenthood

**Déléas-Matthews, Josette**

Women Directors: The Emergence of a New Cinema. Book Review. *Atlantis* 15, No. 2 (Spring 1990):100-102

**Deledda, Grazia**

Cosima. Reviewed by Helen Barolini. *Belles Lettres* 5, No. 3 (Spring 1990):7

**Delegation of Authority.** *See also* Empowerment

Delegating: How to Let Go and Keep Control. Tess Kirby. *Working Woman* (February 1990):32-37

**De Lepervanch, Marie** (joint author). *See* Grosz, Elizabeth A.

**Delhagen, Kate**

Full Speed Ahead. *Women's Sports & Fitness* 12, No. 6 (September 1990):26-28

**Delinquency.** *See* Adolescents – Delinquency

**Delis, Dean C.** and Phillips, Cassandra

The Passion Paradox. *Glamour* (August 1990):214-215+

**Delk, Fannie** (joint editor). *See* DeCosta-Willis, Miriam

**Dellenbaugh, Anne**

Down the Wild River North. Book Review. *The Women's Review of Books* 7, No. 7 (April 1990):16-17

Paddling the River of Life. *The Women's Review of Books* 7, No. 7 (April 1990):16-17

**Dell'Olio, Louis** (about). *See* Fashion Designers, "Gentlemen's Choice"

**Delmar, Viña** (about)

Viña Delmar. Carolyn Banks. *Belles Lettres* 5, No. 3 (Spring 1990):14

**Demaray, Elyse** and Landay, Lori

Senses of Self: Women Writers of the Harlem Renaissance. *Feminist Teacher* 5, No. 2 (Fall 1990):32-33

**Demarchelier, Patrick**

Le Jazz Haute. *Vogue* (August 1990):332-337

**DeMarco, Carolyn**

Do the Right Thing, Eat the Right Thing. *Healthsharing* 11, No. 4 (December 1990):28-30

**DeMaris, Alfred**

The Dynamics of Generational Transfer in Courtship Violence: A Biracial Exploration. *Journal of Marriage and the Family* 52, No. 1 (February 1990):219-231

Interpreting Logistic Regression Results: A Critical Commentary. *Journal of Marriage and the Family* 52, No. 1 (February 1990):271-276

**Demers, Laurence,** McGuire, John L., Phillips, Audrey, and Rubinow, David R.

Premenstrual, Postpartum and Menopausal Mood Disorders. Reviewed by Jeanette Sasmore. *Health Care for Women International* 11, No. 2 (1990):234

**Demetrick, Mary Russo**

Legacy. *Sinister Wisdom* 41 (Summer-Fall 1990):54

Madeline. Poem. *Sinister Wisdom* 41 (Summer-Fall 1990):22

**De Mille, Agnes** (about)

Grande Dame of Dance. Yona Zeldis McDonough. *Harper's Bazaar* (January 1990):55

**Demographic Measurements.** *See* Baby Boom Generation – Demographic Measurements; Mortality Statistics

**De Monteflores, Carmen**

Cantando Bajito/Singing Softly. Reviewed by Erika Smilowitz. *Belles Lettres* 5, No. 2 (Winter 1990):18

Invisible Audiences. *Out/Look* No. 10 (Fall 1990):64-68

**Demos, Vasilikie**

Black Family Studies in the *Journal of Marriage and the Family* and the Issue of Distortion: A Trend Analysis. *Journal of Marriage and the Family* 52, No. 3 (August 1990):603-612

**Dengue Viruses**

Good Health: Lethal Mosquitos. Michael Castleman. *Redbook* 174, No. 6 (April 1990):22-24

**De Nicolo, David**

Vogue Arts: Movies. *Vogue* (September 1990):398-424

**Denicolo, David**

Andie Swings into Stardom. *Glamour* (November 1990):236-237+

Word On Movies. *Glamour* (February 1990):130

Word On . . . Sandra Bernhard. Interview. *Glamour* (March 1990):192

**Denman, Rose Mary**

Let My People In: A Lesbian Minister Tells of Her Struggles to Live Openly and Maintain her Ministry. Reviewed by Penny Perkins. *New Directions for Women* 19, No. 4 (July-August 1990):15

**Denmark–Acquired Immune Deficiency Syndrome**

Changing People's Behavior. *Connexions* 33 (1990):30-31

**Denmark–Status of Women**

The Women's Museum in Denmark. Merete Ipsen and Jette Sandahl. *Journal of Women's History* 2, No. 2 (Fall 1990):168-170

**Denmark–Women's Movement**

The Embodiment of Ugliness and the Logic of Love: The Danish Redstocking Movement. Lynn Walter. *Feminist Review* No. 36 (Autumn 1990):103-126

**Dent, David**

Women in the Military. *Essence* 20, No. 12 (April 1990):41-46

**Dente, Barbara** (about). *See* Fashion Merchandising

**Dentistry**

Dental Questions You Were Afraid to Ask. Tara Flanagan and Ann Ferrar. *Ladies' Home Journal* 107, No. 9 (September 1990):140-143

Is Your Dentist Up-to-Date? Linda J. Heller. *Redbook* 174, No. 5 (March 1990):20-26

**Dentistry–Aesthetics**

Woman Loses Gap, Gains Toothy Grin. Ronni Sandroff. *McCall's* 118, No. 2 (November 1990):60-69

**Denton, Elizabeth**

A Leap of Faith. Short Story. *Iris* 23 (Spring-Summer 1990):17-19

**De Palma, Brian**

Movies: The Bonfire of the Vanities. Reviewed by Graydon Carter. *Vogue* (December 1990):190-194

**Depardieu, Gérard** (about)

Deciphering Depardieu. Paul Chutkow. *Vogue* (December 1990):294-299+

**Department Stores.** *See also* Retail Trade Industry

Fashion Victims. Jill Andresky Fraser. *Savvy Woman* (June 1990):54-57, 84

**Department Stores–Employees**

Counter Cultures: Saleswomen, Managers, and Customers in American Department Stores, 1890-1940. By Susan Porter Benson. Reviewed by Jeanne Allen. *Camera Obscura* No. 22 (January 1990):150-158

Counter Cultures: Saleswomen, Managers and Customers in American Department Stores, 1890-1940. By Susan Porter Benson. Reviewed by Carole Elizabeth Adams. *Gender & History* 2, No. 3 (Autumn 1990):343-348

**DePaulo, Lisa**

Alison Gertz: Champagne, Roses . . . and AIDS. *Mademoiselle* (December 1990):176-179+

**De Pauw, Linda Grant**

Weak Link: The Feminization of the American Military. Book Review. *Minerva* 8, No. 1 (Spring 1990):88-89

**Dependent Behavior.** *See* Learned Helplessness

**Depner, Charlene E.** (joint author). *See* Maccoby, Eleanor E.

**DePorter, Diane**

Young Mother's Story: "I Knew I Had to Survive–For My Daughter's Sake." *Redbook* 175, No. 1 (May 1990):34-36

**Depp, Johnny** (about). *See* Entertainers

**De Pré, Jacqueline** (about)

Jacqueline du Pré: A Life. By Carol Easton. Reviewed by Cecile Latham. *off our backs* 20, No. 9 (October 1990):16

**Depression, Mental.** *See also* Obsessive-Compulsive Disorders

Depression Envy. *Lear's* (December 1990):76-77+

Division of Household Labor, Strain, and Depressive Symptoms among Mexican Americans and Non-Hispanic Whites. Jacqueline M. Golding. *Psychology of Women Quarterly* 14, No. 1 (March 1990):103-117

Good News About the Blues. Susan Carleton. *Working Mother* 13, No. 4 (April 1990):16-22

Health Express: Body & Soul. Maj-Britt Rosenbaum. *Mademoiselle* (January 1990):70

"I Couldn't Cope with Motherhood." Leah Balk. *Working Mother* (November 1990):38-43

Leap into the Light. Barbara Bartocci. *Good Housekeeping* 210, No. 6 (June 1990):52-56

Learned Helplessness: A Factor in Women's Depression. Linda M. Kiefer. *AFFILIA* 5, No. 1 (Spring 1990):21-31

Living on the Edge. Holly Helmstetter. *Family Circle* 103, No. 10 (July 24, 1990):68-70

Moody News: Can a Pill Called Prozac End Depression? Natalie Angier. *Mademoiselle* (April 1990):229, 261-263

Tangled Up in Blues. Elizabeth Wurtzel. *Mademoiselle* (April 1990):228-229, 260-261

Time Out of Mind. William Styron. *Lear's* (August 1990):74-75+

**Depression, Mental–Adolescents**

The Million Adolescent Personality Inventory Profiles of Depressed Adolescents. Marion F. Ehrenberg, David N. Cox, and Raymond F. Koopman. *Adolescence* 25, No. 98 (Summer 1990):415-424

The Prevalence of Depression in High School Students. Marion F. Ehrenberg, David N. Cox, and Raymond F. Koopman. *Adolescence* 25, No. 100 (Winter 1990):905-912

**Depression, Mental–Counseling**

Smile! The Mood Makeover. *Mademoiselle* (December 1990):172-175

Some Greenery for Holiday Blues. John Bradshaw. *Lear's* (December 1990):60

**De Ribes, Jacqueline** (about). *See* Fashion Designers

**Dermansky, Ann**

Descent to Hell and Back. *New Directions for Women* 19, No. 5 (September-October 1990):13

Imprints. *New Directions for Women* 19, No. 6 (November-December 1990):6

The Loony Bin Trip. Book Review. *New Directions for Women* 19, No. 5 (September-October 1990):13

Millett Still a Gadfly. *New Directions for Women* 19, No. 5 (September-October 1990):12-13

**Dermatology**

Banish Blemishes–Fast! Frederic Haberman and Margaret Danbrot. *Redbook* 175, No. 4 (August 1990):20

Skinflicks: Technologies of Care and Repair. Nelson Lee Novick. *Lear's* (October 1990):65

**Derr, Nancy**

Floating in My Mother's Palm. Book Review. *Belles Lettres* 5, No. 4 (Summer 1990):10

Germany East and West: The Twain Meet. *Belles Lettres* 5, No. 4 (Summer 1990):9-10

Lost Weddings. Book Review. *Belles Lettres* 5, No. 4 (Summer 1990):9-10

The Panther Woman: Five Tales from the Cassette Recorder. Book Review. *Belles Lettres* 5, No. 4 (Summer 1990):9

Three Paths to the Lake. Book Review. *Belles Lettres* 5, No. 4 (Summer 1990):10

**Derricotte, Toi**

Captivity. Reviewed by Jan Clausen. *The Women's Review of Books* 7, Nos. 10-11 (July 1990):12-13

**Derron, P. S.**

Health Express: Home Remedies. *Mademoiselle* (February 1990):110

**Derrow, Paula**

Fats: The Good, the Bad and the Deadly. *Mademoiselle* (December 1990):104

**Desai, Amprapali** (joint author). *See* Arora, Uma

**Desai, P. B.** (joint editor). *See* Bose, Ashish

**DeSalvo, Louise**

Coz. Book Review. *New Directions for Women* 19, No. 4 (July-August 1990):14

Disarming Patriarchy. *New Directions for Women* 19, No. 4 (July-August 1990):14

Virginia Woolf: The Impact of Childhood Sexual Abuse on Her Life and Work. Reviewed by Denise M. Marshall. *Belles Lettres* 6, No. 1 (Fall 1990):43-44

Virginia Woolf: The Impact of Childhood Sexual Abuse on Her Life and Work. Reviewed by Florence Rush. *Women's Studies International Forum* 13, No. 3 (1990):276-277

Virginia Woolf: The Impact of Childhood Sexual Abuse on Her Life and Work. Reviewed by Jane Lilienfeld. *Women's Studies International Forum* 13, No. 5 (1990):527-529

Virginia Woolf: The Impact of Childhood Sexual Abuse on Her Life and Work. Reviewed by Julia Robertson. *Resources for Feminist Research* 19, No. 1 (March 1990):36-37

Virginia Woolf: The Impact of Childhood Sexual Abuse on Her Life and Work. Reviewed by Peggy Phelan. *The Women's Review of Books* 7, No. 6 (March 1990):16-17

Virginia Woolf: The Impact of Childhood Sexual Abuse on Her Life and Work. Reviewed by Sydney Janet Kaplan. *NWSA Journal* 2, No. 1 (Winter 1990):124-127

Virginia Woolf and Katharine Furse: An Unpublished Correspondence. *Tulsa Studies in Women's Literature* 9, No. 2 (Fall 1990):228-230

**DeSalvo, Louise,** D'Arcy, Kathleen, and Hogan, Katherine (editors)

Territories of the Voice, Contemporary Stories by Irish Women Writers. Reviewed by Joann Gardner. *The Women's Review of Books* 7, No. 7 (April 1990):24-25

Territories of the Voice: Contemporary Stories by Irish Women Writers. Reviewed by Maxine Rodburg. *Belles Lettres* 5, No. 3 (Spring 1990):2

**De Santis, Lydia** (joint author). *See* Pete, Joanette M.

**De Santis, Marie**

Hate Crimes Bill Excludes Women. *off our backs* 20, No. 5 (May 1990):1

The Middle East Crisis: A Dilemma for Women: Democracy, Kings, and Sexual Apartheid in Saudi Arabia. *off our backs* 20, No. 9 (October 1990):8

Nicaragua: Chamorro's Government Rolls Back Reproductive Rights. *Spare Rib* 217 (October 1990):52

Nicaragua Rolls Back Reproductive Rights. *off our backs* 20, No. 8 (August/September 1990):3

Women's Refuge Faces Funding Cuts. *Spare Rib* 217 (October 1990):45

**Desaulniers, Michelle** (interview)

Mémoire, reconnaissance. Helge Dascher. *Canadian Women's Studies* 11, No. 1 (Spring 1990):75-77

**Descarries, Francine**

L'épouse de LEUR pe4re: Marâtres mode d'emploi. Book Review. *Resources for Feminist Research* 19, No. 2 (June 1990):41

**Descartes, Rene** (about). *See also* Knowledge, Theory of

**Descriptive Video Services**

No More the Pause that Perplexes. J. R. Moehringer. *McCall's* 117, No. 11 (August 1990):64

**DeShazer, Mary K.**

"Sisters in Arms": The Warrior Construct in Writings by Contemporary U.S. Women of Color. *NWSA Journal* 2, No. 3 (Summer 1990):349-373

**Design.** *See also* Craft Arts; Office Layout

Grand Illusions. *Harper's Bazaar* (September 1990):294-299

Julie Rejoicing. *Lear's* (October 1990):106-109

Smooth Moves. *Lear's* (November 1990):118-121

Turning Wood to Good Use. *Lear's* (October 1990):120-125

**Designers.** *See also* Color in Design; Costume Design; Fashion Designers

**Designers – Social Entertaining**

Country Charm. Patricia Beard. *Harper's Bazaar* (October 1990):236

World Apart. Gini Sikes. *Harper's Bazaar* (October 1990):234+

**Desmond, Sharon M.** (joint author). *See* Price, Joy A.

**Desserts.** *See also* Cake; Cookery (Chocolate)

Bake-Shop Secrets. *Ladies' Home Journal* 107, No. 4 (April 1990):192-197

Best Baking Guide. *Family Circle* 103, No. 16 (November 27, 1990):102-119

Better-than-Sex Desserts. *Ladies' Home Journal* 107, No. 3 (March 1990):218-222

Big-Deal Desserts. Maida Heather. *Ladies' Home Journal* 107, No. 9 (September 1990):190-191+

Cookie Superstars. *Ladies' Home Journal* 107, No. 10 (October 1990):196-201

Country-Style Buttermilk Crumb Cake. *Redbook* 174, No. 5 (March 1990):154

Decadent Desserts. Jonell Nash. *Essence* 20, No. 10 (February 1990):85-88+

Fresh Fruit and Fabulous. Holly Sheppard. *McCall's* 118, No. 1 (October 1990):142-144

Happy Halloween Desserts. Donna Meadow. *McCall's* 118, No. 1 (October 1990):140

Light and Easy: Autumn Fruit Compote. *Good Housekeeping* 211, No. 4 (October 1990):132

Mother's Day Delights. *McCall's* 117, No. 8 (May 1990):147

Perfect Summer Desserts. *Ladies' Home Journal* 107, No. 8 (August 1990):138-140

Pumpkin Treats. *Good Housekeeping* 211, No. 4 (October 1990):180-183

Simply Delicious. *Redbook* 175, No. 2 (June 1990):106-111+

Sweet Sensations. *Redbook* 176, No. 1 (November 1990):130-134+

Sweet Surprises. *Ladies' Home Journal* 107, No. 5 (May 1990):190-195

20 Delicious Gifts from Your Kitchen. *Redbook* 176, No. 1 (November 1990):139-154

Warm Desserts for Cold Winter Days. *Ladies' Home Journal* 107, No. 1 (January 1990):144-148

**Desserts, Frozen**

Eat Light: Satisfy Your Cool Cravings. *Redbook* 175, No. 3 (July 1990):128

Outrageous! *Redbook* 175, No. 5 (September 1990):179-186+

Quick Hit: Frozen Fantasy. *Redbook* 175, No. 3 (July 1990):66

**Detectives**

Can These Mysteries Be Solved? Andrea Gross. *Ladies' Home Journal* 107, No. 8 (August 1990):104-106+

**Deutsch, Steven**

Solutions for the New Work Force: Policies for a New Social Contract. Book Review. *Women and Health* 16, Nos. 3/4 (1990):201-205

**Deutschkron, Inge**

Outcast: A Jewish Girl in Wartime Berlin. Reviewed by Myrna Goldenberg. *Belles Lettres* 6, No. 1 (Fall 1990):6-9

**Devaney, Kim** (joint author). *See* Collier, Lee

**De Vault, Christine**

The Sexuality Decision-Making Series for Teens. Reviewed by Peggy Brick. *New Directions for Women* 19, No. 3 (May/June 1990):21

**Devdasis – Goa.** *See* India – Goanese

**Devé, Claire** (about). *See also* Carter, Charla, "European Designers to Watch."

**De Veaux, Alexis**

Forty Fine. *Essence* 20, No. 9 (January 1990):50-52+

Walking into Freedom. *Essence* 21, No. 2 (June 1990):48-53+

**De Veaux, Alexis,** Milloy, Marilyn, and Ross, Michael Erik

Legends in Our Time: Clap Your Hands. *Essence* 21, No. 1 (May 1990):101-122

**Devereaux, Kathryn**

Food for Fuel. *Women's Sports and Fitness* 12, No. 7 (October 1990):24-25

The Green Grocer. *Women's Sports & Fitness* 12, No. 6 (September 1990):24-25

**Devi, Ashapurna**

As Usual. Short story. *Manushi* 57 (March-April 1990):39-42

**Devi, Mahasweta**

The Hunt. Translated by Gayatri Spivak. *Women and Performance: A Journal of Feminist Theory* 5, No. 1, Issue #9 (1990): 61-79

**Devilbiss, M. C.**

Sexism and the War System. Book Review. *Minerva* 8, No. 2 (Summer 1990):79-90

Women in Combat: A Quick Summary of the Arguments on Both Sides. *Minerva* 8, No. 1 (Spring 1990):29-31

**Devine, Eleanore**

You're Standing In My Light and Other Stories. Reviewed by Jennifer L. Sacks. *Belles Lettres* 5, No. 4 (Summer 1990):17

**De Vito, Danny** (about)

Danny De Vito: Reaching New Heights. Michael J. Bandler. *Ladies' Home Journal* 107, No. 1 (January 1990):76-80

**Devor, Holly**

Fantastic Women: Sex, Gender and Transvestism. Book Review. *Resources for Feminist Research* 19, No. 1 (March 1990):11

Gender Blending: Confronting the Limits of Duality. Reviewed by Carol LeMasters. *The Women's Review of Books* 7, No. 9 (June 1990):12

**DeVries, Rachel Guido**

The Accordion. Short Story. *Sinister Wisdom* 41 (Summer-Fall 1990):34-37

Litany on the Equinox. Poem. *Sinister Wisdom* 41 (Summer-Fall 1990):38-39

**Dewey, Joanna** (joint author). *See* Martin, Clarice J.

**de Wolfe, Elsie** (about)

Living. Laurie Schechter. *Vogue* (November 1990):313-315

**Dewson, Molly** (about)

Partner and I: Molly Dewson, Feminism, and New Deal Politics. By Susan Ware. Reviewed by June Purvis. *Women's Studies International Forum* 13, Nos. 1-2 (1990):160-161

**Dexter, Miriam Robbins**

Whence the Goddesses: A Source Book. Reviewed by Deborah Ann Light. *Ms.* 1, No. 2 (September/October 1990):27

**Dey, Susan** and Hurwitz, Joy Sirott

Give Someone Hope – and Help. *Redbook* 176, No. 1 (November 1990):40

**Dharker, Imtiaz**

Purdah. Reviewed by Joyoti Grech. *Spare Rib* No. 211 (April 1990):27

**Dhuibhne, Eilís Ní**

Blood and Water. Reviewed by Patricia Roth Schwartz. *Belles Lettres* 5, No. 3 (Spring 1990):3

**Diabetes**

Attitude Toward Menopause and the Impact of the Menopausal Event on Adult Women with Diabetes Mellitus. Nancy E. White and Judith M. Richter. *Journal of Women and Aging* 2, No. 4 (1990):21-38

Talking with Susan Ruttan: "I'll Always Miss My Sister." Bibliography. Nancy Mills. *Redbook* 174, No. 5 (March 1990):30-34

**Dial-a-Message Telephone Calls.** *See also* Sex Industry

Glamour Guide. Bibliography. *Glamour* (November 1990):87-90

**Dialectic of Enlightenment**

Body and Image Space: Problems and Representability of a Female Dialectic of Enlightenment. Sigrid Weigel. *Australian Feminist Studies* No. 11 (Autumn 1990):1-15

**Diamant, Anita**

Work Daze. *Harper's Bazaar* (October 1990):166-169+

**Diamond, Arlyn** and Edwards, Lee R. (editors)

The Authority of Experience: Essays in Feminist Criticism. Reviewed by Elaine Marks. *Tulsa Studies in Women's Literature* 9, No. 2 (Fall 1990):309-314

**Diamond, Deborah Beroset**

Private Agony, Public Cause. *Ladies' Home Journal* 107, No. 6 (June 1990):124-125+

A Tale of Two Mothers. *Ladies' Home Journal* 107, No. 7 (July 1990):83-85+

**Diamond, Irene** and Kuppler, Lisa

Frontiers of the Imagination: Women, History, and Nature. *Journal of Women's History* 1, No. 3 (Winter 1990):160-180

**Diamond, Irene** and Orenstein, Gloria Feman (editors)

Reweaving the World: The Emergence of Ecofeminism. Reviewed by Greta Gaard. *The Women's Review of Books* 8, No. 2 (November 1990):27-28

**Diamond, Irene** and Quinby, Lee (editors)

Feminism and Foucault: Reflections on Resistance. Reviewed by Constance Balides. *Camera Obscura* No. 22 (January 1990):138-149

Feminism and Foucault: Reflections on Resistance. Reviewed by Ladelle McWhorter. *NWSA Journal* 2, No. 4 (Autumn 1990):677-678

Feminism and Foucault: Reflections on Resistance. Reviewed by Mary Janell Metzger. *Hypatia* 5, No. 3 (Fall 1990):118-124

**Diamond, Jamie**

How Not to Get the D.T.'s When Happy. *Lear's* (September 1990):81-82

Vanity Kills. *Lear's* (January 1990):54-56

**Diamond, Marilyn**

Secret Energy Foods. *Family Circle* 103, No. 12 (September 4, 1990):76+

**Diamond, Sara**

Spiritual Warfare: The Politics of the Christian Right. Reviewed by Ann Baker. *New Directions for Women* 19, No. 1 (January/February 1990):25

**Diamond, Shifra**

Foods to Stay Awake By. *Mademoiselle* (December 1990):106

The Lowdown on Menstrual Problems. *Mademoiselle* (October 1990):120

Talking about Our Generation: The Mademoiselle Poll. *Mademoiselle* (December 1990):161+

**Diana, Princess of Wales** (about)

A Royal Christmas. Andrew Morton. *Good Housekeeping* 211, No. 6 (December 1990):140+

**Diapers**

The Bottom Line. T.J. Ford. *Ms.* 1, No. 1 (July/August 1990):89

Tell Us What You Think: Disposable Diapers. *Glamour* (April 1990):168

This Is What You Thought: Disposable Diapers. *Glamour* (June 1990):167

**DiCaprio, Lisa**

East German Feminists: The Lila Manifesto. *Feminist Studies* 16, No. 3 (Fall 1990):621-636

**Dicharry, Elisabeth K.** (joint author). *See* Higgins, Patricia G.

**Dickens, Charles – Criticism and Interpretation**

Historicisms New and Old: "Charles Dickens" Meets Marxism, Feminism, and West Coast Foucault. Judith Newton. *Feminist Studies* 16, No. 3 (Fall 1990):449-470

**Dickie, Alison**

Cervical Cancer and Smoking. *Healthsharing* 11, No. 3 (June 1990):9

**Dickinson, Emily – Criticism and Interpretation**

Emily Dickinson's "Engulfing" Play: *Antony and Cleopatra.* Judith Farr. *Tulsa Studies in Women's Literature* 9, No. 2 (Fall 1990):231-250

The Encoding of Homoerotic Desire: Emily Dickinson's Letters and Poems to Susan Dickinson, 1850-1886. Ellen Louise Hart. *Tulsa Studies in Women's Literature* 9, No. 2 (Fall 1990):251-272

**Dickinson, Janice** (about)

Model Homes. *Harper's Bazaar* (November 1990):158-163+

**Dickinson, Susan** (about)

The Encoding of Homoerotic Desire: Emily Dickinson's Letters and Poems to Susan Dickinson, 1850-1886. Ellen Louise Hart. *Tulsa Studies in Women's Literature* 9, No. 2 (Fall 1990):251-272

**Dickstein, Ruth** Mills, Victoria A., and Waite, Ellen J.

Women in LC's Terms: A Thesaurus of Library of Congress Subject Headings Related to Women. Reviewed by Mary Ellen S. Capek. *NWSA Journal* 2, No. 3 (Summer 1990):476-484

**Dictionaries**

Webster's First New Intergalactic Wickedary of the English Language. By Mary Daly and Jane Caputi. Reviewed by Mary Ellen S. Capek. *NWSA Journal* 2, No. 3 (Summer 1990):476-484

**Dictionaries – Sexism**

A Note on the Elimination of Sexism in Dictionaries. Morton Benson. *Women & Language* 13, No. 1 (Fall 1990):51

**Diegel, Micki**

Women Who Start Second Families. *Good Housekeeping* 210, No. 5 (May 1990):156-163

**Diet.** *See* Nutrition

**Diets.** *See* Reducing Diets

**Dietz, Mary**

Women and the Ideal Society: Plato's Republic and Modern Myths of Gender. Book Review. *Women & Politics* 10, No. 1 (1990):80-82

**Digby, Anne**

Fasting Girls: The Emergence of Anorexia as a Nervous Disease. Book Review. *Gender & History* 2, No. 3 (Autumn 1990):370-371

**Di Lazzaro, Dalida** (about). *See also* Fashion, "Suprema Donnas"

**Dilke, Emilia** (about)

Writing Inside the Kaleidoscope: Re-Representing Victorian Women Public Figures. Kali A. K. Israel. *Gender & History* 2, No. 1 (Spring 1990):40-48

**Dillard, Annie**

An American Childhood. Reviewed by Deborah Jurdjevic. *Canadian Women's Studies* 11, No. 1 (Spring 1990):110-111

The Writing Life. Reviewed by Suzanne Berne. *Belles Lettres* 5, No. 3 (Spring 1990):6

**Dillard, Annie – Criticism and Interpretation**

"The Waters of Separation": Myth and Ritual in Annie Dillard's *Pilgrim at Tinker Creek.* Jim Cheney. *Journal of Feminist Studies in Religion* 6, No. 1 (Spring 1990):41-63

**Dillingham, Wayne E.**

The Possibility of American Women Becoming Prisoners of War: A Challenge for Behavioral Scientists. *Minerva* 8, No. 4 (Winter 1990):17-22

**Dillon, Millicent**

After Egypt. Reviewed by Scarlet Cheng. *Belles Lettres* 6, No. 1 (Fall 1990):50

**Dillon, Nancy**

The Christmas Eve Caper. *Good Housekeeping* 211, No. 6 (December 1990):70-71+

**Dinerman, Miriam.** *See* Meyer, Carol and Young, Alma (editors), "On the Bias."

**Dinerman, Miriam** (joint editor). *See* Bernard, L. Diane

**Dinkins, Joyce** (about)

New York City's First Lady. Elsie B. Washington. *Essence* 21, No. 5 (September 1990):96-98

**Dinnerstein, Myra** (joint editor). *See* Aiken, Susan Hardy

**Dinur, Esty**

A Wish for Cambodia. *On the Issues* 15 (Summer 1990):22-23+

**Dior, Christian** (about). *See* Fashion Designers

**DiPerna, Paula**

Mopping Up the Mess. *The Women's Review of Books* 7, No. 12 (September 1990):19-20

White Silk and Black Tar: A Journal of the Alaska Oil Spill. Book Review. *The Women's Review of Books* 7, No. 12 (September 1990):19-20

**Disabled**

A Different Parent. Karen Blackford. *Healthsharing* 11, No. 3 (June 1990):20-24

Disability Income: A Case Study. Donna Gallin. *Executive Female* 13, No. 4 (July-August 1990):13-14

Patchwork. Deborah Price. *Belles Lettres* 6, No. 1 (Fall 1990):64-65

Rights of People with Disabilities Clarified. Anne Rauch. *Healthright* 9, No. 3 (May 1990):35-37

Study. Jasmine Marah. *Sinister Wisdom* 42 (Winter 1990-1991):40-41

A View From This Wheelchair. Mary Frances Platt. *off our backs* 20, No. 5 (May 1990):11

Who Do We Think We Are. Pat Isreal. *Healthsharing* 11, No. 3 (June 1990):11

**Disabled – Discrimination**

Accessibility, Male Children Heated Issues at Lesbian Fest. Jorjet Harper. *Hot Wire* 6, No. 1 (January 1990):29+

**Disabled – Education**

Disability Equality in the Classroom – A Human Rights Issue. Micheline Mason. *Gender and Education* 2, No. 3 (1990):363-366

**Disabled – Employment**

Capabilities. Patti Watts. *Executive Female* (May/June 1990):34-36+

**Disabled – Health Care**

Caring for the Disabled Elderly: Who Will Pay? By Alice M. Rivlin, Joshua M. Wiener, Raymond J. Hanley, and Denise A. Spence. Reviewed by Sandy Auburn. *Journal of Women and Aging* 2 No. 3 (1990):113-114

**Disabled – Housing**

Housing for the Disabled. Cathy McPherson. *Canadian Women's Studies* 11, No. 2 (Fall 1990):31-32

Meeting Our Needs: Access for Women with Disabilities. Shirley Masuda. *Canadian Women's Studies* 11, No. 2 (Fall 1990):80-81

**Disabled – Personal Narratives**

Full Circle: Wheel of Misfortune? Chava Willig Levy. *Family Circle* 103, No. 14 (October 16, 1990):192

**Disabled – Psychological Aspects**

Women with Disabilities: Essays in Psychology, Culture and Politics. Edited by Michelle Fine and Adrienne Asch. Reviewed by Hope Landrine. *Psychology of Women Quarterly* 14, No. 3 (September 1990):435-437

**Disabled – Resources**

A Network of Disabled Women. Carolann Barrett. *Woman of Power* 18 (Fall 1990):31-34

**Disabled – Role Models**

Positive Images: Portraits of Women with Disabilities. By Julie Harrison. Reviewed by Judith Pasternak. *On the Issues* 17 (Winter 1990):36-37

**Disabled – Services**

Circle This. Margaret Jaworski. *Family Circle* 103, No. 16 (November 27, 1990):11-12

**Disabled – Services for**

Do's and Don'ts for Helping the Disabled. *Good Housekeeping* 211, No. 3 (September 1990):292

A Ranch Where Miracles Happen. Mike Clary. *McCall's* 117, No. 8 (May 1990):154-160

**Disabled, Violence against**

Violence and Sexual Assault Plague Many Disabled Women. Corbett Joan O'Toole. *New Directions for Women* 19, No. 1 (January/February 1990):17

**Disabled – Women's Movement**

The History of the Disabled Women's Movement in Canada. Meryn Stuart and Glynis Ellerington. *Women and Environments* 12, No. 2 (Spring 1990): 19

Unequal Access: Disabled Women's Exclusion from the Mainstream Women's Movement. Meryn Stuart and Glynis Ellerington. *Women and Environments* 12, No. 2 (Spring 1990): 16-18

**Disabled Children**

Safe in Mother's Arms. Judith Kelman. *Redbook* 175, No. 3 (July 1990):112-114

**Disabled Mothers**

The Reluctant Go-Between. Robert Brody. *Glamour* (October 1990):288+

Tehilah: Our Answered Prayer. Chava Willig Levy. *McCall's* 118, No. 3 (December 1990):138-140

**Disaster Relief**

How to Cope with Disaster. Norman Cousins. *McCall's* 118, No. 1 (October 1990):73-82

**Disasters – Personal Narratives**

We Had Five Minutes to Evacuate Our Apartment. Michael Drinkard and Jill Eisenstadt. *Glamour* (April 1990):270-273+

**Disch, Estelle** and Thompson, Becky

Teaching and Learning from the Heart. *NWSA Journal* 2, No. 1 (Winter 1990):68-78

**Discrimination.** *See also* Employment – Discrimination

Brothers: Is It Always Race or Sex? Stan Clynton Spence. *Essence* 21, No. 6 (October 1990):44

Tell Us What You Think: Are Americans Becoming More Racist? *Glamour* (January 1990):74

**Discrimination – Education**

Academic Discrimination Task Force: Ten Years of Fighting Against Sex Discrimination. *NWSAction* 3, No. 1/2 (Spring 1990): 4-5

The Civil Rights Act of 1990. *NWSAction* 3, No. 1/2 (Spring 1990): 5-6

Success Stories. *NWSAction* 3, No. 1/2 (Spring 1990): 2-4

The Supreme Court Rules in Favor of Opening Tenure Files. Annis Pratt. *NWSAction* 3, No. 1/2 (Spring 1990): 1

**Discrimination in Art**

Racism, Sexism, Still Afflict Art World. Cassandra Langer. *New Directions for Women* 19, No. 1 (January/February 1990):12

**Diseases.** *See also* Children – Diseases; Illness

Diseases Your Doctor May Miss. Bibliography. Stephen Phillip Policoff. *Ladies' Home Journal* 107, No. 6 (June 1990):104-109

Old Diseases, New Concerns. Devera Pine. *Ladies' Home Journal* 107, No. 1 (January 1990):44-51

Watch Out for Strep Throat. Michael Castleman. *Redbook* 176, No. 1 (November 1990):102-103+

**Diseases – Prevention.** *See also* Breast Cancer; Giardiasis; Health Care Policy; Health Education; Mosquitos as Carriers of Disease

The Naked Truth about Fitness. Barbara Ehrenreich. *Lear's* (September 1990):96-99

**Disk Jockeys**

Welcome to the Muthaland. *Spare Rib* No. 212 (May 1990):32-33

**Disposable Diapers.** *See* Diapers

**Di Stefano, Christine**

Reproducing the World: Essays in Feminist Theory. Book Review. *Women & Politics* 10, No. 4 (1990):138-140

**Divakaruni, Chitra**

Searching for the Goddess. *Woman of Power* 15 (Fall-Winter 1990):28-29

Sudha's Story. Poem. *Woman of Power* 18 (Fall 1990):20-21

Visit. Poem. *Woman of Power* 18 (Fall 1990):20

**Diving**

Fitness. Vicki Woods. *Vogue* (April 1990):228-230

**Divorce**

Breaking Out of the Ex-Wife Trap. Sandra Kahn. *Lear's* (December 1990):48-49

Determinants of Divorce: A Review of Research in the Eighties. Lynn K. White. *Journal of Marriage and the Family* 52, No. 4 (November 1990):904-912

Divorce, Remarriage, and Adolescent Substance Use: A Prospective Longitudinal Study. Richard H. Needle, S. Susan Su, and William J. Doherty. *Journal of Marriage and the Family* 52, No. 1 (February 1990):157-169

Divorce, Suicide, and the Mass Media: An Analysis of Differential Identification, 1948-1980. Steven Stack. *Journal of Marriage and the Family* 52, No. 2 (May 1990):553-560

"If Men Are Talking, They Blame It on Women": A Nigerian Woman's Comments on Divorce and Child Custody. Elisha P. Renne. *Feminist Issues* 10, No. 1 (Spring 1990):37-49

Marking Time, Moving Onward. Jennie Nash. *Lear's* (November 1990):80

The Multiple Consequences of Divorce: A Decade Review. Gay C. Kitson and Leslie A. Morgan. *Journal of Marriage and the Family* 52, No. 4 (November 1990):913-924

New Micro-level Data on the Impact of Divorce on Suicide, 1959-1980: A Test of Two Theories. Steven Stack. *Journal of Marriage and the Family* 52, No. 1 (February 1990):119-127

Private Lives. Pamela Redmond Satran. *Family Circle* 103, No. 2 (February 1, 1990):31-32+

The Role of Divorce in Men's Relations with Their Adult Children after Mid-life. Teresa M. Cooney and Peter Uhlenberg. *Journal of Marriage and the Family* 52, No. 3 (August 1990):677-688

Talking with Meredith Baxter-Birney: "Being Single Again Is Scary – and Glorious." Interview. Vicki Jo Radovsky. *Redbook* 175, No. 3 (July 1990):42-44

Wellfleet. Alfred Kazin. *Lear's* (June 1990):76-77+

Women, Work, and Divorce. By Richard R. Peterson. Reviewed by Donna Hodgkins Berardo. *Journal of Marriage and the Family* 52, No. 4 (November 1990):1153

## Divorce – Custody

Brothers: A Father's Joy, A Father's Pain. Calvin Dais. *Essence* 21, No. 8 (December 1990):30

Child Custody and the Politics of Gender. Edited by Carol Smart and Selma Sevenhuijsen. Reviewed by Meg Luxton. *Journal of Marriage and the Family* 52, No. 4 (November 1990):1153-1154

Child Custody and the Politics of Gender. Edited by Carol Smart and Selma Sevenhuijzen. Reviewed by Nancy D. Polikoff. *The Women's Review of Books* 7, No. 9 (June 1990):23-24

Coparenting in the Second Year after Divorce. Eleanor E. Maccoby, Charlene E. Depner, and Robert H. Mnookin. *Journal of Marriage and the Family* 52, No. 1 (February 1990):141-155

Family Justice: Taking the Trauma out of Custody Cases. Bibliography. Liza Nelson. *McCall's* 117, No. 7 (April 1990):27-29

How Could You? Mothers Without Custody of Their Children. By Harriet Edwards. Reviewed by Nancy D. Polikoff. *The Women's Review of Books* 7, No. 9 (June 1990):23-24

In the Name of the Fathers: The Story Behind Child Custody. By Susan Crean. Reviewed by Nancy D. Polikoff. *The Women's Review of Books* 7, No. 9 (June 1990):23-24

## Divorce – Economic Aspects

An Economic Approach to Marital Dissolution in Puerto Rico. Maria E. Canabal. *Journal of Marriage and the Family* 52, No. 2 (May 1990):515-530

The Divorce Revolution: The Unexpected Social and Economics Consequences for Women and Children in America. By Lenore J. Weitzman. Reviewed by Barbara Risman. *Gender and Society* 4, No. 1 (March 1990):105-108

Dollars & Divorce: How to Get What You Deserve. Raoul Lionel Felder. *Harper's Bazaar* (August 1990):144-147

Irreconcilable Differences: Women Defining Class After Divorce and Downward Mobility. Christine E. Grella. *Gender and Society* 4, No. 1 (March 1990):41-55

## Divorce – History

Divorce Patterns in Nineteenth-Century New England. Martin Schultz. *Journal of Family History* 15, No. 1 (January 1990):101-115

Peasant Women and Divorce in Preindustrial Japan. Notes. Laurel L. Cornell. *Signs* 15, No. 4 (Summer 1990):710-732

Putting Asunder: A History of Divorce in Western Society. By Roderick Phillips. Reviewed by A. James Hammerton. *Gender & History* 2, No. 2 (Summer 1990):241-244

## Divorce – Jewish Law

The New, Improved Jewish Divorce: Hers/His. Vicki Hollander. *Lilith* 15, No. 3 (Summer 1990):20-21

## Divorce – Psychological Aspects

Brothers: A Father's Joy, A Father's Pain. Calvin Dais. *Essence* 21, No. 8 (December 1990):30

Divorce History and Self-reported Psychological Distress in Husbands and Wives. Lawrence A. Kurdek. *Journal of Marriage and the Family* 52, No. 3 (August 1990):701-708

How Resentment Can Wreck Divorce. John Bradshaw. *Lear's* (August 1990):57

Suing Dad: Bat Mitzvah in the Divorce Crossfire. Marla Ruth Allison. *Lilith* 15, No. 2 (Spring 1990):23-24

## Divorce – Reform

Women, Families and Equality: Was Divorce Reform A Mistake? Annamay T. Sheppard. *Women's Rights Law Reporter* 12, No. 3 (Fall 1990):143-152

## Divorce – Settlements

Negotiation Divorce Outcomes: Can We Identify Patterns in Divorce Settlements? Jay D. Teachman and Karen Polonko. *Journal of Marriage and the Family* 52, No. 1 (February 1990):129-139

**Divorce – Support Groups**

The Process of Providing Support to Recently Divorced Single Mothers. Mary E. Duffy and Lee Smith. *Health Care for Women International* 11, No. 3 (1990):277-294

**Dixon, Ruth**

Rural Women at Work: Strategies for Development in South Asia. Reviewed by Kalpana Bardhan. *Journal of Women's History* 2, No. 1 (Spring 1990):200-219

**D'Lugo, Carol Clark**

To Love, Honor, and Obey in Colonial Mexico: Conflicts Over Marriage Choice, 1574-1821. Book Review. *Women's Studies International Forum* 13, Nos. 1-2 (1990):161

**Doane, Mary Ann**

The Desire to Desire: The Woman's Film of the 1940s. Reviewed by Paul Rabinowitz. *Feminist Studies* 16, No. 1 (Spring 1990):151-169

**Dobie, Kathy**

Growing Up with Violence. *Vogue* (December 1990):310-315 +

**Dobkin, Alix**

Yahoo Australia! Reviewed by Joanne Stato. *off our backs* 20, No. 9 (October 1990):20

**Dobkin, Alix** (interview)

Hi, Phranc. This Is Alix Calling. Phranc and Alix Dobkin. *Hot Wire* 6, No. 1 (January 1990):16-18 +

**Doctor-Patient Relationships**. *See* Patient-Doctor Relationships

**Documentary Films**. *See also* Riggs, Marlon (about)

In Fading Light. *Spare Rib* No. 209 (February 1990):35

Voices from Gaza: The Inside Story of the Israeli Occupation of Palestine. *Spare Rib* No. 216 (September 1990):33

**Dodd, Alexandra Dundas**

Intimate Adversaries: Cultural Conflict Between Doctors and Women Patients. Reviewed by Margherita Jellinek. *AFFILIA* 5, No. 4 (Winter 1990):108-110

**Dodd, Kathryn**

Cultural Politics and Women's Historical Writing: The Case of Ray Strachey's *The Cause. Women's Studies International Forum* 13, Nos. 1-2 (1990):127-137

**Dodd, Susan**

Hellbent Men and Their Cities. Reviewed by Catherine Francis. *Belles Lettres* 5, No. 4 (Summer 1990):40 +

**Dodder, Richard A.** (joint author). *See* Mitchell, Jim

**Doe, Tonie** and Degen, Paul

Line Drawings: Aphorisms. *Lear's* (February 1990):88-93

**Dogs.** *See also* Pets

Pet Life. Michael W. Fox. *McCall's* 117, No. 7 (April 1990):133; 117, No. 10 (July 1990):111; 118, No. 3 (December 1990):145

Pet News. *Ladies' Home Journal* 107, No. 11 (November 1990):134

Pet News. Nina Keilin. *Ladies' Home Journal* 107, No. 5 (May 1990):124

The Puppy that Didn't Know How to Quit. Roberta Sandler. *Good Housekeeping* 211, No. 4 (October 1990):100

Something to Think about When Choosing a Dog, or Not. Lewis Burke Frumkes. *McCall's* 117, No. 8 (May 1990):58

**Dohaney, M. T.**

The Corrigan Women. Reviewed by Laura M. Robinson. *Atlantis* 15, No. 2 (Spring 1990):98-100

**Doherty, William J.** (joint author). *See* Needle, Richard H.

**Doig, David**

A Place for the Heart. Short Story. *Good Housekeeping* 210, No. 4 (April 1990):98-100

**Dojny, Brooke** (joint author). *See* Barnard, Melanie

**Doke, Larry** (joint author). *See* Miller, Robert P.

**Dolan, Jill**

Feminism and Theatre. Book review. *Signs* 15, No. 4 (Summer 1990):864-869

Interviews with Contemporary Women Playwrights. Book review. *Signs* 15, No. 4 (Summer 1990):864-869

Women in American Theatre. Book review. *Signs* 15, No. 4 (Summer 1990):864-869

**Dolce, Domenico** (about). *See* Italy – Fashion

**Dole, Elizabeth** (about). *See* Dusky, Lorraine

Elizabeth Dole: Southern Charmer. Lorraine Dusky. *McCall's* 117, No. 9 (June 1990):67

The Glass Ceiling: If I Had a Hammer. Patricia O'Toole. *Lear's* (November 1990):29-30

**Dolgin, Janet L.**

Status and Contract in Feminist Legal Theory of the Family: A Reply to Bartlett. *Women's Rights Law Reporter* 12, No. 2 (Summer 1990): 103-113

**Dollimore, Jonathan**

The Cultural Politics of Perversion: Augustine, Shakespeare, Freud, Foucault. *Genders* 8 (Summer 1990):1-16

**Dolls**

Black Like Us: Dolls for Our Kids. Kimberly Knight. *Essence* 21, No. 7 (November 1990):104-109

**Domestic Life.** *See* Family Life

**Domestic Relations.** *See also* Couples; Female-Male Relationships; Sexual Relationships

Ardent Spouse in Search of the Perfect Gift . . . Hugh O'Neill. *McCall's* 118, No. 3 (December 1990):46-48

Couple Time. *Glamour* (April 1990):144

In the Limelight. Arthur J. Robinson, Jr. *Essence* 21, No. 3 (July 1990):34

Long Time Love. Pearl Lewis and Peter Lewis. *Essence* 21, No. 1 (May 1990):139-142+

Private Lives. Sally Helgesen. *Family Circle* 103, No. 8 (June 5, 1990):100-104

Sex and the Married Man. Anthony Brandt. *Lear's* (November 1990):156+

This Working Life: Work Talk: You Always Bore the One You Love. Johanna Schneller. *Working Woman* (May 1990):134

**Domestic Violence.** *See also* Abused Wives; Murder; Violence Against Women

An Analysis of Domestic Violence in Asian American Communities: A Multicultural Approach to Counseling. Christine K. Ho. *Women and Therapy* 9, Nos. 1-2 (1990):129-150

Attributions of Blame for Marital Violence: A Study of Antecedents and Consequences. Bernice Andrews and Chris R. Brewin. *Journal of Marriage and the Family* 52, No. 3 (August 1990):757-767

Battered Women Fill Prisons. Sharon Wyse. *New Directions for Women* 19, No. 2 (March/April 1990):4+

The Battered Women's Movement in Action. Evelyn Tomaszewski. *off our backs* 20, No. 10 (November 1990):1-3

Batterer Still on Police Force. *New Directions for Women* 19, No. 2 (March/April 1990):4

Children of Battered Women. By Peter G. Jaffee, David A. Wolfe, and Susan Kaye Wilson. Reviewed by Sharon Wyse. *On the Issues* 17 (Winter 1990):34-35

Compounding the Triple Jeopardy: Battering in Lesbian of Color Relationships. Valli Kanuha. *Women and Therapy* 9, Nos. 1-2 (1990):169-184

Domestic Tyranny. By Elizabeth Pleck. Reviewed by Jan Faulkner. *AFFILIA* 5, No. 1 (Spring 1990):123-124

Domestic Violence and Sexual Abuse of Children: A Review of Research in the Eighties. Richard J. Gelles and Jon R. Conte. *Journal of Marriage and the Family* 52, No. 4 (November 1990):1045-1058

The Dynamics of Generational Transfer in Courtship Violence: A Biracial Exploration. Alfred DeMaris. *Journal of Marriage and the Family* 52, No. 1 (February 1990):219-231

Family Violence in Cross-cultural Perspective. By David Levinson. Reviewed by Linda E. Saltzman. *Journal of Marriage and the Family* 52, No. 1 (February 1990):280-281

Feminist Perspectives on Wife Abuse. Edited by Kersti Yllo and Michele Bograd. Reviewed by Marcia Bedard. *NWSA Journal* 2, No. 3 (Summer 1990):464-475

Heroes of Their Own Lives: The Politics and History of Family Violence. By Linda Gordon. Reviewed by Joan W. Scott. *Signs* 15, No. 4 (Summer 1990):848-852

Intimate Violence – A Study of Injustice. By Julie Blackman. Reviewed by Freda L. Paltiel. *Women and Health* 16, Nos. 3/4 (1990):196-201

Keeping the Faith: Questions and Answers for the Abused Woman. By Marie M. Fortune. Reviewed by Deborah L. Humphreys. *AFFILIA* 5, No. 2 (Summer 1990):109-111

Legislating Against Violence. *Women in Action* 3 & 4 (1990):43-46

Morphine and Dolly Mixtures. By Carol-Ann Courtney. Reviewed by Penny Simpson. *Spare Rib* No. 209 (February 1990):30

Mother Jailed for Contempt of Court. Maureen O'Hara. *Spare Rib* No. 216 (September 1990):45

Response to Scott. Linda Gordon. *Signs* 15, No. 4 (Summer 1990):852-853

Sibling Violence and Agonistic Interactions among Middle Adolescents. Megan P. Goodwin and Bruce Roscoe. *Adolescence* 25, No. 98 (Summer 1990):451-467

Terrifying Love: Why Battered Women Kill and How Society Responds. By Lenore E. Walker. Reviewed by Marcia Bedard. *NWSA Journal* 2, No. 3 (Summer 1990):464-475

Verbal and Physical Aggression in Marriage. Jan E. Stets. *Journal of Marriage and the Family* 52, No. 2 (May 1990):501-514

Violent Acts and Injurious Outcomes in Married Couples: Methodological Issues in the National Survey of Families and Households. Lisa D. Brush. *Gender and Society* 4, No. 1 (March 1990):56-67

The Violent Family. Edited by Nancy Hitchings. Reviewed by Sandra Bauer. *AFFILIA* 5, No. 1 (Spring 1990):114-115

Women, Policing, and Male Violence: International Perspectives. Edited by Jalna Hanmer, Jill Radford, and Elizabeth A. Stanko. *NWSA Journal* 2, No. 3 (Summer 1990):364-375

Zimbabwe: Opposing Violence. Dolly Vangasayi and Saliwe Matopodzi. *off our backs* 20, No. 7 (July 1990):9

**Domestic Violence – History**

Domestic Tyranny: The Making of American Social Policy Against Family Violence from Colonial Times to the Present. By Elizabeth Pleck. Reviewed by Marcia Bedard. *NWSA Journal* 2, No. 3 (Summer 1990):464-475

Heroes of Their Own Lives: The Politics and History of Family Violence. By Linda Gordon. Reviewed by Marcia Bedard. *NWSA Journal* 2, No. 3 (Summer 1990):464-475

**Domestic Violence – Latin America**

Domestic and Sexual Violence Network Workshop. *Women in Action* 3 & 4 (1990):14

**Domestic Violence – Lesbians**

Lesbian Battery. Mary Suh. *Ms.* 1, No. 2 (September/October 1990):48

**Domestic Workers.** *See* Household Workers

**Domingo, Chris**

"We Are More Than Fourteen": Montreal Mass Femicide. *off our backs* 20, No. 2 (February 1990):10-11

**Dominican Republic – Prostitution**

Dominican Republic: When Prostitution Is Legal. *Women's World* , No. 24 (Winter 1990/91): 41

**Dominican Republic – Status of Women**

The Experience of CIPAF in Documentation. Teresa Peralta. *Women's World* 23 (April 1990):21-22

**Dominican Republic – Violence Against Women**

Everyday Violence. Graciela de la Cruz. *Connexions* 34 (1990):26

**Donawerth, Jane**

Utopian Science: Contemporary Feminist Science Theory and Science Fiction by Women. *NWSA Journal* 2, No. 4 (Autumn 1990):535-557

**Donleavy, J. P.**

A Singular Country. Reviewed by Kent Black. *Harper's Bazaar* (May 1990):80+

**Donnelly, Sally**

Bold Types. *Ms.* 1, No. 3 (November/December 1990):57

**Donofrio, Beverly**

Riding in Cars With Boys: Confessions of a Bad Girl Who Makes Good. Reviewed by Anne Lamott. *Mademoiselle* (August 1990):108

**Donovan, Carrie** (about)

Talking Fashion. Jonathan Van Meter. *Vogue* (September 1990):631-650

**Donovan, Christine**

On the Job. *Family Circle* 103, No. 11 (August 14, 1990):55

**Donovan, Josephine**

Animal Rights and Feminist Theory. Notes. *Signs* 15, No. 2 (Winter 1990):350-375

**Donovan, Mary**

Sex Discrimination in Higher Education and the Professions: An Annotated Bibliography. Review. *Feminist Collections* 11, No. 3 (Spring 1990):15

**Donovan, Mary Ellen** and Ryan, William P.

"I Give So Much and Get So Little." *Working Mother* 13, No. 1 (January 1990):26-31

**Donovan, Mary Ellen** (joint author). *See* Sanford, Linda Tschirhart

**Donovan, Priscilla**

Are You a Right-or Left-Brained Lover? *Redbook* 175, No. 3 (July 1990):84-87

**Donzis, Byron** (about)

The Cowboy as Cosmetician. Karen Stabiner. *Lear's* (January 1990):46-50

**Doppelt, Gabé**

Talking Fashion. *Vogue* (January 1990):229-231+

Talking Fashions. *Vogue* (October 1990):421-436

Talking Parties. *Vogue* (January 1990):232-235+

**Doppelt, Gabé** (editor)

Talking Parties. *Vogue* (December 1990):329-331

**Doran, Terry**, Satterfield, Janet, and Stade, Chris

A Road Well Traveled: Three Generations of Cuban American Women. Reviewed by Vicki L. Ruiz. *NWSA Journal* 2, No. 3 (Summer 1990):490-491

**Dorcey, Mary**

A Noise from the Woodshed. Reviewed by Roisin Ni Mhaille. *Spare Rib* No. 214 (July 1990):23

**Dorcey, Mary** (interview)

The Spaces Between the Words. Nuala Archer. *The Women's Review of Books* 8, No. 3 (December 1990):21-24

**Doress, Paula Brown**

An Interview-Based Exploration of the Motivations and Occupational Aspirations of Chronic Care Workers. *Journal of Women and Aging* 2 No. 3 (1990):93-111

**Dorf, Julie**

On the Theme: Talking with the Editor of the Soviet Union's First Gay and Lesbian Newspaper. Interview. *Out/Look* No. 9 (Summer 1990):55-59

**Dormen, Lesley**

Healthy Love. *Glamour* (October 1990):270-271+

How to Have Fantastic Sex: Know Yourself. *Redbook* 175, No. 4 (August 1990):100-101

Loveplay: The Touching Way to Passion. *Redbook* 175, No. 2 (June 1990):104-105+

The Most Dangerous Relationships a Woman Can Have. *Ladies' Home Journal* 107, No. 9 (September 1990):106-115

Single Again. *Glamour* (September 1990):190-193

**Dornbusch, Sanford M.** and Strober, Myra H. (editors)

Feminism, Children, and the New Families. Reviewed by Ellen B. Bogolub. *AFFILIA* 5, No. 3 (Fall 1990):116-118

**Dorner, Patricia Martinez** (joint author). *See* Silber, Kathleen

**Dorris, Michael**

Books: Coyote Waits. Book review. *Vogue* (July 1990):108-110

**Dos Santos, Judite**

Signs/Signals. Poem. *Heresies* 25 (1990):

**Dotson, Philip** (joint editor). *See* DeCosta-Willis, Miriam

**Double-Bassists**

Charnett Moffett: Bass Hit. Yannick Rice Lamb. *Essence* 21, No. 5 (September 1990):48

**Doucette, Concetta C. Beecher and Stowe.** *Iowa Woman* 9, No. 4 (Winter 1989-90):36-37

**Doudna, Christine**

A Cross Section of Community and Individual Action. Bibliography. *McCall's* 117, No. 8 (May 1990):164-167

Ending the Rape of Our Liberty. Bibliography. *McCall's* 117, No. 8 (May 1990):94-100

**Dougherty, Margot**

Royal Identity Crisis. *Mademoiselle* (August 1990):180-183

**Douglas, Carol Ann**

Love and Politics: Radical Feminist and Lesbian Theories. Reviewed by Barbara Ruth. *Sinister Wisdom* 42 (Winter 1990-1991):117-122

**Douglas, Carol Anne**

Abortion, Class, and Empowerment. *off our backs* 20, No. 2 (February 1990):5

Abortion Bans Mostly Foiled. *off our backs* 20, No. 5 (May 1990):5

After the Stroke. Book Review. *off our backs* 20, No. 10 (November 1990):12

On Boycotting Feminist Books. *off our backs* 20, No. 11 (December 1990):17

Central American Women: Battered in USA. *off our backs* 20, No. 5 (May 1990):3+

Daring to Be Bad: Radical Feminism in American 1967-1975. Book Review. *off our backs* 20, No. 4 (April 1990):16-17

Desert Years: Unlearning the American Dream. Book Review. *off our backs* 20, No. 10 (November 1990):12

Eastern Europe: What's Happening? *off our backs* 20, No. 1 (January 1990):7

Feminism in the Barrios of Costa Rica. *off our backs* 20, No. 3 (March 1990):1-3+

Feminist Theory: Notes from the Third Decade. *off our backs* 20, No. 2 (February 1990):24

Gender and Society. Journal Review. *off our backs* 20, No. 6 (June 1990):17

Inessential Woman. Book Review. *off our backs* 20, No. 4 (April 1990):17-18

Kicking the Habit: A Lesbian Nun Story. Book Review. *off our backs* 20, No. 11 (December 1990):19

Lesbian Philosophies and Cultures. Book Review. *off our backs* 20, No. 9 (October 1990):18-19

Letters From a War Zone. Book Review. *off our backs* 20, No. 1 (January 1990):18-20

Lives of Courage: Women for a New South Africa. Book Review. *off our backs* 20, No. 3 (March 1990):28+

Looking Back on the Last 20 Years. *off our backs* 20, No. 2 (February 1990):15-18

NWSA Workshop: Asian Immigrant Women. *off our backs* 20, No. 8 (August/September 1990):18-19

NWSA Workshop: Women's Studies in China. *off our backs* 20, No. 8 (August/September 1990):

Old Lesbians in Nature. *off our backs* 20, No. 10 (November 1990):12

Passages: Aging Lesbians Meet. *off our backs* 20, No. 5 (May 1990):8

Primate Visions: Gender, Race and Nature in the World of Modern Science. Book Review. *off our backs* 20, No. 7 (July 1990):21-22

Radical Voices. Book Review. *off our backs* 20, No. 4 (April 1990):18

Response to Graffiti: Death Is Not the Answer. *off our backs* 20, No. 6 (June 1990):16

Simone de Beauvoir: A Biography. Book Review. *off our backs* 20, No. 7 (July 1990):20

States Act on Abortion. *off our backs* 20, No. 3 (March 1990):12; 20, No. 4 (April 1990):7

Theories of Sexuality Forum. *off our backs* 20, No. 8 (August/September 1990):17

U.S. out of (fill in the blank). *off our backs* 20, No. 3 (March 1990):23

Women Caught in Crisis. *off our backs* 20, No. 9 (October 1990):8

**Douglas, Carol Anne** (joint author). See Elliott, Farar; Ruby, Jennie

**Douglas, Kirk** (about). See Entertainers

**Douglas, Susan**

When I Breathe There Is a Space: An Interview with Buseje Bailey. *Canadian Women's Studies* 11, No. 1 (Spring 1990):40-42

**Doulton, Meredith** (about)

Monster Mama. Andrew Tilin. *Women's Sports and Fitness* 12, No. 7 (October 1990):16

**Doumato, Lamia**

Architecture and Women: A Bibliography. Reviewed by Pamela H. Simpson. *Woman's Art Journal* 11, No. 2 (Fall 1990-Winter 1991):44-48

**Dove, Rita**

Grace Notes. Reviewed by Jan Clausen. *The Women's Review of Books* 7, Nos. 10-11 (July 1990):12-13

**Dow Chemical Company**. See Morrisonville (Louisiana) – Dow Chemical Company

**Dowd, Maureen**

Patricia Schroeder: Uncompromising Free Spirit. *McCall's* 117, No. 9 (June 1990):64

Run for Your Wife. *Savvy Woman* (September 1990):60-63+

This Working Life: Feminine Wiles Are Back in Business. *Working Woman* (March 1990):158

This Working Life: Sex, Lies and the Business Dinner. *Working Woman* (June 1990):110

**Dowden, Richard** and Houger, Joan

8 Dangerous Breast Cancer Myths. *Redbook* 175, No. 1 (May 1990):114-115

**Dowling, Darlene**

The Grandmother of Time: A Woman's Book of Celebrations, Spells, and Sacred Objects for Every Month of the Year. Book Review. *On the Issues* 16 (Fall 1990):32-33

**Down, Lesley-Anne** (about)

The Stay-at-Home Side of Lesley-Anne Down. Natalie Gittelson. *McCall's* 117, No. 7 (April 1990):20

**Downey, Geraldine** (joint author). See Moen, Phyllis; Tiedje, Linda Beth

**Downey, Robert, Jr.** (about). See also Actors

**Downing, Christine**

Myths and Mysteries of Same-Sex Love. Reviewed by Carol LeMasters. *The Women's Review of Books* 7, No. 6 (March 1990):18-19

Same-Sex Love among the Greek Goddesses. *Woman of Power* 15 (Fall-Winter 1990):50-53

**Downing, Shelley**

Air-Obics. *Women's Sports and Fitness* 12, No. 7 (October 1990):14

**Dowry Deaths**. See India – Violence Against Women

**Doyal, Lesley**

Hazards of Hearth and Home. *Women's Studies International Forum* 13, No. 5 (1990):501-517

Waged Work and Women's Well Being. *Women's Studies International Forum* 13, No. 6 (1990):587-604

**Doyle, James A.**

Beyond Patriarchy: Essays by Men on Pleasure, Power, and Change. Book Review. *Gender and Society* 4, No. 1 (March 1990):117-118

**Drabble, Margaret**

A Natural Curiosity. Reviewed by Rosalind A. Warren. *The Women's Review of Books* 7, No. 5 (February 1990):9

**Drag Queens**. See Transvestites

**Dragu, Margaret** and Harrison, A. S. A.

Revelations: Essays on Striptease and Sexuality. Reviewed by Mariana Valverde. *Atlantis* 15, No. 2 (Spring 1990):115

**Drakulic, Slavenka**

In Their Own Words: Women of Eastern Europe. *Ms.* 1, No. 1 (July/August 1990):36-47

**Drama – History and Criticism**

Having the Last Laugh: Women In Nineteenth Century Bengali Farces. Sumanta Banerjee. *Manushi* No. 59 (July-August 1990):15-20

Women Playwrights in Contemporary Spain and the Male-Dominated Canon. Notes. Patricia W. O'Connor. *Signs* 15, No. 2 (Winter 1990):376-390

**Drama – Social Aspects**

Drama as a Consciousness-Raising Strategy for the Self-Empowerment of Working Women. Elizabeth Torre. *AFFILIA* 5, No. 1 (Spring 1990):49-65

**Dranov, Paula**

The Epi Empire. *Harper's Bazaar* (January 1990):38-44

**Draper, Gail**

Children's Lives as Curriculum. *Heresies* 25 (1990):21-26

**Draper, Polly** (about)

Health and Beauty Special for Busy Bodies. Kathy Henderson. *Redbook* 175, No. 6 (October 1990):79-83

**Dreadlocks**. See Hair Styles

**Dreams**. See Nightmares

**Drefuss, Joel**

Ruin and Reform in Peru. *Lear's* (November 1990):94-97+

**Dreifus, Claudia**

Talking with Valerie Bertinelli: Still Struggling to Save Her Marriage. Interview. *Redbook* 174, No. 6 (April 1990):38-42

**Dress Accessories.** *See also* Brooches; Gucci, Maurizio (about); Paris – Fashion; Purses

Beauty and Fashion Hotline: Touch of Luxe. *Family Circle* 103, No. 17 (December 18, 1990):37-40

Elements. Edited by Candy Pratts Price. *Vogue* (August 1990):152

Elements. *Vogue* (July 1990):72

Elements of Style. Lois Joy Johnson. *Ladies' Home Journal* 107, No. 3 (March 1990):168-173

Fashion Clips. Page Hill Starzinger. *Vogue* (July 1990):36-41; (September 1990):122

Fashion Questions. *Glamour* (October 1990):210

French Accent. *Lear's* (September 1990):134-137

Getting Stoned. *Vogue* (August 1990):300-309

Harvest Gold. *Lear's* (October 1990):114-119

Heart Times. *Glamour* (February 1990):174-175

High Tied. *Harper's Bazaar* (November 1990):132-137

Holiday Gift Guide. Bibliography. *Mademoiselle* (December 1990):62-66

Hot & New Accessories. *Good Housekeeping* 211, No. 4 (October 1990):102-104

The (Key) Chain Gang. Liz Logan. *Mademoiselle* (September 1990):124-127

Let's Talk Fashion: The Status Extras. *Mademoiselle* (January 1990):28-31

The Look of Confidence. *Glamour* (September 1990):278-291

Major Details: Exotic Accessories. *Mademoiselle* (January 1990):138-141

Mixed Metals. *Mademoiselle* (December 1990):146-151

Quick Cachet. *Glamour* (October 1990):280-283

Romantic Gestures. *Vogue* (December 1990):274-281

She Loves New York. *Mademoiselle* (October 1990):142-151

Shine: Accessories. *Vogue* (September 1990):615-619

Special Effects. *Vogue* (August 1990):310-317

Talking Fashion: Fake Out. *Vogue* (September 1990):656

Tie One On. Lois Joy Johnson. *Ladies' Home Journal* 107, No. 8 (August 1990):112-116

Vogue Point of View: First Look at Fall. *Vogue* (August 1990):275

Vogue's Last Look. Edited by Candy Pratts Price. *Vogue* (August 1990):392; (September 1990):674

What They're Wearing. *Glamour* (October 1990):226

**Dressel, Paul L.** and Clark, Ann

A Critical Look at Family Care. *Journal of Marriage and the Family* 52, No. 3 (August 1990):769-782

**Dressing for Success.** *See also* Beauty Culture; Business Entertaining; Maternity Clothes; Suits

Beauty & Fashion Journal. *Ladies' Home Journal* 107, No. 11 (November 1990):49-62

Becoming Skilled, Getting Ahead. Jody Becker. *McCall's* 118, No. 2 (November 1990):38-40

Best-Dressed Days. *Harper's Bazaar* (October 1990):160-165

Career Clothes: The New Ease. *Working Woman* (March 1990):95-121

Career Makeover: "I Needed to Define My Life." Jody Becker. *McCall's* 118, No. 1 (October 1990):31-32

Clothes at Work. *Working Woman* (February 1990):95-101

Dear FC: I Lost My Job. Laurie Fuchs. *Family Circle* 103, No. 13 (September 25, 1990):27-28

Designer Looks at Prices You Can Live with. *Working Woman* (September 1990):169-176

The Dress Advantage. *Working Woman* (September 1990):178-182

Dressing for Special Situations. *Glamour* (May 1990):148-150

Dress Smart. Linda Heller. *Redbook* 175, No. 4 (August 1990):90-94

Dress the Part. *Essence* 21, No. 4 (August 1990):60-65

Executive Essentials. *Harper's Bazaar* (March 1990):150-152

Fashion: Clothes That Lead Double Lives. *Working Woman* (August 1990):74-79

Fashion: Coats that Go Places. *Working Woman* (November 1990):136-141

Fashion: High Profile Style. *Working Woman* (September 1990):159-166

Fashion: Midseason Refreshers. *Working Woman* (January 1990):122-125

Fashion: Smooth Transitions. *Working Woman* (May 1990):98-103

Fashion: Something Personal. *Working Woman* (April 1990):100-105

Fashion: The Plaid Principles. *Working Woman* (October 1990):124-129

Fashion: When White's Just Right. *Working Woman* (June 1990):68-73

Fashion Forward. *Working Woman* (July 1990):86-91

Fashion Makeover. *Redbook* 174, No. 6 (April 1990):96-101

Fashion Questions. *Glamour* (February 1990):140

Fashion Workshop: But Is It Practical? *Glamour* (June 1990):193-196

Fashion Workshop. *Glamour* (February 1990):135-136; (July 1990):131-134

Fashion Workshop: How Much Work-Style does $500 Buy? *Glamour* (November 1990):181-184

Fashion Workshop: Who Would Wear That? *Glamour* (October 1990):205-208

Fashion Workshop: Work Wardrobes. *Glamour* (May 1990):255-228

Gentlemen's Choice. *Savvy Woman* (October 1990):66-73

Glamorous Liaisons. *Mademoiselle* (October 1990):156-161

Highly Toted. *Harper's Bazaar* (October 1990):178-181

Image: Legwork. Andrea Messina. *Working Woman* (August 1990):80-82

Is Your Work Wardrobe the Best it Can Be? *Glamour* (August 1990):106-108

Job Strategies: Don't Let the Heat Defeat You. *Glamour* (June 1990):126

Job Strategies. *Glamour* (January 1990):54-56

Job Strategies: Image Consultants. *Glamour* (February 1990):88-90

Job Strategies. Marilyn Moats Kennedy. *Glamour* (March 1990):111-116

Mind Over Manners. Joni Miller. *Savvy Woman* (July/August 1990):36-38

One Perfect Piece. *Glamour* (March 1990):266-267

The Right Winter Coat for Work. *Glamour* (November 1990):120-122

Stretching the Limits of Fashion. *Glamour* (December 1990):110-114

Style: Black & White in Color. *Essence* 20, No. 12 (April 1990):22

Style: Day into Night. *Essence* 21, No. 8 (December 1990):20

Style at Work. *Glamour* (April 1990):248-255

Style to Go. Lois Barrett. *Essence* 21, No. 5 (September 1990):22-24

The Success Set Gets Casual. *Mademoiselle* (November 1990):188-193

Suitabilities. *Glamour* (February 1990):196-201

Suit Yourself. *Glamour* (June 1990):246-251

Suit Yourself. *Harper's Bazaar* (March 1990):172-179

What to Add to Your Wardrobe This Fall. *Glamour* (October 1990):122-123

Who's *Really* Wearing Shorts to Work? *Glamour* (July 1990):78-80

Working Assets on the Go. *Glamour* (November 1990):244-249

Working Girl U.S.A.: October. *Mademoiselle* (October 1990):141

**Drew, Edwin**

More Than Raindrops. Poem. *Essence* 20, No. 11 (March 1990):126

**Drexel, Burnham Lambert**. *See* Business Failures

**Dreyden, Julia I.** (joint author). *See* Serow, Robert C.

**Dried Flower Arrangement**

Fields of Dreams. *Family Circle* 103, No. 13 (September 25, 1990):76-77

**Drigo, Paola**

Maria Zef. Reviewed by Helen Barolini. *Belles Lettres* 5, No. 3 (Spring 1990):7

Maria Zef. Reviewed by Rita Signorelli-Pappas. *The Women's Review of Books* 7, No. 9 (June 1990):18

**Drinkard, Michael** and Eisenstadt, Jill

We Had Five Minutes to Evacuate Our Apartment. *Glamour* (April 1990):270-273+

**Drinking Water**

How to De-Tox Your Water. Al Ubell and Label Shulman. *Family Circle* 103, No. 15 (November 6, 1990):33-36

Message in a Bottle: Is Your Water Safe to Drink? Karen Keller. *Mademoiselle* (June 1990):121

Water Works Wonders. Kathryn Keller. *Redbook* 175, No. 1 (May 1990):112-113+

**Drinking Water, Bottled**

On the Waterfront. Peter Mehlman. *Savvy Woman* (July/August 1990):82-84

**Driver, Jacqueline D.** (joint author). *See* Kahn, Arnold S.

**Driver Education**. *See* Automobiles – Driver Education

**Drohojowsky, Hunter**

Deconstructive Criticism. *Harper's Bazaar* (March 1990):46

**Drotner, Kirsten**

English Children and Their Magazines, 1751-1945. Reviewed by Penny Tinkler. *Gender and Education* 2, No. 1 (1990):112-113

**Drucker, Joel**

Tennis: Coach in a Box. *Women's Sports & Fitness* 12, No. 6 (September 1990):22

**Drug Abuse.** *See also* Prenatal Influences; Substance Abuse

**Drug Abuse and Crime**

"I Fought the Drug Lords." Monica De Greiff and Guy Gugliotta. *Ladies' Home Journal* 107, No. 2 (February 1990):22-27

**Drug Addiction.** *See* Substance Abuse

**Drugs**

Health Watch. Ruth Winter. *Family Circle* 103, No. 12 (September 4, 1990):51-54

**Drugs, Nonprescription**

How Not to Be Arested for the Sniffles. Bibliography. Randi Londer Gould. *Lear's* (October 1990):48-49

Pharmacy Facts. Gary A. Holt and Cheryl Solimini. *Family Circle* 103, No. 13 (September 25, 1990):116

**Drugs, Prescription.** *See also* Orphan Drugs

Health Dept. Dava Sobel. *Lear's* (January 1990):44

Health Dept. Donna Heiderstadt. *Lear's* (October 1990):70

Pharmacy Facts. Gary A. Holt and Cheryl Solimini. *Family Circle* 103, No. 13 (September 25, 1990):116

**Drug Traffic**

The Ring Around the U.S. Dollar. Patricia O'Toole. *Lear's* (May 1990):29-30

Women and Drugs: The Untold Story. Catherine Breslin. *Ladies' Home Journal* 107, No. 1 (January 1990):89-91+

**Drug Traffic – Opposition**

Colombia's Drug Busting Journalist. María Jimena Duzán *Ms.* 1, No. 1 (July/August 1990):12

**Dual-Career Families.** *See also* Balancing Work and Family Life; Role Strain; Time Management

Checkmates. Ellie McGrath. *Savvy Woman* (January 1990):56-58, 94

Domestic Division of Labor among Working Couples: Does Androgyny Make a Difference? Nancy C. Gunter and B.G. Gunter. *Psychology of Women Quarterly* 14, No. 3 (September 1990):355-370

Making the Most of Two Paychecks. Eleanor Berman. *Working Mother* 13, No. 4 (April 1990):71-81

The Second Shift: Working Parents and the Revolution at Home. By Arlie Hochschild. Reviewed by Lois Braverman. *AFFILIA* 5, No. 4 (Winter 1990):111-113

This Working Life: Confessions of a Monday Lover. Sara Nelson. *Working Woman* (February 1990):128

This Working Life. Kathleen Fury. *Working Woman* (January 1990):144

This Working Life: Work Talk: You Always Bore the One You Love. Johanna Schneller. *Working Woman* (May 1990):134

Women in Dual-Career Families and the Challenge of Retirement. Joy B. Reeves. *Journal of Women and Aging* 2, No. 2 (1990):119-132

**Dubbert, Patricia M.** (joint author). *See* Johnson, Cheryl A.

**Duben, Alan**

Understanding Muslim Households and Families in Late Ottoman Istanbul. *Journal of Family History* 15, No. 1 (January 1990):71-86

**DuBois, Ellen Carol**, Kelly, Gail Paradise, Kennedy, Elizabeth Lapovsky, Korsmeyer, Carolyn W., and Robinson, Lillian S.

Feminist Scholarship: Kindling in the Groves of Academe. Reviewed by Arlene Kaplan Daniels. *Gender and Society* 4, No. 1 (March 1990):96-99

Feminist Scholarship: Kindling in the Groves of America. Reviewed by Carol Lupton. *Gender and Education* 2, No. 2 (1990):251-252

**DuBois, Ellen Carol** and Ruiz, Vicki L. (editors)

Unequal Sisters: A Multicultural Reader in U.S. Women's History. Reviewed by Beverly Guy-Sheftall. *Ms.* 1, No. 1 (July/August 1990):69

Unequal Sisters: A Multicultural Reader in U.S. Women's History. Reviewed by Susan E. Davis. *New Directions for Women* 19, No. 6 (November-December 1990):18

**Dubow, Eric F.** and Luster, Tom

Adjustment of Children Born to Teenage Mothers: The Contribution of Risk and Protective Factors. *Journal of Marriage and the Family* 52, No. 2 (May 1990):393-404

**Dubrovnik (Yugoslavia) – Description and Travel**

Travel: Medieval Magic. Francine Prose. *Savvy Woman* (July/August 1990):78-79

**DuCille, Anne** (joint author). *See* Christian, Barbara

**Ducksworth, Marilyn** (about). *See* Davis, Andrea R., "Power Players"

**Dudar, Eleanor**

Luna. Book Review. *Canadian Women's Studies* 11, No. 1 (Spring 1990):109-110

**Duerst-Lahti, Georgia** and Johnson, Cathy Marie

Gender and Style in Bureaucracy. *Women & Politics* 10, No. 4 (1990):67-120

**Duffy, Ann,** Mandell, Nancy, and Pupo, Norene

Few Choices: Women, Work and Family. Reviewed by Peta Tancred. *Resources for Feminist Research* 19, No. 1 (March 1990):15

**Duffy, Mary E.** and Smith, Lee

The Process of Providing Support to Recently Divorced Single Mothers. *Health Care for Women International* 11, No. 3 (1990):277-294

**Dugdale, Anni**

Beyond Relativism: Moving On – Feminist Struggles. *Australian Feminist Studies* No. 12 (Summer 1990):51-63

**Duigan, John**

Romero. Reviewed by Alba Amaya. *Spare Rib* No. 210 (March 1990):38

**Dukakis, Kitty** and Scovell, Jane

Kitty Dukakis: The True Story. *Good Housekeeping* 211, No. 3 (September 1990):202-213

Now You Know. Reviewed by Elayne Rapping. *The Women's Review of Books* 8, No. 2 (November 1990):5-6

**Duke, Randolph** (about). *See* Fashion Designers, "Battle-Weary Designers"

**Duley, Margot I.**

Changing Our Minds: Feminist Transformations of Knowledge. Book review. *Signs* 15, No. 3 (Spring 1990):648-650

**Dulfer, Candy**

Saxuality. Reviewed by Jennifer Mourin. *Spare Rib* 217 (October 1990):27

**Duluth Women's Health Center.** *See also* Hodgson, Jane (about)

**Dumas, Lynne S.**

The Sibling Gap. *Working Mother* 13, No. 8 (August 1990):36-42

**Dumas, Lynne S.** (joint author). *See* Koltnow, Emily

**Dumon, Wilfried** (joint author). *See* Aldous, Joan

**Dumont, Micheline**

Femmes, culture et révolution. Book Review. *Resources for Feminist Research* 19, No. 2 (June 1990):43

**Dunaway, Faye** (about)

Faye Dunaway: Coming Home to Hollywood. Cliff Jahr. *Ladies' Home Journal* 107, No. 3 (March 1990):80-87

**Dunayer, Joan**

On Speciesist Language. *On the Issues* 17 (Winter 1990):30-31

**Duncan, Isadora** (about). *See also* Love-Letters

After Egypt. By Millicent Dillon. Reviewed by Scarlet Cheng. *Belles Lettres* 6, No. 1 (Fall 1990):50

**Duncan, Sandy** (about)

Sandy Duncan Perks Up "The Hogan Family." Leslie Jay. *Ladies' Home Journal* 107, No. 3 (March 1990):96-98

**Duncker, Patricia** (editor)

In and Out of Time. Reviewed by Annie Hole. *Spare Rib* No. 215 (August 1990):29

**Dundon, Susan**

Diary of a Second Wedding. *McCall's* 117, No. 11 (August 1990):34-43

**Dunham, Katherine** (about). *See* Leadership, "1990 Essence Awards"

**Dunn, Sara**

Voyages of the Valkyries: Recent Lesbian Pornographic Writing. *Feminist Review* No. 34 (Spring 1990):161-170

**Dunnage, Carmen Gloria**

Fifth Latin American and Caribbean Feminist Meeting. *Women in Action* 3 & 4 (1990):3-8

Interview with an Organizer: "We Must Coordinate for the Next Meeting." Interview. *Women in Action* 3 & 4 (1990):9-10

Interview with Bessie Hollants: "We Would Never Have Forgiven Ourselves for Not Speaking Out." Interview. *Women in Action* 3 & 4 (1990):16-17

Women's International Cross-Cultural Exchange. *Women in Action* 3 & 4 (1990):24-29

**Dunnan, Nancy**

Broadcast Finance: The Best on the Airwaves. *Savvy Woman* (February 1990):29-32

A Few Words on Trading Places. Bibliography. *Lear's* (September 1990):32-35

Investing in a World Gone Wide. *Lear's* (May 1990):32-35

The Opening of the American Mind. Bibliography. *Lear's* (November 1990):32-34

Smart Investor: Blue Chips After Black Monday. *Lear's* (February 1990):24-25

Smart Investor: Holding the Ace of Clubs. *Lear's* (August 1990):26-27

Smart Investor: Last-Minute Tax Savings. *Lear's* (March 1990):36-38

Smart Investor: Playing the Global Market. *Lear's* (April 1990):26-28

A Wayfarer's Guide to the Dollar. Bibliography. *Lear's* (July 1990):26-27

When the Dow Turns Down. *Lear's* (October 1990):34-36

The Year of Living Cautiously. *Lear's* (June 1990):38-40

**Dunne, Dominick**

An Inconvenient Woman. Excerpt. Short story. *Ladies' Home Journal* 107, No. 7 (July 1990):48-57

**Dunne, Michael** (joint author). *See* Halford, W. Kim; Raphael, Beverley

**Dunst, Carl J.** (joint author). *See* Cooper, Carolyn S.

**Dunst, Melissa**

Aquatic. *Lear's* (September 1990):128-133

The Cure for Stressed-Out Summer Hair. *Lear's* (September 1990):70-72

The Skinny on Winter Skin. *Lear's* (October 1990):68

**Duong, Anh** (about)

Model Painter. William Norwich. *Vogue* (November 1990):374-379

**Dupiton, Sandra** (about)

Sandra Dupiton Loves to Dance. Martha Southgate. *Essence* 20, No. 10 (February 1990):40

**Du Plessis, Valerie**

Each in Her Own Way: Five Women Leaders of the Developing World. Book Review. *Resources for Feminist Research* 19, No. 1 (March 1990):9

**Dupré, Louise**

Strategies du vertige, trois poe4tes: Nicole Brossard, Madeleine Gagnon, France Théoret. Reviewed by Suzanne Legault. *Canadian Women's Studies* 11, No. 2 (Fall 1990):93-94

**Dupré, Louise** (joint author). *See* Bersianik, Louky

**DuPree, Mary** (about)

A Woman for Lear's: Grace Notes. Jane Howard. *Lear's* (January 1990):132-134

**Dupree, Nathalie**

Nathalie Dupree Cooks Southern Thanksgiving Favorites. *Redbook* 176, No. 1 (November 1990):125-129+

**Duquin, Lorene Hanley** (joint author). *See* Schall, Deborah

**Duras, Marguerite**

Emily L. Reviewed by Marianne Hirsch. *The Women's Review of Books* 8, No. 1 (October 1990):19-20

Practicalities: Marguerite Duras Speaks to Jérôme Beaujour. Reviewed by Marianne Hirsch. *The Women's Review of Books* 8, No. 1 (October 1990):19-20

**Durgin, Leslie** (about)

Boulder Mayor – All in a Day's Work. Susan Bristol-Howard. *Ms.* 1, No. 2 (September/October 1990):90

**Durkee, Rachel** (about). *See* College Students – Leadership

**Durova, Nadezhda**

The Cavalry Maid: The Memoirs of a Woman Soldier of 1812. Reviewed by Rita Victoria Gomez Dearmond. *Gender & History* 2, No. 2 (Summer 1990):229-232

**Durston, Christopher**

The Family and the English Revolution. Reviewed by Cynthia Herrup. *Gender & History* 2, No. 2 (Summer 1990):226-228

**Dusinberre, Juliet**

Alice to the Lighthouse: Children's Books and Radical Experiments in Art. Reviewed by Marcia Jacobson. *Signs* 15, No. 3 (Spring 1990):633-635

**Dusky, Lorraine**

Are You Ready for the '90s? *Working Woman* (January 1990):55

Bright Ideas: Anatomy of a Corporate Revolution. *Working Woman* (July 1990):58-63

Combat Ban Stops Women's Progress, Not Bullets. *McCall's* 117, No. 8 (May 1990):26-28

Elizabeth Dole: Southern Charmer. *McCall's* 117, No. 9 (June 1990):67

And the First Woman President of the United States Will Be . . . *McCall's* 117, No. 12 (September 1990):88-92

How to Boost Your Immune System. *McCall's* 117, No. 12 (September 1990):42-55

How to Eat, Drink and Still Be Merry. *McCall's* 118, No. 3 (December 1990):22

How to Find Companies Where Women Succeed. *Working Woman* (January 1990):81-88

The Lady Is a Thief. *Mademoiselle* (February 1990):168-169+

Progesterone: Safe Antidote for PMS. *McCall's* 118, No. 1 (October 1990):152-156

Sixty-Nine Top Companies for Working Mothers. *Good Housekeeping* 211, No. 2 (August 1990):104-105, 54-56

Women Who Would Be President. *McCall's* 117, No. 9 (June 1990):59-60

You're in the Office Now: The Rules and Regulations of the Work World. *Mademoiselle* (July 1990):130-131, 153-154

**Dutka, Elaine**

Cause Celeb. Bibliography. *McCall's* 118, No. 2 (November 1990):70-72

Cause Celeb. *McCall's* 117, No. 12 (September 1990):112-113

**Dutta, P. K.** and others

Socio-Demographic Profile of Tubectomy Acceptors: An Army Experience. *Journal of Family Welfare* 36, No. 1 (March 1990):56-60

**Dutton, Charles** (about)

Charles Dutton: From Jail to Yale. David Thigpen. *Essence* 21, No. 4 (August 1990):46

**Duvall, Shelley** (about)

The Thinking Woman's Cable. Michele Kort. *Savvy Woman* (November 1990):34-36

**Duzán, María Jimena**

Colombia's Drug Busting Journalist. _Ms.| 1, No. 1 (July/August 1990):12

**Dwellings – Maintenance and Repair**

Every Woman Can . . . Bibliography. *Ladies' Home Journal* 107, No. 11 (November 1990):216-218

Tools & Tips of the Trade. Al Ubell and Label Shulman. *Family Circle* 103, No. 13 (September 25, 1990):139

**Dwellings – Remodeling**

Beat the Clock. John Warde. *Family Circle* 103, No. 6 (April 24, 1990):114+

Decorating Secrets. *Family Circle* 103, No. 13 (September 25, 1990):86-91

Good Housekeeping Home Improvement Guide, 1990. *Good Housekeeping* 210, No. 4 (April 1990):181-226

The House that Love Built. *Glamour* (March 1990):282-285

House Warming. *Redbook* 175, No. 2 (June 1990):114-119

Makeover Your Home . . . for More Warmth & Style. Laurie Tarkan. *Redbook* 176, No. 1 (November 1990):96-101

My Healthy Home. Carolyn B. Noyes. *Ladies' Home Journal* 107, No. 1 (January 1990):110-118

**Dworkin, Andrea**

Israel: Whose Country Is It Anyway? *Ms.* 1, No. 2 (September/October 1990):69-79

Letters From a War Zone. Reviewed by Carol Anne Douglas. *off our backs* 20, No. 1 (January 1990):18-20

Letters from a War Zone: Writings 1976-87. Reviewed by Alice Echols. *The Women's Review of Books* 7, No. 4 (January 1990):5-6

Letters from a War Zone: Writings 1976-1989. Reviewed by Lisa Maher. *Women's Rights Law Reporter* 12, No. 3 (Fall 1990): 209-216

Mercy. Reviewed by Mary Smeeth and Susanne Kappeler. *Spare Rib* 218 (November 1990):27-28

Mercy (excerpt). Short Story. *Spare Rib* 218 (November 1990):28-29

**Dworkin, Andrea** and MacKinnon, Catherine A.

Pornography and Civil Rights: A New Day for Women's Equality. Reviewed by Pauline B. Bart. *NWSA Journal* 2, No. 3 (Summer 1990):516-518

**Dworkin, Andrea** (interview)

Andrea Dworkin: From a War Zone. Elizabeth Braeman and Carol Cox. *off our backs* 20, No. 1 (January 1990):8-9+

**Dwyer, Daisy** and Bruce, Judith (editors)

A Home Divided: Women and Income in the Third World. Reviewed by Eileen Berry. *Women's Studies International Forum* 13, No. 6 (1990):614-617

**Dwyer, Johanna**

The Wise Woman's Diet: Pasta Takes Off Pounds! *Redbook* 175, No. 4 (August 1990):111-120

**Dye, Ellen** and Roth, Susan

Psychotherapists' Knowledge about and Attitudes toward Sexual Assault Victim Clients. *Psychology of Women Quarterly* 14, No. 2 (June 1990):191-212

**Dyhouse, Carol**

Dangerous by Degrees: Women at Oxford and the Somerville College Novelists. Book Review. *Gender and Education* 2, No. 2 (1990):261-262

**Dykewomon, Elana**

Friendship: This Issue. *Sinister Wisdom* 40 (Spring 1990):3 8

Some Things Chava Meyer Says. Poem. *Sinister Wisdom* 42 (Winter 1990-1991):29-31

**Dykewomon, Elana**, Levinkind, Susan, Stoehr, Valerie, Marah, Jasmine, Cardea, Caryatis, and others

Sinister Wisdom Friendship Discussion 12/5/89. *Sinister Wisdom* 40 (Spring 1990):17-35

**Dysfunctional Families.** *See* Child Abuse; Family Violence; Incest; Problem Families; Spouse Abuse

**Dyslexia.** *See also* Attention Deficit Hyperactivity Disorder

# E

**Eads, Winifred E.**

Durable Rustproof Saturday Night. Poem. *Sinister Wisdom* 42 (Winter 1990-1991):92-93

**Eagan, Andrea Boroff**

Choosing Life. *The Women's Review of Books* 7, No. 12 (September 1990):21

Past Due: A Story of Disability, Pregnancy and Birth. Book Review. *The Women's Review of Books* 7, No. 12 (September 1990):21

**Eaglen, Audrey**

The New Women Warriors. *WLW Journal* 14, No. 1 (Fall 1990):13-14

**Eames, Charles (about).** See Muschamp, Herbert

**Earhart, Amelia** (about)

The Sound of Wings: The Life of Amelia Earhart. By Mary S. Lovell. Reviewed by Susan Ware. *The Women's Review of Books* 7, No. 4 (January 1990):7-8

**Ear Infections**

Not Another Ear Infection! David Wessel. *Working Mother* 13, No. 9 (September 1990):76-79

**Earth Communications Office.** See Dutka, Elaine

**Earthquakes.** See Natural Disasters

**Earthworks Group**

Waste Not! *Redbook* 175, No. 2 (June 1990):130-132+

**Easter**

"Here a Duck . . ." Sherry Hemman Hogan. *Good Housekeeping* 210, No. 4 (April 1990):110-113

**Easter Decorations**

Easter Joys. *Redbook* 174, No. 6 (April 1990):30

**Eastern Europe.** See Europe, Eastern

**Eastman, Barbara**

The Other Anna. Short story. *Lear's* (August 1990):116-122

**Eastman, Peggy**

Diaper Set. *Working Mother* (November 1990):122-124; (December 1990):69

Healthy Breasts: What's Normal, What's Not. *Family Circle* 103, No. 9 (June 26, 1990):101-104

**Easton, Carol**

Jacqueline du Pré: A Life. Reviewed by Cecile Latham. *off our backs* 20, No. 9 (October 1990):16

**Easton, S. Boyd**, Shostak, Marjorie, and Konner, Melvin

The Paleolithic Prescription. Reviewed by Lorraine Handler Sirota. *Women and Health* 16, Nos. 3/4 (1990):206-211

**Eating Behavior.** See also Nutrition

Beauty Questions. *Glamour* (October 1990):44

Eater's Digest. *Glamour* (March 1990):295

Fat War. Georgiana Arnold. *Essence* 21, No. 3 (July 1990):52-53+

First Person Singular: Takeout Shakeout. Larry Wallberg. *Savvy Woman* (November 1990):96+

Go Ahead and Eat Cake. Jane Shiyen Chou. *McCall's* 117, No. 10 (July 1990):28-34

Growing Up with a Fat Mom. Linda Neilson. *Glamour* (April 1990):156-160

Junk Food. *Glamour* (August 1990):242-243

Nutrition Makeover. Arlene Fischer. *Redbook* 175, No. 2 (June 1990):135-146

Surprise! The Way You Eat May Be Healthier than You Think. *Glamour* (March 1990):288-290

Weight Watchers Exclusive: Get Your Body Ready for the Beach. Ellie Grossman. *Ladies' Home Journal* 107, No. 6 (June 1990):96-102

When to Give In to Those Food Cravings. Linda J. Heller. *McCall's* 117, No. 11 (August 1990):14

**Eating Disorders.** See also Eating Behavior; Health Education

"Perfect" Bodies to Die for. Bibliography. Judith Warner-Berley. *McCall's* 117, No. 8 (May 1990):64-65

Ready, Set, Go! How to Shape Up Your Kids. Bibliography. Curtis Pesmen. *Ladies' Home Journal* 107, No. 4 (April 1990):89-110

Representation of Hysteria and Eating Disorders. Fiona Place. *Australian Feminist Studies* No. 11 (Autumn 1990):49-59

School Counselors' Knowledge of Eating Disorders. Joy A. Price, Sharon M. Desmond, James H. Price, and Amy Mossing. *Adolescence* 25, No. 100 (Winter 1990):945-947

Why Women Get Addicted to Food. Bibliography. Marie Dawson. *Ladies' Home Journal* 107, No. 9 (September 1990):132-136

Your Body: Confessions of a Food Addict. Nancy Alper. *Family Circle* 103, No. 16 (November 27, 1990):26-29

**Eating Disorders – History**

Fasting Girls: The Emergence of Anorexia as a Nervous Disease. By Joan Jacobs Brumberg. Reviewed by Anne Digby. *Gender & History* 2, No. 3 (Autumn 1990):370-371

**Eber, Irene**

Drops of Honey. Fiction. *Feminist Studies* 16, No. 3 (Fall 1990):607-620

**Eberle, Nancy**

Why We Can't Throw Anything Away. *Ladies' Home Journal* 107, No. 3 (March 1990):66

**Eberstadt, Frederick**

Capital Offense. *Harper's Bazaar* (October 1990):220-221+

**Ebert, Alan**

Chris Evert: My Love Match with Andy. *Good Housekeeping* 211, No. 4 (October 1990):86-90

The Pain and Passion of Quincy Jones. *Essence* 21, No. 7 (November 1990):59-60+

Quincy. *Lear's* (August 1990):64-65

**Ebi-Kryston, Kristie**, Higgins, Millicent W., and Keller, Jacob B.

Health and Other Characteristics of Employed Women and Homemakers in Tecumseh, 1959-1978: Demographic Characteristics, Smoking Habits, Alcohol Consumption, and Pregnancy

Outcomes and Conditions. *Women and Health* 16, No. 2 (1990):5-21

Health and other Characteristics of Employed Women and Homemakers in Tecumseh, 1959-1978: Prevalence of Respiratory and Cardiovascular Symptoms and Illnesses, Mortality Rates and Physical and Physiological Measurements. *Women and Health* 16, No. 2 (1990):23-39

**Echenberg, Havi** and Porter, Bruce

Poverty Stops Equality/Equality Stops Poverty: The Case for Social and Economic Rights. *Canadian Women's Studies* 11, No. 2 (Fall 1990):7-11

**Echols, Alice**

Daring to Be Bad: Radical Feminism in America 1967-1975. Reviewed by Carol Anne Douglas. *off our backs* 20, No. 4 (April 1990):16-17

Daring to Be Bad: Radical Feminism in America 1967-1976. Reviewed by Naomi Weisstein. *Ms.* 1, No. 3 (November/December 1990):54-55

Daring to Be Bad: Radical Feminism in America 1967-1975. Reviewed by Susan E. Davis. *New Directions for Women* 19, No. 5 (September-October 1990):14

Fighting for Feminism. *The Women's Review of Books* 7, No. 4 (January 1990):5-6

Letters from a War Zone: Writings 1976-87. Book Review. *The Women's Review of Books* 7, No. 4 (January 1990):5-6

**Ecker, Martha** (Joint author). *See* Crawley, Donna

**Eckhaus, Phyllis**

Feminist Thought: A Comprehensive Introduction. Book Review. *AFFILIA* 5, No. 3 (Fall 1990):121-122

**Ecofeminism**

Frontiers of the Imagination: Women, History, and Nature. Irene Diamond and Lisa Kuppler. *Journal of Women's History* 1, No. 3 (Winter 1990):160-180

Healing the Wounds: The Promise of Ecofeminism. Edited by Judith Plant. Reviewed by Linda Vance. *NWSA Journal* 2, No. 3 (Summer 1990):485-489

Pornography and Pollution. Patricia H. Hynes. *Women's Studies International Forum* 13, No. 3 (1990):169-176

Reweaving the World: The Emergence of Ecofeminism. Edited by Irene Diamond and Gloria Feman Orenstein. Reviewed by Greta Gaard. *The Women's Review of Books* 8, No. 2 (November 1990):27-28

The Woman I Love Is a Planet; the Planet I Love Is a Tree. Paula Gunn Allen. *Woman of Power* 18 (Fall 1990):5-7

**Ecological Disasters**. *See* Valdez (Alaska) – Oil Spill

**Ecology**. *See also* Ecofeminism; Environmental Sciences

Earth 1990. *Harper's Bazaar* (January 1990):72-77

Earth-Friendly Ecotips. T.J. Ford. *Ms.* 1, No. 2 (September/October 1990):17

Ecological Revolutions: Nature, Gender and Science in New England. By Carolyn Merchant. Reviewed by Linda Vance. *The Women's Review of Books* 7, No. 4 (January 1990):14-15

Environmental Action: Time Is Running Out. Eleanor J. Bader. *On the Issues* 17 (Winter 1990):24-26+

Fire and Rain. Jonathan Weiner. *Lear's* (April 1990):74-79+

Glimpses of the Goddess. Dona Spring. *Woman of Power* 15 (Fall-Winter 1990):77-78

Kids Who Care. Kathryn Watterson. *Working Mother* 13, No. 4 (April 1990):58-62

The State of the Earth. Betsy Carpenter. *Ladies' Home Journal* 107, No. 4 (April 1990):162-164+

**Economic Development**. *See also* Brazil – Debts, Public; United States – Economic Development

**Economic Development – Third World**. *See also* Africa – Economic Assistance; Honduras – Economic Development

Development Crises and Alternative Visions. Ursula Paredes and Georgina Ashworth. *Spare Rib* No. 210 (March 1990):23-25

Development of Africa – Strategies for 1990 and Beyond. *Women's World* 23 (April 1990):35-36

Documentation and Information Activities of CODICE. Wambui Wagacha. *Women's World* 23 (April 1990):23-24

The Global Factory. By Rachel Kamel. Reviewed by Laura McClure. *New Directions for Women* 19, No. 6 (November-December 1990):7

Institute of Southern African Studies. *Women's World* 23 (April 1990):37

**Economic Equality**

Is There a Parent Gap in Pocketbook Politics? Kenneth S. Y. Chew. *Journal of Marriage and the Family* 52, No. 3 (August 1990):723-734

**Economic Forecasting**. *See also* Business Forecasting

Back Talk: Europe '92 and Us. Gregory Simpkins. *Essence* 21, No. 2 (June 1990):114

People Are Talking About . . . *Vogue* (July 1990):89

**Economic Hardship**. *See also* Poverty

Economic Distress and Family Relations: A Review of the Eighties. Patricia Voydanoof. *Journal of Marriage and the Family* 52, No. 4 (November 1990):1099-1115

Linking Economic Hardship to Marital Quality and Instability. Rand D. Conger, Glen H. Elder, Jr., Frederick O. Lorenz, Katherine J. Conger, Ronald L. Simons, and others. *Journal of Marriage and the Family* 52, No. 3 (August 1990):643-656

## Economic Rights

Poverty Stops Equality/Equality Stops Poverty: The Case for Social and Economic Rights. Havi Echenberg and Bruce Porter. *Canadian Women's Studies* 11, No. 2 (Fall 1990):7-11

## Economics – Bibliographies

Reading Lists on Women's Studies in Economics. Barbara R. Bergmann. *Women's Studies Quarterly* 18, Nos. 3-4 (Fall-Winter 1990):75-86

## Economics – Feminist Perspectives

Enterprising Women: Ethnicity, Economy, and Gender Relations. Edited by Sallie Westwood and Parminder Bhachu. Reviewed by Sylvia Walby. *Gender and Society* 4, No. 3 (September 1990):425-427

Feminism and Economics. Barbara R. Bergmann. *Women's Studies Quarterly* 18, Nos. 3-4 (Fall-Winter 1990):68-73

Hidden by the Invisible Hand: Neoclassical Economic Theory and the Textbook Treatment of Race and Gender. Susan F. Feiner and Bruce B. Roberts. *Gender and Society* 4, No. 2 (June 1990):159-181

People and the Debt Crisis. *Women's World* 23 (April 1990):33-34

Sabotaging Their Statistics. Marilyn Waring. *Ms.* 1, No. 1 (July/August 1990):82-83

Women and Recession. Edited by Jill Rubery. Reviewed by Judith Wittner. *Gender and Society* 4, No. 2 (June 1990):258-262

## Economics – Study and Teaching

Confessions of a Feminist Economist: Why I Haven't Yet Taught an Economics Course on Women's Issues. Laurie J. Bassi. *Women's Studies Quarterly* 18, Nos. 3-4 (Fall-Winter 1990):42-45

A Course on Women in the Economy. Carol A. M. Clark. *Women's Studies Quarterly* 18, Nos. 3-4 (Fall-Winter 1990):33-41

Women and Minorities in Introductory Economics Textbooks: 1974 to 1984. Susan F. Feiner and Barbara A. Morgan. *Women's Studies Quarterly* 18, Nos. 3-4 (Fall-Winter 1990):46-67

Women and Work: A Survey of Textbooks. Kathy J. Krynski. *Women's Studies Quarterly* 18, Nos. 3-4 (Fall-Winter 1990):23-31

Women's Roles in the Economy: Teaching the Issues. Barbara R. Bergmann. *Women's Studies Quarterly* 18, Nos. 3-4 (Fall-Winter 1990):6-22

## Economic Value of Women's Work. See also Comparable Worth

Goodbye Paycheck! Hello Apron! Aimee Lee Ball. *Mademoiselle* (January 1990):1363-137+

Stay-at-Home Moms. Josie A. Oppenheim. *Good Housekeeping* 211, No. 3 (September 1990):114+

10 Best Paid Women in America. Anne B. Fisher. *Savvy Woman* (July/August 1990):44-51

## Ecrevan, Marée Dzian

To Grandmother's Bed. Poem. *Sinister Wisdom* 41 (Summer-Fall 1990):118

## Ecuador

Ecuador: Waorani People Fight for Their Life. *Spare Rib* 217 (October 1990):53

## Ecuador – Violence Against Women

Campaign to Confront Violence. Alexandra Ayala Marin. *Connexions* 34 (1990):15

## Edel, Deborah

The Lesbian Herstory Archives: A Statement of Cultural Self-Definition. *Woman of Power* 16 (Spring 1990):22-23

## Edell, Therese (about)

Therese Edell: Composer and Desktop Music Publisher. Sequoia. *Hot Wire* 6, No. 1 (January 1990):48-49+

This Longest Concert: Therese Edell's 40th Birthday Bash. Charlene Ball. *Hot Wire* 6, No. 3 (September 1990):28-29+

## Edelman, Marian Wright (about). See also Leadership, "1990 Women of the Year"

## Edelman, Renée

When Little Sister Means Business. *Working Woman* (February 1990):82-88

## Edelson, Mary Beth (about)

Art Makes Political Waves. Phyllis Rosser. *New Directions for Women* 19, No. 4 (July-August 1990):8

## Edelson, Stuart

Of Torture and Tangents: Consequences of the Robert Mapplethorpe Exhibition. *Out/Look* No. 7 (Winter 1990):52-53

## Edelstein, David

Movies. *Vogue* (May 1990):168-172

## Edemikpong, Ntiense Ben

Women and AIDS. *Women and Therapy* 10, No. 3 (1990):25-34

## Eden, Dawn, Ayres, Joe, and Hopf, Tim

An Analysis of the Mythical Function of Reproductive Advertisements. *Women's Studies in Communication* 12, No. 2 (Fall 1989):77-90

## Edge, Jessie Alma (about)

Prime of Life: Out of Retirement and into Office. Kelly Norton Humphrey. *Family Circle* 103, No. 9 (June 26, 1990):140-142

## Edgerton, Brenda (about). See Davis, Andrea R., "Power Players"

## Edgington, Amy

Critics. Poem. *Heresies* 25 (1990):73

*Quarterly* 18, Nos. 1-2 (Spring-Summer 1990):135-144

Changing Perspectives on Gender. Edited by Helen Burchell and Val Millman. Reviewed by Elisabeth Al-Khalifa. *Gender and Education* 2, No. 2 (1990):241-242

Children's Lives as Curriculum. Gail Draper. *Heresies* 25 (1990):21-26

By Design: Incorporating Feminist Ideas into the Political Theory Curriculum. Barbara Allen. *Feminist Teacher* 5, No. 1 (Spring 1990):15-18

Designing an Inclusive Curriculum: Bringing All Women into the Core. Elizabeth Higginbotham. *Women's Studies Quarterly* 18, Nos. 1-2 (Spring-Summer 1990):7-23

Equal Opportunity Issues in the Context of the National Curriculum: A Black Perspective. Sneh Shah. *Gender and Education* 2, No. 3 (1990):309-318

The Gender Integration Project at Piscataway Township Schools: Quilting a New Pedagogical Patchwork Through Curriculum Re-vision. Verdelle Freeman. *Women's Studies Quarterly* 18, Nos. 1-2 (Spring-Summer 1990):70-77

How Would You Like to Hear Only Half a Story? Ideas for Using Biographies of Historical Women in the Classroom. Shari Steelsmith. *Feminist Teacher* 5, No. 1 (Spring 1990):19-23

Implementing a Whole School Equal Opportunities Policy: A Primary School in Humberside. Sheila Cunnison and Christine Gurevitch. *Gender and Education* 2, No. 3 (1990):283-295

Mathematical Formalism as a Means of Occupational Closure in Computing – Why "Hard" Computing Tends to Exclude Women. Karen Mahony and Brett Van Toen. *Gender and Education* 2, No. 3 (1990):319-331

A Minor of Our Own: A Case for an Academic Program in Women of Color. Lynne Goodstein and LaVerne Gyant. *Women's Studies Quarterly* 18, Nos. 1-2 (Spring-Summer 1990):39-44

The New Jersey Project Enters Its Second Phase. Paula Rothenberg. *Women's Studies Quarterly* 18, Nos. 1-2 (Spring-Summer 1990):119-122

Nonfeminist and Feminist Students at Risk: The Use of Case Study Analysis While Transforming the Postsecondary Curriculum. Joan Poliner Shapiro. *Women's Studies International Forum* 13, No. 6 (1990):553-564

Restructuring the Curriculum: Barriers and Bridges. Barbara Paige-Pointer and Gale Schroeder Auletta. *Women's Studies Quarterly* 18, Nos. 1-2 (Spring-Summer 1990):86-94

Teaching Women's Studies from an International Perspective. Anne Betteridge and Janice Monk. *Women's Studies Quarterly* 18, Nos. 1-2 (Spring-Summer 1990):78-85

Telling Our Stories: The Academy and Change. Judith L. Johnston. *Women's Studies Quarterly* 18, Nos. 3-4 (Fall-Winter 1990):119-126

## Education, Elementary

Get the Teacher on Your Team. Kathy Henderson. *Working Mother* (November 1990):70-74

**Education – Evaluation.** *See also* Schools – Evaluation

## Education – Feminist Perspectives

The Immediate Classroom: Feminist Pedagogy and Peter Brook's *The Empty Space*. Catherine B. Burroughs. *Feminist Teacher* 5, No. 2 (Fall 1990):10-14

Storytelling and Dynamics of Feminist Teaching. Wendy S. Hesford. *Feminist Teacher* 5, No. 2 (Fall 1990):20-24

Teaching Women: Feminism and English Studies. Edited by Ann Thompson and Helen Wilcox. Reviewed by Jane Miller. *Gender and Education* 2, No. 2 (1990):239-240

Within School Walls: The Role of Discipline, Sexuality and the Curriculum. By Ann Marie Wolpe. Reviewed by Katherine M. Clarricoates. *Gender and Education* 2, No. 1 (1990):109-110

## Education – Gender Issues

Co-education – the Disadvantages for Schoolgirls. Averil Burgess. *Gender and Education* 2, No. 1 (1990):91-95

The Female Stranger in a Male School. Maria Pallotta-Chiarolli. *Gender and Education* 2, No. 2 (1990):169-183

Gender Issues and Education. Lesley Johnson. *Australian Feminist Studies* No. 11 (Autumn 1990):17-27

Gender Stereotypes in Children's Books: Their Prevalence and Influence on Cognitive and Affective Development. Sharyl Bender Peterson and Mary Alyce Lach. *Gender and Education* 2, No. 2 (1990):185-197

Girls' Groups as a Component of Anti-Sexist Practice – One Primary School Experience. Diane Reay. *Gender and Education* 2, No. 1 (1990):37-48

Knowledgeable Women: Structuralism and the Reproduction of Elites. By Sara Delamont. Reviewed by Olive Banks. *Gender and Education* 2, No. 1 (1990):97-98

Learning the Hard Way: Women's Oppression in Men's Education. By Taking Liberties Collective. Reviewed by Mary Hughes. *Gender and Education* 2, No. 3 (1990):370-371

Sex Equity in Education: Readings and Strategies. Edited by Anne O'Brien Carelli. Reviewed by Helen Burchell. *Gender and Education* 2, No. 3 (1990):375-377

Towards a Pedagogy of Sexual Difference: Education and Female Genealogy. Anna Maria Piussi. *Gender and Education* 2, No. 1 (1990):81-90

Women and Education: A Canadian Perspective. Edited by Jane S. Gaskell and Arlene Tigar McLaren. Reviewed by Catharine E. Warren. *Gender and Education* 2, No. 1 (1990):102-104

Women Teaching for Change: Gender, Class and Power. By Kathleen Weiler. Reviewed by Sandra Acker. *Gender and Education* 2, No. 1 (1990):105-107

"You're Just Imagining It, Everything's All Right Really, Don't Worry About It": The Position of Women in Surveying Education and Practice. Clara Greed. *Gender and Education* 2, No. 1 (1990):49-61

**Education – Homosexual Issues**

Don't Pass Us By: Keeping Lesbian and Gay Issues on the Agenda. Jane Andrews. *Gender and Education* 2, No. 3 (1990):351-355

Homosexuality and Education. By J. Martin Stafford. Reviewed by Peggy Aggleton. *Gender and Education* 2, No. 2 (1990):247-249

Legalized Invisibility: The Effect of Bill 7 on Lesbian Teachers. Didi Khayatt. *Women's Studies International Forum* 13, No. 3 (1990):185-193

**Education – Legislation**

Human Rights and "Free and Fair Competition": The Significance of European Education Legislation for Girls in the UK. Sheila McIntosh. *Gender and Education* 2, No. 1 (1990):63-79

**Education – Minorities**

Minorities in Higher Education: An Interview with Bambi Ramirez, American Council on Education. Debra Humphreys. *NWSAction* 3, No. 1/2 (Spring 1990): 7-9

**Education – Motivation**

Relations between Early Childhood Care Arrangements and College Students' Psychosocial Development and Academic Performance. Jean M. Ispa, Kathy R. Thornburg, and Mary M. Gray. *Adolescence* 25, No. 99 (Fall 1990):529-542

**Education, Preschool**

Montessori's Warm Way with Babies. Marilyn Gardner. *Working Mother* (November 1990):80-83

**Education – Rural Schools**

A Woman's Place and the Rural School in the United States. Suzanne Clark. *Genders* 8 (Summer 1990):78-90

**Education, Single-Sex**

The Private Eye: Better Dead than Coed. Barbara Grizzuti Harrison. *Mademoiselle* (September 1990):182

The Reform of Girls' Secondary and Higher Education in Victorian England. By Joyce Senders

Pedersen. Reviewed by Felicity Hunt. *Gender & History* 2, No. 1 (Spring 1990):113-114

There's Something About a Convent Girl . . . By Bamboo Productions. Reviewed by Irene Coffey. *Spare Rib* 219 (December 1990-January 1991):35

Working With Boys. Diane Reay. *Gender and Education* 2, No. 3 (1990):269-282

**Education, Special**

What Is Special Education. By John Fish. Reviewed by Sue Woodgate. *Gender and Education* 2, No. 3 (1990):374-375

**Educational Activities**

Are Your Kids Ready for Kindergarten? Kathy Henderson. *Ladies' Home Journal* 107, No. 9 (September 1990):70-72

Crazy Greens. Joel Rapp. *Redbook* 174, No. 5 (March 1990):36-40

What's Happening to Recess? Joanne Oppenheim. *Good Housekeeping* 211, No. 3 (September 1990):162

**Educational Evaluation**

Differences in Extracurricular Activity Participation, Achievement, and Attitudes toward School between Ninth-Grade Students Attending Junior High School and Those Attending Senior High School. Vernon D. Gifford and. *Adolescence* 25, No. 100 (Winter 1990):799-802

**Educational Exchanges. See Study Abroad**

**Educational Opportunity**

Equal Opportunities: Rhetoric or Action. Sue Lees and Maria Scott. *Gender and Education* 2, No. 3 (1990):333-343

Equity in Education. By Walter G. Secade. Reviewed by Anne Walton. *Gender and Education* 2, No. 3 (1990):371-372

Working Towards Equal Opportunity – A Learning Experience. Angela Chronnell. *Gender and Education* 2, No. 3 (1990):345-349

**Educational Toys**

Best for Kids: Gifts Galore that Kids will Adore. Burt Hochberg. *Redbook* 176, No. 2 (December 1990):22-24

Black Like Us: Dolls for Our Kids. Kimberly Knight. *Essence* 21, No. 7 (November 1990):104-109

Toys that Teach. Joy Duckett Cain. *Essence* 21, No. 4 (August 1990):102-104

**Educational Travel.** *See* Study Abroad

**Education Reform Act (Great Britain)**

Equal Opportunities in the New ERA. By NUT Educational Review. Reviewed by Iram Siraj-Blatchford. *Gender and Education* 2, No. 3 (1990):367-368

Equal Opportunity Issues in the Context of the National Curriculum: A Black Perspective. Sneh

Shah. *Gender and Education* 2, No. 3 (1990):309-318

**Edwards, Debra A.** (joint author). *See* Benin, Mary Holland

**Edwards, Elizabeth**

Education Institutions or Extended Families? The Reconstruction of Gender in Women's Colleges in the Late Nineteenth and Early Twentieth Centuries. *Gender and Education* 2, No. 1 (1990):17-35

**Edwards, Harriet**

How Could You? Mothers Without Custody of Their Children. Reviewed by Nancy D. Polikoff. *The Women's Review of Books* 7, No. 9 (June 1990):23-24

**Edwards, Hodee**

Canadian Sunset (A Litany for Fourteen Murdered Women). Poem. *off our backs* 20, No. 3 (March 1990):26-27

**Edwards, Joan** (about)

Cleaning the Environment with a Woman's Touch. Patti Watts. *Executive Female* 13, No. 6 (November-December 1990):6-9

**Edwards, Louise**

Asian Studies Association of Australia 8th Biennial Conference. *Australian Feminist Studies* No. 12 (Summer 1990):113-114

**Edwards, Louise** and Louie, Kam

Women in Chinese Fiction: The Last Ten Years. *Australian Feminist Studies* No. 11 (Autumn 1990):95-112

**Edwards, Owen**

Love Is a Many Splintered Thing. *Savvy Woman* (February 1990):62-64, 92-95

Seen From Within. *Savvy Woman* (January 1990):68-71

**Edwards, Paul N.**

The Army and the Microworld: Computers and the Politics and Gender Identity. *Signs* 16, No. 1 (Autumn 1990):102-127

**Edwards, Rosalind**

Connecting Method and Epistemology: A White Woman Interviewing Black Women. *Women's Studies International Forum* 13, No. 5 (1990):477-490

Feminist Mothers. Book Review. *Women's Studies International Forum* 13, No. 5 (1990):527

The Social Identity of Women. Book Review. *Women's Studies International Forum* 13, No. 6 (1990):611

**Edwards, Ryn**

The Choreographing of Reproductive DNA. *Lesbian Ethics* 4, No. 1 (Spring 1990): 44-51

**Edwards, Sally** (about)

Sallying Forth. Bob Cooper. *Women's Sports and Fitness* 12, No. 7 (October 1990):15

**Egan, Jennifer**

Another Pretty Face. Short story. *Mademoiselle* (December 1990):118-123+

**Egerton, Jayne**

Out but Not Down: Lesbians' Experience of Housing. *Feminist Review* No. 36 (Autumn 1990):75-88

**Eggertson-Tacon, Colleen** (joint author). *See* Miller, A. Therese

**Eggs.** *See* Cookery (Eggs)

**Egypt – Family Planning**

Family Planning and Maternal Health Care in Egypt. Mawaheb T. El-Mouelhy. *Women and Therapy* 10, No. 3 (1990):55-60

**Egypt – History**

Letters from Egypt. By Lucie Duff Gordon. Reviewed by Judith Tucker. *Journal of Women's History* 2, No. 1 (Spring 1990):245-250

**Egypt – Politics and Government**

Guaranteed Seats for Political Representation of Women: The Egyptian Example. Kathleen Howard-Merriam. *Women & Politics* 10, No. 1 (1990):17-42

**Egypt – Women's Movement**

Night of the Staircase. Ada Aharoni and Thea Wolf. *Lilith* 15, No. 4 (Fall 1990):7-9

**Ehrenberg, Margaret**

Women in Prehistory. Reviewed by Karlene Jones-Bley. *NWSA Journal* 2, No. 4 (Autumn 1990):675-677

**Ehrenberg, Marion F.**, Cox, David N., and Koopman, Raymond F.

The Million Adolescent Personality Inventory Profiles of Depressed Adolescents. *Adolescence* 25, No. 98 (Summer 1990):415-424

The Prevalence of Depression in High School Students. *Adolescence* 25, No. 100 (Winter 1990):905-912

**Ehrenfeld, Phyllis**

Leaving Brooklyn. Book Review. *New Directions for Women* 19, No. 1 (January/February 1990):25

Lives of N. J. Women. *New Directions for Women* 19, No. 5 (September-October 1990):20

Past and Promise: Lives of New Jersey Women. Book Review. *New Directions for Women* 19, No. 5 (September-October 1990):20

Three Blind Mice: Two Short Novels. Book Review. *New Directions for Women* 19, No. 2 (March/April 1990):24

**Ehrenreich, Barbara**

Backtalk: Worked Up. *Lear's* (January 1990):125-131

The Naked Truth about Fitness. *Lear's* (September 1990):96-99

Sounds of Silence. *Savvy Woman* (June 1990):51-53

**Eichenbaum, Luise** and Orbach, Susie

Between Women: Love, Envy and Competition in Women's Friendships. Reviewed by Hannah Lerman. *Psychology of Women Quarterly* 14, No. 1 (March 1990):149-150

**Eichler, Margrit**

Nonsexist Research Methods: A Practical Guide. Reviewed by Dorothy L. Steffens and Jane Robbins. *Feminist Collections* 11, No. 2 (Winter 1990):7-9

**Eikenberry, Jill** (about)

Jill. Stephen Farber. *Lear's* (September 1990):86-89

**Eilenberg, Mara**

Family Pictures. Book Review. *The Women's Review of Books* 7, Nos. 10-11 (July 1990):34

Over-extended Family. *The Women's Review of Books* 7, Nos. 10-11 (July 1990):34

**Einstein-Maric, Mileva** (about)

Mileva Einstein-Maric: The Woman Who Did Einstein's Mathematics. Senta Troemel-Ploetz. *Women's Studies International Forum* 13, No. 5 (1990):415-432

**Eisen, George**

Children and Play in the Holocaust: Games among the Shadows. Book Review. *Adolescence* 25, No. 97 (Spring 1990):249

**Eisenberg, Susan**

Another Gift to Women. Poem. *Frontiers* 11, Nos. 2-3 (1990):96

Press Release. Poem. *Frontiers* 11, Nos. 2-3 (1990):97

Progress. Poem. *Frontiers* 11, Nos. 2-3 (1990):97

**Eisenman, Peter** (about). *See* Architecture

**Eisenstadt, Jill** (joint author). *See* Drinkard, Michael

**Eisenstadt, Marvin**, Haynal, André, Rentchnick, Pierre, and De Senarclens, Pierre

Parental Loss and Achievement. Book Review. *Adolescence* 25, No. 98 (Summer 1990):499-500

**Eisenstadter, Ingrid**

It's in the Cards. *Executive Female* 13, No. 6 (November-December 1990):44-47

Sowing the Free Sample. *Executive Female* 13, No. 4 (July-August 1990):11-12

**Eisenstein, Hester**

Tapestries of Life: Women's Work, Women's Consciousness, and the Meaning of Daily Existence. Book Review. *New Directions for Women* 19, No. 3 (May/June 1990):17

Women's Struggles and Strategies. Book Review. *Resources for Feminist Research* 19, No. 1 (March 1990):43-44

**Eisenstein, Paul A.**

In the Driver's Seat. *Family Circle* 103, No. 4 (March 13, 1990):67-69

**Eisenstein, Zillah R.**

The Female Body and the Law. Reviewed by Mary Lyndon Shanley. *NWSA Journal* 2, No. 2 (Spring 1990):308-311

**Eisler, Riane**

The Chalice and the Blade: Our History, Our Future. Reviewed by Ellen M. Shively. *Minerva* 8, No. 2 (Summer 1990):78-79

The Chalice and the Blade. Reviewed by Elaine Norman. *AFFILIA* 5, No. 2 (Summer 1990):102-104

**Eklof, Barbara**

Marmelade Memories. Poem. *Essence* 21, No. 6 (October 1990):126

**Eknilang, Lijon** (joint author). *See* Keju-Johnson, Darlene

**Elder, Gene Wesley**

Portfolio. *Out/Look* No. 7 (Winter 1990):42-43

**Elder, Glen H., Jr.** (joint author). *See* Conger, Rand D.

**Eldridge, Natalie S.** and Gilbert, Lucia A.

Correlates of Relationship Satisfaction in Lesbian Couples. *Psychology of Women Quarterly* 14, No. 1 (March 1990):43-62

**Elected Officials.** *See also* Presidents – United States; State Governments – Elected Officials

Ann Richards: Plain-Speaking Texan. Jody Becker. *McCall's* 117, No. 9 (June 1990):70

Dianne Feinstein: Charismatic Centrist. Jody Becker. *McCall's* 117, No. 9 (June 1990):70-74

Kay Orr: Mrs. Middle America. Jody Becker. *McCall's* 117, No. 9 (June 1990):74

Lunch. Interview. Frances Lear. *Lear's* (April 1990):19-20

Nancy Kassebaum: Heartland Independent. Jane Ciabattari. *McCall's* 117, No. 9 (June 1990):68

Patricia Schroeder: Uncompromising Free Spirit. Maureen Dowd. *McCall's* 117, No. 9 (June 1990):64

Women, Law and Politics: Recruitment Patterns in the Fifty States. Christine B. Williams. *Women & Politics* 10, No. 3 (1990):103-123

The Women Who Run Texas. Molly Ivans. *McCall's* 117, No. 11 (August 1990):98-101 +

**Elected Officials – Homosexuality**

Barney Frank: A Public Man's Private Sins. Barbara Grizzuti Harrison. *Mademoiselle* (February 1990):100

**Elections – Pro-Choice Candidates**

Abortion: Election Turnaround? Anne Summers. *Ms.* 1, No. 2 (September/October 1990):93-94

**Elections – State Offices**

State Elections: Women on the Verge. Nancy Wartik. *Ms.* 1, No. 2 (September/October 1990):92

**Electric Shadow Productions**

Women Watch: Women-Run Companies Create a New Corporate Culture. Patti Watts. *Executive Female* (May/June 1990):10-11

**Electric Shavers**. *See also* Shaving

**Electromagnetic Radiation**. *See* Radiation – Dosage

**Electromagnetic Waves**

Why I Can't Stop Thinking about My Computer. Cindi Leive. *Glamour* (October 1990):162-166

**Electronic Apparatus and Appliances**

State of the Art Electronics. Bibliography. Pamela A. Toussaint. *Essence* 21, No. 3 (July 1990):88-93

**Electronic Office Machines**

Home-Office Wonders. Jeffrey Cohen. *Savvy Woman* (October 1990):28-31

**Elenes, C. Alejandra**

Ethnic Notions. Film review. *Feminist Collections* 11, No. 3 (Spring 1990):9

Fundi: The Story of Ella Baker. Film review. *Feminist Collections* 11, No. 3 (Spring 1990):10-11

Julia de Burgos. Film review. *Feminist Collections* 11, No. 3 (Spring 1990):10

The Lemon Grove Incident. Film review. *Feminist Collections* 11, No. 3 (Spring 1990):9-10

Never Turn Back: The Life of Fanny Lou Hamer. Film review. *Feminist Collections* 11, No. 3 (Spring 1990):10

Watsonville. Film review. *Feminist Collections* 11, No. 3 (Spring 1990):10

**Eliot, George** (about). *See* David, Deirdre

**Elizabeth, Martha**

The Lovers' Kiss. Poem. *Iris* 24 (Fall-Winter 1990):19

**Ellenzweig, Allen**

Picturing the Homoerotic: Gay Images in Photography. *Out/Look* No. 7 (Winter 1990):44-51

**Ellerbee, Linda**

Candid Candice. Interview. *Ladies' Home Journal* 107, No. 6 (June 1990):126-130+

**Ellerington, Glynis** (joint author). *See* Stuart, Meryn

**Ellickson, Judy L.** and Latona, Janet R.

Balancing Personal and Professional Lives: The Unique Concerns of Graduate Students. *Women and Therapy* 9, No. 4 (1990):37-47

**Elliott, Farar**

Courage of Conviction: New Books from Kady and Sarah Schulman. *off our backs* 20, No. 7 (July 1990):13+

NWSA Workshop: Old Women in Art. *off our backs* 20, No. 8 (August/September 1990):18

Panhandling Papers. Book Review. *off our backs* 20, No. 7 (July 1990):13+

People in Trouble. Book Review. *off our backs* 20, No. 7 (July 1990):13+

**Elliott, Farar** and Douglas, Carol Anne

Listen to the Old Women Forum. *off our backs* 20, No. 8 (August/September 1990):17-18

**Elliott, Farar** (joint author). *See* Ruby, Jennie

**Elliott, Gail** (about). *See* Fashion Models

**Elliott, Inger McCabe** (about)

Style. Laurie Tarkan. *Lear's* (March 1990):102-109

**Elliott, Susan**, Gottlieb, Amy, McCaskell, Lisa, and Ruitort, Monica

We Will Not Be Silenced! *Healthsharing* 11, No. 3 (June 1990):3

**Elliott, Teresa** (joint author). *See* Helson, Ravenna

**Ellis, Gary D.** (joint author). *See* White, George L. (Jr.)

**Ellis, Kate**, O'Dair, Barbara, and Tallmer, Abby

Feminism and Pornography. *Feminist Review* No. 36 (Autumn 1990):15-18

**Ellis, Kate Ferguson**

The Contested Castle: Gothic Novels and the Subversion of Domestic Ideology. Reviewed by Judith Wilt. *The Women's Review of Books* 7, No. 9 (June 1990):20

**Ellis, Perry** (about). *See* Fashion Designers

**Ellis, Terry** (about). *See* En Vogue (about)

**Ellis Island (New York) – Immigration Museum**

Circle This. Margaret Jaworski. *Family Circle* 103, No. 13 (September 25, 1990):9-12

**Ellison, Christopher G.**

Family Ties, Friendships, and Subjective Well-being Among Black Americans. *Journal of Marriage and the Family* 52, No. 2 (May 1990):298-310

**Elman, Amy**

Swedish Politics: Women's Subordination in a Gender-Neutral Context. *off our backs* 20, No. 3 (March 1990):4+

**El-Mouelhy, Mawaheb T.**

Family Planning and Maternal Health Care in Egypt. *Women and Therapy* 10, No. 3 (1990):55-60

**Elovich, Richard** (joint author). *See* Hughs, Holly

**El Paso – Mayors.** *See* Texas – Mayors

**El Saadawi, Nawal** (interview)

In Conversation with Nawal El Saadawi. Marcel Farry. *Spare Rib* 217 (October 1990):22-26

**El Salvador.** *See also* Romero, Archbishop Oscar

**El Salvador – Civil War**

El Salvador: Images of War. Photographic essay. Laura McClure. *New Directions for Women* 19, No. 3 (May/June 1990):14-15

If Nicaragua Has Won, El Salvador Will Win. Marta Rodriguez. *Spare Rib* No. 209 (February 1990):44-45

Political Prisoner's Trials. Eleanor J. Bader. *New Directions for Women* 19, No. 3 (May/June 1990):metro 1

The Salvador Beanfield War. *Ms.* 1, No. 1 (July/August 1990):15

Update on El Salvador. Marta Rodriguez. *Spare Rib* No. 212 (May 1990):47-48

**El Salvador – Refugees**

Refugee from El Salvador. Jill Bend. *off our backs* 20, No. 5 (May 1990):1-2

**El Salvador – Status of Women**

A Dream Compels Us: Voices of Salvadoran Women. Edited by New American Press. Reviewed by Lois Wasserspring. *The Women's Review of Books* 7, No. 6 (March 1990):23-24

A Dream Compels Us: Voices of Salvadoran Women. Edited by New Americas Press. Reviewed by Bessy Reyna. *New Directions for Women* 19, No. 5 (September-October 1990):15

Group Fights Oppression. Jennifer Gilbert. *New Directions for Women* 19, No. 6 (November-December 1990):6

**Elwell, Sue Levi**

Standing Again at Sinai: Judaism from a Feminist Perspective. Book review. *Lilith* 15, No. 4 (Fall 1990):33-34

**Elwes, Christina** (about). *See* Social Entertaining

**Emecheta, Buchi**

Bold Type. *Ms.* 1, No. 1 (July/August 1990):68

The Family. Reviewed by Carole Boyce Davies. *Belles Lettres* 6, No. 1 (Fall 1990):20-21

The Family. Reviewed by Elsie B. Washington. *Essence* 21, No. 4 (August 1990):50

The Family. Reviewed by Ernece B. Kelly. *On the Issues* 16 (Fall 1990):32

Gwendolyn. Reviewed by Barbara Burford. *Spare Rib* No. 209 (February 1990):30-31

**Emergency Medical Services.** *See* Disaster Relief

**Emergency Telephone Services.** *See* Telephone – Emergency Reporting Systems

**Emmerichs, Mary Beth**

A History of Their Own: Women in Europe from Prehistory to the Present. Book Review. *Feminist Collections* 11, No. 2 (Winter 1990):3-4

The Women's History of the World. Book Review. *Feminist Collections* 11, No. 2 (Winter 1990):3-4

**Emmerling, Mary**

Mary Emmerling's American Country. *Good Housekeeping* 211, No. 3 (September 1990):221-225

**Emmons, Carol** (joint author). *See* Tiedje, Linda Beth

**Emo, Dretha M.**, Hall, Sharon, and Kern, Darlene

1964: Vietnam and Army Nursing. *Minerva* 8, No. 1 (Spring 1990):49-67

**Emory & Henry College**

Including Women at Emory & Henry College: Evolution of an Inclusive Language Policy. Felicia Mitchell. *Women's Studies Quarterly* 18, Nos. 1-2 (Spring-Summer 1990):222-230

**Emotions.** *See also* Anger; Mood (Psychology)

Getting All Emotional. *Mademoiselle* (June 1990):192-195

In the Spirit: Breaking the Silence. Susan L. Taylor. *Essence* 21, No. 3 (July 1990):49

**Employee Benefits.** *See also* Labor Contracts; Wages

The Bonus Bonanza. Debra Wishik Englander. *Savvy Woman* (October 1990):23-24

Everything's Negotiable. Anna Sobkowski. *Executive Female* (March/April 1990):38-40

The Perk Report. Anita Gates. *Working Woman* (August 1990):62-64

Six Perks That Make Your Salary Worth More. Pamela Kruger. *Working Woman* (January 1990):108-109

**Employee-Employer Relations.** *See also* Management Techniques; Performance Awards; Problem Solving

Career Strategies: Promises, Promises. Can You Make Your Boss Deliver? Adele Scheele. *Working Woman* (July 1990):26-28

Career Strategies: Same Job, New Boss. Can You Make It Work? Adele Scheele. *Working Woman* (June 1990):22-24

Good for Business: A Manager's Hot Line. *Working Woman* (October 1990):33-36; (December 1990):18-23

Job Strategies. Marilyn Moats Kennedy. *Glamour* (April 1990):125-130; (September 1990):149-153

The Makeover of a Manager. Meryl Gordon. *Working Woman* (October 1990):108-111+

Management: Sizing Up Your New Staff. Connie Wallace. *Working Woman* (May 1990):29-32

Managing: Big Changes? How to Stay in Charge. Andrew S. Grove. *Working Woman* (October 1990):38-44

Managing: Office Romance: How to Handle the Heat. Andrew S. Grove. *Working Woman* (December 1990):24-27

Silk Purse Chronicles: The Wages of Spin. Patricia O'Toole. *Lear's* (April 1990):23-24

Surprise! Your New Job isn't the One You Accepted. Marilyn Moats Kennedy. *Glamour* (November 1990):115-116

Why Employees Act the Way They Do: A Manager's Guide to Human Behavior. Eliza Collins. *Working Woman* (December 1990):58-61

Your Brilliant Career. Rebecca Sharp. *Mademoiselle* (June 1990):113

Your Brilliant Career: The Friendship Trap. Rebecca Sharp. *Mademoiselle* (December 1990):100

**Employees, Dismissal of**

Management: How to Fire Someone Without Getting Sued. Deborah L. Jacobs. *Working Woman* (January 1990):24-28

Staying Afloat without Jumping Ship. Sarah Stiansen. *Savvy Woman* (July/August 1990):28-29

**Employees – Psychological Testing**

Alice Down the Rabbit Hole: A Saga. Carol Orlock. *Lear's* (May 1990):36-40

**Employees – Resignation.** *See also* Career Change; Career Management

Strategic Quitting: Pack Your Bags for Greener Pastures. Robert McGarvey. *Executive Female* (March/April 1990):34-36+

You Like Your Job. But Should You Leave It? Ronni Sandroff. *Working Woman* (May 1990):81-85

**Employees – Technological Innovations**

The Introduction of New Technology: Health Implications for Workers. Anne Statham and Ellen Bravo. *Women and Health* 16, No. 2 (1990):105-129

**Employees – Training.** *See also* Crozier, Mary (about); Immigrants – Employment; Industry and Education

A Game Plan for the Future. Pamela Kruger. *Working Woman* (January 1990):74-78

The Smart Office: All Systems Go: How to Manage Technological Change. Sharon Efroymson First. *Working Woman* (April 1990):47-54

**Employee Testing.** *See* Employees – Psychological Testing

**Employer-Employee Relations.** *See* Employee-Employer Relations

**Employment**

How to Get a Raise. Laurie Maynard. *Executive Female* 13, No. 5 (September-October 1990):26

Ingredients for Women's Employment Policy. Edited by Christine E. Bose and Glenna Spitze. Reviewed by Rita Mae Kelly. *Gender and Society* 4, No. 3 (September 1990):429-432

And Still We Rise: African American Women and the U.S. Labor Market. Monica L. Jackson. *Feminist Issues* 10, No. 2 (Fall 1990):55-64

Women and Work: A Survey of Textbooks. Kathy J. Krynski. *Women's Studies Quarterly* 18, Nos. 3-4 (Fall-Winter 1990):23-31

Women's Roles in the Economy: Teaching the Issues. Barbara R. Bergmann. *Women's Studies Quarterly* 18, Nos. 3-4 (Fall-Winter 1990):6-22

**Employment – Day Care Issues**

Sharing Child Care Costs. Ellen Klavan. *Working Mother* (November 1990):52-56

**Employment – Discrimination.** *See also* Affirmative Action; Military Service

Chase Accused of Harassment, and Racism. Andrea Mitchell. *New Directions for Women* 19, No. 1 (January/February 1990):metro4

Close-Up: Don't Use My Name. Martha Nelson. *Savvy Woman* (July/August 1990):5

Corporate Racism: Not Your Imagination. Lloyd Gite. *Glamour* (September 1990):154

Debating Difference: Feminism, Pregnancy and the Workplace. Lise Vogel. *Feminist Studies* 16, No. 1 (Spring 1990):9-32

Discrimination Against Women in New Deal Work Programs. Nancy E. Rose. *AFFILIA* 5, No. 2 (Summer 1990):25-45

Free Advice. Edited by Patti Watts. *Executive Female* (March/April 1990):25-27

Gender Differences in Perceptions of Work: Limited Access to Decision-Making Power and Supervisory Support. Myria Watkins Allen, Joy Hart Seibert, and Ramona R. Rush. *Women's Studies in Communication* 13, No. 2 (Fall 1990):1-20

Gender Segregation in the Workplace: *Plus ça change . . .* Autumn Stanley. *NWSA Journal* 2, No. 4 (Autumn 1990):640-645

Hard-Hatted Women. Edited by Molly Martin. Reviewed by June Axinn. *AFFILIA* 5, No. 2 (Summer 1990):111-112

Hard-Hatted Women: Stories of Struggle and Success in the Trades. Edited by Molly Martin. Reviewed by Autumn Stanley. *NWSA Journal* 2, No. 4 (Autumn 1990):640-645

It's How You Play the Game. Kim Masters. *Working Woman* (May 1990):88-91

Out Box: The "Pretty Woman" Problem. Gail Collins. *Working Woman* (October 1990):160

Over the Edge. Cheryl Gomez-Preston and Jacqueline Trescott. *Essence* 20, No. 11 (March 1990):60-62+

The Reproductive Rights Battle. Sandra Blakeslee. *Working Mother* (December 1990):44-47

Suffer the Working Day: Women in the "Dangerous Trades," 1880-1914. Barbara Harrison. *Women's Studies International Forum* 13, Nos. 1-2 (1990):79-90

Tell Us What You Think: Fetal Protection. *Glamour* (June 1990):168

This Working Life: Sex, Lies and the Business Dinner. Maureen Dowd. *Working Woman* (June 1990):110

Working: Black Women at Work. Josefina Sands. *Essence* 21, No. 1 (May 1990):58-61

**Employment – Equal Opportunity**

On Location: The Housing Department. Anne Other. *Women and Environments* 12, No. 2 (Spring 1990): 26-27

**Employment – Flexible Scheduling**

Escape from the Forty-Hour Workweek. Anne B. Fisher. *Savvy Woman* (March 1990):53-54, 78-80

**Employment – Gender Differences**

The Ideology of Skill: A Case Study. Kathy McDermott. *Australian Feminist Studies* No. 11 (Autumn 1990):61-73

**Employment – History**

Counter Cultures: Saleswomen, Managers and Customers in American Department Stores, 1890-1940. By Susan Porter Benson. Reviewed by Carole Elizabeth Adams. *Gender & History* 2, No. 3 (Autumn 1990):343-348

The White Blouse Revolution: Female Office Workers Since 1870. Edited by Gregory Anderson. Reviewed by Carole Elizabeth Adams. *Gender & History* 2, No. 3 (Autumn 1990):343-348

**Employment – Inside the Home.** *See also* Germany – Employment – Inside the Home

The Home as Workshop: Women as Amateur Nurses and Medical Care Providers. Nona Y. Glazer. *Gender and Society* 4, No. 4 (December 1990):479-499

Homeworking: Myths and Realities. By Sheila Allen and Carol Wolkowitz. Reviewed by Robin Leidner. *Gender and Society* 4, No. 2 (June 1990):262-265

The New Era of Home-Based Work. Edited by Kathleen E. Christensen. Reviewed by Robin Leidner. *Gender and Society* 4, No. 2 (June 1990):262-265

Work in the Family and in the Labor Market: A Cross-national, Reciprocal Analysis. Arne L. Kalleberg and Rachel A. Rosenfeld. *Journal of Marriage and the Family* 52, No. 2 (May 1990):331-346

**Employment, Nontraditional.** *See also* Automobile Mechanics

Gender Differences at Work: Women and Men in Nontraditional Occupations. By Christine Williams. Reviewed by Autumn Stanley. *NWSA Journal* 2, No. 4 (Autumn 1990):640-645

Hard-Hatted Women. Edited by Molly Martin. Reviewed by June Axinn. *AFFILIA* 5, No. 2 (Summer 1990):111-112

The Private Eye: Should Women Have the Right to Fight? Barbara Grizzuti Harrison. *Mademoiselle* (June 1990):114

When Little Sister Means Business. Renée Edelman. *Working Woman* (February 1990):82-88

**Employment, Nontraditional – Gender Discrimination**

Bitter Choices: Blue-Collar Women In and Out of Work. By Ellen Israel Rosen. Reviewed by Autumn Stanley. *NWSA Journal* 2, No. 4 (Autumn 1990):640-645

**Employment – Outside the Home.** *See also* Chicago – History; Employment – Discrimination; Factory Workers – History; Mommy Track; Mothers Working Outside the Home; Quality of Work Life

The Effect of Shift Work on the Quality and Stability of Marital Relations. Lynn K. White and Bruce Keith. *Journal of Marriage and the Family* 52, No. 2 (May 1990):453-462

Employment and Role Satisfaction: Implications for the General Well-Being of Military Wives. Leora N. Rosen, Jeannette R. Ickovics, and Linda Z. Moghadam. *Psychology of Women Quarterly* 14, No. 3 (September 1990):371-385

The Good News about Women and Work and the 90's. Betty Friedan. *Glamour* (March 1990):260-265+

For the Good of Family and Race: Gender, Work, and Domestic Roles in the Black Community, 1880-1930. Notes. Sharon Harley. *Signs* 15, No. 2 (Winter 1990):336-349

Income Generating Programmes for Women: Some Pitfalls. Mira Savara. *Manushi* 58 (May-June 1990):30-33

Labor-Force Reentry Among U.S. Homemakers in Midlife: A Life-Course Analysis. Phyllis Moen, Geraldine Downey, and Niall Bolger. *Gender and Society* 4, No. 2 (June 1990):230-243

Love Among the Ruins. Margaret Carlson. *Savvy Woman* (November 1990):60-63+

Marital Disruption and the Employment of Married Women. Theodore Greenstein. *Journal of Marriage and the Family* 52, No. 3 (August 1990):657-676

Maternal Role of Women in Clerical Jobs in Southern Brazil: Stress and Satisfaction. Afaf I. Meleis, Judith C. Kulig, Eloita Neves Arruda, and Amy Beckman. *Health Care for Women International* 11, No. 4 (1990):369-382

A Matter of Hours: Women, Part-time Work and the Labour Market. By Veronica Beechey and Tessa Perkins. Reviewed by Judith Wittner. *Gender and Society* 4, No. 2 (June 1990):258-262

The Overtime Bind. Diane Cole. *Working Mother* 13, No. 4 (April 1990):34-38

Parental Employment and Family Life: Research in the 1980s. Elizabeth G. Menaghan and Toby L. Parcel. *Journal of Marriage and the Family* 52, No. 4 (November 1990):1079-1098

Parents' Concerns about Their Child's Development: Implications for Fathers' and Mothers' Well-being and Attitudes Toward Work. Ellen Greenberger and Robin O'Neil. *Journal of Marriage and the Family* 52, No. 3 (August 1990):621-635

Prisoners of Work. Suzanne Gordon. *Savvy* (December-January 1991):56-59+

Race and Marital Status Differences in the Labor Force Behavior of Female Family Heads: The Effect of Household Structure. Cynthia Rexroat. *Journal of Marriage and the Family* 52, No. 3 (August 1990):591-601

The Second Shift. By Arlie Hochschild and Ann Machung. Reviewed by Lynne Bravo Rosewater. *Women and Therapy* 9, No. 4 (1990):114-116

The Second Shift: Working Parents and the Revolution at Home. By Arlie Hochschild. Reviewed by Lois Braverman. *AFFILIA* 5, No. 4 (Winter 1990):111-113

The Second Shift: Working Parents and the Revolution at Home. By Arlie Hochschild and Anne Machung. Reviewed by Julie Brines. *Journal of Marriage and the Family* 52, No. 1 (February 1990):278-279

The Seventy-Five Best Companies for Working Mothers. *Working Mother* 13, No. 10 (October 1990):31-64

Sixty-Nine Top Companies for Working Mothers. Lorraine Dusky. *Good Housekeeping* 211, No. 2 (August 1990):104-105, 54-56

Surviving Coming Home. Sandi Kahn Shelton. *Working Mother* (November 1990):105-107

Waged Work and Women's Well Being. Lesley Doyal. *Women's Studies International Forum* 13, No. 6 (1990):587-604

What Pediatricians *Really* Think About Working Mothers. Carin Rubenstein. *Working Mother* 13, No. 4 (April 1990):40-44

Work in the Family and in the Labor Market: A Cross-national, Reciprocal Analysis. Arne L. Kalleberg and Rachel A. Rosenfeld. *Journal of*

*Marriage and the Family* 52, No. 2 (May 1990):331-346

**Employment, Part-Time.** *See also* Employment, Temporary

High School Student Employment in Social Context: Adolescents' Perceptions of the Role of Part-Time Work. David L. Green. *Adolescence* 25, No. 98 (Summer 1990):425-434

Make Money Moonlighting. Lloyd Gite. *Essence* 21, No. 3 (July 1990):28-30

Should You Moonlight? Lloyd Gite. *Glamour* (May 1990):144

**Employment – Relocation**

All the Right Moves. Karen Springen. *Savvy Woman* (February 1990):71-75

The Effect of Group Support on Relocated Corporate and Military Wives: A Secondary Analysis. Kathryn R. Puskar, Gloria Wilson, and Lisa J. Moonis. *Minerva* 8, No. 2 (Summer 1990):36-46

You Haul It. Anna Sobkowski. *Executive Female* 13, No. 4 (July-August 1990):44-45+

**Employment – Supervisors**

Who Makes the Best (and Worst) Boss? Dana Friedman and Ellen Galinsky. *Working Mother* 13, No. 7 (July 1990):56-60

**Employment, Temporary**

Rent-a-Veep. Anita Hussey. *Executive Female* (May/June 1990):14-16

**Employment Agencies.** *See* Ounjian, Marilyn (about)

**Employment and Health**

Health and other Characteristics of Employed Women and Homemakers in Tecumseh, 1959-1978: Demographic Characteristics, Smoking Habits, Alcohol Consumption, and Pregnancy Outcomes and Conditions. Kristie L. Ebi-Kryston and others. *Women and Health* 16, No. 2 (1990):5-21

Health and other Characteristics of Employed Women and Homemakers in Tecumseh, 1959-1978: Prevalence of Respiratory and Cardiovascular Symptoms and Illnesses, Mortality Rates and Physical and Physiological Measurement. Kristie L. Ebi-Kryston and others. *Women and Health* 16, No. 2 (1990):23-39

**Employment Contracts.** *See* Labor Contracts

**Employment, Gender Discrimination**

Justice for All. Armond D. Budish. *Family Circle* 103, No. 10 (July 24, 1990):44+

**Employment Opportunities.** *See also* Career Change; Health Care Occupations – Employment Opportunities; Immigrants – Employment

Back Talk: Owning Our Share. Cheryl F. Wilson. *Essence* 20, No. 12 (April 1990):124

The Brash Pack. Katherine Ann Samon. *Working Woman* (August 1990):66-69

The 25 Hottest Careers. *Working Woman* (July 1990):73-83

How to Come In from the Cold. Anita Gates. *Working Woman* (July 1990):75-78

How to Find Companies Where Women Succeed. Lorraine Dusky. *Working Woman* (January 1990):81-88

Is it Time to Shift Careers? Excerpt. Emily Koltnow and Lynne S. Dumas. *McCall's* 117, No. 12 (September 1990):120-121+

On the Job. JoAnne Alter. *Family Circle* 103, No. 5 (April 3, 1990):22+

The New Professional Temporaries. Kathryn Stechert Black. *Working Mother* (November 1990):58-65

When Your Career's Hot but You're Not. Anita Gates. *Working Woman* (July 1990):80

Working: Red-Hot Jobs. Felicia E. Halpert. *Essence* 20, No. 11 (March 1990):34-37+

The 10 Worst Careers. Anne M. Russell. *Working Woman* (July 1990):82-84

**Employment Practices.** *See* Employment – Discrimination

**Employment Practices – Hiring.** *See also* Employment Opportunities

Alice Down the Rabbit Hole: A Saga. Carol Orlock. *Lear's* (May 1990):36-40

"How I Did It": Creating the Perfect Staff. Elizabeth Perle. *Working Woman* (November 1990):73-76+

**Employment Practices – Recruitment**

The Exchange Rate. Kent R. Davies. *Executive Female* 13, No. 6 (November-December 1990):28-31

**Employment-Related Illness.** *See* Occupational Diseasees

**Employment Security**

Just Do It! Anne B. Fisher. *Savvy Woman* (October 1990):54-57+

Staying Afloat without Jumping Ship. Sarah Stiansen. *Savvy Woman* (July/August 1990):28-29

**Empowerment.** *See also* Advertising – Images of Women; Assertive Behavior; Business Enterrpsies – Ownership; Leadership; Political Activists; Political Power; Reproductive Technologies; Risk Taking

Empowering Women: Leadership Development Strategies on Campus. By Mary Ann Danowitz Sagaria. Reviewed by Linda Forrest. *NWSA Journal* 2, No. 3 (Summer 1990):497-499

Empowering Women: Leadership Development Strategies on Campus. Edited by Mary Ann

Danowitz Sagaria. *Psychology of Women Quarterly* 14, No. 3 (September 1990):439-440

50 Ways to Use Your Power. *Ladies' Home Journal* 107, No. 11 (November 1990):298-302

How to Be the New Kind of Manager. Peter Block. *Working Woman* (July 1990):51-54

Information Is Power. *Women's World* 23 (April 1990):15-17

From Learning Literacy to Regenerating Women's Space: A Story of Women's Empowerment in Nepal. Pramod Parajuli and Elizabeth Enslin. *Women in Action* 1-2 (1990):3-6

Perilous Pastimes. Pamela Kruger. *Working Woman* (February 1990):80-81

The Power of No. Martha E. Thompson. *Feminist Teacher* 5, No. 1 (Spring 1990):24-25

The Profits of Ill Repute. William A. Henry III. *Lear's* (October 1990):152+

Toward the Psychosocial Empowerment of Women. Hiasaura Rubenstein and Sharene K. Lawler. *AFFILIA* 5, No. 3 (Fall 1990):27-38

Turning the Things That Divide Us into Strengths That Unite Us. Rachel Josefowitz Siegel. *Women and Therapy* 9, No. 3 (1990):327-336

Women, Ritual, and Power. Janet L. Jacobs. *Frontiers* I I, Nos. 2-3 (1990).39-44

**Empowerment – Adolescents**

Patterns of Runaway Behavior within a Larger Systems Context: The Road to Empowerment. A. Therese Miller, Colleen Eggertson-Tacon, and Brian Quigg. *Adolescence* 25, No. 98 (Summer 1990):271-289

**Empowerment – Films**

Female Power in the Serial-Queen Melodrama: The Etiology of an Anomaly. Ben Singer. *Camera Obscura* No. 22 (January 1990):91-129

**Emshwiller, Carol**

Verging on the Pertinent. Reviewed by Marcia Tager. *New Directions for Women* 19, No. 1 (January/February 1990):22

**Encyclopedias**

Frauen Lexikon. Edited by Anneliese Lissner, Rita Süssman, and Karin Walter. Reviewed by Marguerite Andersen. *Resources for Feminist Research* 19, No. 1 (March 1990):16

**Endometrial Smears**

Endometrial Smears – A Cautionary Tale. Elaine Russell. *Spare Rib* 217 (October 1990):66

**Energy Conservation.** *See* Recycling (Waste, etc.)

**Engagement**

The Rage to Engage. Lois Smith Brady. *Mademoiselle* (March 1990):174-175, 240

**Engelbrecht, Penelope J.**

"Lifting Belly Is a Language": The Postmodern Lesbian Subject. *Feminist Studies* 16, No. 1 (Spring 1990):85-114

Never Jerk Your Hand Away. Short Story. *Sinister Wisdom* 40 (Spring 1990):102-123

**Engeler, Amy**

Calling a Shade a Shade. *Savvy Woman* (November 1990):44

Giving Up a Baby. *Glamour* (June 1990):252-255+

**Engels, Friedrich** (about)

Engels Revisited: New Feminist Essays. Edited by Janet Sayers, Mary Evans, and Nanneke Redclift. Reviewed by Kathryn Russell. *Signs* 15, No. 2 (Winter 1990):398-400

**Engelstein, Laura**

Lesbian Vignettes: A Russian Triptych from the 1890s. Notes. *Signs* 15, No. 4 (Summer 1990):813-831

**Engineers**

Black Women Engineers and Technologists. Valerie Thomas. *Sage* 6, No. 2 (Fall 1989):24-32

Women in Professional Engineering: The Interaction of Gendered Structures and Values. Ruth Carter and Gill Kirkup. *Feminist Review* No. 35 (Summer 1990):92-101

**Engineers – Personal Narrative**

Trials, Tribulations, Triumphs. Jennie R. Patrick. *Sage* 6, No. 2 (Fall 1989):51-53

**England – History.** See Great Britain – History

**England, Suzanne E.**

Family Leave and Gender Justice. *AFFILIA* 5, No. 2 (Summer 1990):8-24

**Englander, Debra Wishik**

All Tapped Out, No Place to Go. *Savvy Woman* (November 1990):26

The Bonus Bonanza. *Savvy Woman* (October 1990):23-24

Don't Get Ripped Off – Get Smart. *Redbook* 175, No. 1 (May 1990):60-64

Is Your Insurance "Overdressed"? *Savvy Woman* (July/August 1990):24-25

**Engler, Beth** (about)

McCallmanack: Tuning In to Women's Issues. Elizabeth Kolbert. *McCall's* 117, No. 11 (August 1990):62

**Engles, Eric C.**

Datebook/Terrie Williams. Poem. *Essence* 21, No. 5 (September 1990):121

**Enloe, Cynthia**

Bananas, Beaches and Bases: Making Feminist Sense of International Politics. Reviewed by Anne McClintock. *The Women's Review of Books* 7, No. 8 (May 1990):1+

**Enos, Sandra Forsyth**

The Teen Years: Secrets. *Family Circle* 103, No. 13 (September 25, 1990):49-52

**Enos, Sondra Forsyth**

Can This Marriage Be Saved? "My Husband Is Never There for Us." *Ladies' Home Journal* 107, No. 8 (August 1990):12-17

**Enslin, Elizabeth** (joint author). See Parajuli, Pramod

**Entertainers**

Double Play. *Harper's Bazaar* (June 1990):106-109+

Sure Bets. *Harper's Bazaar* (April 1990):115-118

Word On Entertainment. *Glamour* (January 1990):84-85; (February 1990):121-122; (June 1990):183

**Entertaining.** See Business Entertaining; Social Entertaining

**Entertainment Industry.** See also Hawn-Sylbert Movie Company

Lunch. Interview. Frances Lear. *Lear's* (July 1990):17-20

**Entmacher, Joan**

The Social Origins of Private Life: A History of American Families 1600-1900. Book Review. *Women's Studies International Forum* 13, No. 5 (1990):521-522

**Entrepreneurs.** See also Burton, Betsy (about); Business Enterprises – Ownership; Career Management; Lambert, Paula (about); Matthias, Rebecca (about); Organization for Women's Business Development; Owades, Ruth (about); Picasso, Paloma (about); Roberts, Dorothy (about); Success in Business; Wealth Distribution; White, Barbie (about)

Back Talk: Owning Our Share. Cheryl F. Wilson. *Essence* 20, No. 12 (April 1990):124

Business Bulletins. *Executive Female* (March/April 1990):75

Enterprise: Beefing Up a Skinny Business. Janette Scandura. *Working Woman* (February 1990):53-58

Enterprise: How to Find a Market and Make It Yours. Susan Buchsbaum. *Working Woman* (May 1990):39-44

Enterprise: How to Take a Good Business and Make It Better. Mark Stevens. *Working Woman* (March 1990):38-46

Enterprise: The Business Plan That Gets the Loan. Louise Washer. *Working Woman* (January 1990):37-47

Enterprise: They Can Get It for You Wholesale. David E. Gumpert. *Working Woman* (August 1990):33-36

Enterprise: What I Learned from My Mistakes. Susan Peterson. *Working Woman* (June 1990):29-34

Entrepreneurial Edge: Grow, Baby, Grow! Ellie Winninghoff. *Working Woman* (September 1990):101-104

The Entrepreneurial Family Economy: Family Strategies and Self-Employment in Detroit, 1880. Melanie Archer. *Journal of Family History* 15, No. 3 (July 1990):261-283

Entrepreneurs Take It Abroad. Patricia Schiff Estes. *Lear's* (August 1990):28-31

The Epi Empire. Paula Dranov. *Harper's Bazaar* (January 1990):38-44

Female Bonding. Louise Tutelian. *Savvy Woman* (July/August 1990):12

Financial Workshop: Making Your Dream Business a Reality. Mary Rowland. *Working Woman* (January 1990):95-100

First Steps. *Executive Female* (March/April 1990):78; (May/June 1990):74

Forty Under Forty: Women on the Verge of a Major Breakthrough. *Savvy Woman* (June 1990):36-44, 82-83

Incubators Help Hatch Businesses. Doreen Mangan. *Executive Female* (May/June 1990):68-69

Lear's Bulletin. Bibliography. Marion Asnes. *Lear's* (February 1990):36

Married to the Job. Diana Prufer. *Savvy Woman* (June 1990):25-26

Minding Your Own Business. Lorraine Richardson. *Essence* 21, No. 5 (September 1990):39+

Opening Day: We're in Business. Louise Washer. *Working Woman* (May 1990):55-62

Risk-Less: Advice for Entrepreneurs. Ken Sgro. *Executive Female* (May/June 1990):73

Risk-Less Advice for Entrepreneurs. Ken Sgro. *Executive Female* (March/April 1990):77

The Savvy 60: America's Leading Women Business Owners. Edited by Sarah Stiansen. *Savvy Woman* (November 1990):47-52

Six Women Who Changed Their Lives. *Good Housekeeping* 211, No. 1 (July 1990):80-89

Where There's a Will, There's a Way. Joan Delaney. *Executive Female* (March/April 1990):70-71

Windshield Wipers Clean Up. Joan Delaney. *Executive Female* 13, No. 4 (July-August 1990):70-71

Women in Advertising. Bibliography. Nanine Alexander. *Essence* 20, No. 9 (January 1990):35-40

200 Words: Lear's Women Caught in the Act. I. E. Franklin. *Lear's* (February 1990):94-97

**Entwisle, Barbara** and Coles, Catherine M. Demographic Surveys and Nigerian Women. Notes. *Signs* 15, No. 2 (Winter 1990):259-284

**Environment**

Green Watch. *Good Housekeeping* 211, No. 5 (November 1990):111-112

Life in 2010. Sharon Begley. *Family Circle* 103, No. 2 (February 1, 1990):76-77

**Environment – Indoor Pollutants**

The Dark Side of White. Bernadette Vallely. *Healthsharing* 11, No. 3 (June 1990):8

Hidden Health Hazards in Your Home. Linda Mason Hunter. *Family Circle* 103, No. 2 (February 1, 1990):80-81

**Environment – Quality of Life**

Earth Angels. Andrew H. Malcolm. *Family Circle* 103, No. 2 (February 1, 1990):78-79

**Environmental Hazards**

The Bottom Line. T.J. Ford. *Ms.* 1, No. 1 (July/August 1990):89

Earth, Air and Water: Women Fight for the Environment in India. Pamela Philipose. *Healthsharing* 11, No. 1 (December 1989):22-26

Mom Fights Lead Poison. Pat Redmond. *New Directions for Women* 19, No. 3 (May/June 1990):16

PCBs in Inuit Breastmilk. Jo-Ann Lowell. *Healthsharing* 11, No. 1 (December 1989):5

**Environmental Movement.** *See also* Biodegradation; Business – Social Policies; Car Pools; Ecofeminism; Fashion; Great Britain – Environmental Movement; Great Britain – Politics and Government; Recycling (Waste, etc.)

Beyond Global Housekeeping. H. Patricia Hynes. *Ms.* 1, No. 1 (July/August 1990):91-93

Don't Get Bored with Saving the Planet. *Glamour* (September 1990):126

Earth 1990. *Harper's Bazaar* (January 1990):72-77

Environment: 9 Things You Can Do in the '90s to Save the Planet. Bibliography. Jim Jubak and Marie D'Amico. *McCall's* 117, No. 7 (April 1990):34-41

Fire and Rain. Jonathan Weiner. *Lear's* (April 1990):74-79+

Forces for Nature. George Bush. *Harper's Bazaar* (January 1990):72-73+

Green Watch. Bibliography. *Good Housekeeping* 211, No. 3 (September 1990):89-90

Green Watch. *Good Housekeeping* 211, No. 4 (October 1990):127-128

In Land We Trust. Bibliography. Sarah Stiansen. *Savvy Woman* (July/August 1990):23-24

The New Sexy Men: The Politicos. Charla Krupp. *Glamour* (March 1990):190

October 16: World Day of Action Against. *Spare Rib* 217 (October 1990):47-48

Pediatric Healthline. *Ladies' Home Journal* 107, No. 11 (November 1990):142

The Recurring Silent Spring. By H. Patricia Hynes. Reviewed by Sue V. Rosser. *Signs* 15, No. 4 (Summer 1990):872-873

Stars Who Care. JoBeth McDaniel. *Ladies' Home Journal* 107, No. 11 (November 1990):74-80

Stars Who Take Care of the Earth. Linden Gross. *Redbook* 176, No. 1 (November 1990):28-32

The State of the Earth. Betsy Carpenter. *Ladies' Home Journal* 107, No. 4 (April 1990):162-164+

Teaching Children How to Recycle. *Good Housekeeping* 211, No. 3 (September 1990):172

Tell Us What You Think: Disposable Diapers. *Glamour* (April 1990):168

Truth in Fashion. *Glamour* (December 1990):177-178

Twenty-Five Everyday Ways to Help Clean Up Our Planet. Diane MacEachern. *Ladies' Home Journal* 107, No. 4 (April 1990):224

Up Front. *Ladies' Home Journal* 107, No. 9 (September 1990):147-152

Waste Not! Earthworks Group. *Redbook* 175, No. 2 (June 1990):130-132+

A Whole New World: Remaking Masculinity in the Context of the Environmental Movement. Robert W. Connell. *Gender and Society* 4, No. 4 (December 1990):452-478

Woman of Ideas: Hazel Henderson. Susan Chace. *Lear's* (June 1990):98-101+

Women Are Waking Up to their Planet. Patti Jones. *Glamour* (May 1990):270-273+

Women Right Now. *Glamour* (November 1990):99-102

**Environmental Movement – Latin America**

Women and Ecology. *Women in Action* 3 & 4 (1990):47-52

**Environmental Movement – Third World**

Staying Alive: Women, Ecology and Development. By Vandana Shiva. Reviewed by Linda Vance. *NWSA Journal* 2, No. 3 (Summer 1990):485-489

**Environmental Protection – Biosphere Experiment**

Planet Under Glass. Jane Bosveld. *Lear's* (December 1990):84-89+

**Environmental Sciences**

Saving the Earth: New York to Chicago on a Glass of Salt Water. J. R. Moehringer. *McCall's* 117, No. 7 (April 1990):32

**En Vogue** (about)

Born to Sing. Melissa Bedolis. *Mademoiselle* (November 1990):150-153

En Vogue: Styling Style. Deborah Gregory. *Essence* 21, No. 5 (September 1990):47

**Envy**

Idle Chatter. Quentin Crisp. *Lear's* (June 1990):72-73

**Epelbaum, Renee** (Interview)

Renee Epelbaum: Still Struggling for Truth and Justice in Argentina. Rita Falbel and Irena Klepfisz. *Bridges* 1, No. 1 (Spring 1990): 86-95

**Epilepsy**

Diary of a Marriage: Rediscovering the Real Ben. Sylvia Whitman. *McCall's* 117, No. 10 (July 1990):98-100+

A New Dance Step. Lynn Tasker. *Healthsharing* 11, No. 2 (March 1990):14-16

Understanding Epilepsy. *Good Housekeeping* 211, No. 4 (October 1990):251

**Epistemology**. *See also* Feminism – Theory; Knowledge, Theory of

Abstracts: Gender and the Construction of Culture and Knowledge. *Resources for Feminist Research* 19, No. 1 (March 1990):51-66

Epistemological Pluralism: Styles and Voices within the Computer Culture. Sherry Turkle and Seymour Papert. *Signs* 16, No. 1 (Autumn 1990):128-157

Thinking with the Weight of the Earth: Feminist Contributions to an Epistemology of Concreteness. Linda Holler. *Hypatia* 5, No. 1 (Spring 1990):1-23

Transforming Knowledge. By Elizabeth Kamarck Minnich. Reviewed by Gerda Lerner. *The Women's Review of Books* 8, No. 1 (October 1990):10-11

**Epistemology – Psychology**

Approaching a Feminist-Principled Paradigm in the Construction of Personality Theory. Mary B. Ballou. *Women and Therapy* 9, Nos. 1-2 (1990):23-40

**Epistolary Literature**

Discourses of Desire: Gender, Genre, and Epistolary Fictions. By Linda S. Kauffman. Reviewed by Joan Hinde Stewart. *Tulsa Studies in Women's Literature* 9, No. 1 (Spring 1990):149-150

Writing the Female Voice: Essays on Epistolary Literature. Edited by Elizabeth S. Goldsmith. Reviewed by Joan Hinde Stewart. *Tulsa Studies in Women's Literature* 9, No. 1 (Spring 1990):150-152

## Epstein, Cynthia Fuchs

Deceptive Distinctions: Sex, Gender, and the Social Order. Reviewed by Karen K. Kirst-Ashman. *AFFILIA* 5, No. 1 (Spring 1990):116-118

Deceptive Distinctions: Sex, Gender and the Social Order. Reviewed by Debra Renée Kaufman. *Gender and Society* 4, No. 4 (December 1990):

Deceptive Distinctions: Sex, Gender and the Social Order. Reviewed by Janet Zollinger Giele. *Gender and Society* 4, No. 4 (December 1990):553-554

## Epstein, Daniel Mark

Abraham Lincoln's Other Mother. *Good Housekeeping* 210, No. 5 (May 1990):86-89

## Epstein, Edward Jay

Secret of the Airlines. *Lear's* (February 1990):26-30

## Epstein, Julia

Either/Or–Neither/Both: Sexual Ambiguity and the Ideology of Gender. *Genders* 7 (Spring 1990):99-142

Sexual Visions: Images of Gender in Science and Medicine Between the Eighteenth and Twentieth Centuries. Book Review. *The Women's Review of Books* 7, No. 6 (March 1990):13-14

Under the Skin. *The Women's Review of Books* 7, No. 6 (March 1990):13-14

## Epstein, Rachel

Health on Stage. *Healthsharing* 11, No. 2 (March 1990):22-26

## Epstein, Scarlett T. and Watts, Rosemary A. (editors)

The Endless Day: Some Case Material on Asian Rural Women. Reviewed by Kalpana Bardhan. *Journal of Women's History* 2, No. 1 (Spring 1990):200-219

**Equal Access.** *See also* Medical Research

**Equal Opportunity–Employment.** *See also* Employment–Gender Discrimination; Employment Opportunities; Immigrants–Employment

How Pay Equity May Narrow the Salary Gap. Shirley Chan. *Working Woman* (January 1990):107

**Equal Pay for Equal Work.** *See* Wage Equity

## Equal Protection Under the Law

Gender Difference and Gender Disadvantage. Deborah L. Rhode. *Women & Politics* 10, No. 2 (1990):121-135

State Constitutions and Women: Leading or Lagging Agents of Change? Notes. Susan A. MacManus. *Women & Politics* 10, No. 2 (1990):137-151

When Should Differences Make a Difference: A New Approach to the Constitutionality of Gender-

Based Laws. Susan Gluck Mezey. *Women & Politics* 10, No. 2 (1990):105-119

Women, Families and Equality: Was Divorce Reform A Mistake? Annamay T. Sheppard. *Women's Rights Law Reporter* 12, No. 3 (Fall 1990): 143-152

## Erbaugh, Mary

Chinese Women Face Increased Discrimination. *off our backs* 20, No. 3 (March 1990):9+

## Erber-Cadet, Nancy

A History of Their Own: Women in Europe from Pre-history to the Present, Volume 2. Book Review. *New Directions for Women* 19, No. 3 (May/June 1990):18

## Erdrich, Louise

American Horse. Short Story. *Spare Rib* 217 (October 1990):38-43

Baptism of Desire. Reviewed by Annie Finch. *Belles Lettres* 5, No. 4 (Summer 1990):30-31

Best Western. Short Story. *Vogue* (May 1990):288-291, 324

Happy Valentine's Day, Monsieur Ducharme. Short story. *Ladies' Home Journal* 107, No. 2 (February 1990):84+

## Erens, Pamela

Health & Mind. *Glamour* (February 1990):46-51; (June 1990):52; (August 1990):60; (October 1990):60; (December 1990):58

**Eriksson, Brigitte** (joint author). *See* Faderman, Lillian

## Erlen, Judith A. and Holzman, Ian R.

Evolving Issues in Surrogate Motherhood. *Health Care for Women International* 11, No. 3 (1990):319-329

## Erofeev, Victor

Vogue Arts. *Vogue* (November 1990):262+

## Eroticism

Viewpoint: In Praise of Plain White Panties. Peter Richmond. *Glamour* (February 1990):118

## Erotic Literature

Erotica: An Anthology of Women's Writing. Edited by Margaret Reynolds. Reviewed by Maud Sulter. *Spare Rib* 219 (December 1990-January 1991):42-44

Moments of Desire: Sex and Sensuality by Australian Feminist Writers. Edited by Susan Hawthorne and Jenny Pausacker. Reviewed by Susan Sheridan. *Australian Feminist Studies* No. 11 (Autumn 1990):133-135

More Serious Pleasure. Edited by Sheba Collective. Reviewed by Maud Sulter. *Spare Rib* 219 (December 1990-January 1991):42-44

**Errington, Frederick** and Gewertz, Deborah

Cultural Alternatives and a Feminist Anthropology: An Analysis of Culturally Constructed Gender Interests in Papua New Guinea. Reviewed by Debbora Battaglia. *Signs* 15, No. 4 (Summer 1990):869-872

**Errors**

Oops! Susan Jacoby. *Glamour* (July 1990):176-177+

**Erté** (about)

Grand Designs. John McLaughlin. *Harper's Bazaar* (July 1990):84-85+

**Ertman, Martha**

Women and the Law Conference. *off our backs* 20, No. 7 (July 1990):2-5

**Escoffier, Jeffrey**

Inside the Ivory Closet: The Challenges Facing Lesbian and Gay Studies. *Out/Look* No. 10 (Fall 1990):36-37

**Eshe, Aisha**

Sewing Class. Poem. *Heresies* 25 (1990):20

**Espin, Oliva M.**

Empowering Women: Leadership Development Strategies on Campus. Book Review. *Psychology of Women Quarterly* 14, No. 3 (September 1990):439-440

**Espinosa, Dula J.**

Women, Work, and Technology: Transformations. Book Review. *NWSA Journal* 2, No. 3 (Summer 1990):499-501

**Espionage.** *See* Pollard, Anne (about); Rosenberg, Ethel (about)

**Esposito, Phylis** (about). *See* Business Enterprises – Ownership

**Esprit de Corp.** *See* Business Failures

**Esquibel, Catriona**

Debajo del Cielo. Poem. *Frontiers* 11, No. 1 (1990):44-45

**Essays**

Rogue. Kirsten Backstrom. *Trivia* 16/17 (Fall 1990):3-17

**Essence Magazine**

In Celebration of Our Twentieth Anniversary. Edward Lewis. *Essence* 21, No. 1 (May 1990):20-25

Essence: Be an Editor. *Essence* 21, No. 6 (October 1990):98

Graffiti. *Essence* 21, No. 1 (May 1990):208-211

1990 Essence Awards. Bebe Moore Campbell. *Essence* 21, No. 6 (October 1990):55-68

10 Super Fine-Alists. *Essence* 21, No. 3 (July 1990):10-11

**Estate Planning**

Justice for All. Armond D. Bush. *Family Circle* 103, No. 7 (May 15, 1990):33-35

More for Your Money. Barbara Gilder Quint. *Glamour* (September 1990):158-165

**Estefan, Gloria** and Casey, Kathryn

My Miracle. *Ladies' Home Journal* 107, No. 8 (August 1990):99-101+

**Esterline, Mae Handy** (editor)

They Changed Their Worlds: Nine Women of Asia. Reviewed by Kalpana Bardhan. *Journal of Women's History* 2, No. 1 (Spring 1990):200-219

**Esterly, Glenn**

Talking with Peggy Lipton: "My Life Is Starting Over." Interview. *Redbook* 175, No. 6 (October 1990):60-62

**Estes, Patricia Schiff**

Entrepreneurs Take It Abroad. *Lear's* (August 1990):28-31

**Estrogen Replacement Therapy**

Body Briefing: Estrogen Replacement. Marcia Seligson. *Lear's* (March 1990):54-62

The Estrogen Debate. Jane Shiyen Chou and Wendy Murphy. *McCall's* 118, No. 1 (October 1990):157-158

Medinews. *Ladies' Home Journal* 107, No. 6 (June 1990):94

**Etheridge, Melissa** (about)

How Melissa Etheridge Did Not Get Her Start in Women's Music. Toni Armstrong Jr. *Hot Wire* 6, No. 1 (January 1990):24-25

**Ethic of Care.** *See* Caregivers

**Ethics.** *See also* Business Ethics; Fairness; Friendship; Law – Ethics; Medical Ethics; Morality; Trust

Caring: A Feminine Approach to Ethics and Moral Education. By Nel Noddings. Reviewed by Barbara Houston. *Hypatia* 5, No. 1 (Spring 1990):115-119

Caring: A Feminine Approach to Ethics and Moral Education. By Nel Noddings. Reviewed by Claudia Card. *Hypatia* 5, No. 1 (Spring 1990):101-108

Caring: A Feminine Approach to Ethics and Moral Education. By Nel Noddings. Reviewed by Sarah Lucia Hoagland. *Hypatia* 5, No. 1 (Spring 1990):109-114

Ethical Practice in an Unjust World: Educational Evaluation and Social Justice. Gaby Weiner. *Gender and Education* 2, No. 2 (1990):231-238

Feminist Second Thoughts About Free Agency. Paul Benson. *Hypatia* 5, No. 3 (Fall 1990):47-64

"I Wouldn't Let Them Cheat." Sue Collins and Kerry Arquette. *Working Mother* 13, No. 9 (September 1990):36-39

A Question of Morals. Celia Slom. *McCall's* 117, No. 8 (May 1990):70

A Response. Nel Noddings. *Hypatia* 5, No. 1 (Spring 1990):120-126

Scruples: Dish and Tell: Why Do We Talk About Our Friends? Ellen Welty. *Mademoiselle* (February 1990):94

When Friends Give Advice on Love. Carol Lynn Mithers. *Glamour* (February 1990):216

Women and Children First? Barbara Grizzuti Harrison. *Mademoiselle* (December 1990):102

Women and Evil. By Nel Noddings. Reviewed by Berenice Fisher. *The Women's Review of Books* 7, No. 8 (May 1990):21-22

Women and Evil. By Nel Noddings. Reviewed by Sara Ruddick. *New Directions for Women* 19, No. 6 (November-December 1990):24

**Ethics – Study and Teaching**

In Search of an Everyday Morality: The Development of a Measure. Charles M. Shelton and Dan P. McAdams. *Adolescence* 25, No. 100 (Winter 1990):923-943

**Ethiel, Nancy** (joint author). *See* Franzen, Monika

**Ethiopia – Status of Women**

Sweeter Than Honey: Ethiopian Women and Revolution, Testimonies of Tigrayan Women. By Jenny Hammond. Reviewed by Gill Lusk. *The Women's Review of Books* 8, No. 3 (December 1990):13-14

**Ethnic Fashion.** *See* Ethnic Groups – Fashion

**Ethnic Groups**

Reconceptualizing Differences Among Women. Gerda Lerner. *Journal of Women's History* 1, No. 3 (Winter 1990):106-122

**Ethnic Groups – Diversity**

Ethnic and Cultural Diversity: Keys to Power. Julia A. Boyde. *Women and Therapy* 9, Nos. 1-2 (1990):151-167

**Ethnic Groups – Fashion**

Fall Fashion Focus. Patrice McLeod. *Essence* 21, No. 5 (September 1990):20

**Ethnography.** *See also* deCordova, Richard; Papua New Guinea – Anthropology

Can There Be A Feminist Ethnography? Lila Abu-Lughod. *Women and Performance: A Journal of Feminist Theory* 5, No. 1, Issue #9 (1990): 7-27

When Yielding Is Not Consenting: Material and Psychic Determinants of Women's Dominated Consciousness and Some of Their Interpretations in Ethnology, Part 2. Nicole-Claude Mathieu. *Feminist Issues* 10, No. 1 (Spring 1990):51-90

**Etiquette.** *See also* Business Etiquette; Charm; Holidays – Etiquette; Manners; Social Behavior – Humor; Verbal Abuse

Etiquette: Doing It Right. Charlotte Ford. *McCall's* 117, No. 7 (April 1990):130; 117, No. 8 (May 1990):170; 117, No. 9 (June 1990):56-57; 117, No. 10 (July 1990):36; 117, No. 12 (September 1990):34

Etiquette for Every Day. Elizabeth L. Post. *Good Housekeeping* 211, No. 3 (September 1990):62-64; 211, No. 4 (October 1990):52-55

How to Say No! Louise Lague. *Glamour* (November 1990):250-251+

Making the Introduction. Leslie Smith. *Executive Female* 13, No. 4 (July-August 1990):60

Miss Manners' Guide to Excruciatingly Correct Behavior. Judith Martin. *Woman of Power* 17 (Summer 1990):53-55

Saving Grace. Francine Prose. *Savvy Woman* (January 1990):52-55

Scruples: Who's Sorry Later? Ellen Welty. *Mademoiselle* (October 1990):132

**Etra, Jon**

American Original. *Harper's Bazaar* (July 1990):34-36

Haute Bijoux. *Harper's Bazaar* (September 1990):206

Rodeo Days. *Harper's Bazaar* (July 1990):54-57+

Smashing! *Harper's Bazaar* (February 1990):146-147+

World Class. *Harper's Bazaar* (May 1990):33-40

**Ettinger, Shelley**

Holding the Line: Women in the Great Arizona Mine Strike of 1983. Book Review. *New Directions for Women* 19, No. 3 (May/June 1990):17

**Europe, Eastern**

The Bloc Party. Virginia Randall. *Executive Female* 13, No. 5 (September-October 1990):40-41

Eastern Europe: What's Happening? Carol Anne Douglas. *off our backs* 20, No. 1 (January 1990):7

**Europe, Eastern – Status of Women**

Among East European Women: A Reporter's Notebook. Jill Benderly. *On the Issues* 16 (Fall 1990):16-17+

In Their Own Words: Women of Eastern Europe. Slavenka Drakulic. *Ms.* 1, No. 1 (July/August 1990):36-47

**Europe – Fashion**

First-Rate Finds. *Harper's Bazaar* (November 1990):150-157

Puce Becomes You . . . And Other Secrets of European Style. Judy Bachrach. *Savvy Woman* (November 1990):68-71 +

**Europe – History**

A History of Their Own: Women in Europe from Prehistory to the Present. By Bonnie Anderson and Judith Zinsser. Reviewed by Mary Beth Emmerichs. *Feminist Collections* 11, No. 2 (Winter 1990):3-4

A History of Their Own: Women in Europe from Pre-history to the Present, Volume 2. By Bonnie S. Anderson and Judith P. Zinsser. Reviewed by Nancy Erber-Cadet. *New Directions for Women* 19, No. 3 (May/June 1990):18

**Europe – Travel.** *See also* Travel

Travel News. Richard Alleman. *Vogue* (December 1990):228

Yes, You Can Afford to Go to Europe! Bibliography. Stephen Birnbaum. *Good Housekeeping* 211, No. 3 (September 1990):76-81

**Europe – Unification.** *See also* European Economic Community

Curtain Up! Alan Jolis. *Vogue* (March 1990):464-469

**Europe – Women's Studies**

Women's Studies in Europe: Conference Report. Tobe Levin and Jo Myers-Dickinson. *NWSA Journal* 2, No. 1 (Winter 1990):101-104

Women's Studies in Europe: Conference Reports, Part II. Angelika Koster-Lossack and Tobe Levin. *NWSA Journal* 2, No. 2 (Spring 1990):264-268

**European Economic Community**

Back Talk: Europe '92 and Us. Gregory Simpkins. *Essence* 21, No. 2 (June 1990):114

Falling Borders, Rising Hopes: Europe in 1992. Shelley Anderson. *Out/Look* No. 10 (Fall 1990):30-35

The New Concert of Europe. James Chace. *Lear's* (February 1990):99-101

United States of Europe or United Colors of Benetton? Some Feminist Thought on the New Common European Community. Rosi Braidotti and Christien Franken. *Differences* 2, No. 3 (Fall 1990):109-121

**Euthanasia.** *See* Right to Die

**Evangelista, Linda** (about). *See also* Fashion Models

Pretty Woman. Jonathan Van Meter. *Vogue* (October 1990):347 +

**Evangelists.** *See* Bakker, Tammy Faye (about)

**Evans, Betsy** and Nelson, Todd

The Answer Couple. *Glamour* (March 1990):152

**Evans, Elizabeth**

May Sarton Revisited. Reviewed by Loralee MacPike. *NWSA Journal* 2, No. 4 (Autumn 1990):669-674

**Evans, Glen** and Farberow, Norman L.

The Encyclopedia of Suicide. Book Review. *Adolescence* 25, No. 98 (Summer 1990):500

**Evans, Joni** (about)

Lunch. Interview. Frances Lear. *Lear's* (June 1990):19-20

**Evans, Lee** and Bannister, Shelley

Lesbian Violence, Lesbian Victims: How to Identify Battering in Relationships. *Lesbian Ethics* 4, No. 1 (Spring 1990): 52-65

**Evans, Linda Moran** (joint author). *See* Ungaro, Susan

**Evans, Mari**

Speak the Truth to the People. Poem. *Essence* 21, No. 1 (May 1990):206

**Evans, Mary**

The Problem of Gender for Women's Studies. *Women's Studies International Forum* 13, No. 5 (1990):457-462

**Evans, Mary** (joint editor). *See* Sayers, Janet

**Evans, Richard J.**

Comrades and Sisters: Feminism, Socialism and Pacifism in Europe, 1870-1945. Reviewed by Claudia Koonz. *Gender & History* 2, No. 1 (Spring 1990):120-122

**Evans, Sara M.**

Born for Liberty: A History of Women in America. Reviewed by Dana D. Nelson Salvino. *Belles Lettres* 5, No. 3 (Spring 1990):28

Born for Liberty: A History of Women in America. Reviewed by Jo Freeman. *New Directions for Women* 19, No. 2 (March/April 1990):20

**Evans, Sara M.** and Nelson, Barbara J.

Wage Justice: Comparable Worth and the Paradox of Technocratic Reform. Reviewed by Joan Acker. *NWSA Journal* 2, No. 2 (Spring 1990):303-306

Wage Justice: Comparable Worth and the Paradox of Technocratic Reform. Reviewed by Peggy Kahn. *The Women's Review of Books* 7, No. 12 (September 1990):21-23

**Eveline, Joan**

Patriarchy in the Diamond Mines: Women's Work, Research and Affirmative Action. Reviewed by Cora Vellekoop Baldock. *Australian Feminist Studies* No. 12 (Summer 1990):43-49

**Even, Yael**

The Heroine as Hero in Michelangelo's Art. *Woman's Art Journal* 11, No. 1 (Spring-Summer 1990):29-33

**Evert, Chris** (about). *See also* Leadership, "1990 Women of the Year"

Chris Evert: My Love Match with Andy. Alan Ebert. *Good Housekeeping* 211, No. 4 (October 1990):86-90

**Evert, Chris** (interview)

Postscript to a Legendary Rivalry. Ann Smith and Lewis Rothlein. *Women's Sports and Fitness* 12, No. 2 (March 1990):22-25

**Ewald, Janet J.**

Restoring Women to History: Teaching Packets for Integrating Women's History into Courses on Africa, Asia, Latin America, the Caribbean, and the Middle East. Book Review. *Gender & History* 2, No. 3 (Autumn 1990):349-351

**Ewing, Christine** and Klein, Renate

FINNRAGE Conference in Bangladesh. *Connexions* 32 (1990):16-18

**Excimer Lasers.** *See* Lasers in Surgery

**Executives.** *See also* Chief Executive Officers

**Executives – Recruiting**

Lunch. Interview. Frances Lear. *Lear's* (March 1990):25-28

**Executives – Success**

Just Tell Her She Can't. Celia Kuperszmid Lehrman. *Executive Female* (March/April 1990):41-43

**Executives – Training of**

Getting Your MBA on Company Time. Magaly Olivero. *Working Woman* (January 1990):91-92

How to Think Like a CEO for the 90's. Patricia Aburdene. *Working Woman* (September 1990):134-137

**Exercise.** *See also* Aerobic Exercise; Physical Education and Training; Physical Fitness; Physical Fitness Centers; Sports; Stress Relaxation; Stretching Exercises; Travel – Exercise

Beauty & Fashion Journal. *Ladies' Home Journal* 107, No. 2 (February 1990):29-36; 107, No. 11 (November 1990):49-62

Beauty & Health Report: Five Steps to a Flat, Strong Stomach. Andrea Pomerantz Lynn. *Glamour* (April 1990):58

Beauty Questions. *Glamour* (July 1990):26; (August 1990):42

Body Management: Health News. Carl Sherman. *Working Woman* (August 1990):90-93

Bottoms by Jake. Jake Steinfeld. *Ladies' Home Journal* 107, No. 6 (June 1990):38-42

Burn Calories without Exercising. Excerpt. Bryant Stamford and Porter Shimer. *Redbook* 174, No. 6 (April 1990):110-113

Butt Seriously. *Glamour* (March 1990):272-275

Cold Sweat. Marc Bloom. *Women's Sports and Fitness* 12, No. 7 (October 1990):26

Compact Disks, Pelvic Twists. William Harrel. *Lear's* (December 1990):45-46

Contemporary Living: Your Best Body by Summer. *Essence* 20, No. 9 (January 1990):73-78

Crunch. *Glamour* (July 1990):150-151

Elderly Women, Exercise and Healthy Aging. Sandra J. O'Brien and Patricia A. Vertinsky. *Journal of Women and Aging* 2 No. 3 (1990):41-65

Exercise Builds Strong Bones. Diane Debrovner. *McCall's* 118, No. 2 (November 1990):28-32

The Exercise/Illness Connection. David C. Neiman. *Women's Sports and Fitness* 12, No. 2 (March 1990):56-57

Fast-Track Yoga. *Mademoiselle* (November 1990).160-171

Figure Study. *Harper's Bazaar* (August 1990):32 +

A Flat Stomach in 30 Days with Callanetics. Callan Pinckney. *Redbook* 175, No. 2 (June 1990):12-16

Food for Fuel. Kathryn Devereaux. *Women's Sports and Fitness* 12, No. 7 (October 1990):24-25

Great Legs! *Glamour* (September 1990):318-321

Health and Beauty Special for Busy Bodies. Kathy Henderson. *Redbook* 175, No. 6 (October 1990):79-83

Health and Fitness Notes. *Vogue* (August 1990):242

Health Dept. Dava Sobel. *Lear's* (February 1990):54

Health Express: Is Yo-Yo Exercise a No-No? Susan Pocharski. *Mademoiselle* (January 1990):68

Health & Fitness. Bibliography. Stephanie Young. *Glamour* (November 1990):59-66

Health & Fitness. Stephanie Young. *Glamour* (March 1990):57-65; (September 1990):65-72; (October 1990):55-56+; (December 1990):55-56+

Health News. Leslie Granston. *Mademoiselle* (December 1990):112

Health News. Marian Sandmaier. *Working Woman* (December 1990):92

Healthy Attitudes. *Harper's Bazaar* (September 1990):94+

How to Get a Mellow Mindset. Liz Lufkin. *Working Woman* (April 1990):117

Is there an Easy Route to a Better Body? Andrea Pomerantz Lynn. *Glamour* (March 1990):50

Last-Chance Workout. *Family Circle* 103, No. 8 (June 5, 1990):52-53

Lifelong Physical Activity in Midlife and Older Women. Alice J. Dan, JoEllen Wilbur, Cynthia Hedricks, Eileen O'Connor, and Karyn Holm. *Psychology of Women Quarterly* 14, No. 4 (December 1990):531-542

Medical News. Dana Points and Carla Rohlfing. *Family Circle* 103, No. 15 (November 6, 1990):167

Medinews. Joan Lippert. *Ladies' Home Journal* 107, No. 11 (November 1990):152

Medinews. Sally Squires. *Ladies' Home Journal* 107, No. 12 (December 1990):72

Monday, 6:00 A.M.: Some Women Can Hit the Ground Running. *Mademoiselle* (June 1990):182-185

The New Skate Shape-Up. *Mademoiselle* (October 1990):56

Nutrition/Fitness: Exercise: How Much Is Too Much? Jane Shiyen Chou. *McCall's* 117, No. 7 (April 1990):14

Perceived Barriers to Exercise and Weight Control Practices in Community Women. Cheryl A. Johnson, Sheila A. Corrigan, Patricia M. Dubbert, and Sandra E. Gramling. *Women and Health* 16, Nos. 3/4 (1990):177-191

Performance Review: Fitting In Fitness. Karen Behnke and Lorraine Calvacca. *Working Woman* (September 1990):199

The Power Walk. *Mademoiselle* (January 1990):120-121

Prime of Life. *Family Circle* 103, No. 8 (June 5, 1990):124-125+

Relax with Jane Fonda. *Redbook* 174, No. 5 (March 1990):112-113

Roll into Shape. Neil Feineman. *Women's Sports & Fitness* 12, No. 6 (September 1990):50-53

Shall We Dance? *Mademoiselle* (October 1990):180-183

The Sleek Stomach. *Mademoiselle* (December 1990):168-171

10 Steps to a Great Summer Body. *Glamour* (May 1990):280-283

Thin Thighs – In 90 Days or 90 Minutes. Bibliography. *Ladies' Home Journal* 107, No. 9 (September 1990):42-46

Topward Bound. Beth Landman. *Harper's Bazaar* (March 1990):132-148

Update: Your Best Body by Summer. *Essence* 20, No. 11 (March 1990):102; 20, No. 12 (April 1990):98+

Up Front. *Ladies' Home Journal* 107, No. 10 (October 1990):91-96

Warning: When Exercise Is Hazardous to Your Health. Jere Daniel. *Family Circle* 103, No. 14 (October 16, 1990):125-127

Weight Check. *Harper's Bazaar* (August 1990):32-34+

Workouts Without the Work: A Sport-By-Sport Conditioning Guide. Michele Kort. *Women's Sports and Fitness* 12, No. 7 (October 1990):52-55

Your Best Body by Summer Update. *Essence* 20, No. 10 (February 1990):94

Your Body. *Family Circle* 103, No. 11 (August 14, 1990):69-72

**Exercise – Endurance**

Endurance Capacity and Longevity in Women. E. Nygaard, A. Gleerup Madsen, and H. Christensen. *Health Care for Women International* 11, No. 1 (1990):1-10

**Exercise – Equipment and Supplies.** *See also* Home Gyms

Beauty: The Biker Body. *Mademoiselle* (September 1990):62-67

Exercise: The Toll of a New Machine. Holly Reich. *Lear's* (November 1990):62-64

Good Sports: Hot Tips for Working Out in the Cold. Joanne Mattera. *Glamour* (February 1990):58

Great Gear. Diane French. *Women's Sports & Fitness* 12, No. 6 (September 1990):62-63

Great Looks: Bike Off Inches (at Home). *Redbook* 176, No. 2 (December 1990):18

Great Looks: Flatter Any Body. *Redbook* 175, No. 5 (September 1990):16-18

Hot Body Shops. Bibliography. *Harper's Bazaar* (September 1990):98+

Put Your Money Where Your Foot Is: A Guide to Buying Running Shoes. Emily Walzer. *Women's Sports & Fitness* 12, No. 6 (September 1990):36-39

**Exercise Bicycles.** *See* Exercise – Equipment and Supplies

**Exercise Clubs.** *See* Physical Fitness Centers

**Exercise for Children**

Exercises for You and Your Kids. Suzy Prudden. *Good Housekeeping* 211, No. 3 (September 1990):138

Happy Exercise for Healthy Kids. Vic Dante. *McCall's* 117, No. 12 (September 1990):38+

Ready, Set, Go! How to Shape Up Your Kids. Bibliography. Curtis Pesmen. *Ladies' Home Journal* 107, No. 4 (April 1990):89-110

## Exercise Videos

See Jane Run – The Video Workout Revival. Bibliography. Ellen Kunes. *Mademoiselle* (November 1990):194

Video Workouts. *Lear's* (May 1990):26

## Exile

People Who Are "Too Something." Mary Anne Schofield. *Belles Lettres* 5, No. 4 (Summer 1990):43-44

## Explorers

Down the Wild River North. By Constance Helmericks. Reviewed by Anne Dellenbaugh. *The Women's Review of Books* 7, No. 7 (April 1990):16-17

The Magnificent Mountain Women: Adventures in the Colorado Rockies. By Janet Robertson. Reviewed by Judith Niemi. *The Women's Review of Books* 8, No. 1 (October 1990):18-19

Off the Beaten Track: Women Adventurers and Mountaineers in Western Colorado. By Cyndi Smith. Reviewed by Judith Niemi. *The Women's Review of Books* 8, No. 1 (October 1990):18-19

Rambling Gals/Exploring the Scientific Method. Leslie A. Moushey. *Belles Lettres* 5, No. 3 (Spring 1990):10-11

Spinsters Abroad: Victorian Lady Explorers. By Dea Birkett. Reviewed by Helen Callaway. *Women's Studies International Forum* 13, No. 4 (1990):405

Spinsters Abroad: Victorian Lady Explorers. By Dea Birkett. Reviewed by Patricia Lamb. *The Women's Review of Books* 7, No. 5 (February 1990):15

Spinsters Abroad: Victorian Lady Explorers. By Dea Birkett. Reviewed by Sarah Graham-Brown. *Gender & History* 2, No. 3 (Autumn 1990):373-375

A Woman's Trek: What Difference Does Gender Make? Susan L. Blake. *Women's Studies International Forum* 13, No. 4 (1990):347-355

Women into the Unknown: A Sourcebook on Women Explorers and Travelers. By Marion Tinling. Review. *Feminist Collections* 11, No. 3 (Spring 1990):18

**Exposito, Maria Cruz** (joint author). *See* Tally, Justine

**Extermination.** *See* Insect Pests – Control

**Extramarital Affairs.** *See also* Infidelity

Adultery: An Analysis of Love and Betrayal. By Annette Lawson. Reviewed by Lynn Atwater. *Journal of Marriage and the Family* 52, No. 2 (May 1990):564

Affairs of the Heart. Kathleen McCoy. *Redbook* 175, No. 1 (May 1990):128-129+

An Affair to Remember. Chandra Patterson. *Essence* 21, No. 3 (July 1990):59-60+

Can This Marriage Be Saved? "My Husband Is Having an Affair." Margery D. Rosen. *Ladies' Home Journal* 107, No. 4 (April 1990):20-24+

Can You Cheat and Still Be Faithful? Susan Jacoby. *Glamour* (June 1990):224-225+

Do Men Need to Cheat? James Thornton. *Glamour* (December 1990):208-209+

Perceptions on Communication and Sexuality in Marriage in Zimbabwe. Marvellous M. Mhloyi. *Women and Therapy* 10, No. 3 (1990):61-73

Scruples: He Cheated – Do You Rat on the Rat? Ellen Welty. *Mademoiselle* (June 1990):134

Why Women Cheat. Carol Botwin. *Ladies' Home Journal* 107, No. 10 (October 1990):98-102

**Eye – Care and Hygiene.** *See also* Makeup

Beauty: Answers. *Essence* 20, No. 12 (April 1990):17

Beauty and Fashion Hotline: Eye Openers. *Family Circle* 103, No. 9 (June 26, 1990):45

The Best Contact Lenses for You – and Why. Nancy Gagliardi. *Redbook* 175, No. 6 (October 1990):96-97+

Body Briefing: Eyes. Leslie C. Roberts. *Lear's* (April 1990):45-46

The Contact Lens Wearer's Guide to Cosmetics. Stephanie Young. *Glamour* (October 1990):48

Does Your Child Have a Hidden Vision Problem? Steven P. Shelov and Sarah Wernick. *Working Mother* (November 1990):84-88

Eyes Can See Clearly Now: Surgery for the Nearsighted. Cynthia Hacinli. *Mademoiselle* (June 1990):124

Health Department. Leigh Silverman. *Lear's* (May 1990):62; (July 1990):42

Health Notes. *Vogue* (January 1990):124; (September 1990):468

Makeover Your Eyes. *Redbook* 175, No. 6 (October 1990):91-93

Mascara! *Glamour* (July 1990):180-183

**Eye – Laser Surgery**

Sci-Fi Eye Surgery. Marjorie Ingall. *McCall's* 118, No. 2 (November 1990):22

**Eyega, Zeinab** (interview)

Black Women in Sudan. Shay Salomyn. *off our backs* 20, No. 3 (March 1990):8

**Eyeglasses**

Timeless Objects. Kathleen Beckett-Young. *Savvy Woman* (October 1990):38-40

# F

**Fabares, Shelley** (about)

Talking with Shelley Fabares: "I'd Do Anything to Help My Mother." Interview. Ellen Byron. *Redbook* 176, No. 2 (December 1990):38-41

**Fabiano, Sandra** (about)

Presumed Guilty. T. M. Spencer and Jim Brosseau. *Savvy Woman* (October 1990):62-65+

**Fabian Society**

Women's Fabian Tracts. Edited by Sally Alexander. Reviewed by Linda Walker. *Gender & History* 2, No. 2 (Summer 1990):244-246

**Fabrics.** *See* Textile Fabrics

**Face – Care and Hygiene.** *See also* Makeup

Give Yourself a Skincare Makeover. Maggie Morrison. *Redbook* 175, No. 5 (September 1990):170-173

Great Looks: 6 Ways to Younger Skin. Lou Ann Walker. *Redbook* 175, No. 6 (October 1990):16-20

Images: Beauty Answers. Llaura Flynn McCarthy. *Vogue* (September 1990):356

**Facial Massage.** *See* Massage

**Facials.** *See* Face – Care and Hygiene

**Facsimile Transmission.** *See also* Communication; Electronic Office Machines

Memos on the Office Environment. *Working Woman* (April 1990):73-74

**Factory Workers – History.** *See also* Textile Industry

Like a Family: The Making of a Southern Cotton Mill World. By Jacquelyn Dowd Hall and others. Reviewed by Elizabeth Faue. *Signs* 15, No. 2 (Winter 1990):391-394

Once a Cigar Maker: Men, Women and Work Culture in American Cigar Factories, 1900-1919. By Patricia A. Cooper. Reviewed by Elizabeth Faue. *Signs* 15, No. 2 (Winter 1990):391-394

**Faddis, Jon** (about). *See* Music – Jazz

**Faderman, Lillian** and Eriksson, Brigitte

Lesbians in Germany: 1890's to 1920's. Reviewed by Deborah Price. *Belles Lettres* 5, No. 4 (Summer 1990):48-49

**Fahey, Diane**

The Judgement of Paris. Poem. *Hecate* 16, Nos. 1-2 (1990):117

**Failure.** *See* Business Failures

**Failure (Psychology)**

Causal Attributions for Losing as Perceived by Adolescents. Shirley A. Wisniewski and Eugene L. Gaier. *Adolescence* 25, No. 97 (Spring 1990):239-247

**Fain, Jean**

The Silent Killer. Bibliography. *Ladies' Home Journal* 107, No. 3 (March 1990):68-79

**Fairchild, Morgan** (about). *See* Celebrities – Activism

**Fairness**

How Ethical Is American Business? Ronni Sandroff. *Working Woman* (September 1990):113-116

Sexual Ethics: What You Owe a Man You Don't Love. Carol Lynn Mithers. *Glamour* (April 1990):316

The Troubles I've Seen. *Working Woman* (September 1990):129

**Fairy Tales**

Tatterhood and Other Tales. Edited by Ethel Johnston Phelps. Reviewed by Mitzi Myers. *NWSA Journal* 2, No. 2 (Spring 1990):273-281

**Fajitas.** *See* Cookery (Fajitas)

**Fake Fur.** *See* Artificial Fur

**Falbel, Rita**

Two Trees. Song. *Bridges* 1, No. 1 (Spring 1990): 84-85

**Falbel, Rita,** Klepfisz, Irene, and Nevel, Donna

A Handbook for Jewish Women on the Israeli/Palestinian Conflict. Reviewed by Donna Berman. *New Directions for Women* 19, No. 6 (November-December 1990):18

Jewish Women's Call for Peace: A Handbook for Jewish Women on the Israeli/Palestinian Conflict. Reviewed by Lois Levine. *Bridges* 1, No. 2 (Fall 1990): 125

**Falbel, Rita** and Klepfisz, Irena

Renee Epelbaum: Still Struggling for Truth and Justice in Argentina. Interview. *Bridges* 1, No. 1 (Spring 1990): 86-95

**Falconer, Etta Z.**

A Story of Success: The Sciences at Spelman College. *Sage* 6, No. 2 (Fall 1989):36-38

**Falk, Peter** (about)

Peter Falk Reigns in Columbo's Trench Coat. Eric Sherman. *Ladies' Home Journal* 107, No. 3 (March 1990):98-100

**Falletta, JoAnn** (about). *See* Musicians

**Fall Foliage**

The Avid Gardener: Loveliness of Leaves. Leslie Land. *McCall's* 118, No. 1 (October 1990):68

Mother Nature's Fall Spectacular. Bibliography. Stephen Birnbaum. *Good Housekeeping* 211, No. 4 (October 1990):106-108

**Families.** *See also* Divorce; Dual-Career Families

Families. Tamar Jacoby. *Lear's* (April 1990):68-73

Families in Later Life: A Burgeoning Research Area. Timothy H. Brubaker. *Journal of Marriage and the Family* 52, No. 4 (November 1990):959-981

Family Development and the Life Course: Two Perspective on Family Change. Joan Aldous. *Journal of Marriage and the Family* 52, No. 3 (August 1990):517-583

The Family Interpreted: Feminist Theory in Clinical Practice. By Deborah Anna Luepnitz. Reviewed by Shirley Feldman-Summers. *Women and Therapy* 9, No. 4 (1990):116-119

Homeward Bound: American Families in the Cold War Era. By Elaine Tyler May. Reviewed by Susan Ware. *Signs* 16, No. 1 (Autumn 1990):173-175

The Impact of the Family on Health: The Decade in Review. Catherine E. Ross, John Mirowsky, and Karen Goldsteen. *Journal of Marriage and the Family* 52, No. 4 (November 1990):1059-1078

Love Him, Love His Family? Carol Lynn Mithers. *Glamour* (July 1990):194

A Question of Loyalty. Frederick Hermann. *Glamour* (March 1990):286+

Single Women/Family Ties: Life Histories of Older Women. By Katherine R. Allen. Reviewed by Sally A. Lloyd. *Journal of Marriage and the Family* 52, No. 1 (February 1990):281

**Families, African-American.** *See* African-American Families; Family Life – Problems

**Families – Bibliographies**

Bibliography. *Journal of Women's History* 1, No. 3 (Winter 1990):263-276

**Families, Hispanic**

Only Daughter. Sandra Cisneros. *Glamour* (November 1990):256+

**Families – Research Methodologies**

A Brief Response to DeMaris. Jay Teachman and S. Philip Morgan. *Journal of Marriage and the Family* 52, No. 1 (February 1990):277

Gender Issues in Field Research. By Carol A. B. Warren. Reviewed by Sarah H. Matthews. *Journal of Marriage and the Family* 52, No. 1 (February 1990):282

Handbook of Family Measurement Techniques. Edited by John Touliatos, Barry F. Perlmutter, and Murray A. Straus. Reviewed by Mary Ellen Oliveri. *Journal of Marriage and the Family* 52, No. 3 (August 1990):799-800

Interpreting Logistic Regression Results: A Critical Commentary. Alfred DeMaris. *Journal of Marriage and the Family* 52, No. 1 (February 1990):271-276

Knowing Children: Participant Observation with Minors. By Gary Alan Fine and Kent L. Sandstrom. Reviewed by Sarah H. Matthews. *Journal of Marriage and the Family* 52, No. 1 (February 1990):282

Managing Family Data on Multiple Roles and Changing Statuses over Time. Luther B. Otto and Vaughan R. A. Call. *Journal of Marriage and the Family* 52, No. 1 (February 1990):243-248

Violent Acts and Injurious Outcomes in Married Couples: Methodological Issues in the National Survey of Families and Households. Lisa D. Brush. *Gender and Society* 4, No. 1 (March 1990):56-67

**Families – Research Methodology**

Beyond Separate Spheres: Feminism and Family Research. Myra Marx Ferree. *Journal of Marriage and the Family* 52, No. 4 (November 1990):866-884

Marital and Family Enrichment Research: A Decade Review and Look Ahead. Bernard Guerney, Jr. and Pamela Maxson. *Journal of Marriage and the Family* 52, No. 4 (November 1990):1127-1135

Quantitative Research on Marital Quality in the 1980s: A Critical Review. Norval D. Glenn. *Journal of Marriage and the Family* 52, No. 4 (November 1990):818-831

Remarriage and Stepfamily Research in the 1980s: Increased Interest in an Old Family Form. Marilyn Coleman and Lawrence H. Ganong. *Journal of Marriage and the Family* 52, No. 4 (November 1990):925-940

Trends and Directions in Family Research in the 1980s. Felix M. Berardo. *Journal of Marriage and the Family* 52, No. 4 (November 1990):809-817

**Families, Single-Parent.** *See* Divorce – Psychological Aspects; Single Parents

Dysfunction in the Single-Parent and Only-Child Family. Sadi Bayrakal and Teresa M. Kope. *Adolescence* 25, No. 97 (Spring 1990):1-7

The Impact of Parental Loss on Adolescents' Psychosocial Characteristics. Beverley Raphael, Jeff Cubis, Michael Dunne, Terry Lewin, and Brian Kelly. *Adolescence* 25, No. 99 (Fall 1990):689-700

**Family and Education**

Family, School and Society. Edited by Martin Woodhead and Andrea McGrath. Reviewed by C. R. Miller. *Gender and Education* 2, No. 1 (1990):100-102

**Family Finances.** *See also* Finance, Personal; Values

How to Make the Significant Choices. Laura Green. *Lear's* (June 1990):58-59

**Family Illness, Psychology of.** *See* Critically Ill – Family Relationships

**Family Influence.** *See also* Television Programs – Family Influence

The Family Trap. Joan Morgan. *Essence* 21, No. 5 (September 1990):81-82

Health News. Leslie Granston. *Mademoiselle* (November 1990):118

Mama Didn't Lie. Jill Nelson. *Essence* 21, No. 2 (June 1990):61-62+

My Problem: My Sister-in-Law Was Ruining My Marriage. *Good Housekeeping* 211, No. 3 (September 1990):84-87

**Family Law.** *See also* Child Custody; India – Legal System; Law – Feminist Perspectives

Justice For All. Armond D. Budish. *Family Circle* 103, No. 3 (February 20, 1990):41-43

Status and Contract in Feminist Legal Theory of the Family: A Reply to Bartlett. Janet L. Dolgin. *Women's Rights Law Reporter* 12, No. 2 (Summer 1990): 103-113

Stepparents Need Legal Clout. Philip S. Gutis. *McCall's* 117, No. 8 (May 1990):66-67

**Family Leave.** *See* Family Policy; Parental leave

**Family Life.** *See also* Celebrities – Family Life; Father-Daughter Relationships; Mother-Daughter Relationships; Values

Assessment of Work Spillover into Family Life. Stephen A. Small and Dave Riley. *Journal of Marriage and the Family* 52, No. 1 (February 1990):51-61

A Date with Mom. Rae Lynn Barton. *McCall's* 118, No. 1 (October 1990):14

Diary of a Second Wedding. Susan Dundon. *McCall's* 117, No. 11 (August 1990):34-43

Economic Distress and Family Relations: A Review of the Eighties. Patricia Voydanoff. *Journal of Marriage and the Family* 52, No. 4 (November 1990):1099-1115

Family Traditions: The Power of Knowing Who You Are. Susan Brenna. *McCall's* 117, No. 7 (April 1990):76-82

Feminism, Children, and the New Families. Edited by Sanford M. Dornbusch and Myra H. Strober. Reviewed by Ellen B. Bogolub. *AFFILIA* 5, No. 3 (Fall 1990):116-118

<X2>"Guess Who Came to My House." Karen Watson and Nancy Stesin. *Ladies' Home Journal* 107, No. 9 (September 1990):24+

Happy 100th Birthday, Aunt Rose. Kerry McCarthy. *Ladies' Home Journal* 107, No. 7 (July 1990):70-76

His: Spring Training. Daniel Asa Rose. *Glamour* (June 1990):264

How to Talk So Your Kids will Listen. Ray Guarendi. *Redbook* 175, No. 5 (September 1990):150-151+

Ingredients of a Happy Marriage. Alexandra Stoddard. *McCall's* 117, No. 9 (June 1990):140

It's the Weekend: So Why Do You Feel Miserable? Rose Graff. *Working Woman* (March 1990):140-144

Our Families – Then and Now. Joyce A. Ladner. *Essence* 21, No. 1 (May 1990):180-182

Parental Employment and Family Life: Research in the 1980s. Elizabeth G. Menaghan and Toby L.

Parcel. *Journal of Marriage and the Family* 52, No. 4 (November 1990):1079-1098

Parenthood: A Special Report on Families Today. *Ladies' Home Journal* 107, No. 6 (June 1990):71-75

Personal Journal: Married with Children . . . and Still in Love. Anne Mayer. *Ladies' Home Journal* 107, No. 6 (June 1990):110

Rosario. Adan Gettinger-Brizuela. *Out/Look* No. 7 (Winter 1990):25-29

Rose Kennedy at 100. Lester David. *McCall's* 117, No. 8 (May 1990):83-88

**Family Life – Africa.** *See* Africa – Status of Women

**Family Life – Bibliographies**

Havens No More? Discourses of Domesticity. Bonnie Smith. *Gender & History* 2, No. 1 (Spring 1990):98-102

**Family Life – History**

The Family and the English Revolution. By Christopher Durston. Reviewed by Cynthia Herrup. *Gender & History* 2, No. 2 (Summer 1990):226-228

First Person Singular: House Bound. *Savvy Woman* (September 1990):94+

The Gift of Memories. Jane Mattern Vachon. *Ladies' Home Journal* 107, No. 12 (December 1990):78-79

Histoire de la vie Privée, volume 5, De la Premie4re Guerre mondiale à nos jours. Edited by Antoine Prost and Gérard Vincent. Reviewed by Sian Reynolds. *Gender & History* 2, No. 2 (Summer 1990):212-217

Histoire de la vie Privée, volume 4, De la révolution à la Grande Guerre. Edited by Michelle Perrot. Reviewed by Sian Reynolds. *Gender & History* 2, No. 2 (Summer 1990):212-217

The Social Origins of Private Life: A History of American Families 1600-1900. By Stephanie Coontz. Reviewed by Joan Entmacher. *Women's Studies International Forum* 13, No. 5 (1990):521-522

**Family Life – Humor**

Barry Funny. Michael Kiefer. *Ladies' Home Journal* 107, No. 10 (October 1990):78-85

Bob Saget's Funniest Family Stories. Interview. Ellen Byron. *Redbook* 175, No. 5 (September 1990):80-82

10 Reasons to Give a Kid a Hug. Mary Mohler. *Ladies' Home Journal* 107, No. 6 (June 1990):88-89

**Family Life – Problems.** *See also* Child Abuse; Children of Alcoholic Parents; Domestic Violence; Family Structure; Incest; Parenting; Poverty; Problem Families

Answers to Your Questions. Joyce Brothers. *Good Housekeeping* 211, No. 3 (September 1990):214-217; 211, No. 4 (October 1990):111-112

Can This Marriage Be Saved? "He's Always Out with the Guys." Margery D. Rosen. *Ladies' Home Journal* 107, No. 6 (June 1990):12-18

Can This Marriage Be Saved? "My Husband is Never There for Us." Sondra Forsyth Enos. *Ladies' Home Journal* 107, No. 8 (August 1990):12-17

Can This Marriage Be Saved? "There's Something Missing from Our Marriage." Margery D. Rosen. *Ladies' Home Journal* 107, No. 5 (May 1990):12-16

Father Hunger. Michel Marriott. *Essence* 21, No. 7 (November 1990):73-74+

Interiors: The Other Woman. Joan Morgan. *Essence* 21, No. 7 (November 1990):34+

Mind Health. John Tierney. *Vogue* (July 1990):114-119

Mother Love: Lessons in Logic and Lunacy. Rebecca Owens. *Lear's* (May 1990):68-70

The Mothers' Page: His, Mine, Ours. Victoria Ryan. *McCall's* 117, No. 11 (August 1990):9-10

My Problem: I Tried to Live My Teenage Daughter's Life. *Good Housekeeping* 211, No. 4 (October 1990):40-43

Video: The New Family Fix. Katherine Barrett and Richard Greene. *Ladies' Home Journal* 107, No. 2 (February 1990):118-120+

Why I (Still) Want a Wife. Judy Brady. *Ms.* 1, No. 1 (July/August 1990):17

Young Mother's Story: "But for the Grace of God." Deborah Schall and Lorene Hanley Duquin. *Redbook* 176, No. 2 (December 1990):74-80

**Family Life – Role Sharing**

The Secret Strength of Happy Marriages. Annie Gottlieb. *McCall's* 118, No. 3 (December 1990):94-96+

**Family Medicine.** *See also* Pediatrics

Family Doctor. Alan E. Nourse. *Good Housekeeping* 211, No. 3 (September 1990):38-40; 211, No. 4 (October 1990):74

Medical Report: Family Medical History. Victoria Zimet Daly. *Glamour* (February 1990):61-62

Vital Signs. *McCall's* 117, No. 9 (June 1990):16-18; 117, No. 11 (August 1990):24-27

**Family-Owned Business**

Artful Cuisine. Betty Goodwin. *Harper's Bazaar* (July 1990):90-93+

Close Connections. *Harper's Bazaar* (April 1990):61-75

Economies. Marion Asnes. *Lear's* (October 1990):44

Model Gourmets. Jennet Conant. *Harper's Bazaar* (July 1990):94-95+

Stunning Success. Janet Bailey. *Harper's Bazaar* (October 1990):174-175+

When Little Sister Means Business. Renée Edelman. *Working Woman* (February 1990):82-88

**Family Planning.** *See also* Contraception; Egypt – Family Planning; India – Family Planning; Population Control; Pregnancy

Abortion: Empty Womb. Felicia R. Lee. *Essence* 21, No. 1 (May 1990):51-52

Family Planning Handbook for Doctors. Edited by Ronald L. Kleinman. Reviewed by Lynnette Wray. *Healthright* 9, No. 2 (February 1990):38

Making Love, Making Choices. Michele Kort. *Essence* 20, No. 11 (March 1990):57-58

**Family Planning – Asia**

Family Planning in Asia and the Pacific. Kathy Gollan. *Healthright* 9, No. 3 (May 1990):25-28

**Family Planning – Islamic Families**

Fertility and Adoption of Family Planning Among the Muslims of 24 Parganas, West Bengal, Part II. A. K. Ghosh and N. K. Das. *Journal of Family Welfare* 36, No. 1 (March 1990):32-42

**Family Planning – Social Attitudes**

A Comparative Study of Health Distress and Sex Behavioural Attitude of Family Planning Adopters and Non-Adopters. Mahesh Bhargava and Sunita Khajuria. *Journal of Family Welfare* 36, No. 2 (June 1990):23-29

Religion, Social Change and Fertility Behaviour. By R. Jayasree. Reviewed by K. B. Pathak. *Journal of Family Welfare* 36, No. 2 (June 1990):69-70

The Status of Women and Family Planning Acceptance: Some Field Results. Ramamani Sundar. *Journal of Family Welfare* 36, No. 2 (June 1990):60-68

**Family Policy.** *See also* Family Planning; Population Control

Family Leave and Gender Justice. Suzanne E. England. *AFFILIA* 5, No. 2 (Summer 1990):8-24

Family Policy in the 1980s: Controversy and Consensus. Joan Aldous and Wilfried Dumon. *Journal of Marriage and the Family* 52, No. 4 (November 1990):1136-1151

Free-Standing Birth Centers and Medical Control: A Case Study. Kathleen Doherty Turkel. *NWSA Journal* 2, No. 1 (Winter 1990):52-67

Tell Us What You Think: Should Employers Be Required to Provide Family Leave? *Glamour* (September 1990):196

This is What You Thought: Family Leave: Should It Be Mandated? *Glamour* (November 1990):149

Washington Notes: "The Process Stinks." Miranda S. Spivack. *Ms.* 1, No. 2 (September/October 1990):91

## Family Recreation

Are We There Yet? A Guide to Enjoying Car Travel With Your Kids. Marjorie Cohen. *Family Circle* 103, No. 9 (June 26, 1990):117

Fitness. Cynthia Gorney. *Vogue* (December 1990):179-182

## Family Reunions. *See also* Holidays – Psychological Aspects; Traditions

A Country Christmas. *Redbook* 176, No. 2 (December 1990):121-126+

Family Ties & Celebrations. Liza Nelson. *McCall's* 118, No. 2 (November 1990):104-108

Home for the Holidays. *Ladies' Home Journal* 107, No. 12 (December 1990):184-197

Nathalie Dupree Cooks Southern Thanksgiving Favorites. Nathalie Dupree. *Redbook* 176, No. 1 (November 1990):125-129+

Nine Tips to Happier Family Holidays. Gini Kopecky. *Redbook* 176, No. 1 (November 1990):110-111+

Swedish Noel. *Harper's Bazaar* (December 1990):124-125+

A Thanksgiving to Remember. *Ladies' Home Journal* 107, No. 11 (November 1990):232-245

## Family Roles. *See* Gender Roles; Household Labor; Labor, Gender Division of

## Family Size. *See also* China – Population Policy

Family Portrait:"There's Always Room for One More." Sylvia Whitman. *Ladies' Home Journal* 107, No. 3 (March 1990):126-131

Population Policy of China and Its Impact on Family Size and Structure. Hao Cailan. *Journal of Family Welfare* 36, No. 1 (March 1990):7-21

## Family Size – Rural Communities

Determinants of Desired Family Size in Rural Bangladesh: A Two-Stage Analysis. Bashir Ahmed. *Journal of Family Welfare* 36, No. 1 (March 1990):22-31

## Family Size and Achievement

Family Size and Academic Achievement of Children. Varghese I. Cherian. *Journal of Family Welfare* 36, No. 4 (December 1990):56-60

## Family Structure. *See also* African-American Women – History; Household Structure; Nigeria – Gender Roles

Brave New Families: Stories of Democratic Upheaval in Late Twentieth-Century America. By Judith Stacey. Reviewed by Arlene Kaplan Daniels. *The Women's Review of Books* 8, No. 3 (December 1990):14-15

The Entrepreneurial Family Economy: Family Strategies and Self-Employment in Detroit, 1880. Melanie Archer. *Journal of Family History* 15, No. 3 (July 1990):261-283

Evaluations of Family by Youth: Do They Vary as a Function of Family Structure, Gender, and Birth Order? Thomas S. Parish. *Adolescence* 25, No. 98 (Summer 1990):353-356

Family, Feminism, and Race in America. Maxine Baca Zinn. *Gender and Society* 4, No. 1 (March 1990):68-82

Family and Kin – a Few Thoughts. Giovanni Levi. *Journal of Family History* 15, No. 4 (October 1990):567-578

Family Ties, Friendships, and Subjective Well-being Among Black Americans. Christopher, G. Ellison. *Journal of Marriage and the Family* 52, No. 2 (May 1990):298-310

Getting Along with Grandparents. Doris B. Wallace. *Good Housekeeping* 211, No. 3 (September 1990):156+

The Invisible Web: Gender Patterns in Family Relationships. By Marianne Walters, Betty Carter, Peggy Papp, and Olga Silverstein. Reviewed by Ellen B. Bogolub. *AFFILIA* 5, No. 3 (Fall 1990):116-118

A Meta-analytic Review of Family Structure Stereotypes. Lawrence H. Ganong, Marilyn Coleman, and Dennis Mapes. *Journal of Marriage and the Family* 52, No. 2 (May 1990):287-297

Sons, Daughters, and Intergenerational Social Support. Glenna Spitze and John Logan. *Journal of Marriage and the Family* 52, No. 2 (May 1990):420-430

Standing Room Only: A Too-Faraway Grandpa Visits. Meyer Moldeven. *Lilith* 15, No. 1 (Winter 1990):4-5

## Family Structure – History

Family Forms and Domestic Service in Southern Italy from the Seventeenth to the Nineteenth Centuries. Giovanna Da Molin. *Journal of Family History* 15, No. 4 (October 1990):503-527

Female Solitude and Patrilineage: Unmarried Women and Widows during the Eighteenth and Nineteenth Centuries. Maura Palazzi. *Journal of Family History* 15, No. 4 (October 1990):443-459

Out of Wedlock Childbearing in an Ante-Bellum Southern County. Susan Newcomer. *Journal of Family History* 15, No. 3 (July 1990):357-368

The Peasant Family in Northern Italy, 1750-1930: A Reassessment. Pier Paolo Viazzo and Dionigi Albera. *Journal of Family History* 15, No. 4 (October 1990):461-482

The Power of Culture: A Review of the Idea of Africa's Influence on Family Structure in Antebellum America. Antonio McDaniel. *Journal of Family History* 15, No. 2 (April 1990):225-238

## Family Therapy. *See also* Caregiving; Gender Roles; Marriage Counseling

Marriage and Family Therapy: A Decade Review. Fred P. Piercy and Douglas H. Sprenkle. *Journal of*

*Marriage and the Family* 52, No. 4 (November 1990):1116-1126

Our Families, Ourselves. John Bradshaw. *Lear's* (March 1990):85-86

School-Based Social Work and Family Therapy. Thomas L. Millard. *Adolescence* 25, No. 98 (Summer 1990):401-408

**Family Therapy – Feminist Perspectives**

Women, Feminism and Family Therapy. Edited by Lois Braverman. Reviewed by Karen A. Holmes. *AFFILIA* 5, No. 1 (Spring 1990):104-106

Women in Families: A Framework for Family Therapy. Edited by Monica McGoldrick, Carol M. Anderson, and Froma Walsh. Reviewed by Ruth Farber. *AFFILIA* 5, No. 1 (Spring 1990):107-108

**Family Violence.** *See* Child Abuse; Domestic Violence; Violence Against Women

**Fann, Victoria**

Touching Women. *Woman of Power* 18 (Fall 1990):74

**Fantasy**

The Force of Fantasy: Feminism, Mapplethorpe, and Discursive Excess. Judith Butler. *Differences* 2, No. 2 (Summer 1990):105-125

**Farber, Ruth**

Women in Families: A Framework for Family Therapy. Book Review. *AFFILIA* 5, No. 1 (Spring 1990):107-108

**Farber, Stephen**

Jill. *Lear's* (September 1990):86-89

**Farberow, Norman L.** (joint author). *See* Evans, Glen

**Farhoud, Abla**

When I Was Grown Up (Quand j'etais grande). Play. *Women and Performance: A Journal of Feminist Theory* 5, No. 1, Issue #9 (1990): 120-143

**Farhoud, Abla** (about)

Growing . . . Jill MacDougall. *Women and Performance: A Journal of Feminist Theory* 5, No. 1, Issue #9 (1990): 144-155

**Farmanfarmaian, Roxanne**

The Smart Office: Can You Tech It? *Working Woman* (April 1990):58-68

**Farmer, Fannie** (about). *See* Hazard, Jan Turner, "Women Chefs"

**Farmer, Frank F.** (joint author). *See* Papini, Dennis R.

**Farmer, Martin**

Sterling Opportunities. *Executive Female* 13, No. 5 (September-October 1990):42-43

**Farmer, Ruth**

Mistress. Poem. *Sinister Wisdom* 42 (Winter 1990-1991):42-43

The Passage. Poem. *Woman of Power* 16 (Spring 1990):28

**Farnham, Christie** (editor)

The Impact of Feminist Research in the Academy. Reviewed by Arlene Kaplan Daniels. *Gender and Society* 4, No. 1 (March 1990):96-99

**Farr, Cecilia Konchar**

Fragments of Stained Glass. Book Review. *Belles Lettres* 5, No. 2 (Winter 1990):9

Nettie Palmer: Her Private Journal *Fourteen Years*, Poems, Reviews, and Literary Essays. Book Review. *Belles Lettres* 5, No. 2 (Winter 1990):2

**Farr, Judith**

Emily Dickinson's "Engulfing" Play: *Antony and Cleopatra. Tulsa Studies in Women's Literature* 9, No. 2 (Fall 1990):231-250

**Farrell, Laura**

After-Dark Glow. *Harper's Bazaar* (July 1990):78-79

**Farrell, Mary**

Pediatric Healthline. *Ladies' Home Journal* 107, No. 12 (December 1990):64

**Farrell, Suzanne** and Bentley, Toni

Holding on to the Air: An Autobiography. Reviewed by Lynn Garafola. *The Women's Review of Books* 8, No. 3 (December 1990):7-8

**Farrior, Charlotte Ringling** (about). *See* Davis, Andrea R., "Power Players"

**Farry, Marcel**

Censorship – Who's Calling the Shots. *Spare Rib* 219 (December 1990-January 1991):31-32

In Conversation with Nawal El Saadawi. *Spare Rib* 217 (October 1990):22-26

Embryo Research Bill Passed. *Spare Rib* No. 212 (May 1990):44-45

Hands Off the Silcotts. *Spare Rib* No. 210 (March 1990):14-15

Palestine: Massacre at Dome of the Rock. *Spare Rib* 218 (November 1990):12-14

Terror, or Will the Real Terrorists Please Stand Up. Video Review. *Spare Rib* 218 (November 1990):23

Thick as Thieves: Britain and the US in the Gulf. *Spare Rib* No. 216 (September 1990):18-19

**Fashion.** *See also* Beauty Culture; Beauty Standards; Body Image; California – Fashion; Celebrities – Fashion; Chicago – Fashion; Children – Fashion; Clothing and Dress; Costume Jewelry; Ethnic Groups – Fashion; Europe – Fashion; Fashion Designers; Film and Filmmakers; Germany – Fashion; Hair Styles; Holidays – Fashion; Jewelry Makers; Los Angeles – Fashion; Mail-Order Business; Makeup; Nashville – Music;

New York (City) – Fashion; Physical Fitness; Sport Clothes; Textile Fabrics; Travel – Fashion; Washington, D.C. – Fashion; Wedding Costume

Off-Whites are On Again. *Mademoiselle* (January 1990):98-103

One Perfect Piece. *Glamour* (March 1990):266-267

Our Annual Swimsuit Ratings. *Glamour* (June 1990):238-243

Paradise Found. *Harper's Bazaar* (March 1990):166-171

Par Excellence 1990. *Harper's Bazaar* (March 1990):202-207

Paris: Seasonal Perfection. *Harper's Bazaar* (January 1990):120-127

Perfect Whites. *Glamour* (July 1990):170-175

Pleasure Island. *Harper's Bazaar* (June 1990):118-123

Polar Effects. *Vogue* (November 1990):318-326

Portraits in Elegance. *Harper's Bazaar* (August 1990):152-157

The Power of Color. *Ladies' Home Journal* 107, No. 11 (November 1990):64-70

Prelude to Romance. *Glamour* (September 1990):312-315

Print It. *Vogue* (July 1990):162-167

Pure Form. *Harper's Bazaar* (February 1990):114-119

The Quest for the Perfect Winter Coat. Debra Wise. *Glamour* (October 1990):214

Quick Cachet. *Glamour* (October 1990):280-283

Quick Changes. *Harper's Bazaar* (September 1990):308-311

The Quilt Complex. *Mademoiselle* (September 1990):94 +

Radiant Wraps. *Harper's Bazaar* (November 1990):144-149

Ready-to-Go. *Redbook* 174, No. 5 (March 1990):103-107

Ready to Wear: A Clothes Encounter. Richard Atcheson. *Lear's* (October 1990):62-64

A Red Awakening. *Glamour* (February 1990):168-173

Reds: The New Red Revolution. Richard Alleman. *Vogue* (September 1990):552-573

Refinement Redux. *Glamour* (June 1990):256-261

Retroactive. *Harper's Bazaar* (July 1990):74-77

Retro '60s. Suzanne Bersch. *Lear's* (December 1990):108-111

Rich Touches. *Harper's Bazaar* (August 1990):148-157

Rodeo Days. Jon Etra. *Harper's Bazaar* (July 1990):54-57 +

Romantic Gestures. *Vogue* (December 1990):274-281

Saturday Night Style. *Glamour* (August 1990):184-191

Save It for a Rainy Day. *Ladies' Home Journal* 107, No. 4 (April 1990):39

Secrets of Style. *Ladies' Home Journal* 107, No. 11 (November 1990):202-208

Secret Wrap-Ture. *Harper's Bazaar* (May 1990):132-133

See Worthy. *Harper's Bazaar* (May 1990):54

7th On Sale. *Vogue* (September 1990):514

Sew Festive! *Essence* 21, No. 8 (December 1990):50-52

Sew Spring. *Essence* 20, No. 12 (April 1990):59-60

Sexy Marks the Spot. *Mademoiselle* (November 1990):72-76

Sheer Delights. *Lear's* (November 1990):132-135

Shine: Accessories. *Vogue* (September 1990):615-619

Shine: Leathers. *Vogue* (September 1990):610-614

Shine: Metallics. *Vogue* (September 1990):600-609

The Shine Factor. *Lear's* (December 1990):94-101

Shirt Sighted. *Harper's Bazaar* (June 1990):96-99

Shore Thing! *Essence* 21, No. 2 (June 1990):68-73

The Short Cuts. *Essence* 21, No. 3 (July 1990):9

Short Order. *Harper's Bazaar* (October 1990):214-219

The Shorts Circuit. *Harper's Bazaar* (January 1990):86-89

Signature Style. *Harper's Bazaar* (May 1990):144-149

Silver Streak. *Harper's Bazaar* (December 1990):144-151

Simpatico. Nelson W. Aldrich, Jr. *Lear's* (August 1990):90-97

Simple Pleasures. *Harper's Bazaar* (January 1990):128-131

<X2>'60s Something. Jody Shields. *Vogue* (August 1990):292-299

Soft for Day, Bright for Night. *Mademoiselle* (November 1990):56

Soft Petaling. *Harper's Bazaar* (March 1990):242

Softwear. *Essence* 21, No. 5 (September 1990):58-65

Soft Wear. *Lear's* (July 1990):110-115

Softwear. *Redbook* 174, No. 6 (April 1990):85-91

The Kings of Color: Lacroix. Georgina Howell. *Vogue* (September 1990):546-550+

The Kings of Color: Mizrahi. André Leon Talley. *Vogue* (September 1990):532-535

The Kings of Color: Ozbek. Stephanie Mansfield. *Vogue* (September 1990):536-541

The Kings of Color: Versace. Julia Reed. *Vogue* (September 1990):542-545

London after Dark. *Harper's Bazaar* (November 1990):201+

New American Couturiers. Bibliography. Cynthia Heimel. *Vogue* (January 1990):47-61

No Nonsense. Nelson W. Aldrich, Jr. *Lear's* (November 1990):104-107

Partners in Style. *Glamour* (September 1990):304-305

Predictions 1990. *Vogue* (January 1990):146-159

Roehm's Empire. Georgina Howell. *Vogue* (August 1990):352-359+

The '80s. Georgina Howell. *Vogue* (January 1990):214-220

Scented Treasures. Diane Sustandal. *Harper's Bazaar* (October 1990):101-120

Secrets of Style. *Ladies' Home Journal* 107, No. 11 (November 1990):202-208

Shapes of Things to Come. Julie Moline. *Harper's Bazaar* (February 1990):96

Shine: Leathers. *Vogue* (September 1990):610-614

Tailor's Daughter. *Essence* 20, No. 9 (January 1990):17

Top Women Designers. *Essence* 21, No. 3 (July 1990):70-77

View: DKNY. Julia Reed. *Vogue* (December 1990):111-114

View: Image Conscious. Jody Shields. *Vogue* (January 1990):40-42

View: The New Youthquake. Edited by Laurie Schechter. *Vogue* (September 1990):137+

Vogue: Point of View. *Vogue* (January 1990):145

Vogue Point of View: First Look at Fall. *Vogue* (August 1990):275

Vogue Point of View: Global Fashion. *Vogue* (September 1990):513

Vogue Point of View: The New Fashion Sense. *Vogue* (December 1990):247

<X2>"What I Like for Fall": Seven Designers Tell All. *Mademoiselle* (September 1990):90-92

**Fashion Designers–Activism.** *See also* Hamnett, Katherine (about)

7th On Sale. *Vogue* (September 1990):514

**Fashion Industry.** *See* Fashion Merchandising

**Fashion Merchandising.** *See also* Nicole Miller Limited

Fashion Workshop. *Glamour* (August 1990):163-166; (September 1990):227-230

Fashion Workshop: Sale. *Glamour* (December 1990):167-170

Fashion Workshop: What's Coming In, Going Out. *Glamour* (March 1990):201-204

Talking Fashion. Jonathan Van Meter. *Vogue* (September 1990):631-650

Traveling in Style. Debra Michals. *Harper's Bazaar* (July 1990):14-16

**Fashion Models**

Beauty Word of Mouth. *Glamour* (October 1990):37-40

Esmé: Behind the Smile. Lynn Snowden. *Mademoiselle* (June 1990):196-197+

Kim Alexis – First-Rate Mom and Beauty. Beth Weinhouse. *Redbook* 175, No. 1 (May 1990):12-14

Pretty Woman. Jonathan Van Meter. *Vogue* (October 1990):347+

Role Model. Laura Fissinger. *Harper's Bazaar* (August 1990):110-115

Role Models. Lois Joy Johnson. *Ladies' Home Journal* 107, No. 10 (October 1990):172-180

Say Cheese. Marshall Blonsky. *Lear's* (January 1990):70-75

Sexy, S'il Vous Plai3t! *Mademoiselle* (January 1990):126-133

Singular Sensations. *Harper's Bazaar* (March 1990):218-223

Spunky and Punky, Lauren Hutton Says Her Piece. Louise Bernikow. *Lear's* (October 1990):90-93+

Supermodel Cindy Crawford: In the Hot Look of Summer. Lois Joy Johnson. *Ladies' Home Journal* 107, No. 6 (June 1990):132-137

Wild at Heart. David Keeps. *Harper's Bazaar* (August 1990):140-143+

Women Right Now. *Glamour* (May 1990):109-112

**Fassihi, Theresa**

Taking Humor Seriously. *Executive Female* 13, No. 6 (November-December 1990):13-14

**Fat.** *See* Food – Fat Content; Obesity

**Fat Acceptance**

FAT LIP Readers Theatre. Laura Bock. *Woman of Power* 17 (Summer 1990):32-33

Fat Oppression and Psychotherapy: A Feminist Perspective. By Laura S. Brown and Esther D. Rothblum. Reviewed by Carol L. Hill. *Atlantis* 15, No. 2 (Spring 1990):114-115

Fat-Oppressive Attitude and the Feminist Therapist: Fat Oppression. Laura S. Brown. *Woman of Power* 18 (Fall 1990):64-68

Living Large, Getting Fit. E. K. Daufin. *Essence* 21, No. 4 (August 1990):20-25

**Father-Daughter Incest.** *See* Incest

**Father-Daughter Relationships.** *See also* Family-Owned Business

Daddy's Girls and the Fathers Who Adore Them. Eric Goodman. *McCall's* 117, No. 9 (June 1990):94-96+

Father Love. Betty Winston Baye. *Essence* 21, No. 2 (June 1990):34+

Interiors: The Other Woman. Joan Morgan. *Essence* 21, No. 7 (November 1990):34+

Irving Berlin. Mary Ellin Barrett. *Lear's* (June 1990):84-92+

Only Daughter. Sandra Cisneros. *Glamour* (November 1990):256+

**Fathers.** *See also* Divorce–Custody; Parenting

Daddy's Home: Reflections of a Family Man. By Steven Schnur. Reviewed by Rachel Kadish. *Lilith* 15, No. 4 (Fall 1990):34

The Flip Side: Looking for a Few Good Men. Richard Chevat. *Family Circle* 103, No. 9 (June 26, 1990):12

The Teflon Father. Letty Cottin Pogrebin. *Ms.* 1, No. 2 (September/October 1990):95-96

When Dad Won't Discipline. Benjamin Spock. *Redbook* 176, No. 1 (November 1990):38

**Fathers, Adolescent**

Parental Responsibility of African-American Unwed Adolescent Fathers. Kenneth Christmon. *Adolescence* 25, No. 99 (Fall 1990):645-653

**Fathers–Humor**

Laugh with Father. Ellen Byron. *Redbook* 175, No. 2 (June 1990):59-63

**Father-Son Relationships**

Father Hunger. Michel Marriott. *Essence* 21, No. 7 (November 1990):73-74+

His: Spring Training. Daniel Asa Rose. *Glamour* (June 1990):264

Talking with Sylvester Stallone: "My Sons are My Life." Interview. Carol Lynn Mithers. *Redbook* 176, No. 2 (December 1990):32-34

**Fatigue**

Foods to Stay Awake By. Shifra Diamond. *Mademoiselle* (December 1990):106

**Fat Oppression.** *See* Fat Acceptance

**Fats.** *See* Food–Fat Content

**Fat Substitutes.** *See also* Nutrition

Diet News: These Fats Are Guaranteed Fakes. Ellen Kunes. *Mademoiselle* (June 1990):204

**Faue, Elizabeth**

Like a Family: The Making of a Southern Cotton Mill World. Book review. *Signs* 15, No. 2 (Winter 1990):391-394

Once a Cigar Maker: Men, Women and Work Culture in American Cigar Factories, 1900-1919. Book review. *Signs* 15, No. 2 (Winter 1990):391-394

Women Adrift: Independent Wage Earners in Chicago, 1880-1930. Book review. *Signs* 15, No. 2 (Winter 1990):391-394

**Faulkner, Audrey**

On the Lookout: A Model Project in Support of AFFILIA. *AFFILIA* 5, No. 3 (Fall 1990):101-104

**Faulkner, Jan**

Domestic Tyranny. Book Review. *AFFILIA* 5, No. 1 (Spring 1990):123-124

**Faurie, Wanda C.**

Prediction of Length of Hospitalization of Adolescent Psychiatric Inpatients Utilizing the Pd Scale of the MMPI and Demographic Data. *Adolescence* 25, No. 98 (Summer 1990):305-310

**Fausto-Sterling, Anne**

Making Science Masculine. *The Women's Review of Books* 7, No. 7 (April 1990):13-14

The Mind Has No Sex? Women in the Origins of Modern Science. Book Review. *The Women's Review of Books* 7, No. 7 (April 1990):13-14

**Fawcett, Farrah** (about). *See also* Beauty, Personal, "Beauty Bazaar"

Talking with Farrah Fawcett: "I'm My Own Woman." Interview. Glenn Plaskin. *Redbook* 175, No. 4 (August 1990):22-24

**Fax Machines.** *See* Facsimile Transmission

**Fay, Julie**

The Night Before. Poem. *The Women's Review of Books* 7, No. 6 (March 1990):24

The Night of Your Funeral. Poem. *The Women's Review of Books* 7, No. 6 (March 1990):24

**Fay, Mary Ann**

Wild Thorns. Book Review. *Belles Lettres* 5, No. 3 (Spring 1990):12

**Fayer, Joan M.**

Feminist Theory in Practice and Process. Book Review. *Women & Language* 13, No. 2 (Winter 1990):42

**Fear**

The Female Fear. By Margaret T. Gordon and Stephanie Riger. Reviewed by Karen Merriam. *AFFILIA* 5, No. 3 (Fall 1990):114-115

**Fears**

Private Lives. Janice Billingsley. *Family Circle* 103, No. 11 (August 14, 1990):64+

**Fears, Linda**

Bringing Up Baby: A Child's Room that Grows. *Ladies' Home Journal* 107, No. 6 (June 1990):76-78

Recycling Made Easy. Bibliography. *Ladies' Home Journal* 107, No. 10 (October 1990):136-141

**Federal Communications Commission – Pornography Control**

FCC Turns Up Heat on 'Indecent' Radio Content. *Media Report to Women* 18, No. 1 (January/February 1990):4

**Federal Emergency Management Agency.** *See also* Disaster Relief

**Federico, Ellen** (about)

Sowing the Free Sample. Ingrid Eisenstadter. *Executive Female* 13, No. 4 (July-August 1990):11-12

**Feelings.** *See* Emotions

**Feet – Care and Hygiene.** *See* Foot – Care and Hygiene

**Feibleman, Peter**

The Bonsai Connection. *Lear's* (April 1990):38-42

Classic Carly. *Lear's* (December 1990):90-93+

Depression Envy. *Lear's* (December 1990):76-77+

Fired Up, or Fear of Flugging. *Lear's* (July 1990):47-48

How to Be Rude Without Really Trying. *Lear's* (May 1990):49-51

How to Make Love from Potatoes. *Lear's* (November 1990):108-111+

Now, Now, Voyager: A Traveler's Lament. *Lear's* (June 1990):24-26

Relative Time. *Lear's* (October 1990):94-95+

A Sea Change: His Ship Came In. *Lear's* (November 1990):70-72

Total Recoil: Babes at Sea. *Lear's* (January 1990):27-29

Total Recoil: Downstairs, Upstairs. *Lear's* (February 1990):38-41

Total Recoil: How to Look Sick and Stay Healthy. *Lear's* (September 1990):44-46

Total Recoil. *Lear's* (August 1990):53-56

Where's the Beep? *Lear's* (March 1990):48-52

**Feinberg, Harriet**

A Pioneering Dutch Feminist Views Egypt: Aletta Jacobs's Travel Letters. *Feminist Issues* 10, No. 2 (Fall 1990):65-78

**Feineman, Neil**

Roll into Shape. *Women's Sports & Fitness* 12, No. 6 (September 1990):50-53

**Feiner, Susan F.** and Morgan, Barbara A.

Women and Minorities in Introductory Economics Textbooks: 1974 to 1984. *Women's Studies Quarterly* 18, Nos. 3-4 (Fall-Winter 1990):46-67

**Feiner, Susan F.** and Roberts, Bruce B.

Hidden by the Invisible Hand: Neoclassical Economic Theory and the Textbook Treatment of Race and Gender. *Gender and Society* 4, No. 2 (June 1990):159-181

**Feinstein, Dianne** (about)

Dianne Feinstein: Charismatic Centrist. Jody Becker. *McCall's* 117, No. 9 (June 1990):70-74

**Feld, David**

Tables: All Set. Bibliography. *Mademoiselle* (December 1990):68+

**Felder, Leonard**

Private Lives. *Family Circle* 103, No. 12 (September 4, 1990):40+

**Felder, Raoul Lionel**

Dollars & Divorce: How to Get What You Deserve. *Harper's Bazaar* (August 1990):144-147

**Felder, Sara**

In a Cafe. *Lilith* 15, No. 4 (Fall 1990):26-27

**Feldman, Beverly**

Raising Kids with Good Values: 10 Golden Rules. *Redbook* 176, No. 1 (November 1990):116-120

**Feldman, Trude B.**

Secrets of a Happy Marriage. *Family Circle* 103, No. 1 (January 9, 1990):55+

**Feldman-Summers, Shirley**

The Family Interpreted: Feminist Theory in Clinical Practice. Book Review. *Women and Therapy* 9, No. 4 (1990):116-119

**Feldstein, Richard** and Roof, Judith (editors)

Feminism and Psychoanalysis. Reviewed by Joonok Huh. *NWSA Journal* 2, No. 3 (Summer 1990):511-514

**Fellingham, Christine**

Shopping Smart. *Glamour* (June 1990):202+

**Fellman, Anita Clair**

Laura Ingalls Wilder and Rose Wilder Lane: The Politics of a Mother-Daughter Relationship. Notes. *Signs* 15, No. 3 (Spring 1990):535-561

**Felman, Jyl Lynn**

Absence. *Bridges* 1, No. 2 (Fall 1990): 63-68

**Felski, Rita**

Beyond Feminist Aesthetics: Feminist Literature and Social Change. Reviewed by Jane Kneller. *Hypatia* 5, No. 3 (Fall 1990):165-168

**Female Circumcision**

Female Circumcision in Africa: Not Just a Medical Problem. Kathleen Kilday. *Iris* 23 (Spring-Summer 1990):38-43

Female Genital Mutilation: Facts and Strategies for Eradication. Fran P. Hosken. *Woman of Power* 18 (Fall 1990):42-45

U.N. Appeals an International Crime Against Women. *Ms.* 1, No. 1 (July/August 1990):12-13

**Female-Female Relationships**

Best Friends. Debra Kent. *Family Circle* 103, No. 5 (April 3, 1990):62-66

Between Women: Love, Envy and Competition in Women's Friendships. By Luise Eichenbaum and Susie Orbach. Reviewed by Hannah Lerman. *Psychology of Women Quarterly* 14, No. 1 (March 1990):149-150

The Cat Is Back: The Dirty Little Secret of Women's Competition. Elizabeth Kay. *Mademoiselle* (February 1990):120-127

Trashing Women. Rosie Summers. *off our backs* 20, No. 7 (July 1990):22

**Female Friendships.** *See* Female-Female Relationships

**Female Impersonators**

Lana's "Imitation": Melodramatic Repetition and the Gender Performative. Judith Butler. *Genders* 9 (Fall 1990):1-18

**Female-Male Relationships.** *See also* Couples; Domestic Relations; Fighting (Psychology); Men – Psychology; Misogyny; Personal Relationships; Sexual Relationships

About Men. By Phyllis Chesler. Reviewed by Beverly Lowy. *On the Issues* 14 (1990):25

The Answer Couple. Ann Hood and Bob Reiss. *Glamour* (May 1990):136; (July 1990):96-97; (September 1990):166; (November 1990):146-147

The Answer Couple. Betsy Evans and Todd Nelson. *Glamour* (March 1990):152

The Answer Couple. Bob Reiss and Ann Hood. *Glamour* (June 1990):164-165; (August 1990):118-119; (October 1990):141; (December 1990):152-153

Beyond Patriarchy: Essays by Men on Pleasure, Power, and Change. Edited by James A. Doyle. Reviewed by James A. Doyle. *Gender and Society* 4, No. 1 (March 1990):117-118

Boyfriends and Gifts: Present Tense. Ellen Welty. *Mademoiselle* (December 1990):116

Can This Marriage Be Saved? "We're in Love Again." Margery D. Rosen. *Ladies' Home Journal* 107, No. 11 (November 1990):28-34

Casanova Slept Here . . . and You Had to Make the Bed. Judy Bachrach. *Savvy Woman* (June 1990):58-59

Couple Time. *Glamour* (February 1990):104; (March 1990):132; (May 1990):172; (June 1990):142; (July 1990):90; (August 1990):126; (October 1990):148; (November 1990):136

The Dance of Intimacy. By Harriet Goldhor Lerner. Reviewed by Barbara G. Collins. *AFFILIA* 5, No. 3 (Fall 1990):122-124

Editorial: 27 Mini-Gripes That Can Split Any Couple's Seams. *Glamour* (February 1990):72

Falling Out of Love. Susan Jacoby. *Glamour* (November 1990):238+

Flirting for the Fun of it. Louise Lague. *Glamour* (March 1990):242-243+

Give Your Mate a Break. Linda Lee Small. *Working Mother* 13, No. 4 (April 1990):24-28

The Great American Date. *Glamour* (February 1990):176-179

Health & Mind. Pamela Erens. *Glamour* (February 1990):46-51

Healthy Love. Lesley Dormen. *Glamour* (October 1990):270-271+

The Hidden Message Behind Gifts. Linda Lee Small. *Working Mother* (December 1990):14-18

His: Blind Dates. David Seeley. *Mademoiselle* (June 1990):83

How Can Cupid Be So Stupid? Judy Bachrach. *Savvy Woman* (February 1990):56-58, 92

How Early to Bed? The New Sexual Timetables. Ellen Welty. *Mademoiselle* (June 1990):172-173+

How Romance Can Wreck an Office. Salley Shannon. *Working Mother* 13, No. 9 (September 1990):22-27

How to Know it's Over. Meredith Berkman. *Glamour* (November 1990):239

If This Isn't Love, It Could Be a Fix. John Bradshaw. *Lear's* (September 1990):79-80

If You Want Love to Last, Choose Smart. Excerpt. Maurice Yaffé and Elizabeth Fenwick. *Essence* 21, No. 5 (September 1990):85

<X2>"I Give So Much and Get So Little." Mary Ellen Donavan and William P. Ryan. *Working Mother* 13, No. 1 (January 1990):26-31

I'll Lie to Make You Like Me. Skip Hollandsworth. *Mademoiselle* (November 1990):85

Why Can't a Woman Be More Like a Man? John O'Sullivan. *Savvy Woman* (February 1990):59-60, 92

Women, Words, and Men: Excerpts from the Diary of Mary Guion. Martha Tomhave Blauvelt. *Journal of Women's History* 2, No. 2 (Fall 1990):177-184

Women and Love: A Cultural Revolution in Progress. By Shere Hite. Reviewed by Rosemary Coates. *Healthright* 9, No. 2 (February 1990):37

Women Who Work Too Much . . . and the Men Who Love Them. *Mademoiselle* (August 1990):217, 238-240

On Your Own: Can your Relationship Survive This Party Season? Judith Stone. *Glamour* (January 1990):68

On Your Own: Don't Wait for the Last Straw. Judith Stone. *Glamour* (March 1990):122

On Your Own. Judith Stone. *Glamour* (June 1990):146

### Female-Male Relationships – Communication

Image Metaphors of Women and Men in Personal Relationships. William Foster Owen. *Women's Studies in Communication* 12, No. 2 (Fall 1989):37-57

### Female-Male Relationships – Feminist Perspectives

Popular Advice to Women: A Feminist Perspective. Mary Ann Jimenez and Susan Rice. *AFFILIA* 5, No. 3 (Fall 1990):8-26

### Female-Male Relationships – Humor

Farewell, My Hostess. John Leo. *McCall's* 118, No. 2 (November 1990):24

How to Make Love from Potatoes. Peter Feibleman. *Lear's* (November 1990):108-111+

The Prattle of the Sexes. John Leo. *McCall's* 117, No. 7 (April 1990):98-99

### Female Voice

The Acoustic Mirror: The Female Voice in Psychoanalysis and Cinema. By Kaja Silverman. Reviewed by Paula Rabinowitz. *Feminist Studies* 16, No. 1 (Spring 1990):151-169

Shapes of a World Not Realized: Virginia Woolf and the Possibility of a Female Voice. Margaret Mappin. *Australian Feminist Studies* No. 11 (Autumn 1990):75-86

**Feminine Hygiene.** *See* Menstruation

**Feminism.** *See also* African American Women – Feminism; Lawyers – Feminism; Third World Women – Feminism

Beyond Separate Spheres: Feminism and Family Research. Myra Marx Ferree. *Journal of Marriage and the Family* 52, No. 4 (November 1990):866-884

Do You Have to Be a Lesbian to Be a Feminist? Marilyn Frye. *off our backs* 20, No. 8 (August/September 1990):21-23

A Fearful Freedom: Women's Flight from Equality. By Wendy Kaminer. Reviewed by Louise Armstrong. *The Women's Review of Books* 8, No. 2 (November 1990):9-10

Feminism: Freedom from Wifism. By Mia Albright. Reviewed by Margaret Maxwell. *On the Issues* 15 (Summer 1990):29-30

Feminism within American Institutions: Unobtrusive Mobilization in the 1980s. Mary Fainsod Katzenstein. *Signs* 16, No. 1 (Autumn 1990):27-54

Journeys in Our Lives: Learning Feminism. Michelle Brodsky, MyKela Loury, Abby Markowitz, Eden E. Torres, and Lauren Wilson. *NWSA Journal* 2, No. 1 (Winter 1990):79-100

On the New Psychology of Women: A Cautionary View. Marcia C. Westkott. *Feminist Issues* 10, No. 2 (Fall 1990):3-18

Open Letter to Sonia Johnson. Pat Gowens. *off our backs* 20, No. 1 (January 1990):15

A Politics of Intimate Life: A Funny Thing Happened on the Way Through the Eighties. Roberta Hamilton. *Atlantis* 15, No. 2 (Spring 1990):82-89

The Sexual Liberals and the Attack on Feminism. Edited by Dorchen Leidholdt and Janice Raymond. Reviewed by Victoria Kahn. *The Women's Review of Books* 7, No. 5 (February 1990):16

Wake Me When It's Over. Wendy Crisp. *Executive Female* 13, No. 4 (July-August 1990):80

Where the Meanings Are: Feminism and Cultural Spaces. By Catharine Stimpson. Reviewed by Evelyn S. Newlyn. *Women's Studies International Forum* 13, No. 6 (1990):613-614

### Feminism – Bibliographies

Philosophical Feminism: A Bibliographic Guide to Critiques of Science. Alison Wylie, Kathleen Okruhlik, Sandra Morton, and Leslie Thielen-Wilson. *Resources for Feminist Research* 19, No. 2 (June 1990):2-36

### Feminism, Cultural

The Politics of Difference. Hazel V. Carby. *Ms.* 1, No. 2 (September/October 1990):84-85

### Feminism – Ethnography

Can There Be A Feminist Ethnography? Lila Abu-Lughod. *Women and Performance: A Journal of Feminist Theory* 5, No. 1, Issue #9 (1990): 7-27

### Feminism – History

Comrades and Sisters: Feminism, Socialism and Pacifism in Europe, 1870-1945. By Richard J. Evans. Reviewed by Claudia Koonz. *Gender & History* 2, No. 1 (Spring 1990):120-122

History of the Meetings. Ana Maria Portugal. *Women in Action* 3 & 4 (1990):18-19

The Lady and the Tiger: Women's Electoral Activism in New York City Before Suffrage. S. Sara Monoson. *Journal of Women's History* 2, No. 2 (Fall 1990):100-135

<X2>"Men Must Be Educated and Women Must Do It": The National Federation (Later Union) of Women Teachers and Contemporary Feminism 1910-30. Hilda Kean and Alison Oram. *Gender and Education* 2, No. 2 (1990):147-167

A Might-Have-Been: Feminism in Eighteenth-Century France. Catherine Rubinger. *Atlantis* 15, No. 2 (Spring 1990):59-68

NWSA Workshop: Women of Color on Feminist Knowledge. Jennie Ruby. *off our backs* 20, No. 8 (August/September 1990):19-20

A Pioneering Dutch Feminist Views Egypt: Aletta Jacobs's Travel Letters. Harriet Feinberg. *Feminist Issues* 10, No. 2 (Fall 1990):65-78

**Feminism, Marxist**

Revolutionary Popular Feminism in Nicaragua: Articulating Class, Gender, and National Sovereignty. Norma Stoltz Chinchilla. *Gender and Society* 4, No. 3 (September 1990):370-397

**Feminism – Prostitution**

Prostitution and Feminism. *Women's World* , No. 24 (Winter 1990/91): 6-7

**Feminism, Radical**

Authenticity and Fiction in Law: Contemporary Case Studies Exploring Radical Legal Feminism. Sarah Slavin. *Journal of Women's History* 1, No. 3 (Winter 1990):123-159

Daring to Be Bad: Radical Feminism in America 1967-1975. By Alice Echols. Reviewed by Susan E. Davis. *New Directions for Women* 19, No. 5 (September-October 1990):14

Radical Women National Conference: A Cold Shower. Dianne Post. *off our backs* 20, No. 6 (June 1990):10-11

Radical Women National Conference: The Third Wave of Feminism. Roanne Hindin. *off our backs* 20, No. 6 (June 1990):9

**Feminism – Theory.** *See also* Communication – Gender Differences; Engels, Friedrich (about); Knowledge, Theory of; Medical Ethics; Women's Studies

<X2>"Am I That Name?" Feminism and the Category of 'Women' in History. By Denise Riley. Reviewed by Kelly Oliver. *NWSA Journal* 2, No. 4 (Autumn 1990):674-675

Animal Rights and Feminist Theory. Notes. Josephine Donovan. *Signs* 15, No. 2 (Winter 1990):350-375

Between Theory and Fiction: Reflections on Feminism and Classical Scholarship. Ruth Padel. *Gender & History* 2, No. 2 (Summer 1990):198-211

Beyond Women's Issues: Feminism and Social Work. Miriam L. Freeman. *AFFILIA* 5, No. 2 (Summer 1990):72-89

Challenges and Proposals for Feminists in the '90s. *Women in Action* 3 & 4 (1990):20-23

Comment on Hawkesworth's "Knowers, Knowing, Known: Feminist Theory and Claims of Truth." Debra Shogan. *Signs* 15, No. 2 (Winter 1990):424-425

Comment on Hawkesworth's "Knowers, Knowing, Known: Feminist Theory and Claims of Truth." Notes. Susan Hekman. *Signs* 15, No. 2 (Winter 1990):417-419

Conference Call. Barbara Christian, Ann DuCille, Sharon Marcus, Elaine Marks, Nancy K. Miller, and others. *Differences* 2, No. 3 (Fall 1990):52-108

The Difference Within: Feminism and Critical Theory. Edited by Elizabeth Meese and Alice Parker. Reviewed by Amanda Leslie-Spinks. *The Women's Review of Books* 7, No. 8 (May 1990):15-16

Directing Traffic: Subjects, Objects, and the Politics and Exchange. Karen Newman. *Differences* 2, No. 2 (Summer 1990):41-54

Discipline and Vanish: Feminism, the Resistance to Theory, and the Politics of Cultural Studies. Ellen Rooney. *Differences* 2, No. 3 (Fall 1990):14-28

Eccentric Subjects: Feminist Theory and Historical Consciousness. Teresa De Lauretis. *Feminist Studies* 16, No. 1 (Spring 1990):115-150

Epistemological and Methodological Commitments of a Feminist Perspective. Marlene G. Fine. *Women & Language* 13, No. 2 (Winter 1990):35-36

The Everyday World as Problematic: A Feminist Sociology. By Dorothy Smith. Reviewed by Wendy Luttrell. *Signs* 15, No. 3 (Spring 1990):635-640

Feminism and Foucault: Reflections on Resistance. Edited by Irene Diamond and Lee Quinby. Reviewed by Mary Janell Metzger. *Hypatia* 5, No. 3 (Fall 1990):118-124

Feminism and Individualism. Shane Phelan. *Women & Politics* 10, No. 4 (1990):1-18

Feminism and Methodology: Social Science Issues. Edited by Sandra Harding. Reviewed by Susan J. Hekman. *Women & Politics* 10, No. 1 (1990):71-73

Feminism and the Constructions of Knowledge: Speculations on a Subjective Science. Georganne Rundblad. *Women & Language* 13, No. 1 (Fall 1990):53-55

Feminism as Critique: On the Politics of Gender. Edited by Seyla Benhabib and Drucilla Cornell. Reviewed by Mary Janell Metzger. *Hypatia* 5, No. 3 (Fall 1990):118-124

Feminism Unmodified: Discourses on Life and Law. By Catharine A. MacKinnon. Reviewed by Kathleen B. Jones. *Women & Politics* 10, No. 1 (1990):73-76

Feminist Practice and Poststructuralist Theory. By Chris Weedon. Reviewed by Wendy Luttrell. *Signs* 15, No. 3 (Spring 1990):635-640

Feminist Theory: Notes from the Third Decade. Carol Anne Douglas. *off our backs* 20, No. 2 (February 1990):24

Feminist Theory and the Philosophies of Man. By Andrea Nye. Reviewed by Linda Bell. *Hypatia* 5, No. 1 (Spring 1990):127-132

Feminist Theory in Practice and Process. Edited by Micheline R. Malson and others. Reviewed by Joan M. Fayer. *Women & Language* 13, No. 2 (Winter 1990):42

Feminist Thought: A Comprehensive Introduction. By Rosemarie Tong. Reviewed by Phyllis Eckhaus. *AFFILIA* 5, No. 3 (Fall 1990):121-122

Gender and Power. By R. W. Connell. Reviewed by Wendy Luttrell. *Signs* 15, No. 3 (Spring 1990):635-640

Gynocritics/La Gynocritique. Edited by Barbara Godard. Reviewed by Janet M. Paterson. *Resources for Feminist Research* 19, No. 1 (March 1990):19

Inessential Woman. Elizabeth V. Spelman. *Woman of Power* 16 (Spring 1990):24-27

Inessential Woman: Problems of Exclusion in Feminist Thought. By Elizabeth V. Spelman. Reviewed by Elaine Marks. *Tulsa Studies in Women's Literature* 9, No. 2 (Fall 1990):309-314

Interpreting Women's Lives: Feminist Theory and Personal Narratives. Edited by the Personal Narratives Group. Reviewed by Norma Schulman. *Women & Language* 13, No. 2 (Winter 1990):43

The Lie of the Feminist Right Wing Ethic. Shirley Hartwell. *Trivia* 16/17 (Fall 1990):68-80

The Meaning of a Multicultural Perspective for Theory-Building in Feminist Therapy. Laura S. Brown. *Women and Therapy* 9, Nos. 1-2 (1990):1-21

Moments of Writing: Is there a Feminist Auto/Biography? Notes. Liz Stanley. *Gender & History* 2, No. 1 (Spring 1990):58-67

Oppression and Victimization; Choice and Responsibility. Susan Wendell. *Hypatia* 5, No. 3 (Fall 1990):15-46

Paths Toward Diversity: An Intrapsychic Perspective. Susan E. Barrett. *Women and Therapy* 9, Nos. 1-2 (1990):41-52

Politics of Aging: I'm Not Your Mother. Barbara Macdonald. *Ms.* 1, No. 1 (July/August 1990):56-58

Race and Gender in Feminist Theory. Carrie Jane Singleton. *Sage* 6, No. 1 (Summer 1989):12-17

Reply to Hekman. Notes. Mary E. Hawkesworth. *Signs* 15, No. 2 (Winter 1990):420-423

Reply to Shogan. Mary E. Hawkesworth. *Signs* 15, No. 2 (Winter 1990):426-428

Reproducing the World: Essays in Feminist Theory. By Mary O'Brien. Reviewed by Christine Di Stefano. *Women & Politics* 10, No. 4 (1990):138-140

Reproducing the World: Essays in Feminist Theory. By Mary O'Brien. Reviewed by Elizabeth Kamarck Minnich. *Signs* 16, No. 1 (Autumn 1990):177-180

Reproducing the World: Essays in Feminist Theory. By Mary O'Brien. Reviewed by Juanne N. Clarke. *Atlantis* 15, No. 2 (Spring 1990):118

Reproducing the World: Essays in Feminist Theory. By Mary O'Brien. Reviewed by Julia Miles. *Atlantis* 15, No. 2 (Spring 1990):118-120

The Sexual Politics of Meat: A Feminist-Vegetarian Critical Theory. By Carol J. Adams. Reviewed by Kore Archer. *New Directions for Women* 19, No. 4 (July-August 1990):19

Signature Pieces: On the Institution of Authorship. By Peggy Kamuf. Reviewed by Elaine Marks. *Tulsa Studies in Women's Literature* 9, No. 2 (Fall 1990):309-314

Status and Contract in Feminist Legal Theory of the Family: A Reply to Bartlett. Janet L. Dolgin. *Women's Rights Law Reporter* 12, No. 2 (Summer 1990): 103-113

Taking Our Time: Feminist Perspectives on Temporality. Edited by Frieda Johles Forman. Reviewed by Susan S. Arpad. *NWSA Journal* 2, No. 2 (Spring 1990):311-314

Talking Back: Thinking Feminist – Thinking Black. By Bell Hooks. Reviewed by Gesche Peters. *Atlantis* 15, No. 2 (Spring 1990):109-111

Tapestries of Life: Women's Work, Women's Consciousness, and the Meaning of Daily Existence. By Bettina Aptheker. Reviewed by Hester Eisenstein. *New Directions for Women* 19, No. 3 (May/June 1990):17

Tapestries of Life: Women's Work, Women's Consciousness, and the Meaning of Daily Experience. By Bettina Aptheker. Reviewed by Susan S. Arpad. *NWSA Journal* 2, No. 2 (Spring 1990):311-314

<X2>'The Trouble Is It's Ahistorical: The Problem of the Unconscious in Modern Feminist Theory. Rosalind Minsky. *Feminist Review* No. 36 (Autumn 1990):4-14

Toward a Feminist Perspective in Public Administration Theory. Camilla Stivers. *Women & Politics* 10, No. 4 (1990):49-65

Toward a Feminist Theory of the State. By Catharine A. MacKinnon. Reviewed by Eleanor J. Bader. *On the Issues* 14 (1990):26-28

Toward a Feminist Theory of the State. By Catharine MacKinnon. Reviewed by Deborah Schwenck. *Women's Rights Law Reporter* 12, No. 3 (Fall 1990): 205-208

Towards a Politics of Location: Rethinking Marginality. Joan Borsa. *Canadian Women's Studies* 11, No. 1 (Spring 1990):36-39

Using Arendt and Heidegger to Consider Feminist Thinking on Women and Reproductive/Infertility Technologies. Maren Klawiter. *Hypatia* 5, No. 3 (Fall 1990):65-89

Women, Reason, Etc. Miche4le Le Doeuff. *Differences* 2, No. 3 (Fall 1990):1-13

Women, Social Science and Public Policy. Edited by Jacqueline Goodnow and Carole Pateman. Reviewed by Helen Liggett. *Women & Politics* 10, No. 3 (1990):127-129

Women and a New Academy: Gender and Cultural Contexts. By Jean F. O'Barr. Reviewed by Gloria Bowles. *NWSA Journal* 2, No. 2 (Spring 1990):288-290

Women and the Ideal Society: Plato's Republic and Modern Myths of Gender. By Natalie Harris Bluestone. Reviewed by Mary Dietz. *Women & Politics* 10, No. 1 (1990):80-82

### Feminism – Theory – Periodicals

Inscriptions, nos. 3/4 (1900). Reviewed by Irvin Cemil Schick. *Feminist Studies* 16, No. 2 (Summer 1990):345-380

### Feminist Clinics

Does Corporate Giant Fill Health Care Needs Like Feminist Clinics? Jill Benderly. *New Directions for Women* 19, No. 1 (January/February 1990):13

Feminist Clinics Lose Out to Profit-Making Clones. Jill Benderly. *New Directions for Women* 19, No. 1 (January/February 1990):3 +

### Feminist Cultural Studies. See Women's Studies – Curricula

**Feminist Epistemology.** See Epistemology, Feminist; Feminism – Theory

### Feminist Ethics

Beyond Revolt: A Horizon for Feminist Ethics. J. Ralph Lindgren. *Hypatia* 5, No. 1 (Spring 1990):145-150

Further Notes on Feminist Ethics and Pluralism: A Reply to Lindgren. Margaret Urban Walker. *Hypatia* 5, No. 1 (Spring 1990):151-155

**Feminist Movement.** See also Female-Male Relationships – Feminist Perspectives; Greece – Feminist Movement – History; Japan – Feminist Movement; National Organization for Women; South Africa

Claiming the Future. Mary Catherine Bateson. *Lear's* (February 1990):84-87

Editorial: Feminist Paradoxes and the Need for New Agendas. Betty Sancier. *AFFILIA* 5, No. 2 (Summer 1990):5-7

Editorial: On Feminism in Action. Betty Sancier. *AFFILIA* 5, No. 4 (Winter 1990):5-7

Editorial: What's in a Name? Betty Sancier. *AFFILIA* 5, No. 3 (Fall 1990):5-7

Future Feminist Movements. Bell Hooks. *off our backs* 20, No. 2 (February 1990):9

One World Women's Movement. By Chilla Bulbeck. Reviewed by Mamie E. Locke. *Women & Politics* 10, No. 4 (1990):135-136

One World Women's Movement. By Chilla Bulbeck. Reviewed by Shahnaz Khan. *Resources for Feminist Research* 19, No. 1 (March 1990):26

Radical Voices. Edited by Renate D. Klein and Deborah Lynn Steinberg. Reviewed by Carol Anne Douglas. *off our backs* 20, No. 4 (April 1990):18

Rethinking Feminist Organizations. Patricia Yancey Martin. *Gender and Society* 4, No. 2 (June 1990):182-206

Women in the World: 1975-1985, The Women's Decade. Edited by Lynne B. Iglitzin and Ruth Ross. Reviewed by Jane Bayes. *Women & Politics* 10, No. 3 (1990):125-127

### Feminist Movement – History

Love, Friendship, and Feminism in Later 19th-Century England. Philippa Levine. *Women's Studies International Forum* 13, Nos. 1-2 (1990):63-78

The Women's Movement in the Church of England, 1850-1930. By Brian Heeney. Reviewed by John Wolffe. *Gender & History* 2, No. 2 (Summer 1990):236-237

### Feminist Movement – Latin America

Women and Social Change in Latin America. Edited by Elizabeth Jelin. Reviewed by Susana Lastarria-Cornhiel and Wava G. Haney. *Feminist Collections* 12, No. 1 (Fall 1990):9-13

Women-Centered Media Communications within Nicaragua. Angharad N. Valdivia. *Women & Language* 13, No. 1 (Fall 1990):59-63

The Women's Movement in Latin America: Feminism and the Transition to Democracy. Edited by Jane S. Jaquette. Reviewed by Susana Lastarria-Cornhiel and Wava G. Haney. *Feminist Collections* 12, No. 1 (Fall 1990):9-13

### Feminist Movement – Pornography Control

Campaign Against Pornography. Barbara Norden. *Feminist Review* No. 35 (Summer 1990):1-8

Campaign Against Pornography. *Feminist Review* No. 34 (Spring 1990):42-46

Feminism and Pornography. Kate Ellis, Barbara O'Dair, and Abby Tallmer. *Feminist Review* No. 36 (Autumn 1990):15-18

Ideological Contours of the Contemporary Pornography Debate: Divisions and Alliances. Ronald J. Berger, Patricia Searles, and Charles E. Cottle. *Frontiers* 11, Nos. 2-3 (1990):30-38

Washington Jails Nikki Craft for Ripping Up *Esquire*. Lucy Colvin. *off our backs* 20, No. 7 (July 1990):1+

### Feminist Music

Closer to Home. By Jamie Anderson. Reviewed by Lynn Wenzel. *New Directions for Women* 19, No. 3 (May/June 1990):8

### Feminist Organizations

Networking: New Groups. *Women in Action* 3 & 4 (1990):34-35

Women and Ecology. *Women in Action* 3 & 4 (1990):47-52

### Feminist Organizations – Division of Labor

Free Riding, Alternative Organization and Cultural Feminism: The Case of Seneca Women's Peace Camp. Peregrine Schwartz-Shea and Debra D. Burrington. *Women & Politics* 10, No. 3 (1990):1-37

### Feminist Organizations – Funding

Women and Funding. *Women in Action* 3 & 4 (1990):36-42

### Feminist Publications. *See also* Nicaragua – Feminism

Books: World-Class Pleasures. Marilyn French. *Ms.* 1, No. 1 (July/August 1990):66-67

On the Lookout. *AFFILIA* 5, No. 2 (Summer 1990):97-99; 5, No. 4 (Winter 1990):101-104

Prototype Newspaper for Women Circulated at ASNE Convention. *Media Report to Women* 18, No. 3 (May/June 1990):3

### Feminist Publications – Bibliographies

Publications of Interest. Bibliography. *Signs* 15, No. 2 (Winter 1990):429-432; 15, No. 3 (Spring 1990):662-665; 15, No. 4 (Summer 1990):884-886

Resources. *Women in Action* 3 & 4 (1990):62-64

### Feminist Scholarship. *See also* Feminism – Theory; Women's Studies Curricula

Autonomy as Emotion: The Phenomenology of Independence in Academic Women. Niza Yanay and Beverly Birns. *Women's Studies International Forum* 13, No. 3 (1990):249-260

Feminist Cultural Studies: Questions for the 1990s. Anne Balsamo and Paula A. Treichler. *Women & Language* 13, No. 1 (Fall 1990):3-6

Feminist Sociology. By Janet Saltzman. Reviewed by Barbara Lou Fenby. *AFFILIA* 5, No. 1 (Spring 1990):113-114

Jewish Feminist Scholarship Comes of Age. Bibliography. Vanessa Ochs. *Lilith* 15, No. 1 (Winter 1990):8-12

Learning to Say No: Keeping Feminist Research for Ourselves. Belinda Kremer. *Women's Studies International Forum* 13, No. 5 (1990):463-467

Making Jews Visible to Academic Feminists. Cookie Davis. *Lilith* 15, No. 4 (Fall 1990):6

### Feminist Sociology. *See* Feminism – Theory

### Feminist Theology. *See also* Goddess Worship

Gender and Religion: On the Complexity of Symbols. Edited by Caroline Walker Bynum, Stevan Harrell, and Paula Richman. Reviewed by Naomi R. Goldenberg. *Signs* 15, No. 4 (Summer 1990):874-878

Shaping New Vision: Gender and Values in American Culture. Edited by Clarissa W. Atkinson, Constance H. Buchanan, and Margaret R. Miles. Reviewed by Naomi R. Goldenberg. *Signs* 15, No. 4 (Summer 1990):874-878

### Fenby, Barbara Lou

Feminist Sociology. Book Review. *AFFILIA* 5, No. 1 (Spring 1990):113-114

### Fendi, Paola (about). *See* Fashion Designers, "Battle-Weary Designers"

### Fenichell, Stephen

Mark Spitz. *Lear's* (June 1990):102-107

### Fenn, Sherilyn (about)

Slipping into Stardom. Brook Hersey. *Glamour* (October 1990):248-251

### Fennema, Elizabeth (joint author). *See* Hyde, Janet Shibley

### Fenwick, Elizabeth (joint author). *See* Yaffé, Maurice

### Ferber, Elizabeth

Nervous Conditions. Book Review. *New Directions for Women* 19, No. 1 (January/February 1990):22

### Ferguson, Ann

Blood at the Root: Motherhood, Sexuality and Male Dominance. Reviewed by Ellen Jacobs. *Resources for Feminist Research* 19, No. 1 (March 1990):5-6

### Ferguson, J. Barry (about)

Petal Perfection. Mark Matousek. *Harper's Bazaar* (June 1990):136

### Ferguson, J. Barry and Cowan, Tom

A Gathering of Flowers. *McCall's* 117, No. 11 (August 1990):92-96

### Ferguson, Margaret W.

Women in the First Capitalist Society: Experiences in Seventeenth-Century England. Book Review. *Tulsa Studies in Women's Literature* 9, No. 1 (Spring 1990):158-160

### Ferguson, Mary Anne

Carol Burke Ohmann, 1928-1989: A Tribute. *Women's Studies Quarterly* 18, Nos. 3-4 (Fall-Winter 1990):159-160

**Ferguson, Moira** (editor)

The History of Mary Prince: A West Indian Slave, Related by Herself. Reviewed by Jacqui Alexander. *Women's Studies International Forum* 13, Nos. 1-2 (1990):159

**Ferguson, Sarah** (about)

Fergie Gets Real. Susie Pearson. *Ladies' Home Journal* 107, No. 4 (April 1990):155-158+

**Fergusson, David M.**, Horwood, L. John, and Lloyd, Michael

The Effect of Preschool Children on Family Stability. *Journal of Marriage and the Family* 52, No. 2 (May 1990):531-538

**Feria, Delores S.** (editor)

Goodbye to Winter: The Autobiography of Sophie Schmidt-Rodolfo. Reviewed by Barbara M. Posadas. *Women's Studies International Forum* 13, No. 4 (1990):409-410

**Ferra, Lorraine**

Sculpture. Poem. *Iris* 23 (Spring-Summer 1990):36

Woman Ironing (Degas). Poem. *Iris* 23 (Spring-Summer 1990):37

**Ferrar, Ann**

Medinews. *Ladies' Home Journal* 107, No. 2 (February 1990):82

The Whole Birth Catalog. *Ladies' Home Journal* 107, No. 0 (August 1990):46-50

**Ferrar, Ann** (joint author). *See* Flanagan, Tara

**Ferrari, Christina**

Men Who Are Joining the Fight Against Rape. *McCall's* 118, No. 3 (December 1990):71-74+

Planning for the Future: Steps to Take Now. Bibliography. *McCall's* 118, No. 2 (November 1990):85

**Ferrari, Christina** (joint author). *See* Kagan, Julia

**Ferraro, Geraldine** (about)

Ferraro: The Country Is Ready. Anne Summers. *McCall's* 117, No. 9 (June 1990):62-63

**Ferre, Gianfranco** (about). *See* Talley, André Leon

**Ferree, Myra Marx**

Beyond Separate Spheres: Feminism and Family Research. *Journal of Marriage and the Family* 52, No. 4 (November 1990):866-884

**Ferree, Myra Marx** and Hall, Elaine J.

Visual Images of American Society: Gender and Race in Introductory Sociology Textbooks. *Gender and Society* 4, No. 4 (December 1990):500-533

**Ferrier, Carole**

Interview with Pearlie McNeill. *Hecate* 16, Nos. 1-2 (1990):102-110

Questions of Collaboration: Interview with Jackie Huggins and Isabel Tarrago. *Hecate* 16, Nos. 1-2 (1990):140-147

Resisting Authority. *Hecate* 16, Nos. 1-2 (1990):134-139

**Fertility.** *See also* India – Family Planning

The Effect of Birth Spacing on Current Fertility. N. P. Das. *Journal of Family Welfare* 36, No. 4 (December 1990):36-45

Estimation of Potential Fertility Rates by Age-Group for Karnataka State. R. L. Patil. *Journal of Family Welfare* 36, No. 1 (March 1990):3-6

Fertility Patterns Among Soviet Immigrants to Israel: The Role of Cultural Variables. Shalvia Ben-Barak. *Journal of Family History* 15, No. 1 (January 1990):87-100

**Fertility – History**

Italian Fertility: An Historical Account. Massimo Livi Bacci and Marco Breschi. *Journal of Family History* 15, No. 4 (October 1990):385-408

Western Fertility in Mid-Transition: Fertility and Nuptiality in the United States and Selected Nations at the Turn of the Century. Michael R. Haines. *Journal of Family History* 15, No. 1 (January 1990):23-48

What We Can Learn About Fertility Transitions from the New York State Census of 1865? Avery M. Guest. *Journal of Family History* 15, No. 1 (January 1990):49-69

**Fertility, Rural**

Agricultural Modernization, Its Associated Factors and Fertility Behaviour. P. V. Murthy. *Journal of Family Welfare* 36, No. 4 (December 1990):61-66

Socialist Institutions and Wealth Flow Reversal: An Assessment of Post-Revolutionary Chinese Rural Fertility. Kyung-Sup Chang. *Journal of Family History* 15, No. 2 (April 1990):179-200

**Fertility Drugs**

Family Portrait: Three-Million-Dollar Quints. Shana Aborn. *Ladies' Home Journal* 107, No. 2 (February 1990):74-78

**Festa, Susan**

The Heart of the Matter. *Essence* 21, No. 6 (October 1990):25-28

Prevention: A Season for Sneezin'. *Essence* 20, No. 11 (March 1990):24-28

**Fetal Monitoring**

Body Management: Prenatal Testing: The Newest Option. Janice Kaplan. *Working Woman* (January 1990):134-138

Medical Report: A New Prenatal Test. Elisabeth Rosenthal. *Glamour* (June 1990):64-66

Prenatal Testing: Peering into the Womb. Maggie Morrison. *McCall's* 118, No. 1 (October 1990):160-162

Your Pregnancy. Stephanie Young. *Glamour* (November 1990):78; (December 1990):80

**Fighting (Psychology)**

His: Fighting Fair. David McDonough. *Glamour* (December 1990):232

Keep Love Alive: How to Stop Playing the Blame Game. Gail Kessler. *Redbook* 175, No. 4 (August 1990):98-99

Let Me Tell You About Two Fights I've Had with Boyfriends . . . Brook Hersey. *Glamour* (September 1990):332-333+

**Figueira-McDonough, Josefina**

Abortion: Ambiguous Criteria and Confusing Policies. *AFFILIA* 5, No. 4 (Winter 1990):27-54

**Fiji**

White Women in Fiji, 1835-1930: The Ruin of Empire? By Claudia Knapman. Reviewed by Anand A. Yang. *Women's Studies International Forum* 13, No. 4 (1990):407-408

**Fiji – Women's Movement**

Organizing Women in Fiji. Nera Kuckreja Sohoni and Suzanne Messing. *New Directions for Women* 19, No. 3 (May/June 1990):13

**Fildes, Valerie**

Wet Nursing: A History from Antiquity to the Present. Reviewed by Judith S. Lewis. *Gender & History* 2, No. 2 (Summer 1990):232-234

Wet Nursing: A History from Antiquity to the Present. Reviewed by Roe Sybylla. *Australian Feminist Studies* No. 11 (Autumn 1990):129-131

**Filipowicz, Halina**

No Sacred Cows. *The Women's Review of Books* 7, Nos. 10-11 (July 1990):4-6

**Film and Filmmakers.** *See also* Electric Shadow Productions; Film Criticism – Feminist Perspectives; Melodrama in Film; Multimedia Art; Screenplays

All in the Family. Joanne Kaufman. *Ladies' Home Journal* 107, No. 12 (December 1990):106

<X2>*Demon Lover Diary*: Deconstructing Sex, Class, and Cultural Power in Documentary. Patricia R. Zimmermann. *Genders* 8 (Summer 1990):91-109

The Devil & Susan Seidelman. Louise Bernikow. *Lear's* (January 1990):108-111

Do Women Make Better Movies? Ron Rosenbaum. *Mademoiselle* (March 1990):108-110

Feminist Film Aesthetics: A Contextual Approach. Laurie Shrage. *Hypatia* 5, No. 2 (Summer 1990):137-148

Film Fanciers. *Harper's Bazaar* (May 1990):166

Flash in the Clan. Anne Rosenbaum. *Harper's Bazaar* (February 1990):101

French Lessons. Molly Haskell. *Lear's* (July 1990):68-73

Getting Lynched. *Harper's Bazaar* (October 1990):130

The Godfather Diary. Eleanor Coppola. *Vogue* (December 1990):304-309+

Hollywood: By Youth Obsessed. Anna McDonnell. *Mademoiselle* (April 1990):212, 246

Hollywood Melodrama, Douglas Sirk, and the Repression of the Female Subject (*Magnificent Obsession*). Michael Selig. *Genders* 9 (Fall 1990):35-48

Hollywood Royalty. Jerry Lazar. *Mademoiselle* (October 1990):188-191+

The Incredible Shrinking He(r)man: Male Regression, the Male Body, and Film. Tania Modleski. *Differences* 2, No. 2 (Summer 1990):55-75

Iranian Women Filmmakers: A Conference on Contemporary Iranian Cinema. Azadeh. *Spare Rib* No. 210 (March 1990):39

Jewish Film Festival in Moscow. Janis Plotkin. *Bridges* 1, No. 2 (Fall 1990): 109-110

Kinflicks. *Harper's Bazaar* (December 1990):152-153+

Le Jazz Haute. Patrick Demarchelier. *Vogue* (August 1990):332-337

Politics, Perseverance, and Passion from Hollywood. Anne Bromley. *Iris* 23 (Spring-Summer 1990):56-57

A Question of Silence. By Marleen Gorris. Reviewed by Constance Balides. *Feminist Collections* 12, No. 1 (Fall 1990):14-18

Radical Redux. Todd Gold. *Harper's Bazaar* (May 1990):116-119+

<X2>"Role 'Em!": To Get a Part in Hollywood, See These Women. Betsy Israel. *Mademoiselle* (March 1990):104-106

Sharp Shooters. David DeNicolo. *Vogue* (October 1990):384

Vogue Arts. Victor Erofeev. *Vogue* (November 1990):262+

Women Directors: The Emergence of a New Cinema. By Barbara Koenig Quart. Reviewed by Josette Déléas-Matthews. *Atlantis* 15, No. 2 (Spring 1990):100-102

Women Right Now. *Glamour* (November 1990):99-102

**Film and Filmmakers – Africa.** *See also* Ouedraoga, Idrissa

**Film and Filmmakers – Child Audience**

Ethnography and Exhibition: The Child Audience, the Hays Office and Saturday Matinees. Richard deCordova. *Camera Obscura* , No. 23 (May 1990):90-107

**Film and Filmmakers – Education**

Reformers and Spectators: The Film Education Movement in the Thirties. Lea Jacobs. *Camera Obscura* No. 22 (January 1990):29-49

**Film and Filmmakers – History**

Clues, Myths, and the Historical Method. By Carlo Ginzburg. Reviewed by Dana Polan. *Camera Obscura* No. 22 (January 1990):131-137

Feminism and Film History. Patrice Petro. *Camera Obscura* No. 22 (January 1990):9-26

<X2> "The Finest Outside the Loop": Motion Picture Exhibition in Chicago's Black Metropolis, 1905-1928. Mary Carbine. *Camera Obscura* , No. 23 (May 1990): 9-41

**Film and Filmmakers – Images of Women**

Cinema, Censorship and Sexuality, 1909-25. By Annette Kuhn. Reviewed by Sumiko Higashi. *Gender & History* 2, No. 1 (Spring 1990):123-126

The Desire to Desire: The Woman's Film of the 1940s. By Mary Ann Doane. Reviewed by Paul Rabinowitz. *Feminist Studies* 16, No. 1 (Spring 1990):151-169

Unlikely Films, Liberating Roles. Cindy Fuchs. *New Directions for Women* 19, No. 4 (July-August 1990):9

Virulent Machismo Rampant in Vietnam War Films. *New Directions for Women* 19, No. 1 (January/February 1990):10

The Women Who Knew Too Much: Hitchcock and Feminist Theory. By Tania Modleski. Reviewed by Sumiko Higashi. *Gender & History* 2, No. 1 (Spring 1990):123-126

**Film and Filmmakers – Interviews**

Lunch. Interview. Frances Lear. *Lear's* (February 1990):19-22

Marlon Riggs Untied. Interview. Revon Kyle Banneker. *Out/Look* No. 10 (Fall 1990):14-18

Mo' Better Spike. Interview. Jill Nelson. *Essence* 21, No. 4 (August 1990):55 +

Woman, Native, Other: Pratibha Parmar Interviews Trinh T. Minh-ha. Pratibha Parmar. *Feminist Review* No. 36 (Autumn 1990):65-74

**Film Criticism.** *See also* Film Reviews

Beyond Dick Tracy: Summer at the Movies. Brook Hersey. *Glamour* (July 1990):116

The Decontextualization of Abortion: An Analysis of "The Silent Scream." Bonnie A. Haaland. *Women's Studies in Communication* 12, No. 2 (Fall 1989):57-76

Dreams and Dust: Under a Sheltering Sky. Brian Case. *Lear's* (May 1990):90-97

The Hudlins and Kid N' Play Make Movie Magic. Pamela Johnson. *Essence* 20, No. 10 (February 1990):40

Inside Movies: Move Over, Casablanca. Ron Rosenbaum. *Mademoiselle* (January 1990):52-53 +

Jazz Movies: Born Out of a Horn. Geoffrey Wolff. *Lear's* (July 1990):90-95 +

Love Reincarnate. Ron Rosenbaum. *Mademoiselle* (December 1990):84-86

Metropolitan: Self-Doubt Among the Debs. Ron Rosenbaum. *Mademoiselle* (September 1990):162-169

Movies: End to Happy Endings. Lewis Grossberger. *Vogue* (December 1990):196-198

Movies. Geoffrey Ward. *Vogue* (January 1990):94-96

Movies: People – the *Real* Aliens. *Mademoiselle* (February 1990):84-87

Movies: Stairway to Hell. Ron Rosenbaum. *Mademoiselle* (June 1990):104-106

Postcards from the Edge of Mediocrity. Ron Rosenbaum. *Mademoiselle* (November 1990):90-93

Summer Movies. Joanne Kaufman. *Ladies' Home Journal* 107, No. 7 (July 1990):36-40

Tale of a Twisted Sister. Jonathan Van Meter. *Harper's Bazaar* (February 1990):63

Three Men and a Little Lady's Home Journal. Jeff Rovin. *Ladies' Home Journal* 107, No. 12 (December 1990):46-53

Thrill Out. *Harper's Bazaar* (July 1990):80-83

TV's Bill Cosby in Ghost Dad, the Movie. Benilde Little. *Essence* 21, No. 2 (June 1990):38

Violence at the Movies. Brook Hersey. *Glamour* (September 1990):218

Vogue Arts: Movies. Christopher Robbins. *Vogue* (August 1990):216-220

Vogue Arts: Movies. David De Nicolo. *Vogue* (September 1990):398-424

Word on Movies. Brook Hersey. *Glamour* (March 1990):194; (May 1990):208; (September 1990):220; (November 1990):172; (December 1990):160

Word On Movies. Charla Krupp. *Glamour* (April 1990):194

Word on Movies. Charla Krupp. *Glamour* (October 1990):198

Word On Movies. David Denicolo. *Glamour* (February 1990):130

Word On . . . Movies Based on Novels. Brook Hersey. *Glamour* (December 1990):158

You Can't Hurry Love. Phillip Lopate. *Lear's* (July 1990):60-63

**Film Criticism – Feminist Perspectives.** *See also* India – Film Criticism – Feminist Perspectives

Adventures of Goldilocks: Spectatorship, Consumerism and Public Life. Miriam Hansen. *Camera Obscura* No. 22 (January 1990):51-71

Female Power in the Serial-Queen Melodrama: The Etiology of an Anomaly. Ben Singer. *Camera Obscura* No. 22 (January 1990):91-129

Female Spectators: Looking at Film and Television. Edited by E. Deidre Pribram. Reviewed by Sandra Taylor. *Australian Feminist Studies* No. 12 (Summer 1990):127-128

Feminist Visions: Narrative Films by Women. Marilyn Gotschalk. *Feminist Collections* 11, No. 2 (Winter 1990):10-13

Mother Inferior. Georgia Brown. *Lear's* (July 1990):88-89

Oscar Meets the LHJ Lady. Leslie Jay. *Ladies' Home Journal* 107, No. 4 (April 1990):50-54

Reconsidering "Ms. Daisy." Barbara Quart. *Lilith* 15, No. 3 (Summer 1990):29

Technologies of Gender: Essays on Theory, Film, and Fiction. By Teresa de Lauretis. Reviewed by Paula Rabinowitz. *Feminist Studies* 16, No. 1 (Spring 1990):151-169

**Film Festivals.** *See also* Toronto (Canada) – Film Festivals; Venice – Travel

Travel News. Richard Alleman. *Vogue* (January 1990):140

In Visible Colours: Technicolour in a White World. Yasmin Jiwani. *Hot Wire* 6, No. 3 (September 1990):23 +

**Film Festivals – Latin America**

Women and Cinema. *Women in Action* 3 & 4 (1990):61

**Filmgoers**

Adventures of Goldilocks: Spectatorship, Consumerism and Public Life. Miriam Hansen. *Camera Obscura* No. 22 (January 1990):51-71

Reformers and Spectators: The Film Education Movement in the Thirties. Lea Jacobs. *Camera Obscura* No. 22 (January 1990):29-49

**Film Reviews**

An Angel at My Table. *See* Moar, Natasha

The Bonfire of the Vanities. *See* De Palma, Brian

Broken Mirrors. *See* Gorris, Marlene

Celia. *See* Turner, Ann

Chicken Ranch. *See* Broomfield, Nick

Driving Miss Daisy. *See* Beresford, Bruce

Ethnic Notions. *See* Riggs, Marlon

Fundi: The Story of Ella Baker. *See* Grant, Joanne

Ghost. *See* Zucker, Jerry

The Handmaid's Tale. *See* Schlondorff, Volker

Henry V. *See* Branagh, Kenneth

Hero Hiralal. *See* Mehta, Ketan

Julia de Burgos. *See* Garcia Torres, José

Kamikaze Hearts. *See* Bashore, Juliet

The Lemon Grove Incident. *See* Christopher, Frank

Letters to Daddy. *See* Kapoor, Raj

Limit Up. *See* Martini, Richard

Longtime Companion. *See* Rene, Norman

Look Who's Talking. *See* Heckerling, Amy

The Mad Monkey. *See* Trueba, Fernando

Main Azad Hoon: The Politics of Myth and Reality. *See* Anand, Timmu

Men Don't Leave. *See* Brickman, Paul

Mera Pati Sirf Mera Hai. *See* Sethi, Harsh

Miller's Crossing. *See* Coen, Joel and Coen, Ethan

Mo' Better Blues. *See* Lee, Spike

Music Box. *See* Gavras, Costa

Never Turn Back: The Life of Fanny Lou Hamer. *See* Buckley, Bill

Pestonjee. *See* Rao, Vijaya

Pretty Woman. *See* Marshall, Garry

A Private Life. *See* Gerard, Francis

A Question of Silence. *See* Gorris, Marleen

Rihaee. *See* Raje, Aruna

Roger and Me. *See* Moore, Michael

Romero. *See* Duigan, John

Romuald & Juliet. *See* Serrau, Coline

Rosalie Goes Shopping. *See* Adlon, Percy

The Sheltering Sky. *See* Bertolucci, Bernardo

With Silk Wings: Asian American Women at Work. *See* Asian Women United

Stanley and Iris. *See* Ritt, Martin

Surname Viet Given Name Nam. *See* Minh-ha, Trinh T.

Tatie Danielle. *See* Chatiliez, Etienne

Tie Me Up! Tie Me Down!. *See* Almodovar, Pedro

Trop Belle Pour Toi. *See* Blier, Bernard

Watsonville. *See* Silver, John

The Witches. *See* Roeg, Nic

Working Girls. *See* Borden, Lizzie

Yaaba. *See* Ouedraoga, Idrissa

**Films for Children**

Are Horror Movies Too Horrible for Kids? Barbara Smalley. *Redbook* 175, No. 6 (October 1990):36-38

R-Rated Movies: Should Children Watch? Lee Sak. *McCall's* 117, No. 9 (June 1990):48

**Filofax.** *See* Time Management

**Finance, Personal.** *See also* Debt; Financial Planning; Investing

Could You Survive Tough Times. Barbara Gilder Quint. *Family Circle* 103, No. 10 (July 24, 1990):29-30+

Credit Card Capital. Doreen Mangan. *Executive Female* (March/April 1990):74

Fast Cash: Five Ways to Get It. Lynn Brenner. *Working Woman* (August 1990):38-40

First Person Singular: Out of Joint. Ann Banks. *Savvy Woman* (July/August 1990):90+

Gimme Shelter! Deborah Rankin. *Working Mother* (December 1990):30-32

Money: Quick—How Much are You Worth? Julianne Malveaux. *Essence* 21, No. 6 (October 1990):38-41

Money & Friends: If She's Broke, Don't Fix It. Ellen Welty. *Mademoiselle* (January 1990):60

Money Matters. Jack Gillis. *Good Housekeeping* 211, No. 3 (September 1990):92; 211, No. 4 (October 1990):25

The Money Quiz. Daniel Sher. *Working Woman* (January 1990):114

More for Your Money. Barbara Gilder Quint. *Glamour* (March 1990):119-121; (April 1990):132-137; (June 1990):132-135

Prime of Life. Sherrye Henry. *Family Circle* 103, No. 1 (January 9, 1990):29-30

Risk-Less Advice for Entrepreneurs. Ken Sgro. *Executive Female* (March/April 1990):77

A Savings Plan for Spenders. Ellen E. Schultz. *Savvy* (December-January 1991):23-24

Smart Investor: Holding the Ace of Clubs. Nancy Dunnan. *Lear's* (August 1990):26-27

<X2>" The Worst Money Mistake I Ever Made . . ." Barbara Gilder Quint. *Glamour* (July 1990):83-85

Viewpoint: Missing Money. Amy Shapiro. *Glamour* (June 1990):162

<X2> "What's Your Financial Planning IQ?" Donna Gallin. *Executive Female* (May/June 1990):57-59

Your Money. Barbara Gilder Quint. *Family Circle* 103, No. 6 (April 24, 1990):53-54

Your Money. Deborah Rankin. *Family Circle* 103, No. 4 (March 13, 1990):51-52+

Your Money. *Good Housekeeping* 211, No. 3 (September 1990):296; 211, No. 4 (October 1990):252

Your Money. Jan Alexander. *Family Circle* 103, No. 8 (June 5, 1990):25-27

Your Money: Stay Out of the Red This Christmas. Barbara Gilder Quint. *Family Circle* 103, No. 16 (November 27, 1990):45-48

Your Money. *Working Woman* (September 1990):88-90; (October 1990):58-60; (November 1990):81-84; (December 1990):40

On Your Own: Fiscal Fitness. Judith Stone. *Glamour* (August 1990):130

**Financial Institutions.** *See also* Artemis Capital Group, Incorporated

**Financial Occupations**

Outsmarting Wall Street. Ellen Wulfhorst. *Savvy Woman* (November 1990):58

**Financial Planning.** *See also* Annuities; Baby Boom Generation—Financial Planning; Family Finances; Finance, Personal; Income Tax—Planning; Older Adults—Financial Planning; Saving and Investment

All Tapped Out, No Place to Go. Debra Wishik Englander. *Savvy Woman* (November 1990):26

How to Fund Your Dream Business. Claire McIntosh. *Working Woman* (January 1990):100

How to get Credit-Card Savvy. Carol Milano. *Essence* 21, No. 2 (June 1990):32

How to Hire an Attorney. Suzanne B. Laporte. *Working Woman* (August 1990):40-42

Is Your Insurance "Overdressed"? Debra Wishik Englander. *Savvy Woman* (July/August 1990):24-25

Lear's Bulletin. Bibliography. Marion Asnes. *Lear's* (January 1990):38

Lear's Bulletin. Marion Asnes. *Lear's* (March 1990):44; (June 1990):44

Money: Getting Debt-Free in '90. Lisa Collier Cool. *Essence* 20, No. 11 (March 1990):38

More for Your Money. Barbara Gilder Quint. *Glamour* (October 1990):131-134; (November 1990):127-128

More for Your Money: What Should You Do With $1,000 Savings? Barbara Gilder Quint. *Glamour* (January 1990):50-53

The Only Tax Advice You'll Ever Need. Ellen E. Schultz. *Savvy Woman* (November 1990):23-24

The Opening of the American Mind. Bibliography. Nancy Dunnan. *Lear's* (November 1990):32-34

Reality Meets Retirement. Horace Mungin. *Essence* 20, No. 9 (January 1990):30

Smart Investor: Blue Chips After Black Monday. Nancy Dunnan. *Lear's* (February 1990):24-25

The $27,000 Solution. Jennie Nash. *Mademoiselle* (June 1990):164-167+

10 Ways to Increase Your Money Power. Andrea Rock. *Ladies' Home Journal* 107, No. 11 (November 1990):176-180+

**Finch, Annie**

Baptism of Desire. Book Review. *Belles Lettres* 5, No. 4 (Summer 1990):30-31

Green Age. Book Review. *Belles Lettres* 5, No. 4 (Summer 1990):30-31

One Eye on the Sky. *The Women's Review of Books* 7, No. 6 (March 1990):25-26

Poets of Our Time. *Belles Lettres* 5, No. 4 (Summer 1990):30-31

She Rises Like the Sun: Invocations of the Goddess by Contemporary American Women Poets. Book Review. *The Women's Review of Books* 7, No. 6 (March 1990):25-26

Toluca Street. Book Review. *Belles Lettres* 5, No. 4 (Summer 1990):30-31

**Finch, Lyn**

Seduction and Punishment. *Hecate* 16, Nos. 1-2 (1990):8-22

**Findlay, Catherine**

How Criticism Chips Away at a Marriage. *Working Mother* (November 1990):26-30

**Findlen, Barbara**

The Beverly Malibu. Book Review. *Ms.* 1, No. 1 (July/August 1990):69

Bold Types. *Ms.* 1, No. 2 (September/October 1990):29

Culture: A Refuge for Murder. *Ms.* 1, No. 2 (September/October 1990):47

Finding the Lesbians. Book Review. *Ms.* 1, No. 1 (July/August 1990):69

Identity Politics: Lesbian Feminism and the Limits of Community. Book Review. *Ms.* 1, No. 1 (July/August 1990):69

In Search of a Nonviolent Past. *Ms.* 1, No. 2 (September/October 1990):46

**Fine, Gary Alan** and Sandstrom, Kent L.

Knowing Children: Participant Observation with Minors. Reviewed by Sarah H. Matthews. *Journal of Marriage and the Family* 52, No. 1 (February 1990):282

**Fine, Linda**

I Had a Baby After Breast Cancer. *Family Circle* 103, No. 16 (November 27, 1990):94-98

**Fine, Marlene G.**

American Ritual Dramas: Social Rules and Cultural Meanings. Book Review. *Women's Studies International Forum* 13, No. 5 (1990):522-523

Epistemological and Methodological Commitments of a Feminist Perspective. *Women & Language* 13, No. 2 (Winter 1990):35-36

**Fine, Michelle** and Asch, Adrienne (editors)

Women with Disabilities: Essays in Psychology, Culture and Politics. Reviewed by Hope Landrine. *Psychology of Women Quarterly* 14, No. 3 (September 1990):435-437

**Finger, Anne**

Past Due: A Story of Disability, Pregnancy and Birth. Reviewed by Andrea Boroff Eagan. *The Women's Review of Books* 7, No. 12 (September 1990):21

**Fingernails.** *See* Nails (Anatomy) – Care and Hygiene

**Fink, Sue**

True Life Adventure. Reviewed by Diane Stein. *off our backs* 20, No. 7 (July 1990):18-19

**Finke, Nikki**

The Dish on Gish. *Mademoiselle* (April 1990):98-100

**Finn, Janet L.**

Burnout in the Human Services: A Feminist Perspective. *AFFILIA* 5, No. 4 (Winter 1990):55-71

**Finnes, Vi**

We Exist. *Connexions* 34 (1990):31

**Fiocchetto, Rosanna**

Italy. *Feminist Review* No. 34 (Spring 1990):18-22

**Fiori, Gabriella**

Simone Weil: An Intellectual Biography. Reviewed by Johanna Selles-Roney. *Resources for Feminist Research* 19, No. 2 (June 1990):46

**Firearms.** *See also* Handguns

**Firearms – Accidents**

<X2>"Our Most Precious Gift." Bertha Burns. *Ladies' Home Journal* 107, No. 12 (December 1990):22-25

**Firing.** *See also* Employees, Dismissal of

**First, Sharon Efroymson**

The Smart Office: All Systems Go: How to Manage Technological Change. *Working Woman* (April 1990):47-54

**First Husbands.** *See* Political Spouses

**First Ladies.** *See* Governors – United States – Spouses; Political Spouses

**Fischer, Arlene**

Jane Fonda's Lean Routine. *Redbook* 175, No. 6 (October 1990):84-88

From the Mayo Clinic: 12 Tips for a Longer, Healthier Life. *Redbook* 175, No. 5 (September 1990):156-159

New Hope: Doctors are Solving the Mystery of Miscarriage. *Redbook* 174, No. 5 (March 1990):136-137+

Nutrition Makeover. *Redbook* 175, No. 2 (June 1990):135-146

**Fischer, Rita H.** and Isaacs, Florence

Saving Premature Babies. *Good Housekeeping* 211, No. 3 (September 1990):110+

**Fischer, Thomas J.** and Mercer, Marilyn

When Children Have Allergies. *Good Housekeeping* 211, No. 3 (September 1990):142-146

**Fish.** *See* Cookery (Seafood)

**Fish, John**

What Is Special Education. Reviewed by Sue Woodgate. *Gender and Education* 2, No. 3 (1990):374-375

**Fishbein, Eileen Greif**

Predicting Paternal Involvement with a Newborn by Attitude Toward Women's Roles. *Health Care for Women International* 11, No. 1 (1990):109-115

**Fisher, Anne B.**

10 Best Paid Women in America. *Savvy Woman* (July/August 1990):44-51

Escape from the Forty-Hour Workweek. *Savvy Woman* (March 1990):53-54, 78-80

Just Do It! *Savvy Woman* (October 1990):54-57+

Wall Street Women: Women in Power on Wall Street Today. Reviewed by Felicia Kornbluh. *The Women's Review of Books* 7, No. 8 (May 1990):9-10

**Fisher, Berenice**

Banalities of Evil. *The Women's Review of Books* 7, No. 8 (May 1990):21-22

Women and Evil. Book Review. *The Women's Review of Books* 7, No. 8 (May 1990):21-22

**Fisher, Carrie**

The One that Got Away. Excerpt. Short story. *Ladies' Home Journal* 107, No. 9 (September 1990):98-104

**Fisher, Carrie** (about)

Postcards from the Top. Joanne Kaufman. *Ladies' Home Journal* 107, No. 9 (September 1990):96-98+

Straight Up with a Twist. Tim Appelo. *Savvy Woman* (September 1990):56-59+

**Fisher, Graham** and Fisher, Heather

The Forgotten Princess. *Redbook* 175, No. 5 (September 1990):42-44

**Fisher, Heather** (joint author). *See* Fisher, Graham

**Fisher, Jennifer**

The Comic Mirror: Domestic Surveillance in Mary Worth. *Canadian Women's Studies* 11, No. 1 (Spring 1990):60-61

**Fisher, Jo**

Mothers of the Disappeared. Reviewed by Marta Rodriguez. *Spare Rib* No. 212 (May 1990):25

Mothers of the Disappeared. Reviewed by Patricia Hilliard. *New Directions for Women* 19, No. 5 (September-October 1990):15

**Fisher, M. F. K.**

My Grown-Up Ears. *Lear's* (June 1990):144+

**Fisher, Martin** and Abrahms, Sally

Medical Checkups for Teenagers. *Good Housekeeping* 211, No. 3 (September 1990):158-160

**Fishman, Ellen**

Why Women Are Writing Holocaust Memoirs Now. Bibliography. *Lilith* 15, No. 2 (Spring 1990):6-7+

**Fishman, Joan** (about). *See* Title, Stacy

**Fiske, John**

Popular Narrative and Commercial Television. *Camera Obscura* , No. 23 (May 1990): 132-147

**Fissinger, Laura**

Role Model. *Harper's Bazaar* (August 1990):110-115

**Fister, Patricia**

Japanese Women Artists: 1600-1900. Reviewed by Janis Hoogstraten. *Resources for Feminist Research* 19, No. 1 (March 1990):21-22

**Fitness.** *See* Physical Fitness

**FitzGerald, Jennifer**

Virginia Woolf and the Problem of the Subject: Feminine Writing in the Major Novels. Book Review. *Women's Studies International Forum* 13, No. 6 (1990):612-613

**Fitzgerald, Zelda** (about). *See* Love-Letters

**Fitzpatrick, Ellen**

Endless Crusade: Women Social Scientists and Progressive Reform. Reviewed by Barrie Thorne. *The Women's Review of Books* 7, No. 9 (June 1990):22

**Fitzpatrick, Mary Anne** (joint author). *See* Noller, Patricia

**Flags – Mutilation, Defacement, etc.**

Portfolio. Gene Wesley Elder. *Out/Look* No. 7 (Winter 1990):42-43

**Flaherty, Stephen** (joint author). *See* Ahrens, Lynn

**Flanagan, Barbara**

Design Hot Line: The Office that (Almost) Does the Work for You. *Working Woman* (October 1990):112-115

The Way I Want to Live. *Lear's* (October 1990):80-85

**Flanagan, Sabina**

Hildegard of Bingen, 1098-1179: A Visionary Life. Reviewed by Miri Rubin. *Gender & History* 2, No. 3 (Autumn 1990):353-354

Hildegard of Bingen, 1098-1179: A Visionary Life. Reviewed by Phillipa Maddern. *Australian Feminist Studies* No. 12 (Summer 1990):129-130

**Flanagan, Tara** and Ferrar, Ann

Dental Questions You Were Afraid to Ask. *Ladies' Home Journal* 107, No. 9 (September 1990):140-143

**Flanders, Laura**

The Handmaid's Tale. Film review. *New Directions for Women* 19, No. 3 (May/June 1990):7

Machinal. Play review. *New Directions for Women* 19, No. 2 (March/April 1990):13

MADRE Needed More Than Ever. *New Directions for Women* 19, No. 5 (September-October 1990):11+

Military Women and the Media. *New Directions for Women* 19, No. 6 (November-December 1990):1+

Parents Fight Draconian Sentence. *New Directions for Women* 19, No. 2 (March/April 1990):7

Soviet-American Summit Tackles Troubling Issues. *New Directions for Women* 19, No. 4 (July-August 1990):1+

**Flanigan, Beverly**, McLean, Ann, Hall, Chris, and Propp, Veronica

Alcohol Use as a Situational Influence on Young Women's Pregnancy Risk-Taking Behaviors. *Adolescence* 25, No. 97 (Spring 1990):205-214

**Flanner, Janet** (about)

Gene3t: A Biography of Janet Flanner. By Brenda Wineapple. Reviewed by Scarlet Cheng. *Belles Lettres* 5, No. 3 (Spring 1990):8

**Flax, Jane**

Thinking Fragments: Psychoanalysis, Feminism, and Postmodernism in the Contemporary West. Reviewed by Mari Jo Buhle. *The Women's Review of Books* 7, No. 7 (April 1990):23-24

**Flea Markets**

Shopping Smart. Christine Fellingham. *Glamour* (June 1990):202+

**Fleming, Alice**

Quality Mommy Time. *Redbook* 174, No. 6 (April 1990):92-95

**Fleming, Don** and Wernick, Sarah

Little Grownups. *Working Mother* 13, No. 10 (October 1990):24-29

**Fleming, Mali Michelle**

Picnic Perfect. *Essence* 21, No. 3 (July 1990):79-82

**Fletcher, Marjorie H.**

The WRNS: A History of the Women's Royal Naval Service. Reviewed by Peter K. H. Mispelkamp. *Minerva* 8, No. 1 (Spring 1990):86-87

**Fletcher, Suzy H.**

AIDS and Women: An International Perspective. *Health Care for Women International* 11, No. 1 (1990):33-42

**Fletcher, Valerie**

No Accident. Poem. *Women and Therapy* 10, Nos. 1/2 (1990):144-146

**Flewelling, Robert L.** and Bauman, Karl E.

Family Structure as a Predictor of Initial Substance Use and Sexual Intercourse in Early Adolescence. *Journal of Marriage and the Family* 52, No. 1 (February 1990):171-181

**Flexibility.** *See* Joints – Range of Motion

**Flexible Career Patterns.** *See* Balancing Work and Family Life; Career Management

**Flintoff, Anne**

Get Smart! A Woman's Guide to Equality on the Campus. Book Review. *Gender and Education* 2, No. 2 (1990):259

**Flirtation**

Flirting for the Fun of it. Louise Lague. *Glamour* (March 1990):242-243+

**Flisi, Claudia B.**

Progress "All' Italiana." *Ms.* 1, No. 2 (September/October 1990):9

**Floods.** *See* Natural Disasters

**Flores, Toni**

Tapestries of Life: Women's Work, Women's Consciousness, and the Meaning of Daily Experience. Book Review. *Frontiers* 11, Nos. 2-3 (1990):121-122

**Florez, C. Elisa** and Hogan, Dennis P.

Demographic Transition and Life Course Change in Colombia. *Journal of Family History* 15, No. 1 (January 1990):1-21

**Florida – Description and Travel**

Travel: The Florida Fix. Rachel Urquhart and George Kalogerakis. *Vogue* (December 1990):220-226

**Florida Power and Light Company.** *See* Management Techniques

**Florists.** *See also* Flower Arrangement

Floral Flair. *Harper's Bazaar* (March 1990):232-236+

**Flower Arrangement.** *See also* Dried Flower Arrangement; Florists

Long-Stemmed Artistry. Betty Goodwin. *Harper's Bazaar* (March 1990):240

Petal Perfection. Mark Matousek. *Harper's Bazaar* (June 1990):136

**Flowers.** *See also* Mail Order Business

The Avid Gardener: Little Bulbs, Big Rewards. Bibliography. Leslie Land. *McCall's* 117, No. 12 (September 1990):70

A Gathering of Flowers. J. Barry Ferguson and Tom Cowan. *McCall's* 117, No. 11 (August 1990):92-96

Home: Spring Bouquets. Carolyn Noyes. *Ladies' Home Journal* 107, No. 5 (May 1990):86-92

Pretty Enough to Eat. Laurie Ochoa. *Harper's Bazaar* (March 1990):231+

Secrets of a Super Garden. Pamela Guthrie O'Brien. *Ladies' Home Journal* 107, No. 3 (March 1990):149-152

**Flowers, George** (joint author). *See* Nash, Jesse

**Flowers, Juanzetta Shew** (joint author). *See* Gay, Janice Templeton

**Flying Discs (Game)**

Disc Jocks. Susanna Levin. *Women's Sports & Fitness* 12, No. 6 (September 1990):66

**Flynn, Anita** (about)

Weird Science. David Ruben. *Savvy Woman* (November 1990):16

**Flynn, Joyce** and Stricklin, Joyce Occomy (editors)

Frye Street and Environs: The Collected Works of Marita Bonner. Reviewed by Phillipa Kafka. *Sage* 6, No. 2 (Fall 1989):60

**Flynn, Maryclare** (joint author). *See* Chan, Shirley

**Focaccia.** *See* Cookery (Bread)

**Fodor, Iris G.** and Franks, Violet

Women in Midlife and Beyond. *Psychology of Women Quarterly* 14, No. 4 (December 1990):445-449

**Fodor, Iris G.** (joint author). *See* La Sorsa, Valerie A.

**Foglino, Annette**

Trends: No Frills Dining. *Working Woman* (August 1990):42

**Folayan, Ayofemi**

I Am Your Sister: A Tale of Two Conferences. *off our backs* 20, No. 11 (December 1990):1-2

National Black Gay and Lesbian Leadership Forum: A Conference Report. *off our backs* 20, No. 4 (April 1990):2-3

**Foley, Denise**

The Gift of Self-Esteem. *Working Mother* (November 1990):32-36

How to Fire Up an Unmotivated Child. *Working Mother* 13, No. 9 (September 1990):40-48

**Foley, Joseph**

Exposing Darkness to Light: Holly Wright's Vanity Images. *Iris* 23 (Spring-Summer 1990):21-24

**Foley, Mary Jo**

Cancer Organizers Push Feminist Agenda. *New Directions for Women* 19, No. 3 (May/June 1990):1+

Health Research Slights Women. *New Directions for Women* 19, No. 6 (November-December 1990):4-5

**Foley, Michael**

<X2> "Basic Victim Positions" and the Women in Margaret Atwood's *The Handmaid's Tale*. *Atlantis* 15, No. 2 (Spring 1990):50-58

**Foley, Tricia**

Linens, Lace, All Over the Place. Excerpt. *McCall's* 117, No. 12 (September 1990):126-129

**Folk Art.** *See also* Craft Arts

Just Folks. *Redbook* 175, No. 3 (July 1990):108-111

**Folk Literature.** *See also* Jewish Folk Literature; Literary Criticism – Feminist Perspectives

**Folk Music.** *See* Music, Folk

**Follett, Ken**

The Abiding Heart. Short Story. *Good Housekeeping* 211, No. 2 (August 1990):60-69

**Fonda, Jane** (about). *See also* Celebrities – Activism

Jane Fonda's Lean Routine. Arlene Fischer. *Redbook* 175, No. 6 (October 1990):84-88

Relax with Jane Fonda. *Redbook* 174, No. 5 (March 1990):112-113

**Fong, Yem Siu**

The Joy Luck Club. Book Review. *Frontiers* 11, Nos. 2-3 (1990):122-123

**Fonow, Mary Margaret**

Homework: Historical and Contemporary Perspectives on Paid Labor at Home. Book Review. *NWSA Journal* 2, No. 3 (Summer 1990):502-505

Homeworking: Myths and Realities. Book Review. *NWSA Journal* 2, No. 3 (Summer 1990):502-505

**Fontaine, Patricia** (joint author). *See* Gjergingen, Dwenda K.

**Fontana, Victoria**

Today We Will Not Be Invisible or Silent. Poem. *Out/Look* No. 8 (Spring 1990):43

**Foot – Care and Hygiene**

Beauty & Health Report. Andrea Pomerantz Lynn. *Glamour* (June 1990):42

Body Briefing: Feet. Mariana Gosnell. *Lear's* (February 1990):42-44

Heart & Sole: A Complete Guide to Sexy Feet. *Mademoiselle* (June 1990):168-187+

**Football – Accidents and Injuries**

Young Father's Story: "Parents Should Be Warned." Nick Buoniconti and Linda Marsa. *Redbook* 175, No. 5 (September 1990):48-50

**Forbes, Delysia**

Let Reggae Touch Your Soul. *Spare Rib* 217 (October 1990):54-55

No Justice in South Africa. *Spare Rib* 213 (June 1990):43-44

**Ford, Charlotte**

Etiquette: Doing It Right. *McCall's* 117, No. 7 (April 1990):130; 117, No. 8 (May 1990):170; 117, No. 9 (June 1990):56-57; 117, No. 10 (July 1990):36; 117, No. 12 (September 1990):34

**Ford, Faith** (about)

Faith Ford: F. Y. I. Michael J. Bandler. *Ladies' Home Journal* 107, No. 6 (June 1990):130

**Ford, T. J.**

The Bottom Line. *Ms.* 1, No. 1 (July/August 1990):89

Earth-Friendly Ecotips. *Ms.* 1, No. 2 (September/October 1990):17

**Forde, Melanie R.**

Tell Me of Your Secrets, Mary Rose. Poem. *Woman of Power* 16 (Spring 1990):inside front cover

**Ford Foundation**

The Ford Foundation Program on Mainstreaming Minority Women's Studies. Leslie I. Hill. *Women's Studies Quarterly* 18, Nos. 1-2 (Spring-Summer 1990):24-38

**Fordham, Julia**

Porcelain. Reviewed by Elorine Grant. *Spare Rib* No. 209 (February 1990):32

**Fordham, Julia** (about)

Sound Raves. Siobhan Toscano. *Savvy Woman* (October 1990):21

**Forecasting**

Baby Boomer Odyssey. *Lear's* (May 1990):124-125

The Search for Signs of Intelligent Life in the 21st Century. Jane Wagner. *Ms.* 1, No. 3 (November/December 1990):68-71

Trends of the 90's. Mary Ellen Schoonmaker. *Family Circle* 103, No. 1 (January 9, 1990):40-42

**Foreign Investment Policy.** *See also* International Trade Policy

Investing in a World Gone Wide. Nancy Dunnan. *Lear's* (May 1990):32-35

**Foreign Trade Promotion.** *See* Business Travel

**Forman, Frieda J.** (editor)

Taking Our Time: Feminist Perspectives on Temporality. Reviewed by Julia Creet. *Resources for Feminist Research* 19, No. 1 (March 1990):33

Taking Our Time: Feminist Perspectives on Temporality. Reviewed by Susan-Judith Hoffman. *Atlantis* 15, No. 2 (Spring 1990):111-113

Taking Our Time: Feminist Perspectives on Temporality. Reviewed by Susan S. Arpad. *NWSA Journal* 2, No. 2 (Spring 1990):311-314

**Forman, Gail** (joint author). *See* Hedges, Elaine

**Forrest, Kally**

No to Rape. *Connexions* 34 (1990):16

**Forrest, Katherine** (joint author). *See* Ledbetter, Carol

**Forrest, Katherine V.**

The Beverly Malibu. Reviewed by Barbara Findlen. *Ms.* 1, No. 1 (July/August 1990):69

**Forrest, Linda**

Empowering Women: Leadership Development Strategies on Campus. Book Review. *NWSA Journal* 2, No. 3 (Summer 1990):497-499

**Forrest, Mona**

<X2> "Why Should Women Be Engineers When Men Can't?" *off our backs* 20, No. 1 (January 1990):6

**Fortgang, Ilana**

Viewpoint. *Glamour* (September 1990):144

**Fortin, Nina E.** (joint author). *See* Tuchman, Gaye

**Fortino, Denise** (joint author). *See* Grand, Mary Ann

**Fortune, Marie M.**

Keeping the Faith: Questions and Answers for the Abused Woman. Reviewed by Deborah L. Humphreys. *AFFILIA* 5, No. 2 (Summer 1990):109-111

**Fortune, Mary – Anthologies**

The Fortunes of Mary Fortune. Edited by Lucy Sussex. Reviewed by Judith MacBean. *Australian Feminist Studies* No. 12 (Summer 1990):123-125

**Foster, Catherine**

Women for all Seasons: The Story of the Women's International League for Peace and Freedom. Reviewed by Jane S. Gould. *New Directions for Women* 19, No. 4 (July-August 1990):18

**Foster, Thomas**

<X2>"The Very House of Difference": Gender as "Embattled" Standpoint. *Genders* 8 (Summer 1990):17-37

**Foster Care.** *See also* Child Custody

Cast-Off Kids. Joan Smith. *Vogue* (August 1990):324-327+

For Love and Money: Women as Foster Mothers. Brenda Smith and Tina Smith. *AFFILIA* 5, No. 1 (Spring 1990):66-80

Motherhood or Bust: Reflections on the Dreams, and Nightmares of Foster Parenting. Mary Ellen Snodgrass. *On the Issues* 16 (Fall 1990):7-9+

Solomon Says: A Speakout on Foster Care. By Louise Armstrong. Reviewed by Eleanor J. Bader. *On the Issues* 16 (Fall 1990):33-34

Solomon Says: A Speakout on Foster Care. By Louise Armstrong. Reviewed by Nancy D. Polikoff. *The Women's Review of Books* 7, No. 9 (June 1990):23-24

Solomon Says: A Speakout on Foster Care. By Louise Armstrong. Reviewed by Stephanie Stein. *New Directions for Women* 19, No. 3 (May/June 1990):19-20

Susana: The Myth of the "Saved" Child. Naomi Feigelson Chase. *On the Issues* 16 (Fall 1990):10-15+

**Foty, Caroline**

Community Mourns Loss: Sara Deniz Atattimur. *off our backs* 20, No. 3 (March 1990):29

**Foucault, Michel – Criticism and Interpretation**

Feminism and Foucault: Reflections on Resistance. Edited by Irene Diamond and Lee Quinby. Reviewed by Constance Balides. *Camera Obscura* No. 22 (January 1990):138-149

Feminism and Foucault: Reflections on Resistance. Edited by Irene Diamond and Lee Quinby. Reviewed by Ladelle McWhorter. *NWSA Journal* 2, No. 4 (Autumn 1990):677-678

Historicisms New and Old: "Charles Dickens" Meets Marxism, Feminism, and West Coast Foucault. Judith Newton. *Feminist Studies* 16, No. 3 (Fall 1990):449-470

**Foulds, Rosemary**

The Everyday World as Problematic. Book Review. *Women and Environments* 12, No. 2 (Spring 1990): 28

**Fourth of July Celebrations**

An American Celebration. *Family Circle* 103, No. 9 (June 26, 1990):62-65

**Fourth of July Cookery.** *See* Holidays – Cookery

**Fowler, Richard C.** (joint author). *See* Rich, Charles L

**Fowler, Rowena**

Virginia Woolf and Katharine Furse: An Unpublished Correspondence. *Tulsa Studies in Women's Literature* 9, No. 2 (Fall 1990):201-227

**Fox, Bonnie J.**

Selling the Mechanized Household: 70 Years of Ads in *Ladies Home Journal*. *Gender and Society* 4, No. 1 (March 1990):25-40

**Fox, Michael W.**

Pet Life. *McCall's* 117, No. 7 (April 1990):133; 117, No. 8 (May 1990):163; 117, No. 9 (June 1990):124; 117, No. 10 (July 1990):111; 118, No. 2 (November 1990):156; 118, No. 3 (December 1990):145

**Fox, Nicols**

The Other Running Mates: First Ladies. *Lear's* (September 1990):102-105+

**Fox-Genovese, Elizabeth**

Socialist-Feminist American Women's History. *Journal of Women's History* 1, No. 3 (Winter 1990):181-210

**Fraiman, Susan**

Against Gendrification: Agendas for Feminist Scholarship and Teaching in Women's Studies. *Iris* 23 (Spring-Summer 1990):5-9

**Fraisse, Genevie4ve**

Muse de la raison. Reviewed by Mai3r Verthuy. *Resources for Feminist Research* 19, No. 1 (March 1990):25

**Frames.** *See* Picture Frames and Framing

**France – Actors**

Passion Player. Anne-Elisabeth Moutet. *Harper's Bazaar* (August 1990):134-137+

**France – Designers**

European Designers to Watch. Charla Carter. *Vogue* (August 1990):124-150

**France – Feminism**

Sexual Subversions: Three French Feminists. By Elizabeth Grosz. Reviewed by Iris Young. *The Women's Review of Books* 7, No. 8 (May 1990):26

Talking Feminist. Letty Cottin Pogrebin. *On the Issues* 14 (1990):15+

**France – History**

Les Reines de France. By Paule Lejeune. Reviewed by Marie-France Silver. *Resources for Feminist Research* 19, No. 1 (March 1990):31

Muse de la raison. By Genevie4ve Fraisse. Reviewed by Mai3r Verthuy. *Resources for Feminist Research* 19, No. 1 (March 1990):25

Society and Culture in Early Modern France: Eight Essays. By Natalie Davis. Reviewed by Patricia

Crawford. *Australian Feminist Studies* No. 12 (Summer 1990):131-132

Spinners and Weavers of Auffay: Rural Industry and the Sexual Division of Labor in a French Village, 1750-1850. By Gay L. Gullickson. Reviewed by Judith DeGroat. *Gender and Society* 4, No. 2 (June 1990):272-274

Women, Work and the French State: Labour Protection and Social Patriarchy, 1879-1919. By Mary Lynn Stewart. Reviewed by Karen Offen. *Resources for Feminist Research* 19, No. 1 (March 1990):45-46

Women and the Economy of Paris in the Sixteenth Century. Carol Loats. *NWSA Journal* 2, No. 4 (Autumn 1990):684-686

Working Women, Gender, and Industrialization in Nineteenth-Century France: The Case of Lorraine Embroidery Manufacturing. Whitney Walton. *Journal of Women's History* 2, No. 2 (Fall 1990):42-65

### France – History – Feminist Perspectives

Histoire de la vie Privée, volume 5, De la Premie4re Guerre mondiale à nos jours. Edited by Antoine Prost and Gérard Vincent. Reviewed by Sian Reynolds. *Gender & History* 2, No. 2 (Summer 1990):212-217

Histoire de la vie Privée, volume 4, De la révolution à la Grande Guerre. Edited by Michelle Perrot. Reviewed by Sian Reynolds. *Gender & History* 2, No. 2 (Summer 1990):212-217

Sexual Politics in the Career and Legend of Louise Michel. Notes. Marie Marmo Mullaney. *Signs* 15, No. 2 (Winter 1990):300-322

### France – History – Revolution, 1789-1799

The Body and the French Revolution: Sex, Class and Political Culture. By Dorinda Outram. Reviewed by Elisabeth G. Sledziewski. *Gender & History* 2, No. 3 (Autumn 1990):363-365

Citizens: A Chronicle of the French Revolution. By Simon Schama. Reviewed by Susan P. Conner. *Journal of Women's History* 1, No. 3 (Winter 1990):244-260

Femmes, culture et révolution. By Elke Harten and Hans-Christian Harten. Reviewed by Micheline Dumont. *Resources for Feminist Research* 19, No. 2 (June 1990):43

The French Revolution. By George Rudé. Reviewed by Susan P. Conner. *Journal of Women's History* 1, No. 3 (Winter 1990):244-260

The French Revolution. By J. F. Bosher. Reviewed by Susan P. Conner. *Journal of Women's History* 1, No. 3 (Winter 1990):244-260

The Political Culture of the French Revolution, Vol. 2. Edited by Colin Lucas. Reviewed by Susan P. Conner. *Journal of Women's History* 1, No. 3 (Winter 1990):244-260

Women and the Public Sphere in the Age of the French Revolution. By Joan B. Landes. Reviewed by Elisabeth G. Sledziewski. *Gender & History* 2, No. 3 (Autumn 1990):363-365

Women's Memory, Women's History, Women's Political Action: The French Revolution in Retrospect, 1789-1889-1989. Karen Offen. *Journal of Women's History* 1, No. 3 (Winter 1990):211-230

### France – History – Third Republic

L'égalité en marche: La Féminisme français sous la Troisie4me République. By Laurence Klejman and Florence Rochefort. Reviewed by Diane Lamoureux. *Resources for Feminist Research* 19, No. 2 (June 1990):40

### France – Homosexuality

An Interview with Edmund White. Interview. Adam Block. *Out/Look* No. 10 (Fall 1990):56-62

### France – Immigration

<X2>"Fundamentalism" – Haphazardly Used, Never Defined. Liliane Landor. *Spare Rib* No. 209 (February 1990):48

### France, K. L

Health: The Etiquette of Birth Control. *Mademoiselle* (September 1990):187

### France – Prostitution

French Debate on Bordellos. *Women's World* , No. 24 (Winter 1990/91): 50-52

### France – Reproductive Technology

Where to Put Madame X's Ovocytes? Françoise Laborie. *Connexions* 32 (1990):11-13

### France – Travel

Doing Burgundy by Bicycle for Fun. Marcia Seligson. *Lear's* (September 1990):56-59

Riviera Retreat. Diane Sustendal. *Harper's Bazaar* (May 1990):60-68

### France – Violence Against Women

A Testimony Unbinds Many Tongues. Miche4le Le Doeuff. *Connexions* 34 (1990):18-19

### Frances, Esther

Some Thoughts on the Contents of *Hypatia*. *Hypatia* 5, No. 3 (Fall 1990):159-161

### Franchises (Retail Trade)

Economies. Marion Asnes. *Lear's* (November 1990):50

Entrepreneurial Edge. Mark Stevens. *Working Woman* (December 1990):45-48

Franchises Shape Up Kids. *Executive Female* (March/April 1990):76

Mary Poppins to the Rescue. *Executive Female* (May/June 1990):72

**Francis, Catherine**

Hellbent Men and Their Cities. Book Review. *Belles Lettres* 5, No. 4 (Summer 1990):40+

The Hellbent Men They Know. *Belles Lettres* 5, No. 4 (Summer 1990):40+

The People I Know. Book Review. *Belles Lettres* 5, No. 4 (Summer 1990):40+

**Francis, E. Aracelis** (joint author). *See* Peebles-Wilkins, Wilma

**Francis, Joanne Johnston**

Green Pastures. Fiction. *Feminist Studies* 16, No. 1 (Spring 1990):69-83

**Franck, Karen A.** and Ahrentzen, Sherry (editors)

New Households, New Housing. Reviewed by Ellen Vera Allen. *Canadian Women's Studies* 11, No. 2 (Fall 1990):85

**Franco, Jean**

Plotting Women: Gender and Representation in Mexico. Reviewed by Francesca Miller. *NWSA Journal* 2, No. 3 (Summer 1990):514-516

**Franco, Marjorie**

Too Close for Comfort. Short story. *Redbook* 175, No. 4 (August 1990):54-59+

**Frank, Aphra**

Lessons From My Mother's Life. *Glamour* (May 1990):300+

**Frank, Barney** (about)

Barney Frank: A Public Man's Private Sins. Barbara Grizzuti Harrison. *Mademoiselle* (February 1990):100

**Frank, Elizabeth Bales**

Maid of Honor, Inc. *Glamour* (July 1990):86

The Man with a Broken Heart. *Glamour* (November 1990):270

**Frank, Katherine**

A Voyage Out: The Life of Mary Kingsley. Reviewed by Helen Callaway. *Women's Studies International Forum* 13, No. 4 (1990):405

**Frankel, Ellen**

The Classic Tales, 4,000 Years of Jewish Lore. Reviewed by Carole L. Glickfeld. *Lilith* 15, No. 4 (Fall 1990):35

**Frankel, Noralee**

The Southern Side of "Glory": Mississippi African-American Women During the Civil War. *Minerva* 8, No. 3 (Fall 1990):28-36

**Franken, Christien** (joint author). *See* Braidotti, Rosi

**Frankenberg, Ruth**

<X2> "White Women, Racism and Anti-Racism": A Women's Studies Course Exploring Racism and Privilege. *Women's Studies Quarterly* 18, Nos. 1-2 (Spring-Summer 1990):145-153

**Franklin, Aretha** (about). *See also* De Veaux, Alexis, Milloy, Marilyn, and Ross, Michael Erik; Music, Popular

Me and Aretha. Matt Robinson. *Lear's* (May 1990):102-106+

**Franklin, I. E.**

200 Words: Lear's Women Caught in the Act. *Lear's* (February 1990):94-97

**Franks, Violet**

Life Trek: The Odyssey of Adult Development. Book Review. *Journal of Women and Aging* 2 No. 3 (1990):117-118

**Franks, Violet** (joint author). *See* Fodor, Iris G.

**Franzen, Monika** and Ethiel, Nancy

Make Way! A Few Portraits of American Women in Cartoons. *Woman of Power* 17 (Summer 1990):68-73

**Franzway, Suzanne**, Court, Dianne, and Connell, R. W.

Staking a Claim: Feminism, Bureaucracy and the State. Reviewed by Lois Bryson. *Australian Feminist Studies* No. 12 (Summer 1990):133-136

**Fraser, Antonia**

The Warrior Queens. Reviewed by Chitra Pershad Reddin. *Atlantis* 15, No. 2 (Spring 1990):102-103

**Fraser, Jill Andresky**

Fashion Victims. *Savvy Woman* (June 1990):54-57, 84

**Fraser, Laura**

The Cosmetic Surgery Hoax. *Glamour* (February 1990):184-185+

Hodgson's Choice. *Vogue* (July 1990):206-209+

Medical Report: The Mammogram Problem. *Glamour* (December 1990):66-72

RU 486: The "Abortion Pill." *Glamour* (September 1990):316-317+

**Fraser, Nancy**

Gender and History: The Failure of Social Theory in the Age of the Family. Book Review. *NWSA Journal* 2, No. 3 (Summer 1990):505-508

Gender and the Politics of History. Book Review. *NWSA Journal* 2, No. 3 (Summer 1990):505-508

**Fraser, Norah**

One Woman's Journey: Getting Ready to Fight Back. *off our backs* 20, No. 3 (March 1990):25+

**Fraser, Sylvia**

My Father's House. Reviewed by Sandra Butler. *AFFILIA* 5, No. 1 (Spring 1990):110-112

**Fraud.** See Quacks and Quackery; Swindlers and Swindling

**Frazier, Marc**

Crescent City Cuisine: Dining Out in New Orleans. *Harper's Bazaar* (January 1990):134+

**Fredericks, Lynn**

Bottled Blossoms. *Harper's Bazaar* (March 1990):239

Thirst for Knowledge. *Harper's Bazaar* (July 1990):114+

**Frederiksen, Elke** (editor)

Women Writers of Germany, Austria, and Switzerland: An Annotated Bio-Bibliographical Guide. Review. *Feminist Collections* 11, No. 3 (Spring 1990):16

**Free, Suzanne Hamilton**

The Blue Nature. Reviewed by Eleanor J. Bader. *Belles Lettres* 5, No. 2 (Winter 1990):21

**Freedman, Estelle B.**

Small Group Pedagogy: Consciousness Raising in Conservative Times. *NWSA Journal* 2, No. 4 (Autumn 1990):603-623

**Freedman, Estelle B.** (interview)

Fear of Feminism? *The Women's Review of Books* 7, No. 5 (February 1990):25-26

**Freedman, Janet**

Work That Is Real: Perspectives on Feminist Librarianship. *WLW Journal* 14, No. 1 (Fall 1990):3-5

**Freedman, Marcia**

Exile in the Promised Land: A Memoir. Reviewed by Gayle Kirshenbaum. *Ms.* 1, No. 3 (November/December 1990):55

Exile in the Promised Land: A Memoir. Reviewed by Lillian Moed and Tracy Moore. *The Women's Review of Books* 8, No. 3 (December 1990):30

Exile in the Promised Land: A Memoir. Reviewed by Miriyam Glazer. *Belles Lettres* 6, No. 1 (Fall 1990):10-12

Exile in the Promised Land. Reviewed by Donna Berman. *New Directions for Women* 19, No. 6 (November-December 1990):18

Exile in the Promised Land. Reviewed by Margaret Randall. *Bridges* 1, No. 2 (Fall 1990): 121-124

A State of Danger. Video Review. *On the Issues* 15 (Summer 1990):30-31

**Freedman, Rita**

Bodylove. Reviewed by Patricia A. Connor-Greene. *Women and Health* 16, Nos. 3/4 (1990):211-221

**Freedman, Samuel G.**

Small Victories. Excerpt. *McCall's* 117, No. 8 (May 1990):114-118+

**Freedman, Sara**

Among Schoolchildren. Book Review. *The Women's Review of Books* 7, No. 5 (February 1990):1+

The Love of a Good Woman. *The Women's Review of Books* 7, No. 5 (February 1990):1+

**Freedom of Speech.** See also Censorship; Pornography

This is What You Thought: Should There Be Limits on Free Speech? *Glamour* (December 1990):135

**Freeman, Jean Todd**

A Fine Night for Caroling. Short story. *Family Circle* 103, No. 17 (December 18, 1990):56-61

**Freeman, Jo**

Born for Liberty: A History of Women in America. Book Review. *New Directions for Women* 19, No. 2 (March/April 1990):20

**Freeman, Marion** (editor)

Alfonsina Storni: Selected Poems. Reviewed by Zoë Anglesey. *Belles Lettres* 5, No. 2 (Winter 1990):17

**Freeman, Miriam L.**

Beyond Women's Issues: Feminism and Social Work. *AFFILIA* 5, No. 2 (Summer 1990):72-89

**Freeman, Morgan** (about)

Two for the Road. Mark Matousek. *Harper's Bazaar* (January 1990):58

**Freeman, Patricia K.** and Lyons, William

Legislators' Perceptions of Women in State Legislatures. *Women & Politics* 10, No. 4 (1990):121-132

**Freeman, Sue J. M.**

Managing Lives: Corporate Women and Social Change. Reviewed by Felicia Kornbluh. *The Women's Review of Books* 7, No. 8 (May 1990):9-10

**Freeman, Verdelle**

The Gender Integration Project at Piscataway Township Schools: Quilting a New Pedagogical Patchwork Through Curriculum Re-vision. *Women's Studies Quarterly* 18, Nos. 1-2 (Spring-Summer 1990):70-77

**Freeperson, Kathy**

The DeCristo Girls. Short Story. *Sinister Wisdom* 41 (Summer-Fall 1990):23-30

Florida Killer Brings Both Fear and Organizing. *off our backs* 20, No. 9 (October 1990):2-3

Munda. Poem. *Sinister Wisdom* 41 (Summer-Fall 1990):66

**Free Riding.** See Feminist Organizations – Division of Labor

**Freiman, Jane**

Broadway Debut. *Harper's Bazaar* (May 1990):157

A Question of Loyalty. Frederick Hermann. *Glamour* (March 1990):286+

Real Stories of Best Friends. *Glamour* (November 1990):214-219

Scruples: He Cheated–Do You Rat on the Rat? Ellen Welty. *Mademoiselle* (June 1990):134

Sinister Wisdom Friendship Discussion 12/5/89. *Sinister Wisdom* 40 (Spring 1990):17-35

When Friends Give Advice on Love. Carol Lynn Mithers. *Glamour* (February 1990):216

Woman to Woman: Female Friendship in Victorian Fiction. By Tess Cosslett. Reviewed by Susan Hardy Aiken. *Signs* 16, No. 1 (Autumn 1990):188-192

**Friendship–Personal Narratives**

Lunar Eclipse 1989. Sandra Lambert. *Sinister Wisdom* 40 (Spring 1990):72-73

Palabras. Terri de la Peña. *Sinister Wisdom* 40 (Spring 1990):38-39

In a Penal Colony. Loretta Johnson. *Sinister Wisdom* 40 (Spring 1990):15-16

A Sacred Time: Journal Entries (excerpts). Pamela Gray. *Sinister Wisdom* 40 (Spring 1990):64-71

**Fringe Benefits.** *See* Employee Benefits

**Frink, Cheryl Coggins** (joint author). *See* Stacy, Diane

**Frisbees.** *See* Flying Discs (Game)

Fame, Fortune, and Frisbees. Andrew Tilin. *Women's Sports and Fitness* 12, No. 7 (October 1990):14

**Fritz, Leah**

Devotions of a Feminist Atheist. *Ms.* 1, No. 2 (September/October 1990):18-19

**Fritz-Piggott, Jill**

From Fantasy to Reality. *The Women's Review of Books* 7, No. 4 (January 1990):17

At the Gates of the Animal Kingdom. Book Review. *The Women's Review of Books* 7, No. 12 (September 1990):24-26

Light Reading. *The Women's Review of Books* 7, No. 12 (September 1990):24-26

Maasai Days. Book Review. *The Women's Review of Books* 7, No. 4 (January 1990):17

Reliable Light. Book Review. *The Women's Review of Books* 7, No. 12 (September 1990):24-26

The School of Love. Book Review. *The Women's Review of Books* 7, No. 12 (September 1990):24-26

In the Shadow of the Sacred Grove. Book Review. *The Women's Review of Books* 7, No. 4 (January 1990):17

Sweet Talk. Book Review. *The Women's Review of Books* 7, No. 12 (September 1990):24-26

**Froberg, Debra G.** (joint author). *See* Gjergingen, Dwenda K.

**Frodi, Ann,** Grolnick, Wendy, Bridges, Lisa, and Berko, Jacqueline

Infants of Adolescent and Adult Mothers: Two Indices of Socioemotional Development. *Adolescence* 25, No. 98 (Summer 1990):363-374

**Fronefield, Judy Baker**

Sharing Stories: Saving Lives. *Women's Studies Quarterly* 18, Nos. 3-4 (Fall-Winter 1990):168-170

**Frook, John E.**

Found: A Home for Left-Behind Kids. *Family Circle* 103, No. 3 (February 20, 199):84-88

Prisoners at Home. *Family Circle* 103, No. 2 (February 1, 1990):60-62

Women Who Make a Difference: Turning the Town Around. *Family Circle* 103, No. 14 (October 16, 1990):17-19

**Frost, Charles**

A New History of Social Welfare. Book Review. *AFFILIA* 5, No. 3 (Fall 1990):120

**Frost, Kathy** (about)

In From the Cold. Jane Howard. *Lear's* (October 1990):146-150

**Frost, Laurie A.** (joint author). *See* Hyde, Janet Shibley

**Frozen Dinners.** *See* Frozen Foods

**Frozen Foods**

Healthy Cook: Frozen Assets. Mary Beth Jung. *Working Woman* (August 1990):84

**Frueh, Joanna** (joint editor). *See* Raven, Arlene

**Fruit**

Fresh Fruit and Fabulous. Holly Sheppard. *McCall's* 118, No. 1 (October 1990):142-144

Light and Easy: Autumn Fruit Compote. *Good Housekeeping* 211, No. 4 (October 1990):132

**Frumkes, Lewis Burke**

Something to Think about When Choosing a Dog, or Not. *McCall's* 117, No. 8 (May 1990):58

**Frye, Ellen**

The Other Sappho. Reviewed by Kore Archer. *off our backs* 20, No. 7 (July 1990):14

The Other Sappho. Reviewed by Kore Archer. *Sinister Wisdom* 40 (Spring 1990):130-131

**Frye, Marilyn**

Do You Have to Be a Lesbian to Be a Feminist? *off our backs* 20, No. 8 (August/September 1990):21-23

Lesbian Ethics: Toward New Value. Book Review. *Hypatia* 5, No. 3 (Fall 1990):132-137

The Possibility of Lesbian Community. *Lesbian Ethics* 4, No. 1 (Spring 1990): 84-87

A Taste for the Winners. *Savvy Woman* (June 1990):27-28

**Futehally, Shama**

The First Rains. Short Story. *Manushi* No. 59 (July-August 1990):33-42

**Future—Predictions.** *See* Forecasting

# G

**Gaa, John P.** (joint author). *See* Turell, Susan C.

**Gaard, Greta**

Living What We're Thinking. *The Women's Review of Books* 8, No. 2 (November 1990):27-28

Reweaving the World: The Emergence of Ecofeminism. Book Review. *The Women's Review of Books* 8, No. 2 (November 1990):27-28

**Gabbana, Stefano** (about). *See also* Italy—Fashion

**Gadon, Elinor W.**

The Once and Future Goddess: A Symbol for Our Time. Reviewed by Deborah Ann Light. *Ms.* 1, No. 2 (September/October 1990):27

The Once and Future Goddess: A Symbol for Our Time. Reviewed by Jane Caputi. *The Women's Review of Books* 7, No. 8 (May 1990):14-15

The Once and Future Goddess. Reviewed by Cynthia Werthamer. *New Directions for Women* 19, No. 4 (July-August 1990):14

**Gage, Carolyn**

Louisa May Incest, a One-Act Play. *Trivia* 16/17 (Fall 1990):137-156

**Gage, Joan**

After 20 Years, I Met the Daughter I Thought Was Dead. *Good Housekeeping* 210, No. 4 (April 1990):102-109

The Dancin' Grannies. *Good Housekeeping* 211, No. 5 (November 1990):24+

**Gagliardi, N. E.**

Image: Summer Confidence—Makeup that Can Take the Heat. *Working Woman* (June 1990):74-76

**Gagliardi, Nancy**

The Best Contact Lenses for You—and Why. *Redbook* 175, No. 6 (October 1990):96-97+

Beware the New Measles Epidemic. *Redbook* 175, No. 3 (July 1990):34-37

Do You Know His Secret Sexual Fantasies? *Redbook* 175, No. 5 (September 1990):168-169+

**Gagnon, Monika**

Beyond Post-Feminism: The Work of Laura Mulvey and Griselda Pollock. *Canadian Women's Studies* 11, No. 1 (Spring 1990):81-83

**Gaier, Eugene L.** (joint author). *See* Wisniewski, Shirley A.

**Gailey, Christine Ward**

Kinship to Kinship: Gender Hierarchy and State Formation in the Tongan Islands. Reviewed by Mary K. Anglin. *Signs* 15, No. 3 (Spring 1990):642-645

**Gailitis, Margita**

Choice. Poem. *Canadian Women's Studies* 11, No. 2 (Fall 1990):62

Retrograde. Poem. *Canadian Women's Studies* 11, No. 2 (Fall 1990):62

Victorian Lace. Poem. *Canadian Women's Studies* 11, No. 2 (Fall 1990):62

**Gaines, Deborah**

Travel: Last Chance for Summer. Bibliography. *Essence* 21, No. 4 (August 1990):97-98

**Gala, Chetna**

Trying to Give Women Their Due: The Story of Vitner Village. *Manushi* No. 59 (July-August 1990):29-32

**Galas, Judith**

Does "No" Mean "Yes"? *New Directions for Women* 19, No. 6 (November-December 1990):8

**Gales, Ron**

Killing Them Softly. *Working Woman* (November 1990):112-115+

**Galinsky, Ellen**

The Five Biggest Mistakes Most Parents Make. *Ladies' Home Journal* 107, No. 6 (June 1990):80-87

**Galinsky, Ellen** (joint author). *See* Friedman, Dana

**Gallagher, Winifred**

Why Are You the Way You Are? *McCall's* 117, No. 8 (May 1990):78-80

**Gallin, Donna**

Disability Income: A Case Study. *Executive Female* 13, No. 4 (July-August 1990):13-14

<X2> "What's Your Financial Planning IQ?" *Executive Female* (May/June 1990):57-59

**Gallman, Vanessa J.**

Single-Parent Dating: Single . . . with Children. *Essence* 20, No. 12 (April 1990):102-103

**Gallo, Claudia** (joint author). *See* Rubenstein, Carin

**Gallo, Nick**

Rebecca Roe: Getting Tough on Sex Offenders. *McCall's* 117, No. 12 (September 1990):57-58

**Galst, Liz**

Everyday Lesbians. *The Women's Review of Books* 7, No. 4 (January 1990):11

The Mundane and the Monumental. *The Women's Review of Books* 7, No. 8 (May 1990):19

The Names of the Moons of Mars. Book Review. *The Women's Review of Books* 7, No. 4 (January 1990):11

People in Trouble. Book Review. *The Women's Review of Books* 7, No. 8 (May 1990):19

Voyages Out I: Lesbian Short Fiction. Book Review. *The Women's Review of Books* 7, No. 4 (January 1990):11

**Galton, Jean**

Dinner ASAP: Grill Power. *Working Woman* (September 1990):207

A Taste of Summer. *Working Woman* (July 1990):105

**Gambarini, Patricia**

Words and Music for Social Change. *New Directions for Women* 19, No. 5 (September-October 1990):4

**Gamble, Vanessa Northington**

No Medical Miracle. *The Women's Review of Books* 8, No. 3 (December 1990):10-11

Other Women's Children. Book Review. *The Women's Review of Books* 8, No. 3 (December 1990):10-11

**Gambling**

The New Gold Rush. Kathryn Casey. *Ladies' Home Journal* 107, No. 9 (September 1990):160-164 +

**Games.** See also Play

**Games, Board**

Two Lesbian Games. Laura Post. *Hot Wire* 6, No. 2 (May 1990):24-26 +

**Gamman, Lorraine** and Marshment, Margaret (editors)

The Female Gaze. Reviewed by Sumiko Higashi. *Gender & History* 2, No. 1 (Spring 1990):123-126

The Female Gaze: Women as Viewers of Popular Culture. Reviewed by Cynthia Carter. *Resources for Feminist Research* 19, No. 2 (June 1990):41-42

**Gamman, Lorraine** and O'Neill, Gilda

Oxford Twenty Years On: Where Are We Now? *Feminist Review* No. 36 (Autumn 1990):96-102

**Gammon, Carolyn**

Basic Feminist Lessons: Man-hating. *off our backs* 20, No. 3 (March 1990):25

**Gandotra, M. M.** and Das, N. P.

Contraceptive Choice, Shift and Use Continuation: A Prospective Study in Gujarat. *Journal of Family Welfare* 36, No. 3 (September 1990):54-69

**Ganem, Mark**

Italian Nights. *Harper's Bazaar* (April 1990):209-211 +

Vineyard Haven. *Harper's Bazaar* (May 1990):160

**Gangs**

Women Who Make a Difference. Linda Marsa. *Family Circle* 103, No. 15 (November 6, 1990):15-17

**Gannett Foundation – Research Grants**

Women, Men and Media Center Endowed by Gannett Foundation. *Media Report to Women* 18, No. 3 (May/June 1990):1

**Ganong, Lawrence H.**

Strangers in the House. Book Review. *Journal of Marriage and the Family* 52, No. 1 (February 1990):281-282

**Ganong, Lawrence H.,** Coleman, Marilyn, and Mapes, Dennis

A Meta-analytic Review of Family Structure Stereotypes. *Journal of Marriage and the Family* 52, No. 2 (May 1990):287-297

**Ganong, Lawrence H.** (joint author). See Coleman, Marilyn

**Garafola, Lynn**

Holding on to the Air: An Autobiography. Book Review. *The Women's Review of Books* 8, No. 3 (December 1990):7-8

Roses All the Way. *The Women's Review of Books* 8, No. 3 (December 1990):7-8

**Garate, Dama Vasquez** (interview)

Central American Women: Battered in USA. Carol Anne Douglas. *off our backs* 20, No. 5 (May 1990):3 +

**Garb, Maggie**

Information Is Power Chicago Women Know. *New Directions for Women* 19, No. 2 (March/April 1990):12

**Garbage.** See Refuse and Refuse Disposal

**Garber, Marianne Daniels** (joint author). See Garber, Stephen W.

**Garber, Stephen W.** and others

Is Your Child Hyperactive? *Redbook* 175, No. 6 (October 1990):32-35

**Garbo, Greta** (about)

Garbo Talks, In a Manner of Speaking. Antoni Gronowicz. *Lear's* (July 1990):74-87 +

Greta Garbo's "Mysterious" Private Life. Margie Adam. *Out/Look* No. 10 (Fall 1990):25

**Garcia, Andy** (about). See Actors

**Garcia, Guy**

Gods Country. *Harper's Bazaar* (September 1990):128-134

**Garcia, Jane**

Penelope Ann Miller – In Good Shape. *Mademoiselle* (October 1990):92-94

**Garcia, June**

Soul Stylist. *Mademoiselle* (June 1990):92-97

**Garrison, Dee**

Mary Heaton Vorse: The Life of an American Insurgent. Reviewed by Eleanor J. Bader. *Belles Lettres* 5, No. 2 (Winter 1990):13

**Garrison, Zina** (about)

Queen of the Ball. Lloyd Gite. *Essence* 21, No. 3 (July 1990):51+

Zina's Zenith. Josh Young. *Women's Sports and Fitness* 12, No. 4 (May-June 1990):52-56

**Gartner, Dorothy** and Schultz, Nancy M.

Establishing the First Stages of Early Reciprocal Interactions between Mothers and Their Autistic Children. *Women and Therapy* 10, Nos. 1/2 (1990):159-167

**Gartner, Rosemary**

Killing Women: Response to Increased Gender Equality? *Women and Environments* 12, No. 1 (Fall 1989/Winter 1990): 14-16

**Garton, Victoria**

An Open-Trench-Coat Poem for Dirty Boys. Poem. *Heresies* 25 (1990):60

**Garvey, Amy Jacques** (about). *See* Black History

**Garvie, Laurel**

New Projects at Women's Health Clinic. *Healthsharing* 11, No. 2 (March 1990):6

**Gaskell, Jane S.** and McLaren, Arlene Tigar (editors)

Women and Education: A Canadian Perspective. Reviewed by Catharine E. Warren. *Gender and Education* 2, No. 1 (1990):102-104

**Gates, Anita**

Career Management: How to Be the One They Promote. *Working Woman* (October 1990):100-105

How to Come In from the Cold. *Working Woman* (July 1990):75-78

The Perk Report. *Working Woman* (August 1990):62-64

Travel: Get-Smart Getaways. Bibliography. *Essence* 21, No. 5 (September 1990):100-102

When Your Career's Hot but You're Not. *Working Woman* (July 1990):80

**Gaultier, Jean-Paul** (about). *See* Talley, André Leon

**Gaunt, Mary**

Kirkham's Find. Reviewed by Judith MacBean. *Australian Feminist Studies* No. 12 (Summer 1990):123-125

**Gaur, Albertine**

The Perfect Wife: The Orthodox Hindu Woman According to the Stri6dharmapaddhati of Tryambakayajvan. Book Review. *Gender & History* 2, No. 2 (Summer 1990):223-225

Wives of the God-King: The Rituals of the Davada6si6s of Puri. Book Review. *Gender & History* 2, No. 2 (Summer 1990):223-225

**Gavras, Costa**

Music Box. Reviewed by M Hutzpit. *Spare Rib* No. 215 (August 1990):34

**Gay, Janice Templeton,** Flowers, Juanzetta Shew, and Tu, Kuei-Shen

Women's Health Care in China: American Travelers' Views. *Health Care for Women International* 11, No. 1 (1990):65-74

**Gay Academic Union**

Inside the Ivory Closet: The Challenges Facing Lesbian and Gay Studies. Jeffrey Escoffier. *Out/Look* No. 10 (Fall 1990):36-37

**Gayle, Helene** (about). *See* De Veaux, Alexis, Milloy, Marilyn, and Ross, Michael Erik

**Gayle, Nefertiti**

Forwad Out De My African Daughters. Poem. *Spare Rib* No. 210 (March 1990):35

**Gay Rights.** *See also* Homosexuality

Gays Still Banned from Military. Tricia Lootens. *off our backs* 20, No. 4 (April 1990):11

**Gay Rights Activists.** *See also* Acquired Immune Deficiency Syndrome – ACT-UP

An Open Letter to the Gay and Lesbian Community. Holly Hughes and Richard Elovich. *Out/Look* No. 10 (Fall 1990):74-75

Gay Lib vs. AIDS: Averting Civil War in the 1990s. Eric E. Rofes. *Out/Look* No. 8 (Spring 1990):8-17

My America – and Yours: A Letter to US Lesbian and Gay Activists. Dennis Altman. *Out/Look* No. 8 (Spring 1990):62-65

Writers as Activists. Amber Hollibaugh. *Out/Look* No. 10 (Fall 1990):69-72

**Gay Rights Organizations.** *See also* International Lesbian and Gay Association

**Gay Studies**

Inside the Ivory Closet: The Challenges Facing Lesbian and Gay Studies. Jeffrey Escoffier. *Out/Look* No. 10 (Fall 1990):36-37

**Gay Theater.** *See* Theater – Gay Experience

**Geary, Hilary** (about)

Fe3te Accompli. Diane Sustendal. *Harper's Bazaar* (August 1990):176

**Gecas, Viktor** and Seff, Monica A.

Families and Adolescents: A Review of the 1980s. *Journal of Marriage and the Family* 52, No. 4 (November 1990):941-598

**Gediman, Judith S.** and Brown, Linda P.

Birth Bond: Reunions Between Birthparents and Adoptees: What Happens After. Reviewed by Datha Clapper Brack. *New Directions for Women* 19, No. 6 (November-December 1990):25

**Gehry, Frank** (about). *See* Architecture

**Geibel, Victoria**

Telecommuting. *Lear's* (December 1990):102-107

**Geiger, Susan**

What's So Feminist About Doing Women's Oral History? *Journal of Women's History* 2, No. 1 (Spring 1990):169-182

Women and African Nationalism. *Journal of Women's History* 2, No. 1 (Spring 1990):227-244

**Gelb, Joyce** and Klein, Ethel

Women's Movements: Organizing for Change. Reviewed by Joan C. Tronto. *NWSA Journal* 2, No. 3 (Summer 1990):492-495

**Gelles, Judy**

A Family Portrait: A Wife/Mother/Photographer's Revenge. Photo essay. *Ms.* 1, No. 3 (November/December 1990):76-81

**Gelles, Richard J.** and Conte, Jon R.

Domestic Violence and Sexual Abuse of Children: A Review of Research in the Eighties. *Journal of Marriage and the Family* 52, No. 4 (November 1990):1045-1058

**Gemmette, Elizabeth Villiers**

Armed Combat: The Women's Movement Mobilizes Troops in Readiness for the Inevitable Constitutional Attack on the Combat Exclusion for Women in the Military. *Women's Rights Law Reporter* 12, No. 2 (Summer 1990): 89-101

**Gender Bias.** *See* Gender Discrimination

**Gender Differences.** *See also*
Communication – Gender Differences; Genital Herpes; Management Techniques – Gender Differences; Mathematics – Gender Differences; Music, Popular – Gender Differences; Social Entertaining – Home Parties

Boys and Dolls, Girls and Trucks. Julia Kagan. *McCall's* 118, No. 3 (December 1990):88

Deceptive Distinctions: Sex, Gender and the Social Order. By Cynthia Fuchs Epstein. Reviewed by Debra Renée Kaufman. *Gender and Society* 4, No. 4 (December 1990):

Deceptive Distinctions: Sex, Gender and the Social Order. By Cynthia Fuchs Epstein. Reviewed by Janet Zollinger Giele. *Gender and Society* 4, No. 4 (December 1990):553-554

Early Adolescent Age and Gender Differences in Patterns of Emotional Self-Disclosure to Parents and Friends. Dennis R. Papini, Frank F. Farmer, Steven M. Clark, Jill C. Micka, and Jawanda K. Barnett. *Adolescence* 25, No. 100 (Winter 1990):959-976

Gender Comparisons of College Students' Attitudes toward Sexual Behavior. Stephan M. Wilson and Nilufer P. Medora. *Adolescence* 25, No. 99 (Fall 1990):615-627

<X2>*See also* Personality Traits – Gender Differences Risk Taking Behavior – Gender Differences

The Truth About the Sex Gap. Carol Ann Rinzler. *Family Circle* 103, No. 9 (June 26, 1990):57-59

**Gender Discrimination.** *See also*
Employment – Discrimination; Scholastic Aptitude Test – Gender Bias; Universities and Colleges – Sexism

Citizenship in a Woman-Friendly Polity. Notes. Kathleen B. Jones. *Signs* 15, No. 4 (Summer 1990):781-812

Differential Treatment Based on Sex. Karen D. Stout and Michael J. Kelly. *AFFILIA* 5, No. 2 (Summer 1990):60-71

Family Leave and Gender Justice. Suzanne E. England. *AFFILIA* 5, No. 2 (Summer 1990):8-24

Feminism Unmodified: Discourses on Life and Law. By Catharine A. MacKinnon. Reviewed by Kathleen B. Jones. *Women & Politics* 10, No. 1 (1990):73-76

Gender Difference and Gender Disadvantage. Deborah L. Rhode. *Women & Politics* 10, No. 2 (1990):121-135

Out Box: The "Pretty Woman" Problem. Gail Collins. *Working Woman* (October 1990):160

Sex Discrimination in Higher Education and the Professions: An Annotated Bibliography. By Mary Donovan. Review. *Feminist Collections* 11, No. 3 (Spring 1990):15

Strong Mothers, Weak Wives: The Search for Gender Equality. By Miriam M. Johnson. Reviewed by Arline Prigoff. *AFFILIA* 5, No. 2 (Summer 1990):113-114

Women and Politics: An International Perspective. By Vicki Randall. Reviewed by Eleanor E. Zeff. *Women & Politics* 10, No. 3 (1990):135-136

Women and the Constitution: A Bicentennial Perspective. Sandra Day O'Connor. *Women & Politics* 10, No. 2 (1990):5-16

Women as Single Parents: Confronting Institutional Barriers in the Courts, the Workplace, and the Housing Market. Edited by Elizabeth A. Mulroy. Reviewed by Dorothy C. Miller. *AFFILIA* 5, No. 2 (Summer 1990):104-106

**Gender Discrimination, Criminal Justice Administration**

The Wives Take the Heat: Ethel Rosenberg and Anne Pollard. June Barsky. *Lilith* 15, No. 1 (Winter 1990):28-29

Gender Discrimination in Athletics. See also Athletics – Sex Discrimination

Gender Equality. See Separate Spheres; Violence Against Women

Gender Identity. See also Autobiography

Gender Blending: Confronting the Limits of Duality. By Holly Devor. Reviewed by Carol LeMasters. The Women's Review of Books 7, No. 9 (June 1990):12

Gender Trouble: Feminism and the Subversion of Identity. By Judith Butler. Reviewed by Margaret Nash. Hypatia 5, No. 3 (Fall 1990):171-175

Making Faces: The Cosmetics Industry and the Cultural Construction of Gender, 1890-1930. Kathy Peiss. Genders 7 (Spring 1990):143-169

Who Is Laughing Now? The Role of Humour in the Social Construction of Gender. Marlene Mackie. Atlantis 15, No. 2 (Spring 1990):11-26

**Gender Ideology**

Uneven Developments: The Ideological Work of Gender in Mid-Victorian England. By Mary Poovey. Reviewed by Alex Owen. Gender & History 2, No. 2 (Summer 1990):239-241

Gender Marking. See Language – Gender Differences

**Gender Ratio and Socioeconomic Status**

The Socioeconomics of a Female Majority in Eighteenth-Century Bermuda. Notes. Elaine Forman Crane. Signs 15, No. 2 (Winter 1990):231-258

**Gender Representation**

<X2> "The Leg Business": Transgression and Containment in American Burlesque. Robert C. Allen. Camera Obscura , No. 23 (May 1990): 42-69

Gender Roles. See also Family Life; Family Life – Bibliographies; Homemakers; Public Administration – Gender Roles; Schools

Arms and the Enlisted Woman. By Judith Hicks Stiehm. Reviewed by Mary Ann Tetreault. Women & Politics 10, No. 4 (1990):137-138

Deceptive Distinctions: Sex, Gender, and the Social Order. By Cynthia Fuchs Epstein. Reviewed by Karen K. Kirst-Ashman. AFFILIA 5, No. 1 (Spring 1990):116-118

A Delicate Balance: "This is Exactly Where I Want to Be." Margaret Jaworski. Ladies' Home Journal 107, No. 3 (March 1990):162-164

The Effect of Husband's Occupational Attainment on Wife's Achievement. William W. Philliber and Dana Vannoy-Hiller. Journal of Marriage and the Family 52, No. 2 (May 1990):323-329

The Female Role and Menstrual Distress: An Explanation for Inconsistent Evidence. Alfred B. Heilbrun, Jr., Lisa Friedberg, Dawna Wydra, and Alyson L. Worobow. Psychology of Women Quarterly 14, No. 3 (September 1990):403-417

Feminism and Economics. Barbara R. Bergmann. Women's Studies Quarterly 18, Nos. 3-4 (Fall-Winter 1990):68-73

The Flip Side: Looking for a Few Good Men. Richard Chevat. Family Circle 103, No. 9 (June 26, 1990):12

Gender Differences in Spouse Caregiver Strain: Socialization and Role Explanations. Baila Miller. Journal of Marriage and the Family 52, No. 2 (May 1990):311-321

Gender in Intimate Relations. Edited by Barbara J. Risman and Pepper Schwartz. Reviewed by Karen K. Kirst-Ashman. AFFILIA 5, No. 1 (Spring 1990):116-118

Justice, Gender, and the Family. By Susan Moller Okin. Reviewed by Paul William Kingston. Journal of Marriage and the Family 52, No. 2 (May 1990):562-563

Lana's "Imitation": Melodramatic Repetition and the Gender Performative. Judith Butler. Genders 9 (Fall 1990):1-18

Masculinity, Autobiography and History. David Morgan. Gender & History 2, No. 1 (Spring 1990):34-39

Masculinity and Power. By Arthur Brittan. Reviewed by Jeff Hearn. Gender & History 2, No. 3 (Autumn 1990):351-353

Raising Boys, Raising Girls. Lee Salk. McCall's 118, No. 3 (December 1990):84-86

Rousseau's Political Defense of the Sex-roled Family. Penny Weiss and Anne Harper. Hypatia 5, No. 3 (Fall 1990):90-109

Sex Differences in Political Participation: Processes of Change in Fourteen Nations. By Carol A. Christy. Reviewed by Sue Thomas. Women & Politics 10, No. 1 (1990):76-78

In the Spirit: The Feminine Principle. Susan L. Taylor. Essence 21, No. 7 (November 1990):53

Subversive Intent: Gender Politics and the Avant-Garde. By Susan Rubin Suleiman. Reviewed by Lillian S. Robinson. The Women's Review of Books 7, Nos. 10-11 (July 1990):32-33

<X2> "The Very House of Difference": Gender as "Embattled" Standpoint. Thomas Foster. Genders 8 (Summer 1990):17-37

Viewpoint: Being Smart the Woman's Way. Mary-Lou Weisman. Glamour (December 1990):138-140

Women in Colombian Organizations, 1900-1940: A Study in Changing Gender Roles. René De La Pedraja Tomán. Journal of Women's History 2, No. 1 (Spring 1990):98-119

**Gender Roles – Adolescent Attitudes**

Adolescents' Attitudes toward Women's Roles: A Comparison between Israeli Jews and Arabs. Rachel Seginer, Mousa Karayanni, and Mariam M.

Mar'i. *Psychology of Women Quarterly* 14, No. 1 (March 1990):119-133

Comparisons of Female and Male Early Adolescent Sex Role Attitude and Behavior Development. Christine Nelson and Joanne Keith. *Adolescence* 25, No. 97 (Spring 1990):183-204

Relationships between Teenage Smoking and Attitudes toward Women's Rights, Sex Roles, Marriage, Sex and Family. Ingrid Waldron and Diane Lye. *Women and Health* 16, Nos. 3/4 (1990):23-46

**Gender Roles – Africa**

Women and the State in Africa. Edited by Jane L. Parpart and Kathleen A. Staudt. Reviewed by Barbara Lewis. *Women & Politics* 10, No. 1 (1990):82-84

**Gender Roles – History**

Changing Gender Identities in an Industrializing Society: The Case of Norway, 1870-1914. Ida Blom. *Gender & History* 2, No. 2 (Summer 1990):131-147

Gender and History: The Failure of Social Theory in the Age of the Family. By Linda J. Nicholson. Reviewed by Nancy Fraser. *NWSA Journal* 2, No. 3 (Summer 1990):505-508

Gender and the Politics of History. By Joan Wallach Scott. Reviewed by Joan Wallach Scott. *NWSA Journal* 2, No. 3 (Summer 1990):505-508

Sexual Science: The Victorian Construction of Womanhood. By Cynthia Eagle Russett. Reviewed by Nancy Leys Stepan. *Gender & History* 2, No. 3 (Autumn 1990):337-342

Uneven Developments: The Ideological Work of Gender in Mid-Victorian England. By Mary Poovey. Reviewed by Cynthia Wright. *Resources for Feminist Research* 19, No. 1 (March 1990):35-36

Uneven Developments: The Ideological Work of Gender in Mid-Victorian England. By Mary Poovey. Reviewed by Rachel Bowlby. *Tulsa Studies in Women's Literature* 9, No. 2 (Fall 1990):314-317

**Gender Roles – in Families**

Feminism, Children, and the New Families. Edited by Sanford M. Dornbusch and Myra H. Strober. Reviewed by Ellen B. Bogolub. *AFFILIA* 5, No. 3 (Fall 1990):116-118

The Invisible Web: Gender Patterns in Family Relationships. By Marianne Walters, Betty Carter, Peggy Papp, and Olga Silverstein. Reviewed by Ellen B. Bogolub. *AFFILIA* 5, No. 3 (Fall 1990):116-118

Motherhood and Sex Role Development. Mary A. Halas. *Women and Therapy* 10, Nos. 1/2 (1990):227-243

**Gender Roles – Stereotyping**

Hollywood Melodrama, Douglas Sirk, and the Repression of the Female Subject (*Magnificent Obsession*). Michael Selig. *Genders* 9 (Fall 1990):35-48

Never Cry Bull Moose: Of Mooses and Men: The Case of the Scheming Gene. Susan Kray. *Women & Language* 13, No. 1 (Fall 1990):31-37

Old Plans, New Specifications: A Political Reading of the Medical Discourse on Menopause. Roe Sybylla. *Australian Feminist Studies* No. 12 (Summer 1990):95-107

Women and Computers: An Introduction. Ruth Perry and Lisa Greber. *Signs* 16, No. 1 (Autumn 1990):74-101

**Gender Role Stereotyping.** *See also* Gender Discrimination; Sexism

**Gender Studies.** *See also* Tonga – Culture and History

Gender Bias in Scholarship: The Pervasive Prejudice. Edited by Winifred Tomm and Hamilton Gordon. Reviewed by Marilyn Biggerstaff. *AFFILIA* 5, No. 1 (Spring 1990):121-123

Gender Issues in Field Research. By Carol A. B. Warren. Reviewed by Marilyn Biggerstaff. *AFFILIA* 5, No. 1 (Spring 1990):121-123

Mapping the Moral Domain. Edited by Carol Gilligan, Janie Victoria Ward, Jill McLean Taylor, and Betty Bardige. Reviewed by Alison K. Adams. *AFFILIA* 5, No. 3 (Fall 1990):111-113

Meta-analysis and the Psychology of Gender Differences. Janet Shibley Hyde. *Signs* 16, No. 1 (Autumn 1990):55-73

The Problem of Gender for Women's Studies. Mary Evans. *Women's Studies International Forum* 13, No. 5 (1990):457-462

**Genetic Defects.** *See also* Brain

Congenital Disability and Medical Research: The Development of Amniocentesis. Peggy McDonough. *Women and Health* 16, Nos. 3/4 (1990):137-153

**Genetic Defects – Support Groups**

A Guide to Selected National Genetic Voluntary Organizations. By the National Center for Education in Maternal and Child Health. Reviewed by Jeanne Mager Stellman. *Women and Health* 16, No. 1 (1990):115

**Genetic Determinants**

Predisposed and Stuck With It. John Steinbeck IV. *Lear's* (December 1990):56-57

Why Are You the Way You Are? Winifred Gallagher. *McCall's* 117, No. 8 (May 1990):78-80

**Genetic Engineering.** *See also* Reproductive Technologies

The Gene Prophets. Lori Andrews. *Vogue* (January 1990):198-199+

The Rest of Reality. Vandana Shiva. *Ms.* 1, No. 3 (November/December 1990):72-73

**Genetic Screening.** *See also* Fetal Monitoring

The Gene Screen. David Beers. *Vogue* (June 1990):236-237, 278-279

Prenatal Testing: Peering into the Womb. Maggie Morrison. *McCall's* 118, No. 1 (October 1990):160-162

Trial by Genetics. Boston Women's Health Collective. *Ms.* 1, No. 2 (September/October 1990):30

**Genital Herpes.** *See also* Sexually Transmitted Diseases

Genital Herpes: Gender Comparisons and the Disease Experience. Rosemary A. Jadack, Mary L. Keller, and Janet Shibley Hyde. *Psychology of Women Quarterly* 14, No. 3 (September 1990):419-434

**Genital Warts.** *See* Sexually Transmitted Diseases

**Genius**

Haunted by Intellect, Hobbled by Wisdom. Lynn S. Baker. *Lear's* (September 1990):60-64

**Genocide**

Is It Genocide? Karen Grigsby Bates. *Essence* 21, No. 5 (September 1990):76-78+

**George, Diana Hume**

Lynching Women. *Ms.* 1, No. 3 (November/December 1990):58-60

**George, Margaret**

Women in the First Capitalist Society: Experiences in Seventeenth-Century England. Reviewed by Cynthia Herrup. *Gender & History* 2, No. 2 (Summer 1990):226-228

Women in the First Capitalist Society: Experiences in Seventeenth-Century England. Reviewed by Margaret W. Ferguson. *Tulsa Studies in Women's Literature* 9, No. 1 (Spring 1990):158-160

**Gerard, Francis**

A Private Life. Reviewed by Esme Nathan. *Spare Rib* No. 209 (February 1990):35

**Gerber, Merrill Joan**

Bye Bye Baby. Short story. *Redbook* 175, No. 1 (May 1990):48-51+

King of the Hill. Reviewed by Miriam Kalman Harris. *The Women's Review of Books* 7, Nos. 10-11 (July 1990):35

King of the World. Reviewed by Charlotte Zoë Walker. *Belles Lettres* 5, No. 3 (Spring 1990):19

A View of Boston Common. Short Story. *Belles Lettres* 5, No. 3 (Spring 1990):18

**Gerber, Merrill Joan** (interview)

Belles Lettres Interview: Merrill Joan Gerber. Susan Koppelman. *Belles Lettres* 5, No. 3 (Spring 1990):16-17

**Gerberg, Judith**

Workshop: When Change Is In the Air. *Executive Female* (March/April 1990):61-63

**Gergen, Mary M.**

Finished at 40: Women's Development within the Patriarchy. *Psychology of Women Quarterly* 14, No. 4 (December 1990):471-493

**Gerike, Ann E.**

On Gray Hair and Oppressed Brains. *Journal of Women and Aging* 2, No. 2 (1990):35-46

**Germany**

Full Circle: The Wall. Friedl Elaine Bell. *Family Circle* 103, No. 9 (June 26, 1990):154

When Jessica Meets Natasha: A Feminist View of German Reunification. Edda Kerschgens. *Australian Feminist Studies* No. 12 (Summer 1990):15-27

**Germany – Acquired Immune Deficiency Syndrome**

Desire Cannot Be Fragmented. Sabine Marx. *Connexions* 33 (1990):6-9

**Germany – Art History**

Fierce Expressions. Robin Cembalest. *Harper's Bazaar* (September 1990):244-245+

**Germany – Employment – Inside the Home**

<X2> "Housework Made Easy": The Taylorized Housewife in Weimar Germany's Rationalized Economy. Mary Nolan. *Feminist Studies* 16, No. 3 (Fall 1990):549-577

**Germany – Fashion**

Wall to Wall Denim. *Mademoiselle* (September 1990):276-281

**Germany – Feminist Movement**

East German Feminists: The Lila Manifesto. Lisa DiCaprio. *Feminist Studies* 16, No. 3 (Fall 1990):621-636

GDR Women's Culture. *New Directions for Women* 19, No. 3 (May/June 1990):11

The Mothers' Manifesto and Disputes over 'Mütterlichkeit'. Prue Chamberlayne. *Feminist Review* No. 35 (Summer 1990):9-23

**Germany – Filmmaking**

Melodrama and Social Drama in the Early German Cinema. Heide Schlüpmann. *Camera Obscura* No. 22 (January 1990):73-88

**Germany – Homosexuality**

Lesbians in Germany: 1890's to 1920's. By Lillian Faderman and Brigitte Eriksson. Reviewed by Deborah Price. *Belles Lettres* 5, No. 4 (Summer 1990):48-49

**Germany – Nazism – Women's Roles**

Jewish Women in Nazi Germany: Daily Life, Daily Struggles, 1933-1939. Marion A. Kaplan. *Feminist Studies* 16, No. 3 (Fall 1990):579-606

Mothers in the Fatherland. Fred Pelka. *On the Issues* 16 (Fall 1990):26-28+

**Germany – Politics and Government**

Back to the Potsdamer Platz. Richard Atcheson. *Lear's* (April 1990):92-97

Germany Celebrates: Fashion Freedom. *Harper's Bazaar* (September 1990):232-241

The New Concert of Europe. James Chace. *Lear's* (February 1990):99-101

Opposition Activists. *New Directions for Women* 19, No. 3 (May/June 1990):11

What Price Unity? Jill Benderly. *New Directions for Women* 19, No. 3 (May/June 1990):1+

**Germany – Prostitution**

Germany. *Women's World* , No. 24 (Winter 1990/91): 19-21

**Germany – Reproductive Technology**

Homo Erectus. *Connexions* 32 (1990):10

<X2>"Quality Control" of Children. *Connexions* 32 (1990):18-19

Raw Material. Sylvia Groth. *Connexions* 32 (1990):9

**Germany – Status of Women**

The Panther Women: Five Stories from the Cassette Recorder. By Sarah Kirsch. Reviewed by Hilda Scott. *The Women's Review of Books* 7, No. 4 (January 1990):10

Women in East Germany Today. Louise K. Davidson. *off our backs* 20, No. 7 (July 1990):8

**Gero, Joan M.**

Primate Visions: Gender, Race and Nature in the World of Modern Science. Book Review. *Women's Studies International Forum* 13, No. 6 (1990):609-610

**Gershoff, Stanley** and Whitney, Catherine

100 Great Little Tips to Make Healthy Eating Easier. *Redbook* 174, No. 6 (April 1990):120-133

**Gershwin, George**

Vogue Arts: Oh, Kay! Reviewed by Richard Alleman. *Vogue* (December 1990):188-189

**Gertz, Alison** (about)

Alison Gertz: Champagne, Roses . . . and AIDS. Lisa DePaulo. *Mademoiselle* (December 1990):176-179+

**Gertzog, Irwin N.**

Female Suffrage in New Jersey, 1790-1807. *Women & Politics* 10, No. 2 (1990):47-58

**Gerzina, Gretchen Holbrook**

Carrington: A Life. Reviewed by Carolyn Burke. *The Women's Review of Books* 7, No. 5 (February 1990):6-8

**Geschwender, James A.** and Carroll-Seguin, Rita

Exploding the Myth of African-American Progress. Notes. *Signs* 15, No. 2 (Winter 1990):285-299

**Gessen, Masha**

We Have No Sex: Soviet Gays and AIDS in the Era of Glasnost. *Out/Look* No. 9 (Summer 1990):42-54

**Gettinger-Brizuela, Adam**

Rosario. *Out/Look* No. 7 (Winter 1990):25-29

**Getty, Estelle** (about). *See also* Sherman, Eric, "Gabbing with the Golden Girls"

**Gewertz, Deborah** (joint author). *See* Errington, Frederick

**Ghana – Status of Women**

Traffic in Women in Ghana. *Women's World* , No. 24 (Winter 1990/91): 20

Where Do We Stand: African Women of the Diaspora in Kwame Nkrumah's Ghana, 1960. Maceo Crenshaw Dailey, Jr., and Freddye Hill. *Sage* 6, No. 1 (Summer 1989):77-79

**Ghigna, Charles**

Passion's Paradox. Poem. *Good Housekeeping* 211, No. 3 (September 1990):304

**Ghosh, A. K.** and Das, N. K.

Fertility and Adoption of Family Planning Among the Muslims of 24 Parganas, West Bengal, Part II. *Journal of Family Welfare* 36, No. 1 (March 1990):32-42

**Gianoulis, Tina**

Perspective. *Sinister Wisdom* 42 (Winter 1990-1991):69-73

**Giardia Lamblia.** *See* Giardiasis

**Giardiasis**

Good Health: Stomach Distress! Linda Troiano. *Redbook* 175, No. 4 (August 1990):32-34

**Gibbs, Jewelle Taylor**, Huang, Larke Nahme, and associates

Children of Color: Psychological Interventions with Minority Youth. Book Review. *Adolescence* 25, No. 97 (Spring 1990):250

**Giblin, Paul T.** (joint author). *See* Sachs, Barbara A.

**Gibson, Mary**

Between Stangers: Surrogate Mothers, Expectant Fathers, and Brave New Babies. Book Review. *Women and Health* 16, No. 2 (1990):134-137

On the Insensitivity of Women: Science and the Woman Question in Liberal Italy, 1890-1910. *Journal of Women's History* 2, No. 2 (Fall 1990):11-41

**Gibson, Mary Ellis**

New Stories By Southern Women. Reviewed by Junior Bridge. *On the Issues* 15 (Summer 1990):27-28

**Gibson, Mel** (about). *See also* Sexual Attraction, "200 Words"

Talking with Mel Gibson: "My Six Kids Come First." Interview. Carson Jones. *Redbook* 175, No. 4 (August 1990):40-42

**Gibson, Shirley** (about)

Works of Art to Wear. *Essence* 21, No. 6 (October 1990):22

**Giddings, Paula**

Baby of the Family. Book review. *Essence* 20, No. 11 (March 1990):44

Book Marks. Bibliography. *Essence* 21, No. 2 (June 1990):44; 21, No. 4 (August 1990):50; 21, No. 5 (September 1990):52; 21, No. 6 (October 1990):52; 21, No. 7 (November 1990):50; 21, No. 8 (December 1990):38

Book Marks. *Essence* 20, No. 11 (March 1990):44

Book Marks: Taking the Stage. *Essence* 20, No. 10 (February 1990):42

Clover. Book review. *Essence* 21, No. 5 (September 1990):52

Lion in the Lobby: Clarence Mitchell, Jr.'s Struggle for the Passage of Civil Rights Laws. Book review. *Essence* 21, No. 7 (November 1990):50

My Family, The Jacksons. Book review. *Essence* 21, No. 8 (December 1990):38

Terry Williams Takes Drugs Seriously. *Essence* 20, No. 10 (February 1990):42

White Women's Christ and Black Women's Jesus: Feminist Christology and Womanist Response. Book review. *Essence* 21, No. 6 (October 1990):52

**Giddings, Paula** (about). *See* Writers – Interviews, "Graceful Passages"

**Giddle, Cynthia L.**

The Women's Peace Union and the Outlawry of War, 1921-1941. Book Review. *New Directions for Women* 19, No. 5 (September-October 1990):18

WPU: Women Resist War. *New Directions for Women* 19, No. 5 (September-October 1990):18

**Gidycz, Christine A.** and Koss, Mary P.

A Comparison of Group and Individual Sexual Assault Victims. *Psychology of Women Quarterly* 14, No. 3 (September 1990):325-342

**Giele, Janet Zollinger**

Deceptive Distinctions: Sex, Gender and the Social Order. Book Review. *Gender and Society* 4, No. 4 (December 1990):553-554

**Gifford, Kathie Lee** (about)

Star Gazing. Susan Ungaro and Linda Moran Evans. *Family Circle* 103, No. 7 (May 15, 1990):73-74

Star Light, Star Bright. *Family Circle* 103, No. 17 (December 18, 1990):110-115

**Gifford, Vernon D.** and Dean, Margie M.

Differences in Extracurricular Activity Participation, Achievement, and Attitudes toward School between Ninth-Grade Students Attending Junior High School and Those Attending Senior High School. *Adolescence* 25, No. 100 (Winter 1990):799-802

**Gifted Children**

Daydreaming and Curiosity: Stability and Change in Gifted Children and Adolescents. Steven R. Gold and Bruce B. Henderson. *Adolescence* 25, No. 99 (Fall 1990):701-708

Loneliness, Coping Strategies and Cognitive Styles of the Gifted Rural Adolescent. *Adolescence* 25, No. 100 (Winter 1990):977-988

**Gifts to Minors.** *See also* Christmas Gifts

The Early Years. T. Berry Brazelton. *Family Circle* 103, No. 17 (December 18, 1990):84-87

Parents' Journal: 10 Great Gifts for Under $10! Bibliography. Mary Mohler and Margery D. Rosen. *Ladies' Home Journal* 107, No. 12 (December 1990):60-64

**Gigli, Romeo** (about). *See also* Fashion Designers

**Gilbert, Jennifer**

Group Fights Oppression. *New Directions for Women* 19, No. 6 (November-December 1990):6

**Gilbert, Kate**

Crafting Selves: Power, Gender and Discourses of Identity in a Japanese Workplace. Book Review. *The Women's Review of Books* 8, No. 1 (October 1990):5-7

Crested Kimono: Power and Love in the Japanese Business Family. Book Review. *The Women's Review of Books* 8, No. 1 (October 1990):5-7

One Big Happy Family? *The Women's Review of Books* 8, No. 1 (October 1990):5-7

**Gilbert, Lucia A.** (joint author). *See* Eldridge, Natalie S.

**Gilbert, Ronnie**

Love Will Find a Way. Reviewed by Lynn Wenzel. *New Directions for Women* 19, No. 3 (May/June 1990):8

**Gilbert, Ronnie** (about)

AWMAC Banquet Speaker: Ronnie Gilbert. *Hot Wire* 6, No. 2 (May 1990):35

**Gilbert, Sara**

The Psychology of Dieting. Reviewed by Patricia A. Connor-Greene. *Women and Health* 16, Nos. 3/4 (1990):211-221

**Gilbert-Neiss, Connie**

Meet Heidi Jones: The Straight Gay Leader. *Out/Look* No. 8 (Spring 1990):54-55

**Gilchrist, Ellen**

Light Can Be Both Wave and Particle. Reviewed by Valerie Miner. *The Women's Review of Books* 7, No. 7 (April 1990):17-18

**Gilden, K. B.**

Between the Hills and the Sea. Reviewed by Helen Yglesias. *The Women's Review of Books* 7, Nos. 10-11 (July 1990):16-17

**Giles, Dari**

Travel: Spa Vacations. *Essence* 20, No. 9 (January 1990):87-88+

**Giles, Judy**

Second Chance, Second Self? *Gender and Education* 2, No. 3 (1990):357-361

**Giles, Molly**

Maximum Security. Short story. *McCall's* 118, No. 2 (November 1990):119-120+

**Gilford, Dorothy M.** (editor)

The Aging Population in the Twenty-First Century: Statistics for Health Policy. Reviewed by Cheryl H. Kinderknecht. *Journal of Women and Aging* 2 No. 3 (1990):115-116

**Gilkey, Bertha Knox** (about). *See* De Veaux, Alexis, Milloy, Marilyn, and Ross, Michael Erik

**Gill, Mark Stewart**

Deal Her In. *Savvy Woman* (April 1990):19-20

**Gillan, Evelyn**

Grit and Diamonds: Women in Scotland Making History 1980-1990. Book Review. *Spare Rib* No. 214 (July 1990):23

**Gillan, Margaret**

Hush-a-Bye Baby. Video Review. *Spare Rib* 219 (December 1990-January 1991):34

**Gillan, Maria Mazziotti**

Connections. Poem. *Sinister Wisdom* 41 (Summer-Fall 1990):32-33

Public School No. 18: Paterson, New Jersey. Poem. *Sinister Wisdom* 41 (Summer-Fall 1990):8-9

**Gilles de la Tourette's Syndrome.** *See* Policoff, Stephen Phillip, "Diseases Your Doctor May Miss"

**Gillespie, Cynthia K.**

Justifiable Homicide: Battered Women, Self-Defense and the Law. Reviewed by Pamela A. Brown. *AFFILIA* 5, No. 2 (Summer 1990):106-109

**Gillespie, Diane** and Spohn, Cassie

Adolescents' Attitudes Toward Women in Politics: A Follow-up Study. *Women & Politics* 10, No. 1 (1990):1-16

**Gillespie, "Dizzy"** (about). *See* Music – Jazz

**Gillespie, Marcia Ann**

Delusions of Safety. *Ms.* 1, No. 2 (September/October 1990):49-51

**Gillette, Virginia M.**

Love's Rocky Road. *Good Housekeeping* 210, No. 5 (May 1990):182-183

**Gilliam-Mosee, Redenia** (about)

What Goes on Behind the Boardwalk. Janet Gardner. *Savvy Woman* (January 1990):34-36

**Gilligan, Carol** and others (editors)

Mapping the Moral Domain. Reviewed by Alison K. Adams. *AFFILIA* 5, No. 3 (Fall 1990):111-113

**Gillis, Jack**

Money Matters. *Good Housekeeping* 211, No. 3 (September 1990):92; 211, No. 4 (October 1990):25

**Gilman, Charlotte Perkins – Criticism and Interpretation**

The Rape of the Text: Charlotte Gilman's Violation of *Herland*. Kathleen Margaret Lant. *Tulsa Studies in Women's Literature* 9, No. 2 (Fall 1990):291-308

**Gilman, Charlotte Perkins** (about)

To Herland and Beyond: The Life and Work of Charlotte Perkins Gilman. By Ann J. Lane. Reviewed by Mary Titus. *Belles Lettres* 6, No. 1 (Fall 1990):40-42

**Gilman, Hank**

The Social Security Rip-Off. *Working Mother* 13, No. 10 (October 1990):20-23

**Gilman, Michelle** (about)

Woman to Watch. Diane Keaton. *Women's Sports and Fitness* 12, No. 7 (October 1990):57

**Gilman, Rowann**

The One-Inch Solution. *Working Woman* (September 1990):190-192

Summer Indispensables: 17 Super Finds to Order by Phone. *Working Woman* (June 1990):85-86

**Gilmartin, Pat**

Fish and Fetishes: A Victorian Woman on African Rivers. *Women and Environments* 12, No. 2 (Spring 1990): 10-12

**Gilot, Franc2oise**

Picasso, Gilot, Matisse: Daily Life Among the Titans. *Lear's* (August 1990):76-84+

**Gilroy, Beryl**

Boy-Sandwich. Reviewed by Rhonda Cobham. *The Women's Review of Books* 7, Nos. 10-11 (July 1990):29-31

**Gimbutas, Marija**

The Language of the Goddess. Reviewed by Cynthia Werthamer. *New Directions for Women* 19, No. 4 (July-August 1990):14

The Language of the Goddess. Reviewed by Ruby Rohrlich. *The Women's Review of Books* 7, No. 9 (June 1990):14-16

**Gimbutas, Marija** (interview)

Archaeomythology: An Interview with Marija Gimbutas. Joan Marler. *Woman of Power* 15 (Fall-Winter 1990):6-13

**Gingerbread Houses**

Food Forecast. Jean Hewitt. *Family Circle* 103, No. 17 (December 18, 1990):83

Storybook Christmas Houses. Marianne Langan. *McCall's* 118, No. 3 (December 1990):90-93

**Gingras, Anne-Marie**, Maillé, Chantal, and Tardy, Evelyne

Sexes et militantisme. Reviewed by Caroline Andrew. *Resources for Feminist Research* 19, No. 2 (June 1990):45-46

**Ginor, Zvia**

Rediscovering and Creating a Women's Literature. *Lilith* 15, No. 4 (Fall 1990):38

**Ginorio, Angela B.** (joint author). *See* Remick, Helen

**Ginsberg, Alice E.**

Lesbian Ethics. Book Review. *New Directions for Women* 19, No. 1 (January/February 1990):24

**Ginsberg, Susan H.**

Taking the Rush Out of Rush Hour. *Good Housekeeping* 211, No. 3 (September 1990):102

**Ginzberg, Lori**

Standing Again at Sinai: Judaism from a Feminist Perspective. Book Review. *Bridges* 1, No. 2 (Fall 1990): 126-127

**Ginzberg, Ruth**

Reply to Jahren. *Hypatia* 5, No. 1 (Spring 1990):178-180

**Ginzburg, Carlo**

Clues, Myths, and the Historical Method. Reviewed by Dana Polan. *Camera Obscura* No. 22 (January 1990):131-137

**Gioseffi, Daniela**

Women on War and Survival. *On the Issues* 16 (Fall 1990):29-31 +

**Giraffe Project**

What Makes a Giraffe Stand Tall? Ann Medlock. *Lear's* (July 1990):30-31

**Girl Scouts of America.** *See* Hesselbein, Frances (about)

**Gish, Annabeth** (about)

The Dish on Gish. Nikki Finke. *Mademoiselle* (April 1990):98-100

**Gissing, Vera** (about). *See* Holocaust (1939-1945) – Survivors

**Gitanjalishri**

Bel Patra. Short Story. *Manushi* 61 (November-December 1990):37-43

**Gite, Lloyd**

AIDS in the Workplace. *Glamour* (November 1990):116

Corporate Racism: Not Your Imagination. *Glamour* (September 1990):154

Make Money Moonlighting. *Essence* 21, No. 3 (July 1990):28-30

Queen of the Ball. *Essence* 21, No. 3 (July 1990):51 +

Should You Moonlight? *Glamour* (May 1990):144

**Gittelson, Natalie**

The Stay-at-Home Side of Lesley-Anne Down. *McCall's* 117, No. 7 (April 1990):20

Whoopi & Jean Rap. *McCall's* 118, No. 2 (November 1990):110-114

**Gittins, Diana**

A Century of Childhood. Book Review. *Gender and Education* 2, No. 1 (1990):104-105

**Giulietti, Rita** (joint author). *See* Kristiansen, Connie M.

**Givenchy** (about). *See also* Fashion Designers

**Givens, Ron**

Kids' TV: A Report Card. *Ladies' Home Journal* 107, No. 10 (October 1990):72-74

**Giviskos, Lynne**

Cool Salads for Hot Summer Days. *McCall's* 117, No. 9 (June 1990):120

**Gjerdingen, Dwenda K.**, Froberg, Debra G., and Fontaine, Patricia

A Causal Model Describing the Relationship of Women's Postpartum Health to Social Support, Length of Leave, and Complications of Childbirth. *Women and Health* 16, No. 2 (1990):71-87

**Glaser, Elizabeth** (about). *See* Leadership, "1990 Women of the Year"

**Glaser, Milton** (about)

Milton Glaser: The Illusionist. Celia McGee. *Lear's* (September 1990):90-95 +

**Glasgow – Culture**

Scot Free. Julie Moline. *Harper's Bazaar* (June 1990):64 +

**Glasgow, Ellen** (about)

An Epic Life: Novelist and Feminist Ellen Glasgow. Kay Peaslee. *Iris* 24 (Fall-Winter 1990):12-16

**Glasgow, Joanne** (joint editor). *See* Jay, Karla

**Glass Ceiling.** *See also* Career Ladders; Employment – Discrimination

The Glass Ceiling: If I Had a Hammer. Patricia O'Toole. *Lear's* (November 1990):29-30

The Last Barrier. Anne Jardim and Margaret Hennig. *Working Woman* (November 1990):130-134 +

**Glass Craft.** *See* Glassware

**Glassware**

Colored, Cut, or Crystal Clear. Kathryn Lineberger. *Lear's* (November 1990):122-124

**Glaucoma**

Health Department. *Lear's* (June 1990):56

**Glavas, Peggy** (about)

A Real-Life "Norma Rae." Marcia Cohen. *Good Housekeeping* 211, No. 1 (July 1990):98-101

**Glazer, Miriyam**

Desperate for Refuge. *Belles Lettres* 5, No. 3 (Spring 1990):12

Exile in the Promised Land: A Memoir. Book Review. *Belles Lettres* 6, No. 1 (Fall 1990):10-12

The Fringe Is the Most Important Part of the Prayer Shawl. *Belles Lettres* 6, No. 1 (Fall 1990):10-12

God's Ear. Book Review. *Belles Lettres* 6, No. 1 (Fall 1990):10-12

Night Train to Mother. Book Review. *Belles Lettres* 5, No. 3 (Spring 1990):12

Rescued from Oblivion. *Belles Lettres* 5, No. 2 (Winter 1990):7

Standing Again at Sinai: Judaism from a Feminist Perspective. Book Review. *Belles Lettres* 6, No. 1 (Fall 1990):10-12

From That Time and Place, A Memoir 1938-1947. Book Review. *Belles Lettres* 5, No. 2 (Winter 1990):7

**Glazer, Nona Y.**

The Home as Workshop: Women as Amateur Nurses and Medical Care Providers. *Gender and Society* 4, No. 4 (December 1990):479-499

**Glean, Beverley** (about). *See* Irie Dance Company

**Glean, Beverley** (interview)

Let Reggae Touch Your Soul. Delysia Forbes. *Spare Rib* 217 (October 1990):54-55

**Gledhill, Christine** (editor)

Home Is Where the Heart Is: Studies in Melodrama and the Woman's Film. Reviewed by Paula Rabinowitz. *Feminist Studies* 16, No. 1 (Spring 1990):151-169

**Glenn, Evelyn Nakano**

Issei, Nisei, War Bride: Three Generations of Japanese American Women in Domestic Service. Reviewed by Susan Seymour. *Signs* 15, No. 2 (Winter 1990):395-398

**Glenn, Judy**

An Uninsured Women's Center Library . . . It Could Happen to You! *Feminist Collections* 11, No. 2 (Winter 1990):17-18

**Glenn, Norval D.**

Quantitative Research on Marital Quality in the 1980s: A Critical Review. *Journal of Marriage and the Family* 52, No. 4 (November 1990):818-831

**Glenn, Susan**

Daughters of the Shtetl: Life and Labor in the Immigrant Generation. Reviewed by Annelise Orleck. *The Women's Review of Books* 8, No. 3 (December 1990):30-31

**Gleser, Goldine C.** (joint author). *See* Ihilevich, David

**Glickfeld, Carole L.**

The Classic Tales, 4,000 Years of Jewish Lore. Book review. *Lilith* 15, No. 4 (Fall 1990):35

**Global Economy.** *See also* Foreign Investment Policy; International Trade Policy

Smart Investor: Playing the Global Market. Nancy Dunnan. *Lear's* (April 1990):26-28

**Glover, Danny** (about). *See* Actors

**Goal Setting.** *See* Leadership; Organizational Objectives

**Godard, Barbara** (editor)

Gynocritics/La Gynocritique. Reviewed by Janet M. Paterson. *Resources for Feminist Research* 19, No. 1 (March 1990):19

**Godden, Jon** (joint author). *See* Godden, Rumer

**Godden, Rumer** and Godden, Jon

Mercy, Pity, Peace and Love. Reviewed by Nina Mehta. *Belles Lettres* 5, No. 4 (Summer 1990):8

**Goddess Worship**

Amazing Rage. Barbara Mor. *Ms.* 1, No. 1 (July/August 1990):34-35

The Grandmother of Time: A Woman's Book of Celebrations, Spells, and Sacred Objects for Every Month of the Year. By Zsuzsanna E. Budapest. Reviewed by Darlene Dowling. *On the Issues* 16 (Fall 1990):32-33

How I See Her. Genevieve Vaughan. *Woman of Power* 15 (Fall-Winter 1990):62

The Language of the Goddess. By Marija Gimbutas. Reviewed by Cynthia Werthamer. *New Directions for Women* 19, No. 4 (July-August 1990):14

Learning to Dance. Pam McAllister. *Woman of Power* 15 (Fall-Winter 1990):74

The Once and Future Goddess: A Symbol for Our Time. By Elinor W. Gadon. Reviewed by Deborah Ann Light. *Ms.* 1, No. 2 (September/October 1990):27

The Once and Future Goddess: A Symbol for Our Time. By Elinor W. Gadon. Reviewed by Jane Caputi. *The Women's Review of Books* 7, No. 8 (May 1990):14-15

The Once and Future Goddess. By Elinor W. Gadon. Reviewed by Cynthia Werthamer. *New*

*Directions for Women* 19, No. 4 (July-August 1990):14

The Persistence of Female Deities in Patriarchal China. Jordon Paper. *Journal of Feminist Studies in Religion* 6, No. 1 (Spring 1990):25-40

Power Lies in the Stars and Ourselves. Cynthia Werthamer. *New Directions for Women* 19, No. 4 (July-August 1990):8-9

The Presence in the Grove. Jean Mountaingrove. *Woman of Power* 15 (Fall-Winter 1990):80-81

She Rises Life the Sun: Invocations of the Goddess by Contemporary American Women Poets. Edited by Janine Canan. Reviewed by Enid Dame. *Belles Lettres* 5, No. 3 (Spring 1990):9

She Rises Like the Sun: Invocations of the Goddess by Contemporary American Women Poets. Edited by Janine Canan. Reviewed by Annie Finch. *The Women's Review of Books* 7, No. 6 (March 1990):25-26

<X2>"She Want It All": The Sun Goddess in Contemporary Women's Poetry. Patricia Monaghan. *Frontiers* 11, Nos. 2-3 (1990):21-25

Sky Dancer. Tsultrim Allione. *Woman of Power* 15 (Fall-Winter 1990):30-31

Whence the Goddesses: A Source Book. By Miriam Robbins Dexter. Reviewed by Deborah Ann Light. *Ms.* 1, No. 2 (September/October 1990):27

Whose Goddesses Are They? Christina Springer. *New Directions for Women* 19, No. 4 (July-August 1990):4

**Goddess Worship, African**

The Face of Mama is the Blackfaced One. Asungi. *Woman of Power* 15 (Fall-Winter 1990):36-37

Seeking the Goddess in Ancestral Faces. Adele Smith. *Woman of Power* 15 (Fall-Winter 1990):35

**Goddess Worship, Asian**

My Genetic Goddesses. Mitsuye Yamada. *Woman of Power* 15 (Fall-Winter 1990):25-27

**Goddess Worship, Cherokee**

The Grandmothers are Coming Back. Marilou Awiakta. *Woman of Power* 15 (Fall-Winter 1990):41-42

**Goddess Worship, Gaelic**

The Morrigan. Barbara Mor. *Woman of Power* 15 (Fall-Winter 1990):60-61

**Goddess Worship, Indian**

The Embrace of the Mother Goddess. Phoebe Phelps. *Woman of Power* 15 (Fall-Winter 1990):32-34

Searching for the Goddess. Chitra Divakaruni. *Woman of Power* 15 (Fall-Winter 1990):28-29

**Goddess Worship, Mexican**

Re-membering the Goddess. Virginia Sánchez Navarro. *Woman of Power* 15 (Fall-Winter 1990):38-40

**Godley, Georgina** (about). *See* Designers

**Godwin, Rebecca T.**

Thomas. Short Story. *Iris* 24 (Fall-Winter 1990):35-39

**Goel, Uma** (joint author). *See* Singh, Padam

**Gold, Bonnie** and Byron, Ellen

<X2>"School was a Nightmare for Tracey." *Redbook* 174, No. 5 (March 1990):46-49

**Gold – Dress Accessories**

Trading in the New Gold Standard. Diane Clehane. *Lear's* (December 1990):54

**Gold, Fay** (about). *See also* Franklin, I. E., "200 Words"

**Gold, Rozanne** (about)

A Taste for the Winners. Betty Fussell. *Savvy Woman* (June 1990):27-28

**Gold, Steven R.** and Henderson, Bruce B.

Daydreaming and Curiosity: Stability and Change in Gifted Children and Adolescents. *Adolescence* 25, No. 99 (Fall 1990):701-708

**Gold, Todd**

Radical Redux. *Harper's Bazaar* (May 1990):116-119+

**Gold, Tracey** (about)

<X2>"School was a Nightmare for Tracey." Bonnie Gold and Ellen Byron. *Redbook* 174, No. 5 (March 1990):46-49

**Goldberg, Ann**

Body Management: Your Future Face: A Four-Decade Forecast. *Working Woman* (May 1990):111-114

**Goldberg, Barbara**

Go Ahead, Make Her Day. *Savvy Woman* (July/August 1990):60-65+

**Goldberg, Debbie**

Parent Power. *Family Circle* 103, No. 12 (September 4, 1990):91-93

**Goldberg, Kim**

Struggle for Choice on Vancouver Island. *Healthsharing* 11, No. 2 (March 1990):6

**Goldberg, Whoopi** (about)

Whoopi & Jean Rap. Natalie Gittelson. *McCall's* 118, No. 2 (November 1990):110-114

**Goldberger, Avriel H.** (editor)

Woman as Mediatrix: Essays on Nineteenth-Century European Women Writers. Reviewed by Deborah Heller. *Canadian Women's Studies* 11, No. 2 (Fall 1990):90

**Golden, Catherine**

Beatrix Potter: Naturalist Artist. *Woman's Art Journal* 11, No. 1 (Spring-Summer 1990):16-20

**Golden, Gail K.** and Sheinkin, Lynn G.

On the Bias: Leaving Our Father's Houses: Redefining Our Religious Concepts. *AFFILIA* 5, No. 3 (Fall 1990):105-110

**Golden, Stephanie**

Lady versus Low Creature: Old Roots of Current Attitudes toward Homeless Women. *Frontiers* 11, Nos. 2-3 (1990):1-7

**Golden, Susan**

Nursing a Loved One at Home: A Care Giver's Guide. Reviewed by Beverly A. Baldwin. *Journal of Women and Aging* 2, No. 1 (1990):121-123

**Goldenberg, Myrna**

The Alchemy of Survival: One Woman's Journey. Book Review. *Belles Lettres* 6, No. 1 (Fall 1990):6-9

Eva's War: A True Story of Survival. Book Review. *Belles Lettres* 6, No. 1 (Fall 1990):6-9

<X2> (Extra)Ordinary Heroes: Generations of Women Reflect on the Holocaust. *Belles Lettres* 6, No. 1 (Fall 1990):6-9

One, by One, by One: Facing the Holocaust. Book Review. *Belles Lettres* 6, No. 1 (Fall 1990):6-9

Outcast: A Jewish Girl in Wartime Berlin. Book Review. *Belles Lettres* 6, No. 1 (Fall 1990):6-9

Seed of Sarah: Memoirs of a Survivor. Book Review. *Belles Lettres* 6, No. 1 (Fall 1990):6-9

**Goldenberg, Myrna** (joint author). *See* Hedges, Elaine

**Goldenberg, Naomi R.**

Gender and Religion: On the Complexity of Symbols. Book review. *Signs* 15, No. 4 (Summer 1990):874-878

Shaping New Vision: Gender and Values in American Culture. Book review. *Signs* 15, No. 4 (Summer 1990):874-878

**Goldie, Sue M.** (editor)

<X2> "I Have Done My Duty": Florence Nightingale in the Crimean War, 1854-56. Reviewed by June Purvis. *Women's Studies International Forum* 13, Nos. 1-2 (1990):160-161

**Golding, Jacqueline M.**

Division of Household Labor, Strain, and Depressive Symptoms among Mexican Americans and Non-Hispanic Whites. *Psychology of Women Quarterly* 14, No. 1 (March 1990):103-117

**Golding, Sue**

The Difference Within: Feminism and Critical Theory. Book Review. *Resources for Feminist Research* 19, No. 2 (June 1990):39

**Goldingay, Roger** (joint author). *See* Otis, Carol

**Goldman, Anne E.**

<X2> "I Made the Ink": (Literary) Production and Reproduction in *Dessa Rose* and *Beloved*. *Feminist Studies* 16, No. 2 (Summer 1990):313-330

**Goldman, Emma** (about)

Emma Goldman in Exile: From the Russian Revolution to the Spanish Civil War. By Alice Wexler. Reviewed by Eleanor Bader. *Lilith* 15, No. 1 (Winter 1990):7

**Goldman, Juliette** (joint author). *See* Goldman, Ronald

**Goldman, Ronald** and Goldman, Juliette

Show Me Yours: Understanding Children's Sexuality. Reviewed by Rosemary McInnes. *Healthright* 9, No. 2 (February 1990):40

**Gold Miners.** *See* South Africa – Labor

**Goldreich, Gloria**

Mothers. Reviewed by Ruth Schnur. *Lilith* 15, No. 4 (Fall 1990):35

**Goldrich, Laurie**

Express-Lane Cook: An Italian Feast Without Any Fuss. *Working Woman* (February 1990):112

**Golds, Roger** (joint author). *See* Wright, S.

**Goldsby, Jackie**

What It Means to Be Colored Me. *Out/Look* No. 9 (Summer 1990):8-17

**Goldsmith, Elizabeth C.**

A History of Private Life, Vol. III: Passions of the Renaissance. Book Review. *The Women's Review of Books* 7, No. 9 (June 1990):24-25

The Invention of Privacy. *The Women's Review of Books* 7, No. 9 (June 1990):24-25

**Goldsmith, Elizabeth S.** (editor)

Writing the Female Voice: Essays on Epistolary Literature. Reviewed by Joan Hinde Stewart. *Tulsa Studies in Women's Literature* 9, No. 1 (Spring 1990):150-152

**Goldsmith, Judy**

How to Win Friends and Influence Legislators. *Ms.* 1, No. 1 (July/August 1990):90

**Goldsteen, Karen** (joint author). *See* Ross, Catherine E.

**Goldstein, Arnold P.**

The Prepare Curriculum: Teaching Prosocial Competencies. Book Review. *Adolescence* 25, No. 100 (Winter 1990):997

**Goldstein, Elyse**

The Ways We Are: ". . . Who *Has* Made Me a Woman . . ." *Lilith* 15, No. 2 (Spring 1990):32

**Goodman, Melissa**

Men Demystified. *Glamour* (July 1990):162-165

**Goodman, Susan**

Edith Wharton's Mothers and Daughters. *Tulsa Studies in Women's Literature* 9, No. 1 (Spring 1990):127-131

**Goodnow, Jacqueline** and Pateman, Carole (editors)

Women, Social Science and Public Policy. Reviewed by Helen Liggett. *Women & Politics* 10, No. 3 (1990):127-129

**Goodridge, Celeste**

Hints and Disguises: Marianne Moore and Her Contemporaries. Reviewed by Loralee MacPike. *NWSA Journal* 2, No. 4 (Autumn 1990):669-674

**Goodstein, Lynne** and Gyant, LaVerne

A Minor of Our Own: A Case for an Academic Program in Women of Color. *Women's Studies Quarterly* 18, Nos. 1-2 (Spring-Summer 1990):39-44

**Goodwin, Betty**

Artful Cuisine. *Harper's Bazaar* (July 1990):90-93 +

The Foxy Producer. *Mademoiselle* (October 1990):155 +

Long-Stemmed Artistry. *Harper's Bazaar* (March 1990):240

A Perfect 10. *Harper's Bazaar* (May 1990):158

**Goodwin, June**

I Changed My Mind. Poem. *The Women's Review of Books* 8, No. 2 (November 1990):24

Prey. Poem. *The Women's Review of Books* 8, No. 2 (November 1990):24

**Goodwin, Megan P.** and Roscoe, Bruce

Sibling Violence and Agonistic Interactions among Middle Adolescents. *Adolescence* 25, No. 98 (Summer 1990):451-467

**Gorbachev, Raisa** (about)

<X2> "Guess Who Came to My House." Karen Watson and Nancy Stesin. *Ladies' Home Journal* 107, No. 9 (September 1990):24 +

**Gordon, Jaimy**

She Drove Without Stopping. Reviewed by Diana Postlethwaite. *Belles Lettres* 5, No. 4 (Summer 1990):15

**Gordon, Jill**

Beauty Word of Mouth. *Glamour* (September 1990):45-50; (November 1990):37-42; (December 1990):33-36

**Gordon, Kate**

Laughing Beauty. Poem. *Woman of Power* 18 (Fall 1990):15

**Gordon, Linda**

Gender and the Politics of History. Book review. *Signs* 15, No. 4 (Summer 1990):853-858

Heroes of Their Own Lives: The Politics and History of Family Violence. Reviewed by Joan W. Scott. *Signs* 15, No. 4 (Summer 1990):848-852

Heroes of Their Own Lives: The Politics and History of Family Violence. Reviewed by Marcia Bedard. *NWSA Journal* 2, No. 3 (Summer 1990):464-475

Losing Battles. *The Women's Review of Books* 7, No. 6 (March 1990):7-8

The Peaceful Sex? On Feminism and the Peace Movement. *NWSA Journal* 2, No. 4 (Autumn 1990):624-634

Response to Scott. *Signs* 15, No. 4 (Summer 1990):852-853

The Undeserving Poor: From the War on Poverty to the War on Welfare. Book Review. *The Women's Review of Books* 7, No. 6 (March 1990):7-8

**Gordon, Linda** (about)

Response to Gordon. Joan W. Scott. *Signs* 15, No. 4 (Summer 1990):859-860

**Gordon, Lucie Duff**

Letters from Egypt. Reviewed by Judith Tucker. *Journal of Women's History* 2, No. 1 (Spring 1990):245-250

**Gordon, Margaret T.** and Riger, Stephanie

The Female Fear. Reviewed by Karen Merriam. *AFFILIA* 5, No. 3 (Fall 1990):114-115

**Gordon, Mary**

The Other Side. Reviewed by Melanie Kaye-Kantrowitz. *The Women's Review of Books* 7, No. 7 (April 1990):7-9

The Other Side. Reviewed by Scarlet Cheng. *Belles Lettres* 5, No. 3 (Spring 1990):5

**Gordon, Meryl**

The Makeover of a Manager. *Working Woman* (October 1990):108-111 +

<X2> "Who Put *Me* in Charge Anyway?" Confessions of a Rookie Boss. *Mademoiselle* (February 1990):178-179 +

Women Who Work Too Much. *Mademoiselle* (August 1990):214-217, 238

**Gordon, Phyllis** (about)

Women Who Make a Difference. Alice Rindler Shapin. *Family Circle* 103, No. 13 (September 25, 1990):19-23

**Gordon, Pinkie Lee**

Love Considered. Poem. *Essence* 20, No. 11 (March 1990):131

## Gordon, Rebecca

Finding the Lesbians: Personal Accounts from Around the World. Book Review. *The Women's Review of Books* 7, No. 9 (June 1990):7-8

Nice Jewish Girls: A Lesbian Anthology. Book Review. *The Women's Review of Books* 7, No. 9 (June 1990):7-8

The Original Coming Out Stories. Book Review. *The Women's Review of Books* 7, No. 9 (June 1990):7-8

There's Something I've Been Meaning to Tell You. Book Review. *The Women's Review of Books* 7, No. 9 (June 1990):7-8

Twice Blessed: On Being Lesbian, Gay and Jewish. Book Review. *The Women's Review of Books* 7, No. 9 (June 1990):7-8

<X2> "We Are Everywhere." *The Women's Review of Books* 7, No. 9 (June 1990):7-8

## Gordon, Susan

The Write Stuff. *Ladies' Home Journal* 107, No. 2 (February 1990):54

## Gordon, Suzanne

Prisoners of Work. *Savvy* (December-January 1991):56-59+

## Gordon, Tuula

Feminist Mothers. Reviewed by Rosalind Edwards. *Women's Studies International Forum* 13, No. 5 (1990):527

## Gordy, Barbara

Falling Angels. Reviewed by Eleanor J. Bader. *Belles Lettres* 5, No. 3 (Spring 1990):8

## Gore, Lesley (about)

Lesley Gore on k.d. Lang . . . and vice versa. *Ms.* 1, No. 1 (July/August 1990):30-33

## Gore-Booth, Eva (about)

Eva Gore-Booth and Esther Roper: A Biography. By Gifford Lewis. Reviewed by Clare Collins. *Gender & History* 2, No. 1 (Spring 1990):116-118

## Gorney, Cynthia

Fitness. *Vogue* (December 1990):179-182

## Gorov, Lynda

Reform School. *Savvy Woman* (September 1990):64-68+

Vest-Dressed Women. *Savvy Woman* (September 1990):14

## Gorrara, Mary (about)

Against the Odds: Sculptor Mary Gorrara. Luciana Ricciutelli. *Canadian Women's Studies* 11, No. 1 (Spring 1990):100-102

## Gorris, Marleen

A Question of Silence. Reviewed by Constance Balides. *Feminist Collections* 12, No. 1 (Fall 1990):14-18

## Gorris, Marlene (director)

Broken Mirrors. Reviewed by Patricia A. Gozemba. *NWSA Journal* 2, No. 2 (Spring 1990):291-295

## Goscilo, Helena (editor)

Balancing Acts: Contemporary Stories by Russian Women. Reviewed by Jill Benderly. *The Women's Review of Books* 7, Nos. 10-11 (July 1990):19

Balancing Acts: Contemporary Stories by Russsian Women. Reviewed by Judith Deutsch Kornblatt. *Feminist Collections* 11, No. 4 (Summer 1990):3-4

## Goslyn, Anne

Arriving and Caught Up. Music Review. *Spare Rib* 213 (June 1990):35

Like a Version. Record Review. *Spare Rib* No. 212 (May 1990):31

## Gosnell, Mariana

Body Briefing: Feet. *Lear's* (February 1990):42-44

Sleep: The Dynamics of Sweet Dreaming. *Lear's* (January 1990):86-89

## Goss, Julie

Reworking the Rabbi's Role. *Lilith* 15, No. 4 (Fall 1990):16-25

## Gossip. See also Life Styles

Idle Chatter. Quentin Crisp. *Lear's* (June 1990):72-73

one hundred Most Talked-About Women. *Harper's Bazaar* (October 1990):222-225

Scruples: Dish and Tell: Wy Do We Talk About Our Friends? Ellen Welty. *Mademoiselle* (February 1990):94

This Working Life: Meow! Why Men Love a Cat Fight. Alessandra Stanley. *Working Woman* (July 1990):109

Walter Winchell. Liz Smith. *Lear's* (June 1990):74-75+

## Gothic Revival (Literature)

The Contested Castle: Gothic Novels and the Subversion of Domestic Ideology. Kate Ferguson Ellis. Reviewed by Judith Wilt. *The Women's Review of Books* 7, No. 9 (June 1990):20

Gothic Repetition: Husbands, Horrors, and Things That Go Bump in the Night. Notes. Michelle A. Massé. *Signs* 15, No. 4 (Summer 1990):679-709

The Witching Hour. By Anne Rice. Reviewed by Mark Matousek. *Harper's Bazaar* (November 1990):112

**Gotlib, Ian H.** (joint author). *See* Wallace, Pamela M.

**Gottleib, Naomi.** *See* Meyer, Carol and Young, Alma (editors), "On the Bias."

**Gottlieb, Alma** (joint editor). *See* Buckley, Thomas

**Gottlieb, Amy**

Lesbian Sex at Menopause: Better Than Ever. *Healthsharing* 11, No. 4 (December 1990):

**Gottlieb, Amy** (joint author). *See* Elliott, Susan

**Gottlieb, Annie**

The Secret Strength of Happy Marriages. *McCall's* 118, No. 3 (December 1990):94-96+

**Gottschalk, Marilyn**

Feminist Visions: Narrative Films by Women. *Feminist Collections* 11, No. 2 (Winter 1990):10-13

**Gouda, Frances**

Figures of Ill Repute: Representing Prostitution in Nineteenth-Century France. Book Review. *The Women's Review of Books* 7, No. 12 (September 1990):13-14

Men's Fantasies, Women's Realities. *The Women's Review of Books* 7, No. 12 (September 1990):13-14

Women for Hire: Prostitution and Sexuality in France after 1850. Book Review. *The Women's Review of Books* 7, No. 12 (September 1990):13-14

**Gough, Lyn**

As Wise as Serpents: Five Women and an Organization that Changed British Columbia, 1883-1939. Reviewed by Shelley Bosetti-Piché. *Resources for Feminist Research* 19, No. 1 (March 1990):4-5

**Goulart, Frances Sheridan**

Romancing the Stone. *Lear's* (January 1990):32-35

**Gould, Jane S.**

Mother Country: Britain, the Welfare State and Nuclear Pollution. Book Review. *New Directions for Women* 19, No. 1 (January/February 1990):19

Peace, Feminist Goal. *New Directions for Women* 19, No. 4 (July-August 1990):18

Women for all Seasons: The Story of the Women's International League for Peace and Freedom. Book Review. *New Directions for Women* 19, No. 4 (July-August 1990):18

**Gould, Karen**

Writing in the Feminine: Feminism and Experimental Writing in Quebec. Reviewed by Alice Parker. *The Women's Review of Books* 8, No. 3 (December 1990):28-29

**Gould, Lois** (criticism)

A Novelist's Career. Elayne Rapping. *The Women's Review of Books* 7, No. 5 (February 1990):13

**Gould, Randi Londer**

How Not to Be Arrested for the Sniffles. Bibliography. *Lear's* (October 1990):48-49

**Gouma-Peterson, Thalia**

Making Their Mark: Women Artists Move into the Mainstream, 1970-85. Book Review. *Woman's Art Journal* 11, No. 2 (Fall 1990-Winter 1991):38-41

**Gourmelen, Marc** (about). *See* Carter, Charla, "European Designers to Watch."

**Govea, Catalina** (about). *See* Art – Exhibitions, "Racism"

**Government Workers.** *See* Civil Service Workers

**Governors – United States – Mansions**

Inside the Governors' Mansions. Lauren Payne. *Ladies' Home Journal* 107, No. 7 (July 1990):98-104

**Governors – United States – Spouses**

Celestial Reasoning – Ohio's First Lady Talks about Love and Feminism. Janyce Katz. *Ms.* 1, No. 2 (September/October 1990):88

**Gowens, Pat**

Battered Women Are Strong, Wise. *off our backs* 20, No. 1 (January 1990):15+

Open Letter to Sonia Johnson. *off our backs* 20, No. 1 (January 1990):15

**Goyal, Uma** (joint author). *See* Bhatia, M. S.

**Gozemba, Patricia A.**

Broken Mirrors. Film review. *NWSA Journal* 2, No. 2 (Spring 1990):291-295

Chicken Ranch. Film review. *NWSA Journal* 2, No. 2 (Spring 1990):291-295

Working Girls. Film review. *NWSA Journal* 2, No. 2 (Spring 1990):291-295

**Grabska, Elzbieta** (joint author). *See* Kott, Jan

**Grace, Patricia**

Butterflies. Fiction. *Ms.* 1, No. 3 (November/December 1990):44

**Graebner, William**

Coming of Age in Buffalo: Youth and Authority in the Postwar Era. Book Review. *Adolescence* 25, No. 99 (Fall 1990):753

**Graff, E. J.**

The Housemaid's Tale. *The Women's Review of Books* 7, Nos. 10-11 (July 1990):34-35

Mary Reilly. Book Review. *The Women's Review of Books* 7, Nos. 10-11 (July 1990):34-35

**Graff, Rose**

It's the Weekend: So Why Do You Feel Miserable? *Working Woman* (March 1990):140-144

**Graffiti**

Louder Than Words. Jill Posener. *Woman of Power* 17 (Summer 1990):20-23

**Graham, Meredith**

The Scaredy Cats. Short story. *Ladies' Home Journal* 107, No. 2 (February 1990):112-114

**Graham-Brown, Sarah**

Images of Women: The Portrayal of Women in Photography of the Middle East, 1860-1950. Reviewed by Írvin Cemil Schick. *Feminist Studies* 16, No. 2 (Summer 1990):345-380

Images of Women: The Portrayal of Women in Photography of the Middle East, 1860-1950. Reviewed by Wendy Kozol. *Gender & History* 2, No. 1 (Spring 1990):110-113

Spinsters Abroad: Victorian Lady Explorers. Book Review. *Gender & History* 2, No. 3 (Autumn 1990):373-375

**Grahn, Judy**

Lesbian or Gay Writer: Hardly an Alienated Profession. *Out/Look* No. 9 (Summer 1990):38-41

**Grahn, Judy** (editor)

Really Reading Gertrude Stein: A Selected Anthology. Reviewed by Catharine R. Stimpson. *The Women's Review of Books* 7, No. 8 (May 1990):6-7

**Grambs, Jean Dresden**

Women over Forty: Visions and Realities. Reviewed by Rosalind C. Barnett. *Psychology of Women Quarterly* 14, No. 4 (December 1990):618-619

**Gramling, Sandra E.** (joint author). *See* Johnson, Cheryl A.

**Grand, Mary Ann** and Fortino, Denise

I Gave Birth to an Addicted Baby. *Good Housekeeping* 210, No. 4 (April 1990):130-131, 172-178

**Grandparents**

The Early Years. T. Berry Brazelton. *Family Circle* 103, No. 11 (August 14, 1990):41-42 +

Getting Along with Grandparents. Doris B. Wallace. *Good Housekeeping* 211, No. 3 (September 1990):156 +

Grandparents Can Be a Joy (and a Problem). Benjamin Spock. *Redbook* 175, No. 4 (August 1990):30

Interiors: A Swimming Lesson. Jewelle Gomez. *Essence* 21, No. 4 (August 1990):38 +

Standing Room Only: A Too-Faraway Grandpa Visits. Meyer Moldeven. *Lilith* 15, No. 1 (Winter 1990):4-5

**Granston, Leslie**

Can You Eat to Heal? *Mademoiselle* (December 1990):110

Health News. *Mademoiselle* (November 1990):118; (December 1990):112

Red Alert: A Safe Tampon Guide. *Mademoiselle* (October 1990):122

**Grant, Agnes**

Voice in the Blood. *Canadian Women's Studies* 11, No. 1 (Spring 1990):11-14

**Grant, Ali M.**

Taking Space – A More Personal/Political Note. *Women and Environments* 12, No. 1 (Fall 1989/Winter 1990): 17

**Grant, Elorine**

Circle of One. Record Review. *Spare Rib* No. 216 (September 1990):26

Compositions. Music Review. *Spare Rib* No. 215 (August 1990):30

Contribution. Music Review. *Spare Rib* 218 (November 1990):18

Hearts and Flowers. Music Review. *Spare Rib* No. 214 (July 1990):24

Meridian. Theater Review. *Spare Rib* No. 210 (March 1990):36

Paradise. By Ruby Turner. *Spare Rib* No. 209 (February 1990):32

The Women of Brewter Place. Book Review. *Spare Rib* No. 214 (July 1990):22

**Grant, Gwendolyn Goldsby**

Between Us. Bibliography. *Essence* 21, No. 2 (June 1990):26-27

Between Us. *Essence* 20, No. 10 (February 1990):30-; 20, No. 11 (March 1990):30-31; 20, No. 12 (April 1990):30-31; 21, No. 3 (July 1990):26-27; 21, No. 4 (August 1990):30; 31

Between Us. *Essence* 21, No. 5 (September 1990):32-33

Between Us. *Essence* 21, No. 6 (October 1990).30-32

Between Us. *Essence* 21, No. 7 (November 1990):24; 21, No. 8 (December 1990):27

Just Between Us. *Essence* 20, No. 9 (January 1990):26-27 +

**Grant, Jacquelyn**

White Women's Christ and Black Women's Jesus: Feminist Christology and Womanist Response. Reviewed by Paula Giddings. *Essence* 21, No. 6 (October 1990):52

**Grant, James**

Top Gun. *Harper's Bazaar* (October 1990):204-207

**Grant, Joanne** (director)

Fundi: The Story of Ella Baker. Reviewed by C. Alejandra Elenes. *Feminist Collections* 11, No. 3 (Spring 1990):10-11

**Grant, Judith**

The Oppositional Imagination: Feminism, Critique and Political Theory. Book Review. *The Women's Review of Books* 7, No. 4 (January 1990):21-22

Rethinking Desire. *The Women's Review of Books* 7, No. 4 (January 1990):21-22

**Grant, Linda**, Simpson, Layne A., Rong, Xue Lan, and Peters-Golden, Holly

Gender, Parenthood, and Work Hours of Physicians. *Journal of Marriage and the Family* 52, No. 1 (February 1990):39-49

**Grant, Monica**

White Courtesy Phones, Monogamy, and Other . . . Reflections from a Rookie. *Hot Wire* 6, No. 2 (May 1990):46-47

**Grant, Roberta**

How Could I Be So Blind? *Ladies' Home Journal* 107, No. 3 (March 1990):56-62

The New Babysnatchers. *Redbook* 175, No. 1 (May 1990):151-154

**Granville, Evelyn Boyd**

My Life as a Mathematician. *Sage* 6, No. 2 (Fall 1989):44-46

**Graphic Art**. *See* Poster Art

**Graphic Design**

Milton Glaser: The Illusionist. Celia McGee. *Lear's* (September 1990):90-95+

**Gratch, Elizabeth**

How I Wrote *Jubilee* and Other Essays on Life and Literature. Book Review. *The Women's Review of Books* 8, No. 3 (December 1990):29-30

Keeping Faith. *The Women's Review of Books* 8, No. 3 (December 1990):29-30

**Gravenites, Diana**

Shadow Sister. Poem. *Sinister Wisdom* 41 (Summer-Fall 1990):67-70

**Graves, Michael** (about). *See* Architecture

**Gray, Eileen** (about)

Eileen Gray: Architect/Designer. By Peter Adam. Reviewed by Pamela H. Simpson. *Woman's Art Journal* 11, No. 2 (Fall 1990-Winter 1991):44-48

**Gray, Francine du Plessix**

Soviet Women: Walking the Tightrope. Reviewed by Rochelle Ruthchild. *The Women's Review of Books* 8, No. 3 (December 1990):25-26

Soviet Women: Walking the Tightrope. Reviewed by Sandra Pollack. *New Directions for Women* 19, No. 6 (November-December 1990):22

**Gray, Francine du Plessix** (about)

The Winter of Their Discontent. Francine Prose. *Savvy Woman* (March 1990):57-60

**Gray, Francine du Plessix** (interview)

Francine Gray. Susan Jacoby. *Vogue* (March 1990):319, 326, 332

**Gray, Mary M.** (joint author). *See* Ispa, Jean M.

**Gray, Pamela**

Late Irises: A Goodbye Sonnet. Poem. *Sinister Wisdom* 40 (Spring 1990): 71

A Sacred Time: Journal Entries (excerpts). *Sinister Wisdom* 40 (Spring 1990):64-71

**Gray, Paul E.** (interview)

Breaking the Barriers: Women and Minorities in the Sciences. *On the Issues* 15 (Summer 1990):7-9+

**Great Britain**. *See also* Northern Ireland

Surviving the Blues. Edited by Joan Scanlon. Reviewed by Joyoti Grech. *Spare Rib* 219 (December 1990-January 1991):40

**Great Britain – Acquired Immune Deficiency Syndrome**

Beyond Condom-Bound Solutions. Sara Scott. *Connexions* 33 (1990):21-23

HIV-Postive. *Connexions* 33 (1990):14-15

A New Intimacy. *Connexions* 33 (1990):26

<X2>"Pass the Clingfilm, dear!" *Connexions* 33 (1990):28

The Politics of Repression. *Connexions* 33 (1990):2-3

**Great Britain – Africans**

Let it Lie Upon the Table: The Status of Black Women's Biography in the UK. Ziggi Alexander. *Gender & History* 2, No. 1 (Spring 1990):22-33

**Great Britain – Art**. *See also* Butler, Elizabeth Thompson

Images of Victorian Womanhood in English Art. By Susan P. Casteras. Reviewed by Debra N. Mancoff. *Woman's Art Journal* 11, No. 1 (Spring-Summer 1990):42-45

The Other Story: Afro-Asian Artists in Post-War Britain. Rita Keegan. *Spare Rib* No. 209 (February 1990):36

**Great Britain – Art – Exhibitions**

In Focus. Prasanna Probyn. *Spare Rib* No. 210 (March 1990):43

**Great Britain – Caribbean Immigrants**

25 Years of Carnival. *Spare Rib* No. 216 (September 1990):14-17

**Great Britain – Church of England – History**

The Women's Movement in the Church of England, 1850-1930. By Brian Heeney. Reviewed by John Wolffe. *Gender & History* 2, No. 2 (Summer 1990):236-237

**Great Britain – Communications**

Sterling Opportunities. Martin Farmer. *Executive Female* 13, No. 5 (September-October 1990):42-43

**Great Britain – Culture**

English Accents. Mark Matousek. *Harper's Bazaar* (April 1990):198-201+

**Great Britain – Designers**

European Designers to Watch. Charla Carter. *Vogue* (August 1990):124-150

**Great Britain – Education**

Assault Course. Dorothea Smartt. *Sage* 6, No. 1 (Summer 1989):57-58

Equal Opportunities: Rhetoric or Action. Sue Lees and Maria Scott. *Gender and Education* 2, No. 3 (1990):333-343

Human Rights and "Free and Fair Competition": The Significance of European Education Legislation for Girls in the UK. Sheila McIntosh. *Gender and Education* 2, No. 1 (1990):63-79

Implementing a Whole School Equal Opportunities Policy: A Primary School in Humberside. Sheila Cunnison and Christine Gurevitch. *Gender and Education* 2, No. 3 (1990):283-295

Student Loans – Banks Withdraw as Thatcher "Fizzes with Fury." *Spare Rib* No. 209 (February 1990):46

Working With Boys. Diane Reay. *Gender and Education* 2, No. 3 (1990):269-282

**Great Britain – Education – History**

Dangerous by Degrees: Women at Oxford and the Somerville College Novelists. By Susan J. Leonardi. Reviewed by Carol Dyhouse. *Gender and Education* 2, No. 2 (1990):261-262

Education Institutions or Extended Families? The Reconstruction of Gender in Women's Colleges in the Late Nineteenth and Early Twentieth Centuries. Elizabeth Edwards. *Gender and Education* 2, No. 1 (1990):17-35

< X2 > "Men Must Be Educated and Women Must Do It": The National Federation (Later Union) of Women Teachers and Contemporary Feminism 1910-30. Hilda Kean and Alison Oram. *Gender and Education* 2, No. 2 (1990):147-167

Norwood Was a Difficult School. By Jean Lawrence and Margaret Tucker. Reviewed by Susan Lewis. *Gender and Education* 2, No. 1 (1990):116

The Reform of Girls' Secondary and Higher Education in Victorian England. By Joyce Senders Pedersen. Reviewed by Felicity Hunt. *Gender & History* 2, No. 1 (Spring 1990):113-114

**Great Britain – Environmental Movement**

View: Katherine Hamnett. Page Hill Starzinger. *Vogue* (August 1990):111-120

**Great Britain – Feminist Movement**

Cultural Missionaries, Maternal Imperialists, Feminist Allies: British Women Activists in India, 1865-1945. Barbara N. Ramusack. *Women's Studies International Forum* 13, No. 4 (1990):309-321

The De-Eroticization of Women's Liberation: Social Purity Movements and the Revolutionary Feminism of Sheila Jeffreys. Margaret Hunt. *Feminist Review* No. 34 (Spring 1990):23-41

Oxford Twenty Years On: Where Are We Now? Lorraine Gamman and Gilda O'Neill. *Feminist Review* No. 36 (Autumn 1990):96

The White Woman's Burden: British Feminists and the Indian Woman, 1865-1915. Antoinette M. Burton. *Women's Studies International Forum* 13, No. 4 (1990):295-308

**Great Britain – Health Care**

Shielding Women from the Truth: The Story of the Dalkon Shield. Marlene Winfield. *Spare Rib* No. 216 (September 1990):58

**Great Britain – Health Care – History**

Octavia Wilberforce, Pioneer Woman Doctor. By Pat Jalland. Reviewed by Angela V. John. *Gender & History* 2, No. 3 (Autumn 1990):375-377

In Sickness and in Health: The British Experience, 1650-1850. By Roy Porter and Dorothy Porter. Reviewed by Nancy J. Tomes. *Gender & History* 2, No. 3 (Autumn 1990):368-369

**Great Britain – History**

The Autobiographical Subject: Gender and Ideology in Eighteenth-Century England. By Felicity A. Nussbaum. Reviewed by Terri Nickel. *Tulsa Studies in Women's Literature* 9, No. 1 (Spring 1990):143-144

Autobiographical Writings: Women in English Social History, 1800-1914. A Guide to Research, Volume III. Barbara Kanner. *Gender & History* 2, No. 1 (Spring 1990):89-90

Discourse on Popular Culture: Class, Gender and History in Cultural Analysis, 1730 to the Present. By Shiach Morag. Reviewed by Hugh Cunningham. *Gender & History* 2, No. 1 (Spring 1990):110-113

The Family and the English Revolution. By Christopher Durston. Reviewed by Cynthia Herrup. *Gender & History* 2, No. 2 (Summer 1990):226-228

Family Fortunes: Men and Women of the English Middle Class, 1780-1850. By Leonore Davidoff and Catherine Hall. Reviewed by Ellen Jordan. *Signs* 15, No. 3 (Spring 1990):650-652

Family Fortunes: Men and Women of the English Middle Class, 1780-1850. By Leonore Davidoff and Catherine Hall. Reviewed by Mary Louise Adams. *Resources for Feminist Research* 19, No. 1 (March 1990):10-11

Industry of Devotion: The Transformation of Women's Work in England, 1500-1660. By Susan Cahn. Reviewed by Diane Willen. *Gender and Society* 4, No. 2 (June 1990):267-269

Married Women's Separate Property in England, 1660-1833. By Susan Staves. Reviewed by Janice Farrar Thaddeus. *The Women's Review of Books* 8, No. 1 (October 1990):25-26

Myths of Sexuality: Representations of Women in Victorian Britain. By Lynda Nead. Reviewed by Eunice Lipton. *Gender & History* 2, No. 1 (Spring 1990):91-97

<X2>"Neither Pairs Nor Odd": Female Community in Late Nineteenth-Century London. Notes. Deborah Epstein Nord. *Signs* 15, No. 4 (Summer 1990):733-754

Parasexuality and Glamour: The Victorian Barmaid as Cultural Prototype. Peter Bailey. *Gender & History* 2, No. 2 (Summer 1990):148-172

Playing the Game: Sport and the Physical Emancipation of English Women, 1870-1914. By Kathleen E. McCrone. Reviewed by Aniko Varpalotai. *Resources for Feminist Research* 19, No. 1 (March 1990):28

Playing the Game: Sport and the Physical Emancipation of English Women 1870-1914. By Kathleen E. McCrone. Reviewed by Joyce Pedersen. *Gender and Education* 2, No. 1 (1990):107-109

From Private to Public Patriarchy: The Periodisation of British History. Sylvia Walby. *Women's Studies International Forum* 13, Nos. 1-2 (1990):91-104

Property, Power, and Personal Relations: Elite Mothers and Sons in Yorkist and Early Tudor England. Notes. Barbara J. Harris. *Signs* 15, No. 3 (Spring 1990):606-632

On the Trail of Jane the Fool. Denise Selleck. *On the Issues* 14 (1990):22-24+

Uneven Developments: The Ideological Work of Gender in Mid-Victorian England. By Mary Poovey. Reviewed by Alex Owen. *Gender & History* 2, No. 2 (Summer 1990):239-241

Uneven Developments: The Ideological Work of Gender in Mid-Victorian England. By Mary Poovey. Reviewed by Susan Hardy Aiken. *Signs* 16, No. 1 (Autumn 1990):188-192

Vision and Difference: Feminism, Femininity and the History of Art. By Griselda Pollock. Reviewed by Eunice Lipton. *Gender & History* 2, No. 1 (Spring 1990):91-97

Women and Marriage in Nineteenth Century England. By Joan Perkin. Reviewed by A. James Hammerton. *Gender & History* 2, No. 2 (Summer 1990):241-244

Women in the First Capitalist Society: Experiences in Seventeenth-Century England. By Margaret George. Reviewed by Cynthia Herrup. *Gender & History* 2, No. 2 (Summer 1990):226-228

Women in the First Capitalist Society: Experiences in Seventeenth-Century England. By Margaret George. Reviewed by Margaret W. Ferguson. *Tulsa Studies in Women's Literature* 9, No. 1 (Spring 1990):158-160

Writing Inside the Kaleidoscope: Re-Representing Victorian Women Public Figures. Kali A. K. Israel. *Gender & History* 2, No. 1 (Spring 1990):40-48

## Great Britain – Homeless

Surviving Homelessness. Linda King. *Spare Rib* No. 209 (February 1990):38-41

## Great Britain – Homicide

Outrage Protest Anti-Gay Murders. *Spare Rib* No. 216 (September 1990):44

## Great Britain – Household Workers

A Hidden Workforce: Homeworkers in England, 1850-1985. By Shelley Pennington and Belinda Westover. Reviewed by Mary Kinnear. *Resources for Feminist Research* 19, No. 2 (June 1990):37

## Great Britain – Images of Women

Cinema, Censorship and Sexuality, 1909-25. By Annette Kuhn. Reviewed by Sumiko Higashi. *Gender & History* 2, No. 1 (Spring 1990):123-126

The Female Gaze. Edited by Lorraine Gamman and Margaret Marshment. Reviewed by Sumiko Higashi. *Gender & History* 2, No. 1 (Spring 1990):123-126

Women and the Popular Imagination in the Twenties: Flappers and Nymphs. By Billie Melman. Reviewed by Sumiko Higashi. *Gender & History* 2, No. 1 (Spring 1990):123-126

The Women Who Knew Too Much: Hitchcock and Feminist Theory. By Tania Modleski. Reviewed by Sumiko Higashi. *Gender & History* 2, No. 1 (Spring 1990):123-126

## Great Britain – Immigration

The Family. By Buchi Emecheta. Reviewed by Elsie B. Washington. *Essence* 21, No. 4 (August 1990):50

Lai-Ying Must Stay. *Spare Rib* 218 (November 1990):42-43

Woman-Nation-State. Edited by Nira Yuval-Davis and Floya Anthias. Reviewed by Ann Rossiter. *Feminist Review* No. 36 (Autumn 1990):131-134

## Great Britain – Labor Movement – History

Eva Gore-Booth and Esther Roper: A Biography. By Gifford Lewis. Reviewed by Clare Collins. *Gender & History* 2, No. 1 (Spring 1990):116-118

For Labor and For Women: The Women's Labour League, 1906-18. By Christine Collette. Reviewed by Linda Walker. *Gender & History* 2, No. 2 (Summer 1990):244-246

A Singular Marriage: A Labour Love Story in Letters and Diaries. Edited by Jane Cox. Reviewed by Clare Collins. *Gender & History* 2, No. 1 (Spring 1990):116-118

Women's Fabian Tracts. Edited by Sally Alexander. Reviewed by Linda Walker. *Gender & History* 2, No. 2 (Summer 1990):244-246

## Great Britain – Labor Relations

Standing up to the Tories. *Spare Rib* No. 209 (February 1990):16-17

## Great Britain – Legal System

Birmingham 6: Innocent Beyond Any Doubt. Breda Powell. *Spare Rib* 219 (December 1990-January 1991):67

The Heroine's Blazon and Hardwicke's Marriage Act: Commodification for a Novel Market. Katherine Sobba Green. *Tulsa Studies in Women's Literature* 9, No. 2 (Fall 1990):273-290

Judges Overturn Lesbian Custody Ruling. *Spare Rib* No. 216 (September 1990):44

Margaret Thatcher Delays Changes in Child Abuse Law. *Spare Rib* No. 216 (September 1990):45

Mother Jailed for Contempt of Court. Maureen O'Hara. *Spare Rib* No. 216 (September 1990):45

A Sexist and Racist Judiciary. Sara Maguire. *Spare Rib* No. 209 (February 1990):47

When a Woman Says No. O'Hara, Maureen. *Spare Rib* No. 212 (May 1990):12-13

**Great Britain – Lesbianism**

Butch/Femme Obsessions. Susan Ardill and Sue O'Sullivan. *Feminist Review* No. 34 (Spring 1990):79-86

Lesbianism and the Labour Party: The GLC Experience. Ann Tobin. *Feminist Review* No. 34 (Spring 1990):56-66

Out but Not Down: Lesbians' Experience of Housing. Jayne Egerton. *Feminist Review* No. 36 (Autumn 1990):75-88

**Great Britain – Libraries**

Women in Libraries – Ten Years of Independent Organization in the U.K. Heather Watkins. *WLW Journal* 14, No. 1 (Fall 1990):6-8

**Great Britain – Medical Research – Feminist Positions**

Embryo Bill Update. *Spare Rib* No. 209 (February 1990):47

Embryo Research Bill Passed. Marcel Farry. *Spare Rib* No. 212 (May 1990):44-45

**Great Britain – Mental Disorders**

The Female Malady: Women, Madness and English Culture, 1830-1980. Reviewed by Ruth Harris. *Signs* 15, No. 2 (Winter 1990):408-410

**Great Britain – Military – WRNS**

The WRNS: A History of the Women's Royal Naval Service. By Marjorie H. Fletcher. Reviewed by Peter K. H. Mispelkamp. *Minerva* 8, No. 1 (Spring 1990):86-87

**Great Britain – Politics and Government**

The Greening of Sara Parkin. Deborah Stead. *Savvy Woman* (November 1990):64-67+

Labour: Auditioning for the General Election. Sharon Atkin. *Spare Rib* 218 (November 1990):43

Labour's New Policies. Sharon Atkin. *Spare Rib* 213 (June 1990):24-25

The Loony Right Gather at Bournemouth. Veronica Fuller. *Spare Rib* 218 (November 1990):44

Mother Country: Britain, the Welfare State and Nuclear Pollution. By Marilyn Robinson. Reviewed by Jane S. Gould. *New Directions for Women* 19, No. 1 (January/February 1990):19

In the Shadow of Sellafield. *Spare Rib* No. 210 (March 1990):20-22

<X2>"The Men in Grey Suits" say Bye Bye Maggie. Sharon Atkin. *Spare Rib* 219 (December 1990-January 1991):62-64

**Great Britain – Politics and Government – History**

Fractured Faith: Liberal Party Women and the Suffrage Issue in Britain, 1892-1914. Claire Hirshfield. *Gender & History* 2, No. 2 (Summer 1990):173-197

**Great Britain – Poll Tax**

Don't Pay. *Spare Rib* No. 211 (April 1990): 6-11

Poll Tax Greetings from Scotland. Evelyn Ward. *Spare Rib* 219 (December 1990-January 1991):64-65

Poll Tax Update. Lindsay Milligan. *Spare Rib* No. 212 (May 1990):16-18

Poll Tax Update. *Spare Rib* No. 216 (September 1990):46

Wee Papa Girls Rap Against the Tax. *Spare Rib* No. 211 (April 1990):12-14

We're Still Not Paying the Poll Tax. Veronica Fuller. *Spare Rib* 218 (November 1990):11

**Great Britain – Pornography Control**

Campaign Against Pornography. Barbara Norden. *Feminist Review* No. 35 (Summer 1990):1-8

Pornography and Violence: What the 'Experts' Really Say. Lynne Segal. *Feminist Review* No. 36 (Autumn 1990):29-41

Who Watches the Watchwomen?: Feminists Against Censorship. Gillian Rodgerson and Linda Semple. *Feminist Review* No. 36 (Autumn 1990):19-28

**Great Britain – Publishing**

British Publishing. Ellen Mizzell. *Belles Lettres* 6, No. 1 (Fall 1990):62

**Great Britain – Race Relations**

Ain't No Black in the Union Jack. *Spare Rib* No. 216 (September 1990):29-30

Britain: Official Apartheid on Its Way in. Joyoti Grech. *Spare Rib* No. 212 (May 1990):46

Communities of Resistance Challenging Fortress Europe. *Spare Rib* No. 212 (May 1990):6-11

Hands Off the Silcotts. Marcel Farry. *Spare Rib* No. 210 (March 1990):14-15

Racist Murderer Gets Life. *Spare Rib* No. 216 (September 1990):44-45

Southall Responds to Racist Murder. Joyoti Grech. *Spare Rib* No. 209 (February 1990):45-46

Splintered Sisterhood: Antiracism in a Young Women's Project. Clara Connolly. *Feminist Review* No. 36 (Autumn 1990):52-64

Tower Hamlets: BNP Put Forward Candidates in Local Elections. Joyoti Grech. *Spare Rib* No. 212 (May 1990):46

Tower Hamlets Fascists Pop up Again. Joyoti Grech. *Spare Rib* No. 216 (September 1990):46

**Great Britain – Reproductive Rights**

Abortion on Request – One Step Closer. Anne Kane. *Spare Rib* No. 212 (May 1990):44

Action for Parenting and Reproductive Rights. *Spare Rib* 218 (November 1990):42

Britain: Campaign Against Embryo and Human Fertilisation Bill. Alice Henry. *off our backs* 20, No. 4 (April 1990):12

**Great Britain – Royal Family**

Back to School with William and Harry. Penny Junor. *McCall's* 118, No. 1 (October 1990):88-92

Diana's Darlings. Susie Pearson. *Ladies' Home Journal* 107, No. 2 (February 1990):107-110

Diana's Diary. Andrew Morton. *Good Housekeeping* 211, No. 1 (July 1990):112-114, 158-162

Fergie Gets Real. Susie Pearson. *Ladies' Home Journal* 107, No. 4 (April 1990):155-158+

The Forgotten Princess. Graham Fisher and Heather Fisher. *Redbook* 175, No. 5 (September 1990):42-44

The Heir & the Spare. Beth Weinhouse. *Redbook* 175, No. 5 (September 1990):38-42

**Great Britain – Sexuality**

Dangerous Sexualities: Medico-Moral Politics in England Since 1830. By Frank Mort. Reviewed by Chris Waters. *Gender & History* 2, No. 2 (Summer 1990):218-222

**Great Britain – Status of Women**

British Survey Shows Advertising Women Not in Top Jobs. *Media Report to Women* 18, No. 2 (March/April 1990):6-7

Change. *Women's World* 23 (April 1990):43

Enterprising Women. Edited by Sallie Westwood and Parminder Bhachu. Reviewed by Kathryn Ward. *Women's Studies International Forum* 13, No. 5 (1990):523-524

The Third Aspect: An Investigation of U.K. Business Networks. Christine Brookes. *Women's Studies International Forum* 13, No. 6 (1990):577-585

<X2> "We Don't Contravene the Sex Discrimination Act" – Female Students at Journalism

School. Odette Parry. *Gender and Education* 2, No. 1 (1990):3-16

**Great Britain – Taxation**

Abolition of Tax on Workplace Nurseries. Veronica Fuller. *Spare Rib* No. 211 (April 1990):57

**Great Britain – Theater**

Closet Dramas: Homosexual Representation and Class in Postwar British Theater. Alan Sinfield. *Genders* 9 (Fall 1990):112-131

The Hit List: Much Ado About Something. Robert Turnbull. *Harper's Bazaar* (February 1990):47+

Oval House: Weathering the Storms. Susan Hayes. *Spare Rib* No. 212 (May 1990):26

**Great Britain – Travel**

Total Recoil: Downstairs, Upstairs. Peter Feibleman. *Lear's* (February 1990):38-41

**Great Britain – Violence Against Women.** *See also* Rape Victims – Compensation

A Hidden Struggle: Black Women and Violence. Amina Mama. *Connexions* 34 (1990):12-14

A Hidden Struggle: Black Women and Violence. Amina Mama. *Spare Rib* No. 209 (February 1990):8-11

Lai-Ying Must Stay. *Spare Rib* 218 (November 1990):42-43

London Rape Crisis Centre under Threat. *Spare Rib* No. 216 (September 1990):54

Woman to Woman: Dealing with Domestic Violence. *Spare Rib* No. 216 (September 1990):8-13

Women Abusing Women. Ellen Bell. *Connexions* 34 (1990):28-30

**Great Britain – Women's Studies**

Teaching Women: Feminism and English Studies. Edited by Ann Thompson and Helen Wilcox. Reviewed by Gloria Bowles. *NWSA Journal* 2, No. 2 (Spring 1990):288-290

**Greber, Lisa** (joint author). *See* Perry, Ruth

**Grech, Joyoti**

Clearinghouse on Femicide Set Up. *Spare Rib* 219 (December 1990-January 1991):69

Jesus is Indian and Other South African Stories. add. *Spare Rib* No. 210 (March 1990):34

Purdah. add. *Spare Rib* No. 211 (April 1990):27

Putting in the Pickle Where the Jam Should Be. add. *Spare Rib* No. 209 (February 1990):31

Southall Responds to Racist Murder. *Spare Rib* No. 209 (February 1990):45-46

Surviving the Blues. Book Review. *Spare Rib* 219 (December 1990-January 1991):40

Tower Hamlets: BNP Put Forward Candidates in Local Elections. *Spare Rib* No. 212 (May 1990):46

Tower Hamlets Fascists Pop up Again. *Spare Rib* No. 216 (September 1990):46

**Grech, Joyoti** and **Gupta, Tanika**

Shakti: Power of Women. Theater Review. *Spare Rib* 219 (December 1990-January 1991):36

**Greece, Ancient**

The Democratic Body: Prostitution and Citizenship in Classical Athens. David M. Halperin. *Differences* 2, No. 1 (Spring 1990):1-28

Love in the Greek Novel. David Konstan. *Differences* 2, No. 1 (Spring 1990):186-205

Phallos Politikos: Representing the Body Politic in Athens. John J. Winkler. *Differences* 2, No. 1 (Spring 1990):29-45

**Greece, Ancient – Women Writers**

The Woman and the Lyre: Woman Writers in Classical Greece and Rome. By Jane McIntosh Snyder. Reviewed by Katherine Callen King. *Tulsa Studies In Women's Literature* 9, No. 2 (Fall 1990):323-326

**Greece – Feminist Movement – History**

Feminism in Greece Between the Wars: An Anthology. Edited by Effie Avdela and Angelika Psarra. Reviewed by Mary Voyatis. *Gender & History* 2, No. 1 (Spring 1990):122-123

**Greed, Clara**

<X2> "You're Just Imagining It, Everything's All Right Really, Don't Worry About It": The Position of Women in Surveying Education and Practice. *Gender and Education* 2, No. 1 (1990):49-61

**Greeley, Andrew**

Faithful Attraction. *Good Housekeeping* 210, No. 6 (June 1990):132-137

**Green, Anne Bosanko**

One Woman's War: Letters from the Women's Army Corps, 1944-1946. Reviewed by Eleanor Stoddard. *Minerva* 8, No. 4 (Winter 1990):48-53

**Green, Barbara**

The Female Autograph: Theory and Practice of Autobiography from the Tenth to the Twentieth Century. Book Review. *Tulsa Studies in Women's Literature* 9, No. 1 (Spring 1990):135-139

Imaging American Women: Idea and Ideals in Cultural History. Book Review. *Tulsa Studies in Women's Literature* 9, No. 1 (Spring 1990):135-139

Subject to Change: Reading Feminist Writing. Book Review. *Tulsa Studies in Women's Literature* 9, No. 1 (Spring 1990):135-139

**Green, David L**

High School Student Employment in Social Context: Adolescents' Perceptions of the Role of Part-Time Work. *Adolescence* 25, No. 98 (Summer 1990):425-434

**Green, G. Dorsey**

Is Separation Really So Great? *Women and Therapy* 9, Nos. 1-2 (1990):87-104

**Green, Katherine Sobba**

The Heroine's Blazon and Hardwicke's Marriage Act: Commodification for a Novel Market. *Tulsa Studies in Women's Literature* 9, No. 2 (Fall 1990):273-290

**Green, Laura**

How to Make the Significant Choices. *Lear's* (June 1990):58-59

**Green, Sarah**

Inventing Ourselves: Lesbian Life Stories. Book Review. *Feminist Review* No. 34 (Spring 1990):176-177

**Greenberg, David F.**

The Construction of Homosexuality. Reviewed by Leila J. Rupp. *NWSA Journal* 2, No. 2 (Spring 1990):306-308

**Greenberg, Martin** (joint editor). *See* McSherry, Frank, Jr.

**Greenberg, Mary Lou**

Another American Tragedy: The Death of Becky Bell. *On the Issues* 17 (Winter 1990):10-13+

Lost Custody Dooms Child. *New Directions for Women* 19, No. 1 (January/February 1990):18

**Greenberger, Ellen** and O'Neil, Robin

Parents' Concerns about Their Child's Development: Implications for Fathers' and Mothers' Well-being and Attitudes Toward Work. *Journal of Marriage and the Family* 52, No. 3 (August 1990):621-635

**Greendorfer, Susan L**

From "Fair Sex" to Feminism: Sport and the Socialization of Women in the Industrial and Post-Industrial Eras. Book Review. *Gender and Society* 4, No. 1 (March 1990):108-110

**Greene, Beverly**

Sturdy Bridges: The Role of African-American Mothers in the Socialization of African-American Children. *Women and Therapy* 10, Nos. 1/2 (1990):205-225

**Greene, Beverly A.**

What Has Gone Before: The Legacy of Racism and Sexism in the Lives of Black Mothers and Daughters. *Women and Therapy* 9, Nos. 1-2 (1990):207-230

**Greene, Cheryll Y.** and Brown, Marie D. (editors)

Woman Talk. Interviews. *Essence* 21, No. 1 (May 1990):92-96+

**Greene, Gayle**

Family Plots. *The Women's Review of Books* 7, No. 5 (February 1990):8-9

Feminist Fiction, Feminist Form. *Frontiers* 11, Nos. 2-3 (1990):82-88

The Mother/Daughter Plot. Book Review. *The Women's Review of Books* 7, No. 5 (February 1990):8-9

**Greene, Katherine** and Greene, Richard

The Shocking Statistics. *Redbook* 174, No. 5 (March 1990):93+

**Greene, Richard** (joint author). *See* Barrett, Katherine; Greene, Katherine

**Greene, Robert** (about). *See* Perl, Jed, "Vogue Arts: Charmed Lives."

**Greene, Susan** (joint author). *See* Bergman, Miranda

**Greenspan, Nancy Thorndike** (joint author). *See* Greenspan, Stanley I.

**Greenspan, Stanley I.** and Greenspan, Nancy Thorndike

Love Lessons. *Family Circle* 103, No. 1 (January 9, 1990):77+

**Greenstein, Theodore**

Marital Disruption and the Employment of Married Women. *Journal of Marriage and the Family* 52, No. 3 (August 1990):657-676

**Greenwood-Robinson, Maggie**

The Perfect Repetition. *Women's Sports and Fitness* 12, No. 3 (April 1990):30

Periodization: Training for the Peak. *Women's Sports and Fitness* 12, No. 2 (March 1990):12

Strength in Numbers. *Women's Sports and Fitness* 12, No. 4 (May-June 1990):30

**Greer, Germaine**

Daddy, We Hardly Knew You. Reviewed by Jill Conway. *The Women's Review of Books* 7, No. 9 (June 1990):11

**Greer, Sandra C.** (joint author). *See* Beck, Evelyn Torton

**Gregory, Deborah**

Cheryl "Pepsii" Riley: Chapter Two. *Essence* 21, No. 6 (October 1990):47

En Vogue: Styling Style. *Essence* 21, No. 5 (September 1990):47

Joe Morton: Serving Justice. *Essence* 21, No. 4 (August 1990):45

**Gregory, Jamee** (about)

Dinner at Eight. Patricia Beard. *Harper's Bazaar* (August 1990):173+

**Greig, David**

Big Night Out. Reviewed by Dave Burrows. *Healthright* 9, No. 4 (August 1990):47

**Grella, Christine E.**

Irreconcilable Differences: Women Defining Class After Divorce and Downward Mobility. *Gender and Society* 4, No. 1 (March 1990):41-55

**Grewal, Inderpal**

Meatless Days. Book Review. *NWSA Journal* 2, No. 3 (Summer 1990):508-510

**Grewal, Shabnam,** Kay, Jackie, Landor, Liliane, Lewis, Gail, and Parmar, Pratibha (editors)

Charting the Journey: Writings by Black and Third World Women. Reviewed by Amita Handa. *Resources for Feminist Research* 19, No. 2 (June 1990):38

**Grey, Jennifer** (about). *See* Children of Entertainers

**Greydanus, Donald E.** and Shearin, Robert B.

Adolescent Sexuality and Gynecology. Book Review. *Adolescence* 25, No. 99 (Fall 1990):753

**Grief.** *See* Bereavement

**Griew, Kate**

The Pill Protection Plan. Book Review. *Healthright* 9, No. 3 (May 1990):38-39

**Griffin, Annie** (about)

Almost Persuaded. Betty Caplan. *Spare Rib* No. 212 (May 1990):26

**Griffin, William** (joint author). *See* Crane, D. Russell

**Griffith, Melanie** (about). *See also* Actors

Melanie Mellows Out. Bonnie Siegler. *Ladies' Home Journal* 107, No. 10 (October 1990):154-155+

Working Whirl. Jess Bravin. *Harper's Bazaar* (November 1990):170-171

**Griggers, Cathy**

A Certain Tension in the Visual/Cultural Field: Helmut Newton, Deborah Turbeville, and the *Vogue* Fashion Layout. *Differences* 2, No. 2 (Summer 1990):76-104

**Grilling.** *See* Barbecue Cookery

**Grimberg, Salomon**

Frida Kahlo's *Memory*: The Piercing of the Heart by the Arrow of Divine Love. *Woman's Art Journal* 11, No. 2 (Fall 1990-Winter 1991):3-7

**Grimes, Susan**

Ancient Gardens Quilt. Poem. *Women's Studies Quarterly* 18, Nos. 3-4 (Fall-Winter 1990):161-164

**Grimshaw, Patricia**

Paths of Duty: American Missionary Women in Nineteenth-Century Hawaii. Reviewed by Hoda Zaki. *The Women's Review of Books* 7, No. 9 (June 1990):19-20

**Grimshaw, Patricia** and Lake, Marilyn

Two American Conferences. *Australian Feminist Studies* No. 12 (Summer 1990):115-116

**Groyer, Jane**

The Hat. Short story. *Ladies' Home Journal* 107, No. 2 (February 1990):84-88

**Gruau, René**

Haute Heads. *Harper's Bazaar* (April 1990):170-173

**Grudin, Eva**

African America: Images, Ideas, and Realities. *Heresies* 25 (1990):54-56

**Grumet, Madeleine R.**

Bitter Milk: Women and Teaching. Reviewed by Carolyn Steadman. *Gender and Education* 2, No. 2 (1990):249-250

Bitter Milk: Women and Teaching. Reviewed by John Clower. *Feminist Teacher* 5, No. 2 (Fall 1990):34-36

**Grün, Ingolf** (joint author). *See* Hertzler, Ann A.

**Guam – Abortion**

Guam: Territory in Turmoil. Amy Goodman. *On the Issues* 17 (Winter 1990):14-15+

**Guarendi, Ray**

How to Talk So Your Kids will Listen. *Redbook* 175, No. 5 (September 1990):150-151+

**Guatemala – Women's History**

Rigoberta's Narrative and the New Practice of Oral History. Claudia Salazar. *Women & Language* 13, No. 1 (Fall 1990):7-8

**Guberman, Nancy** and Bourgon, Miche4le

Feminist Counselling in Action. Book Review. *Resources for Feminist Research* 19, No. 1 (March 1990):12

**Gucci, Maurizio** (about)

Gucci Again. Georgina Howell. *Vogue* (December 1990):322-327

**Guerney, Bernard, Jr.** and Maxson, Pamela

Marital and Family Enrichment Research: A Decade Review and Look Ahead. *Journal of Marriage and the Family* 52, No. 4 (November 1990):1127-1135

**Guernsey de Zapien, Jill** (joint author). *See* Ide, Bette A.

**Guerrilla Girls**

The Guerrilla Girls. *Ms.* 1, No. 2 (September/October 1990):60-63

**Guest, Avery M.**

What We Can Learn About Fertility Transitions from the New York State Census of 1865? *Journal of Family History* 15, No. 1 (January 1990):49-69

**Guggenheim, Michel** (editor)

Women in French Literature. Reviewed by Anne R. Larsen. *Tulsa Studies in Women's Literature* 9, No. 2 (Fall 1990):329-330

**Gugliotta, Guy** (joint author). *See* De Greiff, Monica

**Guiffré, Guilia** (editor)

A Writing Life. Reviewed by Susan Sheridan. *Australian Feminist Studies* No. 11 (Autumn 1990):133-135

**Guillebaud, John**

Contraception for Women Over 35. *Healthright* 9, No. 4 (August 1990):17-21

**Guillermoprieto, Alma**

Samba. Reviewed by Sally Sommer. *The Women's Review of Books* 7, No. 9 (June 1990):9

**Guion, Mary** (about)

Women, Words, and Men: Excerpts from the Diary of Mary Guion. Martha Tomhave Blauvelt. *Journal of Women's History* 2, No. 2 (Fall 1990):177-184

**Gulati, Leela**

Profiles in Female Poverty: A Study of Five Poor Working Women in Kerala. Reviewed by Kalpana Bardhan. *Journal of Women's History* 2, No. 1 (Spring 1990):200-219

**Gullette, Margaret Morganroth**

Visiting Space: Autumnal Face. *Lear's* (January 1990):136+

**Gullickson, Gay L.**

Spinners and Weavers of Auffay: Rural Industry and the Sexual Division of Labor in a French Village, 1750-1850. Reviewed by Judith DeGroat. *Gender and Society* 4, No. 2 (June 1990):272-274

**Gullotta, Thomas P.** (joint editor). *See* Montemayor, Raymond

**Gumpert, David E.**

Enterprise: They Can Get It for You Wholesale. *Working Woman* (August 1990):33-36

Entrepreneurial Edge: How to Stand Out in a Crowd. *Working Woman* (November 1990):57-63+

**Gun Control.** *See also* Handguns

Full Circle: Ready, Aim, Fire! Sarah Brady. *Family Circle* 103, No. 13 (September 25, 1990):142

**Gunew, Sneja**

Interview: Maxine Hong Kingston. *Hecate* 16, Nos. 1-2 (1990):48-60

**Guns – Accidents.** *See* Firearms – Accidents

**Gunst, Kathy**

10 Great Meals for Small Families. *Redbook* 175, No. 6 (October 1990):129-138

**Gunter, B. G.** (joint author). *See* Gunter, Nancy C.

**Gunter, Nancy C.** and Gunter, B. G.

Domestic Division of Labor among Working Couples: Does Androgyny Make a Difference? *Psychology of Women Quarterly* 14, No. 3 (September 1990):355-370

**Gupta, Nelly Edmondson**

Who Am I? *Ladies' Home Journal* 107, No. 3 (March 1990):160-161+

**Gupta, Nelly Edmondson** (joint author). *See* Snyder, Fran

**Gupta, Tanika**

Barbed Lines. Book Review. *Spare Rib* 218 (November 1990):26

**Gupta, Tanika** (joint author). *See* Grech, Joyoti

**Gurevitch, Christine** (joint author). *See* Cunnison, Sheila

**Gurewitsch, Matthew**

Bolshoi Bravo! *Harper's Bazaar* (July 1990):27

The Faust that Roared. *Harper's Bazaar* (January 1990):116-117

**Gurirab, Joan** (about)

Joan Gurirab: Going Home. Interview. Gwen McKinney. *Essence* 21, No. 6 (October 1990):116-118

**Gutiérrez, Lorraine M.**

Feminist Perspectives on Wife Abuse. Book Review. *AFFILIA* 5, No. 1 (Spring 1990):119-120

**Gutis, Philip S.**

Stepparents Need Legal Clout. *McCall's* 117, No. 8 (May 1990):66-67

Who Are the Psychological Parents? *McCall's* 117, No. 12 (September 1990):66-68

**Guttenberg, Steve** (about). *See also* Film Criticism

**Guttman, Freda** (interview)

An Interview with Freda Guttman, Montreal Artist and Activist. Marguerite Andersen. *Resources for Feminist Research* 19, No. 1 (March 1990):48-50

**Guy, Donna J.**

Public Health, Gender, and Private Morality: Paid Labor and the Formation of the Body Politic in Buenos Aires. *Gender & History* 2, No. 3 (Autumn 1990):297-317

**Guyer, Margaret E.**

Models of Achievement: Reflections of Eminent Women in Psychology, Volume 2. Book Review. *Psychology of Women Quarterly* 14, No. 4 (December 1990):621-623

**Guy-Sheftall, Beverly**

The Black Women's Health Book. Book Review. *Ms.* 1, No. 1 (July/August 1990):68-69

A Fearful Freedom: Women's Flight from Equality. Book Review. *Ms.* 1, No. 1 (July/August 1990):68

Unequal Sisters: A Multicultural Reader in U.S. Women's History. Book Review. *Ms.* 1, No. 1 (July/August 1990):69

**Guy-Sheftall, Beverly** (joint author). *See* Royster, Jacqueline Jones

**Gyant, LaVerne** (joint author). *See* Goodstein, Lynne

**Gymnasiums.** *See also* Physical Fitness Centers

**Gynecological Training Associate Program (GTA)**

Teaching Docs to Improve Gyn Exams. Rosalind Warren. *New Directions for Women* 19, No. 3 (May/June 1990):12

# H

**H. D. – Criticism and Interpretation**

H.D.'s Auto*hetero*graphy. Dianne Chisholm. *Tulsa Studies in Women's Literature* 9, No. 1 (Spring 1990):79-106

**Haaf, Wendy**

Episiotomy Power for Nurses. *Healthsharing* 11, No. 1 (December 1989):8

**Haaland, Bonnie A.**

The Decontextualization of Abortion: An Analysis of "The Silent Scream." *Women's Studies in Communication* 12, No. 2 (Fall 1989):59-76

**Habel, Leo**, Kaye, Katherine, and Lee, Jean

Trends in Reporting of Maternal Drug Abuse and Infant Mortality among Drug-Exposed Infants in New York City. *Women and Health* 16, No. 2 (1990):41-58

**Haberman, Frederic** and Danbrot, Margaret

Banish Blemishes – Fast! *Redbook* 175, No. 4 (August 1990):20

**Hacinli, Cynthia**

A Diet for the Worst Days. *Mademoiselle* (October 1990):120

Eyes Can See Clearly Now: Surgery for the Nearsighted. *Mademoiselle* (June 1990):124

Good (or Bad) to the Last Drop? A Caffeine Update. *Mademoiselle* (November 1990):116

Oops . . . Did You Take Your Pill Today? *Mademoiselle* (September 1990):198

Tummy Trouble: What It's Trying to Tell You. *Mademoiselle* (March 1990):138

**Hacker, Helen**

Opera, or the Undoing of Women. Book Review. *Gender and Society* 4, No. 4 (December 1990):561-563

**Hacker, Marilyn**

Going Back to the River. Reviewed by Judith Barrington. *The Women's Review of Books* 7, Nos. 10-11 (July 1990):28

**Hacker, Sally**

Pleasure, Power and Technology. Reviewed by Annette Burfoot. *Resources for Feminist Research* 19, No. 1 (March 1990):29

Pleasure, Power and Technology: Some Tales of Gender, Engineering and the Cooperative Workplace. Reviewed by Colleen Chesterman. *Australian Feminist Studies* No. 11 (Autumn 1990):123-126

**Hackman, Evette M.**

Food Journal: 100 Low-Fat Foods. *Ladies' Home Journal* 107, No. 4 (April 1990):183-191

**Hadas, Rachel**

The Right to Mourn. Poem. *The Women's Review of Books* 8, No. 3 (December 1990):28

A Week in February. Poem. *The Women's Review of Books* 8, No. 3 (December 1990):28

**Hagell, Elizabeth**

Time for a Change: Women's Health Education in Canadian University Schools of Nursing. *Health Care for Women International* 11, No. 2 (1990):121-131

**Haggis, Jane**

Gendering Colonialism on Colonising Gender? Recent Women's Studies Approaches to White Women and the History of British Colonialism. *Women's Studies International Forum* 13, Nos. 1-2 (1990):105-115

**Hahlweg, Kurt** (joint author). *See* Halford, W. Kim

**Hahn, Jessica** (about)

Jessica Hahn's Strange Odyssey from PTL to Playboy. Mary Zeiss Stange. *Journal of Feminist Studies in Religion* 6, No. 1 (Spring 1990):105-116

**Haile, Barbara J.** and Johnson, Audreye E.

Teaching and Learning about Black Women: The Anatomy of a Course. *Sage* 6, No. 1 (Summer 1989):69-72

**Hailey, B. Jo**, Lalor, Karen M., Hardin, Kimeron N., and Byrne, Heather A.

The Effect of Type of Relationship on Perceived Psychological Distress in Women with Breast Cancer. *Health Care for Women International* 11, No. 3 (1990):359-366

**Haines, Hilary**

Fate Cries Enough. Book Review. *The Women's Review of Books* 7, No. 8 (May 1990):20-21

Following Doctors' Orders. *The Women's Review of Books* 7, No. 8 (May 1990):20-21

The Report of the Committee of Inquiry into Allegations Concerning the Treatment of Cervical Cancer to National Women's Hospital and into Other Related Matters. Book Review. *The Women's Review of Books* 7, No. 8 (May 1990):20-21

Second Opinion: The Politics of Women's Health in New Zealand. Book Review. *The Women's Review of Books* 7, No. 8 (May 1990):20-21

The Unfortunate Experiment. Book Review. *The Women's Review of Books* 7, No. 8 (May 1990):20-21

**Haines, Michael R.**

Western Fertility in Mid-Transition: Fertility and Nuptiality in the United States and Selected Nations at the Turn of the Century. *Journal of Family History* 15, No. 1 (January 1990):23-48

**Hair**

I Capelli Moltissimi. Tasha Belfiore. *Sinister Wisdom* 41 (Summer-Fall 1990):111-113

**Hair – Care and Hygiene.** *See also* Celebrities – Beauty, Personal; Skin – Care and Hygiene

Beauty: Answers. *Essence* 20, No. 10 (February 1990):16; 20, No. 11 (March 1990):19; 21, No. 2 (June 1990):17-18; 21, No. 3 (July 1990):14; 21, No. 5 (September 1990):17; 21, No. 7 (November 1990):16

Beauty: Hydrating Our Hair. *Essence* 21, No. 7 (November 1990):12

Beauty Q & A. *Mademoiselle* (January 1990):24

Beauty Questions. *Glamour* (August 1990):42; (December 1990):42

The Cure for Stressed-Out Summer Hair. Melissa Dunst. *Lear's* (September 1990):70-72

Curly Cues. *Ladies' Home Journal* 107, No. 4 (April 1990):40

Editorial: Roots of Heaven. Frances Lear. *Lear's* (August 1990):136

Go Lighter. Linda Allen Schoen and Paul Lazar. *Redbook* 175, No. 1 (May 1990):18

Great Hair, Great Color. *Family Circle* 103, No. 5 (April 3, 1990):78-82

Great Looks: Go for the Shine! *Redbook* 176, No. 1 (November 1990):22-26

Hair News. *Essence* 21, No. 6 (October 1990):12

Image: Spring Hair Repair. Laurie Linden. *Working Woman* (May 1990):105-108

Images: Hair Answers. Elizabeth Collier. *Vogue* (September 1990):362

Make Waves. *Glamour* (March 1990):277

The Right Brush for Your Hair. *Redbook* 175, No. 1 (May 1990):16

Talking Heads. *Harper's Bazaar* (August 1990):124-125+

Tress Management Made Easy. *Lear's* (July 1990):50

Update: Relaxed Hair. *Essence* 21, No. 5 (September 1990):12-13+

What's Best for Your Hair? Linda Allen Schoen and Paul Lazar. *Redbook* 174, No. 5 (March 1990):18

**Hair – Dyeing and Bleaching**

Beauty Q & A. *Mademoiselle* (November 1990):62

Lavish Lengths. Ellen Breslow. *Harper's Bazaar* (October 1990):53-58+

Look Sensational! *Harper's Bazaar* (September 1990):42+

Make Waves. *Glamour* (March 1990):277

Mess it Up! *Glamour* (July 1990):178-179

Now Cuts for 3 Classic Beauties. *Redbook* 174, No. 5 (March 1990):14-16

Now Makeup & Hair. *Redbook* 175, No. 5 (September 1990):152-155

The One-Inch Solution. Rowann Gilman. *Working Woman* (September 1990):190-192

Quick Change. *Family Circle* 103, No. 10 (July 24, 1990):78-82

Romantic Do's. *Redbook* 175, No. 3 (July 1990):96-99

Rx for RN's: Off-Duty Beauty. *Family Circle* 103, No. 16 (November 27, 1990):78-82

Secret Perms. *McCall's* 118, No. 1 (October 1990):94-100

Serious Hair. *Glamour* (February 1990):180-183

'90s Hair: A Cut Above the Usual. *Lear's* (July 1990):49

The Short Cuts. *Essence* 21, No. 3 (July 1990):9

Simply Beautiful. Lois Joy Johnson. *Ladies' Home Journal* 107, No. 2 (February 1990):124-128

Sisters Go Shorter. *Redbook* 174, No. 6 (April 1990):18

10 Hot Holiday Maneuvers You'll Want to Try Right Now. *Essence* 21, No. 8 (December 1990):8-13

Ten Office Emergencies. *Mademoiselle* (June 1990):46

The Trick Is in the Cut. *Redbook* 175, No. 6 (October 1990):114-117

What's New about Weaves. *Essence* 21, No. 4 (August 1990):12-13

Who Cuts Who. *Harper's Bazaar* (May 1990):71-74+

**Hair Styles and Politics**

Interiors: Is Your Hair Still Political? Audre Lorde. *Essence* 21, No. 5 (September 1990):40+

**Hair Weaves.** *See* Hair Styles

**Haiti – Politics and Government**

Madame la Présidente. Elizabeth Barad. *Ms.* 1, No. 1 (July/August 1990):13

**Halas, Mary A.**

Motherhood and Sex Role Development. *Women and Therapy* 10, Nos. 1/2 (1990):227-243

**Halberstam, Malvina** and Defeis, Elizabeth F.

Women's Legal Rights: International Covenants, An Alternative to ERA? Reviewed by Barbara Stark. *Women's Rights Law Reporter* 12, No. 1 (Spring 1990):51-57

**Haldane, Elizabeth** (about)

Inside Out: Elizabeth Haldane as a Women's Suffrage Survivor in the 1920s and 1930s. Johanna Alberti. *Women's Studies International Forum* 13, Nos. 1-2 (1990):117-125

**Hale, Katherine** (joint author). *See* Switzer, M'Liss

**Hale, Mary M.** and Kelly, Rita Mae (editors)

Gender, Bureaucracy and Democracy: Careers and Equal Opportunity in the Public Sector. Reviewed by Ronald J. Burke. *Atlantis* 15, No. 2 (Spring 1990):116-117

**Hale, Noreen**

Being Old: Seven Women, Seven Views. *Journal of Women and Aging* 2, No. 2 (1990):7-17

**Hale, Sylvia**

The Elusive Promise: The Struggle of Women Development Workers in Rural North India. Reviewed by Sue Ellen Charlton. *Signs* 15, No. 4 (Summer 1990):860-864

**Hales, Dianne**

Elementary Years. *Working Mother* (November 1990):130; (December 1990):72

Health Watch. *Family Circle* 103, No. 6 (April 24, 1990):56-57+

Routines Are Reassuring to Babies. *Working Mother* 13, No. 4 (April 1990):82-85

Stress-Busting Strategies. *Working Mother* 13, No. 9 (September 1990):60-61

**Hales, Dianne** (joint author). *See* Brockman, Elin Schoen

**Haley, Heather Susan**

The Brat from Beverly Hills. Poem. *Heresies* 25 (1990):49

**Halford, W. Kim**, Hahlweg, Kurt, and Dunne, Michael

The Cross-cultural Consistency of Marital Communication Associated with Marital Distress. *Journal of Marriage and the Family* 52, No. 2 (May 1990):487-500

Halitosis. *See* Breath, Offensive

Hall, Arsenio (about). *See* Entertainers; Television Criticism

Hall, Catherine (joint author). *See* Davidoff, Leonore

Hall, Chris (joint author). *See* Flanigan, Beverly

Hall, Elaine J. (joint author). *See* Ferree, Myra Marx

**Hall, Helen** (about)

Female Social Workers in the Second Generation. Janice L. Andrews. *AFFILIA* 5, No. 2 (Summer 1990):46-59

**Hall, Holly**

Clothes Make the Woman. *Belles Lettres* 5, No. 2 (Winter 1990):13

Heavenly Soles: Extraordinary Twentieth-Century Shoes. Book Review. *Belles Lettres* 5, No. 4 (Summer 1990):35+

Men and Women: Dressing the Part. Book Review. *Belles Lettres* 5, No. 2 (Winter 1990):13

**Hall, Jacquelyn Dowd** and others

Like a Family: The Making of a Southern Cotton Mill World. Reviewed by Elizabeth Faue. *Signs* 15, No. 2 (Winter 1990):391-394

**Hall, Joan Joffe**

Remember Who You Are: Stories about Being Jewish. Book review. *Lilith* 15, No. 3 (Summer 1990):6

Twice Blessed: On Being Lesbian, Gay, and Jewish. Book review. *Lilith* 15, No. 3 (Summer 1990):7+

**Hall, Joanne M.**

Alcoholism in Lesbians: Developmental, Symbolic Interactionist, and Critical Perspectives. *Health Care for Women International* 11, No. 1 (1990):89-107

**Hall, Lisa Kahaleole Chang**

After Surgery/Epilepsy Poem #430. Poem. *Sinister Wisdom* 40 (Spring 1990):62-63

Bodily Functions. Poem. *Sinister Wisdom* 40 (Spring 1990):62

If Not Now When? Poem. *Sinister Wisdom* 40 (Spring 1990):62

101 to San Mateo. Poem. *Sinister Wisdom* 40 (Spring 1990):61

Visiting Hours. Poem. *Sinister Wisdom* 40 (Spring 1990):61

**Hall, Mary** (about)

A Woman's Trek: What Difference Does Gender Make? Susan L. Blake. *Women's Studies International Forum* 13, No. 4 (1990):347-355

**Hall, Maureen**

Take Back Four O'Clock. *Women and Environments* 12, No. 2 (Spring 1990): 6-7

Hall, Philippa (joint author). *See* O'Donnell, Carol

**Hall, Radclyffe** (about)

Cutting a Dash: The Dress of Radclyffe Hall and Una Troubridge. Katrina Rolley. *Feminist Review* No. 35 (Summer 1990):54-66

Hall, Sharon (joint author). *See* Emo, Dretha M.

**Hall, Stuart** and Jacques, Martin (editors)

New Times: The Changing Face of Politics in the 1990s. Reviewed by Andrea McRobbie. *Feminist Review* No. 36 (Autumn 1990):127-131

Hall, Susan (joint author). *See* Ledbetter, Carol

**Hall, Trish**

The Joys of Traveling with My Baby. *McCall's* 117, No. 7 (April 1990):10+

**Hall Carpenter Archives Lesbian Oral History Group** (editors)

Inventing Ourselves: Lesbian Life Stories. Reviewed by Jennie Ruby. *off our backs* 20, No. 7 (July 1990):15

**Hall Carpenter Archives/Lesbian Oral History Group** (editors)

Inventing Ourselves: Lesbian Life Stories. Reviewed by Sarah Green. *Feminist Review* No. 34 (Spring 1990):176-177

**Haller, Henry**

"I Cooked for the President." *Ladies' Home Journal* 107, No. 2 (February 1990):162-163

**Hallgarth, Susan A.**

Cather Custody Battles. *The Women's Review of Books* 8, No. 1 (October 1990):23-24

Willa Cather: Double Lives. Book Review. *The Women's Review of Books* 8, No. 1 (October 1990):23-24

**Halloween – Cookery**

Happy Halloween Desserts. Donna Meadow. *McCall's* 118, No. 1 (October 1990):140

It's a Halloween Party! *Glamour* (October 1990):290-294

**Halloween Decorations**

Quick Craft: Trick or Treat? *Family Circle* 103, No. 14 (October 16, 1990):152-158

**Halperin, David M.**

The Democratic Body: Prostitution and Citizenship in Classical Athens. *Differences* 2, No. 1 (Spring 1990):1-28

Halperin, Joel Martin (joint editor). *See* Nguyen-Hong-Nhiem, Lucy

**Halpern, Sue**

Medical Report: Your Medical Records. Bibliography. *Glamour* (September 1990):104-110

**Halpert, Felicia**

Birth Control for Him. *Essence* 21, No. 7 (November 1990):20-22

**Halpert, Felicia E.**

Healing Professions. Bibliography. *Essence* 21, No. 4 (August 1990):32-34

Working: Red-Hot Jobs. *Essence* 20, No. 11 (March 1990):34-37 +

**Halston** (about)

American Original. Jon Etra. *Harper's Bazaar* (July 1990):34-36

Halston: 1932-1990. Liza Minelli and Polly Mellen. *Vogue* (July 1990):62-68

**Halverson, Jayna** (joint author). *See* Spirito, Anthony

**Hamabata, Matthews Masayuki**

Crested Kimono: Power and Love in the Japanese Business Family. Reviewed by Kate Gilbert. *The Women's Review of Books* 8, No. 1 (October 1990):5-7

**Hamalian, Linda**

Have You Met Ms. Jones? *Belles Lettres* 5, No. 4 (Summer 1990):46

How I Became Hettie Jones. Book Review. *Belles Lettres* 5, No. 4 (Summer 1990):46

**Hamazaki, Terrie**

In Canada: The Dialogue Continues. *Spare Rib* No. 216 (September 1990):38-39

**Hamblett, Theora** (about)

The Visionary Paintings of Theora Hamblett. Paul Grootkerk. *Woman's Art Journal* 11, No. 2 (Fall 1990-Winter 1991):19-22

**Hamburg, Joan**

Shopping Smart: Bargain Gifts by Mail. *Family Circle* 103, No. 15 (November 6, 1990):40-43

Shopping Smart. *Family Circle* 103, No. 3 (February 20, 1990):111 +; 103, No. 5 (April 3, 1990):93-94; 103, No. 7 (May 15, 1990):59 +; 103, No. 9 (June 26, 1990):26-28

**Hamelin, Monique**

Femmes et prison. Reviewed by Monique Imbleau. *Resources for Feminist Research* 19, No. 1 (March 1990):14

**Hamer, Diane**

Significant Others: Lesbianism and Psychoanalytic Theory. *Feminist Review* No. 34 (Spring 1990):135

**Hamer, Fanny Lou** (about). *See also* Black History

Never Turn Back: The Life of Fanny Lou Hamer. Directed by Bill Buckley. Reviewed by C. Alejandro Elenes. *Feminist Collections* 11, No. 3 (Spring 1990):10

**Hamer, M. C.** (about). *See* Leadership

**Hamid, Rizu**

Aboriginal Ancestors Journey Home. *Spare Rib* No. 215 (August 1990):22-25

**Hamill, Pete** and Kleiman, Mark A. R.

The Great American Drug Muddle. *Lear's* (March 1990):156-157 +

**Hamilton, Amy** (joint author). *See* Keating, Cricket

**Hamilton, Cathy Johnston**

The Mothers' Page: What Do You Mean My Child's Not Perfect? *McCall's* 117, No. 10 (July 1990):16-18

**Hamilton, Cicely** (about)

Cicely Hamilton, Independent Feminist. Harriet Blodgett. *Frontiers* 11, Nos. 2-3 (1990):99-104

**Hamilton, Gordon** (joint editor). *See* Tomm, Winifred

**Hamilton, J. A.**

Heart Urchin. Poem. *Frontiers* 11, Nos. 2-3 (1990):72-73

Rondônia. Poem. *Frontiers* 11, Nos. 2-3 (1990):73

Silver Pennies. Poem. *Frontiers* 11, Nos. 2-3 (1990):74

**Hamilton, Jon**

The Healthy Family. *Family Circle* 103, No. 4 (March 13, 1990):70 +

**Hamilton, Minard**

Rocking the Ship of State: Toward a Feminist Peace Politics. Book Review. *New Directions for Women* 19, No. 2 (March/April 1990):19

**Hamilton, Paula**

"Inventing the Self": Oral History as Autobiography. *Hecate* 16, Nos. 1-2 (1990):128-133

**Hamilton, Roberta**

A Politics of Intimate Life: A Funny Thing Happened on the Way Through the Eighties. *Atlantis* 15, No. 2 (Spring 1990):82-89

**Ha1mmerle, Christa** (joint author). *See* Bernold, Monika

**Hammerton, A. James**

Putting Asunder: A History of Divorce in Western Society. Book Review. *Gender & History* 2, No. 2 (Summer 1990):241-244

Women and Marriage in Nineteenth Century England. Book Review. *Gender & History* 2, No. 2 (Summer 1990):241-244

**Hammig, Cynthia L** (joint author). *See* Newell, G. Kathleen

**Hammond, Jenny**

Sweeter Than Honey: Ethiopian Women and Revolution, Testimonies of Tigrayan Women. Reviewed by Gill Lusk. *The Women's Review of Books* 8, No. 3 (December 1990):13-14

**Hammonds, Evelynn**

The Black Women's Health Book: Speaking for Ourselves. Book Review. *The Women's Review of Books* 7, No. 9 (June 1990):1-4

**Hanson, Karen**

Dressing Down Dressing Up – The Philosophic Fear of Fashion. *Hypatia* 5, No. 2 (Summer 1990):107-121

**Hanson, Richard A.**

Initial Parenting Attitudes of Pregnant Adolescents and a Comparison with the Decision about Adoption. *Adolescence* 25, No. 99 (Fall 1990):629-643

**Hanson, Sandra L.**

First Births in America: Changes in the Timing of Parenthood. Book Review. *Journal of Marriage and the Family* 52, No. 3 (August 1990):800

**Hånukah**

Hanukah: Lighting the Way to Women's Empowerment. Nina Katz, Amy Sheldon, and Rachel Josefowitz Siegel. *Bridges* 1, No. 2 (Fall 1990): 30-31

Oco Kandelikas. Song. Flory Jogoda. *Bridges* 1, No. 2 (Fall 1990): 32-33

**Hanukkah**

The Art of the Menorah. Phyllis Schiller. *McCall's* 118, No. 3 (December 1990):31-33

Rembrance of Hanukkah Past. Esther J. Ruskay. *Good Housekeeping* 211, No. 6 (December 1990):56 +

**Hanukkah – Cookery**

Hanukkah: The Festival of Lights. *Family Circle* 103, No. 17 (December 18, 1990):48

**Ha-Pi, Asar**

Yoga. *Essence* 20, No. 11 (March 1990):66-67

**Hapke, Laura**

Girls Who Went Wrong: Prostitutes in American Fiction. Reviewed by Nikki Lee Manos. *Belles Lettres* 5, No. 3 (Spring 1990):27

Hungry Hearts and Other Stories. Book Review. *Belles Lettres* 6, No. 1 (Fall 1990):54

Reprints. *Belles Lettres* 5, No. 3 (Spring 1990):22-23; 6, No. 1 (Fall 1990):54-57

Reprints: Women and Work. *Belles Lettres* 5, No. 4 (Summer 1990):33-35

These Modern Women: Autobiographical Essays from the Twenties. Book Review. *Belles Lettres* 6, No. 1 (Fall 1990):54-55

Writing Red: An Anthology of American Women Writers, 1930-1940. Book Review. *Belles Lettres* 6, No. 1 (Fall 1990):55-56

**Happiness**

Happiness: How to get More of it. *Glamour* (December 1990):198-201

**Harasym, Sarah**

Breaking the Sequence: Women's Experimental Fiction. Book Review. *Resources for Feminist Research* 19, No. 1 (March 1990):6-7

**Haraway, Donna**

Primate Visions: Gender, Race, and Nature in the World of Modern Science. Reviewed by Judith Masters. *The Women's Review of Books* 7, No. 4 (January 1990):18-19

Primate Visions: Gender, Race, and Nature in the World of Modern Science. Reviewed by Sandra Harding. *NWSA Journal* 2, No. 2 (Spring 1990):295-298

Primate Visions: Gender, Race and Nature in the World of Modern Science. Reviewed by Carol Anne Douglas. *off our backs* 20, No. 7 (July 1990):21-22

Primate Visions: Gender, Race and Nature in the World of Modern Science. Reviewed by Joan M. Gero. *Women's Studies International Forum* 13, No. 6 (1990):609-610

**Harbert, John C.**

Take 2 Asprin . . . and Call Me in 5 Years. *Family Circle* 103, No. 14 (October 16, 1990):136-138

**Hardin, Kimeron N.** (joint author). *See* Hailey, B. Jo

**Harding, Sandra**

The Permanent Revolution. *The Women's Review of Books* 7, No. 5 (February 1990):17

Primate Visions: Gender, Race, and Nature in the World of Modern Science. Book Review. *NWSA Journal* 2, No. 2 (Spring 1990):295-298

**Harding, Sandra** (editor)

Feminism and Methodology: Social Science Issues. Reviewed by Susan J. Hekman. *Women & Politics* 10, No. 1 (1990):71-73

**Hardwicke Act**

The Heroine's Blazon and Hardwicke's Marriage Act: Commodification for a Novel Market. Katherine Sobba Green. *Tulsa Studies in Women's Literature* 9, No. 2 (Fall 1990):273-290

**Hardy, Jan**

Small Acts. Poem. *Sinister Wisdom* 40 (Spring 1990):36-37

**Harems**

An American Harem. Kathryn Casey. *Ladies' Home Journal* 107, No. 2 (February 1990):116-117 +

The Colonial Harem. By Malek Alloula. Reviewed by Wendy Kozol. *Gender & History* 2, No. 1 (Spring 1990):110-113

Uncovering the Zenana: Visions of Indian Womanhood in Englishwomen's Writings: 1813-1940. Janaki Nair. *Journal of Women's History* 2, No. 1 (Spring 1990):8-34

**Hare-Mustin, Rachel**

Don't Blame Mother: Mending the Mother-Daughter Relationship. Book Review. *Psychology of Women Quarterly* 14, No. 1 (March 1990):143-145

Journal of Feminist Therapy. Periodical review. *Psychology of Women Quarterly* 14, No. 3 (September 1990):440-441

**Hare-Salnave, Barbara** (about). *See* Dent, David

**Haring-Hidore, Marilyn** (joint author). *See* Paludi, Michele A.

**Harjo, Joy**

In Mad Love and War. Reviewed by Margaret Randall. *The Women's Review of Books* 7, Nos. 10-11 (July 1990):17-18

**Harjo, Joy** and Strom, Stephen

Secrets from the Center of the World. Reviewed by Margaret Randall. *The Women's Review of Books* 7, Nos. 10-11 (July 1990):17-18

**Harkin, Margo**

Hush-a-Bye Baby. Reviewed by Margaret Gillan. *Spare Rib* 219 (December 1990-January 1991):34

**Harlem Renaissance**

Senses of Self: Women Writers of the Harlem Renaissance. Elyse Demaray and Lori Landay. *Feminist Teacher* 5, No. 2 (Fall 1990):32-33

Shadowed Dreams: Women's Poetry of the Harlem Renaissance. Edited by Maureen Honey. Reviewed by Lorraine Elena Roses. *The Women's Review of Books* 7, Nos. 10-11 (July 1990):31-32

The Unreadable Black Body: "Conventional" Poetic Form in the Harlem Renaissance. Amitai F. Aviram. *Genders* 7 (Spring 1990):32-46

**Harley, Sharon**

For the Good of Family and Race: Gender, Work, and Domestic Roles in the Black Community, 1880-1930. Notes. *Signs* 15, No. 2 (Winter 1990):336-349

**Harman, Barbara**

Making Artists' Books. *Belles Lettres* 5, No. 4 (Summer 1990):4-5

**Harman, Claire**

Sylvia Townsend Warner: A Biography. Reviewed by Carolyn G. Heilbrun. *The Women's Review of Books* 7, No. 6 (March 1990):8-9

**Harman, Lesley D.**

When a Hostel Becomes a Home – Experiences of Women. Reviewed by Dominique Masson. *Resources for Feminist Research* 19, No. 1 (March 1990):37-38

**Harper, Anne** (joint author). *See* Weiss, Penny

**Harper, Jorjet**

Accessibility, Male Children Heated Issues at Lesbian Fest. *Hot Wire* 6, No. 1 (January 1990):29+

The 1990 AWMAC Conference. *Hot Wire* 6, No. 2 (May 1990):34-35+

The First Annual East Coast Lesbians' Festival. *Hot Wire* 6, No. 1 (January 1990):28+

Sappho: Rediscovering Lesbian Space. *Hot Wire* 6, No. 3 (September 1990):48-49

Southern: The "Live and Let Live" Festival. *Hot Wire* 6, No. 3 (September 1990):40-42

Towards a Lesbian Aesthetic. *Hot Wire* 6, No. 1 (January 1990):14-15+

**Harper, Karen V.**

Power and Gender Issues in Academic Administration: A Study of Directors of BSW Programs. *AFFILIA* 5, No. 1 (Spring 1990):81-93

**Harper, Valerie** (about)

Talking with Valerie Harper. Vicki Jo Radovsky. *Redbook* 175, No. 1 (May 1990):30-32

Valerie Harper: Everything Is Coming Up "Love." Vernon Scott. *Good Housekeeping* 210, No. 6 (June 1990):126-129

**Harragan, Betty Lehan**

Career Advice: Dear Betty Harragan. *Working Woman* (January 1990):32-35; (February 1990):38-43; (March 1990):34-36

**Harrel, William**

Compact Disks, Pelvic Twists. *Lear's* (December 1990):45-46

**Harrell, Sara**

Doing Lunch. Poem. *Executive Female* 13, No. 4 (July-August 1990):51

**Harrell, Stevan** (joint editor). *See* Bynum, Caroline Walker

**Harries, Patrick**

Symbols and Sexuality: Culture and Identity on the Early Witwatersrand Gold Mines. *Gender & History* 2, No. 3 (Autumn 1990):318-336

**Harrington, Mona** (joint author). *See* Aisenberg, Nadya

**Harris, Adrienne E.** and King, Ynestra (editors)

Rocking the Ship of State: Toward a Feminist Peace Politics. Reviewed by Minard Hamilton. *New Directions for Women* 19, No. 2 (March/April 1990):19

**Harris, Alice** (about). *See* De Veaux, Alexis, Milloy, Marilyn, and Ross, Michael Erik

**Harris, Barbara J.**

Property, Power, and Personal Relations: Elite Mothers and Sons in Yorkist and Early Tudor England. Notes. *Signs* 15, No. 3 (Spring 1990):606-632

**Harris, Jana**

The Sourlands. Reviewed by Lee Upton. *Belles Lettres* 5, No. 3 (Spring 1990):24-25

**Harris, Jessica**

Iron Pots and Wooden Spoons. Excerpt. *Essence* 21, No. 6 (October 1990):101-104

**Harris, Lara** (about)

Star 90: Hollywood's Changing Face. *Mademoiselle* (December 1990):32

**Harris, Lynne B.** (joint author). *See* Perkins, H. Wesley

**Harris, Marlys**

What's Wrong with this Picture? *Working Woman* (December 1990):72-76

**Harris, Miriam Kalman**

Claire Myers Spotswood (Owens). *Belles Lettres* 5, No. 2 (Winter 1990):15

King of the Hill. Book Review. *The Women's Review of Books* 7, Nos. 10-11 (July 1990):35

My Jewish Face. Book Review. *Belles Lettres* 6, No. 1 (Fall 1990):12

True to Life. *The Women's Review of Books* 7, Nos. 10-11 (July 1990):35

**Harris, Neil Patrick** (about)

Doogie Houser's Neil Patrick Harris. Curtis Pesmen. *Ladies' Home Journal* 107, No. 5 (May 1990):60

**Harris, Patricia** (joint author). *See* Loxton, Diane

**Harris, Ruth**

The Female Malady: Women, Madness and English Culture, 1830-1980. Book review. *Signs* 15, No. 2 (Winter 1990):408-410

**Harrison, A. S. A.** (joint author). *See* Dragu, Margaret

**Harrison, Barbara**

Suffer the Working Day: Women in the "Dangerous Trades," 1880-1914. *Women's Studies International Forum* 13, Nos. 1-2 (1990):79-90

**Harrison, Barbara Grizzuti**

Barney Frank: A Public Man's Private Sins. *Mademoiselle* (February 1990):100

Can TV Switch Off Bigotry? *Mademoiselle* (November 1990):110

Lewd Music. *Mademoiselle* (October 1990):116

The Private Eye: Better Dead than Coed. *Mademoiselle* (September 1990):182

The Private Eye: Should Women Have the Right to Fight? *Mademoiselle* (June 1990):114

Women and Children First? *Mademoiselle* (December 1990):102

**Harrison, Beppie** (joint author). *See* Romney, Ronna

**Harrison, Cynthia**

From Margin to Mainstream: American Women and Politics Since 1960. Book Review. *NWSA Journal* 2, No. 1 (Winter 1990):139-141

**Harrison, Denise**

Do You Need (or Want) a Master's Degree? *Glamour* (July 1990):76

**Harrison, Jane Ellen** (about)

Jane Ellen Harrison: The Mask and the Self. By Sandra J. Peacock. Reviewed by Janet Howarth. *Gender and Education* 2, No. 2 (1990):246-247

Jane Ellen Harrison: The Mask and the Self. By Sandra J. Peacock. Reviewed by Sandra J. Peacock. *Gender & History* 2, No. 1 (Spring 1990):103-104

**Harrison, Julie**

Positive Images: Portraits of Women with Disabilities. Reviewed by Judith Pasternak. *On the Issues* 17 (Winter 1990):36-37

**Harrison, Wallace K.** (about). *See* Muschamp, Herbert

**Hart, Ellen Louise**

The Encoding of Homoerotic Desire: Emily Dickinson's Letters and Poems to Susan Dickinson, 1850-1886. *Tulsa Studies in Women's Literature* 9, No. 2 (Fall 1990):251-272

**Hart, Kathleen** (joint author). *See* Spirito, Anthony

**Hart, Kitty** (about). *See* Holocaust (1939-1945) – Survivors

**Hart, Lynda**

Making a Spectacle: Feminist Essays on Contemporary Women's Theatre. Reviewed by Catherine Burroughs. *Tulsa Studies in Women's Literature* 9, No. 2 (Fall 1990):326-329

**Hart, Lynda** (editor)

Making A Spectacle: Feminist Essays on Contemporary Women's Theatre. Reviewed by Gail Leondar. *Women and Performance: A Journal of Feminist Theory* 5, No. 1, Issue #9 (1990): 192-193

**Harten, Elke** and Harten, Hans-Christian

Femmes, culture et révolution. Reviewed by Micheline Dumont. *Resources for Feminist Research* 19, No. 2 (June 1990):43

**Harten, Hans-Christian** (joint author). *See* Harten, Elke

**Hartmann, Betsy**

Reproductive Rights and Wrongs: The Global Politics of Population Control and Contraceptive Choice. Reviewed by Peggy L. Chinn. *Signs* 15, No. 2 (Winter 1990):400-405

**Hartmann, Susan M.**

From Margin to Mainstream: American Women and Politics Since 1960. Reviewed by Cynthia

Harrison. *NWSA Journal* 2, No. 1 (Winter 1990):139-141

**Hartung, Beth**

Selective Rejection: How Students Perceive Women's Studies Teachers. *NWSA Journal* 2, No. 2 (Spring 1990):254-263

**Hartwell, Shirley**

The Lie of the Feminist Right Wing Ethic. *Trivia* 16/17 (Fall 1990):68-80

**Harvard Business Review**

Pygmalion in Pinstripes. Sandra Salmans. *Lear's* (April 1990):30-33

**Harvard University**

To Pee or Not to Pee . . . Celebrating Women's History. Irene Davall. *On the Issues* 15 (Summer 1990):20-21

**Harvard University – Law School**. *See also* Bell, Derrick (about)

**Harvard University – Psychology of Women and the Development of Girls Project**

The Importance of Being Eleven. Lindsy Van Gelder. *Ms.* 1, No. 1 (July/August 1990):77-79

**Harvest Festivals – United States**. *See also* Kwanzaa; Thanksgiving Day

**Harvey Girls**

The Harvey Girls, Women Who Opened the West. By Lesley Poling-Kempes. Reviewed by Lynn Wenzel. *New Directions for Women* 19, No. 2 (March/April 1990):15

**Haskell, Molly**

French Lessons. *Lear's* (July 1990):68-73

Seams from a Marriage. *Lear's* (April 1990):58-66

**Hassan, Jamelie**

Women and the State. *Canadian Women's Studies* 11, No. 1 (Spring 1990):25-26

**Hate Crimes**

Hate Crimes Bill Excludes Women. Marie de Santis. *off our backs* 20, No. 6 (June 1990):1

US: Women Excluded from Hate Crimes Bill. *Spare Rib* No. 216 (September 1990):47

**Hathaway, Nancy** (joint author). *See* Lightner, Candy

**Hats**

Haute Heads. René Gruau. *Harper's Bazaar* (April 1990):170-173

We Wear the Crown. *Essence* 21, No. 7 (November 1990):78-85

What They're Wearing. *Glamour* (July 1990):138

**Hatzimanolis, Efi**

The Politics of Nostalgia: Community and Difference in Migrant Writing. *Hecate* 16, Nos. 1-2 (1990):120-127

**Hauck, William E.** (joint author). *See* Moore, J. William

**Hauri, Peter J.** and Linde, Shirley

Can't Sleep? Tired? Tense? *Redbook* 175, No. 1 (May 1990):156-163

**Hautzig, Esther**

Remember Who You Are: Stories about Being Jewish. Reviewed by Joan Joffe Hall. *Lilith* 15, No. 3 (Summer 1990):6

**Haverty, Anne**

Constance Markievicz: An Independent Life. Reviewed by Margaret MacCurtain. *Gender & History* 2, No. 3 (Autumn 1990):365-368

**Hawaii**

Paths of Duty: American Missionary Women in Nineteenth-Century Hawaii. By Patricia Grimshaw. Reviewed by Hoda Zaki. *The Women's Review of Books* 7, No. 9 (June 1990):19-20

**Hawaii – Religion**

Ka'ahumanu, Molder of Change. By Jane L. Silverman. Reviewed by Haunani-Kay Trask. *NWSA Journal* 2, No. 1 (Winter 1990):127-129

**Hawk, Natalyn** (about). *See also* College Students – Leadership

**Hawkesworth, Mary E.**

Reply to Hekman. Notes. *Signs* 15, No. 2 (Winter 1990):420-423

Reply to Shogan. *Signs* 15, No. 2 (Winter 1990):426-428

**Hawkesworth, Mary E.** (about)

Comment on Hawkesworth's "Knowers, Knowing, Known: Feminist Theory and Claims of Truth." Debra Shogan. *Signs* 15, No. 2 (Winter 1990):424-425

Comment on Hawkesworth's "Knowers, Knowing, Known: Feminist Theory and Claims of Truth." Notes. Susan Hekman. *Signs* 15, No. 2 (Winter 1990):417-419

**Hawn, Goldie** (about). *See also* Hawn-Sylbert Movie Company

Happiness Is Goldie's Secret. Melinda Lawrence. *Redbook* 175, No. 3 (July 1990):22-27

Pure Goldie. Kristine McKenna. *Harper's Bazaar* (July 1990):68-73+

**Hawn-Sylbert Movie Company**

Reel Stylishness. Leslie Bennetts. *Lear's* (July 1990):64-67+

**Hawthorne, Susan** and Pausacker, Jenny (editors)

Moments of Desire: Sex and Sensuality by Australian Feminist Writers. Reviewed by Susan Sheridan. *Australian Feminist Studies* No. 11 (Autumn 1990):133-135

**Hayakawa, Noriyo**
Biography, Autobiography and Gender in Japan. *Gender & History* 2, No. 1 (Spring 1990):79-82

**Hayes, Arthur**
Judge Consuelo B. Marshall Holding Court. *Essence* 21, No. 3 (July 1990):37

**Hayes, Darlene** (about)
Darlene Hayes: Producer Plus. Bebe Moore Campbell. *Essence* 21, No. 5 (September 1990):50

**Hayes, E. Kent**
How to Be a Better Parent – Set Limits! *Redbook* 175, No. 4 (August 1990):78-79+

**Hayes, Susan**
Oval House: Weathering the Storms. *Spare Rib* No. 212 (May 1990):26

**Hazan, Marcella** (about)
Italian Spice. Diane Sustendal. *Harper's Bazaar* (July 1990):116

**Hazard, Jan Turner**
Beat-the-Clock Dinners. *Ladies' Home Journal* 107, No. 9 (September 1990):186-188+

Christmas Means Cookies. *Ladies' Home Journal* 107, No. 12 (December 1990):162+

Cuisine of the Sun. *Ladies' Home Journal* 107, No. 8 (August 1990):126-137

Home Cooking. *Ladies' Home Journal* 107, No. 10 (October 1990):184-194

Hot Potatoes! *Ladies' Home Journal* 107, No. 2 (February 1990):139-149

The Lower-Your-Cholesterol Diet. *Ladies' Home Journal* 107, No. 1 (January 1990):128-138

Perfect Summer Parties. *Ladies' Home Journal* 107, No. 6 (June 1990):146-162

Women Chefs' Hall of Fame. *Ladies' Home Journal* 107, No. 11 (November 1990):246-254

World Class Chicken. *Ladies' Home Journal* 107, No. 5 (May 1990):196-202

**Hazard, Jan Turner** (joint author). *See* Payne, Lauren

**Hazardous Wastes.** *See also* Refuse and Refuse Disposal
Green Watch. *Good Housekeeping* 211, No. 4 (October 1990):127-128

Health Watch. Dianne Hales. *Family Circle* 103, No. 6 (April 24, 1990):56-57+

Silk Purse Chronicles: Making an End Run around Armageddon. Patricia O'Toole. *Lear's* (August 1990):21-23

Toxic Nightmare on Main Street. Stephanie Abarbanel. *Family Circle* 103, No. 11 (August 14, 1990):77-80+

**Hazleton, Lesley**
Anatomy of the Year's Best-Seller. *Lear's* (July 1990):28-29

Fast Lane: A Gallant Import. *Lear's* (March 1990):40-42

Fast Lane: Capital Style. *Lear's* (February 1990):32-35

Fast Lane: Care in the Spirit of Summer. *Lear's* (August 1990):24-25

Fast Lane. *Lear's* (January 1990):36

Fast Lane: The Van Is Back in Town. *Lear's* (April 1990):34

Lexus and Infiniti: Luxury for Less. *Lear's* (May 1990):42-44

The Queen of Cars. *Lear's* (December 1990):40-42

Room on the Road Most Taken. *Lear's* (October 1990):41-42

Spotlight on a User-Friendly Car. *Lear's* (November 1990):48

A Tale of Two Mercedes-Benzes. *Lear's* (June 1990):42-43

A Zippy Hatchback in Apple Green. *Lear's* (September 1990):36-37

**Head, Lesley** (joint author). *See* Beck, Wendy

**Headaches**
Serious Headaches. Susan Alai. *Family Circle* 103, No. 15 (November 6, 1990):63-67

Turn Off That Headache! Alan M. Rapoport and Fred D. Sheftell. *Redbook* 175, No. 6 (October 1990):104-105+

**Headhunters.** *See* Executives – Recruiting

**Healing**
Cranial Therapy: Relief at Last. Susan Danese. *Healthsharing* 11, No. 2 (March 1990):27-28

**Health**
Do Muscles Have Memories? Toni Mirosevich. *Trivia* 16/17 (Fall 1990):131-136

The Exercise/Illness Connection. David C. Neiman. *Women's Sports and Fitness* 12, No. 2 (March 1990):56-57

GH/Tums National Survey Results: What Women Really Do to Stay Healthy. *Good Housekeeping* 210, No. 6 (June 1990):28-31

Health on Stage. Rachel Epstein. *Healthsharing* 11, No. 2 (March 1990):22-26

Perfect Health. Deepak Chopra. *Mademoiselle* (August 1990):193-195

Women's Health Questions Answered. By Pat Rush and Ann Rushton. Reviewed by Stefania Siedlecky. *Healthright* 9, No. 4 (August 1990):43

## Health and Employment

Waged Work and Women's Well Being. Lesley Doyal. *Women's Studies International Forum* 13, No. 6 (1990):587-604

## Health and Family Circumstances

Affect Expression, Marital Satisfaction, and Stress Reactivity among Premenopausal Women during a Conflictual Marital Discussion. Marie A. Morell and Robin F. Apple. *Psychology of Women Quarterly* 14, No. 3 (September 1990):387-402

Family Bereavement and Health in Adult Life Course Perspective. H. Wesley Perkins and Lynne B. Harris. *Journal of Marriage and the Family* 52, No. 1 (February 1990):233-241

The Impact of the Family on Health: The Decade in Review. Catherine E. Ross, John Mirowsky, and Karen Goldsteen. *Journal of Marriage and the Family* 52, No. 4 (November 1990):1059-1078

## Health Care. *See also* African-American Women – Health Care; Business Travel – Health Aspects; Exercise; Family Medicine; Great Britain – Health Care – History; Health Education; Health Resorts, Watering Places, etc.; Hospital Care; Hydrotherapy; Patient-Doctor Relationships; Pediatrics; Physical Examination; Skin – Care and Hygiene; Sleep Disorders; Solar Radiation – Physiological Effect; Stress –

Coping Strategies; Stress Relaxation

Allergies: Latest Finds, Best Treatments. Bibliography. Dava Sobel. *Good Housekeeping* 211, No. 3 (September 1990):226-227+

Body Management: Health News. Carl Sherman. *Working Woman* (August 1990):90-93

Body Management: The Executive Workout. Len Kravitz. *Working Woman* (February 1990):115-120

Body Management: The New Fitness Myths – Why You Shouldn't Always Play by the Rules. Ellen Kunes. *Working Woman* (August 1990):87-88

Boston Women's Health Book Collective. *Women's World* 23 (April 1990):51

Community Care Bill Delayed. Marie Pye. *Spare Rib* 217 (October 1990):46-47

8 Dangerous Breast Cancer Myths. Richard Dowden and Joan Houger. *Redbook* 175, No. 1 (May 1990):114-115

Healing from Within. Lisa M. Phipps. *Healthsharing* 11, No. 1 (December 1989):15-16

Healing Technology: Feminist Perspectives. By Kathryn Strother Ratcliff. Reviewed by Demetria Iazzetto. *NWSA Journal* 2, No. 4 (Autumn 1990):664-668

Health: New Cancer Treatments. Vicki Monks. *Vogue* (August 1990):236-240

Health Advice – Before It's too Late. Monica McFadden. *Ms.* 1, No. 3 (November/December 1990):92

Health Express: Home Remedies. P. S. Derron. *Mademoiselle* (February 1990):110

Health News. Marian Sandmaier. *Working Woman* (September 1990):201; (November 1990):148

Health Report: The Sleep Mystique: Could You Get By on Less? Roberta Israeloff. *Working Woman* (September 1990):195-196

Healthy Family. Gary Holt and Joanne Morici. *Family Circle* 103, No. 7 (May 15, 1990):27-30

The Healthy Family. Jon Hamilton. *Family Circle* 103, No. 4 (March 13, 1990):70+

Honoring Our Bodies: The Key to Transformation. Christiane Northrup. *Woman of Power* 18 (Fall 1990):16-19

If You Can't Stand the Heat. Cheryl Solimini. *Family Circle* 103, No. 8 (June 5, 1990):33-36

McCallmanack: Practicing More Humane Medicine. Liza Nelson. *McCall's* 117, No. 9 (June 1990):45

Medical News. Dana Points and Carla Rohlfing. *Family Circle* 103, No. 5 (April 3, 1990):26-27

Medinews. Sally Squires. *Ladies' Home Journal* 107, No. 5 (May 1990):94

Patient's Rights: An Agenda for the Nineties. Maggie Burston. *Healthsharing* 11, No. 3 (June 1990):25-26

Public Health, Gender, and Private Morality: Paid Labor and the Formation of the Body Politic in Buenos Aires. Donna J. Guy. *Gender & History* 2, No. 3 (Autumn 1990):297-317

Specialty Urged in Women's Health. Easy Klein. *New Directions for Women* 19, No. 6 (November-December 1990):1+

Surviving Sniffle Season. Marlene Cimons. *Working Mother* (December 1990):64-66

The Twentieth Anniversary Celebration of *Our Bodies, Ourselves*. Boston Women's Health Book Collective. *Woman of Power* 18 (Fall 1990):8

US: Women of Colour Set Agenda on Women's Health. Pat Redmond. *Spare Rib* 217 (October 1990):53

Vital Signs: Windows to Well-Being. Alexandra Tanski. *McCall's* 117, No. 12 (September 1990):76

Women Right Now. *Glamour* (April 1990):111-112

Women's Health Perspectives: An Annual Review. Edited by Carol J. Luppa and Connie Miller. Reviewed by Margherita Jellinek. *AFFILIA* 5, No. 4 (Winter 1990):108-110

Work Pattern of Women and Its Impact on Health and Nutrition. M. E. Khan, A. K. Tamang, and Bella C. Patel. *Journal of Family Welfare* 36, No. 2 (June 1990):3-22

Young Mother's Story: "A Medical Error Could Cost
Me My Life." Debi Lane. *Redbook* 175, No. 6
(October 1990):64-68

Your Guide to Hospital Care. Lisa Rogak. *Essence*
21, No. 5 (September 1990):29+

### Health Care – Children

Medical Care Use and Expenditures for Children
across Stages of the Family Life Cycle. Peter J.
Cunningham. *Journal of Marriage and the Family*
52, No. 1 (February 1990):197-207

### Health Care – Cross-Cultural Studies

Women and Health: Cross-Cultural Perspectives.
Edited by Patricia Whelehan. Reviewed by
Demetria Iazzetto. *NWSA Journal* 2, No. 4 (Autumn
1990):664-668

### Health Care – Employer Provision

Health Care of Women in the Workplace.
Jacqueline Collins. *Health Care for Women
International* 11, No. 1 (1990):21-32

### Health Care – Medical Histories

Medical Report: Family Medical History. Victoria
Zimet Daly. *Glamour* (February 1990):61-62

### Health Care, Rural

Rural U.S. Women: Traditions and Transitions
Affecting Health Care. Angeline Bushy. *Health Care
for Women International* 11, No. 4 (1990):503-513

### Health Care Activists

Feminism within the Science and Health Care
Professions: Overcoming Resistance. By Sue V.
Rosser. Reviewed by Demetria Iazzetto. *NWSA
Journal* 2, No. 4 (Autumn 1990):664-668

**Health Care Occupations.** *See also* Surgical
Procedures

### Health Care Occupations – Employment
### Opportunities

Healing Professions. Bibliography. Felicia E.
Halpert. *Essence* 21, No. 4 (August 1990):32-34

### Health Care Policy

The Significant Other. Beth Weinhouse. *Savvy
Woman* (October 1990):13-14

### Health Care Policy – India

Fight Disease, Not Patients: AIDS Protest in Delhi.
J. P. Jain, P. S. Sahni, Lalitha S. A., and others.
*Manushi* 58 (May-June 1990):34

**Health Care Services.** *See also* Feminist Clinics

New Projects at Women's Health Clinic. Laurel
Garvie. *Healthsharing* 11, No. 2 (March 1990):6

### Health Care Services – Fees

Feminist Clinics Lose Out to Profit-Making Clones.
Jill Benderly. *New Directions for Women* 19, No. 1
(January/February 1990):3+

### Health Care – Tests

The Healthy Family. Richard Saul Wurman. *Family
Circle* 103, No. 1 (January 9, 1990):l7-18+

### Health Care Workers

An Interview-Based Exploration of the Motivations
and Occupational Aspirations of Chronic Care
Workers. Paula Brown Doress. *Journal of Women
and Aging* 2 No. 3 (1990):93-111

The Healers. *Ladies' Home Journal* 107, No. 11
(November 1990):155-160

Healthworkers and AIDS. Kendra Sundquist.
*Healthright* 9, No. 2 (February 1990):10-12

She Ate Not the Bread of Idleness: Exhaustion Is
Related to Domestic and Salaried Working
Conditions among 539 Québec Hospital Workers.
Daniel Tierney, Patrizia Romito, and Karen
Messing. *Women and Health* 16, No. 1 (1990):21-
42

Standing up to the Tories. *Spare Rib* No. 209
(February 1990):16-17

### Health Care Workers – Acquired Immune
### Deficiency Syndrome

Dr. Lorraine Day: Crusader or Cassandra? Susan
Edmiston. *Glamour* (July 1990):66

**Health Education.** *See also* Allergy; Asthma; Body
Image; Cold (Disease) – Prevention; Consumer
Information; Diseases; Eating Behavior; Eating
Disorders; Food Poisoning; Headaches; Health
Care; Life Styles; Low-Fat Diet; Mammography;
Menopause; National Black Women's Health
Project; Nutrition; Obesity; Overuse Injuries;
Parenting; Pediatrics; Physical Fitness; Reducing
Diets; Salt; Sex Education;

Skin – Care and Hygiene; Sleep Deprivation;
Sunburn; Vitamin Therapy; Weight; Weight Loss

Ask Dr. Mom: Kids, Their Winter Colds . . . and
More. Marianne Neifert. *McCall's* 118, No. 3
(December 1990):44

Ask Dr. Mom: When Children Stutter . . . And
Other Questions. Marianne Neifert. *McCall's* 118,
No. 2 (November 1990):46

Beauty: 10 Affirmations for the 90's. *Essence* 20,
No. 9 (January 1990):9

Beauty and Fashion Hotline: Saving Your Skin.
*Family Circle* 103, No. 14 (October 16, 1990):39-42

Beauty & Health Report: Holiday Sleep Survival
Guide. Stephanie Young. *Glamour* (December
1990):48

Beauty Q & A. *Mademoiselle* (February 1990):48;
(December 1990):53

Beauty Questions. *Glamour* (November 1990):48

Between Us. Bibliography. Gwendolyn Goldsby
Grant. *Essence* 21, No. 6 (October 1990):30-32

Body Briefing: Eyes. Leslie C. Roberts. *Lear's* (April
1990):45-46

The Bottom Line on Beautiful Skin. Stephanie
Young. *Glamour* (November 1990):54

Medical Checkups for Teenagers. Martin Fisher and Sally Abrahms. *Good Housekeeping* 211, No. 3 (September 1990):158-160

Medical News. Dana Points and Carla Rohlfing. *Family Circle* 103, No. 9 (June 26, 1990):30; 103, No. 16 (November 27, 1990):50

Medical Report: The Common Cold Quiz. Michael Castleman. *Glamour* (January 1990):30-35

Medinews. Joan Lippert. *Ladies' Home Journal* 107, No. 7 (July 1990):58; 107, No. 9 (September 1990):138; 107, No. 11 (November 1990):152

Medinews. Sally Squires. *Ladies' Home Journal* 107, No. 5 (May 1990):94; 107, No. 8 (August 1990):30; 107, No. 10 (October 1990):132

Millennium Tremens. Frances Lear. *Lear's* (September 1990):160

Nutrition, Diet & Fitness: What's News Now! *Good Housekeeping* 211, No. 3 (September 1990):266-268; 211, No. 4 (October 1990):194-196

Nutrition Questions. *Glamour* (May 1990):316; (June 1990):272; (October 1990):299

Pediatric Healthline. Mary Farrell. *Ladies' Home Journal* 107, No. 12 (December 1990):64

Prevention: A Season for Sneezin'. Susan Festa. *Essence* 20, No. 11 (March 1990):24-28

Self Center: Health Department. *Lear's* (August 1990):44

Sharing Health in Huron County. Michele Hansen. *Healthsharing* 11, No. 1 (December 1989):7

Skin Care Strategies. *McCall's* 117, No. 8 (May 1990):103-108

Sleep: The Dynamics of Sweet Dreaming. Mariana Gosnell. *Lear's* (January 1990):86-89

Time for a Change: Women's Health Education in Canadian University Schools of Nursing. Elizabeth Hagell. *Health Care for Women International* 11, No. 2 (1990):121-131

Travel: Vacations that Pay Off. Bibliography. *Glamour* (June 1990):171-180

The Twilight Zone. Susan Ince. *Savvy Woman* (November 1990):82-84

Vital Signs. *McCall's* 117, No. 7 (April 1990):43-44; 117, No. 8 (May 1990):38-40; 117, No. 9 (June 1990):16-18; 117, No. 10 (July 1990):22-24; 117, No. 11 (August 1990):24-27; 118, No. 1 (October 1990):46-48

Water Works Wonders. Kathryn Keller. *Redbook* 175, No. 1 (May 1990):112-113+

What Causes Bad Breath? Laura Clark. *Good Housekeeping* 211, No. 4 (October 1990):248

When Should You Be Your Own Doctor? Fran Snyder. *Ladies' Home Journal* 107, No. 2 (February 1990):62-72

Women and Heart Disease. Peter Jaret. *Glamour* (October 1990):68-73

Women's Health: "I Want a Second Opinion." Kathryn Cox and Genell Subak-Sharpe. *Redbook* 175, No. 1 (May 1990):22-28

Your Health: The "Too Much" Syndrome. Dana Points. *Family Circle* 103, No. 17 (December 18, 1990):31-35

**Health Insurance.** *See* Insurance, Health; Older Adults – Health Insurance

**Health Resorts, Watering Places, etc.**

Fitness. Cynthia Gorney. *Vogue* (December 1990):179-182

Girls Just Wanna Work Out. Laura Broadwell. *Women's Sports & Fitness* 12, No. 6 (September 1990):44-48

Hot Body Shops. Bibliography. *Harper's Bazaar* (September 1990):98+

Images: Spas for Solo Vacations. Elizabeth Brous. *Vogue* (December 1990):170-176

Lighten Up: The New Spa Cuisine. *Ladies' Home Journal* 107, No. 5 (May 1990):206-210

Preferred Treatment. Leslie O'Connor. *Harper's Bazaar* (September 1990):102+

The Spa Differential. Carol Isaak Barden. *Lear's* (March 1990):64-67

Spa Guide. Sara Nelson. *Working Woman* (March 1990):146-150

Spa Ritual. *Lear's* (May 1990):22

Spas: Not for Snobs Only. Bibliography. Ellen Kunes. *Mademoiselle* (October 1990):202

Travel: Spa Vacations. Dari Giles. *Essence* 20, No. 9 (January 1990):87-88+

**Healthsharing** (journal)

We Will Not Be Silenced! Susan Elliott, Amy Gottlieb, Lisa McCaskell, and Monica Ruitort. *Healthsharing* 11, No. 3 (June 1990):3

**Health Spas.** *See* Health Resorts, Watering Places, etc.

**Healy, Eloise Klein**

What it was Like the Night Cary Grant Died. Poem. *Out/Look* No. 7 (Winter 1990):74

**Hearing Impairments**

The Reluctant Go-Between. Robert Brody. *Glamour* (October 1990):288+

**Hearn, Jeff**

Masculinity and Power. Book Review. *Gender & History* 2, No. 3 (Autumn 1990):351-353

**Heart – Diseases.** *See also* Health Education

Adolescent Health Status, Behaviors and Cardiovascular Disease. Matthew Adeyanju. *Adolescence* 25, No. 97 (Spring 1990):155-169

Fighting for Three Lives. Julianne Procich. *Ladies' Home Journal* 107, No. 10 (October 1990):22-27 +

The Heart of the Matter. Susan Festa. *Essence* 21, No. 6 (October 1990):25-28

Women and Heart Disease. Peter Jaret. *Glamour* (October 1990):68-73

**Heartney, Eleanor**

Prague's Spring. *Harper's Bazaar* (March 1990):72-85

**Heather, Maida**

Big-Deal Desserts. *Ladies' Home Journal* 107, No. 9 (September 1990):190-191 +

**Heatherly, Gail** (about). *See* Title, Stacy

**Heaton, Caroline** (joint editor). *See* Park, Christine

**Hebald, Carol**

Three Blind Mice: Two Short Novels. Reviewed by Phyllis Ehrenfeld. *New Directions for Women* 19, No. 2 (March/April 1990):24

**Hechler, David**

The Battle and the Backlash: The Child Sexual Abuse War. Book Review. *Adolescence* 25, No. 98 (Summer 1990):501

**Heckerling, Amy**

Look Who's Talking. Reviewed by Jennifer Mourin. *Spare Rib* No. 212 (May 1990):28

**Hedblom, Milda K.**

Women and Power in American Politics. Reviewed by Joan C. Tronto. *NWSA Journal* 2, No. 3 (Summer 1990):492-495

**Hedborg, Jarrett** (about)

Living. Laurie Schechter. *Vogue* (July 1990):133-134

**Hedegaard, Erik**

Get the Picture. *Savvy Woman* (January 1990):72-75, 92-93

Heart Like a Wheel. *Savvy Woman* (June 1990):47-49, 80

The People Picker. *Savvy Woman* (November 1990):14

**Hedges, Elaine**

The Art of Queena Stovall: Images of Country Life. Book Review. *NWSA Journal* 2, No. 2 (Spring 1990):282-287

The Freedom Quilting Bee. Book Review. *NWSA Journal* 2, No. 2 (Spring 1990):282-287

Legacy: The Story of Talula Gilbert Bottoms and Her Quilts. Book Review. *NWSA Journal* 2, No. 2 (Spring 1990):282-287

The Sourcebook for Women Who Create. Book Review. *NWSA Journal* 2, No. 2 (Spring 1990):282-287

**Hedges, Elaine**, Coulter, Sara, Goldenberg, Myrna, and Forman, Gail

Towson State University Community College Curriculum Transformation Project. *Women's Studies Quarterly* 18, Nos. 1-2 (Spring-Summer 1990):122-125

**Hedrick, Joan D.**

Mythical Mothers. *The Women's Review of Books* 7, No. 8 (May 1990):24-25

Sarah Orne Jewett: An American Persephone. Book Review. *The Women's Review of Books* 7, No. 8 (May 1990):24-25

**Hedricks, Cynthia** (joint author). *See* Dan, Alice J.

**Heeney, Brian**

The Women's Movement in the Church of England, 1850-1930. Reviewed by John Wolffe. *Gender & History* 2, No. 2 (Summer 1990):236-237

**Hegi, Ursula**

Floating in My Mother's Palm. Reviewed by Nancy Derr. *Belles Lettres* 5, No. 4 (Summer 1990):10

**Heiderstadt, Donna**

Health Dept. *Lear's* (October 1990):70; (December 1990):58

Insomniacs: Read This and Sleep. *Lear's* (November 1990):55-57

**Helfetz, Julie**

Too Young to Remember. Reviewed by Betty Jean Lifton. *Lilith* 15, No. 1 (Winter 1990):6

**Heilbrun, Alfred B. (Jr.)**, Friedberg, Lisa, Wydra, Dawna, and Worobow, Alyson L.

The Female Role and Menstrual Distress: An Explanation for Inconsistent Evidence. *Psychology of Women Quarterly* 14, No. 3 (September 1990):403-417

**Heilbrun, Carolyn**

Writing a Woman's Life. Reviewed by Elizabeth R. Baer. *Belles Lettres* 5, No. 2 (Winter 1990):4-6 +

**Heilbrun, Carolyn G.**

Sylvia Townsend Warner: A Biography. Book Review. *The Women's Review of Books* 7, No. 6 (March 1990):8-9

Witch Hunt. *The Women's Review of Books* 7, No. 6 (March 1990):8-9

**Heileman, Nancy**

Late Bloomer. Poem. *New Directions for Women* 19, No. 3 (May/June 1990):5

**Heilpern, John**

Vogue Arts: Christmas Gift Books. *Vogue* (December 1990):208-210

**Heimel, Cynthia**

Driving. *Vogue* (September 1990):480-484

New American Couturiers. Bibliography. *Vogue* (January 1990):47-61

**Hein, Hilde** and Korsmeyer, Carolyn

Introduction. *Hypatia* 5, No. 2 (Summer 1990):1-6

**Heinzerling, Lisa**

A New Way of Looking at Violence Against Women. *Glamour* (October 1990):112

**Heisch, Allison**

Ruling Women Out. *The Women's Review of Books* 7, No. 5 (February 1990):23-24

**Hekman, Susan**

Comment on Hawkesworth's "Knowers, Knowing, Known: Feminist Theory and Claims of Truth." Notes. *Signs* 15, No. 2 (Winter 1990):417-419

**Hekman, Susan** (about)

Reply to Hekman. Notes. Mary E. Hawkesworth. *Signs* 15, No. 2 (Winter 1990):420-423

**Hekman, Susan J.**

Feminism and Methodology: Social Science Issues. Book Review. *Women & Politics* 10, No. 1 (1990):71-73

**Heldke, Lisa M.**

A Response to Donald Koch's "Recipes, Cooking, and Conflict." *Hypatia* 5, No. 1 (Spring 1990):165-170

**Helfgott, Esther Altshul**

Jewish Feminism and Identity Politics. *off our backs* 20, No. 5 (May 1990):12-13

**Helgesen, Sally**

Private Lives. *Family Circle* 103, No. 8 (June 5, 1990):100-104

**Hélie-Lucas, Marieme**

Both Left and Right Handed: Arab Women Talk About Their Lives. Book Review. *Connexions* 34 (1990):22-23

**Helland, Janice**

Aztec Imagery in Frida Kahlo's Paintings: Indigenity and Political Commitment. *Woman's Art Journal* 11, No. 2 (Fall 1990-Winter 1991):8-13

**Heller, Deborah**

Woman as Mediatrix: Essays on Nineteenth-Century European Women Writers. Book Review. *Canadian Women's Studies* 11, No. 2 (Fall 1990):90

**Heller, Karen**

A Tasty Guide to Business Dining. *Working Woman* (September 1990):148-149+

Your Money: No Pain, No Gain: How Wall Street Wizards Learned to Invest Their Money. *Working Woman* (June 1990):42-44

**Heller, Karen** and Milward, John

It's a Great Relationship, But Can It Travel? *Mademoiselle* (March 1990):152-154, 238

**Heller, Lee**

Holding the Line: Women in the Great Arizona Mine Strike of 1983. Book Review. *off our backs* 20, No. 5 (May 1990):22

**Heller, Linda J.**

Dress Smart. *Redbook* 175, No. 4 (August 1990):90-94

Is Your Dentist Up-to-Date? *Redbook* 174, No. 5 (March 1990):20-26

When to Give In to Those Food Cravings. *McCall's* 117, No. 11 (August 1990):14

**Hellman, Peter**

She Stoops to Conquer. *Savvy Woman* (March 1990):63-65, 80-83

**Helly, Dorothy O.**

Voices and Echoes: Tales from Colonial Women. Book Review. *Women's Studies International Forum* 13, No. 4 (1990):405-407

Women of the Regiment: Marriage and the Victorian Army. Book Review. *Women's Studies International Forum* 13, No. 4 (1990):405-407

**Helmbold, Lois R.**

Dirty Work. *The Women's Review of Books* 7, No. 8 (May 1990):12-13

Domesticity and Dirt: Housewives and Domestic Servants in the United States, 1920-1945. Book Review. *The Women's Review of Books* 7, No. 8 (May 1990):12-13

Satisfaction Guaranteed: The Making of the American Mass Market. Book Review. *The Women's Review of Books* 7, No. 8 (May 1990):12-13

**Helmericks, Constance**

Down the Wild River North. Reviewed by Anne Dellenbaugh. *The Women's Review of Books* 7, No. 7 (April 1990):16-17

**Helmig, Linda** (joint author). *See* Weidner, Gerdi

**Helmsley, Leona** (about)

Leona's Lament. Cindy Adams. *Ladies' Home Journal* 107, No. 5 (May 1990):80-85+

**Helmstetter, Holly**

Living on the Edge. *Family Circle* 103, No. 10 (July 24, 1990):68-70

**Heloise**

Speaker for the House: The Heloise Helpline. *Good Housekeeping* 211, No. 3 (September 1990):72; 211, No. 4 (October 1990):38

**Helsinger, Elizabeth K.**, Sheets, Robin Lauterbach, and Veeder, Robin

The Woman Question: Society and Literature in Britain and America, 1837-1883. Reviewed by L. J. Abray. *Resources for Feminist Research* 19, No. 1 (March 1990):38-39

**Helson, Ravenna,** Elliott, Teresa, and Leigh, Janet

Number and Quality of Roles: A Longitudinal Personality View. *Psychology of Women Quarterly* 14, No. 1 (March 1990):83-101

**Helson, Ravenna** (joint author). *See* Mitchell, Valory

**Hemminger, Theresa**

Cinderella. Poem. *off our backs* 20, No. 7 (July 1990):19

**Hempel, Amy**

At the Gates of the Animal Kingdom. Reviewed by Jill Fritz-Piggott. *The Women's Review of Books* 7, No. 12 (September 1990):24-26

**Hendel, Yehudit**

Twelve Days in Poland. Excerpt. *Lilith* 15, No. 2 (Spring 1990):16-21

**Henderson, Bruce B.** (joint author). *See* Gold, Steven R.

**Henderson, Gordon** (about). *See* Fashion Designers, "Battle-Weary Designers"

**Henderson, Hazel** (about)

Woman of Ideas: Hazel Henderson. Susan Chace. *Lear's* (June 1990):98-101+

**Henderson, Karla A.** (joint author). *See* Bialeschki, M. Deborah

**Henderson, Kathy**

Are Your Kids Ready for Kindergarten? *Ladies' Home Journal* 107, No. 9 (September 1990):70-72

Get the Teacher on Your Team. *Working Mother* (November 1990):70-74

Health and Beauty Special for Busy Bodies. *Redbook* 175, No. 6 (October 1990):79-83

Why Kids Need to Help. *Working Mother* 13, No. 7 (July 1990):42-47

**Henderson, Randi**

Women Who Make a Difference. *Family Circle* 103, No. 12 (September 4, 1990):19+

**Henderson, Shirley** and Mackay, Alison (editors)

Grit and Diamonds: Women in Scotland Making History 1980-1990. Reviewed by Evelyn Gillan. *Spare Rib* No. 214 (July 1990):23

**Henderson, Stephanie**

Cutting the Cord. Poem. *New Directions for Women* 19, No. 3 (May/June 1990):5

Impasse. Poem. *New Directions for Women* 19, No. 3 (May/June 1990):5

**Hendrix, Harville**

The Four Phases of Marriage. *Family Circle* 103, No. 3 (February 20, 1990):57-58+

Understanding Your Marriage. *Family Circle* 103, No. 6 (April 24, 1990):101+; 103, No. 10 (July 24, 1990):130+

**Hengen, Shannon**

Of Chastity and Power: Elizabethan Literature and the Unmarried Queen. Book Review. *Resources for Feminist Research* 19, No. 2 (June 1990):44-45

From My Guy to Sci-Fi: Genre and Women's Writing in the Postmodern World. Book Review. *Resources for Feminist Research* 19, No. 1 (March 1990):17

**Henggeler, Scott W.**

Delinquency in Adolescence. Book Review. *Adolescence* 25, No. 97 (Spring 1990):250

**Hennig, Margaret** (joint author). *See* Jardim, Anne

**Henry, Alice**

Britain: Campaign Against Embryo and Human Fertilisation Bill. *off our backs* 20, No. 4 (April 1990):12

Child Care – Who Cares? Do Feminists Care? *off our backs* 20, No. 2 (February 1990):12-13

Fighting Wife Abuse in India. *off our backs* 20, No. 3 (March 1990):21

A Formula of Light and Heavy Issues. *off our backs* 20, No. 3 (March 1990):20-21

**Henry, Donna**

Mother Waddles: One Woman's War on Poverty. *Essence* 21, No. 6 (October 1990):48

**Henry, Sara** and Stevenson, Kelly

Picking the Right Shoe for You. *Women's Sports and Fitness* 12, No. 2 (March 1990):29-42

**Henry, Sherrye**

Prime of Life. *Family Circle* 103, No. 1 (January 9, 1990):29-30

**Henry, William A. III**

Maggie Smith. *Lear's* (June 1990):94-97

The Profits of Ill Repute. *Lear's* (October 1990):152+

**Hensman, Rohini**

To Do Something Beautiful (extract). *Spare Rib* 213 (June 1990):9-11

**Hensman, Rohini** (interview)

To Do Something Beautiful: Interview with Rohini Hensman. Rukhsana Ahmad. *Spare Rib* 213 (June 1990):6-8

**Henson, Brenda**

Gulf Coast Women's Festival. *Hot Wire* 6, No. 1 (January 1990):38-39

**Hepburn, Katharine** (about)

Katharine Hepburn at Home. John Bryson. *Good Housekeeping* 211, No. 4 (October 1990):136-139

**Herbal Remedies**

Health: Herbal Tonics. Aimee Lee Ball. *Vogue* (September 1990):454-458

**Herbert, Martha Reed**

Staying Horrified. *Heresies* 25 (1990):90-94

**Herb Gardens**

Parsley, Sage, Rosemary and Thyme. Eleanore Lewis. *Family Circle* 103, No. 9 (June 26, 1990):66-69

**Herbst, Nikki**

Fifth Grade. Poem. *Heresies* 25 (1990):12

**Heredity.** *See* Genetic Determinants

**Herland, Karen**

Montreal Massacre Mobilizes Women Across Canada. *Healthsharing* 11, No. 2 (March 1990):5

**Herman, Stephen**

The Teen Years. *Family Circle* 103, No. 4 (March 13, 1990):171-172

**Herman, Stephen P.**

Relationships: Happy One Day, Sad the Next. *Family Circle* 103, No. 16 (November 27, 1990):53-55

**Hermann, Frederick**

A Question of Loyalty. *Glamour* (March 1990):286+

**Hermann, Mindy**

Eat Well. *Family Circle* 103, No. 2 (February 1, 1990):19+

Magic Foods: Help or Hype? *Family Circle* 103, No. 14 (October 16, 1990):132-134

**Herndon, Calvin** (about)

Anti-Sexist Celebration of Black Women in Literature: *The Sexual Mountain and Black Women Writers* and a Conversation with Calvin Hernton. Gloria Wade-Gayles. *Sage* 6, No. 1 (Summer 1989):45-49

**Heroes**

The Female Hero: A Quest for Healing and Wholeness. Kathleen D. Nobel. *Women and Therapy* 9, No. 4 (1990):3-18

The Heroine as Hero in Michelangelo's Art. Yael Even. *Woman's Art Journal* 11, No. 1 (Spring-Summer 1990):29-33

What Makes a Giraffe Stand Tall? Ann Medlock. *Lear's* (July 1990):30-31

**Heroes in Literature.** *See also* Comic Books, Strips, etc.

Sexuality, Subjectivity, and Reading: Constructing the Heterosexual Heroine in the Late Eighteenth-Century Novel. Lisa L. Moore. *NWSA Journal* 2, No. 4 (Autumn 1990):693-695

**Herpes Zoster**

Health Dept. Leigh Silverman. *Lear's* (September 1990):74

**Herr, Pamela**

Jessie Benton Fremont. Reviewed by Lynn Wenzel. *New Directions for Women* 19, No. 2 (March/April 1990):15

**Herring, Lucy** (about)

A Big Deal Babe. Lois Smith Brady. *Mademoiselle* (October 1990):152-154+

**Herriot, James**

Oscar, the People Cat. *Good Housekeeping* 211, No. 6 (December 1990):88

**Herrly, Abigail** (joint author). *See* Pfluke, Lillian A.

**Herrmann, Marille** (joint author). *See* Bradish, Paula

**Herron, Cindy** (about). *See also* En Vogue (about)

**Herrup, Cynthia**

The Family and the English Revolution. Book Review. *Gender & History* 2, No. 2 (Summer 1990):226-228

Women in the First Capitalist Society: Experiences in Seventeenth-Century England. Book Review. *Gender & History* 2, No. 2 (Summer 1990):226-228

**Hersey, Brook**

Beyond Dick Tracy: Summer at the Movies. *Glamour* (July 1990):116

Cheap Men. *Glamour* (October 1990):300

Let Me Tell You About Two Fights I've Had with Boyfriends . . . *Glamour* (September 1990):332-333+

Love Letters Straight from the Heart. *Glamour* (February 1990):158-161

My Bimbo Boyfriend. *Glamour* (May 1990):318

Sexual Ethics. *Glamour* (September 1990):348

Slipping into Stardom. *Glamour* (October 1990):248-251

Violence at the Movies. *Glamour* (September 1990):218

Will Nancy Survive? *Glamour* (April 1990):192

Word On . . . Kinder, Gentler Male Bonding. *Glamour* (May 1990):206

Word on Movies. *Glamour* (March 1990):194; (May 1990):208; (September 1990):220; (November 1990):172; (December 1990):160

Word On . . . Movies Based on Novels. *Glamour* (December 1990):158

Word On TV's Office Comedies. *Glamour* (June 1990):184

**Hersey, Brook** and Weissinger, Maurice

Word On . . . The Best Music. *Glamour* (December 1990):156

**Hertzberg, Joan F.**

Feminist Psychotherapy and Diversity: Treatment Considerations from a Self Psychology Perspective. *Women and Therapy* 9, No. 3 (1990):275-297

**Hertzler, Ann A.** and Grün, Ingolf

Potential Nutrition Messages in Magazines Read by College Students. *Adolescence* 25, No. 99 (Fall 1990):717-724

**Hesford, Wendy S.**

Storytelling and Dynamics of Feminist Teaching. *Feminist Teacher* 5, No. 2 (Fall 1990):20-24

**Hess, Beth B.**

Aging Parents and Adult Children. Book Review. *Journal of Marriage and the Family* 52, No. 2 (May 1990):566

Invisible Careers: Women Civic Leaders from the Volunteer World. Book Review. *Gender and Society* 4, No. 2 (June 1990):283-284

**Hess, Elizabeth**

Book of Revelations. *The Women's Review of Books* 7, No. 12 (September 1990):10

Patterns of Desire. Book Review. *The Women's Review of Books* 7, No. 12 (September 1990):10

**Hesselbein, Frances** (about)

Thrifty, Kind – and Smart as Hell. Patricia O'Toole. *Lear's* (October 1990):26-30

**Hester, Marianne**

The Dynamics of Male Domination Using the Witch Craze in 16th- and 17th-Century England as a Case Study. *Women's Studies International Forum* 13, Nos. 1-2 (1990):9-19

**Hettena, Charlotte** and Shahinian, Siroon P.

Women and Self-Esteem. Book Review. *Psychology of Women Quarterly* 14, No. 4 (December 1990):620-621

**Heung, Marina**

Common Differences. *The Women's Review of Books* 7, No. 4 (January 1990):8-10

The Forbidden Stitch: An Asian American Women's Anthology. Book Review. *The Women's Review of Books* 7, No. 4 (January 1990):8-10

Making Waves: An Anthology of Writings by and about Asian American Women. Book Review. *The Women's Review of Books* 7, No. 4 (January 1990):8-10

The Piano Tuner. Book Review. *The Women's Review of Books* 7, No. 7 (April 1990):12-13

In Search of the Lost Generation. *The Women's Review of Books* 7, No. 7 (April 1990):12-13

A Story of Women. Film review. *New Directions for Women* 19, No. 3 (May/June 1990):7

Surname Viet Given Name Nam. Film review. *New Directions for Women* 19, No. 1 (January/February 1990):11

True Love. Play review. *New Directions for Women* 19, No. 2 (March/April 1990):13

**Heward, Christine**

Like Father, Like Son: Parental Models and Influences in the Making of Masculinity at an English Public School, 1929-1950. *Women's Studies International Forum* 13, Nos. 1-2 (1990):139-149

**Hewitt, Jean**

Food Forecast. *Family Circle* 103, No. 13 (September 25, 1990):136; 103, No. 15 (November 6, 1990):38; 103, No. 17 (December 18, 1990):83

**Hewitt, Marsha**

Women and Spirituality: Voices of Protest and Promise. Book Review. *Resources for Feminist Research* 19, No. 1 (March 1990):41-42

**Hey, Barbara**

Kids in the Water. *McCall's* 117, No. 10 (July 1990):85-90

**Heyn, Dalma**

The Etiquette of Ending It. *Mademoiselle* (October 1990):80

The Intelligent Woman's Guide to Sex. *Mademoiselle* (June 1990):78

The Intelligent Woman's Guide to Sex: Please Skip the Intimate Details! *Mademoiselle* (January 1990):67

The Intelligent Woman's Guide to Sex: The Waiting-on-a-Man Syndrome. *Mademoiselle* (September 1990):144

The Intelligent Woman's Guide to Sex: 8 Ways to Survive Heartbreak Hell. *Mademoiselle* (February 1990):96

The Myth of the Perfect Couple. *Mademoiselle* (November 1990):80-82

Who, Me, Ambivalent? *Mademoiselle* (December 1990):71-72

**Heyward, Carter**

Speaking of Christ: A Lesbian Feminist Voice. Reviewed by Jacqueline Lapidus. *The Women's Review of Books* 7, No. 9 (June 1990):17-18

Touching Our Strength: The Erotic as Power and the Love of God. Reviewed by Jacqueline Lapidus. *The Women's Review of Books* 7, No. 9 (June 1990):17-18

Touching Our Strength: The Erotic as Power and the Love of God. Reviewed by Penny Perkins. *New Directions for Women* 19, No. 4 (July-August 1990):15

**Hickmore, Mary**

Regrouping for Choice. *Healthsharing* 11, No. 2 (March 1990):8

**Hier, Sally J.**, Korboot, Paula J., and Schweitzer, Robert D.

Social Adjustment and Symptomatology in Two Types of Homeless Adolescents: Runaways and Throwaways. *Adolescence* 25, No. 100 (Winter 1990):761-771

**Hiestand, Emily**

Green the Witch-Hazel Wood. Reviewed by Lee Upton. *Belles Lettres* 5, No. 3 (Spring 1990):24-25

**Higashi, Sumiko**

Cinema, Censorship and Sexuality, 1909-25. Book Review. *Gender & History* 2, No. 1 (Spring 1990):123-126

The Female Gaze. Book Review. *Gender & History* 2, No. 1 (Spring 1990):123-126

Women and the Popular Imagination in the Twenties: Flappers and Nymphs. Book Review. *Gender & History* 2, No. 1 (Spring 1990):123-126

The Women Who Knew Too Much: Hitchcock and Feminist Theory. Book Review. *Gender & History* 2, No. 1 (Spring 1990):123-126

**Higginbotham, Elizabeth**

Changing Our Minds: Feminist Transformations of Knowledge. Book Review. *NWSA Journal* 2, No. 1 (Winter 1990):105-111

Crossing Boundaries: Feminism and the Critique of Knowledge. Book Review. *NWSA Journal* 2, No. 1 (Winter 1990):105-111

Designing an Inclusive Curriculum: Bringing All Women into the Core. *Women's Studies Quarterly* 18, Nos. 1-2 (Spring-Summer 1990):7-23

Learning About Women: Gender, Politics, and Power. Book Review. *NWSA Journal* 2, No. 1 (Winter 1990):105-111

**Higgins, Barbara S.** (joint author). *See* Baranowski, Marc D.

**Higgins, Millicent W.** (joint author). *See* Ebi-Kryston, Kristie

**Higgins, Patricia G.** and Dicharry, Elisabeth K.

Measurement Issues in the Use of the Coopersmith Self-Esteem Inventory with Navajo Women. *Health Care for Women International* 11, No. 3 (1990):251-262

**Higgins, Robin** (about)

An Undying Love. Kasthy Sprayberry Wood. *Ladies' Home Journal* 107, No. 1 (January 1990):96-100

**High Schools**. *See* Schools

**High School Students**. *See* Adolescents; Youth

**Hightower-Coyle, Maryrose**

To Tell the Truth. *McCall's* 118, No. 2 (November 1990):74

**Higonnet, Anne**

Berthe Morisot. Reviewed by Felicia Kornbluh. *The Women's Review of Books* 8, No. 2 (November 1990):13-14

**Hildegard of Bingen** (about)

Hildegard of Bingen, 1098-1179: A Visionary Life. By Sabina Flanagan. Reviewed by Miri Rubin. *Gender & History* 2, No. 3 (Autumn 1990):353-354

Hildegard of Bingen, 1098-1179: A Visionary Life. By Sabina Flanagan. Reviewed by Phillipa Maddern. *Australian Feminist Studies* No. 12 (Summer 1990):129-130

**Hill, Bridget**

Eighteenth Century Women: An Anthology. Reviewed by Patricia Crawford. *Australian Feminist Studies* No. 12 (Summer 1990):131-132

**Hill, Carol L.**

Fat Oppression and Psychotherapy: A Feminist Perspective. Book Review. *Atlantis* 15, No. 2 (Spring 1990):114-115

**Hill, Freddye** (joint author). *See* Dailey, Maceo Crenshaw (Jr.)

**Hill, Ingrid**

Dixie Church Interstate Blues. Reviewed by Suzanne Scott. *Belles Lettres* 5, No. 3 (Spring 1990):20

**Hill, Leslie I.**

Ford Foundation Funds Curriculum Integration Project Mainstreaming Minority Women's Studies. *NWSAction* 3, No. 4 (Winter 1990): 6-7

The Ford Foundation Program on Mainstreaming Minority Women's Studies. *Women's Studies Quarterly* 18, Nos. 1-2 (Spring-Summer 1990):24-38

**Hill, Marcia**

On Creating a Theory of Feminist Therapy. *Women and Therapy* 9, Nos. 1-2 (1990):53-65

**Hill, Veronica**

Blues Angels. *Spare Rib* No. 211 (April 1990):28

Feeling Irie. *Spare Rib* No. 210 (March 1990):16-18

Yaaba. Film Review. *Spare Rib* No. 209 (February 1990):35

**Hill, Wendi E.**

Untitled. Poem. *Essence* 20, No. 11 (March 1990):115

**Hillerman, Tony**

Books: Coyote Waits. Reviewed by Michael Dorris. *Vogue* (July 1990):108-110

**Hilliard, Patricia**

Argentine Mothers' Vigil. *New Directions for Women* 19, No. 5 (September-October 1990):15

Mothers of the Disappeared. Book Review. *New Directions for Women* 19, No. 5 (September-October 1990):15

**Hinckley, David**

Encore! *Lear's* (August 1990):70-71+

**Hindin, Roanne**

Radical Women National Conference: The Third Wave of Feminism. *off our backs* 20, No. 6 (June 1990):9

**Hindle, William H.** (editor)

Breast Disease for Gynecologists. Reviewed by Jeanette Sasmore. *Health Care for Women International* 11, No. 2 (1990):233-234

**Hinduism**

In Defence of Our *Dharma*. Madhu Kishwar. *Manushi* 60 (September-October 1990):2-15

**Hinduism – Status of Women**

The Perfect Wife: The Orthodox Hindu Woman According to the Stri6dharmapaddhati of Tryambakayajvan. By I. Julia Leslie. Reviewed by Albertine Gaur. *Gender & History* 2, No. 2 (Summer 1990):223-225

Wives of the God-King: The Rituals of the Davadasis of Puri. By Frédérique Apffel Marglin. Reviewed by Albertine Gaur. *Gender & History* 2, No. 2 (Summer 1990).223-225

**Hinduism and Law.** *See also* India – Legal System, India – Marriage

**Hindu Law**

What the Law Says. *Manushi* 57 (March-April 1990):2+

**Hine, Darlene Clark**

Black Women in White: Racial Conflict and Cooperation in the Nursing Profession, 1890-1950. Reviewed by Barbara Day. *On the Issues* 15 (Summer 1990):25-26

**Hines, David**

Bondage. Reviewed by Shaila Shah. *Spare Rib* No. 210 (March 1990):36-37

**Hirsch, Kathleen**

Fraternities of Fear: Gang Rape, Male Bonding, and the Silencing of Women. *Ms.* 1, No. 2 (September/October 1990):52-56

**Hirsch, Marianne**

Emily L. Book Review. *The Women's Review of Books* 8, No. 1 (October 1990):19-20

Inside Stories. *The Women's Review of Books* 8, No. 1 (October 1990):19-20

The Mother/Daughter Plot. Reviewed by Gayle Greene. *The Women's Review of Books* 7, No. 5 (February 1990):8-9

Practicalities: Marguerite Duras Speaks to Jérôme Beaujour. Book Review. *The Women's Review of Books* 8, No. 1 (October 1990):19-20

**Hirschfeld, Neal**

The Town That Cleaned Up Its Act. *Family Circle* 103, No. 2 (February 1, 1990):82+

**Hirshfield, Claire**

Fractured Faith: Liberal Party Women and the Suffrage Issue in Britain, 1892-1914. *Gender & History* 2, No. 2 (Summer 1990):173-197

**Hispanic Families**

Hispanic Families in the 1980s: A Decade of Research. William A. Vega. *Journal of Marriage and the Family* 52, No. 4 (November 1990):1015-1024

**Hispanic Families – Mother-Child Relationships**

Maternal Acceptance/Rejection of Mexican Migrant Mothers. Mary Lou de Leon Siantz. *Psychology of Women Quarterly* 14, No. 2 (June 1990):245-254

**Hispanic Women**

Gender, Race, and Culture: Spanish-Mexican Women in the Historiography of Frontier California. Antonia I. Castañeda. *Frontiers* 11, No. 1 (1990):8-20

Latinas of the Americas: A Source Book. By K. Lynn Stoner. Reviewed by Elsa Chaney and Catherine Lundhoff. *Journal of Women's History* 2, No. 1 (Spring 1990):220-226

The Living Legacy of Chicana Performers: Preserving History Through Oral Testimony. Yolanda Broyles-González. *Frontiers* 11, No. 1 (1990):46-52

Not Just Like One of the Family: Chicana Domestics Establishing Professional Relationships with Employers. Mary Romero. *Feminist Issues* 10, No. 2 (Fall 1990):33-41

Rage and Redemption: Reading the Life Story of a Mexican Marketing Woman. Ruth Behar. *Feminist Studies* 16, No. 2 (Summer 1990):223-258

**Hispanic Women – Activism**

Mexican American Women Grassroots Community Activists: "Mothers of East Lost Angeles." Mary Pardo. *Frontiers* 11, No. 1 (1990):1-7

Traditional and Nontraditional Patterns of Female Activism in the United Farm Workers of America, 1962 to 1980. Margaret Rose. *Frontiers* 11, No. 1 (1990):26-32

**Hispanic Women – Child-Rearing Practices**

Maternal Acceptance/Rejection of Mexican Migrant Mothers. Mary Lou de Leon Siantz. *Psychology of Women Quarterly* 14, No. 2 (June 1990):245-254

**Hispanic Women – Education**

The Broken Web: The Educational Experience of Hispanic American Women. By Teresa McKenna and Flora Ida Ortiz. Reviewed by Mary Romero. *Frontiers* 11, No. 1 (1990):86-88

## Hispanic Women – Feminism

Women's Voices Grow Stronger: Politics and Feminism in Latin America. Irene Campos Carr. *NWSA Journal* 2, No. 3 (Summer 1990):450-463

## Hispanic Women – Lesbians

Compañeras: Latina Lesbians (An Anthology). Edited by Juanita Ramos. Reviewed by Marisol Gonzalez. *NWSA Journal* 2, No. 2 (Spring 1990):298-301

## Hispanic Women – Psychology

Division of Household Labor, Strain, and Depressive Symptoms among Mexican Americans and Non-Hispanic Whites. Jacqueline M. Golding. *Psychology of Women Quarterly* 14, No. 1 (March 1990):103-117

## Hispanic Women – Sexuality

The Sexuality of Latinas. Edited by Norma Alarcón, Ana Castillo, and Cherríe Moraga. Reviewed by Marisol Gonzalez. *NWSA Journal* 2, No. 2 (Spring 1990):298-301

## Historians

In Memoriam: Lydia Sklevicky. *Gender & History* 2, No. 3 (Autumn 1990):249-250

## Historiography

Biography, Autobiography and Gender in Japan. Noriyo Hayakawa. *Gender & History* 2, No. 1 (Spring 1990):79-82

British Feminist Histories: An Editorial Introduction. Liz Stanley. *Women's Studies International Forum* 13, Nos. 1-2 (1990):3-7

Cultural Politics and Women's Historical Writing: The Case of Ray Strachey's *The Cause*. Kathryn Dodd. *Women's Studies International Forum* 13, Nos. 1-2 (1990):127-137

Hanging up on Mum or Questions of Everyday Life in the Writing of History. Julia Swindells. *Gender & History* 2, No. 1 (Spring 1990):68-78

"How Could She?" Unpalatable Facts and Feminists' Heroines. Dea Birkett and Julie Wheelwright. *Gender & History* 2, No. 1 (Spring 1990):49-57

Modern English Auto/Biography and Gender: Introduction. Tinne Vammen. *Gender & History* 2, No. 1 (Spring 1990):17-21

The New Historical Synthesis: Women's Biography. Kathleen Barry. *Journal of Women's History* 1, No. 3 (Winter 1990):75-105

From Private to Public Patriarchy: The Periodisation of British History. Sylvia Walby. *Women's Studies International Forum* 13, Nos. 1-2 (1990):91-104

Reconceptualizing Differences Among Women. Gerda Lerner. *Journal of Women's History* 1, No. 3 (Winter 1990):106-122

Recovering Women in History from Feminist Deconstructionism. Liz Stanley. *Women's Studies International Forum* 13, Nos. 1-2 (1990):151-157

Response to Gordon. Joan W. Scott. *Signs* 15, No. 4 (Summer 1990):859-860

Writing Women into History. Gerda Lerner. *Woman of Power* 16 (Spring 1990):6-9

## Historiography – Homosexual Perspectives

Telling (Hi)stories: Rethinking the Lesbian and Gay Historical Imagination. Scott Bravmann. *Out/Look* No. 8 (Spring 1990):68-74

**History.** *See also* Middle Ages – Sexuality

Postmodernism and History: A Reply to Marian Aveling. Kay Schaffer. *Australian Feminist Studies* No. 11 (Autumn 1990):91-94

Reflections on Making. Jane Buyers and Susan Shantz. *Canadian Women's Studies* 11, No. 1 (Spring 1990):27-28

Resisting Amnesia. Adrienne Rich. *Woman of Power* 16 (Spring 1990):15-21

**History, African-American.** *See* Black History

## History – Conferences

The Eighth Berkshire Conference on the History of Women: A Report. Lynn Weiner. *Journal of Women's History* 2, No. 2 (Fall 1990):174-176

Feminist History Conference. Barbara Baird. *Australian Feminist Studies* No. 12 (Summer 1990):117-119

## History – Renaissance

A History of Private Life, Vol. III: Passions of the Renaissance. Edited by Roger Chartier. Reviewed by Elizabeth C. Goldsmith. *The Women's Review of Books* 7, No. 9 (June 1990):24-25

## History – Study and Teaching

How Would You Like to Hear Only Half a Story? Ideas for Using Biographies of Historical Women in the Classroom. Shari Steelsmith. *Feminist Teacher* 5, No. 1 (Spring 1990):19-23

Restoring Women to History: Teaching Packets for Integrating Women's History into Courses on Africa, Asia, Latin America, the Caribbean, and the Middle East. By Iris Berger and others. Reviewed by Janet J. Ewald. *Gender and History* 2, No. 3 (Autumn 1990):349-351

**History of Women.** *See also* African-American Women – History; Feminism – Theory; Feminist Scholarship; Reproductive Choice; Third World Women – History

The Body and the French Revolution: Sex, Class and Political Culture. By Dorinda Outram. Reviewed by Elisabeth G. Sledziewski. *Gender & History* 2, No. 3 (Autumn 1990):363-365

The Chalice and the Blade. By Riane Eisler. Reviewed by Elaine Norman. *AFFILIA* 5, No. 2 (Summer 1990):102-104

The Chalice and the Blade: Our History, Our Future. By Riane Eisler. Reviewed by Ellen M. Shively. *Minerva* 8, No. 2 (Summer 1990):78-79

Fear of Feminism? Estelle Freedman. *The Women's Review of Books* 7, No. 5 (February 1990):25-26

Fresh Evidence, New Witnesses: Finding Women's History. Edited by Margaret Allen, Mary Hutchinson, and Alison Mackinnon. Reviewed by Marilyn Lake. *Australian Feminist Studies* No. 12 (Summer 1990):121-122

On the Front Lines. *Essence* 20, No. 10 (February 1990):45-50

Gender and the Politics of History. By Joan W. Scott. Reviewed by Linda Gordon. *Signs* 15, No. 4 (Summer 1990):853-858

Handbook of American Women's History. Edited by Angela Howard Zophy and Frances Kavenik. Review. *Feminist Collections* 11, No. 3 (Spring 1990):20

A History of Their Own: Women in Europe, from Pre-History to the Present. By Bonnie S. Anderson and Judith P. Zinsser. Reviewed by Janaki Nair. *Gender and Society* 4, No. 4 (December 1990):563-565

A History of Their Own: Women in Europe from Prehistory to the Present. By Bonnie Anderson and Judith Zinsser. Reviewed by Mary Beth Emmerichs. *Feminist Collections* 11, No. 2 (Winter 1990):3-4

A History of Their Own: Women in Europe from Prehistory to the Present. By Bonnie S. Anderson and Judith P. Zinsser. Reviewed by Margaret Saunders. *Iris* 24 (Fall-Winter 1990):60-65

Keep Smiling Through: Women in the Second World War. By Caroline Lang. Reviewed by Fiona Terry. *Gender & History* 2, No. 3 (Autumn 1990):371-373

The Lesbian Herstory Archives: A Statement of Cultural Self-Definition. Deborah Edel. *Woman of Power* 16 (Spring 1990):22-23

The National Women's History Project. Maria Cuevas. *Woman of Power* 16 (Spring 1990):10-14

To Pee or Not to Pee . . . Celebrating Women's History. Irene Davall. *On the Issues* 15 (Summer 1990):20-21

Socialist-Feminist American Women's History. Elizabeth Fox-Genovese. *Journal of Women's History* 1, No. 3 (Winter 1990):181-210

Uncovering a Rich Lesbian Past. Dell Richards. *Hot Wire* 6, No. 2 (May 1990):16+

Unequal Sisters: A Multicultural Reader in U.S. Women's History. Edited by Ellen Carol DuBois and Vicki L. Ruiz. Reviewed by Susan E. Davis. *New Directions for Women* 19, No. 6 (November-December 1990):18

Votes for Women. By Diane Atkinson. Reviewed by Fiona Terry. *Gender & History* 2, No. 3 (Autumn 1990):371-373

What's So Feminist About Doing Women's Oral History? Susan Geiger. *Journal of Women's History* 2, No. 1 (Spring 1990):169-182

Women, Desire, and History. Sonia Johnson. *Woman of Power* 16 (Spring 1990):73-77

Women as Healers: A History of Women and Medicine. By Hilary Bourdillon. Reviewed by Fiona Terry. *Gender & History* 2, No. 3 (Autumn 1990):371-373

Women in the First World War. By Gill Thomas. Reviewed by Fiona Terry. *Gender & History* 2, No. 3 (Autumn 1990):371-373

Women's History and Feminism in China: An Update. Mary Beth Norton. *Journal of Women's History* 2, No. 2 (Fall 1990):166-167

The Women's History of the World. By Rosalind Miles. Reviewed by Mary Beth Emmerichs. *Feminist Collections* 11, No. 2 (Winter 1990):3-4

Women's History/Public History – When the Twain Meet. Jeanne Farr McDonnell. *Journal of Women's History* 2, No. 2 (Fall 1990):171-173

Women's Memory, Women's History, Women's Political Action: The French Revolution in Retrospect, 1789-1989-1989. Karen Offen. *Journal of Women's History* 1, No. 3 (Winter 1990):211-230

## Hitchcock, Alfred – Criticism and Interpretation

The Women Who Knew Too Much: Hitchcock and Feminist Theory. By Tania Modleski. Reviewed by Paula Rabinowitz. *Feminist Studies* 16, No. 1 (Spring 1990):151-169

## Hite, Shere

"I Hope I'm Not Like My Mother." *Women and Therapy* 10, Nos. 1/2 (1990):13-30

Women and Love: A Cultural Revolution in Progress. Reviewed by Rosemary Coates. *Healthright* 9, No. 2 (February 1990):37

## Hittleman, Margo

Words. Poem. *Bridges* 1, No. 2 (Fall 1990): 60-62

## Ho, Chi-Kwan

Gender-Role Perceptions: An Intergenerational Study on Asian-American Women. *NWSA Journal* 2, No. 4 (Autumn 1990):679-681

## Ho, Christine K.

An Analysis of Domestic Violence in Asian American Communities: A Multicultural Approach to Counseling. *Women and Therapy* 9, Nos. 1-2 (1990):129-150

## Hoagland, Sarah Lucia

Caring: A Feminine Approach to Ethics and Moral Education. Book Review. *Hypatia* 5, No. 1 (Spring 1990):109-114

Lesbian Ethics. Reviewed by Alice E. Ginsberg. *New Directions for Women* 19, No. 1 (January/February 1990):24

Lesbian Ethics: Toward New Value. Reviewed by A. Lorraine Ironplow. *NWSA Journal* 2, No. 1 (Winter 1990):142-145

Lesbian Ethics: Toward New Value. Reviewed by Carol Van Kirk. *Hypatia* 5, No. 3 (Fall 1990):147-152

Lesbian Ethics: Toward New Value. Reviewed by Joan Blackwood. *Resources for Feminist Research* 19, No. 1 (March 1990):24

Lesbian Ethics: Toward New Value. Reviewed by María Lugones. *Hypatia* 5, No. 3 (Fall 1990):138-146

Lesbian Ethics: Toward New Value. Reviewed by Marilyn Frye. *Hypatia* 5, No. 3 (Fall 1990):132-137

Some Concerns About Nel Nodding's *Caring*. *Hypatia* 5, No. 1 (Spring 1990):109-114

**Hoagwood, Kimberly**

Blame and Adjustment Among Women Sexually Abused as Children. *Women and Therapy* 9, No. 4 (1990):89-110

**Hoarding of Money.** *See* Misers

**Hoaxes.** *See* Swindlers and Swindling

**Hobbies**

On the Job. Alice Rindler Shapin. *Family Circle* 103, No. 3 (February 20, 1990):25-27

**Hobby, Elaine**

The Ladies: Female Patronage of Restoration Drama. Book Review. *Gender & History* 2, No. 3 (Autumn 1990):359-363

The Prostituted Muse: Images of Women and Women Dramatists, 1642-1737. Book Review. *Gender & History* 2, No. 3 (Autumn 1990):359-363

The Sign of Angellica: Women Writing and Fiction 1660-1800. Book Review. *Gender & History* 2, No. 3 (Autumn 1990):359-363

Virtue of Necessity: English Women's Writing, 1649-1688. Reviewed by Heather Campbell. *Resources for Feminist Research* 19, No. 2 (June 1990):47

**Hochberg, Burt**

Best for Kids: Gifts Galore that Kids will Adore. *Redbook* 176, No. 2 (December 1990):22-24

**Hochschild, Arlie** and Machung, Anne

The Second Shift. Reviewed by Lynne Bravo Rosewater. *Women and Therapy* 9, No. 4 (1990):114-116

The Second Shift: Working Parents and the Revolution at Home. Reviewed by Julie Brines. *Journal of Marriage and the Family* 52, No. 1 (February 1990):278-279

The Second Shift: Working Parents and the Revolution at Home. Reviewed by Lois Braverman. *AFFILIA* 5, No. 4 (Winter 1990):111-113

**Hockey**

Sticking with It. Emily Walzer. *Women's Sports and Fitness* 12, No. 7 (October 1990):66

**Hodges, Laree** (joint author). *See* Kinderknecht, Cheryl H.

**Hodges-Betts, Bobbie**

Recomposing the Samba: A Look at the Contemporary Black Movement in Post-Abolition Brazil. *Sage* 6, No. 1 (Summer 1989):49-51

**Hodgson, Jane** (about)

Hodgson's Choice. Laura Fraser. *Vogue* (July 1990):206-209+

**Hoffert, Sylvia D.**

Private Matters: American Attitudes toward Childbearing and Infant Nurture in the Urban North, 1800-1860. Reviewed by Rickie Solinger. *Women and Health* 16, No. 2 (1990):131-134

**Hoffman, Alice**

Seventh Heaven. Reviewed by Edith Milton. *The Women's Review of Books* 8, No. 3 (December 1990):17-18

Seventh Heaven. Reviewed by Francine Prose. *Savvy Woman* (July/August 1990):20

Seventh Heaven. Reviewed by Laurie Winer. *Vogue* (August 1990):232-234

**Hoffman, Eva**

Lost in Translation: A Life in a New Language. Reviewed by Maria Jastrzebska. *Spare Rib* No. 214 (July 1990):22

Lost in Translation: A Life in a New Languages. Reviewed by Susan P. Willens. *Belles Lettres* 5, No. 2 (Winter 1990):2

**Hoffman, Merle**

On the Issues. *On the Issues* 14 (1990):2-3+; 15 (Summer 1990):2-3+; 16 (Fall 1990):2-3+; 17 (Winter 1990):2-3+

**Hoffman, Ray** (about). *See* D'Amico, Marie and Jubak, Jim

**Hoffman, Ronald** and Albert, Peter J.

Women in the Age of the American Revolution. Reviewed by Elaine Forman Crane. *NWSA Journal* 2, No. 4 (Autumn 1990):661-664

**Hoffman, Susan-Judith**

Taking Our Time: Feminist Perspectives on Temporality. Book Review. *Atlantis* 15, No. 2 (Spring 1990):111-113

**Hoffman, Terri** (about)

Love, Death, & Terri Hoffman. Rosalind Wright. *Good Housekeeping* 211, No. 4 (October 1990):62-69

**Hoffmann, Hans** (about)

Cascade of Color. Brooks Adams. *Harper's Bazaar* (July 1990):30

**Hoff-Wilson, Joan** and Lightman, Marjorie (editors)

Without Precedent: The Life and Career of Eleanor Roosevelt. Reviewed by Sharon Perlman Krefetz. *Women's Studies International Forum* 13, No. 3 (1990):281-283

**Hogan, Dennis P.** (joint author). *See* C. Elisa Florez

**Hogan, Katherine** (joint editor). *See* DeSalvo, Louise

**Hogan, Mary**

Into the Night: A New Visage. *Lear's* (September 1990):68

**Hogan, Sherry Hemman**

"Here a Duck . . ." *Good Housekeeping* 210, No. 4 (April 1990):110-113

**Holcomb, Betty** and Clinton, Linda Hamilton

Family Dream Vacations. *Working Mother* (November 1990):46-51

**Holden, Stephen**

Talking with Carly Simon: "I've Stopped Running from Problems." Interview. *Redbook* 175, No. 3 (July 1990):62-64

**Hole, Annie**

Lesbian Images. add. *Spare Rib* No. 210 (March 1990):35

In and Out of Time. Book Review. *Spare Rib* No. 215 (August 1990):29

**Holidays**. *See also* Time Management; Traditions; *particular holidays*

**Holidays – Clothing and Dress**

All That Glitters. *Essence* 21, No. 8 (December 1990):42-49

**Holidays – Cookery**. *See also* Christmas Cookery; Gingerbread Houses; Social Entertaining

An American Celebration. *Family Circle* 103, No. 9 (June 26, 1990):62-65

Eat Well: Beating Holiday Food Traps. *Family Circle* 103, No. 17 (December 18, 1990):52-54

Have a Great Fourth of July Chicken Cookout. *Redbook* 175, No. 3 (July 1990):69-74

Thanksgiving Cookbook. Marianne Langan. *McCall's* 118, No. 2 (November 1990):123-128+

**Holidays – Decorations**. *See also* Easter Decorations

**Holidays – Etiquette**

Living Beautifully: Holiday Grace Notes. Alexandra Stoddard. *McCall's* 118, No. 3 (December 1990):148

**Holidays – Fashion**

High Style Party Looks. *McCall's* 118, No. 3 (December 1990):79-82

Hot Shots. Lois Joy Johnson. *Ladies' Home Journal* 107, No. 12 (December 1990):152-156

Party! *Glamour* (December 1990):184-191

These Party Dresses Aren't Pricey. *Mademoiselle* (December 1990):54-58

On the Town. *Savvy Woman* (November 1990):72-77

**Holidays – Psychological Aspects**

Calm Down! Beth Thames. *Working Mother* (December 1990):34-39

The Comfort and Joy of Family Rituals. Dena K. Salmon. *Working Mother* (December 1990):48-52

75 Great Ways to Sail Through the Season. *Family Circle* 103, No. 17 (December 18, 1990):145-149

Holiday Health Handbook. Sally Squires. *Ladies' Home Journal* 107, No. 12 (December 1990):76

Holidays are about the Future More than the Past. Mary Catherine Bateson. *McCall's* 118, No. 2 (November 1990):35-37

Nine Tips to Happier Family Holidays. Gini Kopecky. *Redbook* 176, No. 1 (November 1990):110-111+

Private Time. *Glamour* (December 1990):123-124

Some Greenery for Holiday Blues. John Bradshaw. *Lear's* (December 1990):60

The True Spirit of Christmas. Pamela Redmond Satran. *Glamour* (December 1990):228-231+

Your Health: The "Too Much" Syndrome. Dana Points. *Family Circle* 103, No. 17 (December 18, 1990):31-35

On Your Own: Taking Care of Busyiness. Judith Stone. *Glamour* (December 1990):131

**Holistic Health**. *See also* Health Education

Horizons: New Age Rage. Linda Villarosa. *Essence* 20, No. 9 (January 1990):25

**Holistic Medicine**

Health: Herbal Tonics. Aimee Lee Ball. *Vogue* (September 1990):454-458

New Age Health: The M.D.'s vs. the Healers. *Harper's Bazaar* (November 1990):180-183+

**Holland, Janet,** Ramazanoglu, Caroline, and Scott, Sue

Managing Risk and Experiencing Danger: Tensions Between Government AIDS Education Policy and Young Women's Sexuality. *Gender and Education* 2, No. 2 (1990):125-146

**Holland – Prostitution**

Dutch Recommendation on AIDS Policies. *Women's World* , No. 24 (Winter 1990/91): 57-58

Liberal Holland. *Women's World* , No. 24 (Winter 1990/91): 43

**Hollander, Vicki**

The New, Improved Jewish Divorce: Hers/His. *Lilith* 15, No. 3 (Summer 1990):20-21

**Hollandsworth, Skip**

In defense of the Ditz. *Mademoiselle* (September 1990):150

A Guy's-Eye View. *Mademoiselle* (October 1990):122

I'll Lie to Make You Like Me. *Mademoiselle* (November 1990):85

The Road Test: First-Trip-Together Jitters. *Mademoiselle* (December 1990):74-76

Simply Irresistible: The Seven Laws of Desire. *Mademoiselle* (November 1990):136-139

Why I Hate Hunks. *Mademoiselle* (October 1990):86-91

**Hollants, Bessie** (about)

Interview with Bessie Hollants: "We Would Never Have Forgiven Ourselves for Not Speaking Out." Interview. Carmen Gloria Dunnage. *Women in Action* 3 & 4 (1990):16-17

**Holler, Linda**

Thinking with the Weight of the Earth: Feminist Contributions to an Epistemology of Concreteness. *Hypatia* 5, No. 1 (Spring 1990):1-23

**Hollibaugh, Amber**

Creating a Global Sisterhood. *The Women's Review of Books* 7, No. 6 (March 1990):9-10

A Vindication of the Rights of Whores. Book Review. *The Women's Review of Books* 7, No. 6 (March 1990):9-10

Writers as Activists. *Out/Look* No. 10 (Fall 1990):69-72

**Hollins, Frederica** (about)

At Center Stage. Laurie Tarkan. *Lear's* (April 1990):84-91

**Hollister, Beverly** (about). *See also* Beauty, Personal

**Holloway, Gerry**

Women and Marriage in Nineteenth-Century England. Book Review. *Women's Studies International Forum* 13, No. 5 (1990):524

**Holly, Buddy** (about)

Vogue Arts: Theater. Daniel Wolfe. *Vogue* (October 1990):271+

**Holly, Lesley**

Sex Education: Political Issues in Britain and Europe. Book Review. *Gender and Education* 2, No. 2 (1990):243-244

**Hollywood Women's Political Committee.** *See also* Bergman, Marilyn (about)

Lights, Camera, Activism. Ronald Brownstein. *Lear's* (December 1990):78-81+

**Holm, Karyn** (joint author). *See* Dan, Alice J.

**Holmes, Deborah K.**

Structural Causes of Dissatisfaction Among Large-Firm Attorneys: A Feminist Perspective. *Women's Rights Law Reporter* 12, No. 1 (Spring 1990):9-38

**Holmes, Helen Bequaert**

Beyond Conception: The New Politics of Reproduction. Book Review. *The Women's Review of Books* 7, No. 4 (January 1990):20-21

Does *Hypatia* Rock Boats? *Hypatia* 5, No. 3 (Fall 1990):162-164

Reproduction Without Representation? *The Women's Review of Books* 7, No. 4 (January 1990):20-21

In Vitro Fertilization: Building Policy from Laboratories to Legislatures. Book Review. *The Women's Review of Books* 7, No. 4 (January 1990):20-21

**Holmes, Helen B.** (joint author). *See* Corea, Gena

**Holmes, Karen A.**

Feminist Counselling in Action. Book Review. *AFFILIA* 5, No. 1 (Spring 1990):104-106

Women, Feminism and Family Therapy. Book Review. *AFFILIA* 5, No. 1 (Spring 1990):104-106

**Holocaust (1939-1945)**

On the Issues. Merle Hoffman. *On the Issues* 15 (Summer 1990):2-3+

**Holocaust (1939-1945) – Children's Games**

Children and Play in the Holocaust: Games among the Shadows. By George Eisen. Book Review. *Adolescence* 25, No. 97 (Spring 1990):249

**Holocaust (1939-1945) – Survivors**

The Alchemy of Survival: One Woman's Journey. By John E. Mack and Rita S. Rogers. Reviewed by Myrna Goldenberg. *Belles Lettres* 6, No. 1 (Fall 1990):6-9

Eva's War: A True Story of Survival. By Eva Krutein. Reviewed by Myrna Goldenberg. *Belles Lettres* 6, No. 1 (Fall 1990):6-9

One, by One, by One: Facing the Holocaust. By Judith Miller. Reviewed by Myrna Goldenberg. *Belles Lettres* 6, No. 1 (Fall 1990):6-9

Outcast: A Jewish Girl in Wartime Berlin. By Inge Deutschkron. Reviewed by Myrna Goldenberg. *Belles Lettres* 6, No. 1 (Fall 1990):6-9

Seed of Sarah: Memoirs of a Survivor. By Judith Magyar Isaacson. Reviewed by Myrna Goldenberg. *Belles Lettres* 6, No. 1 (Fall 1990):6-9

Too Young to Remember. By Julie Heifetz. Reviewed by Betty Jean Lifton. *Lilith* 15, No. 1 (Winter 1990):6

Why Women Are Writing Holocaust Memoirs Now. Bibliography. Ellen Fishman. *Lilith* 15, No. 2 (Spring 1990):6-7+

**Holoch, Naomi (joint editor).** *See* Nestle, Joan

**Holt, Gary A.** and Solimini, Cheryl

Pharmacy Facts. *Family Circle* 103, No. 13 (September 25, 1990):116

**Holt, Gary** and Morici, Joanne

Healthy Family. *Family Circle* 103, No. 7 (May 15, 1990):27-30

**Holub, Lois**

Who Were the Witches? Bringing the Past to Life. *Woman of Power* 16 (Spring 1990):56-61

**Holzman, Ian R.** (joint author). *See* Erlen, Judith A.

**Home Accidents – Prevention**

Good Health: Food Poisoning Alert! Rosalinda Lawson, Elyse Sosin, and Fran G. Grossman. *Redbook* 176, No. 1 (November 1990):46-57

Redbook's Home Accident-Prevention Guide for Parents. Neal Ashby. *Redbook* 176, No. 2 (December 1990):83-88

**Home-Based Work.** *See also* Child Care

Home Office Wonders. Jeffrey Cohen. *Savvy Woman* (October 1990):28-31

Homework: Historical and Contemporary Perspectives on Paid Labor at Home. Edited by Eileen Boris and Cynthia R. Daniels. Reviewed by Mary Margaret Fonow. *NWSA Journal* 2, No. 3 (Summer 1990):502-505

Homeworking: Myths and Realities. By Sheila Allen and Carol Wolkowitz. Reviewed by Mary Margaret Fonow. *NWSA Journal* 2, No. 3 (Summer 1990):505-505

**Home Birth.** *See* Childbirth – Home Birth

**Home Computers.** *See* Computers

**Home Decoration.** *See* Interior Design

**Home Exchanging**

Travel: Trading Places. Bibliography. Marti Wilson. *Essence* 21, No. 3 (July 1990):94+

**Home Gyms**

Beauty: The Body Shop. *Mademoiselle* (January 1990):16

Exercise: The Toll of a New Machine. Holly Reich. *Lear's* (November 1990):62-64

Great Looks: Bike Off Inches (at Home). *Redbook* 176, No. 2 (December 1990):18

**Home Improvement.** *See* Dwellings – Remodeling

**Homeless**

A Feminist Approach to Working with Homeless Women. Kaaren Strauch Brown and Marjorie Ziefert. *AFFILIA* 5, No. 1 (Spring 1990):6-20

Femmes sans toit ni voix: La problematique des femmes dites sans-abri ou itinerantes. By Françoise-Romaine Ouellette. Reviewed by Dominique Masson. *Canadian Women's Studies* 11, No. 2 (Fall 1990):86

Give Someone Hope – and Help. Susan Dey and Joy Sirott Hurwitz. *Redbook* 176, No. 1 (November 1990):40

Homeless Women and Men: Their Problems and Use of Services. Brent B. Benda and Patrick Dattalo. *AFFILIA* 5, No. 3 (Fall 1990):50-82

Housing Rights . . . For Adults Only? Maureen Callaghan. *Canadian Women's Studies* 11, No. 2 (Fall 1990):61-62

Lady versus Low Creature: Old Roots of Current Attitudes toward Homeless Women. Stephanie Golden. *Frontiers* 11, Nos. 2-3 (1990):1-7

When a Hostel Becomes a Home – Experiences of Women. By Lesley D. Harman. Reviewed by Dominique Masson. *Resources for Feminist Research* 19, No. 1 (March 1990):37-38

Women Together. Action Against Homelessness. *Spare Rib* 217 (October 1990):52

Women Who Make A Difference. Steve Kaplan. *Family Circle* 103, No. 3 (February 20, 1990):15-16+

**Homeless – Adolescents**

Social Adjustment and Symptomatology in Two Types of Homeless Adolescents: Runaways and Throwaways. Sally J. Hier, Paula J. Korboot, and Robert D. Schweitzer. *Adolescence* 25, No. 100 (Winter 1990):761-771

**Homeless – Nutrition**

The Eating Patterns and Problems of Homeless Women. Terry Bunston and Margot Breton. *Women and Health* 16, No. 1 (1990):43-62

**Homemakers.** *See also* Housework

Backtalk: Worked Over. Susan Foy Spratling. *Lear's* (January 1990):124-128

A Delicate Balance: "This Is Exactly Where I Want to Be." Margaret Jaworski. *Ladies' Home Journal* 107, No. 3 (March 1990):162-164

Goodbye Paycheck! Hello Apron! Aimee Lee Ball. *Mademoiselle* (January 1990):1363-137+

Out Box: A Job of One's Own. Gail Collins. *Working Woman* (September 1990):226

Stay-at-Home Moms. Josie A. Oppenheim. *Good Housekeeping* 211, No. 3 (September 1990):114+

**Homemakers Organized for More Employment (H.O.M.E.)**

H.O.M.E.: One Woman's Approach to Society's Problems. Helen M. Stummer. *On the Issues* 15 (Summer 1990):10-15+

**Home Ownership**

Housemates: The New Choice. Elsie B. Washington. *Essence* 21, No. 2 (June 1990):84-86

**Homer, Merlin**

The Art of Emily Carr. Book Review. *Canadian Women's Studies* 11, No. 1 (Spring 1990):106-107

The Life of Emily Carr. Book Review. *Canadian Women's Studies* 11, No. 1 (Spring 1990):106-107

**Home Remedies.** *See also* Herbal Remedies

Health Express: Home Remedies. P. S. Derron. *Mademoiselle* (February 1990):110

Turn Off That Headache! Alan M. Rapoport and Fred D. Sheftell. *Redbook* 175, No. 6 (October 1990):104-105+

**Home Remodeling.** *See* Dwellings – Remodeling

**Home Repair.** *See* Dwellings – Maintenance and Repair

**Home Safety Equipment**

Parenting. Bibliography. *Essence* 21, No. 6 (October 1990):120

**Home Sales.** *See* House Selling

**Home Video Systems.** *See also* Household Electronics

On Screen: Lights! Camera! Action! Eric Burns. *Family Circle* 103, No. 17 (December 18, 1990):152

**Homework.** *See* Child Psychology; Tutoring

**Homi, Julie** (about)

Two Roads to Solo Keyboard Work: Julie Homi and Adrienne Torf. Laura Post. *Hot Wire* 6, No. 2 (May 1990):28-30+

**Homicide.** *See* Murder

**Homoeroticism.** *See also* Mapplethorpe, Robert (about); National Endowment for the Arts

**Homophobia.** *See also* Acquired Immune Deficiency Syndrome and Homophobia; Elected Officials – Homosexuality; National Endowment for the Arts; Police – Homophobia

Combatting Homophobia in Sports. Helen Lenskyj. *off our backs* 20, No. 6 (June 1990):2-3

Fighting Straight Hate. Helen Zia. *Ms.* 1, No. 2 (September/October 1990):47

Heterosexism or Homophobia: The Power of the Language We Use. Joseph H. Neisen. *Out/Look* No. 10 (Fall 1990):36-37

Homophobia: A Weapon of Sexism. By Suzanne Pharr. Reviewed by Claudia Card. *Hypatia* 5, No. 3 (Fall 1990):110-117

Homophobia: A Weapon of Sexism. By Suzanne Pharr. Reviewed by Eleanor Parkhurst. *off our backs* 20, No. 7 (July 1990):16

Homophobia: A Weapon of Sexism. By Suzanne Pharr. Reviewed by Janet E. Robinson. *Women's Studies International Forum* 13, No. 6 (1990):610-611

Homophobia: A Weapon of Sexism. By Suzanne Pharr. Reviewed by Margaret Nash. *Hypatia* 5, No. 3 (Fall 1990):171-175

Homophobia: A Weapon of Sexism. By Suzanne Pharr. Reviewed by Natalie Jane Woodman. *AFFILIA* 5, No. 3 (Fall 1990):124-125

Homophobia Workshop. *off our backs* 20, No. 8 (August/September 1990):17

Outrage Protest Anti-Gay Murders. *Spare Rib* No. 216 (September 1990):44

Taking the Home Out of Homophobia: Black Lesbians Look in Their Own Backyards. Jewelle L. Gomez and Barbara Smith. *Out/Look* No. 8 (Spring 1990):32-37

Talking about It: Homophobia in the Black Community. Jewelle Gomez and Barbara Smith. *Feminist Review* No. 34 (Spring 1990):46-55

Who Speaks for Lesbian/Gay Adolescents: Voices to Be Silenced, Voices to Be Heard. Dean Pierce. *Women & Language* 13, No. 2 (Winter 1990):37-41

**Homophobia – Media and Communications**

ASNE Undertaking Survey of Anti-Gay Attitudes in U.S. Newsrooms. *Media Report to Women* 18, No. 1 (January/February 1990):7-8

**Homosexuality.** *See also* Adolescents – Homosexuality; Celebrities – Homosexuality; Elected Officials – Homosexuality; Gay Rights Activists; Lesbianism; *under particular countries*

All Our Relations. Sawnie E. Morris. *Out/Look* No. 8 (Spring 1990):46-51

The Boys in the Band Come Back. Wendell Ricketts. *Out/Look* No. 9 (Summer 1990):62-67

The Construction of Homosexuality. By David F. Greenberg. Reviewed by Leila J. Rupp. *NWSA Journal* 2, No. 2 (Spring 1990):306-308

Lesbian and Gay People of Colour Gather in London. Natalie Williams. *Spare Rib* 219 (December 1990-January 1991):66-67

Lost Tribal Rites: A Lament. Desmond J. Waite. *Out/Look* No. 9 (Summer 1990):72-73

Myths and Mysteries of Same-Sex Love. By Christine Downing. Reviewed by Carol LeMasters. *The Women's Review of Books* 7, No. 6 (March 1990):18-19

Out of the Closet and Into the Fray: Should Gay Politicians and Celebrities Be Forced to "Come

Out"? Gabriel Rotello, Urvashi Vaid, and Nancy Buermeyer. *On the Issues* 16 (Fall 1990):

Rosario. Adan Gettinger-Brizuela. *Out/Look* No. 7 (Winter 1990):25-29

Same-Sex Love among the Greek Goddesses. Christine Downing. *Woman of Power* 15 (Fall-Winter 1990):50-53

Telling (Hi)stories: Rethinking the Lesbian and Gay Historical Imagination. Scott Bravmann. *Out/Look* No. 8 (Spring 1990):68-74

Ten for Bravery, Zero for Common Sense. Meredith Maran. *Out/Look* No. 7 (Winter 1990):68-72

**Homosexuality – Clothing and Dress**

A Boy's Guide to Feeling Pretty. D-L Alvarez. *Out/Look* No. 8 (Spring 1990):19-20

**Homosexuality – Conferences**

Homosexuality, Which Homosexuality?: Essays from the International Scientific Conference on Lesbian and Gay Studies. By Dennis Altman and others. Reviewed by Alison Oram. *Feminist Review* No. 35 (Summer 1990):121-122

**Homosexuality – Cross-Cultural Studies**

Cross-National Analysis of the Social Construction of Homosexuality and Gender. Saori Kamano. *NWSA Journal* 2, No. 4 (Autumn 1990):696-698

**Homosexuality – Documentary Films**

Out on Tuesday. Pat Coleman. *Spare Rib* No. 210 (March 1990):40

**Homosexuality – History**

Concepts, Experience, and Sexuality. John Boswell. *Differences* 2, No. 1 (Spring 1990):67-87

Therapeutic Arguments and Structures of Desire. Martha Nussbaum. *Differences* 2, No. 1 (Spring 1990):46-66

**Homosexuality – Humor**

List This! Tom Ammiano and Jeanine Strobel. *Out/Look* No. 10 (Fall 1990):63

**Homosexuality – Image in Theater**

Closet Dramas: Homosexual Representation and Class in Postwar British Theater. Alan Sinfield. *Genders* 9 (Fall 1990):112-131

**Homosexuality, Jewish**

Twice Blessed: On Being Lesbian, Gay, and Jewish. Edited by Christie Balka and Andy Rose. Reviewed by Chaia Lehrer. *New Directions for Women* 19, No. 4 (July-August 1990):15

**Homosexuality – Media Portrayal**

'Dykes in the Dailies': How New Zealand Newspapaers Depict Lesbians. *Media Report to Women* 18, No. 3 (May/June 1990):8

**Homosexuality – Personal Narratives**

Coming Out: Out/Look Readers Tell Their Tales. Edited by Debra Chasnoff. *Out/Look* No. 10 (Fall 1990):19-24

A Matter of Personal Pride: A Conversation about Black and White Men Together. Thom Bean. *Out/Look* No. 9 (Summer 1990):70-71

**Homosexuality – Psychoanalytic Theory**

The Psychoanalytic Perspective of Adolescent Homosexuality: A Review. Jon K. Mills. *Adolescence* 25, No. 100 (Winter 1990):913-922

**Honda Accord.** See Automobiles – Purchasing

**Honduras – Economic Development**

Enterprise: Small Successes Yield Big Returns. Brooke Kroeger. *McCall's* 117, No. 11 (August 1990):16-23

**Honey, Maureen** (editor)

Shadowed Dreams: Women's Poetry of the Harlem Renaissance. Reviewed by Lorraine Elena Roses. *The Women's Review of Books* 7, Nos. 10-11 (July 1990):31-32

**Honeymoons**

Travel: Getting Married in Paradise. Bibliography. Stephanie Stokes Oliver. *Essence* 20, No. 10 (February 1990):99-100

**Hong, Ong Teck** (joint author). See Isralowitz, Richard E.

**Hong Kong – Lesbianism**

Opening the Hong Kong Closet. Lenore Norrgard. *Out/Look* No. 7 (Winter 1990):56-61

**Hood, Ann** and Reiss, Bob

The Answer Couple. *Glamour* (May 1990):136; (July 1990):96-97; (September 1990):166; (November 1990):146-147

**Hood, Ann** (joint author). See Reiss, Bob

**Hood, Robin J.** (about)

Filmmakers Robin J. Hood and Penny Joy. Heather Tufts. *Canadian Women's Studies* 11, No. 1 (Spring 1990):94-96

**Hoogstraten, Janis**

Japanese Women Artists: 1600-1900. Book Review. *Resources for Feminist Research* 19, No. 1 (March 1990):21-22

**Hooke, Helen**

Twenty Years of Making Music. *Hot Wire* 6, No. 2 (May 1990):42-43

**Hooker, Alta** (interview)

Sandinistas – Still Making Revolution. *Spare Rib* 219 (December 1990-January 1991):18-20

**Hooks, Bell**

Challenging Men. *Spare Rib* 217 (October 1990):12-15

Feminism and Black Women's Studies. *Sage* 6, No. 1 (Summer 1989):54-56

Future Feminist Movements. *off our backs* 20, No. 2 (February 1990):9

From Skepticism to Feminism. *The Women's Review of Books* 7, No. 5 (February 1990):29

Talking Back: Thinking Feminist – Thinking Black. Reviewed by Gesche Peters. *Atlantis* 15, No. 2 (Spring 1990):109-111

Talking Back: Thinking Feminist, Thinking Black. Reviewed by Nancie E. Caraway. *Sage* 6, No. 2 (Fall 1989):58-59

**Hopkins, Ellen**

No Place to Hide. *Essence* 21, No. 4 (August 1990):66-68+

Purse and Personality. *Mademoiselle* (November 1990):166-167+

This Working Life: Does Your Office Say Bad Things about You? *Working Woman* (April 1990):132

Who Is Felice Schwartz and Why Is She Saying those Terrible Things about Us? *Working Woman* (October 1990):116-120+

**Hopp, Carolyn** (joint author). *See* Hyde, Janet Shibley

**Hoppe, Stephanie** (joint editor). *See* Corrigan, Theresa

**Hopper, Dennis** (about)

Radical Redux. Todd Gold. *Harper's Bazaar* (May 1990):116-119+

**Horak, Heather**

Northampton Activists on Trial. *off our backs* 20, No. 8 (August/September 1990):7

**Hormones**

Are Superovulants Necessary in IVF Procedures? Nick Tonti-Filippini. *Healthright* 9, No. 3 (May 1990):10-13

The Love Hormone. Charlotte Modahl. *Mademoiselle* (November 1990):112

Lupron – New Wonder Drug? Zelda Abramson. *Healthsharing* 11, No. 4 (December 1990):7

Up Front. *Ladies' Home Journal* 107, No. 10 (October 1990):91-96

**Horn, Barbara**

Great Plains Patchwork: A Memoir. Book Review. *Belles Lettres* 5, No. 3 (Spring 1990):23

Letters of a Woman Homesteader. Book Review. *Belles Lettres* 5, No. 3 (Spring 1990):23

A New Home, Who'll Follow? or Glimpses of Western Life. Book Review. *Belles Lettres* 6, No. 1 (Fall 1990):57

Reactions to the West. *Belles Lettres* 5, No. 3 (Spring 1990):23

Windfall and Other Stories. Book Review. *Belles Lettres* 5, No. 3 (Spring 1990):23

**Hornaday, Ann**

Holly Hughes, Playing the Ironies. *Ms.* 1, No. 3 (November/December 1990):64

**Horne, Jean** (about). *See* Leadership, "Achieving Personal Best"

**Horne, Marilyn** (about)

Vogue Arts: Music. David Daniel. *Vogue* (December 1990):204-208

**Horno-Delgado, Asunción**, Ortega, Eliana, Scott, Nina M., and Sternbach, Nancy Saporta (editors)

Breaking Boundaries: Latina Writing and Critical Reading. Reviewed by Cecilia Rodriguez Milanes. *Sage* 6, No. 2 (Fall 1989):65-66

Breaking Boundaries: Latina Writings and Critical Readings. Reviewed by Lourdes Torres. *Women's Studies International Forum* 13, No. 5 (1990):519-520

**Hornosty, Cornelia C.**

Plath. Poem. *Atlantis* 15, No. 2 (Spring 1990):26

**Hornstein-Rabinovitch, Shelley**

The House That Jack Built. *Canadian Women's Studies* 11, No. 1 (Spring 1990):65-67

**Horseman, Joy**

Turn the Radio Down. *Lear's* (March 1990):68

What Will They Try to Sell Me Next? *Lear's* (May 1990):60

**Horsemanship**

A Ranch Where Miracles Happen. Mike Clary. *McCall's* 117, No. 8 (May 1990):154-160

**Horwood, L. John** (joint author). *See* Fergusson, David M.

**Hosiery**

Talking Fashion: Stockings. Vicki Woods. *Vogue* (September 1990):652-654

**Hosken, Fran P.**

Female Genital Mutilation: Facts and Strategies for Eradication. *Woman of Power* 18 (Fall 1990):42-45

**Hoskins, Betty** (joint author). *See* Corea, Gena

**Hospital, Janette Turner**

Charades. Reviewed by Nancy Engbretsen Schaumburger. *Belles Lettres* 5, No. 2 (Winter 1990):14

**Hospital Care.** *See also* Health Care

How to Get Better Care at a Hospital. Candy Schulman. *Glamour* (July 1990):44-47

Personal Hygiene in External Genitalia of Healthy and Hospitalized Elderly Women. Marianne E. Lindell and Henny M. Olsson. *Health Care for Women International* 11, No. 2 (1990):151-158

Your Guide to Hospital Care. Lisa Rogak. *Essence* 21, No. 5 (September 1990):29+

**Hospital Care – Cost**

Code B, for Bothered and Bewildered. Joseph Anthony. *Lear's* (November 1990):42-44

**Hospital Care – Involuntary**

"Dear Dr. M." Karin Singer. *Healthsharing* 11, No. 1 (December 1989):10-14

**Hospital Care – Personal Narratives**

One, Two, Three. Marcy Jacobs. *Sinister Wisdom* 42 (Winter 1990-1991):74-80

**Hospitals**

Les Infirmie4res: de la vocation á la profession. By André Petitat. Reviewed by Jacinthe Michaud. *Resources for Feminist Research* 19, No. 1 (March 1990):20

Vital Signs: Windows to Well-Being. Alexandra Tanski. *McCall's* 117, No. 12 (September 1990):76

**Hostages.** *See* Lebanon – Hostages

**Hotels, Taverns, etc.**

On the Road Again. Bibliography. Monique Burns. *Essence* 21, No. 2 (June 1990):29-30

There's Room at the Inn. Dana Nadel. *Lear's* (December 1990):118-119

Travel: Checking Into Hotel Lust. Bibliography. Liz Logan. *Mademoiselle* (June 1990):68-72

Travel: Hotels Made for Romance. Bibliography. *Glamour* (February 1990):114-117

Travel Bazaar: Scene Stealers. Julie Moline. *Harper's Bazaar* (December 1990):90-96+

**Houde-Quimby, Charlotte** (about)

A Woman for Lear's: Rebirth. Jane Howard. *Lear's* (April 1990):116-119

**Houger, Joan** (joint author). *See* Dowden, Richard

**Houlton, Jennifer**

Innocent Until Proven Otherwise. *Mademoiselle* (June 1990):88

**Housecleaning**

Help! Vicki Lansky. *Family Circle* 103, No. 13 (September 25, 1990):101-102; 103, No. 14 (October 16, 1990):141-142; 103, No. 17 (December 18, 1990):125-126

**House Design**

The Busy Woman's Dream House. *Family Circle* 103, No. 9 (June 26, 1990):83-95

**Household Division of Labor.** *See* Balancing Work and Family Life; Employment – Outside the Home; Housework, Gender Division of

**Household Electronics**

State of the Art Electronics. Bibliography. Pamela A. Toussaint. *Essence* 21, No. 3 (July 1990):88-93

**Household Linens**

Linens, Lace, All Over the Place. Excerpt. Tricia Foley. *McCall's* 117, No. 12 (September 1990):126-129

**Household Repairing.** *See* Dwellings – Maintenance and Repair

**Household Structure**

Dowry, Norms, and Household Formation: A Case Study from North Portugal. Helena Osswald. *Journal of Family History* 15, No. 2 (April 1990):201-224

Race and Marital Status Differences in the Labor Force Behavior of Female Family Heads: The Effect of Household Structure. Cynthia Rexroat. *Journal of Marriage and the Family* 52, No. 3 (August 1990):591-601

Who Lives with Whom? Individual Versus Household Values. Miriam King and Samuel H. Preston. *Journal of Family History* 15, No. 2 (April 1990):117-132

**Household Workers.** *See also* Japanese-American Women – History

Body Politics: Sexuality, Gender, and Domestic Service in Zambia. Karen Tranberg Hansen. *Journal of Women's History* 2, No. 1 (Spring 1990):120-142

The Distinguishing Features of Domestic Service in Italy. Angiolina Arru. *Journal of Family History* 15, No. 4 (October 1990):547-566

Domesticity and Dirt: Housewives and Domestic Servants in the United States, 1920-1945. By Phyllis Palmer. Reviewed by Lois R. Helmbold. *The Women's Review of Books* 7, No. 8 (May 1990):12-13

Hazards of Hearth and Home. Lesley Doyal. *Women's Studies International Forum* 13, No. 5 (1990):501-517

Maids and Madams: Domestic Workers Under Apartheid. By Jacklyn Cock. Reviewed by Stanlie M. James. *Feminist Collections* 12, No. 1 (Fall 1990):3-6

Muchachas No More: Household Workers in Latin America and the Caribbean. Edited by Elsa M. Chaney and Mary Garcia Castro. Reviewed by Diana Brandi. *Women's Studies International Forum* 13, No. 5 (1990):520

Muchachas No More: Household Workers in Latin America and the Caribbean. Edited by Elsa M. Chaney and Mary Garcia Castro. Reviewed by Diana Decker. *off our backs* 20, No. 5 (May 1990):23

Not Just Like One of the Family: Chicana Domestics Establishing Professional Relationships with Employers. Mary Romero. *Feminist Issues* 10, No. 2 (Fall 1990):33-41

Telling Memories Among Southern Women: Domestic Workers and Their Employers in the Segregated South. By Susan Tucker. Reviewed by

Shelley Crisp. *Belles Lettres* 5, No. 2 (Winter 1990):3

**Housemates.** *See* Shared Housing

**House Plants**

Health Dept. Donna Heiderstadt. *Lear's* (October 1990):70

Long-Distance Plant Care. Joel Rapp. *Redbook* 175, No. 4 (August 1990):26

Personal Journal. *Ladies' Home Journal* 107, No. 10 (October 1990):142-146

**Houser, Catherine**

Graver Images. *The Women's Review of Books* 7, No. 4 (January 1990):19-20

Perpetua. Book Review. *The Women's Review of Books* 7, No. 4 (January 1990):19-20

**Houses**

First Person Singular: House Bound. *Savvy Woman* (September 1990):94 +

**Houses – Remodeling.** *See* Dwellings – Remodeling; Interior Design

**Houses – Selling**

Does Your House Have Sales Appeal? Lauren Payne. *Ladies' Home Journal* 107, No. 6 (June 1990):114-118

**House Swapping.** *See* Home Exchanging

**Housework**

Changes in Marriage Associated with the Transition to Parenthood: Individual Differences as a Function of Sex-Role Attitudes and Changes in the Division of Household Labor. Shelley M. MacDermid, Ted L. Huston, and Susan M. McHale. *Journal of Marriage and the Family* 52, No. 2 (May 1990):475-486

The Flip Side: It's a Wash! Stan Stinberg. *Family Circle* 103, No. 14 (October 16, 1990):28-29

GH Institute: Hot Line. *Good Housekeeping* 211, No. 4 (October 1990):206

Handling Everyday Life Problems. Vicki Lansky. *Family Circle* 103, No. 9 (June 26, 1990):98-99

Selling the Mechanized Household: 70 Years of Ads in *Ladies Home Journal*. Bonnie J. Fox. *Gender and Society* 4, No. 1 (March 1990):25-40

Speaker for the House: The Heloise Helpline. Heloise. *Good Housekeeping* 211, No. 3 (September 1990):72; 211, No. 4 (October 1990):38

Teaching Youngsters Household Chores. *Good Housekeeping* 211, No. 3 (September 1990):152

**Housework, Gender Division of**

Division of Household Labor, Strain, and Depressive Symptoms among Mexican Americans and Non-Hispanic Whites. Jacqueline M. Golding. *Psychology of Women Quarterly* 14, No. 1 (March 1990):103-117

Domestic Division of Labor among Working Couples: Does Androgyny Make a Difference? Nancy C. Gunter and B.G. Gunter. *Psychology of Women Quarterly* 14, No. 3 (September 1990):355-370

**Housing**

Women, Human Settlements and Housing. Edited by Caroline O. N. Moser and Linda Peake. Reviewed by Pamela Sayne. *Resources for Feminist Research* 19, No. 1 (March 1990):42-43

Women and Housing: A Research Agenda. Gerda R. Wekerle. *Canadian Women's Studies* 11, No. 2 (Fall 1990):66-67

**Housing – Costs.** *See* Shared Housing

**Housing – Personal Narratives**

Becoming a "Real" Dyke: Employment and Housing. Rue Amana. *Canadian Women's Studies* 11, No. 2 (Fall 1990):43-45

Demolition. Eve Corbel. *Canadian Women's Studies* 11, No. 2 (Fall 1990):51-52

Home Away from Home. Jackie Manthorne. *Canadian Women's Studies* 11, No. 2 (Fall 1990):48-50

Le logement: Point d'ancrage pour un nouveau départ. Françoise Mondor. *Canadian Women's Studies* 11, No. 2 (Fall 1990):46-47

**Housing, Public**

Information Is Power Chicago Women Know. Maggie Garb. *New Directions for Women* 19, No. 2 (March/April 1990):12

**Housing, Rental**

Ce n'est pas la vie en rose. Ruth Pilote. *Canadian Women's Studies* 11, No. 2 (Fall 1990):33-35

Poet Laureate of the Poor: Dorothy O'Connell. Mary Garrett. *Canadian Women's Studies* 11, No. 2 (Fall 1990):36-37

Sexual Harassment of Women Tenants. Sylvia Novac. *Canadian Women's Studies* 11, No. 2 (Fall 1990):58

Tenants Organize! An Interview with Anne Smith. Joyce Watt and Ruth Mott. *Canadian Women's Studies* 11, No. 2 (Fall 1990):29-30

**Housing – Sharing.** *See* Housing Cooperatives; Shared Housing

**Housing and Urban Development, Department of**

She Stoops to Conquer. Peter Hellman. *Savvy Woman* (March 1990):63-65, 80-83

**Housing Cooperatives**

Helping Each Other: A Swedish Perspective. Birgit Krantz. *Canadian Women's Studies* 11, No. 2 (Fall 1990):77-79

L'Arbre de vie. Lucienne Lacasse-Lovsted. *Canadian Women's Studies* 11, No. 2 (Fall 1990):17-18

Mutual Aid and Social Networks: A Feminist-Inspired Housing Co-op in Montreal. Gisele Yasmeen. *Canadian Women's Studies* 11, No. 2 (Fall 1990):25-28

Quality Housing for Women and Children. Myrna Margulies Breitbart. *Canadian Women's Studies* 11, No. 2 (Fall 1990):19-24

**Housing Development**

Global Women and Shelter Network. *Canadian Women's Studies* 11, No. 2 (Fall 1990):41

New Households, New Housing. Edited by Karen A. Franck and Sherry Ahrentzen. Reviewed by Ellen Vera Allen. *Canadian Women's Studies* 11, No. 2 (Fall 1990):85

Women in Toronto Creating Housing: Participation and Process. Pamela Sayne. *Canadian Women's Studies* 11, No. 2 (Fall 1990):38-41

Working on the "Hard" Side. Anne Other. *Canadian Women's Studies* 11, No. 2 (Fall 1990):59-60

**Housing Sales.** *See* House Selling

**Houston, Barbara**

Caring: A Feminine Approach to Ethics and Moral Education. Book Review. *Hypatia* 5, No. 1 (Spring 1990):115-119

Caring and Exploitation. *Hypatia* 5, No. 1 (Spring 1990):115-119

**Houston, Marsha**

Difficult Dialogues: Report on the 1990 Conference on Research in Gender and Communication. *Women & Language* 13, No. 2 (Winter 1990):30-32

**Houston—Politics and Government.** *See also* Texas—Mayors

Lassoing Power. Kathryn Casey. *Savvy Woman* (November 1990):13-14

**Houston, Whitney** (about). *See* Leadership, "1990 Essence Awards"

The Soul of Whitney. Joy Duckett Cain. *Essence* 21, No. 8 (December 1990):54-56

**Houtchens, C. J.**

The Country Girl. *Harper's Bazaar* (January 1990):100-105+

**Howard, Jane**

In From the Cold. *Lear's* (October 1990):146-150

Making the Grade. *Lear's* (November 1990):150-154

A Woman for Lear's: Devotions. *Lear's* (December 1990):128-131

A Woman for Lear's: Downhome. *Lear's* (May 1990):136-139

A Woman for Lear's: Grace Notes. *Lear's* (January 1990):132-134

A Woman for Lear's: Lessons. *Lear's* (March 1990):164-167

A Woman for Lear's: One for the Books. *Lear's* (June 1990):132-135

A Woman for Lear's: Overhaul. *Lear's* (July 1990):120-123

A Woman for Lear's: Rebirth. *Lear's* (April 1990):116-119

A Woman for Lear's: Strong Medicine. *Lear's* (September 1990):156-159

A Woman for Lear's: Taking the Cake. *Lear's* (February 1990):130-132

A Woman for Lear's: Word for Word. *Lear's* (August 1990):132-135

**Howard, Judith A.** and Allen, Carolyn

The Gendered Context of Reading. *Gender and Society* 4, No. 4 (December 1990):534-552

**Howard, Kenneth I.** (joint author). *See* Offer, Daniel

**Howard-Merriam, Kathleen**

Guaranteed Seats for Political Representation of Women: The Egyptian Example. *Women & Politics* 10, No. 1 (1990):17-42

**Howarth, Janet**

Jane Ellen Harrison: The Mask and the Self. Book Review. *Gender and Education* 2, No. 2 (1990):246-247

**Howatson, Marianne**

The New Diversity. *Executive Female* (May/June 1990):18

**Howe, Florence**

Memories of Kate Simon—Dazzling Without Show. *Women's Studies Quarterly* 18, Nos. 3-4 (Fall-Winter 1990):153-158

Poet of History, Poet of Vision. *The Women's Review of Books* 7, Nos. 10-11 (July 1990):41-42

This Is My Century: New and Collected Poems. Book Review. *The Women's Review of Books* 7, Nos. 10-11 (July 1990):41-42

**Howe, Karen G.**

Daughters Discover Their Mothers through Biographies and Genograms: Educational and Clinical Parallels. *Women and Therapy* 10, Nos. 1/2 (1990):31-40

**Howell, Georgina**

Gucci Again. *Vogue* (December 1990):322-327

Jean Seberg. *Vogue* (October 1990):364-375

The Kings of Color: Lacroix. *Vogue* (September 1990):546-550+

Roehm's Empire. *Vogue* (August 1990):352-359+

The '80s. *Vogue* (January 1990):214-220

There's Nothing Like a Dame. *Vogue* (April 1990):378-381, 421

**Howell, Margie** (about)

Up Front. *Ladies' Home Journal* 107, No. 12 (December 1990):101-104

**Howells, Michael** (about)

Prop Artist. *Harper's Bazaar* (November 1990):202+

**Howsam, Leslie**

Women and Industrialization: Gender at Work in Nineteenth-Century England. Book Review. *Atlantis* 15, No. 2 (Spring 1990):106-107

**Hoyles, Celia** (editor)

Girls and Computers: General Issues and Case Studies of Logo in the Mathematics Classroom. Reviewed by Lorraine Cully. *Gender and Education* 2, No. 1 (1990):110-111

**Hoyt, Michael** and Schoonmaker, Mary Ellen

The Friendship Factor. *Family Circle* 103, No. 12 (September 4, 1990):103-104

**Huang, Larke Nahme** (joint author). *See* Gibbs, Jewelle Taylor

**Hub, The**

Hub Holds Out Hope to Teens. Eleanor J. Rader. *New Directions for Women* 19, No. 1 (January/February 1990):metrö+

**Hubbard, Dianne**

Women's Rights in the New Constitution. *Women in Action* 1-2 (1990):24

**Hubbard, Ruth**

The Politics of Women's Biology. Reviewed by Sheila Tobias. *The Women's Review of Books* 8, No. 2 (November 1990):15

**Hubbard, Ruth** and Randall, Margaret

The Shape of Red: Insider/Outsider Reflections. Reviewed by Barbara Ryan. *off our backs* 20, No. 7 (July 1990):17

**Hubbard, Ruth** (interview)

Women's Bodies as Battlegrounds. Kate O'Neill. *Woman of Power* 18 (Fall 1990):10-14

**Hubert, Janet** (about)

Janet Hubert. Benilde Little. *Essence* 21, No. 8 (December 1990):33

**Huck, Shirley** (joint author). *See* Conger, Rand D.

**Huggins, Ericka** (about). *See also* Leadership

**Huggins, Jackie**

International Indigenous Women's Conference. *Australian Feminist Studies* No. 11 (Autumn 1990):113-114

**Huggins, Jackie** (interview)

Questions of Collaboration: Interview with Jackie Huggins and Isabel Tarrago. Carole Ferrier. *Hecate* 16, Nos. 1-2 (1990):140-147

**Hughes, Elizabeth** (about). *See* College Students – Leadership

**Hughes, Holly** (about)

Holly Hughes, Playing the Ironies. Ann Hornaday. *Ms.* 1, No. 3 (November/December 1990):64

**Hughes, Lynn,** Lipke, Kathryn, MacKay, Barbara, Mullen, Cathy, Sacca, Elizabeth, and others

Feminism in Fine Arts Education. *Canadian Women's Studies* 11, No. 1 (Spring 1990):43-45

**Hughes, Mary**

Learning the Hard Way: Women's Oppression in Men's Education. Book Review. *Gender and Education* 2, No. 3 (1990):370-371

**Hughes-Hallett, Lucy**

Cleopatra: Histories, Dreams and Distortions. Reviewed by Marilyn French. *The Women's Review of Books* 8, No. 2 (November 1990):16-17

**Hughs, Holly** and Elovich, Richard

An Open Letter to the Gay and Lesbian Community. *Out/Look* No. 10 (Fall 1990):74-75

**Huh, Joonok**

Between Feminism and Psychoanalysis. Book Review. *NWSA Journal* 2, No. 3 (Summer 1990):511-514

Feminism and Psychoanalysis. Book Review. *NWSA Journal* 2, No. 3 (Summer 1990):511-514

**Huleileh, Serene**

A Mountainous Journey: The Life of Palestine's Outstanding Woman Poet. add. *Spare Rib* No. 216 (September 1990):24

**Human, Pam**

Home Birth. *Spare Rib* No. 209 (February 1990):57

**Human Genome Project**

The Gene Prophets. Lori Andrews. *Vogue* (January 1990):198-199+

**Human Growth Hormone.** *See* Hormones

**Human Papilloma Virus**

Virulent Virus. Elaine M. Hyman. *New Directions for Women* 19, No. 5 (September-October 1990):7+

**Human Rights.** *See* Ethics; Social Values

**Humberstone, Barbara**

Gender, Change and Adventure Education. *Gender and Education* 2, No. 2 (1990):199-215

**Hummingbird Films**

Women HIV and AIDS: Speaking Out in the UK. Reviewed by Judi Wilson. *Spare Rib* 219 (December 1990-January 1991):34-35

**Humor.** *See also* Burlesque; Family Life – Humor; Lesbianism – Humor; Parenting – Humor

The Best of Women's Wit and Humor. Miche4le Brown and Ann O'Connor. *Woman of Power* 17 (Summer 1990):14

A Capital Proposal. Sidney Blumenthal. *Lear's* (August 1990):86-89

Depression Envy. *Lear's* (December 1990):76-77+

Feminist Icons: Buttons, Bumper Stickers, and Graffiti. *Woman of Power* 17 (Summer 1990):30

The Haggard Sense of Humor. Mary Daly. *Woman of Power* 17 (Summer 1990):7-12

Healthy Humor: The Art of Laughing at Ourselves. Melinda Rose. *Woman of Power* 17 (Summer 1990):40-43

Humor as a Professional Tool. Barbara L. Mackoff. *Executive Female* 13, No. 6 (November-December 1990):56-57

Humor in Women's Music. Jamie Anderson. *Hot Wire* 6, No. 1 (January 1990):46-47+

Silverleaf's Choice: An Anthology of Lesbian Humor. Edited by Anne E. Larson and Carole A. Carr. Reviewed by Rosalind Warren. *New Directions for Women* 19, No. 6 (November-December 1990):17

Taking Humor Seriously. Theresa Fassihi. *Executive Female* 13, No. 6 (November-December 1990):13-14

Tales from the Delivery Room. Judith Viorst. *Redbook* 174, No. 6 (April 1990):58-62

Total Recoil. Peter Feibleman. *Lear's* (August 1990):53-56

Who Is Laughing Now? The Role of Humour in the Social Construction of Gender. Marlene Mackie. *Atlantis* 15, No. 2 (Spring 1990):11-26

Women's Humor as Catharsis and Protest. Nancy Walker. *Woman of Power* 17 (Summer 1990):75-80

**Humorists**. *See* Barry, Dave (about)

**Humphrey, Kelly Norton**

Prime of Life: Out of Retirement and into Office. *Family Circle* 103, No. 9 (June 26, 1990):140-142

Prime of Life: The New Recruits. *Family Circle* 103, No. 13 (September 25, 1990):38-40

**Humphreys, Deborah L.**

Keeping the Faith: Questions and Answers for the Abused Woman. Book Review. *AFFILIA* 5, No. 2 (Summer 1990):109-111

**Humphreys, Debra**

Minorities in Higher Education: An Interview with Bambi Ramirez, American Council on Education. *NWSAction* 3, No. 1/2 (Spring 1990): 7-9

Transforming the Curriculum. *NWSAction* 3, No. 4 (Winter 1990): 5-6

Under Attack From the Right. *NWSAction* 3, No. 4 (Winter 1990): 7-8

**Humphries, Steve, Mack, Joanna, and Perks, Robert**

A Century of Childhood. Reviewed by Diana Gittins. *Gender and Education* 2, No. 1 (1990):104-105

**Hunecke, Volker**

The Foundlings of Milan: Abandoned Children and Their Parents from the Seventeenth to the Nineteenth Centuries. Reviewed by Edith Saurer. *Gender & History* 2, No. 3 (Autumn 1990):356-358

**Hung, Bui Sy** (joint author). *See* Phuong, Nguyen Thi Ngoc

**Hungary – Travel.** *See* Budapest

**Hunt, Felicity**

The Reform of Girls' Secondary and Higher Education in Victorian England. Book Review. *Gender & History* 2, No. 1 (Spring 1990):113-114

**Hunt, Margaret**

The De-Eroticization of Women's Liberation: Social Purity Movements and the Revolutionary Feminism of Sheila Jeffreys. *Feminist Review* No. 34 (Spring 1990):23-41

Women and Print Culture: The Construction of Femininity in the Early Periodical. Book Review. *Gender & History* 2, No. 2 (Summer 1990):228-229

**Hunt, Marsha**

Joy. Reviewed by Anne N. Iwobi. *Spare Rib* 217 (October 1990):33

**Hunt, Mary E.**

After the Revolution in Poland Today, Women Still Sweep the Floors. *Lilith* 15, No. 2 (Spring 1990):20

**Hunt, Nancy Rose**

Domesticity and Colonialism in Belgian Africa: Usumbura's *Foyer Social*, 1946-1960. Notes. *Signs* 15, No. 3 (Spring 1990):447-474

"Single Ladies on the Congo": Protestant Missionary Tensions and Voices. *Women's Studies International Forum* 13, No. 4 (1990):395-403

**Hunt, William Holman – Criticism and Interpretation**

Between Dream and Shadow: William Holman Hunt's Lady of Shalott. Sharyn R. Udall. *Woman's Art Journal* 11, No. 1 (Spring-Summer 1990):34-38

**Hunter, Jean E.**

A Daring New Concept: *The Ladies' Home Journal* and Modern Feminism. *NWSA Journal* 2, No. 4 (Autumn 1990):583-602

**Hunter, Linda Mason**

Hidden Health Hazards in Your Home. *Family Circle* 103, No. 2 (February 1, 1990):80-81

**Hunter, Linda Mason** (about). *See also* Dwellings – Remodeling

**Hunter, Pat**

Menopause Without Medicine. Book Review. *Healthright* 9, No. 4 (August 1990):48

Women's Change of Life. Book Review. *Healthright* 9, No. 4 (August 1990):44

**Hurd, Gale Anne** (about). *See* Etra, Jon, "World Class"

**Hurricane Hugo, 1989**

Charleston: Coming Through the Hurricane. Sandra Rhodes. *Ladies' Home Journal* 107, No. 1 (January 1990):16-20

A Hurricane Hits Home. J. Fletcher Robinson. *Essence* 20, No. 12 (April 1990):38

Hurricane! Laura Claverie. *Family Circle* 103, No. 13 (September 25, 1990):78-82

**Hurricanes**. *See* Hurricane Hugo, 1989; Natural Disasters

**Hurshell, Pat**

Opera, or the Undoing of Women. Book Review. *NWSA Journal* 2, No. 1 (Winter 1990):141-142

**Hurst, Jacqui** and Saft, Elizabeth

Cultivated Pleasures: The Art of Romantic Gardening. Reviewed by D. S. Oliver. *The Women's Review of Books* 7, No. 6 (March 1990):21-22

**Hurston, Zora Neale**

A Zora Neale Hurston Sampler. *Woman of Power* 17 (Summer 1990):74

**Hurston, Zora Neale – Criticism and Interpretation**

Narrative Strategies in Zora Neale Hurston's *Dust Tracks on a Road*. Deborah G. Plant. *Sage* 6, No. 1 (Summer 1989):18-23

**Hurt, John** (about). *See* Great Britain – Culture

**Hurwitz, Joy Sirott** (joint author). *See* Dey, Susan

**Husbands of Famous Women**. *See* Celebrities – Spouses

**Huskinson, Janet**

Adults and Children in the Roman Empire. Book Review. *Gender & History* 2, No. 1 (Spring 1990):105-106

**Hussain, Shahnaz Huq** (joint author). *See* Wallace, Ben J.

**Hussey, Anita**

Go Global. *Executive Female* 13, No. 5 (September-October 1990):35-38

Rent-a-Veep. *Executive Female* (May/June 1990):14-16

**Huston, Anjelica** (about)

Riding High. Vicki Woods. *Vogue* (November 1990):356-365

**Huston, Ted L.** (joint author). *See* MacDermid, Shelley M.

**Hutaff, Peggy** (joint author). *See* Martin, Clarice J.

**Hutchens, Rose**

You Must Remember This . . . *Women and Environments* 12, No. 2 (Spring 1990): 20-21

**Hutchings, Nancy** (editor)

The Violent Family. Reviewed by Sandra Bauer. *AFFILIA* 5, No. 1 (Spring 1990):114-115

**Hutchinson, Marcia** (interview)

Transforming Body Image. Carole A. Biederman. *Woman of Power* 18 (Fall 1990):76-80

**Hutchinson, Mary** (joint editor). *See* Allen, Margaret

**Hutson, Jean Blackwell** (about). *See* De Veaux, Alexis, Milloy, Marilyn, and Ross, Michael Erik

**Hutter, Randi**

Muscle Tone. *Harper's Bazaar* (May 1990):140-143

**Hutter, Sarah**

Dial for Help. *Working Mother* (November 1990):45

Take the Kids Cruising. *Working Mother* (December 1990):98-103

**Hutton, Lauren** (about). *See also* Johnson, Lois Joy, "Great Faces"

Spunky and Punky, Lauren Hutton Says Her Piece. Louise Bernikow. *Lear's* (October 1990):90-93 +

Wild at Heart. David Keeps. *Harper's Bazaar* (August 1990):140-143 +

**Hutton, Megan**

Why So Soon? *Healthsharing* 11, No. 4 (December 1990):34

**Hutzpit, M**

Music Box. Film Review. *Spare Rib* No. 215 (August 1990):34

**Hvorostovsky, Dmitri** (about)

Vogue Arts: Music. David Daniel. *Vogue* (September 1990):436-438

**Hyde, Janet Shibley**

Meta-analysis and the Psychology of Gender Differences. *Signs* 16, No. 1 (Autumn 1990):55-73

**Hyde, Janet Shibley**, Fennema, Elizabeth, Ryan, Marilyn, Frost, Laurie A., and Hopp, Carolyn

Gender Comparisons of Mathematics Attitudes and Affect. *Psychology of Women Quarterly* 14, No. 3 (September 1990):299-324

**Hyde, Janet Shibley** (joint author). *See* Jadack, Rosemary A.

**Hyde, Nina** (about)

Fashion Statement. Stephanie Mansfield. *Lear's* (February 1990):52-53

**Hydrotherapy**

Beauty from the Sea. Liza Coleman. *Savvy Woman* (July/August 1990):40-42

Wash and Be Healed: The Water-Cure Movement and Women's Health. By Susan E. Cayleff. Reviewed by Sue Zschoche. *Signs* 15, No. 2 (Winter 1990):414-416

**Hygiene, Personal.** *See also particular parts of the body*

Personal Hygiene in External Genitalia of Healthy and Hospitalized Elderly Women. Marianne E. Lindell and Henny M. Olsson. *Health Care for Women International* 11, No. 2 (1990):151-158

**Hyman, Elaine M.**

Virulent Virus. *New Directions for Women* 19, No. 5 (September-October 1990):7+

**Hynes, H. Patricia**

Beyond Global Housekeeping. *Ms.* 1, No. 1 (July/August 1990):91-93

Pornography and Pollution. *Women's Studies International Forum* 13, No. 3 (1990):169-176

The Recurring Silent Spring. Reviewed by Deborah Jordan. *Australian Feminist Studies* No. 11 (Autumn 1990):127-128

The Recurring Silent Spring. Reviewed by Linda Vance. *NWSA Journal* 2, No. 3 (Summer 1990):485-409

The Recurring Silent Spring. Reviewed by Sue V. Rosser. *Signs* 15, No. 4 (Summer 1990):872-873

**Hynes, H. Patricia** (editor)

Reconstructing Babylon: Essays on Women and Technology. Reviewed by Jalna Hanmer. *Women's Studies International Forum* 13, No. 6 (1990):608-609

Reconstructing Babylon: Essays on Women and Technology. Reviewed by Pat Spallone. *Spare Rib* No. 210 (March 1990):35

**Hynes, Patricia** and Spallone, Patricia

Thirty Years of the Pill. *Spare Rib* No. 214 (July 1990):48-49

**Hypatia** (journal)

Does *Hypatia* Rock Boats? Helen Bequaert Holmes. *Hypatia* 5, No. 3 (Fall 1990):162-164

Some Thoughts on the Contents of *Hypatia*. Esther Frances. *Hypatia* 5, No. 3 (Fall 1990):159-161

**Hypertension.** *See* African-American Women–Health Care; Health Education

**Hypochondria**

No, You Don't Have Cancer: A Reassuring Guide for Hypochondriacs. Ellen Kunes. *Mademoiselle* (June 1990):128

Total Recoil: How to Look Sick and Stay Healthy. Peter Feibleman. *Lear's* (September 1990):44-46

**Hypoglycemia**

Hypoglycemia. Joan Zwozdesky. *Healthsharing* 11, No. 1 (December 1989):27-28

**Hysterectomy**

Don't Ask Your Gynecologist If You Need a Hysterectomy . . . Zelda Abramson. *Healthsharing* 11, No. 3 (June 1990):12-17

Fibroids–Are They Dangerous? Ann Renard. *Redbook* 175, No. 5 (September 1990):28-30

Health. Lynn Payer. *Vogue* (June 1990):152-156

Hidden Death: The Sexual Effects of Hysterectomy. Dorin Schumacher. *Journal of Women and Aging* 2, No. 2 (1990):49-66

The Hysterectomy Epidemic. Nora W. Coffey. *Woman of Power* 18 (Fall 1990):58-60

Loss of the Uterus. Kendra Sundquist. *Healthright* 9, No. 4 (August 1990):29-33

Search for an Alternative. Heather Tucker. *Healthsharing* 11, No. 3 (June 1990):18-19

## I

**Iandoli, Ce Ce**

Viewpoint: The Tyranny of Having It All. *Executive Female* (March/April 1990):29-30

**Iazzetto, Demetria**

Feminism within the Science and Health Care Professions: Overcoming Resistance. Book Review. *NWSA Journal* 2, No. 4 (Autumn 1990):664-668

Healing Technology: Feminist Perspectives. Book Review. *NWSA Journal* 2, No. 4 (Autumn 1990):664-668

Women and Health: Cross-Cultural Perspectives. Book Review. *NWSA Journal* 2, No. 4 (Autumn 1990):664-668

**Iazzetto, Demetria** (joint author). *See* Angela, Angie

**Ice Cream, Ices, etc.**

Outrageous! *Redbook* 175, No. 5 (September 1990):179-186+

**Iceland**

The Viking Riviera. Blanche McCary Boyd. *Vogue* (November 1990):327+

**Ickovics, Jeannette R.** (joint author). *See* Rosen, Leora N.

**Ide, Bette A.**, Tobias, Cynthia, Kay, Margarita, Monk, Janice, and Guernsey de Zapien, Jill

A Comparison of Coping Strategies Used Effectively by Older Anglo and Mexican-American Widows: A Longitudinal Study. *Health Care for Women International* 11, No. 3 (1990):237-249

**Images of Women in the Arts.** *See also* Comic Books, Strips, etc.; Literary Criticism – Feminist Perspectives; Mothers in Films

On the Bias: Seduction. Lynne Tempest. *AFFILIA* 5, No. 4 (Winter 1990):105-107

The Enigma of Woman: Barbara Baynton's *Human Toll.* Rosemary Moore. *Australian Feminist Studies* No. 12 (Summer 1990):83-93

Imaging American Women: Idea and Ideals in Cultural History. By Martha Banta. Reviewed by Barbara Green. *Tulsa Studies in Women's Literature* 9, No. 1 (Spring 1990):135-139

Monstrous Regiment: The Lady Knight in Sixteenth-Century Epic. By Lillian S. Robinson. Reviewed by Marie Cornelia. *Tulsa Studies in Women's Literature* 9, No. 1 (Spring 1990):156-158

The Prostituted Muse: Images of Women and Women Dramatists, 1642-1737. By Jacqueline Pearson. Reviewed by Elaine Hobby. *Gender & History* 2, No. 3 (Autumn 1990):359-363

"Sex as a Weapon": Feminist Rock Music Videos. Robin Roberts. *NWSA Journal* 2, No. 1 (Winter 1990):1-15

Women in Chinese Fiction: The Last Ten Years. Louise Edwards and Kam Louie. *Australian Feminist Studies* No. 11 (Autumn 1990):95-112

Writing Innocence: Fanny Burney's *Evelina* Joanne Cutting-Gray. *Tulsa Studies in Women's Literature* 9, No. 1 (Spring 1990):43-57

**Imamura, Anne E.**

Urban Japanese Housewives: At Home and in the Community. Reviewed by Susan Seymour. *Signs* 15, No. 2 (Winter 1990):395-398

**Imbleau, Monique**

Femmes et prison. Book Review. *Resources for Feminist Research* 19, No. 1 (March 1990):14

**Immarigeon, Russ**

Alternatives to Prison Are Few But Effective. *New Directions for Women* 19, No. 2 (March/April 1990):10

**Immigrants**

Daughters of the Shtetl: Life and Labor in the Immigrant Generation. By Susan Glenn. Reviewed by Annelise Orleck. *The Women's Review of Books* 8, No. 3 (December 1990):30-31

The Fault of Memory: "Southern Italy" in the Imagination of Immigrants and the Lives of Their Children in Italian Harlem, 1920-1945. Robert A. Orsi. *Journal of Family History* 15, No. 2 (April 1990):133-147

Home Is Where My Heart Is. Elizabeth Nunez-Harrell. *Essence* 20, No. 12 (April 1990):36+

Power, Patriarchy, and Gender Conflict in the Vietnamese Immigrant Community. Nazli Kibria. *Gender and Society* 4, No. 1 (March 1990):9-24

Quiet Odyssey: A Pioneer Korean Woman in America. By Mary Paik Lee. Reviewed by Miriam Ching Louie. *Belles Lettres* 6, No. 1 (Fall 1990):27-28

The World of Our Mothers: The Lives of Jewish Immigrant Women. By Sydney Stahl Weinberg. Reviewed by Lynne H. Kleinman. *Gender and Society* 4, No. 1 (March 1990):101-103

**Immigrants – Employment**

Helping Immigrants Adapt Stabilizes a Work Force. Lorraine Calvacca. *Working Woman* (January 1990):84

From Working Daughters to Working Mothers: Immigrant Women in a New England Industrial Community. By Louise Lamphere. Reviewed by Sandra Morgen. *Feminist Studies* 16, No. 1 (Spring 1990):53-67

**Immigrants – Health Problems**

Mental Health Problems of Translocated Women. Barbara Ogur. *Health Care for Women International* 11, No. 1 (1990):43-47

A Reviews of the Health Status of Southeast Asian Refugee Women. Judith C. Kulig. *Health Care for Women International* 11, No. 1 (1990):49-63

**Immigrants – Personal Narratives**

Women Who Chose America. *Glamour* (February 1990):186-189

**Immigrants, Violence against**

Double Jeopardy, Double Courage. Mary Suh. *Ms.* 1, No. 2 (September/October 1990):46

**Immune System**

How to Boost Your Immune System. Lorraine Dusky. *McCall's* 117, No. 12 (September 1990):42-55

How Your Immune System Works. Joan Lippert. *Ladies' Home Journal* 107, No. 10 (October 1990):118-124

Winter Wellness Guide: The Best Defense: Understanding Your Immune System. Hal Straus. *Ladies' Home Journal* 107, No. 1 (January 1990):39-43

**Immunization of Infants.** *See* Vaccination of Infants

**Impersonation.** *See* Spigel, Lynn

**Impostors and Imposture**

Great Impostors. *Harper's Bazaar* (November 1990):55-58

**Impressionism (Art)**

The Looks of Light. Allan Schwartzman. *Harper's Bazaar* (January 1990):118-119+

**Ince, Susan**

The Twilight Zone. *Savvy Woman* (November 1990):82-84

Contraceptive Use Dynamics of Couples Availing of Services from Government Family Planning Clinics: A Case Study of Orissa. M. E. Khan, Bella C. Patel, and R. Chandrasekar. *Journal of Family Welfare* 36, No. 3 (September 1990):18-38

The Effect of Birth Spacing on Current Fertility. N. P. Das. *Journal of Family Welfare* 36, No. 4 (December 1990):36-45

Estimation of Potential Fertility Rates by Age-Group for Karnataka State. R. L. Patil. *Journal of Family Welfare* 36, No. 1 (March 1990):3-6

Fertility and Adoption of Family Planning Among the Muslims of 24 Parganas, West Bengal, Part II. A. K. Ghosh and N. K. Das. *Journal of Family Welfare* 36, No. 1 (March 1990):32-42

How Delaying Marriage and Spacing Births Contributes to Population Control: An Explanation with Illustrations. T. Rajaretnam. *Journal of Family Welfare* 36, No. 4 (December 1990):3-13

The Impact of Infant Mortality on Fertility Behaviour of Women. S. B. Singh Parmar. *Journal of Family Welfare* 36, No. 1 (March 1990):43-47

The Influence of a Community-Based Distribution Programme on Contraceptive Choice. K. Seshagiri Rao. *Journal of Family Welfare* 36, No. 3 (September 1990):86-106

Interrelationship Between Breastfeeding and Lactational Amenorrhoea In a Rural Community of Haryana. M. S. Bhatia and others. *Journal of Family Welfare* 36, No. 4 (December 1990):75-77

Medical Termination of Pregnancy and Concurrent Contraceptive Acceptance. Armin Jamshedji and Narayan Kokate. *Journal of Family Welfare* 36, No. 3 (September 1990):39-53

A New Strategy for Family Welfare in the Corporate Sector. Nina Puri. *Journal of Family Welfare* 36, No. 4 (December 1990):14-19

Population Planning in India: Policy Issues and Research Priorities. Edited by Ashish Bose and P. B. Desai. Reviewed by K. Sivaswamy Srikantan. *Journal of Family Welfare* 36, No. 3 (September 1990):107-110

Religion, Social Change and Fertility Behaviour. By R. Jayasree. Reviewed by K. B. Pathak. *Journal of Family Welfare* 36, No. 2 (June 1990):69-70

Socio-Demographic Profile of Tubectomy Acceptors: An Army Experience. P. K. Dutta, L. S. Vaz, and Harinder Singh. *Journal of Family Welfare* 36, No. 1 (March 1990):56-60

**India – Feminist Movement**

Why I Do Not Call Myself a Feminist. Madhu Kishwar. *Manushi* 61 (November-December 1990):2-8

**India – Film Criticism – Feminist Perspectives**

Letters to Daddy. By Raj Kapoor. Reviewed by Mukul Kesavan. *Manushi* 58 (May-June 1990):43-44

Main Azad Hoon: The Politics of Myth and Reality. By Tinnu Anand. Reviewed by Harsh Sethi. *Manushi* 56 (January-February 1990):43-44

Rihaee. By Aruna Raje. Reviewed by Anu. *Manushi* 57 (March-April 1990):43-44

**India – Health Care**

Impact of Training on the Performance of Traditional Birth Attendants. S. K. Benara and S. K. Chaturvedi. *Journal of Family Welfare* 36, No. 4 (December 1990):32-35

Managerial Skills: A Need for Effective Vaccination Coverage. P. L. Joshi, M. Bhattacharya and B. Raj. *Journal of Family Welfare* 36, No. 2 (June 1990):43-49

The North-South Difference: Contrasting Cultural Traditions of Two Migrant Groups in Delhi. Alaka Basu. *Manushi* 57 (March-April 1990):16-21

Work Pattern of Women and Its Impact on Health and Nutrition. M. E. Khan, A. K. Tamang, and Bella C. Patel. *Journal of Family Welfare* 36, No. 2 (June 1990):3-22

**India – Land Rights**

Narmada People Demand Their Land Rights. Charlotte Sankey. *Spare Rib* 219 (December 1990-January 1991):68-69

**India – Legal System.** *See also* Hindu Law

The Special Marriage Act: Not Special Enough. Ruth Vanita. *Manushi* 58 (May-June 1990):14-21

What the Law Says. *Manushi* 57 (March-April 1990):2+

**India – Marriage**

Inter-District and Inter-Regional Variations In Incidence of Child Marriage Among Females and Its Inter-Censal Changes in Uttar Pradesh. J. N. Srivastava. *Journal of Family Welfare* 36, No. 4 (December 1990):20-31

Marriage and Remarriage Among Bombay Roman Catholics. S. Irudaya Rajan. *Journal of Family Welfare* 36, No. 1 (March 1990):61-79

Socio-Economic Characteristics Influencing Age at Marriage in a Tamil Nadu Village. N. Audiarayana and M. Senthilnayaki. *Journal of Family Welfare* 36, No. 1 (March 1990):48-55

**India – Media and Communications**

Women in Indian Broadcasting. P. C. Chatterji. *Manushi* 61 (November-December 1990):33-36

**India – Migration, Internal**

Developmental Migration: A Processual Analysis of Inter-State Rural-Rural Migration. By B. R. K. Rajw. Reviewed by Shekhar Mukerji. *Journal of Family Welfare* 36, No. 4 (December 1990):78-81

**India – Politics and Government**

In Defence of Our *Dharma*. Madhu Kishwar. *Manushi* 60 (September-October 1990):2-15

The Kashmir Crisis: What Are Our Options? Madhu Kishwar. *Manushi* 58 (May-June 1990):2-8

### India – Poverty

In Defence of Their Livelihood: Hirabehn Parmar and Waste Pickers of Ahmedabad. Elisabeth Bentley. *Manushi* 60 (September-October 1990):16-21

### India – Prostitution

Devadasis in India. *Women's World* , No. 24 (Winter 1990/91): 28-29

The Evolution of a Community: *Devdasis* of Goa. Mario Cabral e Sa. *Manushi* 56 (January-February 1990):25-27

Fight for Prostitutes' Rights as Citizens. Maithri Forum for Women. *Manushi* 58 (May-June 1990):35-36

India: Debate on Prostitution Legislation. *Women's World* , No. 24 (Winter 1990/91): 38-39

A Positive Verdict. Shaila Shah. *Spare Rib* No. 216 (September 1990):36-37

Refracted Reality: The 1935 Calcutta Police Survey of Prostitutes. Notes. Bibliography. Indrani Chatterjee. *Manushi* 57 (March-April 1990):26-36

### India – Reproductive Technology

Genetic Exploitation: Interview with an Eco-Feminist. Theresia Degener. *Connexions* 32 (1990):14-15

### India – Social Science Research – Feminist Perspectives

Learning to Take People Seriously. Madhu Kishwar. *Manushi* 56 (January-February 1990):2-10

### India – Status of Women. *See also* India – Violence Against Women

Akshara. *Women's World* 23 (April 1990):40

The Elusive Promise: The Struggle of Women Development Workers in Rural North India. By Sylvia Hale. Reviewed by Sue Ellen Charlton. *Signs* 15, No. 4 (Summer 1990):860-864

How Elite Is Elite?: Women in the Civil Services. *Manushi* 56 (January-February 1990):18-21

Indian Women and Patriarchy: Conflicts and Dilemmas of Students and Working Women. By Maria Mies. Reviewed by Kalpana Bardhan. *Journal of Women's History* 2, No. 1 (Spring 1990):200-219

Inheritance Rights for Women: A Response to Some Commonly Expressed Fears. Madhu Kishwar and Ruth Vanita. *Manushi* 57 (March-April 1990):3-15

Invisible Hands: Women in Home-Based Production. Edited by Andrea Menefee Singh and Anita Kelles-Viitanen. Reviewed by Kalpana Bardhan. *Journal of Women's History* 2, No. 1 (Spring 1990):200-219

Lifestyle as Resistance: The Case of the Courtesans of Lucknow, India. Veena Taylor Oldenburg. *Feminist Studies* 16, No. 2 (Summer 1990):259-287

May You Be the Mother of a Hundred Sons: A Journey Among the Women of India. By Elisabeth Bumiller. Reviewed by Nina Mehta. *The Women's Review of Books* 8, No. 3 (December 1990):19-20

Multiple Mediations: Feminist Scholarship in the Age of Multinational Reception. Lata Mani. *Women & Language* 13, No. 1 (Fall 1990):56-58

The North-South Difference: Contrasting Cultural Traditions of Two Migrant Groups in Delhi. Alaka Basu. *Manushi* 57 (March-April 1990):16-21

The Perfect Wife: The Orthodox Hindu Woman According to the Stri6dharmapaddhati of Tryambakayajvan. By I. Julia Leslie. Reviewed by Albertine Gaur. *Gender & History* 2, No. 2 (Summer 1990):223-225

Profiles in Female Poverty: A Study of Five Poor Working Women in Kerala. By Leela Gulati. Reviewed by Kalpana Bardhan. *Journal of Women's History* 2, No. 1 (Spring 1990):200-219

Putting Herself into the Picture. Notes. Bibliography. Jyofsna Kapur. *Manushi* 56 (January-February 1990):28-37

The Status of Women and Family Planning Acceptance: Some Field Results. Ramamani Sundar. *Journal of Family Welfare* 36, No. 2 (June 1990):60-68

Struggling with Hope: The Story of Women Fish Vendors of South Kerala. Aleyamma Vijayan. *Manushi* 61 (November-December 1990):9-11

We Will Smash this Prison! Indian Women in Struggle. By Gail Omvedt. Reviewed by Kalpana Bardhan. *Journal of Women's History* 2, No. 1 (Spring 1990):200-219

Wives of the God-King: The Rituals of the Davadasis of Puri. By Frédérique Apffel Marglin. Reviewed by Albertine Gaur. *Gender & History* 2, No. 2 (Summer 1990):223-225

A Woman's Tale. Bonophool. *Manushi* 61 (November-December 1990):32

Women, Work and Property in North-West India. By Ursula Sharma. Reviewed by Kalpana Bardhan. *Journal of Women's History* 2, No. 1 (Spring 1990):200-219

The Working Women's Forum – Through Slum Women's Eyes. Usha Jesudasan. *Women in Action* 1-2 (1990):21-23

### India – Telangana Uprising

"We Were Making History": Women and the Telangana Uprising. Edited by Stree Shakti Sanghathana. Reviewed by Lata Mani. *The Women's Review of Books* 7, No. 9 (June 1990):13-14

**India – Tribes**

All for Survival. P. R. Shukla. *Manushi* 61 (November-December 1990):12-14

**India – Violence Against Women**

Dowry Death. Steve Lerner and Mary Ellin Barrett. *Lear's* (May 1990):98-101+

Fighting Wife Abuse in India. Alice Henry. *off our backs* 20, No. 3 (March 1990):21

How AWAG Dealt with a Rapist. Ila Pathak and Amina Amin. *Manushi* 58 (May-June 1990):37-38

Sex Determination Tests in Surat – A Survey Report. Uma Arora and Amprapali Desai. *Manushi* 60 (September-October 1990):37-38

Victim of Family Conspiracy: The Abduction of Farah. *Manushi* 56 (January-February 1990):11-13

When a Poor Woman Gets Raped. Rupande Ranalal. *Manushi* 60 (September-October 1990):34-36

**India – Women's Movement**

Trying to Give Women Their Due: The Story of Vitner Village. *Manushi* No. 59 (July-August 1990):29-32

**India – Women's Organizations**

A Formula of Light and Heavy Issues. Alice Henry. *off our backs* 20, No. 3 (March 1990):20-21

Income Generating Programmes for Women: Some Pitfalls. Mira Savara. *Manushi* 58 (May-June 1990):30-33

**Indians of North America.** *See also* Navajo Indians

Innu Women and Nation: The Occupation of Nistassinan. Winona LaDuke. *off our backs* 20, No. 10 (November 1990):10+

Strawberry Festival. Greg Sarris. *NWSA Journal* 2, No. 3 (Summer 1990):408-424

**Indians of North America – Art**

Surviving as a Native Woman Artist. Joane Cardinal-Schubert. *Canadian Women's Studies* 11, No. 1 (Spring 1990):50-51

Voice in the Blood. Agnes Grant. *Canadian Women's Studies* 11, No. 1 (Spring 1990):11-14

**Indians of North America – Craft Arts**

Crafting a Tradition. Christine Mather. *McCall's* 118, No. 1 (October 1990):117-120

**Indians of North America – Domestic Violence**

In Search of a Nonviolent Past. Barbara Findlen. *Ms.* 1, No. 2 (September/October 1990):46

**Indians of North America – Housing**

Third World Housing Development and Indigenous People in North America. Winona LaDuke. *Canadian Women's Studies* 11, No. 2 (Fall 1990):12-14

**Indians of North America – Literature**

Voice of First Mother. Paula Gunn Allen. *Ms.* 1, No. 2 (September/October 1990):25-26

**Indians of North America – Personal Narratives**

American Indian Women: Telling Their Lives. By Gretchen M. Bataille and Kathleen Mullen Sands. Reviewed by Manuel G. Gonzales. *Tulsa Studies in Women's Literature* 9, No. 1 (Spring 1990):152-156

Interview with Paula Gunn Allen. Jane Caputi. *Trivia* 16/17 (Fall 1990):50-67

**Indians of North America – Politics and Government**

Justificatory Rhetoric for a Female Political Candidate: A Case Study of Wilma Mankiller. Janis L. King. *Women's Studies in Communication* 13, No. 2 (Fall 1990):21-38

**Indians of North America – Spirituality**

Indian Spiritual Abuse. Andrea Smith. *NWSAction* 3, No. 1/2 (Spring 1990): 35-36

**Indians of North America – Status of Women**

Before the "Trail of Tears." Teresa Amott and Julie Matthaei. *Ms.* 1, No. 3 (November/December 1990):82-83

**Indians of North America in Literature**

Coming-of-Age among Contemporary American Indians as Portrayed in Adolescent Fiction. Carol Markstrom-Adams. *Adolescence* 25, No. 97 (Spring 1990):225-237

**Indigenous Women's Conference**

International Indigenous Women's Conference. Jackie Huggins. *Australian Feminist Studies* No. 11 (Autumn 1990):113-114

**Individualism.** *See also* Feminism – Theory

**Individuality**

Rogue. Kirsten Backstrom. *Trivia* 16/17 (Fall 1990):3-17

**Indonesia – Status of Women**

Women and Work in the Third World: Indonesian Women's Oral Histories. Walter L. Williams. *Journal of Women's History* 2, No. 1 (Spring 1990):183-195

**Indoor Air Pollution.** *See* Air Pollution – Indoors

**Industrial Designers.** *See also* Glaser, Milton (about)

Phone by Krohn. Anne Rosenbaum. *Harper's Bazaar* (February 1990):96

**Industrialization**

Industrialization and Household and Family Life Course Characteristics: Appalachian Kentucky Young Adults in 1880 and 1910. Thomas A. Arcury. *Journal of Family History* 15, No. 3 (July 1990):285-312

Women and Industrialization: Gender at Work in Nineteenth-Century England. By Judy Lown.

Reviewed by Leslie Howsam. *Atlantis* 15, No. 2 (Spring 1990):106-107

Working Women, Gender, and Industrialization in Nineteenth-Century France: The Case of Lorraine Embroidery Manufacturing. Whitney Walton. *Journal of Women's History* 2, No. 2 (Fall 1990):42-65

### Industry – Social Policy

A New Strategy for Family Welfare in the Corporate Sector. Nina Puri. *Journal of Family Welfare* 36, No. 4 (December 1990):14-19

**Industry and Education.** *See also* Technical Education

Getting Your MBA on Company Time. Magaly Olivero. *Working Woman* (January 1990):91-92

Pioneer Intern Program Teaches Basic Work Skills. Janette Scandura. *Working Woman* (January 1990):76

### Inertia (Mechanics)

Inertia. K. C. Cole. *Lear's* (May 1990):112-113 +

**Infant Development.** *See also* Child Development

Everybody Loves a Baby. Shana Aborn and Marianne Wait. *Ladies' Home Journal* 107, No. 3 (March 1990):141-146

How to Read Your Baby's Mind. Peggy Brown. *Working Mother* 13, No. 4 (April 1990):46-49

Hush, Little Baby. Robin Sanders. *Ladies' Home Journal* 107, No. 3 (March 1990):88

It's a New Life – for You, Too! *Redbook* 175, No. 6 (October 1990):28-30

Ready, Set, Crawl! Anne Cassidy. *Working Mother* 13, No. 10 (October 1990):81-85

Routines Are Reassuring to Babies. Dianne Hales. *Working Mother* 13, No. 4 (April 1990):82-85

**Infant Formula.** *See* Infants – Nutrition

**Infant Mortality.** *See* Maternal and Infant Welfare; Mortality Statistics

### Infants

Diaper Set. Peggy Eastman. *Working Mother* (November 1990):122-124; (December 1990):69

How Babies Fall in Love. Eva Conrad. *Working Mother* (December 1990):57-62

The Medical Construction of Gender: Case Management of Intersexed Infants. Suzanne J. Kessler. *Signs* 16, No. 1 (Autumn 1990):3-26

**Infants – Kidnapping.** *See* Kidnapping

**Infants – Mortality.** *See* Mortality Statistics

### Infants – Nutrition

A Feed-Your-Baby Quiz. Michelle Patrick. *Essence* 20, No. 11 (March 1990):104 +

### Infants – Travel

The Joys of Traveling with My Baby. Trish Hall. *McCall's* 117, No. 7 (April 1990):10 +

**Infertility.** *See also* In Vitro Fertilization

Are Superovulants Necessary in IVF Procedures? Nick Tonti-Filippini. *Healthright* 9, No. 3 (May 1990):10-13

The Baby Bust. Monique Burns. *Essence* 21, No. 6 (October 1990):34-35

Failures of Volition: Female Agenda and Infertility in Historical Perspective. Notes. Margarete J. Sandelowski. *Signs* 15, No. 3 (Spring 1990):475-499

Infertility Counselling: Should Surrogacy Be an Option? Sue Craig. *Healthright* 9, No. 2 (February 1990):25-29

Reproductive Slights: What's Happened to Contraceptive Research? Boyd Zenner. *Iris* 24 (Fall-Winter 1990):20-24

Sarah and the Women's Movement: The Experience of Infertility. Dina Afek. *Women and Therapy* 10, Nos. 1/2 (1990):195-203

Sperm Story. Larry Wallberg. *Lear's* (September 1990):100-101

A Tale of Two Mothers. Deborah Beroset Diamond. *Ladies' Home Journal* 107, No. 7 (July 1990):83-85 +

Tehilah: Our Answered Prayer. Chava Willig Levy. *McCall's* 118, No. 3 (December 1990):138-140

Tell Us What You Think: Should Infertility Treatments Be Covered by Insurance? *Glamour* (May 1990):188

Thinking Through Infertility. Jane Covernton. *Healthsharing* 11, No. 1 (December 1989):29-33

This Is What You Thought: Infertility Treatments: Who Pays? *Glamour* (July 1990):99

Will I Be Able to Have a Baby? Judith D. Schwartz. *Glamour* (December 1990):222-223 +

### Infertility – Psychological Aspects

Fault Lines: Infertility and Imperiled Sisterhood. Margarete Sandelowski. *Feminist Studies* 16, No. 1 (Spring 1990):33-51

**Infidelity.** *See also* Extramarital Affairs

What He's Gotta Have It. Bebe Moore Campbell. *Essence* 21, No. 8 (December 1990):60-61 +

### Information Services

International Women's Tribune Center. *Women's World* 23 (April 1990):52

Isis International. *Women's World* 23 (April 1990):49-50

Isis-Women's International Cross-Cultural Exchange. *Women's World* 23 (April 1990):44

Technology: How a Knowledge Detective Can Help You Find Success. Georgene Muller. *Working Woman* (February 1990):44-49

Tech Talk. *Working Woman* (September 1990):94-96

**Information Systems**

Tech Talk. *Working Woman* (December 1990):42

**Ingall, Marjorie**

The Joy of (Protected) Sex. *McCall's* 117, No. 12 (September 1990):76-78

Sci-Fi Eye Surgery. *McCall's* 118, No. 2 (November 1990):22

**Ingram, Angela** (joint editor). *See* Broe, Mary Lynn

**Inheritance**

Inheritance Rights for Women: A Response to Some Commonly Expressed Fears. Madhu Kishwar and Ruth Vanita. *Manushi* 57 (March-April 1990):3-15

**Inheritance Customs.** *See* India – Status of Women; Marriage – Prenuptial Contracts

Inheritance in America: From Colonial Times to the Present. By Carole Shammas, Marylynn Salmon, and Michael Dahlin. Reviewed by Mary M. Schweitzer. *Gender and Society* 4, No. 1 (March 1990):100-101

Wills, Inheritance, and the Moral Order in the Seventeenth-Century Agenais. Gregory Hanlon and Elspeth Carruthers. *Journal of Family History* 15, No. 2 (April 1990):149-161

**Injuries.** *See* Wounds and Injuries

**In-Laws**

Love Him, Love His Family? Carol Lynn Mithers. *Glamour* (July 1990):194

**In Laws – Humor**

Marriage & Humor – a Perfect Union. Judith Viorst. *Redbook* 175, No. 5 (September 1990):72-74

**Innes, Charlotte**

Daughter of Warriors Aids World's Women. *New Directions for Women* 19, No. 1 (January/February 1990):3

Gender Adventure. *New Directions for Women* 19, No. 5 (September-October 1990):17

Lesbians Get Pink-Tagged. *New Directions for Women* 19, No. 2 (March/April 1990):6-7

Sexing the Cherry. Book Review. *New Directions for Women* 19, No. 5 (September-October 1990):17

**Inquisition (Roman Catholic Church).** *See* Venice – Inquisition – History

**Insanity.** *See* Great Britain – Mental Disorders

**Insect Pests – Control**

No Fumes, No Chemicals, No Pests. Alexandra Tanski. *McCall's* 118, No. 2 (November 1990):21

**Insomnia**

Insomniacs: Read This and Sleep. Donna Heiderstadt. *Lear's* (November 1990):55-57

**Inspiration**

In the Spirit: Take Courage! Susan L. Taylor. *Essence* 21, No. 8 (December 1990):41

In the Spirit: The Ties That Bind. Susan L. Taylor. *Essence* 20, No. 12 (April 1990):49

**Institute of Traditional Judaism.** *See also* Judaism, Fundamentalist

**Institutional Discrimination.** *See* Employment – Gender Discrimination

**Insurance**

Is Your Insurance "Overdressed"? Debra Wishik Englander. *Savvy Woman* (July/August 1990):24-25

**Insurance – Automobile.** *See also* Consumer Information

**Insurance, Health**

Code B, for Bothered and Bewildered. Joseph Anthony. *Lear's* (November 1990):42-44

Health: New Cancer Treatments. Vicki Monks. *Vogue* (August 1990):236-240

Tell Us What You Think: Should Infertility Treatments Be Covered by Insurance? *Glamour* (May 1990):188

**Insurance, Life**

More for Your Money. Barbara Gilder Quint. *Glamour* (May 1990):160-162

**Insurance – Long-Term Care**

Don't Be a Victim of Future Shock. Debra Wishik. *Savvy Woman* (January 1990):23-24

**Insurance, Renters'**

More for Your Money. Bibliography. Barbara Gilder Quint. *Glamour* (August 1990):112-114

**Insurance Fraud**

Women Who Make a Difference. Alice Rindler Shapin. *Family Circle* 103, No. 16 (November 27, 1990):17-19

**Intellectual Development.** *See also* Gifted Children

**Intellectual Development – Environmental Factors**

Relations between Early Childhood Care Arrangements and College Students' Psychosocial Development and Academic Performance. Jean M. Ispa, Kathy R. Thornburg, and Mary M. Gray. *Adolescence* 25, No. 99 (Fall 1990):529-542

**Intellectual Development – Gender Differences**

Towards a Feminist Reassessment of Intellectual Virtue. Jane Braaten. *Hypatia* 5, No. 3 (Fall 1990):1-14

The New Wonder Kitchens. *Family Circle* 103, No. 4 (March 13, 1990):88-93

Old Meets New: Kitchens with a Past. *Glamour* (September 1990):334-336

Points of View. *Glamour* (August 1990):236-239

Room for Improvement. Lauren Payne and Karen J. Reisler. *Ladies' Home Journal* 107, No. 5 (May 1990):168-174

Sponge It. *Family Circle* 103, No. 2 (February 1, 1990):76-77

Style. Laurie Tarkan. *Lear's* (March 1990):102-109

Style from Scratch. *Glamour* (May 1990):296-299

Tables: All Set. Bibliography. David Feld. *Mademoiselle* (December 1990):68+

A Timesaver Kitchen. Sally Clark. *McCall's* 117, No. 9 (June 1990):103-111

Top Gun. James Grant. *Harper's Bazaar* (October 1990):204-207

Victorian Decorating. *Family Circle* 103, No. 11 (August 14, 1990):90-96

On the Waterfront. Lauren Payne and Karen J. Reisler. *Ladies' Home Journal* 107, No. 4 (April 1990):166-170

**Interior Lighting.** *See* Lighting, Architectural and Decorative

**International Business Enterprises**

Foreign Intrigue. Anne R. Field. *Savvy Woman* (November 1990):29-32

**International Interdisciplinary Congress of Women – Conferences**

Two American Conferences. Patricia Grimshaw and Marilyn Lake. *Australian Feminist Studies* No. 12 (Summer 1990):115 116

**International Ladies' Garment Workers Union**

Susan Cowell Champions the Union Label. Laura Mansnerus. *McCall's* 117, No. 8 (May 1990):51

**International Lesbian and Gay Association**

Falling Borders, Rising Hopes: Europe in 1992. Shelley Anderson. *Out/Look* No. 10 (Fall 1990):30-35

**International Summit for Women**

International Summit for Women: Many Dimensions of Lesbians and Power. Patricia Tavormina. *off our backs* 20, No. 8 (August/September 1990):24

**International Trade Policy.** *See also* Global Economy

Entrepreneurs Take It Abroad. Patricia Schiff Estes. *Lear's* (August 1990):28-31

**International Travel.** *See* Travel

**International Women's Day Video Festival**

Women's Video Festival to Reach National Audience in April. *Media Report to Women* 18, No. 2 (March/April 1990):7

**International Women's Tribune Center**

Transformation of IWTC's Resource Center. *Women's World* 23 (April 1990):29-32

**Interns.** *See* Business – Internships

**Interpersonal Relations**

Correlates of Relationship Satisfaction in Lesbian Couples. Natalie S. Eldridge and Lucia A. Gilbert. *Psychology of Women Quarterly* 14, No. 1 (March 1990):43-62

The Influence of Gender on Reported Disclosure, Interrogation, and Nonverbal Immediacy in Same-Sex Dyads: An Empirical Study of Uncertainty Reduction Theory. Judith A. Sanders, Richard L. Wiseman, and S. Irene Matz. *Women's Studies in Communication* 13, No. 2 (Fall 1990):85-108

What He Really Wants Is a Dog. By Katie Campbell. Reviewed by Sue Murphy. *Spare Rib* No. 210 (March 1990):34-35

**Interpersonal Relations – Adolescents**

The Contribution of Significant Others to Adolescents' Self-Esteem. Katica Lackovic2-Grgin and Maja Dekovic2. *Adolescence* 25, No. 100 (Winter 1990):839-846

Development or Restoration of Trust in Interpersonal Relationships during Adolescence and Beyond. Christina E. Mitchell. *Adolescence* 25, No. 100 (Winter 1990):847-854

**Interpersonal Relations – Criticism**

Take It Standing Up. Diane Cole. *Executive Female* 13, No. 4 (July-August 1990):16-17

**Interracial Marriage.** *See also* Children, Mixed-Race; Daly, Tyne (about); Interracial Relations

**Interracial Marriage in Literature**

Clover. By Dori Sanders. Reviewed by Paula Giddings. *Essence* 21, No. 5 (September 1990):52

**Interracial Relations**

Black & White Love Affairs. Charla Krupp. *Glamour* (October 1990):194-196

White Boys. Edited by Diane Weathers. *Essence* 20, No. 12 (April 1990):64-66+

**Interviewing.** *See also* Management Techniques

The Art of the Interview. William S. Swan. *Working Woman* (May 1990):96-97

Connecting Method and Epistemology: A White Woman Interviewing Black Women. Rosalind Edwards. *Women's Studies International Forum* 13, No. 5 (1990):477-490

**Intestines – Diseases**

Good Health: Stomach Distress! Linda Troiano. *Redbook* 175, No. 4 (August 1990):32-34

**Intimacy.** *See also* Family Life – Role Sharing

Interstices of Race and Class: Creating Intimacy. Anna Lee. *Lesbian Ethics* 4, No. 1 (Spring 1990): 77-83

A Politics of Intimate Life: A Funny Thing Happened on the Way Through the Eighties. Roberta Hamilton. *Atlantis* 15, No. 2 (Spring 1990):82-89

**Intimacy – Adolescents**

The Development of Intimate Relationships in Late Adolescence. Elizabeth L. Paul and Kathleen M. White. *Adolescence* 25, No. 98 (Summer 1990):375-400

**Intolerance**

L'intolérance: une problem2atique généale. By Lise Noël. Reviewed by Jacinthe Michaud. *Resources for Feminist Research* 19, No. 1 (March 1990):21

**Intrauterine Devices.** *See* Contraception

**Inventors**

Becoming Inventors: Women Who Aspire to Invent. Helene Cummins, Susan A. McDaniel, and Rachelle Sender Beauchamp. *Atlantis* 15, No. 2 (Spring 1990):90-93

Black Women and Inventions. Patricia Carter Sluby. *Sage* 6, No. 2 (Fall 1989):33-35

Invention Begins at Forty: Older Women of the 19th Century as Inventors. Autumn Stanley. *Journal of Women and Aging* 2, No. 2 (1990):133-151

**Investing.** *See also* Business Presentations; Loans; Municipal Bonds; Real Estate Investment; Risk Taking

The Bloc Party. Virginia Randall. *Executive Female* 13, No. 5 (September-October 1990):40-41

Deal Her In. Mark Stewart Gill. *Savvy Woman* (June 1990):19-20

Investing in a World Gone Wide. Nancy Dunnan. *Lear's* (May 1990):32-35

Nest Eggs for the '90s. Ellen Schultz. *Savvy Woman* (June 1990):22-23

Smart Investor: Playing the Global Market. Nancy Dunnan. *Lear's* (April 1990):26-28

The Smart Money Adds a Foreign Accent. Ellen Schultz. *Savvy Woman* (March 1990):25-26

Sterling Opportunities. Martin Farmer. *Executive Female* 13, No. 5 (September-October 1990):42-43

Your Money: No Pain, No Gain: How Wall Street Wizards Learned to Invest Their Money. Karen Heller. *Working Woman* (June 1990):42-44

**Investing – Clubs**

Smart Investor: Holding the Ace of Clubs. Nancy Dunnan. *Lear's* (August 1990):26-27

**Investing – Television**

Broadcast Finance: The Best on the Airwaves. Nancy Dunnan. *Savvy Woman* (February 1990):29-32

**Investment Banking**

Outsmarting Wall Street. Ellen Wulfhorst. *Savvy Woman* (November 1990):58

**In Vitro Fertilization.** *See also* Infertility

To Be Genetically Tied or Not to Be: A Dilemma Posed by the Use of Frozen Embryos. Susan L. Oliff. *Women's Rights Law Reporter* 12, No. 2 (Summer 1990): 115-122

The Exploitation of a Desire: Women's Experiences with In Vitro Fertilisation – An Exploratory Survey. By Renate D. Klein. Reviewed by Jocelynne Scutt. *Women's Studies International Forum* 13, No. 6 (1990):605-608

Motherhood, Ideology, and the Power to Technology: In Vitro Fertilization Use by Adoptive Mothers. Linda S. Williams. *Women's Studies International Forum* 13, No. 6 (1990):543-552

In Vitro Fertilization: Building Policy from Laboratories to Legislatures. By Andrea L. Bonnicksen. Reviewed by Leigh Anne Chavez. *NWSA Journal* 2, No. 4 (Autumn 1990):652-656

In Vitro Fertilization: Building Policy from Laboratories to Legislatures. By Andre L. Bonnicksen. Reviewed by Helen Bequaert Holmes. *The Women's Review of Books* 7, No. 4 (January 1990):20-21

Women with a Fertility Problem. Renate Klein. *Connexions* 32 (1990):22-23

**Ipsen, Merete** and Sandahl, Jette

The Women's Museum in Denmark. *Journal of Women's History* 2, No. 2 (Fall 1990):168-170

**Iran – Status of Women**

Iran: Exiles in Their Own Land. Mahnaz Afkhami. *Ms.* 1, No. 2 (September/October 1990):10

Iranian Women Filmmakers: A Conference on Contemporary Iranian Cinema. Azadeh. *Spare Rib* No. 210 (March 1990):39

**Iraq – International Relations – Kuwait.** *See also* Kuwait – Politics and Government

**Iraq – Politics and Government**

Dateline Kuwait: A Reporter Inside the Gulf Crisis. Caryle Murphy. *Vogue* (December 1990):300-303+

**Ireland.** *See also* Northern Ireland

Irish Feminism – Looking Back, Looking Forward. Marian Larragy. *Spare Rib* No. 215 (August 1990):38-43

Peggy Deery: An Irish Family at War. By Nell McCafferty. Reviewed by Kathleen Gregory Klein. *Belles Lettres* 5, No. 3 (Spring 1990):5

Women in Ireland. By Jennifer Beale. Reviewed by Eleanor J. Bader. *Belles Lettres* 5, No. 3 (Spring 1990):2-3

### Ireland – Artists

Irish Women Artists: From the 18th Century to the Present Day. Edited by Wanda Ryan-Smolin, Elizabeth Mayes, and Jeni Rogers. Reviewed by Hilary Pyle. *Woman's Art Journal* 11, No. 1 (Spring-Summer 1990):45-47

Irish Women Artists: From the 18th Century to the Present Day. Edited by Wanda Ryan-Smolin, Elizabeth Mayes, and Jeni Rogers. Reviewed by Martha Caldwell. *Woman's Art Journal* 11, No. 1 (Spring-Summer 1990):47-49

### Ireland – History – Feminist Perspectives

Constance Markievicz: An Independent Life. By Anne Haverty. Reviewed by Margaret MacCurtain. *Gender & History* 2, No. 3 (Autumn 1990):365-368

Nuns in Nineteenth Century Ireland. By Caitriona Clear. Reviewed by Margaret MacCurtain. *Gender & History* 2, No. 3 (Autumn 1990):365-368

The Women's Suffrage Movement and Irish Society in the Early Twentieth Century. By Cliona Murphy. Reviewed by Margaret MacCurtain. *Gender & History* 2, No. 3 (Autumn 1990):365-368

### Ireland – Music

The Singing and the Crack – the Heart of the People. Julie McNamara. *Spare Rib* 219 (December 1990-January 1991):24-26

### Ireland – Politics and Government

Women and National Liberation. Jo Tully. *Spare Rib* 219 (December 1990-January 1991):48-51

### Ireland – Status of Women

A Belfast Woman. By Mary Beckett. Reviewed by Maureen Murphy. *Feminist Collections* 11, No. 2 (Winter 1990):5-6

Dublin Belles: Conversations with Dublin Women. By Máirín Johnson. Reviewed by Maureen Murphy. *Feminist Collections* 11, No. 2 (Winter 1990):5-6

Dublin Belles. Edited by Mairin Johnston. Reviewed by Susan Swartzlander. *Belles Lettres* 5, No. 3 (Spring 1990):5

I Am of Ireland: Women of the North Speak Out. Elizabeth Shannon. Reviewed by Maureen Murphy. *Feminist Collections* 11, No. 2 (Winter 1990):5-6

Irié (about). *See also* Carter, Charla, "European Designers to Watch."

### Irie Dance Company

Feeling Irie. Veronica Hill. *Spare Rib* No. 210 (March 1990):16-18

### Irigaray, Luce – Criticism and Interpretation

Equality or Divinity – A False Dichotomy? Morny Joy. *Journal of Feminist Studies in Religion* 6, No. 1 (Spring 1990):9-24

The Story of I: Luce Irigaray's Theoretical Masochism. Emily S. Apter. *NWSA Journal* 2, No. 2 (Spring 1990):186-198

### Iris (journal)

Looking Backward and Forward: Celebrating Ten Years of *Iris*. Kristen Rembold and Jennifer G. Shepherd. *Iris* 24 (Fall-Winter 1990):6-9

### Ironplow, A. Lorraine

Lesbian Ethics: Toward New Value. Book Review. *NWSA Journal* 2, No. 1 (Winter 1990):142-145

### Irvin, Patricia L. (about). *See also* Lawyers

### Irwin, Hadley

The Lilith Summer. Reviewed by Mitzi Myers. *NWSA Journal* 2, No. 2 (Spring 1990):273-281

We Are Mesquakie, We Are One. Reviewed by Mitzi Myers. *NWSA Journal* 2, No. 2 (Spring 1990):273-281

### Isaac, Natalie

The Living Tree: A Woman's Response to Shel Silverstein's "The Giving Tree." Poem. *off our backs* 20, No. 7 (July 1990):19

### Isaacs, Florence (joint author). *See* Fischer, Rita H.

### Isaacson, Judith Magyar

Seed of Sarah: Memoirs of a Survivor. Reviewed by Myrna Goldenberg. *Belles Lettres* 6, No. 1 (Fall 1990):6-9

### Isabell, Robert (about). *See also* Florists

### Isaia N.Y.C.. *See* Swan, Phyllis (about)

### Isaksson, Eva (editor)

Women and the Military System. Reviewed by Ursula Barry. *Women's Studies International Forum* 13, No. 3 (1990):281

### Ishiguro, Kazuo

The Remains of the Day. Reviewed by Kent Black. *Harper's Bazaar* (February 1990):50

### Ishii-Kuntz, Masako

Formal Activities for Elderly Women: Determinants of Participation in Voluntary and Senior Center Activities. *Journal of Women and Aging* 2, No. 1 (1990):79-97

### Islam

Female Circumcision in Africa: Not Just a Medical Problem. Kathleen Kilday. *Iris* 23 (Spring-Summer 1990):38-43

### Islam – Family Structure

Understanding Muslim Households and Families in Late Ottoman Istanbul. Alan Duben. *Journal of Family History* 15, No. 1 (January 1990):71-86

### Islam – Status of Women

Both Left and Right Handed: Arab Women Talk About Their Lives. By Bouthaina Shaaban. Reviewed by Marieme Hélie-Lucas. *Connexions* 34 (1990):22-23

Enforcing the Veil. *Connexions* 34 (1990):7

Unearthing the Present. Fatima Mernissi. *Ms.* 1, No. 3 (November/December 1990):74-75

Women Living Under Muslim Laws. *Women's World* 23 (April 1990):45

### Islamic Fundamentalism

"Fundamentalism" – Haphazardly Used, Never Defined. Liliane Landor. *Spare Rib* No. 209 (February 1990):48

Sacred Cows. By Fay Weldon. Reviewed by Clara Connolly. *Feminist Review* No. 35 (Summer 1990):113-117

### Islamic Law. *See also* India – Legal System

### Islamic Women's Organizations – Bibliographies

Muslim Women in Action. *Women's World* 23 (April 1990):54-58

**Ispa, Jean M.,** Thornburg, Kathy R., and Mary M. Gray

Relations between Early Childhood Care Arrangements and College Students' Psychosocial Development and Academic Performance. *Adolescence* 25, No. 99 (Fall 1990):529-542

### Israel – Adolescents

Analysis of a Double-Layered Support System. Rachel Seginer. *Adolescence* 25, No. 99 (Fall 1990):739-752

### Israel, Betsy

"Role 'Em!": To Get a Part in Hollywood, See These Women. *Mademoiselle* (March 1990):104-106

Sexual Ethics: Men from Our Embarrassing Past. *Glamour* (August 1990):248

Sexual Ethics: The Image Game. *Glamour* (December 1990):244

### Israel – Feminism

Building a Movement: Jewish Feminists Speak Out On Israel. Alisa Solomon. *Bridges* 1, No. 1 (Spring 1990): 41-56

### Israel – Feminist Movement

West Bank and Gaza: Occupied Feminism. Gayle Kirshenbaum. *Ms.* 1, No. 2 (September/October 1990):8

### Israel – Immigration

Fertility Patterns Among Soviet Immigrants to Israel: The Role of Cultural Variables. Shalvia Ben-Barak. *Journal of Family History* 15, No. 1 (January 1990):87-100

### Israel, Kali A. K.

Writing Inside the Kaleidoscope: Re-Representing Victorian Women Public Figures. *Gender & History* 2, No. 1 (Spring 1990):40-48

### Israel – Lesbianism

Israel. Spike Pittsberg. *Feminist Review* No. 34 (Spring 1990):14-18

### Israel – Peace Movement

Jewish Women's Call for Peace: A Handbook for Jewish Women on the Israeli/Palestinian Conflict. By Rita Falbel, Irena Klepfisz, and Donna Neval. Reviewed by Lois Levine. *Bridges* 1, No. 2 (Fall 1990): 125

News Shorts. Vanessa Tait. *Spare Rib* No. 209 (February 1990):44

The Next Step. Melanie Kaye/Kantrowitz. *NWSA Journal* 2, No. 2 (Spring 1990):236-244

Two-thousand March for Mideast Peace. Irena Klepfisz. *New Directions for Women* 19, No. 2 (March/April 1990):16

### Israel – Politics and Government

Votes for Women. Hannah Trager. *Journal of Women's History* 2, No. 1 (Spring 1990):196-199

Women and Politics: The Case of Israel. *Women & Politics* 10, No. 1 (1990):43-57

Yael Dayan. Interview. Susan Weidman Schneider. *Lilith* 15, No. 4 (Fall 1990):10-15

### Israel – Reproductive Technology

Legal Conception. Carmel Shalev. *Connexions* 32 (1990):6-7

### Israel – Status of Women

Adolescents' Attitudes toward Women's Roles: A Comparison between Israeli Jews and Arabs. Rachel Seginer, Mousa Karayanni, and Mariam M. Mar'i. *Psychology of Women Quarterly* 14, No. 1 (March 1990):119-133

Israel: Whose Country Is It Anyway? Andrea Dworkin. *Ms.* 1, No. 2 (September/October 1990):69-79

Israeli Women Press for Change. Miriam Benson. *Lilith* 15, No. 4 (Fall 1990):12-13

### Israeli-Arab Relations. *See also* Palestinian Arabs

Exile in the Promised Land. By Marcia Freedman. Reviewed by Donna Berman. *New Directions for Women* 19, No. 6 (November-December 1990):18

A Handbook for Jewish Women on the Israeli/Palestinian Conflict. By Rita Falbel, Irene Klepfisz, and Donna Nevel. Reviewed by Donna Berman. *New Directions for Women* 19, No. 6 (November-December 1990):18

Massacre at Dome of the Rock. Renu Bhullar. *Spare Rib* 218 (November 1990):15-16

Palestine: Massacre at Dome of the Rock. Marcel Farry. *Spare Rib* 218 (November 1990):12-14

Voices from Gaza: The Inside Story of the Israeli Occupation of Palestine. *Spare Rib* No. 216 (September 1990):33

Women for Peace – Dateline, Jerusalem. Penny Rosenwasser. *off our backs* 20, No. 4 (April 1990):4-5

**Israelis – Poland**

Twelve Days in Poland. Excerpt. Yehudit Hendel. *Lilith* 15, No. 2 (Spring 1990):16-21

**Israeloff, Roberta**

The Art of Comforting a Child. *Working Mother* (November 1990):99-103

Health Report: The Sleep Mystique: Could You Get By on Less? *Working Woman* (September 1990):195-196

Why Was I So Afraid of Therapy? *Working Mother* 13, No. 7 (July 1990):18-22

**Isralowitz, Richard E.** and Hong, Ong Teck

Singapore Youth: The Impact of Social Status on Perceptions of Adolescent Problems. *Adolescence* 25, No. 98 (Summer 1990):357-362

**Isreal, Pat**

Who Do We Think We Are. *Healthsharing* 11, No. 3 (June 1990):11

**Istanbul**

Inside Istanbul. Tad Friend. *Vogue* (October 1990):290+

**Istomin, Marta Casals** (about)

Squeeze Play at the Kennedy Center. Alison Cook. *Lear's* (November 1990):88-92+

**Italian-Americans**

On Being Italian-American. An Introspection. Mary Saracino. *Sinister Wisdom* 41 (Summer-Fall 1990):105-110

Commari: Excerpt of a Dialogue. Angie Angela and Demetria Iazzetto. *Sinister Wisdom* 41 (Summer-Fall 1990):82-88

Connections. Mary Anne Bella Mirabella. *Sinister Wisdom* 41 (Summer-Fall 1990):94-100

The Fault of Memory: "Southern Italy" in the Imagination of Immigrants and the Lives of Their Children in Italian Harlem, 1920-1945. Robert A. Orsi. *Journal of Family History* 15, No. 2 (April 1990):133-147

The Italian Jewish Connection, or, The History of America. Joan Capra. *Sinister Wisdom* 41 (Summer-Fall 1990):101-104

The Legacy. Laurie Mattioli. *Sinister Wisdom* 41 (Summer-Fall 1990):58-65

Living as a Sicilian Dyke. Patrizia Tavormina. *Sinister Wisdom* 41 (Summer-Fall 1990):75-78

Photographs of Home. Celine-Marie Pascale. *Sinister Wisdom* 41 (Summer-Fall 1990):90-93

Rose. Jean Rietschel. *Sinister Wisdom* 41 (Summer-Fall 1990):55-57

Two Kinds of People in the World. Darci Cataldo. *Sinister Wisdom* 41 (Summer-Fall 1990):116-117

**Italian Cookery.** *See* Cookery, Italian

**Italy**

Where It All Began: Italy 1954. By Ann Cornelisen. Reviewed by Mary Taylor Simeti. *The Women's Review of Books* 8, No. 1 (October 1990):13-14

**Italy – Culture**

Italian Collective Inspiration for Booklovers Everywhere. Ruby Rohrlich. *New Directions for Women* 19, No. 1 (January/February 1990):16

Suprema Donnas: The Best of Italy. *Lear's* (February 1990):116-125

**Italy – Fashion**

Bravo Armani! *Harper's Bazaar* (February 1990):136-139

Gucci Again. Georgina Howell. *Vogue* (December 1990):322-327

Milan Montage. *Harper's Bazaar* (March 1990):214-217

Shapes of Things to Come. Julie Moline. *Harper's Bazaar* (February 1990):96

**Italy – Fashion Designers**

Milan: Going for Baroque. *Lear's* (July 1990):102-109

Milan's Mellow Mood. *Harper's Bazaar* (January 1990):90-99

**Italy – Feminist Movement**

Progress "All'Italiana." Claudia B. Flisi. *Ms.* 1, No. 2 (September/October 1990):9

**Italy – History**

Age at Marriage in Nineteenth-Century Italy. Rosella Rettaroli. *Journal of Family History* 15, No. 4 (October 1990):409-425

An Introduction to the History of Italian Family Life. Marzio Barbagli and David Kertzer. *Journal of Family History* 15, No. 4 (October 1990):369-383

The Distinguishing Features of Domestic Service in Italy. Angiolina Arru. *Journal of Family History* 15, No. 4 (October 1990):547-566

Family and Kin – a Few Thoughts. Giovanni Levi. *Journal of Family History* 15, No. 4 (October 1990):567-578

Family Forms and Domestic Service in Southern Italy from the Seventeenth to the Nineteenth Centuries. Giovanna Da Molin. *Journal of Family History* 15, No. 4 (October 1990):503-527

Female Solitude and Patrilineage: Unmarried Women and Widows during the Eighteenth and Nineteenth Centuries. Maura Palazzi. *Journal of Family History* 15, No. 4 (October 1990):443-459

On the Insensitivity of Women: Science and the Woman Question in Liberal Italy, 1890-1910. Mary Gibson. *Journal of Women's History* 2, No. 2 (Fall 1990):11-41

Italian Fertility: An Historical Account. Massimo Livi Bacci and Marco Breschi. *Journal of Family History* 15, No. 4 (October 1990):385-408

Land, Kinship, and Consanguineous Marriage in Italy from the Seventeenth to the Nineteenth Centuries. Raul Merzario. *Journal of Family History* 15, No. 4 (October 1990):529-546

The Peasant Family in Northern Italy, 1750-1930: A Reassessment. Pier Paolo Viazzo and Dionigi Albera. *Journal of Family History* 15, No. 4 (October 1990):461-482

Unaccompanied Ladies: Feminist, Italian, and in the Academy. Maurizia Boscagli. *Differences* 2, No. 3 (Fall 1990):122-135

"Where There's No Woman There's No Home": Profile of the Agro-Pastoral Family in Nineteenth-Century Sardinia. Anna Oppo. *Journal of Family History* 15, No. 4 (October 1990):483-502

Women, Family, and the Law, 1750-1942. Chiara Saraceno. *Journal of Family History* 15, No. 4 (October 1990):427-442

**Italy – Lesbianism**

Italy. Rosanna Fiocchetto. *Feminist Review* No. 34 (Spring 1990):18-22

**Italy – Status of Women**

Donna: Women in Italian Culture. Edited by Ada Testaferri. Reviewed by Santo L. Arico. *Canadian Women's Studies* 11, No. 2 (Fall 1990):91

**Italy – Wine and Winemaking**

Vineyard Haven. Mark Ganem. *Harper's Bazaar* (May 1990):160

**Iturbide, Graciela**

Village Mexico. Photographs. *Ms.* 1, No. 1 (July/August 1990):48-53

**Iversen, Joan**

The Mormon-Suffrage Relationship: Personal and Political Quandaries. *Frontiers* 11, Nos. 2-3 (1990):8-16

**Ivins, Molly**

The Women Who Run Texas. *McCall's* 117, No. 11 (August 1990):98-101+

**Ivory Coast – Prostitution**

Ivory Coast: Prostitution in Schools. *Women's World*, No. 24 (Winter 1990/91): 30

**Iwobi, Anne N.**

Joy. Book Review. *Spare Rib* 217 (October 1990):33

And They Didn't Die. Book Review. *Spare Rib* No. 215 (August 1990):28

Zabat: Poetics of a Family Tree. Poems 1986-1989. add. *Spare Rib* No. 209 (February 1990):31

# J

**Jabbour, Hala Deeb**

A Woman of Nazareth. Reviewed by Suha Sabbagh. *The Women's Review of Books* 7, Nos. 10-11 (July 1990):42-43

**Jabs, Carolyn**

How to Raise a Happy Child. *Working Mother* 13, No. 10 (October 1990):67-72

Relax – Seven Ways to Be a Happy, Stress-Free Parent. *Working Mother* 13, No. 1 (January 1990):56-60

**Jack, Dana Crowley** (joint author). *See* Jack, Rand

**Jack, Rand** and Jack, Dana Crowley

Moral Vision and Professional Decisions: The Changing Values of Women and Men Lawyers. Reviewed by Anne Margolis. *The Women's Review of Books* 7, No. 12 (September 1990):17-18

**Jacka, Tamara**

Asian Studies Association of Australia 8th Biennial Conference, Women's Caucus Day. *Australian Feminist Studies* No. 12 (Summer 1990):109-111

**Jackets.** *See* Clothing and Dress

**Jackson, Deborah**

Three in a Bed: Why You Should Sleep with Your Baby. Reviewed by Meg Hand. *Healthright* 9, No. 3 (May 1990):40

**Jackson, Diana R.** (joint author). *See* Beck, Evelyn Torton

**Jackson, Donna**

How to Stay Sweethearts. *Redbook* 176, No. 1 (November 1990):94-95+

**Jackson, Helen**

An Uphill Battle. *Connexions* 33 (1990):4

**Jackson, Janet** (about). *See also* Beauty, Personal, "Beauty Bazaar"

Janet's Nation. David Ritz. *Essence* 20, No. 11 (March 1990):52-54+

Solid Sister. Stephanie Mansfield. *Vogue* (September 1990):574-579+

**Jackson, Jesse** (about). *See* Sexual Attraction, "200 Words"

**Jackson, Kate** (about). *See* Hair Styles

**Jackson, Katherine** and Wiseman, Richard

My Family, The Jacksons. Reviewed by Paula Giddings. *Essence* 21, No. 8 (December 1990):38

**Jackson, Milt** (about). *See* Music – Jazz

**Jackson, Monica L.**

And Still We Rise: African American Women and the U.S. Labor Market. *Feminist Issues* 10, No. 2 (Fall 1990):55-64

**Jacques, Martin** (joint editor). *See* Hall, Stuart

**Jadack, Rosemary A.**, Keller, Mary L., and Hyde, Janet Shibley

Genital Herpes: Gender Comparisons and the Disease Experience. *Psychology of Women Quarterly* 14, No. 3 (September 1990):419-434

**Jaffe, Rona**

Charmed Wives. *Harper's Bazaar* (September 1990):306-307+

**Jaffee, Peter G.**, Wolfe, David A., and Wilson, Susan Kaye

Children of Battered Women. Reviewed by Sharon Wyse. *On the Issues* 17 (Winter 1990):34-35

**Jagoda, Flory**

Oco Kandelikas. Song. *Bridges* 1, No. 2 (Fall 1990): 32-33

**Jaguar Motor Company.** *See* Automobiles – Design and Construction

**Jahr, Cliff**

The Best Bette Yet. *Ladies' Home Journal* 107, No. 1 (January 1990):92-93+

Cher the Unstoppable. *Ladies' Home Journal* 107, No. 11 (November 1990):197+

Faye Dunaway: Coming Home to Hollywood. *Ladies' Home Journal* 107, No. 3 (March 1990):80-87

Tammy at Twilight. *Ladies' Home Journal* 107, No. 7 (July 1990):88-96

A Wild Night with Cybill Shepherd. *Ladies' Home Journal* 107, No. 2 (February 1990):98-104

**Jahren, Neal**

Comments on Ruth Ginzberg's Paper. *Hypatia* 5, No. 1 (Spring 1990):171-177

**Jain, J. P.** and others

Fight Disease, Not Patients: AIDS Protest in Delhi. *Manushi* 58 (May-June 1990):34

**Jalland, Pat**

Octavia Wilberforce, Pioneer Woman Doctor. Reviewed by Angela V. John. *Gender & History* 2, No. 3 (Autumn 1990):375-377

**Jalland, Pat** (editor)

Octavia Wilberforce. Reviewed by Moira Woods. *Women's Studies International Forum* 13, No. 5 (1990):524-525

**Jamaica – Literature**

Bake-Face and Other Guava Stories. By Opal Palmer Adisa. Reviewed by Suzanne Scafe. *Spare Rib* No. 209 (February 1990):31

**James, Ada Lois** (about)

Historical Society Women's Collections to Be Published. Harry Miller. *Feminist Collections* 11, No. 2 (Winter 1990):13-14

**James, Sibyl**

Love Is All. Poem. *Iris* 24 (Fall-Winter 1990):19

Peach Blossoms. Poem. *Iris* 23 (Spring-Summer 1990):inside front cover

**James, Stanlie M.**

Lives of Courage: Women for a New South Africa. Book Review. *Feminist Collections* 12, No. 1 (Fall 1990):3-6

Maids and Madams: Domestic Workers Under Apartheid. Book Review. *Feminist Collections* 12, No. 1 (Fall 1990):3-6

**Jamison, Judith** (about). *See* De Veaux, Alexis, Milloy, Marilyn, and Ross, Michael Erik

**Jamshedji, Armin** and Kokate, Narayan

Medical Termination of Pregnancy and Concurrent Contraceptive Acceptance. *Journal of Family Welfare* 36, No. 3 (September 1990):39-53

**Janis, Carroll** (about). *See* Family-Owned Business

**Janjua, Shahida** (joint author). *See* Seneviratne, Seni

**Jansen, Mary A.**

Intimate Adversaries – Cultural Conflict between Doctors and Women Patients. Book Review. *Psychology of Women Quarterly* 14, No. 3 (September 1990):437-439

**Japan – Business**

Crafting Selves: Power, Gender and Discourses of Identity in a Japanese Workplace. By Dorinne K. Kondo. Reviewed by Kate Gilbert. *The Women's Review of Books* 8, No. 1 (October 1990):5-7

Crested Kimono: Power and Love in the Japanese Business Family. By Matthews Masayuki Hamabata. Reviewed by Kate Gilbert. *The Women's Review of Books* 8, No. 1 (October 1990):5-7

**Japan – Culture and Society**

Images: Japanese Style. Elisabeth Bumiller. *Vogue* (December 1990):147-156

**Japan – Fashion**

Images: Japanese Style. Elisabeth Bumiller. *Vogue* (December 1990):147-156

**Japan – Feminist Movement**

Japanese Women: Rewriting Tradition. Kumiko Makihara. *Lear's* (February 1990):78-83

**Japan – Gender Roles**

A Japanese View of Dependency: What Can Amae Psychology Contribute to Feminist Theory and Therapy. Carla K. Bradshaw. *Women and Therapy* 9, Nos. 1-2 (1990):67-86

Urban Japanese Housewives: At Home and in the Community. By Anne E. Imamura. Reviewed by Susan Seymour. *Signs* 15, No. 2 (Winter 1990):395-398

**Japan – Language – Gender Differences**

Womansword: What Japanese Words Say about Women. By Kittredge Cherry. Reviewed by Mary Ellen S. Capek. *NWSA Journal* 2, No. 3 (Summer 1990):476-484

**Japan – Menopause**

Menopause in Japan Means Konenki. Margaret Lock. *Healthsharing* 11, No. 4 (December 1990):23-25

**Japan – Race Relations**

A Black Woman in Rural Japan. Viki Radden. *Sage* 6, No. 1 (Summer 1989):52-53

**Japan – Status of Women**

Flowers in Salt: The Beginnings of Feminist Consciousness in Modern Japan. By Sharon L. Sievers. Reviewed by Kathleen Uno. *NWSA Journal* 2, No. 1 (Winter 1990):112-119

Japan: "Rapeman" Comics. Natsuko Yamaguchi. *Ms.* 1, No. 3 (November/December 1990):13

Peasant Women and Divorce in Preindustrial Japan. Notes. Laurel L. Cornell. *Signs* 15, No. 4 (Summer 1990):710-732

Reflections on the Way to the Gallows: Rebel Women in Prewar Japan. Edited by Mikiso Hane. Reviewed by Kathleen Uno. *NWSA Journal* 2, No. 1 (Winter 1990):112-119

**Japan – Technology**

The Bonsai Connection. Peter Feibleman. *Lear's* (April 1990):38-42

**Japan – Travel.** *See* Kyoto (Japan) – Description and Travel

**Japan – Women's Movement**

Evolution of the Feminist Movement in Japan. Machiko Matsui. *NWSA Journal* 2, No. 3 (Summer 1990):435-449

**Japanese-American Women – History**

Issei, Nisei, War Bride: Three Generations of Japanese American Women in Domestic Service. By Evelyn Nakano Glenn. Reviewed by Susan Seymour. *Signs* 15, No. 2 (Winter 1990):395-398

**Japanese-American Women in Literature**

Japanese American Women's Life Stories: Maternality in Monica Sone's *Nisei Daughter* and Joy Kogawa's *Obasan*. Shirley Geok-Lin Lim. *Feminist Studies* 16, No. 2 (Summer 1990):289-312

**Japenga, Ann**

The Separatist Revival. *Out/Look* No. 8 (Spring 1990):78-83

**Jaques, Florence Page**

Canoe Country and Snowshoe Country. Reviewed by Margaret Saunders. *Iris* 23 (Spring-Summer 1990):77-76

**Jaquette, Jane S.** (editor)

The Women's Movement in Latin America: Feminism and the Transition to Democracy. Reviewed by Susana Lastarria-Cornhiel and Wava G. Haney. *Feminist Collections* 12, No. 1 (Fall 1990):9-13

**Jardim, Anne** and Hennig, Margaret

The Last Barrier. *Working Woman* (November 1990):130-134+

**Jaret, Peter**

The Healthy Family. *Family Circle* 103, No. 5 (April 3, 1990):34+

Mind Health: Panic. *Vogue* (September 1990):462-467

Pap Tests: Can You Trust Them? *Glamour* (November 1990):68-75

Women and Heart Disease. *Glamour* (October 1990):68-73

**Jarratt, Elizabeth H.**

Feminist Issues in Sport. *Women's Studies International Forum* 13, No. 5 (1990):491-499

**Jarratt, Susan C.**

The First Sophists and Feminism: Discourses of the "Other." *Hypatia* 5, No. 1 (Spring 1990):27-41

**Jastrzebska, Maria**

Lost in Translation: A Life in a New Language. Book Review. *Spare Rib* No. 214 (July 1990):22

**Jaworski, Margaret**

Circle This. *Family Circle* 103, No. 9 (June 26, 1990):9-10; 103, No. 13 (September 25, 1990):9-12; 103, No. 14 (October 16, 1990):11-14; 103, No. 15 (November 6, 1990):9-10; 103, No. 16 (November 27, 1990):11-12

A Delicate Balance: "This Is Exactly Where I Want to Be." *Ladies' Home Journal* 107, No. 3 (March 1990):162-164

Will Daddy Get Better? *Family Circle* 103, No. 14 (October 16, 1990):100-102

**Jay, Karla** and Glasgow, Joanne (editors)

Lesbian Texts and Contexts: Radical Revisions. Reviewed by Elizabeth Wood. *New Directions for Women* 19, No. 6 (November-December 1990):17

**Jay, Leslie**

Oscar Meets the LHJ Lady. *Ladies' Home Journal* 107, No. 4 (April 1990):50-54

Sandy Duncan Perks Up "The Hogan Family." *Ladies' Home Journal* 107, No. 3 (March 1990):96-98

Women of the Years. *Ladies' Home Journal* 107, No. 11 (November 1990):83-92

**Jayasree, R.**

Religion, Social Change and Fertility Behaviour. Reviewed by K. B. Pathak. *Journal of Family Welfare* 36, No. 2 (June 1990):69-70

**Jayaweera, Swarna**

European Women Educators Under the British Colonial Administration in Sri Lanka. *Women's Studies International Forum* 13, No. 4 (1990):323-331

**Jazz.** *See* Music – Jazz

**Jealousy**

The Most Dangerous Relationships a Woman Can Have. Leslie Dormen. *Ladies' Home Journal* 107, No. 9 (September 1990):106-115

Romantic Revenge. Jeannie Ralston. *Glamour* (April 1990):278-279+

"Who's That Blonde – and Why Is My Boyfriend Smiling at Her?" Johanna Schneller. *Mademoiselle* (January 1990):1344-135+

**Jeans, Mary Ellen** (joint author). *See* Brown-Rowat, Beverly

**Jefferson, Denise**

Sam's Secret. *Essence* 21, No. 6 (October 1990):86-88+

**Jefferson, Sharon**

Back Talk: Donor Organs: A Crisis. *Essence* 21, No. 6 (October 1990):146

**Jeffreys, Sheila – Criticism and Interpretation**

The De-Eroticization of Women's Liberation: Social Purity Movements and the Revolutionary Feminism of Sheila Jeffreys. Margaret Hunt. *Feminist Review* No. 34 (Spring 1990):23-41

**Jelin, Elizabeth** (editor)

Women and Social Change in Latin America. Reviewed by Susana Lastarria-Cornhiel and Wava G. Haney. *Feminist Collections* 12, No. 1 (Fall 1990):9-13

**Jellinek, Margherita**

Intimate Adversaries: Cultural Conflict Between Doctors and Women Patients. Book Review. *AFFILIA* 5, No. 4 (Winter 1990):108-110

Women's Health Perspectives: An Annual Review. Book Review. *AFFILIA* 5, No. 4 (Winter 1990):108-110

**Jenkins, Barbara Williams**

Ann Allen Shockley: An Annotated Primary and Secondary Bibliography. Book Review. *Sage* 6, No. 2 (Fall 1989):63-64

**Jenkins, Christine**

True Stories: Biographies of Women for Young Readers. *Feminist Collections* 12, No. 1 (Fall 1990):6-9

**Jenkins, Henry**

"If I Could Speak With Your Sound": Fan Music, Textual Proximity, and Liminal Identification. *Camera Obscura* , No. 23 (May 1990):148-175

**Jenkins, Linda Walsh** (joint editor). *See* Chinoy, Helen Krich

**Jenkins, Mercilee M.**

Teaching the New Majority: Guidelines for Cross-Cultural Communication Between Students and Faculty. *Feminist Teacher* 5, No. 1 (Spring 1990):8-14

**Jennings, Lynn** (about)

Full Speed Ahead. Kate Delhagen. *Women's Sports & Fitness* 12, No. 6 (September 1990):26-28

**Jennings, Maude M.**

How It All Began: Sour Grapes. Play. *Feminist Teacher* 5, No. 2 (Fall 1990):16-19

**Jennings, Maude M.**, Thornburg, Mary Patterson, and Williams, Gari L.

Tell Them a Story. *Feminist Teacher* 5, No. 2 (Fall 1990):15

**Jennings, Thelma**

"Us Colored Women Had to Go Through A Plenty": Sexual Exploitation of African-American Slave Women. *Journal of Women's History* 1, No. 3 (Winter 1990):45-74

**Jensen, Brian** (joint author). *See* Moore, J. William

**Jensen, Larry Cyril** (joint author). *See* Phinney, Virginia G.

**Jensen, Rita**

A Day in the Life. *Ms.* 1, No. 2 (September/October 1990):38-41

**Jesness Inventory**

The MMPI and Jesness Inventory as Measures of Effectiveness on an Inpatient Conduct Disorders Treatment Unit. Gregory Roberts, Kenneth Schmitz, John Pinto, and Stanley Cain. *Adolescence* 25, No. 100 (Winter 1990):989-996

**Jesudasan, Usha**

The Working Women's Forum – Through Slum Women's Eyes. *Women in Action* 1-2 (1990):21-23

**Jet Lag.** *See* Business Travel – Health Aspects

**Jewell, Terri L.**

Barbara Smith and Kitchen Table Women of Color Press. *Hot Wire* 6, No. 2 (May 1990):20-22+

She Who Bears the Thorn. Poem. *Iris* 24 (Fall-Winter 1990):18

Women for All Seasons: Poetry and Prose about Transitions in Women's Lives. Book Review. *New Directions for Women* 19, No. 1 (January/February 1990):25

**Jewelry**

Fashion Faux. *Glamour* (July 1990):140

The Tribe of Dina: A Jewish Women's Anthology. Edited by Melanie Kaye-Kantrowitz and Irena Klepfisz. Reviewed by Julia Wolf Mazow. *Lilith* 15, No. 1 (Winter 1990):6-7

**Jewish Women – Personal Narratives**

Night of the Staircase. Ada Aharoni and Thea Wolf. *Lilith* 15, No. 4 (Fall 1990):7-9

Remember Who You Are: Stories about Being Jewish. By Esther Hautzig. Reviewed by Joan Joffe Hall. *Lilith* 15, No. 3 (Summer 1990):6

Why Women Are Writing Holocaust Memoirs Now. Bibliography. Ellen Fishman. *Lilith* 15, No. 2 (Spring 1990):6-7+

**Jewish Women – Poetry**

Sarah's Daughters Sing: A Sampler of Poems by Jewish Women. Edited by Henny Wenkart. Reviewed by Alicia Ostriker. *Lilith* 15, No. 3 (Summer 1990):6

**Jewish Women – Social Activism.** See also Dayan, Yael (about)

Ernestine L. Rose, Women's Rights Pioneer, 2nd edition. By Yuri Suhl. Reviewed by Rachel Kadish. *Lilith* 15, No. 4 (Fall 1990):34

Israeli Women Press for Change. Miriam Benson. *Lilith* 15, No. 4 (Fall 1990):12-13

A Precious Moment in Chile. Hilary Marcus. *Lilith* 15, No. 4 (Fall 1990):36

**Jezic, Diane Peacock**

Women Composers: A Lost Tradition Found. Reviewed by Ann Armin. *Canadian Women's Studies* 11, No. 1 (Spring 1990):109

Women Composers: The Lost Tradition Found. Reviewed by Priscilla Little. *Iris* 23 (Spring-Summer 1990):74-75

**Jhirad, Susan**

Gender Gaps. *The Women's Review of Books* 7, No. 5 (February 1990):30

**Jibrin, Janis**

Nutrition Now: Move Over, Oat Bran! *Redbook* 175, No. 5 (September 1990):188-191

Stay Slim & Healthy: Snack All Day. *Redbook* 174, No. 5 (March 1990):114-117

**Jie, Zhang**

Heavy Wings. Reviewed by Judy Yung. *Belles Lettres* 6, No. 1 (Fall 1990):30-31

**Jimason, Joanne**

Children's Corner. *Belles Lettres* 5, No. 3 (Spring 1990):15

**Jimenez, Mary Ann** and Rice, Susan

Popular Advice to Women: A Feminist Perspective. *AFFILIA* 5, No. 3 (Fall 1990):8-26

**Jiwani, Yasmin**

In Visible Colours: Technicolour in a White World. *Hot Wire* 6, No. 3 (September 1990):23+

**Jo, Bev,** Strega, Linda, and Ruston

Dykes-Loving-Dykes. Reviewed by Sheila Anne. *off our backs* 20, No. 11 (December 1990):15

**Joanou, Jennifer** (about)

High Profile: Joanous Come Lately. Trish Deitch Rohrer. *Mademoiselle* (December 1990):78

**Joanou, Phil** (about). See Joanou, Jennifer (about)

**Job Layoffs.** See Employees, Dismissal of

**Job Market.** See Employment Opportunities

**Job Retraining.** See Employees – Training

**Job Satisfaction**

Boredom on the Job. Marilyn Moats Kennedy. *Glamour* (October 1990):117

The Work Attachment of Mothers with Preschool Children. Sandra Cotton, John K. Antill, and John D. Cunningham. *Psychology of Women Quarterly* 14, No. 2 (June 1990):255-270

**Job Satisfaction – Gender Differences**

Gender Differences in Perceptions of Work: Limited Access to Decision-Making Power and Supervisory Support. Myria Watkins Allen, Joy Hart Seibert, and Ramona R. Rush. *Women's Studies in Communication* 13, No. 2 (Fall 1990):1-20

**Job Search**

Competitive Edge. *Executive Female* (March/April 1990):14-15

Signed, Sealed, Delivered. Suzanne Weber. *Executive Female* (March/April 1990):36-37

**Job Skills.** See Employees – Training

Solving the Problem at the Source. Ray Marshall. *Working Woman* (January 1990):76-72

**Job Strategies.** See Career Strategies

**Job Stress.** See Occupational Stress

**Job Training – Prison**

No Job Training in Jail. Jana Schroeder. *New Directions for Women* 19, No. 3 (May/June 1990):4

**Johanson, Mary Ann**

Traditions: O Christmas Tree. *McCall's* 118, No. 3 (December 1990):31

**John, Angela V.**

Octavia Wilberforce, Pioneer Woman Doctor. Book Review. *Gender & History* 2, No. 3 (Autumn 1990):375-377

**John, Betty**

Libby, the Alaskan Diaries and Letters of Libby Beaman, 1879-1880. Reviewed by Lynn Wenzel. *New Directions for Women* 19, No. 2 (March/April 1990):14

**Johns, Jasper** (about)

Drawing the Lines. Kristine McKenna. *Harper's Bazaar* (April 1990):196-197+

**Johnson, Angela**

Climb Every Mountain. *off our backs* 20, No. 11 (December 1990):18-19

Extending Shelter. *off our backs* 20, No. 10 (November 1990):14

Nervous Conditions. Book Review. *off our backs* 20, No. 9 (October 1990):17

Response to Graffiti: The Writing on the Wall. *off our backs* 20, No. 6 (June 1990):14-15

**Johnson, Audreye E.** (joint author). See Haile, Barbara J.

**Johnson, Betsey** (about). See Fashion Designers, "Battle-Weary Designers"

**Johnson, Buffie**

Lady of the Beasts. *Woman of Power* 16 (Spring 1990):68-71

**Johnson, Catherine**

Could You Be a Better Friend to Your Husband? *Redbook* 175, No. 5 (September 1990):166-167+

**Johnson, Cathy Marie** (joint author). See Duerst-Lahti, Georgia

**Johnson, Cheryl A.**, Corrigan, Sheila A., Dubbert, Patricia M., and Gramling, Sandra E.

Perceived Barriers to Exercise and Weight Control Practices in Community Women. *Women and Health* 16, Nos. 3/4 (1990):177-191

**Johnson, Dallas E.** (joint author). See Newell, G. Kathleen

**Johnson, Delilah O.** (about). See Lawyers

**Johnson, Joyce**

What Lisa Knew, The Truths and Lies of the Steinberg Case. Reviewed by Marjorie Lipsyte. *New Directions for Women* 19, No. 5 (September-October 1990):10+

**Johnson, Julia Claiborne**

One for the Road: The Very Secret Life of a Solo Traveler. *Mademoiselle* (July 1990):116-117, 154-155

The World's Hippest Office. *Mademoiselle* (May 1990):210-213, 232

**Johnson, Karen** (about). See Dent, David

**Johnson, Lesley**

Gender Issues and Education. *Australian Feminist Studies* No. 11 (Autumn 1990):17-27

**Johnson, Linda Rice** (about). See Family-Owned Business

**Johnson, Lois Joy**

All Grown Up. *Ladies' Home Journal* 107, No. 1 (January 1990):102-108

California Girls. *Ladies' Home Journal* 107, No. 4 (April 1990):172-180

Elements of Style. *Ladies' Home Journal* 107, No. 3 (March 1990):168-173

Great Faces. *Ladies' Home Journal* 107, No. 11 (November 1990):224-228

Great Updates. *Ladies' Home Journal* 107, No. 9 (September 1990):166-174

Hot Shots. *Ladies' Home Journal* 107, No. 12 (December 1990):152-156

The New Naturals. *Ladies' Home Journal* 107, No. 5 (May 1990):178-186

Role Models. *Ladies' Home Journal* 107, No. 10 (October 1990):172-180

Simply Beautiful. *Ladies' Home Journal* 107, No. 2 (February 1990):124-128

Supermodel Cindy Crawford: In the Hot Look of Summer. *Ladies' Home Journal* 107, No. 6 (June 1990):132-137

Tie One On. *Ladies' Home Journal* 107, No. 8 (August 1990):112-116

**Johnson, Loretta**

In a Penal Colony. *Sinister Wisdom* 40 (Spring 1990):15-16

**Johnson, Lyndon Baines** (about). See Love-Letters

**Johnson, Máirín**

Dublin Belles: Conversations with Dublin Women. Reviewed by Maureen Murphy. *Feminist Collections* 11, No. 2 (Winter 1990):5-6

Dublin Belles: Conversations with Dublin Women. Reviewed by Susan Swartzlander. *Belles Lettres* 5, No. 3 (Spring 1990):5

**Johnson, Miriam M.**

Refiguring the Father: New Feminist Readings of Patriarchy. Book Review. *NWSA Journal* 2, No. 4 (Autumn 1990):656-658

Strong Mothers, Weak Wives: The Search for Gender Equality. Reviewed by Arline Prigoff. *AFFILIA* 5, No. 2 (Summer 1990):113-114

**Johnson, Pamela**

The Hudlins and Kid N' Play Make Movie Magic. *Essence* 20, No. 10 (February 1990):40

It's a Hectic World for Debbie Allen. *Essence* 21, No. 2 (June 1990):64-66

**Johnson, Peggy**

Uprising of a Novelist. *The Women's Review of Books* 7, Nos. 10-11 (July 1990):24

**Johnson, Philip** (about)

Master Builders. Karen Stein. *Harper's Bazaar* (August 1990):1668-171+

**Jones, Quincy** (about)

The Pain and Passion of Quincy Jones. Alan Ebert. *Essence* 21, No. 7 (November 1990):59-60+

Quincy. Alan Ebert. *Lear's* (August 1990):64-65

**Jones, Reginald L** (editor)

Black Adolescents. Book Review. *Adolescence* 25, No. 99 (Fall 1990):753

**Jones, Samantha** (about)

Style: The Lady in Lace. *Essence* 20, No. 10 (February 1990):22

**Jones, Ursula M.**

My Homeland. Poem. *Essence* 21, No. 5 (September 1990):114

**Jones-Bley, Karlene**

Women in Prehistory. Book Review. *NWSA Journal* 2, No. 4 (Autumn 1990):675-677

**Jong, Erica**

Any Woman's Blues. Reviewed by Francine Prose. *Savvy Woman* (February 1990):27, 95

**Jordan, Barbara** (about). See De Veaux, Alexis, Milloy, Marilyn, and Ross, Michael Erik

**Jordan, Deborah**

Exposing Nuclear Phallacies. Book Review. *Australian Feminist Studies* No. 11 (Autumn 1990):127-128

Feminist Perspectives on Peace and Education. Book Review. *Australian Feminist Studies* No. 11 (Autumn 1990):127-128

The Recurring Silent Spring. Book Review. *Australian Feminist Studies* No. 11 (Autumn 1990):127-128

**Jordan, Ellen**

Family Fortunes: Men and Women of the English Middle Class, 1780-1850. Book review. *Signs* 15, No. 3 (Spring 1990):650-652

**Jordan, Joyce**

Naming Our Destiny, New and Selected Poems. Reviewed by Susan Sherman. *New Directions for Women* 19, No. 5 (September-October 1990):17

**Jordan, June**

Poem for Obvious Reasons. Poem. *Ms.* 1, No. 1 (July/August 1990):71

**Jordan – Refugee Camps**

Jordan: The Gulf Refugees. Arwa Aamiry. *Ms.* 1, No. 3 (November/December 1990):13

**Jordanova, Ludmilla**

Sexual Visions: Images of Gender in Science and Medicine Between the Eighteenth and Twentieth Centuries. Reviewed by Julia Epstein. *The Women's Review of Books* 7, No. 6 (March 1990):13-14

Sexual Visions: Images of Gender in Science and Medicine Between the Eighteenth and Twentieth

Centuries. Reviewed by Nancy Leys Stepan. *Gender & History* 2, No. 3 (Autumn 1990):337-342

**Jordon, Jennifer**

Interiors: No Bundles of Joy. *Essence* 21, No. 6 (October 1990):42

The Wife. Short story. *Essence* 21, No. 3 (July 1990):66-68+

**Jordon, June** (about)

Woman Talk. Interviews. Edited by Cheryll Y. Greene and Marie D. Brown. *Essence* 21, No. 1 (May 1990):92-96+

**Jorgensen, Lou Ann B.**

A Wider Giving: Women Writing After a Long Silence. Book Review. *Journal of Women and Aging* 2, No. 4 (1990):109-110

**Jorm, A. F.**

A Guide to Understanding Alzheimer's Disease and Related Disorders. Reviewed by Stefania Siedlecky. *Healthright* 9, No. 4 (August 1990):46

**Joseff, Eugene** (about)

Elements: Joseff. Jody Shields. *Vogue* (December 1990):142-144

**Joshi, P. L** and others

Managerial Skills: A Need for Effective Vaccination Coverage. *Journal of Family Welfare* 36, No. 2 (June 1990):43-49

**Journalism.** See also Interviewing; Media and Communications

Eyes of Time: Photojournalism in America. By Marianne Fulton. Reviewed by Harlan Nunn. *On the Issues* 17 (Winter 1990):32-33

"We Don't Contravene the Sex Discrimination Act" – Female Students at Journalism School. Odette Parry. *Gender and Education* 2, No. 1 (1990):3-16

**Journalism – Homosexual Issues**

ASNE Report: Gay, Lesbian Journalists Concerned over Newsroom Roles, Coverage. *Media Report to Women* 18, No. 4 (July-August 1990):4-5

**Journalism – Latin America**

Women in Communications Workshop: Birds of a Feather. Regina Rodriguez. *Women in Action* 3 & 4 (1990):11-13

**Journalism, Tabloid**

Get the Picture. Erik Hedegaard. *Savvy Woman* (January 1990):72-75, 92-93

**Journalists.** See also Donovan, Carrie (about); Television Journalists

Barbara Walters: Media Mover. Jeff Rovin. *Ladies' Home Journal* 107, No. 11 (November 1990):199+

But On-Camera Visibility for Top Women Reporters Declines. *Media Report to Women* 18, No. 2 (March/April 1990):3

Dallas Women Reporting Top Stories Less than One-Third of the Time. *Media Report to Women* 18, No. 1 (January/February 1990):3

Demise of Los Angeles Newspaper Prompts Reminiscences of Pioneer Woman Editor. *Media Report to Women* 18, No. 1 (January/February 1990):6

Gay, Lesbian Journalists Rate Climate, Coverage in Their Newsrooms. *Media Report to Women* 18, No. 3 (May/June 1990):2

Jane's Search for Tomorrow. Jeff Rovin. *Ladies' Home Journal* 107, No. 7 (July 1990):86-87+

Japanese Women: Rewriting Tradition. Kumiko Makihara. *Lear's* (February 1990):78-83

Oakland Exposé: A Hunch Pays Off. Kathleen Tripp. *Ms.* 1, No. 3 (November/December 1990):90

Professional Socialization of Feminist Journalists in the Netherlands. Liesbet van Zoonen. *Women's Studies in Communication* 12, No. 2 (Fall 1989):1-21

Public Policy Seen Improving Gender Balance of Canadian TV Anchors. *Media Report to Women* 18, No. 3 (May/June 1990):7

Swedish Scholar Suggests New Approach to Studying Women in TV News. *Media Report to Women* 18, No. 2 (March/April 1990):8

TV: Broadcast Schmooze. James Kaplan. *Mademoiselle* (June 1990):108

**Journalists – Interviews**

Lunch. Interview. Frances Lear. *Lear's* (September 1990):19-20

The Studs and Charlie Show. Interview. *Lear's* (October 1990):96-99+

**Journalists – Sexual Harassment**

Press Secretary Resigns Over Sexual Remark to Reporter. *Media Report to Women* 18, No. 3 (May/June 1990):7

**Journalists – Sexual Harrassment**

Team Locker Rooms Still Tough Turf for Women Sportswriters. *Media Report to Women* 18, No. 1 (January/February 1990):1-2

**Journals and Diaries**

Anaïs Redux. Ellen Currie. *Lear's* (February 1990):46-48

The Godfather Diary. Eleanor Coppola. *Vogue* (December 1990):304-309+

Lifelines: Women and Writing. Phyllis Theroux. *Lear's* (May 1990):56-58

**Journals and Diaries – Great Britain**

Centuries of Female Days: Englishwomen's Private Diaries. By Harriet Blodgett. Reviewed by Lillian S. Robinson. *Tulsa Studies in Women's Literature* 9, No. 1 (Spring 1990):144-146

**Joy, Morny**

Equality or Divinity – A False Dichotomy? *Journal of Feminist Studies in Religion* 6, No. 1 (Spring 1990):9-24

**Joy, Penny** (about)

Filmmakers Robin J. Hood and Penny Joy. Heather Tufts. *Canadian Women's Studies* 11, No. 1 (Spring 1990):94-96

**Jozwiak, John** (joint author). *See* Thomas, Sandra P.

**Jubak, Jim** and D'Amico, Marie

Environment: 9 Things You Can Do in the '90s to Save the Planet. Bibliography. *McCall's* 117, No. 7 (April 1990):34-41

**Jubak, Jim** (joint author). *See* D'Amico, Marie

**Judaism**

Exile in the Promised Land: A Memoir. By Marcia Freedman. Reviewed by Lillian Moed and Tracy Moore. *The Women's Review of Books* 8, No. 3 (December 1990):30

Exile in the Promised Land: A Memoir. By Marcia Freedman. Reviewed by Miriyam Glazer. *Belles Lettres* 6, No. 1 (Fall 1990):10-12

Rabbinic and Feminist Approaches to Reproductive Technologies. Judith N. Lasker and Harriet L. Parmet. *Journal of Feminist Studies in Religion* 6, No. 1 (Spring 1990):117-130

Reclaiming the Shekhinah. Jane Litwoman. *New Directions for Women* 19, No. 4 (July-August 1990):1+

A Song So Brave. Phyllis Chesler and Joan Roth. *On the Issues* 15 (Summer 1990):19

Standing Again at Sinai: Judaism From a Feminist Perspective. By Judith Plaskow. Reviewed by Alicia Ostriker. *The Women's Review of Books* 7, No. 12 (September 1990):12

Standing Again at Sinai: Judaism from a Feminist Perspective. By Judith Plaskow. Reviewed by Donna Berman. *New Directions for Women* 19, No. 4 (July-August 1990):18

Standing Again at Sinai: Judaism from a Feminist Perspective. By Judith Plaskow. Reviewed by Lori Ginzberg. *Bridges* 1, No. 2 (Fall 1990): 126-127

**Judaism, Fundamentalist**

New Rabbinical College Excludes Women. Lisa Klug. *Lilith* 15, No. 3 (Summer 1990):5

**Judaism – Goddess Worship**

Encountering the Shekhinah. Léah Novick. *Woman of Power* 15 (Fall-Winter 1990):45

**Judaism, Orthodox – Childbirth**

Instructions for the Birthing Team. Sheila Stanger. *Lilith* 15, No. 1 (Winter 1990):21-23

And the Sages Say . . . Gila Berkowitz. *Lilith* 15, No. 1 (Winter 1990):24-25

**Judaism – Rituals.** *See also* Divorce – Jewish Law

. . . And an Anthropologist Says . . . Riv-Ellen Prell. *Lilith* 15, No. 3 (Summer 1990):23

Anxiety 101: Leading the Passover Seder. Jeff Axelbank. *Lilith* 15, No. 2 (Spring 1990):13-15

The Art of the Menorah. Phyllis Schiller. *McCall's* 118, No. 3 (December 1990):31-33

Into the Future with Rituals from Our Past. Susan Schnur. *Lilith* 15, No. 3 (Summer 1990):19

A Midwife's Kaddish. Diane Solomon. *Lilith* 15, No. 3 (Summer 1990):22-23

And the Sages Say . . . Gila Berkowitz. *Lilith* 15, No. 1 (Winter 1990):24-25

Suing Dad: Bat Mitzvah in the Divorce Crossfire. Marla Ruth Allison. *Lilith* 15, No. 2 (Spring 1990):23-24

The Ways We Are: Saying Goodbye to Friends. Jane Litman. *Lilith* 15, No. 1 (Winter 1990):31

The Ways We Are: ". . . Who *Has* Made Me a Woman . . ." Elyse Goldstein. *Lilith* 15, No. 2 (Spring 1990):32

We Rejoice in Our Heritage: Home Rituals for Secular and Humanistic Jews. By Judith Seid. Reviewed by Ruth Kraut. *Bridges* 1, No. 2 (Fall 1990): 128-130

Woman Cantor Breaks Tradition in Yugoslavia. Helen Leneman. *Lilith* 15, No. 2 (Spring 1990):28

**Judaism – Status of Women**

The Cantors Assembly Convention: A Spy Story. Helen Leneman. *Lilith* 15, No. 4 (Fall 1990):37-38

On the Path to Power: Women Decode the Talmud in Their Own Style. Vanessa Ochs. *Lilith* 15, No. 3 (Summer 1990):16-18

Reworking the Rabbi's Role. Julie Goss. *Lilith* 15, No. 4 (Fall 1990):16-25

Standing Again at Sinai: Judaism from a Feminist Perspective. By Judith Plaskow. Reviewed by Sue Levi Elwell. *Lilith* 15, No. 4 (Fall 1990):33-34

**Judges.** *See also* Great Britain – Legal System

Judge Consuelo B. Marshall Holding Court. Arthur Hayes. *Essence* 21, No. 3 (July 1990):37

A Sexist and Racist Judiciary. Sara Maguire. *Spare Rib* No. 209 (February 1990):47

**Judicial System**

Backtalk: The Supremes. Fred Siegel. *Lear's* (February 1990):126-127 +

**Jung, Mary Beth**

Healthy Cook: Frozen Assets. *Working Woman* (August 1990):04

**Junk Bonds**

How I Became a Junk-Bond Airhead. Patricia O'Toole. *Lear's* (June 1990):35-37

More Money: The ABCs of LBOs. Jerome Reinhart. *Executive Female* (March/April 1990):16-18

**Junk Mail.** *See* Advertising, Direct-Mail; Mail-Order Business

**Junor, Penny**

Back to School with William and Harry. *McCall's* 118, No. 1 (October 1990):88-92

**Jurdjevic, Deborah**

An American Childhood. Book Review. *Canadian Women's Studies* 11, No. 1 (Spring 1990):110-111

**Jurich, Anthony P.** (joint author). *See* Newell, G. Kathleen

**Jurik, Nancy**

Women Guarding Men. Book Review. *Gender and Society* 4, No. 1 (March 1990):115-117

**Jurisprudence**

Women and the Law Conference. Martha Ertman. *off our backs* 20, No. 7 (July 1990):2-5

**Jurisprudence – Feminist Perspectives**

Liberating Feminist Jurisprudence. Debra Ratterman. *off our backs* 20, No. 1 (January 1990):12-14

Remaking the Tools: Re-Visioning Rights. Debbie Ratterman. *off our backs* 20, No. 9 (October 1990):12-13

What We Know as Women: A New Look at *Roe v. Wade*. Judith A. Baer. *NWSA Journal* 2, No. 4 (Autumn 1990):558-582

**Juvenile Offenders.** *See* Adolescents – Delinquency

# K

**Kabbani, Rana**

Europe's Myths of Orient. Reviewed by Írvin Cemil Schick. *Feminist Studies* 16, No. 2 (Summer 1990):345-380

**Kachman, Daniel J.** and Mazer, Gilbert E.

Effects of Rational Emotive Education on the Rationality, Neuroticism and Defense Mechanisms of Adolescents. *Adolescence* 25, No. 97 (Spring 1990):131-144

**Kaden, Joan** and McDaniel, Susan A.

Caregiving and Care-Receiving: A Double Bind for Women in Canada's Aging Society. *Journal of Women and Aging* 2 No. 3 (1990):3-26

**Kadic, Bjanka**

The Woman in My Life. *Spare Rib* No. 212 (May 1990):30

**Kadish, Rachel**

Daddy's Home: Reflections of a Family Man. Book review. *Lilith* 15, No. 4 (Fall 1990):34

Ernestine L. Rose, Women's Rights Pioneer, 2nd edition. Book review. *Lilith* 15, No. 4 (Fall 1990):34

What Soviet Anti-Semitism Looks Like Now. *Lilith* 15, No. 4 (Fall 1990):39

**Kadohata, Cynthia**

The Floating World. Reviewed by Shirley Goek-lin Lim. *Belles Lettres* 5, No. 3 (Spring 1990):20

**Kady**

Panhandling Papers. Reviewed by Batya Weinbaum. *NWSA Journal* 2, No. 2 (Spring 1990):323-328

Panhandling Papers. Reviewed by Farar Elliott. *off our backs* 20, No. 7 (July 1990):13 +

**Kafka, Barbara**

Four-Star Ratings. *Family Circle* 103, No. 17 (December 18, 1990):162

Gifts Sweet & Sour. *Family Circle* 103, No. 17 (December 18, 1990):199-200

Savvy School Lunches. *Family Circle* 103, No. 14 (October 16, 1990):162-165

**Kafka, Phillipa**

Frye Street and Environs: The Collected Works of Marita Bonner. Book Review. *Sage* 6, No. 2 (Fall 1989):60

**Kagan, Julia**

Boys and Dolls, Girls and Trucks. *McCall's* 118, No. 3 (December 1990):88

Cybill Shepherd: Doors Keep Opening. *McCall's* 117, No. 10 (July 1990):64-66

**Kagan, Julia and Ferrari, Christina**

Child Labor Laws: What Every Parent Needs to Know. *McCall's* 118, No. 1 (October 1990):106

**Kahlo, Frida – Criticism and Interpretation**

Aztec Imagery in Frida Kahlo's Paintings: Indigenity and Political Commitment. Janice Helland. *Woman's Art Journal* 11, No. 2 (Fall 1990-Winter 1991):8-13

Frida Kahlo's *Memory*: The Piercing of the Heart by the Arrow of Divine Love. Salomon Grimberg. *Woman's Art Journal* 11, No. 2 (Fall 1990-Winter 1991):3-7

**Kahlo, Frida (about)**

Frida Kahlo: The Brush of Anguish. By Martha Zamora. Reviewed by Joan Philpott. *Ms.* 1, No. 2 (September/October 1990):27-28

**Kahn, Arnold S.**

Affirmative Action in Perspective. Book Review. *Psychology of Women Quarterly* 14, No. 1 (March 1990):145-147

**Kahn, Arnold S.**, Presbury, Jack H., Moore, Helen B., and Driver, Jacqueline D.

Characteristics of Accepted versus Rejected Manuscripts. *Psychology of Women Quarterly* 14, No. 1 (March 1990):7-14

**Kahn, Louis** (about). *See* Muschamp, Herbert

**Kahn, Peggy**

Doing Comparable Worth: Gender, Class and Pay Equity. Book Review. *The Women's Review of Books* 7, No. 12 (September 1990):21-23

Wage Justice: Comparable Worth and the Paradox of Technocratic Reform. Book Review. *The Women's Review of Books* 7, No. 12 (September 1990):21-23

Wage Wars. *The Women's Review of Books* 7, No. 12 (September 1990):21-23

A Woman's Wage: Symbolic Meanings and Social Consequences. Book Review. *The Women's Review of Books* 7, No. 12 (September 1990):21-23

**Kahn, Sandra**

Breaking Out of the Ex-Wife Trap. *Lear's* (December 1990):48-49

**Kahn, Susanjill** (joint author). *See* Dykewomon, Elana

**Kahn, Victoria**

Lambasting the Liberals. *The Women's Review of Books* 7, No. 5 (February 1990):16

The Sexual Liberals and the Attack on Feminism. Book Review. *The Women's Review of Books* 7, No. 5 (February 1990):16

**Kahn, Yoel H.**

How We Talk About God. *Bridges* 1, No. 2 (Fall 1990): 25-29

**Kaiser, Sue**

The AIDS Challenge: Prevention Education for Young People. Book Review. *Healthsharing* 11, No. 2 (March 1990):33

**Kalechofsky, Roberta**

Another View of the Middle East: Palestinian Arabs, Yes; PLO, No. *On the Issues* 15 (Summer 1990):18 +

Bodmin, 1329: An Epic Novel of Christians and Jews in the Plague Years. Reviewed by Tracy Scott. *On the Issues* 15 (Summer 1990):25

The Cruel Deception: The Use of Animals in Medical Research. Book Review. *On the Issues* 14 (1990):25-26

Intimate Adversaries: Cultural Conflict Between Doctors and Women Patients. Book Review. *On the Issues* 17 (Winter 1990):33-34

**Kalergis, Mary Motley**

Women Who Chose America. *Glamour* (February 1990):186-189

**Kali for Women** (editors)

Truth Tales: Contemporary Stories by Women Writers of India. Reviewed by Nina Mehta. *Belles Lettres* 6, No. 1 (Fall 1990):23

**Kalleberg, Arne L.** and Rosenfeld, Rachel A.

Work in the Family and in the Labor Market: A Cross-national, Reciprocal Analysis. *Journal of Marriage and the Family* 52, No. 2 (May 1990):331-346

**Kallet, Marilyn**

Frameless Windows, Square of Light. Book Review. *Belles Lettres* 6, No. 1 (Fall 1990):31

Illuminating Kinship. *Belles Lettres* 6, No. 1 (Fall 1990):31

**Kalogerakis, George** (joint author). *See* Urquhart, Rachel

**Kalu, Wilhelmina**

Bereavement and Stress in Career Women. *Women and Therapy* 10, No. 3 (1990):75-87

**Kalyan-Masih, Violet** (joint author). *See* Woodward, John C.

**Kamali, Norma** (about). *See* Fashion Designers, "What I Like for Fall"; Talley, André Leon

**Kamano, Saori**

Cross-National Analysis of the Social Construction of Homosexuality and Gender. *NWSA Journal* 2, No. 4 (Autumn 1990):696-698

**Kamel, Rachel**

The Global Factory. Reviewed by Laura McClure. *New Directions for Women* 19, No. 6 (November-December 1990):7

**Kamen, Paula**

Compassion Comes for the Archbishop. *Ms.* 1, No. 1 (July/August 1990):85-86

Media Exploit Pompon Squad. *New Directions for Women* 19, No. 3 (May/June 1990):16

**Kamerman, Sheila** (joint author). *See* Cadden, Vivian

**Kaminer, Wendy**

A Fearful Freedom: Women's Flight from Equality. Reviewed by Beverly Guy-Sheftall. *Ms.* 1, No. 1 (July/August 1990):68

A Fearful Freedom: Women's Flight from Equality. Reviewed by Louise Armstrong. *The Women's Review of Books* 8, No. 2 (November 1990):9-10

**Kanda, Mikio** (editor)

Widows of Hiroshima: The Life Stories of Nineteen Peasant Wives. Reviewed by Takayo Mukai. *Belles Lettres* 6, No. 1 (Fall 1990):25

**Kandel, Denise B.**

Parenting Styles, Drug Use, and Children's Adjustment in Families of Young Adults. *Journal of Marriage and the Family* 52, No. 1 (February 1990):183-196

**Kandel, Denise B.** (joint author). *See* Rosenbaum, Emily

**Kane, Anne**

Abortion on Request – One Step Closer. *Spare Rib* No. 212 (May 1990):44

**Kane, Deirdre**

Charlotte Bunch Founds The Center for Global Issues and Women's Leadership. *NWSAction* 3, No. 4 (Winter 1990): 8-9

**Kane, Karen**

CD Manufacturing for the Independent Artist. *Hot Wire* 6, No. 1 (January 1990):10-11 +

Stereo Buying for the Novice. *Hot Wire* 6, No. 2 (May 1990):10-11 +

**Kanner, Barbara**

Autobiographical Writings: Women in English Social History, 1800-1914. A Guide to Research, Volume III. *Gender & History* 2, No. 1 (Spring 1990):89-90

**Kanner, Bernice**

The Secret Life of the Female Consumer. *Working Woman* (December 1990):68-71

**Kano, Susan**

Making Peace with Food. Reviewed by Patricia A. Connor-Greene. *Women and Health* 16, Nos. 3/4 (1990):211-221

**Kanter, Rosabeth Moss** (about)

Pygmalion in Pinstripes. Sandra Salmans. *Lear's* (April 1990):30-33

**Kanuha, Valli**

Compounding the Triple Jeopardy: Battering in Lesbian of Color Relationships. *Women and Therapy* 9, Nos. 1-2 (1990):169-184

**Kaplan, Carey**

Goodbye without Leaving. Book Review. *The Women's Review of Books* 8, No. 1 (October 1990):12-13

Starting with Serge. Book Review. *The Women's Review of Books* 8, No. 1 (October 1990):12-13

Unsentimental Educations. *The Women's Review of Books* 8, No. 1 (October 1990):12-13

**Kaplan, Helen Singer**

Bed and Bored? *Redbook* 175, No. 3 (July 1990):100-101 +

How to Have Fantastic Sex: Know Your Body. *Redbook* 175, No. 4 (August 1990):102

The Real Truth about Women and AIDS: How to Eliminate the Risks without Giving Up Love and Sex. Reviewed by Kathryn Quina. *Psychology of Women Quarterly* 14, No. 2 (June 1990):296-298

**Kaplan, James**

All That Junk. *Mademoiselle* (November 1990):106

It Ain't Over Till It's Over. *Mademoiselle* (September 1990):179

Playing Doctor. *Mademoiselle* (December 1990):96

Retire Early! Miss Nothing! *Mademoiselle* (October 1990):110

TV: Broadcast Schmooze. *Mademoiselle* (June 1990):108

**Kaplan, Janet A.**
Unexpected Journeys: The Art and Life of Remedios Varos. Reviewed by Robert J. Belton. *Woman's Art Journal* 11, No. 2 (Fall 1990-Winter 1991):35-36

**Kaplan, Janice**
Body Management: Prenatal Testing: The Newest Option. *Working Woman* (January 1990):134-138

**Kaplan, Marion A.**
Jewish Women in Nazi Germany: Daily Life, Daily Struggles, 1933-1939. *Feminist Studies* 16, No. 3 (Fall 1990):579-606

**Kaplan, Michael**
The Secrets of Super Salespeople (That Everyone Can Use). *Working Woman* (May 1990):92-95+

**Kaplan, Robbie Miller**
Push-Button Resumes. *Executive Female* 13, No. 4 (July-August 1990):35+

**Kaplan, Steve**
Women Who Make A Difference. *Family Circle* 103, No. 3 (February 20, 1990):15-16+

**Kaplan, Sydney Janet**
Literary Daughters. Book Review. *NWSA Journal* 2, No. 1 (Winter 1990):124-127

Virginia Woolf: The Impact of Childhood Sexual Abuse on Her Life and Work. Book Review. *NWSA Journal* 2, No. 1 (Winter 1990):124-127

**Kaplen, Lex** (about)
No Place Like Home. *Harper's Bazaar* (February 1990):76

**Kapoor, Raj**
Letters to Daddy. Reviewed by Mukul Kesavan. *Manushi* 58 (May-June 1990):43-44

**Kapoor, S. K.** (joint author). *See* Singh, Saudan

**Kappeler, Susanne** (joint author). *See* Smeeth, Mary

**Kapur, Jyofsna**
Putting Herself into the Picture. Notes. Bibliography. *Manushi* 56 (January-February 1990):28-37

**Karan, Donna** (about). *See also* Etra, Jon, "World Class"; Fashion Designers, "What I Like for Fall"; Talley, André Leon

More for Less. *Harper's Bazaar* (November 1990):124

View: DKNY. Julia Reed. *Vogue* (December 1990):111-114

**Karate**
Pack a Punch. Therese Iknoian. *Women's Sports and Fitness* 12, No. 7 (October 1990):18

**Karayanni, Mousa** (joint author). *See* Seginer, Rachel

**Karbe, Beth**
For Joan, in 1967. Poem. *Sinister Wisdom* 40 (Spring 1990):76-77

**Kariuki, Priscilla Wanjiru** (joint author). *See* Todd, Judith

**Karlsen, Carol F.**
Witchcraft and the Inquisition in Venice, 1550-1650. Book Review. *Gender & History* 2, No. 3 (Autumn 1990):354-356

**Karp, Lila**
Waiting Game. *The Women's Review of Books* 7, Nos. 10-11 (July 1990):35-36

What Waiting Really Means. Book Review. *The Women's Review of Books* 7, Nos. 10-11 (July 1990):35-36

**Karriem, Jaleelah**
A Poem for Sojourner Truth. Poem. *Essence* 20, No. 11 (March 1990):136

Sunday. Poem. *Essence* 20, No. 11 (March 1990):131

**Karve, Anandibai** (about). *See* India – Status of Women

**Kase, Lori Miller**
Fertile Ground. *Savvy Woman* (September 1990):80-82

**Kashiwa, Anne**
Hitting Your Stride. *Women's Sports and Fitness* 12, No. 4 (May-June 1990):24

**Kashmir**
Escalating Defence Expenditure. Ravi Rikhye. *Manushi* 58 (May-June 1990):9-10

The Kashmir Crisis: What Are Our Options? Madhu Kishwar. *Manushi* 58 (May-June 1990):2-8

**Kasl, Charlotte Davis**
The Twelve-Step Controversy. *Ms.* 1, No. 3 (November/December 1990):30-31

**Kassall, Paula**
Clothes Make the Woman . . . *New Directions for Women* 19, No. 5 (September-October 1990):6

**Kassebaum, Nancy** (about). *See* Dusky, Lorraine
Nancy Kassebaum: Heartland Independent. Jane Ciabattari. *McCall's* 117, No. 9 (June 1990):68

**Kassel, Paula**

Nobody's Coming to Dinner Party. *New Directions for Women* 19, No. 6 (November-December 1990):12

**Kastris, Audrey**

Prime of Life. *Family Circle* 103, No. 6 (April 24, 1990):45+

**Katherine, Amber**

Lizards/Los Padres. Book Review. *Sinister Wisdom* 42 (Winter 1990-1991):127-129

**Katz, Janyce**

Celestial Reasoning – Ohio's First Lady Talks about Love and Feminism. *Ms.* 1, No. 2 (September/October 1990):88

**Katz, John**

Men and Failure. *Glamour* (June 1990):244-245+

**Katz, Michael B.**

The Undeserving Poor: From the War on Poverty to the War on Welfare. Reviewed by Linda Gordon. *The Women's Review of Books* 7, No. 6 (March 1990):7-8

**Katz, Montana** and Vieland, Veronica

Get Smart! A Woman's Guide to Equality on Campus. Reviewed by M. Jane Ayer. *Feminist Collections* 11, No. 3 (Spring 1990):3-4

Get Smart! A Woman's Guide to Equality on the Campus. Reviewed by Anne Flintoff. *Gender and Education* 2, No. 2 (1990):259

**Katz, Nina**, Sheldon, Amy, and Siegel, Rachel Josefowitz

Hanukah: Lighting the Way to Women's Empowerment. *Bridges* 1, No. 2 (Fall 1990): 30-31

**Katz, Sue**

The Iraqi Invasion: An Israeli Perspective. *off our backs* 20, No. 9 (October 1990):9+

**Katzenstein, Mary Fainsod**

Feminism within American Institutions: Unobtrusive Mobilization in the 1980s. *Signs* 16, No. 1 (Autumn 1990):27-54

**Kauffman, Linda S.**

Discourses of Desire: Gender, Genre, and Epistolary Fictions. Reviewed by Joan Hinde Stewart. *Tulsa Studies in Women's Literature* 9, No. 1 (Spring 1990):149-150

**Kaufman, Debra Renée**

Deceptive Distinctions: Sex, Gender and the Social Order. Book Review. *Gender and Society* 4, No. 4 (December 1990):

Women of the New Right. Book Review. *Gender and Society* 4, No. 1 (March 1990):118-120

**Kaufman, Joanne**

All in the Family. *Ladies' Home Journal* 107, No. 12 (December 1990):106

Child Star, Child Addict. *Ladies' Home Journal* 107, No. 3 (March 1990):116-124

Postcards from the Top. *Ladies' Home Journal* 107, No. 9 (September 1990):96-98+

She Never Lets Them See Her Sweat. *Working Woman* (March 1990):80-82

Summer Movies. *Ladies' Home Journal* 107, No. 7 (July 1990):36-40

**Kaufman, Lynne**

My Daughter, Myself. Short story. *Family Circle* 103, No. 14 (October 16, 1990):58-62

**Kaufman, Michael** (editor)

Beyond Patriarchy: Essays by Men on Pleasure, Power, and Change. Reviewed by James A. Doyle. *Gender and Society* 4, No. 1 (March 1990):117-118

**Kaufman, Pamela**

Fitness: Flexibility. *Vogue* (September 1990):366-382

**Kaufman, Shirley**

Milk. Poem. *Lilith* 15, No. 2 (Spring 1990):22

**Kaur, Daljit**

Song for a Sanctuary. Play Review. *Spare Rib* No. 209 (February 1990):33

**Kaur, Nirmaljit** (joint author). See Bhatia, M. S.

**Kavenik, Frances** (joint editor). See Zophy, Angela Howard

**Kawai, Makoto J.**, Miyamoto, Mari, and Miyamoto, Kimio

Five Elderly Dementia Patients Who Played with Dolls. *Journal of Women and Aging* 2, No. 1 (1990):99-107

**Kay, Elizabeth**

The Cat Is Back: The Dirty Little Secret of Women's Competition. *Mademoiselle* (February 1990):120-127

**Kay, Jackie.** See Radio Broadcasting – Plays

Unnatural Passions. Interview. *Spare Rib* No. 209 (February 1990):26-29

**Kay, Jackie** (joint editor). See Grewal, Shabnam

**Kay, Margarita** (joint author). See Ide, Bette A.

**Kaye, Dena**

Little Nell's: Colorado Cuisine. *Harper's Bazaar* (February 1990):186

**Kaye, Elizabeth**

Drug War. *Vogue* (March 1990):354-362

**Kaye, Katherine** (joint author). See Habel, Leo

**Kaye/Kantrowitz, Melanie**

It Ain't Necessarily So . . . *The Women's Review of Books* 7, Nos. 10-11 (July 1990):14

Jasmine. Book Review. *The Women's Review of Books* 7, No. 7 (April 1990):7-9

My Jewish Face. Reviewed by Miriam Kalman Harris. *Belles Lettres* 6, No. 1 (Fall 1990):12

My Jewish Face and Other Stories. Reviewed by Sandra Butler. *Sinister Wisdom* 42 (Winter 1990-1991):122-124

In the New New World. *The Women's Review of Books* 7, No. 7 (April 1990):7-9

The Next Step. *NWSA Journal* 2, No. 2 (Spring 1990):236-244

The Other Side. Book Review. *The Women's Review of Books* 7, No. 7 (April 1990):7-9

Some Pieces of Jewish Left: 1987. *Bridges* 1, No. 1 (Spring 1990): 7-22

What Dinah Thought. Book Review. *The Women's Review of Books* 7, Nos. 10-11 (July 1990):14

**Kaye/Kantrowitz, Melanie** and Klepfisz, Irena

The Tribe of Dina: A Jewish Women's Anthology. Reviewed by Joan Nestle. *Bridges* 1, No. 1 (Spring 1990): 101-102

**Kaye/Kantrowitz, Melanie** and Klepfisz, Irena (editors)

The Tribe of Dina: A Jewish Women's Anthology. Reviewed by Julia Wolf Mazow. *Lilith* 15, No. 1 (Winter 1990):6-7

**Kazanjian, Dodie**

Brides Made. *Vogue* (December 1990):316-321

Koons Crazy. *Vogue* (August 1990):338-343+

New Image. *Vogue* (May 1990):292-298, 320-323

Talking Fashion: Chanel Suit. *Vogue* (August 1990):367-376

**Kazin, Alfred**

Wellfleet. *Lear's* (June 1990):76-77+

**Kean, Hilda** and Oram, Alison

"Men Must Be Educated and Women Must Do It": The National Federation (Later Union) of Women Teachers and Contemporary Feminism 1910-30. *Gender and Education* 2, No. 2 (1990):147-167

**Keane, Mairead** (interview)

Women and National Liberation. Jo Tully. *Spare Rib* 219 (December 1990-January 1991):48-51

**Keane, Molly**

Queen Lear. Reviewed by Barbara Griffith Furst. *Belles Lettres* 5, No. 3 (Spring 1990):4

**Keating, Cricket** and Hamilton, Amy

The Loony Bin Trip. Book Review. *off our backs* 20, No. 11 (December 1990):16

**Keaton, Diane**

Woman to Watch. *Women's Sports and Fitness* 12, No. 7 (October 1990):57

**Keegan, Rita**

The Other Story: Afro-Asian Artists in post-war Britain. *Spare Rib* No. 209 (February 1990):36

**Keeler, Lucy** (about)

Garden as Woman: Creation of Identity in a Turn-of-the-Century Ohio Town. Marilyn Ferris Motz. *NWSA Journal* 2, No. 1 (Winter 1990):35-51

**Keene, Linda Baker** (about). *See* Davis, Andrea R., "Power Players"

**Keeps, David**

The Ode and the New. *Harper's Bazaar* (February 1990):58

Wild at Heart. *Harper's Bazaar* (August 1990):140-143+

**Kefala, Antigone – Criticism and Interpretation**

The Politics of Nostalgia: Community and Difference in Migrant Writing. Efi Hatzimanolis. *Hecate* 16, Nos. 1-2 (1990):120-127

**Keilin, Nina**

Men Trouble. *Ladies' Home Journal* 107, No. 8 (August 1990):84-89

Pet News. *Ladies' Home Journal* 107, No. 2 (February 1990):80; 107, No. 5 (May 1990):124

**Keith, Bruce** (joint author). *See* White, Lynn

**Keith, Carolyn**

On Her Own: Growing Up in the Shadow of the American Dream. Book Review. *AFFILIA* 5, No. 4 (Winter 1990):117-118

**Keith, Joanne** (joint author). *See* Nelson, Christine

**Keju-Johnson, Darlene**, Eknilang, Lijon, and Palacios, Chailang

Pacific Women Speak: The Health Effects of Radiation from Nuclear Testing in the Pacific Islands. *Woman of Power* 18 (Fall 1990):36-41

**Kellam, Geneva**

K.T. Oslin: The True Grit of a Country Charmer. *Lear's* (September 1990):106-109+

**Keller, Jacob B.** (joint author). *See* Ebi-Kryston, Kristie

**Keller, Karen**

Message in a Bottle: Is Your Water Safe to Drink? *Mademoiselle* (June 1990):121

**Keller, Kathryn**

Gaining Weight? Losing Energy? *Redbook* 175, No. 2 (June 1990):120-121+

Water Works Wonders. *Redbook* 175, No. 1 (May 1990):112-113+

**Keller, Mary L.** (joint author). *See* Jadack, Rosemary A.

**Keller, Rosanne**

Beaches I Have Known and Loved. *Lear's* (July 1990):38-39

**Kelles-Viitanen, Anita** (joint editor). *See* Singh, Andrea Menefee

**Kellogg, Mary Alice**

Bicoastal Career. *Harper's Bazaar* (October 1990):176-177+

**Kelly, Angel** (about). *See* Pornography, "A Portrait of Angel"

**Kelly, Brian** (joint author). *See* Raphael, Beverley

**Kelly, Ernece B.**

The Family. Book Review. *On the Issues* 16 (Fall 1990):32

Lives of Courage: Women for a New South Africa. Book Review. *On the Issues* 15 (Summer 1990):26-27

**Kelly, Gail P.**

International Handbook of Women's Education. Review. *Feminist Collections* 11, No. 3 (Spring 1990):16

**Kelly, Gail Paradise** (joint author). *See* DuBois, Ellen Carol

**Kelly, Katie**

The Christmas that Changed My Life. *McCall's* 118, No. 3 (December 1990):65-68+

**Kelly, Liz**

Compensation No Gain. *Spare Rib* No. 209 (February 1990):46-47

Coping with Child Sexual Abuse: A Guide for Teachers. Book Review. *Gender and Education* 2, No. 1 (1990):98-100

Surviving Sexual Violence. Reviewed by Patricia J. Morokoff. *Psychology of Women Quarterly* 14, No. 2 (June 1990):290-292

**Kelly, Liz** and O'Hara, Maureen

Child Sexual Abuse: Let the Children Speak. *Spare Rib* 217 (October 1990):44-45

The Making of Pornography: An Act of Sexual Violence. *Spare Rib* 213 (June 1990):16-19

**Kelly, Michael J.** (joint author). *See* Stout, Karen D.

**Kelly, Rita Mae**

Ingredients for Women's Employment Policy. Book Review. *Gender and Society* 4, No. 3 (September 1990):429-432

**Kelly, Rita Mae** (joint editor). *See* Hale, Mary M.

**Kelly, Susan** and Reddy, Prasuna

Outrageous Fortune. Reviewed by Beverley Raphael. *Healthright* 9, No. 4 (August 1990):41

**Kelman, Judith**

Safe in Mother's Arms. *Redbook* 175, No. 3 (July 1990):112-114

**Kelpfisz, Irena**

A Few Words in the Mother Tongue: Poems Selected and New (1971-1990). Reviewed by Meryl

Altman. *The Women's Review of Books* 8, No. 1 (October 1990):16-18

**Kendall**

Feminine Focus: The New Women Playwrights. Book Review. *The Women's Review of Books* 7, No. 4 (January 1990):15-16

Theatre and Theory. *The Women's Review of Books* 7, No. 4 (January 1990):15-16

**Kendall, Katherine A.**

Always a Sister: The Feminism of Lillian D. Wald. Book Review. *AFFILIA* 5, No. 4 (Winter 1990):113-114

Lillian D. Wald: Progressive Activist. Book Review. *AFFILIA* 5, No. 4 (Winter 1990):113-114

**Kendall, Martha E.**

Elizabeth Cady Stanton. Reviewed by Mitzi Myers. *NWSA Journal* 2, No. 2 (Spring 1990):273-281

**Kenen, Regina H.**

Reproductive Laws for the 1990s. Book Review. *Women and Health* 16, Nos. 3/4 (1990):193-196

**Kennedy, Deborah**

Mary Shelley: Her Life, Her Fiction, Her Monsters. Book Review. *Canadian Women's Studies* 11, No. 2 (Fall 1990):94

**Kennedy, Elizabeth Lapovsky**

Identity Politics: Lesbian Feminism and the Limits of Community. Book Review. *NWSA Journal* 2, No. 3 (Summer 1990):495-497

**Kennedy, Elizabeth Lapovsky** (joint author). *See* DuBois, Ellen Carol

**Kennedy, Florynce**

Color Me Flo: My Hard Life and Good Times. *Woman of Power* 17 (Summer 1990):16-19

**Kennedy, Marilyn Moats**

Boredom on the Job. *Glamour* (October 1990):117

How to Bounce Back from a Mega-Embarrassment. *Glamour* (November 1990):115

Job Strategies: Can You Ask for a Raise Right Now? *Glamour* (February 1990):85-86

Job Strategies. *Glamour* (March 1990):111-116; (April 1990):125-130; (August 1990):99-100; (September 1990):149-153; (December 1990):109

Job Strategies: How Promotable Are You? *Glamour* (May 1990):143

Job Strategies: Surviving a No-Win Situation. *Glamour* (June 1990):121-122

Surprise! Your New Job isn't the One You Accepted. *Glamour* (November 1990):115-116

When to Take Charge, When to Pass Your Boss the Buck. *Glamour* (July 1990):75

**Kennedy, Nigel** (about)

A Plucky Prodigy. Margy Rochlin. *Harper's Bazaar* (February 1990):58

**Kennedy, Rose** (about)

Happy 100th Birthday, Aunt Rose. Kerry McCarthy. *Ladies' Home Journal* 107, No. 7 (July 1990):70-76

Rose Kennedy at 100. Lester David. *McCall's* 117, No. 8 (May 1990):83-88

**Kennedy Center (Washington, D. C.).** *See also* Arts Organizations – Politics

**Kennelly, Laura B.**

Modern Secrets. Book Review. *Belles Lettres* 5, No. 2 (Winter 1990):10

Poets Laureate. *Belles Lettres* 5, No. 2 (Winter 1990):10-11

Skins and Bones. Book Review. *Belles Lettres* 5, No. 2 (Winter 1990):10

Time's Power. Book Review. *Belles Lettres* 5, No. 2 (Winter 1990):10

**Kent, Debra**

Best Friends. *Family Circle* 103, No. 5 (April 3, 1990):62-66

Beyond Thirtysomething. *Working Woman* (September 1990):150-153 +

Living Together: The Truth and the Consequences. *Mademoiselle* (May 1990):201, 236

What You Don't Know About Orgasm Could Thrill You. *Mademoiselle* (February 1990):154-155 +

**Kent, George E.**

A Life of Gwendolyn Brooks. Reviewed by Jacquelyn Y. McLendon. *The Women's Review of Books* 7, Nos. 10-11 (July 1990):26

**Kent, Susan Kingsley**

Equal or Different: Women's Politics, 1800-1914. Book Review. *Gender & History* 2, No. 1 (Spring 1990):114-115

**Kenya – Status of Women**

Women Growing Stronger with Age: The Effect of Status in the United States and Kenya. Judith Todd, Ariella Friedman, and Priscilla Wanjiru Kariuki. *Psychology of Women Quarterly* 14, No. 4 (December 1990):567-577

**Kenzo** (about). *See* Fashion Designers

**Keratotomy, Radial**

Health Notes. *Vogue* (September 1990):468

**Kerber, Linda K.**

"I Have Don . . . Much to Carrey on the Warr": Women and the Shaping of Republican Ideology After the American Revolution. *Journal of Women's History* 1, No. 3 (Winter 1990):231-243

**Kern, Darlene** (joint author). *See* Emo, Dretha M.

**Kerr, Charles**

McBride: Behind the Myth. Book Review. *Healthright* 9, No. 4 (August 1990):45

**Kerschgens, Edda**

When Jessica Meets Natasha: A Feminist View of German Reunification. *Australian Feminist Studies* No. 12 (Summer 1990):15-27

**Kersey, Ethel M.**

Women Philosophers: A Bio-Critical Source Book. Review. *Feminist Collections* 11, No. 3 (Spring 1990):17

**Kertzer, David** (joint author). *See* Barbagli, Marzio

**Kesavan, Mukul**

Letters to Daddy. Film review. *Manushi* 58 (May-June 1990):43-44

**Kessler, Gail**

Keep Love Alive: How to Stop Playing the Blame Game. *Redbook* 175, No. 4 (August 1990):98-99

**Kessler, Marni Reva**

Growing Up with the Impressionists: The Diary of Julie Manet. Book Review. *Woman's Art Journal* 11, No. 1 (Spring-Summer 1990):41-42

**Kessler, Suzanne J.**

The Medical Construction of Gender: Case Management of Intersexed Infants. *Signs* 16, No. 1 (Autumn 1990):3-26

**Kessler-Harris, Alice**

A Woman's Wage: Symbolic Meanings and Social Consequences. Reviewed by Peggy Kahn. *The Women's Review of Books* 7, No. 12 (September 1990):21-23

**Kestenbaum, Clarice J.** and Williams, Daniel T. (editors)

Handbook of Clinical Assessment of Children and Adolescents. Book Review. *Adolescence* 25, No. 99 (Fall 1990):754

**Kestner, Joseph A.**

Mythology and Misogyny: The Social Discourse of Nineteenth-Century British Classical-Subject Painting. Reviewed by Marcia Pointon. *Gender & History* 2, No. 2 (Summer 1990):238-239

**Kevles, Bettyann**

Meat, Morality and Masculinity. *The Women's Review of Books* 7, No. 8 (May 1990):11-12

The Sexual Politics of Meat: A Feminist-Vegetarian Critical Theory. Book Review. *The Women's Review of Books* 7, No. 8 (May 1990):11-12

**Keynes, Milton** and Bunkle, Phillida

Second Opinion: The Politics of Women's Health in New Zealand. Reviewed by Roe Sybylla. *Australian Feminist Studies* No. 11 (Autumn 1990):129-131

**Kindermann, Joni** (joint author). *See* Paludi, Michele A.

**Kindness**

Living Beautifully: Acts of Caring. Alexandra Stoddard. *McCall's* 117, No. 7 (April 1990):136

**King, Andrea**

Big, Beautiful Lips. *Glamour* (April 1990):274-277

**King, B. B.** (about). *See* Music – Jazz

**King, Coretta Scott** (about). *See* De Veaux, Alexis, Milloy, Marilyn, and Ross, Michael Erik

**King, Donna**

"Prostitutes as Pariah in the Age of AIDS": A Content Analysis of Coverage of Women Prostitutes in *The New York Times* and the *Washington Post* September 1985-April 1988. *Women and Health* 16, Nos. 3/4 (1990):155-176

**King, Dorothy E.**

For K G. Poem. *Essence* 20, No. 11 (March 1990):115

Winter Warmth. Poem. *Essence* 21, No. 5 (September 1990):121

**King, Florence**

Ferris Beach. Book Review. *Vogue* (October 1990):271 +

Reflections in a Jaundiced Eye. Reviewed by Scarlet Cheng. *Belles Lettres* 5, No. 2 (Winter 1990):9

**King, Helen**

Jane Ellen Harrison: The Mask and the Self. Book Review. *Gender & History* 2, No. 1 (Spring 1990):103-104

**King, Janet Spencer**

The New Dating Game. *Working Mother* 13, No. 8 (August 1990):18-21

**King, Janis L.**

Justificatory Rhetoric for a Female Political Candidate: A Case Study of Wilma Mankiller. *Women's Studies in Communication* 13, No. 2 (Fall 1990):21-38

**King, Katherine Callen**

The Woman and the Lyre: Woman Writers in Classical Greece and Rome. Book Review. *Tulsa Studies in Women's Literature* 9, No. 2 (Fall 1990):323-326

**King, Linda**

Ghost. Film Review. *Spare Rib* 217 (October 1990):28

A Letter to My Sisters. Poem. *Spare Rib* No. 209 (February 1990):38

Longtime Companion. Film Review. *Spare Rib* 217 (October 1990):28

People in Trouble. Book Review. *Spare Rib* 219 (December 1990-January 1991):41

The Sheltering Sky. Film Review. *Spare Rib* 219 (December 1990-January 1991):28

Surviving Homelessness. *Spare Rib* No. 209 (February 1990):38-41

Wild Women in the Whirlwind: Afra-American Culture and the Contemporary Literary Renaissance. Book Review. *Spare Rib* No. 214 (July 1990):22-23

**King, Marjorie**

American Women's Open Door to Chinese Women: Which Way Does It Open? *Women's Studies International Forum* 13, No. 4 (1990):369-379

**King, Marlene** (about)

A Break for City Kids. Sandy MacDonald. *Family Circle* 103, No. 4 (March 13, 1990):19-22

**King, Martin Luther, Jr.** (about)

Back Talk: Friendship and Betrayal. Armstrong Williams. *Essence* 20, No. 9 (January 1990):110

**King, Mary E.** and Scandura, Janette

Health Report: Customized Stress Control: Identify Your Coping Style. *Working Woman* (October 1990):135-136

**King, Miriam** and Preston, Samuel H.

Who Lives with Whom? Individual Versus Household Values. *Journal of Family History* 15, No. 2 (April 1990):117-132

**King, Reatha Clark**

Becoming a Scientist: An Important Career Decision. *Sage* 6, No. 2 (Fall 1989):47-50

**King, Ursula**

Women and Spirituality: Voices of Protest and Promise. Reviewed by Marsha Hewitt. *Resources for Feminist Research* 19, No. 1 (March 1990):41-42

**King, Ynestra** (joint editor). *See* Harris, Adrienne E.

**Kingsley, Mary** (about)

Fish and Fetishes: A Victorian Woman on African Rivers. Pat Gilmartin. *Women and Environments* 12, No. 2 (Spring 1990): 10-12

A Voyage Out: The Life of Mary Kingsley. By Katherine Frank. Reviewed by Helen Callaway. *Women's Studies International Forum* 13, No. 4 (1990):405

**Kingsolver, Barbara**

Holding the Line: Women in the Great Arizona Mine Strike of 1983. Reviewed by Eleanor J. Bader. *Belles Lettres* 5, No. 4 (Summer 1990):16

Holding the Line: Women in the Great Arizona Mine Strike of 1983. Reviewed by Emily Bass. *The Women's Review of Books* 7, No. 7 (April 1990):9-10

Holding the Line: Women in the Great Arizona Mine Strike of 1983. Reviewed by Lee Heller. *off our backs* 20, No. 5 (May 1990):22

Holding the Line: Women in the Great Arizona Mine Strike of 1983. Reviewed by Shelley Ettinger. *New Directions for Women* 19, No. 3 (May/June 1990):17

Homeland and Other Stories. Reviewed by Michele Clark. *The Women's Review of Books* 7, No. 4 (January 1990):13

Notes from Underground. *The Women's Review of Books* 7, No. 9 (June 1990):21-22

Where the Sun Never Shines: A History of America's Bloody Coal Industry. Book Review. *The Women's Review of Books* 7, No. 9 (June 1990):21-22

**Kingston, Maxine Hong** (interview)

Interview: Maxine Hong Kingston. Sneja Gunew. *Hecate* 16, Nos. 1-2 (1990):48-60

**Kingston, Paul William**

Justice, Gender, and the Family. Book Review. *Journal of Marriage and the Family* 52, No. 2 (May 1990):562-563

**Kinkead, Gwen**

A Fortune in Silk. *Savvy Woman* (January 1990):44-46

**Kinman, Riley** (about). *See* D'Amico, Marie and Jubak, Jim

**Kinnear, Mary**

A Hidden Workforce: Homeworkers in England, 1850-1985. Book Review. *Resources for Feminist Research* 19, No. 2 (June 1990):37

**Kino, Carol**

The Earthquake Took Everything I Owned. *Glamour* (March 1990):161

**Kinsey, Chris** (about)

Cymreictod: Welsh Women. Paintings and Drawings. Penny Simpson. *Spare Rib* No. 211 (April 1990):31

**Kinship Systems**

Gender, Kinship and Rural Work in Colonial Punjab. Michelle Maskiell. *Journal of Women's History* 2, No. 1 (Spring 1990):35-72

**Kinsman, Gary**

The Regulation of Desire: Sexuality in Canada. Reviewed by Chris Waters. *Gender & History* 2, No. 2 (Summer 1990):218-222

**Kipfer, Barbara Ann**

14,000 Things to Be Happy About. Reviewed by Anne Lamott. *Mademoiselle* (May 1990):118

**Kippax, Susan**, Crawford, June, Waldby, Cathy, and Benton, Pam

Women Negotiating Heterosex: Implications for AIDS Prevention. *Women's Studies International Forum* 13, No. 6 (1990):533-542

**Kirby, Carol**

"How I Did It": When Your Image Is Frozen in Time. *Working Woman* (October 1990):53-56

**Kirby, Georgiana Bruce** (about)

Georgiana, Feminist Reformer of the West: The Journal of Georgiana Bruce Kirby. Edited by Carolyn Swift and Judith Steen. *New Directions for Women* 19, No. 2 (March/April 1990):15

**Kirby, Tess**

Delegating: How to Let Go and Keep Control. *Working Woman* (February 1990):32-37

Hands-Off Management. *Executive Female* (March/April 1990):44-45+

**Kirk, Gwyn**

You Can't Kill the Spirit: Stories of Women and Nonviolent Action. Book Review. *Women & Politics* 10, No. 1 (1990):78-80

**Kirk, Joyce F.**

Lives of Courage: Women for a New South Africa. Book Review. *NWSA Journal* 2, No. 4 (Autumn 1990):658-659

**Kirkland, Caroline M.**

A New Home, Who'll Follow? or Glimpses of Western Life. Reviewed by Barbara Horn. *Belles Lettres* 6, No. 1 (Fall 1990):57

**Kirkup, Gill** (joint author). *See* Carter, Ruth

**Kirp, David**

Health. *Vogue* (May 1990):198-204

**Kirsch, Sarah**

The Panther Woman: Five Tales from the Cassette Recorder. Reviewed by Nancy Derr. *Belles Lettres* 5, No. 4 (Summer 1990):9

The Panther Women: Five Stories from the Cassette Recorder. Reviewed by Hilda Scott. *The Women's Review of Books* 7, No. 4 (January 1990):10

**Kirschenbaum, Jill**

The Symmetry of Maya Ying Lin. *Ms.* 1, No. 2 (September/October 1990):20-22

**Kirshenbaum, Gayle**

Abortion: Is There a Doctor in the Clinic? *Ms.* 1, No. 2 (September/October 1990):86-87

A $5 Declaration of Independence. *Ms.* 1, No. 1 (July/August 1990):87

Exile in the Promised Land: A Memoir. Book Review. *Ms.* 1, No. 3 (November/December 1990):55

Mentor Express. *Ms.* 1, No. 3
(November/December 1990):90

West Bank and Gaza: Occupied Feminism. *Ms.* 1,
No. 2 (September/October 1990):8

**Kirshenbaum and Bond**

The World's Hippest Office. Julia Claiborne
Johnson. *Mademoiselle* (May 1990):210-213, 232

**Kirst-Ashman, Karen K.**

Deceptive Distinctions: Sex, Gender, and the Social
Order. Book Review. *AFFILIA* 5, No. 1 (Spring
1990):116-118

Gender in Intimate Relations. Book Review. *AFFILIA*
5, No. 1 (Spring 1990):116-118

**Kisekka, Mere Nakateregga**

AIDS in Uganda as a Gender Issue. *Women and
Therapy* 10, No. 3 (1990):35-53

Gender and Mental Health in Africa. *Women and
Therapy* 10, No. 3 (1990):1-13

**Kishwar, Madhu**

In Defence of Our *Dharma. Manushi* 60
(September-October 1990):2-15

The Kashmir Crisis: What Are Our Options?
*Manushi* 58 (May-June 1990):2-8

Learning to Take People Seriously. *Manushi* 56
(January-February 1990):2-10

Why I Do Not Call Myself a Feminist. *Manushi* 61
(November-December 1990):2-8

Women's Organisations: The Pressure of
Unrealistic Expectations. *Manushi* No. 59 (July-
August 1990):11-14

**Kishwar, Madhu and Vanita, Ruth**

Inheritance Rights for Women: A Response to
Some Commonly Expressed Fears. *Manushi* 57
(March-April 1990):3-15

**Kishwar, Madhu** (joint author). *See* Corea, Gena

**Kiss and Tell** (about)

Drawing the Line. Edited by J. Z. Grover. *Out/Look*
No. 10 (Fall 1990):6-11

**Kissen, Rita M.**

Teaching Agnes Smedley's *Daughter of Earth.*
*NWSA Journal* 2, No. 3 (Summer 1990):425-434

**Kissman, Kris**

Social Support and Gender Role Attitude among
Teenage Mothers. *Adolescence* 25, No. 99 (Fall
1990):709-716

**Kitch, Sally L.**

Chaste Liberation: Celibacy and Female Cultural
Status. Reviewed by Rickie Solinger. *Women and
Health* 16, No. 2 (1990):132-134

**Kitchens – Remodeling**

At Home in the Kitchen. Celia Slom. *McCall's* 117,
No. 9 (June 1990):113-117

Kitchens for People Who Love to Cook. Lauren
Payne and Jan Turner Hazard. *Ladies' Home Journal*
107, No. 3 (March 1990):184-198

Old Meets New: Kitchens with a Past. *Glamour*
(September 1990):334-336

Room for Improvement. Lauren Payne and Karen J.
Reisler. *Ladies' Home Journal* 107, No. 5 (May
1990):168-174

A Timesaver Kitchen. Sally Clark. *McCall's* 117, No.
9 (June 1990):103-111

**Kitson, Gay C.** and Morgan, Leslie A.

The Multiple Consequences of Divorce: A Decade
Review. *Journal of Marriage and the Family* 52, No.
4 (November 1990):913-924

**Kitzinger, Celia**

The Social Construction of Lesbianism. Reviewed
by Helen Lenskyj. *Resources for Feminist Research*
19, No. 1 (March 1990):32

The Social Construction of Lesbianism. Reviewed
by L. Diane Bernard. *AFFILIA* 5, No. 2 (Summer
1990):100-102

**Klaczynski, Paul A.**

Cultural-Developmental Tasks and Adolescent
Development: Theoretical and Methodological
Considerations. *Adolescence* 25, No. 100 (Winter
1990):811-823

**Klass, Perri**

Other Women's Children. Excerpt. Short story.
*Redbook* 176, No. 1 (November 1990):58-70+

Other Women's Children. Reviewed by Vanessa
Northington Gamble. *The Women's Review of Books*
8, No. 3 (December 1990):10-11

A Parent's Ordeal. *Family Circle* 103, No. 6 (April
24, 1990):90-92+

For Women Everywhere. Short story. *Glamour* (July
1990):124-129

**Klass, Perri** (about)

Glamour's First Summer Fiction Issue: Meet the
Authors. *Glamour* (July 1990):121

**Klatch, Rebecca E.**

Women of the New Right. Reviewed by Debra
Renée Kaufman. *Gender and Society* 4, No. 1
(March 1990):118-120

Women of the New Right. Reviewed by Jane
DeHart. *Signs* 15, No. 2 (Winter 1990):405-408

**Klausner, Kim**

On Wearing Skirts. *Out/Look* No. 8 (Spring
1990):18+

**Klavan, Ellen**

Sharing Child Care Costs. *Working Mother*
(November 1990):52-56

**Klawiter, Maren**

Using Arendt and Heidegger to Consider Feminist Thinking on Women and Reproductive/Infertility Technologies. *Hypatia* 5, No. 3 (Fall 1990):65-89

**Kleber, Herbert** (interview)

Drug War. Elizabeth Kaye. *Vogue* (March 1990):354-362

**Klebesadel, Helen**

Medusa Faced. *Woman of Power* 15 (Fall-Winter 1990):58

**Kleiman, Mark A. R.** (joint author). *See* Hamill, Pete

**Klein, Anne** (about). *See also* Fashion Designers

**Klein, Anne C.** (joint author). *See* Brock, Rita Nakashima

**Klein, Calvin** (about). *See also* Fashion Designers; Talley, André Leon

Fast Times. *Harper's Bazaar* (November 1990):138-143

**Klein, Easy**

Specialty Urged in Women's Health. *New Directions for Women* 19, No. 6 (November-December 1990):1+

**Klein, Ethel** (joint author). *See* Gelb, Joyce

**Klein, Kathleen Gregory**

Peggy Deery: An Irish Family at War. Book Review. *Belles Lettres* 5, No. 3 (Spring 1990):5

**Klein, Kristen** (about). *See* College Students – Leadership

**Klein, Michael**

A Stepfather, a Child. Poem. *Out/Look* No. 8 (Spring 1990):57

**Klein, Renate D.**

The Exploitation of a Desire: Women's Experiences with In Vitro Fertilisation – An Exploratory Survey. Reviewed by Jocelynne Scutt. *Women's Studies International Forum* 13, No. 6 (1990):605-608

Infertility: Women Speak Out about Their Experiences of Reproductive Medicine. Reviewed by Jocelynne Scutt. *Women's Studies International Forum* 13, No. 6 (1990):605-608

Women with a Fertility Problem. *Connexions* 32 (1990):22-23

**Klein, Renate D.** and Steinberg, Deborah Lynn (editors)

Radical Voices. Reviewed by Carol Anne Douglas. *off our backs* 20, No. 4 (April 1990):18

**Klein, Renate D.** (joint author). *See* Corea, Gena; Ewing, Christine

**Kleine, Kim**

U.S. Women See Combat in Panama. *off our backs* 20, No. 3 (March 1990):22-23

**Kleinke, Chris L.** and Meyer, Cecilia

Evaluation of Rape Victim by Men and Women with High and Low Belief in a Just World. *Psychology of Women Quarterly* 14, No. 3 (September 1990):343-353

**Klein-Lataud, Christine**

De la lecture and De la critique. Book Review. *Resources for Feminist Research* 19, No. 1 (March 1990):7-8

**Kleinman, Lynne H.**

The World of Our Mothers: The Lives of Jewish Immigrant Women. Book Review. *Gender and Society* 4, No. 1 (March 1990):101-103

**Kleinman, Ronald L.** (editor)

Family Planning Handbook for Doctors. Reviewed by Lynnette Wray. *Healthright* 9, No. 2 (February 1990):38

**Kleinmann, Leanne**

Spins, Skids, Curves and Clutches. *Savvy Woman* (March 1990):30-32

Women and AIDS: Reexamining the Risk. *Glamour* (May 1990):88-92

**Klejman, Laurence** and Rochefort, Florence

L'égalité en marche: La Féminisme français sous la Troisie4me République. Reviewed by Diane Lamoureux. *Resources for Feminist Research* 19, No. 2 (June 1990):40

**Klepfisz, Irena**

Dreams of an Insomniac: Jewish Feminist Essays, Speeches and Diatribes. Reviewed by Evelyn Torton Beck. *Belles Lettres* 6, No. 1 (Fall 1990):2-5

Jewish Feminism 1913: Yente Serdatzky's "Confession." *Bridges* 1, No. 2 (Fall 1990): 77-92

Two-thousand March for Mideast Peace. *New Directions for Women* 19, No. 2 (March/April 1990):16

**Klepfisz, Irena – Criticism and Interpretation**

From Nightmare to Vision: An Introduction to the Essays of Irena Klepfisz. Evelyn Beck Torton. *Belles Lettres* 6, No. 1 (Fall 1990):2-5

**Klepfisz, Irena** (co-interviewer). *See* Falbel, Rita

**Klepfisz, Irena** (joint author). *See* Falbel, Rita; Kaye/Kantrowitz, Melanie

**Klepfisz, Irena** (joint editor). *See* Kaye/Kantrowitz, Melanie (editor)

**Klepfisz, Irene** (joint author). *See* Falbel, Rita

**Klingenberg, Michelle** (joint author). *See* Chan, Shirley

**Klinger, Eric**

Do You Think About Sex Too Much? *Glamour* (September 1990):322-323+

**Klipple, Gary L.** (joint author). *See* Lambert, Vickie A.

**Klitzman, Susan**

Good Work at the Video Display Terminal: A Feminist Ethical Analysis of Changes in Clerical Work. Book Review. *Women and Health* 16, Nos. 3/4 (1990):205-206

**Klug, Lisa**

New Rabbinical College Excludes Women. *Lilith* 15, No. 3 (Summer 1990):5

**Klugman, Barbara**

The Politics of Contraception in South Africa. *Women's Studies International Forum* 13, No. 3 (1990):261-271

**Knapman, Claudia**

White Women in Fiji, 1835-1930: The Ruin of Empire? Reviewed by Anand A. Yang. *Women's Studies International Forum* 13, No. 4 (1990):407-408

**Kneller, Jane**

Beyond Feminist Aesthetics: Feminist Literature and Social Change. Book Review. *Hypatia* 5, No. 3 (Fall 1990):165-168

**Kneupper, Willie Mae**

Love's Labours Quoted. *Lear's* (February 1990):49-50

Women Travelers. *On the Issues* 15 (Summer 1990):24 +

**Knight, Cindy**

State Historical Society of Wisconsin Welcomes Suffragist's Papers. *Feminist Collections* 12, No. 1 (Fall 1990):18-20

**Knight, Gladys** (about). *See* Musicians, Popular, "Repeat Performance"

**Knight, Kimberly**

Afrocentric Gifts. *Essence* 21, No. 8 (December 1990):90

Black Like Us: Dolls for Our Kids. *Essence* 21, No. 7 (November 1990):104-109

**Knoll, Stephen** (about). *See* Beauty Culture, "Who Cuts Who"

**Knoth, Marge**

Slice of Life. *Family Circle* 103, No. 4 (March 13, 1990):N.P.

**Knowlden, Sheila**

Withdrawing from Benzodiazepines. *Healthright* 9, No. 2 (February 1990):13-15

**Knowledge, Theory of.** *See also* Feminism – Theory; Women's Studies

Epistemological and Methodological Commitments of a Feminist Perspective. Marlene G. Fine. *Women & Language* 13, No. 2 (Winter 1990):35-36

Feminism and the Constructions of Knowledge: Speculations on a Subjective Science. Georganne Rundblad. *Women & Language* 13, No. 1 (Fall 1990):53-55

Flight to Objectivity: Essays on Cartesianism and Culture. By Susan R. Bordo. Reviewed by Jacquelyn N. Zita. *Signs* 15, No. 3 (Spring 1990):645-648

**Knowles, Jane Price**

Woman-Defined Motherhood. *Women and Therapy* 10, Nos. 1/2 (1990):1-7

**Knuckles, Jeffrey**

Patience. Poem. *Essence* 21, No. 5 (September 1990):130

**Koch, Donald**

Recipes, Cooking, and Conflict: A Response to Heldke's *Recipes for Theory*. *Hypatia* 5, No. 1 (Spring 1990):156-164

**Koehler-Vandergraaf, Marie** (interview)

About "Joan's Room": Mary Sparling Interviews *Atlantis* Guest Artist Marie Koehler-Vandergraaf. Mary Sparling. *Atlantis* 15, No. 2 (Spring 1990):122-126

**Koenig, Rachel** (joint editor). *See* Betsko, Kathleen

**Koertge, Noretta**

Comments. *Journal of Women's History* 2, No. 2 (Fall 1990):164-165

**Koff, Elissa**, Rierdan, Jill, and Stubbs, Margaret L.

Conceptions and Misconceptions of the Menstrual Cycle. *Women and Health* 16, Nos. 3/4 (1990):119-136

**Kogawa, Joy – Criticism and Interpretation**

Japanese American Women's Life Stories: Maternality in Monica Sone's *Nisei Daughter* and Joy Kogawa's *Obasan*. Shirley Geok-Lin Lim. *Feminist Studies* 16, No. 2 (Summer 1990):289-312

**Kohn, Alfie**

The Top 10 Sex Myths. *Glamour* (October 1990):252-253 +

**Kohn, Jennifer** (joint author). *See* Brown, Karen

**Kohut, David R.** (joint author). *See* Cypess, Sandra Messinger

**Kokate, Narayan** (joint author). *See* Jamshedji, Armin

**Kolata, Gina**

Miracle or Menace? *Redbook* 175, No. 5 (September 1990):174-176 +

**Kolb, Vera**

Body/Politics: Women and the Discourses of Science. Book Review. *Feminist Collections* 11, No. 4 (Summer 1990):4-8

Feminism and Science. Book Review. *Feminist Collections* 11, No. 4 (Summer 1990):4-8

**Kolbert, Elizabeth**

McCallmanack: Tuning In to Women's Issues. *McCall's* 117, No. 11 (August 1990):62

**Kolbert, Kathryn** (joint author). *See* Copelon, Rhonda

**Koltnow, Emily** and Dumas, Lynne S.

Is it Time to Shift Careers? Excerpt. *McCall's* 117, No. 12 (September 1990):120-121+

**Kondo, Dorinne K.**

Crafting Selves: Power, Gender and Discourses of Identity in a Japanese Workplace. Reviewed by Kate Gilbert. *The Women's Review of Books* 8, No. 1 (October 1990):5-7

**Konek, Carol Wolfe**

Dangerous Discussions. *Heresies* 25 (1990):83-86

**Konner, Linda**

Where I Grew Up. *Glamour* (March 1990):174

**Konner, Melvin** (joint author). *See* Easton, S. Boyd

**Konstan, David**

Love in the Greek Novel. *Differences* 2, No. 1 (Spring 1990):186-205

**Koons, Jeff** (about)

Koons Crazy. Dodie Kazanjian. *Vogue* (August 1990):338-343+

**Koonz, Claudia**

Comrades and Sisters: Feminism, Socialism and Pacifism in Europe, 1870-1945. Book Review. *Gender & History* 2, No. 1 (Spring 1990):120-122

**Koonz, Claudia** (interview)

Mothers in the Fatherland. Fred Pelka. *On the Issues* 16 (Fall 1990):26-28+

**Koopman, Raymond F.** (joint author). *See* Ehrenberg, Marion F.

**Kope, Teresa M.** (joint author). *See* Bayrakal, Sadi

**Kopecky, Gini**

Nine Tips to Happier Family Holidays. *Redbook* 176, No. 1 (November 1990):110-111+

**Kopelson, Kevin**

Wilde, Barthes, and the Orgasmics of Truth. *Genders* 7 (Spring 1990):22-31

**Kopp, Wendy** (about). *See also* Leadership, "1990 Women of the Year"

**Koppelman, Susan**

Belles Lettres Interview: Merrill Joan Gerber. *Belles Lettres* 5, No. 3 (Spring 1990):16-17

Civil War Women: American Women Shaped by Conflict in Stories by Alcott, Chopin, Welty and Others. Book Review. *Belles Lettres* 5, No. 4 (Summer 1990):41

Heaviness in the Air. *Belles Lettres* 5, No. 4 (Summer 1990):41

**Korboot, Paula J.** (joint author). *See* Hier, Sally J.

**Korn, Lester** (about)

Lunch. Interview. Frances Lear. *Lear's* (March 1990):25-28

**Kornblatt, Judith Deutsch**

Balancing Acts: Contemporary Stories by Russsian Women. Book Review. *Feminist Collections* 11, No. 4 (Summer 1990):3-4

The Image of Women in Contemporary Soviet Fiction: Selected Short Stories from the U.S.S.R. Book Review. *Feminist Collections* 11, No. 4 (Summer 1990):3-4

**Kornbluh, Felice**

Nice Jewish Girls: A Lesbian Anthology. Book Review. *off our backs* 20, No. 9 (October 1990):15-16

**Kornbluh, Felicia**

Berthe Morisot. Book Review. *The Women's Review of Books* 8, No. 2 (November 1990):13-14

Managing Lives: Corporate Women and Social Change. Book Review. *The Women's Review of Books* 7, No. 8 (May 1990):9-10

The Secret of Her Success. *The Women's Review of Books* 8, No. 2 (November 1990):13-14

Tough at the Top. *The Women's Review of Books* 7, No. 8 (May 1990):9-10

Wall Street Women: Women in Power on Wall Street Today. Book Review. *The Women's Review of Books* 7, No. 8 (May 1990):9-10

**Korn/Ferry International.** *See* Korn, Lester (about)

**Kors, Michael** (about). *See* Fashion Designers, "Gentlemen's Choice"; Fashion Designers, "What I Like for Fall"

**Korsmeyer, Carolyn** (joint author). *See* Hein, Hilde

**Korsmeyer, Carolyn W.** (joint author). *See* DuBois, Ellen Carol

**Korstad, Robert** (joint author). *See* Hall, Jacquelyn Dowd

**Kort, Michele**

The Age of Anonymous. *Essence* 20, No. 11 (March 1990):32

The Epi-Scandal. *Savvy* (December-January 1991):32-34

Making Love, Making Choices. *Essence* 20, No. 11 (March 1990):57-58

The Pick-Up Game. *Women's Sports and Fitness* 12, No. 4 (May-June 1990):68-71

Spinning Their Wheels. *Ms.* 1, No. 1 (July/August 1990):84-85

The Thinking Woman's Cable. *Savvy Woman* (November 1990):34-36

Workouts Without the Work: A Sport-By-Sport Conditioning Guide. *Women's Sports and Fitness* 12, No. 7 (October 1990):52-55

**Koss, Mary P.** (joint author). *See* Gidycz, Christine A.

**Koster-Lossack, Angelika** and Levin, Tobe
Women's Studies in Europe: Conference Reports, Part II. *NWSA Journal* 2, No. 2 (Spring 1990):264-268

**Kotlikoff, Barbara** (about)
One Woman's Office: Essence of Elegance. Leah Rosch. *Working Woman* (January 1990):120-121

**Kott, Andrea**
The Get-Rich-Quick Trick. *Savvy Woman* (September 1990):23-24

**Kott, Jan,** White, Edmund, Grabska, Elzbieta, and Kuryluk, Ewa
The Fabric of Memory, Ewa Kuryluk: Cloth Works, 1978-1987. Reviewed by Danuta Batorsky. *Woman's Art Journal* 11, No. 2 (Fall 1990-Winter 1991):34-35

**Kottner, Ann E.**
An Abyss of Light. Book Review. *The Women's Review of Books* 7, Nos. 10-11 (July 1990):40-41

The Cloning of Joanna May. Book Review. *The Women's Review of Books* 7, Nos. 10-11 (July 1990):40-41

Memories and Visions: Women's Fantasy and Science Fiction. Book Review. *The Women's Review of Books* 7, Nos. 10-11 (July 1990):40-41

The Moonbane Magic. Book Review. *The Women's Review of Books* 7, Nos. 10-11 (July 1990):40-41

New Worlds for Women. *The Women's Review of Books* 7, Nos. 10-11 (July 1990):40-41

Tehanu, the Last Book of Earthsea. Book Review. *The Women's Review of Books* 7, Nos. 10-11 (July 1990):40-41

**Kovel, Ralph** and Kovel, Terry
It's Easy to Collect: Country Pottery. *Redbook* 176, No. 1 (November 1990):196

**Kovel, Terry** (joint author). *See* Kovel, Ralph

**Kovick, Kris** (interview)
Alison Bechdel and Kris Kovick. *Hot Wire* 6, No. 3 (September 1990):12-14+

**Kowaleski-Wallace, Beth** (joint author). *See* Yaeger, Patricia

**Kozhevnikova, Nadezhda**
Home. Short story. *Ladies' Home Journal* 107, No. 5 (May 1990):148-154

**Kozloff, Joyce**
Patterns of Desire. Reviewed by Elizabeth Hess. *The Women's Review of Books* 7, No. 12 (September 1990):10

**Kozol, Wendy**
The Colonial Harem. Book Review. *Gender & History* 2, No. 1 (Spring 1990):110-113

Images of Women: The Portrayal of Women in Photography of the Middle East, 1860-1950. Book Review. *Gender & History* 2, No. 1 (Spring 1990):110-113

**Krakauer, Jon**
High Aspirations. *Women's Sports and Fitness* 12, No. 7 (October 1990):32+

**Kramer, Laura Shapiro**
A Second Chance for Seth. *Family Circle* 103, No. 4 (March 13, 1990):114-116+

**Kramer, Pamela E.** and Lehman, Sheila
Mismeasuring Women: A Critique of Research on Computer Ability and Avoidance. *Signs* 16, No. 1 (Autumn 1990):158-172

**Kranich, Kimberlie A.**
Catalysts of Change: U.S. Periodicals by Women of Color, 1963-1989. *Feminist Teacher* 5, No. 1 (Spring 1990):26-41

**Krantz, Birgit**
Helping Each Other: A Swedish Perspective. *Canadian Women's Studies* 11, No. 2 (Fall 1990):77-79

**Kraushar, Jon** (joint author). *See* Ailes, Roger

**Kraut, Ruth**
We Rejoice in Our Heritage: Home Rituals for Secular and Humanistic Jews. Book Review. *Bridges* 1, No. 2 (Fall 1990): 128-130

**Kravitz, Len**
Body Management: The Executive Workout. *Working Woman* (February 1990):115-120

Getting in Step. *Women's Sports and Fitness* 12, No. 3 (April 1990):18

**Kravitz, Lenny** (about)
Let Love Rule. Carol Cooper. *Essence* 20, No. 10 (February 1990):54-55+

**Kray, Susan**
Never Cry Bull Moose: Of Mooses and Men: The Case of the Scheming Gene. *Women & Language* 13, No. 1 (Fall 1990):31-37

**Krefetz, Sharon Perlman**
Without Precedent: The Life and Career of Eleanor Roosevelt. Book Review. *Women's Studies International Forum* 13, No. 3 (1990):281-283

**Kreiner, Julie A.** (joint author). *See* Nordheim, Christine

**Kreitman, Jill** (about). *See* Title, Stacy

**Kremer, Belinda**
Learning to Say No: Keeping Feminist Research for Ourselves. *Women's Studies International Forum* 13, No. 5 (1990):463-467

**Kumar, P.** (joint author). *See* Singh, Padam

**Kunes, Ellen**

Body Management: The New Fitness Myths – Why You Shouldn't Always Play by the Rules. *Working Woman* (August 1990):87-88

The Buzz on Beef. *Mademoiselle* (December 1990):186

Diet News: How Hollywood Eats. *Mademoiselle* (September 1990):282

Diet News: How to Lose Five Pounds This Month. *Mademoiselle* (January 1990):144

Diet News: Secrets from a Diet Diary. *Mademoiselle* (February 1990):196

Diet News: These Fats Are Guaranteed Fakes. *Mademoiselle* (June 1990):204

No, You Don't Have Cancer: A Reassuring Guide for Hypochondriacs. *Mademoiselle* (June 1990):128

No-Sweat Fitness. *Working Woman* (April 1990):119-120

See Jane Run – The Video Workout Revival. Bibliography. *Mademoiselle* (November 1990):194

Spas: Not for Snobs Only. Bibliography. *Mademoiselle* (October 1990):202

**Kuppler, Lisa** (joint author). *See* Diamond, Irene

**Kurdek, Lawrence A.**

Divorce History and Self-reported Psychological Distress in Husbands and Wives. *Journal of Marriage and the Family* 52, No. 3 (August 1990):701-708

Effects of Child Age on Marital Quality and Distress of Newly Married Mothers and Stepfathers. *Journal of Marriage and the Family* 52, No. 1 (February 1990):81-85

**Kurland, Jeffrey** (about). *See also* Costume Design

**Kurth, Peter**

American Cassandra: The Life of Dorothy Thompson. Reviewed by John Leonard. *Vogue* (June 1990):144-150

**Kurylko, Nathalie**

Where to Live Like a Millionaire. *Savvy Woman* (September 1990):52-53

**Kuryluk, Ewa** (about)

The Fabric of Memory, Ewa Kuryluk: Cloth Works, 1978-1987. By Jan Kott, Edmund White, Elzbieta Grabska, and Ewa Kuryluk. Reviewed by Danuta Batorsky. *Woman's Art Journal* 11, No. 2 (Fall 1990-Winter 1991):34-35

**Kuryluk, Ewa** (joint author). *See* Kott, Jan

**Kutner, Nancy G.** and Brogan, Donna

Gender Roles, Medical Practice Roles, and Ob-Gyn Career Choice: A Longitudinal Study. *Women and Health* 16, Nos. 3/4 (1990):99-117

**Kuwait.** *See also* Persian Gulf War, 1990-1991

**Kuwait – Politics and Government**

Escape from Kuwait. *Glamour* (November 1990):104-108

**Kuwait – United States Ambassador**

Up Front. *Ladies' Home Journal* 107, No. 12 (December 1990):101-104

**Kwanzaa**

Parenting: The Harvest of Kwanzaa. Dee Watts-Jones. *Essence* 21, No. 8 (December 1990):114

**Kyoto (Japan) – Description and Travel**

Kyoto Encounter. Tad Friend. *Vogue* (January 1990):134-138

# L

**Láadan**

Age, Bodily Secretions, Lesbians . . . Developing the Language. Julia Penelope. *Hot Wire* 6, No. 2 (May 1990):18-19+

**LaBelle, Patti** (about). *See* Leadership, "1990 Essence Awards"; Musicians, Popular, "Repeat Performance"

**Labor, Division of.** *See* Feminist Organizations – Division of Labor

**Labor – Gender Differences**

The Ideology of Skill: A Case Study. Kathy McDermott. *Australian Feminist Studies* No. 11 (Autumn 1990):61-73

**Labor and Laboring Classes.** *See* Working Class

**Labor Contracts**

Financial Workshop: Negotiating an Employment Contract. Mary Rowland. *Working Woman* (February 1990):65-68

**Labor Force.** *See* Occupational Trends

**Laborie, Françoise**

Where to Put Madame X's Ovocytes? *Connexions* 32 (1990):11-13

**Labor Laws and Legislation.** *See also* Child Labor

Child Labor Laws: What Every Parent Needs to Know. Julia Kagan and Christina Ferrari. *McCall's* 118, No. 1 (October 1990):106

**Labor Productivity.** *See* Time Management

**Labor Unions.** *See also* International Ladies' Garment Workers Union

Asian Women Workers: Organising, Educating and Solidarity. *Women in Action* 1-2 (1990):7-8

On Boycotting Feminist Books. Carol Anne Douglas. *off our backs* 20, No. 11 (December 1990):17

Caring by the Hour: Women, Work, and Organizing at Duke Medical Center. By Karen Sacks. Reviewed by Sandra Morgen. *Feminist Studies* 16, No. 1 (Spring 1990):53-67

The Diary of a Shirtwaist Striker. By Theresa Serber Malkiel. Reviewed by Annelise Orleck. *The Women's Review of Books* 8, No. 3 (December 1990):30-31

First International Exchange of Women Unionists. Miriam Ching Louie. *off our backs* 20, No. 3 (March 1990):18-19

Holding the Line: Women in the Great Arizona Mine Strike of 1983. By Barbara Kingsolver. Reviewed by Emily Bass. *The Women's Review of Books* 7, No. 7 (April 1990):9-10

Holding the Line: Women in the Great Arizona Mine Strike of 1983. By Barbara Kingsolver. Reviewed by Lee Heller. *off our backs* 20, No. 5 (May 1990):22

Holding the Line: Women in the Great Arizona Mine Strike of 1983. By Barbara Kingsolver. Reviewed by Shelley Ettinger. *New Directions for Women* 19, No. 3 (May/June 1990):17

Labor's Flaming Youth: Telephone Operators and Worker Militancy 1878-1923. By Stephen Norwood. Reviewed by Annelise Orleck. *The Women's Review of Books* 8, No. 3 (December 1990):30-31

Marching Together: Women of the Brotherhood of Sleeping Car Porters. Melinda Chateauvert. *NWSA Journal* 2, No. 4 (Autumn 1990):687-689

Men, Women, and Work: Class, Gender and Protest in the New England Shoe Industry, 1780-1910. By Mary A. Blewett. Reviewed by Louise A. Tilly. *Gender and Society* 4, No. 2 (June 1990):269-272

A Real-Life "Norma Rae." Marcia Cohen. *Good Housekeeping* 211, No. 1 (July 1990):98-101

Rethinking Troubled Relations between Women and Unions: Craft Unionism and Female Activism. Dorothy Sue Cobble. *Feminist Studies* 16, No. 3 (Fall 1990):519-548

Strike Strengthens Women. Miriam Ching Louie. *New Directions for Women* 19, No. 4 (July-August 1990):10

They Would Not Be Moved. Eleanor J. Bader. *Belles Lettres* 5, No. 4 (Summer 1990):16

Traditional and Nontraditional Patterns of Female Activism in the United Farm Workers of America, 1962 to 1980. Margaret Rose. *Frontiers* 11, No. 1 (1990):26-32

Women's Collective Action in the Gallup, New Mexico Coalfields during the 1930s. Katharine Dawson. *NWSA Journal* 2, No. 4 (Autumn 1990):690-692

**La Brasca, Bob**

Marilyn Monroe: The Lost Photographs. *Redbook* 175, No. 6 (October 1990):118-121

**Lacasse-Lovsted, Lucienne**

L'Arbre de vie. *Canadian Women's Studies* 11, No. 2 (Fall 1990):17-18

**Lace and Lace Making.** See also Lace Craft

Amazing Lace. *Harper's Bazaar* (May 1990):110-115

Weekenders. *Redbook* 175, No. 3 (July 1990):104-107

**Lace and Lace-Making**

Amazing Lace. *Harper's Bazaar* (December 1990):87

**Lace Craft**

Linens, Lace, All Over the Place. Excerpt. Tricia Foley. *McCall's* 117, No. 12 (September 1990):126-129

**Lach, Mary Alyce** (joint author). See Peterson, Sharyl Bender

**Lackovic2-Grgin, Katica** and Dekovic2, Maja

The Contribution of Significant Others to Adolescents' Self-Esteem. *Adolescence* 25, No. 100 (Winter 1990):839-846

**Lackow, Manya Prozanskaya**

In the Russian Gymnasia. Excerpt. *Lilith* 15, No. 1 (Winter 1990):15-20

**Lacroix, Christian** (about). See Fashion Designers, "Predictions"; Talley, André Leon

The Kings of Color: Lacroix. Georgina Howell. *Vogue* (September 1990):546-550+

Paris Bouquet. Christopher Petkanas. *Harper's Bazaar* (September 1990):318

**Ladd, Cheryl** (about). See Hair Styles

**Lader, Lawrence**

Margaret Sanger: Militant, Pragmatist, Visionary. *On the Issues* 14 (1990):11-12+

**Ladies' Home Journal**

Never Underestimate the Power of a Woman. Myrna Blyth. *Ladies' Home Journal* 107, No. 11 (November 1990):16-25

**Ladies' Home Journal – Editorial Policy**

A Daring New Concept: The Ladies' Home Journal and Modern Feminism. Jean E. Hunter. *NWSA Journal* 2, No. 4 (Autumn 1990):583-602

**Ladner, Joyce A.**

Black Women as Do-ers: The Social Responsibility of Black Women. *Sage* 6, No. 1 (Summer 1989):87-88

Our Families – Then and Now. *Essence* 21, No. 1 (May 1990):180-182

**LaDuke, Winona**

Innu Women and Nation: The Occupation of Nistassinan. *off our backs* 20, No. 10 (November 1990):10+

Third World Housing Development and Indigenous People in North America. *Canadian Women's Studies* 11, No. 2 (Fall 1990):12-14

**LaFee, Scott**

Desert Dream. *Lear's* (April 1990):50

**LaFortune, Alexa**

Beds I Have Known. *Lear's* (April 1990):48-49

**LaFrance, Marianne**

The Unopposite Sex: The End of the Gender Battle. Book Review. *Psychology of Women Quarterly* 14, No. 3 (September 1990):441-443

**Lagerfeld, Karl** (about). *See also* Fashion Designers, "Predictions"; Perfumes; Talley, André Leon

Belle Chanel. *Harper's Bazaar* (December 1990):136-139

Crossing Borders. Nina Malkin. *Harper's Bazaar* (September 1990):242-243+

View. Laurie Schechter. *Vogue* (January 1990):39

**LaGrone, Oliver**

To Lionel Hampton. Poem. *Essence* 20, No. 11 (March 1990):115

**Lague, Louise**

Flirting for the Fun of it. *Glamour* (March 1990):242-243+

Hair Styles from Hell. *Glamour* (August 1990):198-201

How to Say No! *Glamour* (November 1990):250-251+

10 Things Motherhood has Taught Me. *Glamour* (May 1990):122-131

**Laidlaw, Toni,** Malmo, Cheryl, and associates

Healing Voices. Reviewed by Deborah C. Poff. *Atlantis* 15, No. 2 (Spring 1990):113-114

**Laizner, Andréa Maria** and Jeans, Mary Ellen

Identification of Predictor Variables of a Postpartum Emotional Reaction. *Health Care for Women International* 11, No. 2 (1990):191-207

**Lake, Marilyn**

Fresh Evidence, New Witnesses: Finding Women's History. Book Review. *Australian Feminist Studies* No. 12 (Summer 1990):121-122

**Lake, Marilyn** (joint author). *See* Grimshaw, Patricia

**Lakes, Kerry**

Caution: This Drama Is Not Based on Reality. *off our backs* 20, No. 1 (January 1990):17

**Lakhera, Archana**

Marriage Market. Poem. *Manushi* 56 (January-February 1990):27

**Lalor, Karen M.** (joint author). *See* Hailey, B. Jo

**Lama Foundation.** *See* New Mexico – Lama Foundation

**Lamanna, Dean**

Shanna Reed's "Major" Break. *Ladies' Home Journal* 107, No. 5 (May 1990):58

**Lamanna, Dean** and Leigh, Pamela

We Remember Mama. *Ladies' Home Journal* 107, No. 5 (May 1990):69-72

**Lamb, Patricia**

Spinsters Abroad: Victorian Lady Explorers. Book Review. *The Women's Review of Books* 7, No. 5 (February 1990):15

On the Trail of the Travelers. *The Women's Review of Books* 7, No. 5 (February 1990):15

**Lamb, Yannick Rice**

Charnett Moffett: Bass Hit. *Essence* 21, No. 5 (September 1990):48

**Lambada**

Lambada: The Sexy Way to Shape Up. *Mademoiselle* (June 1990):42-44

**Lambert, Alison**

The Red Furrow. Short Story. *Hecate* 16, Nos. 1-2 (1990):97-101

**Lambert, Clinton E.** (joint author). *See* Lambert, Vickie A.

**Lambert, Nina**

Season of Promise. Short Story. *Good Housekeeping* 210, No. 6 (June 1990):68-75

**Lambert, Paula** (about)

Entrepreneurial Edge: How to Stand Out in a Crowd. David E. Gumpert. *Working Woman* (November 1990):57-63+

**Lambert, Sandra**

Lunar Eclipse 1989. *Sinister Wisdom* 40 (Spring 1990):72-73

**Lambert-Lagacé, Louise**

The Nutrition Challenge for Women: A Guide to Wellness Without Dieting. Reviewed by Jo-Ann Minden. *Healthsharing* 11, No. 1 (December 1989):33-34

**LaMonte, Carla** (about)

Simpatico. Nelson W. Aldrich, Jr. *Lear's* (August 1990):90-97

**Lamott, Anne**

All New People. Reviewed by Lorraine E. McCormack. *Belles Lettres* 5, No. 2 (Winter 1990):12

The Burden of Proof. Book review. *Mademoiselle* (June 1990):98-101

The Dead Girl. Book review. *Mademoiselle* (September 1990):170

14,000 Things to Be Happy About. Book Review. *Mademoiselle* (May 1990):118

Happy None of the Time. *Mademoiselle* (May 1990):118

Kitties Rule. Bibliography. *Mademoiselle* (October 1990):102-104

Riding in Cars With Boys: Confessions of a Bad Girl Who Makes Good. Book Review. *Mademoiselle* (August 1990):108

Room Temperature. Book Review. *Mademoiselle* (April 1990):130

Season's Readings. Bibliography. *Mademoiselle* (December 1990):80-82

What Smart Women Know. Book review. *Mademoiselle* (November 1990):96-99

When Good Things Happen to Bad Girls. *Mademoiselle* (August 1990):108

**Lamoureux, Diane**

L'égalité en marche: La Féminisme français sous la Troisie4me République. Book Review. *Resources for Feminist Research* 19, No. 2 (June 1990):40

**Lampert, Hope**

Career Control: An Owner's Manual. *Working Woman* (September 1990):109-110

**Lamphere, Louise**

From Working Daughters to Working Mothers: Immigrant Women in a New England Industrial Community. Reviewed by Sandra Morgen. *Feminist Studies* 16, No. 1 (Spring 1990):53-67

**Lamude, Kevin G. and Daniels, Tom D.**

Mutual Evaluations of Communication Competence in Superior-Subordinate Relationships: Sex Role Incongruency and Pro-Male Bias. *Women's Studies in Communication* 13, No. 2 (Fall 1990):39-56

**Land, Leslie**

The Avid Gardener: Little Bulbs, Big Rewards. Bibliography. *McCall's* 117, No. 12 (September 1990):70

The Avid Gardener: Loveliness of Leaves. *McCall's* 118, No. 1 (October 1990):68

A Few Words from the Vegetable Patch. *McCall's* 117, No. 11 (August 1990):62-63

Vines: The Architect's Friend. *McCall's* 117, No. 9 (June 1990):45-47

**Landa, Anita**

No Accident: The Voices of Voluntarily Childless Women – An Essay on the Social Construction of Fertility Choices. *Women and Therapy* 10, Nos. 1/2 (1990):139-158

**Landau, Ellen G.** (joint author). *See* Rosen, Randy

**Landay, Lori** (joint author). *See* Demaray, Elyse

**Lander, Louise**

Images of Bleeding: Menstruation as Ideology. Reviewed by Anna Meigs. *Signs* 16, No. 1 (Autumn 1990):180-182

**Landers, Grace**

The Homeless Woman. Poem. *AFFILIA* 5, No. 1 (Spring 1990):1-3

**Landes, Joan B.**

Women and the Public Sphere in the Age of the French Revolution. Reviewed by Elisabeth G. Sledziewski. *Gender & History* 2, No. 3 (Autumn 1990):363-365

**Landi, Ann**

Sex, Lies & Lawsuits. *Mademoiselle* (January 1990):104-105+

**Landman, Beth**

Topward Bound. *Harper's Bazaar* (March 1990):132-148

**Landor, Liliane**

"Fundamentalism" – Haphazardly Used, Never Defined. *Spare Rib* No. 209 (February 1990):48

**Landor, Liliane** (joint editor). *See* Grewal, Shabnam

**Landrieu, Mary** (about) *See* leadership

**Landrine, Hope**

Women with Disabilities: Essays in Psychology, Culture and Politics. Book Review. *Psychology of Women Quarterly* 14, No. 3 (September 1990):435-437

**Landscape Architecture**

Backyards of the Rich and Famous. Lauren Payne. *Ladies' Home Journal* 107, No. 8 (August 1990):118-122

The Small Garden: A Green and Flourishing Refuge. Linda Yang. *McCall's* 117, No. 8 (May 1990):121-124

Vines: The Architect's Friend. Leslie Land. *McCall's* 117, No. 9 (June 1990):45-47

Women Create Gardens in Male Landscapes: A Revisionist Approach to Eighteenth-Century English Garden History. Susan Groag Bell. *Feminist Studies* 16, No. 3 (Fall 1990):471-491

**Land Trusts**

In Land We Trust. Bibliography. Sarah Stiansen. *Savvy Woman* (July/August 1990):23-24

**Land Use.** *See* Land Trusts

**Lane, Alice**

Does Lou Diamond Phillips Have a Flaw? *Mademoiselle* (February 1990):78

**Lane, Ann J.**

To Herland and Beyond: The Life and Work of Charlotte Perkins Gilman. Reviewed by Mary Titus. *Belles Lettres* 6, No. 1 (Fall 1990):40-42

**Lane, Debi**

Young Mother's Story: "A Medical Error Could Cost Me My Life." *Redbook* 175, No. 6 (October 1990):64-68

**Lane, Judith J.** (joint author). *See* Lane, Larry M.

**Lane, Kenneth Jay** (about)

Talking Fashion. Julia Reed. *Vogue* (December 1990):332-334

**Lane, Larry M.** and Lane, Judith J.

The Columbian Patriot: Mercy Otis Warren and the Constitution. *Women & Politics* 10, No. 2 (1990):17-31

**Lane, Maggie**

Literary Daughters. Reviewed by Sydney Janet Kaplan. *NWSA Journal* 2, No. 1 (Winter 1990):124-127

**Lane, Pinkie Gordon**

VII. For You. Poem. *Essence* 20, No. 11 (March 1990):126

**Lane, Rose Wilder** (about). *See also* Wilder, Laura Ingalls (about)

**Lang, Caroline**

Keep Smiling Through: Women in the Second World War. Reviewed by Fiona Terry. *Gender & History* 2, No. 3 (Autumn 1990):371-373

**Lang, Eric** (joint author). *See* Tiedje, Linda Beth

**Lang, Gladys Engel** and Lang, Kurt

Edging Women Out: Victorian Novelists, Publishers, and Social Change. Book Review. *Gender and Society* 4, No. 4 (December 1990):556-558

**lang, k. d.** (about)

The Amazing k. d. lang. Interview. Charla Krupp. *Glamour* (February 1990):124

Lesley Gore on k.d. Lang . . . and vice versa. *Ms.* 1, No. 1 (July/August 1990):30-33

**Lang, Kurt** (joint author). *See* Lang, Gladys Engel

**Lang, Sandra**

Mother and Toddler Groups. *Spare Rib* No. 216 (September 1990):57

**Langan, Marianne**

Holiday Parties Cookbook. *McCall's* 118, No. 3 (December 1990):103-124

Outdoor Eating Cookbook. *McCall's* 117, No. 9 (June 1990):99-101

Pasta Cookbook. *McCall's* 117, No. 12 (September 1990):137-148

Soup and Sandwich Cookbook. *McCall's* 118, No. 1 (October 1990):123-138

Storybook Christmas Houses. *McCall's* 118, No. 3 (December 1990):90-93

Thanksgiving Cookbook. *McCall's* 118, No. 2 (November 1990):123-128+

**Lange, Jessica** (about)

Lange Range. Ross Wetzsteon. *Vogue* (February 1990):192-193, 200

**Langer, Cassandra L.**

Racism, Sexism, Still Afflict Art World. *New Directions for Women* 19, No. 1 (January/February 1990):12

**Langer, Cassandra L.** (joint editor). *See* Raven, Arlene

**Langone, John**

Medical Report: The STD Epidemic. *Glamour* (August 1990):70-74

**Language**

Age, Bodily Secretions, Lesbians . . . Developing the Language. Julia Penelope. *Hot Wire* 6, No. 2 (May 1990):18-19+

Cutting Re/marks. Betsy Warland. *Sinister Wisdom* 42 (Winter 1990-1991):94-112

Lost in Translation: A Life in a New Language. By Eva Hoffman. Reviewed by Maria Jastrzebska. *Spare Rib* No. 214 (July 1990):22

On Speciesist Language. Joan Dunayer. *On the Issues* 17 (Winter 1990):30-31

Universal Grammar. Marlene Nourbese Philip. *Trivia* 16/17 (Fall 1990):34-39

**Language, Business**

So Fellas, Can We Talk? Amy Willard Cross. *Savvy Woman* (March 1990):33-34

**Language, Foreign**

Foreign Language Labs. Robert McGarvey. *Executive Female* 13, No. 5 (September-October 1990):32-34

**Language – Gender Differences.** *See also* Communication – Gender Differences

Difficult Dialogues: Report on the 1990 Conference on Research in Gender and Communication. Marsha Houston. *Women & Language* 13, No. 2 (Winter 1990):30-32

Language, Gender, and Sex in Comparative Perspective. Edited by Susan Philips, Susan Steele, and Christine Tanz. Reviewed by Jackie Urla. *Signs* 15, No. 2 (Winter 1990):412-414

"Lifting Belly Is a Language": The Postmodern Lesbian Subject. Penelope J. Engelbrecht. *Feminist Studies* 16, No. 1 (Spring 1990):85-114

Nu Shu: An Ancient, Secret, Women's Language. Carolyn Lau. *Belles Lettres* 6, No. 1 (Fall 1990):32-35

Speaking Freely: Unlearning the Lies of the Fathers' Tongues. By Julia Penelope. Reviewed by Alida Brill. *Ms.* 1, No. 1 (July/August 1990):70

"Thinking in Things": A Women's Symbol Language. Jennifer Weston. *Trivia* 16/17 (Fall 1990):84-98

Women's Languaging: An Image Word Conjunction. Dyana Werden. *Trivia* 16/17 (Fall 1990):40-49

**Language, Nonsexist**

The Nonsexist Word Finder: A Dictionary of Gender-Free Usage. By Rosalie Maggio. Reviewed by Mary Ellen S. Capek. *NWSA Journal* 2, No. 3 (Summer 1990):476-484

Women of Color and the Core Curriculum: Tools for Transforming the Liberal Arts, Part 2. Susan E. Searing. *Feminist Collections* 11, No. 2 (Winter 1990):15-17

**Language – Sexism**

Heterosexism or Homophobia: The Power of the Language We Use. Joseph H. Neisen. *Out/Look* No. 10 (Fall 1990):36-37

Including Women at Emory & Henry College: Evolution of an Inclusive Language Policy. Felicia Mitchell. *Women's Studies Quarterly* 18, Nos. 1-2 (Spring-Summer 1990):222-230

*Les belles infide4les*/Fidelity or Feminism? The Meaning of Feminist Biblical Translation. Elizabeth A. Castelli. *Journal of Feminist Studies in Religion* 6, No. 2 (Fall 1990):25-39

A Note on the Elimination of Sexism in Dictionaries. Morton Benson. *Women & Language* 13, No. 1 (Fall 1990):51

Sexism in the Chinese Language. Sexist Language – China. *NWSA Journal* 2, No. 4 (Autumn 1990):635-639

**Language and Gender**

A Review of Research on Language and Sex in the Spanish Language. Uwe KJaer Nissen. *Women & Language* 13, No. 2 (Winter 1990):11-29

**Language Skills.** *See* Communication

**Lanker, Brian** (joint author). *See* Bader, Eleanor J.

**Lansbury, Angela** (about)

Positive Moves. Excerpted. *Good Housekeeping* 211, No. 5 (November 1990):172-173

**Lansky, Vicki**

Handling Everyday Life Problems. *Family Circle* 103, No. 9 (June 26, 1990):98-99

Help! *Family Circle* 103, No. 13 (September 25, 1990):101-102; 103, No. 14 (October 16, 1990):141-142; 103, No. 16 (November 27, 1990):100; 103, No. 17 (December 18, 1990):125-126

**Lant, Kathleen Margaret**

The Rape of the Text: Charlotte Gilman's Violation of *Herland*. *Tulsa Studies in Women's Literature* 9, No. 2 (Fall 1990):291-308

**Lantz, Barbara** (about). *See also* Zoli Management Incorporated

**Lapham, Lewis H.**

Burden of the Nouveaux Riches. *Lear's* (May 1990):76-81+

**Lapidus, Jacqueline**

To Love Is to God. *The Women's Review of Books* 7, No. 9 (June 1990):17-18

Speaking of Christ: A Lesbian Feminist Voice. Book Review. *The Women's Review of Books* 7, No. 9 (June 1990):17-18

Touching Our Strength: The Erotic as Power and the Love of God. Book Review. *The Women's Review of Books* 7, No. 9 (June 1990):17-18

**Laporte, Suzanne B.**

How to Hire an Attorney. *Working Woman* (August 1990):40-42

**Laque, Carol Feiser**

Welcome to You See. Poem. *Heresies* 25 (1990):34

**Laredo, Ruth** (about)

Music: Three in Concert. Diane Palacios. *Ms.* 1, No. 1 (July/August 1990):72-73

**Larkin, Judy**

50 Ways to Help Your Child Learn. *Family Circle* 103, No. 12 (September 4, 1990):99-101

**Larragy, Marian**

Irish Feminism – Looking Back, Looking Forward. *Spare Rib* No. 215 (August 1990):38-43

**Larsen, Anne R.**

Women in French Literature. Book Review. *Tulsa Studies in Women's Literature* 9, No. 2 (Fall 1990):329-330

**Larsen, Ester** (about)

Changing People's Behavior. *Connexions* 33 (1990):30-31

**Larsen, Jeanne**

Pomegranate's Story. Short Story. *Iris* 23 (Spring-Summer 1990):46-48

**Larsen, Libby** (about). *See* Composers

**Larson, Anne E.** and Carr, Carole A. (editors)

Silverleaf's Choice: An Anthology of Lesbian Humor. Reviewed by Rosalind Warren. *New Directions for Women* 19, No. 6 (November-December 1990):17

**Larson, C. Kay**

Amazons and Military Maids: Women Who Dressed as Men in Pursuit of Life, Liberty and

Happiness. Book Review. *Minerva* 8, No. 2 (Summer 1990):74-78

Bonny Yank and Ginny Reb. *Minerva* 8, No. 1 (Spring 1990):33-48

**Larson, Jeffry H.** (joint author). *See* Crane, D. Russell

**Larson, Vicki Lord** and McKinley, Nancy L.

Communication Assessment and Intervention Strategies for Adolescents. Book Review. *Adolescence* 25, No. 98 (Summer 1990):501-502

**Lasers in Surgery**

Sci-Fi Eye Surgery. Marjorie Ingall. *McCall's* 118, No. 2 (November 1990):22

**Laskas, Jeanne Marie**

Me! Me! Me! Me! Me! *Glamour* (April 1990):296-297+

**Lasker, Joan** (about)

Quality Time. Jennet Conant. *Harper's Bazaar* (March 1990):30-38

**Lasker, Judith N.** and Parmet, Harriet L. |

Rabbinic and Feminist Approaches to Reproductive Technologies. *Journal of Feminist Studies in Religion* 6, No. 1 (Spring 1990):117-130

**Laskin, David**

Make Room for Daddy. *Redbook* 174, No. 5 (March 1990):122-123+

**La Sorsa, Valerie A.** and Fodor, Iris G.

Adolescent Daughter/Midlife Mother Dyad. *Psychology of Women Quarterly* 14, No. 4 (December 1990):593-606

**Lastarria-Cornhiel, Susana** and Haney, Wava G.

Women and Social Change in Latin America. Book Review. *Feminist Collections* 12, No. 1 (Fall 1990):9-13

The Women's Movement in Latin America: Feminism and the Transition to Democracy. Book Review. *Feminist Collections* 12, No. 1 (Fall 1990):9-13

**Latchkey Children**

The Early Years: After-School Orphans. T. Berry Brazelton. *Family Circle* 103, No. 14 (October 16, 1990):52-56

**Late Childbearing.** *See* Middle-Aged Women – Childbirth

**Latham, Aaron**

Gloria Allred. *Lear's* (June 1990):78-83

**Latham, Cecile**

Attempt to Protect = Contempt? *off our backs* 20, No. 4 (April 1990):10

Failure to Protect = Murder? *off our backs* 20, No. 4 (April 1990):10

Jacqueline du Pré: A Life. Book Review. *off our backs* 20, No. 9 (October 1990):16

**Latici, Elena**

Relationships: "Help! I Married a Big Baby!" *Redbook* 176, No. 2 (December 1990):44-46

**Latin America – Bibliographies**

*Journal of Women's History* 2, No. 2 (Fall 1990):208-211

**Latin America – Documentation Centers**

Documentation Centers Workshop: Our Collective Memory. *Women in Action* 3 & 4 (1990):15

**Latin America – Human Rights**

Elections in Chile: A Facade of Democracy. *Spare Rib* No. 209 (February 1990):22-23

**Latin American and Caribbean Women's Health Network**

Health Networking Programme. Ximena Charnes and Soledad Weinstein. *Women's World* 23 (April 1990):27-28

**Latin American Women**

Recomposing the Samba: A Look at the Contemporary Black Movement in Post-Abolition Brazil. Bobbie Hodges-Betts. *Sage* 6, No. 1 (Summer 1989):49-51

A Road Well Traveled: Three Generations of Cuban American Women. By Terry Doran, Janet Satterfield, and Chris Stade. Reviewed by Vicki L. Ruiz. *NWSA Journal* 2, No. 3 (Summer 1990):490-491

**Latin American Women – Feminist Movement**

Challenges and Proposals for Feminists in the '90s. *Women in Action* 3 & 4 (1990):20-23

Fifth Latin American and Caribbean Feminist Meeting. Carmen Gloria Dunnage. *Women in Action* 3 & 4 (1990):3-8

History of the Meetings. Ana Maria Portugal. *Women in Action* 3 & 4 (1990):18-19

Interview with Bessie Hollants: "We Would Never Have Forgiven Ourselves for Not Speaking Out." Interview. Carmen Gloria Dunnage. *Women in Action* 3 & 4 (1990):16-17

The Women's Movement in Latin America: Feminism and the Transition to Democracy. Edited by Jane S. Jaquette. Reviewed by Susana Lastarria-Cornhiel and Wava G. Haney. *Feminist Collections* 12, No. 1 (Fall 1990):9-13

Women's Social Movements in Latin America. Helen Icken Safa. *Gender and Society* 4, No. 3 (September 1990):354-369

Women's Voices Grow Stronger: Politics and Feminism in Latin America. Irene Campos Carr. *NWSA Journal* 2, No. 3 (Summer 1990):450-463

**Latin American Women – Lesbianism**

Meeting with Repression: 2nd Encuentro Lesbico-Feminista de Latinoamerica y El Caribe. Ana Elena Obando Montserrat Sagot. *off our backs* 20, No. 8 (August/September 1990):2

**Latin American Women – Rural Development**

Rural Women and State Policy: Feminist Perspectives on Latin American Agricultural Development. Edited by Carmen Diana Deere and Magdalena León. Reviewed by Sue Ellen Charlton. *Signs* 15, No. 4 (Summer 1990):860-864

**Latin American Women – Status**

Centro de Documentation Sobre la Mujer. *Women's World* 23 (April 1990):47

Centro de Investigacion Para la Accion Femenina. *Women's World* 23 (April 1990):48

Lucha: The Struggles of Latin American Women. Edited by Connie Weil. Reviewed by Anne Sisson Runyan. *Women's Studies International Forum* 13, No. 5 (1990):520-521

Muchachas No More: Household Workers in Latin America and the Caribbean. Edited by Elsa M. Chaney and Mary Garcia Castro. Reviewed by Judith Rollins. *Gender and Society* 4, No. 3 (September 1990):423-425

Women and Social Change in Latin America. Edited by Elizabeth Jelin. Reviewed by Susana Lastarria-Cornhiel and Wava G. Haney. *Feminist Collections* 12, No. 1 (Fall 1990):9-13

**Latin American Women – Violence**

Legislating Against Violence. *Women in Action* 3 & 4 (1990):43-46

**Latin American Writers**

The Absence of Writing, or How I Almost Became a Spy. Marlene Nourbese Philip. *Trivia* 16/17 (Fall 1990):18-33

**Latin American Writers – Bibliographies**

Women Authors of Hispanic South America: A Bibliography of Literary Criticism and Interpretation. By Sandra Messinger Cypess and others. *Feminist Collections* 11, No. 3 (Spring 1990):15

**Latona, Janet R.** (joint author). *See* Ellickson, Judy L.

**Latour, Marie** (about)

A Story of Women. Directed by Claude Chabrol. Reviewed by Marina Heung. *New Directions for Women* 19, No. 3 (May/June 1990):7

**Lau, Carolyn**

Nu Shu: An Ancient, Secret, Women's Language. *Belles Lettres* 6, No. 1 (Fall 1990):32-35

**Lauber, Lynn**

White Girls. Reviewed by Eleanor J. Bader. *Belles Lettres* 5, No. 3 (Spring 1990):8

**Lauder, Estée** (about)

All About Estée. Julia Reed. *Vogue* (May 1990):268-270, 324

**Lauder, William** (about)

Natural Balance. Jennet Conant. *Harper's Bazaar* (October 1990):200-203 +

**Lauer, Kristin O.** and Murray, Margaret P.

Edith Wharton: An Annotated Secondary Bibliography. Review. *Feminist Collections* 11, No. 3 (Spring 1990):17

**Laundry**

The Flip Side: It's a Wash! Stan Stinberg. *Family Circle* 103, No. 14 (October 16, 1990):28-29

**Lauren, Ralph** (about). *See* Fashion Designers, "Predictions"; Talley, André Leon

**Laurence, Margaret**

Dance on the Earth. Reviewed by Clara Thomas. *Canadian Women's Studies* 11, No. 2 (Fall 1990):87-89

**Lauretis, Teresa de**

Eccentric Subjects: Feminist Theory and Historical Consciousness. *Feminist Studies* 16, No. 1 (Spring 1990):115-150

Technologies of Gender: Essays on Theory, Film, and Fiction. Reviewed by Paula Rabinowitz. *Feminist Studies* 16, No. 1 (Spring 1990):151-169

**Lauter, Estella**

Re-enfranchising Art: Feminist Interventions in the Theory of Art. *Hypatia* 5, No. 2 (Summer 1990):91-106

**Lauter, Estella** (joint author). *See* Krumholz, Linda

**Lauterborn, Bob – Criticism and Interpretation**

Women Changing Ad Business, Says UNC Advertising. *Media Report to Women* 18, No. 1 (January/February 1990):8

**Lavery, Bryony**

Kitchen Matters. Reviewed by Julie McNamara. *Spare Rib* 219 (December 1990-January 1991):38

**Lavut, Karen** and Beer, Frances

Earth Is Our Root: An Interview with Patricia Beatty. *Canadian Women's Studies* 11, No. 1 (Spring 1990):

**Law.** *See also* Violence Against Women – Law and Legislation

**Law – Ethics**

Moral Vision and Professional Decisions: The Changing Values of Women and Men Lawyers. By Jack Rand and Dana Crowley Rand. Reviewed by Anne Margolis. *The Women's Review of Books* 7, No. 12 (September 1990):17-18

**Law – Feminist Perspectives**

Authenticity and Fiction in Law: Contemporary Case Studies Exploring Radical Legal Feminism. Sarah Slavin. *Journal of Women's History* 1, No. 3 (Winter 1990):123-159

Feminism and the Power of Law. By Carol Smart. Reviewed by Anne Margolis. *The Women's Review of Books* 7, No. 12 (September 1990):17-18

Gloria Allred. Aaron Latham. *Lear's* (June 1990):78-83

A Missing Voice in Feminist Legal Theory: The Heterosexual Presumption. Leigh Megan Leonard. *Women's Rights Law Reporter* 12, No. 1 (Spring 1990):39-49

Women's Legal Rights: International Covenants, An Alternative to ERA? By Malvina Halberstam and Elizabeth F. Defeis. Reviewed by Barbara Stark. *Women's Rights Law Reporter* 12, No. 1 (Spring 1990):51-57

**Law–History**

Women, Family, and the Law, 1750-1942. Chiara Saraceno. *Journal of Family History* 15, No. 4 (October 1990):427-442

**Law–Study and Teaching.** *See also* Bell, Derrick (about)

**Law and Women**

Equality and Sex Discrimination Law. By K. O'Donovan and E. Szyszczak. Reviewed by Jennifer Craven-Griffiths. *Gender and Education* 2, No. 3 (1990):373-374

The Female Body and the Law. By Zillah R. Eisenstein. Reviewed by Mary Lyndon Shanley. *NWSA Journal* 2, No. 2 (Spring 1990):308-311

Getting Equal. By C. O'Donnell and P. Hall. Reviewed by Jennifer Craven-Griffiths. *Gender and Education* 2, No. 3 (1990):373-374

Looking for Lesbian Legal Theory–A Surprising Journey. Ruthann Robson. *Sinister Wisdom* 42 (Winter 1990-1991):32-39

She Got 40 Years for Bad Checks. Lynn Wenzel. *New Directions for Women* 19, No. 2 (March/April 1990):5

Women in the Judicial Process. By Beverly B. Cook, Leslie F. Goldstein, Karen O'Connor, and Susette M. Talarico. Reviewed by Joan C. Tronto. *NWSA Journal* 2, No. 3 (Summer 1990):492-495

**Law Firms**

Structural Causes of Dissatisfaction Among Large-Firm Attorneys: A Feminist Perspective. Deborah K. Holmes. *Women's Rights Law Reporter* 12, No. 1 (Spring 1990):9-38

**Lawler, Sharene K.** (joint author). *See* Rubenstein, Hiasaura

**Lawrence, Jean** and Tucker, Margaret

Norwood Was a Difficult School. Reviewed by Susan Lewis. *Gender and Education* 2, No. 1 (1990):116

**Lawrence, Kathleen Rockwell**

Hers: The Nose Job. *Glamour* (September 1990):338+

**Lawrence, Kathleen Walker**

A Corporate Wife after the Ball. *Lear's* (October 1990):58-60

**Lawrence, Melinda**

Happiness Is Goldie's Secret. *Redbook* 175, No. 3 (July 1990):22-27

**Laws, Margaret**

Greed Is Good . . . and Other Management Lessons from Drexel. *Working Woman* (August 1990):70-72

**Lawson, Annette**

Adultery: An Analysis of Love and Betrayal. Reviewed by Lynn Atwater. *Journal of Marriage and the Family* 52, No. 2 (May 1990):564

**Lawson, Rosalinda** and others

Good Health: Food Poisoning Alert! *Redbook* 176, No. 1 (November 1990):46-57

**Lawsuits**

Management: How to Fire Someone Without Getting Sued. Deborah L. Jacobs. *Working Woman* (January 1990):24-28

Sex, Lies & Lawsuits. Ann Landi. *Mademoiselle* (January 1990):104-105+

When You Can Be Sued for Injuries. *Good Housekeeping* 211, No. 3 (September 1990):291

**Lawyers.** *See also* Chicago–Lawyers; Washington, D.C.–Lawyers

Men and Women Lawyers in In-House Legal Departments: Recruitment and Career Patterns. Sharyn L. Roach. *Gender and Society* 4, No. 2 (June 1990):207-219

Women in Law. *Essence* 21, No. 3 (July 1990):38-46

**Lawyers–Fees**

How to Hire an Attorney. Suzanne B. Laporte. *Working Woman* (August 1990):40-42

**Lawyers–Feminism**

Politics, Feminism and Women's Professional Orientations: A Case Study of Women Lawyers. Janet Rosenberg, Harry Perlstadt, and William R. F. Phillips. *Women & Politics* 10, No. 4 (1990):19-48

**Layne, Linda L**

Motherhood Lost: Cultural Dimensions of Miscarriage and Stillbirth in America. *Women and Health* 16, Nos. 3/4 (1990):69-98

**Lazar, Jerry**

Hollywood Royalty. *Mademoiselle* (October 1990):188-191+

**Lazar, Paul** (joint author). *See* Schoen, Linda Allen

**Lazreg, Marnia**

Gender and Politics in Algeria: Unraveling the Religious Paradigm. Notes. *Signs* 15, No. 4 (Summer 1990):755-780

**Lazzaro-Weis, Carol**

The Female *Bildungsroman*: Calling It into Question. *NWSA Journal* 2, No. 1 (Winter 1990):16-34

**Lea, Teresa** (joint author). *See* Cowlishaw, Gillian

**Lead – Toxicology**

Mom Fights Lead Poison. Pat Redmond. *New Directions for Women* 19, No. 3 (May/June 1990):16

**Leadership.** *See also* African-American Women – Leadership; Chief Executives Officers; College Students – Leadership; Elected Officials; Heroes; Management Techniques; Political Activists

Achieving Personal Best: 200 Words on 3 Lear's Women. *Lear's* (June 1990):66

Achieving Personal Best: 200 Words on 4 Lear's Women. *Lear's* (May 1990):20

Back Talk: A Betrayal of Trust. Annette J. Samuels. *Essence* 21, No. 8 (December 1990):142

Back Talk: Where Are Our Future Leaders? Manning Marable. *Essence* 21, No. 7 (November 1990):130

Brave New Girls. Stacy Title. *Mademoiselle* (January 1990):106-109

Elizabeth Dole: Southern Charmer. Lorraine Dusky. *McCall's* 117, No. 9 (June 1990):67

The End of the Big Bad Boss. Anne M. Russell. *Working Woman* (March 1990):79

Executive Agenda. *Working Woman* (October 1990):95-96

Ferraro: The Country Is Ready. Anne Summers. *McCall's* 117, No. 9 (June 1990):62-63

The Fifty Most Powerful Women in America. *Ladies' Home Journal* 107, No. 11 (November 1990):195-200+

Getting Ready to Run the Country. Peggy Simpson. *McCall's* 117, No. 9 (June 1990):62-63+

Good News. Edited by Dana Nasrallah. *Lear's* (December 1990):62-67

How to Think Like a CEO for the 90's. Patricia Aburdene. *Working Woman* (September 1990):134-137

100 Most Talked-About Women. *Harper's Bazaar* (October 1990):222-225

McCall's Editor's Notes. Anne Mollegen Smith. *McCall's* 117, No. 12 (September 1990):85

1990 Essence Awards. Bebe Moore Campbell. *Essence* 21, No. 6 (October 1990):55-68

1990 Women of the Year. *Glamour* (December 1990):96-101

Oakland: Power of the People. Evelyn C. White. *Essence* 21, No. 1 (May 1990):160-164

See the Big Picture? Now Show Your Staff. John Stoltenberg and Claire McIntosh. *Working Woman* (April 1990):84-86+

She Never Lets Them See Her Sweat. Joanne Kaufman. *Working Woman* (March 1990):80-82

The Speech Heard 'Round the World. William Safire. *McCall's* 117, No. 12 (September 1990):94-95

Talent at Work. *Harper's Bazaar* (March 1990):180-191+

Thrifty, Kind – and Smart as Hell. Patricia O'Toole. *Lear's* (October 1990):26-30

Voices of the Decade. Kathryn Casey. *Ladies' Home Journal* 107, No. 1 (January 1990):66-72

Women in the Military. David Dent. *Essence* 20, No. 12 (April 1990):41-46

Women in Washington. *Glamour* (November 1990):92

Women Right Now. *Glamour* (January 1990):46-48; (February 1990):77-80; (March 1990):95-100; (April 1990):111-112; (June 1990):101-106; (July 1990):63-64; (September 1990):131

Women Who Would Be President. Lorraine Dusky. *McCall's* 117, No. 9 (June 1990):59-60

Working it Out in a Downsized World. Patricia O'Toole. *Lear's* (September 1990):29-30

World Class. Jon Etra. *Harper's Bazaar* (May 1990):33-40

On Your Own: Young and In Charge. Judith Stone. *Glamour* (September 1990):178

**Leadership – Politics**

Momentum: Women in American Politics Now. By Ronna Romney and Beppie Harrison. Reviewed by Connie L. Lobur. *Women & Politics* 10, No. 3 (1990):129-130

**Leadership Skills.** *See also* Career Management; Employee-Employer Relations; Management Techniques; Promotions

The Best New Managers will Listen, Motivate, Support. Isn't that Just Like a Woman? Tom Peters. *Working Woman* (September 1990):142-143+

Career Advice: Dear Betty Harragan. Betty Lehan Harragan. *Working Woman* (March 1990):34-36

Get Crazy: How to Have a Breakthrough Idea. Magaly Olivero. *Working Woman* (September 1990):144-147+

Good for Business: A Manager's Hot Line. *Working Woman* (November 1990):41-46

"How Am I Doing?": What Your Boss Can't Tell You. Kent L. Straat and Nellie Sabin. *Working Woman* (August 1990):55-57+

How to Be the Leader They'll Follow. Warren Bennis. *Working Woman* (March 1990):75-78

Management: The Smarter Way to Make Decisions. Pam Miller Withers. *Working Woman* (March 1990):31-32

Management: What Is Your Staff Afraid to Tell You? Elyse T. Tanouye. *Working Woman* (April 1990):35-38

Management Secrets They'll Never Teach You at Business School. Jolie Solomon. *Working Woman* (June 1990):53-54 +

Managers' Shoptalk. *Working Woman* (January 1990):14-20; (February 1990):24-26; (March 1990):24-28; (April 1990):22-28; (May 1990):23-26

The Secrets of Super Salespeople (That Everyone Can Use). Michael Kaplan. *Working Woman* (May 1990):92-95 +

Tech Talk: What Kind of Manager are You? Jon Pepper. *Working Woman* (May 1990):46-52

This Working Life: Feminine Wiles Are Back in Business. Maureen Dowd. *Working Woman* (March 1990):158

**Lear, Frances**

Connectedness. *Lear's* (March 1990):168

Editorial: Roots of Heaven. *Lear's* (August 1990):136

Having It All. *Lear's* (February 1990):136

Lunch. Interview. *Lear's* (January 1990):19-22; (February 1990):19-22; (March 1990):25-28; (April 1990):19-20; (May 1990):17-18; (June 1990):19-20; (July 1990):17-20; (August 1990):15-16; (September 1990):19-20; (October 1990):21-22; (November 1990):23-24; (December 1990):21-24

Millennium Tremens. *Lear's* (September 1990):160

These are a Few of My Positive Things. Poem. *Lear's* (December 1990):132

Welcome to the Club. *Lear's* (May 1990):140

**Learned Helplessness**

Learned Helplessness: A Factor in Women's Depression. Linda M. Kiefer. *AFFILIA* 5, No. 1 (Spring 1990):21-31

**Learning Disabilities.** *See also* Attention Deficit Hyperactivity Disorder; Disabled Children

The Courage to Learn. Bibliography. Rose Marie Semple. *Ladies' Home Journal* 107, No. 11 (November 1990):38-47

**Learning Disabilities – Adolescents**

Transition Goals for Adolescents with Learning Disabilities. By Catherine Trapani. Book Review. *Adolescence* 25, No. 99 (Fall 1990):755

**Learning Motivation.** *See also* Child Psychology

Encouraging Girls to Pursue Math and Science Careers. Bibliography. Celia Slom. *McCall's* 117, No. 8 (May 1990):58-60

Summer Projects for Kids Who Hate School. Patricia Rae Wolff. *McCall's* 117, No. 8 (May 1990):21-24

**Leary, Kathryn D.** (about). *See* Alexander, Nanine

**Leather Garments**

Shine: Leathers. *Vogue* (September 1990):610-614

**Leavy, Jane**

Squeeze Play. Reviewed by Mariah Burton Nelson. *The Women's Review of Books* 7, Nos. 10-11 (July 1990):36

**Lebanon – Civil War**

War's Other Voices: Women Writers on the Lebanese Civil War. By Miriam Cooke. Reviewed by Judith Hicks Stiehm. *Women's Studies International Forum* 13, No. 3 (1990):280-281

**Lebanon – Hostages**

An Undying Love. Kathy Sprayberry Wood. *Ladies' Home Journal* 107, No. 1 (January 1990):96-100

**Le Croy, Craig Winston** (joint author). *See* Ashford, José B.

**Ledbetter, Carol,** Hall, Susan, Swanson, Janice M., and Forrest, Katherine

Readability of Commercial Versus Generic Health Instructions for Condoms. *Health Care for Women International* 11, No. 3 (1990):295-304

**Le Doeuff, Miche4le**

A Testimony Unbinds Many Tongues. *Connexions* 34 (1990):18-19

Women, Reason, Etc. *Differences* 2, No. 3 (Fall 1990):1-13

**Lee, Anna**

Interstices of Race and Class: Creating Intimacy. *Lesbian Ethics* 4, No. 1 (Spring 1990): 77-83

**Lee, B.**

Women Lose Freedom of Choice. *Healthsharing* 11, No. 3 (June 1990):10-11

**Lee, Barbara A.**

Sex Discrimination and the Supreme Court: Implications for Women Faculty. *Women's Studies Quarterly* 18, Nos. 1-2 (Spring-Summer 1990):155-173

**Lee, Brenda** (about). *See also* Transvestism

**Lee, Felicia R.**

Abortion: Empty Womb. *Essence* 21, No. 1 (May 1990):51-52

**Lee, Gary R.** (joint author). *See* Shehan, Constance L.

**Lee, Helen E.**

The Fashion Report. *Savvy Woman* (September 1990):42-44

**Lee, Hermione**

Willa Cather: Double Lives. Reviewed by Susan A. Hallgarth. *The Women's Review of Books* 8, No. 1 (October 1990):23-24

**Lee, Jean** (joint author). *See* Habel, Leo

**Lee, Jid**

Words in Silence: An Exercise in Third World Feminist Criticism. *Frontiers* 11, Nos. 2-3 (1990):66-71

**Lee, Joie** (about)

Joie De Vivre. Martha Southgate. *Savvy Woman* (September 1990):21-22

**Lee, Martin A.** and Solomon, Norman

Unreliable Sources: A Guide to Detecting Bias in News Media. Reviewed by Susan E. Davis. *New Directions for Women* 19, No. 6 (November-December 1990):18

**Lee, Mary Paik**

Quiet Odyssey: A Pioneer Korean Woman in America. Reviewed by Miriam Ching Louie. *Belles Lettres* 6, No. 1 (Fall 1990):27-28

**Lee, Patrick**

Asian Valley Boy: A Monologue. *Out/Look* No. 9 (Summer 1990):18-19

**Lee, Rosemary** (about)

Egg Dances. Christy Adair. *Spare Rib* No. 211 (April 1990):28

**Lee, Sandra Y.**

A Pet a Day . . . *McCall's* 118, No. 3 (December 1990):26-28

**Lee, Spike**

Mo' Better Blues. Reviewed by Esther Bailey. *Spare Rib* 217 (October 1990):29

**Lee, Spike** (about)

Flash in the Clan. Anne Rosenbaum. *Harper's Bazaar* (February 1990):101

Le Jazz Haute. Patrick Demarchelier. *Vogue* (August 1990):332-337

Mo' Better Spike. Interview. Jill Nelson. *Essence* 21, No. 4 (August 1990):55+

**Lee, Thomas R.**, Mancini, Jay A., and Maxwell, Joseph W.

Sibling Relationships in Adulthood: Contact Patterns and Motivations. *Journal of Marriage and the Family* 52, No. 2 (May 1990):431-440

**Lee, Valerie**

Strategies for Teaching Black Women's Literature in a White Cultural Context. *Sage* 6, No. 1 (Summer 1989):74-76

**Leeder, Elaine**

Supermom or Child Abuser? Treatment of the Munchhausen Mother. *Women and Therapy* 9, No. 4 (1990):69-88

**Leedom-Ackerman, Joanne** (joint editor). *See* Coleman, Wanda

**Lees, Sue** and Scott, Maria

Equal Opportunities: Rhetoric or Action. *Gender and Education* 2, No. 3 (1990):333-343

**Lee-Smith, Diana**

Women and Housing in Sub-Saharan Africa. *Canadian Women's Studies* 11, No. 2 (Fall 1990):68-70

**Lefanu, Sarah**

Feminism and Science Fiction. Reviewed by Melissa Scott. *Belles Lettres* 5, No. 4 (Summer 1990):45

**Legal Ethics.** *See* Law – Ethics

**Legault, Suzanne**

Strategies du vertige, trois poe4tes: Nicole Brossard, Madeleine Gagnon, France Théoret. Book Review. *Canadian Women's Studies* 11, No. 2 (Fall 1990):93-94

**Legs**

Beauty & Fashion Journal. *Ladies' Home Journal* 107, No. 6 (June 1990):31-36

Great Legs! *Glamour* (September 1990):318-321

A Leg Up. *Glamour* (November 1990):224-227

'60s Something. Jody Shields. *Vogue* (August 1990):292-299

**LeGuin, Ursula K.**

Tehanu, the Last Book of Earthsea. Reviewed by Ann E. Kottner. *The Women's Review of Books* 7, Nos. 10-11 (July 1990):40-41

**Le Guin, Ursula K.**

The World of Science Fiction. *Ms.* 1, No. 3 (November/December 1990):52-54

**Lehman, Sheila** (joint author). *See* Kramer, Pamela E.

**Lehmann, Jennifer M.**

The Sexual Contract. Book Review. *Journal of Marriage and the Family* 52, No. 2 (May 1990):563-564

**Lehrer, Chaia**

Lesbian and Jewish: An Affirmation. *New Directions for Women* 19, No. 4 (July-August 1990):15

Twice Blessed: On Being Lesbian, Gay, and Jewish. Book Review. *New Directions for Women* 19, No. 4 (July-August 1990):15

**Lehrman, Celia Kuperszmid**

Just Tell Her She Can't. *Executive Female* (March/April 1990):41-43

**Leiblum, Sandra Risa**

Sexuality and the Midlife Woman. *Psychology of Women Quarterly* 14, No. 4 (December 1990):495-508

**Leica Company**

The Beholder. Daniel Grotta. *Lear's* (December 1990):68-75

**Leidholdt, Dorchen** and Raymond, Janice (editors)

The Sexual Liberals and the Attack on Feminism. Reviewed by Victoria Kahn. *The Women's Review of Books* 7, No. 5 (February 1990):16

**Leidholdt, Dorchen** (joint author). *See* Barry, Kathleen L.

**Leidner, Robin**

Homeworking: Myths and Realities. Book Review. *Gender and Society* 4, No. 2 (June 1990):262-265

The New Era of Home-Based Work. Book Review. *Gender and Society* 4, No. 2 (June 1990):262-265

**Leigh, Janet** (joint author). *See* Helson, Ravenna

**Leigh, Jennifer Jason** (about). *See also* Beauty, Personal, "Beauty Bazaar"

Inside People. *Mademoiselle* (January 1990):48-50

Movies. David Edelstein. *Vogue* (May 1990):168-172

**Leigh, Pamela** (joint author). *See* Lamanna, Dean

**Leight, Warren**

His: Trial by Dial – Should You Call Him First? *Mademoiselle* (February 1990):93

Is He Your Boyfriend or Your Baby? *Mademoiselle* (January 1990):62

**Leimbach, Marti**

Big Sister Knows Best. *Mademoiselle* (April 1990):227, 262

Dying Young. Reviewed by Joyce Maynard. *Mademoiselle* (January 1990):56-58

Sex Is Alive and Well. *Harper's Bazaar* (June 1990):70+

**Leimbach, Marti** (about). *See* Leadership, "Talent at Work"

**Leiomyoma uteri**

The Fibroid Epidemic. Evelyn C. White. *Essence* 21, No. 8 (December 1990):22-24

Fibroids – Are They Dangerous? Ann Renard. *Redbook* 175, No. 5 (September 1990):28-30

**Leisure**

All Work and No Play? The Sociology of Women and Leisure. By Rosemary Deem. Reviewed by Susan Maizel Chambre. *Gender and Society* 4, No. 2 (June 1990):281-283

More to Women's Lives Than Work?: A Model for a Course Addressing Women and Leisure. M. Deborah Bialeschki and Karla A. Henderson. *Feminist Teacher* 5, No. 2 (Fall 1990):25-31

**Leisure Activities.** *See also* Recreation

The Busy Life: Weekends with No Regrets. Laurie Tarkan. *Working Woman* (November 1990):150-154

Couple Time. *Glamour* (May 1990):172

3-Day Weekend: Pleasure Clothes. *Glamour* (May 1990):262-269

It's the Weekend: So Why Do You Feel Miserable? Rose Graff. *Working Woman* (March 1990):140-144

Private Time. *Glamour* (March 1990):129-130; (April 1990):141-142; (May 1990):167-168; (July 1990):88-89; (August 1990):121-122; (September 1990):169

Saturday Night Style. *Glamour* (August 1990):184-191

**Leive, Cindi**

Why I Can't Stop Thinking about My Computer. *Glamour* (October 1990):162-166

**Lejeune, Paule**

Les Reines de France. Reviewed by Marie-France Silver. *Resources for Feminist Research* 19, No. 1 (March 1990):31

**Leland, John**

Performance: Multi-Mediator. *Vogue* (January 1990):90-91

**Leloudis, James** (joint author). *See* Hall, Jacquelyn Dowd

**LeMasters, Carol**

Gender Blending: Confronting the Limits of Duality. Book Review. *The Women's Review of Books* 7, No. 9 (June 1990):12

Myths and Mysteries of Same-Sex Love. Book Review. *The Women's Review of Books* 7, No. 6 (March 1990):18-19

Sex in the Age of Death. *The Women's Review of Books* 7, No. 6 (March 1990):18-19

Traitors to Their Sex? *The Women's Review of Books* 7, No. 9 (June 1990):12

**Lemkau, Jeanne** (joint author). *See* Ballantine, Jeanne

**Lende, Karen** (about). *See* Athletes, "The Competitive Edge"

**Leneman, Helen**

The Cantors Assembly Convention: A Spy Story. *Lilith* 15, No. 4 (Fall 1990):37-38

Woman Cantor Breaks Tradition in Yugoslavia. *Lilith* 15, No. 2 (Spring 1990):28

**Lenhart, Maria**

Finances of the Frequent Flyer. *Executive Female* (May/June 1990):40-41

Leno, Jay (about). *See also* Television Programs

Lensink, Judy Nolte (joint editor). *See* Aiken, Susan Hardy

**Lenskyj, Helen**

Beyond Plumbing and Prevention: Feminist Approaches to Sex Education. *Gender and Education* 2, No. 2 (1990):217-230

Combatting Homophobia in Sports. *off our backs* 20, No. 6 (June 1990):2-3

The Social Construction of Lesbianism. Book Review. *Resources for Feminist Research* 19, No. 1 (March 1990):32

Teaching Gender: Sex Education and Sexual Stereotypes. Book Review. *Resources for Feminist Research* 19, No. 1 (March 1990):34

**Lentin, Ronit**

Night Train to Mother. Reviewed by Miriyam Glazer. *Belles Lettres* 5, No. 3 (Spring 1990):12

**Lentz, Kirsten Marthe**

Photo Essay. *Women & Language* 13, No. 1 (Fall 1990):52

**Leo, John**

Farewell, My Hostess. *McCall's* 118, No. 2 (November 1990):24

The Flip Side: Some Assembly Required. *Family Circle* 103, No. 17 (December 18, 1990):43-47

The Prattle of the Sexes. *McCall's* 117, No. 7 (April 1990):98-99

Romance: How to Take It Sitting Down. *McCall's* 117, No. 11 (August 1990):50

Sex, Lies, and Videohabits. *McCall's* 117, No. 9 (June 1990):36

**León, Magdalena** (joint editor). *See* Deere, Carmen Diana

**Leonard, Joan**

Teaching Introductory Feminist Spirituality. *Journal of Feminist Studies in Religion* 6, No. 2 (Fall 1990):121-135

**Leonard, John**

American Cassandra: The Life of Dorothy Thompson. Book Review. *Vogue* (June 1990):144-150

**Leonard, Kenneth E.** (joint editor). *See* Collins, R. Lorraine

**Leonard, Leigh Megan**

A Missing Voice in Feminist Legal Theory: The Heterosexual Presumption. *Women's Rights Law Reporter* 12, No. 1 (Spring 1990):39-49

**Leonarda Productions**

Women Composers and Their Music. Vols. 1 and 2. Reviewed by Priscilla Little. *Iris* 23 (Spring-Summer 1990):74-75

**Leonardi, Susan J.**

Dangerous by Degrees: Women at Oxford and the Somerville College Novelists. Reviewed by Carol Dyhouse. *Gender and Education* 2, No. 2 (1990):261-262

**Leondar, Gail**

Making A Spectacle: Feminist Essays on Contemporary Women's Theatre. Book Review. *Women and Performance: A Journal of Feminist Theory* 5, No. 1, Issue #9 (1990):

**Leon Siantz, Mary Lou de**

Maternal Acceptance/Rejection of Mexican Migrant Mothers. *Psychology of Women Quarterly* 14, No. 2 (June 1990):245-254

**Lerman, Hannah**

Between Women: Love, Envy and Competition in Women's Friendships. Book Review. *Psychology of Women Quarterly* 14, No. 1 (March 1990):149-150

Therapy for Adults Molested as Children: Beyond Survival. Book Review. *Psychology of Women Quarterly* 14, No. 2 (June 1990):192-194

**Lerman, Rhoda**

God's Ear. Reviewed by Miriyam Glazer. *Belles Lettres* 6, No. 1 (Fall 1990):10-12

**Lerner, Gerda**

Reconceptualizing Differences Among Women. *Journal of Women's History* 1, No. 3 (Winter 1990):106-122

To Think Ourselves Free. *The Women's Review of Books* 8, No. 1 (October 1990):10-11

Transforming Knowledge. Book Review. *The Women's Review of Books* 8, No. 1 (October 1990):10-11

Writing Women into History. *Woman of Power* 16 (Spring 1990):6-9

**Lerner, Harriet Goldhor**

The Dance of Intimacy. Reviewed by Barbara G. Collins. *AFFILIA* 5, No. 3 (Fall 1990):122-124

What's a Vulva, Mom? *New Directions for Women* 19, No. 3 (May/June 1990):10

Women Who Read Too Much: Reflections on the Advice-Giving Industry. *The Women's Review of Books* 7, No. 7 (April 1990):15-16

**Lerner, Steve** and Barrett, Mary Ellin

Dowry Death. *Lear's* (May 1990):98-101 +

**Lesbian and Gay Coalition.** *See* New Jersey – Lesbian and Gay Coalition

**Lesbian Art**

Lesbian Tradition. Rachael Field. *Feminist Review* No. 34 (Spring 1990):115-119

## Lesbian Communities

Interstices of Race and Class: Creating Intimacy. Anna Lee. *Lesbian Ethics* 4, No. 1 (Spring 1990): 77-83

The Possibility of Lesbian Community. Marilyn Frye. *Lesbian Ethics* 4, No. 1 (Spring 1990): 84-87

A Trip Through the Women's Communities of Washington D.C. Nancy Seeger and Rena Yount. *Hot Wire* 6, No. 1 (January 1990):40-44+

## Lesbian Conference

Lesbian Conference Sets Bold Agenda. Rosemary Curb. *New Directions for Women* 19, No. 1 (January/February 1990):6

Meeting with Repression: 2nd Encuentro Lesbico-Feminista de Latinoamerica y El Caribe. Ana Elena Obando Montserrat Sagot. *off our backs* 20, No. 8 (August/September 1990):2

National Black Gay and Lesbian Leadership Forum: A Conference Report. Ayofemi Folayan. *off our backs* 20, No. 4 (April 1990):2-3

Passages: Aging Lesbians Meet. Carol Anne Douglas. *off our backs* 20, No. 5 (May 1990):8

Serious Shit at the NLC. Mary Frances Platt. *off our backs* 20, No. 5 (May 1990):10

Spinning on to Atlanta. Rosemary Curb. *off our backs* 20, No. 7 (July 1990):7

## Lesbian Culture

Butch/Femme Obsessions. Susan Ardill and Sue O'Sullivan. *Feminist Review* No. 34 (Spring 1990):79-86

Deviant Dress. Elizabeth Wilson. *Feminist Review* No. 35 (Summer 1990):67-74

I Got This Way From Kissing Girlz. Rebecca Brannon. *Hot Wire* 6, No. 2 (May 1990):36-38

Lesbian Lists. Dell Richards. *Woman of Power* 17 (Summer 1990):64-67

Lesbian Philosophies and Cultures. Edited by Jeffner Allen. Reviewed by Carol Anne Douglas. *off our backs* 20, No. 9 (October 1990):18-19

Lifting Belly: Privacy, Sexuality and Lesbianism. Ruthann Robson. *Women's Rights Law Reporter* 12, No. 3 (Fall 1990): 177-203

Sex, Lies, and Penetration. Jan Brown. *Out/Look* No. 7 (Winter 1990):30-34

Skirting the Issue: Lesbian Fashion for the 1990s. Inge Blackman and Kathryn Perry. *Feminist Review* No. 34 (Spring 1990):67-78

Uncovering a Rich Lesbian Past. Dell Richards. *Hot Wire* 6, No. 2 (May 1990):16+

## Lesbian Ethics

Lesbian Ethics. By Sarah Lucia Hoagland. Reviewed by Alice E. Ginsberg. *New Directions for Women* 19, No. 1 (January/February 1990):24

Lesbian Ethics: Toward New Value. By Sarah Lucia Hoagland. Reviewed by A. Lorraine Ironplow. *NWSA Journal* 2, No. 1 (Winter 1990):142-145

Lesbian Ethics: Toward New Value. By Sarah Lucia Hoagland. Reviewed by Carol Van Kirk. *Hypatia* 5, No. 3 (Fall 1990):147-152

Lesbian Ethics: Toward New Value. By Sarah Lucia Hoagland. Reviewed by María Lugones. *Hypatia* 5, No. 3 (Fall 1990):138-146

Lesbian Ethics: Toward New Value. By Sarah Lucia Hoagland. Reviewed by Marilyn Frye. *Hypatia* 5, No. 3 (Fall 1990):132-137

## Lesbian Feminism

Identity Politics: Lesbian Feminism and the Limits of Community. By Shane Phelan. Reviewed by Barbara Findlen. *Ms.* 1, No. 1 (July/August 1990):69

Identity Politics: Lesbian Feminism and the Limits of Community. By Shane Phelan. Reviewed by Elizabeth Lapovsky Kennedy. *NWSA Journal* 2, No. 3 (Summer 1990):495-497

Identity Politics: Lesbian Feminism and the Limits of Community. By Shane Phelan. Reviewed by Julia Penelope. *The Women's Review of Books* 7, No. 7 (April 1990):11-12

Nice Jewish Girls: A Lesbian Anthology. By Evelyn Torton Beck. Reviewed by Joan Nestle. *Bridges* 1, No. 1 (Spring 1990): 98-101

Why Is This Decade Different from All Other Decades?: A Look at the Rise of Jewish Lesbian Feminism. Faith Rogow. *Bridges* 1, No. 1 (Spring 1990): 67-79

## Lesbian Festival

Accessibility, Male Children Heated Issues at Lesbian Fest. Jorjet Harper. *Hot Wire* 6, No. 1 (January 1990):29+

The First Annual East Coast Lesbians' Festival. Jorjet Harper. *Hot Wire* 6, No. 1 (January 1990):28+

**Lesbianism**. *See also* African-American Women – Lesbianism; Domestic Violence – Lesbians

Cutting Re/marks. Betsy Warland. *Sinister Wisdom* 42 (Winter 1990-1991):94-112

The Dance of Masks. Barbara Smith. *Out/Look* No. 9 (Summer 1990):74-77

Dangerous Discussions. Carol Wolfe Konek. *Heresies* 25 (1990):83-86

Do You Have to Be a Lesbian to Be a Feminist? Marilyn Frye. *off our backs* 20, No. 8 (August/September 1990):21-23

Dykes-Loving-Dykes. By Bev Jo, Linda Strega, and Ruston. Reviewed by Sheila Anne. *off our backs* 20, No. 11 (December 1990):15

Homo Sum. Monique Wittig. *Feminist Issues* 10, No. 1 (Spring 1990):3-11

Lesbian Images. By Jane Rule. Reviewed by Annie Hole. *Spare Rib* No. 210 (March 1990):35

Lesbian Sex at Menopause: Better Than Ever. Amy Gottlieb. *Healthsharing* 11, No. 4 (December 1990):

Love and Politics: Radical Feminist and Lesbian Theories. By Carol Anne Douglas. Reviewed by Barbara Ruth. *Sinister Wisdom* 42 (Winter 1990-1991):117-122

Mapping: Lesbians, AIDS and Sexuality. Sue O'Sullivan and Cindy Patton. *Feminist Review* No. 34 (Spring 1990):120-133

Nice Jewish Girls: A Lesbian Anthology. Edited by Evelyn Torton Beck Reviewed by Rebecca Gordon. *The Women's Review of Books* 7, No. 9 (June 1990):7-8

Out the Other Side: Contemporary Lesbian Writing. Edited by Christine McEwen and Sue O'Sullivan. Reviewed by Becki Ross. *Resources for Feminist Research* 19, No. 1 (March 1990):26-28

The Pleasure Threshold: Looking at Lesbian Pornography on Film. Cherry Smyth. *Feminist Review* No. 34 (Spring 1990):152-159

The Sexual Schism: The British in Barcelona. Sue O'Sullivan. *off our backs* 20, No. 9 (October 1990):10-11

Significant Others: Lesbianism and Psychoanalytic Theory. Diane Hamer. *Feminist Review* No. 34 (Spring 1990):135

The Social Construction of Lesbianism. By Celia Kitzinger. Reviewed by Helen Lenskyj. *Resources for Feminist Research* 19, No. 1 (March 1990):32

The Social Construction of Lesbianism. By Celia Kitzinger. Reviewed by L Diane Bernard. *AFFILIA* 5, No. 2 (Summer 1990):100-102

Twice Blessed: On Being Lesbian, Gay and Jewish. Edited by Christie Balka and Andy Rose. Reviewed by Rebecca Gordon. *The Women's Review of Books* 7, No. 9 (June 1990):7-8

### Lesbianism – Activism

The House That Jill Built: Lesbian Feminist Organizing in Toronto, 1976-1980. Becki Ross. *Feminist Review* No. 35 (Summer 1990):75-91

Lesbianism and the Labour Party: The GLC Experience. Ann Tobin. *Feminist Review* No. 34 (Spring 1990):56-66

### Lesbianism – Archives

International Archives. Alison Read. *Feminist Review* No. 34 (Spring 1990):94-99

The Will to Remember: The Lesbian Herstory Archives of New York. Joan Nestle. *Feminist Review* No. 34 (Spring 1990):86-94

### Lesbianism – Bibliographies

The List: The Top 10 Books. *Out/Look* No. 7 (Winter 1990):5

### Lesbianism – Clothing and Dress

On Wearing Skirts. Kim Klausner. *Out/Look* No. 8 (Spring 1990):18+

### Lesbianism – Coming Out

Coming Out: Out/Look Readers Tell Their Tales. Edited by Debra Chasnoff. *Out/Look* No. 10 (Fall 1990):19-24

Greta Garbo's "Mysterious" Private Life. Margie Adam. *Out/Look* No. 10 (Fall 1990):25

Opening the Hong Kong Closet. Lenore Norrgard. *Out/Look* No. 7 (Winter 1990):56-61

There's Something I've Been Meaning to Tell You . . . By Loralee Pike. Reviewed by Tracy Scott. *New Directions for Women* 19, No. 2 (March/April 1990):24

There's Something I've Been Meaning to Tell You. Edited by Loralee MacPike. Reviewed by Rebecca Gordon. *The Women's Review of Books* 7, No. 9 (June 1990):7-8

### Lesbianism – Domestic Violence

Compounding the Triple Jeopardy: Battering in Lesbian of Color Relationships. Valli Kanuha. *Women and Therapy* 9, Nos. 1-2 (1990):169-184

Lesbian Violence, Lesbian Victims: How to Identify Battering in Relationships. Lee Evans and Shelley Bannister. *Lesbian Ethics* 4, No. 1 (Spring 1990): 52-65

Women Abusing Women. Ellen Bell. *Connexions* 34 (1990):28-30

### Lesbianism – Ethics

Lesbian Ethics: Toward New Value. By Sarah Lucia Hoagland. Reviewed by Joan Blackwood. *Resources for Feminist Research* 19, No. 1 (March 1990):24

### Lesbianism – Housing

Becoming a "Real" Dyke: Employment and Housing. Rue Amana. *Canadian Women's Studies* 11, No. 2 (Fall 1990):43-45

Home Away from Home. Jackie Manthorne. *Canadian Women's Studies* 11, No. 2 (Fall 1990):48-50

Out but Not Down: Lesbians' Experience of Housing. Jayne Egerton. *Feminist Review* No. 36 (Autumn 1990):75-88

### Lesbianism – Humor

List This! Tom Ammiano and Jeanine Strobel. *Out/Look* No. 10 (Fall 1990):63

### Lesbianism – Legal Aspects

Lesbians Get Pink-Tagged. Charlotte Innes. *New Directions for Women* 19, No. 2 (March/April 1990):6-7

Looking for Lesbian Legal Theory – A Surprising Journey. Ruthann Robson. *Sinister Wisdom* 42 (Winter 1990-1991):32-39

A Missing Voice in Feminist Legal Theory: The Heterosexual Presumption. Leigh Megan Leonard. *Women's Rights Law Reporter* 12, No. 1 (Spring 1990):39-49

**Lesbianism – Life Styles.** *See also* Photography – Exhibitions

**Lesbianism – Military Service**

Lesbian Soldiers Tell Their Stories. Johnnie Phelps and Miriam Ben-Shalom. *Minerva* 8, No. 3 (Fall 1990):38-53

**Lesbianism – Personal Narratives**

Finding the Lesbians: Personal Accounts from Around the World. Edited by Julia Penelope and Sarah Valentine. Reviewed by Rebecca Gordon. *The Women's Review of Books* 7, No. 9 (June 1990):7-8

Her Son. Diane Bogus. *Sinister Wisdom* 42 (Winter 1990-1991):86-90

Inventing Ourselves: Lesbian Life Stories. Edited by Hall Carpenter Archives Lesbian Oral History Group. Reviewed by Jennie Ruby. *off our backs* 20, No. 7 (July 1990):15

Inventing Ourselves: Lesbian Life Stories. Edited by the Hall Carpenter Archives/Lesbian Oral History Group. Reviewed by Sarah Green. *Feminist Review* No. 34 (Spring 1990):176-177

Invisible Audiences. Carmen De Monteflores. *Out/Look*, No. 10 (Fall 1990):64-68; No. 10 (Fall 1990):64-68

My Interesting Condition. Jan Clausen. *Out/Look* No. 7 (Winter 1990):10-21

The Original Coming Out Stories. Edited by Julia Penelope and Susan J. Wolfe. Reviewed by Rebecca Gordon. *The Women's Review of Books* 7, No. 9 (June 1990):7-8

Reflections of Midlife Lesbians on Their Adolescence. Barbara E. Sang. *Journal of Women and Aging* 2, No. 2 (1990):111-117

Ten for Bravery, Zero for Common Sense. Meredith Maran. *Out/Look* No. 7 (Winter 1990):68-72

Turning Away From Secrets and Shame. Rosanna Sorella. *Sinister Wisdom* 41 (Summer-Fall 1990):41-44

Waxlips. Helena Lipstadt. *Sinister Wisdom* 42 (Winter 1990-1991):68

What It Means to Be Colored Me. Jackie Goldsby. *Out/Look* No. 9 (Summer 1990):8-17

**Lesbianism – Substance Abuse**

Alcoholism in Lesbians: Developmental, Symbolic Interactionist, and Critical Perspectives. Joanne M. Hall. *Health Care for Women International* 11, No. 1 (1990):89-107

**Lesbianism in Literature**

The Education of Harriet Hatfield. By May Sarton. Reviewed by Pat Coleman. *Spare Rib* No. 210 (March 1990):34

Finding the Lesbians. Edited by Julia Penelope and Sarah Valentine. Reviewed by Barbara Findlen. *Ms.* 1, No. 1 (July/August 1990):69

"Lifting Belly Is a Language": The Postmodern Lesbian Subject. Penelope J. Engelbrecht. *Feminist Studies* 16, No. 1 (Spring 1990):85-114

**Lesbian Literature**

Voyages of the Valkyries: Recent Lesbian Pornographic Writing. Sara Dunn. *Feminist Review* No. 34 (Spring 1990):161-170

**Lesbian Mothers**

Caught between Two Worlds: The Impact of a Child on a Lesbian Couple's Relationship. Eloise Stiglitz. *Women and Therapy* 10, Nos. 1/2 (1990):99-116

Heather Has Two Mommies. By Lesléa Newman. Reviewed by Joanne Stato. *off our backs* 20, No. 3 (March 1990):30

Judges Overturn Lesbian Custody Ruling. *Spare Rib* No. 216 (September 1990):44

Lesbian Parents: Claiming Visibility. Sandra Pollack. *Women and Therapy* 10, Nos. 1/2 (1990):181-194

**Lesbian Relationships**

Correlates of Relationship Satisfaction in Lesbian Couples. Natalie S. Eldridge and Lucia A. Gilbert. *Psychology of Women Quarterly* 14, No. 1 (March 1990):43-62

Friends, Lovers and Passion. Elizabeth Clare. *Sinister Wisdom* 40 (Spring 1990):96-98

Is Separation Really So Great? G. Dorsey Green. *Women and Therapy* 9, Nos. 1-2 (1990):87-104

Lesbian Angels and Other Matters. Jacquelyn N. Zita. *Hypatia* 5, No. 1 (Spring 1990):133-139

Lesbian Love in Limbo. Patricia Roth Schwartz. *off our backs* 20, No. 6 (June 1990):18-20

More Dyke Methods. Joyce Trebilcot. *Hypatia* 5, No. 1 (Spring 1990):140-144

**Lesbian Separatism**

The Possibility of Lesbian Community. Marilyn Frye. *Lesbian Ethics* 4, No. 1 (Spring 1990): 84-87

Separatism Is Not a Luxury: Some Thoughts on Separatism and Class. C. Maria. *Lesbian Ethics* 4, No. 1 (Spring 1990): 66-76

The Separatist Revival. Ann Japenga. *Out/Look* No. 8 (Spring 1990):78-83

Women – and Lesbian – Only Spaces: Thought Into Action. Julia Penelope. *off our backs* 20, No. 5 (May 1990):14-16

On Women's Space. Joanne Stato. *off our backs* 20, No. 9 (October 1990):14

**Lesko, Nancy**

Symbolizing Society: Stories, Rites and Structure in a Catholic High School. Reviewed by Robert Burgess. *Gender and Education* 2, No. 2 (1990):256-257

**Leslie, I. Julia**

The Perfect Wife: The Orthodox Hindu Woman According to the Stri6dharmapaddhati of Tryambakayajvan. Reviewed by Albertine Gaur. *Gender & History* 2, No. 2 (Summer 1990):223-225

**Leslie-Spinks, Amanda**

The Difference Within: Feminism and Critical Theory. Book Review. *The Women's Review of Books* 7, No. 8 (May 1990):15-16

Different Differences. *The Women's Review of Books* 7, No. 8 (May 1990):15-16

**Lessard, Suzannah**

Who Pays for Posterity? *Lear's* (December 1990):120-123

**Lester, Bonnie**

Women and AIDS: A Practical Guide for Those Who Help Others. Reviewed by Kathryn Quina. *Psychology of Women Quarterly* 14, No. 2 (June 1990):296-298

**Lester, David**

Ecological Correlates of Adolescent Attempted Suicide. *Adolescence* 25, No. 98 (Summer 1990):483-485

**Lester, David** and Wilson, C.

Teenage Suicide in Zimbabwe. *Adolescence* 25, No. 100 (Winter 1990):807-809

**Lethbridge, Dona J.**

Use of Contraceptives by Women of Upper Socioeconomic Status. *Health Care for Women International* 11, No. 3 (1990):305-318

**Leto, Denise**

Passion, Danger, Freedom. Poem. *Sinister Wisdom* 41 (Summer-Fall 1990):72-74

We Do the Best I Can: A Series of Portraits. Poem. *Sinister Wisdom* 41 (Summer-Fall 1990):13-18

**Letterman, David** (about). *See* Television Programs

**Letters.** *See also* Love-Letters

Living Beautifully: Letters Sweeten Our Lives. Alexandra Stoddard. *McCall's* 117, No. 8 (May 1990):172

**Letter Writers**

Editorial: This Year, Give Us a Piece of *Your* Mind. *Glamour* (January 1990):58

**Leukemia in Children**

One Mother's Fight for Life. Clarita Fonville Buie. *Family Circle* 103, No. 9 (June 26, 1990):70-74

Young Father's Story: A Portrait of My Daughter. James Aponovich and Sheila Weller. *Redbook* 175, No. 2 (June 1990):36-40

**Leuzzi, Linda**

Nightmares Can Be Good for You. *Ladies' Home Journal* 107, No. 3 (March 1990):64

**Levi, Giovanni**

Family and Kin – a Few Thoughts. *Journal of Family History* 15, No. 4 (October 1990):567-578

**Levin, Susanna**

Disc Jocks. *Women's Sports & Fitness* 12, No. 6 (September 1990):66

**Levin, Tobe** and Myers-Dickinson, Jo

Women's Studies in Europe: Conference Report. *NWSA Journal* 2, No. 1 (Winter 1990):101-104

**Levin, Tobe** (joint author). *See* Koster-Lossack, Angelika

**Levine, James A.**

How Employers are Helping Working Moms. *Good Housekeeping* 211, No. 3 (September 1990):150+

**Levine, Lois**

Jewish Women's Call for Peace: A Handbook for Jewish Women on the Israeli/Palestinian Conflict. Book Review. *Bridges* 1, No. 2 (Fall 1990): 125

**Levine, Philippa**

Love, Friendship, and Feminism in Later 19th-Century England. *Women's Studies International Forum* 13, Nos. 1-2 (1990):63-78

**Levine, Suzanne Braun**

Friendship: The Honesty Frontier. *Ms.* 1, No. 3 (November/December 1990):94-95

**Levinger, Leah** and Adler, Jo

How Children Learn. *Good Housekeeping* 211, No. 3 (September 1990):134+

**Levinkind, Susan** (joint author). *See* Dykewomon, Elana

**Levinson, David**

Family Violence in Cross-cultural Perspective. Reviewed by Linda E. Saltzman. *Journal of Marriage and the Family* 52, No. 1 (February 1990):280-281

**Levinson, Sara** (about)

What's the Big Idea? Sara Nelson. *Working Woman* (July 1990):96-98+

**Levy, Chava Willig**

Full Circle: Wheel of Misfortune? *Family Circle* 103, No. 14 (October 16, 1990):192

Tehilah: Our Answered Prayer. *McCall's* 118, No. 3 (December 1990):138-140

**Levy, Emily**

The Revenge of the Chunky Beef. Short Story. *Sinister Wisdom* 40 (Spring 1990):82-88

**Levy, Karen B.** (joint author). *See* Chrisler, Joan C.

**Levy, Marion Fennelly**

Each in Her Own Way: Five Women Leaders of the Developing World. Reviewed by Valerie de Plessis. *Resources for Feminist Research* 19, No. 1 (March 1990):9

**Lew, Julie**

Ruth Brinker's Meals Feed Body and Soul. *McCall's* 117, No. 7 (April 1990):23

**Lewin, Terry** (joint author). *See* Raphael, Beverley

**Lewis, Ann F.**

AT&T, the Bishops and Other Bad Connections. *Ms.* 1, No. 1 (July/August 1990):88

**Lewis, Barbara**

Women and the State in Africa. Book Review. *Women & Politics* 10, No. 1 (1990):82-84

**Lewis, Carl** (about). *See* Athletes, "The Competitive Edge"

**Lewis, Deborah Shaw** and Lewis, Gregg

What's the Most Stressful Job in the World? *Redbook* 175, No. 6 (October 1990):102-103+

**Lewis, Debra**

When Love Turns Violent. *Glamour* (August 1990):234-235

**Lewis, Debra J.**

Just Give Us the Money: A Discussion of Wage Discrimination and Pay Equity. Reviewed by Stella Lord. *Resources for Feminist Research* 19, No. 1 (March 1990):22

**Lewis, Earlene** (joint musician). *See* Adegbalola, Gaye

**Lewis, Edith** (joint author). *See* Taylor, Robert Joseph

**Lewis, Edward**

In Celebration of Our Twentieth Anniversary. *Essence* 21, No. 1 (May 1990):20-25

**Lewis, Eleanore**

Parsley, Sage, Rosemary and Thyme. *Family Circle* 103, No. 9 (June 26, 1990):66-69

**Lewis, Gail**

Audre Lorde: Vignettes and Mental Conversations. *Feminist Review* No. 34 (Spring 1990):100-114

**Lewis, Gail** (joint editor). *See* Grewal, Shabnam

**Lewis, Gifford**

Eva Gore-Booth and Esther Roper: A Biography. Reviewed by Clare Collins. *Gender & History* 2, No. 1 (Spring 1990):116-118

**Lewis, Gregg** (joint author). *See* Lewis, Deborah Shaw

**Lewis, Jo Ann**

Moroccan Idyll. *Harper's Bazaar* (February 1990):166-167+

Prints of Darkness. *Harper's Bazaar* (May 1990):56+

**Lewis, Joanne** (about). *See also* Franklin, I. E., "200 Words"

**Lewis, Judith S.**

Wet Nursing: A History from Antiquity to the Present. Book Review. *Gender & History* 2, No. 2 (Summer 1990):232-234

**Lewis, Lisa A.**

Gender Politics and MTV: Voicing the Difference. Reviewed by Alida Brill. *Ms.* 1, No. 1 (July/August 1990):70

Gender Politics and MTV: Voicing the Difference. Reviewed by Jane Caputi. *The Women's Review of Books* 8, No. 3 (December 1990):27

**Lewis, Magda A. Gere**

Canadian Women: A History. Book Review. *Women's Studies International Forum* 13, Nos. 1-2 (1990):162

**Lewis, Pearl** and Lewis, Peter

Long Time Love. *Essence* 21, No. 1 (May 1990):139-142+

**Lewis, Peter** (joint author). *See* Lewis, Pearl

**Lewis, Samella** (about). *See* De Veaux, Alexis, Milloy, Marilyn, and Ross, Michael Erik

**Lewis, Sara**

Mothers Make Mistakes. Short story. *Redbook* 174, No. 5 (March 1990):52-59

**Lewis, Susan**

Norwood Was a Difficult School. Book Review. *Gender and Education* 2, No. 1 (1990):116

**Liability (Law)**

When You Can Be Sued for Injuries. *Good Housekeeping* 211, No. 3 (September 1990):291

**Libel Suits.** *See* Trials (libel)

**Librarians**

Work That Is Real: Perspectives on Feminist Librarianship. Janet Freedman. *WLW Journal* 14, No. 1 (Fall 1990):3-5

**Library of Congress – Subject Headings**

Women in LC's Terms: A Thesaurus of Library of Congress Subject Headings Related to Women. By Ruth Dickstein, Victoria A. Mills, and Ellen J. Waite. Reviewed by Mary Ellen S. Capek. *NWSA Journal* 2, No. 3 (Summer 1990):476-484

**Licad, Cecile** (about). *See* Musicians

**Lichtenstein, Grace**

Fitness: Wilderness Sports. Bibliography. *Vogue* (January 1990):80-83

Giving Disneyland a Run for Its Money. *Savvy Woman* (February 1990):42-45

Witness to Freedom. *Savvy Woman* (July/August 1990):56-59+

**Lida, David**

External Affairs. Bibliography. *Harper's Bazaar* (April 1990):78-82

Mary Reilly. Book Review. *Harper's Bazaar* (February 1990):108-110

**Liddington, Jill**

The Long Road to Greenham: Feminism and Anti-Militarism in Britain since 1820. Reviewed by Jo Vellacott. *Resources for Feminist Research* 19, No. 2 (June 1990):44

**Liebach, Renate**

Message from Romania. *Spare Rib* No. 209 (February 1990):23-24

**Lieff, Ann** (about)

Enterprise: How to Take a Good Business and Make It Better. Mark Stevens. *Working Woman* (March 1990):38-46

**Life Cycles**

Family Development and the Life Course: Two Perspective on Family Change. Joan Aldous. *Journal of Marriage and the Family* 52, No. 3 (August 1990):517-583

New Evidence on the Timing of Early Life-Course Transitions: The United States 1900 to 1980. David Stevens. *Journal of Family History* 15, No. 2 (April 1990):163-178

Women in Midlife and Beyond. Iris G. Fodor and Violet Franks. *Psychology of Women Quarterly* 14, No. 4 (December 1990):445-449

Women's Prime of Life: Is It the 50s? Valory Mitchell and Ravenna Helson. *Psychology of Women Quarterly* 14, No. 4 (December 1990):451-470

**Life History Writing**

Life (H)istory Writing: The Relationship between Talk and Text. Margaret Somerville. *Australian Feminist Studies* No. 12 (Summer 1990):29-42

Rage and Redemption: Reading the Life Story of a Mexican Marketing Woman. Ruth Behar. *Feminist Studies* 16, No. 2 (Summer 1990):223-258

**Life Insurance.** *See* Insurance, Life

**Life-Saving.** *See* Rescues

**Life Styles.** *See also* Financial Planning; Homosexuality; Lesbianism; Orderliness

The Buy-Buy Babes. Jill Neimark. *Mademoiselle* (February 1990):174-175+

The Childless Executive: By Choice or By Default? Stephani Cook. *Working Woman* (November 1990):126-129+

Families. Tamar Jacoby. *Lear's* (April 1990):68-73

February Is a Great Month to . . . Bibliography. *Glamour* (February 1990):149

Inside Books: Lifestyles of the Rich and Shameless. Joyce Maynard. *Mademoiselle* (February 1990):88+

Interiors: No Bundles of Joy. Jennifer Jordon. *Essence* 21, No. 6 (October 1990):42

January Is a Great Month to . . . *Glamour* (January 1990):101

Need to Know. Christine Logan Wright. *Mademoiselle* (June 1990):86

The Paleolithic Prescription. By S. Boyd Eaton, Marjorie Shostak, and Melvin Konner. Reviewed by Lorraine Handler Sirota. *Women and Health* 16, Nos. 3/4 (1990):206-211

The Separatist Revival. Ann Japenga. *Out/Look* No. 8 (Spring 1990):78-83

Style: Keep It Pure and Simple. Alexandra Stoddard. *McCall's* 117, No. 11 (August 1990):126

Talking about Our Generation: The Mademoiselle Poll. Shifra Diamond. *Mademoiselle* (December 1990):161+

Tapestries of Life: Women's Work, Women's Consciousness, and the Meaning of Daily Life. By Bettina Aptheker. Reviewed by Elizabeth Dane. *AFFILIA* 5, No. 4 (Winter 1990):110-111

Tapestries of Life: Women's Work, Women's Consciousness, and the Meaning of Daily Life. By Bettina Aptheker. Reviewed by Linda Roman. *On the Issues* 15 (Summer 1990):28-29

They've Got to Have It: The Twentysomethings Take Over. Jill Nelmark. *Mademoiselle* (December 1990):158-160

You Can Reverse Aging: How Anti-Aging Clinics Turn Back the Clock. Anne Cassidy. *Family Circle* 103, No. 14 (October 16, 1990):118-122

**Lifshitz, Leatrice H.** (editor)

Her Soul Beneath the Bone: Women's Poetry on Breast Cancer. Reviewed by Alison Townsend. *The Women's Review of Books* 7, No. 8 (May 1990):16

**Lifton, Betty Jean**

Too Young to Remember. Book review. *Lilith* 15, No. 1 (Winter 1990):6

**Liggett, Helen**

Women, Social Science and Public Policy. Book Review. *Women & Politics* 10, No. 3 (1990):127-129

**Light, Beth** (joint author). *See* Prentice, Alison

**Light, Deborah Ann**

The Book of J. Book Review. *Ms.* 1, No. 2 (September/October 1990):27

The Illegitimacy of Jesus: A Feminist Theological Interpretation of the Infancy Narratives. Book Review. *Ms.* 1, No. 2 (September/October 1990):27

The Once and Future Goddess: A Symbol for Our Time. Book Review. *Ms.* 1, No. 2 (September/October 1990):27

Whence the Goddesses: A Source Book. Book Review. *Ms.* 1, No. 2 (September/October 1990):27

**Light, Judith** (about)

Eat Light: How Judith Got Light. Kathleen Mackay. *Redbook* 175, No. 5 (September 1990):26

**Lighting, Architectural and Decorative**

Living Beautifully: Let in the Light, Brighten Your Home. Alexandra Stoddard. *McCall's* 117, No. 10 (July 1990):136

**Lightman, Marjorie** (joint editor). *See* Hoff-Wilson, Joan

**Lightner, Candy** and Hathaway, Nancy

The Other Side of Sorrow. Excerpt. *Ladies' Home Journal* 107, No. 9 (September 1990):158-159+

**Lila Manifesto**

East German Feminists: The Lila Manifesto. Lisa DiCaprio. *Feminist Studies* 16, No. 3 (Fall 1990):621-636

**Lilien, Copie** (about). *See* Entrepreneurs

**Lilienfeld, Jane**

Feminist Literary History. Book Review. *Women's Studies International Forum* 13, Nos. 1-2 (1990):165-166

Virginia Woolf: The Impact of Childhood Sexual Abuse on Her Life and Work. Book Review. *Women's Studies International Forum* 13, No. 5 (1990):527-529

**Lilith Feminist History Conference**

Feminist History Conference. Barbara Baird. *Australian Feminist Studies* No. 12 (Summer 1990):117-119

**Lim, Shirley Goek-Lin**

The Floating World. Book Review. *Belles Lettres* 5, No. 3 (Spring 1990):20

Japanese American Women's Life Stories: Maternality in Monica Sone's *Nisei Daughter* and Joy Kogawa's *Obasan. Feminist Studies* 16, No. 2 (Summer 1990):289-312

The Longman Anthology of World Literature by Women, 1875-1975. Book Review. *The Women's Review of Books* 7, Nos. 10-11 (July 1990):15-16

Modern Secrets. Reviewed by Laura B. Kennelly. *Belles Lettres* 5, No. 2 (Winter 1990):10

Welcome Presences, Unwelcome Absences. *The Women's Review of Books* 7, Nos. 10-11 (July 1990):15-16

**Lim, Shirley Goek-Lin** and Tsutakawa, Mayumi (editors)

The Forbidden Stitch: An Asian American Women's Anthology. Reviewed by Marina Heung. *The Women's Review of Books* 7, No. 4 (January 1990):8-10

**Lin, Maya Ying** (about)

The Symmetry of Maya Ying Lin. Jill Kirschenbaum. *Ms.* 1, No. 2 (September/October 1990):20-22

**Lincoln, Sarah Bush** (about)

Abraham Lincoln's Other Mother. Daniel Mark Epstein. *Good Housekeeping* 210, No. 5 (May 1990):86-89

**Lincoln Town Car.** *See* Automobiles – Design and Construction

**Lind, Mary Ann**

The Compassionate Memsahibs: Welfare Activities of British Women in India, 1900-1947. Reviewed by Anand A. Yang. *Women's Studies International Forum* 13, No. 4 (1990):407-408

**Linde, Shirley** (joint author). *See* Hauri, Peter J.

**Lindell, Marianne E.** and Olsson, Henny M.

Personal Hygiene in External Genitalia of Healthy and Hospitalized Elderly Women. *Health Care for Women International* 11, No. 2 (1990):151-158

**Linden, Amy**

Barbara Brandon: A Comic Strip about Us. *Essence* 20, No. 11 (March 1990):46

**Linden, Laurie**

Image: Spring Hair Repair. *Working Woman* (May 1990):105-108

**Lindgren, J. Ralph**

Beyond Revolt: A Horizon for Feminist Ethics. *Hypatia* 5, No. 1 (Spring 1990):145-150

**Lindholm, Marika**

Working Parents: Transformation in Gender Roles and Public Policies in Sweden. Book Review. *Journal of Marriage and the Family* 52, No. 2 (May 1990):564-565

**Lindner, Lawrence**

Nutrition Now: Bone Up on Beef. *Redbook* 174, No. 5 (March 1990):157-162

**Lindquist, Barbara** (joint author). *See* Molnar, Alex

**Lindsay, Beverly**

Cross-Cultural Perspectives on Women in Higher Education. *Sage* 6, No. 1 (Summer 1989):92-96

**Lindvall, Michael L.**

A Child Is Born. *Good Housekeeping* 211, No. 6 (December 1990):116-118

**Line and Staff Organization.** *See* Delegation of Authority

**Lineberger, Kathryn**

Colored, Cut, or Crystal Clear. *Lear's* (November 1990):122-124

Knocking on Wood. *Lear's* (October 1990):138

What Lisa Knew, The Truths and Lies of the Steinberg Case. Book Review. *New Directions for Women* 19, No. 5 (September-October 1990):10+

**Lipton, Eunice**

Myths of Sexuality: Representations of Women in Victorian Britain. Book Review. *Gender & History* 2, No. 1 (Spring 1990):91-97

Vision and Difference: Feminism, Femininity and the History of Art. Book Review. *Gender & History* 2, No. 1 (Spring 1990):91-97

Women, Pleasure, and Painting (e.g., Boucher). *Genders* 7 (Spring 1990):69-86

**Lipton, Peggy** (about)

Talking with Peggy Lipton: "My Life Is Starting Over." Interview. Glenn Esterly. *Redbook* 175, No. 6 (October 1990):60-62

**Lisle, Laurie**

Louise Nevelson: A Passionate Life. Reviewed by Arlene Raven. *The Women's Review of Books* 8, No. 1 (October 1990):14-15

Louise Nevelson: A Passionate Life. Reviewed by Joan Philpott. *Ms.* 1, No. 2 (September/October 1990):28

**Lissner, Anneliese,** Su1ssman, Rita, and Walter, Karin (editors)

Frauen Lexikon. Reviewed by Marguerite Andersen. *Resources for Feminist Research* 19, No. 1 (March 1990):16

**Listfield, Emily**

Lucy. Book Review. *Harper's Bazaar* (October 1990):82

**Literacy.** *See* Illiteracy

**Literart Criticism – Feminist Perspectives**

Feminine Perspectives and Narrative Points of View. Ismay Barwell. *Hypatia* 5, No. 2 (Summer 1990):63-75

**Literary Criticism**

Abandoned Women and Poetic Tradition. By Lawrence Lipking. Reviewed by Herbert F. Tucker. *Iris* 23 (Spring-Summer 1990):71-73

Book Bazaar: Tale Spinners. Brenda Cullerton. *Harper's Bazaar* (December 1990):98

The Changing Subject and the Politics of Theory. R. Radhakrishnan. *Differences* 2, No. 2 (Summer 1990):126-152

The Difference Within: Feminism and Critical Theory. Edited by Elizabeth Meese and Alice Parker. Reviewed by Sue Golding. *Resources for Feminist Research* 19, No. 2 (June 1990):39

Inside Books: Lifestyles of the Rich and Shameless. Joyce Maynard. *Mademoiselle* (February 1990):88+

Word On Books. Bibliography. Laura Mathews. *Glamour* (April 1990):196

Word On Books. Laura Mathews. *Glamour* (January 1990):86; (February 1990):132; (June 1990):188

**Literary Criticism – Deconstruction**

The First Sophists and Feminism: Discourses of the "Other." Susan C. Jarratt. *Hypatia* 5, No. 1 (Spring 1990):27-41

A Spurious Set (Up): "Fetching Females" and "Seductive" Theories in *Phaedrus*, "Plato's Pharmacy," and *Spurs*. Katherine Cummings. *Genders* 8 (Summer 1990):38-61

**Literary Criticism – Feminist Perspectives.** *See also* Children's Literature; Feminism – Theory

Between Theory and Fiction: Reflections on Feminism and Classical Scholarship. Ruth Padel. *Gender & History* 2, No. 2 (Summer 1990):198-211

The Blackman's Guide to Understanding the Blackwoman. By Shahrazad Ali. Reviewed by Iyanla Vanzant. *Essence* 21, No. 5 (September 1990):55

Book Marks. Bibliography. Paula Giddings. *Essence* 21, No. 5 (September 1990):52; 21, No. 6 (October 1990):52

The Borders of Ethical, Erotic, and Artistic Possibilities in *Little Women*. Notes. Ann B. Murphy. *Signs* 15, No. 3 (Spring 1990):562-585

Conference Report. Carmel Macdonald-Grahame and Jane Southwell. *Hecate* 16, Nos. 1-2 (1990):184-192

Contemporary Women's Fiction: Narrative Practice and Feminist Theory. By Paulina Palmer. Reviewed by Alice Hall Petry. *Tulsa Studies in Women's Literature* 9, No. 2 (Fall 1990):332-334

Desire and Domestic Fiction: A Political History of the Novel. By Nancy Armstrong. Reviewed by Katharine M. Rogers. *Signs* 15, No. 4 (Summer 1990):878-882

Double-dealing Fictions. Sarah Schuyler. *Genders* 9 (Fall 1990):75-92

The Female *Bildungsroman*: Calling It into Question. Carol Lazzaro-Weis. *NWSA Journal* 2, No. 1 (Winter 1990):16-34

Feminist Literary History. By Janet Todd. Reviewed by Jane Lilienfeld. *Women's Studies International Forum* 13, Nos. 1-2 (1990):165-166

Gothic Repetition: Husbands, Horrors, and Things That Go Bump in the Night. Notes. Michelle A. Massé. *Signs* 15, No. 4 (Summer 1990):679-709

Havens No More? Discourses of Domesticity. Bonnie Smith. *Gender & History* 2, No. 1 (Spring 1990):98-102

Intellectual Women and Victorian Patriarchy: Harriet Martineau, Elizabeth Barrett Browning, George Eliot. By Deirdre David. Reviewed by Katharine M. Rogers. *Signs* 15, No. 4 (Summer 1990):878-882

Is There a Feminist Aesthetic? Marilyn French. *Hypatia* 5, No. 2 (Summer 1990):33-42

The List: The Top 10 Books. *Out/Look* No. 7 (Winter 1990):5

New Reference Works in Women's Studies. *Feminist Collections* 11, No. 2 (Winter 1990):20-25; 12, No. 1 (Fall 1990):25-33

Poetics and Politics: The Defiant Muse. Darby Tench. *Iris* 24 (Fall-Winter 1990):49-53

Popular Advice to Women: A Feminist Perspective. Mary Ann Jimenez and Susan Rice. *AFFILIA* 5, No. 3 (Fall 1990):8-26

Reading "Snow White": The Mother's Story. Notes. Shuli Barzilai. *Signs* 15, No. 3 (Spring 1990):515-534

Reading the Body in Contemporary Culture: An Annotated Bibliography. Anne Balsamo. *Women & Language* 13, No. 1 (Fall 1990):64-85

Rediscovering and Creating a Women's Literature. Zvia Ginor. *Lilith* 15, No. 4 (Fall 1990):38

Resources. *Women in Action* 3 & 4 (1990):62-64

Romance and the Erotics of Property: Mass-Market Fiction for Women. By Jan Cohn. Reviewed by Katharine M. Rogers. *Signs* 15, No. 4 (Summer 1990):878-882

Season's Readings. Bibliography. Anne Lamott. *Mademoiselle* (December 1990):80-82

Subject to Change: Reading Feminist Writing. By Nancy K. Miller. Reviewed by Barbara Green. *Tulsa Studies in Women's Literature* 9, No. 1 (Spring 1990):135-139

True Stories: Biographies of Women for Young Readers. Christine Jenkins. *Feminist Collections* 12, No. 1 (Fall 1990):6-9

Woman, Morality, and Fiction. Jenefer Robinson and Stephanie Ross. *Hypatia* 5, No. 2 (Summer 1990):76-90

Women of the Left Bank: Paris, 1900-1940. By Shari Benstock. Reviewed by Megan Roughley. *Gender & History* 2, No. 1 (Spring 1990):118-120

Words in Silence: An Exercise in Third World Feminist Criticism. Jid Lee. *Frontiers* 11, Nos. 2-3 (1990):66-71

Writing for Their Lives. By Gillian Hanscombe and Virginia L. Smyers. Reviewed by Megan Roughley. *Gender & History* 2, No. 1 (Spring 1990):118-120

## Literary Genres – Gender Roles

Gender, Genre and Narrative Pleasure. Edited by Derek Longhurst. Reviewed by Maureen Reddy. *The Women's Review of Books* 7, No. 7 (April 1990):25-26

Gender, Genre and Narrative Pleasure. Edited by Derek Longhurst. Reviewed by Sandra Taylor. *Australian Feminist Studies* No. 12 (Summer 1990):127-128

Literature. *See also* Children's Literature; Jewish Women – Literature

Fourth International Book Fare, June 1990. Eleanor J. Bader. *Belles Lettres* 6, No. 1 (Fall 1990):59-61

## Literature – Addresses, Essays, Lectures. *See also* Engels, Friedrich (about)

Comrades and Sisters: Feminism, Socialism and Pacifism in Europe, 1870-1945. By Richard J. Evans. Reviewed by Claudia Koonz. *Gender & History* 2, No. 1 (Spring 1990):120-122

Report from the Zora Neale Hurston Society Conference. Kamili Anderson. *Belles Lettres* 6, No. 1 (Fall 1990):63

## Literature – Africa – Images of Women

The Goddess O4sdotun as a Paradigm for African Feminist Criticism. Diedre L. Bádéjodot. *Sage* 6, No. 1 (Summer 1989):27-32

## Literature, African-American

Wild Women in the Whirlwind: Afra-American Culture and the Contemporary Literary Renaissance. Edited by Joanne M. Braxton and Andrée Nicola McLaughlin. Reviewed by Linda King. *Spare Rib* No. 214 (July 1990):22-23

## Literature – African-American

Wild Women In the Whirlwind: Afra-American Culture and the Contemporary Literary Renaissance. Edited by Joanne M. Braxton and Andrée Nicola McLaughlin. Reviewed by doris davenport. *WRB* 7, Nos. 10-11 (July 1990):36-37

## Literature – Anthologies

Eighteenth Century Women: An Anthology. By Bridget Hill. Reviewed by Patricia Crawford. *Australian Feminist Studies* No. 12 (Summer 1990):131-132

## Literature – Arabic

Opening the Gates: A Century of Arab Feminist Writing. Edited by Margot Badran and Miriam Cooke. Reviewed by Lina Mansour. *Spare Rib* No. 214 (July 1990):36-41

## Literature – Asia – Study and Teaching

The Politics and Pedagogy of Asian Literatures in American Universities. Rey Chow. *Differences* 2, No. 3 (Fall 1990):29-51

## Literature – Australia

A Writer's Friends and Associates: Notes from the Correspondence in the Zora Cross Papers. Julia Saunders. *Hecate* 16, Nos. 1-2 (1990):90-96

Zora Cross's Entry into Australian Literature. Michael Sharkey. *Hecate* 16, Nos. 1-2 (1990):65-89

## Literature – China

Red Ivy, Green Earth Mother. By Ai Bei. Reviewed by Helen Zia. *Ms.* 1, No. 3 (November/December 1990):56

Women in Chinese Fiction: The Last Ten Years. Louise Edwards and Kam Louie. *Australian Feminist Studies* No. 11 (Autumn 1990):95-112

## Literature – Collections

Breaking the Sequence: Women's Experimental Fiction. Edited by Ellen G. Friedman and Miriam Fuchs. Reviewed by Sarah Harasym. *Resources for Feminist Research* 19, No. 1 (March 1990):6-7

The Longman Anthology of World Literature by Women, 1875-1975. Edited by Marian Arkin and Barbara Shollar. Reviewed by Shirley Goek-Lin Lim. *The Women's Review of Books* 7, Nos. 10-11 (July 1990):15-16

The Meridian Anthology of Early Women Writers: British Literary Women from Aphra Behn to Maria Edgeworth 1660-1800. Edited by Katherine M. Rogers and William McCarthy. Reviewed by Ann B. Shteir. *Canadian Women's Studies* 11, No. 2 (Fall 1990):91-92

Women's Writing in Exile. Edited by Mary Lynn Broe and Angela Ingram. Reviewed by doris davenport. *The Women's Review of Books* 7, Nos. 10-11 (July 1990):36-37

## Literature, Feminist

Books: World-Class Pleasures. Marilyn French. *Ms.* 1, No. 1 (July/August 1990):66-67

Feminist Fiction, Feminist Form. Gayle Greene. *Frontiers* 11, Nos. 2-3 (1990):82-88

Feminist Literature: New Boom for Publishers. Mary Mackay. *Iris* 24 (Fall-Winter 1990):34

"She Want It All": The Sun Goddess in Contemporary Women's Poetry. Patricia Monaghan. *Frontiers* 11, Nos. 2-3 (1990):21-25

## Literature – French Language

Mariama Bâ: Parallels, Convergence, and Interior Space. Obioma Nnaemeka. *Feminist Issues* 10, No. 1 (Spring 1990):13-35

## Literature – Germany

Germany East and West: The Twain Meet. Nancy Derr. *Belles Lettres* 5, No. 4 (Summer 1990):9-10

## Literature – Great Britain

British Women Writers: An Anthology. Edited by Dale Spender and Janet Todd. Reviewed by Katherine M. Rogers. *Belles Lettres* 5, No. 3 (Spring 1990):25

Literary Daughters. By Maggie Lane. Reviewed by Sydney Janet Kaplan. *NWSA Journal* 2, No. 1 (Winter 1990):124-127

The Meridian Anthology of Early Women Writers: British Literary Women from Aphra Behn to Maria Edgeworth 1660-1800. Edited by Katherine M. Rogers and William McCarthy. Reviewed by Ann B. Shteir. *Canadian Women's Studies* 11, No. 2 (Fall 1990):91-92

Patchwork. Deborah Price. *Belles Lettres* 5, No. 2 (Winter 1990):20-21

## Literature – Great Britain – History and Criticism

Of Chastity and Power: Elizabethan Literature and the Unmarried Queen. By Philippa Berry. Reviewed by Shannon Hengen. *Resources for Feminist Research* 19, No. 2 (June 1990):44-45

Half Savage and Hardy and Free: Women and Rural Radicalism in the Nineteenth-Century Novel. By Judith Weissman. Reviewed by Susan Hardy Aiken. *Signs* 16, No. 1 (Autumn 1990):188-192

Images of Adolescence in English Literature: The Middle Ages to the Modern Period. Claudio Violato and Arthur J. Wiley. *Adolescence* 25, No. 98 (Summer 1990):253-264

The Ladies: Female Patronage of Restoration Drama. By David Roberts. Reviewed by Elaine Hobby. *Gender & History* 2, No. 3 (Autumn 1990):359-363

The Prostituted Muse: Images of Women and Women Dramatists, 1642-1737. By Jacqueline Pearson. Reviewed by Elaine Hobby. *Gender & History* 2, No. 3 (Autumn 1990):359-363

Sexuality, Subjectivity, and Reading: Constructing the Heterosexual Heroine in the Late Eighteenth-Century Novel. Lisa L. Moore. *NWSA Journal* 2, No. 4 (Autumn 1990):693-695

The Sign of Angellica: Women, Writing, and Fiction, 1660-1800. By Janet Todd. Reviewed by Ann B. Shteir. *Canadian Women's Studies* 11, No. 2 (Fall 1990):91-92

The Sign of Angellica: Women, Writing and Fiction 1660-1800. By Janet Todd. Reviewed by Elaine Hobby. *Gender & History* 2, No. 3 (Autumn 1990):359-363

Uncovering the Zenana: Visions of Indian Womanhood in Englishwomen's Writings: 1813-1940. Janaki Nair. *Journal of Women's History* 2, No. 1 (Spring 1990):8-34

Virtue of Necessity: English Women's Writing, 1649-1688. By Elaine Hobby. Reviewed by Heather Campbell. *Resources for Feminist Research* 19, No. 2 (June 1990):47

## Literature – Greece

Love in the Greek Novel. David Konstan. *Differences* 2, No. 1 (Spring 1990):186-205

## Literature – Ireland

Territories of the Voice, Contemporary Stories by Irish Women Writers. Edited by Louise DeSalvo, Kathleen D'Arcy, and Katherine Hogan. Reviewed by Joann Gardner. *The Women's Review of Books* 7, No. 7 (April 1990):24-25

## Literature – Japan

Aspects of Love in Contemporary Novels by Japanese Women. Orie Muta. *Hecate* 16, Nos. 1-2 (1990):151-163

**Literature – Latin America**

Breaking Boundaries: Latina Writings and Critical Readings. Edited by Asunción Horno-Delgado, Eliana Ortega, Nina M. Scott, and Nancy Saporta Sternbach. Reviewed by Lourdes Torres. *Women's Studies International Forum* 13, No. 5 (1990):519-520

**Literature – Latin Language**

This Sex Which Is Not One: De-Constructing Ovid's Hermaphrodite. Georgia Nugent. *Differences* 2, No. 1 (Spring 1990):160-185

**Literature, Lesbian – History and Criticism**

The Safe Sea of Women: Lesbian Fiction 1969-1989. By Bonnie Zimmerman. Reviewed by Jan Clausen. *The Women's Review of Books* 8, No. 2 (November 1990):7-8

**Literature, Popular**

From My Guy to Sci-Fi: Genre and Women's Writing in the Postmodern World. Edited by Helen Carr. Reviewed by Maureen Reddy. *The Women's Review of Books* 7, No. 7 (April 1990):25-26

**Literature, Proletarian**

Ending Difference/Different Endings: Class, Closure, and Collectivity in Women's Proletarian Fiction. Paula Rabinowitz. *Genders* 8 (Summer 1990):62-77

**Literature – Romance**

Adjustment Is the Key – Postmarital Romance in Indian Popular Fiction. Amita Tyagi and Patricia Uberoi. *Manushi* 61 (November-December 1990):15-21

Good-Bye Heathcliff: Changing Heroes, Heroines, Roles, and Values in Women's Category Romances. By Mariam Darce Frenier. Reviewed by Eleanor Ty. *Atlantis* 15, No. 2 (Spring 1990):96-98

Reading the Romance: Women, Patriarchy and Popular Literature. By Janice A. Radway. Reviewed by Judy Simons. *Women's Studies International Forum* 13, No. 3 (1990):277

The Reverend Idol and Other Parsonage Secrets: Women Write Romances about Ministers, 1880-1950. Ann-Janine Morey. *Journal of Feminist Studies in Religion* 6, No. 1 (Spring 1990):87-103

**Literature – South Africa**

Jesus Is Indian and Other South African Stories. By Agnes Sam. Reviewed by Joyoti Grech. *Spare Rib* No. 210 (March 1990):34

**Literature – Soviet Union**

Balancing Acts: Contemporary Stories by Russian Women. Edited by Helena Goscilo. Reviewed by Judith Deutsch Kornblatt. *Feminist Collections* 11, No. 4 (Summer 1990):3-4

The Image of Women in Contemporary Soviet Fiction: Selected Short Stories from the U.S.S.R. Edited by Sigrid McLaughlin. Reviewed by Judith Deutsch Kornblatt. *Feminist Collections* 11, No. 4 (Summer 1990):3-4

**Literature – Spain – History and Criticism.** *See also* Spain – Writers

**Literature – Spanish Language**

Stratagems of the Strong, Stratagems of the Weak: Autobiographical Prose of the Seventeenth-Century Hispanic Convent. Electa Arenal and Stacey Schlau. *Tulsa Studies in Women's Literature* 9, No. 1 (Spring 1990):25-42

**Literature – Status of Women**

Edging Women Out: Victorian Novelists, Publishers, and Social Change. By Gaye Tuchman and Nina E. Fortin. Reviewed by Gladys Engel Lang and Kurt Lang. *Gender and Society* 4, No. 4 (December 1990):556-558

Edging Women Out: Victorian Novelists, Publishers, and Social Change. By Gaye Tuchman and Nina E. Fortin. Reviewed by Jane Nardin. *Gender and Society* 4, No. 4 (December 1990):558-561

**Literature – Study and Teaching**

Canto, Locura y Poesia. Olivia Castellano. *The Women's Review of Books* 7, No. 5 (February 1990):18-20

Class Struggle. Linda Bamber. *The Women's Review of Books* 7, No. 5 (February 1990):20-21

Novels of Initiation: A Guidebook for Teaching Literature to Adolescents. By David Peck. Book Review. *Adolescence* 25, No. 100 (Winter 1990):999-1000

Teaching Agnes Smedley's *Daughter of Earth*. Rita M. Kissen. *NWSA Journal* 2, No. 3 (Summer 1990):425-434

A Thematic Approach to Teaching *The Bluest Eye*. Margaret G. Lloyd. *Sage* 6, No. 1 (Summer 1989):59-62

Women of Color and the Core Curriculum: Tools for Transforming the Liberal Arts, Part 4. Susan F. Searing. *Feminist Collections* 12, No. 1 (Fall 1990):21-24

Writing Cultures: An Interdisciplinary Approach to Developing Cross-Cultural Courses. Kathleen Mullen Sands. *Women's Studies Quarterly* 18, Nos. 3-4 (Fall-Winter 1990):100-118

**Literature – Third World**

At the Receiving End: Reading "Third" World Texts in a "First" World Context. Anuradha Dingwaney Needham. *Women's Studies Quarterly* 18, Nos. 3-4 (Fall-Winter 1990):91-99

**Literature – United States – History and Criticism**

Girls Who Went Wrong: Prostitutes in American Fiction. By Laura Hapke. Reviewed by Nikki Lee Manos. *Belles Lettres* 5, No. 3 (Spring 1990):27

**Lithgow, John** (about). *See* Entertainers

**Lithography**

June Wayne's Quantum Aesthetics. Ruth Weisberg. *Woman's Art Journal* 11, No. 1 (Spring-Summer 1990):4-8

**Litman, Jane**

The Ways We Are: Saying Goodbye to Friends. *Lilith* 15, No. 1 (Winter 1990):31

**Litoff, Judy Barrett** and Smith, David C. (editors)

Miss You: The World War II Letters of Barbara Wooddall Taylor and Charles E. Taylor. Reviewed by Mary Anne Schofield. *Belles Lettres* 5, No. 4 (Summer 1990):39

**Little, Benilde**

Derrick Bell: Harvard's Conscience. *Essence* 21, No. 7 (November 1990):44

Janet Hubert. *Essence* 21, No. 8 (December 1990):33

Randy Crawford: Jazzy Rhythm 'n Blues. *Essence* 21, No. 4 (August 1990):48

Robert Johnson: The Eyes Behind BET. *Essence* 21, No. 7 (November 1990):48

TV's Bill Cosby in Ghost Dad, the Movie. *Essence* 21, No. 2 (June 1990):38

**Little, Priscilla**

Women Composers: The Lost Tradition Found. Book Review. *Iris* 23 (Spring-Summer 1990):74-75

Women Composers and Their Music. Vols. 1 and 2. Music Review. *Iris* 23 (Spring-Summer 1990):74-75

**Littrell, John M.** (joint author). *See* Littrell, Mary Ann

**Littrell, Mary Ann**, Damhorst, Mary Lynn, and Littrell, John M.

Clothing Interests, Body Satisfaction, and Eating Behavior of Adolescent Females: Related or Independent Dimensions? *Adolescence* 25, No. 97 (Spring 1990):77-95

**Litwoman, Jane**

Reclaiming the Shekhinah. *New Directions for Women* 19, No. 4 (July-August 1990):1+

**Lively, Penelope** (criticism)

Penelope Lively's *Moon Tiger*: A Feminist "History of the World." Mary Hurley Moran. *Frontiers* 11, Nos. 2-3 (1990):89-95

**Livingston, Carole Rose**

Two Prayers. Song. *Bridges* 1, No. 1 (Spring 1990):82-83

**Living Wills**

Do You Need a Living Will? *Good Housekeeping* 211, No. 4 (October 1990):248

**Llongueras, Luis** (about). *See* Spain – Culture and Society

**Lloyd, Margaret G.**

A Thematic Approach to Teaching *The Bluest Eye*. *Sage* 6, No. 1 (Summer 1989):59-62

**Lloyd, Michael** (joint author). *See* Fergusson, David M.

**Lloyd, Nancy**

With a Fly's Eye, Whale's Wit and Woman's Heart: Animals and Women. Book Review. *On the Issues* 16 (Fall 1990):32

**Lloyd, Sally A.**

Single Women/Family Ties: Life Histories of Older Women. Book Review. *Journal of Marriage and the Family* 52, No. 1 (February 1990):281

**Lo, Fulang**

Morning Breeze: A True Story of China's Cultural Revolution. Reviewed by Mitzi Myers. *NWSA Journal* 2, No. 2 (Spring 1990):273-281

Morning Breeze. Reviewed by Scarlet Cheng. *Belles Lettres* 5, No. 2 (Winter 1990):9

**Loans**. *See also* Credit

Fast Cash: Five Ways to Get It. Lynn Brenner. *Working Woman* (August 1990):38-40

How to Fund Your Dream Business. Claire McIntosh. *Working Woman* (January 1990):100

Seed Capital. Doreen Mangan. *Executive Female* (May/June 1990):70

**Loats, Carol**

Women and the Economy of Paris in the Sixteenth Century. *NWSA Journal* 2, No. 4 (Autumn 1990):684-686

**Lobbying**

How to Win Friends and Influence Legislators. Judy Goldsmith. *Ms.* 1, No. 1 (July/August 1990):90

**Lobo, J.** (joint author). *See* Singh, Saudan

**Lobur, Connie L.**

Momentum: Women in American Politics Now. Book Review. *Women & Politics* 10, No. 3 (1990):129-130

**Loch-Wouters, Marge**

Children's Cornucopia. *WLW Journal* 14, No. 1 (Fall 1990):15

**Lock, Margaret**

Menopause in Japan Means Konenki. *Healthsharing* 11, No. 4 (December 1990):23-25

**Locke, Mamie E.**

One World Women's Movement. Book Review. *Women & Politics* 10, No. 4 (1990):135-136

From Three-Fifths to Zero: Implications of the Constitution for African-American Women, 1787-1870. *Women & Politics* 10, No. 2 (1990):33-46

**Loda, Katherine E.**

Russian Women's Studies: Essays on Sexism in Soviet Culture. Book Review. *Women's Studies International Forum* 13, No. 3 (1990):273

**Loeffelholz, Mary**

Posing the Woman Citizen: The Contradictions of Stanton's Feminism. *Genders* 7 (Spring 1990):87-98

**Loewenstein, Andrea Freud**

Troubled Times. *The Women's Review of Books* 7, Nos. 10-11 (July 1990):22-23

**Loft, Lenore**

Eve Reconceived: Religious Perspectives in Feminist Children's Literature in France. *Women's Studies International Forum* 13, No. 3 (1990):221-228

Slavery and the French Revolutionists (1788-1805). Book Review. *Women's Studies International Forum* 13, Nos. 1-2 (1990):160

**Logan, John** (joint author). *See* Spitze, Glenna

**Logan, Julie**

The Cos-medics. *Harper's Bazaar* (January 1990):38

How a Man's Age Changes His Outlook on Love. *Glamour* (April 1990):256-259

**Logan, Liz**

The (Key) Chain Gang. *Mademoiselle* (September 1990):124-127

Travel: Checking Into Hotel Lust. Bibliography. *Mademoiselle* (June 1990):68-72

**Logan, Richard** (about). *See* Oakland, CA – Political Activists

**Logen, Onnie Lee**

Motherwit: An Alabama Midwife's Story. Reviewed by Shelley Crisp. *Belles Lettres* 5, No. 2 (Winter 1990):3

**Lokhorst, Marion**

Quebec Nurses' Strike. *Healthsharing* 11, No. 1 (December 1989):9

**Lomax, Melanie** (about). *See* De Veaux, Alexis, Milloy, Marilyn, and Ross, Michael Erik

**London Rape Crisis Centre**

London Rape Crisis Centre under Threat. *Spare Rib* No. 216 (September 1990):54

**London (U.K.)**

City Fare. Carla Carlisle. *Harper's Bazaar* (November 1990):204

London after Dark. *Harper's Bazaar* (November 1990):201 +

Our Sisters' London: Feminist Walking Tours. By Katherine Sturtevant. Reviewed by Anna Davin. *The Women's Review of Books* 8, No. 1 (October 1990):11-12

Prop Artist. *Harper's Bazaar* (November 1990):202 +

**Loneliness**

Predictors of Loneliness in Older Women and Men. Cornelia Beck, Cathleen Schultz, Chris Gorman Walton, and Robert Walls. *Journal of Women and Aging* 2, No. 1 (1990):3-31

**Long, Monica**

Silence. Poem. *Hecate* 16, Nos. 1-2 (1990):62

**Long, Patricia**

Thin Promises. *Vogue* (October 1990):400-401 +

**Long, Priscilla**

Where the Sun Never Shines: A History of America's Bloody Coal Industry. Reviewed by Barbara Kingsolver. *The Women's Review of Books* 7, No. 9 (June 1990):21-22

**Longbotham, Lori**

Food Advisory. *Working Woman* (October 1990):147

**Longevity**

Endurance Capacity and Longevity in Women. E. Nygaard, A. Gleerup Madsen, and H. Christensen. *Health Care for Women International* 11, No. 1 (1990):1-10

**Longhurst, Derek** (editor)

Gender, Genre and Narrative Pleasure. Reviewed by Maureen Reddy. *The Women's Review of Books* 7, No. 7 (April 1990):25-26

Gender, Genre and Narrative Pleasure. Reviewed by Sandra Taylor. *Australian Feminist Studies* No. 12 (Summer 1990):127-128

**Lootens, Tricia**

Gays Still Banned from Military. *off our backs* 20, No. 4 (April 1990):11

Male Students in Women's Studies. *off our backs* 20, No. 8 (August/September 1990):20 +

**Lopata, Helena Z.**

On Their Own: Widows and Widowhood in the American Southwest, 1848-1939. Book Review. *Gender and Society* 4, No. 1 (March 1990):103-105

**Lopate, Phillip**

You Can't Hurry Love. *Lear's* (July 1990):60-63

**Lord, Shirley**

Beauty Clips. *Vogue* (January 1990):64; (July 1990):74; (August 1990):154; (September 1990):296; (December 1990):146

Beauty's New Nature. *Vogue* (October 1990):394-398

Images: Flawless Skin. *Vogue* (January 1990):67-70

Images: The Penciled Face. *Vogue* (August 1990):169

Images. *Vogue* (October 1990):193 +

The Seductive Face. *Vogue* (September 1990):594-599

The Seven Ages of Skin. *Vogue* (January 1990):208-213

**Lord, Stella**

Just Give Us the Money: A Discussion of Wage Discrimination and Pay Equity. Book Review. *Resources for Feminist Research* 19, No. 1 (March 1990):22

**Lorde, Audre**

Apartheid U.S.A. Reviewed by Jacqueline E. Wade. *NWSA Journal* 2, No. 2 (Spring 1990):315-319

A Burst of Light. Reviewed by Batya Weinbaum. *NWSA JournalNWSA Journal* 2, No. 3 (Summer 1990): 2, No. 2 (Spring 1990):323-328

I Am Your Sister: Black Women Organizing across Sexualities. Reviewed by Jacqueline E. Wade. *NWSA Journal* 2, No. 2 (Spring 1990):315-319

Interiors: Is Your Hair Still Political? *Essence* 21, No. 5 (September 1990):40+

Women on Trains. Poem. *Ms.* 1, No. 2 (September/October 1990):64

**Lorde, Audre – Criticism and Interpretation**

Audre Lorde: Vignettes and Mental Conversations. Gail Lewis. *Feminist Review* No. 34 (Spring 1990):100-114

I Am Your Sister: A Tale of Two Conferences. Ayofemi Folayan. *off our backs* 20, No. 11 (December 1990):1-2

**Lorde, Audre** (about). *See* Writers – Interviews, "Graceful Passages"

A Radio Profile of Audre Lorde. By Jennifer Abod. Reviewed by Jacqui Alexander. *NWSA Journal* 2, No. 1 (Winter 1990):129-131

**Lorde, Audre** (conference)

I Am Your Sister Celeconference: Tribute to Audre Lorde. Joanne Stato. *off our backs* 20, No. 11 (December 1990):2-5+

**Loren, Sophia** (about)

Viva Sophia! Christopher Andersen. *Ladies' Home Journal* 107, No. 4 (April 1990):58-62

**Lorenz, Frederick O.** (joint author). *See* Conger, Rand D.

**Los Angeles – Celebrities**

California Girls. Lois Joy Johnson. *Ladies' Home Journal* 107, No. 4 (April 1990):172-180

**Los Angeles – Fashion**

Style: The L.A. Law. *Mademoiselle* (October 1990):192-201

**Los Angeles – Motion Picture Industry**

Hollywood Royalty. Jerry Lazar. *Mademoiselle* (October 1990):188-191+

**Los Angeles – Public Schools**

The Fear of Feminization: Los Angeles High Schools in the Progressive Era. Victoria Bissell Brown. *Feminist Studies* 16, No. 3 (Fall 1990):493-518

**Los Angeles – Shopping.** *See also* Shopping

**Los Angeles – Television Producers and Directors**

The Foxy Producer. Betty Goodwin. *Mademoiselle* (October 1990):155+

**Los Angeles – Youth Intervention Program**

Women Who Make a Difference. Linda Marsa. *Family Circle* 103, No. 15 (November 6, 1990):15-17

**Losing.** *See* Failure (Psychology)

**Lothinie4re-Harwood, Susanne de**

L'autre oeil: Le nu féminin dans l'art masculin. Book Review. *Canadian Women's Studies* 11, No. 1 (Spring 1990):106

**Lou, Barbara**

Your Stress Points. *Family Circle* 103, No. 5 (April 3, 1990):49-53

**Louie, Kam** (joint author). *See* Edwards, Louise

**Louie, Miriam Ching**

The Far East Comes Near: Autobiographical Accounts of Southeast Asian Students in America. Book Review. *Belles Lettres* 6, No. 1 (Fall 1990):27-28

First International Exchange of Women Unionists. *off our backs* 20, No. 3 (March 1990):18-19

Odysseys. *Belles Lettres* 6, No. 1 (Fall 1990):27-28

Quiet Odyssey: A Pioneer Korean Woman in America. Book Review. *Belles Lettres* 6, No. 1 (Fall 1990):27-28

Strike Strengthens Women. *New Directions for Women* 19, No. 4 (July-August 1990):10

**Loulan, JoAnn** (interview)

Education as Entertainment: Lesbian Sexpert JoAnn Loulan. Toni Armstrong Jr. *Hot Wire* 6, No. 1 (January 1990):3-5+

**Loury, MyKela** (joint author). *See* Brodsky, Michelle

**Love.** *See also* Sexual Attraction

Falling Out of Love. Susan Jacoby. *Glamour* (November 1990):238+

Love's Labours Quoted. Willie Mae Kneupper. *Lear's* (February 1990):49-50

My Funny Valentine. Robin Reif. *Glamour* (February 1990):206

The Passion Paradox. Dean C. Delis and Cassandra Phillips. *Glamour* (August 1990):214-215+

Romance. A. Alvarez. *Lear's* (November 1990):98-99+

In the Spirit: One Love. Susan L. Taylor. *Essence* 20, No. 10 (February 1990):53

**Love, Monie** (interview)

Down to Earth. Esther Bailey. *Spare Rib* 218 (November 1990):38-39

**Love, Patricia** and Robinson, Jo

Daughters Who Can't Get Away. *Glamour* (May 1990):294-295+

**Love, Susan M.**

Dr. Susan Love's Breast Book. *Good Housekeeping* 210, No. 6 (June 1990):168–169, 255-261

Dr. Susan Love's Breast Book. Reviewed by Alida Brill. *Ms.* 1, No. 1 (July/August 1990):70

**Love in Films**

You Can't Hurry Love. Phillip Lopate. *Lear's* (July 1990):60-63

**Love-Letters**

Love Letters Straight from the Heart. Brook Hersey. *Glamour* (February 1990):158-161

By Love Possessed. *Harper's Bazaar* (February 1990):178-181

**Lovell, Khalida** (about)

Solo Mothering. *Essence* 20, No. 11 (March 1990):97-98

**Lovell, Mary S.**

The Sound of Wings: The Life of Amelia Earhart. Reviewed by Susan Ware. *The Women's Review of Books* 7, No. 4 (January 1990):7-8

**Low, Nancy** (about)

Cleaning the Environment with a Woman's Touch. Patti Watts. *Executive Female* 13, No. 6 (November-December 1990):6-9

**Low-Cholesterol Diet.** *See also* Nutrition–Advertisements

The Lower-Your-Cholesterol Diet. Jan Turner Hazard. *Ladies' Home Journal* 107, No. 1 (January 1990):128-138

**Lowe, Graham S.**

Women in the Administrative Revolution. Reviewed by Anne Statham. *Gender and Society* 4, No. 1 (March 1990):113-115

**Lowell, Joann**

Networking at CRIAW. *Healthsharing* 11, No. 2 (March 1990):8

**Lowell, Jo-Ann**

PCBs in Inuit Breastmilk. *Healthsharing* 11, No. 1 (December 1989):5

**Low-Fat Diet.** *See also* Desserts; Eating Behavior; Food–Fat Content; Nutrition; Reducing Diets

Cook Like a Pro: The Slim Chef's Dummer Party Tips. *Family Circle* 103, No. 9 (June 26, 1990):48-50

Diet News: These Fats Are Guaranteed Fakes. Ellen Kunes. *Mademoiselle* (June 1990):204

East Meets West. *Ladies' Home Journal* 107, No. 9 (September 1990):192

Eater's Digest. *Glamour* (July 1990):193; (November 1990):262

Eat Well: Beating Holiday Food Traps. *Family Circle* 103, No. 17 (December 18, 1990):52-54

Fats: The Good, the Bad and the Deadly. Paula Derrow. *Mademoiselle* (December 1990):104

Food & Health. *Glamour* (September 1990):344

Food Journal: 100 Low-Fat Foods. Evette M. Hackman. *Ladies' Home Journal* 107, No. 4 (April 1990):183-191

Hamming It Up: Great Low-Calorie Dishes. Karen Sethre White. *McCall's* 117, No. 11 (August 1990):120

Health Department. Leigh Silverman. *Lear's* (July 1990):42

Health Dept. Donna Heiderstadt. *Lear's* (December 1990):58

Leaner Ways to Eat. *Glamour* (May 1990):302-306

Lighten Up: The New Spa Cuisine. *Ladies' Home Journal* 107, No. 5 (May 1990):206-210

Low-Fat Cooking: Fast, Fabulous Fajitas. *Family Circle* 103, No. 15 (November 6, 1990):58

Nutrinews. *Ladies' Home Journal* 107, No. 12 (December 1990):198

Nutripoints. Roy E. Vartabedian and Kathy Matthews. *Ladies' Home Journal* 107, No. 2 (February 1990):38-43

Nutrition Now: Move Over, Oat Bran! Janis Jibrin. *Redbook* 175, No. 5 (September 1990):188-191

Oat-Bran Entrées: Savory and Slimming. *McCall's* 117, No. 7 (April 1990):125

Pure Food. *Lear's* (January 1990):80-85

The Ultimate Low-Fat Cookbook. *Ladies' Home Journal* 107, No. 11 (November 1990):259-272

Weight Check. *Harper's Bazaar* (August 1990):32-34+

**Lown, Judy**

Women and Industrialization: Gender at Work in Nineteenth-Century England. Reviewed by Leslie Howsam. *Atlantis* 15, No. 2 (Spring 1990):106-107

**Lowy, Beverly**

About Men. Book Review. *On the Issues* 14 (1990):25

The One You Call Sister. Book Review. *On the Issues* 15 (Summer 1990):27

Women and Madness. Book Review. *On the Issues* 14 (1990):25

**Loxton, Diane** and Harris, Patricia

Job Evaluation and Broadbanding in the Western Australian Public Service. Reviewed by Cora Vellekoop Baldock. *Australian Feminist Studies* No. 12 (Summer 1990):43-49

**Lucas, Colin** (editor)

The Political Culture of the French Revolution, Vol. 2. Reviewed by Susan P. Conner. *Journal of Women's History* 1, No. 3 (Winter 1990):244-260

**Lucas, Eugenie A.**

State Feminism: Norwegian Women and the Welfare State. *Feminist Issues* 10, No. 2 (Fall 1990):43-53

**Lucas, Helen** (interview)

Conversation Fragments: Helen Lucas. Meg Luxton and Shelagh Wilkinson. *Canadian Women's Studies* 11, No. 1 (Spring 1990):92

**Lucey, Helen** (joint author). *See* Walkerdine, Valerie

**Lucht, John** (about). *See* Career Management

**Luepnitz, Deborah Anna**

The Family Interpreted: Feminist Theory in Clinical Practice. Reviewed by Shirley Feldman-Summers. *Women and Therapy* 9, No. 4 (1990):116-119

Feminism and Psychoanalytic Theory. Book Review. *The Women's Review of Books* 7, No. 8 (May 1990):17-18

Psychoanalysis and/or Feminism. *The Women's Review of Books* 7, No. 8 (May 1990):17-18

**Lufkin, Liz**

How to Get a Mellow Mindset. *Working Woman* (April 1990):117

Slow Down, You Move Too Fast: The Time-Sickness Cure. *Working Woman* (April 1990):111-112

**Luggage**

Baggage Claim. *Mademoiselle* (October 1990):226

**Lugones, María**

Hispaneando y Lesbiando: On Sarah Hoagland's Lesbian Ethics. *Hypatia* 5, No. 3 (Fall 1990):138-146

Lesbian Ethics: Toward New Value. Book Review. *Hypatia* 5, No. 3 (Fall 1990):138-146

**Lumet, Jenny** (about). *See* Children of Entertainers

**Lunchbox Cookery**

Savvy School Lunches. Barbara Kafka. *Family Circle* 103, No. 14 (October 16, 1990):162-165

**Lund, Diane**

Don't Get Pregnant – Or Else. *Good Housekeeping* 210, No. 4 (April 1990):119, 228-230

**Lunden, Joan** (about). *See also* Television Journalists – Networking

Star Gazing. Ellen Sherman. *Family Circle* 103, No. 1 (January 9, 1990):33-34

**Lundhoff, Catherine** (joint author). *See* Chaney, Elsa

**Lundquist, Anne**

Small Girl at the Chesapeake. Poem. *Sinister Wisdom* 42 (Winter 1990-1991):113

**Luppa, Carol J.** and Miller, Connie (editors)

Women's Health Perspectives: An Annual Review. Reviewed by Margherita Jellinek. *AFFILIA* 5, No. 4 (Winter 1990):108-110

**Lupton, Carol**

Feminist Scholarship: Kindling in the Groves of America. Book Review. *Gender and Education* 2, No. 2 (1990):251-252

Gender Issues in Field Research. Book Review. *Gender and Education* 2, No. 2 (1990):251-252

**Lupus**

Circle This. Margaret Jaworski. *Family Circle* 103, No. 14 (October 16, 1990):11-14

**Luria, Zella**

Journal of Women and Aging. Periodical review. *Psychology of Women Quarterly* 14, No. 4 (December 1990):617

**Lurie, Alison**

A Curious Haunting. Short story. *Redbook* 175, No. 6 (October 1990):40-52

Face of the '90s. *Lear's* (January 1990):61-69

**Lusardi, Lee A.**

Power Talk. *Working Woman* (July 1990):92-94

**Lusk, Gill**

The Bitter with the Sweet. *The Women's Review of Books* 8, No. 3 (December 1990):13-14

Sweeter Than Honey: Ethiopian Women and Revolution, Testimonies of Tigrayan Women. Book Review. *The Women's Review of Books* 8, No. 3 (December 1990):13-14

**Luster, Tom** (joint author). *See* Dubow, Eric F.

**Luttrell, Wendy**

The Everyday World as Problematic: A Feminist Sociology. Book review. *Signs* 15, No. 3 (Spring 1990):635-640

Feminist Practice and Poststructuralist Theory. Book review. *Signs* 15, No. 3 (Spring 1990):635-640

Gender and Power. Book review. *Signs* 15, No. 3 (Spring 1990):635-640

**Luxton, Meg**

Child Custody and the Politics of Gender. Book Review. *Journal of Marriage and the Family* 52, No. 4 (November 1990):1153-1154

**Luxton, Meg** and Wilkinson, Shelagh

Conversation Fragments: Helen Lucas. *Canadian Women's Studies* 11, No. 1 (Spring 1990):92

**MacDougall, Jill** (joint author). *See* Burns, Judy

**MacDowell, Andie** (about). *See also* Beauty, Personal, "Beauty Bazaar"

Andie Swings into Stardom. David Denicolo. *Glamour* (November 1990):236-237+

**MacEachern, Diane**

Twenty-Five Everyday Ways to Help Clean Up Our Planet. *Ladies' Home Journal* 107, No. 4 (April 1990):224

**Macera, C. A.** (joint author). *See* Cokkinades, Vilma E.

**Macera, Caroline A.**

Women and Exercise: Physiology and Sports Medicine. Book Review. *Women and Health* 16, No. 2 (1990):137-138

**Machitun**

Three Mary's and a Rose. Reviewed. *Spare Rib* 219 (December 1990-January 1991):37

**Machung, Ann** (joint author). *See* Hochschild, Arlie

**Mack, Joanna** (joint author). *See* Humphries, Steve

**Mack, John E.** and Rogers, Rita S.

The Alchemy of Survival: One Woman's Journey. Reviewed by Myrna Goldenberg. *Belles Lettres* 6, No. 1 (Fall 1990):6-9

**MacKay, Barbara** (joint author). *See* Hughes, Lynn

**Mackay, Kathleen**

Eat Light: How Judith Got Light. *Redbook* 175, No. 5 (September 1990):26

**Mackay, Mary**

Feminist Literature: New Boom for Publishers. *Iris* 24 (Fall-Winter 1990):34

**Mackay, Noreen Ash**

Are They Selling Her Lips: Advertising and Identity. Book Review. *On the Issues* 17 (Winter 1990):

**Mackenzie, Fiona**

Geography of Gender in the Third World. Book Review. *Resources for Feminist Research* 19, No. 1 (March 1990):18

**Mackey, Judith**

Winning Over Women: The Tobacco Industry Takes Aim. *Women in Action* 1-2 (1990):17-19

**Mackey, Marlene C.**

Women's Choice of Childbirth Setting. *Health Care for Women International* 11, No. 2 (1990):175-189

**Mackie, Marlene**

Who Is Laughing Now? The Role of Humour in the Social Construction of Gender. *Atlantis* 15, No. 2 (Spring 1990):11-26

**Mackinnon, Alison** (joint editor). *See* Allen, Margaret

**MacKinnon, Catharine A.**

Feminism Unmodified: Discourses on Life and Law. Reviewed by Kathleen B. Jones. *Women & Politics* 10, No. 1 (1990):73-76

Toward a Feminist Theory of the State. Reviewed by Deborah Schwenck. *Women's Rights Law Reporter* 12, No. 3 (Fall 1990): 205-208

Toward a Feminist Theory of the State. Reviewed by Eleanor J. Bader. *On the Issues* 14 (1990):26-28

Toward a Feminist Theory of the State. Reviewed by Emily M. Calhoun. *Frontiers* 11, Nos. 2-3 (1990):120-121

**MacKinnon, Catherine A.** (joint author). *See* Dworkin, Andrea

**Mackoff, Barbara L.**

Humor as a Professional Tool. *Executive Female* 13, No. 6 (November-December 1990):56-57

**MacLachlan, Kyle** (about)

Can He Bake a Cherry Pie? Meredith Brody and Christine Logan Wright. *Mademoiselle* (September 1990):248-249+

**MacLaine, Shirley** (about). *See also* Beauty, Personal, "Beauty Bazaar"

**Maclay, K. T.**

Close Shaves. *Lear's* (November 1990):78

Fashion Design in a Bottle. *Lear's* (November 1990):74

Perfume Envy: His for Her. *Lear's* (November 1990):77

**MacLeod, Linda**

The City for Women: No Safe Place. *Women and Environments* 12, No. 1 (Fall 1989/Winter 1990): 6-7

**MacLeod, Sandra**

Childcare and Access: Women in Tertiary Education in Scotland. Book Review. *Gender and Education* 2, No. 3 (1990):377-378

**MacManus, Susan A.**

State Constitutions and Women: Leading or Lagging Agents of Change? Notes. *Women & Politics* 10, No. 2 (1990):137-151

**MacNaughton, Robin**

Horoscopes: November. *Harper's Bazaar* (November 1990):218

**MacPhee, Susan C.**

Talking Peace: The Women's International Peace Conference. Reviewed by Anne Sisson Runyan. *Atlantis* 15, No. 2 (Spring 1990):107-109

**MacPike, Loralee**

Hints and Disguises: Marianne Moore and Her Contemporaries. Book Review. *NWSA Journal* 2, No. 4 (Autumn 1990):669-674

May Sarton Revisited. Book Review. *NWSA Journal* 2, No. 4 (Autumn 1990):669-674

Sarah Orne Jewett: An American Persephone. Book Review. *NWSA Journal* 2, No. 4 (Autumn 1990):669-674

**MacPike, Loralee** (editor)

There's Something I've Been Meaning to Tell You. Reviewed by Rebecca Gordon. *The Women's Review of Books* 7, No. 9 (June 1990):7-8

**MADD.** *See* Mothers Against Drunk Driving

**Maddern, Phillipa**

Hildegard of Bingen, 1098-1179: A Visionary Life. Book Review. *Australian Feminist Studies* No. 12 (Summer 1990):129-130

Medieval Prostitution. Book Review. *Australian Feminist Studies* No. 12 (Summer 1990):129-130

**Madhubuti, Haki**

Black Men: Single, Obsolete, and Dangerous? Reviewed by Maceo Crenshaw Dailey, Jr. *Sage* 6, No. 2 (Fall 1989):66-67

**Madhubuti, Haki R.**

The B Network. Poem. *Essence* 21, No. 5 (September 1990):114

A Bonding (For Susan and Kephra). Poem. *Essence* 21, No. 5 (September 1990):134

Mothers. Poem. *Essence* 20, No. 11 (March 1990):136

**Madison (Wisconsin).** *See also* Urban Living

Giving in to the Good Life. Lorrie Moore. *Savvy Woman* (September 1990):50-51+

**Madness.** *See* Mental Disorders

**Madonna** (about). *See also* Beauty Standards; Leadership, "1990 Women of the Year"; Sexual Attraction

Eye on . . . Madonna. *Harper's Bazaar* (June 1990):100-105+

Living to Tell: Madonna's Resurrection of the Fleshly. Susan McClary. *Genders* 7 (Spring 1990):1-21

Madonna Flexes Her Muscles. Richard Price. *Ladies' Home Journal* 107, No. 11 (November 1990):198+

Who's That Girl? Irene Coffey. *Spare Rib* 219 (December 1990-January 1991):27

**Madoo-Lengermann, Patricia** and Niebrugge-Brantley, Jill

Life/Lines: Theorizing Women's Autobiography. Book Review. *Tulsa Studies in Women's Literature* 9, No. 1 (Spring 1990):133-135

**MADRE**

MADRE Needed More Than Ever. Laura Flanders. *New Directions for Women* 19, No. 5 (September-October 1990):11+

**Madsen, A. Gleerup** (joint author). *See* Nygaard, E.

**Magazines.** *See* Periodicals

**Magder, Ruth**

America and I: Short Stories by American Jewish Women Writers. Book Review. *Belles Lettres* 6, No. 1 (Fall 1990):13

Let's Hear It for the Klopstocks. *Belles Lettres* 6, No. 1 (Fall 1990):13

**Maggio, Rosalie**

The Nonsexist Word Finder: A Dictionary of Gender-Free Usage. Reviewed by Mary Ellen S. Capek. *NWSA Journal* 2, No. 3 (Summer 1990):476-484

**Magnuson, Ann** (about)

Word On the Most Intriguing Boss on TV. Charla Krupp. *Glamour* (June 1990):186

**Maguire, Sara**

Rape in Marriage: Make It a Crime. *Spare Rib. See also* Rape – Law and Legislation

A Sexist and Racist Judiciary. *Spare Rib* No. 209 (February 1990):47

**Mahan, Sue**

Partial Justice: Women in State Prisons, 1800-1935. Book Review. *NWSA Journal* 2, No. 2 (Spring 1990):320-323

Walltappings: An Anthology of Writings by Women Prisoners. Book Review. *NWSA Journal* 2, No. 2 (Spring 1990):320-323

**Maher, Lisa**

Letters from a War Zone: Writings 1976-1989. Book Review. *Women's Rights Law Reporter* 12, No. 3 (Fall 1990): 209-216

**Mahon, Phyllis** (interview)

Waiting for the Angel. *Spare Rib* 218 (November 1990):30-31

**Mahony, Karen** and Van Toen, Brett

Mathematical Formalism as a Means of Occupational Closure in Computing – Why "Hard" Computing Tends to Exclude Women. *Gender and Education* 2, No. 3 (1990):319-331

**Mahood, Linda**

The Magdalene's Friend: Prostitution and Social Control in Glasgow, 1869-1890. *Women's Studies International Forum* 13, Nos. 1-2 (1990):49-61

**Maier, Frank**

A Final Gift. *Ladies' Home Journal* 107, No. 3 (March 1990):102-111

11 Quick Beauty Updates. *Glamour* (March 1990):238-241

Reggie Wells, Man of a Thousand Faces. Elsie B. Washington. *Essence* 21, No. 2 (June 1990):10

Rethinking Pink. *Mademoiselle* (February 1990):170-173

Retro '60s. Suzanne Bersch. *Lear's* (December 1990):108-111

The Return of Glamour. Laurie Tarkan. *Lear's* (September 1990):66

Rx for RN's: Off-Duty Beauty. *Family Circle* 103, No. 16 (November 27, 1990):78-82

The Seductive Face. Shirley Lord. *Vogue* (September 1990):594-599

Sheer Blues. *Harper's Bazaar* (April 1990):180-183

Simply Beautiful. *Lear's* (March 1990):132-137

Simply Beautiful. Lois Joy Johnson. *Ladies' Home Journal* 107, No. 2 (February 1990):124-128

The Skinny on Winter Skin. Melissa Dunst. *Lear's* (October 1990):68

Soft for Day, Bright for Night. *Mademoiselle* (November 1990):56

Sports Makeup Goes the Distance. *Lear's* (June 1990):30

Spring Eye-Openers. *Harper's Bazaar* (March 1990):120-124

Stay Light! *Harper's Bazaar* (June 1990):110-113

Summer Beauty News: Soft & Sexy. *Redbook* 175, No. 3 (July 1990):77-83

2 Sunny, Sexy Makeups. *Glamour* (May 1990):260-261

Take five! *Redbook* 174, No. 5 (March 1990):108-111

Ten Makeup Tricks Even a Beauty Klutz Can Do. *Mademoiselle* (October 1990):42

Trading in the New Gold Standard. Diane Clehane. *Lear's* (December 1990):54

Trendsetters. *Harper's Bazaar* (September 1990):44-48

What a Beautiful Wedding! *Redbook* 175, No. 3 (July 1990):14-16

What's In a Name? Liza Coleman. *Savvy Woman* (November 1990):42-43

**Makihara, Kumiko**
Japanese Women: Rewriting Tradition. *Lear's* (February 1990):78-83

**Malaysia – Childbirth**
"I Was Afraid to Cut the Umbilical Cord." *Connexions* 32 (1990):8

**Malcolm, Andrew H.**
Earth Angels. *Family Circle* 103, No. 2 (February 1, 1990):78-79

**Malcolm X** (about)
Back Talk: With Respect to Malcolm. Ron Daniels. *Essence* 20, No. 10 (February 1990):126

**Malcom, Shirley**
Increasing the Participation of Black Women in Science and Technology. *Sage* 6, No. 2 (Fall 1989):15-17

**Male-Female Relationships.** *See* Female-Male Relationships

**Malevich, Kazimir** (about)
Malevich. Rosamond Bernier. *Vogue* (September 1990):588-593 +

**Malik, Afshan N.**
Shaitan & the Chappal. Short Story. *Spare Rib* No. 211 (April 1990):18-19

**Malkiel, Theresa Serber**
The Diary of a Shirtwaist Striker. Reviewed by Annelise Orleck. *The Women's Review of Books* 8, No. 3 (December 1990):30-31

**Malkin, Nina**
Crossing Borders. *Harper's Bazaar* (September 1990):242-243 +

Image: The Business Traveler's Beauty Advisory. *Working Woman* (March 1990):122-124

Image: True Colors – Makeup That's Tailor-Made for You. *Working Woman* (February 1990):104-106

Inside Music. *Mademoiselle* (January 1990):54; (February 1990):90

Manhattan Purists. *Harper's Bazaar* (January 1990):34

Trade Secrets. Bibliography. *Harper's Bazaar* (September 1990):82

**Malmo, Cheryl** (joint author). *See* Laidlaw, Toni
**Malone, Joan**
Marijuana Makes a Comeback. *Mademoiselle* (October 1990):184-187

**Malone, Maggie**
Ladies in Waiting. *Savvy* (December-January 1991):14

**Malone, Michelle** (about). *See also* Music – Rock
**Malovich, Natalie J.** and Stake, Jayne E.
Sexual Harassment on Campus: Individual Differences in Attitudes and Beliefs. *Psychology of Women Quarterly* 14, No. 1 (March 1990):63-81

**Maloy, Kate**
Pep Talk! *Redbook* 175, No. 3 (July 1990):102-103 +

**Malpede, Karen**

To Hell and Back. *The Women's Review of Books* 8, No. 1 (October 1990):7-8

The Loony-Bin Trip. Book Review. *The Women's Review of Books* 8, No. 1 (October 1990):7-8

**Malson, Micheline R.** and others (editors)

Feminist Theory in Practice and Process. Reviewed by Joan M. Fayer. *Women & Language* 13, No. 2 (Winter 1990):42

**Malveaux, Julianne**

Back Talk: Eat Those Dirty Words! *Essence* 20, No. 11 (March 1990):146

Maxine Waters: Woman of the House. *Essence* 21, No. 7 (November 1990):55-56+

Money: Premarital "Insurance." *Essence* 20, No. 10 (February 1990):32+

Money: Quick—How Much are You Worth? *Essence* 21, No. 6 (October 1990):38-41

Oakland: Back to the Future. *Essence* 21, No. 1 (May 1990):157-159

**Mama, Amina**

A Hidden Struggle: Black Women and Violence. *Connexions* 34 (1990):12-14

A Hidden Struggle: Black Women and Violence. *Spare Rib* No. 209 (February 1990):8-11

**Mama, Robin Sakina** (joint author). *See* Nuccio, Kathleen E.

**Mammography**

Breast Cancer: New Hope in the '90s. Maxine Abrams. *Good Housekeeping* 211, No. 4 (October 1990):77-80

Facing Fears about Mammograms. Ronni Sandroff. *McCall's* 117, No. 12 (September 1990):25-29

Health Dept. Dava Sobel. *Lear's* (January 1990):44

Health Dept. Leigh Silverman. *Lear's* (September 1990):74

Healthy Breasts: What's Normal, What's Not. Peggy Eastman. *Family Circle* 103, No. 9 (June 26, 1990):101-104

Mammography Screening: Is It Safe? *Ms.* 1, No. 2 (September/October 1990):31

Medical Report: The Mammogram Problem. Laura Fraser. *Glamour* (December 1990):66-72

Prevention: Breast Intentions. Annette M. Brown. *Essence* 20, No. 9 (January 1990):21-22

What Doctors Aren't Saying. *Glamour* (May 1990):94

**Mamonova, Tatyana**

Russian Women's Studies: Essays on Sexism in Soviet Culture. Reviewed by Elizabeth Waters. *Australian Feminist Studies* No. 11 (Autumn 1990):117-120

Russian Women's Studies: Essays on Sexism in Soviet Culture. Reviewed by Katherine E. Loda. *Women's Studies International Forum* 13, No. 3 (1990):273

Russian Women's Studies: Essays on Sexism in Soviet Culture. Reviewed by Norma Noonan. *Women & Politics* 10, No. 4 (1990):133-134

**Man, Prehistoric.** *See* History, Ancient—Feminist Perspectives

**Management Techniques.** *See also* Business—Social Policies; Career Management; Employees, Dismissal of; Entrepreneurs; Leadership Skills; Office Management; Performance Appraisal

The Best New Managers will Listen, Motivate, Support. Isn't that Just Like a Woman? Tom Peters. *Working Woman* (September 1990):142-143+

Bright Ideas: Anatomy of a Corporate Revolution. Lorraine Dusky. *Working Woman* (July 1990):58-63

Career Advice: Dear Betty Harragan. Betty Lehan Harragan. *Working Woman* (January 1990):32-35; (February 1990):38-43; (March 1990):34-36

Career Workshop: How to Work Faster, Smarter. *Working Woman* (April 1990):77

Competitive Edge. *Executive Female* (March/April 1990):14-15

Delegating: How to Let Go and Keep Control. Tess Kirby. *Working Woman* (February 1990):32-37

Executive Agenda. *Working Woman* (September 1990):130-131; (October 1990):95-96

Good for Business: A Manager's Hot Line. *Working Woman* (September 1990):62-66; (October 1990):33-36

Greed Is Good . . . and Other Management Lessons from Drexel. Margaret Laws. *Working Woman* (August 1990):70-72

Hands-Off Management. Tess Kirby. *Executive Female* (March/April 1990):44-45+

"How I Did It": Creating the Perfect Staff. Elizabeth Perle. *Working Woman* (November 1990):73-76+

How Should You Criticize Your Boss? Carefully. Hendrie Weisinger. *Working Woman* (February 1990):90-91+

How to Be the Leader They'll Follow. Warren Bennis. *Working Woman* (March 1990):75-78

How to Be the New Kind of Manager. Peter Block. *Working Woman* (July 1990):51-54

"Just Do It": The New Job Strategy. Nancy K. Austin. *Working Woman* (April 1990):78-80+

Killing Them Softly. Ron Gales. *Working Woman* (November 1990):112-115+

The Makeover of a Manager. Meryl Gordon. *Working Woman* (October 1990):108-111+

Management: Sizing Up Your New Staff. Connie Wallace. *Working Woman* (May 1990):29-32

Management: The Death of Hierarchy. Nancy K. Austin. *Working Woman* (July 1990):22-25

Management: The Smarter Way to Make Decisions. Pam Miller Withers. *Working Woman* (March 1990):31-32

Management: What Is Your Staff Afraid to Tell You? Elyse T. Tanouye. *Working Woman* (April 1990):35-38

Management: What's the Right Thing? Everyday Ethical Dilemmas. Andrew S. Grove. *Working Woman* (June 1990):16-20

Managers' Shoptalk. *Working Woman* (January 1990):14-20; (February 1990):24-26; (March 1990):24-28; (April 1990):22-28; (May 1990):23-26; (June 1990):10-14; (July 1990):13-21; (August 1990):18-22

Managing: Big Changes? How to Stay in Charge. Andrew S. Grove. *Working Woman* (October 1990):38-44

Managing: How to Get Your Staff Psyched. Nancy K. Austin. *Working Woman* (September 1990):68-73

Managing: Race Against Time – and Win. Nancy K. Austin. *Working Woman* (November 1990):48-54

The New Breed of Leaders: Taking Charge in a Different Way. Michele Morris. *Working Woman* (March 1990):73-75

The New Corporate Survival Guide: Can You Thrive in Your Company? Thomas L. Quick. *Working Woman* (July 1990):45-48

"Who Put *Me* in Charge Anyway?" Confessions of a Rookie Boss. Meryl Gordon. *Mademoiselle* (February 1990):178-179+

Why Employees Act the Way They Do: A Manager's Guide to Human Behavior. Eliza Collins. *Working Woman* (December 1990):58-61

**Management Techniques – Gender Differences**

Power Talk. Lee A. Lusardi. *Working Woman* (July 1990):92-94

**Management Techniques – Humor**

This Working Life: Feminine Wiles Are Back in Business. Maureen Dowd. *Working Woman* (March 1990):158

**Management Theory.** *See* Organizational Theory; Power Structure

**Mancini, Jay A.** (editor)

Aging Parents and Adult Children. Reviewed by Beth B. Hess. *Journal of Marriage and the Family* 52, No. 2 (May 1990):566

**Mancini, Jay A.** (joint author). *See* Lee, Thomas R.

**Mancoff, Debra N.**

Images of Victorian Womanhood in English Art. Book Review. *Woman's Art Journal* 11, No. 1 (Spring-Summer 1990):42-45

**Mandel, Barrett J.** (joint author). *See* Yellen, Judith

**Mandela, Nelson** (about)

Mandela the Man. *Ms.* 1, No. 1 (July/August 1990):15

In the Spirit: Take Courage! Susan L. Taylor. *Essence* 21, No. 8 (December 1990):41

In the Spirit: The Power of Commitment. Susan L. Taylor. *Essence* 21, No. 2 (June 1990):47

Walking into Freedom. Alexis De Veaux. *Essence* 21, No. 2 (June 1990):48-53+

Winnie and Nelson Mandela: Rising Above the Hype. Elean Thomas. *Spare Rib* No. 212 (May 1990):36-39

**Mandela, Winnie**

When a Woman Is A Rock. *Spare Rib* No. 210 (March 1990):6-10

**Mandela, Winnie** (about). *See also under* De Veaux, Alexis, Milloy, Marilyn, and Ross, Michael Erik; Leadership, "1990 Essence Awards"

The Persecution of Nomzamo Winnie Mandela. *Spare Rib* 217 (October 1990):49-50

Winnie and Nelson Mandela: Rising Above the Hype. Elean Thomas. *Spare Rib* No. 212 (May 1990):36-39

**Mandell, Nancy**

Best Friends and Marriage: Exchange Among Women. Book Review. *Journal of Marriage and the Family* 52, No. 3 (August 1990):802-803

**Mandell, Nancy** (joint author). *See* Duffy, Ann

**Mandla, Nolthando**

No Reforming Apartheid. *Spare Rib* 219 (December 1990-January 1991):20-23

**Manet, Julie** (about)

Growing Up with the Impressionists: The Diary of Julie Manet. Edited by Rosalind de Boland Roberts and Jane Roberts. Reviewed by Marni Reva Kessler. *Woman's Art Journal* 11, No. 1 (Spring-Summer 1990):41-42

**Mangan, Doreen**

Avoid a Cash Crunch. *Executive Female* 13, No. 5 (September-October 1990):70-71

Building a Bank Alliance. *Executive Female* 13, No. 4 (July-August 1990):74

Business Pitches that Score. *Executive Female* (March/April 1990):72-73

Check It Out. *Executive Female* 13, No. 4 (July-August 1990):72-73

Credit Card Capital. *Executive Female* (March/April 1990):74

Incubators Help Hatch Businesses. *Executive Female* (May/June 1990):68-69

Is It Time to Clone Your Company? *Executive Female* 13, No. 5 (September-October 1990):68-69

More Money: How One Small Supplier Grappled with the Campeau Giant. *Executive Female* (March/April 1990):18-19

People Leasing. *Executive Female* 13, No. 6 (November-December 1990):72-73

Seed Capital. *Executive Female* (May/June 1990):70

What Is Your Company Worth? *Executive Female* 13, No. 6 (November-December 1990):74

**Mangan, J. A.** and Park, Roberta J. (editors)

From "Fair Sex" to Feminism: Sport and the Socialization of Women in the Industrial and Post-Industrial Eras. Reviewed by Susan L. Greendorfer. *Gender and Society* 4, No. 1 (March 1990):108-110

**Mani, Lata**

On the Boundaries of Struggle. *The Women's Review of Books* 7, No. 9 (June 1990):13-14

Multiple Mediations: Feminist Scholarship in the Age of Multinational Receptiion. *Feminist Review* No. 35 (Summer 1990):24-41

Multiple Mediations: Feminist Scholarship in the Age of Multinational Reception. *Women & Language* 13, No. 1 (Fall 1990):56-58

"We Were Making History": Women and the Telangana Uprising. Book Review. *The Women's Review of Books* 7, No. 9 (June 1990):13-14

**Manicuring.** See Hand–Care and Hygiene; Nails (Anatomy)–Care and Hygiene

**Mankiller, Wilma** (about)

Justificatory Rhetoric for a Female Political Candidate: A Case Study of Wilma Mankiller. Janis L. King. *Women's Studies in Communication* 13, No. 2 (Fall 1990):21-38

**Manners.** See also Charm; Etiquette; Gossip; Verbal Abuse

Money & Friends: If She's Broke, Don't Fix It. Ellen Welty. *Mademoiselle* (January 1990):60

A Tasty Guide to Business Dining. Karen Heller. *Working Woman* (September 1990):148-149+

We Need a Manners Makeover. Amy Willard Cross. *Glamour* (April 1990):146

**Manners–Humor**

How to Be Rude Without Really Trying. Peter Feibleman. *Lear's* (May 1990):49-51

**Manning, Kenneth**

Roger Arliner Young. *Sage* 6, No. 2 (Fall 1989):3-7

**Manos, Nikki Lee**

Fallen Women's Studies. *Belles Lettres* 5, No. 3 (Spring 1990):27

Girls Who Went Wrong: Prostitutes in American Fiction. Book Review. *Belles Lettres* 5, No. 3 (Spring 1990):27

**Mansell, Alice**

Towards a Feminist Visual Practice. *Canadian Women's Studies* 11, No. 1 (Spring 1990):29-30

**Mansell, Chris**

Mother Us. Poem. *Hecate* 16, Nos. 1-2 (1990):116

**Mansfield, Phyllis Kernoff** (joint author). See Yu, Lucy C.

**Mansfield, Stephanie**

Fashion Statement. *Lear's* (February 1990):52-53

The Kings of Color: Ozbek. *Vogue* (September 1990):536-541

Solid Sister. *Vogue* (September 1990):574-579+

Sophia Coppola. *Vogue* (April 1990):126-130

View. *Vogue* (June 1990):70-72, 82

**Mansnerus, Laura**

Susan Cowell Champions the Union Label. *McCall's* 117, No. 8 (May 1990):51

**Mansour, Lina**

The Dance of Amel Denhaooine Miller. *Spare Rib* 213 (June 1990):30-31

Opening the Gates: A Century of Arab Feminist Writing. Book Review. *Spare Rib* No. 214 (July 1990):36-41

**Manthorne, Jackie**

Fourteen Women Killed in Montreal. *off our backs* 20, No. 1 (January 1990):1+

Home Away from Home. *Canadian Women's Studies* 11, No. 2 (Fall 1990):48-50

**Manzi, Alice**

A Sculptural Odyssey. *Woman of Power* 15 (Fall-Winter 1990):47-49

**Maori–Political Activism**

The Maori Struggle Continues–Ke Whawhai tonu matou. Ake! Ake! Ake! Matiria Pura and Robyn Short. *Spare Rib* No. 211 (April 1990):20-21

**Mapes, Dennis** (joint author). See Ganong, Lawrence H.

**MAPI.** See Million Adolescent Personality Inventory (MAPI)

**Mappin, Margaret**

Shapes of a World Not Realized: Virginia Woolf and the Possibility of a Female Voice. *Australian Feminist Studies* No. 11 (Autumn 1990):75-86

**Mapplethorpe, Robert** (about)

Picturing the Homoerotic: Gay Images in Photography. Allen Ellenzweig. *Out/Look* No. 7 (Winter 1990):44-51

Of Torture and Tangents: Consequences of the Robert Mapplethorpe Exhibition. Stuart Edelson. *Out/Look* No. 7 (Winter 1990):52-53

**Marable, Manning**

Back Talk: Where Are Our Future Leaders? *Essence* 21, No. 7 (November 1990):130

**Maracle, Lee**

Nobody Home. *Trivia* 16/17 (Fall 1990):108-118

**Marah, Jasmine**

Study. *Sinister Wisdom* 42 (Winter 1990-1991):40-41

**Marah, Jasmine** (joint author). *See* Dykewomon, Elana

**Maraini, Dacia** (about)

Feminist Theory as Practice: Italian Feminism and the Work of Teresa de Lauretis and Dacia Maraini. Itala T. C. Rutter. *Women's Studies International Forum* 13, No. 6 (1990):565-575

**Maran, Meredith**

Ten for Bravery, Zero for Common Sense. *Out/Look* No. 7 (Winter 1990):68-72

**Marcelino, Elizabeth Protacio**

Towards Understanding the Psychology of the Filipino. *Women and Therapy* 9, Nos. 1-2 (1990):105-128

**March, Olivia** (about)

Financial Workshop: Making Your Dream Business a Reality. Mary Rowland. *Working Woman* (January 1990):95-100

**Marcow, Vivien** (joint author). *See* McKim, Elizabeth

**Marcus, Hilary**

A Precious Moment in Chile. *Lilith* 15, No. 4 (Fall 1990):36

**Marcus, Robert F.** (joint author). *See* Masselam, Venus S.

**Marcus, Sharon** (joint author). *See* Christian, Barbara

**Marfan Syndrome.** *See* Policoff, Stephen Phillip, "Diseases Your Doctor May Miss"

**Marginality**

Towards a Politics of Location: Rethinking Marginality. Joan Borsa. *Canadian Women's Studies* 11, No. 1 (Spring 1990):36-39

**Marglin, Frédérique Apffel**

Wives of the God-King: The Rituals of the Davada6si6s of Puri. Reviewed by Albertine Gaur. *Gender & History* 2, No. 2 (Summer 1990):223-225

**Margolies, Janet**

Give Your Best. Bibliography. *Ladies' Home Journal* 107, No. 12 (December 1990):108-121

**Margolies, Liz**

Cracks in the Frame: Feminism and the Boundaries of Therapy. *Women and Therapy* 9, No. 4 (1990):19-35

**Margolis, Anne**

Feminism and the Power of Law. Book Review. *The Women's Review of Books* 7, No. 12 (September 1990):17-18

Moral Vision and Professional Decisions: The Changing Values of Women and Men Lawyers. Book Review. *The Women's Review of Books* 7, No. 12 (September 1990):17-18

The Weighted Scales of Justice. *The Women's Review of Books* 7, No. 12 (September 1990):17-18

**Margulies, Stephen**

Crossing the Border: Poetry in Charlottesville. *Iris* 23 (Spring-Summer 1990):14-16

**Mar'i, Mariam M.** (joint author). *See* Seginer, Rachel

**Maria, C.**

Separatism Is Not a Luxury: Some Thoughts on Separatism and Class. C. Maria. *Lesbian Ethics* 4, No. 1 (Spring 1990): 66-76

**Marijuana**

Marijuana Makes a Comeback. Joan Malone. *Mademoiselle* (October 1990):184-187

**Marin, Alexandra Ayala**

Campaign to Confront Violence. *Connexions* 34 (1990):15

**Marketing**

Entrepreneurial Edge: How to Stand Out in a Crowd. David E. Gumpert. *Working Woman* (November 1990):57-63+

**Marketing and Sales Occupations.** *See also* Selling

Charismatic Capitalism: Direct Selling Organizations in America. By Nicole Woolsey Biggart. Reviewed by Diane Barthel. *Gender and Society* 4, No. 2 (June 1990):266-267

**Market Research.** *See also* Consumer Behavior; Management Techniques

Enterprise: How to Find a Market and Make It Yours. Susan Buchsbaum. *Working Woman* (May 1990):39-44

"How I Did It": When Your Image Is Frozen in Time. Carol Kirby. *Working Woman* (October 1990):53-56

**Markievicz, Constance** (about)

Constance Markievicz: An Independent Life. By Anne Haverty. Reviewed by Margaret MacCurtain. *Gender & History* 2, No. 3 (Autumn 1990):365-368

**Markowitz, Abby** (joint author). *See* Brodsky, Michelle

**Marks, Cynthia**

Health: Birth Control. *Mademoiselle* (September 1990):188-198

**Marks, Elaine**

The Authority of Experience: Essays in Feminist Criticism. Book Review. *Tulsa Studies in Women's Literature* 9, No. 2 (Fall 1990):309-314

Inessential Woman: Problems of Exclusion in Feminist Thought. Book Review. *Tulsa Studies in Women's Literature* 9, No. 2 (Fall 1990):309-314

Women Analyze Women in France, England, and the United States. Book Review. *NWSA Journal* 2, No. 1 (Winter 1990):131-134

**Marks, Elaine** (joint author). *See* Christian, Barbara

**Marks, Jane**

Nobody's Child. *Family Circle* 103, No. 15 (November 6, 1990):90-94

**Marks, Laurie J.**

The Moonbane Magic. Reviewed by Ann E. Kottner. *The Women's Review of Books* 7, Nos. 10-11 (July 1990):40-41

**Marks, Shula**

Not Either an Experimental Doll. Reviewed by Gwendolyn Mikell. *Belles Lettres* 5, No. 3 (Spring 1990):13-14

**Marks, Shula** (editor)

Not Either an Experimental Doll: The Separate Worlds of Three South African Women. Reviewed by Elaine Salo. *Women's Studies International Forum* 13, No. 3 (1990):274-275

Not Either an Experimental Doll: The Separate Worlds of Three South African Women. Reviewed by Sheila Tlou. *Women's Studies International Forum* 13, No. 4 (1990):408

**Marks, Tracy**

Rediscovering the Muse. *Woman of Power* 15 (Fall-Winter 1990):55-57

**Markstrom-Adams, Carol**

Coming-of-Age among Contemporary American Indians as Portrayed in Adolescent Fiction. *Adolescence* 25, No. 97 (Spring 1990):225-237

**Marlene**

Music as Activism. *Hot Wire* 6, No. 2 (May 1990):53

**Marler, Joan**

Archaeomythology: An Interview with Marija Gimbutas. *Woman of Power* 15 (Fall-Winter 1990):6-13

**Marquez, Teresa** (joint editor). *See* Rebolledo, Tey Diana

**Marriage**. *See also* Communication; Domestic Relations; Japan – Gender Roles

Changing Patterns of Marriage. Larry Bumpass, James Sweet, and Teresa Castro Martin. *Journal of Marriage and the Family* 52, No. 3 (August 1990):747-756

Faithful Attraction. Andrew Greeley. *Good Housekeeping* 210, No. 6 (June 1990):132-137

The Four Phases of Marriage. Harville Hendrix. *Family Circle* 103, No. 3 (February 20, 1990):57-58+

Holy Matrimony! Jeannie Ralston. *Mademoiselle* (March 1990):176-178, 240

How Criticism Chips Away at a Marriage. Catherine Findlay. *Working Mother* (November 1990):26-30

La fin du mariage? jeunes couples des annees' 80. By Françoise Battagliola. Reviewed by Denise Veillette. *Resources for Feminist Research* 19, No. 1 (March 1990):15-16

Marital Noncohabitation: Separation Does Not Make the Heart Grow Fonder. Ronald R. Rindfuss and Elizabeth Hervey Stephen. *Journal of Marriage and the Family* 52, No. 1 (February 1990):259-269

Marriage and Family Therapy. A Decade Review. Fred P. Piercy and Douglas H. Sprenkle. *Journal of Marriage and the Family* 52, No. 4 (November 1990):1116-1126

Mate Selection Patterns of Men and Women in Personal Advertisements: New Bottle, Old Wine. Aysan Sev'er. *Atlantis* 15, No. 2 (Spring 1990):70-76

Men and the "M" Word. John Colapinto. *Mademoiselle* 142-145; (December 1990):

Private Lives. Barbara Mathias. *Family Circle* 103, No. 7 (May 15, 1990):53-55

Seams from a Marriage. Molly Haskell. *Lear's* (April 1990):58-66

Understanding Your Marriage. Harville Hendrix. *Family Circle* 103, No. 6 (April 24, 1990):101+; 103, No. 10 (July 24, 1990):130+

What a Baby Does to a Marriage. Carla Cantor. *Working Mother* 13, No. 7 (July 1990):25-31

**Marriage – Africa**

African Feminism(s) and the Question of Marital and Non-Marital Loneliness and Intimacy. E. Imafedia Okhamafe. *Sage* 6, No. 1 (Summer 1989):33-39

**Marriage, Arranged**

Love Matches and Arranged Marriages: A Chinese Replication. Xu Xiaohe and Martin King Whyte. *Journal of Marriage and the Family* 52, No. 3 (August 1990):709-722

## Marriage – Communication

The Cross-cultural Consistency of Marital Communication Associated with Marital Distress. W. Kim Halford, Kurt Hahlweg, and Michael Dunne. *Journal of Marriage and the Family* 52, No. 2 (May 1990):487-500

Marital Communication in the Eighties. Patricia Noller and Mary Ann Fitzpatrick. *Journal of Marriage and the Family* 52, No. 4 (November 1990):832-843

## Marriage – Counseling. See also Extramarital Affairs; Time Management

Affairs of the Heart. Kathleen McCoy. *Redbook* 175, No. 1 (May 1990):128-129+

An Affair to Remember. Chandra Patterson. *Essence* 21, No. 3 (July 1990):59-60+

"Anything They Can Do, We Can Do Better": Couples in Competition. Sam Johnson. *Mademoiselle* (June 1990):186-187+

Bed and Bored? Helen Singer Kaplan. *Redbook* 175, No. 3 (July 1990):100-101+

Can This Marriage Be Saved? "After Sixteen Years of Marriage, I'm Still a Virgin." Corinne Clements. *Ladies' Home Journal* 107, No. 9 (September 1990):18-22

Can This Marriage Be Saved? "He's Always Out with the Guys." Margery D. Rosen. *Ladies' Home Journal* 107, No. 6 (June 1990):12-18

Can This Marriage Be Saved? "He's There for Everyone Except Me." Margery D. Rosen. *Ladies' Home Journal* 107, No. 3 (March 1990):10-21

Can This Marriage Be Saved? "I Can Never Make Him Happy." Margery D. Rosen. *Ladies' Home Journal* 107, No. 12 (December 1990):14-21+

Can This Marriage Be Saved? "I Just Don't Respect Him Anymore." Ellen Switzer. *Ladies' Home Journal* 107, No. 10 (October 1990):14-20

Can This Marriage Be Saved? "My Husband Doesn't Want to Make Love." Margery D. Rosen. *Ladies' Home Journal* 107, No. 1 (January 1990):10-14

Can This Marriage Be Saved? "My Husband Is Having an Affair." Margery D. Rosen. *Ladies' Home Journal* 107, No. 4 (April 1990):20-24+

Can This Marriage Be Saved? "My Husband Is Never There for Us." Sondra Forsyth Enos. *Ladies' Home Journal* 107, No. 8 (August 1990):12-17

Can This Marriage Be Saved? "My Husband Keeps Calling Those Sex Hotlines." Margery D. Rosen. *Ladies' Home Journal* 107, No. 7 (July 1990):14-20

Can This Marriage Be Saved? "There's Something Missing from Our Marriage." Margery D. Rosen. *Ladies' Home Journal* 107, No. 5 (May 1990):12-16

Can This Marriage Be Saved? "We Can't Stop Fighting." Margery D. Rosen. *Ladies' Home Journal* 107, No. 2 (February 1990):14-20

Can This Marriage Be Saved? "We're in Love Again." Margery D. Rosen. *Ladies' Home Journal* 107, No. 11 (November 1990):28-34

Can We Work It Out? Evette Porter. *Essence* 20, No. 10 (February 1990):56-58+

Could You Be a Better Friend to Your Husband? Catherine Johnson. *Redbook* 175, No. 5 (September 1990):166-167+

Cycles of Desire. Dorothy Glasser Weiss. *Glamour* (May 1990):278-279+

Don't Be His Mother. Excerpt. Barbara De Angelis. *Redbook* 174, No. 5 (March 1990):130-131+

Don't Settle – Sizzle! Dorothy Glasser Weiss. *Redbook* 175, No. 1 (May 1990):120-121+

His: Fighting Fair. David McDonough. *Glamour* (December 1990):232

How to Make the Significant Choices. Laura Green. *Lear's* (June 1990):58-59

How to Stay Sweethearts. Donna Jackson. *Redbook* 176, No. 1 (November 1990):94-95+

If You Want Love to Last, Choose Smart. Excerpt. Maurice Yaffé and Elizabeth Fenwick. *Essence* 21, No. 5 (September 1990):85

Ingredients of a Happy Marriage. Alexandra Stoddard. *McCall's* 117, No. 9 (June 1990):140

Keep Love Alive: How to Stop Playing the Blame Game. Gail Kessler. *Redbook* 175, No. 4 (August 1990):98-99

Loveplay: The Touching Way to Passion. Lesley Dormen. *Redbook* 175, No. 2 (June 1990):104-105+

Love Therapy. *Harper's Bazaar* (December 1990):140-143

Mind Health. John Tierney. *Vogue* (July 1990):114-119

My Problem: My Sister-in-Law Was Ruining My Marriage. *Good Housekeeping* 211, No. 3 (September 1990):84-87

Pep Talk! Kate Maloy. *Redbook* 175, No. 3 (July 1990):102-103+

Personal Journal: Important Insights into the Way We Feel. *Ladies' Home Journal* 107, No. 4 (April 1990):120-124

Private Lives: Are You Too Tired for Sex? Barbara De Angelis. *Family Circle* 103, No. 14 (October 16, 1990):32-37

Relationships: "Help! I Married a Big Baby!" Elena Latici. *Redbook* 176, No. 2 (December 1990):44-46

Reunited. Elaine C. Ray. *Essence* 20, No. 10 (February 1990):69-72

The Secret Strength of Happy Marriages. Annie Gottlieb. *McCall's* 118, No. 3 (December 1990):94-96+

Sex & Health. Shirley Zussman. *Glamour* (December 1990):246

The Shameful Shock Waves of Rage. John Bradshaw. *Lear's* (June 1990):63

Stay Close! Anne Mayer. *Redbook* 175, No. 3 (July 1990):94-95+

The Way We Are. Lois Wyse. *Good Housekeeping* 211, No. 4 (October 1990):264

What Makes a Couple Happy? Ayala M. Pines. *Redbook* 174, No. 6 (April 1990):102-103+

Why Women Cheat. Carol Botwin. *Ladies' Home Journal* 107, No. 10 (October 1990):98-102

**Marriage – Dowry.** *See* India – Violence Against Women

**Marriage – Gender Roles**

Equal Partners: Successful Women in Marriage. By Dana Vannoy-Hiller and William W. Philliber. Reviewed by Lesley J. Watson. *Women and Environments* 12, No. 2 (Spring 1990): 29-30

Love Among the Ruins. Margaret Carlson. *Savvy Woman* (November 1990):60-63+

Strong Mothers, Weak Wives. The Search for Gender Equality. By Miriam M. Johnson. Reviewed by Arline Prigoff. *AFFILIA* 5, No. 2 (Summer 1990):113-114

Tactics That Get Him to Help Out. Sherry Amatenstein. *Family Circle* 103, No. 5 (April 3, 1990):89-91

**Marriage – History**

Age at Marriage in Nineteenth-Century Italy. Rosella Rettaroli. *Journal of Family History* 15, No. 4 (October 1990):409-425

Land, Kinship, and Consanguineous Marriage in Italy from the Seventeenth to the Nineteenth Centuries. Raul Merzario. *Journal of Family History* 15, No. 4 (October 1990):529-546

Lewis Henry Morgan and the Prohibition of Cousin Marriage in the United States. Martin Ottenheimer. *Journal of Family History* 15, No. 3 (July 1990):325-334

The Market for Marriage in Colonial Queensland. Katie Spearritt. *Hecate* 16, Nos. 1-2 (1990):23-42

Marriage in Pre-Industrial Warsaw in the Light of Demographic Studies. Cezary Kuklo. *Journal of Family History* 15, No. 3 (July 1990):239-259

Putting Asunder: A History of Divorce in Western Society. By Roderick Phillips. Reviewed by A. James Hammerton. *Gender & History* 2, No. 2 (Summer 1990):241-244

Western Fertility in Mid-Transition: Fertility and Nuptiality in the United States and Selected Nations

at the Turn of the Century. Michael R. Haines. *Journal of Family History* 15, No. 1 (January 1990):23-48

Women and Marriage in Nineteenth-Century England. By Joan Perkin. Reviewed by Gerry Holloway. *Women's Studies International Forum* 13, No. 5 (1990):524

Women and Marriage in Nineteenth Century England. Reviewed by A. James Hammerton. *Gender & History* 2, No. 2 (Summer 1990):241-244

**Marriage – Humor**

Marriage & Humor – a Perfect Union. Judith Viorst. *Redbook* 175, No. 5 (September 1990):72-74

**Marriage, Interracial**

Mixed Blood: Intermarriage and Ethnic Identity in Twentieth Century America. By Paul R. Spickard. Reviewed by Ronald C. Johnson. *Journal of Marriage and the Family* 52, No. 3 (August 1990):803

New Trends in Black American Interracial Marriage: The Social Structural Context. M. Belinda Tucker and Claudia Mitchell-Kernan. *Journal of Marriage and the Family* 52, No. 1 (February 1990):209-218

**Marriage – Personal Narratives**

Diary of a Marriage: Rediscovering the Real Ben. Sylvia Whitman. *McCall's* 117, No. 10 (July 1990):98-100+

**Marriage – Prenuptial Contracts**

Money: Premarital "Insurance." Julianne Malveaux. *Essence* 20, No. 10 (February 1990):32+

The Special Marriage Act: Not Special Enough. Ruth Vanita. *Manushi* 58 (May-June 1990):14-21

**Marriage – Rape.** *See* Rape – Law and Legislation

**Marriage – Satisfaction.** *See also* Marriage – Counseling

Affect Expression, Marital Satisfaction, and Stress Reactivity among Premenopausal Women during a Conflictual Marital Discussion. Marie A. Morell and Robin F. Apple. *Psychology of Women Quarterly* 14, No. 3 (September 1990):387-402

Are You a Right-or Left-Brained Lover? Priscilla Donovan. *Redbook* 175, No. 3 (July 1990):84-87

Coping Efforts and Marital Satisfaction: Measuring Marital Coping and Its Correlates. Marilyn L. Bowman. *Journal of Marriage and the Family* 52, No. 2 (May 1990):463-474

Couple Time. *Glamour* (March 1990):132

The Effect of Shift Work on the Quality and Stability of Marital Relations. Lynn K. White and Bruce Keith. *Journal of Marriage and the Family* 52, No. 2 (May 1990):453-462

His: Love and Thunderbolts. David Meyer. *Glamour* (August 1990):240

The Katharine Hepburn School of Love. Hugh O'Neill. *McCall's* 118, No. 1 (October 1990):52-58

Linking Economic Hardship to Marital Quality and Instability. Rand D. Conger, Glen H. Elder, Jr., Frederick O. Lorenz, Katherine J. Conger, Ronald L. Simons, and others. *Journal of Marriage and the Family* 52, No. 3 (August 1990):643-656

Marital Adjustment During the Transition to Parenthood: Stability and Predictors of Change. Pamela M. Wallace and Ian H. Gotlib. *Journal of Marriage and the Family* 52, No. 1 (February 1990):21-29

Marital and Family Enrichment Research: A Decade Review and Look Ahead. Bernard Guerney, Jr. and Pamela Maxson. *Journal of Marriage and the Family* 52, No. 4 (November 1990):1127-1135

Marital Disruption and the Employment of Married Women. Theodore Greenstein. *Journal of Marriage and the Family* 52, No. 3 (August 1990):657-676

Marriage as Partnership. *Glamour* (July 1990):70

Patterns of Marital Change across the Transition to Parenthood: Pregnancy to Three Years Postpartum. Jay Belsky and Michael Rovine. *Journal of Marriage and the Family* 52, No. 1 (February 1990):5-19

Personal Journal: Married with Children . . . and Still in Love. Anne Mayer. *Ladies' Home Journal* 107, No. 6 (June 1990):110

Quantitative Research on Marital Quality in the 1980s: A Critical Review. Norval D. Glenn. *Journal of Marriage and the Family* 52, No. 4 (November 1990):818-831

Religious Heterogamy, Religiosity, and Marital Happiness: The Case of Catholics. Constance L. Shehan, E. Wilbur Bock, and Gary R. Lee. *Journal of Marriage and the Family* 52, No. 1 (February 1990):73-79

Withdrawal, Hostility, and Displeasure in Satisfied and Dissatisfied Marriages. Linda J. Roberts and Lowell J. Krokoff. *Journal of Marriage and the Family* 52, No. 1 (February 1990):95-105

**Marriage – Virginity Tests**

The Virginity Test: A Bridal Nightmare. Sriani Basnayake. *Journal of Family Welfare* 36, No. 2 (June 1990):50-59

**Marriage Age**

Age at Marriage in Nineteenth-Century Italy. Rosella Rettaroli. *Journal of Family History* 15, No. 4 (October 1990):409-425

Inter-District and Inter-Regional Variations in Incidence of Child Marriage Among Females and Its Inter-Censal Changes in Uttar Pradesh. J. N. Srivastava. *Journal of Family Welfare* 36, No. 4 (December 1990):20-31

Socio-Economic Characteristics Influencing Age at Marriage in a Tamil Nadu Village. N. Audiarayana and M. Senthilnayaki. *Journal of Family Welfare* 36, No. 1 (March 1990):48-55

**Marriage and Religion**

Marriage and Remarriage Among Bombay Roman Catholics. S. Irudaya Rajan. *Journal of Family Welfare* 36, No. 1 (March 1990):61-79

**Marriage Ceremonies.** *See* Wedding Ceremonies

**Marriage Customs.** *See also* Mormon Church – Marriage Customs; Traditions; Wedding Ceremonies

Honor Thy Marriage (and Anniversary). Judith Viorst. *Redbook* 175, No. 2 (June 1990):48-51

**Marriage Proposals**

Jake: A Man's Opinion. *Glamour* (December 1990):132

**Marriott, Michel**

Father Hunger. *Essence* 21, No. 7 (November 1990):73-74+

**Marrs, Caroline**

Group Profiles. *Women in Action* 1-2 (1990):26-30

**Marsa, Linda**

Women Who Make a Difference. *Family Circle* 103, No. 15 (November 6, 1990):15-17

**Marsa, Linda** (joint author). *See* Buoniconti, Nick

**Marshall, Consuelo B.** (about)

Judge Consuelo B. Marshall Holding Court. Arthur Hayes. *Essence* 21, No. 3 (July 1990):37

**Marshall, Denise M.**

The Line of the Sun. Book Review. *Belles Lettres* 5, No. 2 (Winter 1990):16

Messengers to the New World. *Belles Lettres* 5, No. 2 (Winter 1990):16

Tyrannies, Servilities, and Psychic Space. *Belles Lettres* 6, No. 1 (Fall 1990):43-44

Virginia Woolf: The Impact of Childhood Sexual Abuse on Her Life and Work. Book Review. *Belles Lettres* 6, No. 1 (Fall 1990):43-44

**Marshall, Esmé** (about)

Esmé: Behind the Smile. Lynn Snowden. *Mademoiselle* (June 1990):196-197+

**Marshall, Garry**

Pretty Woman. Reviewed by Sue Murphy. *Spare Rib* No. 212 (May 1990):28

**Marshall, Linda Elovitz**

Treating Herself with Kindness. *Lear's* (August 1990):40-42

**Marshall, Ray**

Solving the Problem at the Source. *Working Woman* (January 1990):76-72

**Marshment, Margaret** (joint editor). *See* Gamman, Lorraine

**Martin, Ann M.** (about)

Baby-Sitting Nights, Preteen Days. Kathleen Brady. *McCall's* 118, No. 2 (November 1990):57-58

**Martin, Charles L.**

Resources. *Executive Female* (May/June 1990):48

**Martin, Clarice J.**, Dewey, Joanna, Hutaff, Peggy, and Schaberg, Jane

Womanist Interpretation of the New Testament: The Quest for Holistic and Inclusive Translation and Interpretation. *Journal of Feminist Studies in Religion* 6, No. 2 (Fall 1990):41-85

**Martin, Emily**

The Woman in the Body: A Cultural Analysis of Reproduction. Reviewed by Roe Sybylla. *Australian Feminist Studies* No. 11 (Autumn 1990):129-131

**Martin, Judith**

Miss Manners' Guide to Excruciatingly Correct Behavior. *Woman of Power* 17 (Summer 1990):53-55

**Martin, Lynn** (about). *See also* Leadership

**Martin, Molly** (editor)

Hard-Hatted Women. Reviewed by June Axinn. *AFFILIA* 5, No. 2 (Summer 1990):111-112

Hard-Hatted Women: Stories of Struggle and Success in the Trades. Reviewed by Autumn Stanley. *NWSA Journal* 2, No. 4 (Autumn 1990):640-645

**Martin, Patricia Yancey**

The Organization Family: Work and Family Linkages in the U.S. Military. Book Review. *Journal of Marriage and the Family* 52, No. 2 (May 1990):565-566

Rethinking Feminist Organizations. *Gender and Society* 4, No. 2 (June 1990):182-206

**Martin, Ruth**

Witchcraft and the Inquisition in Venice, 1550-1650. Reviewed by Carol F. Karlsen. *Gender & History* 2, No. 3 (Autumn 1990):354-356

**Martin, Teresa Castro** (joint author). *See* Bumpass, Larry

**Martin, Theodora Penny**

The Sound of Our Own Voices: Women's Study Clubs, 1860-1910. Reviewed by Angela Howard Zophy. *Signs* 15, No. 2 (Winter 1990):410-411

**Martin, Valerie**

Mary Reilly. Reviewed by David Lida. *Harper's Bazaar* (February 1990):108-110

Mary Reilly. Reviewed by E. J. Graff. *The Women's Review of Books* 7, Nos. 10-11 (July 1990):34-35

**Martinac, Paula**

The One You Call Sister. Reviewed by Rosalind Warren. *New Directions for Women* 19, No. 4 (July-August 1990):19

**Martinac, Paula** and Tomaso, Carla

Voyages Out I: Lesbian Short Fiction. Reviewed by Liz Galst. *The Women's Review of Books* 7, No. 4 (January 1990):11

**Martinac, Paula** (editor)

The One You Call Sister. Reviewed by Beverly Lowy. *On the Issues* 15 (Summer 1990):27

The One You Call Sister. Reviewed by Lynne M. Constantine. *Belles Lettres* 5, No. 3 (Spring 1990):6

**Martindale, Sherri**

Voices from Prison. *New Directions for Women* 19, No. 3 (May/June 1990):6

**Martineau, Harriet** (about). *See* David, Deirdre

**Martini, Richard**

Limit Up. Reviewed by Esther Bailey. *Spare Rib* No. 214 (July 1990):32

**Martlew, Gillian** and Silver, Shelley

The Pill Protection Plan. Reviewed by Kate Griew. *Healthright* 9, No. 3 (May 1990):38-39

**Martz, Larry**

Anatomy of a High. *Mademoiselle* (May 1990):161, 243

**Marx, Sabine**

Desire Cannot Be Fragmented. *Connexions* 33 (1990):6-9

**Mascara.** *See* Makeup

**Masculinity.** *See also* Men – Psychology

The Incredible Shrinking He(r)man: Male Regression, the Male Body, and Film. Tania Modleski. *Differences* 2, No. 2 (Summer 1990):55-75

Like Father, Like Son: Parental Models and Influences in the Making of Masculinity at an English Public School, 1929-1950. Catherine Heward. *Women's Studies International Forum* 13, Nos. 1-2 (1990):139-149

A Whole New World: Remaking Masculinity in the Context of the Environmental Movement. Robert W. Connell. *Gender and Society* 4, No. 4 (December 1990):452-478

**Masculinity – History – Feminist Perspectives**

Masculinity and Power. By Arthur Brittan. Reviewed by Jeff Hearn. *Gender & History* 2, No. 3 (Autumn 1990):351-353

**Masia, Seth** (joint author). *See* McCloy, Marjorie

**Maskiell, Michelle**

Gender, Kinship and Rural Work in Colonial Punjab. *Journal of Women's History* 2, No. 1 (Spring 1990):35-72

**Mason, Catherine**

AIDS and its Metaphors. Book Review. *Healthright* 9, No. 4 (August 1990):40

Psychology and Parenthood. Book Review. *Healthright* 9, No. 4 (August 1990):42

**Mason, Micheline**

Disability Equality in the Classroom – A Human Rights Issue. *Gender and Education* 2, No. 3 (1990):363-366

**Mason, Pam**

Allanah Myles. Music Review. *Spare Rib* 213 (June 1990):35

Baby M/Q.E.D. *Spare Rib* No. 216 (September 1990):30

The Captain Swing Review. Music Review. *Spare Rib* No. 214 (July 1990):24

**Mason, Patience**

Recovering from the War. Reviewed by Susanne Carter. *Minerva* 8, No. 3 (Fall 1990):73-77

**Mason, Ruth**

Foodculture: A Window Onto Women's Lives. *Lilith* 15, No. 1 (Winter 1990):26-27

**Mason-John, Valerie**

Postcard from Paradise. Music Review. *Spare Rib* 218 (November 1990):18

**Massachusetts – State Legislation**

The Presence of Women Candidates and the Role of Gender in Campaigns for the State Legislature in an Urban Setting: The Case of Massachusetts. Barbara Burrell. *Women & Politics* 10, No. 3 (1990):85-102

**Massachussets Institute of Technology – Mobile Robotics Group.** *See* Robotics

**Massage**

Hands On. Laura Flynn McCarthy. *Vogue* (April 1990):376, 421

The Masseuse. Cynthia Waring. *Woman of Power* 18 (Fall 1990):75

Saving Face with a Hot New Treatment. Karen Dawson. *Lear's* (October 1990):66

Touching Women. Victoria Fann. *Woman of Power* 18 (Fall 1990):74

**Massé, Michelle A.**

Gothic Repetition: Husbands, Horrors, and Things That Go Bump in the Night. Notes. *Signs* 15, No. 4 (Summer 1990):679-709

**Masselam, Venus S.**, Marcus, Robert F., and Stunkard, Clayton L.

Parent-Adolescent Communication, Family Functioning, and School Performance. *Adolescence* 25, No. 99 (Fall 1990):737

**Masserman, Jules H.** and Uribe, Victor M.

Adolescent Sexuality. Book Review. *Adolescence* 25, No. 99 (Fall 1990):754

**Massey, Renelle** (joint author). *See* Walfish, Steven

**Massing, Michael**

Crack! Girls Like You on Drugs Like That. *Mademoiselle* (May 1990):159-161

**Mass Media.** *See* Media and Communications

**Masson, Dominique**

Femmes sans toit ni voix: La problematique des femmes dites sans-abri ou itinerantes. Book Review. *Canadian Women's Studies* 11, No. 2 (Fall 1990):86

Personnes âgées et logement. Book Review. *Canadian Women's Studies* 11, No. 2 (Fall 1990):86-87

When a Hostel Becomes a Home – Experiences of Women. Book Review. *Resources for Feminist Research* 19, No. 1 (March 1990):37-38

**Masson, Jeffrey** (about)

Lunch. Interview. Frances Lear. *Lear's* (December 1990):21-24

**Mass Transit Street Theater**

Interviews Transformed into Play for Street Theater. Judith Pasternak. *New Directions for Women* 19, No. 1 (January/February 1990):metrö+

**Mastectomy.** *See* Breast Cancer

Living with Loss, Dreaming of Lace. Mimi Schwartz. *Lear's* (October 1990):54-56

**Masters, Judith**

Natural Selection, Cultural Construction. *The Women's Review of Books* 7, No. 4 (January 1990):18-19

Primate Visions: Gender, Race, and Nature in the World of Modern Science. Book Review. *The Women's Review of Books* 7, No. 4 (January 1990):18-19

**Masters, Kim**

It's How You Play the Game. *Working Woman* (May 1990):88-91

**Masuda, Shirley**

Meeting Our Needs: Access for Women with Disabilities. *Canadian Women's Studies* 11, No. 2 (Fall 1990):80-81

**Matchmakers.** *See also* Blind Dates

The Meet Market. Peter Wilkinson. *Savvy Woman* (July/August 1990):52-55+

**Maternal Age.** *See* Middle-Aged Women – Childbirth

**Maternal and Infant Welfare.** *See also* Industry – Social Policy; Prenatal Influences

Better Beginnings: The LHJ Guide to Pregnancy. Beth Weinhouse and Barbara Burgower. *Ladies' Home Journal* 107, No. 8 (August 1990):35-42

Family Planning and Maternal Health Care in Egypt. Mawaheb T. El-Mouelhy. *Women and Therapy* 10, No. 3 (1990):55-60

Fighting for Three Lives. Julianne Procich. *Ladies' Home Journal* 107, No. 10 (October 1990):22-27+

It's a New Life – for You, Too! *Redbook* 175, No. 6 (October 1990):28-30

Saving Premature Babies. Rita H. Fischer and Florence Isaacs. *Good Housekeeping* 211, No. 3 (September 1990):110+

Your Pregnancy. Bibliography. Stephanie Young. *Glamour* (May 1990):80

Your Pregnancy. Stephanie Young. *Glamour* (March 1990):74; (July 1990):40; (August 1990):64; (October 1990):74

**Maternity Clothes**

An Eastern Solution to the Western Waist. Christine K. Van De Velde. *Savvy Woman* (July/August 1990):30-35

**Maternity Leave**

Back to Work After the Baby. Susan Schneider. *Working Mother* 13, No. 8 (August 1990):28-35

Government Fights Maternity Leave Reforms. *Spare Rib* 217 (October 1990):45

**Mathematics**

Black Women Mathematicians: In Short Supply. Sylvia Bozeman. *Sage* 6, No. 2 (Fall 1989):18-23

**Mathematics – Gender Differences**

Gender Comparisons of Mathematics Attitudes and Affect. Janet Shibley Hyde, Elizabeth Fennema, Marilyn Ryan, Laurie A. Frost, and Carolyn Hopp. *Psychology of Women Quarterly* 14, No. 3 (September 1990):299-324

**Mathematics – Personal Narrative**

My Life as a Mathematician. Evelyn Boyd Granville. *Sage* 6, No. 2 (Fall 1989):44-46

**Mather, Christine**

Crafting a Tradition. *McCall's* 118, No. 1 (October 1990):117-120

**Matheson, Clare**

Fate Cries Enough. Reviewed by Hilary Haines. *The Women's Review of Books* 7, No. 8 (May 1990):20-21

**Mathews, John**

Tools of Change: New Technology and the Democratisation of Work. Reviewed by Cora

Vellekoop Baldock. *Australian Feminist Studies* No. 12 (Summer 1990):43-49

**Mathews, Laura**

Word On Books. Bibliography. *Glamour* (April 1990):196

Word on Books. Bibliography. *Glamour* (March 1990):196; (May 1990):210; (August 1990):160; (September 1990):222; (November 1990):174; (December 1990):162

Word On Books. *Glamour* (January 1990):86; (February 1990):132; (June 1990):188

Word on Books. *Glamour* (October 1990):200

**Mathias, Barbara**

Private Lives. *Family Circle* 103, No. 7 (May 15, 1990):53-55

**Mathias, Timothy** (about)

The Boy Who Beat the Odds. Edward J. Sylvester. *Ladies' Home Journal* 107, No. 1 (January 1990):94-95+

**Mathieu, Nicole-Claude**

When Yielding Is Not Consenting: Material and Psychic Determinants of Women's Dominated Consciousness and Some of Their Interpretations in Ethnology, Part 2. *Feminist Issues* 10, No. 1 (Spring 1990):51-90

**Matisse, Henri – Criticism and Interpretation**

Engendering Imaginary Modernism. Henri Matisse's *Bonheur de vivre*. Margaret Werth. *Genders* 9 (Fall 1990):49-74

**Matisse, Henri** (about)

Matisse's Eastern Eden. Jed Perl. *Vogue* (March 1990):430-433, 524

Moroccan Idyll. Jo Ann Lewis. *Harper's Bazaar* (February 1990):166-167+

Picasso, Gilot, Matisse: Daily Life Among the Titans. Franc2oise Gilot. *Lear's* (August 1990):76-84+

**Matopodzi, Saliwe** (joint author). *See* Vengasayi, Dolly

**Matousek, Mark**

Calls of the Wild. Bibliography. *Harper's Bazaar* (July 1990):18-22

English Accents. *Harper's Bazaar* (April 1990):198-201+

Gallows Humor. Bibliography. *Harper's Bazaar* (September 1990):200-204

Petal Perfection. *Harper's Bazaar* (June 1990):136

Sure Shot. *Harper's Bazaar* (March 1990):212-213+

Two for the Road. *Harper's Bazaar* (January 1990):58

The Witching Hour. Book Review. *Harper's Bazaar* (November 1990):112

**Matsakis, Aphrodite**

Vietnam Wives. Reviewed by Susanne Carter. *Minerva* 8, No. 3 (Fall 1990):73-77

**Matson, Suzanne**

Woman with Distaff. Poem. *Iris* 24 (Fall-Winter 1990):54

**Matsui, Machiko**

Evolution of the Feminist Movement in Japan. *NWSA Journal* 2, No. 3 (Summer 1990):435-449

**Matsumoto, Valerie**

Making Face, Making Soul/Haciendo Caras: Creative and Critical Perspectives by Women of Color. Book Review. *The Women's Review of Books* 8, No. 2 (November 1990):1 +

From Silence to Resistance. *The Women's Review of Books* 8, No. 2 (November 1990):1 +

**Mattel, Incorporated.** *See* Barad, Jill (about)

**Mattera, Joanne**

Good Sports. *Glamour* (April 1990):82; (June 1990):78

Good Sports: Hot Tips for Working Out in the Cold. *Glamour* (February 1990):58

Good Sports: Mind Games. *Glamour* (December 1990):76

Good Sports: Take Your Workout on Vacation. *Glamour* (September 1990):92

Women and Cars: On a Roll. *Glamour* (May 1990):254-259

**Matthaei, Julie** (joint author). *See* Teresa Amott

**Matthews, Kathy** (joint author). *See* Vartabedian, Roy E.

**Matthews, Nicole**

Vampires. Short Story. *Hecate* 16, Nos. 1-2 (1990):111-114

**Matthews, Sarah H.**

Gender Issues in Field Research. Book Review. *Journal of Marriage and the Family* 52, No. 1 (February 1990):282

Knowing Children: Participant Observation with Minors. Book Review. *Journal of Marriage and the Family* 52, No. 1 (February 1990):282

**Matthias, Rebecca** (about)

Enterprise: The Start-Up: Treading Water until Your Ship Comes In. Elizabeth Birkelund Oberbeck. *Working Woman* (April 1990):41-44

**Matthiessen, Peter** (about)

Calls of the Wild. Bibliography. Mark Matousek. *Harper's Bazaar* (July 1990):18-22

**Mattioli, Laurie**

The Legacy. *Sinister Wisdom* 41 (Summer-Fall 1990):58-65

**Mattox, Cheryl Warren**

Shake It to the One That You Love the Best. Reviewed by Lynn Wenzel. *New Directions for Women* 19, No. 5 (September-October 1990):6

**Matz, S. Irene** (joint author). *See* Sanders, Judith A.

**Mauri, Marleyne**

Sleep and the Reproductive Cycle: A Review. *Health Care for Women International* 11, No. 4 (1990):409-421

**Max Factor Museum of Beauty**

History in the Makeup. Margy Rochlin. *Savvy Woman* (November 1990):18

**Maxims.** *See* Aphorisms and Apothegms

**Maxson, Pamela** (joint author). *See* Guerney, Bernard, Jr.

**Maxwell, Joseph W.** (joint author). *See* Lee, Thomas R.

**Maxwell, Margaret**

Feminism: Freedom from Wifism. Book Review. *On the Issues* 15 (Summer 1990):29-30

**May, Elaine Tyler**

Homeward Bound: American Families in the Cold War Era. Reviewed by Susan Ware. *Signs* 16, No. 1 (Autumn 1990):173-175

**May, Kathy**

Ascension. Poem. *Iris* 24 (Fall-Winter 1990):54

**Mayberry, Linda J.** (joint author). *See* Affonso, Dyanne D.

**Mayer, Anne**

Personal Journal: Married with Children . . . and Still in Love. *Ladies' Home Journal* 107, No. 6 (June 1990):110

Stay Close! *Redbook* 175, No. 3 (July 1990):94-95 +

**Mayer, Melanie J.**

Klondike Women, True Tales of the 1897-98 Gold Rush. Reviewed by Lynn Wenzel. *New Directions for Women* 19, No. 2 (March/April 1990):14

**Mayes, Elizabeth** (joint editor). *See* Ryan-Smolin, Wanda

**Mayfield, Kimberly**

Crazy at 13. Poem. *Frontiers* 11, Nos. 2-3 (1990):108

Death in Drowning. Poem. *Frontiers* 11, Nos. 2-3 (1990):110

A Girl. Poem. *Frontiers* 11, Nos. 2-3 (1990):109

**Maynard, Joyce**

Dying Young. Book review. *Mademoiselle* (January 1990):56-58

Inside Books: Lifestyles of the Rich and Shameless. *Mademoiselle* (February 1990):88 +

Love Is a Many Splintered Thing. *Mademoiselle* (March 1990):112-114

**Maynard, Laurie**

How to Get a Raise. *Executive Female* 13, No. 5 (September-October 1990):26

**Maynard, Mary** (joint author). *See* Coles, Bob

**Maynard, Valerie** (about). *See* Artists

**Mayo, Lisa** (interview)

Spiderwoman Theater. Carolann Barrett. *Woman of Power* 17 (Summer 1990):34-37

**Mayo Clinic.** *See also* Health Education

**Mayors.** *See also* Texas – Mayors

Boulder Mayor – All in a Day's Work. Susan Bristol-Howard. *Ms.* 1, No. 2 (September/October 1990):90

Women Watch: Votes of Confidence for Two First-Time Mayors. Patti Watts. *Executive Female* (March/April 1990):6-7

**Mazer, Gilbert E.** (joint author). *See* Kachman, Daniel J.

**Mazow, Julia Wolf**

The Tribe of Dina: A Jewish Women's Anthology. Book review. *Lilith* 15, No. 1 (Winter 1990):6-7

**Mbele, Nyami** (interview)

No Reforming Apartheid. Nolthando Mandla. *Spare Rib* 219 (December 1990-January 1991):20-23

**McAlevey, Peter**

On the Road Again. *Savvy Woman* (July/August 1990):25-26

**McAllister, Pam**

Learning to Dance. *Woman of Power* 15 (Fall-Winter 1990):74

You Can't Kill the Spirit: Stories of Women and Nonviolent Action. Reviewed by Gwyn Kirk. *Women & Politics* 10, No. 1 (1990):78-80

**McBay, Shirley M.** (interview)

Breaking the Barriers: Women and Minorities in the Sciences. *On the Issues* 15 (Summer 1990):7-9+

**McBride, Elissa** (about). *See* Title, Stacy

**McCafferty, Nell**

Peggy Deery: An Irish Family at War. Reviewed by Kathleen Gregory Klein. *Belles Lettres* 5, No. 3 (Spring 1990):5

**McCallen, Brian**

Fairways to Heaven. *Harper's Bazaar* (March 1990):56-62

**McCall's Magazine**

What's Causing the Changes in McCall's. Anne Mollegen Smith. *McCall's* 117, No. 7 (April 1990):59

**McCandless, Amy Thompson**

Maintaining the Spirit and Tone of Robust Manliness: The Battle Against Coeducation at

Southern Colleges and Universities, 1890-1940. *NWSA Journal* 2, No. 2 (Spring 1990):199-216

**McCann, Janet**

The Meeting. Poem. *Atlantis* 15, No. 2 (Spring 1990):58

Pictures of Doors. Poem. *Frontiers* 11, Nos. 2-3 (1990):106

Sister Rat. Poem. *Frontiers* 11, Nos. 2-3 (1990):107

Why Grandmother Never Learned English. Poem. *Frontiers* 11, Nos. 2-3 (1990):105

**McCarthy, Kerry**

Happy 100th Birthday, Aunt Rose. *Ladies' Home Journal* 107, No. 7 (July 1990):70-76

**McCarthy, Laura Flynn**

The Beauty News You Can Use. *Working Woman* (December 1990):88-90

Body Management: Contraception for the '90s. *Working Woman* (January 1990):129-132+

Hands On. *Vogue* (April 1990):376, 421

Images: Beauty Answers. *Vogue* (January 1990):78; (August 1990):180; (September 1990):356

Images: Hair Answers, Beauty Answers. *Vogue* (July 1990):84-86

Images: Hair Answers. *Vogue* (January 1990):76; (August 1990):189

Youth – Or Consequences? The Truth About the New Aging Antidotes. *Working Woman* (May 1990):116-118

**McCarthy, Margaret**

Do Clothes Make the Wo(Man)? *New Directions for Women* 19, No. 4 (July-August 1990):20

Tranformations: Crossdressers and Those Who Love Them. Book Review. *New Directions for Women* 19, No. 4 (July-August 1990):20

**McCarthy, Mary – Criticism and Interpretation**

I'll Tell You No Lies: Mary McCarthy's *Memories of a Catholic Girlhood* and the Fictions of Authority. Barbara Rose. *Tulsa Studies in Women's Literature* 9, No. 1 (Spring 1990):107-126

**McCarthy, Mary** (about)

Ode to a Woman Well at Ease: Mary McCarthy, 1912-1989. Eileen Simpson. *Lear's* (April 1990):136+

McCarthy, William (joint editor). See Rogers, Katherine M.

McCarty, Kim and Michael (about). See Goodwin, Betty, "Artful Cuisine"

McCaskell, Lisa (joint author). See Elliott, Susan

McClanahan, Rue (about). See also Sherman, Eric, "Gabbing with the Golden Girls"

McClary, Susan

Living to Tell: Madonna's Resurrection of the Fleshly. Genders 7 (Spring 1990):1-21

McClintock, Anne

Bananas, Beaches and Bases: Making Feminist Sense of International Politics. Book Review. The Women's Review of Books 7, No. 8 (May 1990):1+

Dangerous Liaisons. The Women's Review of Books 7, No. 8 (May 1990):1+

McClintock, Barbara (criticism)

Universality and Difference: O'Keeffe and McClintock. San MacColl. Hypatia 5, No. 2 (Summer 1990):149-157

McCloy, Marjorie

First Resorts. Women's Sports and Fitness 12, No. 7 (October 1990):47-51

McCloy, Marjorie and Masia, Seth

Ladies' Choice. Women's Sports and Fitness 12, No. 7 (October 1990):38-45

McCloy, Marjorie and Taggart, Sophie

Weight Training Back in Action. Women's Sports & Fitness 12, No. 6 (September 1990):18

McCloy, Marjorie (joint author). See Raia, James

McCluggage, Denise

On the Road: Car Care for the Couldn't-Care-Less. Glamour (June 1990):110

McClure, Laura

El Salvador: Images of War. Photographic essay. New Directions for Women 19, No. 3 (May/June 1990):14-15

Global Exploitation. New Directions for Women 19, No. 6 (November-December 1990):7

The Global Factory. Book Review. New Directions for Women 19, No. 6 (November-December 1990):7

Women Protected Out of Jobs. New Directions for Women 19, No. 1 (January/February 1990):1

McComas, Maggie

The Eco-Executive. Savvy Woman (October 1990):33-37

McConnel, Patricia

Sing Soft, Sing Loud. Reviewed by Lee Upton. Belles Lettres 5, No. 3 (Spring 1990):25

Sing Soft, Sing Loud. Reviewed by Martha Boethel. New Directions for Women 19, No. 2 (March/April 1990):18

McCorkle, Jill

Ferris Beach. Reviewed by Florence King. Vogue (October 1990):271+

McCorkle, Susannah

No More Blues. Reviewed by Lynn Wenzel. New Directions for Women 19, No. 5 (September-October 1990):6

McCormack, Lorraine E.

All New People. Book Review. Belles Lettres 5, No. 2 (Winter 1990):12

McCormick, Ruth

Women and Social Work: Toward a Woman-Centered Practice. Book Review. AFFILIA 5, No. 3 (Fall 1990):118-120

McCoy, Kathleen

Affairs of the Heart. Redbook 175, No. 1 (May 1990):128-129+

Private Lives: You and Your Mom. Family Circle 103, No. 17 (December 18, 1990):74-81

McCracken, LuAnn

"The synthesis of my being": Autobiography and the Reproduction of Identity in Virginia Woolf. Tulsa Studies in Women's Literature 9, No. 1 (Spring 1990):59-78

McCrone, Kathleen E.

Playing the Game: Sport and the Physical Emancipation of English Women, 1870-1914. Reviewed by Aniko Varpalotai. Resources for Feminist Research 19, No. 1 (March 1990):28

Playing the Game: Sport and the Physical Emancipation of English Women 1870-1914. Reviewed by Joyce Pedersen. Gender and Education 2, No. 1 (1990):107-109

McCrory, Moy

The Fading Shrine (excerpts). Spare Rib No. 215 (August 1990):12-16

McCrory, Moy (interview)

Hijacked Spirituality and Buried Herstories. Maude Casey. Spare Rib No. 215 (August 1990):8-11

McDaniel, Antonio

The Power of Culture: A Review of the Idea of Africa's Influence on Family Structure in Antebellum America. Journal of Family History 15, No. 2 (April 1990):225-238

McDaniel, JoBeth

Stars Who Care. Ladies' Home Journal 107, No. 11 (November 1990):74-80

McDaniel, Susan A. (joint author). *See* Helene Cummins; Kaden, Joan

McDermott, David (about). *See* Perl, Jed, "Vogue Arts: Charmed Lives."

McDermott, Kathy

The Ideology of Skill: A Case Study. *Australian Feminist Studies* No. 11 (Autumn 1990):61-73

McDonald's Corporation

October 16: World Day of Action Against. *Spare Rib* 217 (October 1990):47-48

McDonaugh, Eileen Lorenzi

The Significance of the Nineteenth Amendment: A New Look at Civil Rights, Social Welfare, and Woman Suffrage Alignments in the Progressive Era. *Women & Politics* 10, No. 2 (1990):59-94

McDonnell, Anna

Hollywood: By Youth Obsessed. *Mademoiselle* (April 1990):212, 246

McDonnell, Jeanne Farr

Women's History/Public History – When the Twain Meet. *Journal of Women's History* 2, No. 2 (Fall 1990):171-173

McDonough, David

His: Fighting Fair. *Glamour* (December 1990):232

McDonough, Peggy

Congenital Disability and Medical Research: The Development of Amniocentesis. *Women and Health* 16, Nos. 3/4 (1990):137-153

McDonough, Yona Zeldis

Grande Dame of Dance. *Harper's Bazaar* (January 1990):55

Prime-Time Affairs. *Harper's Bazaar* (August 1990):50

McDowell, Deborah E. (interview)

Saving the Text: An Interview with Deborah E. McDowell. Kimberly Connor. *Iris* 23 (Spring-Summer 1990):25-30

McEachern, Susan

Feminism, Family and Photography. *Canadian Women's Studies* 11, No. 1 (Spring 1990):14-15

McEachron, Ann E. (joint author). *See* Bolton, Frank

McEvilley, Thomas (joint author). *See* Rosen, Randy

McEwen, Christine and O'Sullivan, Sue (editors)

Out the Other Side: Contemporary Lesbian Writing. Reviewed by Becki Ross. *Resources for Feminist Research* 19, No. 1 (March 1990):26-28

McFadden, Margaret

Boston Teenagers Debate the Woman Question, 1837-1838. Notes. *Signs* 15, No. 4 (Summer 1990):832-847

McFadden, Monica

Health Advice – Before It's too Late. *Ms.* 1, No. 3 (November/December 1990):92

McFall, Lynne

The One True Story of the World. Reviewed by Diana Postlethwaite. *Belles Lettres* 5, No. 4 (Summer 1990):15

McFarland, Dennis

The Music Room (excerpt). *Vogue* (April 1990):391-393, 420

McGarvey, Robert

Foreign Language Labs. *Executive Female* 13, No. 5 (September-October 1990):32-34

Gift Rap. *Executive Female* 13, No. 6 (November-December 1990):33-34

Rehearsing for Success. *Executive Female* 13, No. 1 (January-February 1990):34-37

Strategic Quitting: Pack Your Bags for Greener Pastures. *Executive Female* (March/April 1990):34-36 +

McGee, Celia

Milton Glaser: The Illusionist. *Lear's* (September 1990):90-95 +

McGehee, Peter

The End of the Season. Short story. *Out/Look* No. 7 (Winter 1990):36-41

McGinnis, James (joint author). *See* McGinnis, Kathleen

McGinnis, Kathleen and McGinnis, James

Parenting for Peace and Justice: Ten Years Later. Book Review. *Adolescence* 25, No. 100 (Winter 1990):998

McGinnis, Lila

Crowded Honeymoon. Short Story. *Good Housekeeping* 210, No. 4 (April 1990):134-135

McGinnis, Mary

From My Eyes. Poem. *Woman of Power* 18 (Fall 1990):30

To My Eyes. Poem. *Woman of Power* 18 (Fall 1990):30

McGoldrick, Monica and others (editors)

Women in Families: A Framework for Family Therapy. Reviewed by Ruth Farber. *AFFILIA* 5, No. 1 (Spring 1990):107-108

McGough, Peter (about). *See also* Perl, Jed, "Vogue Arts: Charmed Lives."

McGovern, Elizabeth (about). *See also* Actors

The Mystery of McGovern. Michael Kilian. *Mademoiselle* (July 1990):56, 144

The Dress Circle. *Harper's Bazaar* (April 1990):94-103

Grand Designs. *Harper's Bazaar* (July 1990):84-85 +

A Nose for Business. *Harper's Bazaar* (January 1990):32

**McLaughlin, Sigrid** (editor)

The Image of Women in Contemporary Soviet Fiction: Selected Short Stories from the USSR. Reviewed by Jill Benderly. *The Women's Review of Books* 7, Nos. 10-11 (July 1990):19

The Image of Women in Contemporary Soviet Fiction: Selected Short Stories from the U.S.S.R. Reviewed by Judith Deutsch Kornblatt. *Feminist Collections* 11, No. 4 (Summer 1990):3-4

**McLean, Ann** (joint author). *See* Flanigan, Beverly

**McLendon, Jacquelyn Y.**

A Life of Gwendolyn Brooks. Book Review. *The Women's Review of Books* 7, Nos. 10-11 (July 1990):26

Poet of Black and Tan. *The Women's Review of Books* 7, Nos. 10-11 (July 1990):26

**McLeod, Patrice**

Fall Fashion Focus. *Essence* 21, No. 5 (September 1990):20

**McMillan, Margaret**

Women of the Raj. Reviewed by Anand A. Yang. *Women's Studies International Forum* 13, No. 4 (1990):407-408

**McMillan, Terry**

Disappearing Acts. Reviewed by C. J. Walker. *New Directions for Women* 19, No. 5 (September-October 1990):19

Looking for Mr. Right. *Essence* 20, No. 10 (February 1990):34 +

**McMullen, Barbara E.** and McMullen, John F.

The Latest PC Power: All Plugged In. *Lear's* (December 1990):36-37

**McMullen, John F.** (joint author). *See* McMullen, Barbara E.

**McNamara, Jo Ann**

Carnal Knowing: Female Nakedness and Religious Meaning in the Christian West. Book Review. *The Women's Review of Books* 8, No. 1 (October 1990):21-22

How Women Became Sex Objects. *The Women's Review of Books* 8, No. 1 (October 1990):21-22

**McNamara, Julie**

Kitchen Matters. Theater Review. *Spare Rib* 219 (December 1990-January 1991):38

The Singing and the Crack – the Heart of the People. *Spare Rib* 219 (December 1990-January 1991):24-26

**McNamara, Mary**

Recovering from Recovery. *Glamour* (November 1990):176

**McNamee, Louise** (about). *See also* Success in Business, "Talent at work"

Killing Them Softly. Ron Gales. *Working Woman* (November 1990):112-115 +

**McNaughton, Cath**

Quebec Women: A History. Book Review. *Women's Studies International Forum* 13, Nos. 1-2 (1990):162-163

**McNeill, Pearlie** (interview)

Interview with Pearlie McNeill. Carole Ferrier. *Hecate* 16, Nos. 1-2 (1990):102-110

**McNichol, Kristy** (about)

Kristy McNichol Finds a Full Life on Empty Nest. Mark Morrison. *Ladies' Home Journal* 107, No. 3 (March 1990):100

**McPhail, Margaret** (joint author). *See* Adamson, Nancy

**McPherson, Cathy**

Housing for the Disabled. *Canadian Women's Studies* 11, No. 2 (Fall 1990):31-32

**McQuaid, Matilda** (joint editor). *See* Berkeley, Ellen Perry

**McQuilkin, Jill**

The Busy Life: Presentation Is Everything. *Working Woman* (September 1990):202-205

**McQuillan, Susan**

Low-Fat Cooking: Trim the Fat, Not the Flavor. *Family Circle* 103, No. 13 (September 25, 1990):55-58

Quick, Quicker Menus. *Family Circle* 103, No. 17 (December 18, 1990):179-184

**McRaney, Gerald** (about)

What's Hot on TV: At Ease with Gerald McRaney. Jim Calio. *Ladies' Home Journal* 107, No. 5 (May 1990):56-58

**McRobbie, Andrea**

New Times: The Changing Face of Politics in the 1990s. Book Review. *Feminist Review* No. 36 (Autumn 1990):127-131

**McSherry, Frank, Jr.,** Waugh, Charles G., and Greenberg, Martin (editors)

Civil War Women: American Women Shaped by Conflict in Stories by Alcott, Chopin, Welty and Others. Reviewed by Susan Koppelman. *Belles Lettres* 5, No. 4 (Summer 1990):41

**McSpadden, Holly A.**

Las Mujeres Hablan: An Anthology of Nuevo Mexicana Writers. Book Review. *Frontiers* 11, No. 1 (1990):89-90

**McWhorter, Ladelle**

Feminism and Foucault: Reflections on Resistance. Book Review. *NWSA Journal* 2, No. 4 (Autumn 1990):677-678

**Mead, Margaret** (about). *See also* Papua New Guinea – Anthropology

**Meadow, Donna**

Elegant First Courses. *McCall's* 118, No. 2 (November 1990):136

Flavor to Relish All Year Long. *McCall's* 117, No. 11 (August 1990):116

Happy Halloween Desserts. *McCall's* 118, No. 1 (October 1990):140

**Measles.** *See also* Diseases

Beware the New Measles Epidemic. Nancy Gagliardi. *Redbook* 175, No. 3 (July 1990):34-37

**Meat.** *See* Cookery (Meat)

**Mechanics.** *See* Automobile Mechanics

**Media and Communications**

Against the Odds: Welfare Mothers Publish Newspaper. Pat Redmond. *New Directions for Women* 19, No. 1 (January/February 1990):8

The Female Gaze: Women as Viewers of Popular Culture. Edited by Lorraine Gamman and Margaret Marshment. Reviewed by Cynthia Carter. *Resources for Feminist Research* 19, No. 2 (June 1990):41-42

Female Spectators: Looking at Film and Television. Edited by E. Deidre Pribam. Reviewed by Cynthia Carter. *Resources for Feminist Research* 19, No. 2 (June 1990):41-42

Military Women and the Media. Laura Flanders. *New Directions for Women* 19, No. 6 (November-December 1990):1+

Visual Images of American Society: Gender and Race in Introductory Sociology Textbooks. Myra Marx Ferree and Elaine J. Hall. *Gender and Society* 4, No. 4 (December 1990):500-533

WIFP Introduces Booklet Series on Women and Communication. *Media Report to Women* 18, No. 6 (November-December 1990):6

Women's Media: The Way to Revolution. Martha Leslie Allen. *off our backs* 20, No. 2 (February 1990):14+

**Media and Communications – Bias**

Gay, Lesbian Journalists Rate Climate, Coverage in Their Newsrooms. *Media Report to Women* 18, No. 3 (May/June 1990):2

Unreliable Sources: A Guide to Detecting Bias in News Media. By Martin A. Lee and Norman Solomon. Reviewed by Susan E. Davis. *New Directions for Women* 19, No. 6 (November-December 1990):18

**Media and Communications – Discrimination**

Age Bias in Media Industry Complicating Career Paths. *Media Report to Women* 18, No. 5 (September-October 1990):3-4

Baseball Pitcher Uses Sexual Comment to Decline Interview with Reporter. *Media Report to Women* 18, No. 5 (September-October 1990):2-3

National Association of Black Journalists Forms Task Force on Women. *Media Report to Women* 18, No. 6 (November-December 1990):6

TRNDA Survey Shows Little Change for Women in Newsrooms. *Media Report to Women* 18, No. 5 (September-October 1990):1

**Media and Communications – Educational Programs**

Media Matter: TV Use in Childhood and Adolescence. By Karl Erik Rosengren and Sven Windahl. Book Review. *Adolescence* 25, No. 100 (Winter 1990):1000-1001

**Media and Communications – Images of Women**

The Comic Mirror: Domestic Surveillance in Mary Worth. Jennifer Fisher. *Canadian Women's Studies* 11, No. 1 (Spring 1990):60-61

Exploding the Beauty Myth. Naomi Wolfe. *Spare Rib* 218 (November 1990):6-10

The Female Gaze. Edited by Lorraine Gamman and Margaret Marshment. Reviewed by Sumiko Higashi. *Gender & History* 2, No. 1 (Spring 1990):123-126

Gender Differentiation in *The New York Times*, 1885 and 1985: Some Surprises. *Media Report to Women* 18, No. 2 (March/April 1990):3-4

*Media and Values* Magazine Produces Special Issue on Women and Media. *Media Report to Women* 18, No. 2 (March/April 1990):7

The Media Construct a Menstrual Monster: A Content Analysis of PMS Articles in the Popular Press. Joan C. Chrisler and Karen B. Levy. *Women and Health* 16, No. 2 (1990):89-104

Military Women in Film, TV, Media: Invisible, Sexually Stereotyped. *Media Report to Women* 18, No. 3 (May/June 1990):6-7

When Is a Mother Not a Mother? The Baby M Case. Bilbiography. Sonia Jaffe Robbins. *Women & Language* 13, No. 1 (Fall 1990):41-46

Women, Men and Media Center Endowed by Gannett Foundation. *Media Report to Women* 18, No. 3 (May/June 1990):1

Women and Print Culture: The Construction of Femininity in the Early Periodical. By Kathryn Shevelow. Reviewed by Margaret Hunt. *Gender & History* 2, No. 2 (Summer 1990):228-229

Women and the Popular Imagination in the Twenties: Flappers and Nymphs. By Billie Melman. Reviewed by Sumiko Higashi. *Gender & History* 2, No. 1 (Spring 1990):123-126

**Media and Communications – Propaganda**

This Working Life: The World According to P.R. Gail Collins. *Working Woman* (August 1990):98

**Media and Communications – Research**

Research Roundup. *Media Report to Women* 18, No. 5 (September-October 1990):6-8

**Media and Communications – Status of Women**

ANPA Issues 1990 Report on Women and Minority Employment at Newspapers. *Media Report to Women* 18, No. 4 (July-August 1990):3-4

Broadcasters See Ebbing of Sexism, More Clout for Women in News. *Media Report to Women* 18, No. 3 (May/June 1990):8-9

Broadcast Networking. Jennet Conant. *Working Woman* (August 1990):58-61

Little Improvement Noted in Women's Page One Status. *Media Report to Women* 18, No. 3 (May/June 1990):3-4

NFPW Study: Women Grossly Underrepresented in Newspaper Content, Editorial Decisions. *Media Report to Women* 18, No. 4 (July-August 1990):2-3

Study Finds Nearly 70% of Denver Women Journalists See Sexism at Work. *Media Report to Women* 18, No. 2 (March/April 1990):4-5

Study of Newspaper Business Sections: Still a Male Domain. *Media Report to Women* 10, No. 3 (May/June 1990):5

Women Could Dominate News Director Positions Early in 21st Century. *Media Report to Women* 18, No. 2 (March/April 1990):2-3

Women in Broadcasting Going It Alone, Magazine Says. *Media Report to Women* 18, No. 5 (September-October 1990):1-2

Women TV Network Correspondents Report Only 15% of News Stories. *Media Report to Women* 18, No. 6 (November-December 1990):1

**Media and Communications – Stereotyping.** *See* Television Programs – Stereotyping

**Media and Communications – Wage Equity**

PRSA Adopts Policy Statement Affirming Equal Opportunity for Women. *Media Report to Women* 18, No. 2 (March/April 1990):1-2

Why Meryl Streep Earns So Much Less than Sylvester Stalone. Charla Krupp. *Glamour* (July 1990):114-115

WICI Survey Finds Media Salaries for Women Depressed throughout Careers. *Media Report to Women* 18, No. 3 (May/June 1990):5-6

**Media and Values** (periodical)

*Media and Values* Magazine Produces Special Issue on Women and Media. *Media Report to Women* 18, No. 2 (March/April 1990):7

**Medical Care.** *See* Health Care; Holistic Medicine; Maternal and Infant Welfare; Obstetrics

**Medical Emergencies**

When Should You Be Your Own Doctor? Fran Snyder. *Ladies' Home Journal* 107, No. 2 (February 1990):62-72

**Medical Ethics.** *See also* Health Care; Medical Records; Patient-Doctor Relationships; Reproductive Choice; Right to Die

The Cosmetic Surgery Hoax. Laura Fraser. *Glamour* (February 1990):184-185+

Embryos, Ethics and Women's Rights. Edited by Elaine Hoffman Baruch, Amadeo F. D'Adamo, Jr. and Joni Seager. Reviewed by Sonia G. Austrian. *AFFILIA* 5, No. 3 (Fall 1990):113-114

Health News: Dangerous Doctors and Phony Cures. Rita Baron-Faust. *Redbook* 175, No. 6 (October 1990):54-59

Is There a Right Reason for Having a Baby? Michael Specter. *Glamour* (August 1990):96

Mapping the Moral Domain. Edited by Carol Gilligan, Janie Victoria Ward, Jill McLean Taylor, and Betty Bardige. Reviewed by Alison K. Adams. *AFFILIA* 5, No. 3 (Fall 1990):111-113

Radical Conceptions: Reproductive Technologies and Feminist Theories. Susan Behuniak-Long. *Women & Politics* 10, No. 3 (1990):39-64

Surgery: Weighing the Options. Leigh Silverman. *Lear's* (June 1990):48-50

This Is What You Thought. *Glamour* (January 1990):73

Whose Life Is More Important: An Animal's or a Child's? Alice Steinbach. *Glamour* (January 1990):1440-141+

**Medical Quacks.** *See* Quacks and Quackery

**Medical Records**

Medical Report: Your Medical Records. Bibliography. Sue Halpern. *Glamour* (September 1990):104-110

**Medical Research.** *See also* Brain; Genetic Determinants; Human Genome Project; Orphan Drugs

Cancer Organizers Push Feminist Agenda. Mary Jo Foley. *New Directions for Women* 19, No. 3 (May/June 1990):1+

Conquering Cancer. *Harper's Bazaar* (August 1990):46+

The Cruel Deception: The Use of Animals in Medical Research. By Robert Sharpe. Reviewed by Roberta Kalechofsky. *On the Issues* 14 (1990):25-26

Fertile Ground. Lori Miller Kase. *Savvy Woman* (September 1990):80-82

A Final Gift. Frank Maier. *Ladies' Home Journal* 107, No. 3 (March 1990):102-111

Health & Mind. Pamela Erens. *Glamour* (August 1990):60

Health Research Slights Women. Mary Jo Foley. *New Directions for Women* 19, No. 6 (November-December 1990):4-5

How Your Immune System Works. Joan Lippert. *Ladies' Home Journal* 107, No. 10 (October 1990):118-124

Is Health Equity on the Way? Boston Women's Health Book Collective. *Ms.* 1, No. 3 (November/December 1990):25

Medical News. Dana Points and Carla Rohlfing. *Family Circle* 103, No. 17 (December 18, 1990):72

Medical Studies On Women are Urgently Needed. *Glamour* (March 1990):146

Miracle or Menace? Gina Kolata. *Redbook* 175, No. 5 (September 1990):174-176+

New Gains in Cancer Therapy. Irene Nyborg-Andersen. *Ladies' Home Journal* 107, No. 5 (May 1990):66

Playing with Time. Rita Baron-Faust. *Harper's Bazaar* (August 1990):46+

The Significant Other. Beth Weinhouse. *Savvy Woman* (October 1990):13-14

The Silent Killer. Bibliography. Jean Fain. *Ladies' Home Journal* 107, No. 3 (March 1990):68-79

Silk Purse Chronicles: The High Cost of Orphan Drugs. Patricia O'Toole. *Lear's* (February 1990):22-23

**Medical Schools**

Staying Horrified. Martha Reed Herbert. *Heresies* 25 (1990):90-94

**Medical Sciences – Employment Opportunities.** *See also* Health Care Occupations – Employment Opportunities

**Medical Termination of Pregnancy Act – India.** *See* India – Abortion Laws

**Medicare**

Older Women's Health and Financial Vulnerability: Implications of the Medicare Benefit Structure. Shoshanna Sofaer and Emily Abel. *Women and Health* 16, Nos. 3/4 (1990):47-67

**Medicine.** *See* Health Care; Medical Research; Medical Sciences; Patient-Doctor Relationship

**Medicine, Preventive.** *See* Health Care

From the Mayo Clinic: 12 Tips for a Longer, Healthier Life. Arlene Fischer. *Redbook* 175, No. 5 (September 1990):156-159

A Pet a Day . . . Sandra Y. Lee. *McCall's* 118, No. 3 (December 1990):26-28

Take 2 Asprin . . .and Call Me in 5 Years. John C. Harbert. *Family Circle* 103, No. 14 (October 16, 1990):136-138

**Medicine as a Profession**

Gender Roles, Medical Practice Roles, and Ob-Gyn Career Choice: A Longitudinal Study. Nancy G. Kutner and Donna Brogan. *Women and Health* 16, Nos. 3/4 (1990):99-117

Women as Healers: A History of Women and Medicine. By Hilary Bourdillon. Reviewed by Fiona Terry. *Gender & History* 2, No. 3 (Autumn 1990):371-373

**Meditation**

In the Spirit: Staying Centered. Susan L. Taylor. *Essence* 21, No. 4 (August 1990):53

**Medjuck, Sheva**

Ethnicity and Feminism: Two Solitudes? *Atlantis* 15, No. 2 (Spring 1990):1-10

**Medlock, Ann**

What Makes a Giraffe Stand Tall? *Lear's* (July 1990):30-31

**Medora, Nilufer P.** (joint author). *See* Wilson, Stephan M.

**Meduri, Avanthi** (joint author). *See* Burns, Judy

**Medusa**

Medusa and the Female Gaze. Susan R. Bowers. *NWSA Journal* 2, No. 2 (Spring 1990):217-235

**Meehan, Fiona**

The Factory Girls. Theater Review. *Spare Rib* 218 (November 1990):24

**Meehan, Mary** (about)

Inviting Chintz & Prints. Robert Turnbull. *Harper's Bazaar* (April 1990):206-207+

**Meese, Elizabeth** and Parker, Alice (editors)

The Difference Within: Feminism and Critical Theory. Reviewed by Amanda Leslie-Spinks. *The Women's Review of Books* 7, No. 8 (May 1990):15-16

The Difference Within: Feminism and Critical Theory. Reviewed by Sue Golding. *Resources for Feminist Research* 19, No. 2 (June 1990):39

**Meetings.** *See also* Communication; Employee-Employer Relations; Planning

**Mehlman, Peter**

The New Sexy. *Harper's Bazaar* (February 1990):120-127+

On the Waterfront. *Savvy Woman* (July/August 1990):82-84

**Mehta, Ketan**

Hero Hiralal. Reviewed by Ruth Vanita. *Manushi* 61 (November-December 1990):44

**Mehta, Nina**

May You Be the Mother of a Hundred Sons: A Journey Among the Women of India. Book Review. *The Women's Review of Books* 8, No. 3 (December 1990):19-20

Mercy, Pity, Peace and Love. Book Review. *Belles Lettres* 5, No. 4 (Summer 1990):8

The Proverbial Scent of Incense. *Belles Lettres* 6, No. 1 (Fall 1990):23

Stranger in a Strange Land. *The Women's Review of Books* 8, No. 3 (December 1990):19-20

Truth Tales: Contemporary Stories by Women Writers of India. Book Review. *Belles Lettres* 6, No. 1 (Fall 1990):23

**Meigs, Anna**

Blood Magic: The Anthropology of Menstruation. Book Review. *Signs* 16, No. 1 (Autumn 1990):180-182

Images of Bleeding: Menstruation as Ideology. Book Review. *Signs* 16, No. 1 (Autumn 1990):180-182

**Meister, Barbara**

Rediscovery: Louise Colet. *Belles Lettres* 5, No. 4 (Summer 1990):18-20

**Melanesia – Women's Roles**

The Gender of the Gift: Problems with Women and Problems with Society in Melanesia. By Marilyn Strathern. Reviewed by Gillian Cowlishaw. *Australian Feminist Studies* No. 11 (Autumn 1990):121-122

**Melanin.** *See* Melanism

**Melanism**

Mysteries of Melanin. Bibliography. Allison Abner. *Essence* 21, No. 7 (November 1990):30-31

**Melanoma.** *See also* Skin Cancer

**Melby, Janet N.** (joint author). *See* Conger, Rand D.; Simons, Ronald L.

**Meleis, Afaf L.,** Kulig, Judith C., Arruda, Eloita Neves, and Beckman, Amy

Maternal Role of Women in Clerical Jobs in Southern Brazil: Stress and Satisfaction. *Health Care for Women International* 11, No. 4 (1990):369-382

**Mellen, Polly** (joint author). *See* Minnelli, Liza

**Mellor, Anne K.**

Mary Shelley: Her Life, Her Fiction, Her Monsters. Reviewed by Deborah Kennedy. *Canadian Women's Studies* 11, No. 2 (Fall 1990):94

**Melman, Billie**

Women and the Popular Imagination in the Twenties: Flappers and Nymphs. Reviewed by Sumiko Higashi. *Gender & History* 2, No. 1 (Spring 1990):123-126

**Melodrama in Film**

Female Power in the Serial-Queen Melodrama: The Etiology of an Anomaly. Ben Singer. *Camera Obscura* No. 22 (January 1990):91-129

Home Is Where the Heart Is: Studies in Melodrama and the Woman's Film. Edited by Christine Gledhill.

Reviewed by Paula Rabinowitz. *Feminist Studies* 16, No. 1 (Spring 1990):151-169

Melodrama and Social Drama in the Early German Cinema. Heide Schlüpmann. *Camera Obscura* No. 22 (January 1990):73-88

**Melville, Pauline**

Shape-Shifter. Reviewed by Sue Murphy. *Spare Rib* No. 211 (April 1990):27

**Memphis State University – Center for Research on Women**

Center for Research on Women/Memphis State University Research Clearinghouse on Women of Color and Southern Women. *Women's Studies Quarterly* 18, Nos. 1-2 (Spring-Summer 1990):117-119

**Men – Psychology.** *See also* Masculinity; Sexual Relationships

The Answer Couple. Ann Hood and Bob Reiss. *Glamour* (May 1990):136; (July 1990):96-97; (September 1990):166; (November 1990):146-147

The Answer Couple. Betsy Evans and Todd Nelson. *Glamour* (March 1990):152

The Answer Couple. Bob Reiss and Ann Hood. *Glamour* (August 1990):118-119; (October 1990):141; (December 1990):152-153

Brothers: It Begins with Me. Michael Saunders. *Essence* 21, No. 4 (August 1990):40-41

Brothers: I Want to Cry. G. Modele Clarke. *Essence* 21, No. 7 (November 1990):38-39

Brothers: Tears of a Stepfather. Hector V. Lino, Jr. *Essence* 21, No. 5 (September 1990):42

Cheap Men. Brook Hersey. *Glamour* (October 1990):300

The Children I Almost Had. David Mills. *Essence* 20, No. 10 (February 1990):36

Could You Be a Better Friend to Your Husband? Catherine Johnson. *Redbook* 175, No. 5 (September 1990):166-167+

In defense of the Ditz. Skip Hollandsworth. *Mademoiselle* (September 1990):150

Do Men Need to Cheat? James Thornton. *Glamour* (December 1990):208-209+

Do You Know His Secret Sexual Fantasies? Nancy Gagliardi. *Redbook* 175, No. 5 (September 1990):168-169+

Easy Ways to Help Him Be a Sexier Lover. Kathryn Stechert Black. *Redbook* 175, No. 6 (October 1990):112-113+

Evaluation of Rape Victim by Men and Women with High and Low Belief in a Just World. Chris L. Kleinke and Cecilia Meyer. *Psychology of Women Quarterly* 14, No. 3 (September 1990):343-353

Fraternities of Fear: Gang Rape, Male Bonding, and the Silencing of Women. Kathleen Hirsch. *Ms.* 1, No. 2 (September/October 1990):52-56

His: Love and Thunderbolts. David Meyer. *Glamour* (August 1990):240

How a Man's Age Changes His Outlook on Love. Julie Logan. *Glamour* (April 1990):256-259

I'll Lie to Make You Like Me. Skip Hollandsworth. *Mademoiselle* (November 1990):85

The Intelligent Woman's Guide to Sex. Dalma Heyn. *Mademoiselle* (June 1990):78

Is He Mr. Right? Or Mr. Right-for-Now? Candace Bushnell. *Mademoiselle* (February 1990):186-187

Jake: A Man's Opinion. *Glamour* (February 1990):108; (March 1990):140-143; (May 1990):174-180; (August 1990):134-136; (September 1990):184-186

Male Angst . . . And Women Who Live Through It. Mary Kay Blakely. *Lear's* (August 1990):72-73+

A Man's Wallet. *Glamour* (October 1990):151-152

The Man with a Broken Heart. Elizabeth Bales Frank. *Glamour* (November 1990):270

Men: Solving the Puzzle. Barbara DeAngelis. *Ladies' Home Journal* 107, No. 5 (May 1990):116-118+

Men and Damage Control. Judith Stone. *Glamour* (November 1990):144

Men and Failure. John Katz. *Glamour* (June 1990):244-245+

Men and the "M" Word. John Colapinto. *Mademoiselle* (December 1990):142-145

Men Demystified. Melissa Goodman. *Glamour* (July 1990):162-165

Men & Romance. Neil Chesanow. *Glamour* (February 1990):166-167+

Men Trouble. Nina Keilin. *Ladies' Home Journal* 107, No. 8 (August 1990):84-89

Relationships: "Help! I Married a Big Baby!" Elena Latici. *Redbook* 176, No. 2 (December 1990):44-46

Simply Irresistible: The Seven Laws of Desire. Skip Hollandsworth. *Mademoiselle* (November 1990):136-139

Stag Is a Drag. *Glamour* (November 1990):140-143

The Top 10 Sex Myths. Alfie Kohn. *Glamour* (October 1990):252-253+

Vanity Kills. Jamie Diamond. *Lear's* (January 1990):54-56

What Makes a Woman Sexy? Sherry Suib Cohen. *Ladies' Home Journal* 107, No. 11 (November 1990):116-123

What Men Envy about Women. Frank Conroy. *Glamour* (March 1990):252-253+

What Men Fear Most: Girl Talk. Jean Gonick. *Glamour* (August 1990):226-227+

What Smart Women Know. By Steven Carter and Julia Sokol. Reviewed by Anne Lamott. *Mademoiselle* (November 1990):96-99

**Men, Single**

Stag Is a Drag. *Glamour* (November 1990):140-143

**Men, Single – Humor**

A Man's Wallet. *Glamour* (October 1990):151-152

**Menaghan, Elizabeth G.** and Parcel, Toby L.

Parental Employment and Family Life: Research in the 1980s. *Journal of Marriage and the Family* 52, No. 4 (November 1990):1079-1098

**Men and Women's Club**

Rational Sex or Spiritual Love? The Men and Women's Club of the 1880s. Lucy Bland. *Women's Studies International Forum* 13, Nos. 1-2 (1990):33-48

**Menarche**

The Experience of Menarche. J. Weisgarber and J. W. Osborne. *Atlantis* 15, No. 2 (Spring 1990):27-39

Menarche: Responses of Early Adolescent Females. Arlene McGrory. *Adolescence* 25, No. 98 (Summer 1990):265-270

**Menchu, Rigoberta** (about). *See also* Third World Women – Oral History

**Mendola, Mary**

Sidewalk Spirituality Embraces the Divine in All. *New Directions for Women* 19, No. 4 (July-August 1990):6

**Mendonc3a, Nana**

Brazil. *Feminist Review* No. 34 (Spring 1990):8-11

**Meningitis.** *See* Diseases

**Mennen, Ferol E.**

Dilemmas and Demands: Working with Adult Survivors of Sexual Abuse. *AFFILIA* 5, No. 4 (Winter 1990):72-86

**Mennitt, Patricia**

Health Express: Low Fat, High Hype: The Great Food-Label Scam. *Mademoiselle* (February 1990):102-106

**Menon, Lakshmi**

Classification Systems: Need, Rationale and Basis. *Women's World* 23 (April 1990):18-20

**Menopause**

Attitude Toward Menopause and the Impact of the Menopausal Event on Adult Women with Diabetes Mellitus. Nancy E. White and Judith M. Richter. *Journal of Women and Aging* 2, No. 4 (1990):21-38

Body Briefing: Estrogen Replacement. Marcia Seligson. *Lear's* (March 1990):54-62

The Colours of Menopause. Margaret de Souza. *Healthsharing* 11, No. 4 (December 1990):14-17

Commentary on "Sexuality and the Midlife Woman." Ellen Cole and Esther Rothblum. *Psychology of Women Quarterly* 14, No. 4 (December 1990):509-512

Conceptions and Misconceptions of the Menstrual Cycle. Elissa Koff, Jill Rierdan, and Margaret L. Stubbs. *Women and Health* 16, Nos. 3/4 (1990):119-136

Do the Right Thing, Eat the Right Thing. Carolyn DeMarco. *Healthsharing* 11, No. 4 (December 1990):28-30

Hot Flashes. Ann Voda. *Healthsharing* 11, No. 4 (December 1990):13

Medical News. Dana Points and Carla Rohlfing. *Family Circle* 103, No. 16 (November 27, 1990):50

Menopause and You. Bibliography. *Essence* 21, No. 2 (June 1990):20-22

Menopause Resources. Janine O'Leary Cobb. *Healthsharing* 11, No. 4 (December 1990):26-27

Menopause Without Medicine. By Linda Ojeda. Reviewed by Pat Hunter. *Healthright* 9, No. 4 (August 1990):48

Old Plans, New Specifications: A Political Reading of the Medical Discourse on Menopause. Roe Sybylla. *Australian Feminist Studies* No. 12 (Summer 1990):95-107

The Take-Charge Patient. Bibliography. Andrea Atkins. *Ladies' Home Journal* 107, No. 11 (November 1990):163-174

The Wisdom of Menopause. Janine O'Leary Cobb. *Healthsharing* 11, No. 4 (December 1990):8-12

Women's Change of Life. By Leonard Mervyn. Reviewed by Pat Hunter. *Healthright* 9, No. 4 (August 1990):44

**Menopause – Narratives**

Why So Soon? Megan Hutton. *Healthsharing* 11, No. 4 (December 1990):34

**Menopause – Sexuality**

A Season for Sex. Gail Weber. *Healthsharing* 11, No. 4 (December 1990):18-22

**Menorah.** *See also* Hanukkah

**Men Psychology**

Career Strategies: Male Bonding: Can You Beat It? Adele Scheele. *Working Woman* (December 1990):30-32

**Menstruation.** *See also* Menarche; Premenstrual Syndrome; Tampons; Toxic Shock Syndrome

Blood Magic: The Anthropology of Menstruation. Edited by Thomas Buckley and Alma Gottlieb. Reviewed by Anna Meigs. *Signs* 16, No. 1 (Autumn 1990):180-182

Conceptions and Misconceptions of the Menstrual Cycle. Elissa Koff, Jill Rierdan, and Margaret L. Stubbs. *Women and Health* 16, Nos. 3/4 (1990):119-136

A Diet for the Worst Days. Cynthia Hacinli. *Mademoiselle* (October 1990):120

A Guy's-Eye View. Skip Hollandsworth. *Mademoiselle* (October 1990):122

Health: What's Your Period I.Q.? Janet Siroto. *Mademoiselle* (October 1990):118

Images of Bleeding: Menstruation as Ideology. By Louise Lander. Reviewed by Anna Meigs. *Signs* 16, No. 1 (Autumn 1990):180-182

Lifeblood: A New Image for Menstruation. By Margaret Sheffield and Sheila Bewley. Reviewed by Lee Collier and Kim Devaney. *Healthright* 9, No. 2 (February 1990):39

The Lowdown on Menstrual Problems. Shifra Diamond. *Mademoiselle* (October 1990):120

Questionnaire Studies of Paramenstrual Symptoms. John T.E. Richardson. *Psychology of Women Quarterly* 14, No. 1 (March 1990):15-42

Viewpoint. Ilana Fortgang. *Glamour* (September 1990):144

What You *Don't* Know about Your Period. Bibliography. Fran Snyder. *Ladies' Home Journal* 107, No. 5 (May 1990):108-114

**Menstruation – Cross-Cultural Studies**

Religious Influence on Menstrual Attitudes and Symptoms. Barbara Olasov Rothbaum and Joan Jackson. *Women and Health* 16, No. 1 (1990):63-78

**Menstruation – Exercise and**

Menstrual Dysfunction among Habitual Runners. Vilma E. Cokkinades, C.A. Macera, and R.R. Pate. *Women and Health* 16, No. 2 (1990):59-69

**Menstruation – Psychological Aspects**

Cardiovascular Stress Reactivity and Mood during the Menstrual Cycle. Gerdi Weidner and Linda Helmig. *Women and Health* 16, Nos. 3/4 (1990):5-21

The Female Role and Menstrual Distress: An Explanation for Inconsistent Evidence. Alfred B. Heilbrun, Jr., Lisa Friedberg, Dawna Wydra, and Alyson L. Worobow. *Psychology of Women Quarterly* 14, No. 3 (September 1990):403-417

**Mental Depression**

Social Skills and Depression in Adolescent Suicide Attempters. Anthony Spirito, Kathleen hart, James Overholser, and Jayna Halverson. *Adolescents* 25, No. 99 (Fall 1990):543-552

**Mental Disorders.** *See also*
Adolescents – Psychology; Behavior Disorders;
Depression, Mental; Great Britain – Mental
Disorders; Panic Disorders

Brave New Brain. Nancy C. Andreasen. *Vogue*
(January 1990):196-199+

The Oppression of Caring: Women Caregivers of
Relatives with Mental Illness. Anna Scheyetl.
*AFFILIA* 5, No. 1 (Spring 1990):32-48

The Private Terror of a Panic Attack. Leigh
Silverman. *Lear's* (August 1990):36-39

Who Am I? Nelly Edmondson Gupta. *Ladies' Home
Journal* 107, No. 3 (March 1990):160-161+

Women and Madness. By Phyllis Chesler.
Reviewed by Beverly Lowy. *On the Issues* 14
(1990):25

**Mental Disorders – Recovery**

Enter Password: Recovery. By Elly Bulkin. Reviewed
by Rebecca Ripley. *Sinister Wisdom* 42 (Winter
1990-1991):124-126

**Mental Health**

Resisting Psychiatry. Angela Browne. *Healthsharing*
11, No. 2 (March 1990):17-21

**Mental Health – Gender Differences**

Gender and Mental Health in Africa. Mere
Kakateregga Kisekka. *Women and Therapy* 10, No.
3 (1990):1-13

**Mental Health – Religion and**

Mental Health Aspects of Zar for Women in Sudan.
Edith H. Grotberg. *Women and Therapy* 10, No. 3
(1990):15-24

**Mentally Handicapped Children – Adoption**

Finding Homes for Jewish Babies. Toby Axelrod.
*Lilith* 15, No. 3 (Summer 1990):4-5

**Mentoring**

Mentor Express. Gayle Kirshenbaum. *Ms.* 1, No. 3
(November/December 1990):90

Mentoring and Being Mentored: Issues of Sex,
Power, and Politics for Older Women. Michele A.
Paludi, Deborah Meyers, Joni Kindermann, Hilda
Speicher, and Marilyn Haring-Hidore. *Journal of
Women and Aging* 2 No. 3 (1990):81-92

Update: News, Trends, and Vital Statistics About
Women. *Executive Female* (March/April 1990):8-10

**Mentors in Business.** *See also* Support Systems

In-House Mentors Keep Training Costs Down.
Claire McIntosh. *Working Woman* (January
1990):68

**Mercedes-Benz Motor Company.** *See*
Automobiles – Purchasing

**Mercer, Calvin**

Walker's Critique of Religion in *The Color Purple*.
*Sage* 6, No. 1 (Summer 1989):24-26

**Mercer, Marilyn** (joint author). *See* Fischer,
Thomas J.

**Mercer, Susan O.** (joint editor). *See* Garner, J.
Dianne

**Merchant, Carolyn**

Ecological Revolutions: Nature, Gender and Science
in New England. Reviewed by Linda Vance. *The
Women's Review of Books* 7, No. 4 (January
1990):14-15

**Merck, Mandy** (interview)

Lesbians Hit Prime Time. *Spare Rib* 213 (June
1990):39-42

**Meredith, Philip**

Sex Education: Political Issues in Britain and Europe.
Reviewed by Lesley Holly. *Gender and Education* 2,
No. 2 (1990):243-244

**Meriwether, Louise** (about). *See*
Writers – Interviews, "Graceful Passages"

**Mernissi, Fatima**

Doing Daily Battle: Interviews with Moroccan
Women. Reviewed by Susan Schaefer Davis. *Belles
Lettres* 5, No. 3 (Spring 1990):12

Unearthing the Present. *Ms.* 1, No. 3
(November/December 1990):74-75

**Merriam, Karen**

The Female Fear. Book Review. *AFFILIA* 5, No. 3
(Fall 1990):114-115

**Merrifield, Helen**

Little Fox. Poem. *Hecate* 16, Nos. 1-2 (1990):115-
116

**Merrit, Susan**

The Power of Support Groups. *Working Mother* 13,
No. 5 (May 1990):24-26

**Merritt, Myra** (about). *See* Musicians

**Merrow, John**

Schools for Tomorrow. *Working Mother* 13, No. 8
(August 1990):66-71

**Merton, Vikki**

Transformations. Poem. *Frontiers* 11, Nos. 2-3
(1990):98

**Mertus, Julie A.**

Fake Abortion Clinics: The Threat to Reproductive
Self-Determination. *Women and Health* 16, No. 1
(1990):95-113

**Mervyn, Leonard**

Women's Change of Life. Reviewed by Pat Hunter.
*Healthright* 9, No. 4 (August 1990):44

**Meryman, Richard**

Carol Burnett. *Lear's* (August 1990):60-63+

**Merzario, Raul**

Land, Kinship, and Consanguineous Marriage in
Italy from the Seventeenth to the Nineteenth

Centuries. *Journal of Family History* 15, No. 4 (October 1990):529-546

**Meschery, Joanne** (about)

A Woman for Lear's: One for the Books. Jane Howard. *Lear's* (June 1990):132-135

**Mescus, Janet** (about). *See* Dent, David

**Mesnier, Roland** (about)

Cook Like a Pro: Hail to the Chef. *Family Circle* 103, No. 14 (October 16, 1990):66-68

**Messer-Davidow, Ellen**

Changing the System: The Board of Trustees Caper. *Women's Studies Quarterly* 18, Nos. 3-4 (Fall-Winter 1990):136-146

**Messina, Andrea**

Good Show: How to Look Your Best When You Feel Your Worst. *Working Woman* (June 1990):68-73

Image: Legwork. *Working Woman* (August 1990):80-82

**Messina, Louise**

50 Cookie Jars. *Good Housekeeping* 211, No. 4 (October 1990):146-149+

**Messina, Maria**

A House in the Shadows. Reviewed by Helen Barolini. *Belles Lettres* 5, No. 3 (Spring 1990):7

**Messing, Karen** (joint author). *See* Tierney, Daniel

**Messing, Suzanne**

Feminist Philanthropy: Young, Vital and Growing. *New Directions for Women* 19, No. 4 (July-August 1990):11

Founding Mother Takes New Steps. *New Directions for Women* 19, No. 4 (July-August 1990):10

SisterSerpents Strike Abortion Foes. *New Directions for Women* 19, No. 1 (January/February 1990):11

**Messing, Suzanne** (joint author). *See* Sohoni, Nera Kuckreja

**Messinger, Lisa Mintz**

Georgia O'Keeffe. Reviewed by Barbara Buhler Lynes. *Belles Lettres* 5, No. 4 (Summer 1990):3-4

**Metaphysics**

A Spurious Set (Up): "Fetching Females" and "Seductive" Theories in *Phaedrus*, "Plato's Pharmacy," and *Spurs*. Katherine Cummings. *Genders* 8 (Summer 1990):38-61

**Metcalf, Wendy**

Short Story. *Spare Rib* No. 209 (February 1990):39

**Metropolitan Museum of Art.** *See* New York (City) – Metropolitan Museum of Art

**Metz, Gayle** (about)

The Get-Rich-Quick Trick. Andrea Kott. *Savvy Woman* (September 1990):23-24

**Metz, Kristen**

Passionate Differences: A Working Model for Cross-Cultural Communication. *Journal of Feminist Studies in Religion* 6, No. 1 (Spring 1990):131-151

**Metzger, Deena**

What Dinah Thought. Excerpt. Short story. *Lilith* 15, No. 2 (Spring 1990):8-12

What Dinah Thought. Reviewed by Melanie Kaye/Kantrowitz. *The Women's Review of Books* 7, Nos. 10-11 (July 1990):14

**Metzger, Mary Janell**

Double Gestures: Feminist Critiques and the Search for a Useable Practice. *Hypatia* 5, No. 3 (Fall 1990):118-124

Feminism and Foucault: Reflections on Resistance. Book Review. *Hypatia* 5, No. 3 (Fall 1990):118-124

Feminism as Critique: On the Politics of Gender. Book Review. *Hypatia* 5, No. 3 (Fall 1990):118-124

**Mewshaw, Elizabeth A.** (joint author). *See* Lambert, Vickie A.

**Mexico – Art**

Aztec Imagery in Frida Kahlo's Paintings: Indigenity and Political Commitment. Janice Helland. *Woman's Art Journal* 11, No. 2 (Fall 1990-Winter 1991):8-13

Mexico's Visual Culture. Roberta Smith. *Vogue* (October 1990):256+

**Mexico, Colonial**

To Love, Honor, and Obey in Colonial Mexico: Conflicts Over Marriage Choice, 1574-1821. By Patricia Seed. Reviewed by Carol Clark D'Lugo. *Women's Studies International Forum* 13, Nos. 1-2 (1990):161

**Mexico – Intercultural Documentation Center.** *See* Hollants, Bessie (about)

**Mexico – Photographs**

Village Mexico. Graciela Iturbide. *Ms.* 1, No. 1 (July/August 1990):48-53

**Mexico – Revolution of 1910**

Women School Teachers in the Mexican Revolution: The Story of Reyna's Braids. Mary Kay Vaughan. *Journal of Women's History* 2, No. 1 (Spring 1990):143-168

**Mexico – Status of Women**

Plotting Women: Gender and Representation in Mexico. By Jean Franco. Reviewed by Francesca Miller. *NWSA Journal* 2, No. 3 (Summer 1990):514-516

**Mexico – Travel**

Blame it on the Heat Wave. Sara Nelson. *Glamour* (July 1990):152-153+

**Mexico – Violence Against Women**

Women Force a Government Response. Elizabeth Shrader Cox. *Connexions* 34 (1990):4-5

**Mexico – Yucatán Peninsula**

Gods Country. Guy Garcia. *Harper's Bazaar* (September 1990):128-134

**Meyer, Beryl**

Makeup's New Look: Less Is More. *Working Woman* (April 1990):106-108

**Meyer, Carol** and Young, Alma (editors)

On the Bias. *AFFILIA* 5, No. 1 (Spring 1990):97-102

**Meyer, Carol H.**. *See also* Meyer, Carol and Young, Alma (editors), "On the Bias"

**Meyer, Cecilia** (joint author). *See* Kleinke, Chris L.

**Meyer, David**

His: Love and Thunderbolts. *Glamour* (August 1990):240

**Meyerowitz, Joanne J.**

Sexual Geography and Gender Economy: The Furnished Room Districts of Chicago, 1890-1930. *Gender & History* 2, No. 3 (Autumn 1990):274-296

Women Adrift: Independent Wage Earners in Chicago, 1880-1930. Reviewed by Elizabeth Faue. *Signs* 15, No. 2 (Winter 1990):391-394

**Meyers, Deborah** (joint author). *See* Paludi, Michele A.

**Meyers, Ruth S.** (editor)

Embers: Stories for a Changing World. Reviewed by Mitzi Myers. *NWSA Journal* 2, No. 2 (Spring 1990):273-281

**Mezey, Susan Gluck**

When Should Differences Make a Difference: A New Approach to the Constitutionality of Gender-Based Laws. *Women & Politics* 10, No. 2 (1990):105-119

**Mhaille, Roisin Ni**

A Noise from the Woodshed. Book Review. *Spare Rib* No. 214 (July 1990):23

**Mhloyi, Marvellous M.**

Perceptions on Communication and Sexuality in Marriage in Zimbabwe. *Women and Therapy* 10, No. 3 (1990):61-73

**Michals, Debra**

Traveling in Style. *Harper's Bazaar* (July 1990):14-16

**Michaud, Jacinthe**

Les Infirmières: de la vocation à la profession. Book Review. *Resources for Feminist Research* 19, No. 1 (March 1990):20

L'intolérance: une problemàtique généale. Book Review. *Resources for Feminist Research* 19, No. 1 (March 1990):21

**Michel, Louise** (about)

Sexual Politics in the Career and Legend of Louise Michel. Notes. Marie Marmo Mullaney. *Signs* 15, No. 2 (Winter 1990):300-322

**Michel, Sonya**

Arms and the Woman: War, Gender, and Literary Representation. Book Review. *The Women's Review of Books* 7, No. 6 (March 1990):26-27

Not So Innocent Bystanders. *The Women's Review of Books* 7, No. 6 (March 1990):26-27

**Michelangelo – Criticism and Interpretation**

The Heroine as Hero in Michelangelo's Art. Yael Even. *Woman's Art Journal* 11, No. 1 (Spring-Summer 1990):29-33

**Michie, Helena**

The Greatest Story (N)ever Told: The Spectacle of Recantation. *Genders* 9 (Fall 1990):19-34

**Micka, Jill C.** (joint author). *See* Papini, Dennis R.

**Mickens, Ronald**

Black Women in Science and Technology: A Selected Bibliography. *Sage* 6, No. 2 (Fall 1989):54

**Microwave Cookery**

Elegant First Courses. Donna Meadow. *McCall's* 118, No. 2 (November 1990):136

Flavor to Relish All Year Long. Donna Meadow. *McCall's* 117, No. 11 (August 1990):116

The Healthy Microwave Cookbook. Marie Simmons. *Ladies' Home Journal* 107, No. 10 (October 1990):203-208

Microwave Cookbook. *Good Housekeeping* 211, No. 3 (September 1990):257-258

The Microwave Cookbook. *Good Housekeeping* 211, No. 4 (October 1990):199-200

Microwave Safety. *Good Housekeeping* 211, No. 3 (September 1990):154 +

The Most-Common Cooking Mistakes. *Ladies' Home Journal* 107, No. 4 (April 1990):210-214

Summer Micro-Raves. *Ladies' Home Journal* 107, No. 7 (July 1990):128-132

Super Soups, Hot or Cold. *McCall's* 117, No. 7 (April 1990):123

**Midcalf, Sumica**

August 28. Poem. *off our backs* 20, No. 7 (July 1990):19

Untitled. Poem. *off our backs* 20, No. 7 (July 1990):19

**Midcareer Change.** *See* Career Change

**Middle Age.** *See also* Occupational Mobility – Middle Age; Sexuality – Middle Age

Finished at 40: Women's Development within the Patriarchy. Mary M. Gergen. *Psychology of Women Quarterly* 14, No. 4 (December 1990):471-493

Midlife Women's Political Consciousness: Case Studies of Psychosocial Development and Political Commitment. Abigail J. Stewart and Sharon Gold-

Steinberg. *Psychology of Women Quarterly* 14, No. 4 (December 1990):543-566

Women in Midlife and Beyond. Iris G. Fodor and Violet Franks. *Psychology of Women Quarterly* 14, No. 4 (December 1990):445-449

Women over Forty: Visions and Realities. By Jean Dresden Grambs. Reviewed by Rosalind C. Barnett. *Psychology of Women Quarterly* 14, No. 4 (December 1990):618-619

Women's Prime of Life: Is It the 50s? Valory Mitchell and Ravenna Helson. *Psychology of Women Quarterly* 14, No. 4 (December 1990):451-470

### Middle Age – Cross-Cultural Studies

Women Growing Stronger with Age: The Effect of Status in the United States and Kenya. Judith Todd, Ariella Friedman, and Priscilla Wanjiru Kariuki. *Psychology of Women Quarterly* 14, No. 4 (December 1990):567-577

### Middle Age – Health Issues

Lifelong Physical Activity in Midlife and Older Women. Alice J. Dan, JoEllen Wilbur, Cynthia Hedricks, Eileen O'Connor, and Karyn Holm. *Psychology of Women Quarterly* 14, No. 4 (December 1990):531-542

### Middle Age – Parenting

Adolescent Daughter/Midlife Mother Dyad. Valerie A. La Sorsa and Iris G. Fodor. *Psychology of Women Quarterly* 14, No. 4 (December 1990):593-606

### Middle-Aged Women – Childbirth

Brother-to-Be! At 24? Terry Nelson. *Essence* 20, No. 11 (March 1990):42

I Had a Baby After Breast Cancer. Linda Fine. *Family Circle* 103, No. 16 (November 27, 1990):94-98

Late Expectations. *Harper's Bazaar* (August 1990):38+

Postponing Motherhood. Margie Patlak. *Glamour* (March 1990):68-70

Vital Signs. *McCall's* 117, No. 10 (July 1990):22-24

### Middle-Aged Women – Health

A Causal Analysis of Employment and Health in Midlife Women. Pamela K. Adelmann, Toni C. Antonucci, Susan E. Crohan, and Lerita M. Coleman. *Women and Health* 16, No. 1 (1990):5-20

### Middle Ages – Sexuality

Law, Sex, and Christian Society in Medieval Europe. By James A. Brundage. Reviewed by Michael B. Schwarz. *Out/Look* No. 7 (Winter 1990):76-81

### Middle East – Bibliographies

*Journal of Women's History* 2, No. 2 (Fall 1990):202-208

### Middle Eastern Women – History

The Colonial Harem. By Malek Alloula. Reviewed by Wendy Kozol. *Gender & History* 2, No. 1 (Spring 1990):110-113

Images of Women: The Portrayal of Women in Photography of the Middle East, 1860-1950. By Sarah Graham-Brown. Reviewed by Írvin Cemil Schick. *Feminist Studies* 16, No. 2 (Summer 1990):345-380

Images of Women: The Portrayal of Women in Photography of the Middle East, 1860-1950. By Sarah Graham-Brown. Reviewed by Wendy Kozol. *Gender & History* 2, No. 1 (Spring 1990):110-113

### Middle Eastern Women – Political Power

Guaranteed Seats for Political Representation of Women: The Egyptian Example. Kathleen Howard-Merriam. *Women & Politics* 10, No. 1 (1990):17-42

### Middleton, David L.

Toni Morrison: An Annotated Bibliography. Reviewed by Danílle K. Taylor-Guthrie. *Sage* 6, No. 2 (Fall 1989):64-65

### Midler, Bette (about)

The Best Bette Yet. Cliff Jahr. *Ladies' Home Journal* 107, No. 1 (January 1990):92-93+

Bette's Best Diet Yet. Glenn Plaskin. *Family Circle* 103, No. 9 (June 26, 1990):33-34

Talking with Bette Midler: What Makes Bette Laugh? Interview. Alan W. Petrucelli. *Redbook* 175, No. 5 (September 1990):76-78

### Midlife Crisis

Male Angst . . . And Women Who Live Through It. Mary Kay Blakely. *Lear's* (August 1990):72-73+

### Midwifery. *See also* Houde-Quimby, Charlotte (about)

"I Was Afraid to Cut the Umbilical Cord." *Connexions* 32 (1990):8

Midwives: Talking about a Revolution. Helen Zia. *Ms.* 1, No. 3 (November/December 1990):91

Motherwit: An Alabama Midwife's Story. By Onnie Lee Logan. Reviewed by Shelley Crisp. *Belles Lettres* 5, No. 2 (Winter 1990):3

### Midwives – Training

Impact of Training on the Performance of Traditional Birth Attendants. S. K. Benara and S. K. Chaturvedi. *Journal of Family Welfare* 36, No. 4 (December 1990):32-35

### Mies, Maria

Indian Women and Patriarchy: Conflicts and Dilemmas of Students and Working Women. Reviewed by Kalpana Bardhan. *Journal of Women's History* 2, No. 1 (Spring 1990):200-219

Women's Studies: Science, Violence and Responsibility. *Women's Studies International Forum* 13, No. 5 (1990):433-441

**Mieses, Stanley**

Centennial Cheer. *Harper's Bazaar* (September 1990):208

**Migraine.** *See* Headaches

**Migration, Rural – India**

Developmental Migration: A Processual Analysis of Inter-State Rural-Rural Migration. By B. R. K. Rajw. Reviewed by Shekhar Mukerji. *Journal of Family Welfare* 36, No. 4 (December 1990):78-81

**Mihopoulos, Effie**

The Midwives. Poem. *Frontiers* 11, Nos. 2-3 (1990):17-20

**Mikell, Gwendolyn**

Kick of a Dying Horse. *Belles Lettres* 5, No. 3 (Spring 1990):13-14

Lives of Courage: Women of a New South Africa. Book Review. *Belles Lettres* 5, No. 3 (Spring 1990):13-14

Not Either an Experimental Doll. Book Review. *Belles Lettres* 5, No. 3 (Spring 1990):13-14

**Mikulski, Barbara** (about). *See* Leadership, "1990 Women of the Year"

**Milan – Fashion.** *See* Italy – Designers

**Milan – Interior Design**

Living. Charla Carter. *Vogue* (September 1990):501-507

**Milan – Shopping.** *See* Shopping

**Milan – Social History**

The Foundlings of Milan: Abandoned Children and Their Parents from the Seventeenth to the Nineteenth Centuries. By Volker Hunecke. Reviewed by Edith Saurer. *Gender & History* 2, No. 3 (Autumn 1990):356-358

**Milanes, Cecilia Rodriguez**

Breaking Boundaries: Latina Writing and Critical Reading. Book Review. *Sage* 6, No. 2 (Fall 1989):65-66

**Milano, Carol**

How to get Credit-Card Savvy. *Essence* 21, No. 2 (June 1990):32

**Mile, Siân**

Femme Foetal: The Construction/Destruction of Female Subjectivity in *Housekeeping*, or NOTHING GAINED. *Genders* 8 (Summer 1990):129-136

**Miles, Angela**

Reproducing the World: Essays in Feminist Theory. Book Review. *Atlantis* 15, No. 2 (Spring 1990):118-120

**Miles, Margaret**

Carnal Knowing: Female Nakedness and Religious Meaning in the Christian West. Reviewed by Jo Ann McNamara. *The Women's Review of Books* 8, No. 1 (October 1990):21-22

**Miles, Margaret R.** (joint editor). *See* Atkinson, Clarissa W.

**Miles, Martha** (joint author). *See* Adams, Gail

**Miles, Rosalind**

The Women's History of the World. Reviewed by Mary Beth Emmerichs. *Feminist Collections* 11, No. 2 (Winter 1990):3-4

**Military Combat**

Armed Combat: The Women's Movement Mobilizes Troops in Readiness for the Inevitable Constitutional Attack on the Combat Exclusion for Women in the Military. *Women's Rights Law Reporter* 12, No. 2 (Summer 1990): 89-101

Combat Ban Stops Women's Progress, Not Bullets. Lorraine Dusky. *McCall's* 117, No. 8 (May 1990):26-28

Combat Exclusion: Military Necessity or Another Name for Bigotry. Paul E. Roush. *Minerva* 8, No. 3 (Fall 1990):1-15

The Private Eye: Should Women Have the Right to Fight? Barbara Grizzuti Harrison. *Mademoiselle* (June 1990):114

Women at Arms: The Combat Controversy. Francine D'Amico. *Minerva* 8, No. 2 (Summer 1990):1-19

Women in Combat: A Quick Summary of the Arguments on Both Sides. M. C. Devilbiss. *Minerva* 8, No. 1 (Spring 1990):29-31

Women Pilots in Combat: Attitudes of Male and Female Pilots. Patricia M. Shields, Landon Curry, and Janet Nichols. *Minerva* 8, No. 2 (Summer 1990):21-35

Women Under Fire. Andrea Gross. *Ladies' Home Journal* 107, No. 12 (December 1990):93-97

**Military Leadership**

The Warrior Queens. By Antonia Fraser. Reviewed by Chitra Pershad Reddin. *Atlantis* 15, No. 2 (Spring 1990):102-103

**Military Service.** *See also* Military Combat; Prostitution – Military

Arms and the Enlisted Woman. By Judith Hicks Stiehm. Reviewed by Jennifer Ring. *Women's Studies International Forum* 13, No. 5 (1990):525-526

Arms and the Enlisted Woman. By Judith Hicks Stiehm. Reviewed by Mary Ann Tetreault. *Women & Politics* 10, No. 4 (1990):137-138

Arms and the Woman: War, Gender, and Literary Representation. Edited by Helen M. Cooper, Adrienne Auslander Munich, and Susan Merrill Squier. Reviewed by Sonya Michel. *The Women's Review of Books* 7, No. 6 (March 1990):26-27

The Army and the Microworld: Computers and the Politics and Gender Identity. Paul N. Edwards. *Signs* 16, No. 1 (Autumn 1990):102-127

Black, Female and in Uniform: An African-American Woman in the United States Army, 1973-1979. Brenda L. Moore. *Minerva* 8, No. 2 (Summer 1990):62-66

Combat Ban Stops Women's Progress, Not Bullets. Lorraine Dusky. *McCall's* 117, No. 8 (May 1990):26-28

Female Naval Reservists During World War II: A Historiographical Essay. Regina T. Akers. *Minerva* 8, No. 2 (Summer 1990):55-61

Gays Still Banned from Military. Tricia Lootens. *off our backs* 20, No. 4 (April 1990):11

The Military: More Than Just a Job? Edited by Charles C. Moskos and Frank R. Wood. Reviewed by Dorothy Schneider and Carl Schneider. *Minerva* 8, No. 4 (Winter 1990):44-48

Military Women and the Media. Laura Flanders. *New Directions for Women* 19, No. 6 (November-December 1990):1+

The New Women Warriors. *WLW Journal* 14, No. 1 (Fall 1990):13-14

The Organization Family: Work and Family Linkages in the U.S. Military. Edited by Gary L. Bowen and Dennis K. Orthner. Reviewed by Patricia Yancey Martin. *Journal of Marriage and the Family* 52, No. 2 (May 1990):565-566

Sexual Harassment in the Military. Nancy G. Wilds. *Minerva* 8, No. 4 (Winter 1990):1-16

The Spirit of Molly Marine. Erika S. Nau. *Minerva* 8, No. 4 (Winter 1990):23-29

Up Front. *Ladies' Home Journal* 107, No. 11 (November 1990):127-132

U.S. out of (fill in the blank). Carol Anne Douglas. *off our backs* 20, No. 3 (March 1990):23

U.S. Women See Combat in Panama. Kim Kleine. *off our backs* 20, No. 3 (March 1990):22-23

Weak Link: The Feminization of the American Military. By Brian Mitchell. Reviewed by Linda Grant De Pauw. *Minerva* 8, No. 1 (Spring 1990):88-89

Women and Their Wartime Roles. Mary Ann Attebury. *Minerva* 8, No. 1 (Spring 1990):11-28

Women and the Military System. Edited by Eva Isaksson. Reviewed by Ursula Barry. *Women's Studies International Forum* 13, No. 3 (1990):281

Women in the Military. David Dent. *Essence* 20, No. 12 (April 1990):41-46

Women Under Fire. Andrea Gross. *Ladies' Home Journal* 107, No. 12 (December 1990):93-97

## Military Service – Family Issues

The Effect of Group Support on Relocated Corporate and Military Wives: A Secondary Analysis. Kathryn R. Puskar, Gloria Wilson, and Lisa J. Moonis. *Minerva* 8, No. 2 (Summer 1990):36-46

Employment and Role Satisfaction: Implications for the General Well-Being of Military Wives. Leora N. Rosen, Jeannette R. Ickovics, and Linda Z. Moghadam. *Psychology of Women Quarterly* 14, No. 3 (September 1990):371-385

International Relocation: Women's Coping Methods. Kathryn R. Puskar. *Health Care for Women International* 11, No. 3 (1990):263-276

Women of the Regiment: Marriage and the Victorian Army. By Myna Trustram. Reviewed by Dorothy O. Helly. *Women's Studies International Forum* 13, No. 4 (1990):405-407

## Military Service – History

Amazons and Military Maids: Women Who Dressed as Men in Pursuit of Life, Liberty and Happiness. By Julie Wheelwright. Reviewed by C. Kay Larson. *Minerva* 8, No. 2 (Summer 1990):74-78

Amazons and Military Maids: Women Who Dressed as Men in the Pursuit of Life, Liberty and the Pursuit of Happiness. By Julie Wheelwright. Reviewed by Rita Victoria Gomez Dearmond. *Gender & History* 2, No. 2 (Summer 1990):229-232

The Cavalry Maid: The Memoirs of a Woman Soldier of 1812. By Nadezhda Durova. Reviewed by Rita Victoria Gomez Dearmond. *Gender & History* 2, No. 2 (Summer 1990):229-232

The Tradition of Female Transvestism in Early Modern Europe. Rudolf M. Dekker and Lotte C. Van de Pol. Reviewed by Rita Victoria Gomez Dearmond. *Gender & History* 2, No. 2 (Summer 1990):229-232

## Military Service – Homosexuality

Lesbian Soldiers Tell Their Stories. Johnnie Phelps and Miriam Ben-Shalom. *Minerva* 8, No. 3 (Fall 1990):38-53

## Military Service – Media Portrayal

Military Women in Film, TV, Media: Invisible, Sexually Stereotyped. *Media Report to Women* 18, No. 3 (May/June 1990):6-7

## Military Service – Personal Narratives

How It All Came Out: The Story of Florence Steinberg. Eleanor Stoddard. *Minerva* 8, No. 3 (Fall 1990):55-72

Life's High Spot. Amber Tullar. *Minerva* 8, No. 1 (Spring 1990):68-81

## Military Service – Sexism

Sexism and the War System. By Betty A. Reardon. Reviewed by M. C. Devilbiss. *Minerva* 8, No. 2 (Summer 1990):79-90

Sexism in the Military: Reality Echoed in Haldeman's *Forever War* and Herbert's *God Emperor of Dune*. Cynthia A. Wright. *Minerva* 8, No. 3 (Fall 1990):16-27

## Milken, Michael (about)

How I Became a Junk-Bond Airhead. Patricia O'Toole. *Lear's* (June 1990):35-37

**Millais, John Everett** (criticism)

*The Order of Release* and *Peace Concluded*: Millais's Reversal of a Victorian Formula. Elaine Shefer. *Woman's Art Journal* 11, No. 2 (Fall 1990-Winter 1991):30-33

**Millard, Thomas L.**

School-Based Social Work and Family Therapy. *Adolescence* 25, No. 98 (Summer 1990):401-408

**Miller, A. Therese**, Eggertson-Tacon, Colleen, and Quigg, Brian

Patterns of Runaway Behavior within a Larger Systems Context: The Road to Empowerment. *Adolescence* 25, No. 98 (Summer 1990):271-289

**Miller, Annetta**

The Big T(hrill) Personality: Why Some Like It Hot. *Working Woman* (February 1990):76-78

**Miller, Annetta** and Kruger, Pamela

The New Old Boy. *Working Woman* (April 1990):94-96

**Miller, Baila**

Gender Differences in Spouse Caregiver Strain: Socialization and Role Explanations. *Journal of Marriage and the Family* 52, No. 2 (May 1990):311-321

**Miller, Barbara** (joint author). *See* Miller, Robin L.

**Miller, Brent C.** and Moore, Kristin A.

Adolescent Sexual Behavior, Pregnancy, and Parenting: Research Through the 1980s. *Journal of Marriage and the Family* 52, No. 4 (November 1990):1025-1044

**Miller, C. R.**

Family, School and Society. Book Review. *Gender and Education* 2, No. 1 (1990):100-102

**Miller, Carol** (about)

Meet Carol Miller: Reader of the Year. Eleanor Berman. *Working Mother* 13, No. 5 (May 1990):18-22

**Miller, Constance** (about). *See* De Veaux, Alexis, Milloy, Marilyn, and Ross, Michael Erik

**Miller, Dorothy C.**

Women as Single Parents: Confronting Institutional Barriers in the Courts, the Workplace, and the Housing Market. Book Review. *AFFILIA* 5, No. 2 (Summer 1990):104-106

**Miller, Francesca**

Plotting Women: Gender and Representation in Mexico. Book Review. *NWSA Journal* 2, No. 3 (Summer 1990):514-516

**Miller, Harry**

Historical Society Women's Collections to Be Published. *Feminist Collections* 11, No. 2 (Winter 1990):13-14

**Miller, Henry** (about). *See also* Love-Letters

**Miller, Jane**

Teaching Women: Feminism and English Studies. Book Review. *Gender and Education* 2, No. 2 (1990):239-240

**Miller, Jay** (editor)

Coyote Stories. Reviewed by Alanna Brown. *The Women's Review of Books* 8, No. 2 (November 1990):19-20

Mourning Dove, A Salishan Autobiography. Reviewed by Alanna Brown. *The Women's Review of Books* 8, No. 2 (November 1990):19-20

**Miller, Joni**

Mind Over Manners. *Savvy Woman* (July/August 1990):36-38

**Miller, Judith**

One, by One, by One: Facing the Holocaust. Reviewed by Myrna Goldenberg. *Belles Lettres* 6, No. 1 (Fall 1990):6-9

**Miller, May**

Collected Poems of May Miller. Reviewed by Kimberly Wallace Sanders. *Sage* 6, No. 2 (Fall 1989):62-63

**Miller, Nancy K.**

Subject to Change: Reading Feminist Writing. Reviewed by Barbara Green. *Tulsa Studies in Women's Literature* 9, No. 1 (Spring 1990):135-139

**Miller, Nancy K.** (joint author). *See* Christian, Barbara

**Miller, Penelope Ann** (about)

Penelope Ann Miller – In Good Shape. Jane Garcia. *Mademoiselle* (October 1990):92-94

**Miller, Robert P.**, Cosgrove, Jean M., and Doke, Larry

Motivating Adolescents to Reduce Their Fines in a Token Economy. *Adolescence* 25, No. 97 (Spring 1990):97-104

**Miller, Robin, L.** and Miller, Barbara

Mothering the Biracial Child: Bridging the Gaps between African-American and White Parenting Styles. *Women and Therapy* 10, Nos. 1/2 (1990):169-179

**Miller, Sally M.**

The World of Our Mothers: The Lives of Jewish Immigrant Women. Book Review. *NWSA Journal* 2, No. 2 (Spring 1990):301-303

**Miller, Sue**

Family Pictures. Excerpt. Short story. *Ladies' Home Journal* 107, No. 6 (June 1990):62-68

Family Pictures. Reviewed by Francine Prose. *Savvy Woman* (July/August 1990):20

Family Pictures. Reviewed by Mara Eilenberg. *The Women's Review of Books* 7, Nos. 10-11 (July 1990):34

**Millett, Kate**

The Loony-Bin Trip. Reviewed by Ann Dermansky. *New Directions for Women* 19, No. 5 (September-October 1990):13

The Loony Bin Trip. Reviewed by Cricket Keating and Amy Hamilton. *off our backs* 20, No. 11 (December 1990):16

The Loony-Bin Trip. Reviewed by Karen Malpede. *The Women's Review of Books* 8, No. 1 (October 1990):7-8

**Millett, Kate (about)**

Millett Still a Gadfly. Ann Dermansky. *New Directions for Women* 19, No. 5 (September-October 1990):12-13

**Milligan, Lindsay**

Poll Tax Update. *Spare Rib* No. 212 (May 1990):16-18

**Million Adolescent Personality Inventory (MAPI)**

The Million Adolescent Personality Inventory Profiles of Depressed Adolescents. Marion F. Ehrenberg, David N. Cox, and Raymond F. Koopman. *Adolescence* 25, No. 98 (Summer 1990):415-424

**Millman, Val** (joint editor). *See* Burchell, Helen

**Milloy, Marilyn**

Sisters Helping Sisters. *Essence* 21, No. 6 (October 1990):83-84+

A Very Special Gift. *Essence* 21, No. 8 (December 1990):62-64+

**Milloy, Marilyn** (joint author). *See* De Veaux, Alexis

**Mills, David**

The Children I Almost Had. *Essence* 20, No. 10 (February 1990):36

**Mills, Donna** (about). *See* Dutka, Elaine

**Mills, Jon K.**

The Psychoanalytic Perspective of Adolescent Homosexuality: A Review. *Adolescence* 25, No. 100 (Winter 1990):913-922

**Mills, Nancy**

Talking with Susan Ruttan: "I'll Always Miss My Sister." Bibliography. *Redbook* 174, No. 5 (March 1990):30-34

**Mills, Sally** (about)

A Woman for Lear's: Overhaul. Jane Howard. *Lear's* (July 1990):120-123

**Mills, Stephanie** (about). *See* Musicians, Popular, "Repeat Performance"

**Mills, Victoria A.** (joint author). *See* Dickstein, Ruth

**Milner, Judith** and Blyth, Eric

Coping with Child Sexual Abuse: A Guide for Teachers. Reviewed by Liz Kelly. *Gender and Education* 2, No. 1 (1990):98-100

**Milojevic, Sanja**

Where Wives Are Never Battered . . . *Connexions* 34 (1990):6

**Milton, Edith**

Fantasies of Suburbia. *The Women's Review of Books* 8, No. 3 (December 1990):17-18

Seventh Heaven. Book Review. *The Women's Review of Books* 8, No. 3 (December 1990):17-18

**Milva** (about). *See also* Fashion, "Suprema Donnas"

**Milward, John** (joint author). *See* Heller, Karen

**Min, Katherine**

The Girl Who Loved Dylan. Short Story. *Iris* 24 (Fall-Winter 1990):46-48

**Mind/Body Split**

The Mind/Body Link. Stephen Phillip Policoff. *Ladies' Home Journal* 107, No. 10 (October 1990):126-130

**Minden, Jo-Ann**

The Nutrition Challenge for Women: A Guide to Wellness Without Dieting. Book Review. *Healthsharing* 11, No. 1 (December 1989):33-34

**Miner, Valerie**

Calling Homes: Working-Class Women's Writings. Book Review. *The Women's Review of Books* 7, No. 12 (September 1990):1-4

In a Class By Themselves. *The Women's Review of Books* 7, No. 12 (September 1990):1-4

Light Can Be Both Wave and Particle. Book Review. *The Women's Review of Books* 7, No. 7 (April 1990):17-18

Middle-Class Moods. *The Women's Review of Books* 7, No. 7 (April 1990):17-18

Ordinary Love and Good Will. Book Review. *The Women's Review of Books* 7, No. 7 (April 1990):17-18

**Miners**

Cheers for Mavis Williams. Elayne Clift. *New Directions for Women* 19, No. 3 (May/June 1990):3

**Minh-ha, Trinh T.** (about)

Woman, Native, Other: Pratibha Parmar Interviews Trinh T. Minh-ha. Pratibha Parmar. *Feminist Review* No. 36 (Autumn 1990):65-74

**Minh-ha, Trinh T.** (director)

Surname Viet Given Name Nam. Reviewed by Marina Heung. *New Directions for Women* 19, No. 1 (January/February 1990):11

**Miniature Electronic Equipment**

Telecommuting. Victoria Geibel. *Lear's* (December 1990):102-107

**Miniaturization.** *See* Miniature Electronic Equipment

**Mining Industry – Working Conditions**

Advocate Battles for Safety in Mines and Poultry Plants. Elayne Clift. *New Directions for Women* 19, No. 3 (May/June 1990):3

**Mink, Gwendolyn**

Good Intentions. *The Women's Review of Books* 7, No. 12 (September 1990):23-24

Settlement Folk: Social Thought and the American Settlement Movement, 1885-1930. Book Review. *The Women's Review of Books* 7, No. 12 (September 1990):23-24

**Minnelli, Liza** (about)

LIZA. James Servin. *Harper's Bazaar* (August 1990):130-133+

**Minnelli, Liza** and Mellen, Polly

Halston: 1932-1990. *Vogue* (July 1990):62-68

**Minnesota Multiphasic Personality Inventory (MMPI)**

The MMPI and Jesness Inventory as Measures of Effectiveness on an Inpatient Conduct Disorders Treatment Unit. Gregory Roberts, Kenneth Schmitz, John Pinto, and Stanley Cain. *Adolescence* 25, No. 100 (Winter 1990):989-996

MMPI Profiles of Adolescent Substance Abusers in Treatment. Steven Walfish, Renelle Massey, and Anton Krone. *Adolescence* 25, No. 99 (Fall 1990):567-572

**Minnich, E.,** O'Barr, J., and Rosenfeld, R. (editors)

Reconstructing the Academy: Women's Education and Women's Studies. Reviewed by Sara Delamont. *Gender and Education* 2, No. 2 (1990):245-246

**Minnich, Elizabeth Kamarck**

Reproducing the World: Essays in Feminist Theory. Book Review. *Signs* 16, No. 1 (Autumn 1990):177-180

Transforming Knowledge. Reviewed by Gerda Lerner. *The Women's Review of Books* 8, No. 1 (October 1990):10-11

**Minnick, Molly** (about). *See* Casey, Kathryn, "Voices of the Decade"

**Minor, Kit**

A Passion for Friends. Book Review. *Women and Therapy* 9, No. 4 (1990):120-122

**Minorities.** *See also* African-American Women; Hispanic Women; Women of Color

ANPA Issues 1990 Report on Women and Minority Employment at Newspapers. *Media Report to Women* 18, No. 4 (July-August 1990):3-4

Breaking the Barriers: Women and Minorities in the Sciences. Paul E. Gray and Shirley M. McBay. *On the Issues* 15 (Summer 1990):7-9+

**Minorities – Scholarships, Fellowships, etc.** *See also* Scholarships

Education: Financing Your College Dreams. Bibliography. *Essence* 20, No. 12 (April 1990):34

**Minorities in Television**

Can TV Switch Off Bigotry? Barbara Grizzuti Harrison. *Mademoiselle* (November 1990):110

**Minority Executives**

Free Advice. Edited by Patti Watts. *Executive Female* (March/April 1990):25-27

**Minow-Pinkney, Makiko**

Virginia Woolf and the Problem of the Subject: Feminine Writing in the Major Novels. Reviewed by Jennifer FitzGerald. *Women's Studies International Forum* 13, No. 6 (1990):612-613

**Minsky, Rosalind**

'The Trouble Is It's Ahistorical: The Problem of the Unconscious in Modern Feminist Theory. *Feminist Review* No. 36 (Autumn 1990):4-14

**Minstrel Show.** *See* Burlesque

**Mirabella, Mary Anne Bella**

Connections. *Sinister Wisdom* 41 (Summer-Fall 1990):94-100

**Mirkin, Gabe** (joint author). *See* Shangold, Mona

**Mirosevich, Toni**

Do Muscles Have Memories? *Trivia* 16/17 (Fall 1990):131-136

**Mirowsky, John** (joint author). *See* Ross, Catherine E.

**Miscarriage.** *See* Pregnancy, Incomplete

**Misers**

Cheap Men. Brook Hersey. *Glamour* (October 1990):300

**Miskimins, R. W.**

A Theoretical Model for the Practice of Residential Treatment. *Adolescence* 25, No. 100 (Winter 1990):867-890

**Misogyny**

The Blackman's Guide to Understanding the Blackwoman. By Shahrazad Ali. Reviewed by Iyanla Vanzant. *Essence* 21, No. 5 (September 1990):55

**Mispelkamp, Peter K. H.**

The WRNS: A History of the Women's Royal Naval Service. Book Review. *Minerva* 8, No. 1 (Spring 1990):86-87

**Miss America, 1990**

Head Turner. Joy Duckett Cain. *Essence* 20, No. 9 (January 1990):54-55

**Misselwitz, Helke** (interview)

Looking for Spring. Karen Rosenberg. *The Women's Review of Books* 7, Nos. 10-11 (July 1990):6-7

## Missing Children

"Have You Seen My Son?" Patricia Wetterling. *Ladies' Home Journal* 107, No. 3 (March 1990):22-32

## Missionaries

African-American Women Missionaries and European Imperialism in Southern Africa, 1880-1920. Sylvia M. Jacobs. *Women's Studies International Forum* 13, No. 4 (1990):381-394

American Women's Open Door to Chinese Women: Which Way Does It Open? Marjorie King. *Women's Studies International Forum* 13, No. 4 (1990):369-379

Paths of Duty: American Missionary Women in Nineteenth-Century Hawaii. By Patricia Grimshaw. Reviewed by Hoda Zaki. *The Women's Review of Books* 7, No. 9 (June 1990):19-20

"Single Ladies on the Congo": Protestant Missionary Tensions and Voices. Nancy Rose Hunt. *Women's Studies International Forum* 13, No. 4 (1990):395-403

## Missionaries, Medical

Opportunities for Women: The Development of Professional Women's Medicine in Canton, China, 1879-1901. Sara W. Tucker. *Women's Studies International Forum* 13, No. 4 (1990):357-368

## Mission Home Movement

Relations of Rescue: The Search for Female Authority in the American West, 1874-1939. By Peggy Pascoe. Reviewed by Lillian Schlissel. *The Women's Review of Books* 7, No. 12 (September 1990):18

Mitchal, Saundra (about). *See* Davis, Andrea R., "Power Players"

## Mitchell, Andrea

Chase Accused of Harassment, and Racism. *New Directions for Women* 19, No. 1 (January/February 1990):metro4

## Mitchell, Brian

Weak Link: The Feminization of the American Military. Reviewed by Linda Grant De Pauw. *Minerva* 8, No. 1 (Spring 1990):88-89

## Mitchell, Celeste

In the Driver's Seat: Families Pick the Winners. *Family Circle* 103, No. 15 (November 6, 1990):156

## Mitchell, Christina E.

Development or Restoration of Trust in Interpersonal Relationships during Adolescence and Beyond. *Adolescence* 25, No. 100 (Winter 1990):847-854

## Mitchell, Clarence, Jr. (about)

Lion in the Lobby: Clarence Mitchell, Jr.'s Struggle for the Passage of Civil Rights Laws. By Denton Watson. Reviewed by Paula Giddings. *Essence* 21, No. 7 (November 1990):50

## Mitchell, Felicia

Including Women at Emory & Henry College: Evolution of an Inclusive Language Policy. *Women's Studies Quarterly* 18, Nos. 1-2 (Spring-Summer 1990):222-230

**Mitchell, Jim**, Dodder, Richard A., and Norris, Terry D.

Neutralization and Delinquency: A Comparison by Sex and Ethnicity. *Adolescence* 25, No. 98 (Summer 1990):487-497

**Mitchell, Valory** and Helson, Ravenna

Women's Prime of Life: Is It the 50s? *Psychology of Women Quarterly* 14, No. 4 (December 1990):451-470

**Mitchell-Kernan, Claudia** (joint author). *See* Tucker, M. Belinda

**Mitchinson, Wendy** (joint author). *See* Prentice, Alison

## Mithers, Carol Lynn

Just One Peek. *Glamour* (January 1990):160

Love Him, Love His Family? *Glamour* (July 1990):194

Loving a Man Who Is "Different." *Glamour* (March 1990):296

Sexual Ethics. *Glamour* (June 1990):274

Sexual Ethics: What You Owe a Man You Don't Love. *Glamour* (April 1990):316

Talking with Sylvester Stallone: "My Sons are My Life." Interview. *Redbook* 176, No. 2 (December 1990):32-34

Teri Garr Gets Serious (Sort of). Interview. *Redbook* 175, No. 4 (August 1990):66-68

When Friends Give Advice on Love. *Glamour* (February 1990):216

**Mitsubishi Motor Company.** *See also* Automobiles—Purchasing

**Miyake, Issey** (about). *See* Fashion Designers

**Miyamoto, Kimio** (joint author). *See* Kawai, Makoto J.

**Miyamoto, Mari** (joint author). *See* Kawai, Makoto J.

**Mizrahi, Isaac** (about). *See* Fashion Designers, "Gentlemen's Choice"; Fashion Designers, "Predictions"; Talley, André Leon

The Kings of Color: Mizrahi. André Leon Talley. *Vogue* (September 1990):532-535

## Mizzell, Ellen

British Publishing. *Belles Lettres* 6, No. 1 (Fall 1990):62

**MMPI.** *See* Minnesota Multiphasic Personality Inventory (MMPI)

**Mnookin, Robert H.** (joint author). *See* Maccoby, Eleanor E.

**Moar, Natasha**

An Angel at My Table. Film Review. *Spare Rib* 218 (November 1990):19

Between Friends. add. *Spare Rib* No. 216 (September 1990):25

Family News. Book Review. *Spare Rib* No. 215 (August 1990):29

Matilda's Mistake. Book Review. *Spare Rib* 217 (October 1990):33

Primavera. Book Review. *Spare Rib* 213 (June 1990):28

Revenge. Book Review. *Spare Rib* 219 (December 1990-January 1991):41

**Modahl, Charlotte**

The Love Hormone. *Mademoiselle* (November 1990):112

**Modell, John**

Into One's Own: From Youth to Adulthood in the United States, 1920-1975. Reviewed by Jeylan T. Mortimer. *Journal of Marriage and the Family* 52, No. 2 (May 1990):561-562

**Models, Fashion.** *See* Fashion Models

**Models – Interior Design**

Model Homes. *Harper's Bazaar* (November 1990):158-163+

**Modernism (Art)**

Art: Modernism. Herbert Muschamp. *Vogue* (January 1990):118-120

**Modjeska, Drusilla** (editor)

Inner Cities: Australian Women's Memory of Place. Reviewed by Susan Sheridan. *Australian Feminist Studies* No. 11 (Autumn 1990):133-135

**Modleski, Tania**

The Incredible Shrinking He(r)man: Male Regression, the Male Body, and Film. *Differences* 2, No. 2 (Summer 1990):55-75

The Women Who Knew Too Much: Hitchcock and Feminist Theory. Reviewed by Paula Rabinowitz. *Feminist Studies* 16, No. 1 (Spring 1990):151-169

The Women Who Knew Too Much: Hitchcock and Feminist Theory. Reviewed by Sumiko Higashi. *Gender & History* 2, No. 1 (Spring 1990):123-126

**Moed, Lillian** and Moore, Tracy

Ahead of Her Time. *The Women's Review of Books* 8, No. 3 (December 1990):30

Exile in the Promised Land: A Memoir. Book Review. *The Women's Review of Books* 8, No. 3 (December 1990):30

**Moehringer, J. R.**

No More the Pause that Perplexes. *McCall's* 117, No. 11 (August 1990):64

Saving the Earth: New York to Chicago on a Glass of Salt Water. *McCall's* 117, No. 7 (April 1990):32

**Moen, Phyllis**

Working Parents: Transformation in Gender Roles and Public Policies in Sweden. Reviewed by Marika Lindholm. *Journal of Marriage and the Family* 52, No. 2 (May 1990):564-565

**Moen, Phyllis,** Downey, Geraldine, and Bolger, Niall

Labor-Force Reentry Among U.S. Homemakers in Midlife: A Life-Course Analysis. *Gender and Society* 4, No. 2 (June 1990):230-243

**Moffett, Charnett** (about)

Charnett Moffett: Bass Hit. Yannick Rice Lamb. *Essence* 21, No. 5 (September 1990):48

**Moggach, Deborah**

Stolen. Reviewed by Rukhsana Ahmad. *Spare Rib* No. 209 (February 1990):34

**Moghadam, Linda Z.** (joint author). *See* Rosen, Leora N.

**Mohammad, Farah** (about)

Victim of Family Conspiracy: The Abduction of Farah. *Manushi* 56 (January-February 1990):11-13

**Mohan, Dinesh**

The Hazardous Working Conditions of Rural Women. *Manushi* No. 59 (July-August 1990):25-28

Scientists and War and Peace. *Manushi* 58 (May-June 1990):11-13

**Mohan, Philip J.**

The Effect of Maternal Employment on Mormon and Non-Mormon Adolescents. *Adolescence* 25, No. 100 (Winter 1990):831-837

**Mohanty, Chandra T.** and Mohanty, Satya P.

Contradictions of Colonialism. *The Women's Review of Books* 7, No. 6 (March 1990):19-21

Recasting Women: Essays in Colonial History. Book Review. *The Women's Review of Books* 7, No. 6 (March 1990):19-21

**Mohanty, Satya P.** (joint author). *See* Mohanty, Chandra T.

**Mohler, Mary**

10 Reasons to Give a Kid a Hug. *Ladies' Home Journal* 107, No. 6 (June 1990):88-89

**Mohler, Mary** and Rosen, Margery D.

Parents' Journal: 10 Great Gifts for Under $10! Bibliography. *Ladies' Home Journal* 107, No. 12 (December 1990):60-64

Parents' Journal. *Ladies' Home Journal* 107, No. 2 (February 1990):52; 107, No. 4 (April 1990):82-87; 107, No. 5 (May 1990):138-144; 107, No. 7 (July

1990):78-80; 107, No. 8 (August 1990):70; 107, No. 9 (September 1990):86

Parents' Journal: Peace at Last! *Ladies' Home Journal* 107, No. 11 (November 1990):138

**Moldenhauer, Judith A.**

Architecture: A Place for Women. Book Review. *The Women's Review of Books* 7, No. 6 (March 1990):29-30

Women's Ways of Building. *The Women's Review of Books* 7, No. 6 (March 1990):29-30

**Moldeven, Meyer**

Standing Room Only: A Too-Faraway Grandpa Visits. *Lilith* 15, No. 1 (Winter 1990):4-5

**Moline, Julie**

Scot Free. *Harper's Bazaar* (June 1990):64+

Shapes of Things to Come. *Harper's Bazaar* (February 1990):96

Travel Bazaar: Scene Stealers. *Harper's Bazaar* (December 1990):90-96+

**Molnar, Alex** and Lindquist, Barbara

Changing Problem Behavior in Schools. Book Review. *Adolescence* 25, No. 100 (Winter 1990):998

**Mommy Track**

Who Is Felice Schwartz and Why Is She Saying those Terrible Things about Us? Ellen Hopkins. *Working Woman* (October 1990):116-120+

**Momsen, Janet H.** and Townsend, Janet (editors)

Geography of Gender in the Third World. Reviewed by Fiona Mackenzie. *Resources for Feminist Research* 19, No. 1 (March 1990):18

**Monaghan, Patricia**

Salve Regina: Salvaging the Queen. *Woman of Power* 15 (Fall-Winter 1990):46

"She Want It All": The Sun Goddess in Contemporary Women's Poetry. *Frontiers* 11, Nos. 2-3 (1990):21-25

**Monagle, Katie**

On the Legislative Front. *Ms.* 1, No. 2 (September/October 1990):45

South Africa: Enough Is Enough. *Ms.* 1, No. 2 (September/October 1990):11

**Mondor, Françoise**

Le logement: Point d'ancrage pour un nouveau départ. *Canadian Women's Studies* 11, No. 2 (Fall 1990):46-47

**Monet, Claude** (about). *See* Impressionism (Art)

**Money.** *See also* Credit; Loans; Saving and Investment

The Money Quiz. Daniel Sher. *Working Woman* (January 1990):114

Shopping Smart. Joan Hamburg. *Family Circle* 103, No. 3 (February 20, 1990):111+

**Money Laundering**

The Ring Around the U.S. Dollar. Patricia O'Toole. *Lear's* (May 1990):29-30

**Money Management.** *See* Finance, Personal

**Monk, Janice** (joint author). *See* Betteridge, Anne; Ide, Bette A.

**Monks, Vicki**

Health: New Cancer Treatments. *Vogue* (August 1990):236-240

**Monogamy.** *See* Infidelity

**Monoson, S. Sara**

The Lady and the Tiger: Women's Electoral Activism in New York City Before Suffrage. *Journal of Women's History* 2, No. 2 (Fall 1990):100-135

**Monroe, Marilyn** (about)

Marilyn Monroe: The Lost Photographs. Bob La Brasca. *Redbook* 175, No. 6 (October 1990):118-121

**Monstrous Regiment** (about)

Monstrous Regiment: 15 Years. By Betty Caplan. *Spare Rib* No. 210 (March 1990):37

**Montana, Claude** (about). *See* Talley, André Leon

**Montand, Yves** (about). *See* Sexual Attraction, "200 Words"

**Monteflores, Carmen de**

Singing Softly/Cantando Bajito. Reviewed by Electa Arenal and Martha T. Zingo. *New Directions for Women* 19, No. 3 (May/June 1990):24

**Montemayor, Raymond**, Adams, Gerald R., and Gullotta, Thomas P. (editors)

From Childhood to Adolescence: A Transitional Period? Book Review. *Adolescence* 25, No. 99 (Fall 1990):754

**Montessori**

Montessori's Warm Way with Babies. Marilyn Gardner. *Working Mother* (November 1990):80-83

**Mood (Psychology)**

Smile! The Mood Makeover. *Mademoiselle* (December 1990):172-175

**Moog, Carol**

Are They Selling Her Lips: Advertising and Identity. Reviewed by Noreen Ash Mackay. *On the Issues* 17 (Winter 1990):

**Moonis, Lisa J.** (joint author). *See* Puskar, Kathryn R.

**Moonlighting**

Make Money Moonlighting. Lloyd Gite. *Essence* 21, No. 3 (July 1990):28-30

Should You Moonlight? Lloyd Gite. *Glamour* (May 1990):144

**Moore, Brenda L.**

Black, Female and in Uniform: An African-American Woman in the United States Army, 1973-1979. *Minerva* 8, No. 2 (Summer 1990):62-66

**Moore, Dudley** (about)

A Perfect 10. Betty Goodwin. *Harper's Bazaar* (May 1990):158

**Moore, Helen B.** (joint author). *See* Kahn, Arnold S.

**Moore, Henrietta L**

Feminism and Anthropology. Reviewed by Gillian Cowlishaw. *Australian Feminist Studies* No. 11 (Autumn 1990):121-122

**Moore, J. William,** Jensen, Brian, and Hauck, William E.

Decision-Making Processes of Youth. *Adolescence* 25, No. 99 (Fall 1990):583-592

**Moore, Kristin A.** (joint author). *See* Miller, Brent C.

**Moore, Lisa L**

Sexuality, Subjectivity, and Reading: Constructing the Heterosexual Heroine in the Late Eighteenth-Century Novel. *NWSA Journal* 2, No. 4 (Autumn 1990):693-695

**Moore, Lorrie**

Giving in to the Good Life. *Savvy Woman* (September 1990):50-51+

**Moore, Marianne – Criticism and Interpretation**

Hints and Disguises: Marianne Moore and Her Contemporaries. By Celeste Goodridge. Reviewed by Loralee MacPike. *NWSA Journal* 2, No. 4 (Autumn 1990):669-674

**Moore, Mary** (about)

She Never Lets Them See Her Sweat. Joanne Kaufman. *Working Woman* (March 1990):80-82

**Moore, Michael**

Roger and Me. Reviewed by Esther Bailey. *Spare Rib* No. 212 (May 1990):28

**Moore, Rachelle** (joint author). *See* Cypess, Sandra Messinger

**Moore, Rosemary**

The Enigma of Woman: Barbara Baynton's *Human Toll. Australian Feminist Studies* No. 12 (Summer 1990):83-93

**Moore, Ruth**

Rich in Spirit. Short story. *Redbook* 176, No. 2 (December 1990):62-72

**Moore, Sylvia**

New Images of the Nude. *New Directions for Women* 19, No. 6 (November-December 1990):24

The Nude: A New Perspective. Book Review. *New Directions for Women* 19, No. 6 (November-December 1990):24

**Moore, Tracy** (joint author). *See* Moed, Lillian

**Moose.** *See* Animal Behavior

**Moose, Ruth**

Dreaming in Color. Reviewed by Janet Zandy. *Belles Lettres* 6, No. 1 (Fall 1990):58

The Wreath Ribbon Quilt. Reviewed by Janet Zandy. *Belles Lettres* 6, No. 1 (Fall 1990):58

**Mor, Barbara**

Amazing Rage. *Ms.* 1, No. 1 (July/August 1990):34-35

The Morrigan. *Woman of Power* 15 (Fall-Winter 1990):60-61

From My Forehead. Poem. *Woman of Power* 18 (Fall 1990):15

**Moraga, Cherríe**

La Ofrenda. Short story. *Out/Look* No. 10 (Fall 1990):50-53

**Moraga, Cherríe** (joint editor). *See* Alarcón, Norma

**Morales, Aurora Levins**

Silent Dancing: A Partial Remembrance of a Puerto Rican Childhood. Book Review. *The Women's Review of Books* 8, No. 3 (December 1990):9-10

Under the Mango Tree. *The Women's Review of Books* 8, No. 3 (December 1990):9-10

**Morality.** *See also* Ethics

Can You Cheat and Still Be Faithful? Susan Jacoby. *Glamour* (June 1990):224-225+

Viewpoint: We *Are* Good – Deep Down. Liv Ullmann. *Glamour* (January 1990):70

**Moran, Elaine**

A Walk Through Women's History. *Iris* 23 (Spring-Summer 1990):35

**Moran, Mary C.** (about)

Women Watch: Votes of Confidence for Two First-Time Mayors. Patti Watts. *Executive Female* (March/April 1990):6-7

**Moran, Mary Hurley**

Penelope Lively's *Moon Tiger*: A Feminist "History of the World." *Frontiers* 11, Nos. 2-3 (1990):89-95

**Moran, Mary** (joint author). *See* Morgen, Sandra

**Morano, Elizabeth**

Sonia Delaunay: Art into Fashion. Reviewed by Sherry Buckberrough. *Woman's Art Journal* 11, No. 1 (Spring-Summer 1990):39-41

**Morell, Marie A.** and Apple, Robin F.

Affect Expression, Marital Satisfaction, and Stress Reactivity among Premenopausal Women during a Conflictual Marital Discussion. *Psychology of Women Quarterly* 14, No. 3 (September 1990):387-402

**Morey, Ann-Janine**

The Reverend Idol and Other Parsonage Secrets: Women Write Romances about Ministers, 1880-1950. *Journal of Feminist Studies in Religion* 6, No. 1 (Spring 1990):87-103

**Morgan, Barbara A.** (joint author). *See* Feiner, Susan F.

**Morgan, David**

Masculinity, Autobiography and History. *Gender & History* 2, No. 1 (Spring 1990):34-39

**Morgan, Elizabeth** (about)

Women Right Now. *Glamour* (March 1990):95-100

**Morgan, Joan**

Back Talk: The Struggle Is Ours. *Essence* 21, No. 1 (May 1990):216

The Family Trap. *Essence* 21, No. 5 (September 1990):81-82

Interiors: The Other Woman. *Essence* 21, No. 7 (November 1990):34+

Lorna Simpson: Words of Art. *Essence* 21, No. 8 (December 1990):36

**Morgan, Julia** (about)

Julia Morgan, Architect. By Sarah Holmes Boutelle. Reviewed by Pamela H. Simpson. *Woman's Art Journal* 11, No. 2 (Fall 1990-Winter 1991):44-48

**Morgan, Leslie A.** (joint author). *See* Kitson, Gay C.

**Morgan, Melizma**

The Secret Keeper. Short Story. *Sinister Wisdom* 42 (Winter 1990-1991):10-21

**Morgan, Robin**

Can the Women's Movement Reach You? *Ms.* 1, No. 3 (November/December 1990):92

Chai Ling Talks with Robin Morgan. *Ms.* 1, No. 2 (September/October 1990):12-16

The Found Season. Poem. *The Women's Review of Books* 7, No. 4 (January 1990):16

The Heart Balloon. Poem. *Woman of Power* 16 (Spring 1990):5

Upstairs in the Garden: Poems Selected and New (1968-1988). Reviewed by Meryl Altman. *The Women's Review of Books* 8, No. 1 (October 1990):16-18

**Morgan, S. Philip** (joint author). *See* Furstenberg, Frank F.; Rindfuss, Ronald R.; Teachman, Jay

**Morgan, Sally**

My Place. Reviewed by Susanna Sloat. *Belles Lettres* 5, No. 2 (Winter 1990):7

**Morgen, Sandra**

Caring by the Hour: Women, Work, and Organizing at Duke Medical Center. Book Review. *Feminist Studies* 16, No. 1 (Spring 1990):53-67

Women's Work and Chicano Families: Cannery Workers of the Santa Clara Valley. Book Review. *Feminist Studies* 16, No. 1 (Spring 1990):53-67

From Working Daughters to Working Mothers: Immigrant Women in a New England Industrial Community. Book Review. *Feminist Studies* 16, No. 1 (Spring 1990):53-67

**Morgen, Sandra** and Moran, Mary

Transforming Introductory Anthropology: The American Anthropological Association Project on Gender and the Curriculum. *Women's Studies Quarterly* 18, Nos. 1-2 (Spring-Summer 1990):95-103

**Morgen, Sandra** (joint editor). *See* Bookman, Ann

**Morice, Laura**

Inside Hot! *Mademoiselle* (January 1990):40

Move Over, Rambo: There's a New Sly in Town. *Mademoiselle* (February 1990):176-177+

**Morici, Joanne** (joint author). *See* Holt, Gary

**Morisot, Berthe** (about)

Berthe Morisot. By Anne Higonnet. Reviewed by Felicia Kornbluh. *The Women's Review of Books* 8, No. 2 (November 1990):13-14

**Moritz, Marguerite J.**

Waiting for Prime Time: The Women of Television News. Book Review. *Frontiers* 11, Nos. 2-3 (1990):124

**Mormon Church – Marriage Customs**

An American Harem. Kathryn Casey. *Ladies' Home Journal* 107, No. 2 (February 1990):116-117 +

**Mormon Church – Women's Roles**

The Mormon-Suffrage Relationship: Personal and Political Quandaries. Joan Iversen. *Frontiers* 11, Nos. 2-3 (1990):8-16

**Mormons – Family Relations**

The Effect of Maternal Employment on Mormon and Non-Mormon Adolescents. Philip J. Mohan. *Adolescence* 25, No. 100 (Winter 1990):831-837

**Morocco – Status of Women**

Doing Daily Battle: Interviews with Moroccan Women. By Fatima Mernissi. Reviewed by Susan Schaefer Davis. *Belles Lettres* 5, No. 3 (Spring 1990):12

**Morocco – Travel.** *See also* Tangier (Morocco) – Description and Travel

**Morokoff, Patricia J.**

Surviving Sexual Violence. Book Review. *Psychology of Women Quarterly* 14, No. 2 (June 1990):290-292

**Morolo, Winnie**

Thula Sana Lwaml. Poem. *Spare Rib* No. 215 (August 1990):19

**Morrigan** (Goddess)

Amazing Rage. Barbara Mor. *Ms.* 1, No. 1 (July/August 1990):34-35

**Morris, Bonnie**

Anti-Semitism in the Women's Movement: A Jewish Lesbian Speaks. *off our backs* 20, No. 11 (December 1990):12-13

How I (Almost) Met Martina Navratilova. *Hot Wire* 6, No. 3 (September 1990):22

**Morris, Larry** (joint author). *See* Bolton, Frank

**Morris, Mark** (about)

Vogue Arts: Dance. David Daniel. *Vogue* (November 1990):284+

**Morris, Mary**

The Waiting Room. Reviewed by Faye Moskowitz. *Belles Lettres* 5, No. 2 (Winter 1990):10-11

The Wall. Short story. *Vogue* (September 1990):580-583+

**Morris, Mary** (interview)

Belles Lettres Interview: Mary Morris. Suzanne Scott and Lynne M. Constantine. *Belles Lettres* 5, No. 2 (Winter 1990):11

**Morris, Michele**

Finding the Guts to Go. Interview. *Working Woman* (May 1990):86+

The New Breed of Leaders: Taking Charge in a Different Way. *Working Woman* (March 1990):73-75

**Morris, Michelle**

Bernard Shaw: Anchoring the World. *Essence* 21, No. 7 (November 1990):42

**Morris, Robert Lee** (about)

World Apart. Gini Sikes. *Harper's Bazaar* (October 1990):234+

**Morris, Sawnie E.**

All Our Relations. *Out/Look* No. 8 (Spring 1990):46-51

**Morrison, Maggie**

Give Yourself a Skincare Makeover. *Redbook* 175, No. 5 (September 1990):170-173

Prenatal Testing: Peering into the Womb. *McCall's* 118, No. 1 (October 1990):160-162

Women Get Less Sleep Than Men. *McCall's* 117, No. 11 (August 1990):44-49

**Morrison, Mark**

Kristy McNichol Finds a Full Life on Empty Nest. *Ladies' Home Journal* 107, No. 3 (March 1990):100

**Morrison, Toni**

The Way Down. Poem. *Ms.* 1, No. 1 (July/August 1990):29

**Morrison, Toni – Criticism and Interpretation**

Critical Essays on Toni Morrison. By Nellie Y. McKay. Reviewed by Claudia Tate. *Tulsa Studies in Women's Literature* 9, No. 2 (Fall 1990):317-321

"I Made the Ink": (Literary) Production and Reproduction in *Dessa Rose* and *Beloved*. Anne E. Goldman. *Feminist Studies* 16, No. 2 (Summer 1990):313-330

A Thematic Approach to Teaching *The Bluest Eye*. Margaret G. Lloyd. *Sage* 6, No. 1 (Summer 1989):59-62

**Morrison, Toni** (about). *See* De Veaux, Alexis, Milloy, Marilyn, and Ross, Michael Erik

Toni Morrison: An Annotated Bibliography. By David L. Middleton. Reviewed by Danille K. Taylor-Guthrie. *Sage* 6, No. 2 (Fall 1989):64-65

**Morrisonville (Louisiana) – Dow Chemical Company**

Silk Purse Chronicles: Making an End Run around Armageddon. Patricia O'Toole. *Lear's* (August 1990):21-23

**Morrone, Wenda Wardell** (joint author). *See* Muscari, Ann

**Morse, Janice M.**

"Euch, Those Are for Your Husband!": Examination of Cultural Values and Assumptions Associated with Breast-Feeding. *Health Care for Women International* 11, No. 2 (1990):223-232

**Mort, Frank**

Dangerous Sexualities: Medico-Moral Politics in England Since 1830. Reviewed by Chris Waters. *Gender & History* 2, No. 2 (Summer 1990):218-222

**Mortality Statistics**

Breaking the Age Barrier: The Lifestyle Connection. *Family Circle* 103, No. 14 (October 16, 1990):115-117

The Impact of Infant Mortality on Fertility Behaviour of Women. S. B. Singh Parmar. *Journal of Family Welfare* 36, No. 1 (March 1990):43-47

Trends in Reporting of Maternal Drug Abuse and Infant Mortality among Drug-Exposed Infants in New York City. Leo Habel, Katherine Kaye, and Jean Lee. *Women and Health* 16, No. 2 (1990):41-58

**Mortgages**

The Check's in the Mail – Or Is It? Ellen Schultz. *Savvy Woman* (January 1990):26-27

**Mortimer, Jeylan T.**

Into One's Own: From Youth to Adulthood in the United States, 1920-1975. Book Review. *Journal of Marriage and the Family* 52, No. 2 (May 1990):561-562

**Morton, Andrew**

Diana's Diary. *Good Housekeeping* 211, No. 1 (July 1990):112-114, 158-162

A Royal Christmas. *Good Housekeeping* 211, No. 6 (December 1990):140+

**Morton, Joe** (about)

Joe Morton: Serving Justice. Deborah Gregory. *Essence* 21, No. 4 (August 1990):45

**Morton, Sandra** (joint author). *See* Wylie, Alison

**Mosbacher, Georgette** (about). *See* Cosmetics Industry, "The Beauty Queens"

**Moscow– Grocery Trade**

Inside Moscow's Grocery Stores. Vivian Cadden. *McCall's* 117, No. 10 (July 1990):78-82

**Moscow–** *Theme* "Newspaper

On the Theme: Talking with the Editor of the Soviet Union's First Gay and Lesbian Newspaper. Interview. Julie Dorf. *Out/Look* No. 9 (Summer 1990):55-59

**Moser, Caroline O. N.** and Peake, Linda (editors)

Women, Human Settlements and Housing. Reviewed by Pamela Sayne. *Resources for Feminist Research* 19, No. 1 (March 1990):42-43

**Moses, Rebecca** (about). *See* Fashion Designers, "Battle-Weary Designers"; Fashion Designers, "What I Like for Fall"

**Moses, Yolanda**

. . . But Some of Us Are (Still) Brave. *The Women's Review of Books* 7, No. 5 (February 1990):31-32

**Moskos, Charles C.** and Wood, Frank R. (editors)

The Military: More Than Just a Job? Reviewed by Dorothy Schneider and Carl Schneider. *Minerva* 8, No. 4 (Winter 1990):44-48

**Moskowitz, Faye**

The Waiting Room. Book Review. *Belles Lettres* 5, No. 2 (Winter 1990):10-11

**Mosley, Gail**

My Lumpectomy. *Good Housekeeping* 210, No. 4 (April 1990):78-82

**Mosquitos as Carriers of Disease**

Good Health: Lethal Mosquitos. Michael Castleman. *Redbook* 174, No. 6 (April 1990):22-24

**Moss, Thylias**

Dennis' Sky Leopard. Poem. *Iris* 24 (Fall-Winter 1990):18

**Mossing, Amy** (joint author). *See* Price, Joy A.

**Mother-Blaming**

Mother-Blaming and Clinical Theory. Janet L. Surrey. *Women and Therapy* 10, Nos. 1/2 (1990):83-87

Mother-Hatred and Mother-Blaming: What Electra Did to Clytemnestra. Phyllis Chesler. *Women and Therapy* 10, Nos. 1/2 (1990):71-81

Old Women as Mother Figures. Rachel Josefowitz Siegel. *Women and Therapy* 10, Nos. 1/2 (1990):89-97

**Mother-Daughter Relationships.** *See also* Parenting

Adolescent Daughter/Midlife Mother Dyad. Valerie A. La Sorsa and Iris G. Fodor. *Psychology of Women Quarterly* 14, No. 4 (December 1990):593-606

Beauty Heritage. *Harper's Bazaar* (August 1990):116-121+

Daughters Discover Their Mothers through Biographies and Genograms: Educational and Clinical Parallels. Karen G. Howe. *Women and Therapy* 10, Nos. 1/2 (1990):31-40

Democracy in the Kitchen: Regulating Mothers and Socialising Daughters. By Valerie Walkerdine and Helen Lucey. Reviewed by Bronwyn Davies. *Gender and Education* 2, No. 1 (1990):113-115

Don't Blame Mother: Mending the Mother-Daughter Relationship. By Paula Caplan. Reviewed by Rachel Hare-Mustin. *Psychology of Women Quarterly* 14, No. 1 (March 1990):143-145

Don't Blame Mother: Mending the Mother-Daughter Relationship. By Paula J. Caplan. Reviewed by Barbara G. Collins. *AFFILIA* 5, No. 3 (Fall 1990):122-124

Don't Blame Mother: Mending the Mother-Daughter Relationship. By Paula J. Caplan. Reviewed by Denise Miller Garman. *Iris* 24 (Fall-Winter 1990):67-68

Don't Blame Mother: Mending the Mother-Daughter Relationship. By Paula J. Caplan. Reviewed by Michele Clark. *Women and Therapy* 9, No. 4 (1990):112-114

Francesca Ranieri Tramontana 1887-1963. Frances Tramontana Patchett. *Sinister Wisdom* 41 (Summer-Fall 1990):19-21

How to Have a More Loving Relationship with Your Mom. Victoria Secunda. *Redbook* 175, No. 1 (May 1990):138-139+

"I Hope I'm Not Like My Mother." Shere Hite. *Women and Therapy* 10, Nos. 1/2 (1990):13-30

The Language of Love and Guilt: Mother-Daughter Relationships from a Cross-cultural Perspective. By Ruth Wodak and Muriel Schulz. Reviewed by Gisele Thibault. *Resources for Feminist Research* 19, No. 1 (March 1990):23-24

Laura Ingalls Wilder and Rose Wilder Lane: The Politics of a Mother-Daughter Relationship. Notes. Anita Clair Fellman. *Signs* 15, No. 3 (Spring 1990):535-561

Legacy. Mary Russo Demetrick. *Sinister Wisdom* 41 (Summer-Fall 1990):54

Lessons From My Mother's Life. Aphra Frank. *Glamour* (May 1990):300+

Making Mother-Blaming Visible: The Emperor's New Clothes. Paula J. Caplan. *Women and Therapy* 10, Nos. 1/2 (1990):61-70

Mama Didn't Lie. Jill Nelson. *Essence* 21, No. 2 (June 1990):61-62 +

The Mother/Daughter Plot. By Marianne Hirsch. Reviewed by Gayle Greene. *The Women's Review of Books* 7, No. 5 (February 1990):8-9

Mourning the Myth of Mother/hood: Reclaiming Our Mothers' Legacies. Martha A. Robbins. *Women and Therapy* 10, Nos. 1/2 (1990):41-59

My Daughter, the Little Princess. Catherine Peck. *McCall's* 117, No. 12 (September 1990):31-32

My Daughter and Me: Déjà Vu All Over Again. Jane Adams. *Lear's* (May 1990):72-74

Nothing in Common. Lois Smith Brady. *Mademoiselle* (March 1990):208-209, 247-248

Private Lives: You and Your Mom. Kathleen McCoy. *Family Circle* 103, No. 17 (December 18, 1990):74-81

Reassessing Mother Blame in Incest. Notes. Janet Liebman Jacobs. *Signs* 15, No. 3 (Spring 1990):500-514

Talking with Valerie Harper. Vicki Jo Radovsky. *Redbook* 175, No. 1 (May 1990):30-32

Trust Me, Trust Me. Ann F. Caron. *Good Housekeeping* 211, No. 5 (November 1990):87-88

What Has Gone Before: The Legacy of Racism and Sexism in the Lives of Black Mothers and Daughters. Beverly A. Greene. *Women and Therapy* 9, Nos. 1-2 (1990):207-230

Young Mother's Story: "I Knew I Had to Survive – For My Daughter's Sake." Diane DePorter. *Redbook* 175, No. 1 (May 1990):34-36

**Mother-Daughter Relationships – Poems**

The Gold Taloned Mirrors. Pat Andrus. *Women and Therapy* 10, Nos. 1/2 (1990):11

I Was in Hawaii. Pat Andrus. *Women and Therapy* 10, Nos. 1/2 (1990):9-10

**Motherhood.** *See* Parenthood

**Mothering.** *See* Parenting

**Mothers.** *See also* Surrogate Mothers

The American Mother: A Landmark Survey for the 1990s. Margery D. Rosen. *Ladies' Home Journal* 107, No. 5 (May 1990):132-136

Motherly Devotion. Pat Ross. *McCall's* 117, No. 8 (May 1990):47-48

Starring Moms. Barbara Carlin. *Family Circle* 103, No. 7 (May 15, 1990):80-85

Why a Good Mother May Be Better than Perfect. Anne Mollegen Smith. *McCall's* 117, No. 8 (May 1990):77

**Mothers – Personal Narratives**

"I Hope I'm Not Like My Mother." Shere Hite. *Women and Therapy* 10, Nos. 1/2 (1990):13-30

**Mothers Against Drunk Driving.** *See also* Dutka, Elaine; School Buses – Accidents

The Other Side of Sorrow. Excerpt. Candy Lightner and Nancy Hathaway. *Ladies' Home Journal* 107, No. 9 (September 1990):158-159 +

**Mothers in Films**

Mother Inferior. Georgia Brown. *Lear's* (July 1990):88-89

**Mothers in Literature**

Mother-Hatred and Mother-Blaming: What Electra Did to Clytemnestra. Phyllis Chesler. *Women and Therapy* 10, Nos. 1/2 (1990):71-81

**Mothers' Manifesto**

The Mothers' Manifesto and Disputes over 'Mütterlichkeit'. Prue Chamberlayne. *Feminist Review* No. 35 (Summer 1990):9-23

**Mother-Son Relationships**

Captain of the Ship. James Clayton. *Essence* 21, No. 2 (June 1990):36

Property, Power, and Personal Relations: Elite Mothers and Sons in Yorkist and Early Tudor England. Notes. Barbara J. Harris. *Signs* 15, No. 3 (Spring 1990):606-632

We Remember Mama. Dean Lamanna and Pamela Leigh. *Ladies' Home Journal* 107, No. 5 (May 1990):69-72

**Mothers Working Outside the Home.** *See also* Balancing Work and Family Life; Maternity Clothes; Mommy Track; Time Management

Backtalk: Worked Up. Barbara Ehrenreich. *Lear's* (January 1990):125-131

A Delicate Balance: "The Trick Is Not to Panic." Robin Sanders. *Ladies' Home Journal* 107, No. 3 (March 1990):163-166

The Effect of Maternal Employment on Mormon and Non-Mormon Adolescents. Philip J. Mohan. *Adolescence* 25, No. 100 (Winter 1990):831-837

Free Advice. Edited by Patti Watts. *Executive Female* (May/June 1990):23-26

How Employers are Helping Working Moms. James A. Levine. *Good Housekeeping* 211, No. 3 (September 1990):150 +

How Is Your Work Affecting Your Health, Your Family, Your Life? *McCall's* 117, No. 9 (June 1990):29-34

More for Your Money. Bibliography. Barbara Gilder Quint. *Glamour* (August 1990):112-114

Opinion Makers: Working Mothers Should . . . *Redbook* 174, No. 6 (April 1990):70

Polling America: Where's a Woman's Place? Ernie Anastos. *Family Circle* 103, No. 14 (October 16, 1990):74-77

Precious Moments. Jennet Conant. *Harper's Bazaar* (March 1990):21-22

The Work Attachment of Mothers with Preschool Children. Sandra Cotton, John K. Antill, and John D. Cunningham. *Psychology of Women Quarterly* 14, No. 2 (June 1990):255-270

You're Pregnant? You're Fired. Ira Wolfman. *Savvy Woman* (September 1990):13-14

**Motivation.** *See also* Education – Motivation

The Fine Art of Using Money as a Motivator. Connie Wallace. *Working Woman* (January 1990):126-127+

**Mott, Ruth** (joint author). *See* Watt, Joyce

**Motz, Marilyn Ferris**

Garden as Woman: Creation of Identity in a Turn-of-the-Century Ohio Town. *NWSA Journal* 2, No. 1 (Winter 1990):35-51

**Mountain Climbing**

Climb Every Mountain. Angela Johnson. *off our backs* 20, No. 11 (December 1990):18-19

**Mountaineering**

High Aspirations. Jon Krakauer. *Women's Sports and Fitness* 12, No. 7 (October 1990):32+

**Mountaingrove, Jean**

The Presence in the Grove. *Woman of Power* 15 (Fall-Winter 1990):80-81

**Mountaingrove, Ruth**

Intricate Passions. Book Review. *off our backs* 20, No. 11 (December 1990):13

**Mourin, Jennifer**

Days of Open Hand. Record Review. *Spare Rib* No. 212 (May 1990):31

Look Who's Talking. Film Review. *Spare Rib* No. 212 (May 1990):28

Saxuality. Music Review. *Spare Rib* 217 (October 1990):27

The Sweet Keeper. Record Review. *Spare Rib* No. 210 (March 1990):41

**Mourning Dove** (about)

Mourning Dove, A Salishan Autobiography. Edited by Jay Miller. Reviewed by Alanna Brown. *The Women's Review of Books* 8, No. 2 (November 1990):19-20

**Moushey, Leslie A.**

Rambling Gals/Exploring the Scientific Method. *Belles Lettres* 5, No. 3 (Spring 1990):10-11

**Moutet, Anne-Elisabeth**

French Revolutionary. *Harper's Bazaar* (April 1990):204-205+

Passion Player. *Harper's Bazaar* (August 1990):134-137+

**Movie Criticism.** *See* Film Criticism; Film Reviews

**Movies.** *See* Film and Filmmakers

**Moynahan, Molly**

Sleeping Alone. Short Story. *Mademoiselle* (April 1990):178-187

**Ms. Foundation for Women**

Founding Mother Takes New Steps. Suzanne Messing. *New Directions for Women* 19, No. 4 (July-August 1990):10

**Muccia, Caterina**

Tips on Trips. *Family Circle* 103, No. 14 (October 16, 1990):174

**Muchnic, Suzanne**

Family Reunion. *Harper's Bazaar* (June 1990):36

The Starker Image. *Harper's Bazaar* (April 1990):132

**Mud Flower Collective, The**

God's Fierce Whimsy – Christian Feminism and Theological Education. Reviewed by Joanne Stato. *off our backs* 20, No. 8 (August/September 1990):26-27+

**Mueller, Kay E.** and Powers, William G.

Parent-Child Sexual Discussion: Perceived Communicator Style and Subsequent Behavior. *Adolescence* 25, No. 98 (Summer 1990):469-482

**Mueller, Lisel**

International Film Festival. Poem. *Iris* 23 (Spring-Summer 1990):36

Waving from Shore. Reviewed by Shirley Anders. *Iris* 24 (Fall-Winter 1990):66-67

**Mugler, Thierry** (about). *See also* Etra, Jon, "World Class"

**Muhich, Lisa** (interview)

Innerviews. Diane French. *Women's Sports and Fitness* 12, No. 7 (October 1990):56

**Mukai, Takayo**

A Discrimination Conveniently Covert. *Belles Lettres* 6, No. 1 (Fall 1990):29

The River with No Bridge. Book Review. *Belles Lettres* 6, No. 1 (Fall 1990):29

Widows of Hiroshima: The Life Stories of Nineteen Peasant Wives. Book Review. *Belles Lettres* 6, No. 1 (Fall 1990):25

**Mukerji, Shekhar**

Developmental Migration: A Processual Analysis of Inter-State Rural-Rural Migration. Book Review. *Journal of Family Welfare* 36, No. 4 (December 1990):78-81

**Mukherjee, Bharati**

Jasmine. Reviewed by Melanie Kaye-Kantrowitz. *The Women's Review of Books* 7, No. 7 (April 1990):7-9

**Mullaney, Marie Marmo**

Sexual Politics in the Career and Legend of Louise Michel. Notes. *Signs* 15, No. 2 (Winter 1990):300-322

**Mullen, Cathy** (joint author). *See* Hughes, Lynn

**Muller, Georgene**

Technology: How a Knowledge Detective Can Help You Find Success. *Working Woman* (February 1990):44-49

**Mullis, Ann** (joint author). *See* Youngs, George A. (Jr.)

**Mullis, Ron** (joint author). *See* Youngs, George A. (Jr.)

**Mulroy, Elizabeth A.** (editor)

Women as Single Parents: Confronting Institutional Barriers in the Courts, the Workplace, and the Housing Market. Reviewed by Dorothy C. Miller. *AFFILIA* 5, No. 2 (Summer 1990):104-106

**Multimedia Art.** *See also* Performance Art

Feminist Visions: Words and Pictures. Linda Shult. *Feminist Collections* 11, No. 4 (Summer 1990):9-10

**Multinational Corporations.** *See also* Global Economy

The Bonsai Connection. Peter Feibleman. *Lear's* (April 1990):38-42

**Multiple Births**

Family Portrait: Three-Million-Dollar Quints. Shana Aborn. *Ladies' Home Journal* 107, No. 2 (February 1990):74-78

**Multiple Personality**

Who Am I? Nelly Edmondson Gupta. *Ladies' Home Journal* 107, No. 3 (March 1990):160-161+

**Multiple Roles and Health.** *See also* Role Strain

Number and Quality of Roles: A Longitudinal Personality View. Ravenna Helson, Teresa Elliott, and Janet Leigh. *Psychology of Women Quarterly* 14, No. 1 (March 1990):83-101

**Mulvey, Laura** (criticism)

Beyond Post-Feminism: The Work of Laura Mulvey and Griselda Pollock. Monika Gagnon. *Canadian Women's Studies* 11, No. 1 (Spring 1990):81-83

**Mumford, Laura Stempel**

Women's Issues: An Annotated Bibliography. Review. *Feminist Collections* 11, No. 3 (Spring 1990):17

**Munch, Edvard** (about)

Prints of Darkness. Jo Ann Lewis. *Harper's Bazaar* (May 1990):56+

**Mundigo, A.** (joint author). *See* Phillips, James F.

**Mungin, Horace**

Reality Meets Retirement. *Essence* 20, No. 9 (January 1990):30

**Munich, Adrienne Auslander** (joint editor). *See* Cooper, Helen M.

**Municipal Bonds**

Female Bonding. Louise Tutelian. *Savvy Woman* (July/August 1990):12

**Muñiz-Huberman, Angelina**

Enclosed Garden. Reviewed by Barbara Benham. *Belles Lettres* 5, No. 2 (Winter 1990):18

**Munk, Erika**

Sex . . . Violence . . . Rite of Passage? *Lear's* (November 1990):112-115+

**Munnings, Frances**

Sidelined. *Women's Sports & Fitness* 12, No. 6 (September 1990):40-43

**Munro, Alice**

Friend of My Youth. Reviewed by Rosalind A. Warren. *The Women's Review of Books* 7, No. 8 (May 1990):8-9

Friend of My Youth. Reviewed by Suzanne Berne. *Belles Lettres* 5, No. 4 (Summer 1990):21-22

**Murder.** *See also* Cults; Salcido, Angela (about); Self-Defense

Daddy's Girl. Susan Edmiston. *Glamour* (November 1990):228-231+

Justifiable Homicide: Battered Women, Self-Defense and the Law. By Cynthia K. Gillespie. Reviewed by Pamela A. Brown. *AFFILIA* 5, No. 2 (Summer 1990):106-109

By Love Obsessed: The Shocking Story of a Real-Life Fatal Attraction. John Colapinto. *Mademoiselle* (August 1990):188-191, 230-232

The Perfect Marriage That Ended in Murder. *Good Housekeeping* 210, No. 5 (May 1990):166, 219-220

When Battered Women Kill. By Angela Browne. Reviewed by Pamela A. Brown. *AFFILIA* 5, No. 2 (Summer 1990):106-109

**Murdoch, Iris**

The Message to the Planet. Reviewed by Nancy Engbretsen Schaumburger. *Belles Lettres* 5, No. 4 (Summer 1990):23

**Murdock, Richard T.** (joint author). *See* White, George L. (Jr.)

**Murphy, Ann B.**

The Borders of Ethical, Erotic, and Artistic Possibilities in *Little Women*. Notes. *Signs* 15, No. 3 (Spring 1990):562-585

**Murphy, Caryle**

Dateline Kuwait: A Reporter Inside the Gulf Crisis. *Vogue* (December 1990):300-303+

**Murphy, Cliona**

The Women's Suffrage Movement and Irish Society in the Early Twentieth Century. Reviewed by

Margaret MacCurtain. *Gender & History* 2, No. 3 (Autumn 1990):365-368

**Murphy, John. M.**

"To Create a Race of Thoroughbreds": Margaret Sanger and *The Birth Control Review*. *Women's Studies in Communication* 13, No. 1 (Spring 1990): 23-45

**Murphy, Mary** (joint author). *See* Hall, Jacquelyn Dowd

**Murphy, Maureen**

A Belfast Woman. Book Review. *Feminist Collections* 11, No. 2 (Winter 1990):5-6

Dublin Belles: Conversations with Dublin Women. Book Review. *Feminist Collections* 11, No. 2 (Winter 1990):5-6

I Am of Ireland: Women of the North Speak Out. Book Review. *Feminist Collections* 11, No. 2 (Winter 1990):5-6

**Murphy, Patrick T.**

The Little Boy Nobody Wanted. *Good Housekeeping* 211, No. 4 (October 1990):135+

**Murphy, Sue**

Lulu. Theater Review. *Spare Rib* 217 (October 1990):31

The Mad Monkey. Film Review. *Spare Rib* 219 (December 1990-January 1991):28

Men Don't Leave. Film Review. *Spare Rib* No. 216 (September 1990):32

Pretty Woman. Film Review. *Spare Rib* No. 212 (May 1990):28

In the Red Kitchen. Book Review. *Spare Rib* 213 (June 1990):28-29

Shape-Shifter. add. *Spare Rib* No. 211 (April 1990):27

Stanley and Iris. Film Review. *Spare Rib* No. 214 (July 1990):30-31

*Stanley and Iris*: Hollywood's Latest Cop Out. *Spare Rib* No. 214 (July 1990):30-31

Storia 4: Green. Short Stories. add. *Spare Rib* No. 212 (May 1990):25

Trop Belle Pour Toi (Too Beautiful for You). Film Review. *Spare Rib* No. 211 (April 1990):30

What He Really Wants Is a Dog. add. *Spare Rib* No. 210 (March 1990):34-35

**Murphy, Wendy** (joint author). *See* Chou, Jane Shiyen

**Murphy, Zacki**

Entertaining: Special Settings. *Family Circle* 103, No. 16 (November 27, 1990):59-60

**Murray, Janet Horowitz**

Clothing the Emperors. *The Women's Review of Books* 7, No. 9 (June 1990):6

What I Saw at the Revolution: A Political Life in the Reagan Era. Book Review. *The Women's Review of Books* 7, No. 9 (June 1990):6

**Murray, Margaret P.** (joint author). *See* Lauer, Kristin O.

**Murray, Melissa**

Changelings. Reviewed by Patricia Roth Schwartz. *Belles Lettres* 5, No. 3 (Spring 1990):3

**Murthy, P. V.**

Agricultural Modernization, Its Associated Factors and Fertility Behaviour. *Journal of Family Welfare* 36, No. 4 (December 1990):61-66

**Muscari, Ann** and Morrone, Wanda Wardell

Every Minute Doesn't Count. *Family Circle* 103, No. 1 (January 9, 1990):85+

**Muschamp, Herbert**

Art: Modernism. *Vogue* (January 1990):118-120

Oil and Water. *Vogue* (July 1990):200-205+

**Muscle Strength**

Muscle Tone. Randi Hutter. *Harper's Bazaar* (May 1990):140-143

**Muses**

Rediscovering the Muse. Tracy Marks. *Woman of Power* 15 (Fall-Winter 1990):55-57

**Musgrave, Susan**

Family Plot. Poem. *Iris* 23 (Spring-Summer 1990):37

**Music.** *See also* Burlesque; Feminist Music; Songs

Learning to Play. Joan Herbst Shapiro. *Heresies* 25 (1990):80-82

Music as Activism. Marlene. *Hot Wire* 6, No. 2 (May 1990):53

Private Time. *Glamour* (October 1990):145-146

Sonia Johnson Speaks of Creating a "Women's World." Sonia Johnson. *Hot Wire* 6, No. 3 (September 1990):37-39

Words and Music for Social Change. Patricia Gambarini. *New Directions for Women* 19, No. 5 (September-October 1990):4

**Music—Africa.** *See also* Chewaluza, Mataya Clifford; Khotso House Trio

**Music—Blues**

Blues Angels. Veronica Hill. *Spare Rib* No. 211 (April 1990):28

**Music, Classical**

Yes, Mendelssohn Was a Woman. Lynn Wenzel. *New Directions for Women* 19, No. 1 (January/February 1990):9

**Music, Classical—Opera**

The Faust that Roared. Matthew Gurewitsch. *Harper's Bazaar* (January 1990):116-117

Opéra, or the Undoing of Women. By Catherine Clément. Reviewed by Helen Hacker. *Gender and Society* 4, No. 4 (December 1990):561-563

Opera, or the Undoing of Women. By Catherine Clement. Reviewed by Pat Hurshell. *NWSA Journal* 2, No. 1 (Winter 1990):141-142

Vogue Arts: Music. David Daniel. *Vogue* (September 1990):436-438; (December 1990):204-208

## Music – Country and Western

Country Goes to Town. Julia Reed and Bruce Weber. *Vogue* (July 1990):176-195 +

K.T. Oslin: The True Grit of a Country Charmer. Geneva Kellam. *Lear's* (September 1990):106-109 +

## Music – Feminist Perspectives

Humor in Women's Music. Jamie Anderson. *Hot Wire* 6, No. 1 (January 1990):46-47 +

Towards a Lesbian Aesthetic. Jorjet Harper. *Hot Wire* 6, No. 1 (January 1990):14-15 +

Women's Music and the Divine Proportion. Kay Gardner. *Hot Wire* 6, No. 2 (May 1990):50-52 +

## Music – Folk

Familiar Faces. By Peggy Seeger. Reviewed by Lynn Wenzel. *New Directions for Women* 19, No. 3 (May/June 1990):8

"If I Could Speak With Your Sound": Fan Music, Textual Proximity, and Liminal Identification. Henry Jenkins. *Camera Obscura* , No. 23 (May 1990): 148-175

## Music – Jazz

Jazz in Women. *Spare Rib* No. 214 (July 1990):6-11

Jazz Movies: Born Out of a Horn. Geoffrey Wolff. *Lear's* (July 1990):90-95 +

Mama Said There'd Be Days Like This – My Life in the Jazz World. Reviewed by Robyn Archer. *Feminist Review* No. 35 (Summer 1990):123-124

Mood Music. *Harper's Bazaar* (April 1990):174-179

**Music – New Orleans.** *See* New Orleans – Music

**Music, Popular.** *See also* Clooney, Rosemary (about); Rhythm and Blues Music; Scotland – Music, Popular; Zydeco Music

The Amazing k. d. lang. Interview. Charla Krupp. *Glamour* (February 1990):124

Anything Goes: Reclaiming the Songs of Cole Porter. Christian Wright. *Mademoiselle* (November 1990):94

Born to Sing. Melissa Bedolis. *Mademoiselle* (November 1990):150-153

Classic Carly. Peter Feibleman. *Lear's* (December 1990):90-93 +

En Vogue: Styling Style. Deborah Gregory. *Essence* 21, No. 5 (September 1990):47

Love Will Find a Way. By Ronnie Gilbert. Reviewed by Lynn Wenzel. *New Directions for Women* 19, No. 3 (May/June 1990):8

Madonna Flexes Her Muscles. Richard Price. *Ladies' Home Journal* 107, No. 11 (November 1990):198 +

Not Just a Pretty Face. David Ritz. *Essence* 21, No. 5 (September 1990):72-74

The Ode and the New. David Keeps. *Harper's Bazaar* (February 1990):58

One Nation Under a Groove. Christian Wright. *Mademoiselle* (December 1990):95

The Pain and Passion of Quincy Jones. Alan Ebert. *Essence* 21, No. 7 (November 1990):59-60 +

Solid Sister. Stephanie Mansfield. *Vogue* (September 1990):574-579 +

Soul Stylist. June Garcia. *Mademoiselle* (June 1990):92-97

Sound Raves. Siobhan Toscano. *Savvy Woman* (October 1990):21

Vogue Arts: The Lady's Got Soul. Nick Coleman. *Vogue* (August 1990):210-214

Welcome to the Muthaland. *Spare Rib* No. 212 (May 1990):32-33

What's Hot: Music's Legendary Ladies. *Ladies' Home Journal* 107, No. 6 (June 1990):44-48

Word On . . . *Glamour* (October 1990):191-192

Word On . . . The Best Music. Brook Hersey and Maurice Weissinger. *Glamour* (December 1990):156

Word On . . . Willson Phillips. Charla Krupp. *Glamour* (May 1990):204

## Music, Popular – Gender Differences

"Stylistic Ensembles" on a Different Pitch: A Comparative Analysis of Men's and Women's Rugby Songs. Elizabeth Wheatley. *Women & Language* 13, No. 1 (Fall 1990):21-26

**Music – Rap.** *See also* Popular Culture

Down to Earth. Esther Bailey. *Spare Rib* 218 (November 1990):38-39

Lewd Music. Barbara Grizzuti Harrison. *Mademoiselle* (October 1990):116

2 Live Crew Lyrics Raise Problem of Censorship vs. Obscenity. *Media Report to Women* 18, No. 4 (July-August 1990):1-2

Music: Welcome to the Funhouse. Jill Pearlman. *Vogue* (July 1990):90-93

Never Trust a Big Butt and a Smile. Tricia Rose. *Camera Obscura* , No. 23 (May 1990): 108-131

Women Rap Back. Michele Wallace. *Ms.* 1, No. 3 (November/December 1990):61

Women Right Now. Bibliography. *Glamour* (October 1990):103-110

## Music, Religious

Rhythm and the Frame Drum: Attributes of the Goddess. Layne Redmond. *Woman of Power* 15 (Fall-Winter 1990):20-23

## Music – Rhythm and Blues

Saffire: The Uppity Blues Women. By Gaye Adegbalola, Earlene Lewis, and Ann Rabson. Reviewed by Lynn Wenzel. *New Directions for Women* 19, No. 3 (May/June 1990):8

## Music – Rock

Girls with Guitars. Karen Schoemer. *Mademoiselle* (October 1990):112

Group Pushes Nonsexist Rock. Wickie Stamps. *New Directions for Women* 19, No. 1 (January/February 1990):7

Just Me and the Boys? Women in Local-Level Rock and Roll. Stephen B. Groce and Margaret Cooper. *Gender and Society* 4, No. 2 (June 1990):220-229

Living to Tell: Madonna's Resurrection of the Fleshly. Susan McClary. *Genders* 7 (Spring 1990):1-21

She Rockers Live at the Fridge. Esther Bailey. *Spare Rib* No. 209 (February 1990):32

Son of Sexism. Karen Schoemer. *Mademoiselle* (May 1990):128-130

"Women in Rock Music" Revisited: A Response to Sawchuk's Critique in *Atlantis*, Vol 14, no. 2. Emily Nett. *Atlantis* 15, No. 2 (Spring 1990):77-00

## Musical Instruments

The Accordion: Out of the Closet and into Your Hands! Karen Beth. *Hot Wire* 6, No. 2 (May 1990):40-41 +

## Music Festivals. See also Salzburg
(Austria) – Mozart Festival, 1991

Doing the Festivals: Or, How I Spent My Summer. Cathy Andrews. *Hot Wire* 6, No. 3 (September 1990):43 +

1989 Festival Photos. *Hot Wire* 6, No. 1 (January 1990):34-35

1990 Festival Photos. *Hot Wire* 6, No. 3 (September 1990):32-33

The Fifth National Women's Choral Festival. Cathy Roma. *Hot Wire* 6, No. 2 (May 1990):44-45

Gulf Coast Women's Festival. Brenda Henson. *Hot Wire* 6, No. 1 (January 1990):38-39

July. *Glamour* (July 1990):143

The Michigan Festival Concert Band. Kay Creech. *Hot Wire* 6, No. 1 (January 1990):32-33 +

The National Women's Music Festival: Bringing Non-Dominant Women to Full Boil. Christina Springer. *off our backs* 20, No. 5 (May 1990):9

Neophyte at Michigan. Aj Fugh-Berman. *off our backs* 20, No. 10 (November 1990):11 +

Report from Albuquerque: Wiminfest '89. Paula Walowitz. *Hot Wire* 6, No. 1 (January 1990):36-37

Southern: The "Live and Let Live" Festival. Jorjet Harper. *Hot Wire* 6, No. 3 (September 1990):40-42

## Musicians. See also Composers; Singers; Violinists

Four to Jam. Judy Simmons. *Ms.* 1, No. 2 (September/October 1990):23

Lesley Gore on k.d. Lang . . . and vice versa. *Ms.* 1, No. 1 (July/August 1990):30-33

Music: Three in Concert. Diane Palacios. *Ms.* 1, No. 1 (July/August 1990):72-73

My Miracle. Gloria Estefan and Kathryn Casey. *Ladies' Home Journal* 107, No. 8 (August 1990):99-101 +

Who's On in Classical Music. *Glamour* (July 1990):68

Wild Women Don't Have the Blues. Produced by Carole van Falkenburg and Christie Dall. Reviewed by Lynn Wenzel. *New Directions for Women* 19, No. 3 (May/June 1990):9

## Musicians – Personal Narratives

Grace Notes from Holly Near. *Ms.* 1, No. 3 (November/December 1990):62

## Musicians, Popular. See also Double-Bassists

Angela Winbush Takes Care of Business. Carol Cooper. *Essence* 20, No. 10 (February 1990):39

Basia – Coming to America. Karen Schoemer. *Mademoiselle* (September 1990):160

Billy Idol – Rebel With a New Cause. Karen Schoemer. *Mademoiselle* (September 1990):174

Book Marks. Bibliography. Paula Giddings. *Essence* 21, No. 8 (December 1990):38

Cheryl "Pepsii" Riley: Chapter Two. Deborah Gregory. *Essence* 21, No. 6 (October 1990):47

Inside Music. Nina Malkin. *Mademoiselle* (January 1990):54; (February 1990):90

Janet's Nation. David Ritz. *Essence* 20, No. 11 (March 1990):52-54 +

Luther Here and Now. David Ritz. *Essence* 21, No. 7 (November 1990):66-68 +

Me and Aretha. Matt Robinson. *Lear's* (May 1990):102-106 +

My Family, The Jacksons. By Katherine Jackson and Richard Wiseman. Reviewed by Paula Giddings. *Essence* 21, No. 8 (December 1990):38

Naturally Natalie. Elsie B. Washington. *Essence* 21, No. 6 (October 1990):14-17

Regina Belle: Showing Us the Way. Carol Cooper. *Essence* 20, No. 11 (March 1990):44

Repeat Performance. Carol Cooper. *Essence* 21, No. 1 (May 1990):144-148

The Soul of Whitney. Joy Duckett Cain. *Essence* 21, No. 8 (December 1990):54-56

### Musicians, Popular – Interviews

Talking with Carly Simon: "I've Stopped Running from Problems." Interview. Stephen Holden. *Redbook* 175, No. 3 (July 1990):62-64

### Musicians in Film

Vocal Heroes. David Thigpen. *Harper's Bazaar* (November 1990):172-175

### Music Industry

Maurice Starr: The General. Jesse Nash and George Flowers. *Essence* 21, No. 8 (December 1990):34

### Music Reviews

Allanah Myles. *See* Myles, Allanah

All For Freedom. *See* Sweet Honey in the Rock

All Hail Queen Latifah. *See* Telstar Video Entertainment

Arriving and Caught Up. *See* Palm, Anna

The Captain Swing Review. *See* Shocked, Michelle

Compositions. *See* Baker, Anita

Contribution. *See* Paris, Mica

Drum Drama. *See* Tyler, Edwina Lee

Familiar Faces. *See* Seeger, Peggy

Freedom to Love. *See* Nolan, Faith

Hearts and Flowers. *See* Armatrading, Joan

If You See a Dream. *See* Roderick, Libby

Love Will Find a Way. *See* Gilbert, Ronnie

Music: The Blue Nile. Karen Schoemer. *Mademoiselle* (June 1990):98-101

No More Blues. *See* McCorkle, Susannah

Postcard from Paradise. *See* Compilation

Saffire: The Uppity Blues Women. *See* Adegbalola, Gaye

Saxuality. *See* Dulfer, Candy

Shake It to the One That You Love the Best. *See* Mattox, Cheryl Warren

Sky Dances. *See* Near, Holly

Things Here Are Different. *See* Sobule, Jill

True Life Adventure. *See* Fink, Sue

Two Nice Girls. *See* Rough Trade

Women Composers and Their Music, Vols. 1 and 2. *See* Leonarda Productions

Yahoo Australia!. *See* Dobkin, Alix

### Music Videos

Gender Politics and MTV: Voicing the Difference. By Lisa A. Lewis. Reviewed by Alida Brill. *Ms.* 1, No. 1 (July/August 1990):70

"Sex as a Weapon": Feminist Rock Music Videos. Robin Roberts. *NWSA Journal* 2, No. 1 (Winter 1990):1-15

### Musil, Caryn McTighe

Belief Against the Odds. *NWSAction* 3, No. 3 (Fall 1990): 5

Rivers, Swamps, and Vanishing Ponds. *NWSAction* 3, No. 4 (Winter 1990): 2-4

### Musil, Caryn McTighe (about)

Caryn McTighe Musil Resigns After Six Years as Director. Nancy Seale Osborne. *NWSAction* 3, No. 4 (Winter 1990):

### Musiol, Marie-Jeanne

L'autre oeil: Le nu féminin dans l'art masculin. Reviewed by Susanne de Lothinie4re-Harwood. *Canadian Women's Studies* 11, No. 1 (Spring 1990):106

### Musto, Michael

Fantasy Land. *Harper's Bazaar* (July 1990):42-53

### Muta, Orie

Aspects of Love in Contemporary Novels by Japanese Women. *Hecate* 16, Nos. 1-2 (1990):151-163

### Muthaland

Welcome to the Muthaland. *Spare Rib* No. 212 (May 1990):32-33

### Muti, Ornella (about). *See* Celebrities – Business Ownership

### Myers, Gay Nagle

Get Up and Go. *Family Circle* 103, No. 4 (March 13, 1990):N.P.

### Myers, Mitzi

An Outbreak of Peace. Book Review. *NWSA Journal* 2, No. 2 (Spring 1990):273-281

Books for Today's Young Readers: An Annotated Bibliography of Recommended Fiction for Ages 10-14. Book Review. *NWSA Journal* 2, No. 2 (Spring 1990):273-281

Elizabeth Cady Stanton. Book Review. *NWSA Journal* 2, No. 2 (Spring 1990):273-281

Embers: Stories for a Changing World. Book Review. *NWSA Journal* 2, No. 2 (Spring 1990):273-281

Green March Moons. Book Review. *NWSA Journal* 2, No. 2 (Spring 1990):273-281

The Lilith Summer. Book Review. *NWSA Journal* 2, No. 2 (Spring 1990):273-281

Morning Breeze: A True Story of China's Cultural Revolution. Book Review. *NWSA Journal* 2, No. 2 (Spring 1990):273-281

Tatterhood and Other Tales. Book Review. *NWSA Journal* 2, No. 2 (Spring 1990):273-281

We Are Mesquakie, We Are One. Book Review. *NWSA Journal* 2, No. 2 (Spring 1990):273-281

**Myers-Dickinson, Jo** (joint author). *See* Levin, Tobe

**Myles, Allanah**

Allanah Myles. Reviewed by Pam Mason. *Spare Rib* 213 (June 1990):35

**Myles, Allanah** (about). *See also* Music – Rock

**Mysticism**

Equality or Divinity – A False Dichotomy? Morny Joy. *Journal of Feminist Studies in Religion* 6, No. 1 (Spring 1990):9-24

**Mythology – Images of Women**

Medusa and the Female Gaze. Susan R. Bowers. *NWSA Journal* 2, No. 2 (Spring 1990):217-235

Sappho's Gaze: Fantasies of a Goddess and Young Man. Eva Stehle. *Differences* 2, No. 1 (Spring 1990):88-125

**Mythology – Africa**

The Goddess Osun as a Paradigm for African Feminist Criticism. Diedre L. Bádéjot. *Sage* 6, No. 1 (Summer 1989):27-32

# N

**Nabili, Marva.** *See* Azadeh, "Iranian Women Filmmakers"

**Nachum, Nancy**

Peaceniks. *Sinister Wisdom* 42 (Winter 1990-1991):49-52

**Nadel, Dana**

There's Room at the Inn. *Lear's* (December 1990):118-119

**Nadler, Lawrence B. and Nadler, Marjorie Keeshan**

Perceptions of Sex Differences in Classroom Communication. *Women's Studies in Communication* 13, No. 1 (Spring 1990): 46-65

**Nadler, Marjorie Keeshan** (joint author). *See* Nadler, Lawrence B.

**Nagel, Paul C.**

The Adams Women: Abigail and Louisa Adams, Their Sisters and Daughters. Reviewed by Elaine Forman Crane. *NWSA Journal* 2, No. 4 (Autumn 1990):661-664

**Nails – Care and Hygiene**

4 Ways to Look Party-Perfect. *Ladies' Home Journal* 107, No. 12 (December 1990):37-44

**Nails (Anatomy) – Care and Hygiene.** *See also* Skin – Care and Hygiene

Autumn Forecast I: In the Buff. Laurie Tarkan. *Lear's* (August 1990):49

Baby Your Nails. *Redbook* 175, No. 6 (October 1990):98-101

Beauty: Answers. *Essence* 20, No. 11 (March 1990):19; 21, No. 6 (October 1990):18; 21, No. 8 (December 1990):16

Beauty: The At-Home Hand Spa. *Mademoiselle* (September 1990):86

Beauty: The World in Your Hands. *Essence* 20, No. 9 (January 1990):10-11

Beauty Word of Mouth. *Glamour* (March 1990):37-40

Hands. Jody Shields. *Vogue* (August 1990):346-351

Hands-On Style. Cheryl Solimini. *Working Woman* (July 1990):100-102

Nail Care. *Essence* 21, No. 5 (September 1990):14

A Perfect Ten. Debra A. Ward. *McCall's* 117, No. 11 (August 1990):12

**Nair, Janaki**

A History of Their Own: Women in Europe, from Pre-History to the Present. Book Review. *Gender and Society* 4, No. 4 (December 1990):563-565

Uncovering the Zenana. Visions of Indian Womanhood in Englishwomen's Writings: 1813-1940. *Journal of Women's History* 2, No. 1 (Spring 1990):8-34

**Naisbitt, John** (about)

Lunch. Interview. Frances Lear. *Lear's* (October 1990):21-22

**Naishan, Cheng**

The Piano Tuner. Reviewed by Marina Heung. *The Women's Review of Books* 7, No. 7 (April 1990):12-13

**Names.** *See also* Verbal Abuse

Namesakes! Kathleen Brady. *McCall's* 117, No. 8 (May 1990):51-52

Women of Color and the Core Curriculum: Tools for Transforming the Liberal Arts, Part 2. Susan E. Searing. *Feminist Collections* 11, No. 2 (Winter 1990):15-17

**Namibia**

Namibian Independence Day. *Spare Rib* No. 212 (May 1990):46

**Namibia – Politics and Government**

Birthing a Nation. *Ms.* 1, No. 1 (July/August 1990):14

Joan Gurirab: Going Home. Interview. Gwen McKinney. *Essence* 21, No. 6 (October 1990):116-118

De Klerk's "Reforms" – Unfinished Business. *Spare Rib* No. 209 (February 1990): 21-22

A Private Life. Film Review. *Spare Rib* No. 209 (February 1990):35

**National Archives – Center for Electronic Records**

Electronic Records at the National Archives: Resources for Women's Studies. Margaret O. Adams. *NWSA Journal* 2, No. 2 (Spring 1990):269-272

**National Association for the Advancement of Colored People.** *See also* Civil Rights Movement

**National Association of Black and White Men Together**

A Matter of Personal Pride: A Conversation about Black and White Men Together. Thom Bean. *Out/Look* No. 9 (Summer 1990):70-71

**National Black Women's Health Project**

Health Care for the Whole Woman. Liza Nelson. *McCall's* 118, No. 3 (December 1990):35

"Sisters in Session." Lisa Diane White. *New Directions for Women* 19, No. 5 (September-October 1990):8

Women of Color Set Agenda. Pat Redmond. *New Directions for Women* 19, No. 5 (September-October 1990):1+

**National Center for Education in Maternal and Child Health**

A Guide to Selected National Genetic Voluntary Organizations. Reviewed by Jeanne Mager Stellman. *Women and Health* 16, No. 1 (1990):115

**National Child Support Advocacy Coalition.** *See* Child Support

**National Coalition for Seat Belts on School Buses.** *See* School Buses – Accidents

**National Commission on Orphan Diseases.** *See* Policoff, Stephen Phillip, "Diseases Your Doctor May Miss"

**National Commission on Working Women – Wider Opportunities for Women**

Fall 1989 TV Season 'Takes Two Steps Bac,' Says NCWW/WOW. *Media Report to Women* 18, No. 1 (January/February 1990):4-5

**National Coordinating Council of Salvadoran Women**

Group Fights Oppression. Jennifer Gilbert. *New Directions for Women* 19, No. 6 (November-December 1990):6

**National Debt.** *See* Brazil – Debts, Public

**National Education Association.** *See also* Schools – Evaluation

**National Endowment for the Arts**

An Open Letter to the Gay and Lesbian Community. Holly Hughes and Richard Elovich. *Out/Look* No. 10 (Fall 1990):74-75

Censorship: NEA Denies Grants to Lesbians and Gays. Robin Sawyer. *off our backs* 20, No. 8 (August/September 1990):5

The NEA Is the Least of It. Barbara Smith. *Ms.* 1, No. 3 (November/December 1990):65-67

**National Institute of Health.** *See* Medical Research

**National Institutes of Health (NIH)**

Is Health Equity on the Way? Boston Women's Health Book Collective. *Ms.* 1, No. 3 (November/December 1990):25

Medical Studies on Women Are Urgently Needed. *Glamour* (March 1990):146

**Nationalism**

Rabindranath Tagore on Nationalism. Rabindranath Tagore. *Manushi* 58 (May-June 1990):13

**Nationalism, African**

Women and African Nationalism. Susan Geiger. *Journal of Women's History* 2, No. 1 (Spring 1990):227-244

**Nationalism, African-American**

Africa on My Mind: Gender, Counter Discourse and African-American Nationalism. E. Frances White. *Journal of Women's History* 2, No. 1 (Spring 1990):73-97

**National Leadership Coalition on AIDS – Workplace Resource Center**

AIDS in the Workplace. Lloyd Gite. *Glamour* (November 1990):116

**National Lesbian Conference (NLC)**

Lesbian Conference Sets Bold Agenda. Rosemary Curb. *New Directions for Women* 19, No. 1 (January/February 1990):6

**National Organization for Rare Disorders.** *See* Policoff, Stephen Phillip, "Diseases Your Doctor May Miss"

**National Organization for Women**

NOW Confronts Racism. Eleanor J. Bader. *New Directions for Women* 19, No. 6 (November-December 1990):3+

NOW Seeks Racial Diversity. Eleanor J. Bader. *New Directions for Women* 19, No. 6 (November-December 1990):11

NOW's National Conference. Robin Sawyer. *off our backs* 20, No. 8 (August/September 1990):4

Then and Now: From Epiphany to Excess. Margaret Carlson. *Lear's* (February 1990):72-77

**National Parenting Center**

The Good Mother. Penny Colman. *Ladies' Home Journal* 107, No. 1 (January 1990):36

**National Welfare Rights Organization**

Biting the Hand that Feeds Them: Organizing Women on Welfare at the Grass Roots Level. By

Jacqueline Pope. Reviewed by Margaret Nielsen. *AFFILIA* 5, No. 4 (Winter 1990):115

**National Woman Suffrage Association.** *See* Suffrage Movement – History

**National Women's Mailing List**

Can the Women's Movement Reach You? Robin Morgan. *Ms.* 1, No. 3 (November/December 1990):92

**National Women's Studies Association**

Belief Against the Odds. Caryn McTighe Musil. *NWSAction* 3, No. 3 (Fall 1990): 5

First Feminist of Ohio Opens NWSA '90. Dagmar Celeste. *NWSAction* 3, No. 3 (Fall 1990): 1-3

A Letter from Ruby Sales. Ruby N. Sales. *off our backs* 20, No. 8 (August/September 1990):25

NWSA: Troubles Surface at Conference. Jennie Ruby, Farar Elliott, and Carol Anne Douglas. *off our backs* 20, No. 8 (August/September 1990):1+

Racism at the NWSA: A Letter from White Women. *off our backs* 20, No. 10 (November 1990):17-18

Reflections on NWSA '90. Patsy Schweickart. *NWSAction* 3, No. 3 (Fall 1990): 3-4

Under Attack From the Right. Debra Humphreys. *NWSAction* 3, No. 4 (Winter 1990): 7-8

**National Women's Studies Association – Future**

Rivers, Swamps, and Vanishing Ponds. Caryn McTighe Musil. *NWSAction* 3, No. 4 (Winter 1990): 2-4

**National Women's Studies Association Conferences – Student Caucus Meetings**

Journeys in Our Lives: Learning Feminism. Michelle Brodsky, MyKela Loury, Abby Markowitz, Eden E. Torres, and Lauren Wilson. *NWSA Journal* 2, No. 1 (Winter 1990):79-100

**Native Americans.** *See* Indians of North America

**Natural Disasters.** *See also* Hurricane Hugo, 1989; Rescues

Charleston: Coming Through the Hurricane. Sandra Rhodes. *Ladies' Home Journal* 107, No. 1 (January 1990):16-20

How to Cope with Disaster. Norman Cousins. *McCall's* 118, No. 1 (October 1990):73-82

A Hurricane Hits Home. J. Fletcher Robinson. *Essence* 20, No. 12 (April 1990):38

San Francisco: Shaken but Undefeated. Cindy Hampton. *Ladies' Home Journal* 107, No. 1 (January 1990):16+

**Natural Products**

Flower Power. *Glamour* (October 1990):244-247

Manhattan Purists. Nina Malkin. *Harper's Bazaar* (January 1990):34

**Natural Resources**

Forces for Nature. George Bush. *Harper's Bazaar* (January 1990):72-73+

**Nau, Erika S.**

The Spirit of Molly Marine. *Minerva* 8, No. 4 (Winter 1990):23-29

**Navajo Indians**

Measurement Issues in the Use of the Coopersmith Self-Esteem Inventory with Navajo Women. Patricia G. Higgins and Elisabeth K. Dicharry. *Health Care for Women International* 11, No. 3 (1990):251-262

**Navajo Indians in Literature**

Books: Coyote Waits. By Tony Hillerman. Reviewed by Michael Dorris. *Vogue* (July 1990):108-110

**Navarro, Virginia Sánchez**

Re-membering the Goddess. *Woman of Power* 15 (Fall-Winter 1990):38-40

**Naves, Elaine Kalman**

Tears: A Yom Kippur Story. Short story. *Lilith* 15, No. 4 (Fall 1990):30-32

**Navratilova, Martina**

Back from Burnout. *Glamour* (May 1990):212

**Navratilova, Martina** (about)

How I (Almost) Met Martina Navratilova. Bonnie Morris. *Hot Wire* 6, No. 3 (September 1990):22

**Navratilova, Martina** (interview)

Postscript to a Legendary Rivalry. Ann Smith and Lewis Rothlein. *Women's Sports and Fitness* 12, No. 2 (March 1990):22-25

**Naylor, Gloria**

Mama Day. Reviewed by Adele S. Newson. *Sage* 6, No. 2 (Fall 1989):56-57

The Women of Brewster Place. Reviewed by Elorine Grant. *Spare Rib* No. 214 (July 1990):22

**Naylor, Gloria** (about). *See* Writers – Interviews, "Graceful Passages"

**Nead, Lynda**

The Female Nude: Pornography, Art, and Sexuality. Notes. *Signs* 15, No. 2 (Winter 1990):323-335

Myths of Sexuality: Representations of Women in Victorian Britain. Reviewed by Eunice Lipton. *Gender & History* 2, No. 1 (Spring 1990):91-97

**Neal, Arthur G.** (joint author). *See* Groat, H. Theodore

**Near, Holly**

Grace Notes from Holly Near. *Ms.* 1, No. 3 (November/December 1990):62

Sky Dances. Reviewed by Jill Benderly. *On the Issues* 14 (1990):28-29

**Near, Holly** and Richardson, Derk

Fire in the Rain . . . Singer in the Storm: An Autobiography of Holly Near. Reviewed by Lynn Wenzel. *New Directions for Women* 19, No. 5 (September-October 1990):14

Fire in the Rain . . . Singer in the Storm. Reviewed by Cynthia M. Serrano. *The Women's Review of Books* 8, No. 2 (November 1990):18-19

Fire in the Rain . . . Singer in the Storm (excerpts). *Hot Wire* 6, No. 3 (September 1990):3-5+

**Near, Holly** (interview)

Holly Near. Toni Armstrong Jr. *Hot Wire* 6, No. 3 (September 1990):2-5+

**Nebraska – Political Representation**

Adolescents' Attitudes Toward Women in Politics: A Follow-up Study. Diane Gillespie and Cassie Spohn. *Women & Politics* 10, No. 1 (1990):1-16

**Nebraska Sociological Feminist Collective**

A Feminist Ethic for Social Science Research. Reviewed by Dorothy L. Steffens and Jane Robbins. *Feminist Collections* 11, No. 2 (Winter 1990):7-9

**Neck**

The Best-Dressed Neck. *Mademoiselle* (November 1990):149

**Needham, Anuradha Dingwaney**

At the Receiving End: Reading "Third" World Texts in a "First" World Context. *Women's Studies Quarterly* 18, Nos. 3-4 (Fall-Winter 1990):91-99

**Needham, Wilma** (criticism)

Operations in the Sphere of the Vulgar: The Work of Wilma Needham. Carol Williams. *Canadian Women's Studies* 11, No. 1 (Spring 1990):56-59

**Needle, Richard H.**, Su, S. Susan, and Doherty, William J.

Divorce, Remarriage, and Adolescent Substance Use: A Prospective Longitudinal Study. *Journal of Marriage and the Family* 52, No. 1 (February 1990):157-169

**Negotiation.** *See* Wages – Negotiation

**Negotiation (in Business).** *See also* Wages – Negotiation

Financial Workshop: Negotiating an Employment Contract. Mary Rowland. *Working Woman* (February 1990):65-68

The Negotiating Art: You Can Always Get What You Want. Ellen J. Belzer. *Working Woman* (April 1990):98-99+

**Negri, Sharon**

Searching Ruby's Hands. Poem. *Iris* 23 (Spring-Summer 1990):20

**Negrón-Muntaner, Frances**

The Wait/Espera. Poem. *Sinister Wisdom* 42 (Winter 1990-1991):82-84

**Neifert, Marianne**

Ask Dr. Mom: Kids, Their Winter Colds . . . and More. *McCall's* 118, No. 3 (December 1990):44

Ask Dr. Mom. *McCall's* 117, No. 7 (April 1990):8; 117, No. 8 (May 1990):19; 117, No. 9 (June 1990):10; 117, No. 11 (August 1990):28; 118, No. 1 (October 1990):36-37

Ask Dr. Mom: When Children Stutter . . . And Other Questions. *McCall's* 118, No. 2 (November 1990):46

**Neilson, Linda**

Growing Up with a Fat Mom. *Glamour* (April 1990):156-160

**Neilson, Melany**

Even Mississippi. Reviewed by Shelley Crisp. *Belles Lettres* 5, No. 2 (Winter 1990):3

**Neimark, Jill**

The Buy-Buy Babes. *Mademoiselle* (February 1990):174-175+

Stretch: The No-Fail Guide to Big Career Jumps. *Working Woman* (November 1990):116-117

They've Got to Have It: The Twentysomethings Take Over. *Mademoiselle* (December 1990):158-160

**Neimark, Paul**

My Kingdom for a Horse. *Executive Female* 13, No. 4 (July-August 1990):22 34

**Neipris, Ellen** (about). *See* Title, Stacy

**Neisen, Joseph H.**

Heterosexism or Homophobia: The Power of the Language We Use. *Out/Look* No. 10 (Fall 1990):36-37

**Nekola, Charlotte** (joint editor). *See* Rabinowitz, Paula

**Nelson, Barbara J.** (joint author). *See* Evans, Sara M.

**Nelson, Christine** and Keith, Joanne

Comparisons of Female and Male Early Adolescent Sex Role Attitude and Behavior Development. *Adolescence* 25, No. 97 (Spring 1990):183-204

**Nelson, James Lindemann** (joint author). *See* Boyer, Jeannine Ross

**Nelson, Janet**

The Learning Curve. *Women's Sports and Fitness* 12, No. 3 (April 1990):70-71

**Nelson, Jill**

Back from Crack. *Essence* 20, No. 9 (January 1990):57-58+

Mama Didn't Lie. *Essence* 21, No. 2 (June 1990):61-62+

Mo' Better Spike. Interview. *Essence* 21, No. 4 (August 1990):55+

**Nelson, Linda**

Poetry. Poems. *Out/Look* No. 9 (Summer 1990):69

**Nelson, Liza**

Family Justice: Taking the Trauma out of Custody Cases. Bibliography. *McCall's* 117, No. 7 (April 1990):27-29

Family Ties & Celebrations. *McCall's* 118, No. 2 (November 1990):104-108

Health Care for the Whole Woman. *McCall's* 118, No. 3 (December 1990):35

McCallmanack: Practicing More Humane Medicine. *McCall's* 117, No. 9 (June 1990):45

**Nelson, Margaret K.**

Mothering Others' Children: The Experiences of Family Day-Care Providers. Notes. *Signs* 15, No. 3 (Spring 1990):586-605

**Nelson, Mariah Burton**

Squeeze Play. Book Review. *The Women's Review of Books* 7, Nos. 10-11 (July 1990):36

Striking Out. *The Women's Review of Books* 7, Nos. 10-11 (July 1990):36

**Nelson, Martha**

Close-Up: Don't Use My Name. *Savvy Woman* (July/August 1990):5

**Nelson, Mary** (joint editor). *See* Quackenbush, Marcia

**Nelson, Peter**

The Good Daughter. Short story. *Redbook* 174, No. 5 (March 1990):60-64+

**Nelson, Robert J.**

Willa Cather and France: In Search of the Lost Language. Reviewed by Patrick W. Shaw. *Tulsa Studies in Women's Literature* 9, No. 2 (Fall 1990):337-339

**Nelson, Sara**

Blame it on the Heat Wave. *Glamour* (July 1990):152-153+

Love's Power Plays. *Glamour* (January 1990):148-149+

Memoir of an AIDS Volunteer. *Lilith* 15, No. 1 (Winter 1990):13-14

Spa Guide. *Working Woman* (March 1990):146-150

This Working Life: Confessions of a Monday Lover. *Working Woman* (February 1990):128

What's the Big Idea? *Working Woman* (July 1990):96-98+

**Nelson, Sara** (joint author). *See* Clark, Shauna

**Nelson, Terry**

Brother-to-Be! At 24? *Essence* 20, No. 11 (March 1990):42

**Nelson, Todd** (joint author). *See* Evans, Betsy

**Nepal – Literacy**

From Learning Literacy to Regenerating Women's Space: A Story of Women's Empowerment in Nepal. Pramod Parajuli and Elizabeth Enslin. *Women in Action* 1-2 (1990):3-6

**Nepal – Politics and Government**

Witness to Freedom. Grace Lichtenstein. *Savvy Woman* (July/August 1990):56-59+

Women and the Democracy Movement in Nepal. Hsila Yami. *Manushi* 60 (September-October 1990):29-33

**Nepal – Status of Women**

Dangerous Wives and Sacred Sisters: Social and Symbolic Roles of High-Caste Women in Nepal. By Lynn Bennett. Reviewed by Kalpana Bardhan. *Journal of Women's History* 2, No. 1 (Spring 1990):200-219

**Nepomiatzi, Helene** (about). *See also* Carter, Charla, "European Designers to Watch."

**Nervous Disorders.** *See* Mental Disorders

**Nestle, Joan**

Nice Jewish Girls: A Lesbian Anthology. Book Review. *Bridges* 1, No. 1 (Spring 1990): 98-101

The Tribe of Dina: A Jewish Women's Anthology. Book Review. *Bridges* 1, No. 1 (Spring 1990): 101-102

Twice Blessed: On Being Lesbian, Gay *and* Jewish. Book Review. *Bridges* 1, No. 1 (Spring 1990): 102-104

The Will to Remember: The Lesbian Herstory Archives of New York. *Feminist Review* No. 34 (Spring 1990):86-94

**Nestle, Joan** and Holoch, Naomi (editors)

Women on Women: An Anthology of American Lesbian Short Fiction. Reviewed by Jennie Ruby. *off our backs* 20, No. 7 (July 1990):15

**Nestle Co.**

Nestle Boycott Speeds Up. *Spare Rib* No. 216 (September 1990):46

**Netherlands – Film and Filmmakers**

A Question of Silence. By Marleen Gorris. Reviewed by Constance Balides. *Feminist Collections* 12, No. 1 (Fall 1990):14-18

**Netherlands – Media and Communication**

Professional Socialization of Feminist Journalists in the Netherlands. Liesbet van Zoonen. *Women's Studies in Communication* 12, No. 2 (Fall 1989):1-21

**Netherlands – Prostitution**

Netherlands. *Women's World* , No. 24 (Winter 1990/91): 21

**Nett, Emily**

"Women in Rock Music" Revisited: A Response to Sawchuk's Critique in *Atlantis*, Vol 14, no. 2. *Atlantis* 15, No. 2 (Spring 1990):77-80

**Networking.** *See also* Career Management; Support Systems; Television Journalists – Networking

Documentation and Communication: Strategies for Networking and Change. *Women's World* 23 (April 1990):8-12

Editorial: On Feminism in Action. Betty Sancier. *AFFILIA* 5, No. 4 (Winter 1990):5-7

Lear's Bulletin. Marion Asnes. *Lear's* (August 1990):32

Mother and Toddler Groups. Sandra Lang. *Spare Rib* No. 216 (September 1990):57

Networking: It's All Fun and Games. Leslie Smith. *Executive Female* 13, No. 6 (November-December 1990):59-60

Networking. Leslie Smith. *Executive Female* 13, No. 5 (September-October 1990):57

Networking: Playing to Win: A Conference Preview. Leslie Smith. *Executive Female* (May/June 1990):50

Psst! The New Way to Network Is . . . Softly. Cynthia Crossen. *Working Woman* (September 1990):154-156

Update: News, Trends, and Vital Statistics About Women. *Executive Female* (March/April 1990):8-10

Why Network? *Women's World* 23 (April 1990):6-7

**Networks, Business**

Networking: Special Interest Networks. Leslie Smith. *Executive Female* (March/April 1990):53

The Third Aspect: An Investigation of U.K. Business Networks. Christine Brookes. *Women's Studies International Forum* 13, No. 6 (1990):577-585

**Networks, Social**

Networking: New Groups. *Women in Action* 3 & 4 (1990):34-35

Women's International Cross-Cultural Exchange. Carmen Gloria Dunnage. *Women in Action* 3 & 4 (1990):24-29

**Networks, Social – Adolescents**

Analysis of a Double-Layered Support System. Rachel Seginer. *Adolescence* 25, No. 99 (Fall 1990):739-752

**Neustein, Sherry** (about)

Lost Custody Dooms Child. Mary Lou Greenberg. *New Directions for Women* 19, No. 1 (January/February 1990):18

**Neuville, Charlotte** (about). *See* Talley, André Leon

**Nevel, Donna** (joint author). *See* Falbel, Rita

**Nevelson, Louise** (about)

Louise Nevelson: A Passionate Life. By Laurie Lisle. Reviewed by Arlene Raven. *The Women's Review of Books* 8, No. 1 (October 1990):14-15

Louise Nevelson: A Passionate Life. By Laurie Lisle. Reviewed by Joan Philpott. *Ms.* 1, No. 2 (September/October 1990):28

**Neverdon-Morton, Cynthia**

Afro-American Women of the South and the Advancement of the Race, 1895-1925. Reviewed by Wilma Peebles-Wilkins. *AFFILIA* 5, No. 1 (Spring 1990):108-110

**Neville, C. J.**

The Dévotes: Women and Church in Seventeenth-Century France. Book Review. *Atlantis* 15, No. 2 (Spring 1990):104-106

**New Age Movement**

New Age Health: The M.D.'s vs. the Healers. *Harper's Bazaar* (November 1990):180-183+

New Age or Armageddon? Monica Sjöö. *Woman of Power* 16 (Spring 1990):62-67

**New Americas Press** (editor)

A Dream Compels Us: Voices of Salvadoran Women. Reviewed by Bessy Reyna. *New Directions for Women* 19, No. 5 (September-October 1990):15

A Dream Compels Us: Voices of Salvadoran Women. Reviewed by Lois Wasserspring. *The Women's Review of Books* 7, No. 6 (March 1990):23-24

**Newcomb, Michael** (joint author). *See* Wyatt, Gail Elizabeth

**Newcomer, Susan**

Out of Wedlock Childbearing in an Ante-Bellum Southern County. *Journal of Family History* 15, No. 3 (July 1990):357-368

**New Deal Work Programs.** *See* United States – History

**Newell, G. Kathleen,** Hammig, Cynthia L., Jurich, Anthony P., and Johnson, Dallas E.

Self-Concept as a Factor in the Quality of Diets of Adolescent Girls. *Adolescence* 25, No. 97 (Spring 1990):117-130

**New England States – Christmas Decorations**

A New England Christmas. Lauren Payne. *Ladies' Home Journal* 107, No. 12 (December 1990):138-143

**New Historicism**

Historicisms New and Old: "Charles Dickens" Meets Marxism, Feminism, and West Coast Foucault. Judith Newton. *Feminist Studies* 16, No. 3 (Fall 1990):449-470

**Newington, Nina Crow**

Harvest of Ghosts (excerpts). Short Story. *Sinister Wisdom* 40 (Spring 1990):79-81

**New Jersey – Education**

The New Jersey Project Enters Its Second Phase. Paula Rothenberg. *Women's Studies Quarterly* 18, Nos. 1-2 (Spring-Summer 1990):119-122

**New Jersey – Lesbian and Gay Coalition**

Meet Heidi Jones: The Straight Gay Leader. Connie Gilbert-Neiss. *Out/Look* No. 8 (Spring 1990):54-55

**New Jersey – Suffrage – History**

Female Suffrage in New Jersey, 1790-1807. Irwin N. Gertzog. *Women & Politics* 10, No. 2 (1990):47-58

**Newlyn, Evelyn S.**

Where the Meanings Are: Feminism and Cultural Spaces. Book Review. *Women's Studies International Forum* 13, No. 6 (1990):613-614

**Newman, Amy**

Aestheticism, Feminism, and the Dynamics of Reversal. *Hypatia* 5, No. 2 (Summer 1990):20-32

**Newman, Felice**

In Memorium: Anne Pride. *off our backs* 20, No. 9 (October 1990):21

**Newman, Karen**

Directing Traffic: Subjects, Objects, and the Politics and Exchange. *Differences* 2, No. 2 (Summer 1990):41-54

**Newman, Leslea**

Heather Has Two Mommies. Reviewed by Joanne Stato. *off our backs* 20, No. 3 (March 1990):30

Secrets. Reviewed by Rosalind Warren. *New Directions for Women* 19, No. 6 (November-December 1990):17

**New Mexico – History**

Women's Collective Action in the Gallup, New Mexico Coalfields during the 1930s. Katharine Dawson. *NWSA Journal* 2, No. 4 (Autumn 1990):690-692

**New Mexico – Lama Foundation**

All Our Relations. Sawnie E. Morris. *Out/Look* No. 8 (Spring 1990):46-51

**New Orleans – Music**

The Bayou Beat. Mimi Read. *Harper's Bazaar* (January 1990):136+

**New Orleans – Restaurants**

Crescent City Cuisine: Dining Out in New Orleans. Marc Frazier. *Harper's Bazaar* (January 1990):134+

**New Products.** *See* Cosmetics Industry; Miniature Electronic Equipment

**Newson, Adele S.**

Mama Day. Book Review. *Sage* 6, No. 2 (Fall 1989):56-57

**Newspapers.** *See* Media and Communications

**Newton, Judith**

Historicisms New and Old: "Charles Dickens" Meets Marxism, Feminism, and West Coast Foucault. *Feminist Studies* 16, No. 3 (Fall 1990):449-470

**Newton-John, Olivia** (about). *See* Celebrities – Activism

**New Year's Resolutions**

Beauty: 10 Affirmations for the 90's. *Essence* 20, No. 9 (January 1990):9

January Is a Great Month to . . . *Glamour* (January 1990):101

**New York (City) – Crime.** *See* Central Park (New York, N.Y.) – Crime

**New York (City) – Culture and Society**

Broadway Debut. Jane Freiman. *Harper's Bazaar* (May 1990):157

Centennial Cheer. Stanley Mieses. *Harper's Bazaar* (September 1990):208

Hour Town. *Harper's Bazaar* (September 1990):141-198

Putting Out the Bonfire. Jim Sleeper. *Lear's* (February 1990):108-115

Russian House. *Harper's Bazaar* (November 1990):206

Shopping Spree. Helen Lee Schifter. *Harper's Bazaar* (October 1990):62-64+

**New York (City) – Disasters**

We Had Five Minutes to Evacuate Our Apartment. Michael Drinkard and Jill Eisenstadt. *Glamour* (April 1990):270-273+

**New York (City) – Employment**

A Big Deal Babe. Lois Smith Brady. *Mademoiselle* (October 1990):152-154+

**New York (City) – Fashion**

She Loves New York. *Mademoiselle* (October 1990):142-151

**New York (City) – Fashion Designers**

New York Collections: Body Heat. *Harper's Bazaar* (January 1990):106-115

New York Nights. *Lear's* (March 1990):112-121

**New York (City) – Gay Men's Health Crisis**

Memoir of an AIDS Volunteer. Sara Nelson. *Lilith* 15, No. 1 (Winter 1990):13-14

**New York (City) – Lesbian Herstory Archives**

The Will to Remember: The Lesbian Herstory Archives of New York. Joan Nestle. *Feminist Review* No. 34 (Spring 1990):86-94

**New York (City) – Metropolitan Museum of Art – Exhibitions**

Family Reunion. Suzanne Muchnic. *Harper's Bazaar* (June 1990):36

Vogue Arts: Design. André Leon Talley. *Vogue* (December 1990):200-202

**New York (City) – Metropolitan Opera**

The Faust that Roared. Matthew Gurewitsch. *Harper's Bazaar* (January 1990):116-117

**New York (City) – Police**

"Gay Party at Police Station." *Out/Look* No. 8 (Spring 1990):44-45

**New York (City) – Politics and Government.** *See also* Dinkins, Joyce (about)

**New York (City) – Restaurants**

Food. Jeffrey Steingarten. *Vogue* (September 1990):486-498

**New York (City) – Social Life and Customs**

Talking Out of Town: Rotten to the Core. Tracy Young. *Vogue* (August 1990):382

**New York (City) – Substance Abuse**

Trends in Reporting of Maternal Drug Abuse and Infant Mortality among Drug-Exposed Infants in New York City. Leo Habel, Katherine Kaye, and Jean Lee. *Women and Health* 16, No. 2 (1990):41-58

**New York City Ballet**

Stepping Up. Julia Szabo. *Harper's Bazaar* (February 1990):72

**New York (State) – Abortion Rights**

New York: Reclaiming Choice Territory. Amy Capen. *Ms.* 1, No. 2 (September/October 1990):92

**New York Times, The**

Gender Differentiation in *The New York Times*, 1885 and 1985: Some Surprises. *Media Report to Women* 18, No. 2 (March/April 1990):3-4

**New York Times Book Review** (journal)

Patchwork. Deborah Price. *Belles Lettres* 5, No. 3 (Spring 1990):26-27

**New Zealand.** *See* Maori

**New Zealand – Health**

Fate Cries Enough. By Clare Matheson. Reviewed by Hilary Haines. *The Women's Review of Books* 7, No. 8 (May 1990):20-21

The Report of the Committee of Inquiry into Allegations Concerning the Treatment of Cervical Cancer at National Women's Hospital and into Other Related Matters. Reviewed by Hilary Haines.

*The Women's Review of Books* 7, No. 8 (May 1990):20-21

Second Opinion: The Politics of Women's Health in New Zealand. By Phillida Bunkle. Reviewed by Hilary Haines. *The Women's Review of Books* 7, No. 8 (May 1990):20-21

The Unfortunate Experiment. By Sandra Coney. Reviewed by Hilary Haines. *The Women's Review of Books* 7, No. 8 (May 1990):20-21

**New Zealand – Health Care**

Second Opinion: The Politics of Women's Health in New Zealand. By Milton Keynes and Phillida Bunkle. Reviewed by Roe Sybylla. *Australian Feminist Studies* No. 11 (Autumn 1990):129-131

**New Zealand – Media and Communications**

'Dykes in the Dailies': How New Zealand Newspapaers Depict Lesbians. *Media Report to Women* 18, No. 3 (May/June 1990):8

**New Zealand – Prostitution**

Avant-Garde or Traitors of the Women's Movement? *Women's World* , No. 24 (Winter 1990/91): 49

**Ng, Wendy L**

Responding to Violence on Campus. Book Review. *NWSA Journal* 2, No. 4 (Autumn 1990):660-661

**Ngcobo, Lauretta**

And They Didn't Die. Reviewed by Anne N. Iwobi. *Spare Rib* No. 215 (August 1990):28

**Ngcobo, Nadipha**

Violence Against Women. *Women In Action* 1-2 (1990):25-26

**Nguyen-Hong-Nhiem, Lucy** and Halpern, Joel Martin (editors)

The Far East Comes Near: Autobiographical Accounts of Southeast Asian Students in America. Reviewed by Miriam Ching Louie. *Belles Lettres* 6, No. 1 (Fall 1990):27-28

**Nicaragua.** *See also* Sandinistas

**Nicaragua – Acquired Immune Deficiency Syndrome**

Moving Forward Together. *Connexions* 33 (1990):13

**Nicaragua – Elections**

Report from Nicaragua. Millie Thayer. *Spare Rib* No. 210 (March 1990):12-14

US Electoral Politricks. Holly Sklar. *Spare Rib* No. 212 (May 1990):20-23

**Nicaragua – Feminism**

Revolutionary Popular Feminism in Nicaragua: Articulating Class, Gender, and National Sovereignty. Norma Stoltz Chinchilla. *Gender and Society* 4, No. 3 (September 1990):370-397

Women-Centered Media Communications within Nicaragua. Angharad N. Valdivia. *Women & Language* 13, No. 1 (Fall 1990):59-63

### Nicaragua – Politics and Government

Flowers for Violeta. Dennis Covington. *Vogue* (August 1990):318-323+

Nicaragua After the Elections. Linda Clements. *off our backs* 20, No. 4 (April 1990):1+

Sweet Victory. Anne Arrarte. *Ladies' Home Journal* 107, No. 7 (July 1990):44-47

### Nicaragua – Prostitution

Nicaragua: From the Bordellos to the Streets. *Women's World* , No. 24 (Winter 1990/91): 42

### Nicaragua – Rape

A Developing Legal System Grapples with an Ancient Problem: Rape in Nicaragua. Beth Stephens. *Women's Rights Law Reporter* 12, No. 2 (Summer 1990): 69-88

### Nicaragua – Reproductive Rights

Nicaragua: Chamorro's Government Rolls Back Reproductive Rights. Marie de Santis. *Spare Rib* 217 (October 1990):52

Nicaragua Rolls Back Reproductive Rights. Marie de Santis. *off our backs* 20, No. 8 (August/September 1990):3

### Nichols, Grace

I Is a Long-Memoried Woman. *Spare Rib* 218 (November 1990):20-22

**Nichols, Janet** (joint author). *See* Sheilds, Patricia M.

### Nichols-Casebolt, Ann

For Reasons of Poverty: A Critical Analysis of the Public Child Welfare System in the United States. Book Review. *Journal of Marriage and the Family* 52, No. 3 (August 1990):801-802

### Nicholson, Linda J.

Gender and History: The Failure of Social Theory in the Age of the Family. Reviewed by Nancy Fraser. *NWSA Journal* 2, No. 3 (Summer 1990):505-508

### Nickel, Terri

The Autobiographical Subject: Gender and Ideology in Eighteenth-Century England. Book Review. *Tulsa Studies in Women's Literature* 9, No. 1 (Spring 1990):143-144

### Nicol, Bill

McBride: Behind the Myth. Reviewed by Charles Kerr. *Healthright* 9, No. 4 (August 1990):45

### Nicole Miller Limited

More Money: How One Small Supplier Grappled with the Campeau Giant. Doreen Mangan. *Executive Female* (March/April 1990):18-19

**Niebrugge-Brantley, Jill** (joint reviewer). *See* Madoo-Lengermann, Patricia

### Niederman, Sharon

A Quilt of Words: Women's Diaries, Letters, and Original Accounts of Life in the Southwest, 1860-1960. Reviewed by Lynn Wenzel. *New Directions for Women* 19, No. 2 (March/April 1990):15

### Nielsen, Margaret

Biting the Hand that Feeds Them: Organizing Women on Welfare at the Grass Roots Level. Book Review. *AFFILIA* 5, No. 4 (Winter 1990):115

### Nieman, David C.

The Exercise/Illness Connection. *Women's Sports and Fitness* 12, No. 2 (March 1990):56-57

### Niemann, Linda

Boomer: Railroad Memoirs. Reviewed by Wendy Chapkis. *The Women's Review of Books* 7, No. 7 (April 1990):6-7

### Niemi, Judith

Fear of the Wilderness. *Woman of Power* 18 (Fall 1990):82-83

The Magnificent Mountain Women: Adventures in the Colorado Rockies. Book Review. *The Women's Review of Books* 8, No. 1 (October 1990):18-19

Off the Beaten Track: Women Adventurers and Mountaineers in Western Colorado. Book Review. *The Women's Review of Books* 8, No. 1 (October 1990):18-19

Reaching Their Peak. *The Women's Review of Books* 8, No. 1 (October 1990):18-19

### Nigeria – Adult Education

Nigerian Women's Quest for Role Fulfillment. Judith D.C. Osuala. *Women and Therapy* 10, No. 3 (1990):89-98

### Nigeria – Gender Roles

Demographic Surveys and Nigerian Women. Notes. Barbara Entwisle and Catherine M. Coles. *Signs* 15, No. 2 (Winter 1990):259-284

### Nigeria – Status of Women

"If Men Are Talking, They Blame It on Women": A Nigerian Woman's Comments on Divorce and Child Custody. Elisha P. Renne. *Feminist Issues* 10, No. 1 (Spring 1990):37-49

### Nightengale, Sharon

Day Help. Poem. *Essence* 21, No. 5 (September 1990):118

### Nightingale, Florence (about)

"I Have Done My Duty": Florence Nightingale in the Crimean War, 1854-56. Edited by Sue M. Goldie. Reviewed by June Purvis. *Women's Studies International Forum* 13, Nos. 1-2 (1990):160-161

### Nightmares

Into the Nightmare. Jane Bosveld. *Mademoiselle* (November 1990):114

Nightmares Can Be Good for You. Linda Leuzzi. *Ladies' Home Journal* 107, No. 3 (March 1990):64

**Nin, Anaïs** (about)

Anaïs Redux. Ellen Currie. *Lear's* (February 1990):46-48

**Nissan Motors.** *See* Automobiles – Purchasing

**Nissen, Uwe Kjaer**

A Review of Research on Language and Sex in the Spanish Language. *Women & Language* 13, No. 2 (Winter 1990):11-29

**Nixon, Will**

How to Host a Business Bash that's Not a Bore. *Working Woman* (November 1990):122-125

**Nixon, Will** and Goldstein, Judy

Save Time! *Redbook* 175, No. 4 (August 1990):86-87

**Njeri, Itabari**

What's Love Got to Do With It? Short story. *Essence* 20, No. 10 (February 1990):64-66 +

**Nkwinti, Koleka** (interview)

No to Rape. Kally Forrest. *Connexions* 34 (1990):16

**Nnaemeka, Obioma**

Mariama Bâ: Parallels, Convergence, and Interior Space. *Feminist Issues* 10, No. 1 (Spring 1990):13-35

**Nobadula, Thembi** (interview)

South African Women Return Home. *Spare Rib* No. 215 (August 1990):20-21

**Nobel, Kathleen D.**

The Female Hero: A Quest for Healing and Wholeness. *Women and Therapy* 9, No. 4 (1990):3-18

**Nochlin, Linda**

Women, Art, and Power and Other Essays. Reviewed by Whitney Chadwick. *Woman's Art Journal* 11, No. 2 (Fall 1990-Winter 1991):37-38

**Noddings, Nel**

Caring: A Feminine Approach to Ethics and Moral Education. Reviewed by Barbara Houston. *Hypatia* 5, No. 1 (Spring 1990):115-119

Caring: A Feminine Approach to Ethics and Moral Education. Reviewed by Claudia Card. *Hypatia* 5, No. 1 (Spring 1990):101-108

Caring: A Feminine Approach to Ethics and Moral Education. Reviewed by Sarah Lucia Hoagland. *Hypatia* 5, No. 1 (Spring 1990):109-114

A Response. *Hypatia* 5, No. 1 (Spring 1990):120-126

Women and Evil. Reviewed by Berenice Fisher. *The Women's Review of Books* 7, No. 8 (May 1990):21-22

Women and Evil. Reviewed by Sara Ruddick. *New Directions for Women* 19, No. 6 (November-December 1990):24

**Noël, Lise**

L'intolérance: une problem2atique généale. Reviewed by Jacinthe Michaud. *Resources for Feminist Research* 19, No. 1 (March 1990):21

**Noel, Nancy L**

Clara Barton: Professional Angel. Book review. *Signs* 15, No. 3 (Spring 1990):640-642

Ordered to Care: The Dilemma of American Nursing, 1850-1945. Book review. *Signs* 15, No. 3 (Spring 1990):640-642

**Noel, Rachel B.** (about). *See* De Veaux, Alexis, Milloy, Marilyn, and Ross, Michael Erik

**Noggle, Anne**

For God, Country and the Thrill of It. Reviewed by Pat Pateman. *Minerva* 8, No. 2 (Summer 1990):73-74

**Nolan, Faith**

Freedom to Love. Reviewed by Jill Benderly. *On the Issues* 14 (1990):29

**Nolan, Mary**

"Housework Made Easy": The Taylorized Housewife in Weimar Germany's Rationalized Economy. *Feminist Studies* 16, No. 3 (Fall 1990):549-577

**Nolan, Sarah M.**

"How I Did It": Selling Your Idea to Management. *Working Woman* (September 1990):83-85

**Noller, Patricia** and Fitzpatrick, Mary Anne

Marital Communication in the Eighties. *Journal of Marriage and the Family* 52, No. 4 (November 1990):832-843

**Nompondwana, Lydia** (interview)

No Justice in South Africa. Delysia Forbes. *Spare Rib* 213 (June 1990):43-44

**Nonkin, Lesley Jane** (editor)

Upfront. *Vogue* (August 1990):81-86; (September 1990):109-114; (December 1990):87-90

**Nonprofit Organizations.** *See also* Arts Organizations; Hesselbein, Frances (about)

**Nonprofit Organizations – Funding**

Women and Funding. *Women in Action* 3 & 4 (1990):36-42

**Nontenja, Luvuyo Don Garcia**

Speak. Poem. *Women in Action* 1-2 (1990):16

**Nontraditional Employment.** *See* Employment, Nontraditional

**Nonviolence**

You Can't Kill the Spirit: Stories of Women and Nonviolent Action. By Pam McAllister. Reviewed by

Gwyn Kirk. *Women & Politics* 10, No. 1 (1990):78-80

**Noonan, Norma**

Russian Women's Studies: Essays on Sexism in Soviet Culture. Book Review. *Women & Politics* 10, No. 4 (1990):133-134

**Noonan, Peggy**

What I Saw at the Revolution: A Political Life in the Reagan Era. Reviewed by Janet Horowitz Murray. *The Women's Review of Books* 7, No. 9 (June 1990):6

**Noonan, Peggy** (interview)

A Thousand Points to Write: Peggy Noonan on Getting a Speach Started and Keeping It Going. Interview. Christine Reinhardt. *Working Woman* (November 1990):120+

**Nord, Christine Winquist** (joint author). *See* Peterson, James L.

**Nord, Deborah Epstein**

The High Price of Free Love. *The Women's Review of Books* 8, No. 3 (December 1990):5-7

"Neither Pairs Nor Odd": Female Community in Late Nineteenth-Century London. Notes. *Signs* 15, No. 4 (Summer 1990):733-754

The New Women and the Old Men: Love, Sex, and the Woman Question. Book Review. *The Women's Review of Books* 8, No. 3 (December 1990):5-7

**Norden, Barbara**

Campaign Against Pornography. *Feminist Review* No. 35 (Summer 1990):1-8

**Nordheim, Christine** and Kreiner, Julie A.

Michelle Shocked on Coming Out. *Hot Wire* 6, No. 3 (September 1990):20-21

**Norman, Elaine**

The Chalice and the Blade. Book Review. *AFFILIA* 5, No. 2 (Summer 1990):102-104

**Norman, Robert J.**

Cause and Management of Miscarriage. *Healthright* 9, No. 4 (August 1990):22-24

**Norrgard, Lenore**

Opening the Hong Kong Closet. *Out/Look* No. 7 (Winter 1990):56-61

**Norris, Jane** (editor)

Daughters of the Elderly: Building Partnerships in Caregiving. Reviewed by Shirley L. Patterson. *Journal of Women and Aging* 2, No. 1 (1990):123-124

**Norris, Terry D.** (joint author). *See* Mitchell, Jim

**North, Percy**

America's Favorite Female Artist. *Belles Lettres* 5, No. 4 (Summer 1990):2-3

Georgia O'Keeffe. Book Review. *Belles Lettres* 5, No. 4 (Summer 1990):2-3

O'Keeffe, Stieglitz and the Critics, 1916-1929. Book Review. *Belles Lettres* 5, No. 4 (Summer 1990):2-3

**North Atlantic Treaty Organization**

Innu Women and Nation: The Occupation of Nistassinan. Winona LaDuke. *off our backs* 20, No. 10 (November 1990):10+

**North Dakota – History**

Day In, Day Out: Women's Lives in North Dakota. Edited by Bjorn Benson, Elizabeth Hampsten, and Kathryn Sweney. Reviewed by Jane M. Pederson. *NWSA Journal* 2, No. 3 (Summer 1990):519-520

**Northern Ireland**

Abortion in Northern Ireland: Report of an International Tribunal. By Northern Ireland Abortion Law Reform Association. Reviewed by Ruth Riddick. *Women's Studies International Forum* 13, No. 3 (1990):273-274

I Am of Ireland: Women of the North Speak Out. By Elizabeth Shannon. Reviewed by Eleanor J. Bader. *Belles Lettres* 5, No. 3 (Spring 1990):2-3

**Northern Ireland – Falls Women's Centre**

Falls Women's Centre Fights Sectarian Vote. *Spare Rib* No. 209 (February 1990):45

**Northern Ireland – Political Protest**

No More Bloody Sundays. Rita O'Reilly. *Spare Rib* No. 209 (February 1990):46

**Northern Ireland – Violence**

Collusion, Raids and the Cult of Fear. *Spare Rib* No. 209 (February 1990):18-20

Geraldine Skillen Convicted. *Spare Rib* No. 212 (May 1990):46

Winchester 3 Freed. *Spare Rib* No. 212 (May 1990):45

**Northern Ireland Abortion Law Reform Association**

Abortion in Northern Ireland: Report of an International Tribunal. Reviewed by Ruth Riddick. *Women's Studies International Forum* 13, No. 3 (1990):273-274

**Northern Women's Centre**

The Centre of the Backlash – Montreal. Joan Baril. *off our backs* 20, No. 4 (April 1990):13-15

**Northrop, Margaretta**

Ways of Caring. *Vogue* (November 1990):368-369

**Northrup, Christiane**

Honoring Our Bodies: The Key to Transformation. *Woman of Power* 18 (Fall 1990):16-19

**Northwest Women's Center.** *See* Philadelphia (Pa.) – Northwest Women's Center

**Norton, Mary Beth**

Women's History and Feminism in China: An Update. *Journal of Women's History* 2, No. 2 (Fall 1990):166-167

**Norville, Deborah** (about). *See also* Television Journalists – Networking

Deborah Norville: Southern Belle or Steel Magnolia? Charla Krupp. *Glamour* (November 1990):168-170

**Norway – Acquired Immune Deficiency Syndrome**

"When Penis Equals Sexuality." *Connexions* 33 (1990):11-12

**Norway – History – Feminist Perspectives**

Changing Gender Identities in an Industrializing Society: The Case of Norway, 1870-1914. Ida Blom. *Gender & History* 2, No. 2 (Summer 1990):131-147

**Norway – Prostitution**

We Exist. Vi Finnes. *Connexions* 34 (1990):31

**Norway – Status of Women**

State Feminism: Norwegian Women and the Welfare State. Eugenie A. Lucas. *Feminist Issues* 10, No. 2 (Fall 1990):43-53

**Norwich, William**

Model Painter. *Vogue* (November 1990):374-379

**Norwood, Stephen**

Labor's Flaming Youth: Telephone Operators and Worker Militancy 1878-1923. Reviewed by Annelise Orleck. *The Women's Review of Books* 8, No. 3 (December 1990):30-31

**Nosebleed**

Healthwatch: Nosebleeds. Dava Sobel. *Ladies' Home Journal* 107, No. 3 (March 1990):92

**Nostalgia**

Motherly Devotion. Pat Ross. *McCall's* 117, No. 8 (May 1990):47-48

**Notgrass, Cindy M.** (joint author). *See* Wyatt, Gail Elizabeth

**Nottingham, Suzanne**

Ski Lifts. *Women's Sports and Fitness* 12, No. 7 (October 1990):20-21

**Notting Hill Carnival.** *See* West Indians – Festivals

**Nourse, Alan E.**

Family Doctor. *Good Housekeeping* 211, No. 3 (September 1990):38-40; 211, No. 4 (October 1990):74

**Novac, Sylvia**

Not Seen, Not Heard: Women and Housing Policy. *Canadian Women's Studies* 11, No. 2 (Fall 1990):53-57

Sexual Harassment of Women Tenants. *Canadian Women's Studies* 11, No. 2 (Fall 1990):58

**Novel – History and Criticism.** *See also* Gothic Revival (Literature); Literary Criticism – Feminist Perspectives

Books: Picturing Will. By Ann Beattie. Reviewed by Gene Lyons. *Vogue* (January 1990):106-110

Clover. By Dori Sanders. Reviewed by Paula Giddings. *Essence* 21, No. 5 (September 1990):52

The Great Letter E. Reviewed by Pamela Renner. *Lilith* 15, No. 3 (Summer 1990):24

Mary Reilly. By Valerie Martin. Reviewed by David Lida. *Harper's Bazaar* (February 1990):108-110

Mothers. By Gloria Goldreich. Reviewed by Ruth Schnur. *Lilith* 15, No. 4 (Fall 1990):35

The Remains of the Day. By Kazuo Ishiguro. Reviewed by Kent Black. *Harper's Bazaar* (February 1990):50

Seventh Heaven. By Alice Hoffman. Reviewed by Laurie Winer. *Vogue* (August 1990):232-234

A Singular Country. By J. P. Donleavy. Reviewed by Kent Black. *Harper's Bazaar* (May 1990):80+

**Novel, Romantic**

O My Cordelia. Donna Baker. *Good Housekeeping* 211, No. 5 (December 1990):235-238+

**Novel – History and Criticism**

Imagining Our Lives: The Novelist as Historian. Bettina Aptheker. *Woman of Power* 16 (Spring 1990):32-35

**Novello, Antonia** (about)

The Country Doctor. Leslie Phillips. *Savvy Woman* (July/August 1990):11-12

**Novels**

Marie Laveau, Voodoo Queen. Jewell Parker Rhodes. *Feminist Studies* 16, No. 2 (Summer 1990):331-344

**Novick, Léah**

Encountering the Shekhinah. *Woman of Power* 15 (Fall-Winter 1990):45

Shekhinah. Poem. *Woman of Power* 15 (Fall-Winter 1990):44

**Novick, Nelson Lee**

Skinflicks: Technologies of Care and Repair. *Lear's* (October 1990):65

**NOW.** *See* National Organization for Women

**Nowakowski, Patty**

Young Mother's Story: "How Could I Let Them Separate My Twins?" *Redbook* 175, No. 3 (July 1990):38-41

**Noyes, Carolyn**

Home: Spring Bouquets. *Ladies' Home Journal* 107, No. 5 (May 1990):86-92

**Noyes, Carolyn B.**

My Healthy Home. *Ladies' Home Journal* 107, No. 1 (January 1990):110-118

**Nuccio, Kathleen E.** and Mama, Robin Sakina

Effects of Fetal Protection Policies on Women Workers. *AFFILIA* 5, No. 3 (Fall 1990):39-49

**Nuclear Power**

Exposing Nuclear Phallacies. Edited by Diana E. H. Russell. Reviewed by Deborah Jordan. *Australian Feminist Studies* No. 11 (Autumn 1990):127-128

**Nuclear Power – Environmental and Health Aspects**

In the Shadow of Sellafield. *Spare Rib* No. 210 (March 1990):20-22

**Nuclear Weapons Testing**

Pacific Women Speak: The Health Effects of Radiation from Nuclear Testing in the Pacific Islands. Darlene Keju-Johnson, Lijon Eknilang, and Chailang Palacios. *Woman of Power* 18 (Fall 1990):36-41

**Nude, The**

The Female Nude: Pornography, Art. and Sexuality. Notes. Lynda Nead. *Signs* 15, No. 2 (Winter 1990):323-335

**Nugent, Georgia**

This Sex Which Is Not One: De-Constructing Ovid's Hermaphrodite. *Differences* 2, No. 1 (Spring 1990):160-185

**Nunez-Harrell, Elizabeth**

Home Is Where My Heart Is. *Essence* 20, No. 12 (April 1990):36+

**Nunn, Harlan**

Eyes of Time: Photojournalism in America. Book Review. *On the Issues* 17 (Winter 1990):32-33

**Nunn, Pamela Gerrish**

Crossing Over: Feminism and Art of Social Concern. Book Review. *Woman's Art Journal* 11, No. 2 (Fall 1990-Winter 1991):42-44

Feminist Art Criticism, An Anthology. Book Review. *Woman's Art Journal* 11, No. 2 (Fall 1990-Winter 1991):42-44

**Nunnalee, Karolyn**

Patty's Legacy. Bibliography. *Ladies' Home Journal* 107, No. 4 (April 1990):28-36

**Nuns**

The Crisis of Legacy: Life Review Interviews with Elderly Women Religious. Mary Alice Wolf. *Journal of Women and Aging* 2 No. 3 (1990):67-79

**Nuns – Ireland – History**

Nuns in Nineteenth Century Ireland. By Caitriona Clear. Reviewed by Margaret MacCurtain. *Gender & History* 2, No. 3 (Autumn 1990):365-368

**Nuns – Personal Narratives**

Stratagems of the Strong, Stratagems of the Weak: Autobiographical Prose of the Seventeenth-Century Hispanic Convent. Electa Arenal and Stacey Sclau. *Tulsa Studies in Women's Literature* 9, No. 1 (Spring 1990):25-42

**Nurmi, Jari-Erik**

Adolescents' Orientation to the Future: Development of Interests and Plans, and Related Attributions and Affects, in the Life-Span Context. Book Review. *Adolescence* 25, No. 99 (Fall 1990):755

**Nurseries.** *See* Children – Rooms

**Nursing**

Dimensions of Nurse and Patient Roles in Labor. Janet I. Beaton. *Health Care for Women International* 11, No. 4 (1990):393-408

Episiotomy Power for Nurses. Wendy Haaf. *Healthsharing* 11, No. 1 (December 1989):8

Self-Attitudes and Behavioral Characteristics of Type A and B Female Registered Nurses. Sandra P. Thomas and John Jozwiak. *Health Care for Women International* 11, No. 4 (1990):477-489

Trying It on for Size: Mutual Support in Role Transition for Pregnant Teens and Student Nurses. Judith Wuest. *Health Care for Women International* 11, No. 4 (1990):383-392

**Nursing – Ethics**

A Comment on Fry's "The Role of Caring in a Theory of Nursing Ethics." Jeannine Ross Boyer and James Lindemann Nelson. *Hypatia* 5, No. 3 (Fall 1990):153-158

**Nursing – History.** *See also* Barton, Clara (about)

Angels and Citizens: British Women as Military Nurses, 1854-1914. By Anne Summers. Reviewed by Peri Rosenfeld. *Gender and Society* 4, No. 2 (June 1990):274-276

Ordered to Care: The Dilemma of American Nursing, 1850-1945. By Susan M. Reverby. Reviewed by Peri Rosenfeld. *Gender and Society* 4, No. 2 (June 1990):274-276

**Nursing – History – United States**

Black Women in White: Racial Conflict and Cooperation in the Nursing Profession, 1890-1950. By Darlene Clark Hine. Reviewed by Barbara Day. *On the Issues* 15 (Summer 1990):25-26

Ordered to Care: The Dilemma of American Nursing, 1850-1945. By Susan Reverby. Reviewed by Nancy L. Noel. *Signs* 15, No. 3 (Spring 1990):640-642

**Nursing Aides**

An Interview-Based Exploration of the Motivations and Occupational Aspirations of Chronic Care Workers. Paula Brown Doress. *Journal of Women and Aging* 2 No. 3 (1990):93-111

**Nursing Homes**

Gray Matters. Bibliography. Monique Burns. *Essence* 20, No. 12 (April 1990):77-79

**Nursing Homes – Personal Narratives**

Women In a Nursing Home: Living with Hope and Meaning. Claire M. Brody. *Psychology of Women Quarterly* 14, No. 4 (December 1990):579-592

**Nursing Schools**

Time for a Change: Women's Health Education in Canadian University Schools of Nursing. Elizabeth Hagell. *Health Care for Women International* 11, No. 2 (1990):121-131

**Nussbaum, Felicity A.**

The Autobiographical Subject: Gender and Ideology in Eighteenth-Century England. Reviewed by Terri Nickel. *Tulsa Studies in Women's Literature* 9, No. 1 (Spring 1990):143-144

**Nussbaum, Karen** (joint author). *See* Sweeny, John J.

**Nussbaum, Martha**

Therapeutic Arguments and Structures of Desire. *Differences* 2, No. 1 (Spring 1990):46-66

**NUT Educational Review**

Equal Opportunities in the New ERA. Reviewed by Iram Siraj-Blatchford. *Gender and Education* 2, No. 3 (1990):367-368

**Nutrition.** *See also* Aging; Breakfasts and Brunches; Breast Cancer; Christmas – Parties; Cookery; Food; Food – Fat Content; Health Education; Homeless – Nutrition; Immune System; Low Fat Diet; Skin – Care and Hygiene; Vitamin Therapy

Beef Is Back. *Ladies' Home Journal* 107, No. 9 (September 1990):194+

The Buzz on Beef. Ellen Kunes. *Mademoiselle* (December 1990):186

Can You Eat to Heal? Leslie Granston. *Mademoiselle* (December 1990):110

Cleansing Diet Recipes. Jonell Nash. *Essence* 20, No. 9 (January 1990):80-83+

Cuisine of the Sun. Jan Turner Hazard. *Ladies' Home Journal* 107, No. 8 (August 1990):126-137

A Diet for the Worst Days. Cynthia Hacinli. *Mademoiselle* (October 1990):120

Diet News: How Hollywood Eats. Ellen Kunes. *Mademoiselle* (September 1990):282

Diet News: How to Lose Five Pounds This Month. Ellen Kunes. *Mademoiselle* (January 1990):144

Diet Q & A. *Mademoiselle* (June 1990):206; (October 1990):204

Dinner ASAP: Grill Power. Jean Galton. *Working Woman* (September 1990):207

Dinner on a Bed. *Glamour* (April 1990):304-305

Do the Right Thing, Eat the Right Thing. Carolyn DeMarco. *Healthsharing* 11, No. 4 (December 1990):28-30

Easy as Pie. *Ladies' Home Journal* 107, No. 1 (January 1990):122-126

Eater's Digest. *Glamour* (March 1990):295; (June 1990):270; (November 1990):262

Eat Right, Be Healthier, Live Longer. Jane Shiyen Chou. *McCall's* 117, No. 8 (May 1990):32

Eat Well: Wheat vs. Oats. Mindy Hermann. *Family Circle* 103, No. 2 (February 1, 1990):19+

Fish for Life. Valerie Vaz. *Essence* 21, No. 2 (June 1990):75-78

Fish Stories. *Ladies' Home Journal* 107, No. 4 (April 1990):199-203

Food Advisory. Densie Webb. *Working Woman* (November 1990):157

Food Advisory. Lori Longbotham. *Working Woman* (October 1990):147

Food Forecast. Jean Hewitt. *Family Circle* 103, No. 15 (November 6, 1990):38

Food & Health. *Glamour* (September 1990):344

Food News. Valerie Vaz. *Essence* 21, No. 8 (December 1990):100

Foods to Stay Awake By. Shifra Diamond. *Mademoiselle* (December 1990):106

Go Ahead and Eat Cake. Jane Shiyen Chou. *McCall's* 117, No. 10 (July 1990):28-34

The Good News about Snacking. *Glamour* (January 1990):158

Health News. Marian Sandmaier. *Working Woman* (September 1990):201

Healthy Cook: Frozen Assets. Mary Beth Jung. *Working Woman* (August 1990):84

The Healthy Microwave Cookbook. Marie Simmons. *Ladies' Home Journal* 107, No. 10 (October 1990):203-208

Home Cooking. Jan Turner Hazard. *Ladies' Home Journal* 107, No. 10 (October 1990):184-194

Hot Diggity! *Redbook* 175, No. 4 (August 1990):96-97+

Hot Potatoes! Jan Turner Hazard. *Ladies' Home Journal* 107, No. 2 (February 1990):139-149

How Does Your Sandwich Stack Up? *Good Housekeeping* 211, No. 4 (October 1990):178

How Safe Is Our Food? Excerpt. Tufts University School of Nutrition. *Ladies' Home Journal* 107, No. 6 (June 1990):168-173

How to Eat, Drink and Still Be Merry. Lorraine Dusky. *McCall's* 118, No. 3 (December 1990):22

Junk Food. *Glamour* (August 1990):242-243

Just Saying No, No, No to the Sizzle. Toby Cohen. *Lear's* (October 1990):76

Leaner Ways to Eat. *Glamour* (May 1990):302-306

Magic Foods: Help or Hype? Mindy Hermann. *Family Circle* 103, No. 14 (October 16, 1990):132-134

Medinews. Sally Squires. *Ladies' Home Journal* 107, No. 8 (August 1990):30

No-Cook Suppers. *Ladies' Home Journal* 107, No. 8 (August 1990):143-147

Nutrinews. Densie Webb. *Ladies' Home Journal* 107, No. 10 (October 1990):210-212

Nutripoints. Roy E. Vartabedian and Kathy Matthews. *Ladies' Home Journal* 107, No. 2 (February 1990):38-43; 107, No. 3 (March 1990):48+

Nutrition, Diet & Fitness: What's News Now! *Good Housekeeping* 211, No. 3 (September 1990):266-268; 211, No. 4 (October 1990):194-196

The Nutrition Challenge for Women: A Guide to Wellness Without Dieting. By Louise Lambert-Lagacé. Reviewed by Jo-Ann Minden. *Healthsharing* 11, No. 1 (December 1989):33-34

Nutrition/Fitness: Exercise: How Much Is Too Much? Jane Shiyen Chou. *McCall's* 117, No. 7 (April 1990):14

Nutrition Makeover. Arlene Fischer. *Redbook* 175, No. 2 (June 1990):135-146

Nutrition Now: The Perfect Salad. *Redbook* 175, No. 3 (July 1990):116-121

Nutrition Now: 7 Vitamins & Minerals Women Need Most. Mona Sue Boyd. *Redbook* 175, No. 4 (August 1990):124-130

Nutrition Now: Wake Up and Smile. *Redbook* 174, No. 5 (March 1990):164-171

Nutrition Questions. *Glamour* (May 1990):316; (June 1990):272; (October 1990):299

100 Great Little Tips to Make Healthy Eating Easier. Stanley Gershoff and Catherine Whitney. *Redbook* 174, No. 6 (April 1990):120-133

Party Quiche! *Redbook* 176, No. 2 (December 1990):148

The P.E.P Diet: The Perfect Eating Plan for Life. Susan Male Smith. *Family Circle* 103, No. 14 (October 16, 1990):128-130

Pleasing Your Picky Eaters. Carin Rubenstein and Claudia Gallo. *Working Mother* 13, No. 1 (January 1990):79-84

Postpatriarchal Eating. *Ms.* 1, No. 1 (July/August 1990):59

Pure Food. *Lear's* (January 1990):80-85

Saturday Night Supper: Sautéed Chicken. *Glamour* (March 1990):293

Savor the Flavor of Fall. *Family Circle* 103, No. 14 (October 16, 1990):106-108

Savvy School Lunches. Barbara Kafka. *Family Circle* 103, No. 14 (October 16, 1990):162-165

Secret Energy Foods. Marilyn Diamond. *Family Circle* 103, No. 12 (September 4, 1990):76+

Shortcut Nutrition. *Glamour* (November 1990):258-261

Skillet Spareribs. *Redbook* 175, No. 5 (September 1990):194

Slim Pork. *Redbook* 175, No. 1 (May 1990):140-148

Stay Slim & Healthy: Snack All Day. Janis Jibrin. *Redbook* 174, No. 5 (March 1990):114-117

Supermarket Diet. Densie Webb. *Redbook* 175, No. 1 (May 1990):100

Surprise! The Way You Eat May Be Healthier than You Think. *Glamour* (March 1990):288-290

10 Great Meals for Small Families. Kathy Gunst. *Redbook* 175, No. 6 (October 1990):129-138

The Ten Most Underrated Foods. *Glamour* (February 1990):210-211

12 Great Meals for Small Families. Melanie Barnard and Brooke Dojny. *Redbook* 174, No. 5 (March 1990):141-152

Vital Signs. *McCall's* 117, No. 7 (April 1990):43-44

Your Protein Profile. Jane E. Brody. *Family Circle* 103, No. 11 (August 14, 1990):57+

**Nutrition – Adolescents**

Clothing Interests, Body Satisfaction, and Eating Behavior of Adolescent Females: Related or Independent Dimensions? Mary Ann Littrell, Mary Lynn Damhorst, and John M. Littrell. *Adolescence* 25, No. 97 (Spring 1990):77-95

Self-Concept as a Factor in the Quality of Diets of Adolescent Girls. G. Kathleen Newell, Cynthia L. Hammig, Anthony P. Jurich, and Dallas E. Johnson. *Adolescence* 25, No. 97 (Spring 1990):117-130

**Nutrition – Advertisements**

Health Express: Low Fat, High Hype: The Great Food-Label Scam. Patricia Mennitt. *Mademoiselle* (February 1990):102-106

Potential Nutrition Messages in Magazines Read by College Students. Ann A. Hertzler and Ingolf Grün. *Adolescence* 25, No. 99 (Fall 1990):717-724

**Nuytten, Bruno** (director)

Camille Claudel. Reviewed by Judy Simmons. *Ms.* 1, No. 1 (July/August 1990):74-75

**Nyabongo, Elizabeth**

Elizabeth of Toro: The Odyssey of an African Princess. Reviewed by Carole Boyce Davies. *Belles Lettres* 5, No. 3 (Spring 1990):13

**Nyborg-Andersen, Irene**

"I Slipped on the Ice." *Ladies' Home Journal* 107, No. 1 (January 1990):52-56

New Gains in Cancer Therapy. *Ladies' Home Journal* 107, No. 5 (May 1990):66

**Nyborg-Andersen, Irene** (joint author). *See* Chittum, Samme

**Nyden-Rodstein, Barbara** (about)

A Faucet Firm Lands in Hot Water. Joan Delaney. *Executive Female* 13, No. 6 (November-December 1990):70-71

**Nye, Andrea**

Feminist Theory and the Philosophies of Man. Reviewed by Linda Bell. *Hypatia* 5, No. 1 (Spring 1990):127-132

**Nye, Louise Klimpton**

The Witches. *Spare Rib* No. 214 (July 1990):32

**Nygaard, E.,** Madsen, A. Gleerup, and Christensen, H.

Endurance Capacity and Longevity in Women. *Health Care for Women International* 11, No. 1 (1990):1-10

# O

**Oakland, Calif.**

Oakland Highlights. Lillian Broadous II. *Essence* 21, No. 1 (May 1990):166-170

**Oakland, Calif. – Political Activists**

Oakland: Back to the Future. Julianne Malveaux. *Essence* 21, No. 1 (May 1990):157-159

Oakland: Power of the People. Evelyn C. White. *Essence* 21, No. 1 (May 1990):160-164

**Oakley, Ann**

Matilda's Mistake. Reviewed by Natasha Moar. *Spare Rib* 217 (October 1990):33

**Oates, Joyce Carol**

Possession. Book Review. *Vogue* (November 1990):274+

**O'Barr, Jean F.**

Women and a New Academy: Gender and Cultural Contexts. Reviewed by Gloria Bowles. *NWSA Journal* 2, No. 2 (Spring 1990):288-290

**O'Barr, Jean F.** (editor)

Women and a New Academy: Gender and Cultural Contexts. Reviewed by M. Jane Ayer. *Feminist Collections* 11, No. 3 (Spring 1990):3-4

O'Barr, J. (joint editor). *See* Minnich, E.

**Oberbeck, Elizabeth Birkelund**

Enterprise: The Start-Up: Treading Water until Your Ship Comes In. *Working Woman* (April 1990):41-44

**Obesity.** *See also* Children – Obesity; Weight Loss

Fat War. Georgiana Arnold. *Essence* 21, No. 3 (July 1990):52-53+

Fear of Fat: How Young Can It Start? Lee Salk. *McCall's* 117, No. 11 (August 1990):65

Growing Up with a Fat Mom. Linda Neilson. *Glamour* (April 1990):156-160

Health Notes. *Vogue* (July 1990):112

Talking with Delta Burke: "Nothing Matters but Our Love." Interview. Jerry Buck. *Redbook* 174, No. 6 (April 1990):34-36

Weighing Your Risks. *Glamour* (September 1990):306-309

**Obituaries**

Levin, Nora. *Lilith* 15, No. 2 (Spring 1990):28

Ohmann, Carol Burke. *Women's Studies Quarterly* 18, Nos. 3-4 (Fall-Winter 1990):159-160

Simon, Kate. *Women's Studies Quarterly* 18, Nos. 3-4 (Fall-Winter 1990):153-158

Wischnitzer, Rachel. *Lilith* 15, No. 2 (Spring 1990):28

Yost, Barbara Ann. *Minerva* 8, No. 2 (Summer 1990):67-71

**O'Brien, Edna**

The High Road. Reviewed by Mary Titus. *Belles Lettres* 5, No. 3 (Spring 1990):4

**O'Brien, Kate**

The Ante-Room. Reviewed by Kathleene West. *Belles Lettres* 5, No. 3 (Spring 1990):4

The Land of Spices. Reviewed by Kathleene West. *Belles Lettres* 5, No. 3 (Spring 1990):4

**O'Brien, Mary**

Reproducing the World: Essays in Feminist Theory. Reviewed by Christine Di Stefano. *Women & Politics* 10, No. 4 (1990):138-140

Reproducing the World: Essays in Feminist Theory. Reviewed by Elizabeth Kamarck Minnich. *Signs* 16, No. 1 (Autumn 1990):177-180

Reproducing the World: Essays in Feminist Theory. Reviewed by Juanne N. Clarke. *Atlantis* 15, No. 2 (Spring 1990):118

Reproducing the World: Essays in Feminist Theory. Reviewed by Julia Miles. *Atlantis* 15, No. 2 (Spring 1990):118-120

**O'Brien, Pamela Guthrie**

Secrets of a Super Garden. *Ladies' Home Journal* 107, No. 3 (March 1990):149-152

**O'Brien, Sandra J.** and Vertinsky, Patricia A.

Elderly Women, Exercise and Healthy Aging. *Journal of Women and Aging* 2 No. 3 (1990):41-65

**O'Brien, Tim**

Field Trip. Short story. *McCall's* 117, No. 11 (August 1990):78-79

**Obscenity.** *See also* Pornography

X Rated: When Hardcore Hits Home. Nancy Shulins. *Family Circle* 103, No. 16 (November 27, 1990):63-69

**Obsessive-Compulsive Disorders**

Personal Journal. Bibliography. *Ladies' Home Journal* 107, No. 9 (September 1990):122-126

**Obstetrics**

The Whole Birth Catalog. Ann Ferrar. *Ladies' Home Journal* 107, No. 8 (August 1990):46-50

**Occupational Health and Safety**

Advocate Battles for Safety in Mines and Poultry Plants. Elayne Clift. *New Directions for Women* 19, No. 3 (May/June 1990):3

The Hazardous Working Conditions of Rural Women. Dinesh Mohan. *Manushi* No. 59 (July-August 1990):25-28

Hazards of Hearth and Home. Lesley Doyal. *Women's Studies International Forum* 13, No. 5 (1990):501-517

Health and Fitness Notes. *Vogue* (December 1990):215

Health Care of Women in the Workplace. Jacqueline Collins. *Health Care for Women International* 11, No. 1 (1990):21-32

Health News. Marian Sandmaier. *Working Woman* (November 1990):148

How to Rid Your Company of VDT Health Hazards. Shirley Chan. *Working Woman* (March 1990):52

Is Your Office Making You Sick? Charles Piller and Michael Castleman. *Redbook* 174, No. 6 (April 1990):114-115+

Is Your Office Making You Sick? Patricia Canole. *Executive Female* (May/June 1990):32-33+

Medinews. Sally Squires. *Ladies' Home Journal* 107, No. 4 (April 1990):112-118

Suffer the Working Day: Women in the "Dangerous Trades," 1880-1914. Barbara Harrison. *Women's Studies International Forum* 13, Nos. 1-2 (1990):79-90

This Is What You Thought: Whose Job Is Fetal Protection? *Glamour* (August 1990):139

Why I Can't Stop Thinking about My Computer. Cindi Leive. *Glamour* (October 1990):162-166

Women Protected Out of Jobs. Laura McClure. *New Directions for Women* 19, No. 1 (January/February 1990):1

**Occupational Mobility – Middle Age**

Career Developments and Transitions of Middled-Aged Women. Rosalie J. Ackerman. *Psychology of*

*Women Quarterly* 14, No. 4 (December 1990):513-530

**Occupational Status.** *See also* Power Structure

**Occupational Stress.** *See also* Balancing Work and Family Life; Employees – Resignation; Stress

Attention Working Women: Rate Your Stress Life. *Redbook* 175, No. 2 (June 1990):83-90

Bereavement and Stress in Career Women. Wilhelmina Kalu. *Women and Therapy* 10, No. 3 (1990):75-87

Burnout in the Human Services: A Feminist Perspective. Janet L. Finn. *AFFILIA* 5, No. 4 (Winter 1990):55-71

Can Getting Mad Get the Job Done? Kathryn Stechert Black. *Working Woman* (March 1990):86-90

Career Strategies: Burned Out. Can You Get Fired Up Again? Adele Scheele. *Working Woman* (October 1990):46-48

Health Report: Customized Stress Control: Identify Your Coping Style. Mary E. King and Janette M. Scandura. *Working Woman* (October 1990):135-136

Medical News. Dana Points and Carla Rohlfing. *Family Circle* 103, No. 13 (September 25, 1990):24

Mid-Course Correction. A'Lelia Bundles. *Essence* 20, No. 9 (January 1990):28+

She Ate Not the Bread of Idleness: Exhaustion Is Related to Domestic and Salaried Working Conditions among 539 Québec Hospital Workers. Daniel Tierney, Patrizia Romito, and Karen Messing. *Women and Health* 16, No. 1 (1990):21-42

**Occupational Training.** *See also* Employees – Training; Immigrants – Employment; Industry and Education

**Occupational Trends**

Are You Ready for the '90s? Lorraine Dusky. *Working Woman* (January 1990):55

Why It Won't Be Business as Usual. Ronni Sandroff. *Working Woman* (January 1990):58-62

**Ochoa, Laurie**

Pretty Enough to Eat. *Harper's Bazaar* (March 1990):231+

**Ochs, Vanessa**

Jewish Feminist Scholarship Comes of Age. Bibliography. *Lilith* 15, No. 1 (Winter 1990):8-12

On the Path to Power: Women Decode the Talmud in Their Own Style. *Lilith* 15, No. 3 (Summer 1990):16-18

**O'Connell, Agnes N.** and Russo, Nancy Felipe (editors)

Models of Achievement: Reflections of Eminent Women in Psychology, Volume 2. Reviewed by

Margaret E. Guyer. *Psychology of Women Quarterly* 14, No. 4 (December 1990):621-623

**O'Connell, Dorothy** (about)

Poet Laureate of the Poor: Dorothy O'Connell. Mary Garrett. *Canadian Women's Studies* 11, No. 2 (Fall 1990):36-37

**O'Connell, Sanjida**

Come the Revolution. Short Story. *Spare Rib* 219 (December 1990-January 1991):54-56

**O'Connor, Ann** (joint author). *See* Brown, Miche4le

**O'Connor, Denise**

Between Feminism and Psychoanalysis. Book Review. *Feminist Review* No. 34 (Spring 1990):171-175

**O'Connor, Eileen** (joint author). *See* Dan, Alice J.

**O'Connor, Karen** and Segal, Jeffrey A.

Justice Sandra Day O'Connor and the Supreme Court's Reaction to Its First Female Member. *Women & Politics* 10, No. 2 (1990):95-104

**O'Connor, Karen** (joint author). *See* Cook, Beverly B.

**O'Connor, Leslie**

Preferred Treatment. *Harper's Bazaar* (September 1990):102+

**O'Connor, Patricia W.**

Women Playwrights in Contemporary Spain and the Male-Dominated Canon. Notes. *Signs* 15, No. 2 (Winter 1990):376-390

**O'Connor, Sandra Day**

Women and the Constitution: A Bicentennial Perspective. *Women & Politics* 10, No. 2 (1990):5-16

**O'Connor, Sandra Day** (about)

Justice Sandra Day O'Connor and the Supreme Court's Reaction to Its First Female Member. Karen O'Connor and Jeffrey A. Segal. *Women & Politics* 10, No. 2 (1990):95-104

**O'Connor, Sinéad** (about). *See* Entertainers

**O'Dair, Barbara** (joint author). *See* Ellis, Kate

**Odendahl, Teresa**

Charity Begins at Home: Generosity and Self-Interest Among the Philanthropic Elite. Reviewed by Mary Ellen Capek. *The Women's Review of Books* 8, No. 3 (December 1990):12-13

**Odetta** (about). *See* Musicians, Popular, "Repeat Performance"

**Odom, Mary Ann** (about)

"How I Did It": Homing In on the Hottest Trends. *Working Woman* (December 1990):35-36

**O'Donnell, Carol** and Hall, Philippa

Getting Equal: Labour Market Regulation and Women's Work. Reviewed by Cora Vellekoop

Baldock. *Australian Feminist Studies* No. 12 (Summer 1990):43-49

Getting Equal. Reviewed by Jennifer Craven-Griffiths. *Gender and Education* 2, No. 3 (1990):373-374

**O'Donovan, K.** and Szyszczak, E.

Equality and Sex Discrimination Law. Reviewed by Jennifer Craven-Griffiths. *Gender and Education* 2, No. 3 (1990):373-374

**Offen, Karen**

Women, Work and the French State: Labour Protection and Social Patriarchy, 1879-1919. Book Review. *Resources for Feminist Research* 19, No. 1 (March 1990):45-46

Women's Memory, Women's History, Women's Political Action: The French Revolution in Retrospect, 1789-1889-1989. *Journal of Women's History* 1, No. 3 (Winter 1990):211-230

**Offer, Daniel**, Ostrov, Eric, Howard, Kenneth I., and Atkinson, Robert

The Teenage World: Adolescents' Self-Image in Ten Countries. Book Review. *Adolescence* 25, No. 100 (Winter 1990):999

**Office Decoration**

One Woman's Office: Essence of Elegance. Leah Rosch. *Working Woman* (January 1990):120-121

**Office Environment.** *See* Air Pollution – Indoors; Quality of Work Life

**Office Equipment and Supplies**

Cruise in the Fast Lane. George L. Beiswinger. *Executive Female* (May/June 1990):30-31+

**Office Layout.** *See also* Home-Based Work

Design Hot Line: The Office that (Almost) Does the Work for You. Barbara Flanagan. *Working Woman* (October 1990):112-115

Get Organized. Regina Baraban. *Working Woman* (January 1990):116-119

Memos on the Office Environment. *Working Woman* (February 1990):70-72; (March 1990):65-68; (August 1990):51-52

**Office Machines.** *See* Electronic Office Machines

**Office Management**

How to Manage Office Friction. Andrew S. Grove. *Working Woman* (August 1990):24-26

Memos on the Office Environment. *Working Woman* (May 1990):77-78; (June 1990):49-50; (July 1990):67-70

Private Time. *Glamour* (January 1990):62-63

**Office Parties**

Out Box: Office-Party Perverts. Gail Collins. *Working Woman* (November 1990):176

Over-40 & Better than Ever! *Harper's Bazaar* (August 1990):101

Prime of Life. Andrea Jolles. *Family Circle* 103, No. 4 (March 13, 1990):58+

Women As They Age: Challenge, Opportunity, and Triumph. Edited by J. Dianne Garner and Susan O. Mercer. Reviewed by Judith G. Gonyea. *AFFILIA* 5, No. 4 (Winter 1990):116-117

**Older Adults – Abuse.** *See* Adams, Aileen (about)

**Older Adults – Activism**

Prime of Life: Out of Retirement and into Office. Kelly Norton Humphrey. *Family Circle* 103, No. 9 (June 26, 1990):140-142

Prime of Life: Sixtysomething . . . *Family Circle* 103, No. 14 (October 16, 1990):46-48

Prime of Life: The New Recruits. Kelly Norton Humphrey. *Family Circle* 103, No. 13 (September 25, 1990):38-40

**Older Adults – Activities**

Being Old: Seven Women, Seven Views. Noreen Hale. *Journal of Women and Aging* 2, No. 2 (1990):7-17

The Dancin' Grannies. Joan Gage. *Good Housekeeping* 211, No. 5 (November 1990):24+

Five Elderly Dementia Patients Who Played with Dolls. Makoto J. Kawai, Mari Miyamoto, and Kimio Miyamoto. *Journal of Women and Aging* 2, No. 1 (1990):99-107

Formal Activities for Elderly Women: Determinants of Participation in Voluntary and Senior Center Activities. Masako Ishii-Kuntz. *Journal of Women and Aging* 2, No. 1 (1990):79-97

Inventing Freedom: The Positive Poetic "Mutterings" of Older Women. Jo C. Searles. *Journal of Women and Aging* 2, No. 2 (1990):153-160

Invention Begins at Forty: Older Women of the 19th Century as Inventors. Autumn Stanley. *Journal of Women and Aging* 2, No. 2 (1990):133-151

Older Women: Surviving and Thriving: A Manual for Group Leaders. By Ruth Harriet Jacobs. Reviewed by Joan H. Carder. *Journal of Women and Aging* 2, No. 1 (1990):125-126

**Older Adults – Care.** *See also* Parents, Aged

Family Leave and Gender Justice. Suzanne E. England. *AFFILIA* 5, No. 2 (Summer 1990):8-24

Gray Matters. Bibliography. Monique Burns. *Essence* 20, No. 12 (April 1990):77-79

Women in a Nursing Home: Living with Hope and Meaning. Claire M. Brody. *Psychology of Women Quarterly* 14, No. 4 (December 1990):579-592

**Older Adults – Discrimination**

Age Bias in Media Industry Complicating Career Paths. *Media Report to Women* 18, No. 5 (September-October 1990):3-4

On Gray Hair and Oppressed Brains. Ann E. Gerike. *Journal of Women and Aging* 2, No. 2 (1990):35-46

Listen to the Old Women Forum. Farar Elliott and Carol Anne Douglas. *off our backs* 20, No. 8 (August/September 1990):17-18

Media Checklist for Decoding Images in Print and Video Media. *Media Report to Women* 18, No. 5 (September-October 1990):4-5

Mentoring and Being Mentored: Issues of Sex, Power, and Politics for Older Women. Michele A. Paludi, Deborah Meyers, Joni Kindermann, Hilda Speicher, and Marilyn Haring-Hidore. *Journal of Women and Aging* 2 No. 3 (1990):81-92

Old Women as Mother Figures. Rachel Josefowitz Siegel. *Women and Therapy* 10, Nos. 1/2 (1990):89-97

Politics of Aging: I'm Not Your Mother. Barbara Macdonald. *Ms.* 1, No. 1 (July/August 1990):56-58

Women and Varieties of Ageism. Evelyn R. Rosenthal. *Journal of Women and Aging* 2, No. 2 (1990):1-6

**Older Adults – Economic Status**

Poverty Among Black Elderly Women. Vanessa Wilson-Ford. *Journal of Women and Aging* 2, No. 4 (1990):5-20

Women Who Make a Difference. Mary Beth Sammons. *Family Circle* 103, No. 11 (August 14, 1990):17-19

**Older Adults – Financial Planning.** *See also* Wills

A Few Words on Trading Places. Bibliography. Nancy Dunnan. *Lear's* (September 1990):32-35

Gender Differences in Retirement Planning Among Educators: Implications for Practice with Older Women. Virginia Richardson. *Journal of Women and Aging* 2 No. 3 (1990):27-40

Older Women's Health and Financial Vulnerability: Implications of the Medicare Benefit Structure. Shoshanna Sofaer and Emily Abel. *Women and Health* 16, Nos. 3/4 (1990):47-67

Planning for the Future: Steps to Take Now. Bibliography. Christina Ferrari. *McCall's* 118, No. 2 (November 1990):85

**Older Adults – Health Care.** *See also* Medicare

Adjusting to Chronic Disease: The Osteoporotic Woman. Karen A. Roberto. *Journal of Women and Aging* 2, No. 1 (1990):33-47

The Aging Population in the Twenty-First Century: Statistics for Health Policy. Edited by Dorothy M. Gilford. Reviewed by Cheryl H. Kinderknecht.

*Journal of Women and Aging* 2 No. 3 (1990):115-116

Elderly Women, Exercise and Healthy Aging. Sandra J. O'Brien and Patricia A. Vertinsky. *Journal of Women and Aging* 2 No. 3 (1990):41-65

Predictors of Health Status of Mid-Life Women: Implications for Later Adulthood. Sandra P. Thomas. *Journal of Women and Aging* 2, No. 1 (1990):49-77

Predictors of Loneliness in Older Women and Men. Cornelia Beck, Cathleen Schultz, Chris Gorman Walton, and Robert Walls. *Journal of Women and Aging* 2, No. 1 (1990):3-31

**Older Adults – Health Insurance**

Women Who Make a Difference. Alice Rindler Shapin. *Family Circle* 103, No. 16 (November 27, 1990):17-19

**Older Adults – Housing**

Personnes âgées et logement. By Ghislaine Paquin, Jacinthe Aubin, and Marie Boivin. Reviewed by Dominique Masson. *Canadian Women's Studies* 11, No. 2 (Fall 1990):86-87

**Older Adults – Media Portrayal**

Reconsidering "Ms. Daisy." Barbara Quart. *Lilith* 15, No. 3 (Summer 1990):29

**Older Adults – Relationships**

Friendships Among Old Women. Ruth Harriet Jacobs. *Journal of Women and Aging* 2, No. 2 (1990):19-32

Love and Work After 60: An Integration of Personal and Professional Growth Within a Long-Term Marriage. Rachel Josefowitz Siegel. *Journal of Women and Aging* 2, No. 2 (1990):69-79

Remarriage in Later Life: A Critique and Review of the Literature. Jean A. Steitz and Karen G. Welker. *Journal of Women and Aging* 2, No. 4 (1990):81-90

**Older Adults – Sexuality**

Endless Desire. Susan Crain Bakos. *Harper's Bazaar* (August 1990):36

Hidden Death: The Sexual Effects of Hysterectomy. Dorin Schumacher. *Journal of Women and Aging* 2, No. 2 (1990):49-66

**Older Adults – Stereotyping**

Media Stereotyping: A Comparison of the Way Elderly Women and Men Are Portrayed on Prime-Time Television. JoEtta A. Vernon, J. Allen Williams, Jr., Terri Phillips, and Janet Wilson. *Journal of Women and Aging* 2, No. 4 (1990):55-68

We Are Not Your Mothers: Report on Two Groups of Women Over Sixty. Rachel Josefowitz Siegel. *Journal of Women and Aging* 2, No. 2 (1990):81-89

**Older Mothers.** *See* Middle-Aged Women – Childbirth

**Older Students.** *See* Adult Students

**Old Girl Networks.** *See* Networking; Professional Women's Groups

**Olds, Sally Wendkos** and Papalia, Diane E.

Are Kids Growing Up Too Fast? *Redbook* 174, No. 5 (March 1990):91-92 +

**Olesen, Virginia**

Self-Assessment and Change in One's Profession: Notes on the Phenomenology of Aging Among Mid-Life Women. *Journal of Women and Aging* 2, No. 4 (1990):69-79

**Oliff, Susan L.**

To Be Genetically Tied or Not to Be: A Dilemma Posed by the Use of Frozen Embryos. *Women's Rights Law Reporter* 12, No. 2 (Summer 1990): 115-122

**Oliker, Stacey J.**

Best Friends and Marriage: Exchange Among Women. Reviewed by Nancy Mandell. *Journal of Marriage and the Family* 52, No. 3 (August 1990):802-803

Best Friends and Marriage. Reviewed by E. Kay Trimberger. *The Women's Review of Books* 7, No. 5 (February 1990):10-11

**Olivacce, Beverley** (about). *See* Fashion Designers, "Top Women Designers"

**Oliver, D. S.**

Cultivated Pleasures: The Art of Romantic Gardening. Book Review. *The Women's Review of Books* 7, No. 6 (March 1990):21-22

Everyday Magic. *The Women's Review of Books* 8, No. 2 (November 1990):23-24

Garden Varieties. *The Women's Review of Books* 7, No. 6 (March 1990):21-22

The Scented Garden: Choosing, Growing and Using the Plants that Bring Fragrance to Your Life, Home and Table. Book Review. *The Women's Review of Books* 7, No. 6 (March 1990):21-22

Wheel of the Year: Living the Magical Life. Book Review. *The Women's Review of Books* 8, No. 2 (November 1990):23-24

Women's Rituals: A Sourcebook. Book Review. *The Women's Review of Books* 8, No. 2 (November 1990):23-24

**Oliver, Kelly**

"Am I That Name?" Feminism and the Category of 'Women' in History. Book Review. *NWSA Journal* 2, No. 4 (Autumn 1990):674-675

Death and Dissymmetry: The Politics of Coherence in the Book of Judges. Book Review. *Hypatia* 5, No. 3 (Fall 1990):169-171

**Oliver, Stephanie Stokes**

Parenting: The Middle Passage. *Essence* 21, No. 1 (May 1990):186

Travel: Getting Married in Paradise. Bibliography. *Essence* 20, No. 10 (February 1990):99-100

**Oliveri, Mary Ellen**

Handbook of Family Measurement Techniques. Book Review. *Journal of Marriage and the Family* 52, No. 3 (August 1990):799-800

**Olivero, Magaly**

Get Crazy: How to Have a Breakthrough Idea. *Working Woman* (September 1990):144-147+

Getting Your MBA on Company Time. *Working Woman* (January 1990):91-92

**Olmos, Edward James** (about). *See* Dutka, Elaine

**O'Loughlin, Michael** (joint author). *See* Kuhn, Deanna

**Olsen, Joseph A.** (joint author). *See* Phinney, Virginia G.

**Olsson, Henny M.** (joint author). *See* Lindell, Marianne E.

**Omolade, Barbara**

It's a Family Affair: The Real Lives of Black Single Mothers. Reviewed by Jacqueline E. Wade. *NWSA Journal* 2, No. 2 (Spring 1990):315-319

**Omvedt, Gail**

We Will Smash this Prison! Indian Women in Struggle. Reviewed by Kalpana Bardhan. *Journal of Women's History* 2, No. 1 (Spring 1990):200-219

**O'Neal, Kathleen M.**

An Abyss of Light. Reviewed by Ann E. Kottner. *The Women's Review of Books* 7, Nos. 10-11 (July 1990):40-41

**O'Neal, Ryan** (about). *See* Celebrities - Life Styles

**O'Neil, Robin** (joint author). *See* Greenberger, Ellen

**O'Neill, Gilda** (joint author). *See* Gamman, Lorraine

**O'Neill, Hugh**

Ardent Spouse in Search of the Perfect Gift . . . *McCall's* 118, No. 3 (December 1990):46-48

The Katharine Hepburn School of Love. *McCall's* 118, No. 1 (October 1990):52-58

**O'Neill, Kate**

Women's Bodies as Battlegrounds. *Woman of Power* 18 (Fall 1990):10-14

**Only Children.** *See* Single-Child Family

**On the Issues** (journal)

On the Issues Goes Quarterly. *On the Issues* 17 (Winter 1990):29

**On the Line**

Words and Music for Social Change. Patricia Gambarini. *New Directions for Women* 19, No. 5 (September-October 1990):4

**Opera.** *See* Music, Classical - Opera

**Operation Brotherhood** (about)

Women Who Make a Difference. Mary Beth Sammons. *Family Circle* 103, No. 11 (August 14, 1990):17-19

**Oppenheim, Joanne**

What's Happening to Recess? *Good Housekeeping* 211, No. 3 (September 1990):162

**Oppenheim, Josie A.**

Stay-at-Home Moms. *Good Housekeeping* 211, No. 3 (September 1990):114+

**Oppenheimer, Judy**

Private Demons: The Life of Shirley Jackson. Reviewed by Deborah Price. *Belles Lettres* 5, No. 4 (Summer 1990):49

**Oppo, Anna**

"Where There's No Woman There's No Home": Profile of the Agro-Pastoral Family in Nineteenth-Century Sardinia. *Journal of Family History* 15, No. 4 (October 1990):483-502

**Oracle (Arizona) - Biosphere II**

Planet Under Glass. Jane Bosveld. *Lear's* (December 1990):184-89+

**Oral Contraceptives.** *See* Contraception

**Oral History.** *See also* Third World Women - Oral History

Interpreting Women's Lives: Feminist Theory and Personal Narratives. Edited by the Personal Narratives Group. Reviewed by Norma Schulman. *Women & Language* 13, No. 2 (Winter 1990):43

"Inventing the Self": Oral History as Autobiography. Paula Hamilton. *Hecate* 16, Nos. 1-2 (1990):128-133

The Living Legacy of Chicana Performers: Preserving History Through Oral Testimony. Yolanda Broyles-González. *Frontiers* 11, No. 1 (1990):46-52

What's So Feminist About Doing Women's Oral History? Susan Geiger. *Journal of Women's History* 2, No. 1 (Spring 1990):169-182

Women and Work in the Third World: Indonesian Women's Oral Histories. Walter L. Williams. *Journal of Women's History* 2, No. 1 (Spring 1990):183-195

**Oral Tradition**

Baby of the Family. By Tina McElroy Ansa. Reviewed by Paula Giddings. *Essence* 20, No. 11 (March 1990):44

Book Marks. Paula Giddings. *Essence* 20, No. 11 (March 1990):44

Poets: Keeping the Vision Alive. Angela Kinamore. *Essence* 21, No. 1 (May 1990):205

**Oram, Alison**

Homosexuality, Which Homosexuality?: Essays from the International Scientific Conference on Lesbian and Gay Studies. Book Review. *Feminist Review* No. 35 (Summer 1990):121-122

**Oram, Alison** (joint author). *See* Kean, Hilda

**Orbach, Israel**

Children Who Don't Want to Live: Understanding and Treating the Suicidal Child. Book Review. *Adolescence* 25, No. 97 (Spring 1990):251

**Orderliness.** *See also* Time Management

Beat the Clock. Stephanie Culp. *Family Circle* 103, No. 1 (January 9, 1990):119-121

Get Reorganized! *Redbook* 174, No. 6 (April 1990):73-82

Help! Vicki Lansky. *Family Circle* 103, No. 13 (September 25, 1990):101-102; 103, No. 14 (October 16, 1990):141-142

High Profile: Happiness Is a Warm Filofax. Jacqueline Wasser. *Mademoiselle* (September 1990):154+

Home Free: Of Keepsakes and God Pots. Betty Fussell. *Lear's* (November 1990):58-60

Shopping Smart. Joan Hamburg. *Family Circle* 103, No. 5 (April 3, 1990):93-94

This Working Life: Does Your Office Say Bad Things about You? Ellen Hopkins. *Working Woman* (April 1990):132

What a Difference a Day Makes! Claire McIntosh. *Working Woman* (April 1990):83

**Ordination of Women.** *See* Religious Discrimination

**O'Reilly, Jane**

How It All Turned Out. *Lear's* (March 1990):75-81

**O'Reilly, Rita**

No More Bloody Sundays. *Spare Rib* No. 209 (February 1990):46

**Orenstein, Gloria Feman** (joint editor). *See* Diamond, Irene

**Orenstein, Peggy**

Images: Body Care. Bibliography. *Vogue* (January 1990):72-74

The Politics of Birth Control. *Glamour* (October 1990):264-267+

Women at Risk. *Vogue* (November 1990):370-371+

**Organ Donors**

Back Talk: Donor Organs: A Crisis. Sharon Jefferson. *Essence* 21, No. 6 (October 1990):146

Campaigning Against the Trafficking of Human Organs. *Women's World*, No. 24 (Winter 1990/91): 31-32

On Donor Babies. Barbara Katz Rothman. *On the Issues* 17 (Winter 1990):23+

A Final Gift. Frank Maier. *Ladies' Home Journal* 107, No. 3 (March 1990):102-111

A Leap of Faith. Donna E. Boetig. *Family Circle* 103, No. 17 (December 18, 1990):116-120

**Organization.** *See also* Orderliness

Get Control of Clutter. Eleanor Berman. *Working Mother* 13, No. 8 (August 1990):50-51

Save Time! Will Nixon and Judy Goldstein. *Redbook* 175, No. 4 (August 1990):86-87

**Organizational Objectives.** *See also* Organizational Theory; Time Management

Managing: How to Get Your Staff Psyched. Nancy K. Austin. *Working Woman* (September 1990):68-73

See the Big Picture? Now Show Your Staff. John Stoltenberg and Claire McIntosh. *Working Woman* (April 1990):84-86+

Set Your Goals and Make Them Happen. Sandy Sheehy. *Working Woman* (April 1990):81-82+

**Organizational Theory.** *See also* Power Structure

Hierarchies, Jobs, Bodies: A Theory of Gendered Organizations. Joan Acker. *Gender and Society* 4, No. 2 (June 1990):139-158

Management: The Death of Hierarchy. Nancy K. Austin. *Working Woman* (July 1990):22-25

Rethinking Feminist Organizations. Patricia Yancey Martin. *Gender and Society* 4, No. 2 (June 1990):182-206

Working it Out in a Downsized World. Patricia O'Toole. *Lear's* (September 1990):29-30

**Organization for Women's Business Development**

Enterprise: Small Successes Yield Big Returns. Brooke Kroeger. *McCall's* 117, No. 11 (August 1990):16-23

**Organizations.** *See also* Communication in Organizations

Women's Movements: Organizing for Change. By Joyce Gelb and Ethel Klein. *NWSA Journal* 2, No. 3 (Summer 1990):492-495

Women's Organisations: The Pressure of Unrealistic Expectations. Madhu Kishwar. *Manushi* No. 59 (July-August 1990):11-14

**Orgasm**

How to Have Fantastic Sex: Know Your Body. Helen Singer Kaplan. *Redbook* 175, No. 4 (August 1990):102

How to Have Fantastic Sex: Know Yourself. Lesley Dormen. *Redbook* 175, No. 4 (August 1990):100-101

Jake: A Man's Opinion. *Glamour* (September 1990):184-186

What You Don't Know About Orgasm Could Thrill You. Debra Kent. *Mademoiselle* (February 1990):154-155+

**Orlando—Walt Disney World**

Fantasy Land. Michael Musto. *Harper's Bazaar* (July 1990):42-53

**Orleck, Annelise**

Daughters of the Shtetl: Life and Labor in the Immigrant Generation. Book Review. *The Women's Review of Books* 8, No. 3 (December 1990):30-31

The Diary of a Shirtwaist Striker. Book Review. *The Women's Review of Books* 8, No. 3 (December 1990):30-31

Fire and Grace: The Life of Rose Pastor Stokes. Book Review. *The Women's Review of Books* 7, No. 9 (June 1990):25-26

Labor's Flaming Youth: Telephone Operators and Worker Militancy 1878-1923. Book Review. *The Women's Review of Books* 8, No. 3 (December 1990):30-31

A Militant and a Millionaire. *The Women's Review of Books* 7, No. 9 (June 1990):25-26

In Search of Alliances. *The Women's Review of Books* 8, No. 3 (December 1990):31-32

**Orlock, Carol**

Alice Down the Rabbit Hole: A Saga. *Lear's* (May 1990):36-40

When the Clock Strikes 98.6—Relax! *Lear's* (September 1990):51-55

**Ornamental Fishes.** *See also* Aquarium Fishes

**O'Roak, Debra** (about)

Women Who Make a Difference: Turning the Town Around. John E. Frook. *Family Circle* 103, No. 14 (October 16, 1990):17-19

**Orozco, Cynthia E.**

Getting Started in Chicana Studies. *Women's Studies Quarterly* 18, Nos. 1-2 (Spring-Summer 1990):46-69

**Orphan Drugs**

Diseases Your Doctor May Miss. Bibliography. Stephen Phillip Policoff. *Ladies' Home Journal* 107, No. 6 (June 1990):104-109

Silk Purse Chronicles: The High Cost of Orphan Drugs. Patricia O'Toole. *Lear's* (February 1990):22-23

**Orphans.** *See* Romania—Children

**Orr, Kay** (about)

Kay Orr: Mrs. Middle America. Jody Becker. *McCall's* 117, No. 9 (June 1990):74

**Orsi, Robert A.**

The Fault of Memory: "Southern Italy" in the Imagination of Immigrants and the Lives of Their Children in Italian Harlem, 1920-1945. *Journal of Family History* 15, No. 2 (April 1990):133-147

**Ortega, Eliana** (joint editor). *See* Horno-Delgado, Asunción

**Orthner, Dennis K.** (joint editor). *See* Bowen, Gary L.

**Orthodontics, Corrective**

Medinews. Ann Ferrar. *Ladies' Home Journal* 107, No. 2 (February 1990):82

**Orthodox Judaism.** *See* Judaism, Orthodox

**Ortiz, Flora Ida** (joint author). *See* McKenna Teresa

**Osborne, J. W.** (joint author). *See* Weisgarber, J.

**Osborne, Kay** (about). *See also* Watts, Patti (editor), "Free Advice."

**Osborne, Nancy Seale**

Caryn McTighe Musil Resigns After Six Years as Director. *NWSAction* 3, No. 4 (Winter 1990): 1-2

**Oslin, K. T.** (about)

K. T. Oslin: The True Grit of a Country Charmer. Geneva Kollam. *Lear's* (September 1990):106-109+

**Osswald, Helena**

Dowry, Norms, and Household Formation: A Case Study from North Portugal. *Journal of Family History* 15, No. 2 (April 1990):201-224

**Ostenk, Annemiek** and Wilkens, Linda (editors)

Voorplanting Als Bio-Industrie. Reviewed by Rosi Braidotti. *Women's Studies International Forum* 13, No. 5 (1990):529

**Osteoporosis.** *See also* Estrogen Replacement Therapy

Adjusting to Chronic Disease: The Osteoporotic Woman. Karen A. Roberto. *Journal of Women and Aging* 2, No. 1 (1990):33-47

Health Notes. *Vogue* (January 1990):124

Osteoporosis: A Health Issue for Women. Michelle M. Alberts. *Health Care for Women International* 11, No. 1 (1990):11-19

Osteoporosis. Lyn Friedli. *Spare Rib* No. 209 (February 1990):58

**Osteoporosis—Prevention**

Exercise Builds Strong Bones. Diane Debrovner. *McCall's* 118, No. 2 (November 1990):28-32

**Osterud, Nancy Grey**

American Autobiographies. *Gender & History* 2, No. 1 (Spring 1990):83-87

**Ostriker, Alicia**

Green Age. Reviewed by Annie Finch. *Belles Lettres* 5, No. 4 (Summer 1990):30-31

From a New Past to a New Future. *The Women's Review of Books* 7, No. 12 (September 1990):12

Sarah's Daughters Sing: A Sampler of Poems by Jewish Women. Book review. *Lilith* 15, No. 3 (Summer 1990):6

Standing Again at Sinai: Judaism From a Feminist Perspective. Book Review. *The Women's Review of Books* 7, No. 12 (September 1990):12

**Ostrov, Eric** (joint author). *See* Offer, Daniel

**Osuala, Judith D. C.**

Nigerian Women's Quest for Role Fulfillment. *Women and Therapy* 10, No. 3 (1990):89-98

**O'Sullivan, John**

Why Can't a Woman Be More Like a Man? *Savvy Woman* (February 1990):59-60, 92

**O'Sullivan, Sue**

The Sexual Schism: The British in Barcelona. *off our backs* 20, No. 9 (October 1990):10-11

**O'Sullivan, Sue** and Patton, Cindy

Mapping: Lesbians, AIDS and Sexuality. *Feminist Review* No. 34 (Spring 1990):120-133

**O'Sullivan, Sue** (joint author). *See* Ardill, Susan

**O'Sullivan, Sue** (joint editor). *See* McEwen, Christine

**Other, Anne**

On Location: The Housing Department. *Women and Environments* 12, No. 2 (Spring 1990): 26-27

Working on the "Hard" Side. *Canadian Women's Studies* 11, No. 2 (Fall 1990):59-60

**Otis, Carol** and Goldingay, Roger

Sports Medicine: Hot Tips. *Women's Sports & Fitness* 12, No. 6 (September 1990):10

**O'Toole, Corbett Joan**

Violence and Sexual Assault Plague Many Disabled Women. *New Directions for Women* 19, No. 1 (January/February 1990):17

**O'Toole, Patricia**

The Glass Ceiling: If I Had a Hammer. *Lear's* (November 1990):29-30

How Do You Build a $44 Million Company? *Working Woman* (April 1990):88-92

How I Became a Junk-Bond Airhead. *Lear's* (June 1990):35-37

Making a List and Checking It Twice. *Lear's* (December 1990):29-30

Private Connives. *Lear's* (August 1990):98-101

The Ring Around the U.S. Dollar. *Lear's* (May 1990):29-30

Saving Grace: Leave It to Boomer? *Lear's* (July 1990):22-23

Silk Purse Chronicles. *Lear's* (March 1990):32-34

Silk Purse Chronicles: Making an End Run around Armageddon. *Lear's* (August 1990):21-23

Silk Purse Chronicles: The High Cost of Orphan Drugs. *Lear's* (February 1990):22-23

Silk Purse Chronicles: The Wages of Spin. *Lear's* (April 1990):23-24

Thrifty, Kind – and Smart as Hell. *Lear's* (October 1990):26-30

Working it Out in a Downsized World. *Lear's* (September 1990):29-30

**Ottenheimer, Martin**

Lewis Henry Morgan and the Prohibition of Cousin Marriage in the United States. *Journal of Family History* 15, No. 3 (July 1990):325-334

**Otto, Luther B.** and Call, Vaughan R. A.

Managing Family Data on Multiple Roles and Changing Statuses over Time. *Journal of Marriage and the Family* 52, No. 1 (February 1990):243-248

**Ouedraoga, Idrissa**

Yaaba. Reviewed by Veronica Hill. *Spare Rib* No. 209 (February 1990):35

**Ouellette, Franc1oise-Romaine**

Femmes sans toit ni voix: La problematique des femmes dites sans-abri ou itinerantes. Reviewed by Dominique Masson. *Canadian Women's Studies* 11, No. 2 (Fall 1990):86

**Oumano, Elena**

About Face: Beyond Cosmetic Surgery. *Lear's* (July 1990):35-36

**Ounjian, Marilyn** (about)

Business Is Better the Second Time Around. Joan Delaney. *Executive Female* (May/June 1990):66-67

**Outdoor Cookery.** *See also* Barbecue Cookery

America Entertains. Phyllis Schiller. *McCall's* 117, No. 10 (July 1990):112

Have a Great Fourth of July Chicken Cookout. *Redbook* 175, No. 3 (July 1990):69-74

Lite Eating: Bread Winners. *McCall's* 117, No. 10 (July 1990):114

Outdoor Eating Cookbook. Marianne Langan. *McCall's* 117, No. 9 (June 1990):99-101

Perfect Summer Parties. Jan Turner Hazard. *Ladies' Home Journal* 107, No. 6 (June 1990):146-162

Picnic Perfect. Mali Michelle Fleming. *Essence* 21, No. 3 (July 1990):79-82

Picnic Salad Pack-Alongs. *McCall's* 117, No. 10 (July 1990):116

Picnic Time! Jonell Nash. *Essence* 21, No. 3 (July 1990):84-87

Sandwiches that Sizzle. *Glamour* (September 1990):340-341 +

Summer Barbecue Cookbook. *McCall's* 117, No. 10 (July 1990):103-107 +

**Outlaw, Louise Lee**

Isn't It Romantic? Short Story. *Good Housekeeping* 211, No. 1 (July 1990):116-117

**Outlet Stores**

Shopping Smart: What's New in Off-Price? Bibliography. Debra Wise. *Glamour* (September 1990):272

The Year's First Fashion Bargains. *Glamour* (January 1990):142-147

**Out/Look Magazine**

Editorial: Let's Get National. Debra Chasnoff. *Out/Look* No. 10 (Fall 1990):3-5

**Outram, Dorinda**

The Body and the French Revolution: Sex, Class and Political Culture. Reviewed by Elisabeth G. Sledziewski. *Gender & History* 2, No. 3 (Autumn 1990):363-365

**Out Write – First National Lesbian and Gay Writers Conference, 1990**

Lesbian or Gay Writer: Hardly an Alienated Profession. Judy Grahn. *Out/Look* No. 9 (Summer 1990):38-41

**Oval House** (about)

Oval House: Weathering the Storms. Susan Hayes. *Spare Rib* No. 212 (May 1990):26

**Ovarian Cancer**

New Clues to a Cure. Louise Tutelian. *Savvy Woman* (March 1990):76-77

The Silent Killer. Bibliography. Jean Fain. *Ladies' Home Journal* 107, No. 3 (March 1990):68-79

**Overachievement.** *See also* Balancing Work and Family Life; Workaholics

Mid-Course Correction. A'Lelia Bundles. *Essence* 20, No. 9 (January 1990):28 +

**Overholser, James** (joint author). *See* Spirito, Anthony

**Over-the-Counter Drugs.** *See* Nonprescription Drugs

**Overuse Injuries**

Medinews. Sally Squires. *Ladies' Home Journal* 107, No. 4 (April 1990):112-118

**Owades, Ruth** (about)

A Catalog Comes Up Roses. Ellie McGrath. *Savvy Woman* (September 1990):38-40

**Owen, Alex**

Uneven Developments: The Ideological Work of Gender in Mid-Victorian England. Book Review. *Gender & History* 2, No. 2 (Summer 1990):239-241

**Owen, Patricia** (joint author). *See* Berk, Bernice

**Owen, William Foster**

Image Metaphors of Women and Men in Personal Relationships. *Women's Studies in Communication* 12, No. 2 (Fall 1989):37-57

**Owens, Lakisha**

Windows. Poem. *Heresies* 25 (1990):18

**Owens, Rebecca**

Mother Love: Lessons in Logic and Lunacy. *Lear's* (May 1990):68-70

**Oxdemir, Burcu**

Like Committing Crimes, and You? *off our backs* 20, No. 3 (March 1990):24

**Ozbek, Rifat** (about)

The Kings of Color: Ozbek. Stephanie Mansfield. *Vogue* (September 1990):536-541

# P

**Pacific Islands**

Listen to the Tangata Whenua. *Spare Rib* 217 (October 1990):50

Pacific Women Speak: The Health Effects of Radiation from Nuclear Testing in the Pacific Islands. Darlene Keju-Johnson, Lijon Eknilang, and Chailang Palacios. *Woman of Power* 18 (Fall 1990):36-41

**Pacific Islands – Family Planning**

Family Planning in Asia and the Pacific. Kathy Gollan. *Healthright* 9, No. 3 (May 1990):25-28

**Pacifism**

Pacifism and Care. Victoria Davion. *Hypatia* 5, No. 1 (Spring 1990):90-100

The Women's Peace Union and the Outlawry of War, 1921-1941. By Harriet Hyman Alonso. Reviewed by Cynthia L. Giddle. *New Directions for Women* 19, No. 5 (September-October 1990):18

**Packer, Nancy Huddleston**

The Women Who Walk. Reviewed by Ann L. McLaughlin. *Belles Lettres* 5, No. 2 (Winter 1990):14

**Paczensky, Susanne V.**

In a Semantic Fog: How to Confront the Accusation That Abortion Equals Killing. *Women's Studies International Forum* 13, No. 3 (1990):177-184

**Padel, Ruth**

Between Theory and Fiction: Reflections on Feminism and Classical Scholarship. *Gender & History* 2, No. 2 (Summer 1990):198-211

**Pagels, Elaine**

Adam, Eve, and the Serpent. Reviewed by Michael B. Schwarz. *Out/Look* No. 7 (Winter 1990):76-81

Adam, Eve and the Serpent. Reviewed by Elizabeth A. Clark. *Gender & History* 2, No. 1 (Spring 1990):106-109

**Paige-Pointer, Barbara** and Auletta, Gale Schroeder

Restructuring the Curriculum: Barriers and Bridges. *Women's Studies Quarterly* 18, Nos. 1-2 (Spring-Summer 1990):86-94

**Pain.** *See also* Backache; Health Education

The Healthy Family. Peter Jaret. *Family Circle* 103, No. 5 (April 3, 1990):34+

Serious Headaches. Susan Alai. *Family Circle* 103, No. 15 (November 6, 1990):63-67

**Painter, Charlotte**

A Wider Giving: Women Writing After a Long Silence. Reviewed by Lou Ann B. Jorgensen. *Journal of Women and Aging* 2, No. 4 (1990):109-110

**Painter, Nell Irvin**

Sojourner Truth in Life and Memory: Writing the Biography of an American Exotic. *Gender & History* 2, No. 1 (Spring 1990):3-16

**Painting**

Tools & Tips of the Trade. Al Ubell and Label Shulman. *Family Circle* 103, No. 13 (September 25, 1990):139

**Pakistan – Government and Politics**

Benazir Bhutto Defeated at the Polls. Rukhsana Ahmad. *Spare Rib* 218 (November 1990):45

**Pakistan – History.** *See* Kashmir – History

**Pakistan – International Relations – India**

Scientists and War and Peace. Dinesh Mohan. *Manushi* 58 (May-June 1990):11-13

**Pakistan – Politics and Government**

Benazir Bhutto: Her Rise, Fall – and Rise? Shazia Rafi. *Ms.* 1, No. 3 (November/December 1990):16-20

Pakistan: A Constitutional Coup. Rukhsana Ahmad. *Spare Rib* No. 216 (September 1990):20-23

**Pakistan – Status of Women**

Meatless Days. By Sara Suleri. Reviewed by Inderpal Grewal. *NWSA Journal* 2, No. 3 (Summer 1990):508-510

Pakistani Women: Socioeconomic and Demographic Profile. Edited by Nasra Shah. Reviewed by Kalpana Bardhan. *Journal of Women's History* 2, No. 1 (Spring 1990):200-219

**Palacios, Chailang** (joint author). *See* Keju-Johnson, Darlene

**Palacios, Diane**

Music: Three in Concert. *Ms.* 1, No. 1 (July/August 1990):72-73

**Palazzi, Maura**

Female Solitude and Patrilineage: Unmarried Women and Widows during the Eighteenth and Nineteenth Centuries. *Journal of Family History* 15, No. 4 (October 1990):443-459

**Palca, Alfred**

Uneasy Pieces: Trials of an Unproduced Screenwriter. *Lear's* (July 1990):54-59+

**Palcy, Euzhan** (interview)

Putting Apartheid on Screen. Talking with Euzhan Palcy. *Spare Rib* No. 209 (February 1990):12-15

**Palestine – History**

Domestic Life in Palestine. By Mary Eliza Rogers. Reviewed by Judith Tucker. *Journal of Women's History* 2, No. 1 (Spring 1990):245-250

**Palestinian Arabs**

Another View of the Middle East: Palestinian Arabs, Yes; PLO, No. Roberta Kalechofsky. *On the Issues* 15 (Summer 1990):18+

Palestine: Remembering Sabra and Shatila. Samar Alami. *Spare Rib* 217 (October 1990):51

Passionate Differences: A Working Model for Cross-Cultural Communication. Kristen Metz. *Journal of Feminist Studies in Religion* 6, No. 1 (Spring 1990):131-151

**Palestinian Arabs – Feminism**

West Bank and Gaza: Occupied Feminism. Gayle Kirshenbaum. *Ms.* 1, No. 2 (September/October 1990):8

**Palestinian Arabs – Intifada**

Palestine: New Wave of Repression – New Wave of Resistance. *Spare Rib* 213 (June 1990):26-27

A State of Danger. By Haim Bresheet. Reviewed by Marcia Freedman. *On the Issues* 15 (Summer 1990):30-31

From Stones to Statehood: The Palestinian Uprising. By Phyllis Bennis and Neal Cassidy. Reviewed by Eleanor J. Bader. *On the Issues* 15 (Summer 1990):16-17+

On the Third Anniversary of the Intifada. Samar Alami. *Spare Rib* 219 (December 1990-January 1991):52-53

Women in Black: Weekly Vigils Against the Israeli Occupation. Bill Strubbe. *On the Issues* 15 (Summer 1990):18

**Paley, Grace**

Two Ways of Telling. *Ms.* 1, No. 3 (November/December 1990):41-44

**Palladino, Diane** and Stephenson, Yanela

Perceptions of Sexual Self: Their Impact on Relationships Between Lesbian and Heterosexual Women. *Women and Therapy* 9, No. 3 (1990):231-253

**Pallot, Judith**

Mothers of Misery, Child Abandonment in Russia. Book Review. *Gender & History* 2, No. 3 (Autumn 1990):358-359

**Pallotta-Chiarolli, Maria**

The Female Stranger in a Male School. *Gender and Education* 2, No. 2 (1990):169-183

**Palm, Anna**

Arriving and Caught Up. Reviewed by Anne Goslyn. *Spare Rib* 213 (June 1990):35

**Palmeira, Rosemary** (editor)

Poems of Birth and Motherhood. *Spare Rib* No. 212 (May 1990):57

**Palmer, Nettie** (about)

Nettie Palmer. Edited by Vivian Smith. Reviewed by Barbara Brook. *Women's Studies International Forum* 13, No. 3 (1990):275-276

Nettie Palmer: Her Private Journal *Fourteen Years*, Poems, Reviews, and Literary Essays. Edited by Vivian Smith. Reviewed by Cecilia Konchar Farr. *Belles Lettres* 5, No. 2 (Winter 1990):2

**Palmer, Paulina**

Contemporary Women's Fiction: Narrative Practice and Feminist Theory. Reviewed by Alice Hall Petry. *Tulsa Studies in Women's Literature* 9, No. 2 (Fall 1990):332-334

**Palmer, Phyllis**

Domesticity and Dirt: Housewives and Domestic Servants in the United States, 1920-1945. Reviewed by Lois R. Helmbold. *The Women's Review of Books* 7, No. 8 (May 1990):12-13

**Paltiel, Freda L.**

Feminist Perspectives on Wife Abuse. Book Review. *Women and Health* 16, Nos. 3/4 (1990):196-201

Intimate Violence—A Study of Injustice. Book Review. *Women and Health* 16, Nos. 3/4 (1990):196-201

**Paludi, Michele A.**, Meyers, Deborah, Kindermann, Joni, Speicher, Hilda, and Haring-Hidore, Marilyn

Mentoring and Being Mentored: Issues of Sex, Power, and Politics for Older Women. *Journal of Women and Aging* 2 No. 3 (1990):81-92

**Pam, Susan**

Curl Up and Dye. Reviewed by Janice Shinebourne. *Spare Rib* 217 (October 1990):31-32

**Pan-Africanism**

Dishes from Africa and the Diaspora. Jonell Nash. *Essence* 21, No. 6 (October 1990):107-108+

**Panama—Invasion**

U.S. Women See Combat in Panama. Kim Kleine. *off our backs* 20, No. 3 (March 1990):22-23

US Invades Panama. *Spare Rib* No. 209 (February 1990):42-43

**Panic Disorders**

"Doctor, Am I Having a Heart Attack?" Dava Sobel. *Good Housekeeping* 210, No. 5 (May 1990):78-82

Mind Health: Panic. Peter Jaret. *Vogue* (September 1990):462-467

The Private Terror of a Panic Attack. Leigh Silverman. *Lear's* (August 1990):36-39

**Panno, Laura** (about). *See* Fashion, "Suprema Donnas"

**Papalia, Diane E.** (joint author). *See* Olds, Sally Wendkos

**Paper, Jordon**

The Persistence of Female Deities in Patriarchal China. *Journal of Feminist Studies in Religion* 6, No. 1 (Spring 1990):25-40

**Papert, Seymour** (joint author). *See* Turkle, Sherry

**Papini, Dennis R.**, Farmer, Frank F., Clark, Steven M., Micka, Jill C., and Barnett, Jawanda K.

Early Adolescent Age and Gender Differences in Patterns of Emotional Self-Disclosure to Parents and Friends. *Adolescence* 25, No. 100 (Winter 1990):959-976

**Pap Smear**

Pap Tests: Can You Trust Them? Peter Jaret. *Glamour* (November 1990):68-75

**Papua-New Guinea—Anthropology**

Cultural Alternatives and a Feminist Anthropology: An Analysis of Culturally Constructed Gender Interests in Papua New Guinea. By Frederick Errington and Deborah Gewertz. Reviewed by Debbora Battaglia. *Signs* 15, No. 4 (Summer 1990):869-872

**Papua-New Guinea—Status of Women**

Papua New Guinea and the "Aquatic Continent." Margaret M. Taylor. *Ms.* 1, No. 3 (November/December 1990):14-15

**Paquette, Patricia**

A Bandage in One Hand and a Bible in the Other: The Story of Captain Sally L. Tompkins (CSA). *Minerva* 8, No. 2 (Summer 1990):47-54

**Paquin, Ghislaine**, Aubin, Jacinthe, and Boivin, Marie

Personnes âgées et logement. Reviewed by Dominique Masson. *Canadian Women's Studies* 11, No. 2 (Fall 1990):86-87

**Parajuli, Pramod** and Enslin, Elizabeth

From Learning Literacy to Regenerating Women's Space: A Story of Women's Empowerment in Nepal. *Women in Action* 1-2 (1990):3-6

**Paramenstrual Symptomatology.** *See* Menstruation

**Parcel, Toby L.** (joint author). *See* Menaghan, Elizabeth G.

**Pardeck, Jean A.** and Pardeck, John T.

Family Factors Related to Adolescent Autonomy. *Adolescence* 25, No. 98 (Summer 1990):311-319

**Pardeck, John T.** (joint author). *See* Pardeck, Jean A.

**Pardo, Mary**

Mexican American Women Grassroots Community Activists: "Mothers of East Lost Angeles." *Frontiers* 11, No. 1 (1990):1-7

**Paredes, Ursula** and Ashworth, Georgina

Development Crises and Alternative Visions. *Spare Rib* No. 210 (March 1990):23-25

**Parental Leave.** *See* Family Policy

**Parent-Child Relationships**

Daddy, We Hardly Knew You. By Germaine Greer. Reviewed by Jill Conway. *The Women's Review of Books* 7, No. 9 (June 1990):11

Daughters Who Can't Get Away. Patricia Love and Jo Robinson. *Glamour* (May 1990):294-295+

Dimensions of the Family Environment as Perceived by Children: A Multidimensional Scaling Analysis. Paul R. Amato. *Journal of Marriage and the Family* 52, No. 3 (August 1990):613-620

The Effect of Social Support on Adolescent Mothers' Styles of Parent-Child Interaction as Measured on Three Separate Occasions. kCarolyn S. Cooper, Carl J. Dunst, and Sherra D. Vance. *Adolescence* 25, No. 97 (Spring 1990):49-57

Establishing the First Stages of Early Reciprocal Interactions between Mothers and Their Autistic Children. Dorothy Gartner and Nancy M. Schultz. *Women and Therapy* 10, Nos. 1/2 (1990):159-167

Families and Adolescents: A Review of the 1980s. Viktor Gecas and Monica A. Seff. *Journal of Marriage and the Family* 52, No. 4 (November 1990):941-598

Infants of Adolescent and Adult Mothers: Two Indices of Socioemotional Development. Ann Frodi, Wendy Grolnick, Lisa Bridges, and Jacqueline Berko. *Adolescence* 25, No. 98 (Summer 1990):363-374

The Likelihood of Parent-Adult Child Coresidence: Effects of Family Structure and Parental Characteristics. William S. Aquilino. *Journal of Marriage and the Family* 52, No. 2 (May 1990):405-419

Parental and Nonparental Child Care and Children's Socioemotional Development: A Decade in Review. Jay Belsky. *Journal of Marriage and the Family* 52, No. 4 (November 1990):884-903

Private Lives. Leonard Felder. *Family Circle* 103, No. 12 (September 4, 1990):40+

The Role of Divorce in Men's Relations with Their Adult Children after Mid-life. Teresa M. Cooney and Peter Uhlenberg. *Journal of Marriage and the Family* 52, No. 3 (August 1990):677-688

The Teen Years. Neta Jackson. *Family Circle* 103, No. 7 (May 15, 1990):66+

Women and Elderly Parents: Moral Controversy in an Aging Society. Stephen G. Post. *Hypatia* 5, No. 1 (Spring 1990):83-89

**Parenthood.** *See also* Surrogate Mothers

The Effect of Preschool Children on Family Stability. David M. Fergusson, L. John Horwood, and Michael Lloyd. *Journal of Marriage and the Family* 52, No. 2 (May 1990):531-538

Effects of Child Age on Marital Quality and Distress of Newly Married Mothers and Stepfathers. Lawrence A. Kurdek. *Journal of Marriage and the Family* 52, No. 1 (February 1990):81-85

Feminist Mothers. By Tuula Gordon. Reviewed by Rosalind Edwards. *Women's Studies International Forum* 13, No. 5 (1990):527

First Births in America: Changes in the Timing of Parenthood. By Ronald R. Rindfuss, S. Philip Morgan, and Gary Swicegood. Reviewed by Sandra L. Hanson. *Journal of Marriage and the Family* 52, No. 3 (August 1990):800

Gender, Parenthood, and Work Hours of Physicians. Linda Grant, Layne A. Simpson, Xue Lan Rong, and Holly Peters-Golden. *Journal of Marriage and the Family* 52, No. 1 (February 1990):39-49

Is There a Parent Gap in Pocketbook Politics? Kenneth S. Y. Chew. *Journal of Marriage and the Family* 52, No. 3 (August 1990):723-734

Marital Adjustment During the Transition to Parenthood: Stability and Predictors of Change. Pamela M. Wallace and Ian H. Gotlib. *Journal of Marriage and the Family* 52, No. 1 (February 1990):21-29

Motherhood: What It Does to Your Mind. By Jane Price. Reviewed by Datha Clapper Brack. *New Directions for Women* 19, No. 2 (March/April 1990):24

Motherhood and Sex Role Development. Mary A. Halas. *Women and Therapy* 10, Nos. 1/2 (1990):227-243

The Mother Myth: A Feminist Analysis of Post Partum Depression. Debbie Field. *Healthsharing* 11, No. 1 (December 1989):17-21

Mothers with Chronic Illness: A Predicament of Social Construction. Sally E. Thorne. *Health Care for Women International* 11, No. 2 (1990):209-221

Patterns of Marital Change across the Transition to Parenthood: Pregnancy to Three Years Postpartum. Jay Belsky and Michael Rovine. *Journal of Marriage and the Family* 52, No. 1 (February 1990):5-19

Psychology and Parenthood. By Jean Gross. Reviewed by Catherine Mason. *Healthright* 9, No. 4 (August 1990):42

Star Gazing. Susan Ungaro and Linda Moran Evans. *Family Circle* 103, No. 7 (May 15, 1990):73-74

What's Behind the Mommy Wars? *Working Mother* 13, No. 10 (October 1990):74-79

Woman-Defined Motherhood. Jane Price Knowles. *Women and Therapy* 10, Nos. 1/2 (1990):1-7

**Parenting.** *See also* Adolescents as Parents; African-American Families – Parenting; Automobiles – Touring; Balancing Work and Family Life; Child Psychology; Educational Activities; Family Life; Father-Son Relationships; Gender Roles; Grandparents; Health Education; Homemakers; Infants – Nutrition; Lesbian Mothers; Middle Age – Parenting; Mother-Daughter Relationships; Single Parents; Stepfamilies; Stress – Coping Strategies; Time Management

Adolescent Rebellion . . . Or Sheer Defiance? Lee Salk. *McCall's* 117, No. 10 (July 1990):56

Adolescent Sexual Behavior, Pregnancy, and Parenting: Research Through the 1980s. Brent C. Miller and Kristin A. Moore. *Journal of Marriage and the Family* 52, No. 4 (November 1990):1025-1044

Are Kids Growing Up Too Fast? Sally Wendkos Olds and Diane E. Papalia. *Redbook* 174, No. 5 (March 1990):91-92+

Are You an Overprotective Parent? Bernice Berk and Patricia Owen. *Good Housekeeping* 211, No. 3 (September 1990):100+

Are You Spoiling Your Child? Anne Cassidy. *Working Mother* 13, No. 5 (May 1990):34-46

The Art of Comforting a Child. Roberta Israeloff. *Working Mother* (November 1990):99-103

Ask Dr. Mom. Marianne Neifert. *McCall's* 117, No. 7 (April 1990):8; 117, No. 8 (May 1990):19; 117, No. 9 (June 1990):10; 117, No. 11 (August 1990):28; 118, No. 1 (October 1990):36-37

Ask Dr. Mom: When Children Stutter . . . And Other Questions. Marianne Neifert. *McCall's* 118, No. 2 (November 1990):46

Babies, Birds and Bees. Lee Salk. *McCall's* 117, No. 8 (May 1990):65

Back Talk: An Education Agenda. Adelaide Sanford. *Essence* 21, No. 4 (August 1990):126

Beat the Clock. Patricia Rodriguez. *Family Circle* 103, No. 4 (March 13, 1990):181

Boost Your Child's Self-Confidence. Benjamin Spock. *Redbook* 174, No. 6 (April 1990):32

Comment on Suleiman's "On Maternal Splitting." Raquel Portillo Bauman. *Signs* 15, No. 3 (Spring 1990):653-655

Contemporary Living: Families. Bibliography. *Essence* 21, No. 4 (August 1990):75-84

Coparenting in the Second Year after Divorce. Eleanor E. Maccoby, Charlene E. Depner, and Robert H. Mnookin. *Journal of Marriage and the Family* 52, No. 1 (February 1990):141-155

A Date with Mom. Rae Lynn Barton. *McCall's* 118, No. 1 (October 1990):14

Dear Mom, I Lost My Retainers. Gayle Lea Brown. *McCall's* 118, No. 3 (December 1990):14-21

Dial for Help. Sarah Hutter. *Working Mother* (November 1990):45

Diana's Darlings. Susie Pearson. *Ladies' Home Journal* 107, No. 2 (February 1990):107-110

A Different Parent. Karen Blackford. *Healthsharing* 11, No. 3 (June 1990):20-24

Does Your Child Feel Second-Rate? Benjamin Spock. *Redbook* 175, No. 1 (May 1990):38

On Donor Babies. Barbara Katz Rothman. *On the Issues* 17 (Winter 1990):23+

Don't Let Your Good Baby Turn into a Terrible Toddler! Anne Cassidy. *Working Mother* (November 1990):90-97

Early Patterns of Maternal Attachment. Judith Rivinus Fuller. *Health Care for Women International* 11, No. 4 (1990):433-446

The Early Years: Mom Loves You More. T. Berry Brazelton. *Family Circle* 103, No. 9 (June 26, 1990):41-43

The Early Years. T. Berry Brazelton. *Family Circle* 103, No. 2 (February 1, 1990):37-39; 103, No. 5 (April 3, 1990):42+; 103, No. 10 (July 24, 1990):42; 103, No. 15 (November 6, 1990):49-54

Everybody Loves a Baby. Shana Aborn and Marianne Wait. *Ladies' Home Journal* 107, No. 3 (March 1990):141-146

Every Minute Doesn't Count. Ann Muscari and Wenda Wardell Morrone. *Family Circle* 103, No. 1 (January 9, 1990):85+

A Family Portrait: A Wife/Mother/Photographer's Revenge. Photo essay. *Ms.* 1, No. 3 (November/December 1990):76-81

Father Knows Best??? Mom Knows Better. Teryl Zarnow. *Redbook* 175, No. 2 (June 1990):112-113+

Feeding Right From the Start. Kathleen Braden. *Family Circle* 103, No. 1 (January 9, 1990):78+

The Five Biggest Mistakes Most Parents Make. Ellen Galinsky. *Ladies' Home Journal* 107, No. 6 (June 1990):80-87

Frequency of Illness in Mother-Infant Dyads. L. Colette Jones and Peggy Parks. *Health Care for Women International* 11, No. 4 (1990):461-475

Get the Teacher on Your Team. Kathy Henderson. *Working Mother* (November 1990):70-74

The Gift of Self-Esteem. Denise Foley. *Working Mother* (November 1990):32-36

The Good Mother. Penny Colman. *Ladies' Home Journal* 107, No. 1 (January 1990):36

Grandparents Can Be a Joy (and a Problem). Benjamin Spock. *Redbook* 175, No. 4 (August 1990):30

The Heir & the Spare. Beth Weinhouse. *Redbook* 175, No. 5 (September 1990):38-42

Homework: Should Parents Help? Lee Salk. *McCall's* 118, No. 2 (November 1990):56

How Babies Fall in Love. Eva Conrad. *Working Mother* (December 1990):57-62

How Children Learn. Leah Levinger and Jo Adler. *Good Housekeeping* 211, No. 3 (September 1990):134+

How to Be a Better Parent—Set Limits! E. Kent Hayes. *Redbook* 175, No. 4 (August 1990):78-79+

How to Boost Your Child's Self-Esteem. Lawrence Balter. *Ladies' Home Journal* 107, No. 11 (November 1990):106-109

How to Civilize a Smart-Mouthed Child. Francine Prose. *Working Mother* 13, No. 7 (July 1990):49-50

How to Fire Up an Unmotivated Child. Denise Foley. *Working Mother* 13, No. 9 (September 1990):40-48

How to Make Your Home a Whine-Free Zone. Salley Shannon. *Working Mother* 13, No. 4 (April 1990):51-57

How to Raise a Friendly Kind of Kid. Linda Lee Small. *Working Mother* 13, No. 8 (August 1990):45-49

How to Raise a Happy Child. Carolyn Jabs. *Working Mother* 13, No. 10 (October 1990):67-72

How to Talk So Your Kids will Listen. Ray Guarendi. *Redbook* 175, No. 5 (September 1990):150-151+

Hush, Little Baby. Robin Sanders. *Ladies' Home Journal* 107, No. 3 (March 1990):88

The Joys of Traveling with My Baby. Trish Hall. *McCall's* 117, No. 7 (April 1990):10+

Kids of Summer 1990. *Good Housekeeping* 210, No. 6 (June 1990):83-120

Lend a Helping Hand. Benjamin Spock. *Redbook* 176, No. 2 (December 1990):30

Love Lessons. Stanley I. Greenspan and Nancy Thorndike Greenspan. *Family Circle* 103, No. 1 (January 9, 1990):77+

Make Room for Daddy. David Laskin. *Redbook* 174, No. 5 (March 1990):122-123+

Mother and Toddler Groups. Sandra Lang. *Spare Rib* No. 216 (September 1990):57

Mother & Child. *Good Housekeeping* 211, No. 4 (October 1990):82-84

Motherhood or Bust: Reflections on the Dreams, and Nightmares of Foster Parenting. Mary Ellen Snodgrass. *On the Issues* 16 (Fall 1990):7-9+

Mothering Others' Children: The Experiences of Family Day-Care Providers. Notes. Margaret K. Nelson. *Signs* 15, No. 3 (Spring 1990):586-605

The Mothers' Page: A House Full of Kids. Lisa Passey Boynton. *McCall's* 117, No. 9 (June 1990):6-8

The Mothers' Page: What Do You Mean My Child's Not Perfect? *McCall's* 117, No. 10 (July 1990):16-18

My Daughter, the Little Princess. Catherine Peck. *McCall's* 117, No. 12 (September 1990):31-32

My Daughter and Me: Déjà Vu All Over Again. Jane Adams. *Lear's* (May 1990):72-74

My Pet Theory. Benjamin Spock. *Redbook* 175, No. 5 (September 1990):46

My Problem: I Tried to Live My Teenage Daughter's Life. *Good Housekeeping* 211, No. 4 (October 1990):40-43

One Mother's Story: Why Didn't I? Penny Colman. *Ladies' Home Journal* 107, No. 3 (March 1990):90

Our Families, Ourselves: Addiction of the Narcissistically Deprived. John Bradshaw. *Lear's* (January 1990):40-41

Our Families, Ourselves. John Bradshaw. *Lear's* (March 1990):85-86

Parenthood: A Special Report on Families Today. *Ladies' Home Journal* 107, No. 6 (June 1990):71-75

Parenting: A Collective Job Description. Karen Lior. *Women and Environments* 12, No. 2 (Spring 1990):8-9

Parenting: An Advocate for Adoption. Bibliography. Joy Duckett Cain. *Essence* 21, No. 7 (November 1990):110

Parenting. Bibliography. *Essence* 21, No. 3 (July 1990):96; 21, No. 6 (October 1990):120

Parenting. *Essence* 20, No. 11 (March 1990):106

Parenting: Fat Facts. Andrea R. Davis. *Essence* 21, No. 2 (June 1990):95

Parenting: Learning to Let Go. Valerie Wilson Wesley. *Essence* 21, No. 1 (May 1990):188

Parenting: The Middle Passage. Stephanie Stokes Oliver. *Essence* 21, No. 1 (May 1990):186

What's the Best Advice You Can Give New Moms? Judith Viorst. *Redbook* 175, No. 1 (May 1990):40-43

What to Do When . . . Bruce J. McIntosh and Dava Sobel. *Good Housekeeping* 211, No. 3 (September 1990):132+

When a Parent Plays Favorites. Lee Salk. *McCall's* 117, No. 12 (September 1990):68

When Dad Won't Discipline. Benjamin Spock. *Redbook* 176, No. 1 (November 1990):38

Who Are the Psychological Parents? Philip S. Gutis. *McCall's* 117, No. 12 (September 1990):66-68

Why Are You the Way You Are? Winifred Gallagher. *McCall's* 117, No. 8 (May 1990):78-80

Women Who Start Second Families. Micki Diegel. *Good Housekeeping* 210, No. 5 (May 1990):156-163

## Parenting – Humor

The Flip Side. Louis Phillips. *Family Circle* 103, No. 15 (November 6, 1990):262-29

Getting Through. Trish Vradenburg. *Ladies' Home Journal* 107, No. 11 (November 1990):140

PB & J: One Mother's Story. Anne Sheffield. *Ladies' Home Journal* 107, No. 8 (August 1990):72

A Survival Handbook for Moms. Paddy Yost. *Good Housekeeping* 211, No. 3 (September 1990):130+

10 Reasons to Give a Kid a Hug. Mary Mohler. *Ladies' Home Journal* 107, No. 6 (June 1990):88-89

What Kids Say (When They Think You're Not Listening). Judith Viorst. *Redbook* 174, No. 5 (March 1990):42-45

## Parenting – Mixed-Race Children

Mothering the Biracial Child: Bridging the Gaps between African-American and White Parenting Styles. Robin L. Miller and Barbara Miller. *Women and Therapy* 10, Nos. 1/2 (1990):169-179

## Parenting – Role Division

Daddy's Girls and the Fathers Who Adore Them. Eric Goodman. *McCall's* 117, No. 9 (June 1990):94-96+

Husband and Wife Differences in Determinants of Parenting: A Social Learning/Exchange Model of Parental Behavior. Ronald L. Simons, Les B. Whitbeck, Rand D. Conger, and Janet N. Melby. *Journal of Marriage and the Family* 52, No. 2 (May 1990):375-392

Parental Responsibility of African-American Unwed Adolescent Fathers. Kenneth Christmon. *Adolescence* 25, No. 99 (Fall 1990):645-653

Predicting Paternal Involvement with a Newborn by Attitude Toward Women's Roles. Eileen Greif Fishbein. *Health Care for Women International* 11, No. 1 (1990):109-115

Social Support and Gender Role Attitude among Teenage Mothers. Kris Kissman. *Adolescence* 25, No. 99 (Fall 1990):709-716

## Parenting – Stress

Stress Experienced by Mothers of Young Children. L. Joan Brailey. *Health Care for Women International* 11, No. 3 (1990):347-358

## Parenting – Support Groups

The Effect of Social Support on Adolescent Mothers' Styles of Parent-Child Interaction as Measured on Three Separate Occasions. kCarolyn S. Cooper, Carl J. Dunst, and Sherra D. Vance. *Adolescence* 25, No. 97 (Spring 1990):49-57

## Parenting – Values and Behavior

Defining Child Maltreatment: Ratings of Parental Behaviors. Bruce Roscoe. *Adolescence* 25, No. 99 (Fall 1990):517-528

Initial Parenting Attitudes of Pregnant Adolescents and a Comparison with the Decision about Adoption. Richard A. Hanson. *Adolescence* 25, No. 99 (Fall 1990):629-643

Parenting Attitudes of Adolescent and Older Mothers. Marc D. Baranowski, Gary L. Schilmoeller, and Barbara S. Higgins. *Adolescence* 25, No. 100 (Winter 1990):781-790

Parenting for Peace and Justice: Ten Years Later. By Kathleen McGinnis and James McGinnis. Book Review. *Adolescence* 25, No. 100 (Winter 1990):998

## Parents, Aged. *See also* Older Adults

The Daughter Track. *Glamour* (May 1990):94

Encounters with Angels. Sophy Burnham. *McCall's* 118, No. 3 (December 1990):76-77

A Few Words on Trading Places. Bibliography. Nancy Dunnan. *Lear's* (September 1990):32-35

The Last Taboo. Andrea Gross. *Ladies' Home Journal* 107, No. 4 (April 1990):144-148

Our Parents Growing Older. Jane Ciabattari. *McCall's* 118, No. 2 (November 1990):81-88+

Planning for the Future: Steps to Take Now. Bibliography. Christina Ferrari. *McCall's* 118, No. 2 (November 1990):85

## Parents of Disabled Children

Safe in Mother's Arms. Judith Kelman. *Redbook* 175, No. 3 (July 1990):112-114

A Woman Today: A Home for Patty. Diane Stacy and Cheryl Coggins Frink. *Ladies' Home Journal* 107, No. 5 (May 1990):20-26

## Parikh, Manju

Sex-Selective Abortions in India: Parental Choice or Sexist Discrimination? *Feminist Issues* 10, No. 2 (Fall 1990):19-32

**Paris – Art**

Kitsch and Tell. Nadine Frey. *Harper's Bazaar* (February 1990):82

**Paris – Description and Travel**

Travel: Paris: The European City You Can Afford. Bibliography. *Glamour* (March 1990):177-179

**Paris – Fashion.** *See also particular designers*

Appareled Like the Spring: The French Collections. *Lear's* (February 1990):61-71

Haute Bijoux. Jon Etra. *Harper's Bazaar* (September 1990):206

Paris: Seasonal Perfection. *Harper's Bazaar* (January 1990):120-127

Paris' Beau Ideal. *Lear's* (August 1990):108-115

Paris Match. *Harper's Bazaar* (April 1990):136

Paris Soir. *Harper's Bazaar* (April 1990):216

Show Stoppers. *Harper's Bazaar* (April 1990):140-149

**Paris – Le Cordon Bleu**

Upper Crusts. Christopher Petkanas. *Harper's Bazaar* (July 1990):113 +

**Paris, Mica**

Contribution. Reviewed by Elorine Grant. *Spare Rib* 218 (November 1990):18

**Paris, Sherri**

Manhood and Politics: A Feminist Reading in Political Theory. Book Review. *Hypatia* 5, No. 3 (Fall 1990):175-180

**Paris – Social Life and Customs.** *See also* Shopping

Night Visions. Christopher Petkanas. *Harper's Bazaar* (October 1990):233 +

Paris Bouquet. Christopher Petkanas. *Harper's Bazaar* (September 1990):318

Paris Charm. Charla Carter. *Harper's Bazaar* (February 1990):140-143 +

Talking Parties. *Vogue* (September 1990):662

**Parish, Thomas S.**

Evaluations of Family by Youth: Do They Vary as a Function of Family Structure, Gender, and Birth Order? *Adolescence* 25, No. 98 (Summer 1990):353-356

**Paris Review**

The Paris Review Anthology. Edited by George Plimpton. Reviewed by Deborah Price. *Belles Lettres* 5, No. 4 (Summer 1990):47-48

**Park, Christine** and Heaton, Caroline (editors)

Close Company: Stories of Mothers and Daughters. Reviewed by Lynne M. Constantine. *Belles Lettres* 5, No. 3 (Spring 1990):6

**Park, Roberta J.** (joint editor). *See* Mangan, J. A.

**Parker, Alice**

Holograms of Desire. *The Women's Review of Books* 8, No. 3 (December 1990):28-29

Writing in the Feminine: Feminism and Experimental Writing in Quebec. Book Review. *The Women's Review of Books* 8, No. 3 (December 1990):28-29

**Parker, Alice** (joint editor). *See* Meese, Elizabeth

**Parker, Corey** (about)

Corey Parker: *Thirtysomething*'s Younger Man. Jennie Nash. *Mademoiselle* (February 1990):80

**Parker, Pat** (about)

Pat Parker: A Tribute. Lyndie Brimstone. *Feminist Review* No. 34 (Spring 1990):4-7

**Parker, Sarah Jessica** (about)

Romantic Do's. *Redbook* 175, No. 3 (July 1990):96-99

**Parkhurst, Eleanor**

The Cutting Edge of Sexism: Reflections on Male Dominance; Violence; and Most Especially Homophobia. *off our backs* 20, No. 7 (July 1990):16

Homophobia: A Weapon of Sexism. Book Review. *off our backs* 20, No. 7 (July 1990):16

**Parkin, Sara** (about)

The Greening of Sara Parkin. Deborah Stead. *Savvy Woman* (November 1990):64-67 +

**Parks, Mary Anderson**

A Small Battle. Short story. *AFFILIA* 5, No. 2 (Summer 1990):90-96

**Parks, Peggy** (joint author). *See* Jones, L. Colette

**Parks-Satterfield, Deb**

Naps . . . The Politics of Hair (excerpts). Short Story. *Sinister Wisdom* 42 (Winter 1990-1991):54-58

**Parmar, Pratibha**

Woman, Native, Other: Pratibha Parmar Interviews Trinh T. Minh-ha. *Feminist Review* No. 36 (Autumn 1990):65-74

**Parmar, Pratibha** (joint editor). *See* Grewal, Shabnam

**Parmar, S. B. Singh**

The Impact of Infant Mortality on Fertility Behaviour of Women. *Journal of Family Welfare* 36, No. 1 (March 1990):43-47

**Parmet, Harriet L.** (joint author). *See* Lasker, Judith N.

**Parpart, Jane L.** and Staudt, Kathleen A. (editors)

Women and the State in Africa. Reviewed by Barbara Lewis. *Women & Politics* 10, No. 1 (1990):82-84

**Parrots**

Pet Life. Michael W. Fox. *McCall's* 117, No. 8 (May 1990):163

**Parry, Odette**

"We Don't Contravene the Sex Discrimination Act" – Female Students at Journalism School. *Gender and Education* 2, No. 1 (1990):3-16

**Parthenogenesis**

The Choreographing of Reproductive DNA. Ryn Edwards. *Lesbian Ethics* 4, No. 1 (Spring 1990): 44-51

Lesbian Rebirth. Chris Sitka. *Lesbian Ethics* 4, No. 1 (Spring 1990): 4-27

The Selfish Sperm Theory. Jesse Cougar. *Lesbian Ethics* 4, No. 1 (Spring 1990): 28-43

9 Somewhat Queer and Wonderful Facts About Animal Reproduction. Excerpt. Dell Richards. *Out/Look* No. 8 (Spring 1990):56

**Parties.** *See also* Social Entertaining

Black-Tie Anxiety: The Agony and Ecstasy of Dressing Up. *Mademoiselle* (December 1990):126-129

The Busy Life: Presentation Is Everything. Jill McQuilkin. *Working Woman* (September 1990):202-205

Confessions of a Beauty Sinner. *Mademoiselle* (December 1990):152-155

How to Host a Business Bash that's Not a Bore. Will Nixon. *Working Woman* (November 1990):122-125

It's a Halloween Party! *Glamour* (October 1990):290-294

For Night: Dress Whites. *Mademoiselle* (December 1990):130-135

Weekends: Designing the Perfect Party. Leah Rosch. *Working Woman* (March 1990):133-137

**Parties – Fashion**

Beauty and Fashion Hotline: Touch of Luxe. *Family Circle* 103, No. 17 (December 18, 1990):37-40

**Partnership.** *See also* Naisbitt, John (about)

Opening Day: We're in Business. Louise Washer. *Working Woman* (May 1990):55-62

Partners in Style. *Glamour* (September 1990):304-305

Top Gun. James Grant. *Harper's Bazaar* (October 1990):204-207

Trouble at the Top? How to Stay Out of It. Ellen Rapp. *Working Woman* (June 1990):60

The War of the Bosses. Ellen Rapp. *Working Woman* (June 1990):57-59

**Parton, Dolly** (about)

Dolly's House. Lauren Payne. *Ladies' Home Journal* 107, No. 9 (September 1990):176-179

**Part-time Employment.** *See* Employment, Part-time

**Pascale, Celine-Marie**

Photographs of Home. *Sinister Wisdom* 41 (Summer-Fall 1990):90-93

**Pascall, Gillian**

Social Policy: A Feminist Analysis. Reviewed by Roberta M. Spalter-Roth. *Gender and Society* 4, No. 1 (March 1990):111-113

**Paschke, Ed** (about)

The Starker Image. Suzanne Muchnic. *Harper's Bazaar* (April 1990):132

**Pascoe, Peggy**

At the Crossroads of Culture. *The Women's Review of Books* 7, No. 5 (February 1990):22-23

Relations of Rescue: The Search for Female Authority in the American West, 1874-1939. Reviewed by Lillian Schlissel. *The Women's Review of Books* 7, No. 12 (September 1990):18

**Passover – Customs and Practices**

Anxiety 101: Leading the Passover Seder. Jeff Axelbank. *Lilith* 15, No. 2 (Spring 1990):13-15

**Pasta.** *See* Cookery (Pasta)

**Pastan, Linda**

Yahrzeit Candle. Poem. *Lilith* 15, No. 1 (Winter 1990):27

**Paster, Darrell L**

A State of Shock: Recollections of Romania. *On the Issues* 16 (Fall 1990):19-21

**Pasternak, Judith**

Interviews Transformed into Play for Street Theater. *New Directions for Women* 19, No. 1 (January/February 1990):metrö+

Positive Images: Portraits of Women with Disabilities. Video Review. *On the Issues* 17 (Winter 1990):36-37

**Patchett, Frances Tramontana**

Francesca Ranieri Tramontana 1887-1963. *Sinister Wisdom* 41 (Summer-Fall 1990):19-21

**Pate, R. R.** (joint author). *See* Cokkinades, Vilma E.

**Patel, Bella C.** (joint author). *See* Khan, M. E.

**Pateman, Carole**

The Sexual Contract. Reviewed by Jennifer M. Lehmann. *Journal of Marriage and the Family* 52, No. 2 (May 1990):563-564

The Sexual Contract. Reviewed by Mary Lyndon Shanley. *Signs* 16, No. 1 (Autumn 1990):183-187

**Pateman, Carole** (joint editor). *See* Goodnow, Jacqueline

**Pateman, Pat**

For God, Country and the Thrill of It. Book Review. *Minerva* 8, No. 2 (Summer 1990):73-74

**Paterson, Janet M.**

Gynocritics/La Gynocritique. Book Review. *Resources for Feminist Research* 19, No. 1 (March 1990):19

**Pathak, Ila** and Amin, Amina

How AWAG Dealt with a Rapist. *Manushi* 58 (May-June 1990):37-38

**Pathak, K. B.**

Religion, Social Change and Fertility Behaviour. Book Review. *Journal of Family Welfare* 36, No. 2 (June 1990):69-70

**Patient-Doctor Relationships.** *See also* Health Care; Privacy Rights

Intimate Adversaries: Cultural Conflict Between Doctors and Women Patients. By Alexandra Dundas Dodd. Reviewed by Margherita Jellinek. *AFFILIA* 5, No. 4 (Winter 1990):108-110

Intimate Adversaries – Cultural Conflict between Doctors and Women Patients. By Alexandra Dundas Todd. Reviewed by Mary A. Jansen. *Psychology of Women Quarterly* 14, No. 3 (September 1990):437-439

McCallmanack: Practicing More Humane Medicine. Liza Nelson. *McCall's* 117, No. 9 (June 1990):45

The Take-Charge Patient. Bibliography. Andrea Atkins. *Ladies' Home Journal* 107, No. 11 (November 1990):163-174

Teaching Docs to Improve Gyn Exams. Rosalind Warren. *New Directions for Women* 19, No. 3 (May/June 1990):12

**Patil, R. L**

Estimation of Potential Fertility Rates by Age-Group for Karnataka State. *Journal of Family Welfare* 36, No. 1 (March 1990):3-6

**Patitz, Tatjana** (about). *See also* Fashion Models, "Singular Sensations"

**Patlak, Margie**

Postponing Motherhood. *Glamour* (March 1990):68-70

**Patnaik, Eira**

"Madam, May I Have a Word with You?" *Sage* 6, No. 1 (Summer 1989):66

**Patriarchy.** *See also* Great Britain – History

**Patriarchy – Feminist Perspectives**

On the Bias: Leaving Our Father's Houses: Redefining Our Religious Concepts. Gail K. Golden and Lynn G. Sheinkin. *AFFILIA* 5, No. 3 (Fall 1990):105-110

Refiguring the Father: New Feminist Readings of Patriarchy. By Patricia Yaeger and Beth Kowaleski-Wallace. Reviewed by Miriam M. Johnson. *NWSA Journal* 2, No. 4 (Autumn 1990):656-658

**Patriarchy – Women's Roles.** *See also* Judaism; Religious Discrimination

. . . And an Anthropologist Says . . . Riv-Ellen Prell. *Lilith* 15, No. 3 (Summer 1990):23

Into the Future with Rituals from Our Past. Susan Schnur. *Lilith* 15, No. 3 (Summer 1990):19

The New, Improved Jewish Divorce: Hers/His. Vicki Hollander. *Lilith* 15, No. 3 (Summer 1990):20-21

Our Lives, Circa 1919. Maxine Schwartz Seller. *Lilith* 15, No. 4 (Fall 1990):42

On the Path to Power: Women Decode the Talmud in Their Own Style. Vanessa Ochs. *Lilith* 15, No. 3 (Summer 1990):16-18

What the Law Says. *Manushi* 57 (March-April 1990):2 +

**Patrick, Jennie R.**

Trials, Tribulations, Triumphs. *Sage* 6, No. 2 (Fall 1989):51-53

**Patrick, Michelle**

A Feed-Your-Baby Quiz. *Essence* 20, No. 11 (March 1990).104 +

Parenting: The Taming of the Twos. *Essence* 21, No. 5 (September 1990):106-108

**Patrick, Sharon L** (about)

Patrick's Rainbow. Lynn Braz. *Executive Female* 13, No. 6 (November-December 1990):50 +

**Patriotism**

Rabindranath Tagore on Nationalism. Rabindranath Tagore. *Manushi* 58 (May-June 1990):13

**Patterson, Casey**

Living in the Fast Lane. *Women's Sports and Fitness* 12, No. 2 (March 1990):14-15

**Patterson, Chandra**

An Affair to Remember. *Essence* 21, No. 3 (July 1990):59-60 +

**Patterson, Rosalyn**

Black Women in the Biological Sciences. *Sage* 6, No. 2 (Fall 1989):8-14

**Patterson, Shirley L**

Daughters of the Elderly: Building Partnerships in Caregiving. Book Review. *Journal of Women and Aging* 2, No. 1 (1990):123-124

**Patterson, Yolanda Astarita**

Simone de Beauvoir and the Demystification of Motherhood. Reviewed by Sonia Jaffe Robbins. *New Directions for Women* 19, No. 3 (May/June 1990):20

**Patwardhan, Leelabai** (about). *See also*
India – Status of Women

**Patychuk, Dianne**

Shrink Resistant: The Struggle Against Psychiatry in
Canada. Book Review. *Healthsharing* 11, No. 2
(March 1990):32

**Paul, Elizabeth L.** and White, Kathleen M.

The Development of Intimate Relationships in Late
Adolescence. *Adolescence* 25, No. 98 (Summer
1990):375-400

**Paul, Ellen Frankel**

Equity and Gender: The Comparable Worth
Debate. Reviewed by Faye Crosby. *Psychology of
Women Quarterly* 14, No. 1 (March 1990):147-148

**Pauley, Jane** (about). *See also* Leadership, "1990
Women of the Year"; Television
Journalists – Networking

Here *Today* Gone Tomorrow: When Jane Pauley
*Should* Have Quit. Claire McIntosh. *Working
Woman* (May 1990):82-83

Jane Pauley's Prime Time. Gail Collins. *Savvy*
(December-January 1991):52-54+

Jane's Search for Tomorrow. Jeff Rovin. *Ladies'
Home Journal* 107, No. 7 (July 1990):86-87+

**Pausacker, Jenny** (joint editor). *See* Hawthorne,
Susan

**Paxton, Nancy L.**

Feminism Under the Raj: Complicity and
Resistance in the Writings of Flora Annie Steel and
Annie Besant. *Women's Studies International
Forum* 13, No. 4 (1990):333-346

**Pay Equity.** *See* Wage Equity

**Payer, Lynn**

Health. *Vogue* (June 1990):152-156

**Paylor, Sheryl Hill**

Women of Color in the United States: A Guide to
the Literature. Book Review. *Sage* 6, No. 2 (Fall
1989):57-58

**Payne, Lauren**

Backyards of the Rich and Famous. *Ladies' Home
Journal* 107, No. 8 (August 1990):118-122

Does Your House Have Sales Appeal? *Ladies'
Home Journal* 107, No. 6 (June 1990):114-118

Dolly's House. *Ladies' Home Journal* 107, No. 9
(September 1990):176-179

The House of Our Dreams. *Ladies' Home Journal*
107, No. 10 (October 1990):162-165

A House Without a Man Is Still a Home. *Ladies'
Home Journal* 107, No. 11 (November 1990):210-
215

Inside the Governors' Mansions. *Ladies' Home
Journal* 107, No. 7 (July 1990):98-104

A New England Christmas. *Ladies' Home Journal*
107, No. 12 (December 1990):138-143

**Payne, Lauren** and Hazard, Jan Turner

Kitchens for People Who Love to Cook. *Ladies'
Home Journal* 107, No. 3 (March 1990):184-198

**Payne, Lauren** and Reisler, Karen J.

Room for Improvement. *Ladies' Home Journal* 107,
No. 5 (May 1990):168-174

On the Waterfront. *Ladies' Home Journal* 107, No.
4 (April 1990):166-170

**Payton, Sarah**

Kamikaze Hearts. Film Review. *Spare Rib* No. 215
(August 1990):35

Portrait of a Marriage. Video Review. *Spare Rib* 217
(October 1990):30

Steel Magnolias. Film Review. *Spare Rib* No. 211
(April 1990):30

**Peace Corps**

Prime of Life: The New Recruits. Kelly Norton
Humphrey. *Family Circle* 103, No. 13 (September
25, 1990):38-40

**Peace Movements**

Feminist Perspectives on Peace and Education. By
Birgit Brock Utne. Reviewed by Deborah Jordan.
*Australian Feminist Studies* No. 11 (Autumn
1990):127-128

The Long Road to Greenham: Feminism and Anti-
Militarism in Britain since 1820. By Jill Liddington.
Reviewed by Jo Vellacott. *Resources for Feminist
Research* 19, No. 2 (June 1990):44

Maternal Thinking: Towards a Politics of Peace. By
Sara Ruddick. Reviewed by Jean P. Rumsey.
*Hypatia* 5, No. 3 (Fall 1990):125-131

Painting for Peace: Break the Silence Mural Project.
Miranda Bergman, Susan Greene, Dina Redman,
and Marlene Tobias. *Bridges* 1, No. 2 (Fall 1990):
39-57

The Peaceful Sex? On Feminism and the Peace
Movement. Linda Gordon. *NWSA Journal* 2, No. 4
(Autumn 1990):624-634

Peaceniks. Nancy Nachum. *Sinister Wisdom* 42
(Winter 1990-1991):49-52

The Politics of Violence. Charlotte Bunch. *On the
Issues* 16 (Fall 1990):25

Rocking the Ship of State: Toward a Feminist Peace
Politics. Edited by Adrienne E. Harris and Ynestra
King. Reviewed by Minard Hamilton. *New
Directions for Women* 19, No. 2 (March/April
1990):19

Talking Peace: The Women's International Peace
Conference. By Susan C. MacPhee. Reviewed by
Anne Sisson Runyan. *Atlantis* 15, No. 2 (Spring
1990):107-109

Women on War and Survival. Daniela Gioseffi. *On the Issues* 16 (Fall 1990):29-31+

**Peacock, Sandra J.**

Jane Ellen Harrison: The Mask and the Self. Reviewed by Janet Howarth. *Gender and Education* 2, No. 2 (1990):246-247

Jane Ellen Harrison: The Mask and the Self. Reviewed by Sandra J. Peacock. *Gender & History* 2, No. 1 (Spring 1990):103-104

**Peake, Linda**

Women's Work: Incorporating Gender Into Theories of Urban-Social Change. *Women and Environments* 12, No. 1 (Fall 1989/Winter 1990): 18-20

**Peake, Linda** (joint editor). *See* Moser, Caroline O. N.

**Peanut Butter**

Good Food: Peanut Butter Celebration! *Good Housekeeping* 211, No. 3 (September 1990):252-255

**Pearlman, Jill**

Music: Welcome to the Funhouse. *Vogue* (July 1990):90-93

**Pears**

Pick a Perfect Pear. *Family Circle* 103, No. 14 (October 16, 1990).104-105

**Pearson, Carol S.**, Shavlik, Donna L., and Touchton, Judith G. (editors)

Educating the Majority: Women Challenge Tradition in Higher Education. Reviewed by Gloria Bowles. *NWSA Journal* 2, No. 2 (Spring 1990):288-290

**Pearson, Jacqueline**

The Prostituted Muse: Images of Women and Women Dramatists, 1642-1737. Reviewed by Elaine Hobby. *Gender & History* 2, No. 3 (Autumn 1990):359-363

**Pearson, Susie**

Diana's Darlings. *Ladies' Home Journal* 107, No. 2 (February 1990):107-110

Fergie Gets Real. *Ladies' Home Journal* 107, No. 4 (April 1990):155-158+

**Peaslee, Kay**

An Epic Life: Novelist and Feminist Ellen Glasgow. *Iris* 24 (Fall-Winter 1990):12-16

**Peck, Catherine**

My Daughter, the Little Princess. *McCall's* 117, No. 12 (September 1990):31-32

**Peck, David**

Novels of Initiation: A Guidebook for Teaching Literature to Adolescents. Book Review. *Adolescence* 25, No. 100 (Winter 1990):999-1000

**Pecukonis, Edward V.**

A Cognitive/Affective Empathy Training Program as a Function of Ego Development in Aggressive Adolescent Females. *Adolescence* 25, No. 97 (Spring 1990):59-76

**Pedersen, Joyce**

Playing the Game: Sport and the Physical Emancipation of English Women 1870-1914. Book Review. *Gender and Education* 2, No. 1 (1990):107-109

**Pedersen, Joyce Senders**

The Reform of Girls' Secondary and Higher Education in Victorian England. Reviewed by Felicity Hunt. *Gender & History* 2, No. 1 (Spring 1990):113-114

**Pederson, Jane M.**

Day In, Day Out: Women's Lives in North Dakota. Book Review. *NWSA Journal* 2, No. 3 (Summer 1990):519-520

**Pediatrics.** *See also* Child Development; Children – Obesity

Ask Dr. Mom: Kids, Their Winter Colds . . . and More. Marianne Neifert. *McCall's* 118, No. 3 (December 1990):44

Ask Dr. Mom. Marianne Neifert. *McCall's* 117, No. 7 (April 1990):8; 117, No. 8 (May 1990):19; 117, No. 9 (June 1990):10; 117, No. 11 (August 1990):28; 118, No. 1 (October 1990):36-37

Health Watch: Fever. Dava Sobel. *Ladies' Home Journal* 107, No. 2 (February 1990):56

Healthwatch: Nosebleeds. Dava Sobel. *Ladies' Home Journal* 107, No. 3 (March 1990):92

Medinews. Bibliography. Sally Squires. *Ladies' Home Journal* 107, No. 1 (January 1990):84

Pediatric Healthline. *Ladies' Home Journal* 107, No. 9 (September 1990):90; 107, No. 11 (November 1990):142

Pediatric Healthline. Mary Farrell. *Ladies' Home Journal* 107, No. 12 (December 1990):64

Understanding Kids. Lawrence Balter. *Ladies' Home Journal* 107, No. 10 (October 1990):76

What Pediatricians *Really* Think About Working Mothers. Carin Rubenstein. *Working Mother* 13, No. 4 (April 1990):40-44

When Children Have Allergies. Thomas J. Fischer and Marilyn Mercer. *Good Housekeeping* 211, No. 3 (September 1990):142-146

**Peebles-Wilkins, Wilma**

Afro-American Women of the South and the Advancement of the Race, 1895-1925. Book Review. *AFFILIA* 5, No. 1 (Spring 1990):108-110

**Peebles-Wilkins, Wilma** and Francis, E. Aracelis

Two Outstanding Women in Social Welfare History: Mary Church Terrell and Ida B. Wells-Barnett. *AFFILIA* 5, No. 4 (Winter 1990):87-100

**Peet, Phyllis**

The Art Education of Emily Sartain. *Woman's Art Journal* 11, No. 1 (Spring-Summer 1990):9-15

**Peiss, Kathy**

Making Faces: The Cosmetics Industry and the Cultural Construction of Gender, 1890-1930. *Genders* 7 (Spring 1990):143-169

**Pelc, Mary DeLorenzo**

The Dream Book: An Anthology of Writings by Italian-American Women. Book Review. *Sinister Wisdom* 41 (Summer-Fall 1990):79-81

**Pelka, Fred**

Mothers in the Fatherland. *On the Issues* 16 (Fall 1990):26-28+

**Pellini, Donatella** (about). *See* Milan – Interior Design

**Pelton, Leroy H.**

For Reasons of Poverty: A Critical Analysis of the Public Child Welfare System in the United States. Reviewed by Ann Nichols-Casebolt. *Journal of Marriage and the Family* 52, No. 3 (August 1990):801-802

**Penelope, Julia**

Age, Bodily Secretions, Lesbians . . . Developing the Language. *Hot Wire* 6, No. 2 (May 1990):18-19+

A Case of Mistaken Identity. *The Women's Review of Books* 7, No. 7 (April 1990):11-12

Identity Politics: Lesbian Feminism and the Limits of Community. Book Review. *The Women's Review of Books* 7, No. 7 (April 1990):11-12

Speaking Freely: Unlearning the Lies of the Fathers' Tongues. Reviewed by Alida Brill. *Ms.* 1, No. 1 (July/August 1990):70

Women – and Lesbian – Only Spaces: Thought Into Action. *off our backs* 20, No. 5 (May 1990):14-16

**Penelope, Julia** and Valentine, Sarah (editors)

Finding the Lesbians: Personal Accounts from Around the World. Reviewed by Rebecca Gordon. *The Women's Review of Books* 7, No. 9 (June 1990):7-8

Finding the Lesbians. Reviewed by Barbara Findlen. *Ms.* 1, No. 1 (July/August 1990):69

**Penelope, Julia** and Wolfe, Susan J. (editors)

The Original Coming Out Stories. Reviewed by Rebecca Gordon. *The Women's Review of Books* 7, No. 9 (June 1990):7-8

**Penn, Shana**

Platonic Dialogue? *The Women's Review of Books* 7, No. 6 (March 1990):28-29

Sex and Other Sacred Games: Love, Desire, Power and Possession. Book Review. *The Women's Review of Books* 7, No. 6 (March 1990):28-29

**Pennington, Shelley** and Westover, Belinda

A Hidden Workforce: Homeworkers in England, 1850-1985. Reviewed by Mary Kinnear. *Resources for Feminist Research* 19, No. 2 (June 1990):37

**People's Republic of China.** *See* China

**Pepe, Sheila**

To Soar: Interview with Nancy Spero. *Trivia* 16/17 (Fall 1990):119-127

**Pepper, Jon**

Tech Talk: What Kind of Manager are You? *Working Woman* (May 1990):46-52

**Peralta, Teresa**

The Experience of CIPAF in Documentation. *Women's World* 23 (April 1990):21-22

**Perdue, Theda**

Indians, Outlaws, and Angie Debo. Film review. *NWSA Journal* 2, No. 4 (Autumn 1990):646-649

**Perfectionism**

Are You Too Good? Kathryn Stechert Black. *Glamour* (March 1990):164-167

**Performance Appraisal.** *See also* Career Management; Employee Benefits; Promotions; Wages

"How Am I Doing?": What Your Boss Can't Tell You. Kent L. Straat and Nellie Sabin. *Working Woman* (August 1990):55-57+

Stretch: The No-Fail Guide to Big Career Jumps. Jill Neimark. *Working Woman* (November 1990):116-117

**Performance Art**

In a Cafe. *Lilith* 15, No. 4 (Fall 1990):26-27

Holly Hughes, Playing the Ironies. Ann Hornaday. *Ms.* 1, No. 3 (November/December 1990):64

Performance: Multi-Mediator. John Leland. *Vogue* (January 1990):90-91

**Performance Awards**

Bright Ideas: Anatomy of a Corporate Revolution. Lorraine Dusky. *Working Woman* (July 1990):58-63

**Perfumes**

Beauty: Business Scents. Teri Agins. *Essence* 20, No. 11 (March 1990):20-23

Beauty: Enduring Scents. *Essence* 21, No. 1 (May 1990):46-48

Beauty Clips. Shirley Lord. *Vogue* (September 1990):296; (December 1990):146

Beauty & Fashion Journal. *Ladies' Home Journal* 107, No. 12 (December 1990):29-32

Beauty Word of Mouth. *Glamour* (October 1990):37-40

Eau de Summer Scents: Coming Up Light. *Lear's* (June 1990):28

Fashion Design in a Bottle. K. T. Maclay. *Lear's* (November 1990):74

Florientals in Bloom. *Essence* 21, No. 5 (September 1990):19

Fragrance: The Five Pleasure Principles. *Mademoiselle* (November 1990):178-181

French Savoir Faire. *Harper's Bazaar* (May 1990):126-131+

His or Hers? *Glamour* (December 1990):224-227

Holiday Gifts of Scent. *Essence* 21, No. 8 (December 1990):18

Images: Bottled Fantasy. Jonathan Van Meter. *Vogue* (September 1990):342-344

Perfume Envy: His for Her. K. T. Maclay. *Lear's* (November 1990):77

Perfume Options. Debra A. Ward. *McCall's* 118, No. 3 (December 1990):24

Scented Treasures. Diane Sustandal. *Harper's Bazaar* (October 1990):101-120

Scentiment. Kathleen Beckett-Young. *Lear's* (November 1990):136-139

Top Honors. *Harper's Bazaar* (September 1990):316

Uncommon Scents. Diane Sustendal. *Harper's Bazaar* (September 1990):315+

**Periodical Reviews**

Journal of Feminist Therapy. *See* Hare-Mustin, Rachel T.

Journal of Women and Aging. *See* Luria, Zella

Periodical Notes. *Feminist Collections* 11, No. 2 (Winter 1990):26-29; 11, No. 4 (Summer 1990):19-21; 12, No. 1 (Fall 1990):33-36

Skipping Stones: A Multi-ethnic Children's Forum. *off our backs* 20, No. 3 (March 1990):30-31

**Periodicals.** *See also* Wigwag Magazine

Catalysts of Change: U.S. Periodicals by Women of Color, 1963-1989. Kimberly Kranich. *Feminist Teacher* 5, No. 1 (Spring 1990):26-41

Characteristics of Accepted versus Rejected Manuscripts. Arnold S. Kahn, Jack H. Presbury, Helen B. Moore, and Jacqueline D. Driver. *Psychology of Women Quarterly* 14, No. 1 (March 1990):7-14

Second Survey of Magazines Shows No Improvement in Coverage of Women. *Media Report to Women* 18, No. 6 (November-December 1990):4-5

U.S. Women's Magazines: In Search of an Audience. *Media Report to Women* 18, No. 5 (September-October 1990):5

Welcome to the Club. Frances Lear. *Lear's* (May 1990):140

Women Pictures on Only 14% of *Time* Magazine Covers since 1923, Study Finds. *Media Report to Women* 18, No. 1 (January/February 1990):3-4

Women's Magazines Regressing to 'Submissive Domesticity,' Writer Says. *Media Report to Women* 18, No. 1 (January/February 1990):7

**Periodicals—Advertising**

Sex, Lies and Advertising. Gloria Steinem. *Ms.* 1, No. 1 (July/August 1990):18-28

**Periodicals—Bibliographies**

New and Newly Discovered Periodicals. *Feminist Collections* 11, No. 3 (Spring 1990):21-23

Special Issues of Periodicals. *Feminist Collections* 11, No. 3 (Spring 1990):23-24

**Periodicals—History—Feminist Perspectives**

Women and Print Culture: The Construction of Femininity In the Early Periodical. By Kathryn Shevelow. Reviewed by Margaret Hunt. *Gender & History* 2, No. 2 (Summer 1990):228-229

**Periodicals—Images of Women**

A Certain Tension in the Visual/Cultural Field: Helmut Newton, Deborah Turbeville, and the *Vogue* Fashion Layout. Cathy Griggers. *Differences* 2, No. 2 (Summer 1990):76-104

**Perkin, Joan**

Women and Marriage in Nineteenth Century England. Reviewed by A. James Hammerton. *Gender & History* 2, No. 2 (Summer 1990):241-244

Women and Marriage in Nineteenth-Century England. Reviewed by Gerry Holloway. *Women's Studies International Forum* 13, No. 5 (1990):524

**Perkins, H. Wesley and Harris, Lynne B.**

Family Bereavement and Health in Adult Life Course Perspective. *Journal of Marriage and the Family* 52, No. 1 (February 1990):233-241

**Perkins, Penny**

Film Makers on Hot Topics. *New Directions for Women* 19, No. 2 (March/April 1990):metrö

Is the Church Revelvant? *New Directions for Women* 19, No. 4 (July-August 1990):15

Let My People In: A Lesbian Minister Tells of Her Struggles to Live Openly and Maintain her Ministry. Book Review. *New Directions for Women* 19, No. 4 (July-August 1990):15

Through the Wire. Play review. *New Directions for Women* 19, No. 2 (March/April 1990):metrö

Through the Wire. Video Review. *On the Issues* 15 (Summer 1990):31

Touching Our Strength: The Erotic as Power and the Love of God. Book Review. *New Directions for Women* 19, No. 4 (July-August 1990):15

**Perkins, Tessa** (joint author). *See* Beechey, Veronica

**Perks.** *See* Employee Benefits

**Perks, Robert** (joint author). *See* Humphries, Steve

**Perl, Jed**

Culture Shock. *Vogue* (October 1990):377-378

Gold Rush. *Vogue* (February 1990):216, 225

Matisse's Eastern Eden. *Vogue* (March 1990):430-433, 524

Vogue Arts: Art. *Vogue* (November 1990):260+

Vogue Arts: Charmed Lives. *Vogue* (August 1990):224-232

**Perle, Elizabeth**

"How I Did It": Creating the Perfect Staff. *Working Woman* (November 1990):73-76+

**Perlmutter, Barry F.** (joint editor). *See* Touliatos, John

**Perlstadt, Harry** (joint author). *See* Rosenberg, Janet

**Permanent Waving.** *See* Hair Styles

**Perrot, Michelle** (editor)

Histoire de la vie Privée, volume 4, De la révolution à la Grande Guerre. Reviewed by Sian Reynolds. *Gender & History* 2, No. 2 (Summer 1990):212-217

**Perry, Julia Amanda** (about)

Black Women Blaze Musical Trails. Lynn Wenzel. *New Directions for Women* 19, No. 1 (January/February 1990):9

**Perry, Kathryn** (joint author). *See* Blackman, Inge

**Perry, Ruth** and Greber, Lisa

Women and Computers: An Introduction. *Signs* 16, No. 1 (Autumn 1990):74-101

**Persian Gulf War, 1990-1991**

Arab State Pays Heavy Price for Opposing US. *Spare Rib* 219 (December 1990-January 1991):14-18

Dateline Kuwait: A Reporter Inside the Gulf Crisis. Caryle Murphy. *Vogue* (December 1990):300-303+

The Iraqi Invasion: An Israeli Perspective. Sue Katz. *off our backs* 20, No. 9 (October 1990):9+

Jordan: The Gulf Refugees. Arwa Aamiry. *Ms.* 1, No. 3 (November/December 1990):13

The Middle East Crisis: A Dilemma for Women: Democracy, Kings, and Sexual Apartheid in Saudi Arabia. Marie de Santis. *off our backs* 20, No. 9 (October 1990):8

Not Home for the Holidays. *Family Circle* 103, No. 17 (December 18, 1990):88-90

Thick as Thieves: Britain and the US in the Gulf. Marcel Farry. *Spare Rib* No. 216 (September 1990):18-19

Women Caught in Crisis. Carol Anne Douglas. *off our backs* 20, No. 9 (October 1990):8

Women Under Fire. Andrea Gross. *Ladies' Home Journal* 107, No. 12 (December 1990):93-97

**Personal Appearance**

Every Face has a Secret. Laura Rosetree. *Redbook* 174, No. 6 (April 1990):54-56

Woman Loses Gap, Gains Toothy Grin. Ronni Sandroff. *McCall's* 118, No. 2 (November 1990):60-69

**Personal Computers.** *See* Computers

**Personal Hygiene**

Images: Body Care. Bibliography. Peggy Orenstein. *Vogue* (January 1990):72-74

**Personality Traits.** *See also* Charm

Purse and Personality. Ellen Hopkins. *Mademoiselle* (November 1990):166-167+

**Personality Traits – Gender Differences**

The Big T(hrill) Personality: Why Some Like It Hot. Annetta Miller. *Working Woman* (February 1990):76-78

**Personal Management.** *See* Time Management

**Personal Narratives.** *See* Autobiography; Journals and Diaries; Oral History

**Personal Narratives Group** (editor)

Interpreting Women's Lives: Feminist Theory and Personal Narratives. Reviewed by Elizabeth R. Baer. *Belles Lettres* 5, No. 2 (Winter 1990):4-6+

Interpreting Women's Lives: Feminist Theory and Personal Narratives. Reviewed by Norma Schulman. *Women & Language* 13, No. 2 (Winter 1990):43

**Personal Relationships.** *See also* Female-Male Relationships

Can We Work It Out? Evette Porter. *Essence* 20, No. 10 (February 1990):56-58+

Getting All Emotional. *Mademoiselle* (June 1990):192-195

Looking for Mr. Right. Terry McMillan. *Essence* 20, No. 10 (February 1990):34+

Never Can Say Goodbye. Karen Grigsby Bates. *Essence* 20, No. 10 (February 1990):61-62

Real Stories of Best Friends. *Glamour* (November 1990):214-219

What He's Gotta Have It. Bebe Moore Campbell. *Essence* 21, No. 8 (December 1990):60-61+

**Personal Space.** *See also* Privacy

Living Beautifully: What Every Woman Needs: A Place to Call Her Own. Alexandra Stoddard. *McCall's* 117, No. 12 (September 1990):164

**Pertillar, Lisa Ann** (about). *See* College Students – Leadership

**Pertschuk, Michael**

Tanning Addiction. *Vogue* (June 1990):216

**Peru – Politics and Government**

Ruin and Reform in Peru. Joel Drefuss. *Lear's* (November 1990):94-97 +

**Peru – Prostitution**

Prostitution in Peru's Amazon Region. *Women's World* , No. 24 (Winter 1990/91): 36

**Peru – Status of Women**

Sellers and Servants: Working Women in Lima, Peru. By Ximena Bunster and Elsa M. Chaney. Reviewed by Doris P. Slesinger. *Gender and Society* 4, No. 3 (September 1990):421-423

**Perversion**

The Cultural Politics of Perversion: Augustine, Shakespeare, Freud, Foucault. Jonathan Dollimore. *Genders* 8 (Summer 1990):1-16

**Pesmen, Curtis**

Doogie Houser's Neil Patrick Harris. *Ladies' Home Journal* 107, No. 5 (May 1990):60

Ready, Set, Go! How to Shape Up Your Kids. Bibliography. *Ladies' Home Journal* 107, No. 4 (April 1990):89-110

**Pesticides**

No Fumes, No Chemicals, No Pests. Alexandra Tanski. *McCall's* 118, No. 2 (November 1990):21

The Recurring Silent Spring. By H. Patricia Hynes. Reviewed by Linda Vance. *NWSA Journal* 2, No. 3 (Summer 1990):485-489

The Recurring Silent Spring. By Patricia Hynes. Reviewed by Deborah Jordan. *Australian Feminist Studies* No. 11 (Autumn 1990):127-128

**Pests – Control.** *See* Insect Pests – Control

**Pete, Joanette M.** and De Santis, Lydia

Sexual Decision Making in Young Black Adolescent Females. *Adolescence* 25, No. 97 (Spring 1990):145-154

**Peters, Barbara McGarry**

Suite Dreams. *Executive Female* (March/April 1990):46-48 +

**Peters, Colette**

Treasure Chests. *Ladies' Home Journal* 107, No. 12 (December 1990):160 +

**Peters, Gesche**

Talking Back: Thinking Feminist – Thinking Black. Book Review. *Atlantis* 15, No. 2 (Spring 1990):109-111

**Peters, Paula**

Planned Parenthood Opens in Charlottesville. *Iris* 24 (Fall-Winter 1990):11

**Peters, Tom**

The Best New Managers will Listen, Motivate, Support. Isn't that Just Like a Woman? *Working Woman* (September 1990):142-143 +

**Peters-Golden, Holly** (joint author). *See* Grant, Linda

**Peterson, James L.** and Nord, Christine Winquist

The Regular Receipt of Child Support: A Multistep Process. *Journal of Marriage and the Family* 52, No. 2 (May 1990):539-551

**Peterson, Jean Treloggen**

Sibling Exchanges and Complementarity in the Philippine Highlands. *Journal of Marriage and the Family* 52, No. 2 (May 1990):441-451

**Peterson, Richard R.**

Women, Work, and Divorce. Reviewed by Donna Hodgkins Berardo. *Journal of Marriage and the Family* 52, No. 4 (November 1990):1153

**Peterson, Sharyl Bender** and Lach, Mary Alyce

Gender Stereotypes in Children's Books: Their Prevalence and Influence on Cognitive and Affective Development. *Gender and Education* 2, No. 2 (1990):185-197

**Peterson, Sonja**

Hidden Blessing. Short Story. *Good Housekeeping* 211, No. 6 (December 1990):154-155

**Peterson, Susan**

Enterprise: What I Learned from My Mistakes. *Working Woman* (June 1990):29-34

**Petherbridge, Deanna** (about)

Themata: New Drawings by Deanna Petherbridge. Katy Deepwell. *Spare Rib* No. 210 (March 1990):42

**Petitat, André**

Les Infirmie4res: de la vocation á la profession. Reviewed by Jacinthe Michaud. *Resources for Feminist Research* 19, No. 1 (March 1990):20

**Petkanas, Christopher**

Night Visions. *Harper's Bazaar* (October 1990):233 +

Paris Bouquet. *Harper's Bazaar* (September 1990):318

Upper Crusts. *Harper's Bazaar* (July 1990):113 +

**Petro, Patrice**

Feminism and Film History. *Camera Obscura* No. 22 (January 1990):9-26

**Petrucci, Judy** (about)

Women Watch: Votes of Confidence for Two First-Time Mayors. Patti Watts. *Executive Female* (March/April 1990):6-7

**Petrucelli, Alan W.**

Talking with Bette Midler: What Makes Bette Laugh? Interview. *Redbook* 175, No. 5 (September 1990):76-78

Talking with Victoria Principal: "I'm in Great Shape." Interview. *Redbook* 175, No. 6 (October 1990):72-74

**Petry, Alice Hall**

Contemporary Women's Fiction: Narrative Practice and Feminist Theory. Book Review. *Tulsa Studies in Women's Literature* 9, No. 2 (Fall 1990):332-334

**Pets.** *See also* Aquarium Fishes; Birds, Ornamental; Cats; Children and Pets; Dogs

The Flip Side. Patricia Volk. *Family Circle* 103, No. 11 (August 14, 1990):27+

Pet Life. Michael W. Fox. *McCall's* 117, No. 7 (April 1990):133; 117, No. 8 (May 1990):163; 117, No. 9 (June 1990):124; 118, No. 2 (November 1990):156

Pet News. Nina Keilin. *Ladies' Home Journal* 107, No. 2 (February 1990):80; 107, No. 5 (May 1990):124

The Puppy that Didn't Know How to Quit. Roberta Sandler. *Good Housekeeping* 211, No. 4 (October 1990):100

**Pets – Humor**

Something to Think about When Choosing a Dog, or Not. Lewis Burke Frumkes. *McCall's* 117, No. 8 (May 1990):58

**Pets – Social Aspects**

A Pet a Day . . . Sandra Y. Lee. *McCall's* 118, No. 3 (December 1990):26-28

**Pet Therapy.** *See* Pets – Social Aspects

**Pfau, Michael and Burgoon, Michael**

Inoculation in Political Campaigns and Gender. *Women's Studies in Communication* 13, No. 1 (Spring 1990): 1-21

**Pfeiffer, Michelle** (about). *See* Sexual Attraction

**Pflaum, Rosalynd**

Grand Obsession: Madame Curie and Her World. Reviewed by Margaret N. Rogers. *The Women's Review of Books* 7, No. 12 (September 1990):27-28

**Pfluke, Lillian A.** and Herrly, Abigail

Indomitable. Book Review. *Minerva* 8, No. 1 (Spring 1990):83-86

**Pharr, Suzanne**

Homophobia: A Weapon of Sexism. Reviewed by Claudia Card. *Hypatia* 5, No. 3 (Fall 1990):110-117

Homophobia: A Weapon of Sexism. Reviewed by Eleanor Parkhurst. *off our backs* 20, No. 7 (July 1990):16

Homophobia: A Weapon of Sexism. Reviewed by Janet E. Robinson. *Women's Studies International Forum* 13, No. 6 (1990):610-611

Homophobia: A Weapon of Sexism. Reviewed by Margaret Nash. *Hypatia* 5, No. 3 (Fall 1990):171-175

Homophobia: A Weapon of Sexism. Reviewed by Natalie Jane Woodman. *AFFILIA* 5, No. 3 (Fall 1990):124-125

**Phelan, Peggy**

Growing Up Abused. *The Women's Review of Books* 7, No. 6 (March 1990):16-17

Virginia Woolf: The Impact of Childhood Sexual Abuse on Her Life and Work. Book Review. *The Women's Review of Books* 7, No. 6 (March 1990):16-17

Virginia Woolf and the Fictions of Psychoanalysis. Book Review. *The Women's Review of Books* 7, No. 6 (March 1990):16-17

**Phelan, Peggy** (joint author). *See* Burns, Judy

**Phelan, Shane**

Feminism and Individualism. *Women & Politics* 10, No. 4 (1990):1-18

Identity Politics: Lesbian Feminism and the Limits of Community. Reviewed by Barbara Findlen. *Ms.* 1, No. 1 (July/August 1990):69

Identity Politics: Lesbian Feminism and the Limits of Community. Reviewed by Elizabeth Lapovsky Kennedy. *NWSA Journal* 2, No. 3 (Summer 1990):495-497

Identity Politics: Lesbian Feminism and the Limits of Community. Reviewed by Julia Penelope. *The Women's Review of Books* 7, No. 7 (April 1990):11-12

**Phelps, Ethel Johnston** (editor)

Tatterhood and Other Tales. Reviewed by Mitzi Myers. *NWSA Journal* 2, No. 2 (Spring 1990):273-281

**Phelps, Johnnie** and Ben-Shalom, Miriam

Lesbian Soldiers Tell Their Stories. *Minerva* 8, No. 3 (Fall 1990):38-53

**Phelps, Phoebe**

The Embrace of the Mother Goddess. *Woman of Power* 15 (Fall-Winter 1990):32-34

**Pheterson, Gail** (editor)

A Vindication of the Rights of Whores. Reviewed by Amber Hollibaugh. *The Women's Review of Books* 7, No. 6 (March 1990):9-10

A Vindication of the Rights of Whores. Reviewed by Penny Skillman. *Belles Lettres* 5, No. 3 (Spring 1990):11

**Philadelphia – Northwest Women's Center**

On the Picket Lines: Defending Abortion Rights. Excerpt. Christie Balka. *Lilith* 15, No. 1 (Winter 1990):4

**Philadelphia, PA – MOVE**

Free Ramona Africa. Free MOVE. *Spare Rib* No. 212 (May 1990):48

<X1> **Philadelphia Experiment.** *See* Support Systems

## Philanthropy

Burden of the Nouveaux Riches. Lewis H. Lapham. *Lear's* (May 1990):76-81 +

Charity Begins at Home: Generosity and Self-Interest Among the Philanthropic Elite. By Teresa Odendahl. Reviewed by Mary Ellen Capek. *The Women's Review of Books* 8, No. 3 (December 1990):12-13

Feminist Philanthropy: Young, Vital and Growing. Suzanne Messing. *New Directions for Women* 19, No. 4 (July-August 1990):11

## Philip, Marlene Nourbese

The Absence of Writing, or How I Almost Became a Spy. *Trivia* 16/17 (Fall 1990):18-33

Harriet's Daughter. Reviewed by Rhonda Cobham. *The Women's Review of Books* 7, Nos. 10-11 (July 1990):29-31

Universal Grammar. *Trivia* 16/17 (Fall 1990):34-39

## Philipose, Pamela

Earth, Air and Water: Women Fight for the Environment in India. *Healthsharing* 11, No. 1 (December 1989):22-26

## Philippines

Towards Understanding the Psychology of the Filipino. Elizabeth Protacio Marcelino. *Women and Therapy* 9, Nos. 1 2 (1990):105-128

## Philippines – Family Structure

Sibling Exchanges and Complementarity in the Philippine Highlands. Jean Treloggen Peterson. *Journal of Marriage and the Family* 52, No. 2 (May 1990):441-451

## Philippines – Prostitution

Women Organizing: The Philippines: Prostitutes Unite. *Women in Action* 3 & 4 (1990):53-55

## Philippines – Status of Women

Center for Women's Resources. *Women's World* 23 (April 1990):41

Women in Development. *Women in Action* 1-2 (1990):13-15

## Philippines – Violence Against Women

Manobo Women Speak. *Connexions* 34 (1990):21

## Philippines – Women's Movement

A Profile in Documentation Work: In the Service of Women's Movement. La-Rainne Abad-Sarmiento. *Women's World* 23 (April 1990):25-22

## Philips, Susan and others (editors)

Language, Gender, and Sex in Comparative Perspective. Reviewed by Jackie Urla. *Signs* 15, No. 2 (Winter 1990):412-414

## Philliber, William W. and Vannoy-Hiller, Dana

The Effect of Husband's Occupational Attainment on Wife's Achievement. *Journal of Marriage and the Family* 52, No. 2 (May 1990):323-329

## Philliber, William W. (joint author). *See* Vannoy-Hiller, Dana

## Phillips, Audrey (joint author). *See* Demers, Laurence

## Phillips, Cassandra (joint author). *See* Delis, Dean C.

## Phillips, James F. and others

The Correlates of Continuity in Contraceptive Use. *Journal of Family Welfare* 36, No. 3 (September 1990):3-17

## Phillips, Leslie

The Country Doctor. *Savvy Woman* (July/August 1990):11-12

## Phillips, Lou Diamond (about)

Does Lou Diamond Phillips Have a Flaw? Alice Lane. *Mademoiselle* (February 1990):78

## Phillips, Louis

The Flip Side. *Family Circle* 103, No. 15 (November 6, 1990):262-29

## Phillips, Martha (about). *See also* Family-Owned Business, "Close Connections"

## Phillips, Norah

Male Artists Upstairs, Females in the Basement. *Canadian Women's Studies* 11, No. 1 (Spring 1990):103

## Phillips, Roderick

Putting Asunder: A History of Divorce in Western Society. Reviewed by A. James Hammerton. *Gender & History* 2, No. 2 (Summer 1990):241-244

## Phillips, Terri (joint author). *See* Vernon, JoEtta A.

## Phillips, William R. F. (joint author). *See* Rosenberg, Janet

## Philosophers

Women Philosophers: A Bio-Critical Source Book. By Ethel M. Kersey. Review. *Feminist Collections* 11, No. 3 (Spring 1990):17

## Philosophy

Lesbian Philosophies and Cultures. Edited by Jeffner Allen. Reviewed by Elizabeth Wood. *New Directions for Women* 19, No. 6 (November-December 1990):17

Spiraling into the Nineties: An Invitation to Outercourse. Mary Daly. *Woman of Power* 17 (Summer 1990):6-12

## Philosophy – Feminist Perspectives. *See also* Knowledge, Theory of

Analogy as Destiny: Cartesian Man and the Woman Reader. Carol H. Cantrell. *Hypatia* 5, No. 2 (Summer 1990):7-19

Dressing Down Dressing Up – The Philosophic Fear of Fashion. Karen Hanson. *Hypatia* 5, No. 2 (Summer 1990):107-121

Feminism and Individualism. Shane Phelan. *Women & Politics* 10, No. 4 (1990):1-18

Inessential Woman. By Elizabeth Spelman. Reviewed by Carol Anne Douglas. *off our backs* 20, No. 4 (April 1990):17-18

Women and the Ideal Society: Plato's Republic and Modern Myths of Gender. By Natalie Harris Bluestone. Reviewed by Mary Dietz. *Women & Politics* 10, No. 1 (1990):80-82

**Philpott, Joan**

Frida Kahlo: The Brush of Anguish. Book Review. *Ms.* 1, No. 2 (September/October 1990):27-28

Louise Nevelson: A Passionate Life. Book Review. *Ms.* 1, No. 2 (September/October 1990):28

**Phinney, Virginia G.**, Jensen, Larry Cyril, Olsen, Joseph A., and Cundick, Bert

The Relationship between Early Development and Psychosexual Behaviors in Adolescent Females. *Adolescence* 25, No. 98 (Summer 1990):321-332

**Phipps, Lisa M.**

Healing from Within. *Healthsharing* 11, No. 1 (December 1989):15-16

**Phoenix, Ann**

Invented Lives: Narratives of Black Women 1860-1960. Book Review. *Gender and Education* 2, No. 2 (1990):252-254

**Photographers.** *See also* Artists

Lorna Simpson: Words of Art. Joan Morgan. *Essence* 21, No. 8 (December 1990):36

**Photographs.** *See also* Actors – Photographs; Children – Photographs; Middle Eastern Women – History

Body & Soul. Francesco Scavullo. *Harper's Bazaar* (October 1990):192-199

Chosen Images: A Decade of Jewish Feminism. Joan E. Biren. *Bridges* 1, No. 1 (Spring 1990): 57-66

Photo Essay. Kirsten Marthe Lentz. *Women & Language* 13, No. 1 (Fall 1990):52

The Woman in My Life: Photography of Women. *Feminist Review* No. 36 (Autumn 1990):42-51

**Photography.** *See also* Cameras; Weddings – Photography

Candid Camera. Robin Cembalest. *Harper's Bazaar* (November 1990):88-92

Crossing Borders. Nina Malkin. *Harper's Bazaar* (September 1990):242-243 +

Feminism, Family and Photography. Susan McEachern. *Canadian Women's Studies* 11, No. 1 (Spring 1990):14-15

Man Ray. David Shapiro. *Harper's Bazaar* (September 1990):292-293 +

Memories. *Glamour* (February 1990):202-205

Painting with Light. Kristine McKenna. *Harper's Bazaar* (March 1990):208-209 +

Portraits en regard. Francine Dagenais. *Canadian Women's Studies* 11, No. 1 (Spring 1990):18-21

Prague's Spring. Eleanor Heartney. *Harper's Bazaar* (March 1990):72-85

Seen From Within. Owen Edwards. *Savvy Woman* (January 1990):68-71

Sure Shot. Mark Matousek. *Harper's Bazaar* (March 1990):212-213 +

**Photography – Exhibitions**

Drawing the Line. Edited by J. Z. Grover. *Out/Look* No. 10 (Fall 1990):6-11

Picturing the Homoerotic: Gay Images in Photography. Allen Ellenzweig. *Out/Look* No. 7 (Winter 1990):44-51

Of Torture and Tangents: Consequences of the Robert Mapplethorpe Exhibition. Stuart Edelson. *Out/Look* No. 7 (Winter 1990):52-53

The Woman in My Life. Bjanka Kadic. *Spare Rib* No. 212 (May 1990):30

**Phranc** (interview)

Hi, Phranc. This Is Alix Calling. Phranc and Alix Dobkin. *Hot Wire* 6, No. 1 (January 1990):16-18 +

**Phuong, Nguyen Thi Ngoc**, Hung, Bui Sy, Schecter, Arnold, and Vu, Dan Quoc

Dioxin Levels in Adipose Tissues of Hospitalized Women Living in the South of Vietnam in 1984-89 with a Brief Review of Their Clinical Histories. *Women and Health* 16, No. 1 (1990):79-93

**Physical Education and Training.** *See also* Physical Fitness

Body Management: The Executive Workout. Len Kravitz. *Working Woman* (February 1990):115-120

Getting Faster, Faster. Owen Anderson. *Women's Sports & Fitness* 12, No. 6 (September 1990):30-32

Sports Medicine: Hot Tips. Carol Otis and Roger Goldingay. *Women's Sports & Fitness* 12, No. 6 (September 1990):10

Tennis: Coach in a Box. Joel Drucker. *Women's Sports & Fitness* 12, No. 6 (September 1990):22

**Physical Education Facilities.** *See also* Physical Fitness Centers

**Physical Examination**

Take 2 Asprin . . . and Call Me in 5 Years. John C. Harbert. *Family Circle* 103, No. 14 (October 16, 1990):136-138

**Physical Fitness.** *See also* Aerobic Exercise; Celebrities – Beauty, Personal; Exercise; Exercise for Children; Joints – Range of Motion; Physical Education and Training; Walking; Weight Loss

Beauty: The Body Shop. *Mademoiselle* (January 1990):16

Body Image. Mary Kay Blakely. *Lear's* (January 1990):52-53

Body Management: The New Fitness Myths – Why You Shouldn't Always Play by the Rules. Ellen Kunes. *Working Woman* (August 1990):87-88

Bottoms by Jake. Jake Steinfeld. *Ladies' Home Journal* 107, No. 6 (June 1990):38-42

Countdown to Summer. *Ladies' Home Journal* 107, No. 5 (May 1990):37-54

Fitness. Jani Scandura. *Vogue* (October 1990):232+

Fitness and Flexibility. James Servin. *Harper's Bazaar* (January 1990):46

Fitness Notes. *Vogue* (January 1990):84

A Flat Stomach in 30 Days with Callanetics. Callan Pinckney. *Redbook* 175, No. 2 (June 1990):12-16

Health and Fitness. Bibliography. Stephanie Young. *Glamour* (January 1990):26-29

Health & Fitness. Stephanie Young. *Glamour* (February 1990):43-44; (April 1990):69-74

Living Large, Getting Fit. E. K. Daufin. *Essence* 21, No. 4 (August 1990):20-25

Loosen Up! Janette M. Scandura. *Redbook* 175, No. 1 (May 1990):116-119

The Naked Truth about Fitness. Barbara Ehrenreich. *Lear's* (September 1990):96-99

No-Sweat Fitness. Ellen Kunes. *Working Woman* (April 1990):119-120

Performance Review: Going Places, Staying Healthy. Karen Behnke and Lorraine Calvacca. *Working Woman* (October 1990):139

The Sleek Stomach. *Mademoiselle* (December 1990):168-171

Slim Down for Summer. *Family Circle* 103, No. 7 (May 15, 1990):09+

The Spa Differential. Carol Isaak Barden. *Lear's* (March 1990):64-67

Star Gazing. *Family Circle* 103, No. 4 (March 13, 1990):81-82

Video Workouts. *Lear's* (May 1990):26

Warning: When Exercise Is Hazardous to Your Health. Jere Daniel. *Family Circle* 103, No. 14 (October 16, 1990):125-127

**Physical Fitness Centers.** *See also* Physical Fitness for Children

Enterprise: Beefing Up a Skinny Business. Janette Scandura. *Working Woman* (February 1990):53-58

Girls Just Wanna Work Out. Laura Broadwell. *Women's Sports & Fitness* 12, No. 6 (September 1990):44-48

Spa Guide. Sara Nelson. *Working Woman* (March 1990):146-150

**Physical Fitness for Children**

Franchises Shape Up Kids. *Executive Female* (March/April 1990):76

**Physicians**

Gender, Parenthood, and Work Hours of Physicians. Linda Grant, Layne A. Simpson, Xue Lan Rong, and Holly Peters-Golden. *Journal of Marriage and the Family* 52, No. 1 (February 1990):39-49

Gender Roles, Medical Practice Roles, and Ob-Gyn Career Choice: A Longitudinal Study. Nancy G. Kutner and Donna Brogan. *Women and Health* 16, Nos. 3/4 (1990):99-117

Octavia Wilberforce, Pioneer Woman Doctor. By Pat Jalland. Reviewed by Angela V. John. *Gender & History* 2, No. 3 (Autumn 1990):375-377

**Physicians in Television**

Playing Doctor. James Kaplan. *Mademoiselle* (December 1990):96

**Physics.** *See also* Space Sciences

Spaced Out: Into New Dimensions. K. C. Cole. *Lear's* (March 1990):110-111

**Physiology**

Facts about the Human Body. *Good Housekeeping* 211, No. 4 (October 1990):247

**Picasso, Pablo** (about)

Picasso, Gilot, Matisse: Daily Life Among the Titans. Franc2oise Gilot. *Lear's* (August 1990):76-84+

**Picasso, Paloma** (about). *See* Cosmetics Industry, "The Beauty Queens"

The Busy Life: Design for Living. Kathleen Beckett-Young. *Working Woman* (October 1990):140-144

No Nonsense. Nelson W. Aldrich, Jr. *Lear's* (November 1990):104-107

**Pici, Joe**

Cross My Heart. Short story. *Redbook* 175, No. 3 (July 1990):57-60

**Picnicking.** *See also* Outdoor Cookery

Fired Up, or Fear of Flugging. Peter Feibleman. *Lear's* (July 1990):47-48

Picnic Perfect. Mali Michelle Fleming. *Essence* 21, No. 3 (July 1990):79-82

Picnic Salad Pack-Alongs. *McCall's* 117, No. 10 (July 1990):116

Picnic Time! Jonell Nash. *Essence* 21, No. 3 (July 1990):84-87

**Picone, Gennaro** (about)

Southern Exposure. Colette Rossant. *Harper's Bazaar* (April 1990):212

**Picture Frames and Framing**

Art on the Edge. Brooks Adams. *Vogue* (July 1990):94-99

Representation of Hysteria and Eating Disorders. *Australian Feminist Studies* No. 11 (Autumn 1990):49-59

**Planned Parenthood**

Faye: The Leader Women Are Waiting For? Lois Romano. *Glamour* (February 1990):194-195+

Planned Parenthood Opens in Charlottesville. Paula Peters. *Iris* 24 (Fall-Winter 1990):11

**Planning.** *See also* Small Business; Time Management

Set Your Goals and Make Them Happen. Sandy Sheehy. *Working Woman* (April 1990):81-82+

Tech Talk: How to Build a Better Meeting – The On-Line Advantage. Carol Bialkowski. *Working Woman* (July 1990):40-42

"What's Your Financial Planning IQ?" Donna Gallin. *Executive Female* (May/June 1990):57-59

**Plant, Deborah G.**

Narrative Strategies in Zora Neale Hurston's *Dust Tracks on a Road. Sage* 6, No. 1 (Summer 1989):18-23

**Plant, Judith** (editor)

Healing the Wounds: The Promise of Ecofeminism. Reviewed by Linda Vance. *NWSA Journal* 2, No. 3 (Summer 1990):485-489

**Plant, Mike**

Triathalon: A Training Schedule for Mortals. *Women's Sports and Fitness* 12, No. 2 (March 1990):47-51

**Plaskin, Glenn**

Bette's Best Diet Yet. *Family Circle* 103, No. 9 (June 26, 1990):33-34

Ivanna's Heartache. *Ladies' Home Journal* 107, No. 5 (May 1990):75-78+

Talking with Farrah Fawcett: "I'm My Own Woman." Interview. *Redbook* 175, No. 4 (August 1990):22-24

**Plaskow, Judith**

Standing Again at Sinai: Judaism From a Feminist Perspective. Reviewed by Alicia Ostriker. *The Women's Review of Books* 7, No. 12 (September 1990):12

Standing Again at Sinai: Judaism from a Feminist Perspective. Reviewed by Donna Berman. *New Directions for Women* 19, No. 4 (July-August 1990):18

Standing Again at Sinai: Judaism from a Feminist Perspective. Reviewed by Lori Ginzberg. *Bridges* 1, No. 2 (Fall 1990): 126-127

Standing Again at Sinai: Judaism from a Feminist Perspective. Reviewed by Miriyam Glazer. *Belles Lettres* 6, No. 1 (Fall 1990):10-12

Standing Again at Sinai: Judaism from a Feminist Perspective. Reviewed by Sue Levi Elwell. *Lilith* 15, No. 4 (Fall 1990):33-34

**Plastic Surgery.** *See also* Cosmetic Surgery

Hers: The Nose Job. Kathleen Rockwell Lawrence. *Glamour* (September 1990):338+

Surgery Stars. Lorraine Daigneault. *Harper's Bazaar* (August 1990):128-129+

Surgical Shaping. Carol Isaak Barden. *Harper's Bazaar* (August 1990):45+

**Plath, Sylvia** (about)

Bitter Fame: A Life of Sylvia Plath. By Anne Stevenson. Reviewed by Janice M. Cauwels. *New Directions for Women* 19, No. 1 (January/February 1990):20

**Plato** (about). *See* Philosophy – Feminist Perspectives

**Platt, Linda** (about). *See* Fashion Designers, "What I Like for Fall"

**Platt, Mary Frances**

Serious Shit at the NLC. *off our backs* 20, No. 5 (May 1990):10

A View From This Wheelchair. *off our backs* 20, No. 5 (May 1990):11

**Platt, Tom** (about). *See* Fashion Designers, "What I Like for Fall"

**Play**

Full Circle: Vidiot Box. Tricia Tunstall. *Family Circle* 103, No. 16 (November 27, 1990):146

**Play Reviews**

A Few Good Men. By Aaron Sorkin. Reviewed by Kent Black. *Harper's Bazaar* (February 1990):50

**Plays.** *See also* Performance Art

How It All Began: Sour Grapes. Maude M. Jennings. *Feminist Teacher* 5, No. 2 (Fall 1990):16-19

Louisa May Incest, a One-Act Play. Carolyn Gage. *Trivia* 16/17 (Fall 1990):137-156

When I Was Grown Up (Quand j'etais grande). Abla Farhoud. *Women and Performance: A Journal of Feminist Theory* 5, No. 1, Issue #9 (1990): 120-143

**Playwrights**

Feminine Focus: The New Women Playwrights. Edited by Enoch Brater. Reviewed by Kendall. *The Women's Review of Books* 7, No. 4 (January 1990):15-16

Plays on the Radio. *Spare Rib* No. 216 (September 1990):28

The Wendy Chronicles. Kent Black. *Harper's Bazaar* (March 1990):154-162

Women Playwrights in Contemporary Spain and the Male-Dominated Canon. Notes. Patricia W. O'Connor. *Signs* 15, No. 2 (Winter 1990):376-390

**Playwrights – Interviews**

Interviews with Contemporary Women Playwrights. Edited by Kathleen Betsko and Rachel Koenig. Reviewed by Jill Dolan. *Signs* 15, No. 4 (Summer 1990):864-869

**Pleck, Elizabeth**

Domestic Tyranny. Reviewed by Jan Faulkner. *AFFILIA* 5, No. 1 (Spring 1990):123-124

Domestic Tyranny: The Making of American Social Policy Against Family Violence from Colonial Times to the Present. Reviewed by Marcia Bedard. *NWSA Journal* 2, No. 3 (Summer 1990):464-475

**Plimpton, George** (editor)

The Paris Review Anthology. Reviewed by Deborah Price. *Belles Lettres* 5, No. 4 (Summer 1990):47-48

**Plimpton, Martha** (about)

Inside People. *Mademoiselle* (January 1990):48-50

**Plotkin, Janis**

Jewish Film Festival in Moscow. *Bridges* 1, No. 2 (Fall 1990): 109-110

**Plotnick, Robert D.**

Welfare and Out-of-Wedlock Childbearing: Evidence from the 1980s. *Journal of Marriage and the Family* 52, No. 3 (August 1990):735-746

**PMS.** *See* Premenstrual Syndrome

**Pocahontas** (about)

Grandmothers of a New World. Beth Brant. *Woman of Power* 16 (Spring 1990):40-47

**Pocharski, Susan**

Health Express: Is Yo-Yo Exercise a No-No? *Mademoiselle* (January 1990):68

**Pocock, Barbara** (editor)

Demanding Skill: Women and Technical Education in Australia. Reviewed by Autumn Stanley. *NWSA Journal* 2, No. 4 (Autumn 1990):640-645

**Poems**

Adler, Fran

Begot. *Bridges* 1, No. 1 (Spring 1990): 31

Switchback. *Bridges* 1, No. 1 (Spring 1990): 31

Agosin, Marjorie

Poems. *Lilith* 15, No. 3 (Summer 1990):13-14

Akiwumi, Viki

Ancient Rite. *Essence* 20, No. 11 (March 1990):125

Alexander, Estella Conwill

Cosmic Iconography. *Essence* 20, No. 11 (March 1990):129

Amos, Emma

Beating the Odds. *Heresies* 25 (1990):74

Anderson, Candy

Too Many Faces of Me. *New Directions for Women* 19, No. 3 (May/June 1990):5

Andrus, Pat

The Gold-Taloned Mirrors. *Women and Therapy* 10, Nos. 1/2 (1990):11

I Was in Hawaii. *Women and Therapy* 10, Nos. 1/2 (1990):9-10

Angelou, Maya

Our Grandmothers. *Ms.* 1, No. 3 (November/December 1990):22-23

Arcana, Judith

Return. *Bridges* 1, No. 2 (Fall 1990): 23

Atungaye, Monifa

Callers. *Essence* 20, No. 12 (April 1990):109

Ghost Dancing. *Essence* 20, No. 11 (March 1990):129

Azpadu, Dodici

Omertà. *Sinister Wisdom* 41 (Summer-Fall 1990):71

Back, Rachel Tzvia

A Second Sara. *Bridges* 1, No. 2 (Fall 1990): 59

From the Watertower. *Bridges* 1, No. 2 (Fall 1990): 93-94

Bagby, Rachel

*Woman of Power* 15 (Fall-Winter 1990):19

Bariteau, Corinne Adria

Home at Last! *Good Housekeeping* 211, No. 4 (October 1990):220

Love and Romance. *Good Housekeeping* 211, No. 3 (September 1990):304

Barrett, Carol

Fear of Feathers. *The Women's Review of Books* 7, No. 5 (February 1990):14

The Robbery of Rosalind Franklin. *The Women's Review of Books* 7, No. 5 (February 1990):14

Barrows, Anita

Movements toward form. *Bridges* 1, No. 2 (Fall 1990): 95-99

Bergland, Martha

The Birds Not Only Be But Mean. *Iris* 23 (Spring-Summer 1990):37

Berta, Renée

The Power in Young Girls. *Frontiers* 11, Nos. 2-3 (1990):80-81

Bradford, Michael

The Legend of Nelson Mandela. *Essence* 20, No. 11 (March 1990):133

Breeze, Jean Binta

Natural High. *Spare Rib* No. 212 (May 1990):57

Broumas, Olga

The Choir. *Ms.* 1, No. 2 (September/October 1990):front cover

Bruining, Anne Mi Ok

Stones in Somerville. *Sinister Wisdom* 40 (Spring 1990):91-93

Bufkin, Regina

The Reluctant Feminist. *Feminist Review* No. 35 (Summer 1990):109-110

Burd, Jennifer

Keep. *Iris* 24 (Fall-Winter 1990):55

Burke, Anne. Postcards. *Canadian Women's Studies* 11, No. 2 (Fall 1990):82

Burke, Colleen. The Edge of It. *Hecate* 16, Nos. 1-2 (1990):63

Caine, Shulamith Wechter

She Thinks of the Word *Stay. Women's Studies Quarterly* 18, Nos. 3-4 (Fall-Winter 1990):89

Unlearning the Syntax. *Women's Studies Quarterly* 18, Nos. 3-4 (Fall-Winter 1990):89

Cannon, Maureen

To Kathy, Reading. *Good Housekeeping* 211, No. 2 (August 1990):172

New Daughter. *Good Housekeeping* 211, No. 2 (August 1990):172

Cantrell, Mary

In Autumn. *Iowa Woman* 9, No. 4 (Winter 1989-90):26

Capone, Janet

In Answer to Their Questions. *Sinister Wisdom* 41 (Summer-Fall 1990):122-127

Caris, Jane

Snow Change. *Iris* 24 (Fall-Winter 1990):54

Carlin, Lisa

The Significance of Stones. *Sinister Wisdom* 42 (Winter 1990-1991):47-48

Cartier, Marie

A Manual for Survival. *Heresies* 25 (1990):17

Cervantes, Lorna Dee. Pleiades from the Cables of Genocide. *Frontiers* 11, No. 1 (1990):22-23

Cervantes, Lorna Dee. The Levee: Letter to No One. *Frontiers* 11, No. 1 (1990):21

Chalmer, Judith

Judith Uncovers Susanna. *Bridges* 1, No. 2 (Fall 1990): 24

Stone Bubbles. *Atlantis* 15, No. 2 (Spring 1990):80

Chang, Diana

In Two. *Ms.* 1, No. 1 (July/August 1990):83

Chitgopekar, Nilima M.

The Bitch. *Manushi* 58 (May-June 1990):36

Chrystos

Savage Eloquence. *Woman of Power* 16 (Spring 1990):inside back cover

Clifton, Lucille

Female. *Essence* 21, No. 5 (September 1990):132

Collins, Martha

Girls. *The Women's Review of Books* 7, No. 9 (June 1990):24

Party. *The Women's Review of Books* 7, No. 9 (June 1990):24

Corey, Anne

Plain Geometry. *Sinister Wisdom* 40 (Spring 1990):99-100

Cortez, Jayne

If the Drum Is a Woman. *Essence* 21, No. 5 (September 1990):118

Push Back the Catastrophes. *Essence* 21, No. 1 (May 1990):205

Craft, Sheila

The General Was a Lady. *Minerva* 8, No. 4 (Winter 1990):54-55

Cumming, Patricia

Snow Blind. *The Women's Review of Books* 7, No. 8 (May 1990):18

Song. *The Women's Review of Books* 7, No. 8 (May 1990):18

Cuomo, Chris

The Wax Problem. *Sinister Wisdom* 41 (Summer-Fall 1990):114-115

Dalton, Anne B.

Eidetic Images. *Sinister Wisdom* 42 (Winter 1990-1991):85

Dambroff, Susan

Tell Me of Your Secrets, Mary Rose. *Woman of Power* 16 (Spring 1990):inside front cover

Freeperson, Kathy

Munda. *Sinister Wisdom* 41 (Summer-Fall 1990):66

Gailitis, Margita. Choice. *Canadian Women's Studies* 11, No. 2 (Fall 1990):62

Gailitis, Margita. Retrograde. *Canadian Women's Studies* 11, No. 2 (Fall 1990):62

Gailitis, Margita. Victorian Lace. *Canadian Women's Studies* 11, No. 2 (Fall 1990):62

Garton, Victoria

An Open-Trench-Coat Poem for Dirty Boys. *Heresies* 25 (1990):60

Gayle, Nefertiti

Forwad Out De My African Daughters. *Spare Rib* No. 210 (March 1990):35

Ghigna, Charles

Passion's Paradox. *Good Housekeeping* 211, No. 3 (September 1990):304

Gillan, Maria Mazziotti

Connections. *Sinister Wisdom* 41 (Summer-Fall 1990):32-33

Public School No. 18: Paterson, New Jersey. *Sinister Wisdom* 41 (Summer-Fall 1990):8-9

Goodwin, June

I Changed My Mind. *The Women's Review of Books* 8, No. 2 (November 1990):24

Prey. *The Women's Review of Books* 8, No. 2 (November 1990):24

Gordon, Kate

Laughing Beauty. *Woman of Power* 18 (Fall 1990):15

Gordon, Pinkie Lee

Love Considered. *Essence* 20, No. 11 (March 1990):131

Gravenites, Diana

Shadow Sister. *Sinister Wisdom* 41 (Summer-Fall 1990):67-70

Gray, Pamela

Late Irises: A Goodbye Sonnet. *Sinister Wisdom* 40 (Spring 1990): 71

Grimes, Susan

Ancient Gardens Quilt. *Women's Studies Quarterly* 18, Nos. 3-4 (Fall-Winter 1990):161-164

Hadas, Rachel

The Right to Mourn. *The Women's Review of Books* 8, No. 3 (December 1990):28

A Week in February. *The Women's Review of Books* 8, No. 3 (December 1990):28

Haley, Heather Susan

The Brat from Beverly Hills. *Heresies* 25 (1990):49

Hall, Lisa Kahaleole Chang

After Surgery/Epilepsy Poem #430. *Sinister Wisdom* 40 (Spring 1990):62-63

Bodily Functions. *Sinister Wisdom* 40 (Spring 1990):62

If Not Now When? *Sinister Wisdom* 40 (Spring 1990):62

101 to San Mateo. *Sinister Wisdom* 40 (Spring 1990):61

Visiting Hours. *Sinister Wisdom* 40 (Spring 1990):61

Hamilton, J. A.

Heart Urchin. *Frontiers* 11, Nos. 2-3 (1990):72-73

Rondônia. *Frontiers* 11, Nos. 2-3 (1990):73

Silver Pennies. *Frontiers* 11, Nos. 2-3 (1990):74

Hardy, Jan

Small Acts. *Sinister Wisdom* 40 (Spring 1990):36-37

Harrell, Sara

Doing Lunch. *Executive Female* 13, No. 4 (July-August 1990):51

Healy, Eloise Klein

What it was Like the Night Cary Grant Died. *Out/Look* No. 7 (Winter 1990):74

Heileman, Nancy

Late Bloomer. *New Directions for Women* 19, No. 3 (May/June 1990):5

Hemminger, Theresa

Cinderella. *off our backs* 20, No. 7 (July 1990):19

Henderson, Stephanie

Cutting the Cord. *New Directions for Women* 19, No. 3 (May/June 1990):5

Impasse. *New Directions for Women* 19, No. 3 (May/June 1990):5

Herbst, Nikki

Fifth Grade. *Heresies* 25 (1990):12

Hill, Wendi E.

Untitled. *Essence* 20, No. 11 (March 1990):115

Hittleman, Margo

Poem. *Bridges* 1, No. 2 (Fall 1990): 60-62

Hornosty, Cornelia C.

Plath. *Atlantis* 15, No. 2 (Spring 1990):26

Isaac, Natalie

The Living Tree: A Woman's Response to Shel Silverstein's "The Giving Tree." *off our backs* 20, No. 7 (July 1990):19

James, Sibyl

Love Is All. *Iris* 24 (Fall-Winter 1990):19

Peach Blossoms. *Iris* 23 (Spring-Summer 1990):inside front cover

Jewell, Terri L.

She Who Bears the Thorn. *Iris* 24 (Fall-Winter 1990):18

Jones, Ursula M.

My Homeland. *Essence* 21, No. 5 (September 1990):114

Jordan, June

Poem for Obvious Reasons. *Ms.* 1, No. 1 (July/August 1990):71

Karbe, Beth

For Joan, in 1967. *Sinister Wisdom* 40 (Spring 1990):76-77

Karriem, Jaleelah

A Poem for Sojourner Truth. *Essence* 20, No. 11 (March 1990):136

Karriem, Jaleelah. *Essence* 20, No. 11 (March 1990):131

Kaufman, Shirley

Milk. *Lilith* 15, No. 2 (Spring 1990):22

Khalil, Sameeha S. Untitled. *Spare Rib* 218 (November 1990):17

Khephra

The Dream. *Essence* 21, No. 8 (December 1990):129

Talking Drums #1. *Essence* 20, No. 11 (March 1990):125

King, Dorothy E.

For K G. *Essence* 20, No. 11 (March 1990):115

Winter Warmth. *Essence* 21, No. 5 (September 1990):121

King, Linda

A Letter to My Sisters No. 209 (February 1990):38

Klein, Michael

A Stepfather, a Child. *Out/Look* No. 8 (Spring 1990):57

Knuckles, Jeffrey

Patience. *Essence* 21, No. 5 (September 1990):130

Kumar, K. G.

The Road to Thottapally. *Manushi* 60 (September-October 1990):26-28

LaGrone, Oliver

To Lionel Hampton. *Essence* 20, No. 11 (March 1990):115

Lakhera, Archana

Marriage Market. *Manushi* 56 (January-February 1990):27

Landers, Grace

The Homeless Woman. *AFFILIA* 5, No. 1 (Spring 1990):1-3

Lane, Pinkie Gordon

VII. For You. *Essence* 20, No. 11 (March 1990):126

Laque, Carol Feiser

Welcome to You See. *Heresies* 25 (1990):34

Laubach, Tonya

To Margi, in winter. *Feminisms* 3, No. 1 (January/February 1990):11

Trapeze Days. *Feminisms* 3, No. 1 (January/February 1990):11

Lear, Frances

These are a Few of My Positive Things. *Lear's* (December 1990):132

Leto, Denise

Passion, Danger, Freedom. *Sinister Wisdom* 41 (Summer-Fall 1990):72-74

We Do the Best I Can: A Series of Portraits. *Sinister Wisdom* 41 (Summer-Fall 1990):13-18

Long, Monica. Silence. *Hecate* 16, Nos. 1-2 (1990):62

Lorde, Audre

Women on Trains. *Ms.* 1, No. 2 (September/October 1990):64

Lundquist, Anne

Small Girl at the Chesapeake. *Sinister Wisdom* 42 (Winter 1990-1991):113

Madhubuti, Haki

Mothers. *Essence* 20, No. 11 (March 1990):136

Madhubuti, Haki R.

I Am Tired of Being Angry. *Heresies* 25 (1990):27

Piercy, Marge

For Each Age, Its Amulet. *Ms.* 1, No. 2 (September/October 1990):32

Place, Fiona

Media, Discourse, and Power. *Women & Language* 13, No. 1 (Fall 1990):9-20

Powell, Amanda

After the Phone Call. *The Women's Review of Books* 7, No. 7 (April 1990):19

Horseradish. *The Women's Review of Books* 7, No. 7 (April 1990):19

Powell, Leslie

Poems. *Out/Look* No. 10 (Fall 1990):81

Pressman, Stephanie

Ravens. *Bridges* 1, No. 2 (Fall 1990): 34

A Wedding. *Bridges* 1, No. 2 (Fall 1990): 35-38

Prince, Heather

Anniversary Request. *Canadian Women's Studies* 11, No. 1 (Spring 1990):68

Untitled. *Canadian Women's Studies* 11, No. 1 (Spring 1990):68

Racette, E. A.

Untitled. *Heresies* 25 (1990):10

Randall, Mary Carol

Commitment. *Sinister Wisdom* 40 (Spring 1990):10-14

Ravikovitch, Dahlia

Hide and Seek. *Lilith* 15, No. 1 (Winter 1990):27

Reti, Ingrid

Duologue. *Journal of Women and Aging* 2, No. 2 (1990):109

Reality? *Journal of Women and Aging* 2, No. 2 (1990):47

At Sixty-One. *Journal of Women and Aging* 2, No. 2 (1990):91

Reyes, Lina Sagaral

'Storya. *Women in Action* 3 & 4 (1990):60

Rich, Adrienne

Untitled. *Ms.* 1, No. 1 (July/August 1990):29

Richardson, Mariah L.

For Bay. *Essence* 21, No. 6 (October 1990):137

Hair. *Woman of Power* 18 (Fall 1990):15

Rickel, Boyer

Downpour. *Out/Look* No. 7 (Winter 1990):75

Riemer, Ruby

The Old Great Round. *Hypatia* 5, No. 1 (Spring 1990):24-26

Robinson, Nelcia

Creation Fire. *Women in Action* 1-2 (1990):2

Robson, Ruthann

Lesbian Lesbian. *Out/Look* No. 10 (Fall 1990):26-29

Rodgers, Carolyn M.

The Black Heart as Ever Green. *Essence* 21, No. 5 (September 1990):114

Earth Is Not the World, Nor All Its Beauty. *Essence* 21, No. 5 (September 1990):121

Shout. *Essence* 21, No. 1 (May 1990):205

Rodgers, Margaret

O Canada (a feminist version). *Atlantis* 15, No. 2 (Spring 1990):10

O Canada (sung in two colour harmony). *Atlantis* 15, No. 2 (Spring 1990):10

Rosenwasser, Rena

Berlin Nights. *Trivia* 16/17 (Fall 1990):80-83

Rule, Bernadette

Cut Flowers for Linda. *Canadian Women's Studies* 11, No. 1 (Spring 1990):42

Salaam, Kalamu ya

Young Mother Blues #1/T.'s tune. *Iris* 24 (Fall-Winter 1990):IFC

Samson, Stacie

Mixed Blood. *Sinister Wisdom* 41 (Summer-Fall 1990):45-46

Sánchez, Elba Rosario. Premonición. *Frontiers* 11, No. 1 (1990):65

Sanchez, Sonia

An Anthem (For the ANC and Brandywine Peace Community). *Essence* 21, No. 5 (September 1990):125

Haiku. *Essence* 21, No. 5 (September 1990):118

Poem No. 8. *Essence* 21, No. 1 (May 1990):205

Sapphire

American Dreams. *Sinister Wisdom* 42 (Winter 1990-1991):22-28

Sappho

Ode to Aphrodite. *off our backs* 20, No. 7 (July 1990):14

Fountains Weren't Meant to Be Predictable. *Hecate* 16, Nos. 1-2 (1990):119

There Is Always One Who Is Different. *Hecate* 16, Nos. 1-2 (1990):119

Thomas, Elean

Sheroes and Heroes.*Spare Rib* No. 210 (March 1990):10

Thompson, Cath

Recently, It Has Occurred to Me. *Sinister Wisdom* 40 (Spring 1990):94-95

Tóth, Eva

The Creation of the World. *Feminist Review* No. 36 (Autumn 1990):93-94

Wanted. *Feminist Review* No. 36 (Autumn 1990):92

tova

Does It Hurt? *Bridges* 1, No. 2 (Fall 1990): 69-73

Tuqan, Fadwa

Between Ebb and Flow. *Spare Rib* No. 216 (September 1990):24

Van Gerven, Claudia

Artemis-Callisto: She Is Not Afraid. *Frontiers* 11, Nos. 2-3 (1990):59-60

How to Write a Love Poem: Instructions for Dr. Williams. *Frontiers* 11, Nos. 2-3 (1990):62-64

She Has Taken Up Writing. *Frontiers* 11, Nos. 2-3 (1990):65

The Spirit String. *Frontiers* 11, Nos. 2-3 (1990):61

Varley, Jane

First Detasseling. *Iowa Woman* 9, No. 4 (Winter 1989-90):23

Varma, Archana

The Cost. *Manushi* 57 (March-April 1990):37

Poems. *Manushi* 58 (May-June 1990):26-29

Some Poems. *Manushi* 56 (January-February 1990):14-17

Varmar, Archana

Fear. *Manushi* 61 (November-December 1990):28-31

Veno, Aro

Baccalà. *Sinister Wisdom* 41 (Summer-Fall 1990):120

Viorst, Judith

Earrings. *McCall's* 117, No. 11 (August 1990):90-91

Vollmer, Judith

Father's Magic Trick. *The Women's Review of Books* 8, No. 1 (October 1990):22

The Nuclear Accident at SL 1, Idaho Falls, 1961. *The Women's Review of Books* 8, No. 1 (October 1990):22

Wagner, Anneliese

Requiem for Oma Berta. *Lilith* 15, No. 4 (Fall 1990):28

Walker, Alice

Did This Happen to Your Mother? Did Your Sister Throw Up a Lot? *Spare Rib* 218 (November 1990):26

Even as I Hold You. *Essence* 21, No. 5 (September 1990):110

Malcolm. *Essence* 21, No. 1 (May 1990):205

Ndebele. *Ms.* 1, No. 3 (November/December 1990):45

Warn, Emily

The Word Between the World and God. *Bridges* 1, No. 1 (Spring 1990): 30

Weinbaum, Batya

The Chess Game. *Feminist Review* No. 36 (Autumn 1990):95

Weiss, Jill

*Women and Environments* 12, No. 2 (Spring 1990): 15

Wheatley, Pat

A Subversive. *Canadian Women's Studies* 11, No. 1 (Spring 1990):64

Whitman, Lee Miriam

Four Poems in the Voice of Eve. *Bridges* 1, No. 1 (Spring 1990): 39-40

Williams, Sherley Anne

The Lessons of This Decade. *Essence* 21, No. 5 (September 1990):112

Wilson, Budge

For Glynis Reaching the Age of 21. *Canadian Women's Studies* 11, No. 2 (Fall 1990):83

Yeager, Ann Lowrey

Songs of Lost Children. *AFFILIA* 5, No. 4 (Winter 1990):119

Young, Lélia

Aimer ou La Centaure. *Canadian Women's Studies* 11, No. 1 (Spring 1990):89

Jour. *Canadian Women's Studies* 11, No. 1 (Spring 1990):89

Sans titre. *Canadian Women's Studies* 11, No. 1 (Spring 1990):89

Youngblood, Julia

Silent Shards. *Out/Look* No. 8 (Spring 1990):40

Zamora, Daisy

Death's Makeup. *The Women's Review of Books* 7, Nos. 10-11 (July 1990):21

Zettell, Susan

Masks. *Atlantis* 15, No. 2 (Spring 1990):93

Ziety, Ann

The Man Tells Her. *Spare Rib* No. 209 (February 1990):39

Zipter, Yvonne

Finding the Hot Wire. *Hot Wire* 6, No. 3 (September 1990):7

Zulu, Itibari M.

Deliverance. *Essence* 21, No. 4 (August 1990):120

Zumwalt, Nancy

Alcestis. *Feminist Review* No. 35 (Summer 1990):111-112

**Poetry**

Poets: Keeping the Vision Alive. Angela Kinamore. *Essence* 21, No. 1 (May 1990):205

Zabat: Poetics of a Family Tree. Poems 1986-1989. By Maud Sulter. Reviewed by Anne Iwobi. *Spare Rib* No. 209 (February 1990):31

**Poetry – Collections**

Sarah's Daughters Sing: A Sampler of Poems by Jewish Women. Edited by Henny Wenkart. Reviewed by Alicia Ostriker. *Lilith* 15, No. 3 (Summer 1990):6

Women for All Seasons: Poetry and Prose about Transitions in Women's Lives. Edited by Wanda Coleman and Joanne Leedom-Ackerman. Reviewed by Terri Lynn Jewell. *New Directions for Women* 19, No. 1 (January/February 1990):25

**Poetry – Criticism and Interpretation**

The Unreadable Black Body: "Conventional" Poetic Form in the Harlem Renaissance. Amitai F. Aviram. *Genders* 7 (Spring 1990):32-46

Poets. *See also* Webber, Storme

Crossing the Border: Poetry in Charlottesville. Stephen Margulies. *Iris* 23 (Spring-Summer 1990):14-16

Inventing Freedom: The Positive Poetic "Mutterings" of Older Women. Jo C. Searles. *Journal of Women and Aging* 2, No. 2 (1990):153-160

Pat Parker: A Tribute. Lyndie Brimstone. *Feminist Review* No. 34 (Spring 1990):4-7

**Poff, Deborah C.**

Healing Voices. Book Review. *Atlantis* 15, No. 2 (Spring 1990):113-114

**Pogrebin, Letty Cottin**

Friends: Who We Like, Why We Like Them and What We Do with Them. Reviewed by Eleanor Bader. *Lilith* 15, No. 3 (Summer 1990):6-7

Priorities: It's About Time! *Family Circle* 103, No. 16 (November 27, 1990):34-40

Talking Feminist. *On the Issues* 14 (1990):15+

The Teflon Father. *Ms.* 1, No. 2 (September/October 1990):95-96

**Pohl, Frances K.**

"The World Wall: A Vision of the Future Without Fear": An Interview with Judith F. Baca. *Frontiers* 11, No. 1 (1990):33-43

**Pointon, Marcia**

Mythology and Misogyny: The Social Discourse of Nineteenth-Century British Classical-Subject Painting. Book Review. *Gender & History* 2, No. 2 (Summer 1990):238-239

**Points, Dana**

Your Health: The "Too Much" Syndrome. *Family Circle* 103, No. 17 (December 18, 1990):31-35

**Points, Dana and Rohlfing, Carla**

Medical News. *Family Circle* 103, No. 5 (April 3, 1990):26-27

**Points, Dana** and Rohlfing, Carla

Medical News. *Family Circle* 103, No. 9 (June 26, 1990):30; 103, No. 13 (September 25, 1990):24; 103, No. 15 (November 6, 1990):167; 103, No. 16 (November 27, 1990):50; 103, No. 17 (December 18, 1990):72

**Poitier, Sidney** (about)

Sidney Poitier. Joan Barthel. *Lear's* (November 1990):100-103+

**Polan, Dana**

Clues, Myths, and the Historical Method. Book Review. *Camera Obscura* No. 22 (January 1990):131-137

**Poland – Anti-Semitism.** *See also* Auschwitz (Poland) – Carmelite Convent

Twelve Days in Poland. Excerpt. Yehudit Hendel. *Lilith* 15, No. 2 (Spring 1990):16-21

**Poland – History**

Marriage in Pre-Industrial Warsaw in the Light of Demographic Studies. Cezary Kuklo. *Journal of Family History* 15, No. 3 (July 1990):239-259

**Poland, Marilyn L.** (joint author). *See* Sachs, Barbara A.

**Poland – Status of Women**

The "Liberation" of Economic Necessity: Women in Poland. Ewa Stajkowska Setaro. *Iris* 24 (Fall-Winter 1990):40-43

**Poland – Women's Roles**

After the Revolution in Poland Today, Women Still Sweep the Floors. Mary E. Hunt. *Lilith* 15, No. 2 (Spring 1990):20

**Police – Homophobia**

"Gay Party at Police Station." *Out/Look* No. 8 (Spring 1990):44-45

**Policoff, Stephen Phillip**

Diseases Your Doctor May Miss. Bibliography. *Ladies' Home Journal* 107, No. 6 (June 1990):104-109

The Mind/Body Link. *Ladies' Home Journal* 107, No. 10 (October 1990):126-130

**Polikoff, Nancy D.**

Child Custody and the Politics of Gender. Book Review. *The Women's Review of Books* 7, No. 9 (June 1990):23-24

Fathers' Rights, Mothers' Wrongs. *The Women's Review of Books* 7, No. 9 (June 1990):23-24

How Could You? Mothers Without Custody of Their Children. Book Review. *The Women's Review of Books* 7, No. 9 (June 1990):23-24

In the Name of the Fathers: The Story Behind Child Custody. Book Review. *The Women's Review of Books* 7, No. 9 (June 1990):23-24

Solomon Says: A Speakout on Foster Care. Book Review. *The Women's Review of Books* 7, No. 9 (June 1990):23-24

**Poling-Kempes, Lesley**

The Harvey Girls, Women Who Opened the West. Reviewed by Lynn Wenzel. *New Directions for Women* 19, No. 2 (March/April 1990):15

**Political Activism.** *See also* Hollywood Women's Political Committee

How to Win Friends and Influence Legislators. Judy Goldsmith. *Ms.* 1, No. 1 (July/August 1990):90

Marilyn Bergman, the Way She Is. David Rieff. *Lear's* (December 1990):82-83 +

Mexican American Women Grassroots Community Activists: "Mothers of East Lost Angeles." Mary Pardo. *Frontiers* 11, No. 1 (1990):1-7

The Profits of Ill Repute. William A. Henry III. *Lear's* (October 1990):152 +

Reproducing the World: Essays in Feminist Theory. By Mary O'Brien. Reviewed by Christine Di Stefano. *Women & Politics* 10, No. 4 (1990):138-140

Women and the Public Sphere in the Age of the French Revolution. By Joan B. Landes. Reviewed by Elisabeth G. Sledziewski. *Gender & History* 2, No. 3 (Autumn 1990):363-365

Women Who Make a Difference: Turning the Town Around. John E. Frook. *Family Circle* 103, No. 14 (October 16, 1990):17-19

You Can't Kill the Spirit: Stories of Women and Nonviolent Action. By Pam McAllister. Reviewed by Gwyn Kirk. *Women & Politics* 10, No. 1 (1990):78-80

**Political Activism – Gender Differences**

Is Political Activism Still a "Masculine" Endeavor? Gender Comparisons among High School Political Activists. Nancy Romer. *Psychology of Women Quarterly* 14, No. 2 (June 1990):229-243

**Political Activists.** *See also* Activism; Activists; Davis, Angela Y. (about); Gay Rights Activists; Goldman, Emma (about); Hair Styles and Politics; International Lesbian and Gay Association; Oakland, CA – Political Activists; Parkin, Sara (about); Waters, Maxine (about)

A Belfast Woman. By Mary Beckett. Reviewed by Maureen Murphy. *Feminist Collections* 11, No. 2 (Winter 1990):5-6

Derrick Bell: Harvard's Conscience. Benilde Little. *Essence* 21, No. 7 (November 1990):44

Dublin Belles: Conversations with Dublin Women. By Máirín Johnson. Reviewed by Maureen Murphy. *Feminist Collections* 11, No. 2 (Winter 1990):5-6

Family Politics. Ellie McGrath. *Savvy Woman* (October 1990):16

And the First Woman President of the United States Will Be . . . Lorraine Dusky. *McCall's* 117, No. 12 (September 1990):88-92

A Guerrilla Grapples with AIDS. Herbert Daniel. *Out/Look* No. 8 (Spring 1990):27-30

I Am of Ireland: Women of the North Speak Out. Elizabeth Shannon. Reviewed by Maureen Murphy. *Feminist Collections* 11, No. 2 (Winter 1990):5-6

Lassoing Power. Kathryn Casey. *Savvy Woman* (November 1990):13-14

McCall's Editor's Notes. Anne Mollegen Smith. *McCall's* 117, No. 12 (September 1990):85

Women in Public: From Banners to Ballots, 1825-1880. By Mary Ryan. Reviewed by Ruth Rosen. *The Women's Review of Books* 7, No. 9 (June 1990):10-11

**Political Campaigns**

Campaign '90 Tip Sheet. Mary Thom. *Ms.* 1, No. 1 (July/August 1990):89

Inoculation in Political Campaigns and Gender. Michael Pfau and Michael Burgoon. *Women's Studies in Communication* 13, No. 1 (Spring 1990):1-21

**Political Candidates**

Legislators' Perceptions of Women in State Legislatures. Patricia K. Freeman and William Lyons. *Women & Politics* 10, No. 4 (1990):121-132

The Presence of Women Candidates and the Role of Gender in Campaigns for the State Legislature in an Urban Setting: The Case of Massachusetts. Barbara Burrell. *Women & Politics* 10, No. 3 (1990):85-102

Women, Law and Politics: Recruitment Patterns in the Fifty States. Christine B. Williams. *Women & Politics* 10, No. 3 (1990):103-123

**Political Consciousness**

Midlife Women's Political Consciousness: Case Studies of Psychosocial Development and Political Commitment. Abigail J. Stewart and Sharon Gold-Steinberg. *Psychology of Women Quarterly* 14, No. 4 (December 1990):543-566

**Political Conservatism.** *See also* Right Wing Organizations

**Political Husbands.** *See* Political Spouses

**Political Leaders.** *See also* Elected Officials; Leadership

Up Front. *Ladies' Home Journal* 107, No. 11 (November 1990):127-132

**Political Leaders - France.** *See also* Michel, Louise (about)

**Political Participation.** *See also* Citizenship; Political Candidates; Suffrage Movement

Female Suffrage in New Jersey, 1790-1807. Irwin N. Gertzog. *Women & Politics* 10, No. 2 (1990):47-58

From Margin to Mainstream: American Women and Politics Since 1960. By Susan M. Hartmann. Reviewed by Cynthia Harrison. *NWSA Journal* 2, No. 1 (Winter 1990):139-141

My Brain's Not Blond. Cybill Shepherd. *Ms.* 1, No. 3 (November/December 1990):84-85

Women, Political Action, and Political Participation. By Virginia Sapiro. Reviewed by Joan C. Tronto. *NWSA Journal* 2, No. 3 (Summer 1990):492-495

**Political Participation - Cross-Cultural Studies**

Sex Differences in Political Participation: Processes of Change in Fourteen Nations. By Carol A. Christy. Reviewed by Sue Thomas. *Women & Politics* 10, No. 1 (1990):76-78

**Political Participation - History - Feminist Perspectives**

Equal or Different: Women's Politics, 1800-1914. Edited by Jane Rendall. Reviewed by Susan Kingsley Kent. *Gender & History* 2, No. 1 (Spring 1990):114-115

**Political Power.** *See also* Judicial System; Middle Eastern Women - Political Power

Learning About Women: Gender, Politics, and Power. Edited by Jill K. Conway, Susan C. Bourque,

and Joan W. Scott. Reviewed by Elizabeth Higginbotham. *NWSA Journal* 2, No. 1 (Winter 1990):105-111

Momentum: Women in American Politics Now. By Ronna Romney and Beppie Harrison. Reviewed by Connie L. Lobur. *Women & Politics* 10, No. 3 (1990):129-130

Women, Power and Policy: Toward the Year 2000. Edited by Ellen Boneparth and Emily Stoper. Reviewed by Joan Hulse Thompson. *Women & Politics* 10, No. 3 (1990):133-134

Women and Politics: An International Perspective. By Vicki Randall. Reviewed by Eleanor E. Zeff. *Women & Politics* 10, No. 3 (1990):135-136

Women and Politics: The Case of Israel. *Women & Politics* 10, No. 1 (1990):43-57

Women and Power in American Politics. By Milka K. Hedblom. Reviwed by Joan C. Tronto. *NWSA Journal* 2, No. 3 (Summer 1990):492-495

Women and the Politics of Empowerment. Edited by Ann Bookman and Sandra Morgen. Reviewed by Sue Tolleson Rinehart. *Women & Politics* 10, No. 3 (1990):131-132

**Political Prisoners.** *See also* El Salvador - Civil War

Gulag, U.S.A. Bonnie Allen. *Ms.* 1, No. 1 (July/August 1990):76

Parents Fight Draconian Sentence. Laura Flanders. *New Directions for Women* 19, No. 2 (March/April 1990):7

Through the Wire. By Nina Rosenblum and Alexandra White. Reviewed by Penny Perkins. *New Directions for Women* 19, No. 2 (March/April 1990):metrö

**Political Representation.** *See also* Elected Officials; Political Candidates

**Political Sciences - Study and Teaching.** *See also* China - Political Sciences - Study and Teaching

**Political Spouses.** *See also* Presidents - United States - Spouses

Kitty Dukakis: The True Story. Kitty Dukakis and Jane Scovell. *Good Housekeeping* 211, No. 3 (September 1990):202-213

New York City's First Lady. Elsie B. Washington. *Essence* 21, No. 5 (September 1990):96-98

The Other Running Mates: First Ladies. Nicols Fox. *Lear's* (September 1990):102-105 +

Out Box: A Job of One's Own. Gail Collins. *Working Woman* (September 1990):226

Run for Your Wife. Maureen Dowd. *Savvy Woman* (September 1990):60-63 +

**Political Theory**

By Design: Incorporating Feminist Ideas into the Political Theory Curriculum. Barbara Allen. *Feminist Teacher* 5, No. 1 (Spring 1990):15-18

Feminist Second Thoughts About Free Agency. Paul Benson. *Hypatia* 5, No. 3 (Fall 1990):47-64

Homo Sum. Monique Wittig. *Feminist Issues* 10, No. 1 (Spring 1990):3-11

Manhood and Politics: A Feminist Reading in Political Theory. By Wendy Brown. Reviewed by Sherri Paris. *Hypatia* 5, No. 3 (Fall 1990):175-180

Nobody Home. Lee Maracle. *Trivia* 16/17 (Fall 1990):108-118

Women and Counter-Power. Edited by Yolande Cohen. Reviewed by Linda Christiansen-Ruffman. *Resources for Feminist Research* 19, No. 1 (March 1990):39-40

Women's Rights, Feminism, and Politics in the United States. By Mary Lyndon Shanley. Reviewed by Joan C. Tronto. *NWSA Journal* 2, No. 3 (Summer 1990):492-495

**Political Theory – Feminist Perspectives**

Manhood and Politics: A Feminist Reading in Political Theory. By Wendy Brown. Reviewed by Judith Wagner DeCew. *Women's Studies International Forum* 13, No. 3 (1990):279-280

Manhood and Politics: A Feminist Reading in Political Theory. By Wendy Brown. Reviewed by Mary Lyndon Shanley. *Signs* 16, No. 1 (Autumn 1990):183-187

Maternal Thinking: Towards a Politics of Peace. By Sara Ruddick. Reviewed by Evelyne Accad. *Women's Studies International Forum* 13, No. 5 (1990):526-527

The Oppositional Imagination: Feminism, Critique and Political Theory. By Joan Elizabeth Cocks. Reviewed by Judith Grant. *The Women's Review of Books* 7, No. 4 (January 1990):21-22

The Sexual Contract. By Carole Pateman. Reviewed by Mary Lyndon Shanley. *Signs* 16, No. 1 (Autumn 1990):183-187

Toward a Feminist Theory of the State. By Catharine A. MacKinnon. Reviewed by Emily M. Calhoun. *Frontiers* 11, Nos. 2-3 (1990):120-121

**Political Wives.** *See* Political Spouses

**Politicians.** *See* Elected Officials

**Politics**

See How They Run. Anna Sobkowski. *Executive Female* 13, No. 5 (September-October 1990):14-16+

What I Saw at the Revolution: A Political Life in the Reagan Era. Peggy Noonan. Reviewed by Janet Horowitz Murray. *The Women's Review of Books* 7, No. 9 (June 1990):6

**Politics, International**

Bananas, Beaches and Bases: Making Feminist Sense of International Politics. By Cynthia Enloe. Reviewed by Anne McClintock. *The Women's Review of Books* 7, No. 8 (May 1990):1+

**Politics – New Right**

Women of the New Right. By Rebecca E. Klatch. Reviewed by Debra Renée Kaufman. *Gender and Society* 4, No. 1 (March 1990):118-120

**Politics, Radical**

Radical Politics in a Reactionary Age: The Unmaking of Rosika Schwimmer, 1914-1930. Beth S. Wenger. *Journal of Women's History* 2, No. 2 (Fall 1990):66-99

**Politics and Government**

"I Have Don . . . Much to Carrey on the Warr": Women and the Shaping of Republican Ideology After the American Revolution. Linda K. Kerber. *Journal of Women's History* 1, No. 3 (Winter 1990):231-243

**Polke, Sigmar** (about)

Vogue Arts: Art. Jed Perl. *Vogue* (November 1990):260+

**Pollack, Sandra**

Biased View of Soviet Women. *New Directions for Women* 19, No. 6 (November-December 1990):22

Lesbian Parents: Claiming Visibility. *Women and Therapy* 10, Nos. 1/2 (1990):181-194

Soviet Women: Walking the Tightrope. Book Review. *New Directions for Women* 19, No. 6 (November-December 1990):22

**Pollard, Anne** (about)

The Wives Take the Heat: Ethel Rosenberg and Anne Pollard. June Barsky. *Lilith* 15, No. 1 (Winter 1990):28-29

**Pollard, Jonathan** (about). *See also* Pollard, Anne (about)

**Polley, Paulette** (about). *See also* Casey, Kathryn, "Voices of the Decade"

**Pollock, Griselda**

Vision and Difference: Feminism, Femininity and the History of Art. Reviewed by Eunice Lipton. *Gender & History* 2, No. 1 (Spring 1990):91-97

**Pollock, Griselda** (criticism)

Beyond Post-Feminism: The Work of Laura Mulvey and Griselda Pollock. Monika Gagnon. *Canadian Women's Studies* 11, No. 1 (Spring 1990):81-83

**Poll Tax**

Poll Tax Cuts. *Spare Rib* 217 (October 1990):46

**Pollution**

Green Watch. *Good Housekeeping* 211, No. 4 (October 1990):127-128

**Pollution – Indoors**

Hidden Health Hazards in Your Home. *Family Circle* 103, No. 2 (February 1, 1990):80-81

**Polonko, Karen** (joint author). *See* Teachman, Jay D.

**Polygamy**

An American Harem. Kathryn Casey. *Ladies' Home Journal* 107, No. 2 (February 1990):116-117+

**Ponce, Mary Helen**

The Color Red. *Frontiers* 11, No. 1 (1990):25

On Mending. *Frontiers* 11, No. 1 (1990):24-25

The Wedding. Reviewed by Charlotte Zoë Walker. *Belles Lettres* 5, No. 2 (Winter 1990):17

**Pool, Gail**

Angels on Toast. Book Review. *The Women's Review of Books* 7, Nos. 10-11 (July 1990):20

The Golden Spur. Book Review. *The Women's Review of Books* 7, Nos. 10-11 (July 1990):20

Living by Her Wit. *The Women's Review of Books* 7, Nos. 10-11 (July 1990):20

The Locusts Have No King. Book Review. *The Women's Review of Books* 7, Nos. 10-11 (July 1990):20

The Wicked Pavilion. Book Review. *The Women's Review of Books* 7, Nos. 10-11 (July 1990):20

**Poovey, Mary**

Uneven Developments: The Ideological Work of Gender in Mid-Victorian England. Reviewed by Alex Owen. *Gender & History* 2, No. 2 (Summer 1990):239-241

Uneven Developments: The Ideological Work of Gender in Mid-Victorian England. Reviewed by Cynthia Wright. *Resources for Feminist Research* 19, No. 1 (March 1990):35-36

Uneven Developments: The Ideological Work of Gender in Mid-Victorian England. Reviewed by Rachel Bowlby. *Tulsa Studies in Women's Literature* 9, No. 2 (Fall 1990):314-317

Uneven Developments: The Ideological Work of Gender in Mid-Victorian England. Reviewed by Susan Hardy Aiken. *Signs* 16, No. 1 (Autumn 1990):188-192

**Pope, Jacqueline**

Biting the Hand that Feeds Them: Organizing Women on Welfare at the Grass Roots Level. Reviewed by Margaret Nielsen. *AFFILIA* 5, No. 4 (Winter 1990):115

**Popowich, Coreen** (joint author). *See* Smith, Linda

**Popular Culture.** *See also* Book Lists; Essence Magazine; Literary Criticism – Feminist Perspectives; Social Trends; Television Programs; Video Reviews

All That Junk. James Kaplan. *Mademoiselle* (November 1990):106

August. Bibliography. *Glamour* (August 1990):183

Black & White Love Affairs. Charla Krupp. *Glamour* (October 1990):194-196

Circle This. Margaret Jaworski. *Family Circle* 103, No. 9 (June 26, 1990):9-10

Cosby vs. The Simpsons: Is TV Programming Your Family? Ira Wolfman. *Family Circle* 103, No. 14 (October 16, 1990):79-85

Driven to Question: What Is a Car, Anyway? Nancy Slonim Aronie. *Lear's* (April 1990):52

Driving. Cynthia Heimel. *Vogue* (September 1990):480-484

The Encyclopedia of Bad Taste. By Jane Stern and Michael Stern. Reviewed by Francine Prose. *Savvy Woman* (November 1990):20-21

Forum. Beverly Sills. *McCall's* 117, No. 12 (September 1990):21-22

G Notes. *Glamour* (December 1990):183

Graffiti. *Essence* 20, No. 9 (January 1990):103-105; 20, No. 10 (February 1990):120; 20, No. 11 (March 1990):140; 20, No. 12 (April 1990):118

Guessing Your Age. Tracy Young. *Vogue* (July 1990):224

It Ain't Over Till It's Over. James Kaplan. *Mademoiselle* (September 1990):179

Kitsch and Tell. Nadine Frey. *Harper's Bazaar* (February 1990):82

March Is a Great Month to . . . *Glamour* (March 1990):229

Need to Know. Christine Logan Wright. *Mademoiselle* (June 1990):86

November: G Notes. *Glamour* (November 1990):199

Out of the Ordinary. Robin Cembalest. *Harper's Bazaar* (October 1990):146-150

People Are Talking About. Julia Reed. *Vogue* (August 1990):209; (September 1990):393

People Are Talking About. *Vogue* (December 1990):185

September. *Glamour* (September 1990):277

Sure Bets. *Harper's Bazaar* (April 1990):115-118

Talking Out of Turn: Frock Around the Clock. Tracy Young. *Vogue* (September 1990):658

Television: Behind the Screens at TV's Funniest New Show. Bibliography. Jill Rachlin. *Ladies' Home Journal* 107, No. 6 (June 1990):54-59

Turned-On TV. Tracy Young. *Vogue* (September 1990):584-587

Upfront. Edited by Lesley Jane Nonkin. *Vogue* (August 1990):81-86; (September 1990):109-114; (December 1990):87-90

Vogue Arts: In Brief. *Vogue* (December 1990):212

What They're Doing. *Glamour* (August 1990):178

Women and Cars: On a Roll. Joanne Mattera. *Glamour* (May 1990):254-259

Women of the Years. Leslie Jay. *Ladies' Home Journal* 107, No. 11 (November 1990):83-92

Women Right Now. *Glamour* (August 1990):89-94

Word On . . . *Glamour* (March 1990):189; (May 1990):203; (July 1990):113; (August 1990):155-158; (September 1990):215; (October 1990):191-192; (December 1990):155

Word On Movies. David Denicolo. *Glamour* (February 1990):130

Word On TV's Office Comedies. Brook Hersey. *Glamour* (June 1990):184

**Popular Music.** *See* Music, Popular

**Population Control.** *See also* Contraception; Reproductive Technologies

How Delaying Marriage and Spacing Births Contributes to Population Control: An Explanation with Illustrations. T. Rajaretnam. *Journal of Family Welfare* 36, No. 4 (December 1990):3-13

**Population Control – Research**

Population Planning in India: Policy Issues and Research Priorities. Edited by Ashish Bose and P. B. Desai. Reviewed by K. Sivaswamy Srikantan. *Journal of Family Welfare* 36, No. 3 (September 1990):107-110

**Population Distribution – Marketing Research**

Beyond Thirtysomething. Debra Kent. *Working Woman* (September 1990):150-153+

**Population Policy.** *See also* Family Planning; Fertility

**Pork.** *See* Cookery (Meat)

**Pornography.** *See also* Nude, The; Obscenity; *particular countries*; Violence Against Women

Boycott Athena "Porn" Bookshops. Maureen O'Hara. *Spare Rib* 219 (December 1990-January 1991):64

FCC Turns Up Heat on 'Indecent' Radio Content. *Media Report to Women* 18, No. 1 (January/February 1990):4

Fighting Porn in Scotland. Maggie C. Sinclair. *Spare Rib* 219 (December 1990-January 1991):65

The Force of Fantasy: Feminism, Mapplethorpe, and Discursive Excess. Judith Butler. *Differences* 2, No. 2 (Summer 1990):105-125

The Making of Pornography: An Act of Sexual Violence. *Spare Rib* 213 (June 1990):16-19

Men Against Pornography. Clodagh Corcoran. *Spare Rib* 217 (October 1990):47

Pornography and Civil Rights: A New Day for Women's Equality. By Andrea Dworkin and Catherine A. MacKinnon. Reviewed by Pauline B.

Bart. *NWSA Journal* 2, No. 3 (Summer 1990):516-518

Pornography and Pollution. Patricia H. Hynes. *Women's Studies International Forum* 13, No. 3 (1990):169-176

A Portrait of Angel. Bebe Moore Campbell. *Essence* 21, No. 7 (November 1990):63-64+

Sex, Lust & Videotapes. Roberto Santiago. *Essence* 21, No. 7 (November 1990):62-64+

**Pornography – Feminist Perspectives**

Pornography and Social Policy: Three Feminist Approaches. Barbara G. Collins. *AFFILIA* 5, No. 4 (Winter 1990):8-26

**Pornography, Lesbian**

The Pleasure Threshold: Looking at Lesbian Pornography on Film. Cherry Smyth. *Feminist Review* No. 34 (Spring 1990):152-159

Voyages of the Valkyries: Recent Lesbian Pornographic Writing. Sara Dunn. *Feminist Review* No. 34 (Spring 1990):161-170

**Porter, Bruce** (joint author). *See* Echenberg, Havi

**Porter, Cathy**

Larissa Reisner. Reviewed by June Purvis. *Women's Studies International Forum* 13, Nos. 1-2 (1990):160-161

**Porter, Cole** (about)

Anything Goes: Reclaiming the Songs of Cole Porter. Christian Wright. *Mademoiselle* (November 1990):94

**Porter, Dorothy** (joint author). *See* Porter, Roy

**Porter, Evette**

Can We Work It Out? *Essence* 20, No. 10 (February 1990):56-58+

Faith Ringgold: Every Quilt Tells a Story. *Essence* 21, No. 1 (May 1990):78

Women in the Arts. Bibliography. *Essence* 21, No. 1 (May 1990):80-86

**Porter, Laura Spencer** (about)

Forerunners: Laura Spencer Porter. Jennifer G. Shepherd. *Iris* 24 (Fall-Winter 1990):58-59

**Porter, Roy** and Porter, Dorothy

In Sickness and in Health: The British Experience, 1650-1850. Reviewed by Nancy J. Tomes. *Gender & History* 2, No. 3 (Autumn 1990):368-369

**Portugal, Ana Maria**

History of the Meetings. *Women in Action* 3 & 4 (1990):18-19

**Portugal – Marriage Customs**

Dowry, Norms, and Household Formation: A Case Study from North Portugal. Helena Osswald. *Journal of Family History* 15, No. 2 (April 1990):201-224

**Posadas, Barbara M.**

Goodbye to Winter: The Autobiography of Sophie Schmidt-Rodolfo. Book Review. *Women's Studies International Forum* 13, No. 4 (1990):409-410

**Posener, Jill**

Louder Than Words. *Woman of Power* 17 (Summer 1990):20-23

**Possession – Spirit**

Ritual Grievance: The Language of Woman? Susan Slyomovics. *Women and Performance: A Journal of Feminist Theory* 5, No. 1, Issue #9 (1990): 53-60

**Post, Dianne**

Interindependence: A New Concept in Relationships. *Lesbian Ethics* 4, No. 1 (Spring 1990): 88-92

Radical Women National Conference: A Cold Shower. *off our backs* 20, No. 6 (June 1990):10-11

**Post, Elizabeth L.**

Etiquette for Every Day. *Good Housekeeping* 211, No. 3 (September 1990):62-64; 211, No. 4 (October 1990):52-55

**Post, Laura**

Maiden Voyage: The First Olivia Cruise. *Hot Wire* 6, No. 3 (September 1990):26-27 +

Sonia Johnson. *Hot Wire* 6, No. 3 (September 1990):30-39

Two Lesbian Games. *Hot Wire* 6, No. 2 (May 1990):24-26 +

Two Roads to Solo Keyboard Work: Julie Homi and Adrienne Torf. *Hot Wire* 6, No. 2 (May 1990):28-30 +

**Post, Stephen G.**

Women and Elderly Parents: Moral Controversy in an Aging Society. *Hypatia* 5, No. 1 (Spring 1990):83-89

**Poster Art**

Art Acts Up: A Graphic Response to AIDS. Excerpt. Douglas Crimp. *Out/Look* No. 9 (Summer 1990):22-30

**Postlethwaite, Diana**

The One True Story of the World. Book Review. *Belles Lettres* 5, No. 4 (Summer 1990):15

On the Road. *Belles Lettres* 5, No. 4 (Summer 1990):15

She Drove Without Stopping. Book Review. *Belles Lettres* 5, No. 4 (Summer 1990):15

**Postmodernism**

Aestheticism, Feminism, and the Dynamics of Reversal. Amy Newman. *Hypatia* 5, No. 2 (Summer 1990):20-32

Thinking Fragments: Psychoanalysis, Feminism, and Postmodernism in the Contemporary West. By

Jane Flax. Reviewed by Mari Jo Buhle. *The Women's Review of Books* 7, No. 7 (April 1990):23-24

Thinking with the Weight of the Earth: Feminist Contributions to an Epistemology of Concreteness. Linda Holler. *Hypatia* 5, No. 1 (Spring 1990):1-23

**Postpartum Emotions.** *See* Childbirth – Postpartum Emotions

**Potash, Cricket**

Seize the Time. *Heresies* 25 (1990):14-16

**Potash, Marlin S.**

You Can Change Your Life. *Good Housekeeping* 211, No. 4 (October 1990):94-96

**Potatoes.** *See also* Cookery (Vegetables)

**Potratz, Julie** (about). *See also* Art – Exhibitions, "Racism"

**Potter, Beatrix** (about)

Beatrix Potter: Naturalist Artist. Catherine Golden. *Woman's Art Journal* 11, No. 1 (Spring-Summer 1990):16-20

**Pottery**

Crafting a Tradition. Christine Mather. *McCall's* 118, No. 1 (October 1990):117-120

It's Easy to Collect: Country Pottery. Ralph Kovel and Terry Kovel. *Redbook* 176, No. 1 (November 1990):196

**Potts, Annie** (about). *See* Television Programs

**Potts, Malcolm**

The Origin of the Attitudes. *Healthright* 9, No. 3 (May 1990):29-33

**Potts, Malcolm** (interview)

Fertility Control in the 90s – An Interview with Malcolm Potts. Jo Calluy. *Healthright* 9, No. 2 (February 1990):21-24

**Poulin, Lucy** (about)

H.O.M.E.: One Woman's Approach to Society's Problems. Helen M. Stummer. *On the Issues* 15 (Summer 1990):10-15 +

**Poultry Industry – Working Conditions**

Advocate Battles for Safety in Mines and Poultry Plants. Elayne Clift. *New Directions for Women* 19, No. 3 (May/June 1990):3

**Poverty.** *See also* Economic Hardship; Family Life – Problems; Waddles, Charleszetta "Mother" (about)

Dependency and Poverty: Old Problems in a New World. By June Axinn and Mark Stern. Reviewed by Mimi Abramovitz. *Journal of Women and Aging* 2, No. 4 (1990):111-113

Living Without Choices. Helen M. Stummer. *On the Issues* 17 (Winter 1990):16-22 +

The Poverty Industry. Theresa Funiciello. *Ms.* 1, No. 3 (November/December 1990):33-40

Poverty Stops Equality/Equality Stops Poverty: The Case for Social and Economic Rights. Havi Echenberg and Bruce Porter. *Canadian Women's Studies* 11, No. 2 (Fall 1990):7-11

For Reasons of Poverty: A Critical Analysis of the Public Child Welfare System in the United States. By Leroy H. Pelton. Reviewed by Ann Nichols-Casebolt. *Journal of Marriage and the Family* 52, No. 3 (August 1990):801-802

The Undeserving Poor: From the War on Poverty to the War on Welfare. By Michael B. Katz. Reviewed by Linda Gordon. *The Women's Review of Books* 7, No. 6 (March 1990):7-8

Young Mother's Story: "We Count Our Blessings Every Day." Stephanie Sermuksnis. *Redbook* 176, No. 1 (November 1990):42-44

**Poverty – Gender Differences**

American Women in Poverty. By Paul E. Zopf, Jr. Reviewed by Emily Stoper. *Women & Politics* 10, No. 4 (1990):140-141

**Poverty – Reproductive Choice**

The Future of Reproductive Choice for Poor Women and Women of Color. Dorothy E. Roberts. *Women's Rights Law Reporter* 12, No. 2 (Summer 1990): 59-67

**Powell, Amanda**

After the Phone Call. Poem. *The Women's Review of Books* 7, No. 7 (April 1990):19

Horseradish. Poem. *The Women's Review of Books* 7, No. 7 (April 1990):19

**Powell, Breda**

Birmingham 6: Innocent Beyond Any Doubt. *Spare Rib* 219 (December 1990-January 1991):67

**Powell, Dawn**

Angels on Toast. Reviewed by Gail Pool. *The Women's Review of Books* 7, Nos. 10-11 (July 1990):20

The Golden Spur. Reviewed by Gail Pool. *The Women's Review of Books* 7, Nos. 10-11 (July 1990):20

The Locusts Have No King. Reviewed by Gail Pool. *The Women's Review of Books* 7, Nos. 10-11 (July 1990):20

The Wicked Pavilion. Reviewed by Gail Pool. *The Women's Review of Books* 7, Nos. 10-11 (July 1990):20

**Powell, Ivor** and Brooks, Philip

The Other Afrikaners. *Vogue* (July 1990):1196-199+

**Powell, Leslie**

Poems. *Out/Look* No. 10 (Fall 1990):81

**Powell, Nancy** (about)

Affairs to Remember. Maureen Sajbel. *Harper's Bazaar* (August 1990):174+

**Power.** *See* Masculinity – History – Feminist Perspectives; Political Power

**Power, Jane**

Jailed Women Have Day in Court. *New Directions for Women* 19, No. 2 (March/April 1990):9

**Powers, William G.** (joint author). *See* Mueller, Kay E.

**Power Structure**

The Last Barrier. Anne Jardim and Margaret Hennig. *Working Woman* (November 1990):130-134+

Power and Gender Issues in Academic Administration: A Study of Directors of BSW Programs. Karen V. Harper. *AFFILIA* 5, No. 1 (Spring 1990):81-93

**Prakash, V.** (joint author). *See* Sachar, R. K.

**Pratt, Annis**

The Supreme Court Rules in Favor of Opening Tenure Files. *NWSAction* 3, No. 1/2 (Spring 1990): 1

**Pratt, Minnie Bruce**

Crime Against Nature. Reviewed by Jan Clausen. *The Women's Review of Books* 7, Nos. 10-11 (July 1990):12-13

**Pratt, Minnie Bruce** (about)

Minnie Bruce Pratt Wins Lamont Prize. Yvonne Zipter. *Hot Wire* 6, No. 1 (January 1990):43

**Pregnancy.** *See also* In Vitro Fertilization

Better Beginnings: The LHJ Guide to Pregnancy. Beth Weinhouse and Barbara Burgower. *Ladies' Home Journal* 107, No. 8 (August 1990):35-42

Cause and Management of Miscarriage. Robert J. Norman. *Healthright* 9, No. 4 (August 1990):22-24

The Five Most Common Maternity Myths. *Ladies' Home Journal* 107, No. 8 (August 1990):44

From Here to Maternity. Maxine Lipner. *Essence* 21, No. 3 (July 1990):24

The Pregnant Professional. Anna Sobkowski. *Executive Female* 13, No. 1 (January-February 1990):29-33

Sex Determination Tests in Surat – A Survey Report. Uma Arora and Amprapali Desai. *Manushi* 60 (September-October 1990):37-38

The Tentative Pregnancy – Prenatal Diagnosis and the Future of Motherhood. By Barbara Katz Rothman. Reviewed by Hilda Bastion. *Healthright* 9, No. 4 (August 1990):42-43

Your Pregnancy. Bibliography. Stephanie Young. *Glamour* (May 1990):80

Your Pregnancy. Stephanie Young. *Glamour* (February 1990):55; (March 1990):74; (April 1990):86; (July 1990):40; (August 1990):64; (September 1990):100; (October 1990):74; (November 1990):78; (December 1990):80

Press. Joan C. Chrisler and Karen B. Levy. *Women and Health* 16, No. 2 (1990):89-104

PMS Update. Bibliography. Stephanie Young. *Glamour* (April 1990):94-98

Progesterone: Safe Antidote for PMS. Lorraine Dusky. *McCall's* 118, No. 1 (October 1990):152-156

Women's Health News. *Redbook* 175, No. 5 (September 1990):32-36

**Prenatal Care.** *See also* Maternal and Infant Welfare

**Prenatal Influences**

"We are So Lucky to Have Him." Catherline Breslin. *Ladies' Home Journal* 107, No. 12 (December 1990):136+

**Prenatal Tests.** *See* Fetal Monitoring

**Prentice, Alison,** Bourne, Paula, Brandt, Gail Cuthbert, Light, Beth, Mitchinson, Wendy, and others

Canadian Women: A History. Reviewed by Magda A. Gere Lewis. *Women's Studies International Forum* 13, Nos. 1-2 (1990):162

**Presbury, Jack H.** (joint author). *See* Kahn, Arnold S.

**Prescod, Marsha**

3010: A Space Idiocy. Short Story. *Spare Rib* 218 (November 1990):34-37

The Rise of Aretha Tubman VI: An African History Book. *Spare Rib* No. 212 (May 1990):14-15

Sleeping Dogs. Short Story. *Spare Rib* 213 (June 1990):20-22

**Presidents – United States.** *See also* Leadership

And the First Woman President of the United States Will Be . . . Lorraine Dusky. *McCall's* 117, No. 12 (September 1990):88-92

Getting Ready to Run the Country. Peggy Simpson. *McCall's* 117, No. 9 (June 1990):62-63+

The Speech Heard 'Round the World. William Safire. *McCall's* 117, No. 12 (September 1990):94-95

Women Who Would Be President. Lorraine Dusky. *McCall's* 117, No. 9 (June 1990):59-60

**Presidents – United States – Chefs**

"I Cooked for the President." Henry Haller. *Ladies' Home Journal* 107, No. 2 (February 1990):162-163

**Presidents, United States – Spouses.** *See also* Political Spouses

**Presidents – United States – Spouses**

Barbara Bush: First Lady, First Class. Cindy Adams. *Ladies' Home Journal* 107, No. 11 (November 1990):196+

At Home with Barbara Bush. Alison Cook. *Ladies' Home Journal* 107, No. 3 (March 1990):157-159+

The Other Running Mates: First Ladies. Nicols Fox. *Lear's* (September 1990):102-105+

**Presley, Elvis – Impersonators**

Communicating With the Dead: Elvis as Medium. Lynn Spigel. *Camera Obscura* , No. 23 (May 1990): 176-205

**Presley, Elvis** (about)

A Gift from Elvis. Melle Starsen. *Ladies' Home Journal* 107, No. 8 (August 1990):18-22

**Press – Propaganda.** *See* Media and Communications – Propaganda

**Pressman, Stephanie**

Ravens. Poem. *Bridges* 1, No. 2 (Fall 1990): 34

A Wedding. Poem. *Bridges* 1, No. 2 (Fall 1990): 35-38

**Preston, Samuel H.** (joint author). *See* King, Miriam

**Pribble, Victoria** (about). *See* Zoli Management Incorporated

**Pribram, E. Deidre** (editor)

Female Spectators: Looking at Film and Television. Reviewed by Cynthia Carter. *Resources for Feminist Research* 19, No. 2 (June 1990):41-42

Female Spectators: Looking at Film and Television. Reviewed by Sandra Taylor. *Australian Feminist Studies* No. 12 (Summer 1990):127-128

**Price, Candy Pratts**

Fall Shoe Report: Feet First. *Vogue* (July 1990):45-57

**Price, Candy Pratts** (editor)

Elements. *Vogue* (August 1990):152; (September 1990):290

Vogue's Last Look. *Vogue* (August 1990):392; (September 1990):674; (December 1990):344

**Price, Deborah**

Lesbians in Germany: 1890's to 1920's. Book Review. *Belles Lettres* 5, No. 4 (Summer 1990):48-49

The Paris Review Anthology. Book Review. *Belles Lettres* 5, No. 4 (Summer 1990):47-48

Patchwork. *Belles Lettres* 5, No. 2 (Winter 1990):20-21; 5, No. 3 (Spring 1990):26; 5, No. 4 (Summer 1990):47-49; 6, No. 1 (Fall 1990):64-65

Private Demons: The Life of Shirley Jackson. Book Review. *Belles Lettres* 5, No. 4 (Summer 1990):49

**Price, Florence** (about)

Black Women Blaze Musical Trails. Lynn Wenzel. *New Directions for Women* 19, No. 1 (January/February 1990):9

**Price, James H.** (joint author). *See* Price, Joy A.

**Price, Jane**

Motherhood: What It Does to Your Mind. Reviewed by Datha Clapper Brack. *New Directions for Women* 19, No. 2 (March/April 1990):24

**Price, Joan**

A Vision of Radiance. *Woman of Power* 18 (Fall 1990):62-63

**Price, Joy A.,** Desmond, Sharon M., Price, James H., and Mossing, Amy

School Counselors' Knowledge of Eating Disorders. *Adolescence* 25, No. 100 (Winter 1990):945-947

**Price, Leontyne** (about). *See* De Veaux, Alexis, Milloy, Marilyn, and Ross, Michael Erik; Leadership, "1990 Essence Awards"

**Price, Richard**

Madonna Flexes Her Muscles. *Ladies' Home Journal* 107, No. 11 (November 1990):198+

**Price, Susan**

Stars in Aspen. *Ladies' Home Journal* 107, No. 12 (December 1990):54-59

**Pride, Anne** (about)

In Memorium: Anne Pride. Felice Newman. *off our backs* 20, No. 9 (October 1990):21

**Pride and Vanity.** *See* Narcissism

**Prigoff, Arline**

Strong Mothers, Weak Wives: The Search for Gender Equality. Book Review. *AFFILIA* 5, No. 2 (Summer 1990):113-114

**Primatology**

Primate Visions: Gender, Race, and Nature in the World of Modern Science. By Donna Haraway. Reviewed by Sandra Harding. *NWSA Journal* 2, No. 2 (Spring 1990):295-298

**Prince, Heather**

Anniversary Request. Poem. *Canadian Women's Studies* 11, No. 1 (Spring 1990):68

Untitled. Poem. *Canadian Women's Studies* 11, No. 1 (Spring 1990):68

**Prince, Joyce** and Adams, Margaret E.

The Psychology of Childbirth. Reviewed by Andrea Robertson. *Healthright* 9, No. 2 (February 1990):39

**Principal, Victoria** (about)

Talking with Victoria Principal: "I'm in Great Shape." Interview. Alan W. Petrucelli. *Redbook* 175, No. 6 (October 1990):72-74

**Pringle, Rosemary**

Secretaries Talk Sexuality, Power and Work. Reviewed by Colleen Chesterman. *Australian Feminist Studies* No. 11 (Autumn 1990):123-126

**Priorities.** *See also* Time Management

Priorities: It's About Time! Letty Cottin Pogrebin. *Family Circle* 103, No. 16 (November 27, 1990):34-40

10 Things Motherhood Has Taught Me. Louise Lague. *Glamour* (May 1990):122-131

On Your Own: Fiscal Fitness. Judith Stone. *Glamour* (August 1990):130

**Prison**

Femmes et prison. By Monique Hamelin. Reviewed by Monique Imbleau. *Resources for Feminist Research* 19, No. 1 (March 1990):14

In a Penal Colony. Loretta Johnson. *Sinister Wisdom* 40 (Spring 1990):15-16

Through the Wire. By Daedalus Productions. Reviewed by Penny Perkins. *On the Issues* 15 (Summer 1990):31

Women Guarding Men. By Lynn E. Zimmer. Reviewed by Nancy Jurik. *Gender and Society* 4, No. 1 (March 1990):115-117

**Prisoners**

Machinal. By Sophie Treadwell. Reviewed by Laura Flanders. *New Directions for Women* 19, No. 2 (March/April 1990):13

Partial Justice: Women in State Prisons, 1800-1935. By Nicole Hahn Rafter. Reviewed by Sue Mahan. *NWSA Journal* 2, No. 2 (Spring 1990):320-323

Record Numbers of Women in Prison. Pat Redmond. *New Directions for Women* 19, No. 2 (March/April 1990):1+

She Got 40 Years for Bad Checks. Lynn Wenzel. *New Directions for Women* 19, No. 2 (March/April 1990):5

Sing Soft, Sing Loud. By Patricia McConnel. Reviewed by Martha Boethel. *New Directions for Women* 19, No. 2 (March/April 1990):18

Walltappings: An Anthology of Writings by Women Prisoners. Edited by Judith A. Scheffler. Reviewed by Sue Mahan. *NWSA Journal* 2, No. 2 (Spring 1990):320-323

**Prisoners – Battered Women**

Battered Women Fill Prisons. Sharon Wyse. *New Directions for Women* 19, No. 2 (March/April 1990):4+

Batterer Still on Police Force. *New Directions for Women* 19, No. 2 (March/April 1990):4

**Prisoners – Child Custody**

Jailed Mothers Risk Losing Their Kids. Linda Roman. *New Directions for Women* 19, No. 2 (March/April 1990):3

**Prisoners – Homophobia**

Lesbians Get Pink-Tagged. Charlotte Innes. *New Directions for Women* 19, No. 2 (March/April 1990):6-7

Minsky. *Feminist Review* No. 36 (Autumn 1990):4-14

Women Analyze Women in France, England, and the United States. Edited by Elaine Hoffman Baruch and Lucienne J. Serrano. *NWSA Journal* 2, No. 1 (Winter 1990):131-134

### Psychological Distress

Divorce History and Self-reported Psychological Distress in Husbands and Wives. Lawrence A. Kurdek. *Journal of Marriage and the Family* 52, No. 3 (August 1990):701-708

The Effect of Type of Relationship on Perceived Psychological Distress in Women with Breast Cancer. B. Jo Hailey, Karen M. Lalor, Kimeron M. Hardin, and Heather A. Byrne. *Health Care for Women International* 11, No. 3 (1990):359-366

### Psychological Growth

From Childhood to Adolescence: A Transitional Period? Edited by Raymond Montemayor, Gerald R. Adams, and Thomas P. Tullotta. Book Review. *Adolescence* 25, No. 99 (Fall 1990):754

Infants of Adolescent and Adult Mothers: Two Indices of Socioemotional Development. Ann Frodi, Wendy Grolnick, Lisa Bridges, and Jacqueline Berko. *Adolescence* 25, No. 98 (Summer 1990):363-374

### Psychological Testing

Number and Quality of Roles: A Longitudinal Personality View. Ravenna Helson, Teresa Elliott, and Janet Leigh. *Psychology of Women Quarterly* 14, No. 1 (March 1990):83-101

### Psychologists

Barbara Strudler Wallston: Pioneer of Contemporary Feminist Psychology, 1943-1987. Nancy Felipe Russo. *Psychology of Women Quarterly* 14, No. 2 (June 1990):277-287

Health & Mind. Pamela Erens. *Glamour* (October 1990):60

Models of Achievement: Reflections of Eminent Women in Psychology, Volume 2. Edited by Agnes N. O'Connell and Nancy Felipe Russo. *Psychology of Women Quarterly* 14, No. 4 (December 1990):621-623

Psychology. *See also* Men – Psychology

Meta-analysis and the Psychology of Gender Differences. Janet Shibley Hyde. *Signs* 16, No. 1 (Autumn 1990):55-73

On the New Psychology of Women: A Cautionary View. Marcia C. Westkott. *Feminist Issues* 10, No. 2 (Fall 1990):3-18

### Psychology – Feminist Perspectives

Contextual History: A Framework for Re-Placing Women in the History of Psychology. Janis S. Bohan. *Psychology of Women Quarterly* 14, No. 2 (June 1990):213-227

Cracks in the Frame: Feminism and the Boundaries of Therapy. Liz Margolies. *Women and Therapy* 9, No. 4 (1990):19-35

Developing a Feminist Model for Clinical Consultation: Combining Diversity and Commonality. Sandra J. Coffman. *Women and Therapy* 9, No. 3 (1990):255-273

Diversifying Feminist Theory and Practice: Broadening the Concept of Victimization. Lynne Bravo Rosewater. *Women and Therapy* 9, No. 3 (1990):299-311

The Female Hero: A Quest for Healing and Wholeness. Kathleen D. Nobel. *Women and Therapy* 9, No. 4 (1990):3-18

Feminist Frameworks: Retrospect and Prospect. *Psychology of Women Quarterly* 14, No. 1 (March 1990):1-5

A Japanese View of Dependency: What Can Amae Psychology Contribute to Feminist Theory and Therapy. Carla K. Bradshaw. *Women and Therapy* 9, Nos. 1-2 (1990):67-86

White Feminist Therapist and Anti-Racism. Elizabeth J. Rave. *Women and Therapy* 9, No. 3 (1990):313-326

### Psychology – Publications

Characteristics of Accepted versus Rejected Manuscripts. Arnold S. Kahn, Jack H. Presbury, Helen B. Moore, and Jacqueline D. Driver. *Psychology of Women Quarterly* 14, No. 1 (March 1990):7-14

### Psychology – Separation

Is Separation Really So Great? G. Dorsey Green. *Women and Therapy* 9, Nos. 1-2 (1990):87-104

### Psychology – Sikolohiyang Pilipino

Towards Understanding the Psychology of the Filipino. Elizabeth Protacio Marcelino. *Women and Therapy* 9, Nos. 1-2 (1990):105-128

### Psychology – Study and Teaching

Integrating Issues of Gender, Race, and Ethnicity into Experimental Psychology and Other Social-Science Methodology Courses. Donna Crawley and Martha Ecker. *Women's Studies Quarterly* 18, Nos. 1-2 (Spring-Summer 1990):105-116

Psychology of Children. *See* Child Psychology

Psychology of Women. *See also* Infertility

Finished at 40: Women's Development within the Patriarchy. Mary M. Gergen. *Psychology of Women Quarterly* 14, No. 4 (December 1990):471-493

The Futility of Magical Thinking. John Bradshaw. *Lear's* (July 1990):52

Mother-Blaming and Clinical Theory. Janet L. Surrey. *Women and Therapy* 10, Nos. 1/2 (1990):83-87

Premenstrual, Postpartum and Menopausal Mood Disorders. By Laurence Demers, John L. McGuire,

Audrey Phillips, and David R. Rubinow. Reviewed by Jeanette Sasmore. *Health Care for Women International* 11, No. 2 (1990):234

The Psychology of the Female Body. By Jane M. Ussher. Reviewed by Lorelei Cederstrom. *Resources for Feminist Research* 19, No. 1 (March 1990):30-31

The Psychology of the Female Body. By Jane Ussher. Reviewed by Roe Sybylla. *Australian Feminist Studies* No. 11 (Autumn 1990):129-131

Self-Attitudes and Behavioral Characteristics of Type A and B Female Registered Nurses. Sandra P. Thomas and John Jozwiak. *Health Care for Women International* 11, No. 4 (1990):477-489

Why We Can't Throw Anything Away. Nancy Eberle. *Ladies' Home Journal* 107, No. 3 (March 1990):66

**Psychology of Women – History**

Contextual History: A Framework for Re-Placing Women in the History of Psychology. Janis S. Bohan. *Psychology of Women Quarterly* 14, No. 2 (June 1990):213-227

**Psychology of Women – Study and Teaching**

Daughters Discover Their Mothers through Biographies and Genograms: Educational and Clinical Parallels. Karen G. Howe. *Women and Therapy* 10, Nos. 1/2 (1990):31-40

**Psychotherapy.** *See also* Cognitive Therapy; Group Therapy

Can Psychotherapists Hurt You? By Judy Striano. Reviewed by Cheryl Brown Travis. *Psychology of Women Quarterly* 14, No. 1 (March 1990):148-149

On Creating a Theory of Feminist Therapy. Marcia Hill. *Women and Therapy* 9, Nos. 1-2 (1990):53-65

Developing a Feminist Model for Clinical Consultation: Combining Diversity and Commonality. Sandra J. Coffman. *Women and Therapy* 9, No. 3 (1990):255-273

Feminist Counselling in Action. By Jocelyn Chaplin. Reviewed by Nancy Guberman and Miche4le Bourgon. *Resources for Feminist Research* 19, No. 1 (March 1990):12

Feminist Psychotherapy and Diversity: Treatment Considerations from a Self Psychology Perspective. Joan F. Hertzberg. *Women and Therapy* 9, No. 3 (1990):275-297

Healing Voices. By Toni Laidlaw, Cheryl Malmo, and Associates. Reviewed by Deborah C. Poff. *Atlantis* 15, No. 2 (Spring 1990):113-114

Knowing Herself: Women Tell Their Stories in Psychotherapy. By Joan Hamerman Robbins. Reviewed by Sharland Trotter. *The Women's Review of Books* 8, No. 3 (December 1990):20-21

Our Turn. Angela Browne. *Healthsharing* 11, No. 3 (June 1990):8

Role Conflict: Coping With Work in A Community Mental Health Centre. Jan Steele. *Women and Environments* 12, No. 2 (Spring 1990): 24-25

Sarah and the Women's Movement: The Experience of Infertility. Dina Afek. *Women and Therapy* 10, Nos. 1/2 (1990):195-203

In Search of Solutions: A New Direction in Psychotherapy. By William Hudson O'Hanlon and Michele Weiner-Davis. Book Review. *Adolescence* 25, No. 100 (Winter 1990):999

Shrink Resistant: The Struggle Against Psychiatry in Canada. Edited by Bonnie Burstow and Don Weitz. Reviewed by Dianne Patychuk. *Healthsharing* 11, No. 2 (March 1990):32

**Psychotherapy – Client-Therapist Relations**

Fat-Oppressive Attitude and the Feminist Therapist: Fat Oppression. Laura S. Brown. *Woman of Power* 18 (Fall 1990):64-68

Sex in the Therapy Hour: A Case of Professional Incest. By Carolyn Bates and Annette Brodsky. Reviewed by Julia A. Sherman. *Psychology of Women Quarterly* 14, No. 2 (June 1990):289-290

**Psychotherapy – Cross-Cultural Perspectives**

The Meaning of a Multicultural Perspective for Theory-Building in Feminist Therapy. Laura S. Brown. *Women and Therapy* 9, Nos. 1-2 (1990):1-21

**Psychotherapy – Munchhausen Syndrome**

Supermom or Child Abuser? Treatment of the Munchhausen Mother. Elaine Leeder. *Women and Therapy* 9, No. 4 (1990):69-88

**Psychotherapy – Periodicals**

Journal of Feminist Therapy. Reviewed by Rachel T. Hare-Mustin. *Psychology of Women Quarterly* 14, No. 3 (September 1990):440-441

**Psychotherapy – Personal Narratives**

Why Was I So Afraid of Therapy? Roberta Israeloff. *Working Mother* 13, No. 7 (July 1990):18-22

**Psychotherapy – Rape Victims**

Psychotherapists' Knowledge about and Attitudes toward Sexual Assault Victim Clients. Ellen Dye and Susan Roth. *Psychology of Women Quarterly* 14, No. 2 (June 1990):191-212

**Psychotherapy – Women of Color**

Ethnic and Cultural Diversity: Keys to Power. Julia A. Boyde. *Women and Therapy* 9, Nos. 1-2 (1990):151-167

**Puberty**

Brink of Womanhood. Irene Tiersten. *New Directions for Women* 19, No. 5 (September-October 1990):7

**Public Administration – Feminist Perspectives**

Toward a Feminist Perspective in Public Administration Theory. Camilla Stivers. *Women & Politics* 10, No. 4 (1990):49-65

**Public Administration – Gender Roles**

Gender and Style in Bureaucracy. Georgia Duerst-Lahti and Cathy Marie Johnson. *Women & Politics* 10, No. 4 (1990):67-120

**Public Health.** *See* Health Care; Occupational Health and Safety

**Public Policy**

Social Policy: A Feminist Analysis. By Gillian Pascall. Reviewed by Roberta M. Spalter-Roth. *Gender and Society* 4, No. 1 (March 1990):111-113

**Public Relations.** *See also* Customer Service

Gender Gap Persists in Compensation for Public Relations Professionals. *Media Report to Women* 18, No. 4 (July-August 1990):5

Public Relations Textbooks Offer Skewed Image of Women in PR. *Media Report to Women* 18, No. 1 (January/February 1990):6-7

**Public Relations – Business**

This Working Life: The World According to P.R. Gail Collins. *Working Woman* (August 1990):98

**Public Relations Society of America – Task Force on the Status of Women**

PRSA Adopts Policy Statement Affirming Equal Opportunity for Women. *Media Report to Women* 18, No. 2 (March/April 1990):1-2

**Public Service.** *See* Civil Service Workers; Public Administration

**Public Speaking**

Public-Speaking Survival Strategies: How to Make an Audience Love You. Roger Ailes and Jon Kraushar. *Working Woman* (November 1990):118-119+

Say the Magic Words. Laurel Touby. *Working Woman* (November 1990):120+

**Publishers and Publishing**

Barbara Smith and Kitchen Table Women of Color Press. Terri L. Jewell. *Hot Wire* 6, No. 2 (May 1990):20-22+

Barbara Wilson Talks About: Feminist Publishing, Crime and Punishment. June Thomas. *off our backs* 20, No. 1 (January 1990):10-11

Bold Types. Sally Donnelly. *Ms.* 1, No. 3 (November/December 1990):57

Lunch. Interview. Frances Lear. *Lear's* (June 1990):19-20

The New Diversity. Marianne Howatson. *Executive Female* (May/June 1990):18

Reprint Rights, Reprint Wrongs. Carol Barash. *The Women's Review of Books* 7, No. 5 (February 1990):11-12

Therese Edell: Composer and Desktop Music Publisher. Sequoia. *Hot Wire* 6, No. 1 (January 1990):48-49+

**Publishers and Publishing – Bibliographies**

Guide to Women Book Publishers in the United States for 1988/89. By Jenny Wren. Review. *Feminist Collections* 11, No. 3 (Spring 1990):19

**Puerto Rico**

Silent Dancing: A Partial Remembrance of a Puerto Rican Childhood. By Judith Ortiz Cofer. Reviewed by Aurora Levins Morales. *The Women's Review of Books* 8, No. 3 (December 1990):9-10

**Puerto Rico – Divorce**

An Economic Approach to Marital Dissolution in Puerto Rico. Maria E. Canabal. *Journal of Marriage and the Family* 52, No. 2 (May 1990):515-530

**Puerto Rico – Manufacturing**

Export-Oriented Industrialization and the Demand for Female Labor: Puerto Rican Women in the Manufacturing Sector, 1952-1980. Palmira N. Ríos. *Gender and Society* 4, No. 3 (September 1990):321-337

**Puerto Rico – Violence Against Women**

When Does a Law Work Too Well? Norma Valle. *Connexions* 34 (1990):20-21

**Puka, Bill**

The Liberation of Caring: A Different Voice for Gilligan's "Different Voice." *Hypatia* 5, No. 1 (Spring 1990):58-82

**Pullinger, Kate**

Is There Poll Tax After Death? Short Story. *Spare Rib* 217 (October 1990):16-17

**Pumpkin.** *See* Cookery (Vegetables)

**Pupo, Norene** (joint author). *See* Duffy, Ann

**Pura, Matiria** and Short, Robyn

The Maori Struggle Continues – Ke Whawhai tonu matou. Ake! Ake! Ake! *Spare Rib* No. 211 (April 1990):20-21

**Puri, Nina**

A New Strategy for Family Welfare in the Corporate Sector. *Journal of Family Welfare* 36, No. 4 (December 1990):14-19

**Purses**

Purse and Personality. Ellen Hopkins. *Mademoiselle* (November 1990):166-167+

**Purvis, June**

"I Have Done My Duty": Florence Nightingale in the Crimean War, 1854-56. Book Review. *Women's Studies International Forum* 13, Nos. 1-2 (1990):160-161

Larissa Reisner. Book Review. *Women's Studies International Forum* 13, Nos. 1-2 (1990):160-161

Partner and I: Molly Dewson, Feminism, and New Deal Politics. Book Review. *Women's Studies International Forum* 13, Nos. 1-2 (1990):160-161

**Pusateri, D. M.**

Feng Shui. *Executive Female* 13, No. 5 (September-October 1990):47-50

**Pusateri, D. M.** (joint author). *See* Weber, Suzanne

**Puskar, Kathryn R.**

International Relocation: Women's Coping Methods. *Health Care for Women International* 11, No. 3 (1990):263-276

**Puskar, Kathryn R.**, Wilson, Gloria, and Moonis, Lisa J.

The Effect of Group Support on Relocated Corporate and Military Wives: A Secondary Analysis. *Minerva* 8, No. 2 (Summer 1990):36-46

**Putman, Andrée** (about)

French Revolutionary. Anne-Elisabeth Moutet. *Harper's Bazaar* (April 1990):204-205 +

**Pye, Marie**

Community Care Bill Delayed. *Spare Rib* 217 (October 1990):46-47

**Pyle, Hilary**

The "Daemon Fantasy" in Alicia Boyle's Paintings. *Woman's Art Journal* 11, No. 1 (Spring-Summer 1990):21-25

Irish Women Artists: From the 18th Century to the Present Day. Book Review. *Woman's Art Journal* 11, No. 1 (Spring-Summer 1990):45-47

# Q

**Quackenbush, Marcia**, Nelson, Mary, and Clark, Kay (editors)

The AIDS Challenge: Prevention Education for Young People. Reviewed by Sue Kaiser. *Healthsharing* 11, No. 2 (March 1990):33

**Quacks and Quackery**

Health News: Dangerous Doctors and Phony Cures. Rita Baron-Faust. *Redbook* 175, No. 6 (October 1990):54-59

**Quality of Work Life.** *See also* Computer Technology; Employees – Resignation; Occupational Stress; Office Layout; Performance Awards

Design Hot Line: The Office that (Almost) Does the Work for You. Barbara Flanagan. *Working Woman* (October 1990):112-115

Memos on the Office Environment. *Working Woman* (February 1990):70-72; (March 1990):65-68; (May 1990):77-78; (June 1990):49-50; (July 1990):67-70; (August 1990):51-52

**Quart, Barbara Koenig**

Reconsidering "Ms. Daisy." *Lilith* 15, No. 3 (Summer 1990):29

Women Directors: The Emergence of a New Cinema. Reviewed by Josette Déléas-Matthews. *Atlantis* 15, No. 2 (Spring 1990):100-102

**Québec – Health Care**

She Ate Not the Bread of Idleness: Exhaustion Is Related to Domestic and Salaried Working Conditions among 539 Québec Hospital Workers. Daniel Tierney, Patrizia Romito, and Karen Messing. *Women and Health* 16, No. 1 (1990):21-42

**Queenan, Joe**

The Business Person's Essential Library. Bibliography. *Working Woman* (November 1990):101-106

**Queen Latifah** (about). *See* Musicians, Popular, "Repeat Performance"

**Queiro-Tajalli, Irene.** *See* Meyer, Carol and Young, Alma (editors), "On the Bias"

**Quick, Thomas L**

The New Corporate Survival Guide: Can You Thrive in Your Company? *Working Woman* (July 1990):45-48

**Quigg, Brian** (joint author). *See* Miller, A. Therese

**Quilting**

Faith Ringgold: Every Quilt Tells a Story. Evette Porter. *Essence* 21, No. 1 (May 1990):78

The Freedom Quilting Bee. By Nancy Callahan. Reviewed by Elaine Hedges. *NWSA Journal* 2, No. 2 (Spring 1990):282-287

The Quilt Complex. *Mademoiselle* (September 1990):94 +

**Quina, Kathryn**

The Real Truth about Women and AIDS: How to Eliminate the Risks without Giving Up Love and Sex. Book Review. *Psychology of Women Quarterly* 14, No. 2 (June 1990):296-298

Women and AIDS: A Practical Guide for Those Who Help Others. Book Review. *Psychology of Women Quarterly* 14, No. 2 (June 1990):296-298

Women and AIDS. Book Review. *Psychology of Women Quarterly* 14, No. 2 (June 1990):296-298

**Quinby, Lee** (joint editor). *See* Diamond, Irene

**Quindlen, Anna**

Full Circle: God Bless Us Everyone! *Family Circle* 103, No. 17 (December 18, 1990):208

**Quinn, Danny, Francesco, and Lorenzo** (about). *See also* Children of Entertainers

**Quinn-Musgrove, Sandra L**

Extended Care-Giving: The Experience of Surviving Spouses. *Journal of Women and Aging* 2, No. 2 (1990):93-107

**Quint, Barbara Gilder**

Bill Collectors: How Much Can They Harass You? *Glamour* (February 1990):95-96

Could You Survive Tough Times. *Family Circle* 103, No. 10 (July 24, 1990):29-30 +

More for Your Money. Bibliography. *Glamour* (August 1990):112-114

More for Your Money. *Glamour* (March 1990):119-121; (April 1990):132-137; (May 1990):160-162; (June 1990):132-135; (September 1990):158-165; (October 1990):131-134; (November 1990):127-128; (December 1990):118-121

More for Your Money: What Should You Do With $1,000 Savings? *Glamour* (January 1990):50-53

Prime of Life. *Family Circle* 103, No. 11 (August 14, 1990):49+

"The Worst Money Mistake I Ever Made . . ." *Glamour* (July 1990):83-85

Your Money. *Family Circle* 103, No. 1 (January 9, 1990):24+; 103, No. 6 (April 24, 1990):53-54

Your Money: Stay Out of the Red This Christmas. *Family Circle* 103, No. 16 (November 27, 1990):45-48

**Quintuplets.** *See* Multiple Births

**Quitting.** *See* Employees – Resignation

**Quotations.** *See* Love

# R

**Rabinovitz, Lauren**

Temptations of Pleasure: Nickelodeons, Amusement Parks, and the Sights of Female Sexuality. *Camera Obscura*, No. 23 (May 1990): 70-89

**Rabinowitz, Paula**

The Acoustic Mirror: The Female Voice in Psychoanalysis and Cinema. Book Review. *Feminist Studies* 16, No. 1 (Spring 1990):151-169

The Desire to Desire: The Woman's Film of the 1940s. Book Review. *Feminist Studies* 16, No. 1 (Spring 1990):151-169

Ending Difference/Different Endings: Class, Closure, and Collectivity in Women's Proletarian Fiction. *Genders* 8 (Summer 1990):62-77

Home Is Where the Heart Is: Studies in Melodrama and the Woman's Film. Book Review. *Feminist Studies* 16, No. 1 (Spring 1990):151-169

Technologies of Gender: Essays on Theory, Film, and Fiction. Book Review. *Feminist Studies* 16, No. 1 (Spring 1990):151-169

The Women Who Knew Too Much: Hitchcock and Feminist Theory. Book Review. *Feminist Studies* 16, No. 1 (Spring 1990):151-169

**Rabinowitz, Paula** and Nekola, Charlotte (editors)

Writing Red: An Anthology of American Women Writers, 1930-1940. Reviewed by Laura Hapke. *Belles Lettres* 6, No. 1 (Fall 1990):55-56

**Rable, George**

Civil Wars: Women and the Crisis of Southern Nationalism. Reviewed by Jane E. Schultz. *The*

*Women's Review of Books* 7, No. 8 (May 1990):23-24

**Rabson, Ann** (joint musician). *See* Adegbalola, Gaye

**Race, Class, and Gender Studies.** *See also* African-American Women – History

Assault Course. Dorothea Smartt. *Sage* 6, No. 1 (Summer 1989):57-58

Exploding the Myth of African-American Progress. Notes. James A. Geschwender and Rita Carroll-Seguin. *Signs* 15, No. 2 (Winter 1990):285-299

Family, Feminism, and Race in America. Maxine Baca Zinn. *Gender and Society* 4, No. 1 (March 1990):68-82

Race and Gender in Feminist Theory. Carrie Jane Singleton. *Sage* 6, No. 1 (Summer 1989):12-17

**Race Discrimination.** *See* Discrimination; Racism

**Race Relations**

Connecting Method and Epistemology: A White Woman Interviewing Black Women. Rosalind Edwards. *Women's Studies International Forum* 13, No. 5 (1990):477-490

Teaching the New Majority: Guidelines for Cross-Cultural Communication Between Students and Faculty. Mercilee M. Jenkins. *Feminist Teacher* 5, No. 1 (Spring 1990):8-14

**Race Relations – Stereotyping**

Brothers: Is It Always Race or Sex? Stan Clynton Spence. *Essence* 21, No. 6 (October 1990):44

**Race Relations in Literature**

A Peach Farmer's Harvest: Book Royalties. Wendy Cole. *McCall's* 118, No. 2 (November 1990):49

**Racette, E. A.**

Untitled. Poem. *Heresies* 25 (1990):10

**Rachlin, Jill**

Television: Behind the Screens at TV's Funniest New Show. Bibliography. *Ladies' Home Journal* 107, No. 6 (June 1990):54-59

**Rachlin, Jill** and others

School Smarts: Help Your Children Make the Grade. *Ladies' Home Journal* 107, No. 9 (September 1990):61-68

**Racial Stereotypes**

Can TV Switch Off Bigotry? Barbara Grizzuti Harrison. *Mademoiselle* (November 1990):110

Ethnic Notions. Directed by Marlon Riggs. Reviewed by C. Alejandra Elenes. *Feminist Collections* 11, No. 3 (Spring 1990):9

**Racing.** *See* Bicycle Racing–Training; Running Races

**Racism.** *See also* Discrimination

Apartheid U.S.A. By Audre Lorde. Reviewed by Jacqueline E. Wade. *NWSA Journal* 2, No. 2 (Spring 1990):315-319

Back Talk: A Betrayal of Trust. Annette J. Samuels. *Essence* 21, No. 8 (December 1990):142

Brothers: It Begins with Me. Michael Saunders. *Essence* 21, No. 4 (August 1990):40-41

The Construction, Deconstruction, and Reconstruction of Difference. Paula Rothenberg. *Hypatia* 5, No. 1 (Spring 1990):42-57

Corporate Racism: Not Your Imagination. Lloyd Gite. *Glamour* (September 1990):154

A Dialogue on Race. Rosemary L. Bray. *Glamour* (August 1990):220-221+

Ethnicity and Feminism: Two Solitudes? Sheva Medjuck. *Atlantis* 15, No. 2 (Spring 1990):1-10

Forum: "What If We Made Racism a Woman's Issue . . ." Johnnetta B. Cole. *McCall's* 118, No. 1 (October 1990):39-40

"How Do I Explain Racism to My Son?" Allison Davis. *Working Mother* 13, No. 4 (April 1990):30-33

"Madam, May I Have a Word with You?" Elra Patnaik. *Sage* 6, No. 1 (Summer 1989):66

Media Watch. Marie Shear. *New Directions for Women* 19, No. 1 (January/February 1990):7

NOW Confronts Racism. Eleanor J. Bader. *New Directions for Women* 19, No. 6 (November-December 1990):3+

NWSA: Troubles Surface at Conference. Jennie Ruby, Farar Elliott, and Carol Anne Douglas. *off our backs* 20, No. 8 (August/September 1990):1+

Our Common Enemy Our Common Cause. By Merle Woo. Reviewed by Jacqueline E. Wade. *NWSA Journal* 2, No. 2 (Spring 1990):315-319

Racism at the NWSA: A Letter from White Women. *off our backs* 20, No. 10 (November 1990):17-18

Tell Us What You Think: Are Americans Becoming More Racist? *Glamour* (January 1990):74

This Is What You Thought: Racial Incidents. *Glamour* (March 1990):171

White Feminist Therapist and Anti-Racism. Elizabeth J. Rave. *Women and Therapy* 9, No. 3 (1990):313-326

**Racism in the Arts**

Anti-Sexist Celebration of Black Women in Literature: *The Sexual Mountain and Black Women Writers* and a Conversation with Calvin Hernton. Gloria Wade-Gayles. *Sage* 6, No. 1 (Summer 1989):45-49

The NEA Is the Least of It. Barbara Smith. *Ms.* 1, No. 3 (November/December 1990):65-67

**Radden, Viki**

A Black Woman in Rural Japan. *Sage* 6, No. 1 (Summer 1989):52-53

**Rader, Eleanor J.**

Hub Holds Out Hope to Teens. *New Directions for Women* 19, No. 1 (January/February 1990):metrö+

**Radford, Jill** (joint editor). *See* Hanmer, Jalna

**Radhakrishnan, R.**

The Changing Subject and the Politics of Theory. *Differences* 2, No. 2 (Summer 1990):126-152

**Radial Keratotomy.** *See* Keratotomy, Radial

**Radiation.** *See also* Nuclear Power

**Radiation–Health Hazards**

Radiation Update: Danger in the Schoolyard. Paul Brodeur. *Family Circle* 103, No. 13 (September 25, 1990):61-67

Young Mother's Story: "A Medical Error Could Cost Me My Life." Debi Lane. *Redbook* 175, No. 6 (October 1990):64-68

**Radiation–Safety Measures**

Radiation Alert: Will Flying Give You Cancer? *Glamour* (May 1990):196

**Radical Women National Conference**

Radical Women National Conference: A Cold Shower. Dianne Post. *off our backs* 20, No. 6 (June 1990):10-11

Radical Women National Conference: The Third Wave of Feminism. Roanne Hindin. *off our backs* 20, No. 6 (June 1990):9

**Radin, Norma** (joint author). *See* Danziger, Sandra K.

**Radio Broadcasting.** *See also* Albany (New York)–WAMC Public Radio

How to Get Airplay on Noncommercial Radio. Kay Gardner. *Hot Wire* 6, No. 3 (September 1990):50-51

Radio News Director to Collect $700,000 after Being Butt of Sex Jokes on Air. *Media Report to Women* 18, No. 2 (March/April 1990):3

**Radio Broadcasting–Commercials**

A Voice in the Crowd. Craig Bloom. *Lear's* (October 1990):100-103

**Radio Broadcasting–Plays**

Plays on the Radio. *Spare Rib* No. 216 (September 1990):28

**Radio Talk Shows.** *See* Talk Shows

**Radner, Hilary**

Quality Television and Feminine Narcissism: The Shrew and the Covergirl. *Genders* 8 (Summer 1990):110-128

**Randall, Margaret**

Exile in the Promised Land. Book Review. *Bridges* 1, No. 2 (Fall 1990): 121-124

In Mad Love and War. Book Review. *The Women's Review of Books* 7, Nos. 10-11 (July 1990):17-18

Nothing to Lose. *The Women's Review of Books* 7, Nos. 10-11 (July 1990):17-18

Secrets from the Center of the World. Book Review. *The Women's Review of Books* 7, Nos. 10-11 (July 1990):17-18

When Art Meets Politics: Three Worlds, Three Stories. *The Women's Review of Books* 7, Nos. 10-11 (July 1990):21-22

**Randall, Margaret** (joint author). *See* Hubbard, Ruth

**Randall, Mary Carol**

Commitment. Poem. *Sinister Wisdom* 40 (Spring 1990):10-14

**Randall, Vicki**

Women and Politics: An International Perspective. Reviewed by Eleanor E. Zeff. *Women & Politics* 10, No. 3 (1990):135-136

**Randall, Virginia**

The Bloc Party. *Executive Female* 13, No. 5 (September-October 1990):40-41

**Randolph, Liz** (about)

Radio News Director to Collect $700,000 after Being Butt of Sex Jokes on Air. *Media Report to Women* 18, No. 2 (March/April 1990):3

**Rankin, Deborah**

Gimme Shelter! *Working Mother* (December 1990):30-32

Your Money. *Family Circle* 103, No. 4 (March 13, 1990):51-52+

**Ransel, David L.**

Mothers of Misery, Child Abandonment in Russia. Reviewed by Judith Pallot. *Gender & History* 2, No. 3 (Autumn 1990):358-359

**Rao, K. Seshagiri**

The Influence of a Community-Based Distribution Programme on Contraceptive Choice. *Journal of Family Welfare* 36, No. 3 (September 1990):86-106

**Rao, Vijaya**

Pestonjee. Reviewed by Ruth Vanita. *Manushi* 60 (September-October 1990):44

**Rape.** *See also* Hate Crimes; Sex Crimes; Violence Against Women

Alleged Rape–Woman Jailed. Maureen O'Hara. *Spare Rib* 219 (December 1990-January 1991):66

Defining Rape. By Linda Bookover Bourque. Reviewed by Gloria Cowan. *Psychology of Women Quarterly* 14, No. 2 (June 1990):294-296

Ending the Rape of Our Liberty. Bibliography. Christine Doudna. *McCall's* 117, No. 8 (May 1990):94-100

Fraternity Gang Rape: Sex, Brotherhood, and Privilege on Campus. By Peggy Reeves Sanday. Reviewed by Marjorie Lipsyte. *New Directions for Women* 19, No. 6 (November-December 1990):22

The Greatest Story (N)ever Told: The Spectacle of Recantation. Helena Michie. *Genders* 9 (Fall 1990):19-34

How AWAG Dealt with a Rapist. Ila Pathak and Amina Amin. *Manushi* 58 (May-June 1990):37-38

On the Issues. Merle Hoffman. *On the Issues* 17 (Winter 1990):2-3+

Men Who Are Joining the Fight Against Rape. Christina Ferrari. *McCall's* 118, No. 3 (December 1990):71-74+

No to Rape. Kally Forrest. *Connexions* 34 (1990):16

Readers Speak Out: "Get Tougher on Rapists." *Redbook* 175, No. 6 (October 1990):160

Six Countries: Women March Against Rape. *Spare Rib* 217 (October 1990):52-53

When a Woman Says No. O'Hara, Maureen. *Spare Rib* No. 212 (May 1990):12-13

Yes to Action. *Connexions* 34 (1990):16-17

Young But Not Innocent. Beth Weinhouse. *Redbook* 174, No. 6 (April 1990):135-139

**Rape–Acquaintance**

The Glamour Report: Campus Rape. Le Anne Schreiber. *Glamour* (September 1990):292-295+

**Rape–College Students**

Fraternities of Fear: Gang Rape, Male Bonding, and the Silencing of Women. Kathleen Hirsch. *Ms.* 1, No. 2 (September/October 1990):52-56

Media Exploit Pompon Squad. Paula Kamen. *New Directions for Women* 19, No. 3 (May/June 1990):16

**Rape–Counseling**

London Rape Crisis Centre under Threat. *Spare Rib* No. 216 (September 1990):54

**Rape–Group**

A Comparison of Group and Individual Sexual Assault Victims. Christine A. Gidycz and Mary P. Koss. *Psychology of Women Quarterly* 14, No. 3 (September 1990):325-342

Sex . . . Violence . . . Rite of Passage? Erika Munk. *Lear's* (November 1990):112-115+

**Rape, Incestuous**

A Testimony Unbinds Many Tongues. Miche4le Le Doeuff. *Connexions* 34 (1990):18-19

**Rape – Law and Legislation**

A Developing Legal System Grapples with an Ancient Problem: Rape in Nicaragua. Beth Stephens. *Women's Rights Law Reporter* 12, No. 2 (Summer 1990): 69-88

Rape in Marriage: Make It a Crime. Sara Maguire. *Spare Rib* No. 216 (September 1990):44

**Rape – Media Presentation**

TV Rape: Television's Communication of Cultural Attitudes toward Rape. Susan L. Brinson. *Women's Studies in Communication* 12, No. 2 (Fall 1989):23-36

**Rape – Psychological Effects**

Internal and External Mediators of Women's Rape Experiences. Gail Elizabeth Wyatt, Cindy M. Notgrass, and Michael Newcomb. *Psychology of Women Quarterly* 14, No. 2 (June 1990):153-176

**Rape Victims**

Evaluation of Rape Victim by Men and Women with High and Low Belief in a Just World. Chris L. Kleinke and Cecilia Meyer. *Psychology of Women Quarterly* 14, No. 3 (September 1990):343-353

When a Poor Woman Gets Raped. Rupande Ranalal. *Manushi* 60 (September-October 1990):34-36

**Rape Victims – Compensation**

Compensation No Gain. Liz Kelly. SR No. 209 (February 1990):46-47

**Rape Victims – Narratives**

Rape: My Story. By Jill Saward. Reviewed by Maureen O'Hara. *Spare Rib* 219 (December 1990-January 1991):39-40

**Rape Victims – Personal Narratives**

The Woman Who Had to Speak Out. Marianne Jacobbi. *Good Housekeeping* 211, No. 2 (August 1990):82-89

**Rape Victims – Rights**

Naming the Rape Victim: Poll Says Most People Opposed. *Media Report to Women* 18, No. 3 (May/June 1990):6

This Is What You Thought: Should the Press Publish Rape Victims' Names? *Glamour* (September 1990):195

Victims of Rape Lose Benefits. *Spare Rib* 217 (October 1990):45-46

**Raphael, Bette-Jane**

The Flip Side. *Family Circle* 103, No. 2 (February 1, 1990):17

**Raphael, Beverley**

Outrageous Fortune. Book Review. *Healthright* 9, No. 4 (August 1990):41

**Raphael, Beverley,** Cubis, Jeff, Dunne, Michael, Lewin, Terry, and Kelly, Brian

The Impact of Parental Loss on Adolescents' Psychosocial Characteristics. *Adolescence* 25, No. 99 (Fall 1990):689-700

**Raphael, Phyllis**

First Thoughts on My Second Marriage. *Lear's* (June 1990):52-53

**Rapley, Elizabeth**

The Dévotes: Women and Church in Seventeenth-Century France. Reviewed by C. J. Neville. *Atlantis* 15, No. 2 (Spring 1990):104-106

**Rap Music.** *See* Music – Rap

**Rapoport, Alan M.** and Sheftell, Fred D.

Turn Off That Headache! *Redbook* 175, No. 6 (October 1990):104-105 +

**Rapp, Ellen**

Trouble at the Top? How to Stay Out of It. *Working Woman* (June 1990):60

The War of the Bosses. *Working Woman* (June 1990):57-59

**Rapp, Joel**

Crazy Greens. *Redbook* 174, No. 5 (March 1990):36-40

Long-Distance Plant Care. *Redbook* 175, No. 4 (August 1990):26

**Rapp, Rayna** (joint editor). *See* Kruks, Sonia

**Rapping, Elayne**

American Nightmare. *The Women's Review of Books* 8, No. 2 (November 1990):5-6

A Novelist's Career. *The Women's Review of Books* 7, No. 5 (February 1990):13

Now You Know. Book Review. *The Women's Review of Books* 8, No. 2 (November 1990):5-6

**Raque, Sally**

You've Come a Long Way, Ladies. *Women's Sports and Fitness* 12, No. 4 (May-June 1990):61-66

**Rare Diseases.** *See* Diseases

**Rashad, Phylicia** (about). *See* Johnson, Lois Joy, "Great Faces"

**Rastafari Movement.** *See* Hair Styles and Politics

**Ratcliff, Kathryn Strother**

Healing Technology: Feminist Perspectives. Reviewed by Demetria Iazzetto. *NWSA Journal* 2, No. 4 (Autumn 1990):664-668

**Rathbone, Irene**

We That Were Young. Reviewed by Bonnie Kime Scott. *Tulsa Studies in Women's Literature* 9, No. 2 (Fall 1990):339-342

**Rathge, Richard** (joint author). *See* Youngs, George A. (Jr.)

**Rational-Emotive Psychotherapy**

Effects of Rational Emotive Education on the Rationality, Neuroticism and Defense Mechanisms of Adolescents. Daniel J. Kachman and Gilbert E. Mazer. *Adolescence* 25, No. 97 (Spring 1990):131-144

**Rationality**

Women, Reason, Etc. Miche4le Le Doeuff. *Differences* 2, No. 3 (Fall 1990):1-13

**Rattazzi, Delfina** (about). *See also* Fashion, "Suprema Donnas"

**Ratterman, Debbie**

Remaking the Tools: Re-Visioning Rights. *off our backs* 20, No. 9 (October 1990):12-13

**Ratterman, Debra**

Liberating Feminist Jurisprudence. *off our backs* 20, No. 1 (January 1990):12-14

**Rauch, Anne**

Rights of People with Disabilities Clarified. *Healthright* 9, No. 3 (May 1990):35-37

**Raudsepp, Eugene**

Career Management: Are You Flexible Enough to Succeed? *Working Woman* (October 1990):106-107

Will You Find Management Fulfilling? *Executive Female* 13, No. 4 (July-August 1990):57-59

**Rauschenberg, Robert** (about)

Collage Barrage. Thomas Connors. *Harper's Bazaar* (December 1990):50

**Rave, Elizabeth J.**

White Feminist Therapist and Anti-Racism. *Women and Therapy* 9, No. 3 (1990):313-326

**Raven, Arlene**

Crossing Over: Feminism and Art of Social Concern. Reviewed by Pamela Gerrish Nunn. *Woman's Art Journal* 11, No. 2 (Fall 1990-Winter 1991):42-44

Just the Facts. *The Women's Review of Books* 8, No. 1 (October 1990):14-15

Louise Nevelson: A Passionate Life. Book Review. *The Women's Review of Books* 8, No. 1 (October 1990):14-15

**Raven, Arlene**, Langer, Cassandra L., and Frueh, Joanna (editors)

Feminist Art Criticism, An Anthology. Reviewed by Pamela Gerrish Nunn. *Woman's Art Journal* 11, No. 2 (Fall 1990-Winter 1991):42-44

**Raven, Marsha** (about)

Blues Angels. Veronica Hill. *Spare Rib* No. 211 (April 1990):28

**Ravikovitch, Dahlia**

Hide and Seek. Poem. *Lilith* 15, No. 1 (Winter 1990):27

**Ray, Elaine C.**

Reunited. *Essence* 20, No. 10 (February 1990):69-72

25 Travel Tips. *Essence* 20, No. 12 (April 1990):96

**Ray, Man** (about)

Man Ray. David Shapiro. *Harper's Bazaar* (September 1990):292-293+

**Raymond, Barbara**

Rescued by Love. *Redbook* 176, No. 2 (December 1990):116-118+

**Raymond, Barbara Bisantz**

A Special Dad. *Good Housekeeping* 210, No. 6 (June 1990):76-78

**Raymond, Janice**

The Chilling of Reproductive Choice. *On the Issues* 14 (1990):7-9

**Raymond, Janice G.**

A Passion for Friends. Reviewed by Kit Minor. *Women and Therapy* 9, No. 4 (1990):120-122

**Raymond, Janice** (interview)

Embryo Research & Rambo Technology. *Spare Rib* No. 211 (April 1990):14-17

**Raymond, Janice** (joint author). *See* Corea, Gena

**Raymond, Janice** (joint editor). *See* Leidholdt, Dorchen

**Razors.** *See* Shaving

**Read, Alison**

International Archives. *Feminist Review* No. 34 (Spring 1990):94-99

**Read, Mimi**

The Bayou Beat. *Harper's Bazaar* (January 1990):136+

**Readership Surveys.** *See also* Adult Development; Career-Family Conflict; Crime; Diapers; Freedom of Speech; Infertility; Mothers; Pregnancy Discrimination; Privacy Rights; Racism; Rape; Rape Victims; Right to Die

Attention Working Women: Rate Your Stress Life. *Redbook* 175, No. 2 (June 1990):83-90

Business Ethics: What Are Your Personal Standards? *Working Woman* (February 1990):61-62

Editorial: This Year, Give Us a Piece of *Your* Mind. *Glamour* (January 1990):58

Essence: Be an Editor. *Essence* 21, No. 6 (October 1990):98

The Great Astrology Test. *Ladies' Home Journal* 107, No. 1 (January 1990):58-65

How Is Your Work Affecting Your Health, Your Family, Your Life? *McCall's* 117, No. 9 (June 1990):29-34

Personal Journal: Important Insights into the Way We Feel. *Ladies' Home Journal* 107, No. 4 (April 1990):120-124

Sex and the Savvy Woman. Gail Collins. *Savvy Woman* (July/August 1990):66-69

Talking about Our Generation: The Mademoiselle Poll. Shifra Diamond. *Mademoiselle* (December 1990):161+

Tell Us What You Think: Is Sex Overrated in Women's Lives? *Glamour* (February 1990):112

Tell Us What You Think: Should There be Limits on Free Speech? *Glamour* (October 1990):160

Tell Us What You Think: Telephone Privacy. *Glamour* (March 1990):172

This Is What You Thought: Drugs. *Glamour* (February 1990):111

This Is What You Thought: Gay Celebrities: Should Private Lives Be Made Public? *Glamour* (October 1990):159

This Is What You Thought: How's Your Sex Life? *Glamour* (April 1990):167

This Is What You Thought: Infertility Treatments: Who Pays? *Glamour* (July 1990):99

This Is What You Thought: Racial Incidents. *Glamour* (March 1990):171

This Is What You Thought: Who's Calling? *Glamour* (May 1990):187

## Reading

The Gendered Context of Reading. Judith A. Howard and Carolyn Allen. *Gender and Society* 4, No. 4 (December 1990):534-552

## Reading Disability

What to Do When a Child Won't Read. Lee Salk. *McCall's* 117, No. 7 (April 1990):31

## Real Economy System for Teens (REST)

The "Rest" Program: A New Treatment System for the Oppositional Defiant Adolescent. David B. Stein and Edward D. Smith. *Adolescence* 25, No. 100 (Winter 1990):891-904

## Real Estate

Giving Disneyland a Run for Its Money. Grace Lichtenstein. *Savvy Woman* (February 1990):42-45

**Real Estate Investment.** *See also* Condominiums; Houses – Selling

A Blessing on Both Your Houses. Siobhan Toscano. *Savvy Woman* (September 1990):24-28

More for Your Money. Barbara Gilder Quint. *Glamour* (October 1990):131-134

**Reardon, Betty A.**

Sexism and the War System. Reviewed by M. C. Devilbiss. *Minerva* 8, No. 2 (Summer 1990):79-90

**Reay, Diane**

Girls' Groups as a Component of Anti-Sexist Practice – One Primary School Experience. *Gender and Education* 2, No. 1 (1990):37-48

Working With Boys. *Gender and Education* 2, No. 3 (1990):269-282

**Rebolledo, Tey Diana,** Gonzales-Berry, Erlinda, and Marquez, Teresa (editors)

Las Mujeres Hablan: An Anthology of Nuevo Mexicana Writers. Reviewed by Holly A. McSpadden. *Frontiers* 11, No. 1 (1990):89-90

**Recalls.** *See* Product Recall

**Recesses.** *See also* Educational Activities

## Recording Industry

CD Manufacturing for the Independent Artist. Karen Kane. *Hot Wire* 6, No. 1 (January 1990):10-11+

## Record Reviews

Circle of One. *See* Adams, Oleta

Days of Open Hand. *See* Vega, Suzanne

Like a Version. *See* Two Nice Girls

Paradise. *See* Turner, Ruby

Porcelain. *See* Fordham, Julia

The Sweet Keeper. *See* Tikaram, Tanita

Women of Africa. *See* Chewaluza, Mataya Clifford

**Recreation.** *See also* Leisure Activities

March Is a Great Month to . . . *Glamour* (March 1990):229

Private Time. *Glamour* (November 1990):133

Time-Out: Simple Pleasures. *Ladies' Home Journal* 107, No. 4 (April 1990):136-142

**Recycling Industry.** *See also* Recycling (Waste, etc.)

**Recycling (Waste, etc.).** *See also* Refuse and Refuse Disposal

The Eco-Executive. Maggie McComas. *Savvy Woman* (October 1990):33-37

5 Plans to Solve the Garbage Mess. Marie D'Amico and Jim Jubak. *McCall's* 117, No. 11 (August 1990):52-60

Glamour Guide. Bibliography. *Glamour* (October 1990):89-98

The Green Grocer. Kathryn Devereaux. *Women's Sports & Fitness* 12, No. 6 (September 1990):24-25

Recycling: Any Office Can. Alice Rindler Shapin. *Working Mother* 13, No. 9 (September 1990):30-34

Recycling Made Easy. Bibliography. Linda Fears. *Ladies' Home Journal* 107, No. 10 (October 1990):136-141

Teaching Children How to Recycle. *Good Housekeeping* 211, No. 3 (September 1990):172

The Town That Cleaned Up Its Act. Neal Hirschfeld. *Family Circle* 103, No. 2 (February 1, 1990):82+

Waste Not! *Redbook* 176, No. 1 (November 1990):34-36

**Redclift, Nanneke** (joint editor). *See* Sayers, Janet

Reddin, Chitra Pershad

The Warrior Queens. Book Review. *Atlantis* 15, No. 2 (Spring 1990):102-103

**Reddy, Maureen**

Gender, Genre and Narrative Pleasure. Book Review. *The Women's Review of Books* 7, No. 7 (April 1990):25-26

From My Guy to Sci-Fi: Genre and Women's Writing in the Postmodern World. Book Review. *The Women's Review of Books* 7, No. 7 (April 1990):25-26

The Politics of Pop. Lit. *The Women's Review of Books* 7, No. 7 (April 1990):25-26

**Reddy, Prasuna** (joint author). *See* Kelly, Susan

**Redfern, Bernice**

Women of Color in the United States: A Guide to the Literature. Reviewed by Sheryl Hill Paylor. *Sage* 6, No. 2 (Fall 1989):57-58

**Redford, Robert** (about)

Home Decorating: Robert Redford's Rocky Mountain Crafts. *Redbook* 175, No. 6 (October 1990):70

**Redman, Dina** (joint author). *See* Bergman, Miranda

**Redmond, Layne**

Rhythm and the Frame Drum: Attributes of the Goddess. *Woman of Power* 15 (Fall-Winter 1990):20-23

**Redmond, Pat**

Against the Odds: Welfare Mothers Publish Newspaper. *New Directions for Women* 19, No. 1 (January/February 1990):8

Mom Fights Lead Poison. *New Directions for Women* 19, No. 3 (May/June 1990):16

Record Numbers of Women in Prison. *New Directions for Women* 19, No. 2 (March/April 1990):1+

US: Women of Colour Set Agenda on Women's Health. *Spare Rib* 217 (October 1990):53

Women and Crime: Not Much Is Known. *New Directions for Women* 19, No. 3 (May/June 1990):6

Women of Color Set Agenda. *New Directions for Women* 19, No. 5 (September-October 1990):1+

**Redstocking Movement – Denmark**

The Embodiment of Ugliness and the Logic of Love: The Danish Redstocking Movement. Lynn Walter. *Feminist Review* No. 36 (Autumn 1990):103-126

**Reducing Diets.** *See also* Obesity

Bette's Best Diet Yet. Glenn Plaskin. *Family Circle* 103, No. 9 (June 26, 1990):33-34

Diet News. C. Wayne Callaway and Catherine Whitney. *Redbook* 175, No. 1 (May 1990):20

Diet News: Don't Be Fooled. *Redbook* 174, No. 6 (April 1990):26-28

Diet News: Feel Fuller Longer. *Redbook* 174, No. 5 (March 1990):28

Diet News: How Hollywood Eats. Ellen Kunes. *Mademoiselle* (September 1990):282

Diet News: How to Lose Five Pounds This Month. Ellen Kunes. *Mademoiselle* (January 1990):144

Diet News: Secrets from a Diet Diary. Ellen Kunes. *Mademoiselle* (February 1990):196

Diet Q & A. *Mademoiselle* (February 1990):198; (June 1990):206; (October 1990):204; (November 1990):196; (December 1990):188

Eat Light: Have a Thin Thanksgiving. *Redbook* 176, No. 1 (November 1990):174

Fat City. Sarah Stiansen. *Savvy* (December-January 1991):49-51+

Food Advisory. Densie Webb. *Working Woman* (November 1990):157

GH Rates Those Famous Diets. *Good Housekeeping* 211, No. 3 (September 1990):289-290

Jane Fonda's Lean Routine. Arlene Fischer. *Redbook* 175, No. 6 (October 1990):84-88

Medical News. Dana Points and Carla Rohlfing. *Family Circle* 103, No. 9 (June 26, 1990):30

The P.E.P Diet: The Perfect Eating Plan for Life. Susan Male Smith. *Family Circle* 103, No. 14 (October 16, 1990):128-130

The Psychology of Dieting. By Sara Gilbert. Reviewed by Patricia A. Connor-Greene. *Women and Health* 16, Nos. 3/4 (1990):211-221

Redbook's New Wise Woman's Diet: "We Lost – and How!" *Redbook* 175, No. 4 (August 1990):105-110

Stay Slim & Healthy: Snack All Day. Janis Jibrin. *Redbook* 174, No. 5 (March 1990):114-117

Supermarket Diet. Densie Webb. *Redbook* 175, No. 1 (May 1990):100

Ten Pounds Off by Christmas. *Family Circle* 103, No. 15 (November 6, 1990):158-162

Thin Promises. Patricia Long. *Vogue* (October 1990):400-401 +

The Wise Woman's Diet: Pasta Takes Off Pounds! Johanna Dwyer. *Redbook* 175, No. 4 (August 1990):111-120

**Reed, Ann** (about)

Ann Reed: TKO Over His Purple Badness Prince at Awards Night. *Hot Wire* 6, No. 3 (September 1990):30-31

**Reed, Emmie Dell** (about). *See* Leadership

**Reed, Julia**

All About Estée. *Vogue* (May 1990):268-270, 324

Fashion and Society. *Vogue* (October 1990):388-393 +

The Kings of Color: Versace. *Vogue* (September 1990):542-545

People Are Talking About. *Vogue* (August 1990):209; (September 1990):393; (December 1990):185

Talking Fashion. *Vogue* (December 1990):332-334

View: DKNY. *Vogue* (December 1990):111-114

View: Joan Chen. *Vogue* (September 1990):214-218

What Ever Happened to Privacy? *Vogue* (February 1990):316-321, 354

Winona Ryder: Letting Loose. *Vogue* (December 1990):290-293

**Reed, Julia** and Weber, Bruce

Country Goes to Town. *Vogue* (July 1990):176-195 +

**Reed, Shanna** (about)

Shanna Reed's "Major" Break. Dean Lamanna. *Ladies' Home Journal* 107, No. 5 (May 1990):58

**Reentry Students.** *See* Adult Students

**Reese, Karen**

"Mommy, Please Come Get Me!" *Ladies' Home Journal* 107, No. 6 (June 1990):20-22 +

**Reeves, Joy B.**

Women in Dual-Career Families and the Challenge of Retirement. *Journal of Women and Aging* 2, No. 2 (1990):119-132

**Reeves, Michelle** (about)

Michelle Reeves: A True Winner. *Essence* 21, No. 3 (July 1990):12

**Refugees – Personal Narratives**

In the Russian Gymnasia. Excerpt. Manya Prozanskaya Lackow. *Lilith* 15, No. 1 (Winter 1990):15-20

**Refuse and Refuse Disposal.** *See also* Business – Social Policies

Environment: 9 Things You Can Do in the '90s to Save the Planet. Bibliography. Jim Jubak and Marie D'Amico. *McCall's* 117, No. 7 (April 1990):34-41

5 Plans to Solve the Garbage Mess. Marie D'Amico and Jim Jubak. *McCall's* 117, No. 11 (August 1990):52-60

Glamour Guide. *Glamour* (August 1990):79-84

Green Watch. Bibliography. *Good Housekeeping* 211, No. 3 (September 1990):89-90

Recycling Made Easy. Bibliography. Linda Fears. *Ladies' Home Journal* 107, No. 10 (October 1990):136-141

Viewpoint. Ilana Fortgang. *Glamour* (September 1990):144

Waste Not! Earthworks Group. *Redbook* 175, No. 2 (June 1990):130-132 +

Women Are Waking Up to Their Planet. Patti Jones. *Glamour* (May 1990):270-273 +

Your Environment: The Good, the Bad, the Biodegradable. Sharon Begley. *Family Circle* 103, No. 14 (October 16, 1990):71-72

**Reggie, Denis** (about)

Two on the Aisle. *Harper's Bazaar* (June 1990):135 +

**Regna, Joseph**

Teaching Technology from a Feminist Perspective: A Practical Guide. Book Review. *Signs* 16, No. 1 (Autumn 1990):175-177

**Rehabilitation**

The Accident. Beverly Beyette. *Family Circle* 103, No. 12 (September 4, 1990):80-82

**Reich, Holly**

Exercise: The Toll of a New Machine. *Lear's* (November 1990):62-64

**Reid-Dove, Allyson**

Seven Black-Owned Island Guest Houses. *Essence* 20, No. 12 (April 1990):89-92

**Reider, Ines** and Ruppelt, Patricia (editors)

AIDS: The Women. Reviewed by Christine Pierce. *NWSA Journal* 2, No. 1 (Winter 1990):134-139

**Reif, Robin**

My Funny Valentine. *Glamour* (February 1990):206

**Reinhardt, Christine**

A Thousand Points to Write: Peggy Noonan on Getting a Speech Started and Keeping It Going. Interview. *Working Woman* (November 1990):120 +

**Reinhart, Jerome**

More Money: The ABCs of LBOs. *Executive Female* (March/April 1990):16-18

**Reisler, Karen J.** (joint author). See Payne, Lauren

**Reisner, Larissa** (about)

Larissa Reisner. By Cathy Porter. Reviewed by June Purvis. *Women's Studies International Forum* 13, Nos. 1-2 (1990):160-161

**Reiss, Bob** and Hood, Ann

The Answer Couple. *Glamour* (June 1990):164-165; (August 1990):118-119; (October 1990):141; (December 1990):152-153

**Reiss, Bob** (joint author). See Hood, Ann

**Reith, Kathryn**

It's Not Just a Job, It's a Sport. *Women's Sports & Fitness* 12, No. 6 (September 1990):58-59

Teamwork. *Women's Sports and Fitness* 12, No. 4 (May-June 1990):78

**Reith, Kathryn M.**

Reading, Running and Arithmetic. *Women's Sports and Fitness* 12, No. 7 (October 1990):60

**Reitz, Rosetta**

Dinah Washington: Long Live the Queen! *Hot Wire* 6, No. 3 (September 1990):34-36+

Ethel Waters. *Hot Wire* 6, No. 1 (January 1990):20-22+

**Relationship Addiction.** See also Female-Male Relationships – Feminist Perspectives

**Relationships.** See Female-Male Relationships; Personal Relationships

**Relativity (Physics) – Humor**

Relative Time. Peter Feibleman. *Lear's* (October 1990):94-95+

**Religion.** See also Missionaries; Yoruba – Religion

How We Talk About God. Yoel H. Kahn. *Bridges* 1, No. 2 (Fall 1990): 25-29

Speaking of Christ: A Lesbian Feminist Voice. By Carter Heyward. Reviewed by Jacqueline Lapidus. *The Women's Review of Books* 7, No. 9 (June 1990):17-18

Touching Our Strength: The Erotic as Power and the Love of God. By Carter Heyward. Reviewed by Jacqueline Lapidus. *The Women's Review of Books* 7, No. 9 (June 1990):17-18

**Religion, African-American**

Let the Church Say Amen! Pearl Cleage. *Essence* 20, No. 12 (April 1990):69-70+

**Religion – Feminist Perspectives.** See also Feminist Theology

On the Bias: Leaving Our Father's Houses: Redefining Our Religious Concepts. Gail K. Golden and Lynn G. Sheinkin. *AFFILIA* 5, No. 3 (Fall 1990):105-110

Refiguring the Father: New Feminist Readings of Patriarchy. By Patricia Yaeger and Beth Kowaleski-Wallace. Reviewed by Miriam M. Johnson. *NWSA Journal* 2, No. 4 (Autumn 1990):656-658

**Religion – Holidays.** See also Church and State

**Religion – Study and Teaching**

Sunday School: The Formation of an American Institution, 1790-1880. By Anne M. Boylan. Reviewed by Lee Chambers-Schiller. Book Review. *Gender & History* 2, No. 2 (Summer 1990):235-236

Teaching Introductory Feminist Spirituality. Joan Leonard. *Journal of Feminist Studies in Religion* 6, No. 2 (Fall 1990):121-135

**Religion and Family**

Religion and Family in the 1980s: Discovery and Development. Darwin L. Thomas and Marie Cornwall. *Journal of Marriage and the Family* 52, No. 4 (November 1990):983-992

Religious Heterogamy, Religiosity, and Marital Happiness: The Case of Catholics. Constance L. Shehan, E. Wilbur Bock, and Gary R. Lee. *Journal of Marriage and the Family* 52, No. 1 (February 1990):73-79

**Religion and Politics – Algeria**

Gender and Politics in Algeria: Unraveling the Religious Paradigm. Notes. Marnia Lazreg. *Signs* 15, No. 4 (Summer 1990):755-780

**Religion and Race**

Walker's Critique of Religion in *The Color Purple*. Calvin Mercer. *Sage* 6, No. 1 (Summer 1989):24-26

**Religious Discrimination.** See also Patriarchy – Women's Roles

The Cantors Assembly Convention: A Spy Story. Helen Leneman. *Lilith* 15, No. 4 (Fall 1990):37-38

New Rabbinical College Excludes Women. Lisa Klug. *Lilith* 15, No. 3 (Summer 1990):5

Reworking the Rabbi's Role. Julie Goss. *Lilith* 15, No. 4 (Fall 1990):16-25

Standing Again at Sinai: Judaism from a Feminist Perspective. By Judith Plaskow. Reviewed by Sue Levi Elwell. *Lilith* 15, No. 4 (Fall 1990):33-34

The Ways We Are: ."..Who Has Made Me a Woman . . ." Elyse Goldstein. *Lilith* 15, No. 2 (Spring 1990):32

**Religious Orders.** See Nuns

**Religious Practices.** See also Judaism – Rituals; Passover – Customs and Practices; Sexual Repression

Religious Influence on Menstrual Attitudes and Symptoms. Barbara Olasov Rothbaum and Joan Jackson. *Women and Health* 16, No. 1 (1990):63-78

**Relocation**

International Relocation: Women's Coping Methods. Kathryn R. Puskar. *Health Care for Women International* 11, No. 3 (1990):263-276

Fake Abortion Clinics: The Threat to Reproductive Self-Determination. Julie A. Mertus. *Women and Health* 16, No. 1 (1990):95-113

The Future of Reproductive Choice for Poor Women and Women of Color. Dorothy E. Roberts. *Women's Rights Law Reporter* 12, No. 2 (Summer 1990): 59-67

The Glamour Report: Here Come the Pregnancy Police. Susan Edmiston. *Glamour* (August 1990):202-205+

Hodgson's Choice. Laura Fraser. *Vogue* (July 1990):206-209+

On the Picket Lines: Defending Abortion Rights. Excerpt. Christie Balka. *Lilith* 15, No. 1 (Winter 1990):4

### Reproductive Choice – Activism

Calling All Students: S.O.S. Organizes Prochoice Actions. Hilary Illick. *New Directions for Women* 19, No. 1 (January/February 1990):4

Daughter's Zeal Revives Mother's Activist Spirit. Vivan Scheinmann. *New Directions for Women* 19, No. 1 (January/February 1990):18

Four Jailed in Court Demo. Laura Schere. *New Directions for Women* 19, No. 3 (May/June 1990):metrö

My Brain's Not Blond. Cybill Shepherd. *Ms.* 1, No. 3 (November/December 1990).84-85

Saving Choice: Youth Organizes to Oppose Parental Consent and Notification. *On the Issues* 14 (1990):21

We Have Met the Enemy and They Are Us. Mary Thom. *Ms.* 1, No. 1 (July/August 1990):79

### Reproductive Rights

Precedent and Progress: The Impending Crisis of Fetal Rights. Katherine A. White. *Women & Language* 13, No. 1 (Fall 1990):47-49

Pregnant Drug Users Face Jail. Eleanor J. Bader. *New Directions for Women* 19, No. 2 (March/April 1990):1+

Reproductive Laws for the 1990s. Edited by Sherrill Cohen and Nadine Taub. Reviewed by Regina H. Kenen. *Women and Health* 16, Nos. 3/4 (1990):193-196

The Reproductive Rights Battle. Sandra Blakeslee. *Working Mother* (December 1990):44-47

Romania: Pregnancy Police. *off our backs* 20, No. 2 (February 1990):6-7

Women of Color Set Agenda. Pat Redmond. *New Directions for Women* 19, No. 5 (September-October 1990):1+

Women's Bodies: Sacred Essence in Physical Form. Rebecca Wells Windinwood. *Woman of Power* 18 (Fall 1990):54-56

Women's Global Network for Reproductive Rights. *Women's World* 23 (April 1990):46

### Reproductive Technologies. See also
Abortion – Sex Selection; Surrogate Mothers

Beyond Conception: The New Politics of Reproduction. By Patricia Spallone. Reviewed by Leigh Anne Chavez. *NWSA Journal* 2, No. 4 (Autumn 1990):652-656

Beyond Relativism: Moving On – Feminist Struggles. Ann Dugdale. *Australian Feminist Studies* No. 12 (Summer 1990):51-63

Body Management: Prenatal Testing: The Newest Option. Janice Kaplan. *Working Woman* (January 1990):134-138

A Child at ANY Price? Robyn Rowland. *Connexions* 32 (1990):3-5, 30-31

Debating Reproductive Technologies. Paula Bradish and Marille Herrmann. *Connexions* 32 (1990):26-28

Embryos, Ethics and Women's Rights. Edited by Elaine Hoffman Baruch, Amadeo F. D'Adamo, Jr. and Joni Seager. Reviewed by Sonia G. Austrian. *AFFILIA* 5, No. 3 (Fall 1990):113-114

Fault Lines: Infertility and Imperiled Sisterhood. Margarete Sandelowski. *Feminist Studies* 16, No. 1 (Spring 1990):33-51

FINNRAGE Conference In Bangladesh. Christine Ewing and Renate Klein. *Connexions* 32 (1990):16-18

Infertility: Women Speak Out about Their Experiences of Reproductive Medicine. By Renate D. Klein. Reviewed by Jocelynne Scutt. *Women's Studies International Forum* 13, No. 6 (1990):605-608

Man-Made Women: How New Reproductive Technologies Affect Women. By Gena Corea and others. Reviewed by Peggy L. Chinn. *Signs* 15, No. 2 (Winter 1990):400-405

Rabbinic and Feminist Approaches to Reproductive Technologies. Judith N. Lasker and Harriet L. Parmet. *Journal of Feminist Studies in Religion* 6, No. 1 (Spring 1990):117-130

Radical Conceptions: Reproductive Technologies and Feminist Theories. Susan Behuniak-Long. *Women & Politics* 10, No. 3 (1990):39-64

Recreating Motherhood: Ideology and Technology in a Patriarchal Society. By Barbara Katz Rothman. Reviewed by Laura R. Woliver. *Women's Studies International Forum* 13, No. 5 (1990):529-530

Reproductive Rights and Wrongs: The Global Politics of Population Control and Contraceptive Choice. By Betsy Hartmann. Reviewed by Peggy L. Chinn. *Signs* 15, No. 2 (Winter 1990):400-405

Reproductive Technologies: Gender, Motherhood and Medicine. Edited by Michelle Stanworth.

Reviewed by Peggy L. Chinn. *Signs* 15, No. 2 (Winter 1990):400-405

Using Arendt and Heidegger to Consider Feminist Thinking on Women and Reproductive/Infertility Technologies. Maren Klawiter. *Hypatia* 5, No. 3 (Fall 1990):65-89

Young Mother's Story: "How Could I Let Them Separate My Twins?" Patty Nowakowski. *Redbook* 175, No. 3 (July 1990):38-41

**Reproductive Technologies – Laws and Legislation**

To Be Genetically Tied or Not to Be: A Dilemma Posed by the Use of Frozen Embryos. Susan L. Oliff. *Women's Rights Law Reporter* 12, No. 2 (Summer 1990): 115-122

**Reproductive Technology**

Questionnaire Studies of Paramenstrual Symptoms. John T.E. Richardson.*Psychology of Women Quarterly* 14, No. 1 (March 1990):15-42

**Rescues**

"Mommy, Please Come Get Me!" Karen Reese. *Ladies' Home Journal* 107, No. 6 (June 1990):20-22 +

**Research Clearinghouse on Women of Color and Southern Women**

Center for Research on Women/Memphis State University Research Clearinghouse on Women of Color and Southern Women. *Women's Studies Quarterly* 18, Nos. 1-2 (Spring-Summer 1990):117-119

**Research Methodology**

The Art of the Interview. William S. Swan. *Working Woman* (May 1990):96-97

Body/Politics: Women and the Discourses of Science. Edited by Mary Jacobus and others. Reviewed by Vera Kolb. *Feminist Collections* 11, No. 4 (Summer 1990):4-8

The Effects of Feminist Approaches on Research Methodologies. Edited by Winnie Tomm. Reviewed by Dorothy L. Steffens and Jane Robbins. *Feminist Collections* 11, No. 2 (Winter 1990):7-9

Feminism and Science. Edited by Nancy Tuana. Reviewed by Vera Kolb. *Feminist Collections* 11, No. 4 (Summer 1990):4-8

A Feminist Ethic for Social Science Research. By Nebraska Sociological Feminist Collective. Reviewed by Dorothy L. Steffens and Jane Robbins. *Feminist Collections* 11, No. 2 (Winter 1990):7-9

Feminist Scholarship: Kindling in the Groves of Academe. By Ellen Carol DuBois, Gail Paradise Kelly, Elizabeth Lapovsky Kennedy, Carolyn W. Korsmeyer, and Lillian S. Robinson. Reviewed by Arlene Kaplan Daniels. *Gender and Society* 4, No. 1 (March 1990):96-99

Feminist Scholarship: Kindling in the Groves of America. By Ellen Carol DuBois, Gail Paradise Kelly,

Elizabeth Lapovsky Kennedy, Carolyn W. Korsmeyer, and Lillian S. Robinson. Reviewed by Carol Lupton. *Gender and Education* 2, No. 2 (1990):251-252

Gender Issues in Field Research. By Carol A. B. Warren. Reviewed by Carol Lupton. *Gender and Education* 2, No. 2 (1990):251-252

Gender Issues in Field Research. By Carol A. B. Warren. Reviewed by Dorothy L. Steffens and Jane Robbins. *Feminist Collections* 11, No. 2 (Winter 1990):7-9

The Impact of Feminist Research in the Academy. Edited by Christie Farnham. Reviewed by Arlene Kaplan Daniels. *Gender and Society* 4, No. 1 (March 1990):96-99

The Mind Has No Sex? Women in the Origins of Modern Science. By Londa Schiebinger. Reviewed by Nancy Leys Stepan. *Gender & History* 2, No. 3 (Autumn 1990):337-342

Nonsexist Research Methods: A Practical Guide. By Margrit Eichler. Reviewed by Dorothy L. Steffens and Jane Robbins. *Feminist Collections* 11, No. 2 (Winter 1990):7-9

Sexual Visions: Images of Gender in Science and Medicine Between the Eighteenth and Twentieth Centuries. By Ludmilla Jordanova. Reviewed by Nancy Leys Stepan. *Gender & History* 2, No. 3 (Autumn 1990):337-342

**Resolution Trust Corporation**

Economies. Marion Asnes. *Lear's* (December 1990):44

**Resorts**. *See also* Hotels, Taverns, etc.; Vacations

Riviera Retreat. Diane Sustendal. *Harper's Bazaar* (May 1990):60-68

Travel: Away with the Kids. Bibliography. *Essence* 21, No. 2 (June 1990):91-92

Travel. Bibliography. *Glamour* (August 1990):143-152; (December 1990):143-146

Travel: Last Chance for Summer. Bibliography. Deborah Gaines. *Essence* 21, No. 4 (August 1990):97-98

Travel: The Best Country Inns for Fall Weekend Getaways. Bibliography. *Glamour* (September 1990):205-208

Travel: Where to Chill Out. *Glamour* (July 1990):103-106

**Restaurant Management**

Trends: No Frills Dining. Annette Foglino. *Working Woman* (August 1990):42

**Restaurants**. *See also* New Orleans – Restaurants

Artful Cuisine. Betty Goodwin. *Harper's Bazaar* (July 1990):90-93 +

Eating Out: Get a Great Fish Dinner. *Glamour* (April 1990):306

Eating Out: Glamour Rates the Guidebooks. Bibliography. *Glamour* (August 1990):246

Eating Out: Good Food for Fewer $$$. *Glamour* (September 1990):342

Food. Jeffrey Steingarten. *Vogue* (September 1990):486-498

Global Kitchens. Regina Schrambling. *Savvy Woman* (November 1990):78-80

Little Nell's: Colorado Cuisine. Dena Kaye. *Harper's Bazaar* (February 1990):186

Model Gourmets. Jennet Conant. *Harper's Bazaar* (July 1990):94-95 +

**Restivo, Mary Ann** (about). *See* Fashion Designers, "What I Like for Fall"

Mary Ann Restivo: Subtle Chic. *Lear's* (June 1990):108-111

**Retail Trade Industry**

A Day in the Life of a Victoria's Secret. Mimi Swartz. *Mademoiselle* (April 1990):238-239, 264

Fashion Fax. *Glamour* (April 1990):242

**Retarded Children – Adoption.** *See* Mentally Handicapped Children – Adoption

**Reti, Ingrid**

Duologue. Poem. *Journal of Women and Aging* 2, No. 2 (1990):109

Reality? Poem. *Journal of Women and Aging* 2, No. 2 (1990):47

At Sixty-One. Poem. *Journal of Women and Aging* 2, No. 2 (1990):91

**Retirement**

Prime of Life. Audrey Kastris. *Family Circle* 103, No. 6 (April 24, 1990):45 +

Reality Meets Retirement. Horace Mungin. *Essence* 20, No. 9 (January 1990):30

Women in Dual-Career Families and the Challenge of Retirement. Joy B. Reeves. *Journal of Women and Aging* 2, No. 2 (1990):119-132

**Retirement – Planning for**

Gender Differences in Retirement Planning Among Educators: Implications for Practice with Older Women. Virginia Richardson. *Journal of Women and Aging* 2 No. 3 (1990):27-40

Nest Eggs for the '90s. Ellen Schultz. *Savvy Woman* (June 1990):22-23

**Retirement Income.** *See* Older Adults – Financial Planning

**Retreats.** *See* Personal Space

**Rettaroli, Rosella**

Age at Marriage in Nineteenth-Century Italy. *Journal of Family History* 15, No. 4 (October 1990):409-425

**Reverby, Susan M.**

Ordered to Care: The Dilemma of American Nursing, 1850-1945. Reviewed by Nancy L. Noel. *Signs* 15, No. 3 (Spring 1990):640-642

Ordered to Care: The Dilemma of American Nursing, 1850-1945. Reviewed by Peri Rosenfeld. *Gender and Society* 4, No. 2 (June 1990):274-276

**Rexroat, Cynthia**

Race and Marital Status Differences in the Labor Force Behavior of Female Family Heads: The Effect of Household Structure. *Journal of Marriage and the Family* 52, No. 3 (August 1990):591-601

**Reyes, Lina Sagaral**

'Storya. Poem. *Women in Action* 3 & 4 (1990):60

**Reyes, María de la Luz**

Mamacita Mía: Her Three Lives. *Frontiers* 11, No. 1 (1990):53-59

**Reyna, Bessy**

A Dream Compels Us: Voices of Salvadoran Women. Book Review. *New Directions for Women* 19, No. 5 (September-October 1990):15

Landscapes of a New Land: Short Fiction by Latin American Women. Book Review. *New Directions for Women* 19, No. 5 (September-October 1990):15

Latin American Women Speak in Fact, Fiction. *New Directions for Women* 19, No. 5 (September-October 1990):15

**Reynolds, Margaret** (editor)

Erotica: An Anthology of Women's Writing. Reviewed by Maud Sulter. *Spare Rib* 219 (December 1990-January 1991):42-44

**Reynolds, Sarah**

Fine Art Cookies. *McCall's* 118, No. 3 (December 1990):98-100 +

Herbal Pasta. *McCall's* 118, No. 2 (November 1990):131-132

**Reynolds, Sian**

Histoire de la vie Privée, volume 5, De la Premie4re Guerre mondiale à nos Jours. Book Review. *Gender & History* 2, No. 2 (Summer 1990):212-217

Histoire de la vie Privée, volume 4, De la révolution à la Grande Guerre. Book Review. *Gender & History* 2, No. 2 (Summer 1990):212-217

**Rhode, Deborah L.**

Gender Difference and Gender Disadvantage. *Women & Politics* 10, No. 2 (1990):121-135

**Rhodes, Jewell Parker**

Marie Laveau, Voodoo Queen. Novel excerpt. *Feminist Studies* 16, No. 2 (Summer 1990):331-344

**Rhodes, Sandra**

Charleston: Coming Through the Hurricane. *Ladies' Home Journal* 107, No. 1 (January 1990):16-20

**Rhone, Sylvia** (about). *See* Davis, Andrea R., "Power Players"

Rap-Sody & Blues. Andrea Davis. *Executive Female* (May/June 1990):44-46

**Rhythm and Blues Music**

Randy Crawford: Jazzy Rhythm 'n Blues. Benilde Little. *Essence* 21, No. 4 (August 1990):48

**Ricciutelli, Luciana**

Against the Odds: Sculptor Mary Gorrara. *Canadian Women's Studies* 11, No. 1 (Spring 1990):100-102

**Rice, Anne**

The Witching Hour. Reviewed by Mark Matousek. *Harper's Bazaar* (November 1990):112

**Rice, Susan** (joint author). *See* Jimenez, Mary Ann

**Rice-Marko, Debbie** (about)

In the Driver's Seat. Maxine Lipner. *Executive Female* 13, No. 1 (January-February 1990):26-28

**Rich, Adrienne**

Changing Our Own Words. Book Review. *Bridges* 1, No. 2 (Fall 1990): 111-120

Muriel Rukeyser, 1913-1978: "Poet . . . Woman . . . American . . . Jew." *Bridges* 1, No. 1 (Spring 1990): 23-26

Resisting Amnesia. *Woman of Power* 16 (Spring 1990):15-21

She. Poem. *Ms.* 1, No. 1 (July/August 1990):29

Time's Power. Reviewed by Judith Vollmer. *The Women's Review of Books* 7, No. 6 (March 1990):12-13

Time's Power. Reviewed by Laura B. Kennelly. *Belles Lettres* 5, No. 2 (Winter 1990):10

Wild Women in the Whirlwind. Book Review. *Bridges* 1, No. 2 (Fall 1990): 111-120

**Rich, Barbara**

Bedrock. Book Review. *The Women's Review of Books* 7, Nos. 10-11 (July 1990):25-26

Chloe and Olivia. Book Review. *The Women's Review of Books* 7, Nos. 10-11 (July 1990):25-26

Friendship Interruptus. *The Women's Review of Books* 7, Nos. 10-11 (July 1990):25-26

**Rich, Charles L,** Sherman, Miriam, and Fowler, Richard C.

San Diego Suicide Study: The Adolescents. *Adolescence* 25, No. 100 (Winter 1990):855-865

**Rich, Cynthia**

Desert Years: Unlearning the American Dream. Reviewed by Carol Anne Douglas. *off our backs* 20, No. 10 (November 1990):12

**Richards, Ann** (about)

Ann Richards: Plain-Speaking Texan. Jody Becker. *McCall's* 117, No. 9 (June 1990):70

**Richards, Dell**

Lesbian Lists. *Woman of Power* 17 (Summer 1990):64-67

9 Somewhat Queer and Wonderful Facts About Animal Reproduction. Excerpt. *Out/Look* No. 8 (Spring 1990):56

Uncovering a Rich Lesbian Past. *Hot Wire* 6, No. 2 (May 1990):16+

**Richards, Lily**

The Seductive Mother. *Lear's* (October 1990):86-89+

**Richards, Lloyd** (about). *See* Popular Culture

**Richardson, Derk** (joint author). *See* Near, Holly

**Richardson, Diane**

Women and AIDS. Reviewed by Kathryn Quina. *Psychology of Women Quarterly* 14, No. 2 (June 1990):296-298

**Richardson, Glenn E.** (joint author). *See* White, George L. (Jr.)

**Richardson, John T. E.**

Questionnaire Studies of Paramenstrual Symptoms. *Psychology of Women Quarterly* 14, No. 1 (March 1990):15-42

**Richardson, Lorraine**

Minding Your Own Business. *Essence* 21, No. 5 (September 1990):39+

**Richardson, Mariah L**

For Bay. Poem. *Essence* 21, No. 6 (October 1990):137

Hair. Poem. *Woman of Power* 18 (Fall 1990):15

**Richardson, Virginia**

Gender Differences in Retirement Planning Among Educators: Implications for Practice with Older Women. *Journal of Women and Aging* 2 No. 3 (1990):27-40

**Richman, Michele**

"Womanship" Opens New Horizons. *Iris* 24 (Fall-Winter 1990):44

**Richman, Paula** (joint editor). *See* Bynum, Caroline Walker

**Richmond, Peter**

Viewpoint: In Praise of Plain White Panties. *Glamour* (February 1990):118

**Richmond, Robyn** and Wakefield, Denis (editors)

AIDS and Other Sexually Transmitted Diseases. Reviewed by Lynne Wray. *Healthright* 9, No. 3 (May 1990):38

**Richter, Judith M.** (joint author). *See* White, Nancy E.

**Rickel, Boyer**

Downpour. Poem. *Out/Look* No. 7 (Winter 1990):75

**Ricketts, David**

Eat Well. *Family Circle* 103, No. 6 (April 24, 1990):39-40+

**Ricketts, Patsy** (interview)

Let Reggae Touch Your Soul. Delysia Forbes. *Spare Rib* 217 (October 1990):54-55

**Ricketts, Wendell**

The Boys in the Band Come Back. *Out/Look* No. 9 (Summer 1990):62-67

**Ricks, M. Stephanie**

The Black Women's Health Book: Speaking for Ourselves. Book Review. *Belles Lettres* 5, No. 4 (Summer 1990):27-28

I Know I Am Important, Because I Feel It. *Belles Lettres* 5, No. 4 (Summer 1990):27-28

**Riddick, Ruth**

Abortion in Northern Ireland: Report of an International Tribunal. Book Review. *Women's Studies International Forum* 13, No. 3 (1990):273-274

**Ridesharing.** *See* Car Pools

**Riedmann, Agnes**

Changing Family Life in East Africa: Women and Children at Risk. Book Review. *Journal of Marriage and the Family* 52, No. 4 (November 1990):1155

**Rieff, David**

Marilyn Bergman, the Way She Is. *Lear's* (December 1990):82-83+

**Riegert, Peter** (about)

Word On Entertainment. *Glamour* (April 1990):189

**Riemer, Ruby**

The Old Great Round. Poem. *Hypatia* 5, No. 1 (Spring 1990):24-26

**Rierdan, Jill** (joint author). *See* Koff, Elissa

**Rietschel, Jean**

Rose. *Sinister Wisdom* 41 (Summer-Fall 1990):55-57

**Riger, Stephanie** (joint author). *See* Gordon, Margaret T.

**Rigg, Diana** (about)

Vogue Arts: Television. Cathleen Schine. *Vogue* (October 1990):260+

**Riggins, Lois** (about)

A Woman for Lear's: Downhome. Jane Howard. *Lear's* (May 1990):136-139

**Riggs, Marlon** (about)

Marlon Riggs Untied. Interview. Revon Kyle Banneker. *Out/Look* No. 10 (Fall 1990):14-18

**Riggs, Marlon** (director)

Ethnic Notions. Reviewed by C. Alejandra Elenes. *Feminist Collections* 11, No. 3 (Spring 1990):9

**Right to Die**

Do You Need a Living Will? *Good Housekeeping* 211, No. 4 (October 1990):248

Full Circle: One Last Wish. Betty Rollin. *Family Circle* 103, No. 15 (November 6, 1990):170

Private Agony, Public Cause. Deborah Beroset Diamond. *Ladies' Home Journal* 107, No. 6 (June 1990):124-125+

This Is What You Thought. *Glamour* (January 1990):73

**Right to Life.** *See* Abortion – Opposition

**Right Wing Ethic**

The Lie of the Feminist Right Wing Ethic. Shirley Hartwell. *Trivia* 16/17 (Fall 1990):68-80

**Right Wing Organizations**

Women of the New Right. By Rebecca E. Klatch. Reviewed by Jane DeHart. *Signs* 15, No. 2 (Winter 1990):405-408

**Rikhye, Ravi**

Escalating Defence Expenditure. *Manushi* 58 (May-June 1990):9-10

**Riley, Cheryl "Pepsii"** (about)

Cheryl "Pepsii" Riley: Chapter Two. Deborah Gregory. *Essence* 21, No. 6 (October 1990):47

**Riley, Dave** (joint author). *See* Small, Stephen A.

**Riley, Denise**

"Am I That Name?" Feminism and the Category of 'Women' in History. Reviewed by Kelly Oliver. *NWSA Journal* 2, No. 4 (Autumn 1990):674-675

**Riley, Jocelyn** (about)

Feminist Visions: Words and Pictures. Linda Shult. *Feminist Collections* 11, No. 4 (Summer 1990):9-10

**Rindfuss, Ronald R.**, Morgan, S. Philip, and Swicegood, Gary

First Births in America: Changes in the Timing of Parenthood. Reviewed by Sandra L. Hanson. *Journal of Marriage and the Family* 52, No. 3 (August 1990):800

**Rindfuss, Ronald R.** and Stephen, Elizabeth Hervey

Marital Noncohabitation: Separation Does Not Make the Heart Grow Fonder. *Journal of Marriage and the Family* 52, No. 1 (February 1990):259-269

**Rinehart, Sue Tolleson**

Women and the Politics of Empowerment. Book Review. *Women & Politics* 10, No. 3 (1990):131-132

**Ring, Jennifer**

Arms and the Enlisted Woman. Book Review. *Women's Studies International Forum* 13, No. 5 (1990):525-526

**Ringgold, Faith** (about)

Faith Ringgold: Every Quilt Tells a Story. Evette Porter. *Essence* 21, No. 1 (May 1990):78

**Ringwald, Molly** (about). *See also* Actors

**Rinzler, Carol Ann**

Eat Well. *Family Circle* 103, No. 8 (June 5, 1990):40+

The Truth About the Sex Gap. *Family Circle* 103, No. 9 (June 26, 1990):57-59

**Ríos, Palmira N.**

Export-Oriented Industrialization and the Demand for Female Labor: Puerto Rican Women in the Manufacturing Sector, 1952-1980. *Gender and Society* 4, No. 3 (September 1990):321-337

**Ripley, Rebecca**

Enter Password: Recovery. Book Review. *Sinister Wisdom* 42 (Winter 1990-1991):124-126

**Ripp, Judith**

Mind Over Body. *Lear's* (January 1990):100-103

**Risbourg, Pascale** (about). *See also* Carter, Charla, "European Designers to Watch."

**Risk Taking.** *See also* Career Change; Entrepreneurs

The Get-Rich-Quick Trick. Andrea Kott. *Savvy Woman* (September 1990):23-24

How to Tell a Smart Risk from a Dumb One. Jeannette R. Scollard. *Working Woman* (February 1990):78-79

Perilous Pastimes. Pamela Kruger. *Working Woman* (February 1990):80-81

Where the Scares Are: 8 Risky Businesses. Shirley Chan, Maryclare Flynn, and Michelle Klingenberg. *Working Woman* (February 1990):81

**Risk Taking – Gender Differences**

The Big T(hrill) Personality: Why Some Like It Hot. Annetta Miller. *Working Woman* (February 1990):76-78

**Risman, Barbara**

The Divorce Revolution: The Unexpected Social and Economics Consequences for Women and Children in America. Book Review. *Gender and Society* 4, No. 1 (March 1990):105-108

**Risman, Barbara J.** and Schwartz, Pepper (editors)

Gender in Intimate Relations. Reviewed by Karen K. Kirst-Ashman. *AFFILIA* 5, No. 1 (Spring 1990):116-118

**Ritchie, Jane**

Women and Smoking: A Lethal Deception. *Women's Studies International Forum* 13, No. 3 (1990):201-208

**Rites.** *See* Ritual

**Ritt, Martin**

Stanley and Iris. Reviewed by Sue Murphy. *Spare Rib* No. 214 (July 1990):30-31

**Ritual**

American Ritual Dramas: Social Rules and Cultural Meanings. By Mary Jo Deegan. Reviewed by Marlene G. Fine. *Women's Studies International Forum* 13, No. 5 (1990):522-523

The Comfort and Joy of Family Rituals. Dena K. Salmon. *Working Mother* (December 1990):48-52

Tapestries of Life: Women's Work, Women's Consciousness, and the Meaning of Daily Experience. By Bettina Aptheker. Reviewed by Toni Flores. *Frontiers* 11, Nos. 2-3 (1990):121-122

"The Waters of Separation": Myth and Ritual in Annie Dillard's *Pilgrim at Tinker Creek*. Jim Cheney. *Journal of Feminist Studies in Religion* 6, No. 1 (Spring 1990):41-63

Wheel of the Year: Living the Magical Life. By Pauline Campanelli. Reviewed by D. S. Oliver. *The Women's Review of Books* 8, No. 2 (November 1990):23-24

Women, Ritual, and Power. Janet L. Jacobs. *Frontiers* 11, Nos. 2-3 (1990):39-44

Women's Rituals: A Sourcebook. By Barbara G. Walker. Reviewed by D. S. Oliver. *The Women's Review of Books* 8, No. 2 (November 1990):23-24

**Ritz, David**

Janet's Nation. *Essence* 20, No. 11 (March 1990):52-54+

Luther Here and Now. *Essence* 21, No. 7 (November 1990):66-68+

Not Just a Pretty Face. *Essence* 21, No. 5 (September 1990):72-74

**Rivera, Raquel**

Learning the Arts at University. *Canadian Women's Studies* 11, No. 1 (Spring 1990):46-47

**Rivlin, Alice M.**, Wiener, Joshua M., Hanley, Raymond J., and Spence, Denise A.

Caring for the Disabled Elderly: Who Will Pay? Reviewed by Sandy Auburn. *Journal of Women and Aging* 2 No. 3 (1990):113-114

**Rix, Sara E.** (editor)

The American Women, 1990-1991: A Status Report. Reviewed by Susan E. Davis. *New Directions for Women* 19, No. 6 (November-December 1990):18

**Rizzo, Betty**

The Piozzi Letters, Correspondence of Hester Lynch Piozzi, 1784-1821 (Formerly Mrs. Thrale), Volume 1, 1784-1791. Book Review. *Tulsa Studies in Women's Literature* 9, No. 1 (Spring 1990):147-149

**Roach, Mary**

Cholesterol. *Vogue* (May 1990):300-301, 323

**Roach, Sharyn L.**

Men and Women Lawyers in In-House Legal Departments: Recruitment and Career Patterns. *Gender and Society* 4, No. 2 (June 1990):207-219

**Robbins, Christopher**

Vogue Arts: Movies. *Vogue* (August 1990):216-220

**Robbins, Fred**

China Beach's Dana Delany. Interview. *McCall's* 117, No. 8 (May 1990):42

**Robbins, Jane** (joint reviewer). *See* Steffens, Dorothy L.

**Robbins, Joan Hamerman**

Knowing Herself: Women Tell Their Stories in Psychotherapy. Reviewed by Sharland Trotter. *The Women's Review of Books* 8, No. 3 (December 1990):20-21

**Robbins, Martha A.**

Mourning the Myth of Mother/hood: Reclaiming Our Mothers' Legacies. *Women and Therapy* 10, Nos. 1/2 (1990):41-59

**Robbins, Sonia Jaffe**

Simone de Beauvoir and the Demystification of Motherhood. Book Review. *New Directions for Women* 19, No. 3 (May/June 1990):20

When Is a Mother Not a Mother? The Baby M Case. Bilbiography. *Women & Language* 13, No. 1 (Fall 1990):41-46

**Roberto, Karen A.**

Adjusting to Chronic Disease: The Osteoporotic Woman. *Journal of Women and Aging* 2, No. 1 (1990):33-47

**Roberts, Bruce B.** (joint author). *See* Feiner, Susan F.

**Roberts, David**

The Ladies: Female Patronage of Restoration Drama. Reviewed by Elaine Hobby. *Gender & History* 2, No. 3 (Autumn 1990):359-363

**Roberts, Dorothy** (about)

How Do You Build a $44 Million Company? Patricia O'Toole. *Working Woman* (April 1990):88-92

**Roberts, Dorothy E.**

The Future of Reproductive Choice for Poor Women and Women of Color. *Women's Rights Law Reporter* 12, No. 2 (Summer 1990): 59-67

**Roberts, Gregory,** Schmitz, Kenneth, Pinto, John, and Cain, Stanley

The MMPI and Jesness Inventory as Measures of Effectiveness on an Inpatient Conduct Disorders Treatment Unit. *Adolescence* 25, No. 100 (Winter 1990):989-996

**Roberts, Helen**

The Everyday World as Problematic. Book Review. *Gender and Education* 2, No. 1 (1990):117-118

**Roberts, Jane** (joint editor). *See* Roberts, Rosalind de Boland

**Roberts, Julia** (about). *See also* Beauty, Personal

Woman of Character. Tom Christie. *Vogue* (April 1990):394-398, 421

Word On Entertainment. *Glamour* (April 1990):189

**Roberts, Leslie C.**

Body Briefing: Eyes. *Lear's* (April 1990):45-46

**Roberts, Lillian** (about). *See* De Veaux, Alexis, Milloy, Marilyn, and Ross, Michael Erik

**Roberts, Linda J.** and Krokoff, Lowell J.

Withdrawal, Hostility, and Displeasure in Satisfied and Dissatisfied Marriages. *Journal of Marriage and the Family* 52, No. 1 (February 1990):95-105

**Roberts, Michele**

In the Red Kitchen. Reviewed by Sue Murphy. *Spare Rib* 213 (June 1990):28-29

**Roberts, Robin**

"Sex as a Weapon": Feminist Rock Music Videos. *NWSA Journal* 2, No. 1 (Winter 1990):1-15

**Roberts, Rosalind de Boland** and Roberts, Jane (editors)

Growing Up with the Impressionists: The Diary of Julie Manet. Reviewed by Marni Reva Kessler. *Woman's Art Journal* 11, No. 1 (Spring-Summer 1990):41-42

**Robertson, Andrea**

Preparing for Birth. Reviewed by Elizabeth Andrew. *Healthright* 9, No. 2 (February 1990):36

The Psychology of Childbirth. Book Review. *Healthright* 9, No. 2 (February 1990):39

**Robertson, Janet**

The Magnificent Mountain Women: Adventures in the Colorado Rockies. Reviewed by Judith Niemi. *The Women's Review of Books* 8, No. 1 (October 1990):18-19

**Robertson, Joan F.**

Alcohol and the Family. Book Review. *Journal of Marriage and the Family* 52, No. 4 (November 1990):1154-1155

**Robertson, Judith**

Virginia Woolf: The Impact of Childhood Sexual Abuse on Her Life and Work. Book Review.

*Resources for Feminist Research* 19, No. 1 (March 1990):36-37

**Robinson, Andrea** (about)

The Natural. Susan Caminiti. *Working Woman* (September 1990):138-141+

**Robinson, Arthur J., Jr.**

In the Limelight. *Essence* 21, No. 3 (July 1990):34

**Robinson, Audrey** (about). *See also* College Students – Leadership

**Robinson, Bryan E.**

Working with Children of Alcoholics: The Practitioner's Handbook. Book Review. *Adolescence* 25, No. 100 (Winter 1990):1000

**Robinson, Dawn** (about). *See also* En Vogue (about)

**Robinson, J. Fletcher**

A Hurricane Hits Home. *Essence* 20, No. 12 (April 1990):38

**Robinson, Janet E.**

Homophobia: A Weapon of Sexism. Book Review. *Women's Studies International Forum* 13, No. 6 (1990):610-611

**Robinson, Jenefer** and Ross, Stephanie

Woman, Morality, and Fiction. *Hypatia* 5, No. 2 (Summer 1990):76-90

**Robinson, Jo** (joint author). *See* Love, Patricia

**Robinson, Laura M.**

The Corrigan Women. Book Review. *Atlantis* 15, No. 2 (Spring 1990):98-100

**Robinson, Lillian S.**

Centuries of Female Days: Englishwomen's Private Diaries. Book Review. *Tulsa Studies in Women's Literature* 9, No. 1 (Spring 1990):144-146

Monstrous Regiment: The Lady Knight in Sixteenth-Century Epic. Reviewed by Marie Cornelia. *Tulsa Studies in Women's Literature* 9, No. 1 (Spring 1990):156-158

At Play in the Mind-Fields. *The Women's Review of Books* 7, Nos. 10-11 (July 1990):32-33

Subversive Intent: Gender Politics and the Avant-Garde. Book Review. *The Women's Review of Books* 7, Nos. 10-11 (July 1990):32-33

**Robinson, Lillian S.** (joint author). *See* DuBois, Ellen Carol

**Robinson, Lou**

Rapport. Fiction. *Trivia* 16/17 (Fall 1990):128-130

**Robinson, Marilyn**

Mother Country: Britain, the Welfare State and Nuclear Pollution. Reviewed by Jane S. Gould. *New Directions for Women* 19, No. 1 (January/February 1990):19

**Robinson, Marilynne – Criticism and Interpretation**

Femme Foetal: The Construction/Destruction of Female Subjectivity in *Housekeeping,* or NOTHING GAINED. Siân Mile. *Genders* 8 (Summer 1990):129-136

**Robinson, Marilynne** (interview)

Belles Lettres Interview: Marilynne Robinson. Kay Bonetti. *Belles Lettres* 6, No. 1 (Fall 1990):36-39

**Robinson, Matt**

Me and Aretha. *Lear's* (May 1990):102-106+

**Robinson, Nelcia**

Creation Fire. Poem. *Women in Action* 1-2 (1990):2

**Robinson, Rita**

The Joys of Tooling Around. *Lear's* (June 1990):54

**Robinson, Roxana Barry**

Georgia O'Keeffe. Reviewed by Percy North. *Belles Lettres* 5, No. 4 (Summer 1990):2-3

**Robotham, Rosemarie**

Jesse. Short story. *Essence* 21, No. 4 (August 1990):70-72+

**Robotics**

Weird Science. David Ruben. *Savvy Woman* (November 1990):16

**Robson,** Georgeson, and Beck (editors)

The Women Writers' Handbook. Reviewed by Margaretta Jolly. *Spare Rib* No. 215 (August 1990):28-29

**Robson, Jocelyn** (joint author). *See* Alcock, Beverley

**Robson, Ruthann**

Eye of the Hurricane. Reviewed by Marge Piercy. *The Women's Review of Books* 7, No. 8 (May 1990):22

Lesbian Lesbian. Poem. *Out/Look* No. 10 (Fall 1990):26-29

Lifting Belly: Privacy, Sexuality and Lesbianism. *Women's Rights Law Reporter* 12, No. 3 (Fall 1990): 177-203

Looking for Lesbian Legal Theory – A Surprising Journey. *Sinister Wisdom* 42 (Winter 1990-1991):32-39

**Rochefort, Florence** (joint author). *See* Klejman, Laurence

**Rochlin, Margy**

First Person Singular: House Bound. *Savvy Woman* (September 1990):94+

History in the Makeup. *Savvy Woman* (November 1990):18

A Plucky Prodigy. *Harper's Bazaar* (February 1990):58

**Rogak, Lisa**

Your Guide to Hospital Care. *Essence* 21, No. 5 (September 1990):29+

**Rogers, Jeni** (joint editor). *See* Ryan-Smolin, Wanda

**Rogers, Katherine M.**

British Women Writers: An Anthology. Book Review. *Belles Lettres* 5, No. 3 (Spring 1990):25

Desire and Domestic Fiction: A Political History of the Novel. Book review. *Signs* 15, No. 4 (Summer 1990):878-882

Incidents in the Life of a Slave Girl. Book Review. *Belles Lettres* 5, No. 2 (Winter 1990):6

Intellectual Women and Victorian Patriarchy: Harriet Martineau, Elizabeth Barrett Browning, George Eliot. Book review. *Signs* 15, No. 4 (Summer 1990):878-882

The Plight of Intellectual Women. *Belles Lettres* 5, No. 3 (Spring 1990):25

Romance and the Erotics of Property: Mass-Market Fiction for Women. Book review. *Signs* 15, No. 4 (Summer 1990):878-882

The Slave Narrative: Its Place in American History. Book Review. *Belles Lettres* 5, No. 2 (Winter 1990):6

In Their Own Words. *Belles Lettres* 5, No. 2 (Winter 1990):6

**Rogers, Katherine M.** and McCarthy, William (editors)

The Meridian Anthology of Early Women Writers: British Literary Women from Aphra Behn to Maria Edgeworth 1660-1800. Reviewed by Ann B. Shteir. *Canadian Women's Studies* 11, No. 2 (Fall 1990):91-92

**Rogers, Margaret N.**

Grand Obsession: Madame Curie and Her World. Book Review. *The Women's Review of Books* 7, No. 12 (September 1990):27-28

A Scientific Dynasty. *The Women's Review of Books* 7, No. 12 (September 1990):27-28

**Rogers, Mary Eliza**

Domestic Life in Palestine. Reviewed by Judith Tucker. *Journal of Women's History* 2, No. 1 (Spring 1990):245-250

**Rogers, Rita S.** (joint author). *See* Mack, John E.

**Rogers, Theresa** (about). *See* Fashion Designers, "Top Women Designers"

**Rogow, Faith**

Why Is This Decade Different from All Other Decades?: A Look at the Rise of Jewish Lesbian Feminism. *Bridges* 1, No. 1 (Spring 1990): 67-79

**Rogues and Vagabonds in Literature**

Rogue. Kirsten Backstrom. *Trivia* 16/17 (Fall 1990):3-17

**Rohlfing, Carla**

The Healthy Family. *Family Circle* 103, No. 3 (February 20, 1990):37-39

Your Body. *Family Circle* 103, No. 10 (July 24, 1990):53-54+

**Rohlfing, Carla** (joint author). *See* Points, Dana

**Rohrer, Trish Deitch**

High Profile: Joanous Come Lately. *Mademoiselle* (December 1990):78

**Rohrlich, Ruby**

Italian Collective Inspiration for Booklovers Everywhere. *New Directions for Women* 19, No. 1 (January/February 1990):16

The Language of the Goddess. Book Review. *The Women's Review of Books* 7, No. 9 (June 1990):14-16

Prehistoric Puzzles. *The Women's Review of Books* 7, No. 9 (June 1990):14-16

**Role Expectations – Gender Differences**

In the Spirit: The Feminine Principle. Susan L. Taylor. *Essence* 21, No. 7 (November 1990):53

**Role Models**

Reading to Our Daughters (and Sons): Are There Any Role Models Out There? Kristen Staby Rembold. *Iris* 23 (Spring-Summer 1990):64-65

Who Do Our Kids Most Admire? *Good Housekeeping* 211, No. 3 (September 1990):174

Women Right Now. *Glamour* (September 1990):131

**Role Satisfaction**

Employment and Role Satisfaction: Implications for the General Well-Being of Military Wives. Leora N. Rosen, Jeannette R. Ickovics, and Linda Z. Moghadam. *Psychology of Women Quarterly* 14, No. 3 (September 1990):371-385

**Role Strain.** *See also* Dual-Career Families; Multiple Roles and Health

Managing Family Data on Multiple Roles and Changing Statuses over Time. Luther B. Otto and Vaughan R. A. Call. *Journal of Marriage and the Family* 52, No. 1 (February 1990):243-248

**Roller Skating**

The New Skate Shape-Up. *Mademoiselle* (October 1990):56

Roll into Shape. Neil Feineman. *Women's Sports & Fitness* 12, No. 6 (September 1990):50-53

**Rolley, Katrina**

Cutting a Dash: The Dress of Radclyffe Hall and Una Troubridge. *Feminist Review* No. 35 (Summer 1990):54-66

**Rollin, Betty**

Full Circle: One Last Wish. *Family Circle* 103, No. 15 (November 6, 1990):170

**Rollins, Judith**

Muchachas No More: Household Workers in Latin America and the Caribbean. Book Review. *Gender and Society* 4, No. 3 (September 1990):423-425

**Rollins, Tim** (about)

Art: Bronx Revival. Paul Taylor. *Vogue* (January 1990):114-117

**Rolls-Royce.** *See* Automobiles – Design and Construction

**Roma, Cathy**

The Fifth National Women's Choral Festival. *Hot Wire* 6, No. 2 (May 1990):44-45

**Roman, Linda**

Despite Quake Damage, Women's Building Essential Haven. *New Directions for Women* 19, No. 1 (January/February 1990):6

Jailed Mothers Risk Losing Their Kids. *New Directions for Women* 19, No. 2 (March/April 1990):3

RU 486: Another Look. *New Directions for Women* 19, No. 6 (November-December 1990):4

Tapestries of Life: Women's Work, Women's Consciousness, and the Meaning of Daily Life. Book Review. *On the Issues* 15 (Summer 1990):28-29

**Roman Catholic Church**

Eve Reconceived: Religious Perspectives in Feminist Children's Literature in France. Lenore Loft. *Women's Studies International Forum* 13, No. 3 (1990):221-228

**Roman Catholic Church – Ecclesial Base Communities**

Women's Participation in the Brazilian "People's Church": A Critical Appraisal. Sonia E. Alvarez. *Feminist Studies* 16, No. 2 (Summer 1990):381-408

**Roman Catholic Church – Remarriage**

Marriage and Remarriage Among Bombay Roman Catholics. S. Irudaya Rajan. *Journal of Family Welfare* 36, No. 1 (March 1990):61-79

**Roman Catholic Church – Women's Roles**

The Dévotes: Women and Church in Seventeenth-Century France. By Elizabeth Rapley. Reviewed by C. J. Neville. *Atlantis* 15, No. 2 (Spring 1990):104-106

**Romance.** *See also* Female-Male Relationships; Love

The Etiquette of Ending It. Dalma Heyn. *Mademoiselle* (October 1990):80

How to Stay Sweethearts. Donna Jackson. *Redbook* 176, No. 1 (November 1990):94-95+

Love Letters Straight from the Heart. Brook Hersey. *Glamour* (February 1990):158-161

Romance. A. Alvarez. *Lear's* (November 1990):98-99+

**Roman Empire – Status of Women.** *See* Rome – Empire, 30 B.C.-476 A.D. – Status of Women

**Romania**

Romania: Pregnancy Police. *off our backs* 20, No. 2 (February 1990):6-7

**Romania – Children**

Boundless Love. Eileen McHenry. *Ladies' Home Journal* 107, No. 12 (December 1990):132-136+

Rescued by Love. Barbara Raymond. *Redbook* 176, No. 2 (December 1990):116-118+

A State of Shock: Recollections of Romania. Darrell L. Paster. *On the Issues* 16 (Fall 1990):19-21

**Romania – Politics and Government**

Message from Romania. Renate Liebach. *Spare Rib* No. 209 (February 1990):23-24

**Romano, Lois**

Faye: The Leader Women Are Waiting For? *Glamour* (February 1990):194-195+

**Rombauer, Irma** (about). *See* Hazard, Jan Turner, "Women Chefs"

**Rome, Classical – Women Writers**

The Woman and the Lyre: Woman Writers in Classical Greece and Rome. By Jane McIntosh Snyder. Reviewed by Katherine Callen King. *Tulsa Studies in Women's Literature* 9, No. 2 (Fall 1990):323-326

**Rome – Empire, 30 B.C.-476 A.D. – Status of Women**

Adults and Children in the Roman Empire. By Thomas Wiedemann. Reviewed by Janet Huskinson. *Gender & History* 2, No. 1 (Spring 1990):105-106

Patrons, Not Priests: Gender and Power in Late Ancient Christianity. Elizabeth A. Clark. *Gender & History* 2, No. 3 (Autumn 1990):253-273

**Romer, Nancy**

Is Political Activism Still a "Masculine" Endeavor? Gender Comparisons among High School Political Activists. *Psychology of Women Quarterly* 14, No. 2 (June 1990):229-243

**Romero, Archbishop Oscar** (about)

Romero. By John Duigan. Reviewed by Alba Amaya. *Spare Rib* No. 210 (March 1990):38

**Romero, Mary**

The Broken Web: The Educational Experience of Hispanic American Women. Book Review. *Frontiers* 11, No. 1 (1990):86-88

Not Just Like One of the Family: Chicana Domestics Establishing Professional Relationships with Employers. *Feminist Issues* 10, No. 2 (Fall 1990):33-41

**Romito, Patrizia** (joint author). *See* Tierney, Daniel

**Romney, Ronna** and Harrison, Beppie

Momentum: Women in American Politics Now. Reviewed by Connie L. Lobur. *Women & Politics* 10, No. 3 (1990):129-130

**Rong, Xue Lan** (joint author). *See* Grant, Linda

**Rony, Dorothy**

The First Wave. *Belles Lettres* 5, No. 2 (Winter 1990):12

Making Waves: An Anthology of Writings By and About Asian American Women. Book Review. *Belles Lettres* 5, No. 2 (Winter 1990):12

Without Ceremony. Book Review. *Belles Lettres* 5, No. 2 (Winter 1990):12

**Ronyoung, Kim**

Clay Walls. Reviewed by Roberta L. Chew. *Belles Lettres* 6, No. 1 (Fall 1990):26-27

**Roof, Judith** (joint editor). *See* Feldstein, Richard

**Roommates.** *See also* Shared Housing

**Rooney, Ellen**

Discipline and Vanish: Feminism, the Resistance to Theory, and the Politics of Cultural Studies. *Differences* 2, No. 3 (Fall 1990):14-28

**Rooney, Frances**

Living in Clumps. *Women and Environments* 12, No. 2 (Spring 1990): 4-5

**Roosevelt, Eleanor** (about)

Without Precedent: The Life and Career of Eleanor Roosevelt. Edited by Joan Hoff-Wilson and Marjorie Lightman. Reviewed by Sharon Perlman Krefetz. *Women's Studies International Forum* 13, No. 3 (1990):281-283

**Root, Maria P. P.**

Resolving "Other" Status: Identity Development of Biracial Individuals. *Women and Therapy* 9, Nos. 1-2 (1990):185-205

Therapy for Adults Molested as Children: Beyond Survival. Book Review. *Women and Therapy* 9, No. 4 (1990):123-125

**Roper, Esther** (about). *See also* Gore-Booth, Eva (about)

**Rosa, Gladys M.** (about). *See also* Watts, Patti (editor), "Free Advice."

**Rosch, Leah**

One Woman's Office: Essence of Elegance. *Working Woman* (January 1990):120-121

Switching Careers and Getting a Good Reception. *Working Woman* (February 1990):92-93+

Weekends: Designing the Perfect Party. *Working Woman* (March 1990):133-137

**Roscoe, Bruce**

Defining Child Maltreatment: Ratings of Parental Behaviors. *Adolescence* 25, No. 99 (Fall 1990):517-528

**Roscoe, Bruce** and Kruger, Tammy L.

AIDS: Late Adolescents' Knowledge and Its Influence on Sexual Behavior. *Adolescence* 25, No. 97 (Spring 1990):39-48

**Roscoe, Bruce** (joint author). *See* Goodwin, Megan P.

**Rose, Andy** (joint editor). *See* Balka, Christie

**Rose, Barbara**

I'll Tell You No Lies: Mary McCarthy's *Memories of a Catholic Girlhood* and the Fictions of Authority. *Tulsa Studies in Women's Literature* 9, No. 1 (Spring 1990):107-126

**Rose, Charlie** (about)

The Studs and Charlie Show. Interview. *Lear's* (October 1990):96-99+

**Rose, Daniel Asa**

His: Spring Training. *Glamour* (June 1990):264

**Rose, Ernestine L.** (about)

Ernestine L. Rose, Women's Rights Pioneer, 2nd edition. By Yuri Suhl. Reviewed by Rachel Kadish. *Lilith* 15, No. 4 (Fall 1990):34

Forerunners: Ernestine Rose. Rachel Garfield. *Iris* 23 (Spring-Summer 1990):62-63

**Rose, Margaret**

Traditional and Nontraditional Patterns of Female Activism in the United Farm Workers of America, 1962 to 1980. *Frontiers* 11, No. 1 (1990):26-32

**Rose, Melinda**

Healthy Humor: The Art of Laughing at Ourselves. *Woman of Power* 17 (Summer 1990):40-43

**Rose, Nancy E.**

Discrimination Against Women in New Deal Work Programs. *AFFILIA* 5, No. 2 (Summer 1990):25-45

**Rose, Phyllis**

Jazz Cleopatra: Josephine Baker in Her Time. Reviewed by Mindy Aloff. *The Women's Review of Books* 7, No. 4 (January 1990):1+

Jazz Cleopatra: Josephine Baker in Her Time. Reviewed by Perdita Schaffner. *New Directions for Women* 19, No. 3 (May/June 1990):25

**Rose, Tricia**

Never Trust a Big Butt and a Smile. *Camera Obscura*, No. 23 (May 1990): 108-131

**Rosen, Ellen Israel**

Bitter Choices: Blue-Collar Women In and Out of Work. Reviewed by Autumn Stanley. *NWSA Journal* 2, No. 4 (Autumn 1990):640-645

**Rosen, Leora N.**, Ickovics, Jeannette R., and Moghadam, Linda Z.

Employment and Role Satisfaction: Implications for the General Well-Being of Military Wives. *Psychology of Women Quarterly* 14, No. 3 (September 1990):371-385

**Rosen, Margery D.**

The American Mother: A Landmark Survey for the 1990s. *Ladies' Home Journal* 107, No. 5 (May 1990):132-136

Can This Marriage Be Saved? "He's Always Out with the Guys." *Ladies' Home Journal* 107, No. 6 (June 1990):12-18

Can This Marriage Be Saved? "He's There for Everyone Except Me." *Ladies' Home Journal* 107, No. 3 (March 1990):10-21

Can This Marriage Be Saved? "I Can Never Make Him Happy." *Ladies' Home Journal* 107, No. 12 (December 1990):14-21+

Can This Marriage Be Saved? "My Husband Doesn't Want to Make Love." *Ladies' Home Journal* 107, No. 1 (January 1990):10-14

Can This Marriage Be Saved? "My Husband Is Having an Affair." *Ladies' Home Journal* 107, No. 4 (April 1990):20-24+

Can This Marriage Be Saved? "My Husband Keeps Calling Those Sex Hotlines." *Ladies' Home Journal* 107, No. 7 (July 1990):14-20

Can This Marriage Be Saved? "There's Something Missing from Our Marriage." *Ladies' Home Journal* 107, No. 5 (May 1990):12-16

Can This Marriage Be Saved? "We Can't Stop Fighting." *Ladies' Home Journal* 107, No. 2 (February 1990):14-20

Can This Marriage Be Saved? "We're in Love Again." *Ladies' Home Journal* 107, No. 11 (November 1990):28-34

**Rosen, Margery D.** (joint author). *See* Mohler, Mary

**Rosen, Paul M.** (joint author). *See* Walsh, Barent W.

**Rosen, Randy**, Landau, Ellen G., Tomkins, Calvin, Stein, Judith E., Wooster, Ann-Sargeant, and others

Making Their Mark: Women Artists Move into the Mainstream, 1970-85. Reviewed by Thalia Gouma-Peterson. *Woman's Art Journal* 11, No. 2 (Fall 1990-Winter 1991):38-41

**Rosen, Ruth**

Getting Out of the House. *The Women's Review of Books* 7, No. 9 (June 1990):10-11

Women in Public: From Banners to Ballots, 1825-1880. Book Review. *The Women's Review of Books* 7, No. 9 (June 1990):10-11

**Rosenbaum, Anne**

Flash in the Clan. *Harper's Bazaar* (February 1990):101

Phone by Krohn. *Harper's Bazaar* (February 1990):96

**Rosenbaum, Emily** and Kandel, Denise B.

Early Onset of Adolescent Sexual Behavior and Drug Involvement. *Journal of Marriage and the Family* 52, No. 3 (August 1990):783-798

**Rosenbaum, Maj-Britt**

Doctor, Doctor. *Mademoiselle* (June 1990):132; (November 1990):120; (December 1990):114

Health Express: Body and Soul. *Mademoiselle* (February 1990):116

Health Express: Body & Soul. *Mademoiselle* (January 1990):70

**Rosenbaum, Maj-Britt** and Sills, Judith

Doctor, Doctor. *Mademoiselle* (September 1990):202; (October 1990):130

**Rosenbaum, Ron**

Buying As a Religious Experience. *Mademoiselle* (May 1990):112-114

Do Women Make Better Movies? *Mademoiselle* (March 1990):108-110

The Handmaid's Tale. Film Review. *Mademoiselle* (May 1990):112-114

Henry V. Film Review. *Mademoiselle* (April 1990):139-142

Inside Movies: Move Over, Casablanca. *Mademoiselle* (January 1990):52-53+

Love Reincarnate. *Mademoiselle* (December 1990):84-86

Metropolitan: Self-Doubt Among the Debs. Film review. *Mademoiselle* (September 1990):162-169

Miller's Crossing. Film review. *Mademoiselle* (October 1990):98-101

Movies: People – the *Real* Aliens. *Mademoiselle* (February 1990):84-87

Movies: Stairway to Hell. *Mademoiselle* (June 1990):104-106

Postcards from the Edge of Mediocrity. *Mademoiselle* (November 1990):90-93

Rosalie Goes Shopping. Film Review. *Mademoiselle* (May 1990):112-114

**Rosenberg, David** (translator)

The Book of J. Reviewed by Deborah Ann Light. *Ms.* 1, No. 2 (September/October 1990):27

**Rosenberg, Ethel** (about)

The Wives Take the Heat: Ethel Rosenberg and Anne Pollard. June Barsky. *Lilith* 15, No. 1 (Winter 1990):28-29

**Rosenberg, Janet** and others

Politics, Feminism and Women's Professional Orientations: A Case Study of Women Lawyers. *Women & Politics* 10, No. 4 (1990):19-48

**Rosenberg, Julius** (about). *See* Rosenberg, Ethel (about)

**Rosenberg, Karen**

Looking for Spring. *The Women's Review of Books* 7, Nos. 10-11 (July 1990):6-7

**Rosenblum, Nina** and White, Alexandra

Through the Wire. Reviewed by Penny Perkins. *New Directions for Women* 19, No. 2 (March/April 1990):metrö

**Rosenfeld, Peri**

Angels and Citizens: British Women as Military Nurses, 1854-1914. Book Review. *Gender and Society* 4, No. 2 (June 1990):274-276

Ordered to Care: The Dilemma of American Nursing, 1850-1945. Book Review. *Gender and Society* 4, No. 2 (June 1990):274-276

**Rosenfeld, Rachel A.** (joint author). *See* Kalleberg, Arne L.

**Rosenfeld, R.** (joint editor). *See* Minnich, E.

**Rosengren, Karl Erik** and Windahl, Sven

Media Matter: TV Use in Childhood and Adolescence. Book Review. *Adolescence* 25, No. 100 (Winter 1990):1000-1001

**Rosenthal, Elisabeth**

Medical Report: A New Prenatal Test. *Glamour* (June 1990):64-66

**Rosenthal, Evelyn R.**

Women and Varieties of Ageism. *Journal of Women and Aging* 2, No. 2 (1990):1-6

**Rosenwasser, Penny**

Women for Peace – Dateline, Jerusalem. *off our backs* 20, No. 4 (April 1990):4-5

**Rosenwasser, Rena**

Berlin Nights. Poem. *Trivia* 16/17 (Fall 1990):80-83

**Roses, Lorraine Elena**

Renaissance Women. *The Women's Review of Books* 7, Nos. 10-11 (July 1990):31-32

Shadowed Dreams: Women's Poetry of the Harlem Renaissance. Book Review. *The Women's Review of Books* 7, Nos. 10-11 (July 1990):31-32

**Rosetree, Laura**

Every Face has a Secret. *Redbook* 174, No. 6 (April 1990):54-56

**Rosewater, Lynne Bravo**

Diversifying Feminist Theory and Practice: Broadening the Concept of Victimization. *Women and Therapy* 9, No. 3 (1990):299-311

The Second Shift. Book Review. *Women and Therapy* 9, No. 4 (1990):114-116

**Ross, Becki**

The House That Jill Built: Lesbian Feminist Organizing in Toronto, 1976-1980. *Feminist Review* No. 35 (Summer 1990):75-91

Out the Other Side: Contemporary Lesbian Writing. Book Review. *Resources for Feminist Research* 19, No. 1 (March 1990):26-28

**Ross, Catherine E.**, Mirowsky, John, and Goldsteen, Karen

The Impact of the Family on Health: The Decade in Review. *Journal of Marriage and the Family* 52, No. 4 (November 1990):1059-1078

**Ross, Diana** (about). *See* Musicians, Popular, "Repeat Performance"

**Ross, Herbert**

Steel Magnolias. Reviewed by Sarah Payton. *Spare Rib* No. 211 (April 1990):30

**Ross, Michael Erik** (joint author). *See* De Veaux, Alexis

**Ross, Pat**

Boxes for Our Treasures. *McCall's* 117, No. 10 (July 1990):93-96

It's the Mix that Refreshes: Formal Country. *McCall's* 117, No. 7 (April 1990):91-96

Motherly Devotion. *McCall's* 117, No. 8 (May 1990):47-48

**Ross, Ruth** (joint editor). *See* Iglitzin, Lynne B.

**Ross, Stephanie** (joint author). *See* Robinson, Jenefer

**Rossant, Colette**

Southern Exposure. *Harper's Bazaar* (April 1990):212

**Rossellini, Isabella** (about). *See also* Beauty, Personal, "Beauty Bazaar"; Johnson, Lois Joy, "Great Faces"

**Rosser, Phyllis**

Artist's Work Reclaims the Female Body. *New Directions for Women* 19, No. 1 (January/February 1990):10+

Art Makes Political Waves. *New Directions for Women* 19, No. 4 (July-August 1990):8

**Rosser, Phyllis** (joint author). *See* Wolfe, Leslie R.

**Rosser, Sue V.**

Feminism within the Science and Health Care Professions: Overcoming Resistance. Reviewed by Demetria Iazzetto. *NWSA Journal* 2, No. 4 (Autumn 1990):664-668

The Recurring Silent Spring. Book review. *Signs* 15, No. 4 (Summer 1990):872-873

**Royster, Jacqueline Jones** and Guy-Sheftall, Beverly

Reflections on the Spelman College Inaugural Symposium: The Empowerment of Black Women. *Sage* 6, No. 1 (Summer 1989):84

**Rozen, Sydney Craft** (joint author). *See* Bernstein, Albert J.

**RU 486**. *See* Contraception – RU 486

**Ruben, David**

Weird Science. *Savvy Woman* (November 1990):16

**Rubenstein, Carin**

Sex and the Working Mother. *Working Mother* 13, No. 5 (May 1990):54-60

What Pediatricians *Really* Think About Working Mothers. *Working Mother* 13, No. 4 (April 1990):40-44

**Rubenstein, Carin** and Gallo, Claudia

Pleasing Your Picky Eaters. *Working Mother* 13, No. 1 (January 1990):79-84

**Rubenstein, Hiasaura** and Lawler, Sharene K.

Toward the Psychosocial Empowerment of Women. *AFFILIA* 5, No. 3 (Fall 1990):27-38

**Rubery, Jill** (editor)

Women and Recession. Reviewed by Judith Wittner. *Gender and Society* 4, No. 2 (June 1990):258-262

**Rubin, Lillian**

Erotic Wars: What Happened to the Sexual Revolution? Reviewed by Jewelle Gomez. *The Women's Review of Books* 8, No. 3 (December 1990):1+

**Rubin, Miri**

Hildegard of Bingen, 1098-1179: A Visionary Life. Book Review. *Gender & History* 2, No. 3 (Autumn 1990):353-354

**Rubinger, Catherine**

A Might-Have-Been: Feminism in Eighteenth-Century France. *Atlantis* 15, No. 2 (Spring 1990):59-68

**Rubinow, David R.** (joint author). *See* Demers, Laurence

**Rubinstein, Ruth P.**

Beauty Secrets: Women and the Politics of Appearance. Book Review. *Gender and Society* 4, No. 1 (March 1990):110-111

Paris Fashion: A Cultural History. Book Review. *Woman's Art Journal* 11, No. 1 (Spring-Summer 1990):49-50

**Ruby, Jennie**

Inventing Ourselves: Lesbian Life Stories. Book Review. *off our backs* 20, No. 7 (July 1990):15

Lesbian Stories . . . Lesbian Lives. *off our backs* 20, No. 7 (July 1990):15

McMartin Preschool Case: Learning from Experience. *off our backs* 20, No. 4 (April 1990):10-11

NWSA Workshop: Women of Color on Feminist Knowledge. *off our backs* 20, No. 8 (August/September 1990):19-20

What Is *off our backs*? *off our backs* 20, No. 2 (February 1990):1-3

Women on Women: An Anthology of American Lesbian Short Fiction. Book Review. *off our backs* 20, No. 7 (July 1990):15

**Ruby, Jennie,** Elliott, Farar, and Douglas, Carol Anne

NWSA: Troubles Surface at Conference. *off our backs* 20, No. 8 (August/September 1990):1+

**Ruby, Jennie** (joint author). *See* Stato, Joanne

**Ruddick, Sara**

Maternal Thinking: Towards a Politics of Peace. Reviewed by Evelyne Accad. *Women's Studies International Forum* 13, No. 5 (1990):526-527

Maternal Thinking: Towards a Politics of Peace. Reviewed by Jean P. Rumsey. *Hypatia* 5, No. 3 (Fall 1990):125-131

The Root of all Evil? *New Directions for Women* 19, No. 6 (November-December 1990):24

Women and Evil. Book Review. *New Directions for Women* 19, No. 6 (November-December 1990):24

**Rudé, George**

The French Revolution. Reviewed by Susan P. Conner. *Journal of Women's History* 1, No. 3 (Winter 1990):244-260

**Rudet, Jacqueline**. *See* Radio Broadcasting – Plays

**Rudnick, Lois**

Feminist on the Frontier. *The Women's Review of Books* 7, No. 7 (April 1990):22

Mary Austin: Songs of a Maverick. Book Review. *The Women's Review of Books* 7, No. 7 (April 1990):22

**Rudnick, Paul**

Cher Madness. *Vogue* (December 1990):282-289

**Rudolf, Patricia**

Is Your Back Fit to Bare? *Redbook* 175, No. 2 (June 1990):128-129

**Ruether, Rosemary Radford** (joint author). *See* Brock, Rita Nakashima

**Ruff Family (about)**. *See also* Valdez (Alaska) – Oil Spills

**Rugby Football – Bawdy Songs**

"Stylistic Ensembles" on a Different Pitch: A Comparative Analysis of Men's and Women's Rugby Songs. Elizabeth Wheatley. *Women & Language* 13, No. 1 (Fall 1990):21-26

**Ruggiero, Chris**

Teaching Women's Studies: The Repersonalization of Our Politics. *Women's Studies International Forum* 13, No. 5 (1990):469-475

**Ruitort, Monica** (joint author). *See* Elliott, Susan

**Ruiz, Vicki L.**

A Road Well Traveled: Three Generations of Cuban American Women. Book Review. *NWSA Journal* 2, No. 3 (Summer 1990):490-491

**Ruiz, Vicki L.** (joint editor). *See* DuBois, Ellen Carol

**Rukeyser, Muriel**

Muriel Rukeyser: Under Forty. Essay. *Bridges* 1, No. 1 (Spring 1990): 26-29

**Rukeyser, Muriel** (about)

Muriel Rukeyser, 1913-1978: "Poet . . . Woman . . . American . . . Jew." Adrienne Rich. *Bridges* 1, No. 1 (Spring 1990): 23-26

**Rule, Bernadette**

Cut Flowers for Linda. Poem. *Canadian Women's Studies* 11, No. 1 (Spring 1990):42

**Rule, Jane**

After the Fire. Reviewed by Tracy Scott. *New Directions for Women* 19, No. 1 (January/February 1990):24

Lesbian Images. Reviewed by Annie Hole. *Spare Rib* No. 210 (March 1990):35

**Rumsey, Jean P.**

Constructing *Maternal Thinking. Hypatia* 5, No. 3 (Fall 1990):125-131

Maternal Thinking: Towards a Politics of Peace. Book Review. *Hypatia* 5, No. 3 (Fall 1990):125-131

**Runaway Youth.** *See* Adolescents, Runaway

**Rundblad, Georganne**

Feminism and the Constructions of Knowledge: Speculations on a Subjective Science. *Women & Language* 13, No. 1 (Fall 1990):53-55

**Running**

Slow Down, You Move Too Fast. Gordon Bakoulis Bloch. *Women's Sports and Fitness* 12, No. 3 (April 1990):24

Trail Mix. Gordon Bakoulis Bloch. *Women's Sports and Fitness* 12, No. 4 (May-June 1990):28

**Running – Health Aspects**

Menstrual Dysfunction among Habitual Runners. Vilma E. Cokkinades, C.A. Macera, and R.R. Pate. *Women and Health* 16, No. 2 (1990):59-69

**Running Races**

Everywhere to Run. Bob Cooper. *Women's Sports & Fitness* 12, No. 6 (September 1990):33

Full Speed Ahead. Kate Delhagen. *Women's Sports & Fitness* 12, No. 6 (September 1990):26-28

Getting Faster, Faster. Owen Anderson. *Women's Sports & Fitness* 12, No. 6 (September 1990):30-32

**Running Shoes**

Put Your Money Where Your Foot Is: A Guide to Buying Running Shoes. Emily Walzer. *Women's Sports & Fitness* 12, No. 6 (September 1990):36-39

**Runyan, Anne Sisson**

Lucha: The Struggles of Latin American Women. Book Review. *Women's Studies International Forum* 13, No. 5 (1990):520-521

Talking Peace: The Women's International Peace Conference. Book Review. *Atlantis* 15, No. 2 (Spring 1990):107-109

**Runyeon, Jennifer** (about)

Windshield Wipers Clean Up. Joan Delaney. *Executive Female* 13, No. 4 (July-August 1990):70-71

**Runyon, Kim** (about). *See* Entrepreneurs

**Rupp, Leila J.**

The Construction of Homosexuality. Book Review. *NWSA Journal* 2, No. 2 (Spring 1990):306-308

Public Prudery, Private Passion. *The Women's Review of Books* 7, No. 7 (April 1990):20

Searching the Heart: Women, Men, and Romantic Love in Nineteenth-Century America. Book Review. *The Women's Review of Books* 7, No. 7 (April 1990):20

**Ruppelt, Patricia** (joint editor). *See* Reider, Ines

**Rural Development.** *See also* Bangladesh – Status of Women; India – Status of Women; Latin American Women – Rural Development

**Rural Living**

The Flip Side. Margery Cunninghamn. *Family Circle* 103, No. 8 (June 5, 1990):30-31

**Rural Society**

The Invisible Resource: Women and Work in Rural Bangladesh. By Ben J. Wallace, Rosie Mujid Ahsan, Shahnaz Huq Hussain, and Ekramul Ahsan. Reviewed by Sue Ellen Charlton. *Signs* 15, No. 4 (Summer 1990):860-864

**Rural Women.** *See also* India – Health Care

The Hazardous Working Conditions of Rural Women. Dinesh Mohan. *Manushi* No. 59 (July-August 1990):25-28

Learning to Take People Seriously. Madhu Kishwar. *Manushi* 56 (January-February 1990):2-10

**Rush, Florence**

Virginia Woolf: The Impact of Childhood Sexual Abuse on Her Life and Work. Book Review. *Women's Studies International Forum* 13, No. 3 (1990):276-277

**Rush, Pat** and Rushton, Ann

Women's Health Questions Answered. Reviewed by Stefania Siedlecky. *Healthright* 9, No. 4 (August 1990):43

**Rush, Ramona R.** (joint author). *See* Allen, Myria Watkins

**Rushton, Ann** (joint author). *See* Rush, Pat

**Ruskay, Esther J.**

Rembrance of Hanukkah Past. *Good Housekeeping* 211, No. 6 (December 1990):56+

**Russell, Anne M.**

The End of the Big Bad Boss. *Working Woman* (March 1990):79

Office Tech: More Power to Them. *Working Woman* (October 1990):63-68

The 10 Worst Careers. *Working Woman* (July 1990):82-84

**Russell, Anne M.** (editor)

Working Woman 11th Annual Salary Survey, 1990. *Working Woman* (January 1990):105-112

**Russell, Diana E. H.**

From Expert Witness to Jail Inmate. *off our backs* 20, No. 10 (November 1990):4

Lives of Courage: Women for a New South Africa. Reviewed by Carol Anne Douglas. *off our backs* 20, No. 3 (March 1990):28+

Lives of Courage: Women for a New South Africa. Reviewed by Ernece B. Kelly. *On the Issues* 15 (Summer 1990):26-27

Lives of Courage: Women for a New South Africa. Reviewed by Joyce F. Kirk. *NWSA Journal* 2, No. 4 (Autumn 1990):658-659

Lives of Courage: Women for a New South Africa. Reviewed by Stanlie M. James. *Feminist Collections* 12, No. 1 (Fall 1990):3-6

Lives of Courage: Women of a New South Africa. Reviewed by Gwendolyn Mikell. *Belles Lettres* 5, No. 3 (Spring 1990):13-14

**Russell, Diana E. H.** and Caputi, Jane

Canadian Massacre: It Was Political. *New Directions for Women* 19, No. 2 (March/April 1990):17

**Russell, Diana E. H.** (editor)

Exposing Nuclear Phallacies. Reviewed by Deborah Jordan. *Australian Feminist Studies* No. 11 (Autumn 1990):127-128

**Russell, Diana E. H.** (joint author). *See* Caputi, Jane

**Russell, Elaine**

Endometrial Smears – A Cautionary Tale. *Spare Rib* 217 (October 1990):66

**Russell, Kathryn**

Engels Revisited: New Feminist Essays. Book review. *Signs* 15, No. 2 (Winter 1990):398-400

**Russett, Cynthia Eagle**

Sexual Science: The Victorian Construction of Womanhood. Reviewed by Nancy Leys Stepan. *Gender & History* 2, No. 3 (Autumn 1990):337-342

**Russo, Nancy Felipe**

Barbara Strudler Wallston: Pioneer of Contemporary Feminist Psychology, 1943-1987. *Psychology of Women Quarterly* 14, No. 2 (June 1990):277-287

**Russo, Nancy Felipe** (joint editor). *See* O'Connell, Agnes N.

**Ruston** (joint author). *See* Jo, Bev

**Rutgers University – School of Social Work**

On the Lookout: A Model Project in Support of AFFILIA. Audrey Faulkner. *AFFILIA* 5, No. 3 (Fall 1990):101-104

**Ruth, Barbara**

Love and Politics: Radical Feminist and Lesbian Theories. Book Review. *Sinister Wisdom* 42 (Winter 1990-1991):117-122

**Ruthchild, Rochelle**

Gray Eminence. *The Women's Review of Books* 8, No. 3 (December 1990):25-26

Ideology Is Destiny? *The Women's Review of Books* 7, No. 6 (March 1990):15

Soviet Women: Walking the Tightrope. Book Review. *The Women's Review of Books* 8, No. 3 (December 1990):25-26

A Turn Toward the Future. *The Women's Review of Books* 7, Nos. 10-11 (July 1990):8-9

Women and Ideology in the Soviet Union. Book Review. *The Women's Review of Books* 7, No. 6 (March 1990):15

**Ruttan, Susan** (about)

Talking with Susan Ruttan: "I'll Always Miss My Sister." Bibliography. Nancy Mills. *Redbook* 174, No. 5 (March 1990):30-34

**Rutter, Itala T. C.**

Feminist Theory as Practice: Italian Feminism and the Work of Teresa de Lauretis and Dacia Maraini. *Women's Studies International Forum* 13, No. 6 (1990):565-575

**Ryan, Barbara**

Insiders, Outsiders and Where the Lines Are Drawn. *off our backs* 20, No. 7 (July 1990):17

The Shape of Red: Insider/Outsider Reflections. Book Review. *off our backs* 20, No. 7 (July 1990):17

**Ryan, Margaret** (joint author). *See* Wright, S.

**Ryan, Marilyn** (joint author). *See* Hyde, Janet Shibley

**Ryan, Mary**

Women in Public: From Banners to Ballots, 1825-1880. Reviewed by Ruth Rosen. *The Women's Review of Books* 7, No. 9 (June 1990):10-11

**Ryan, Meg** (about). *See* Beauty, Personal, "Beauty Bazaar"

**Ryan, Victoria**

The Mothers' Page: His, Mine, Ours. *McCall's* 117, No. 11 (August 1990):9-10

**Ryan, William P.** (joint author). *See* Donovan, Mary Ellen

**Ryan-Smolin, Wanda,** Mayes, Elizabeth, and Rogers, Jeni (editors)

Irish Women Artists: From the 18th Century to the Present Day. Reviewed by Hilary Pyle. *Woman's Art Journal* 11, No. 1 (Spring-Summer 1990):45-47

Irish Women Artists: From the 18th Century to the Present Day. Reviewed by Martha Caldwell. *Woman's Art Journal* 11, No. 1 (Spring-Summer 1990):47-49

**Ryder, Winona** (about). *See also* Beauty, Personal, "Beauty Bazaar"

Winona Ryder: Letting Loose. Julia Reed. *Vogue* (December 1990):290-293

# S

**S. A., Lalitha** (joint author). *See* Jain, J. P.

**Saar, Betye** (about). *See also* Artists

**Sabatini, Gabriela** (about). *See also* Athletes, "The Competitive Edge"

**Sabbagh, Suha**

My Life Story: The Autobiography of a Berber Woman. Book Review. *The Women's Review of Books* 7, Nos. 10-11 (July 1990):42-43

Tales of Exile. *The Women's Review of Books* 7, Nos. 10-11 (July 1990):42-43

A Woman of Nazareth. Book Review. *The Women's Review of Books* 7, Nos. 10-11 (July 1990):42-43

**Sabin, Nellie** (joint author). *See* Straat, Kent L.

**Sacca, Elizabeth** (joint author). *See* Hughes, Lynn

**Sacchi, Virginia Will**

Two to Four from 9 to 5: The Adventures of a Day Care Provider. Book Review. *Iris* 24 (Fall-Winter 1990):65-66

**Sachar, R. K.** and others

Sex Selective Fertility Control. *Journal of Family Welfare* 36, No. 2 (June 1990):30-35

**Sachs, Barbara A.,** Poland, Marilyn L., and Giblin, Paul T.

Enhancing the Adolescent Reproductive Process: Efforts to Implement a Program for Black Adolescent Fathers. *Health Care for Women International* 11, No. 4 (1990):447-460

**Sacks, Jennifer L.**

You're Standing In My Light and Other Stories. Book Review. *Belles Lettres* 5, No. 4 (Summer 1990):17

**Sacks, Karen**

Caring by the Hour: Women, Work, and Organizing at Duke Medical Center. Reviewed by Sandra Morgen. *Feminist Studies* 16, No. 1 (Spring 1990):53-67

**Sackville West, Vita** (about)

Portrait of a Marriage. Reviewed by Sarah Payton. *Spare Rib* 217 (October 1990):30

**Safa, Helen Icken**

Women's Social Movements in Latin America. *Gender and Society* 4, No. 3 (September 1990):354-369

**Safety.** *See also* Children – Safety; Crime Prevention

Glamour Guide. *Glamour* (June 1990):83-88

Take Back Four O'Clock| Maureen Hall. *Women and Environments* 12, No. 2 (Spring 1990): 6-7

**Safford, Betty C.**

Comment on Zita's Review of *The Science Question in Feminism. Hypatia* 5, No. 1 (Spring 1990):181-182

**Safire, William**

The Speech Heard 'Round the World. *McCall's* 117, No. 12 (September 1990):94-95

**Saft, Elizabeth** (joint author). *See* Hurst, Jacqui

**Sagaria, Mary Ann Danowitz** (editor)

Empowering Women: Leadership Development Strategies on Campus. Reviewed by Linda Forrest. *NWSA Journal* 2, No. 3 (Summer 1990):497-499

Empowering Women: Leadership Development Strategies on Campus. Reviewed by Oliva M. Espin. *Psychology of Women Quarterly* 14, No. 3 (September 1990):439-440

**Saget, Bob** (about)

Bob Saget's Funniest Family Stories. Interview. Ellen Byron. *Redbook* 175, No. 5 (September 1990):80-82

**Sagot, Ana Elena Obando Montserrat**

Meeting with Repression: 2nd Encuentro Lesbico-Feminista de Latinoamerica y El Caribe. *off our backs* 20, No. 8 (August/September 1990):2

**Sagot, Ana Elena Obando Montserrat** (interview)

Feminism in the Barrios of Costa Rica. Carol Anne Douglas. *off our backs* 20, No. 3 (March 1990):1-3+

**Sahag, John** (about). *See also* Beauty Culture, "Who Cuts Who"

**Sahgal, Nayantara**

Storm in Chandigarh. Reviewed by Marina Budhos. *Belles Lettres* 6, No. 1 (Fall 1990):24-25

**Sahni, P. S.** (joint author). *See* Jain, J. P.

**Sailing**

Good Sports. Joanne Mattera. *Glamour* (June 1990):78

**St. Valentine's Day – Cookery**

Sweet Nothings. Elaine Gonzales. *Ladies' Home Journal* 107, No. 2 (February 1990):158-160

**Saint James, Susan** (about)

Star Gazing. *Family Circle* 103, No. 4 (March 13, 1990):81-82

**Saint Laurent, Yves** (about). *See also under* Fashion Designers; Fashion Designers, "Predictions"; Talley, André Leon

Haute Bijoux. Jon Etra. *Harper's Bazaar* (September 1990):206

New Year's Yves. *Vogue* (January 1990):186-189

**Sajbel, Maureen**

Affairs to Remember. *Harper's Bazaar* (August 1990):174+

Best Boutiques. *Harper's Bazaar* (October 1990):67-80

**Salaam, Kalamu ya**

Young Mother Blues #1/T.'s tune. Poem. *Iris* 24 (Fall-Winter 1990):IFC

**Salads**

Main-Dish Salads. *Ladies' Home Journal* 107, No. 7 (July 1990):114-118

Nutrition Now: The Perfect Salad. *Redbook* 175, No. 3 (July 1990):116-121

**Salaries.** *See* Wages

**Salazar, Claudia**

Rigoberta's Narrative and the New Practice of Oral History. *Women & Language* 13, No. 1 (Fall 1990):7-8

**Salcido, Angela** (about)

Angela. Shirley Steshinsky. *Glamour* (March 1990):268-271+

**Salem, Dorothy C.**

Black Women's Studies: A White Woman's Personal Journey. *Sage* 6, No. 1 (Summer 1989):67-68

**Salerno-Sonnenberg, Nadja** (about). *See also* Musicians

**Sales**

Sales or Service? Paul Brooks. *Executive Female* 13, No. 5 (September-October 1990):53-54

**Sales, Ruby**

A Letter from Ruby Sales. *off our backs* 20, No. 8 (August/September 1990):25

**Sales, Ruby** (interview)

In Our Own Words. *The Women's Review of Books* 7, No. 5 (February 1990):24-25

**Salesmanship.** *See* Selling

**Sales Presentations.** *See* Selling

**Saline, Carol**

The Philadelphia Experiment. *Lear's* (March 1990):94-101

**Salisbury, Jan** (joint author). *See* Remick, Helen

**Salk, Lee**

Adolescent Rebellion . . . Or Sheer Defiance? *McCall's* 117, No. 10 (July 1990):56

After-School Jobs: Are They Good for Kids? *McCall's* 118, No. 1 (October 1990):102-106

Babies, Birds and Bees. *McCall's* 117, No. 8 (May 1990):65

Fear of Fat: How Young Can It Start? *McCall's* 117, No. 11 (August 1990):65

Homework: Should Parents Help? *McCall's* 118, No. 2 (November 1990):56

Raising Boys, Raising Girls. *McCall's* 118, No. 3 (December 1990):84-86

R-Rated Movies: Should Children Watch? *McCall's* 117, No. 9 (June 1990):48

What to Do When a Child Won't Read. *McCall's* 117, No. 7 (April 1990):31

When a Parent Plays Favorites. *McCall's* 117, No. 12 (September 1990):68

**Salmans, Sandra**

Pygmalion in Pinstripes. *Lear's* (April 1990):30-33

**Salmon, Dena K.**

The Comfort and Joy of Family Rituals. *Working Mother* (December 1990):48-52

Twenty-One Ways to Soothe a Baby. *Working Mother* 13, No. 9 (September 1990):70-74

**Salmon, Marylynn** (joint author). *See* Shammas, Carole

**Salo, Elaine**

Not Either an Experimental Doll: The Separate Worlds of Three South African Women. Book Review. *Women's Studies International Forum* 13, No. 3 (1990):274-275

**Salomyn, Shay**

Black Women in Sudan. *off our backs* 20, No. 3 (March 1990):8

**Salt**

Food: Salt. Jeffrey Steingarten. *Vogue* (August 1990):266-272

**Salter, Mary Jo**

Unfinished Painting. Reviewed by Lee Upton. *Belles Lettres* 5, No. 3 (Spring 1990):24-25

**Saltpaw, C. R.**

Back Talk: Corporate Sisters. *Essence* 21, No. 3 (July 1990):114

**Saltzman, Janet**

Feminist Sociology. Reviewed by Barbara Lou Fenby. *AFFILIA* 5, No. 1 (Spring 1990):113-114

**Saltzman, Linda E.**

Family Violence in Cross-cultural Perspective. Book Review. *Journal of Marriage and the Family* 52, No. 1 (February 1990):280-281

**Salvatore, Diane**

A Memory of Dancing. Short story. *Ladies' Home Journal* 107, No. 3 (March 1990):132-138

Where the Heart Is. Short story. *Redbook* 176, No. 2 (December 1990):54-60

**Salvino, Dana D. Nelson**

Born for Liberty: A History of Women in America. Book Review. *Belles Lettres* 5, No. 3 (Spring 1990):28

Declaration of Interdependence. *Belles Lettres* 5, No. 3 (Spring 1990):28

**Salwen, Laura V.**

The Myth of the Wicked Stepmother. *Women and Therapy* 10, Nos. 1/2 (1990):117-125

**Salzburg (Austria) – Mozart Festival, 1991**

Sounds of Music. Bibliography. Diana Burgwyn. *Harper's Bazaar* (November 1990):74+

**Salzman, Jeff** (joint author). *See* Calano, Jimmy

**Sam, Agnes.** *See* Radio Broadcasting – Plays

Jesus Is Indian and Other South African Stories. Reviewed by Joyoti Grech. *Spare Rib* No. 210 (March 1990):34

**Sammons, Mary Beth**

Woman Who Make a Difference. *Family Circle* 103, No. 11 (August 14, 1990):17-19

**Samon, Katherine Ann**

Apartment Life, 1990. *Mademoiselle* (April 1990):220-221, 256-259, 264

The Brash Pack. *Working Woman* (August 1990):66-69

**Samson, Stacie**

Mixed Blood. Poem. *Sinister Wisdom* 41 (Summer-Fall 1990):45-46

**Samuels, Annette J.**

Back Talk: A Betrayal of Trust. *Essence* 21, No. 8 (December 1990):142

**Samundra, Shashi**

The Cover-Up. Short story. *Manushi* 56 (January-February 1990):38-39

**San Antonio – Mayors.** *See* Texas – Mayors

**Sánchez, Elba Rosario**

Premonición. Poem. *Frontiers* 11, No. 1 (1990):65

**Sanchez, Sonia**

An Anthem (For the ANC and Brandywine Peace Community). Poem. *Essence* 21, No. 5 (September 1990):125

Haiku. Poem. *Essence* 21, No. 5 (September 1990):118

Poem No. 8. Poem. *Essence* 21, No. 1 (May 1990):205

**Sanchez, Sonia** (about). *See* Writers – Interviews, "Graceful Passages"

**Sancier, Betty.** *See also* Meyer, Carol and Young, Alma (editors), "On the Bias."

Editorial: Feminist Paradoxes and the Need for New Agendas. *AFFILIA* 5, No. 2 (Summer 1990):5-7

Editorial: On Feminism in Action. *AFFILIA* 5, No. 4 (Winter 1990):5-7

Editorial: Promoting Reproductive Rights in 1990. *AFFILIA* 5, No. 1 (Spring 1990):5

Editorial: What's in a Name? *AFFILIA* 5, No. 3 (Fall 1990):5-7

**Sand, George** (about)

The Thinking Bosom. Barbara Griffith Furst. *Belles Lettres* 5, No. 2 (Winter 1990):8

**Sandahl, Jette** (joint author). *See* Ipsen, Merete

**Sandar, Ramamani**

The Status of Women and Family Planning Acceptance: Some Field Results. *Journal of Family Welfare* 36, No. 2 (June 1990):60-68

**Sanday, Peggy Reeves**

Fraternity Gang Rape: Sex, Brotherhood, and Privilege on Campus. Reviewed by Marjorie Lipsyte. *New Directions for Women* 19, No. 6 (November-December 1990):22

**Sandelowski, Margarete J.**

Failures of Volition: Female Agenda and Infertility in Historical Perspective. Notes. *Signs* 15, No. 3 (Spring 1990):475-499

Fault Lines: Infertility and Imperiled Sisterhood. *Feminist Studies* 16, No. 1 (Spring 1990):33-51

**Sanders, Dori**

Clover. Reviewed by Jane Smiley. *Vogue* (April 1990):278-281

Clover. Reviewed by Paula Giddings. *Essence* 21, No. 5 (September 1990):52

**Sanders, Dori** (about)

A Peach Farmer's Harvest: Book Royalties. Wendy Cole. *McCall's* 118, No. 2 (November 1990):49

**Sanders, Judith A.,** Wiseman, Richard L., and Matz, S. Irene

The Influence of Gender on Reported Disclosure, Interrogation, and Nonverbal Immediacy in Same-Sex Dyads: An Empirical Study of Uncertainty

Reduction Theory. *Women's Studies in Communication* 13, No. 2 (Fall 1990):85-108

**Sanders, Kimberly Wallace**

Collected Poems of May Miller. Book Review. *Sage* 6, No. 2 (Fall 1989):62-63

**Sanders, Leslie**

Their Place on the Stage: Black Women Playwrights in America. Book Review. *Canadian Women's Studies* 11, No. 1 (Spring 1990):108-109

**Sanders, Marlene** and Rock, Marcia

Waiting for Prime Time: The Women of Television News. Reviewed by Marguerite J. Moritz. *Frontiers* 11, Nos. 2-3 (1990):124

**Sanders, Robin**

A Delicate Balance: "The Trick Is Not to Panic." *Ladies' Home Journal* 107, No. 3 (March 1990):163-166

Hush, Little Baby. *Ladies' Home Journal* 107, No. 3 (March 1990):88

**Sanders, Rose M.** (about). *See* De Veaux, Alexis, Milloy, Marilyn, and Ross, Michael Erik

**San Diego (CA) – Suicide Study**

San Diego Suicide Study: The Adolescents. Charles L. Rich, Miriam Sherman, and Richard C. Fowler. *Adolescence* 25, No. 100 (Winter 1990):855-865

**Sandinistas**

Report from Nicaragua. Millie Thayer. *Spare Rib* No. 210 (March 1990):12-14

Sandinistas – Still Making Revolution. *Spare Rib* 219 (December 1990-January 1991):18-20

**Sandler, Bunny** (about)

Conflict in Academia: Why Was Bunny Sandler Sacked? Peggy Simpson. *Ms.* 1, No. 3 (November/December 1990):86-87

**Sandler, Roberta**

The Puppy that Didn't Know How to Quit. *Good Housekeeping* 211, No. 4 (October 1990):100

**Sandlin, Martha** (joint producer). *See* Abrash, Barbara

**Sandmaier, Marian**

Health Express News. *Mademoiselle* (February 1990):112-114

Health News. Bibliography. *Mademoiselle* (October 1990):124

Health News. *Mademoiselle* (June 1990):130; (September 1990):200

Health News. *Working Woman* (September 1990):201; (November 1990):148; (December 1990):92

**Sandroff, Ronni**

Facing Fears about Mammograms. *McCall's* 117, No. 12 (September 1990):25-29

How Ethical Is American Business? *Working Woman* (September 1990):113-116

Why It Won't Be Business as Usual. *Working Woman* (January 1990):58-62

Woman Loses Gap, Gains Toothy Grin. *McCall's* 118, No. 2 (November 1990):60-69

You Like Your Job. But Should You Leave It? *Working Woman* (May 1990):81-85

**Sands, Josefina**

Working: Black Women at Work. *Essence* 21, No. 1 (May 1990):58-61

**Sands, Kathleen Mullen**

Writing Cultures: An Interdisciplinary Approach to Developing Cross-Cultural Courses. *Women's Studies Quarterly* 18, Nos. 3-4 (Fall-Winter 1990):100-118

**Sands, Kathleen Mullen** (joint author). *See* Bataille, Gretchen M.

**Sandstrom, Kent L.** (joint author). *See* Fine, Gary Alan

**Sandwiches.** *See* Cookery (Sandwiches)

Sandwiches that Sizzle. *Glamour* (September 1990):340-341+

**Sanford, Adelaide**

Back Talk: An Education Agenda. *Essence* 21, No. 4 (August 1990):126

**Sanford, Adelaide L.** (about). *See* De Veaux, Alexis, Milloy, Marilyn, and Ross, Michael Erik

**Sanford, Barbara**

A Package From My Father: Remembering and Recovering From Childhood Sexual Abuse. *Women and Environments* 12, No. 2 (Spring 1990): 13-15

**Sanford, Linda Tschirhart** and Donovan, Mary Ellen

Women and Self-Esteem. Reviewed by Charlotte Hettena and Siroon P. Shahinian. *Psychology of Women Quarterly* 14, No. 4 (December 1990):620-621

**Sanford, Winifred M.**

Windfall and Other Stories. Reviewed by Barbara Horn. *Belles Lettres* 5, No. 3 (Spring 1990):23

**San Francisco – Earthquake, 1989**

The Earthquake Took Everything I Owned. Carol Kino. *Glamour* (March 1990):161

San Francisco: Shaken but Undefeated. Cindy Hampton. *Ladies' Home Journal* 107, No. 1 (January 1990):16+

**San Francisco – Women's Building**

Despite Quake Damage, Women's Building Essential Haven. Linda Roman. *New Directions for Women* 19, No. 1 (January/February 1990):6

**Sang, Barbara E.**

Reflections of Midlife Lesbians on Their Adolescence. *Journal of Women and Aging* 2, No. 2 (1990):111-117

**Sangari, KumKum** and Vaid, Sudesh (editors)

Recasting Women: Essays in Colonial History. Reviewed by Chandra T. Mohanty and Satya P. Mohanty. *The Women's Review of Books* 7, No. 6 (March 1990):19-21

**Sanger, Margaret** (about)

Margaret Sanger: An Alternate View. Jill Benderly. *On the Issues* 14 (1990):13

Margaret Sanger: Militant, Pragmatist, Visionary. Lawrence Lader. *On the Issues* 14 (1990):11-12+

"To Create a Race of Thoroughbreds:" Margaret Sanger and *The Birth Control Review*. John M. Murphy. *Women's Studies in Communication* 13, No. 1 (Spring 1990): 23-45

**Sangster, Joan**

Dreams of Equality: Women on the Canadian Left, 1920-1950. Reviewed by Clare Collins. *Resources for Feminist Research* 19, No. 1 (March 1990):8

**Sankey, Charlotte**

Narmada People Demand Their Land Rights. *Spare Rib* 219 (December 1990-January 1991):68-69

**Santa Fe Performing Arts School and Company**

At Center Stage. Laurie Tarkan. *Lear's* (April 1990):84-91

**Santiago, Roberto**

Sex, Lust & Videotapes. *Essence* 21, No. 7 (November 1990):62-64+

**Sapiro, Virginia**

Women, Political Action, and Political Participation. Reviewed by Joan C. Tronto. *NWSA Journal* 2, No. 3 (Summer 1990):492-495

**Sapphire**

American Dreams. Poem. *Sinister Wisdom* 42 (Winter 1990-1991):22-28

**Sappho**

Ode to Aphrodite. Poem. *off our backs* 20, No. 7 (July 1990):14

**Sappho – Criticism and Interpretation**

Sappho's Gaze: Fantasies of a Goddess and Young Man. Eva Stehle. *Differences* 2, No. 1 (Spring 1990):88-125

**Sappho** (about)

The Other Sappho. By Ellen Frye. Reviewed by Kore Archer. *off our backs* 20, No. 7 (July 1990):14

Sappho: Rediscovering Lesbian Space. Jorjet Harper. *Hot Wire* 6, No. 3 (September 1990):48-49

**Sara**

ASL Interpreting for Concerts: What Producers Should Know. *Hot Wire* 6, No. 3 (September 1990):18-19+

**Sarabhai, Mallika**

Shakti: Power of Women. Reviewed by Joyoti Grech and Tanika Gupta. *Spare Rib* 219 (December 1990-January 1991):36

**Saraceno, Chiara**

Women, Family, and the Law, 1750-1942. *Journal of Family History* 15, No. 4 (October 1990):427-442

**Saracino, Mary**

On Being Italian-American: An Introspection. *Sinister Wisdom* 41 (Summer-Fall 1990):105-110

**Sarkozi, Julie**

So, She Came Here. Poem. *Hecate* 16, Nos. 1-2 (1990):61-62

Untitled. Poem. *Hecate* 16, Nos. 1-2 (1990):64

**Sarris, Greg**

Strawberry Festival. *NWSA Journal* 2, No. 3 (Summer 1990):408-424

**Sartain, Emily** (about)

The Art Education of Emily Sartain. Phyllis Peet. *Woman's Art Journal* 11, No. 1 (Spring-Summer 1990):9-15

**Sarton, May**

After the Stroke. Reviewed by Carol Anne Douglas. *off our backs* 20, No. 10 (November 1990):12

The Education of Harriet Hatfield. Reviewed by Pat Coleman. *Spare Rib* No. 210 (March 1990):34

**Sarton, May** (about)

May Sarton Revisited. By Elizabeth Evans. Reviewed by Loralee MacPike. *NWSA Journal* 2, No. 4 (Autumn 1990):669-674

**Sasmore, Jeanette**

Breast Disease for Gynecologists. Book Review. *Health Care for Women International* 11, No. 2 (1990):233-234

Premenstrual, Postpartum and Menopausal Mood Disorders. Book Review. *Health Care for Women International* 11, No. 2 (1990):234

**Sati**. *See* Suttee

**Satire**

Asian Valley Boy: A Monologue. Patrick Lee. *Out/Look* No. 9 (Summer 1990):18-19

**Satow, Susan** (joint author). *See* Beard, Lillian McLean

**Satran, Pamela Redmond**

How to *Really* Enjoy Your Kids. *Ladies' Home Journal* 107, No. 11 (November 1990):146-151

Private Lives. *Family Circle* 103, No. 2 (February 1, 1990):31-32+

6 Rules for Summer Lovers. *Glamour* (May 1990):248-249+

Shop Smart. *Redbook* 175, No. 4 (August 1990):95

Shortcuts to Life. *Glamour* (June 1990):234-236

The True Spirit of Christmas. *Glamour* (December 1990):228-231+

**Satterfield, Janet** (joint author). *See* Doran, Terry

**Saudi Arabia.** *See also* Persian Gulf War, 1990-1991

**Saudi Arabia – Persian Gulf War, 1990-1991**

Escape from Kuwait. *Glamour* (November 1990):104-108

**Saudi Arabia – Status of Women**

The Middle East Crisis: A Dilemma for Women: Democracy, Kings, and Sexual Apartheid in Saudi Arabia. Marie de Santis. *off our backs* 20, No. 9 (October 1990):8

**Saunders, Beatrice.** *See* Meyer, Carol and Young, Alma (editors), "On the Bias."

**Saunders, Constance** (about). *See* Fashion Designers, "Top Women Designers"

**Saunders, Edward J.** and Saunders, Jeanne A.

Drug Therapy in Pregnancy: The Lessons of Diethylstilbestrol, Thalidomide, and Bendectin. *Health Care for Women International* 11, No. 4 (1990):423-432

**Saunders, Gil**

The Nude: A New Perspective. Reviewed by Sylvia Moore. *New Directions for Women* 19, No. 6 (November-December 1990):24

**Saunders, Jeanne A.** (joint author). *See* Saunders, Edward J.

**Saunders, Julia**

A Writer's Friends and Associates: Notes from the Correspondence in the Zora Cross Papers. *Hecate* 16, Nos. 1-2 (1990):90-96

**Saunders, Kate** (editor)

Revenge. Reviewed by Natasha Moar. *Spare Rib* 219 (December 1990-January 1991):41

**Saunders, Kay**

Recent Women's Studies Scholarship, 1: History. *Hecate* 16, Nos. 1-2 (1990):171-183

**Saunders, Margaret**

Canoe Country and Snowshoe Country. Book Review. *Iris* 23 (Spring-Summer 1990):77-76

A History of Their Own: Women in Europe from Prehistory to the Present. Book Review. *Iris* 24 (Fall-Winter 1990):60-65

**Saunders, Michael**

Brothers: It Begins with Me. *Essence* 21, No. 4 (August 1990):40-41

**Saura, Carlos** (about). *See* Spain – Culture and Society

**Saurer, Edith**

The Foundlings of Milan: Abandoned Children and Their Parents from the Seventeenth to the Nineteenth Centuries. Book Review. *Gender & History* 2, No. 3 (Autumn 1990):356-358

**Sauter, Sandra** (about)

Feng Shui. D. M. Pusateri. *Executive Female* 13, No. 5 (September-October 1990):47-50

**Savara, Mira**

Income Generating Programmes for Women: Some Pitfalls. *Manushi* 58 (May-June 1990):30-33

**Saving and Investment.** *See also* Financial Planning; Investing; Junk Bonds; Stocks

Awaiting a Nine-Percent Solution. Susan Scherreik. *Lear's* (November 1990):36-38

Economies. Bibliography. Marion Asnes. *Lear's* (September 1990):42

Economies. Marion Asnes. *Lear's* (October 1990):44; (November 1990):50; (December 1990):44

Lear's Bulletin. Bibliography. Marion Asnes. *Lear's* (January 1990):38

Lear's Bulletin. Marion Asnes. *Lear's* (March 1990):44; (April 1990):36; (July 1990):32; (August 1990):32

More for Your Money. Barbara Gilder Quint. *Glamour* (May 1990):160-162; (December 1990):118-121

More for Your Money: What Should You Do With $1,000 Savings? Barbara Gilder Quint. *Glamour* (January 1990):50-53

Saving Grace: Leave It to Boomer? Patricia O'Toole. *Lear's* (July 1990):22-23

Smart Investor: Last-Minute Tax Savings. Nancy Dunnan. *Lear's* (March 1990):36-38

10 Ways to Increase Your Money Power. Andrea Rock. *Ladies' Home Journal* 107, No. 11 (November 1990):176-180+

" The Worst Money Mistake I Ever Made . . ." Barbara Gilder Quint. *Glamour* (July 1990):83-85

When the Dow Turns Down. Nancy Dunnan. *Lear's* (October 1990):34-36

The Year of Living Cautiously. Nancy Dunnan. *Lear's* (June 1990):38-40

Your Money. Barbara Gilder Quint. *Family Circle* 103, No. 1 (January 9, 1990):24+

Your Money. *Good Housekeeping* 211, No. 3 (September 1990):296; 211, No. 4 (October 1990):252

Your Money. *Working Woman* (September 1990):88-90; (October 1990):58-60; (November 1990):81-84; (December 1990):40

**Saving and Thrift**

Why We Can't Throw Anything Away. Nancy Eberle. *Ladies' Home Journal* 107, No. 3 (March 1990):66

**Savoca, Nancy** (director)

True Love. Reviewed by Marina Heung. *New Directions for Women* 19, No. 2 (March/April 1990):13

**Saward, Jill**

Rape: My Story. Reviewed by Maureen O'Hara. *Spare Rib* 219 (December 1990-January 1991):39-40

**Sawer, Marian**

Sisters in Suits. Reviewed by Lois Bryson. *Australian Feminist Studies* No. 12 (Summer 1990):133-136

**Sawyer, Diane** (about). *See also* Television Journalists—Networking

**Sawyer, Robin**

Censorship: NEA Denies Grants to Lesbians and Gays. *off our backs* 20, No. 8 (August/September 1990):5

NOW's National Conference. *off our backs* 20, No. 8 (August/September 1990):4

**Saxton, Marsha** (interview)

A Network of Disabled Women. Carolann Barrett. *Woman of Power* 18 (Fall 1990):31-34

**Sayers, Janet** and others (editors)

Engels Revisited: New Feminist Essays. Reviewed by Kathryn Russell. *Signs* 15, No. 2 (Winter 1990):398-400

**Sayings.** *See* Aphorisms and Apothegms

**Sayne, Pamela**

Housing Language, Housing Reality? *Canadian Women's Studies* 11, No. 2 (Fall 1990):6

Women, Human Settlements and Housing. Book Review. *Resources for Feminist Research* 19, No. 1 (March 1990):42-43

Women in Toronto Creating Housing: Participation and Process. *Canadian Women's Studies* 11, No. 2 (Fall 1990):38-41

**Scaasi, Arnold** (about). *See* Fashion Designers, "Battle-Weary Designers"

**Scadron, Arlene** (editor)

On Their Own: Widows and Widowhood in the American Southwest, 1848-1939. Reviewed by Manuel G. Gonzales. *Tulsa Studies in Women's Literature* 9, No. 1 (Spring 1990):152-156

**Scafe, Suzanne**

Bake-Face and Other Guava Stories. add. *Spare Rib* No. 209 (February 1990):31

**Scafuro, Adele**

Discourses of Sexual Violation in Mythic Accounts and Dramatic Versions of "The Girl's Tragedy." *Differences* 2, No. 1 (Spring 1990):126-159

**Scales-Trent, Judy**

Bodies of Water. Book Review. *The Women's Review of Books* 7, No. 12 (September 1990):15

Produced and Abandoned. *The Women's Review of Books* 7, No. 12 (September 1990):15

**Scandinavia—Feminist Movement**

Feminism in Scandinavia. Beth Reba Weise. *off our backs* 20, No. 3 (March 1990):5-7

**Scandron, Arlene** (editor)

On Their Own: Widows and Widowhood in the American Southwest, 1848-1939. Reviewed by Helena Z. Lopata. *Gender and Society* 4, No. 1 (March 1990):103-105

**Scandura, Janette**

Enterprise: Beefing Up a Skinny Business. *Working Woman* (February 1990):53-58

Loosen Up! *Redbook* 175, No. 1 (May 1990):116-119

Pioneer Intern Program Teaches Basic Work Skills. *Working Woman* (January 1990):76

**Scandura, Janette** (joint author). *See* King, Mary E.

**Scandura, Jani**

Fitness. *Vogue* (October 1990):232+

My Year Without Sex. *Mademoiselle* (July 1990):85-87

**Scanlon, Joan** (editor)

Surviving the Blues. Reviewed by Joyoti Grech. *Spare Rib* 219 (December 1990-January 1991):40

**Scarves**

High Tied. *Harper's Bazaar* (November 1990):132-137

Tie One On. Lois Joy Johnson. *Ladies' Home Journal* 107, No. 8 (August 1990):112-116

**Scates, Maxine**

Toluca Street. Reviewed by Annie Finch. *Belles Lettres* 5, No. 4 (Summer 1990):30-31

**Scavullo, Francesco**

Body & Soul. *Harper's Bazaar* (October 1990):192-199

**Schaberg, Jane**

The Illegitimacy of Jesus: A Feminist Theological Interpretation of the Infancy Narratives. Reviewed by Deborah Ann Light. *Ms.* 1, No. 2 (September/October 1990):27

**Schaberg, Jane** (joint author). *See* Martin, Clarice J.

**Schafer, Sylvia** (joint author). *See* Christian, Barbara

**Schaffer, Kay**

Postmodernism and History: A Reply to Marian Aveling. *Australian Feminist Studies* No. 11 (Autumn 1990):91-94

**Schaffner, Perdita**

Jazz Cleopatra: Josephine Baker in Her Time. Book Review. *New Directions for Women* 19, No. 3 (May/June 1990):25

**Schall, Deborah** and Duquin, Lorene Hanley

Young Mother's Story: "But for the Grace of God." *Redbook* 176, No. 2 (December 1990):74-80

**Schama, Simon**

Citizens: A Chronicle of the French Revolution. Reviewed by Susan P. Conner. *Journal of Women's History* 1, No. 3 (Winter 1990):244-260

**Schatz, Carol**

London, Paris, Rome: Dressing Native. *Mademoiselle* (September 1990):140

Trains: All Aboard for Romance. Bibliography. *Mademoiselle* (October 1990):76-78

**Schaumburger, Nancy Engbretsen**

Charades. Book Review. *Belles Lettres* 5, No. 2 (Winter 1990):14

Her Infinite Variety. *Belles Lettres* 5, No. 4 (Summer 1990):23

The Message to the Planet. Book Review. *Belles Lettres* 5, No. 4 (Summer 1990):23

**Schechter, Laurie**

Living. *Vogue* (July 1990):133-134; (November 1990):313-315

View. *Vogue* (January 1990):39

Vogue's View. *Vogue* (October 1990):131+; (November 1990):121+

**Schechter, Laurie** (editor)

Living: Christmas in the Country. *Vogue* (December 1990):241-245

View: Katherine Hamnett. *Vogue* (August 1990):111-120

View: The New Youthquake. *Vogue* (September 1990):137+

**Schecter, Arnold** (joint author). *See* Phuong, Nguyen Thi Ngoc

**Scheele, Adele**

Career Strategies: Burned Out. Can You Get Fired Up Again? *Working Woman* (October 1990):46-48

Career Strategies: Male Bonding: Can You Beat It? *Working Woman* (December 1990):30-32

Career Strategies: Promises, Promises. Can You Make Your Boss Deliver? *Working Woman* (July 1990):26-28

Career Strategies: Same Job, New Boss. Can You Make It Work? *Working Woman* (June 1990):22-24

Career Strategies: Should You Push Hard for a Promotion? *Working Woman* (May 1990):34-37

Career Strategies: The Flash Factor: Can You Electrify Your Image? *Working Woman* (September 1990):76-78

Career Strategies: The Power of Small Talk: How to Schmooze Successfully. *Working Woman* (November 1990):67-68

Career Strategies: Your Boss Just Stole Your Idea. Can You Get It Back? *Working Woman* (April 1990):30-32

You've Fallen Out of Favor. Can You Win It Back? *Working Woman* (August 1990):28-30

**Scheffler, Judith A.** (editor)

Walltappings: An Anthology of Writings by Women Prisoners. Reviewed by Sue Mahan. *NWSA Journal* 2, No. 2 (Spring 1990):320-323

**Scheinmann, Vivan**

Daughter's Zeal Revives Mother's Activist Spirit. *New Directions for Women* 19, No. 1 (January/February 1990):18

**Schenck, Celeste** (joint editor). *See* Brodzki, Bella

**Schenk, Leslee**

Tour de Tater. *Women's Sports and Fitness* 12, No. 7 (October 1990):29-31

**Schere, Laura**

Four Jailed in Court Demo. *New Directions for Women* 19, No. 3 (May/June 1990):metrö

**Scherreik, Susan**

Awaiting a Nine-Percent Solution. *Lear's* (November 1990):36-38

**Scheyetl, Anna**

The Oppression of Caring: Women Caregivers of Relatives with Mental Illness. *AFFILIA* 5, No. 1 (Spring 1990):32-48

**Schichor, Aric**, Beck, Arne, Bernstein, Bruce, and Crabtree, Ben

Seat Belt Use and Stress in Adolescents. *Adolescence* 25, No. 100 (Winter 1990):773-779

**Schick, Írvin Cemil**

The Colonial Harem. Book Review. *Feminist Studies* 16, No. 2 (Summer 1990):345-380

Europe's Myths of Orient. Book Review. *Feminist Studies* 16, No. 2 (Summer 1990):345-380

Images of Women: The Portrayal of Women in Photography of the Middle East, 1860-1950. Book Review. *Feminist Studies* 16, No. 2 (Summer 1990):345-380

Inscriptions, nos. 3/4 (1988). Periodical review. *Feminist Studies* 16, No. 2 (Summer 1990):345-380

**Schiebinger, Londa**

The Mind Has No Sex? Women in the Origins of Modern Science. Reviewed by Anne Fausto-Sterling. *The Women's Review of Books* 7, No. 7 (April 1990):13-14

The Mind Has No Sex? Women in the Origins of Modern Science. Reviewed by Nancy Leys Stepan. *Gender & History* 2, No. 3 (Autumn 1990):337-342

**Schiffer, Claudia** (about)

Autumn Beauty. *Harper's Bazaar* (September 1990):246-249

Sexy, S'il Vous Plai3t! *Mademoiselle* (January 1990):126-133

**Schifter, Helen Lee**

Shopping Spree. *Harper's Bazaar* (October 1990):62-64+

**Schiller, Phyllis**

America Entertains. *McCall's* 117, No. 10 (July 1990):112

The Art of the Menorah. *McCall's* 118, No. 3 (December 1990):31-33

**Schilmoeller, Gary L.** (joint author). *See* Baranowski, Marc D.

**Schindler, Rick**

Classics Illustrated Redux. *McCall's* 117, No. 8 (May 1990):62

**Schine, Cathleen**

Vogue Arts: Television. *Vogue* (August 1990):222-224; (September 1990):434-436; (October 1990):260+

**Schlau, Stacey** (joint author). *See* Arenal, Electa

**Schlissel, Lillian**

Far from Home: Families of the Westward Journey. Reviewed by Lynn Wenzel. *New Directions for Women* 19, No. 2 (March/April 1990):14

Relations of Rescue: The Search for Female Authority in the American West, 1874-1939. Book Review. *The Women's Review of Books* 7, No. 12 (September 1990):18

Saved from a Fate Worse Than Death? *The Women's Review of Books* 7, No. 12 (September 1990):18

**Schlondorff, Volker**

The Handmaid's Tale. Reviewed by Laura Flanders. *New Directions for Women* 19, No. 3 (May/June 1990):7

The Handmaid's Tale. Reviewed by Rukhsana Ahmad. *Spare Rib* 218 (November 1990):19

**Schlüpmann, Heide**

Melodrama and Social Drama in the Early German Cinema. *Camera Obscura* No. 22 (January 1990):73-88

**Schmidt, Erik**

Dropped from the Pack. *Women's Sports and Fitness* 12, No. 3 (April 1990):44-55

**Schmidt, Joanne**

She Came to Stay. Book Review. *Belles Lettres* 6, No. 1 (Fall 1990):46

Trio Life Goes Adrift. *Belles Lettres* 6, No. 1 (Fall 1990):46

**Schmidt, L. J.** (joint author). *See* White, George L. (Jr.)

**Schmidt-Rodolfo, Sophie** (about)

Goodbye to Winter: The Autobiography of Sophie Schmidt-Rodolfo. Edited by Delores S. Feria. Reviewed by Barbara M. Posadas. *Women's Studies International Forum* 13, No. 4 (1990):409-410

**Schmitz, Betty** (joint author). *See* Beck, Evelyn Torton

**Schmitz, Kenneth** (joint author). *See* Roberts, Gregory

**Schnatter, Mary Jo**

The After-Sex Pill. *McCall's* 118, No. 3 (December 1990):26

**Schneberg, Willa**

Collect Call from a Pay Phone in a "Maon Olim." Poem. *Bridges* 1, No. 1 (Spring 1990): 36

Expanded/Extended Memory. Poem. *Bridges* 1, No. 1 (Spring 1990): 38

Kaddish for Felix Nussbaum (1904-1944). Poem. *Bridges* 1, No. 1 (Spring 1990): 32-33

Not the Lecture. Poem. *Bridges* 1, No. 1 (Spring 1990): 34

One Friday at the Spatz's. Poem. *Bridges* 1, No. 1 (Spring 1990): 35

The Oral Tradition. Poem. *Bridges* 1, No. 1 (Spring 1990): 37

**Schneider, Carl** (joint author). *See* Schneider, Dorothy

**Schneider, Claudine** (about). *See* Leadership

**Schneider, Dorothy** and Schneider, Carl

The Military: More Than Just a Job? Book Review. *Minerva* 8, No. 4 (Winter 1990):44-48

**Schneider, Susan**

Back to Work After the Baby. *Working Mother* 13, No. 8 (August 1990):28-35

The Trade in Sticky Fingers. *Lear's* (September 1990):38-40

**Schneider, Susan Weidman**

The Anti-Choice Movement: Bad News for Jews. *Lilith* 15, No. 3 (Summer 1990):8-11

Yael Dayan. Interview. *Lilith* 15, No. 4 (Fall 1990):10-15

**Schneller, Johanna**

This Working Life: Work Talk: You Always Bore the One You Love. *Working Woman* (May 1990):134

"Who's That Blonde – and Why Is My Boyfriend Smiling at Her?" *Mademoiselle* (January 1990):1344-135+

**Schnur, Ruth**

Mothers. Book review. *Lilith* 15, No. 4 (Fall 1990):35

**Schnur, Steven**

Daddy's Home: Reflections of a Family Man. Reviewed by Rachel Kadish. *Lilith* 15, No. 4 (Fall 1990):34

**Schnur, Susan**

Into the Future with Rituals from Our Past. *Lilith* 15, No. 3 (Summer 1990):19

Killing Our Sorrows. Bibliography. *Lilith* 15, No. 3 (Summer 1990):15

Marjorie Agosin: A Woman, a Jew and a Chilean. *Lilith* 15, No. 3 (Summer 1990):12

**Schoemer, Karen**

Basia – Coming to America. *Mademoiselle* (September 1990):160

Billy Idol – Rebel With a New Cause. *Mademoiselle* (September 1990):174

Girls with Guitars. *Mademoiselle* (October 1990):112

Music: The Blue Nile. *Mademoiselle* (June 1990):98-101

Son of Sexism. *Mademoiselle* (May 1990):128-130

**Schoemperlen, Diane**

The Wrong Men. Short story. *Mademoiselle* (February 1990):128-131

**Schoen, Linda Allen** and Lazar, Paul

Go Lighter. *Redbook* 175, No. 1 (May 1990):18

What's Best for Your Hair? *Redbook* 174, No. 5 (March 1990):18

**Schofield, Mary Anne**

Arms and the Woman: War, Gender, and Literary Representation. Book Review. *Belles Lettres* 5, No. 4 (Summer 1990):38-39

Miss You: The World War II Letters of Barbara Wooddall Taylor and Charles E. Taylor. Book Review. *Belles Lettres* 5, No. 4 (Summer 1990):39

People Who Are "Too Something." *Belles Lettres* 5, No. 4 (Summer 1990):43-44

War as Women Saw It. *Belles Lettres* 5, No. 4 (Summer 1990):38-39

Wave Me Goodbye: Stories of the Second World War. Book Review. *Belles Lettres* 5, No. 4 (Summer 1990):38-39

Women's Writing in Exile. Book Review. *Belles Lettres* 5, No. 4 (Summer 1990):43-44

**Scholarship – Feminist Perspectives**

Against Gendrification: Agendas for Feminist Scholarship and Teaching in Women's Studies. Susan Fraiman. *Iris* 23 (Spring-Summer 1990):5-9

Multiple Mediations: Feminist Scholarship in the Age of Multinational Reception. Lata Mani. *Feminist Review* No. 35 (Summer 1990):24-41

**Scholarships**

Education: Steps to Studying Smart. Bibliography. *Essence* 21, No. 6 (October 1990):36

**Scholastic Aptitude Test**

The SAT Gender Gap. Excerpt. Leslie R. Wolfe and Phyllis Rosser. *Women & Language* 13, No. 2 (Winter 1990):2-10

**School Buses – Accidents**

Patty's Legacy. Bibliography. Karolyn Nunnalee. *Ladies' Home Journal* 107, No. 4 (April 1990):28-36

**School Districts – Finance**

Who Pays for Posterity? Suzannah Lessard. *Lear's* (December 1990):120-123

**School Promotion.** *See* Promotion (School)

**School Retention.** *See* Promotion (School)

**Schools.** *See also* Segregation in Education

**Schools, Catholic**

The Female Stranger in a Male School. Maria Pallotta-Chiarolli. *Gender and Education* 2, No. 2 (1990):169-183

Symbolizing Society: Stories, Rites and Structure in a Catholic High School. By Nancy Lesko. Reviewed by Robert Burgess. *Gender and Education* 2, No. 2 (1990):256-257

**Schools – Discipline**

Changing Problem Behavior in Schools. By Alex Molnar and Barbara Lindquist. Book Review. *Adolescence* 25, No. 100 (Winter 1990):998

**Schools – Evaluation.** *See also* Chicago – Schools

High Marks. Beth Brophy. *Ladies' Home Journal* 107, No. 12 (December 1990):122-127+

How to Solve Our Teacher Shortage. Eric Goodman. *McCall's* 117, No. 12 (September 1990):104-110+

Parenting: Taking Back Our Schools. Valerie Wilson Wesley. *Essence* 20, No. 10 (February 1990):102+

**Schools – Gender Relations**

Fostering Positive Race, Class, and Gender Dynamics in the Classroom. Lynn Weber Cannon.

*Women's Studies Quarterly* 18, Nos. 1-2 (Spring-Summer 1990):126-134

The Gender Integration Project at Piscataway Township Schools: Quilting a New Pedagogical Patchwork Through Curriculum Re-vision. Verdelle Freeman. *Women's Studies Quarterly* 18, Nos. 1-2 (Spring-Summer 1990):70-77

**Schools – Gender Roles**

The Fear of Feminization: Los Angeles High Schools in the Progressive Era. Victoria Bissell Brown. *Feminist Studies* 16, No. 3 (Fall 1990):493-518

**Schools – Race Relations**

Fostering Positive Race, Class, and Gender Dynamics in the Classroom. Lynn Weber Cannon. *Women's Studies Quarterly* 18, Nos. 1-2 (Spring-Summer 1990):126-134

"White Women, Racism and Anti-Racism": A Women's Studies Course Exploring Racism and Privilege. Ruth Frankenberg. *Women's Studies Quarterly* 18, Nos. 1-2 (Spring-Summer 1990):145-153

**Schools – Student Activities**

Differences in Extracurricular Activity Participation, Achievement, and Attitudes toward School between Ninth-Grade Students Attending Junior High School and Those Attending Senior High School. Vernon D. Gifford. *Adolescence* 25, No. 100 (Winter 1990):799-802

**Schools, Traveling. See also** Study Abroad

**Schoonmaker, Mary Ellen**

Trends of the 90's. *Family Circle* 103, No. 1 (January 9, 1990):40-42

**Schoonmaker, Mary Ellen** (joint author). *See* Hoyt, Michael

**Schor, Mira**

On Failure and Anonymity. *Heresies* 25 (1990):7-9

**Schor, Sandra**

The Great Letter E. Reviewed by Pamela Renner. *Lilith* 15, No. 3 (Summer 1990):24

**Schott, Penelope S.**

On the Edge of Visible Light. Poem. *Iris* 23 (Spring-Summer 1990):inside back cover

Read This to Your Daughter. *Lear's* (June 1990):64-65

**Schrambling, Regina**

Global Kitchens. *Savvy Woman* (November 1990):78-80

**Schreiber, Le Anne**

The Glamour Report: Campus Rape. *Glamour* (September 1990):292-295+

**Schroeder, Jana**

No Job Training in Jail. *New Directions for Women* 19, No. 3 (May/June 1990):4

**Schroeder, Patricia** (about). *See also* Dusky, Lorraine; Leadership, "1990 Women of the Year"

Patricia Schroeder: Uncompromising Free Spirit. Maureen Dowd. *McCall's* 117, No. 9 (June 1990):64

**Schulman, Barbara**

Harassing the Harassers. *The Women's Review of Books* 7, No. 5 (February 1990):27

**Schulman, Candy**

How to get Better Care at a Hospital. *Glamour* (July 1990):44-47

**Schulman, Michael**

What Money Can't Buy. *Working Mother* (December 1990):41-43

**Schulman, Norma**

Interpreting Women's Lives: Feminist Theory and Personal Narratives. Book Review. *Women & Language* 13, No. 2 (Winter 1990):43

**Schulman, Sarah**

After Delores. Reviewed by Linda Semple. *Feminist Review* No. 35 (Summer 1990):119-121

People in Trouble. Reviewed by Farar Elliott. *off our backs* 20, No. 7 (July 1990):13+

People in Trouble. Reviewed by Linda King. *Spare Rib* 219 (December 1990-January 1991):41

People in Trouble. Reviewed by Liz Galst. *The Women's Review of Books* 7, No. 8 (May 1990):19

**Schulman, Sarah** (interview)

Troubled Times. Andrea Freud Loewenstein. *The Women's Review of Books* 7, Nos. 10-11 (July 1990):22-23

**Schultz, Ellen**

The Check's in the Mail – Or Is It? *Savvy Woman* (January 1990):26-27

Nest Eggs for the '90s. *Savvy Woman* (June 1990):22-23

The Only Tax Advice You'll Ever Need. *Savvy Woman* (November 1990):23-24

The Smart Money Adds a Foreign Accent. *Savvy Woman* (March 1990):25-26

**Schultz, Ellen E.**

Among the Bogóbo. *Savvy* (December-January 1991):90

A Savings Plan for Spenders. *Savvy* (December-January 1991):23-24

**Schultz, Jane E.**

Civil Wars: Women and the Crisis of Southern Nationalism. Book Review. *The Women's Review of Books* 7, No. 8 (May 1990):23-24

Defeat on All Fronts. *The Women's Review of Books* 7, No. 8 (May 1990):23-24

**Schultz, Martin**

Divorce Patterns in Nineteenth-Century New England. *Journal of Family History* 15, No. 1 (January 1990):101-115

**Schultz, Nancy M.** (joint author). *See* Gartner, Dorothy

**Schulz, Muriel** (joint author). *See* Wodak, Ruth

**Schulz, Phillip Stephen**

As American as Apple Pie. Excerpt. *Ladies' Home Journal* 107, No. 4 (April 1990):205-208

**Schumacher, Dorin**

Hidden Death: The Sexual Effects of Hysterectomy. *Journal of Women and Aging* 2, No. 2 (1990):49-66

**Schuman, Joan**

Friendly Definitions. Poem. *Sinister Wisdom* 40 (Spring 1990):101

**Schur, Edwin M.**

The Americanization of Sex. Reviewed by Patricia MacCorquodale. *Journal of Marriage and the Family* 52, No. 1 (February 1990):279-280

**Schuyler, Sarah**

Double-dealing Fictions. *Genders* 9 (Fall 1990):75-92

**Schwartz, Felice** (about)

Who Is Felice Schwartz and Why Is She Saying those Terrible Things about Us? Ellen Hopkins. *Working Woman* (October 1990):116-120+

**Schwartz, Gil**

The Big Issue: Safety, Not Size. *Mademoiselle* (October 1990):166-167+

"Hi! I'm Calling from the Car Phone!."..And Other Breaches of High-Tech Etiquette. *Working Woman* (December 1990):66-67

**Schwartz, Judith D.**

Will I Be Able to Have a Baby? *Glamour* (December 1990):222-223+

**Schwartz, Lynn Sharon**

Leaving Brooklyn. Reviewed by Phyllis Ehrenfeld. *New Directions for Women* 19, No. 1 (January/February 1990):25

**Schwartz, Mimi**

Living with Loss, Dreaming of Lace. *Lear's* (October 1990):54-56

**Schwartz, Patricia Roth**

Bitterness and Truth. *Belles Lettres* 5, No. 3 (Spring 1990):3

Blood and Water. Book Review. *Belles Lettres* 5, No. 3 (Spring 1990):3

Changelings. Book Review. *Belles Lettres* 5, No. 3 (Spring 1990):3

Different Kinds of Love. Book Review. *Belles Lettres* 5, No. 3 (Spring 1990):3

With a Fly's Eye, Whale's Wit, and Woman's Heart. Book Review. *Belles Lettres* 5, No. 2 (Winter 1990):12

Lesbian Love in Limbo. *off our backs* 20, No. 6 (June 1990):18-20

My Head Is Opening. Book Review. *Belles Lettres* 5, No. 3 (Spring 1990):3

The Names of the Moons of Mars. Reviewed by Liz Galst. *The Women's Review of Books* 7, No. 4 (January 1990):11

**Schwartz, Pepper** (joint editor). *See* Risman, Barbara J.

**Schwartzman, Allan**

The Looks of Light. *Harper's Bazaar* (January 1990):118-119+

**Schwartzman, Julie**

A Way With Women. Short story. *Mademoiselle* (September 1990):208-214+

**Schwartz-Shea, Peregrine** and Burrington, Debra D.

Free Riding, Alternative Organization and Cultural Feminism: The Case of Seneca Women's Peace Camp. *Women & Politics* 10, No. 3 (1990):1-37

**Schwarz, Evalee** (about)

When a Widow Takes the Helm in a Male-Dominated Industry. Patti Watts. *Executive Female* 13, No. 4 (July-August 1990):18-21

**Schwarz, Michael B.**

Adam, Eve, and the Serpent. Book Review. *Out/Look* No. 7 (Winter 1990):76-81

The Body and Society: Men, Women, and Sexual Renunciation in Early Christianity. Book Review. *Out/Look* No. 7 (Winter 1990):76-81

Law, Sex, and Christian Society in Medieval Europe. Book Review. *Out/Look* No. 7 (Winter 1990):76-81

**Schwarzenegger, Arnold** (about)

Talking with Arnold Schwarzenegger: Tough Man, Tender Heart. Interview. Sally Ogle Davis. *Redbook* 175, No. 5 (September 1990):84-86

**Schweickart, Patsy**

Reflections on NWSA '90. *NWSAction* 3, No. 3 (Fall 1990): 3-4

**Schweitzer, Mary M.**

Inheritance in America: From Colonial Times to the Present. Book Review. *Gender and Society* 4, No. 1 (March 1990):100-101

**Schweitzer, Robert D.** (joint author). *See* Hier, Sally J.

**Schwenck, Deborah**

Toward a Feminist Theory of the State. Book Review. *Women's Rights Law Reporter* 12, No. 3 (Fall 1990): 205-208

**Schweninger, Loren**

Property-Owning Free African-American Women in the South, 1800-70. *Journal of Women's History* 1, No. 3 (Winter 1990):13-44

**Schwimmer, Rosika** (about)

Radical Politics in a Reactionary Age: The Unmaking of Rosika Schwimmer, 1914-1930. Beth S. Wenger. *Journal of Women's History* 2, No. 2 (Fall 1990):66-99

**Science.** See also Research Methodology

Breaking the Barriers: Women and Minorities in the Sciences. Paul E. Gray and Shirley M. McBay. *On the Issues* 15 (Summer 1990):7-9+

Comment on Zita's Review of *The Science Question in Feminism*. Betty C. Safford. *Hypatia* 5, No. 1 (Spring 1990):181-182

On the Insensitivity of Women: Science and the Woman Question in Liberal Italy, 1890-1910. Mary Gibson. *Journal of Women's History* 2, No. 2 (Fall 1990):11-41

Primate Visions: Gender, Race, and Nature in the World of Modern Science. By Donna Haraway. Reviewed by Judith Masters. *The Women's Review of Books* 7, No. 4 (January 1990):18-19

Primate Visions: Gender, Race and Nature in the World of Modern Science. By Donna Haraway. Reviewed by Carol Anne Douglas. *off our backs* 20, No. 7 (July 1990):21-22

Primate Visions: Gender, Race and Nature in the World of Modern Science. By Donna Haraway. Reviewed by Joan M. Gero. *Women's Studies International Forum* 13, No. 6 (1990):609-610

**Science – Bibliographies**

Black Women in Science and Technology: A Selected Bibliography. Ronald Mickens. *Sage* 6, No. 2 (Fall 1989):54

**Science – Feminist Perspectives**

Analogy as Destiny: Cartesian Man and the Woman Reader. Carol H. Cantrell. *Hypatia* 5, No. 2 (Summer 1990):7-19

Beyond Relativism: Moving On – Feminist Struggles. Ann Dugdale. *Australian Feminist Studies* No. 12 (Summer 1990):51-63

Body/Politics: Women and the Discourses of Science. Edited by Mary Jacobus and others. Reviewed by Vera Kolb. *Feminist Collections* 11, No. 4 (Summer 1990):4-8

Comments on Ruth Ginzberg's Paper. Neal Jahren. *Hypatia* 5, No. 1 (Spring 1990):171-177

Feminism and Science. Edited by Nancy Tuana. Reviewed by Vera Kolb. *Feminist Collections* 11, No. 4 (Summer 1990):4-8

Feminism and the Constructions of Knowledge: Speculations on a Subjective Science. Georganne Rundblad. *Women & Language* 13, No. 1 (Fall 1990):53-55

Men, Power and the Exploitation of Women. Jalna Hanmer. *Women's Studies International Forum* 13, No. 5 (1990):443-456

The Mind Has No Sex? Women in the Origins of Modern Science. By Londa Schiebinger. Reviewed by Nancy Leys Stepan. *Gender & History* 2, No. 3 (Autumn 1990):337-342

Philosophical Feminism: A Bibliographic Guide to Critiques of Science. Alison Wylie, Kathleen Okruhlik, Sandra Morton, and Leslie Thielen-Wilson. *Resources for Feminist Research* 19, No. 2 (June 1990):2-36

Sexual Science: The Victorian Construction of Womanhood. By Cynthia Eagle Russett. Reviewed by Nancy Leys Stepan. *Gender & History* 2, No. 3 (Autumn 1990):337-342

Sexual Visions: Images of Gender in Science and Medicine Between the Eighteenth and Twentieth Centuries. By Ludmilla Jordanova. Reviewed by Nancy Leys Stepan. *Gender & History* 2, No. 3 (Autumn 1990):337-342

Utopian Science: Contemporary Feminist Science Theory and Science Fiction by Women. Jane Donawerth. *NWSA Journal* 2, No. 4 (Autumn 1990):535-557

Women's Studies: Science, Violence and Responsibility. Maria Mies. *Women's Studies International Forum* 13, No. 5 (1990):433-441

**Science – History**

The Mind Has No Sex? Women in the Origins of Modern Science. By Londa Schiebinger. Reviewed by Anne Fausto-Sterling. *The Women's Review of Books* 7, No. 7 (April 1990):13-14

Sexual Visions: Images of Gender in Science and Medicine Between the Eighteenth and Twentieth Centuries. By Ludmilla Jordanova. Reviewed by Julia Epstein. *The Women's Review of Books* 7, No. 6 (March 1990):13-14

**Science – Personal Narrative**

Becoming a Scientist: An Important Career Decision. Reatha Clark King. *Sage* 6, No. 2 (Fall 1989):47-50

A Life in Science: Research and Service. Jewel Plummer Cobb. *Sage* 6, No. 2 (Fall 1989):39-43

**Science – Study and Teaching.** See also Robotics

The Development of Scientific Thinking Skills. By Deanna Kuhn, Eric Amsel, and Michael O'Loughlin. Book Review. *Adolescence* 25, No. 98 (Summer 1990):501

Encouraging Girls to Pursue Math and Science Careers. Bibliography. Celia Slom. *McCall's* 117, No. 8 (May 1990):58-60

Increasing the Participation of Black Women in Science and Technology. Shirley Malcom. *Sage* 6, No. 2 (Fall 1989):15-17

Parenting. *Essence* 20, No. 9 (January 1990):90

Saving the Earth: New York to Chicago on a Glass of Salt Water. J. R. Moehringer. *McCall's* 117, No. 7 (April 1990):32

Spaced Out: Into New Dimensions. K. C. Cole. *Lear's* (March 1990):110-111

A Story of Success: The Sciences at Spelman College. Etta Z. Falconer. *Sage* 6, No. 2 (Fall 1989):36-38

### Science – Feminist Perspectives

Reply to Jahren. Ruth Ginzberg. *Hypatia* 5, No. 1 (Spring 1990):178-180

### Science Fiction

Academics in Outer Space. Melissa Scott. *Belles Lettres* 5, No. 4 (Summer 1990):45

Alien to Femininity: Speculative Fiction and Feminist Theory. By Marleen S. Barr. Reviewed by Hoda M. Zaki. *Women's Studies International Forum* 13, No. 3 (1990):277-279

Beyond Elves and Warrior Women: Broadening the Boundaries of Speculative Fiction. Joanne Stato and Jennie Ruby. *off our backs* 20, No. 5 (May 1990):18-19

Feminist Utopias. By Frances Bartkowski. Reviewed by Karen Axness. *Feminist Collections* 11, No. 3 (Spring 1990):5-7

Memories and Visions: Women's Fantasy and Science Fiction. Edited by Susanna Sturgis. Reviewed by Joanne Stato. *off our backs* 20, No. 5 (May 1990):17+

From My Guy to Sci-Fi: Genre and Women's Writing in the Postmodern World. Edited by Helen Carr. Reviewed by Shannon Hengen. *Resources for Feminist Research* 19, No. 1 (March 1990):17

Utopian Science: Contemporary Feminist Science Theory and Science Fiction by Women. Jane Donawerth. *NWSA Journal* 2, No. 4 (Autumn 1990):535-557

The World of Science Fiction. Ursula K. Le Guin. *Ms.* 1, No. 3 (November/December 1990):52-54

Worlds Within Women: Myth and Mythmaking in Fantastic Literature by Women. By Thelma J. Shinn. Reviewed by Hoda M. Zaki. *Women's Studies International Forum* 13, No. 3 (1990):277-279

**Scientific Method.** *See* Animal Behavior; Research Methodology; Science

### Scollard, Jeannette R.

How to Tell a Smart Risk from a Dumb One. *Working Woman* (February 1990):78-79

### Scotland

Grit and Diamonds: Women in Scotland Making History 1980-1990. Edited by Shirley Henderson and Alison Mackay. Reviewed by Evelyn Gillan. *Spare Rib* No. 214 (July 1990):23

### Scotland – Description and Travel

Highland Fling. *Harper's Bazaar* (December 1990):106-119

Scot Free. Julie Moline. *Harper's Bazaar* (June 1990):64+

### Scotland – Music, Popular

Music: The Blue Nile. Karen Schoemer. *Mademoiselle* (June 1990):98-101

### Scotland – Prostitution

The Magdalene's Friend: Prostitution and Social Control in Glasgow, 1869-1890. Linda Mahood. *Women's Studies International Forum* 13, Nos. 1-2 (1990):49-61

### Scotland – Status of Women

Childcare and Access: Women in Tertiary Education in Scotland. By Gill Scott. Reviewed by Sandra MacLeod. *Gender and Education* 2, No. 3 (1990):377-378

### Scotland – Suicide

Ecological Correlates of Adolescent Attempted Suicide. David Lester. *Adolescence* 25, No. 98 (Summer 1990):483-485

### Scott, Bonnie Kime

Not So Quiet. Book Review. *Tulsa Studies in Women's Literature* 9, No. 2 (Fall 1990):339-342

We That Were Young. Book Review. *Tulsa Studies in Women's Literature* 9, No. 2 (Fall 1990):339-342

**Scott, Gail** (joint author). *See* Bersianik, Louky

### Scott, Gill

Childcare and Access: Women in Tertiary Education in Scotland. Reviewed by Sandra MacLeod. *Gender and Education* 2, No. 3 (1990):377-378

### Scott, Hilda

The Panther Women: Five Stories from the Cassette Recorder. Book Review. *The Women's Review of Books* 7, No. 4 (January 1990):10

The Women Behind the Wall. *The Women's Review of Books* 7, No. 4 (January 1990):10

### Scott, Holland

Chic Expertise. *Harper's Bazaar* (October 1990):170-173+

### Scott, Joan W.

Gender and the Politics of History. Reviewed by Linda Gordon. *Signs* 15, No. 4 (Summer 1990):853-858

Gender and the Politics of History. Reviewed by Nancy Fraser. *NWSA Journal* 2, No. 3 (Summer 1990):505-508

Heroes of Their Own Lives: The Politics and History of Family Violence. Book review. *Signs* 15, No. 4 (Summer 1990):848-852

Response to Gordon. *Signs* 15, No. 4 (Summer 1990):859-860

**Scott, Joan W.** (about)

Response to Scott. Linda Gordon. *Signs* 15, No. 4 (Summer 1990):852-853

**Scott, Joan W.** (joint author). *See* Christian, Barbara

**Scott, Joan W.** (joint editor). *See* Conway, Jill K.

**Scott, Maria** (joint author). *See* Lees, Sue

**Scott, Melissa**

Academics in Outer Space. *Belles Lettres* 5, No. 4 (Summer 1990):45

Feminism and Science Fiction. Book Review. *Belles Lettres* 5, No. 4 (Summer 1990):45

Memories and Visions: Women's Fantasy and Science Fiction. Book Review. *Belles Lettres* 5, No. 4 (Summer 1990):45

**Scott, Nina M.** (joint editor). *See* Horno-Delgado, Asunción

**Scott, Sara**

Beyond Condom-Bound Solutions. *Connexions* 33 (1990):21-23

**Scott, Sue** (joint author). *See* Holland, Janet

**Scott, Suzanne**

Dixie Church Interstate Blues. Book Review. *Belles Lettres* 5, No. 3 (Spring 1990):20

Sister Gin. Book Review. *Belles Lettres* 5, No. 3 (Spring 1990):22

**Scott, Suzanne** and Constantine, Lynne M.

Belles Lettres Interview. *Belles Lettres* 5, No. 4 (Summer 1990):24-26

Belles Lettres Interview: Mary Morris. *Belles Lettres* 5, No. 2 (Winter 1990):11

**Scott, Tracy**

After the Fire. Book Review. *New Directions for Women* 19, No. 1 (January/February 1990):24

Bodmin, 1329: An Epic Novel of Christians and Jews in the Plague Years. Book Review. *On the Issues* 15 (Summer 1990):25

The Dog Collar Murders. Book Review. *New Directions for Women* 19, No. 5 (September-October 1990):20

There's Something I've Been Meaning to Tell You . . . Book Review. *New Directions for Women* 19, No. 2 (March/April 1990):24

**Scott, Vernon**

Delta Burke: "Learning to Be Happy the Way I Am." *Good Housekeeping* 210, No. 5 (May 1990):165, 245-246

Valerie Harper: Everything Is Coming Up "Love." *Good Housekeeping* 210, No. 6 (June 1990):126-129

We Talk to Connie Sellecca. *Good Housekeeping* 211, No. 5 (November 1990):158-161

Widowed. Excerpted. *Good Housekeeping* 211, No. 5 (November 1990):163+

**Scott, Willard**

Willard Scott's Breakfast Book. *Ladies' Home Journal* 107, No. 3 (March 1990):201-216

**Scovell, Jane** (joint author). *See* Dukakis, Kitty

**Screenplays**

Uneasy Pieces: Trials of an Unproduced Screenwriter. Alfred Palca. *Lear's* (July 1990):54-59+

**Screenwriters – Personal Narratives.** *See* Writers – Personal Narratives

**Scripts.** *See* Screenplays

**Sculling.** *See* Rowing

**Sculptors.** *See also* Artists

A Sculptural Odyssey. Alice Manzi. *Woman of Power* 15 (Fall-Winter 1990):47-49

The Symmetry of Maya Ying Lin. Jill Kirschenbaum. *Ms.* 1, No. 2 (September/October 1990):20-22

**Scutt, Jocelynne**

The Exploitation of a Desire: Women's Experiences with In Vitro Fertilisation – An Exploratory Survey. Book Review. *Women's Studies International Forum* 13, No. 6 (1990):605-608

Infertility: Women Speak Out about Their Experiences of Reproductive Medicine. Book Review. *Women's Studies International Forum* 13, No. 6 (1990):605-608

**Seafood.** *See also* Cookery (Seafood)

Sea Fare. Jonell Nash. *Essence* 21, No. 2 (June 1990):80-82

**Seaforth, Sybil**

Growing Up With Miss Milly. Reviewed by Rhonda Cobham. *The Women's Review of Books* 7, Nos. 10-11 (July 1990):29-31

**Seager, Joni** (joint editor). *See* Baruch, Elaine Hoffman

**Searing, Susan E.**

Women of Color and the Core Curriculum: Tools for Transforming the Liberal Arts, Part 2. *Feminist Collections* 11, No. 2 (Winter 1990):15-17

Women of Color and the Core Curriculum: Tools for Transforming the Liberal Arts, Part 3. *Feminist Collections* 11, No. 4 (Summer 1990):11-16

Women of Color and the Core Curriculum: Tools for Transforming the Liberal Arts, Part 4. *Feminist Collections* 12, No. 1 (Fall 1990):21-24

**Searles, Jo C.**

Inventing Freedom: The Positive Poetic "Mutterings" of Older Women. *Journal of Women and Aging* 2, No. 2 (1990):153-160

**Searles, John S.** (joint editor). *See* Collins, R. Lorraine

**Searles, Patricia** (joint author). *See* Berger, Ronald J.

**Seasonal Affective Disorder**

Mind Health. Erica Goode. *Vogue* (February 1990):230, 235

**Seat Belts.** *See* Automobiles – Safety – Seat Belts

**Seattle – King County Prosecutor's Office – Special Assault Unit.** *See* Roe, Rebecca (about)

**Seberg, Jean** (about) Jean Seberg. Georgina Howell. *Vogue:*(October 1990):364-375

**Secade, Walter G.**

Equity in Education. Reviewed by Anne Walton. *Gender and Education* 2, No. 3 (1990):371-372

**Secondhand Trade.** *See also* Flea Markets

**Second Homes.** *See also* Condominiums

A Blessing on Both Your Houses. Siobhan Toscano. *Savvy Woman* (September 1990):24-28

**Second Marriage.** *See* Remarriage

**Secretaries – Personal Narratives**

Secretaries Talk Sexuality, Power and Work. By Rosemary Pringle. Reviewed by Colleen Chesterman. *Australian Feminist Studies* No. 11 (Autumn 1990):123-126

**Secunda, Victoria**

How to Have a More Loving Relationship with Your Mom. *Redbook* 175, No. 1 (May 1990):138-139+

**Sedaris, David**

Caesura. Short story. *Out/Look* No. 8 (Spring 1990):58-61

**Sedgwick, Kyra** (about)

Bright Face, Big Future. Jeff Yarbrough. *Harper's Bazaar* (February 1990):54

**Seed, Patricia**

To Love, Honor, and Obey in Colonial Mexico: Conflicts Over Marriage Choice, 1574-1821. Reviewed by Carol Clark D'Lugo. *Women's Studies International Forum* 13, Nos. 1-2 (1990):161

**Seeger, Nancy** and Yount, Rena

A Trip Through the Women's Communities of Washington D.C. *Hot Wire* 6, No. 1 (January 1990):40-44+

**Seeger, Peggy**

Familiar Faces. Reviewed by Lynn Wenzel. *New Directions for Women* 19, No. 3 (May/June 1990):8

**Seeley, David**

His: Blind Dates. *Mademoiselle* (June 1990):83

Women Who Work Too Much . . . and the Men Who Love Them. *Mademoiselle* (August 1990):217, 238-240

**Seese, June Akers**

What Waiting Really Means. Reviewed by Lila Karp. *The Women's Review of Books* 7, Nos. 10-11 (July 1990):35-36

**Seff, Monica A.** (joint author). *See* Gecas, Viktor

**Segal, Jeffrey A.** (joint author). *See* O'Connor, Karen

**Segal, Lynne**

Pornography and Violence: What the 'Experts' Really Say. *Feminist Review* No. 36 (Autumn 1990):29-41

**Seginer, Rachel**

Analysis of a Double-Layered Support System. *Adolescence* 25, No. 99 (Fall 1990):739-752

**Seginer, Rachel,** Karayanni, Mousa, and Mar'i, Mariam M.

Adolescents' Attitudes toward Women's Roles: A Comparison between Israeli Jews and Arabs. *Psychology of Women Quarterly* 14, No. 1 (March 1990):119-133

**Segregation**

"The Finest Outside the Loop": Motion Picture Exhibition in Chicago's Black Metropolis, 1905-1928. Mary Carbine. *Camera Obscura* , No. 23 (May 1990): 9-41

**Segregation in Education**

Britain: Official Apartheid on Its Way in. Joyoti Grech. *Spare Rib* No. 212 (May 1990):46

The Lemon Grove Incident. Directed by Frank Christopher. Reviewed by C. Alejandra Elenes. *Feminist Collections* 11, No. 3 (Spring 1990):9-10

**Seibert, Joy Hart** (joint author). *See* Allen, Myria Watkins

**Seid, Judith**

We Rejoice in Our Heritage: Home Rituals for Secular and Humanistic Jews. Reviewed by Ruth Kraut. *Bridges* 1, No. 2 (Fall 1990): 128-130

**Seidelman, Susan** (about)

The Devil & Susan Seidelman. Louise Bernikow. *Lear's* (January 1990):108-111

**Seideman, Ruth Young**

Effects of a Premenstrual Syndrome Education Program on Premenstrual Symptomatology. *Health Care for Women International* 11, No. 4 (1990):491-501

**Sekhon, Kuldip Singh** (about)

Communities of Resistance Challenging Fortress Europe. *Spare Rib* No. 212 (May 1990):6-11

Southall Responds to Racist Murder. Joyoti Grech. *Spare Rib* No. 209 (February 1990):45-46

**Sekoff, Roy**

Jon Cryer, Your Big Break Is Calling. *Mademoiselle* (January 1990):44

How to Make Yourself a Stronger Person. Claire Berman. *Ladies' Home Journal* 107, No. 11 (November 1990):96-104

Interiors: A Swimming Lesson. Jewelle Gomez. *Essence* 21, No. 4 (August 1990):38+

Measurement Issues in the Use of the Coopersmith Self-Esteem Inventory with Navajo Women. Patricia G. Higgins and Elisabeth K. Dicharry. *Health Care for Women International* 11, No. 3 (1990):251-262

Our Families, Ourselves. John Bradshaw. *Lear's* (April 1990):55-56

In the Spirit: A Fresh Start. Susan L. Taylor. *Essence* 20, No. 9 (January 1990):43

Ten Steps to Self-Esteem. Monique Burns. *Essence* 21, No. 4 (August 1990):57-58

Women and Self-Esteem. By Linda Tschirhart Sanford and Mary Ellen Donovan. Reviewed by Charlotte Hettena and Siroon P. Shahinian. *Psychology of Women Quarterly* 14, No. 4 (December 1990):620-621

**Self-Help Techniques.** *See also* Behavior Change; Child Psychology; Consumer Information; Counseling; Depression, Mental – Counseling; Environmental Movement; Exercise; Female-Male Relationships; Home Remedies; Illness – Psychological Aspects; Leadership Skills; Literary Criticism – Feminist Perspectives; Management Techniques; Meditation; Parenting; Self-Determination; Self-Esteem; Self-Presentation; Sex Education; Stress – Coping Strategies; Stress Relaxation

The Age of Anonymous. Michele Kort. *Essence* 20, No. 11 (March 1990):32

Between Us. Gwendolyn Goldsby Grant. *Essence* 20, No. 10 (February 1990):30-; 31

Couple Time. *Glamour* (April 1990):144

Etiquette: Doing It Right. Charlotte Ford. *McCall's* 117, No. 8 (May 1990):170

Every Woman Can . . . Bibliography. *Ladies' Home Journal* 107, No. 11 (November 1990):216-218

Face It: Stress Shows! *Glamour* (October 1990):272-275

The Futility of Magical Thinking. John Bradshaw. *Lear's* (July 1990):52

GH Institute: Hot Line. *Good Housekeeping* 211, No. 4 (October 1990):206

Glamour Guide. *Glamour* (April 1990):103-107

Handling Everyday Life Problems. Vicki Lansky. *Family Circle* 103, No. 9 (June 26, 1990):98-99

Happiness: How to get More of it. *Glamour* (December 1990):198-201

Health Express News. Marian Sandmaier. *Mademoiselle* (February 1990):112-114

How to Know it's Over. Meredith Berkman. *Glamour* (November 1990):239

The Intelligent Woman's Guide to Sex: The Waiting-on-a-Man Syndrome. Dalma Heyn. *Mademoiselle* (September 1990):144

Lovetalk: The Quickest Way to Better Sex. Steven Carter and Julia Sokol. *Redbook* 174, No. 6 (April 1990):108-109+

No, You Don't Have Cancer: A Reassuring Guide for Hypochondriacs. Ellen Kunes. *Mademoiselle* (June 1990):128

Personal Journal. *Ladies' Home Journal* 107, No. 10 (October 1990):142-146

The Short-Order Spa. Marianne Wait. *Ladies' Home Journal* 107, No. 9 (September 1990):128

Sisters Helping Sisters. Marilyn Milloy. *Essence* 21, No. 6 (October 1990):83-84+

Speaker for the House: The Heloise Helpline. Heloise. *Good Housekeeping* 211, No. 3 (September 1990):72

Staying Cool When the Stakes are High. Diane Cole. *Working Woman* (February 1990):80

What Makes a Couple Happy? Ayala M. Pines. *Redbook* 174, No. 6 (April 1990):102-103+

What Smart Women Know. By Steven Carter and Julia Sokol. Reviewed by Anne Lamott. *Mademoiselle* (November 1990):96-99

Women Who Read Too Much: Reflections on the Advice-Giving Industry. Harriet Goldhor Lerner. *The Women's Review of Books* 7, No. 7 (April 1990):15-16

Your Brilliant Career: It's New, It's Improved, It's You! Rebecca Sharp. *Mademoiselle* (November 1990):109

On Your Own: Feeling Fifteen Again. Judith Stone. *Glamour* (February 1990):107

**Selfish Behavior.** *See* Narcissism

**Self-Mutilation**

Self-Mutilation: Theory. By Barent W. Walsh and Paul M. Rosen. Book Review. *Adolescence* 25, No. 97 (Spring 1990):251-252

**Self-Presentation.** *See also* Office Politics

Capabilities. Patti Watts. *Executive Female* (May/June 1990):34-36+

Career Strategies: The Flash Factor: Can You Electrify Your Image? Adele Scheele. *Working Woman* (September 1990):76-78

Competitive Edge. *Executive Female* (March/April 1990):14-15

Dear FC: I Lost My Job. Laurie Fuchs. *Family Circle* 103, No. 13 (September 25, 1990):27-28

Does Your Image Need Fine-Tuning? Colleen Sullivan. *Working Woman* (November 1990):142-144

Executive Agenda. *Working Woman* (November 1990):109-110

Good Show: How to Look Your Best When You Feel Your Worst. Andrea Messina. *Working Woman* (October 1990):130-132

Job Strategies: Image Consultants. *Glamour* (February 1990):88-90

Shortcuts to Life. Pamela Redmond Satran. *Glamour* (June 1990):234-236

**Self-Promotion.** *See* Self-Presentation

**Self-Sacrifice.** *See also* Caregiving

Thoughts on Caretaking: Shuck Off the Yoke. John Bradshaw. *Lear's* (May 1990):67

**Selig, Michael**

Hollywood Melodrama, Douglas Sirk, and the Repression of the Female Subject (*Magnificent Obsession*). *Genders* 9 (Fall 1990):35-48

**Seligson, Marcia**

Body Briefing: Estrogen Replacement. *Lear's* (March 1990):54-62

Doing Burgundy by Bicycle for Fun. *Lear's* (September 1990):56-59

**Sell, Ingrid**

Seizing Power to Regenerate the Earth. *New Directions for Women* 19, No. 4 (July-August 1990):3

**Sellafield Nuclear Power Plant.** *See* Great Britain – Nuclear Power

**Sellecca, Connie** (about)

We Talk to Connie Sellecca. Vernon Scott. *Good Housekeeping* 211, No. 5 (November 1990):158-161

**Selleck, Denise**

On the Trail of Jane the Fool. *On the Issues* 14 (1990):22-24+

**Selleck, Tom** (about). *See* Film Criticism

**Seller, Maxine Schwartz**

Our Lives, Circa 1919. *Lilith* 15, No. 4 (Fall 1990):42

**Selles-Roney, Johanna**

Simone Weil: An Intellectual Biography. Book Review. *Resources for Feminist Research* 19, No. 2 (June 1990):46

**Selling**

The Secrets of Super Salespeople (That Everyone Can Use). Michael Kaplan. *Working Woman* (May 1990):92-95+

What Are Your Best Tactics for Making a Sale to a Tough Client? Patti Watts and Shelley Garcia.

*Executive Female* 13, No. 5 (September-October 1990):8-12

**Seltzer, Anne-Marie R.**

Sporting Women Play the Field. *New Directions for Women* 19, No. 4 (July-August 1990):12-13

**Selzer, Richard**

Follow Your Heart. Short story. *Redbook* 175, No. 5 (September 1990):52-62

**Semiotics**

Sex and Semiotic Confusion: Report from Moscow. Elizabeth Waters. *Australian Feminist Studies* No. 12 (Summer 1990):1-14

**Semizorova, Nina** (about)

Dance. David Daniel. *Vogue* (July 1990):100-106

**Semple, Linda**

After Delores. Book Review. *Feminist Review* No. 35 (Summer 1990):119-121

The Dog Collar Murders. Book Review. *Feminist Review* No. 35 (Summer 1990):119-121

**Semple, Linda** (joint author). *See* Rodgerson, Gillian

**Semple, Rose Marie**

The Courage to Learn. Bibliography. *Ladies' Home Journal* 107, No. 11 (November 1990):38-47

**Seneca (New York) – Women's Peace Camp**

Free Riding, Alternative Organization and Cultural Feminism: The Case of Seneca Women's Peace Camp. Peregrine Schwartz-Shea and Debra D. Burrington. *Women & Politics* 10, No. 3 (1990):1-37

**Senegal – Description and Travel**

Travel: Scenes of Senegal. Sherley Anne Williams. *Essence* 20, No. 11 (March 1990):110-112

**Seneviratne, Seni, Chowdhury, Maya, and Janjua, Shahida**

Putting in the Pickle Where the Jam Should Be. Reviewed by Joyoti Grech. *Spare Rib* No. 209 (February 1990):31

**Senthilnayaki, M.** (joint author). *See* Audiarayana, N.

**Separate Spheres.** *See also* Employment – Outside the Home

Editorial: Feminist Paradoxes and the Need for New Agendas. Betty Sancier. *AFFILIA* 5, No. 2 (Summer 1990):5-7

The "Space" Behind the Dialogue: The Gender-Coding of Space on *Cheers*. Notes. Charles Acland. *Women & Language* 13, No. 1 (Fall 1990):38-40

Women's History/Public History – When the Twain Meet. Jeanne Farr McDonnell. *Journal of Women's History* 2, No. 2 (Fall 1990):171-173

**Separation-Individuation (Psychology)**

Adolescent Separation-Individuation and Family Transitions. Jill A. Daniels. *Adolescence* 25, No. 97 (Spring 1990):105-116

**Sequoia**

Therese Edell: Composer and Desktop Music Publisher. *Hot Wire* 6, No. 1 (January 1990):48-49+

**Serdatzky, Yente**

Vide/Confession. In English and Yiddish. *Bridges* 1, No. 2 (Fall 1990): 77-92

**Sermuksnis, Stephanie**

Young Mother's Story: "We Count Our Blessings Every Day." *Redbook* 176, No. 1 (November 1990):42-44

**Serow, Robert C.** and Dreyden, Julia I.

Community Service among College and University Students: Individual and Institutional Relationships. *Adolescence* 25, No. 99 (Fall 1990):553-566

**Serrano, Cynthia M.**

Fire in the Rain . . . Singer in the Storm. Book Review. *The Women's Review of Books* 8, No. 2 (November 1990):18-19

Singing for the Revolution. *The Women's Review of Books* 8, No. 2 (November 1990):18-19

**Serrano, Lucienne J.** (joint editor). *See* Baruch, Elaine Hoffman

**Serrau, Coline**

Romuald & Juliet. Reviewed by Esther Bailey. *Spare Rib* No. 216 (September 1990):32-33

**Servin, James**

Fitness and Flexibility. *Harper's Bazaar* (January 1990):46

LIZA. *Harper's Bazaar* (August 1990):130-133+

Prime Time Provocateurs. *Harper's Bazaar* (March 1990):67-68

**Setaro, Ewa Stajkowska**

The "Liberation" of Economic Necessity: Women in Poland. *Iris* 24 (Fall-Winter 1990):40-43

**Sethi, Harsh**

Main Azad Hoon: The Politics of Myth and Reality. Film review. *Manushi* 56 (January-February 1990):43-44

Mera Pati Sirf Mera Hai. Film Review. *Manushi* No. 59 (July-August 1990):43-44

**Seto, Thelma**

This Shame Is a Carnivore. Poem. *Sinister Wisdom* 42 (Winter 1990-1991):44-46

**Setouchi, Harumi**

The End of Summer. Reviewed by Cathie Brettschneider. *Belles Lettres* 5, No. 3 (Spring 1990):20

**Setton, Ruth Knafo**

America and I: Short Stories by American Jewish Women Writers. Book review. *Lilith* 15, No. 4 (Fall 1990):33

**Sevenhuijzen, Selma** (joint editor). *See* Smart, Carol

**Sev'er, Aysan**

Mate Selection Patterns of Men and Women in Personal Advertisements: New Bottle, Old Wine. *Atlantis* 15, No. 2 (Spring 1990):70-76

**Sewing.** *See also* Craft Arts

Beauty and Fashion Hotline: What's In/What's Out. *Family Circle* 103, No. 13 (September 25, 1990):43-44

Country Cottage. *Family Circle* 103, No. 14 (October 16, 1990):88-93

Sew and Go! *Family Circle* 103, No. 17 (December 18, 1990):164-166

Sew Festive! *Essence* 21, No. 8 (December 1990):50-52

Sew Spring. *Essence* 20, No. 12 (April 1990):59-60

Tote-All Picnic Set. *Family Circle* 103, No. 9 (June 26, 1990):108-111

**Sex, Tantric**

Sex Can Be Spiritual. Robin Bennett. *New Directions for Women* 19, No. 4 (July-August 1990):7

**Sex – Teenage**

Polling America. Ernie Anastos. *Family Circle* 103, No. 12 (September 4, 1990):37-39

**Sex Crimes.** *See also* Rape

Rebecca Roe: Getting Tough on Sex Offenders. Nick Gallo. *McCall's* 117, No. 12 (September 1990):57-58

**Sex Discrimination.** *See* Discrimination; Gender Discrimination

**Sex Discrimination in Employment.** *See* Employment – Gender Discrimination

**Sex Education.** *See also* Acquired Immune Deficiency Syndrome – Education; Adolescents – Psychology; Childbirth; Contraception; Fibrocystic Disease; Menopause; Pap Smear; Pregnancy; Premenstrual Syndrome; Sexuality – Dysfunction

The After-Sex Pill. Mary Jo Schnatter. *McCall's* 118, No. 3 (December 1990):26

Attitudes: The Sexual Revolution. Karen Grigsby Bates. *Essence* 21, No. 1 (May 1990):54-56

Babies, Birds and Bees. Lee Salk. *McCall's* 117, No. 8 (May 1990):65

The Baby Bust. Monique Burns. *Essence* 21, No. 6 (October 1990):34-35

Between Us. Bibliography. Gwendolyn Goldsby Grant. *Essence* 21, No. 2 (June 1990):26-27; 21, No. 4 (August 1990):30; 21, No. 5 (September 1990):32-33; 21, No. 7 (November 1990):24; 21, No. 8 (December 1990):27

Between Us. Gwendolyn Goldsby Grant. *Essence* 20, No. 11 (March 1990):30-31; 20, No. 12 (April 1990):30-31

Beyond Plumbing and Prevention: Feminist Approaches to Sex Education. Helen Lenskyj. *Gender and Education* 2, No. 2 (1990):217-230

Can This Marriage Be Saved? "I Just Don't Respect Him Anymore." Ellen Switzer. *Ladies' Home Journal* 107, No. 10 (October 1990):14-20

Contraception for Men. *Good Housekeeping* 211, No. 3 (September 1990):295

Cycles of Desire. Dorothy Glasser Weiss. *Glamour* (May 1990):278-279+

Doctor, Doctor. Maj-Britt Rosenbaum. *Mademoiselle* (June 1990):132; (November 1990):120

Don't Be His Mother. Excerpt. Barbara De Angelis. *Redbook* 174, No. 5 (March 1990):130-131+

Do You Know His Secret Sexual Fantasies? Nancy Gagliardi. *Redbook* 175, No. 5 (September 1990):168-169+

Do You Think About Sex Too Much? Eric Klinger. *Glamour* (September 1990):322-323+

Easy Ways to Help Him Be a Sexier Lover. Kathryn Stechert Black. *Redbook* 175, No. 6 (October 1990):112-113+

Endless Desire. Susan Crain Bakos. *Harper's Bazaar* (August 1990):36

The Estrogen Debate. Jjane Shiyen Chou and Wendy Murphy. *McCall's* 118, No. 1 (October 1990):157-158

The Five Most Common Maternity Myths. *Ladies' Home Journal* 107, No. 8 (August 1990):44

A Guy's-Eye View. Skip Hollandsworth. *Mademoiselle* (October 1990):122

Health: Birth Control. Cynthia Marks. *Mademoiselle* (September 1990):188-198

Health: The Etiquette of Birth Control. K. L. France. *Mademoiselle* (September 1990):187

Health: What's Your Period I.Q.? Janet Siroto. *Mademoiselle* (October 1990):118

Health Express: Body and Soul. Maj-Britt Rosenbaum. *Mademoiselle* (February 1990):116

Health Express: Body & Soul. Maj-Britt Rosenbaum. *Mademoiselle* (January 1990):70

Health & Fitness. Stephanie Young. *Glamour* (February 1990):43-44

Health & Mind. Pamela Erens. *Glamour* (February 1990):46-51

Health News. Marian Sandmaier. *Mademoiselle* (June 1990):130; (September 1990):200

From Here to Maternity. Maxine Lipner. *Essence* 21, No. 3 (July 1990):24

How to Have Fantastic Sex: Know Your Body. Helen Singer Kaplan. *Redbook* 175, No. 4 (August 1990):102

How to Have Fantastic Sex: Know Yourself. Lesley Dormen. *Redbook* 175, No. 4 (August 1990):100-101

I Tested HIV-Positive. Marlene Cimons. *Essence* 20, No. 12 (April 1990):72-75

The Joy of (Protected) Sex. Marjorie Ingall. *McCall's* 117, No. 12 (September 1990):76-78

Just Between Us. Gwendolyn Goldsby Grant. *Essence* 20, No. 9 (January 1990):26-27+

The Love Hormone. Charlotte Modahl. *Mademoiselle* (November 1990):112

Loveplay: The Touching Way to Passion. Lesley Dormen. *Redbook* 175, No. 2 (June 1990):104-105+

Lovetalk: The Quickest Way to Better Sex. Steven Carter and Julia Sokol. *Redbook* 174, No. 6 (April 1990):100-109 I

The Lowdown on Menstrual Problems. Shifra Diamond. *Mademoiselle* (October 1990):120

Medical Report: A New Prenatal Test. Elisabeth Rosenthal. *Glamour* (June 1990):64-66

Medinews. Sally Squires. *Ladies' Home Journal* 107, No. 10 (October 1990):132

Menopause and You. Bibliography. *Essence* 21, No. 2 (June 1990):20-22

Oops . . . Did You Take Your Pill Today? Cynthia Hacinli. *Mademoiselle* (September 1990):198

Pep Talk! Kate Maloy. *Redbook* 175, No. 3 (July 1990):102-103+

PMS Update. Bibliography. Stephanie Young. *Glamour* (April 1990):94-98

Private Lives: Are You Too Tired for Sex? Barbara De Angelis. *Family Circle* 103, No. 14 (October 16, 1990):32-37

Reducing the Risk: Building Skills to Prevent Pregnancy. By Richard P. Barth. Reviewed by Peggy Brick. *New Directions for Women* 19, No. 3 (May/June 1990):21

Safe Sex for Bad Backs. Jane Shiyen Chou. *McCall's* 117, No. 10 (July 1990):60

Sex and the Married Man. Anthony Brandt. *Lear's* (November 1990):156+

Sex Drive: A User's Guide. Monique Burns. *Essence* 21, No. 4 (August 1990):29

Sex Education: Political Issues in Britain and Europe. By Philip Meredith. Reviewed by Lesley Holly. *Gender and Education* 2, No. 2 (1990):243-244

Sex & Health. Shirley Zussman. *Glamour* (January 1990):163; (February 1990):219; (March 1990):298; (April 1990):318; (May 1990):320; (June 1990):276; (July 1990):195; (August 1990):250; (November 1990):272; (December 1990):246

Sex & Health. Shirlley Zussman. *Glamour* (September 1990):86

Sex Play – Is It Okay? Benjamin Spock. *Redbook* 175, No. 3 (July 1990):30

The Sexuality Decision-Making Series for Teens. By Christine De Vault. Reviewed by Peggy Brick. *New Directions for Women* 19, No. 3 (May/June 1990):21

"Talk to My Mom about Sex? No Way!" Ruth K. Westheimer. *Redbook* 175, No. 2 (June 1990):28-32

Teaching Gender: Sex Education and Sexual Stereotypes. By Tricia Szirom. Reviewed by Ann Marie Wolpe. *Gender and Education* 2, No. 2 (1990):254-255

Teaching Gender: Sex Education and Sexual Stereotypes. By Tricia Szirom. Reviewed by Helen Lenskyj. *Resources for Feminist Research* 19, No. 1 (March 1990):34

This Is What You Thought: How's Your Sex Life? *Glamour* (April 1990):167

The Top 10 Sex Myths. Alfie Kohn. *Glamour* (October 1990):252-253+

What's a Vulva, Mom? Harriet Goldhor Lerner. *New Directions for Women* 19, No. 3 (May/June 1990):10

What You Don't Know About Orgasm Could Thrill You. Debra Kent. *Mademoiselle* (February 1990):154-155+

What You *Don't* Know about Your Period. Bibliography. Fran Snyder. *Ladies' Home Journal* 107, No. 5 (May 1990):108-114

Will I Be Able to Have a Baby? Judith D. Schwartz. *Glamour* (December 1990):222-223+

Women and AIDS: Reexamining the Risk. Leanne Kleinmann. *Glamour* (May 1990):88-92

Women's Health: "I Want a Second Opinion." Kathryn Cox and Genell Subak-Sharpe. *Redbook* 175, No. 1 (May 1990):22-28

Women's Health News. *Redbook* 175, No. 5 (September 1990):32-36

Your Pregnancy. Stephanie Young. *Glamour* (February 1990):55; (April 1990):86

**Sex Education – Home**

Family Interactions and Sex Education in the Home. S. Elizabeth Baldwin and Madelon Visintainer Baranoski. *Adolescence* 25, No. 99 (Fall 1990):573-582

Parent-Child Sexual Discussion: Perceived Communicator Style and Subsequent Behavior. Kay E. Mueller and William G. Powers. *Adolescence* 25, No. 98 (Summer 1990):469-482

**Sex/Gender Systems.** *See also* Power Structure; Religion and Politics – Algeria

**Sex Industry.** *See* Pornography

Can This Marriage Be Saved? "My Husband Keeps Calling Those Sex Hotlines." Margery D. Rosen. *Ladies' Home Journal* 107, No. 7 (July 1990):14-20

**Sexism.** *See also* Misogyny

The Construction, Deconstruction, and Reconstruction of Difference. Paula Rothenberg. *Hypatia* 5, No. 1 (Spring 1990):42-57

Ethnicity and Feminism: Two Solitudes? Sheva Medjuck. *Atlantis* 15, No. 2 (Spring 1990):1-10

A Good Year for Bitching. *Glamour* (December 1990):104

Homophobia: A Weapon of Sexism. By Suzanne Pharr. Reviewed by Natalie Jane Woodman. *AFFILIA* 5, No. 3 (Fall 1990):124-125

The New Old Boy. Annetta Miller and Pamela Kruger. *Working Woman* (April 1990):94-96

Russian Women's Studies: Essays on Sexism in Soviet Culture. By Tatyana Mamonova. Reviewed by Norma Noonan. *Women & Politics* 10, No. 4 (1990):133-134

Sex, Lust & Videotapes. Roberto Santiago. *Essence* 21, No. 7 (November 1990):62-64+

Son of Sexism. Karen Schoemer. *Mademoiselle* (May 1990):128-130

**Sexism in Language.** *See* Language – Sexism

**Sexism in Literature**

Anti-Sexist Celebration of Black Women in Literature: *The Sexual Mountain and Black Women Writers* and a Conversation with Calvin Hernton. Gloria Wade-Gayles. *Sage* 6, No. 1 (Summer 1989):45-49

**Sexism in Music**

Women Rap Back. Michele Wallace. *Ms.* 1, No. 3 (November/December 1990):61

**Sex Objects**

The Big Issue: Safety, Not Size. Gil Schwartz. *Mademoiselle* (October 1990):166-167+

The Truth about Breasts: A Beauty & Health Guide. *Mademoiselle* (October 1990):164-165

Young Mother's Story: "My Boss Ordered Me to Sleep with Him." Shauna Clark and Sara Nelson. *Redbook* 174, No. 6 (April 1990):64-67

**Sexual Harassment – College Students**

Sexual Harassment on Campus: Individual Differences in Attitudes and Beliefs. Natalie J. Malovich and Jayne E. Stake. *Psychology of Women Quarterly* 14, No. 1 (March 1990):63-81

**Sexual Identity**

The Dance of Masks. Barbara Smith. *Out/Look* No. 9 (Summer 1990):74-77

Either/Or – Neither/Both: Sexual Ambiguity and the Ideology of Gender. Julia Epstein. *Genders* 7 (Spring 1990):99-142

Lost Tribal Rites: A Lament. Desmond J. Waite. *Out/Look* No. 9 (Summer 1990):72-73

My Interesting Condition. Jan Clausen. *Out/Look* No. 7 (Winter 1990):10-21

Perceptions of Sexual Self: Their Impact on Relationships Between Lesbian and Heterosexual Women. Diane Palladino and Yanela Stephenson. *Women and Therapy* 9, No. 3 (1990):231-253

The Search for Acceptance: Consumerism, Sexuality, and Self among American Women. By Jerry Jacobs. Reviewed by Jeanne Ballantine and Jeanne Lemkau. *Psychology of Women Quarterly* 14, No. 3 (September 1990):443-444

This Sex Which Is Not One: De-Constructing Ovid's Hermaphrodite. Georgia Nugent. *Differences* 2, No. 1 (Spring 1990):160-185

**Sexuality**

The Americanization of Sex. By Edwin M. Schur. Reviewed by Patricia MacCorquodale. *Journal of Marriage and the Family* 52, No. 1 (February 1990):279-280

Blood at the Root: Motherhood, Sexuality and Male Dominance. By Ann Ferguson. Reviewed by Ellen Jacobs. *Resources for Feminist Research* 19, No. 1 (March 1990):5-6

Carnal Knowing: Female Nakedness and Religious Meaning in the Christian West. By Margaret Miles. Reviewed by Jo Ann McNamara. *The Women's Review of Books* 8, No. 1 (October 1990):21-22

Don't Settle – Sizzle! Dorothy Glasser Weiss. *Redbook* 175, No. 1 (May 1990):120-121+

Education as Entertainment: Lesbian Sexpert JoAnn Loulan. Toni Armstrong Jr. *Hot Wire* 6, No. 1 (January 1990):3-5+

Erotic Wars: What Happened to the Sexual Revolution? By Lillian Rubin. Reviewed by Jewelle Gomez. *The Women's Review of Books* 8, No. 3 (December 1990):1+

Family Structure as a Predictor of Initial Substance Use and Sexual Intercourse in Early Adolescence. Robert L. Flewelling and Karl E. Bauman. *Journal of*

*Marriage and the Family* 52, No. 1 (February 1990):171-181

How Early to Bed? The New Sexual Timetables. Ellen Welty. *Mademoiselle* (June 1990):172-173+

Lifting Belly: Privacy, Sexuality and Lesbianism. Ruthann Robson. *Women's Rights Law Reporter* 12, No. 3 (Fall 1990): 177-203

No Cleavage Required! Getting to the Soul of Sex Appeal. Ellen Welty. *Mademoiselle* (April 1990):198-201, 263

The Occidental Alice. Nancy Armstrong. *Differences* 2, No. 2 (Summer 1990):3-40

Pillow Talk. Janet Siroto. *Mademoiselle* (October 1990):162-163+

The Regulation of Desire: Sexuality in Canada. By Gary Kinsman. Reviewed by Chris Waters. *Gender & History* 2, No. 2 (Summer 1990):218-222

Sex, Lies, and Penetration. Jan Brown. *Out/Look* No. 7 (Winter 1990):30-34

Sex and the Savvy Woman. Gail Collins. *Savvy Woman* (July/August 1990):66-69

Sex Is Alive and Well. Marti Leimbach. *Harper's Bazaar* (June 1990):70+

Sexual Confidence: Women's New Attitudes, New Outlooks. *Glamour* (January 1990):128-133+

The Sexual Contract. By Carole Pateman. Reviewed by Jennifer M. Lehmann. *Journal of Marriage and the Family* 52, No. 2 (May 1990):563-564

Tell Us What You Think: Is Sex Overrated in Women's Lives? *Glamour* (February 1990):112

Temptations of Pleasure: Nickelodeons, Amusement Parks, and the Sights of Female Sexuality. Lauren Rabinovitz. *Camera Obscura* , No. 23 (May 1990): 70-89

Theories of Sexuality Forum. Carol Anne Douglas. *off our backs* 20, No. 8 (August/September 1990):17

The Truth About the Sex Gap. Carol Ann Rinzler. *Family Circle* 103, No. 9 (June 26, 1990):57-59

Women Negotiating Heterosex: Implications for AIDS Prevention. Susan Kippax, June Crawford, Cathy Waldby, and Pam Benton. *Women's Studies International Forum* 13, No. 6 (1990):533-542

**Sexuality – Dysfunction**

Bed and Bored? Helen Singer Kaplan. *Redbook* 175, No. 3 (July 1990):100-101+

Can This Marriage Be Saved? "After Sixteen Years of Marriage, I'm Still a Virgin." Corinne Clements. *Ladies' Home Journal* 107, No. 9 (September 1990):18-22

Can This Marriage Be Saved? "My Husband Doesn't Want to Make Love." Margery D. Rosen. *Ladies' Home Journal* 107, No. 1 (January 1990):10-14

## Sexuality – History

Adam, Eve, and the Serpent. By Elaine Pagels. Reviewed by Michael B. Schwarz. *Out/Look* No. 7 (Winter 1990):76-81

The Body and Society: Men, Women, and Sexual Renunciation in Early Christianity. By Peter Brown. Reviewed by Michael B. Schwarz. *Out/Look* No. 7 (Winter 1990):76-81

Concepts, Experience, and Sexuality. John Boswell. *Differences* 2, No. 1 (Spring 1990):67-87

Consuming Desire: Sexual Science and the Emergence of a Culture of Abundance, 1871-1914. By Lawrence Birken. Reviewed by Chris Waters. *Gender & History* 2, No. 2 (Summer 1990):218-222

Dangerous Sexualities: Medico-Moral Politics in England Since 1830. By Frank Mort. Reviewed by Chris Waters. *Gender & History* 2, No. 2 (Summer 1990):218-222

Daughters of the Game: Troilus and Cressida and the Sexual Discourse of 16th-Century England. Virginia Mason Vaughan. *Women's Studies International Forum* 13, No. 3 (1990):209-220

Myths of Sexuality: Representations of Women in Victorian Britain. By Lynda Nead. Reviewed by Eunice Lipton. *Gender & History* 2, No. 1 (Spring 1990):91-97

The Origin of the Attitudes. Malcolm Potts. *Healthright* 9, No. 3 (May 1990):29-33

Parasexuality and Glamour: The Victorian Barmaid as Cultural Prototype. Peter Bailey. *Gender & History* 2, No. 2 (Summer 1990):148-172

Searching the Heart: Women, Men, and Romantic Love in Nineteenth-Century America. By Karen Lystra. Reviewed by Leila J. Rupp. *The Women's Review of Books* 7, No. 7 (April 1990):20

Sexual Geography and Gender Economy: The Furnished Room Districts of Chicago, 1890-1930. Joanne Meyerowitz. *Gender & History* 2, No. 3 (Autumn 1990):274-296

Therapeutic Arguments and Structures of Desire. Martha Nussbaum. *Differences* 2, No. 1 (Spring 1990):46-66

## Sexuality – Middle Age

Commentary on "Sexuality and the Midlife Woman." Ellen Cole and Esther Rothblum. *Psychology of Women Quarterly* 14, No. 4 (December 1990):509-512

Sexuality and the Midlife Woman. Sandra Risa Leiblum. *Psychology of Women Quarterly* 14, No. 4 (December 1990):495-508

## Sexuality – Survey

Sex and the Working Mother. Carin Rubenstein. *Working Mother* 13, No. 5 (May 1990):54-60

## Sexuality and Menopause

A Season for Sex. Gail Weber. *Healthsharing* 11, No. 4 (December 1990):18-22

## Sexuality in the Theater

"The Leg Business": Transgression and Containment in American Burlesque. Robert C. Allen. *Camera Obscura* , No. 23 (May 1990): 42-69

**Sexually Transmitted Diseases**. *See also* Acquired Immune Deficiency Syndrome; Human Papilloma Virus

AIDS and Other Sexually Transmitted Diseases. Edited by Robyn Richmond and Denis Wakefield. Reviewed by Lynne Wray. *Healthright* 9, No. 3 (May 1990):38

Health Dept. *Lear's* (November 1990):82

Health News. Bibliography. Marian Sandmaier. *Mademoiselle* (October 1990):124

Medical Report: The STD Epidemic. John Langone. *Glamour* (August 1990):70-74

## Sexually Transmitted Diseases – Legal Aspects

Sex, Lies & Lawsuits. Ann Landi. *Mademoiselle* (January 1990):104-105 +

## Sexually Transmitted Diseases – Prevention

Body Management: Contraception for the '90s. Laura Flynn McCarthy. *Working Woman* (January 1990):129-132 +

## Sexually Transmitted Diseases, Prevention

Falling in Love with Condoms. Lyn Stoker. *Healthright* 9, No. 4 (August 1990):35-37

**Sexual Politics**. *See also* Gender Roles; MacKinnon, Catharine; Power Structure; Religion and Politics – Algeria; Reproductive Technologies

The New Women and the Old Men: Love, Sex, and the Woman Question. By Ruth Brandon. Reviewed by Deborah Epstein Nord. *The Women's Review of Books* 8, No. 3 (December 1990):5-7

The Social Construction of Lesbianism. By Celia Kitzinger. Reviewed by L. Diane Bernard. *AFFILIA* 5, No. 2 (Summer 1990):100-102

**Sexual Relationships**. *See also* Dating Customs; Extramarital Affairs; Female-Male Relationships; Personal Relationships

Couples: 10 Reasons to Pair Off. Ellen Welty. *Mademoiselle* (September 1990):242-247

Couple Time. *Glamour* (January 1990):64

In Defense of the Ditz. Skip Hollandsworth. *Mademoiselle* (September 1990):150

Does "No" Mean "Yes"? Judith Galas. *New Directions for Women* 19, No. 6 (November-December 1990):8

The Etiquette of Ending It. Dalma Heyn. *Mademoiselle* (October 1990):80

His: Trial by Dial – Should You Call Him First? Warren Leight. *Mademoiselle* (February 1990):93

How a Man's Age Changes His Outlook on Love. Julie Logan. *Glamour* (April 1990):256-259

The Intelligent Woman's Guide to Sex: Please Skip the Intimate Details! Dalma Heyn. *Mademoiselle* (January 1990):67

The Intelligent Woman's Guide to Sex: The Waiting-on-a-Man Syndrome. Dalma Heyn. *Mademoiselle* (September 1990):144

The Intelligent Woman's Guide to Sex: eight Ways to Survive Heartbreak Hell. Dalma Heyn. *Mademoiselle* (February 1990):96

Jake: A Man's Opinion. *Glamour* (April 1990):148-150

The Myth of the Perfect Couple. Dalma Heyn. *Mademoiselle* (November 1990):80-82

The Road Test: First-Trip-Together Jitters. Skip Hollandsworth. *Mademoiselle* (December 1990):74-76

Romantic Revenge. Jeannie Ralston. *Glamour* (April 1990):278-279+

Scruples: Make a Match, Play With Fire? Ellen Welty. *Mademoiselle* (September 1990):204

**Sexual Relationships – Humor**

Romance: How to Take It Sitting Down. John Leo. *McCall's* 117, No. 11 (August 1990):50

Sex, Lies, and Videohabits. John Leo. *McCall's* 117, No. 9 (June 1990):36

**Sexual Repression.** *See also* Asceticism

Adam, Eve and the Serpent. By Elaine Pagels. Reviewed by Elizabeth A. Clark. *Gender & History* 2, No. 1 (Spring 1990):106-109

**Sexual Repression – History.** *See also* Middle Ages – Sexuality

**Sexual Violence.** *See also* Rape; Violence Against Women

Daddy's Girl. Susan Edmiston. *Glamour* (November 1990):228-231+

Pornography and Violence: What the 'Experts' Really Say. Lynne Segal. *Feminist Review* No. 36 (Autumn 1990):29-41

Surviving Sexual Violence. By Liz Kelly. Reviewed by Patricia J. Morokoff. *Psychology of Women Quarterly* 14, No. 2 (June 1990):290-292

**Seymour, Jane** (about). *See also* Celebrities – Activism; Johnson, Lois Joy, "Great Faces"

Where I Grew Up. Linda Konner. *Glamour* (March 1990):174

**Seymour, Susan**

Issei, Nisei, War Bride: Three Generations of Japanese American Women in Domestic Service.

Book review. *Signs* 15, No. 2 (Winter 1990):395-398

Urban Japanese Housewives: At Home and in the Community. Book review. *Signs* 15, No. 2 (Winter 1990):395-398

**Sgro, Ken**

Risk-Less: Advice for Entrepreneurs. *Executive Female* (May/June 1990):73

Risk-Less Advice for Entrepreneurs. *Executive Female* (March/April 1990):77

**Shaaban, Bouthaina**

Both Left and Right Handed: Arab Women Talk About Their Lives. Reviewed by Marieme Hélie-Lucas. *Connexions* 34 (1990):22-23

**Shadbolt, Doris**

The Art of Emily Carr. Reviewed by Merlin Homer. *Canadian Women's Studies* 11, No. 1 (Spring 1990):106-107

**Shaffer, David R.**

Developmental Psychology: Childhood and Adolescence (2nd ed.). Book Review. *Adolescence* 25, No. 100 (Winter 1990):1001

**Shah, Deepa**

Stalking Shadows. Short story. *Manushi* 56 (January-February 1990):40-42

**Shah, Nasra** (editor)

Pakistani Women: Socioeconomic and Demographic Profile. Reviewed by Kalpana Bardhan. *Journal of Women's History* 2, No. 1 (Spring 1990):200-219

**Shah, Shaila**

Bondage. Theater Review. *Spare Rib* No. 210 (March 1990):36-37

**Shah, Sneh**

Equal Opportunity Issues in the Context of the National Curriculum: A Black Perspective. *Gender and Education* 2, No. 3 (1990):309-318

**Shahinian, Siroon P.** (joint author). *See* Hettena, Charlotte

**Shaikh, Karimabibi** (about)

"How We Poor Women Work Together": Profile of Karimabibi Shaikh. Elisabeth Bentley. *Manushi* No. 59 (July-August 1990):2-10

**Shakeshaft, Charol**

Women in Educational Administration. Reviewed by Anne Statham. *Gender and Society* 4, No. 1 (March 1990):113-115

**Shakespeare, Margaret**

The Busy Life: The Career, the Husband, the Kids and Everything. *Working Woman* (December 1990):94-98

**Shakespeare, William – Criticism and Interpretation**

Daughters of the Game: Troilus and Cressida and the Sexual Discourse of 16th-Century England. Virginia Mason Vaughan. *Women's Studies International Forum* 13, No. 3 (1990):209-220

Emily Dickinson's "Engulfing" Play: *Antony and Cleopatra*. Judith Farr. *Tulsa Studies in Women's Literature* 9, No. 2 (Fall 1990):231-250

**Shalev, Carmel**

Birth Power: The Case for Surrogacy. Reviewed by Leigh Anne Chavez. *NWSA Journal* 2, No. 4 (Autumn 1990):652-656

Legal Conception. *Connexions* 32 (1990):6-7

**Shalifeh, Sahar**

Wild Thorns. Reviewed by Mary Ann Fay. *Belles Lettres* 5, No. 3 (Spring 1990):12

**Shammas, Carole**, Salmon, Marylynn, and Dahlin, Michael

Inheritance in America: From Colonial Times to the Present. Reviewed by Mary M. Schweitzer. *Gender and Society* 4, No. 1 (March 1990):100-101

**Shange, Ntozake** (about). *See* Musicians, Popular, "Repeat Performance"; Writers – Interviews, "Graceful Passages"

**Shangold, Mona** and Mirkin, Gabe

Women and Exercise: Physiology and Sports Medicine. Reviewed by Caroline A. Macera. *Women and Health* 16, No. 2 (1990):137-138

**Shanley, Mary Lyndon**

The Female Body and the Law. Book Review. *NWSA Journal* 2, No. 2 (Spring 1990):308-311

Manhood and Politics: A Feminist Reading in Political Theory. Book Review. *Signs* 16, No. 1 (Autumn 1990):183-187

The Sexual Contract. Book Review. *Signs* 16, No. 1 (Autumn 1990):183-187

Women's Rights, Feminism, and Politics in the United States. Reviewed by Joan C. Tronto. *NWSA Journal* 2, No. 3 (Summer 1990):492-495

**Shannon, Elizabeth**

I Am of Ireland: Women of the North Speak Out. Reviewed by Eleanor J. Bader. *Belles Lettres* 5, No. 3 (Spring 1990):2-3

I Am of Ireland: Women of the North Speak Out. Reviewed by Maureen Murphy. *Feminist Collections* 11, No. 2 (Winter 1990):5-6

**Shannon, Salley**

How Romance Can Wreck an Office. *Working Mother* 13, No. 9 (September 1990):22-27

How to Make Your Home a Whine-Free Zone. *Working Mother* 13, No. 4 (April 1990):51-57

**Shantz, Susan** (joint author). *See* Buyers, Jane

**Shapin, Alice Rindler**

On the Job. *Family Circle* 103, No. 3 (February 20, 1990):25-27

Recycling: Any Office Can. *Working Mother* 13, No. 9 (September 1990):30-34

Women Who Make a Difference. *Family Circle* 103, No. 13 (September 25, 1990):19-23; 103, No. 16 (November 27, 1990):17-19

**Shapiro, Alice**

The Art of Education. Poem. *Heresies* 25 (1990):5

**Shapiro, Amy**

Viewpoint: Missing Money. *Glamour* (June 1990):162

**Shapiro, David**

Man Ray. *Harper's Bazaar* (September 1990):292-293+

**Shapiro, Joan Herbst**

Learning to Play. *Heresies* 25 (1990):80-82

**Shapiro, Joan Poliner**

Nonfeminist and Feminist Students at Risk: The Use of Case Study Analysis While Transforming the Postsecondary Curriculum. *Women's Studies International Forum* 13, No. 6 (1990):553-564

**Shapiro, Vivian** (about). *See* Watts, Patti (editor), "Free Advice."

**Shared Housing**

Housemates: The New Choice. Elsie B. Washington. *Essence* 21, No. 2 (June 1990):84-86

**Sharkey, Michael**

Zora Cross's Entry into Australian Literature. *Hecate* 16, Nos. 1-2 (1990):65-89

**Sharma, Ursula**

Women, Work and Property in North-West India. Reviewed by Kalpana Bardhan. *Journal of Women's History* 2, No. 1 (Spring 1990):200-219

**Sharp, Paula**

The Woman Who Was Not All There. Reviewed by Eleanor J. Bader. *Belles Lettres* 5, No. 2 (Winter 1990):13

**Sharp, Rebecca**

Your Brilliant Career: Back to Graduate School? *Mademoiselle* (October 1990):114

Your Brilliant Career: It's New, It's Improved, It's You! *Mademoiselle* (November 1990):109

Your Brilliant Career. *Mademoiselle* (June 1990):113

Your Brilliant Career: Must a Business Lunch Be All Business? *Mademoiselle* (February 1990):99

Your Brilliant Career: Pet Peeves. *Mademoiselle* (September 1990):180

Your Brilliant Career: The Friendship Trap. *Mademoiselle* (December 1990):100

**Sharpe, Robert**

The Cruel Deception: The Use of Animals in Medical Research. Reviewed by Roberta Kalechofsky. *On the Issues* 14 (1990):25-26

**Shaving**

Close Shaves. K. T. Maclay. *Lear's* (November 1990):78

**Shavlik, Donna L.** (joint editor). *See* Pearson, Carol S.

**Shaw, Bernard** (about)

Bernard Shaw: Anchoring the World. Michelle Morris. *Essence* 21, No. 7 (November 1990):42

**Shaw, Jenny**

Teachers, Gender and Careers. Book Review. *Gender and Education* 2, No. 2 (1990):242-243

**Shaw, Patrick W.**

Willa Cather and France: In Search of the Lost Language. Book Review. *Tulsa Studies in Women's Literature* 9, No. 2 (Fall 1990):337-339

**Shcherbina, Tatiana**

Untitled. Poem. *The Women's Review of Books* 7, Nos. 10-11 (July 1990):9

**Shcherbina, Tatiana** (interview)

A Turn Toward the Future. Rochelle Ruthchild. *The Women's Review of Books* 7, Nos. 10-11 (July 1990):8-9

**Shear, Marie**

Media Watch. *New Directions for Women* 19, No. 1 (January/February 1990):7

**Shearin, Robert B.** (joint author). *See* Greydanus, Donald E.

**Sheba Collective** (editors)

More Serious Pleasure. Reviewed by Maud Sulter. *Spare Rib* 219 (December 1990-January 1991):42-44

**Sheehy, Sandy**

The Business-Pleasure Trip. *Working Woman* (June 1990):89-95

Set Your Goals and Make Them Happen. *Working Woman* (April 1990):81-82+

**Sheets, Robin Lauterbach**

Ellen Terry: Player in Her Time. Book Review. *Tulsa Studies in Women's Literature* 9, No. 1 (Spring 1990):163-165

**Sheets, Robin Lauterbach** (joint author). *See* Helsinger, Elizabeth K.

**Shefer, Elaine**

*The Order of Release* and *Peace Concluded*: Millais's Reversal of a Victorian Formula. *Woman's Art Journal* 11, No. 2 (Fall 1990-Winter 1991):30-33

**Sheffield, Anne**

PB & J: One Mother's Story. *Ladies' Home Journal* 107, No. 8 (August 1990):72

**Sheffield, Margaret** and Bewley, Sheila

Lifeblood: A New Image for Menstruation. Reviewed by Lee Collier and Kim Devaney. *Healthright* 9, No. 2 (February 1990):39

**Sheftell, Fred D.** (joint author). *See* Rapoport, Alan M.

**Shehan, Constance L.,** Bock, E. Wilbur, and Lee, Gary R.

Religious Heterogamy, Religiosity, and Marital Happiness: The Case of Catholics. *Journal of Marriage and the Family* 52, No. 1 (February 1990):73-79

**Sheinkin, Lynn G.** (joint author). *See* Golden, Gail K.

**Sheldon, Amy** (joint author). *See* Katz, Nina

**Sheldon, Sidney**

Memories of Midnight. Short story. *Good Housekeeping* 211, No. 3 (September 1990):46-59

**Shelley, Mary** (about)

Mary Shelley: Her Life, Her Fiction, Her Monsters. By Anne K. Mellor. Reviewed by Deborah Kennedy. *Canadian Women's Studies* 11, No. 2 (Fall 1990):94

**Shellfish**

Ultimate Shrimp Rolls. Holly Sheppard. *McCall's* 118, No. 1 (October 1990):108-110

**Shelov, Steven P.** and Wernick, Sarah

Does Your Child Have a Hidden Vision Problem? *Working Mother* (November 1990):84-88

**Shelton, Charles M.** and McAdams, Dan P.

In Search of an Everyday Morality: The Development of a Measure. *Adolescence* 25, No. 100 (Winter 1990):923-943

**Shelton, Sandi Kahn**

Surviving Coming Home. *Working Mother* (November 1990):105-107

**Shenton, Joan**

Dispatches: The AIDS Catch. Reviewed by Judi Wilson. *Spare Rib* No. 215 (August 1990):32-33

**Shepherd, Cybill**

My Brain's Not Blond. *Ms.* 1, No. 3 (November/December 1990):84-85

**Shepherd, Cybill** (about)

Cybill Shepherd: Doors Keep Opening. Julia Kagan. *McCall's* 117, No. 10 (July 1990):64-66

A Wild Night with Cybill Shepherd. Cliff Jahr. *Ladies' Home Journal* 107, No. 2 (February 1990):98-104

**Shields, Jody**

Elements: Joseff. *Vogue* (December 1990):142-144

Hands. *Vogue* (August 1990):346-351

Images: History of the Hairdresser. *Vogue* (July 1990):77-83

'60s Something. *Vogue* (August 1990):292-299

View: Image Conscious. *Vogue* (January 1990):40-42

**Shields, Patricia M.**, Curry, Landon, and Nichols, Janet

Women Pilots in Combat: Attitudes of Male and Female Pilots. *Minerva* 8, No. 2 (Summer 1990):21-35

**Shimer, Porter** (joint author). *See* Stamford, Bryant

**Shinebourne, Janice**

Curl Up and Dye. Theater Review. *Spare Rib* 217 (October 1990):31-32

**Shingles.** *See* Herpes Zoster

**Shinn, Thelma J.**

Worlds Within Women: Myth and Mythmaking in Fantastic Literature by Women. Reviewed by Hoda M. Zaki. *Women's Studies International Forum* 13, No. 3 (1990):277-279

**Shiva, Vandana**

The Myth of the Miracle Seeds. *Women in Action* 1-2 (1990):11-12

The Rest of Reality. *Ms.* 1, No. 3 (November/December 1990):72-73

Staying Alive: Women, Ecology and Development. Reviewed by Linda Vance. *NWSA Journal* 2, No. 3 (Summer 1990):485-489

**Shiva, Vandana** (interview)

Genetic Exploitation: Interview with an Eco-Feminist. Theresia Degener. *Connexions* 32 (1990):14-15

**Shively, Ellen M.**

The Chalice and the Blade: Our History, Our Future. Book Review. *Minerva* 8, No. 2 (Summer 1990):78-79

**Shocked, Michelle**

The Captain Swing Review. Reviewed by Pam Mason. *Spare Rib* No. 214 (July 1990):24

**Shocked, Michelle** (interview)

Michelle Shocked on Coming Out. Christine Nordheim and Julie A. Kreiner. *Hot Wire* 6, No. 3 (September 1990):20-21

**Shockley, Ann Allen** (about)

Ann Allen Shockley: An Annotated Primary and Secondary Bibliography. By Rita B. Dandridge. Reviewed by Barbara Williams Jenkins. *Sage* 6, No. 2 (Fall 1989):63-64

**Shockley, Ann Allen** (editor)

Afro-American Women Writers, 1746-1933: An Anthology and Critical Guide. Reviewed by Claudia Tate. *Tulsa Studies in Women's Literature* 9, No. 2 (Fall 1990):317-321

**Shoemaker, Pamela**

Rap Sheet. *Heresies* 25 (1990):61

**Shoes.** *See also* Foot – Care and Hygiene

Details. *Lear's* (July 1990):96-101

Fall Shoe Report: Feet First. Candy Pratts Price. *Vogue* (July 1990):45-57

Great Looks: Soft Steps. *Redbook* 175, No. 6 (October 1990):22-26

Heavenly Soles: Extraordinary Twentieth-Century Shoes. By Mary Trasko. Reviewed by Holly Hall. *Belles Lettres* 5, No. 4 (Summer 1990):35+

Step in Time. Stacey Okun. *Savvy Woman* (November 1990):38-40

What They're Wearing. *Glamour* (July 1990):138

**Shoes, Athletic**

Athletic Footwear Keeps the Nation on Its Toes. *Executive Female* 13, No. 6 (November-December 1990):76

Picking the Right Shoe for You. Sara Henry and Kelly Stevenson. *Women's Sports and Fitness* 12, No. 2 (March 1990):29-42

**Shogan, Debra**

Comment on Hawkesworth's "Knowers, Knowing, Known: Feminist Theory and Claims of Truth." *Signs* 15, No. 2 (Winter 1990):424-425

**Shogan, Debra** (about)

Reply to Shogan. Mary E. Hawkesworth. *Signs* 15, No. 2 (Winter 1990):426-428

**Shollar, Barbara** (joint editor). *See* Arkin, Marian

**Shope, Kimberly Ann**

Song. Short Story. *Good Housekeeping* 210, No. 6 (June 1990):143-145

**Shoplifting**

The Trade in Sticky Fingers. Susan Schneider. *Lear's* (September 1990):38-40

**Shopping.** *See also* Consumer Information; New York (City) – Culture and Society; Travel Costs

Beauty and Fashion Hotline: Catalog Chic. *Family Circle* 103, No. 16 (November 27, 1990):31-32

Best Boutiques. Maureen Sajbel. *Harper's Bazaar* (October 1990):67-80

Eat Light: Fabulous Mail-Order Finds. *Redbook* 176, No. 2 (December 1990):150

Fabulous Fashion Finds. *Family Circle* 103, No. 14 (October 16, 1990):94-99

Fashion Fax. Bibliography. *Glamour* (January 1990):98

Fashion Fax. *Glamour* (February 1990):144-146

Fashion Workshop: How Much Work-Style does $500 Buy? *Glamour* (November 1990):181-184

Fashion Workshop: Sale. *Glamour* (December 1990):167-170

Great Gear. Diane French. *Women's Sports & Fitness* 12, No. 6 (September 1990):62-63

How to Shop, When to Stop. *Ladies' Home Journal* 107, No. 10 (October 1990):38-46

How to Shop Like a Pro. *Ladies' Home Journal* 107, No. 3 (March 1990):42-44+

Inside Hot! Laura Morice. *Mademoiselle* (January 1990):40

A Little Shop Talk. *Mademoiselle* (January 1990):142

More Splash than Cash. *Harper's Bazaar* (November 1990):131

Objects of Desire. *Harper's Bazaar* (December 1990):59-78

Real Steals: 50 Finds Under $50. *Family Circle* 103, No. 9 (June 26, 1990):76-81

Shopping Smart: Bargain Gifts by Mail. Joan Hamburg. *Family Circle* 103, No. 15 (November 6, 1990):40-43

Shopping Smart. Christine Fellingham. *Glamour* (June 1990):202 ɪ

Shopping Smart: What's New in Off-Price? Bibliography. Debra Wise. *Glamour* (September 1990):272

Shopping Until You Can't Stop. John Bradshaw. *Lear's* (October 1990):75

Shop Smart. Pamela Redmond Satran. *Redbook* 175, No. 4 (August 1990):95

Something Special. *Glamour* (November 1990):232-235

1-800-STYLE. *Glamour* (August 1990):222-225

Summer Indispensables: 17 Super Finds to Order by Phone. Rowann Gilman. *Working Woman* (June 1990):85-86

Talking Fashion: Chanel Suit. Dodie Kazanjian. *Vogue* (August 1990):367-376

What Will They Try to Sell Me Next? Joy Horseman. *Lear's* (May 1990):60

Women Right Now. *Glamour* (May 1990):109-111

The Year's First Fashion Bargains. *Glamour* (January 1990):142-147

**Short, Randall**

Theater: A Few Good Men. Theater review. *Vogue* (January 1990):98

**Short, Robyn** (joint author). *See* Pura, Matiria

**Short Stories**

3010: A Space Idiocy. Marsha Prescod. *Spare Rib* 218 (November 1990):34-37

The Abiding Heart. Ken Follett. *Good Housekeeping* 211, No. 2 (August 1990):60-69

The Accordion. Rachel Guido DeVries. *Sinister Wisdom* 41 (Summer-Fall 1990):34-37

The Age of Lead. Short story. Margaret Atwood. *Lear's* (September 1990):114-119+

Along Came Love. Helen Lewis Coffer. *Good Housekeeping* 211, No. 5 (November 1990):138-141

American Horse. Louise Erdrich. *Spare Rib* 217 (October 1990):38-43

An Inconvenient Woman. Excerpt. Short story. Dominick Dunne. *Ladies' Home Journal* 107, No. 7 (July 1990):48-57

Another Pretty Face. Short story. Jennifer Egan. *Mademoiselle* (December 1990):118-123+

An Unmarried Man. Short story. Lisa Zeidner. *Mademoiselle* (November 1990):126-131

The Bare Truth. Short story. Tom Bodett. *Redbook* 175, No. 5 (September 1990):64-66+

Becoming Somebody's Mother. Short story. Laurie Colwin. *Redbook* 175, No. 3 (July 1990):46-54

Belly Dancers' Reunion. Phyllis Barber. *Frontiers* 11, Nos. 2-3 (1990):75-79

Bel Patra. Gitanjalishri. *Manushi* 61 (November-December 1990):37-43

Bodies at Sea. By Erin McGraw. Reviewed by Marcia Tager. *New Directions for Women* 19, No. 1 (January/February 1990):22

Boomerang Love. Excerpt. Short story. Jimmy Buffett. *Ladies' Home Journal* 107, No. 4 (April 1990):72-77+

Bringing It All Back Home Again. Short story. Laurie Colwin. *McCall's* 117, No. 8 (May 1990):110-112+

Bunch of Keys. R. Chudamani. *Manushi* 60 (September-October 1990):39-43

Bye Bye Baby. Short story. Merrill Joan Gerber. *Redbook* 175, No. 1 (May 1990):48-51+

Caesura. Short story. David Sedaris. *Out/Look* No. 8 (Spring 1990):58-61

Cartographies. By Maya Sonenberg. Reviewed by Marcia Tager. *New Directions for Women* 19, No. 1 (January/February 1990):22

Come the Revolution. Sanjida O'Connell. *Spare Rib* 219 (December 1990-January 1991):54-56

The Cookie Rebellion. Short story. Will Stanton. *Redbook* 176, No. 1 (November 1990):74-82

The Cover-Up. Short story. Shashi Samundra. *Manushi* 56 (January-February 1990):38-39

Cross My Heart. Short story. Joe Pici. *Redbook* 175, No. 3 (July 1990):57-60

Crowded Honeymoon. Lila McGinnis. *Good Housekeeping* 210, No. 4 (April 1990):134-135

A Curious Haunting. Short story. Alison Lurie. *Redbook* 175, No. 6 (October 1990):40-52

Daneshvar's Playhouse. By Simin Daneshvar. Reviewed by Marcia Tager. *New Directions for Women* 19, No. 1 (January/February 1990):22

Dark Deceiver. Short story. Sharleen Cooper Cohen. *Good Housekeeping* 211, No. 4 (October 1990):209-230+

Days of Awe. Maxine Rodburg. *Belles Lettres* 6, No. 1 (Fall 1990):14-19

The DeCristo Girls. Kathy Freeperson. *Sinister Wisdom* 41 (Summer-Fall 1990):23-30

Di's Double. Short story. Alan Brown. *Redbook* 174, No. 6 (April 1990):44-53+

Doll Baby. Short story. Deborah Joy Corey. *Mademoiselle* (October 1990):134-136+

To Do Something Beautiful (extract). Rohini Hensman. *Spare Rib* 213 (June 1990):9-11

The End of the Season. Short story. Peter McGehee. *Out/Look* No. 7 (Winter 1990):36-41

Family Pictures. Excerpt. Short story. Sue Miller. *Ladies' Home Journal* 107, No. 6 (June 1990):62-68

Field Trip. Short story. Tim O'Brien. *McCall's* 117, No. 11 (August 1990):78-79

A Fine Night for Caroling. Short story. Jean Todd Freeman. *Family Circle* 103, No. 17 (December 18, 1990):56-61

The First Rains. Shama Futehally. *Manushi* No. 59 (July-August 1990):33-42

Follow Your Heart. Short story. Richard Selzer. *Redbook* 175, No. 5 (September 1990):52-62

Gemini. Merle Collins. *Spare Rib* No. 216 (September 1990):40-43

The Girl Called Samantha. Isobel Stewart. *Good Housekeeping* 211, No. 2 (August 1990):112-113

The Girl of His Dreams. Marian Bates. *Good Housekeeping* 211, No. 5 (November 1990):168-169

The Girl Who Loved Dylan. Katherine Min. *Iris* 24 (Fall-Winter 1990):46-48

The Good Daughter. Short story. Peter Nelson. *Redbook* 174, No. 5 (March 1990):60-64+

By the Grace of Shasthi. Short story. Rajshekhar Basu. *Manushi* 58 (May-June 1990):39-42

Happy Valentine's Day, Monsieur Ducharme. Short story. Louise Erdich. *Ladies' Home Journal* 107, No. 2 (February 1990):84+

"Harry, My Mom's Boyfriend." Short story. Robin Hansen. *Redbook* 174, No. 6 (April 1990):150-154

Harvest of Ghosts (excerpts). Nina Crow Newington. *Sinister Wisdom* 40 (Spring 1990):79-81

The Hat. Short story. Jane Groyer. *Ladies' Home Journal* 107, No. 2 (February 1990):84-88

Heart-Work. Short story. Roberta Silman. *McCall's* 117, No. 7 (April 1990):49-57

Hidden Blessing. Sonja Peterson. *Good Housekeeping* 211, No. 6 (December 1990):154-155

Holy Music. Short story. Bebe Moore Campbell. *Essence* 21, No. 8 (December 1990):58-59+

Home. Short story. Nadezhda Kozhevnikova. *Ladies' Home Journal* 107, No. 5 (May 1990):148-154

How I Get Started in a Life of Crime. Gila Svirsky. *Sinister Wisdom* 40 (Spring 1990):48-60

How It Went in the West. Matthew T. Jones. *Good Housekeeping* 210, No. 6 (June 1990):138-143

The Hunt. Mahasweta Devi. Translated by Gayatri Spivak. *Women and Performance: A Journal of Feminist Theory* 5, No. 1, Issue #9 (1990): 61-79

Isn't It Romantic? Louise Lee Outlaw. *Good Housekeeping* 211, No. 1 (July 1990):116-117

Is There Poll Tax After Death? Kate Pullinger. *Spare Rib* 217 (October 1990):16-17

Italy. Janet Capone. *Sinister Wisdom* 41 (Summer-Fall 1990):47-53

Jesse. Short story. Rosemarie Robotham. *Essence* 21, No. 4 (August 1990):70-72+

Journey to Love. Jane Roberts Woods. *Good Housekeeping* 211, No. 2 (August 1990):155-172, 184-190, 196-203

Just a Matter of Time. Short story. Joey Wauters. *Redbook* 175, No. 1 (May 1990):54-59

Kate's Story. Excerpt. Short story. Maggie Skye. *Good Housekeeping* 211, No. 3 (September 1990):277-288+

A Kind of Flying. Short story. Ron Carlson. *McCall's* 117, No. 11 (August 1990):69-74

King's Oak. Excerpt. Short story. Anne Rivers Siddons. *Ladies' Home Journal* 107, No. 10 (October 1990):108-115

The Lamp: A Parable About Art and Class and the Function of Kishinev in the Jewish Imagination.

Irena Klepfisz. *Bridges* 1, No. 1 (Spring 1990): 96-97

The Language of Bees. Short story. Kelly Cherry. *McCall's* 117, No. 12 (September 1990):132-135+

La Ofrenda. Short story. Cherríe Moraga. *Out/Look* No. 10 (Fall 1990):50-53

Laundering Money. Short story. Barbara Shulgasser. *Glamour* (July 1990):123+

A Leap of Faith. Elizabeth Denton. *Iris* 23 (Spring-Summer 1990):17-19

Leapole Lester. Heather Cyr. *Good Housekeeping* 210, No. 6 (June 1990):145-146

Lessons in Love. Isobel Stewart. *Good Housekeeping* 210, No. 6 (June 1990):176-177

Love's Rocky Road. Virginia M. Gillette. *Good Housekeeping* 210, No. 5 (May 1990):182-183

The Marrying Kind. Kate Braestrup. *Mademoiselle* (March 1990):160-167, 234

Mars Bar. Short story. Mary Wings. *Out/Look* No. 9 (Summer 1990):32-35

Matchmaking Angels. Short story. Pearl Canick Solomon. *Redbook* 176, No. 2 (December 1990):48-53

Maximum Security. Short story. Molly Giles. *McCall's* 118, No. 2 (November 1990):119-120+

Memories of Midnight. Short story. Sidney Sheldon. *Good Housekeeping* 211, No. 3 (September 1990):46-59

A Memory of Dancing. Short story. Diiane Salvatore. *Ladies' Home Journal* 107, No. 3 (March 1990):132-138

Mercy (excerpt). Andrea Dworkin. *Spare Rib* 218 (November 1990):28-29

Monkey Mountain Morning. Bobbie Trotter. *Minerva* 8, No. 4 (Winter 1990):56-59

Mothers Make Mistakes. Short story. Sara Lewis. *Redbook* 174, No. 5 (March 1990):52-59

The Mother Who Never Was. Short story. Lisa K. Buchanan. *Mademoiselle* (June 1990):136-138+

The Music Room (excerpt). Dennis McFarland. *Vogue* (April 1990):391-393, 420

My Child Forever. Short story. Andrew Borders. *Redbook* 175, No. 4 (August 1990):60-68

My Daughter, Myself. Short story. Lynne Kaufman. *Family Circle* 103, No. 14 (October 16, 1990):58-62

My Day Off. Jane Routley. *Hecate* 16, Nos. 1-2 (1990):164-166

Naps . . . The Politics of Hair (excerpts). Deb Parks-Satterfield. *Sinister Wisdom* 42 (Winter 1990-1991):54-58

Never Jerk Your Hand Away. Penelope J. Engelbrecht. *Sinister Wisdom* 40 (Spring 1990):102-123

The Nickel Plan. Short story. Jane Smiley. *McCall's* 118, No. 1 (October 1990):112-114+

No Shuttle to Central Vermont. Michele Clark. *Bridges* 1, No. 2 (Fall 1990): 15-21

From *Notes to My Sisters*. Moni Lai Storz. *Hecate* 16, Nos. 1-2 (1990):43-47

One, Please. Laura Cunningham. *Mademoiselle* (August 1990):148, 232-235

The One that Got Away. Excerpt. Short story. Carrie Fisher. *Ladies' Home Journal* 107, No. 9 (September 1990):98-104

The Other Anna. Short story. Barbara Eastman. *Lear's* (August 1990):116-122

Other Women's Children. Excerpt. Short story. Perri Klass. *Redbook* 176, No. 1 (November 1990):58-70+

Personal Testimony. Short story. Lynna Williams. *Lear's* (January 1990):116-121

A Place for the Heart. David Doig. *Good Housekeeping* 210, No. 4 (April 1990):98-100

The Plains of Passage. Excerpt. Short story. Jean Auel. *Ladies' Home Journal* 107, No. 11 (November 1990):184-193

Pomegranate's Story. Jeanne Larsen. *Iris* 23 (Spring-Summer 1990):46-48

Precious. Short story. Lois Wyse. *Redbook* 175, No. 2 (June 1990):42-44

The Red Furrow. Alison Lambert. *Hecate* 16, Nos. 1-2 (1990):97-101

Remember the Oranges. Short story. Gerald R. Toner. *Ladies' Home Journal* 107, No. 12 (December 1990):84-92

The Revenge of the Chunky Beef. Emily Levy. *Sinister Wisdom* 40 (Spring 1990):82-88

Rich in Spirit. Short story. Ruth Moore. *Redbook* 176, No. 2 (December 1990):62-72

The Rise of Aretha Tubman VI: An African History Book. Marsha Prescod. *Spare Rib* No. 212 (May 1990):14-15

Sarah. Mary A. White. *Sinister Wisdom* 40 (Spring 1990):40-47

The Scaredy Cats. Short story. Meredith Graham. *Ladies' Home Journal* 107, No. 2 (February 1990):112-114

The Scarlet Thread. Evelyn Anthony. *Good Housekeeping* 211, No. 1 (July 1990):163-180, 192-198, 205-206

Season of Promise. Nina Lambert. *Good Housekeeping* 210, No. 6 (June 1990):68-75

The Secret Keeper. Melizma Morgan. *Sinister Wisdom* 42 (Winter 1990-1991):10-21

September. Rosamunde Pilcher. *Good Housekeeping* 210, No. 5 (May 1990):241-244, 248-250, 261-275

Shaitan & the Chappal. Short Story. Afshan N. Malik. *Spare Rib* No. 211 (April 1990):18-19

She JUST Can't Talk. Barbara Wels. *Hecate* 16, Nos. 1-2 (1990):148-150

Sleeping Alone. Molly Moynahan. *Mademoiselle* (April 1990):178-187

Sleeping Dogs. Marsha Prescod. *Spare Rib* 213 (June 1990):20-22

A Small Battle. Short story. Mary Anderson Parks. *AFFILIA* 5, No. 2 (Summer 1990):90-96

Some Pieces of Jewish Left: 1987. Melanie Kaye/Kantrowitz. *Bridges* 1, No. 1 (Spring 1990): 7-22

Song. Kimberly Ann Shope. *Good Housekeeping* 210, No. 6 (June 1990):143-145

Special Interests. Linda Cashdan. *Good Housekeeping* 210, No. 6 (June 1990):219-245, 262-267

Squandering the Blue. Short story. Kate Braverman. *Lear's* (March 1990):122-125+

Stalking Shadows. Short story. Deepa Shah. *Manushi* 56 (January-February 1990):40-42

Subject to Diary. Short story. Fay Weldon. *Lear's* (April 1990):112-115+

Such Good Friends. Short story. J. California Cooper. *Essence* 21, No. 1 (May 1990):150-154+

A Sweet Memory. Short story. Robley Wilson, Jr. *Redbook* 174, No. 5 (March 1990):172-174

Take Her Dancing. Short story. Michael C. White. *Redbook* 175, No. 4 (August 1990):44-50

Tears: A Yom Kippur Story. Short story. Elaine Kalman Naves. *Lilith* 15, No. 4 (Fall 1990):30-32

Theodora. Excerpt. Short story. Barbara Taylor Bradford. *Ladies' Home Journal* 107, No. 8 (August 1990):90-97

Thinking West. Short story. Shylah Boyd. *McCall's* 117, No. 11 (August 1990):75-77

Thomas. Rebecca T. Godwin. *Iris* 24 (Fall-Winter 1990):35-39

Too Close for Comfort. Short story. Marjorie Franco. *Redbook* 175, No. 4 (August 1990):54-59+

Traveling with Married Men. Elizabeth Tippens. *Mademoiselle* (May 1990):150-154, 228-230

Tres Mujeres. Terri de la Peña. *Frontiers* 11, No. 1 (1990):60-64

Trip to the City (from my point of view). Jennifer Vacchiano. *Women's Studies Quarterly* 18, Nos. 3-4 (Fall-Winter 1990):165-167

As Usual. Short story. Ashapurna Devi. *Manushi* 57 (March-April 1990):39-42

Vampires. Nicole Matthews. *Hecate* 16, Nos. 1-2 (1990):111-114

Verging on the Pertinent. By Carol Emshwiller. Reviewed by Marcia Tager. *New Directions for Women* 19, No. 1 (January/February 1990):22

A View of Boston Common. Merrill Joan Gerber. *Belles Lettres* 5, No. 3 (Spring 1990):18

Vinnie's Angel. Susan Thaler. *Good Housekeeping* 211, No. 6 (December 1990):62+

The Virgin of Polish Hill. Carolyn Banks. *Belles Lettres* 5, No. 4 (Summer 1990):11-14

Voyage of the Heart. Short story. Florence Jane Soman. *Good Housekeeping* 211, No. 4 (October 1990):150-151

The Wall. Short story. Mary Morris. *Vogue* (September 1990):580-583+

The Watching Shadows. Michael Allegretto. *Good Housekeeping* 210, No. 4 (April 1990):231-249, 259-273

A Way With Women. Short story. Julie Schwartzman. *Mademoiselle* (September 1990):208-214+

Weight. Short story. Margaret Atwood. *Vogue* (August 1990):328-331+

What Dinah Thought. Excerpt. Short story. Deena Metzger. *Lilith* 15, No. 2 (Spring 1990):8-12

What's Love Got to Do With It? Short story. Itabari Njeri. *Essence* 20, No. 10 (February 1990):64-66+

What They're Missing. Michele Connelly. *Sinister Wisdom* 42 (Winter 1990-1991):59-67

What They Write About in Other Countries. Mary Sojourner. *Heresies* 25 (1990):38-48

When First He Kissed Me. Short story. Amy Belding Brown. *Good Housekeeping* 211, No. 4 (October 1990):70-72

Where the Heart Is. Short story. Diane Salvatore. *Redbook* 176, No. 2 (December 1990):54-60

The Wife. Short story. Jennifer Jordon. *Essence* 21, No. 3 (July 1990):66-68+

For Women Everywhere. Short story. Perri Klass. *Glamour* (July 1990):124-129

The Wrong Men. Short story. Diane Schoemperlen. *Mademoiselle* (February 1990):128-131

## Short Stories – History and Criticism

America and I: Short Stories by American Jewish Women Writers. Edited by Joyce Antler. Reviewed by Ruth Knafo Setton. *Lilith* 15, No. 4 (Fall 1990):33·

**Shostak, Elizabeth**

Liberation Struggle. *The Women's Review of Books* 8, No. 2 (November 1990):26

The Same Sea as Every Summer. Book Review. *The Women's Review of Books* 8, No. 2 (November 1990):26

**Shostak, Marjorie** (joint author). *See* Easton, S. Boyd

**Showalter, Elaine**

The Female Malady: Women, Madness and English Culture, 1830-1980. Reviewed by Ruth Harris. *Signs* 15, No. 2 (Winter 1990):408-410

**Showalter, Elaine** (editor)

These Modern Women: Autobiographical Essays from the Twenties. Reviewed by Laura Hapke. *Belles Lettres* 6, No. 1 (Fall 1990):54-55

**Showers, Margi** (about). *See also* Entrepreneurs

**Shrage, Laurie**

Feminist Film Aesthetics: A Contextual Approach. *Hypatia* 5, No. 2 (Summer 1990):137-148

**Shrimps.** *See* Cookery (Seafood)

**Shriver, Maria** (about). *See also* Television Journalists – Networking

**Shteir, Ann B.**

The Meridian Anthology of Early Women Writers: British Literary Women from Aphra Behn to Maria Edgeworth 1660-1800. Book Review. *Canadian Women's Studies* 11, No. 2 (Fall 1990):91-92

The Sign of Angellica: Women, Writing, and Fiction, 1660-1800. Book Review. *Canadian Women's Studies* 11, No. 2 (Fall 1990):91-92

**Shukla, P. R.**

All for Survival. *Manushi* 61 (November-December 1990):12-14

**Shulgasser, Barbara**

Laundering Money. Short story. *Glamour* (July 1990):123+

**Shulgasser, Barbara** (about)

Glamour's First Summer Fiction Issue: Meet the Authors. *Glamour* (July 1990):121

**Shulins, Nancy**

Obsessed. *Family Circle* 103, No. 8 (June 5, 1990):57-59

X Rated: When Hardcore Hits Home. *Family Circle* 103, No. 16 (November 27, 1990):63-69

**Shulman, Alix Kates**

Burning Questions. Reviewed by Lynn Wenzel. *New Directions for Women* 19, No. 3 (May/June 1990):23

**Shulman, Alix Kates – Criticism and Interpretation**

A Decade Later Burning Questions Remain Unanswered. Lynn Wenzel. *New Directions for Women* 19, No. 3 (May/June 1990):23

**Shulman, Label** (joint author). *See* Ubell, Al

**Shult, Linda**

An Encyclopedic Undertaking. *Feminist Collections* 11, No. 3 (Spring 1990):11-12

Feminist Visions: Words and Pictures. *Feminist Collections* 11, No. 4 (Summer 1990):9-10

**Shultz, Cathleen** (joint author). *See* Beck, Cornelia

**Sibling Relationships.** *See also* Sister-Brother Relationships

The Early Years: Mom Loves You More. T. Berry Brazelton. *Family Circle* 103, No. 9 (June 26, 1990):41-43

Sibling Exchanges and Complementarity in the Philippine Highlands. Jean Treloggen Peterson. *Journal of Marriage and the Family* 52, No. 2 (May 1990):441-451

Sibling Relationships in Adulthood: Contact Patterns and Motivations. Thomas R. Lee, Jay A. Mancini, and Joseph W. Maxwell. *Journal of Marriage and the Family* 52, No. 2 (May 1990):431-440

Sibling Violence and Agonistic Interactions among Middle Adolescents. Megan P. Goodwin and Bruce Roscoe. *Adolescence* 25, No. 98 (Summer 1990):451-467

**Siblings**

The Sibling Gap. Lynne S. Dumas. *Working Mother* 13, No. 8 (August 1990):36-42

**Sibling Temperaments**

The One You Call Sister. Edited by Paula Martinac. Reviewed by Beverly Lowry. *On the Issues* 15 (Summer 1990):27

**Siddons, Anne Rivers**

King's Oak. Excerpt. Short story. *Ladies' Home Journal* 107, No. 10 (October 1990):108-115

**Sidel, Ruth**

On Her Own: Growing Up in the Shadow of the American Dream. Reviewed by Carolyn Keith. *AFFILIA* 5, No. 4 (Winter 1990):117-118

On Her Own: Growing Up in the Shadow of the American Dream. Reviewed by Deborah Solomon. *The Women's Review of Books* 7, No. 7 (April 1990):1+

On Her Own: Growing Up in the Shadow of the American Dream. Reviewed by Martha Boethel. *New Directions for Women* 19, No. 6 (November-December 1990):20

**SIDS.** *See* Sudden Infant Death Syndrome

**Siedlecky, Stefania**

A Guide to Understanding Alzheimer's Disease and Related Disorders. Book Review. *Healthright* 9, No. 4 (August 1990):46

Women's Health Questions Answered. Book Review. *Healthright* 9, No. 4 (August 1990):43

**Siegal, Aranka** (about). *See* Holocaust (1939-1945) – Survivors

**Siegel, Dorothy G.** (joint author). *See* Sherill, Jan M.

**Siegel, Fred**

Backtalk: The Supremes. *Lear's* (February 1990):126-127 +

**Siegel, Jessica** (about)

Small Victories. Excerpt. Samuel G. Freedman. *McCall's* 117, No. 8 (May 1990):114-118 +

**Siegel, Rachel Josefowitz**

Love and Work After 60: An Integration of Personal and Professional Growth Within a Long-Term Marriage. *Journal of Women and Aging* 2, No. 2 (1990):69-79

Old Women as Mother Figures. *Women and Therapy* 10, Nos. 1/2 (1990):89-97

Turning the Things That Divide Us into Strengths That Unite Us. *Women and Therapy* 9, No. 3 (1990):327-336

We Are Not Your Mothers: Report on Two Groups of Women Over Sixty. *Journal of Women and Aging* 2, No. 2 (1990):81-89

**Siegel, Rachel Josefowitz** (joint author). *See* Katz, Nina

**Siegler, Bonnie**

Jamie Lee Curtis. *McCall's* 117, No. 9 (June 1990):23

Melanie Mellows Out. *Ladies' Home Journal* 107, No. 10 (October 1990):154-155 +

Twin Peaks' Joan Chen: Success Came American-Style. *McCall's* 118, No. 1 (October 1990):34

**Siegler, Bonnie** (joint author). *See* Casey, Kathryn

**Sien, Bettianne Shoney**

Lizards/Los Padres. Reviewed by Amber Katherine. *Sinister Wisdom* 42 (Winter 1990-1991):127-129

**Sievers, Sharon L.**

Flowers in Salt: The Beginnings of Feminist Consciousness in Modern Japan. Reviewed by Kathleen Uno. *NWSA Journal* 2, No. 1 (Winter 1990):112-119

**Signorelli-Pappas, Rita**

Maria Zef. Book Review. *The Women's Review of Books* 7, No. 9 (June 1990):18

Tales of the Disinherited. *The Women's Review of Books* 7, No. 9 (June 1990):18

**Sikes, Gini**

World Apart. *Harper's Bazaar* (October 1990):234 +

**Silber, Kathleen** and Dorner, Patricia Martinez

Children of Open Adoption. Reviewed by Datha Clapper Brack. *New Directions for Women* 19, No. 6 (November-December 1990):25

**Silcott, George** (about)

Hands Off the Silcotts. Marcel Farry. *Spare Rib* No. 210 (March 1990):14-15

**Silence**

Challenging Men. Bell Hooks. *Spare Rib* 217 (October 1990):12-15

**Sills, Beverly**

Forum. *McCall's* 117, No. 12 (September 1990):21-22

**Sills, Judith** (joint author). *See* Rosenbaum, Maj-Britt

**Silman, Roberta**

Heart-Work. Short story. *McCall's* 117, No. 7 (April 1990):49-57

**Silver, John**

Watsonville. Reviewed by C. Alejandra Elenes. *Feminist Collections* 11, No. 3 (Spring 1990):10

**Silver, Marie-France**

Les Reines de France. Book Review. *Resources for Feminist Research* 19, No. 1 (March 1990):31

**Silver, Shelley** (joint author). *See* Martlew, Gillian

**Silverman, Jane L.**

Ka'ahumanu, Molder of Change. Reviewed by Haunani-Kay Trask. *NWSA Journal* 2, No. 1 (Winter 1990):127-129

**Silverman, Kaja**

The Acoustic Mirror: The Female Voice in Psychoanalysis and Cinema. Reviewed by Paula Rabinowitz. *Feminist Studies* 16, No. 1 (Spring 1990):151-169

**Silverman, Leigh**

Health Department. *Lear's* (May 1990):62; (July 1990):42

Health Deptartment. *Lear's* (September 1990):74

The Private Terror of a Panic Attack. *Lear's* (August 1990):36-39

Surgery: Weighing the Options. *Lear's* (June 1990):48-50

**Silvermoon, Flash**

Enough Is Enough. Poem. *off our backs* 20, No. 9 (October 1990):2

**Silver-Plated Ware, Victorian**

Silver Plate Grabs the Spotlight. Sally Clark. *McCall's* 117, No. 9 (June 1990):55

**Simeti, Mary Taylor**

From a Vanished World. *The Women's Review of Books* 8, No. 1 (October 1990):13-14

Where It All Began: Italy 1954. Book Review. *The Women's Review of Books* 8, No. 1 (October 1990):13-14

**Simko, Alison**

Catch of the Season. *Savvy Woman* (November 1990):56

**Simmons, Judy**

Camille Claudel. Film review. *Ms.* 1, No. 1 (July/August 1990):74-75

Four to Jam. *Ms.* 1, No. 2 (September/October 1990):23

**Simmons, Marie**

Come for the Weekend. *Working Woman* (June 1990):79-82 +

The Healthy Microwave Cookbook. *Ladies' Home Journal* 107, No. 10 (October 1990):203-208

The Sensible Salad. *Working Woman* (May 1990):130

**Simon, Carly** (about)

Classic Carly. Peter Feibleman. *Lear's* (December 1990):90-93 +

Talking with Carly Simon: "I've Stopped Running from Problems." Interview. Stephen Holden. *Redbook* 175, No. 3 (July 1990):62-64

What's Hot: Music's Legendary Ladies. *Ladies' Home Journal* 107, No. 6 (June 1990):44-48

**Simon, Kate** (about)

Memories of Kate Simon – Dazzling Without Show. Florence Howe. *Women's Studies Quarterly* 18, Nos. 3-4 (Fall-Winter 1990):153-158

**Simone, Nina** (about). *See* De Veaux, Alexis, Milloy, Marilyn, and Ross, Michael Erik

**Simons, Judy**

Reading the Romance: Women, Patriarchy and Popular Literature. Book Review. *Women's Studies International Forum* 13, No. 3 (1990):277

**Simons, Ronald L**, Whitbeck, Les B., Conger, Rand D., and Melby, Janet N.

Husband and Wife Differences in Determinants of Parenting: A Social Learning/Exchange Model of Parental Behavior. *Journal of Marriage and the Family* 52, No. 2 (May 1990):375-392

**Simons, Ronald L** (joint author). *See* Conger, Rand D.

**Simpkins, Gregory**

Back Talk: Europe '92 and Us. *Essence* 21, No. 2 (June 1990):114

**Simpson, Coreen** (about). *See* Fashion Designers, "Top Women Designers"

**Simpson, Eileen**

Ode to a Woman Well at Ease: Mary McCarthy, 1912-1989. *Lear's* (April 1990):136 +

**Simpson, Layne A.** (joint author). *See* Grant, Linda

**Simpson, Lorna** (about)

Lorna Simpson: Words of Art. Joan Morgan. *Essence* 21, No. 8 (December 1990):36

**Simpson, Pamela H.**

Architecture: A Place for Women. Book Review. *Woman's Art Journal* 11, No. 2 (Fall 1990-Winter 1991):44-48

Architecture and Women: A Bibliography. Book Review. *Woman's Art Journal* 11, No. 2 (Fall 1990-Winter 1991):44-48

Eileen Gray: Architect/Designer. Book Review. *Woman's Art Journal* 11, No. 2 (Fall 1990-Winter 1991):44-48

Julia Morgan, Architect. Book Review. *Woman's Art Journal* 11, No. 2 (Fall 1990-Winter 1991):44-48

The Lady Architects, Lois Lilley Howe, Eleanor Manning and Mary Almy, 1913-1937. Book Review. *Woman's Art Journal* 11, No. 2 (Fall 1990-Winter 1991):48

**Simpson, Peggy**

Conflict in Academia: Why Was Bunny Sandler Sacked? *Ms.* 1, No. 3 (November/December 1990):86-87

Getting Ready to Run the Country. *McCall's* 117, No. 9 (June 1990):62-63 +

**Simpson, Penny**

Cymreictod: Welsh Women. Paintings and Drawings by Chris Kinsey. *Spare Rib* No. 211 (April 1990):31

Exchanges: Poems by Women in Wales. add. *Spare Rib* No. 216 (September 1990):25

Morphine and Dolly Mixtures. add. *Spare Rib* No. 209 (February 1990):30

On My Life: Women's Writing from Wales. Book Review. *Spare Rib* 213 (June 1990):29

**Sinclair, Maggie C.**

Fighting Porn in Scotland. *Spare Rib* 219 (December 1990-January 1991):65

**Sinfield, Alan**

Closet Dramas: Homosexual Representation and Class in Postwar British Theater. *Genders* 9 (Fall 1990):112-131

**Singapore – Culture and Society**

Singapore Youth: The Impact of Social Status on Perceptions of Adolescent Problems. Richard E. Isralowitz and Ong Teck Hong. *Adolescence* 25, No. 98 (Summer 1990):357-362

**Singer, Ben**

Female Power in the Serial-Queen Melodrama: The Etiology of an Anomaly. *Camera Obscura* No. 22 (January 1990):91-129

**Singer, Karin**

"Dear Dr. M." *Healthsharing* 11, No. 1 (December 1989):10-14

**Singerman, Deborah**

Australia: Lesbian Discrimination Fought. *off our backs* 20, No. 7 (July 1990):9

**Singers.** *See also* Musicians, Popular

Encore! David Hinckley. *Lear's* (August 1990):70-71+

**Singh, Andrea Menefee** and Kelles-Viitanen, Anita (editors)

Invisible Hands: Women in Home-Based Production. Reviewed by Kalpana Bardhan. *Journal of Women's History* 2, No. 1 (Spring 1990):200-219

**Singh, Harinder** (joint author). *See* Dutta, P. K.

**Singh, Padam** and others

Adoption of Family Planning Practices and Associated Factors in Pararganj Area of Delhi. *Journal of Family Welfare* 36, No. 2 (June 1990):36-42

**Singh, Saudan** and others

Interrelationship Between Breastfeeding and Lactational Amenorrhoea in a Rural Community of Haryana. *Journal of Family Welfare* 36, No. 4 (December 1990):75-77

**Single-Child Family**

Dysfunction in the Single-Parent and Only-Child Family. Sadi Bayrakal and Teresa M. Kope. *Adolescence* 25, No. 97 (Spring 1990):1-7

**Single Mothers.** *See* Single Parents

**Singleness.** *See also* Life Styles; Single Women

**Single Parents.** *See also* Stoppi, Isa (about); Tynan, Kathleen (about)

A House Without a Man Is Still a Home. Lauren Payne. *Ladies' Home Journal* 107, No. 11 (November 1990):210-215

Interiors: Mama's Legacy. Billie Jean Young. *Essence* 21, No. 8 (December 1990):28

"Let's Not Forget the Children" Bibliography. Susan Speir. *Ladies' Home Journal* 107, No. 7 (July 1990):22-27

The Process of Providing Support to Recently Divorced Single Mothers. Mary E. Duffy and Lee Smith. *Health Care for Women International* 11, No. 3 (1990):277-294

Single-Parent Dating: Single . . . with Children. Vanessa J. Gallman. *Essence* 20, No. 12 (April 1990):102-103

Solo Mothering. *Essence* 20, No. 11 (March 1990):97-98

Women as Single Parents: Confronting Institutional Barriers in the Courts, the Workplace, and the Housing Market. Edited by Elizabeth A. Mulroy. Reviewed by Dorothy C. Miller. *AFFILIA* 5, No. 2 (Summer 1990):104-106

**Single Parents, African-American**

It's a Family Affair: The Real Lives of Black Single Mothers. By Barbara Omolade. Reviewed by Jacqueline E. Wade. *NWSA Journal* 2, No. 2 (Spring 1990):315-319

**Single Parents – Housing**

Le logement: Point d'ancrage pour un nouveau départ. Françoise Mondor. *Canadian Women's Studies* 11, No. 2 (Fall 1990):46-47

**Single-Sex Education.** *See* Education, Single-Sex

**Singleton, Carrie Jane**

Race and Gender in Feminist Theory. *Sage* 6, No. 1 (Summer 1989):12-17

**Single Women**

"Neither Pairs Nor Odd": Female Community in Late Nineteenth-Century London. Notes. Deborah Epstein Nord. *Signs* 15, No. 4 (Summer 1990):733-754

Single Again. Lesley Dormen. *Glamour* (September 1990):190-193

**Single Women – Vacations**

Images: Spas for Solo Vacations. Elizabeth Brous. *Vogue* (December 1990):170-176

**Siraj-Blatchford, Iram**

Equal Opportunities in the New ERA. Book Review. *Gender and Education* 2, No. 3 (1990):367-368

**Sirota, Lorraine Handler**

The Paleolithic Prescription. Book Review. *Women and Health* 16, Nos. 3/4 (1990):206-211

**Siroto, Janet**

Health: What's Your Period I.Q.? *Mademoiselle* (October 1990):118

Natural Beauties. *Harper's Bazaar* (January 1990):78-85

Pillow Talk. *Mademoiselle* (October 1990):162-163+

**Sissel, Sandy** (joint director). *See* Broomfield, Nick

**Sister-Brother Relationships**

High Profile: Joanous Come Lately. Trish Deitch Rohrer. *Mademoiselle* (December 1990):78

**Sister Netifa**

Woman Determined. Reviewed. *Spare Rib* No. 216 (September 1990):26

**Sisters**

Big Sister Knows Best. Marti Leimbach. *Mademoiselle* (April 1990):227, 262

Go Away, Little Girl. Tania Aebi. *Mademoiselle* (April 1990):227, 262

The One You Call Sister. By Paula Martinac. Reviewed by Rosalind Warren. *New Directions for Women* 19, No. 4 (July-August 1990):19

**SisterSerpents**

SisterSerpents Strike Abortion Foes. Suzanne Messing. *New Directions for Women* 19, No. 1 (January/February 1990):11

**Sitka, Chris**

Lesbian Rebirth. *Lesbian Ethics* 4, No. 1 (Spring 1990): 4-27

**Sjöblad, Christina**

The Lund Project on Women's Autobiographies and Diaries in Sweden. *Gender & History* 2, No. 1 (Spring 1990):87-88

**Sjogren's Syndrome.** *See* Policoff, Stephen Phillip, "Diseases Your Doctor May Miss"

**Sjöö, Monica**

New Age or Armageddon? *Woman of Power* 16 (Spring 1990):62-67

**Skelly, Flora**

Legal-Eagle Affairs. *Mademoiselle* (October 1990):154-155+

**Skevington, Suzanne** and Baker, Deborah (editors)

The Social Identity of Women. Reviewed by Rosalind Edwards. *Women's Studies International Forum* 13, No. 6 (1990):611

**Skiing**

Fitness: Wilderness Sports. Bibliography. Grace Lichtenstein. *Vogue* (January 1990):80-83

Ski Lifts. Suzanne Nottingham. *Women's Sports and Fitness* 12, No. 7 (October 1990):20-21

**Skiing – Equipment**

Ladies' Choice. Marjorie McCloy and Seth Masia. *Women's Sports and Fitness* 12, No. 7 (October 1990):38-45

**Skilled Labor.** *See* Labor, Skilled

**Skillen, Geraldine** (about)

Geraldine Skillen Convicted. *Spare Rib* No. 212 (May 1990):46

**Skillman, Penny**

Life "In the Life." *Belles Lettres* 5, No. 3 (Spring 1990):11

A Vindication of the Rights of Whores. Book Review. *Belles Lettres* 5, No. 3 (Spring 1990):11

Working. Book Review. *Belles Lettres* 5, No. 3 (Spring 1990):11

**Skin – Care and Hygiene.** *See also* Beauty, Personal; Makeup; Nails (Anatomy) – Care and Hygiene; Suntan Products

About Face: Beyond Cosmetic Surgery. Elena Oumano. *Lear's* (July 1990):35-36

Aquatic. Melissa Dunst. *Lear's* (September 1990):128-133

Banish Blemishes – Fast! Frederic Haberman and Margaret Danbrot. *Redbook* 175, No. 4 (August 1990):20

Beach Beauty. *Harper's Bazaar* (June 1990):28-35

Beauty: Answers. *Essence* 20, No. 9 (January 1990):14; 20, No. 12 (April 1990):17; 21, No. 2 (June 1990):17-18; 21, No. 3 (July 1990):14; 21, No. 6 (October 1990):18; 21, No. 8 (December 1990):16

Beauty: Put Your Best Face Forward. Mary-Ellen Banashek. *Essence* 20, No. 10 (February 1990):12-13+

Beauty and Fashion Hotline: Saving Your Skin. *Family Circle* 103, No. 14 (October 16, 1990):39-42

Beauty Buys and Bargains. *Mademoiselle* (January 1990):18-20

Beauty Clinic: Department Stores: A Giveaway Guide. *Mademoiselle* (January 1990):22

Beauty from the Sea. Liza Coleman. *Savvy Woman* (July/August 1990):40-42

Beauty & Health Report. Andrea Pomerantz Lynn. *Glamour* (June 1990):42

The Beauty News You Can Use. Laura Flynn McCarthy. *Working Woman* (December 1990):88-90

Beauty Q & A. *Mademoiselle* (January 1990):24; (June 1990):50; (October 1990):68; (November 1990):62; (December 1990):53

Beauty Questions. *Glamour* (January 1990):22; (February 1990):34; (May 1990):54-58; (June 1990):38; (September 1990):56; (October 1990):44; (November 1990):48; (December 1990):42

Beauty Word of Mouth. *Glamour* (February 1990):27-30; (May 1990):41-46; (June 1990):31-34; (July 1990):19-22

Body Management: Your Future Face: A Four-Decade Forecast. Ann Goldberg. *Working Woman* (May 1990):111-114

The Bottom Line on Beautiful Skin. Stephanie Young. *Glamour* (November 1990):54

Burns, Bites and Rashes. Mark Deitch. *Working Mother* 13, No. 7 (July 1990):80-83

Clean Is Sexy: Skin Care Goes Back to Nature. *Mademoiselle* (February 1990):188-191

The Cos-medics. Julie Logan. *Harper's Bazaar* (January 1990):38

Cover-Ups. Laurie Tarkan. *Lear's* (June 1990):126-131

A Day at the Beach. *McCall's* 117, No. 9 (June 1990):81-92

The $5 Face. *Mademoiselle* (January 1990):116-119

Give Yourself a Skincare Makeover. Maggie Morrison. *Redbook* 175, No. 5 (September 1990):170-173

Glamour Guide. Bibliography. *Glamour* (February 1990):65-69

Great Looks: 6 Ways to Younger Skin. Lou Ann Walker. *Redbook* 175, No. 6 (October 1990):16-20

Great Skin Now. *Glamour* (April 1990):284-287

Images: Beauty Answers. Elizabeth Collier. *Vogue* (December 1990):166

Images: Beauty Answers. Laura Flynn McCarthy. *Vogue* (January 1990):78

Images: Beauty Answers. Llaura Flynn McCarthy. *Vogue* (September 1990):356

Images: Flawless Skin. Shirley Lord. *Vogue* (January 1990):67-70

Images: Hair Answers, Beauty Answers. Laura Flynn McCarthy. *Vogue* (July 1990):84-86

Images. Shirley Lord. *Vogue* (October 1990):193+

Is Your Back Fit to Bare? Patricia Rudolf. *Redbook* 175, No. 2 (June 1990):128-129

The Latest Overnight Sensation. Karen Dawson. *Lear's* (November 1990):76

Let Yourself Glow! *Redbook* 176, No. 1 (November 1990):112-115

Nail Care. *Essence* 21, No. 5 (September 1990):14

Native Sun. Patricia Mason Woods. *Essence* 21, No. 3 (July 1990):20-23

Preferred Treatment. Leslie O'Connor. *Harper's Bazaar* (September 1990):102+

Rich Girl Beauty, Real Girl Price. *Mademoiselle* (January 1990):110-115

Saving Face with a Hot New Treatment. Karen Dawson. *Lear's* (October 1990):66

Sensitive Skin. Mary-Ellen Banashek. *Essence* 20, No. 9 (January 1990):68-70+

The Seven Ages of Skin. Shirley Lord. *Vogue* (January 1990):208-213

Skin: Research, Revelations, and Refinements. Laurie Tarkan. *Lear's* (January 1990):91-95

Skin Care. Jennet Conant. *Harper's Bazaar* (February 1990):160-165+

Skin Care Now. *Working Mother* 13, No. 5 (May 1990):49-52

Skin Care Strategies. *McCall's* 117, No. 8 (May 1990):103-108

Skinflicks: Technologies of Care and Repair. Nelson Lee Novick. *Lear's* (October 1990):65

The Skinny on Winter Skin. Melissa Dunst. *Lear's* (October 1990):68

Skin Savers. *Harper's Bazaar* (August 1990):126-127+

Stay Light! *Harper's Bazaar* (June 1990):110-113

Sun Care: Day One. *Harper's Bazaar* (April 1990):184-185

5 Sunless Ways to a Golden Tan. *Glamour* (May 1990):284-285

Tan. Jeannie Ralston. *Vogue* (March 1990):242-244, 248

Tanning Addiction. Michael Pertschuk. *Vogue* (June 1990):216

Treat Yourself Well. *Redbook* 174, No. 5 (March 1990):132-135

4 Ways to Look Party-Perfect. *Ladies' Home Journal* 107, No. 12 (December 1990):37-44

What's In a Name? Liza Coleman. *Savvy Woman* (November 1990):42-43

Youth—Or Consequences? The Truth About the New Aging Antidotes. Laura Flynn McCarthy. *Working Woman* (May 1990):116-118

**Skin Cancer**

A Cancer Answer: The New Melanoma Vaccine. Doris Day. *Mademoiselle* (January 1990):70

A Deadly Skin Cancer on the Rise. Beth Weinhouse. *Redbook* 175, No. 2 (June 1990):20-24

Health & Fitness. Bibliography. Stephanie Young. *Glamour* (May 1990):63-74

Self Center: Health Department. *Lear's* (August 1990):44

**Skin Color**

Beauty: Color Me Black. *Essence* 21, No. 7 (November 1990):14-15

Mysteries of Melanin. Bibliography. Allison Abner. *Essence* 21, No. 7 (November 1990):30-31

**Ski Resorts**

First Resorts. Marjorie McCloy. *Women's Sports and Fitness* 12, No. 7 (October 1990):47-51

Head for the Hills. Bibliography. Khephra Burns. *Essence* 21, No. 8 (December 1990):108-112

Stars in Aspen. Susan Price. *Ladies' Home Journal* 107, No. 12 (December 1990):54-59

**Skis and Skiing.** *See also* Aspen

The Ski-and-be-Seen Scene. *Harper's Bazaar* (February 1990):26-38

**Skis and Skiing – Equipment and Supplies**

Apre4s, Of Course. *Mademoiselle* (November 1990):172-177

**Sklar, Holly**

US Electoral Politricks. *Spare Rib* No. 212 (May 1990):20-23

**Sklevicky, Lydia** (about)

In Memoriam: Lydia Sklevicky. *Gender & History* 2, No. 3 (Autumn 1990):249-250

**Skye, Maggie**

Kate's Story. Excerpt. Short story. *Good Housekeeping* 211, No. 3 (September 1990):277-288+

**Slavery**

Slave Women in Caribbean Society, 1650-1838. By Barbara Bush. Reviewed by Rosalyn Terborg-Penn. *The Women's Review of Books* 8, No. 1 (October 1990):8-9

"Us Colored Women Had to Go Through A Plenty": Sexual Exploitation of African-American Slave Women. Thelma Jennings. *Journal of Women's History* 1, No. 3 (Winter 1990):45-74

**Slavery – Narratives**

The History of Mary Prince: A West Indian Slave, Related by Herself. Edited by Moira Ferguson. Reviewed by Jacqui Alexander. *Women's Studies International Forum* 13, Nos. 1-2 (1990):159

Incidents in the Life of a Slave Girl. By Harriet A. Jacobs. Reviewed by Katherine M. Rogers. *Belles Lettres* 5, No. 2 (Winter 1990):6

Moral Experience in Harriet Jacobs's Incidents in the Life of a Slave Girl. Sarah Way Sherman. *NWSA Journal* 2, No. 2 (Spring 1990):167-185

The Slave Narrative: Its Place in American History. By Marion Wilson Starling. Reviewed by Katherine M. Rogers. *Belles Lettres* 5, No. 2 (Winter 1990):6

**Slavery, Sexual.** *See* Trafficking in Women

**Slavin, Sarah**

Authenticity and Fiction in Law: Contemporary Case Studies Exploring Radical Legal Feminism. *Journal of Women's History* 1, No. 3 (Winter 1990):123-159

**Sledziewski, Elisabeth G.**

The Body and the French Revolution: Sex, Class and Political Culture. Book Review. *Gender & History* 2, No. 3 (Autumn 1990):363-365

Women and the Public Sphere in the Age of the French Revolution. Book Review. *Gender & History* 2, No. 3 (Autumn 1990):363-365

**Sleep**

Sleep and the Reproductive Cycle: A Review. Marleyne Mauri. *Health Care for Women International* 11, No. 4 (1990):409-421

**Sleep Deprivation**

Beauty & Health Report: Holiday Sleep Survival Guide. Stephanie Young. *Glamour* (December 1990):48

Can't Sleep? Tired? Tense? Peter J. Hauri and Shirley Linde. *Redbook* 175, No. 1 (May 1990):156-163

Health Report: The Sleep Mystique: Could You Get By on Less? Roberta Israeloff. *Working Woman* (September 1990):195-196

The Late Show: A Healthy Girl's Guide to the Benefits of Staying Awake. *Mademoiselle* (February 1990):156-159

Medinews. Sally Squires. *Ladies' Home Journal* 107, No. 3 (March 1990):114

Sleep: The Dynamics of Sweet Dreaming. Mariana Gosnell. *Lear's* (January 1990):86-89

Snooze News. *Essence* 20, No. 12 (April 1990):32

Women Get Less Sleep Than Men. Maggie Morrison. *McCall's* 117, No. 11 (August 1990):44-49

**Sleep Disorders**

Insomniacs: Read This and Sleep. Donna Heiderstadt. *Lear's* (November 1990):55-57

Into the Nightmare. Jane Bosveld. *Mademoiselle* (November 1990).114

The Twilight Zone. Susan Ince. *Savvy Woman* (November 1990):82-84

**Sleeper, Jim**

Putting Out the Bonfire. *Lear's* (February 1990):108-115

**Slesinger, Doris P.**

Sellers and Servants: Working Women in Lima, Peru. Book Review. *Gender and Society* 4, No. 3 (September 1990):421-423

**Sligh, Clarissa**

On Being an American Black Student. *Heresies* 25 (1990):29-33

**Sloat, Suzanna**

My Place. Book Review. *Belles Lettres* 5, No. 2 (Winter 1990):7

A School for "Young Ladies of Color." *Belles Lettres* 6, No. 1 (Fall 1990):47

A Whole-Souled Woman: Prudence Crandall and the Education of Black Women. Book Review. *Belles Lettres* 6, No. 1 (Fall 1990):47

**Slom, Celia**

Carpooling Incentives Aim at Americans Who Solo (Or: Baby, You Can Drive My Car). *McCall's* 117, No. 8 (May 1990):63

Dial 911: Computers Shrink Emergency Response Times. *McCall's* 117, No. 8 (May 1990):56

Encouraging Girls to Pursue Math and Science Careers. Bibliography. *McCall's* 117, No. 8 (May 1990):58-60

At Home in the Kitchen. *McCall's* 117, No. 9 (June 1990):113-117

A Question of Morals. *McCall's* 117, No. 8 (May 1990):70

Sue Cischke: Driving Smart. *McCall's* 118, No. 1 (October 1990):60-62

Two Needs, One Day-Care Center. *McCall's* 117, No. 10 (July 1990):56

**Sluby, Patricia Carter**

Black Women and Inventions. *Sage* 6, No. 2 (Fall 1989):33-35

**Slutsky, Laura** (about)

The People Picker. Erik Hedegaard. *Savvy Woman* (November 1990):14

**Slyomovics, Susan**

Ritual Grievance: The Language of Woman? *Women and Performance: A Journal of Feminist Theory* 5, No. 1, Issue #9 (1990): 53-60

**Slyomovics, Susan** (joint author). *See* Burns, Judy

**Small, Linda Lee**

Give Your Mate a Break. *Working Mother* 13, No. 4 (April 1990):24-28

The Hidden Message Behind Gifts. *Working Mother* (December 1990):14-18

How to Raise a Friendly Kind of Kid. *Working Mother* 13, No. 8 (August 1990):45-49

**Small, Stephen A.**, and Riley, Dave

Assessment of Work Spillover into Family Life. *Journal of Marriage and the Family* 52, No. 1 (February 1990):51-61

**Small Business.** *See also* Entrepreneurs; Mail Order Business; Market Research; Partnership

Enterprise: The Business Plan That Gets the Loan. Louise Washer. *Working Woman* (January 1990):37-47

First Steps. *Executive Female* (May/June 1990):74

**Smalley, Barbara**

Are Horror Movies Too Horrible for Kids? *Redbook* 175, No. 6 (October 1990):36-38

**Small Groups – Research**

Small Group Pedagogy: Consciousness Raising in Conservative Times. Estelle B. Freedman. *NWSA Journal* 2, No. 4 (Autumn 1990):603-623

**Small Towns.** *See* City and Town Life

**Smart, Carol**

Feminism and the Power of Law. Reviewed by Anne Margolis. *The Women's Review of Books* 7, No. 12 (September 1990):17-18

**Smart, Carol** and Sevenhuijsen, Selma (editors)

Child Custody and the Politics of Gender. Reviewed by Meg Luxton. *Journal of Marriage and the Family* 52, No. 4 (November 1990):1153-1154

**Smart, Carol** and Sevenhuijzen, Selma (editors)

Child Custody and the Politics of Gender. Reviewed by Nancy D. Polikoff. *The Women's Review of Books* 7, No. 9 (June 1990):23-24

**Smart, Jean** (about). *See also* Television Programs

**Smartt, Dorothea**

Assault Course. *Sage* 6, No. 1 (Summer 1989):57-58

**Smedley, Agnes – Criticism and Interpretation**

Teaching Agnes Smedley's *Daughter of Earth*. Rita M. Kissen. *NWSA Journal* 2, No. 3 (Summer 1990):425-434

**Smeeth, Mary** and Kappeler, Susanne

Mercy. Book Review. *Spare Rib* 218 (November 1990):27-28

**Smiley, Jane**

Buster Midnight's Cafe. Book Review. *Vogue* (April 1990):278-281

Clover. Book Review. *Vogue* (April 1990):278-281

Finding Signs. Book Review. *Vogue* (April 1990):278-281

The Nickel Plan. Short story. *McCall's* 118, No. 1 (October 1990):112-114+

Ordinary Love and Good Will. Reviewed by Valerie Miner. *The Women's Review of Books* 7, No. 7 (April 1990):17-18

Then She Found Me. Book Review. *Vogue* (April 1990):278-281

**Smilowitz, Erika**

Cantando Bajito/Singing Softly. Book Review. *Belles Lettres* 5, No. 2 (Winter 1990):18

The Orchid House. Book Review. *Belles Lettres* 5, No. 2 (Winter 1990):18

Undiscovered Islands. *Belles Lettres* 5, No. 2 (Winter 1990):18

**Smith, Adele**

Seeking the Goddess in Ancestral Faces. *Woman of Power* 15 (Fall-Winter 1990):35

**Smith, Andrea**

Indian Spiritual Abuse. *NWSAction* 3, No. 1/2 (Spring 1990): 35-36

**Smith, Andres** (about). *See* Athletes, "The Competitive Edge"

**Smith, Ann** and Rothlein, Lewis

Postscript to a Legendary Rivalry. *Women's Sports and Fitness* 12, No. 2 (March 1990):22-25

**Smith, Anne** (interview)

Tenants Organize! An Interview with Anne Smith. Joyce Watt and Ruth Mott. *Canadian Women's Studies* 11, No. 2 (Fall 1990):29-30

**Smith, Anne Mollegen**

McCall's Editor's Notes. *McCall's* 117, No. 12 (September 1990):85

What's Causing the Changes in McCall's. *McCall's* 117, No. 7 (April 1990):59

Why a Good Mother May Be Better than Perfect. *McCall's* 117, No. 8 (May 1990):77

**Smith, Barbara**

The Dance of Masks. *Out/Look* No. 9 (Summer 1990):74-77

The NEA Is the Least of It. *Ms.* 1, No. 3 (November/December 1990):65-67

**Smith, Barbara** (about). *See also* Writers – Interviews, "Graceful Passages"

Barbara Smith and Kitchen Table Women of Color Press. Terri L. Jewell. *Hot Wire* 6, No. 2 (May 1990):20-22 +

**Smith, Barbara** (joint author). *See* Gomez, Jewelle L.

**Smith, Bonnie**

Havens No More? Discourses of Domesticity. *Gender & History* 2, No. 1 (Spring 1990):98-102

**Smith, Brenda** and Smith, Tina

For Love and Money: Women as Foster Mothers. *AFFILIA* 5, No. 1 (Spring 1990):66-80

**Smith, Cyndi**

Off the Beaten Track: Women Adventurers and Mountaineers in Western Colorado. Reviewed by Judith Niemi. *The Women's Review of Books* 8, No. 1 (October 1990):18-19

**Smith, David C.** (joint editor). *See* Litoff, Judy Barrett

**Smith, Dorothy**

The Everyday World as Problematic: A Feminist Sociology. Reviewed by Wendy Luttrell. *Signs* 15, No. 3 (Spring 1990):635-640

The Everyday World as Problematic. Reviewed by Rosemary Foulds. *Women and Environments* 12, No. 2 (Spring 1990): 28

**Smith, Dorothy E.**

The Everyday World as Problematic. Reviewed by Helen Roberts. *Gender and Education* 2, No. 1 (1990):117-118

**Smith, Edward D.** (joint author). *See* Stein, David B.

**Smith, Geri**

I.O.U. $115 Billion. *Savvy Woman* (October 1990):58-61 +

**Smith, Hazel**

Not a Man to Match Her: The Marketing of a Prime Minister. Book Review. *Spare Rib* No. 215 (August 1990):28-29

**Smith, Helen Zenna**

Not So Quiet. Reviewed by Bonnie Kime Scott. *Tulsa Studies in Women's Literature* 9, No. 2 (Fall 1990):339-342

**Smith, Jaclyn** (about). *See also* Hair Styles

Jaclyn Smith: "I'm Still the Marrying Kind." Christopher Andersen. *Ladies' Home Journal* 107, No. 8 (August 1990):62-66

**Smith, Joan**

Cast-Off Kids. *Vogue* (August 1990):324-327 +

**Smith, Lee** (joint author). *See* Duffy, Mary E.

**Smith, Leslie**

Making the Introduction. *Executive Female* 13, No. 4 (July-August 1990):60

Networking. *Executive Female* 13, No. 5 (September-October 1990):57

Networking: It's All Fun and Games. *Executive Female* 13, No. 6 (November-December 1990):59-60

Networking: Playing to Win: A Conference Preview. *Executive Female* (May/June 1990):50

Networking: Special Interest Networks. *Executive Female* (March/April 1990):33

**Smith, Linda** and Popowich, Coreen

Women in Active Recovery. *Healthsharing* 11, No. 1 (December 1989):5

**Smith, Liz**

Walter Winchell. *Lear's* (June 1990):74-75 +

**Smith, Maggie** (about). *See also* Great Britain – Culture

Maggie Smith. William A. Henry III. *Lear's* (June 1990):94-97

There's Nothing Like a Dame. Georgina Howell. *Vogue* (April 1990):378-381, 421

**Smith, Mary Perry** (about). *See also* Leadership

**Smith, Roberta**

Mexico's Visual Culture. *Vogue* (October 1990):256 +

**Smith, Sidonie**

A Poetics of Women's Autobiography: Marginality and the Fictions of Self-Representation. Reviewed by Elizabeth R. Baer. *Belles Lettres* 5, No. 2 (Winter 1990):4-6 +

A Poetics of Women's Autobiography: Marginality and the Fictions of Self-Representation. Reviewed by Linda Wagner-Martin. *Tulsa Studies in Women's Literature* 9, No. 1 (Spring 1990):139-142

Self, Subject, and Resistance: Marginalities and Twentieth-Century Autobiographical Practice. *Tulsa Studies in Women's Literature* 9, No. 1 (Spring 1990):11-24

**Smith, Sinjin** (about). *See* Athletes, "The Competitive Edge"

**Smith, Susan Male**

The P.E.P Diet: The Perfect Eating Plan for Life. *Family Circle* 103, No. 14 (October 16, 1990):128-130

**Smith, Thomas Ewin**

Parental Separation and the Academic Self-Concepts of Adolescents: An Effort to Solve the Puzzle of Separation Effects. *Journal of Marriage and the Family* 52, No. 1 (February 1990):107-118

**Smith, Tina** (joint author). *See* Smith, Brenda

**Smith, Vivian** (editor)

Nettie Palmer: Her Private Journal *Fourteen Years*, Poems, Reviews, and Literary Essays. Reviewed by Cecilia Konchar Farr. *Belles Lettres* 5, No. 2 (Winter 1990):2

Nettie Palmer. Reviewed by Barbara Brook. *Women's Studies International Forum* 13, No. 3 (1990):275-276

**Smits, Marina**

Hands. Poem. *Canadian Women's Studies* 11, No. 1 (Spring 1990):68

Perpetrator. Poem. *Canadian Women's Studies* 11, No. 1 (Spring 1990):68

**Smoking**

Cervical Cancer and Smoking. Alison Dickie. *Healthsharing* 11, No. 3 (June 1990):9

Health Dept. Donna Heiderstadt. *Lear's* (December 1990):58

Imprints. Ann Dermansky. *New Directions for Women* 19, No. 6 (November-December 1990):6

Slow Poison: The Cigarette Blitz. *Manushi* No. 59 (July-August 1990):20

Smoking vs. Women. Boston Women's Health Book Collective. *Ms.* 1, No. 1 (July/August 1990):54-55

Winning Over Women: The Tobacco Industry Takes Aim. Judith Mackey. *Women in Action* 1-2 (1990):17-19

Women and Smoking: A Lethal Deception. Jane Ritchie. *Women's Studies International Forum* 13, No. 3 (1990):201-208

**Smoking – Adolescents**

Relationships between Teenage Smoking and Attitudes toward Women's Rights, Sex Roles, Marriage, Sex and Family. Ingrid Waldron and Diane Lye. *Women and Health* 16, Nos. 3/4 (1990):23-46

State-by-State Report: Laws to Stop Kids from Smoking. *Good Housekeeping* 211, No. 4 (October 1990):245-246

**Smothers, Ella** (about)

Style: Portrait in Fast Motion. *Essence* 21, No. 4 (August 1990):18

**Smyers, Virginia L.** (joint author). *See* Hanscombe, Gillian

**Smyth, Cherry**

Oranges Are Not the Only Fruit. Television Play Review. *Spare Rib* No. 209 (February 1990):34

The Pleasure Threshold: Looking at Lesbian Pornography on Film. *Feminist Review* No. 34 (Spring 1990):152-159

**Snack Foods**

The Good News about Snacking. *Glamour* (January 1990):158

**Snodgrass, Mary Ellen**

Motherhood or Bust: Reflections on the Dreams, and Nightmares of Foster Parenting. *On the Issues* 16 (Fall 1990):7-9+

**Snowden, Lynn**

Esmé: Behind the Smile. *Mademoiselle* (June 1990):196-197+

**Snowe, Olympia** (about). *See also* Leadership

**Snyder, Fran**

What You *Don't* Know about Your Period. Bibliography. *Ladies' Home Journal* 107, No. 5 (May 1990):108-114

When Should You Be Your Own Doctor? *Ladies' Home Journal* 107, No. 2 (February 1990):62-72

**Snyder, Fran** and Gupta, Nelly Edmondson

America's Contraceptive Gap. *Ladies' Home Journal* 107, No. 6 (June 1990):186

**Snyder, Jane McIntosh**

The Woman and the Lyre: Woman Writers in Classical Greece and Rome. Reviewed by Johanna H. Stuckey. *Canadian Women's Studies* 11, No. 2 (Fall 1990):89-90

The Woman and the Lyre: Woman Writers in Classical Greece and Rome. Reviewed by Katherine Callen King. *Tulsa Studies in Women's Literature* 9, No. 2 (Fall 1990):323-326

**Sobek, María Herrera** and Viramontes, Helena María (editors)

Chicana Creativity and Criticism: Charting New Frontiers in American Literature. Reviewed by Cordelia (Chávez) Candelaria. *Frontiers* 11, No. 1 (1990):85-86

**Sobel, Dava**

Allergies: Latest Finds, Best Treatments. Bibliography. *Good Housekeeping* 211, No. 3 (September 1990):226-227+

Cheers? The Sobering News About Women and Alcohol. *Mademoiselle* (May 1990):138

"Doctor, Am I Having a Heart Attack?" *Good Housekeeping* 210, No. 5 (May 1990):78-82

Health Department. *Lear's* (March 1990):70

Health Dept. *Lear's* (January 1990):44; (February 1990):54

Health Watch: Fever. *Ladies' Home Journal* 107, No. 2 (February 1990):56

Healthwatch: Nosebleeds. *Ladies' Home Journal* 107, No. 3 (March 1990):92

**Sobel, Dava** (joint author). *See* McIntosh, Bruce J.

**Sobkowski, Anna**

Everything's Negotiable. *Executive Female* (March/April 1990):38-40

The Pregnant Professional. *Executive Female* 13, No. 1 (January-February 1990):29-33

See How They Run. *Executive Female* 13, No. 5 (September-October 1990):14-16+

You Haul It. *Executive Female* 13, No. 4 (July-August 1990):44-45+

**Sobule, Jill**

Things Here Are Different. Reviewed. *Spare Rib* No. 215 (August 1990):30

**Social Behavior** *See also* Conduct of Life; Social Skills

Etiquette for Every Day. Elizabeth L. Post. *Good Housekeeping* 211, No. 3 (September 1990):62-64; 211, No. 4 (October 1990):52-55

Scruples: I've Got a (Style) Secret. Ellen Welty. *Mademoiselle* (November 1990):124

Scruples: Who's Sorry Later? Ellen Welty. *Mademoiselle* (October 1990):132

Women and Children First? Barbara Grizzuti Harrison. *Mademoiselle* (December 1990):102

**Social Behavior – Humor**

Farewell, My Hostess. John Leo. *McCall's* 118, No. 2 (November 1990):24

**Social Change**

The Everyday World as Problematic. By Dorothy Smith. Reviewed by Rosemary Foulds. *Women and Environments* 12, No. 2 (Spring 1990): 28

**Social Change – Activism**

The Peaceful Sex? On Feminism and the Peace Movement. Linda Gordon. *NWSA Journal* 2, No. 4 (Autumn 1990):624-634

**Social Class.** *See* Class Structure

**Social Diseases.** *See* Sexually Transmitted Diseases

**Social Entertaining.** *See also* Business Entertaining; Caterers and Catering; Children – Parties; Cookery – Equipment and Supplies;

Designers – Social Entertaining; Family Reunions; Holidays – Cookery; Manners; Thanksgiving Day

Affairs to Remember. Maureen Sajbel. *Harper's Bazaar* (August 1990):174+

America Entertains. Phyllis Schiller. *McCall's* 117, No. 10 (July 1990):112

Art and Leisure: Good Talk. John McLaughlin. *Harper's Bazaar* (February 1990):144-145+

Black-Tie Anxiety: The Agony and Ecstasy of Dressing Up. *Mademoiselle* (December 1990):126-129

The Busy Life: Presentation Is Everything. Jill McQuilkin. *Working Woman* (September 1990):202-205

Come for the Weekend. Marie Simmons. *Working Woman* (June 1990):79-82+

Come Over for Brunch. *Glamour* (January 1990):150-155

Couple Time. *Glamour* (June 1990):142

Dinner at Eight. Patricia Beard. *Harper's Bazaar* (August 1990):173+

Eating In: How to Stock This Year's Bar. *Glamour* (December 1990):242

Entertaining: Special Settings. Zacki Murphy. *Family Circle* 103, No. 16 (November 27, 1990):59-60

Festive Food. Dee Dee Dailey. *Essence* 21, No. 8 (December 1990):102-106+

Fe3te Accompli. Diane Sustendal. *Harper's Bazaar* (August 1990):176

Food for Family Gatherings. Valerie Vaz. *Essence* 21, No. 4 (August 1990):86-87

Glamour Guide. *Glamour* (January 1990):37-41

High Style Party Looks. *McCall's* 118, No. 3 (December 1990):79-82

Holiday Parties Cookbook. Marianne Langan. *McCall's* 118, No. 3 (December 1990):103-124

Lite Eating: Bread Winners. *McCall's* 117, No. 10 (July 1990):114

Living Beautifully: Give Your House a Holiday Glow. Alexandra Stoddard. *McCall's* 118, No. 2 (November 1990):168

Living Beautifully: Holiday Grace Notes. Alexandra Stoddard. *McCall's* 118, No. 3 (December 1990):148

Party! *Glamour* (December 1990):184-191

Perfect Summer Parties. Jan Turner Hazard. *Ladies' Home Journal* 107, No. 6 (June 1990):146-162

Rocky Mountain High. Diane Tegmeyer. *Harper's Bazaar* (February 1990):185+

Saturday Night Supper: A French "Pizza." *Glamour* (October 1990):296

Saturday Night Supper: Pork Chops with Cider. *Glamour* (February 1990):214

75 Great Ways to Sail Through the Season. *Family Circle* 103, No. 17 (December 18, 1990):145-149

Smashing! Jon Etra. *Harper's Bazaar* (February 1990):146-147+

Star Quality. Deborah Sroloff. *Harper's Bazaar* (February 1990):148-149

A Summer Buffet. Jonell Nash. *Essence* 21, No. 4 (August 1990):88-92+

Tables: All Set. Bibliography. David Feld. *Mademoiselle* (December 1990):68+

Talking Fashion: Mimi. Kevin Allman. *Vogue* (August 1990):378-380

That's Entertainment! Diane Sustendal. *Harper's Bazaar* (January 1990):133+

These Party Dresses Aren't Pricey. *Mademoiselle* (December 1990):54-58

We Need a Manners Makeover. Amy Willard Cross. *Glamour* (April 1990):146

On Your Own: Can your Relationship Survive This Party Season? Judith Stone. *Glamour* (January 1990):68

## Social Entertaining – Home Parties

"Why Do Women Do Such Womenly Things?" The Genre and Socio-historical Analogs of Home Parties. Sheila J. Sullivan. *Women's Studies in Communication* 13, No. 1 (Spring 1990): 66-91

## Social Environments

Living in Clumps. Frances Rooney. *Women and Environments* 12, No. 2 (Spring 1990): 4-5

## Social History

Total Recoil. Peter Feibleman. *Lear's* (August 1990):53-56

Women of the Years. Leslie Jay. *Ladies' Home Journal* 107, No. 11 (November 1990):83-92

## Social Identity

The Social Identity of Women. Edited by Suzanne Skevington and Deborah Baker. Reviewed by Rosalind Edwards. *Women's Studies International Forum* 13, No. 6 (1990):611

"The Very House of Difference": Gender as "Embattled" Standpoint. Thomas Foster. *Genders* 8 (Summer 1990):17-37

## Socialism

Promissory Notes: Women in the Transition to Socialism. Edited by Sonia Kruks, Rayna Rapp, and Marilyn B. Young. Reviewed by Bettina Aptheker. *New Directions for Women* 19, No. 5 (September-October 1990):19

Socialist-Feminist American Women's History. Elizabeth Fox-Genovese. *Journal of Women's History* 1, No. 3 (Winter 1990):181-210

## Socialism – Feminist Perspectives

When Jessica Meets Natasha: A Feminist View of German Reunification. Edda Kerschgens. *Australian Feminist Studies* No. 12 (Summer 1990):15-27

## Socialist Feminism

Identity Politics and the Hierarchy of Oppression: A Comment. Linda Briskin. *Feminist Review* No. 35 (Summer 1990):102-108

New Times: The Changing Face of Politics in the 1990s. Edited by Stuart Hall and Martin Jacques. Reviewed by Andrea McRobbie. *Feminist Review* No. 36 (Autumn 1990):127-131

## Socialization

Cohort Replacement and Changes in Parental Socialization Values. Duane F. Alwin. *Journal of Marriage and the Family* 52, No. 2 (May 1990):347-360

The Liberation of Caring: A Different Voice for Gilligan's "Different Voice." Bill Puka. *Hypatia* 5, No. 1 (Spring 1990):58-82

## Socialization – Cross-Cultural Studies

Sturdy Bridges: The Role of African-American Mothers in the Socialization of African-American Children. Beverly Greene. *Women and Therapy* 10, Nos. 1/2 (1990):205-225

**Social Problems.** *See* Domestic Violence; Homelessness; Substance Abuse; Unemployment

## Social Purity Movement

The De-Eroticization of Women's Liberation: Social Purity Movements and the Revolutionary Feminism of Sheila Jeffreys. Margaret Hunt. *Feminist Review* No. 34 (Spring 1990):23-41

## Social Responsibility

Black Women as Do-ers: The Social Responsibility of Black Women. Joyce A. Ladner. *Sage* 6, No. 1 (Summer 1989):87-88

**Social Science Research.** *See also* Research Methodology

Deceptive Distinctions: Sex, Gender, and the Social Order. By Cynthia Fuchs Epstein. Reviewed by Karen K. Kirst-Ashman. *AFFILIA* 5, No. 1 (Spring 1990):116-118

Endless Crusade: Women Social Scientists and Progressive Reform. By Ellen Fitzpatrick. Reviewed by Barrie Thorne. *The Women's Review of Books* 7, No. 9 (June 1990):22

Feminism and Methodology: Social Science Issues. Edited by Sandra Harding. Reviewed by Susan J. Hekman. *Women & Politics* 10, No. 1 (1990):71-73

A Feminist Ethic for Social Science Research. By Nebraska Sociological Feminist Collective. Reviewed by Dorothy L. Steffens and Jane Robbins. *Feminist Collections* 11, No. 2 (Winter 1990):7-9

Gender Bias in Scholarship: The Pervasive Prejudice. Edited by Winifred Tomm and Hamilton Gordon. Reviewed by Marilyn Biggerstaff. *AFFILIA* 5, No. 1 (Spring 1990):121-123

Gender in Intimate Relations. Edited by Barbara J. Risman and Pepper Schwartz. Reviewed by Karen K. Kirst-Ashman. *AFFILIA* 5, No. 1 (Spring 1990):116-118

Gender Issues in Field Research. By Carol A. B. Warren. Reviewed by Dorothy L. Steffens and Jane Robbins. *Feminist Collections* 11, No. 2 (Winter 1990):7-9

Gender Issues in Field Research. By Carol A. B. Warren. Reviewed by Marilyn Biggerstaff. *AFFILIA* 5, No. 1 (Spring 1990):121-123

On the Lookout. Edited by L. Diane Bernard and Miriam Dinerman. *AFFILIA* 5, No. 1 (Spring 1990):94-96

Nonsexist Research Methods: A Practical Guide. By Margrit Eichler. Reviewed by Dorothy L. Steffens and Jane Robbins. *Feminist Collections* 11, No. 2 (Winter 1990):7-9

The Possibility of American Women Becoming Prisoners of War: A Challenge for Behavioral Scientists. Wayne E. Dillingham. *Minerva* 8, No. 4 (Winter 1990):17-22

Women and the Politics of Empowerment. Edited by Ann Bookman and Sandra Morgen. Reviewed by Sue Tolleson Rinehart. *Women & Politics* 10, No. 3 (1990):131-132

**Social Sciences and Policy**

Women, Social Science and Public Policy. Edited by Jacqueline Goodnow and Carole Pateman. Reviewed by Helen Liggett. *Women & Politics* 10, No. 3 (1990):127-129

**Social Security**

The Social Security Rip-Off. Hank Gilman. *Working Mother* 13, No. 10 (October 1990):20-23

**Social Skills.** See also Self-Help Techniques

Career Strategies: The Power of Small Talk: How to Schmooze Successfully. Adele Scheele. *Working Woman* (November 1990):67-68

Couple Time. *Glamour* (November 1990):136

Etiquette: Doing It Right. Charlotte Ford. *McCall's* 117, No. 7 (April 1990):130; 117, No. 10 (July 1990):36; 117, No. 12 (September 1990):34

Glamour Guide. *Glamour* (March 1990):85-89

How to Bounce Back from a Mega-Embarrassment. Marilyn Moats Kennedy. *Glamour* (November 1990):115

How to Say No! Louise Lague. *Glamour* (November 1990):250-251+

Living Beautifully: Letters Sweeten Our Lives. Alexandra Stoddard. *McCall's* 117, No. 8 (May 1990):172

Oops! Susan Jacoby. *Glamour* (July 1990):176-177+

**Social Status**

Charmed Wives. Rona Jaffe. *Harper's Bazaar* (September 1990):306-307+

Portraits in Elegance. *Harper's Bazaar* (August 1990):152-157

Singapore Youth: The Impact of Social Status on Perceptions of Adolescent Problems. Richard E. Isralowitz and Ong Teck Hong. *Adolescence* 25, No. 98 (Summer 1990):357-362

**Social Structure.** See also Life Styles

**Social Trends.** See also Fashion; Popular Culture

Circle This. Margaret Jaworski. *Family Circle* 103, No. 9 (June 26, 1990):9-10; 103, No. 13 (September 25, 1990):9-12; 103, No. 15 (November 6, 1990):9-10

People Are Talking About. Julia Reed. *Vogue* (August 1990):209; (September 1990):393

People Are Talking About. *Vogue* (December 1990):185

Romance: How to Take It Sitting Down. John Leo. *McCall's* 117, No. 11 (August 1990):50

Talking Out of Turn: Frock Around the Clock. Tracy Young. *Vogue* (September 1990):658

Upfront. Edited by Lesley Jane Nonkin. *Vogue* (September 1990):109-114, (December 1990):87-90

**Social Values.** See also Activism; Children – Social Values; Fairness; Traditions; Trust; Volunteer Work

A Dialogue on Race. Rosemary L. Bray. *Glamour* (August 1990):220-221+

The Earthquake Took Everything I Owned. Carol Kino. *Glamour* (March 1990):161

Editorial: *People's* Rights Above Animal Rights. *Glamour* (June 1990):92

Forum. Beverly Sills. *McCall's* 117, No. 12 (September 1990):21-22

Health & Mind. Pamela Erens. *Glamour* (June 1990):52

Viewpoint: Being Smart the Woman's Way. Mary-Lou Weisman. *Glamour* (December 1990):138-140

Why We're Really Good at Heart. *Glamour* (September 1990):302-303+

**Social Welfare.** See also Caregiving

**Social Welfare – History.** See also African-American Women – History

A New History of Social Welfare. By Phyllis J. Day. Reviewed by Charles Frost. *AFFILIA* 5, No. 3 (Fall 1990):120

**Social Welfare – Reform**

The Poverty Industry. Theresa Funiciello. *Ms.* 1, No. 3 (November/December 1990):33-40

**Social Work**

Beyond Women's Issues: Feminism and Social Work. Miriam L. Freeman. *AFFILIA* 5, No. 2 (Summer 1990):72-89

Differential Treatment Based on Sex. Karen D. Stout and Michael J. Kelly. *AFFILIA* 5, No. 2 (Summer 1990):60-71

Female Social Workers in the Second Generation. Janice L. Andrews. *AFFILIA* 5, No. 2 (Summer 1990):46-59

Women and Social Work: Toward a Woman-Centered Practice. By Jaina Hanmer and Daphne Statham. Reviewed by Ruth McCormick. *AFFILIA* 5, No. 3 (Fall 1990):118-120

**Social Work – Burnout**

Burnout in the Human Services: A Feminist Perspective. Janet L. Finn. *AFFILIA* 5, No. 4 (Winter 1990):55-71

**Society Balls.** *See also* Charity Balls

Maestros of Mood. *Harper's Bazaar* (December 1990):176+

Pretty in White. *Harper's Bazaar* (December 1990):174+

**Society for International Development**

Development of Africa – Strategies for 1990 and Beyond. *Women's World* 23 (April 1990):35-36

**Sociobiology**

Sociobiology and the Social Sciences. Edited by Robert W. Bell and Nancy J. Bell. Reviewed by Jetse Sprey. *Journal of Marriage and the Family* 52, No. 4 (November 1990):1152-1153

**Socioeconomic Status.** *See* Gender Ratio and Socioeconomic Status

**Sociology**

Directing Traffic: Subjects, Objects, and the Politics and Exchange. Karen Newman. *Differences* 2, No. 2 (Summer 1990):41-54

The Everyday World as Problematic. By Dorothy E. Smith. Reviewed by Helen Roberts. *Gender and Education* 2, No. 1 (1990):117-118

Feminist Sociology. By Janet Saltzman. Reviewed by Barbara Lou Fenby. *AFFILIA* 5, No. 1 (Spring 1990):113-114

**Sociology of Sport.** *See* Sports – Sociological Aspects

**Sodomy Laws.** *See* Homosexuality – Laws and Legislation

**Sofaer, Shoshanna** and Abel, Emily

Older Women's Health and Financial Vulnerability: Implications of the Medicare Benefit Structure. *Women and Health* 16, Nos. 3/4 (1990):47-67

**Sofat, R.** (joint author). *See* Sachar, R. K.

**Softball**

Looking for Her Field of Dreams. Nancy Slonim Aronie. *Lear's* (July 1990):40

**Sohoni, Nera Kuckreja** and Messing, Suzanne

Organizing Women in Fiji. *New Directions for Women* 19, No. 3 (May/June 1990):13

**Sojourner, Mary**

What They Write About in Other Countries. Short Story. *Heresies* 25 (1990):38-48

**Sok-kyong, Kang,** Chi-won, Kim, and Chong-hui, O

Words of Farewell: Stories by Korean Women Writers. Reviewed by Marilyn Chandler. *The Women's Review of Books* 7, Nos. 10-11 (July 1990):27

**Sokol, Julia** (joint author). *See* Carter, Steven

**Solar Radiation – Physiological Effect**

Screening the New Sunscreens. Lorraine Calvacca. *Working Woman* (May 1990):120-123

Skin: Research, Revelations, and Refinements. Laurie Tarkan. *Lear's* (January 1990):91-95

Sun Care: Day One. *Harper's Bazaar* (April 1990):184-185

**Solbiati, Vittorio** (about). *See* Milan – Interior Design

**Solimini, Cheryl**

Hands-On Style. *Working Woman* (July 1990):100-102

If You Can't Stand the Heat. *Family Circle* 103, No. 8 (June 5, 1990):33-36

Making Better Bodies. *Family Circle* 103, No. 14 (October 16, 1990):113-114

**Solimini, Cheryl** (joint author). *See* Holt, Gary A.

**Solinger, Rickie**

Chaste Liberation: Celibacy and Female Cultural Status. Book Review. *Women and Health* 16, No. 2 (1990):132-134

The Girl Nobody Loved: Psychological Explanations for White Single Pregnancy in the Pre-*Roe v. Wade* Era, 1945-1965. *Frontiers* 11, Nos. 2-3 (1990):45-54

Private Matters: American Attitudes toward Childbearing and Infant Nurture in the Urban North, 1800-1860. Book Review. *Women and Health* 16, No. 2 (1990):131-134

"Wake Up Little Susie": Single Pregnancy and Race in the Pre-*Roe v. Wade* Era. *NWSA Journal* 2, No. 4 (Autumn 1990):682-683

**Solnicki, Jill**

Storm Brewing. Poem. *Atlantis* 15, No. 2 (Spring 1990):58

**Solomon, Alisa**

Building a Movement: Jewish Feminists Speak Out On Israel. *Bridges* 1, No. 1 (Spring 1990): 41-56

**Solomon, Deborah**

Alone at Last. *The Women's Review of Books* 7, No. 7 (April 1990):1+

Composing a Life. Book Review. *The Women's Review of Books* 7, No. 12 (September 1990):26-27

On Her Own: Growing Up in the Shadow of the American Dream. Book Review. *The Women's Review of Books* 7, No. 7 (April 1990):1+

To Live the Examined Life. *The Women's Review of Books* 7, No. 12 (September 1990):26-27

**Solomon, Diane**

A Midwife's Kaddish. *Lilith* 15, No. 3 (Summer 1990):22-23

**Solomon, Jolie**

Management Secrets They'll Never Teach You at Business School. *Working Woman* (June 1990):53-54+

**Solomon, Norman** (joint author). *See* Lee, Martin A.

**Solomon, Pearl Canick**

Matchmaking Angels. Short story. *Redbook* 176, No. 2 (December 1990):148 53

**Solorzano, Lucia**

What to Do if Your Child Hates the Teacher. *Ladies' Home Journal* 107, No. 9 (September 1990):73-78

**Solorzano, Lucia and Atkins, Andrea**

Will Staying Back Help or Hurt? *Ladies' Home Journal* 107, No. 9 (September 1990):80-82

**Soman, Florence Jane**

Voyage of the Heart. Short story. *Good Housekeeping* 211, No. 4 (October 1990):150-151

**Somerville, Margaret**

Life (H)istory Writing: The Relationship between Talk and Text. *Australian Feminist Studies* No. 12 (Summer 1990):29-42

**Sommer, Sally**

In the Culture of Carnival. *The Women's Review of Books* 7, No. 9 (June 1990):9

Samba. Book Review. *The Women's Review of Books* 7, No. 9 (June 1990):9

**Sone, Monica – Criticism and Interpretation**

Japanese American Women's Life Stories: Maternality in Monica Sone's *Nisei Daughter* and Joy Kogawa's *Obasan*. Shirley Geok-Lin Lim. *Feminist Studies* 16, No. 2 (Summer 1990):289-312

**Sonenberg, Maya**

Cartographies. Reviewed by Marcia Tager. *New Directions for Women* 19, No. 1 (January/February 1990):22

**Song, Cathy**

Frameless Windows, Square of Light. Reviewed by Marilyn Kallet. *Belles Lettres* 6, No. 1 (Fall 1990):31

**Songs**

Oco Kandelikas. Flory Jagoda. *Bridges* 1, No. 2 (Fall 1990): 32-33

Smoke of the Battle. Laura Wetzler. *Bridges* 1, No. 1 (Spring 1990): 80-81

Two Prayers. Carole Rose Livingston. *Bridges* 1, No. 1 (Spring 1990): 82-83

Two Trees. Rita Falbel. *Bridges* 1, No. 1 (Spring 1990): 84-85

**Sonnenberg, Nadja** (about)

Music: Three in Concert. Diane Palacios. *Ms.* 1, No. 1 (July/August 1990):72-73

**Sontag, Susan**

AIDS and its Metaphors. Reviewed by Catherine Mason. *Healthright* 9, No. 4 (August 1990):40

**Sophists**

The First Sophists and Feminism: Discourses of the "Other." Susan C. Jarratt. *Hypatia* 5, No. 1 (Spring 1990):27-41

**Sorella, Naja** (joint author). *See* Dykewomon, Elana

**Sorella, Rosanna**

Turning Away From Secrets and Shame. *Sinister Wisdom* 41 (Summer-Fall 1990):41-44

**Sorenson, Jacki**

A Legend's Views and New Tapes to Use. *Women's Sports and Fitness* 12, No. 2 (March 1990):20-21

**Sorkin, Aaron**

A Few Good Men. Reviewed by Kent Black. *Harper's Bazaar* (February 1990):50

Theater: A Few Good Men. Reviewed by Randall Short. *Vogue* (January 1990):98

**Sorrel, Lorraine**

Child Care – Who Cares? Does Congress Care? *off our backs* 20, No. 2 (February 1990):13+

Congress Disapproves The Dinner Party. *off our backs* 20, No. 9 (October 1990):21

What Women Are Worth. *off our backs* 20, No. 2 (February 1990):4+

**Sosin, Elyse** (joint author). *See* Lawson, Rosalinda

**Soul Music.** *See also* Musicians, Popular

**Sound – Equipment and Supplies**

CD Manufacturing for the Independent Artist. Karen Kane. *Hot Wire* 6, No. 1 (January 1990):10-11+

Stereo Buying for the Novice. Karen Kane. *Hot Wire* 6, No. 2 (May 1990):10-11+

Soup. *See* Cookery (Soup)

**South, Molly** (about)

Giving Disneyland a Run for Its Money. Grace Lichtenstein. *Savvy Woman* (February 1990):42-45

**South Africa**

Lives of Courage: Women for a New South Africa. By Diana E. H. Russell. Reviewed by Carol Anne Douglas. *off our backs* 20, No. 3 (March 1990):28 +

Lives of Courage: Women for a New South Africa. By Diana E. H. Russell. Reviewed by Ernece B. Kelly. *On the Issues* 15 (Summer 1990):26-27

Lives of Courage: Women for a New South Africa. By Diana E. H. Russell. Reviewed by Stanlie M. James. *Feminist Collections* 12, No. 1 (Fall 1990):3-6

Lives of Courage: Women for a New South Africa. By Diana E.H. Russell. Reviewed by Joyce F. Kirk. *NWSA Journal* 2, No. 4 (Autumn 1990):658-659

Lives of Courage: Women of a New South Africa. By Diana E. H. Russell. Reviewed by Gwendolyn Mikell. *Belles Lettres* 5, No. 3 (Spring 1990):13-14

Namibia and South Africa: Women Speak Out. *Women in Action* 3 & 4 (1990):57-59

No Justice in South Africa. Delysia Forbes. *Spare Rib* 213 (June 1990):43-44

Not Either an Experimental Doll. By Shula Marks. Reviewed by Gwendolyn Mikell. *Belles Lettres* 5, No. 3 (Spring 1990):13-14

Not Either an Experimental Doll: The Separate Worlds of Three South African Women. Edited by Shula Marks. Reviewed by Elaine Salo. *Women's Studies International Forum* 13, No. 3 (1990):274-275

South African Women Return Home. *Spare Rib* No. 215 (August 1990):20-21

**South Africa – Apartheid**

Apartheid Continues. Esme Nathan. *Spare Rib* No. 212 (May 1990):48

Maids and Madams: Domestic Workers Under Apartheid. By Jacklyn Cock. Reviewed by Stanlie M. James. *Feminist Collections* 12, No. 1 (Fall 1990):3-6

Namibia: On the Road to Freedom. Gwen McKinney. *Essence* 21, No. 6 (October 1990):111-114+

The Other Afrikaners. Ivor Powell and Philip Brooks. *Vogue* (July 1990):1196-199+

Putting Apartheid on Screen. Talking with Euzhan Palcy. *Spare Rib* No. 209 (February 1990):12-15

In the Spirit: The Power of Commitment. Susan L. Taylor. *Essence* 21, No. 2 (June 1990):47

When a Woman Is a Rock. Winnie Mandela. *Spare Rib* No. 210 (March 1990):6-10

**South Africa – Colonialism**

African-American Women Missionaries and European Imperialism in Southern Africa, 1880-1920. Sylvia M. Jacobs. *Women's Studies International Forum* 13, No. 4 (1990):381-394

**South Africa – Contraception**

The Politics of Contraception in South Africa. Barbara Klugman. *Women's Studies International Forum* 13, No. 3 (1990):261-271

**South Africa – Labor Movement**

Gender, Race, and Political Empowerment: South African Canning Workers, 1940-1960. Iris Berger. *Gender and Society* 4, No. 3 (September 1990):398-420

Symbols and Sexuality: Culture and Identity on the Early Witwatersrand Gold Mines. Patrick Harries. *Gender & History* 2, No. 3 (Autumn 1990):318-336

**South Africa – Political Protest**

Redemption Songs. *Spare Rib* No. 210 (March 1990):26-27

**South Africa – Politics and Government**

De Klerk's "Reforms" – Unfinished Business. Esme Nathan. *Spare Rib* No. 209 (February 1990): 21-22

Walking into Freedom. Alexis De Veaux. *Essence* 21, No. 2 (June 1990):48-53 +

**South Africa – Status of Women**

Not Either an Experimental Doll: The Separate Worlds of Three South African Women. Edited by Shula Marks. Reviewed by Sheila Tlou. *Women's Studies International Forum* 13, No. 4 (1990):408

**South Africa – Violence**

Buthelezi and De Klerk in League. Esme Nathan. *Spare Rib* No. 216 (September 1990):47-48

**South Africa – Violence Against Women**

No to Rape. Kally Forrest. *Connexions* 34 (1990):16

South Africa: Enough Is Enough. Katie Monagle. *Ms.* 1, No. 2 (September/October 1990):11

Yes to Action. *Connexions* 34 (1990):16-17

**South Carolina – Hurricanes**

Hurricane! Laura Claverie. *Family Circle* 103, No. 13 (September 25, 1990):78-82

**Southern States – Status of Women.** *See also* Factory Workers – History

Hard Times Cotton Mill Girls: Personal Histories of Womanhood and Poverty in the South. By Victoria Byerly. Reviewed by Patricia Hill Collins. *Gender and Society* 4, No. 3 (September 1990):427-429

Maintaining the Spirit and Tone of Robust Manliness: The Battle Against Coeducation at Southern Colleges and Universities, 1890-1940. Amy Thompson McCandless. *NWSA Journal* 2, No. 2 (Spring 1990):199-216

Property-Owning Free African-American Women in the South, 1800-70. Loren Schweninger. *Journal of Women's History* 1, No. 3 (Winter 1990):13-44

**Southgate, Martha**

Bill Cosby–Living with Heartbreak. *Redbook* 175, No. 2 (June 1990):52-54+

Joie De Vivre. *Savvy Woman* (September 1990):21-22

Sandra Dupiton Loves to Dance. *Essence* 20, No. 10 (February 1990):40

**South Korea–Prostitution**

As For South Korea . . . *Women's World* , No. 24 (Winter 1990/91): 22

**Southwell, Jane** (joint author). *See* Macdonald-Grahame, Carmel

**South West Africa People's Organization.** *See* Namibia–Politics and Government

**Souvenirs (Keepsakes)**

Home Free: Of Keepsakes and God Pots. Betty Fussell. *Lear's* (November 1990):58-60

**Souza, Margaret de**

The Colours of Menopause. *Healthsharing* 11, No. 4 (December 1990):14-17

**Soviet Union**

Francine Gray. Susan Jacoby. *Vogue* (March 1990):319, 326, 332

Soviet-American Summit Tackles Troubling Issues. Laura Flanders. *New Directions for Women* 19, No. 4 (July-August 1990): I +

The Winter of Their Discontent. Francine Prose. *Savvy Woman* (March 1990):57-60

**Soviet Union–Anti-Semitism**

What Soviet Anti-Semitism Looks Like Now. Rachel Kadish. *Lilith* 15, No. 4 (Fall 1990):39

**Soviet Union–Art History**

Malevich. Rosamond Bernier. *Vogue* (September 1990):588-593+

**Soviet Union–Culture and Society**

Family Reunion. Suzanne Muchnic. *Harper's Bazaar* (June 1990):36

Mothers of Misery, Child Abandonment in Russia. By David L. Ransel. Reviewed by Judith Pallot. *Gender & History* 2, No. 3 (Autumn 1990):358-359

Reds: The New Red Revolution. Richard Alleman. *Vogue* (September 1990):552-573

**Soviet Union–Economic Development**

Inside Moscow's Grocery Stores. Vivian Cadden. *McCall's* 117, No. 10 (July 1990):78-82

**Soviet Union–Education**

In the Russian Gymnasia. Excerpt. Manya Prozanskaya Lackow. *Lilith* 15, No. 1 (Winter 1990):15-20

**Soviet Union–Homosexuality**

Lesbian Vignettes: A Russian Triptych from the 1890s. Notes. Laura Engelstein. *Signs* 15, No. 4 (Summer 1990):813-831

On the Theme: Talking with the Editor of the Soviet Union's First Gay and Lesbian Newspaper. Interview. Julie Dorf. *Out/Look* No. 9 (Summer 1990):55-59

We Have No Sex: Soviet Gays and AIDS in the Era of Glasnost. Masha Gessen. *Out/Look* No. 9 (Summer 1990):42-54

**Soviet Union–Media and Communications.** *See also* Moscow–*Theme* Newspaper

**Soviet Union–Status of Women**

Balancing Acts: Contemporary Stories by Russsian Women. Edited by Helena Goscilo. Reviewed by Judith Deutsch Kornblatt. *Feminist Collections* 11, No. 4 (Summer 1990):3-4

Feminists Despite Themselves: Women in Ukranian Community Life, 1884-1939. By Martha Bohachevsky-Chomiak. Reviewed by Frances Swyripa. *Resources for Feminist Research* 19, No. 1 (March 1990):13

The Image of Women in Contemporary Soviet Fiction: Selected Short Stories from the U.S.S.R. Edited by Sigrid McLaughlin. Reviewed by Judith Deutsch Kornblatt. *Feminist Collections* 11, No. 4 (Summer 1990):3-4

Russian Women's Studies: Essays on Sexism in Soviet Culture. By Tatyana Mamonova. Reviewed by Elizabeth Waters. *Australian Feminist Studies* No. 11 (Autumn 1990):117-120

Russian Women's Studies: Essays on Sexism in Soviet Culture. By Tatyana Mamonova. Reviewed by Katherine E. Loda. *Women's Studies International Forum* 13, No. 3 (1990):273

Russian Women's Studies: Essays on Sexism in Soviet Culture. By Tatyana Mamonova. Reviewed by Norma Noonan. *Women & Politics* 10, No. 4 (1990):133-134

Sex and Semiotic Confusion: Report from Moscow. Elizabeth Waters. *Australian Feminist Studies* No. 12 (Summer 1990):1-14

Soviet Women: Walking the Tightrope. By Francine du Plessix Gray. Reviewed by Rochelle Ruthchild. *The Women's Review of Books* 8, No. 3 (December 1990):25-26

Soviet Women: Walking the Tightrope. By Francine du Plessix Gray. Reviewed by Sandra Pollack. *New Directions for Women* 19, No. 6 (November-December 1990):22

Women and Ideology in the Soviet Union. By Mary Buckley. Reviewed by Rochelle Ruthchild. *The Women's Review of Books* 7, No. 6 (March 1990):15

Women and Politics in the USSR: Consciousness Raising and Soviet Women's Groups. By Genia K.

Browning. Reviewed by Elizabeth Waters. *Australian Feminist Studies* No. 11 (Autumn 1990):117-120

**Spacek, Sissy** (about)

The Country Girl. C. J. Houtchens. *Harper's Bazaar* (January 1990):100-105+

**Space Sciences**

Inertia. K. C. Cole. *Lear's* (May 1990):112-113+

**Spader, James** (about)

The Trouble With Jimmy. *Vogue* (November 1990):380-383

**Spain – Culture and Society**

Spain's Reign. *Harper's Bazaar* (August 1990):78-94

**Spain – Writers**

Las Románticas: Women Writers and Subjectivity in Spain, 1835-1850. By Susan Kirkpatrick. Reviewed by James D. Fernández. *Tulsa Studies in Women's Literature* 9, No. 2 (Fall 1990):321-323

Women Playwrights in Contemporary Spain and the Male-Dominated Canon. Notes. Patricia W. O'Connor. *Signs* 15, No. 2 (Winter 1990):376-390

**Spallone, Patricia**

Beyond Conception: The New Politics of Reproduction. Reviewed by Helen Bequaert Holmes. *The Women's Review of Books* 7, No. 4 (January 1990):20-21

Beyond Conception: The New Politics of Reproduction. Reviewed by Leigh Anne Chavez. *NWSA Journal* 2, No. 4 (Autumn 1990):652-656

Reconstructing Babylon: Women and Technology. Book Review. *Spare Rib* No. 210 (March 1990):35

**Spallone, Patricia** (joint author). *See* Hynes, Patricia

**Spalter-Roth, Roberta M.**

Social Policy: A Feminist Analysis. Book Review. *Gender and Society* 4, No. 1 (March 1990):111-113

**Spanish Language – Gender Markings**

A Review of Research on Language and Sex in the Spanish Language. Uwe Kjaer Nissen. *Women & Language* 13, No. 2 (Winter 1990):11-29

**Sparling, Mary**

About "Joan's Room": Mary Sparling Interviews *Atlantis* Guest Artist Marie Koehler-Vandergraaf. *Atlantis* 15, No. 2 (Spring 1990):122-126

**Spas.** *See* Health Resorts, Watering Places, etc.

**Spearritt, Katie**

The Market for Marriage in Colonial Queensland. *Hecate* 16, Nos. 1-2 (1990):23-42

**Spears, Heather**

Every Woman's Guide to Hysterectomy. Poem. *Canadian Women's Studies* 11, No. 2 (Fall 1990):42

**Special Interest Networks.** *See* Networks

**Special Olympics**

Queen for a Day: The Royal Treatment. *Family Circle* 103, No. 9 (June 26, 1990):55

**Specter, Michael**

Is There a Right Reason for Having a Baby? *Glamour* (August 1990):96

**Spector, Janet D.**

The Minnesota Plan II: A Project to Improve the University Environment for Women Faculty, Administrators, and Academic Professional Staff. *Women's Studies Quarterly* 18, Nos. 1-2 (Spring-Summer 1990):189-205

**Speechwriting**

A Thousand Points to Write: Peggy Noonan on Getting a Speach Started and Keeping It Going. Interview. Christine Reinhardt. *Working Woman* (November 1990):120+

**Speicher, Hilda** (joint author). *See* Paludi, Michele A.

**Speir, Susan**

"Let's Not Forget the Children" Bibliography. *Ladies' Home Journal* 107, No. 7 (July 1990):22-27

**Spektor, Mira Josefowitz**

Sonnet. Poem. *Journal of Women and Aging* 2, No. 2 (1990):67

Untitled. Poem. *Journal of Women and Aging* 2, No. 2 (1990):33-34

**Spelman, Elizabeth V.**

Inessential Woman: Problems of Exclusion in Feminist Thought. Reviewed by Elaine Marks. *Tulsa Studies in Women's Literature* 9, No. 2 (Fall 1990):309-314

Inessential Woman. Reviewed by Carol Anne Douglas. *off our backs* 20, No. 4 (April 1990):17-18

Inessential Woman. *Woman of Power* 16 (Spring 1990):24-27

**Spelman College**

A Story of Success: The Sciences at Spelman College. Etta Z. Falconer. *Sage* 6, No. 2 (Fall 1989):36-38

**Spelman College – Inaugural Symposium**

*Another Day Will Find Us Brave*: Inaugural Address, November 6, 1988. Johnnetta B. Cole *Sage* 6, No. 1 (Summer 1989):85-86

Reflections on the Spelman College Inaugural Symposium: The Empowerment of Black Women. Jacqueline Jones Royster and Beverly Guy-Sheftall. *Sage* 6, No. 1 (Summer 1989):84

**Spence, Catherine Helen**

Mr. Hogarth's Will. Reviewed by Judith MacBean. *Australian Feminist Studies* No. 12 (Summer 1990):123-125

In the Spirit: Going the Distance. Susan L. Taylor. *Essence* 21, No. 6 (October 1990):71

In the Spirit: In Our Own Image. Susan L. Taylor. *Essence* 21, No. 1 (May 1990):91

In the Spirit: One Love. Susan L. Taylor. *Essence* 20, No. 10 (February 1990):53

In the Spirit: Shaping the Future. Susan L. Taylor. *Essence* 20, No. 11 (March 1990):51

In the Spirit: Staying Centered. Susan L. Taylor. *Essence* 21, No. 4 (August 1990):53

In the Spirit: The Ties That Bind. Susan L. Taylor. *Essence* 20, No. 12 (April 1990):49

Spiritual Journey. Beverly Weston and Bebe Moore Campbell. *Essence* 21, No. 6 (October 1990):94-96+

Touching Our Strength: The Erotic as Power and the Love of God. By Carter Heyward. Reviewed by Penny Perkins. *New Directions for Women* 19, No. 4 (July-August 1990):15

Using Your "Mind Sight." Iyanla Vanzant. *Essence* 21, No. 5 (September 1990):36

Women and Spirituality: Voices of Protest and Promise. By Ursula King. Reviewed by Marsha Hewitt. *Resources for Feminist Research* 19, No. 1 (March 1990):41-42

**Spirituality—Teaching**
Teaching Introductory Feminist Spirituality. Joan Leonard. *Journal of Feminist Studies in Religion* 6, No. 2 (Fall 1990):121-135

**Spitz, Mark** (about)
Mark Spitz. Stephen Fenichell. *Lear's* (June 1990):102-107

**Spitzack, Carol** (joint author). *See* Carter, Kathryn

**Spitze, Glenna** and Logan, John
Sons, Daughters, and Intergenerational Social Support. *Journal of Marriage and the Family* 52, No. 2 (May 1990):420-430

**Spitze, Glenna** (joint editor). *See* Bose, Christine E.

**Spivack, Miranda S.**
Supreme Court: Double Trouble for Repro Rights? *Ms.* 1, No. 3 (November/December 1990):89

Washington Notes: "The Process Stinks." *Ms.* 1, No. 2 (September/October 1990):91

**Spivak, Gayatri Chakravorty**
In Other Worlds: Essays in Cultural Politics. Reviewed by Susan Hardy Aiken. *NWSA Journal* 2, No. 1 (Winter 1990):145-147

**Spivak, Gayatri Chakravorty** (Interview)
*Women and Performance: A Journal of Feminist Theory* 5, No. 1, Issue #9 (1990): 80-92

**Spizman, Robyn Freedman** (joint author). *See* Garber, Stephen W.

**Spock, Benjamin**
Boost Your Child's Self-Confidence. *Redbook* 174, No. 6 (April 1990):32

Does Your Child Feel Second-Rate? *Redbook* 175, No. 1 (May 1990):38

Grandparents Can Be a Joy (and a Problem). *Redbook* 175, No. 4 (August 1990):30

Lend a Helping Hand. *Redbook* 176, No. 2 (December 1990):30

My Pet Theory. *Redbook* 175, No. 5 (September 1990):46

Sex Play—Is It Okay? *Redbook* 175, No. 3 (July 1990):30

When Dad Won't Discipline. *Redbook* 176, No. 1 (November 1990):38

**Spohn, Cassie** (joint author). *See* Gillespie, Diane

Sponge. *See* Contraception

**Sport Clothes**
Apre4s, Of Course. *Mademoiselle* (November 1990):172-177

Great Looks: Flatter Any Body. *Redbook* 175, No. 5 (September 1990):16-18

High-Impact Fashions/Low Impact Sports. *Lear's* (January 1990):104-107

Lady Blues: The New Nauticals Just *Look* Rich. *Mademoiselle* (January 1990):86-91

Par Excellence 1990. *Harper's Bazaar* (March 1990):202-207

**Sports.** *See also* Athletics; Bicycling; Rock Climbing; Roller Skating; Tennis; Winter Sports
Calendar. *Women's Sports & Fitness* 12, No. 6 (September 1990):15

Combatting Homophobia in Sports. Helen Lenskyj. *off our backs* 20, No. 6 (June 1990):2-3

The Competitive Edge. *Harper's Bazaar* (June 1990):49-54

Disc Jocks. Susanna Levin. *Women's Sports & Fitness* 12, No. 6 (September 1990):66

Double Your Pleasure. James Raia and Marjorie McCloy. *Women's Sports & Fitness* 12, No. 6 (September 1990):20

From "Fair Sex" to Feminism: Sport and the Socialization of Women in the Industrial and Post-Industrial Eras. Edited by J. A. Mangan and Robert J. Park. Reviewed by Susan L. Greendorfer. *Gender and Society* 4, No. 1 (March 1990):108-110

Fitness. Rachel Urquhart. *Vogue* (August 1990):191-200

Good Sports. Joanne Mattera. *Glamour* (April 1990):82; (June 1990):78

Good Sports: Take Your Workout on Vacation. Joanne Mattera. *Glamour* (September 1990):92

Health and Fitness Notes. *Vogue* (December 1990):215

Living Well. *Women's Sports & Fitness* 12, No. 6 (September 1990):12-14

Looking for Her Field of Dreams. Nancy Slonim Aronie. *Lear's* (July 1990):40

Sporting Women Play the Field. Anne-Marie R. Seltzer. *New Directions for Women* 19, No. 4 (July-August 1990):12-13

Thoughts on Skimming the Waters. Rebecca Busselle. *Lear's* (October 1990):50-52

TV Sports Study: Women Are Humorous Sex Objects in Stands, Missing as Athletes. *Media Report to Women* 18, No. 6 (November-December 1990):3

**Sports—Accidents and Injuries.** *See also* Aquatic Sports—Safety; Football—Accidents and Injuries

Keeping Your Child Safe. Mark Widome and Anne Cassidy. *Good Housekeeping* 211, No. 3 (September 1990):148+

**Sports—Employment Opportunities.** *See also* Athletics—Career Opportunities

**Sports—Journalism**

Baseball Pitcher Uses Sexual Comment to Decline Interview with Reporter. *Media Report to Women* 18, No. 5 (September-October 1990):2-3

Insults to Women Sportswriters Rock Sports Journalism, Teams. *Media Report to Women* 18, No. 6 (November-December 1990):3-4

**Sports—Sociological Aspects**

"Stylistic Ensembles" on a Different Pitch: A Comparative Analysis of Men's and Women's Rugby Songs. Elizabeth Wheatley. *Women & Language* 13, No. 1 (Fall 1990):21-26

**Sports—Training**

Good Sports: Mind Games. Joanne Mattera. *Glamour* (December 1990):76

**Sports Facilities.** *See* Health Resorts, Watering-Places, etc.; Physical Fitness Centers

**Sports for Children**

Kids in the Water. Barbara Hey. *McCall's* 117, No. 10 (July 1990):85-90

**Sports Medicine**

Sports Medicine: Hot Tips. Carol Otis and Roger Goldingay. *Women's Sports & Fitness* 12, No. 6 (September 1990):10

Women and Exercise: Physiology and Sports Medicine. By Mona Shangold and Gabe Mirkin. Reviewed by Caroline A. Macera. *Women and Health* 16, No. 2 (1990):137-138

**Sportswriters**

Team Locker Rooms Still Tough Turf for Women Sportswriters. *Media Report to Women* 18, No. 1 (January/February 1990):1-2

**Spotswood, Claire Myers (Owens) (about)**

Claire Myers Spotswood (Owens). Miriam Kalman Harris. *Belles Lettres* 5, No. 2 (Winter 1990):15

**Spouse Abuse.** *See also* Domestic Violence; Violence Against Women

Feminist Perspectives on Wife Abuse. Edited by Kersti Yllo and Michele Bograd. Reviewed by Freda L. Paltiel. *Women and Health* 16, Nos. 3/4 (1990):196-201

Perceptions of Wife Abuse: Effects of Gender, Attitudes toward Women, and Just-World Beliefs among College Students. Connie M. Kristiansen and Rita Giulietti. *Psychology of Women Quarterly* 14, No. 2 (June 1990):177-189

**Spratling, Susan Foy**

Backtalk: Worked Over. *Lear's* (January 1990):124-128

**Sprenkle, Douglas H.** (joint author). *See* Piercy, Fred P.

**Sprey, Jetse**

Sociobiology and the Social Sciences. Book Review. *Journal of Marriage and the Family* 52, No. 4 (November 1990):1152-1153

**Spring, Dona**

Glimpses of the Goddess. *Woman of Power* 15 (Fall-Winter 1990):77-78

**Springen, Karen**

All the Right Moves. *Savvy Woman* (February 1990):71-75

When Divorce Rocks a Company. *Savvy Woman* (March 1990):34-38

**Springer, Christina**

The National Women's Music Festival: Bringing Non-Dominant Women to Full Boil. *off our backs* 20, No. 5 (May 1990):9

Whose Goddesses Are They? *New Directions for Women* 19, No. 4 (July-August 1990):4

Wishlist. Poem. *Sinister Wisdom* 42 (Winter 1990-1991):8-9

**Springer, Judy**

Goddesses Unite: The Making of a Mural. *Canadian Women's Studies* 11, No. 1 (Spring 1990):97-98

**Spruill, D. Lynn** (about). *See also* Texas—Mayors

**Squier, Susan Merrill**

Each Dream, I Struggle. Poem. *The Women's Review of Books* 7, No. 12 (September 1990):20

Hepatitis. Poem. *The Women's Review of Books* 7, No. 12 (September 1990):20

**Squier, Susan Merrill** (joint editor). See Cooper, Helen M.

**Squires, Sally**

Get Your Child to Sleep Through the Night. *Working Mother* 13, No. 8 (August 1990):72-76

Holiday Health Handbook. *Ladies' Home Journal* 107, No. 12 (December 1990):76

Medinews. Bibliography. *Ladies' Home Journal* 107, No. 1 (January 1990):84

Medinews. *Ladies' Home Journal* 107, No. 3 (March 1990):114; 107, No. 4 (April 1990):112-118; 107, No. 5 (May 1990):94; 107, No. 8 (August 1990):30; 107, No. 10 (October 1990):132; 107, No. 12 (December 1990):72

**Srikantan, K. Sivaswamy**

Population Planning in India: Policy Issues and Research Priorities. Book Review. *Journal of Family Welfare* 36, No. 3 (September 1990):107-110

**Sri Lanka – British Occupation**

European Women Educators Under the British Colonial Administration in Sri Lanka. Swarna Jayaweera. *Women's Studies International Forum* 13, No. 4 (1990):323-331

**Sri Lanka – Marriage Customs**

The Virginity Test: A Bridal Nightmare. Sriani Basnayake. *Journal of Family Welfare* 36, No. 2 (June 1990):50-59

**Srivastava, J. N.**

Inter-District and Inter-Regional Variations in Incidence of Child Marriage Among Females and Its Inter-Censal Changes in Uttar Pradesh. *Journal of Family Welfare* 36, No. 4 (December 1990):20-31

**Sroloff, Deborah**

Star Quality. *Harper's Bazaar* (February 1990):148-149

**St. Andrews, B. A.**

Cat's Eye. Book Review. *Belles Lettres* 5, No. 3 (Spring 1990):9

Requiem for an Age. *Belles Lettres* 5, No. 3 (Spring 1990):9

**St. John, Barbara A.**

How to Make an Excellent Teacher. *Heresies* 25 (1990):57

**Stabiner, Karen**

The Cowboy as Cosmetician. *Lear's* (January 1990):46-50

**Stacey, Judith**

Brave New Families: Stories of Democratic Upheaval in Late Twentieth-Century America. Reviewed by Arlene Kaplan Daniels. *The Women's Review of Books* 8, No. 3 (December 1990):14-15

**Stack, Steven**

Divorce, Suicide, and the Mass Media: An Analysis of Differential Identification, 1948-1980. *Journal of Marriage and the Family* 52, No. 2 (May 1990):553-560

New Micro-level Data on the Impact of Divorce on Suicide, 1959-1980: A Test of Two Theories. *Journal of Marriage and the Family* 52, No. 1 (February 1990):119-127

**Stacy, Diane** and Frink, Cheryl Coggins

A Woman Today: A Home for Patty. *Ladies' Home Journal* 107, No. 5 (May 1990):20-26

**Stade, Chris** (joint author). See Doran, Terry

**Stafford, Beth** (editor)

Directory of Women's Studies Programs and Library Resources. Review. *Feminist Collections* 11, No. 3 (Spring 1990):18

**Stafford, J. Martin**

Homosexuality and Education. Reviewed by Peggy Aggleton. *Gender and Education* 2, No. 2 (1990):247-249

**Stafford, Jean** (about)

Jean Stafford: The Savage Heart. By Charlotte Margolis Goodman. Reviewed by Emily Toth. *The Women's Review of Books* 8, No. 3 (December 1990):15-16

Jean Stafford: The Savage Heart. By Charlotte Margolis Goodman. Reviewed by Mary Titus. *Belles Lettres* 6, No. 1 (Fall 1990):40-42

**Stahl, Lesley** (about). See Television Journalists – Networking

**Stake, Jayne E.** (joint author). See Malovich, Natalie J.

**Staller, Ilona** (about). See Kazanjian, Dodie, "Koons Crazy."

**Stallone, Sylvester** (about)

Move Over, Rambo: There's a New Sly in Town. Laura Morice. *Mademoiselle* (February 1990):176-177+

Talking with Sylvester Stallone: "My Sons are My Life." Interview. Carol Lynn Mithers. *Redbook* 176, No. 2 (December 1990):32-34

**Stamford, Bryant** and Shimer, Porter

Burn Calories without Exercising. Excerpt. *Redbook* 174, No. 6 (April 1990):110-113

**Stamps, Wickie**

Group Pushes Nonsexist Rock. *New Directions for Women* 19, No. 1 (January/February 1990):7

**Stange, Mary Zeiss**

Jessica Hahn's Strange Odyssey from PTL to Playboy. *Journal of Feminist Studies in Religion* 6, No. 1 (Spring 1990):105-116

**Stanger, Sheila**

Instructions for the Birthing Team. *Lilith* 15, No. 1 (Winter 1990):21-23

**Stanko, Elizabeth A.** (joint editor). *See* Hanmer, Jalna

**Stanley, Alessandra**

This Working Life: Meow! Why Men Love a Cat Fight. *Working Woman* (July 1990):109

**Stanley, Autumn**

Gender Segregation in the Workplace: *Plus ça change . . . NWSA Journal* 2, No. 4 (Autumn 1990):640-645

Invention Begins at Forty: Older Women of the 19th Century as Inventors. *Journal of Women and Aging* 2, No. 2 (1990):133-151

**Stanley, Liz**

British Feminist Histories: An Editorial Introduction. *Women's Studies International Forum* 13, Nos. 1-2 (1990):3-7

Moments of Writing: Is there a Feminist Auto/Biography? Notes. *Gender & History* 2, No. 1 (Spring 1990):58-67

Recovering Women in History from Feminist Deconstructionism. *Women's Studies International Forum* 13, Nos. 1-2 (1990):151-157

**Stansfield, Lisa** (about)

Soul Stylist. June Garcia. *Mademoiselle* (June 1990):92-97

Vogue Arts: The Lady's Got Soul. Nick Coleman. *Vogue* (August 1990):210-214

**Stanton, Domna C.** (editor)

The Female Autograph: Theory and Practice of Autobiography from the Tenth to the Twentieth Century. Reviewed by Barbara Green. *Tulsa Studies in Women's Literature* 9, No. 1 (Spring 1990):135-139

**Stanton, Donna** (editor)

The Female Autobiograph: Theory and Practice of Autobiography from the Tenth to the Twentieth Centuries. Reviewed by Elizabeth R. Baer. *Belles Lettres* 5, No. 2 (Winter 1990):4-6+

**Stanton, Elizabeth Cady** (about)

Elizabeth Cady Stanton. By Martha E. Kendall. Reviewed by Mitzi Myers. *NWSA Journal* 2, No. 2 (Spring 1990):273-281

Posing the Woman Citizen: The Contradictions of Stanton's Feminism. Mary Loeffelholz. *Genders* 7 (Spring 1990):87-98

**Stanton, Will**

The Cookie Rebellion. Short story. *Redbook* 176, No. 1 (November 1990):74-82

**Stanworth, Michelle** (editor)

Reproductive Technologies: Gender, Motherhood and Medicine. Reviewed by Peggy L. Chinn. *Signs* 15, No. 2 (Winter 1990):400-405

**Stapleton, Jean** (about)

Whoopi & Jean Rap. Natalie Gittelson. *McCall's* 118, No. 2 (November 1990):110-114

**Stark, Barbara**

Women's Legal Rights: International Covenants, An Alternative to ERA? Book Review. *Women's Rights Law Reporter* 12, No. 1 (Spring 1990):51-57

**Starling, Marion Wilson**

The Slave Narrative: Its Place in American History. Reviewed by Katherine M. Rogers. *Belles Lettres* 5, No. 2 (Winter 1990):6

**Starr, Maurice** (about)

Maurice Starr: The General. Jesse Nash and George Flowers. *Essence* 21, No. 8 (December 1990):34

**Starr, Tama** (about)

Live from Times Square. Paul Tough. *Savvy* (December-January 1991):16

**Starsen, Melle**

A Gift from Elvis. *Ladies' Home Journal* 107, No. 8 (August 1990):18-22

**Starwoman, Athena**

Horoscope. *Vogue* (January 1990):128-133; (July 1990):120-122

**Starzinger, Page Hill**

The Cutting Edge. Bibliography. *Vogue* (July 1990):168-175

Fashion Clips. *Vogue* (January 1990):34; (July 1990):36-41; (August 1990):102-107; (September 1990):122; (December 1990):102

View. *Vogue* (June 1990):66-68

**State Constitutions.** *See* Constitutions, State

**State Governments.** *See also* Constitutions, State

**State Governments – Elected Officials**

Legislators' Perceptions of Women in State Legislatures. Patricia K. Freeman and William Lyons. *Women & Politics* 10, No. 4 (1990):121-132

**State Governors' Mansions.** *See* Governors – United States – Mansions

**Staten, Marjorie A.** (about). *See* Legal System

**State Religion.** *See* Church and State; Religious Discrimination

**Statham, Anne**

Pushing the Limits: The Female Administrative Aspirant. Book Review. *Gender and Society* 4, No. 1 (March 1990):113-115

Women in Educational Administration. Book Review. *Gender and Society* 4, No. 1 (March 1990):113-115

Women in the Administrative Revolution. Book Review. *Gender and Society* 4, No. 1 (March 1990):113-115

**Statham, Anne** and Bravo, Ellen

The Introduction of New Technology: Health Implications for Workers. *Women and Health* 16, No. 2 (1990):105-129

**Statham, Daphne** (joint author). *See* Hanmer, Jaina

**Stato, Joanne**

All For Freedom. Music Review. *off our backs* 20, No. 5 (May 1990):20-21

God's Fierce Whimsy – Christian Feminism and Theological Education. Book Review. *off our backs* 20, No. 8 (August/September 1990):26-27+

"Great Women" In Abundance. *off our backs* 20, No. 3 (March 1990):31

Heather Has Two Mommies. Book Review. *off our backs* 20, No. 3 (March 1990):30

I Am Your Sister Celeconference: Tribute to Audre Lorde. *off our backs* 20, No. 11 (December 1990):2-5+

Memories and Visions: Women's Fantasy and Science Fiction. Book Review. *off our backs* 20, No. 5 (May 1990):17+

Montreal Gynocide. *off our backs* 20, No. 1 (January 1990):1

Mud Flower Collective: Challenging Theological Education. *off our backs* 20, No. 8 (August/September 1990):26-27+

Roadwork. Poem. *off our backs* 20, No. 2 (February 1990):23

Skipping Stones: A Multi-ethnic Children's Forum. Journal Review. *off our backs* 20, No. 3 (March 1990):30-31

Sweet Honey in the Rock's First Children's Album: All For Freedom. *off our backs* 20, No. 5 (May 1990):20-21

Volunteer. Poem. *off our backs* 20, No. 2 (February 1990):23

On Women's Space. *off our backs* 20, No. 9 (October 1990):14

Yahoo Australia! Music Review. *off our backs* 20, No. 9 (October 1990):20

**Stato, Joanne** and Ruby, Jennie

Beyond Elves and Warrior Women: Broadening the Boundaries of Speculative Fiction. *off our backs* 20, No. 5 (May 1990):18-19

**Status of Women.** *See* Africa, Status of Women; Christianity – Status of Women; Islam, Status of Women; Judaism, Status of Women; Media and Communications – Status of Women; *under particular countries*

**Staudt, Kathleen A.** (joint editor). *See* Parpart, Jane L.

**Staves, Susan**

Married Women's Separate Property in England, 1660-1833. Reviewed by Janice Farrar Thaddeus. *The Women's Review of Books* 8, No. 1 (October 1990):25-26

**Stead, Deborah**

The Greening of Sara Parkin. *Savvy Woman* (November 1990):64-67+

**Steadman, Carolyn**

Bitter Milk: Women and Teaching. Book Review. *Gender and Education* 2, No. 2 (1990):249-250

**Steel, Danielle** (about). *See also* Etra, Jon, "World Class"

**Steel, Flora Annie** (criticism)

Feminism Under the Raj: Complicity and Resistance in the Writings of Flora Annie Steel and Annie Besant. Nancy L. Paxton. *Women's Studies International Forum* 13, No. 4 (1990):333-346

**Steele, Jan**

Role Conflict: Coping With Work in A Community Mental Health Centre. *Women and Environments* 12, No. 2 (Spring 1990): 24-25

**Steele, Susan** (joint editor). *See* Philips, Susan

**Steele, Valerie**

Paris Fashion: A Cultural History. Reviewed by Ruth P. Rubinstein. *Woman's Art Journal* 11, No. 1 (Spring-Summer 1990):49-50

**Steele, Valerie** (joint editor). *See* Kidwell, Claudia Brush

**Steelsmith, Shari**

How Would You Like to Hear Only Half a Story? Ideas for Using Biographies of Historical Women in the Classroom. *Feminist Teacher* 5, No. 1 (Spring 1990):19-23

**Steenburgen, Mary** (about)

Mary Steenburgen: Ahead to the Future. Michael J. Bandler. *Ladies' Home Journal* 107, No. 7 (July 1990):38-40

**Steffe, Cynthia** (about)

Desiging Woman. Joan Delaney. *Executive Female* 13, No. 5 (September-October 1990):66-67

**Steffens, Dorothy L.** and Robbins, Jane

The Effects of Feminist Approaches on Research Methodologies. Book Review. *Feminist Collections* 11, No. 2 (Winter 1990):7-9

A Feminist Ethic for Social Science Research. Book Review. *Feminist Collections* 11, No. 2 (Winter 1990):7-9

Stepparents Need Legal Clout. Philip S. Gutis. *McCall's* 117, No. 8 (May 1990):66-67

Strangers in the House. By William R. Beer. Reviewed by Lawrence H. Ganong. *Journal of Marriage and the Family* 52, No. 1 (February 1990):281-282

**Stephanie, Princess of Monaco**

Royal Identity Crisis. Margot Dougherty. *Mademoiselle* (August 1990):180-183

**Stephen, Elizabeth Hervey** (joint author). *See* Rindfuss, Ronald R.

**Stephen Family – Genealogy**

The Symonds and Stephen Families. *Tulsa Studies in Women's Literature* 9, No. 2 (Fall 1990):228

**Stephens, Beth**

A Developing Legal System Grapples with an Ancient Problem: Rape in Nicaragua. *Women's Rights Law Reporter* 12, No. 2 (Summer 1990): 69-88

**Stephens, Malvina** (about). *See also* Leadership

**Stephens, Mariflo**

Making It Up as We Go Along. *Iris* 24 (Fall-Winter 1990):56-57

**Stephenson, Yanela** (joint author). *See* Palladino, Diane

**Stepmothers in Literature**. *See also* Literary Criticism – Feminist Perspectives

**Sterility**. *See also* Infertility

**Sterilization**. *See also* Contraception; Contraception – Tubal Sterilization; India – Family Planning

Birth Control for Him. Felicia Halpert. *Essence* 21, No. 7 (November 1990):20-22

Sterilization Anxiety and Fertility Control in the Later Years of Childbearing. H. Theodore Groat, Arthur G. Neal, and Jerry W. Wicks. *Journal of Marriage and the Family* 52, No. 1 (February 1990):249-258

Tying the Tubes. By Catherine de Costa. Reviewed by Sue Craig. *Healthright* 9, No. 4 (August 1990):46-47

The Ultimate Birth Control. Kelly Costigan. *Savvy Woman* (January 1990):84-85

**Stern, Jane** and Stern, Michael

The Encyclopedia of Bad Taste. Reviewed by Francine Prose. *Savvy Woman* (November 1990):20-21

**Stern, Mark** (joint author). *See* Axinn, June

**Stern, Michael** (joint author). *See* Stern, Jane

**Sternbach, Nancy Saporta** (joint editor). **See** Horno-Delgado, Asunción

**Stesin, Nancy** (joint author). *See* Rachlin, Jill; Watson, Karen

**Stets, Jan E.**

Verbal and Physical Aggression in Marriage. *Journal of Marriage and the Family* 52, No. 2 (May 1990):501-514

**Stevens, David**

New Evidence on the Timing of Early Life-Course Transitions: The United States 1900 to 1980. *Journal of Family History* 15, No. 2 (April 1990):163-178

**Stevens, Mark**

Enterprise: How Customer Service Built a Business. *Working Woman* (July 1990):31-38

Enterprise: How to Take a Good Business and Make It Better. *Working Woman* (March 1990):38-46

Entrepreneurial Edge. *Working Woman* (December 1990):45-48

**Stevenson, Anne**

Bitter Fame: A Life of Sylvia Plath. Reviewed by Janice M. Cauwels. *New Directions for Women* 19, No. 1 (January/February 1990):20

**Stevenson, Kelly** (joint author). *See* Henry, Sara

**Stewart, Abigail J.** and Gold-Steinberg, Sharon

Midlife Women's Political Consciousness: Case Studies of Psychosocial Development and Political Commitment. *Psychology of Women Quarterly* 14, No. 4 (December 1990):543-566

**Stewart, Dave** (about). *See* Leadership

**Stewart, Elinore Pruitt**

Letters of a Woman Homesteader. Reviewed by Barbara Horn. *Belles Lettres* 5, No. 3 (Spring 1990):23

**Stewart, Isobel**

The Girl Called Samantha. Short Story. *Good Housekeeping* 211, No. 2 (August 1990):112-113

Lessons in Love. Short Story. *Good Housekeeping* 210, No. 6 (June 1990):176-177

**Stewart, Joan Hinde**

Discourses of Desire: Gender, Genre, and Epistolary Fictions. Book Review. *Tulsa Studies in Women's Literature* 9, No. 1 (Spring 1990):149-150

Writing the Female Voice: Essays on Epistolary Literature. Book Review. *Tulsa Studies in Women's Literature* 9, No. 1 (Spring 1990):150-152

**Stewart, Martha** (about). *See* Etra, Jon, "World Class"

**Stewart, Mary Lynn**

Women, Work and the French State: Labour Protection and Social Patriarchy, 1879-1919. Reviewed by Karen Offen. *Resources for Feminist Research* 19, No. 1 (March 1990):45-46

**Stiansen, Sarah**

Beyond the Bake Sale. *Savvy* (December-January 1991):13-14

Fat City. *Savvy* (December-January 1991):49-51+

In Land We Trust. Bibliography. *Savvy Woman* (July/August 1990):23-24

Staying Afloat without Jumping Ship. *Savvy Woman* (July/August 1990):28-29

Staying on Top. *Savvy Woman* (November 1990):54-55

**Stiansen, Sarah** (editor)

The Savvy 60: America's Leading Women Business Owners. *Savvy Woman* (November 1990):47-52

**Stieglitz, Maria**

T.V. Men: Wimps or What? *Lilith* 15, No. 3 (Summer 1990):28-29

**Stiehm, Judith Hicks**

Arms and the Enlisted Woman. Reviewed by Jennifer Ring. *Women's Studies International Forum* 13, No. 5 (1990):525-526

Arms and the Enlisted Woman. Reviewed by Mary Ann Tetreault. *Women & Politics* 10, No. 4 (1990):137-138

War's Other Voices: Women Writers on the Lebanese Civil War. Book Review. *Women's Studies International Forum* 13, No. 3 (1990):280-281

**Stiglitz, Eloise**

Caught between Two Worlds: The Impact of a Child on a Lesbian Couple's Relationship. *Women and Therapy* 10, Nos. 1/2 (1990):99-116

**Stillbirth.** *See* Pregnancy, Incomplete

**Stimpson, Catharine**

Where the Meanings Are: Feminism and Cultural Spaces. Reviewed by Evelyn S. Newlyn. *Women's Studies International Forum* 13, No. 6 (1990):613-614

**Stimpson, Catharine R.**

Going to Be Flourishing. *The Women's Review of Books* 7, No. 8 (May 1990):6-7

Really Reading Gertrude Stein: A Selected Anthology. Book Review. *The Women's Review of Books* 7, No. 8 (May 1990):6-7

**Stinberg, Stan**

The Flip Side: It's a Wash! *Family Circle* 103, No. 14 (October 16, 1990):28-29

**Stineman, Esther Lanigan**

Mary Austin: Song of a Maverick. Reviewed by Mary Titus. *Belles Lettres* 6, No. 1 (Fall 1990):40-42

Mary Austin: Songs of a Maverick. Reviewed by Lois Rudnick. *The Women's Review of Books* 7, No. 7 (April 1990):22

**Stinginess.** *See* Misers

**Stinson, Susan**

Band Class Collaboration. Poem. *Sinister Wisdom* 40 (Spring 1990):78

**Stivers, Camilla**

Toward a Feminist Perspective in Public Administration Theory. *Women & Politics* 10, No. 4 (1990):49-65

**Stockings.** *See* Hosiery

**Stock Markets**

Wall Street Women: Women in Power on Wall Street Today. By Anne B. Fisher. Reviewed by Felicia Kornbluh. *The Women's Review of Books* 7, No. 8 (May 1990):9-10

Your Money: No Pain, No Gain: How Wall Street Wizards Learned to Invest Their Money. Karen Heller. *Working Woman* (June 1990):42-44

**Stock Markets – Leveraged Buyouts**

More Money: The ABCs of LBOs. Jerome Reinhart. *Executive Female* (March/April 1990):16-18

**Stockmyer, John** and Williams, Robert

Life Trek: The Odyssey of Adult Development. Reviewed by Violet Franks. *Journal of Women and Aging* 2 No. 3 (1990):117-118

**Stocks**

Smart Investor: Blue Chips After Black Monday. Nancy Dunnan. *Lear's* (February 1990):24-25

When the Dow Turns Down. Nancy Dunnan. *Lear's* (October 1990):34-36

**Stoddard, Alexandra**

Ingredients of a Happy Marriage. *McCall's* 117, No. 9 (June 1990):140

Living Beautifully: Acts of Caring. *McCall's* 117, No. 7 (April 1990):136

Living Beautifully: Give Your House a Holiday Glow. *McCall's* 118, No. 2 (November 1990):168

Living Beautifully: Holiday Grace Notes. *McCall's* 118, No. 3 (December 1990):148

Living Beautifully: Let in the Light, Brighten Your Home. *McCall's* 117, No. 10 (July 1990):136

Living Beautifully: Letters Sweeten Our Lives. *McCall's* 117, No. 8 (May 1990):172

Living Beautifully: Make Time to Do It Now! *McCall's* 118, No. 1 (October 1990):164

Living Beautifully: What Every Woman Needs: A Place to Call Her Own. *McCall's* 117, No. 12 (September 1990):164

Style: Keep It Pure and Simple. *McCall's* 117, No. 11 (August 1990):126

**Stoddard, Eleanor**

How It All Came Out: The Story of Florence Steinberg. *Minerva* 8, No. 3 (Fall 1990):55-72

My War: WWII – As Experienced by One Woman Soldier. Book Review. *Minerva* 8, No. 4 (Winter 1990):48-53

One Woman's War: Letters from the Women's Army Corps, 1944-1946. Book Review. *Minerva* 8, No. 4 (Winter 1990):48-53

**Stoehr, Valerie** (joint author). *See* Dykewomon, Elana

**Stoker, Lyn**

Falling in Love with Condoms. *Healthright* 9, No. 4 (August 1990):35-37

**Stokes, Deborah Lockwood**

Married Again. Poem. *Essence* 20, No. 11 (March 1990):126

**Stokes, Rose Pastor**

Fire and Grace: The Life of Rose Pastor Stokes. By Arthur Zipser and Pearl Zipser. Reviewed by Annelise Orleck. *The Women's Review of Books* 7, No. 9 (June 1990):25-26

**Stoltenberg, John** and McIntosh, Claire

See the Big Picture? Now Show Your Staff. *Working Woman* (April 1990):84-86 +

**Stomach Ailments**

Tummy Trouble: What It's Trying to Tell You. Cynthia Hacinli. *Mademoiselle* (March 1990):138

**Stone, Dee Wallace**

"My Baby Is a Miracle!" *Working Mother* 13, No. 1 (January 1990):32-34

**Stone, Ellen**

The Year of Seeking Purity. Poem. *Bridges* 1, No. 2 (Fall 1990): 22

**Stone, Judith**

Happiness: How to get More of it. *Glamour* (December 1990):198-201

Joint Venture. *Glamour* (October 1990):154

Living with Loose Ends. *Glamour* (May 1990):184

Men and Damage Control. *Glamour* (November 1990):144

Toning Down for the Nineties. *Glamour* (July 1990):95

On Your Own: Can your Relationship Survive This Party Season? *Glamour* (January 1990):68

On Your Own: Don't Wait for the Last Straw. *Glamour* (March 1990):122

On Your Own: Feeling Fifteen Again. *Glamour* (February 1990):107

On Your Own: Fiscal Fitness. *Glamour* (August 1990):130

On Your Own. *Glamour* (June 1990):146

On Your Own: Option Overload. *Glamour* (April 1990):154

On Your Own: Taking Care of Busyiness. *Glamour* (December 1990):131

On Your Own: Young and In Charge. *Glamour* (September 1990):178

**Stone, Laurie**

Starting with Serge. Reviewed by Carey Kaplan. *The Women's Review of Books* 8, No. 1 (October 1990):12-13

**Stone, Merlin**

Goddess as Guidess. *Woman of Power* 15 (Fall-Winter 1990):16-18

**Stone, Susan** (about)

A Woman for Lear's: Lessons. Jane Howard. *Lear's* (March 1990):164-167

**Stoner, K. Lynn**

Latinas of the Americas: A Source Book. Reviewed by Elsa Chaney and Catherine Lundhoff. *Journal of Women's History* 2, No. 1 (Spring 1990):220-226

**Stoper, Emily**

American Women in Poverty. Book Review. *Women & Politics* 10, No. 4 (1990):140-141

**Stoper, Emily** (joint editor). *See* Boneparth, Ellen

**Stoppi, Isa** (about)

Lunch. Interview. Frances Lear. *Lear's* (January 1990):19-22

**Storage in the Home.** *See also* Boxes, Ornamental

Get Reorganized! *Redbook* 174, No. 6 (April 1990):73-82

2 People, 2 Wardrobes, Too Much! *Glamour* (April 1990):298-300

**Storey, Eileen** (about)

A Woman for Lear's: Strong Medicine. Jane Howard. *Lear's* (September 1990):156-159

**Storytelling**

Pandora's Jar Re-Opened: Storytelling and Feminism. Alexandria Lippincott. *Woman of Power* 16 (Spring 1990):36-39, 83

Storytelling and Dynamics of Feminist Teaching. Wendy S. Hesford. *Feminist Teacher* 5, No. 2 (Fall 1990):20-24

**Stryker, Sandy** (joint author). *See* Bingham, Mindy

**Stuart, Meryn** and Ellerington, Glynis

The History of the Disabled Women's Movement in Canada. *Women and Environments* 12, No. 2 (Spring 1990): 19

Unequal Access: Disabled Women's Exclusion from the Mainstream Women's Movement. *Women and Environments* 12, No. 2 (Spring 1990): 16-18

**Stuart, Richard B.** and Jacobson, Barbara

Weight, Sex and Marriage. Reviewed by Patricia A. Connor-Greene. *Women and Health* 16, Nos. 3/4 (1990):211-221

**Stubbs, Margaret L.** (joint author). *See* Koff, Elissa

**Stuckey, Johanna H.**

The Woman and the Lyre: Woman Writers in Classical Greece and Rome. Book Review. *Canadian Women's Studies* 11, No. 2 (Fall 1990):89-90

**Student Financial Aid.** *See also* Scholarships

**Students Organizing Students (SOS)**

Calling All Students: S.O.S. Organizes Prochoice Actions. Hilary Illick. *New Directions for Women* 19, No. 1 (January/February 1990):4

**Study Abroad**

Travel: Get-Smart Getaways. Bibliography. Anita Gates. *Essence* 21, No. 5 (September 1990):100-102

**Stummer, Helen M.**

H.O.M.E.: One Woman's Approach to Society's Problems. *On the Issues* 15 (Summer 1990):10-15 +

Living Without Choices. *On the Issues* 17 (Winter 1990):16-22 +

**Stunkard, Clayton L.** (joint author). *See* Masselam, Venus S.

**Sturgis, Susanna**

Bulkin's *Password* Explores Abuse, Healing. *off our backs* 20, No. 7 (July 1990):12

Enter Password: Recovery. Book Review. *off our backs* 20, No. 7 (July 1990):12

**Sturgis, Susanna** (editor)

Memories and Visions: Women's Fantasy and Science Fiction. Reviewed by Ann E. Kottner. *The Women's Review of Books* 7, Nos. 10-11 (July 1990):40-41

Memories and Visions: Women's Fantasy and Science Fiction. Reviewed by Joanne Stato. *off our backs* 20, No. 5 (May 1990):17 +

Memories and Visions: Women's Fantasy and Science Fiction. Reviewed by Melissa Scott. *Belles Lettres* 5, No. 4 (Summer 1990):45

**Sturgis, Susanna** (interview)

Beyond Elves and Warrior Women: Broadening the Boundaries of Speculative Fiction. Joanne Stato and Jennie Ruby. *off our backs* 20, No. 5 (May 1990):18-19

**Sturgis, Susanna J.**

Mimi's Revenge. Fiction. *Trivia* 16/17 (Fall 1990):99-107

**Sturtevant, Katherine**

Our Sisters' London: Feminist Walking Tours. Reviewed by Anna Davin. *The Women's Review of Books* 8, No. 1 (October 1990):11-12

**Style.** *See* Fashion

**Styron, William**

Time Out of Mind. *Lear's* (August 1990):74-75 +

**Su, S. Susan** (joint author). *See* Needle, Richard H.

**Subak-Sharpe, Genell** (joint author). *See* Cox, Kathryn

**Subjectivity, Female**

Femme Foetal: The Construction/Destruction of Female Subjectivity in *Housekeeping,* or NOTHING GAINED. Siân Mile. *Genders* 8 (Summer 1990):129-136

**Substance Abuse.** *See also* Adolescents – Substance Abuse; Health Education

The Age of Anonymous. Michele Kort. *Essence* 20, No. 11 (March 1990):32

Anatomy of a High. Larry Martz. *Mademoiselle* (May 1990):161, 243

Back from Crack. Jill Nelson. *Essence* 20, No. 9 (January 1990):57-58 +

Between Us. Bibliography. Gwendolyn Goldsby Grant. *Essence* 21, No. 3 (July 1990):26-27

Bill Cosby – Living with Heartbreak. Bill Cosby. *Redbook* 175, No. 2 (June 1990):52-54 +

Clooney! Joan Barthel. *Lear's* (February 1990):102-107 +

Could You Stop Drinking for a Month? Susan Jacoby. *Glamour* (April 1990):288-289 +

Drug War. Elizabeth Kaye. *Vogue* (March 1990):354-362

Early Onset of Adolescent Sexual Behavior and Drug Involvement. Emily Rosenbaum and Denise B. Kandel. *Journal of Marriage and the Family* 52, No. 3 (August 1990):783-798

Kitty Dukakis: The True Story. Kitty Dukakis and Jane Scovell. *Good Housekeeping* 211, No. 3 (September 1990):202-213

Marijuana Makes a Comeback. Joan Malone. *Mademoiselle* (October 1990):184-187

Narc in a Can. *Executive Female* 13, No. 6 (November-December 1990):24

Parenting Styles, Drug Use, and Children's Adjustment in Families of Young Adults. Denise B. Kandel. *Journal of Marriage and the Family* 52, No. 1 (February 1990):183-196

Sounds of Silence. Barbara Ehrenreich. *Savvy Woman* (June 1990):51-53

This Is What You Thought: Drugs. *Glamour* (February 1990):111

Trends in Reporting of Maternal Drug Abuse and Infant Mortality among Drug-Exposed Infants in New York City. Leo Habel, Katherine Kaye, and Jean Lee. *Women and Health* 16, No. 2 (1990):41-58

Women and Drugs: The Untold Story. Catherine Breslin. *Ladies' Home Journal* 107, No. 1 (January 1990):89-91+

**Substance Abuse—Crack**

Crack! Girls Like You on Drugs Like That. Michael Massing. *Mademoiselle* (May 1990):159-161

**Substance Abuse—Prevention**

Innocent Casualties in the War on Drugs. Betsy Swart. *On the Issues* 17 (Winter 1990):27-28+

**Substance Abuse—Public Policy**

The Great American Drug Muddle. Pete Hamill and Mark A. R. Kleiman. *Lear's* (March 1990):156-157+

**Substance Abuse—Treatment**

A Natural Therapies Approach to Minor Tranquilliser Withdrawal. Ginny Codd. *Healthright* 9, No. 2 (February 1990):16-20

Withdrawing from Benzodiazepines. Sheila Knowlden. *Healthright* 9, No. 2 (February 1990):13-15

Women in Active Recovery. Linda Smith and Coreen Popowich. *Healthsharing* 11, No. 1 (December 1989):5

**Suburbs**

L'aménagement des banlieues et le quotidien des femmes actives. Denise Roy. *Canadian Women's Studies* 11, No. 2 (Fall 1990):71-75

**Success**

Achieving Personal Best: 200 Words on 3 Lear's Women. *Lear's* (June 1990):66

Achieving Personal Best: 200 Words on 4 Lear's Women. *Lear's* (May 1990):20

Personal Journal. *Ladies' Home Journal* 107, No. 11 (November 1990):110-114

You Must Remember This . . . Rose Hutchens. *Women and Environments* 12, No. 2 (Spring 1990):20-21

**Success in Business.** *See also* Burton, Betsy (about); Business—Mergers and Acquisitions; Business Failures; Business Leaders; Career Management; Entrepreneurs; Lieff, Ann (about); March, Olivia (about); Market Research;

Performance Appraisal; Picasso, Paloma (about); Promotions; Risk Taking; Robinson, Andrea (about); Social Skills; Wealth Distribution

Breaking and Entering: How Girls Like You Get Dream Jobs. Irene Daria. *Mademoiselle* (September 1990):272-275+

Catch of the Season. Alison Simko. *Savvy Woman* (November 1990):56

Enterprise: How Customer Service Built a Business. Mark Stevens. *Working Woman* (July 1990):31-38

Free Advice. Patti Watts and Shelley Garcia. *Executive Female* 13, No. 1 (January-February 1990):41-44

Power Players. Andrea R. Davis. *Essence* 20, No. 11 (March 1990):71-84

Rehearsing for Success. Robert McGarvey. *Executive Female* 13, No. 1 (January-February 1990):34-37

Staying on Top. Sarah Stiansen. *Savvy Woman* (November 1990):54-55

Talent at Work. *Harper's Bazaar* (March 1990):180-191+

**Sudan—Feminist Movement**

Black Women in Sudan. Shay Salomyn. *off our backs* 20, No. 3 (March 1990):8

**Sudan—Zar Cult**

Mental Health Aspects of Zar for Women in Sudan. Edith H. Grotberg. *Women and Therapy* 10, No. 3 (1990):15-24

**Sudden Infant Death Syndrome**

Parenting. *Essence* 20, No. 11 (March 1990):106

**Suffrage Movement.** *See also* African-American Women—History; James, Ada Lois (about); New Jersey—Suffrage—History; United States Constitution—19th Amendment

Boston Teenagers Debate the Woman Question, 1837-1838. Notes. Margaret McFadden. *Signs* 15, No. 4 (Summer 1990):832-847

Equal or Different: Women's Politics, 1800-1914. Edited by Jane Rendall. Reviewed by Susan Kingsley Kent. *Gender & History* 2, No. 1 (Spring 1990):114-115

Fractured Faith: Liberal Party Women and the Suffrage Issue in Britain, 1892-1914. Claire Hirshfield. *Gender & History* 2, No. 2 (Summer 1990):173-197

Inside Out: Elizabeth Haldane as a Women's Suffrage Survivor in the 1920s and 1930s. Johanna Alberti. *Women's Studies International Forum* 13, Nos. 1-2 (1990):117-125

The Mormon-Suffrage Relationship: Personal and Political Quandaries. Joan Iversen. *Frontiers* 11, Nos. 2-3 (1990):8-16

Posing the Woman Citizen: The Contradictions of Stanton's Feminism. Mary Loeffelholz. *Genders* 7 (Spring 1990):87-98

A Reevaluation of "The Problem of Surplus Women" in 19th-Century England: The Case of the 1851 Census. Judith Worsnop. *Women's Studies International Forum* 13, Nos. 1-2 (1990):21-31

The Spectacle of Women: Imagery of the Suffrage Campaign 1907-1914. By Lisa Tickner. Reviewed by Lynne Walker. *Woman's Art Journal* 11, No. 2 (Fall 1990-Winter 1991):48-50

State Historical Society of Wisconsin Welcomes Suffragist's Papers. Cindy Knight. *Feminist Collections* 12, No. 1 (Fall 1990):18-20

Votes for Women. By Diane Atkinson. Reviewed by Fiona Terry. *Gender & History* 2, No. 3 (Autumn 1990):371-373

Votes for Women. Hannah Trager. *Journal of Women's History* 2, No. 1 (Spring 1990):196-199

Women in Pacific Northwest History. By Karen J. Blair. Reviewed by Karen J. Blair. *New Directions for Women* 19, No. 2 (March/April 1990):14-15

The Women's Suffrage Movement and Irish Society in the Early Twentieth Century. By Cliona Murphy. Reviewed by Margaret MacCurtain. *Gender & History* 2, No. 3 (Autumn 1990):365-368

**Sugarman, Carole**

Eat Well. *Family Circle* 103, No. 4 (March 13, 1990):34+

**Suh, Mary**

Double Jeopardy, Double Courage. *Ms.* 1, No. 2 (September/October 1990):46

Guess Who's Not Coming to Dinner. *Ms.* 1, No. 2 (September/October 1990):87

Lesbian Battery. *Ms.* 1, No. 2 (September/October 1990):48

The Many Sins of "Miss Saigon." Play review. *Ms.* 1, No. 3 (November/December 1990):63

Webster—One Year and Many Battles Later. *Ms.* 1, No. 1 (July/August 1990):87

**Suhl, Yuri**

Ernestine L. Rose, Women's Rights Pioneer, 2nd edition. Reviewed by Rachel Kadish. *Lilith* 15, No. 4 (Fall 1990):34

**Suice—Children**

Children Who Don't Want to Live: Understanding and Treating the Suicidal Child. By Israel Orbach. Book Review. *Adolescence* 25, No. 97 (Spring 1990):251

**Suicide.** *See also* Adolescents—Suicide

Divorce, Suicide, and the Mass Media: An Analysis of Differential Identification, 1948-1980. Steven Stack. *Journal of Marriage and the Family* 52, No. 2 (May 1990):553-560

The Encyclopedia of Suicide. By Glen Evans and Norman L. Farberow. Book Review. *Adolescence* 25, No. 98 (Summer 1990):500

New Micro-level Data on the Impact of Divorce on Suicide, 1959-1980: A Test of Two Theories. Steven Stack. *Journal of Marriage and the Family* 52, No. 1 (February 1990):119-127

**Suits**

Suitable Suits. *Savvy Woman* (September 1990):70-75

**Suleiman, Susan Rubin**

Reply to Bauman. *Signs* 15, No. 3 (Spring 1990):656-659

Subversive Intent: Gender Politics and the Avant-Garde. Reviewed by Lillian S. Robinson. *The Women's Review of Books* 7, Nos. 10-11 (July 1990):32-33

**Suleiman, Susan Rubin** (about)

Comment on Suleiman's "On Maternal Splitting." Raquel Portillo Bauman. *Signs* 15, No. 3 (Spring 1990):653-655

**Suleri, Sara**

Meatless Days. Reviewed by Inderpal Grewal. *NWSA Journal* 2, No. 3 (Summer 1990):508-510

**Sullivan, Colleen**

Does Your Image Need Fine-Tuning? *Working Woman* (November 1990):142-144

**Sullivan, Kathleen** (about). *See also* Television Journalists—Networking

**Sullivan, Sheila J.**

"Why Do Women Do Such Womenly Things?" The Genre and Socio-historical Analogs of Home Parties. *Women's Studies in Communication* 13, No. 1 (Spring 1990): 66-91

**Sulter, Maud**

Erotica: An Anthology of Women's Writing. Book Review. *Spare Rib* 219 (December 1990-January 1991):42-44

More Serious Pleasure. Book Review. *Spare Rib* 219 (December 1990-January 1991):42-44

Zabat: Poetics of a Family Tree. Poems 1986-1989. Reviewed by Anne Iwobi. *Spare Rib* No. 209 (February 1990):31

**Sumii, Sue**

The River with No Bridge. Reviewed by Takayo Mukai. *Belles Lettres* 6, No. 1 (Fall 1990):29

**Summer Resorts.** *See also* Fashion

Blame it on the Heat Wave. Sara Nelson. *Glamour* (July 1990):152-153+

**Summers, Anne**

Abortion: Election Turnaround? *Ms.* 1, No. 2 (September/October 1990):93-94

Angels and Citizens: British Women as Military Nurses, 1854-1914. Reviewed by Peri Rosenfeld. *Gender and Society* 4, No. 2 (June 1990):274-276

Ferraro: The Country Is Ready. *McCall's* 117, No. 9 (June 1990):62-63

**Summers, Rosie**

Trashing Women. *off our backs* 20, No. 7 (July 1990):22

**Sunburn.** *See also* Skin – Care and Hygiene; Skin Cancer; Solar Radiation – Physiological Effect

Beauty & Health Report. Stephanie Young. *Glamour* (July 1990):28

**Sunday Schools**

Sunday School: The Formation of an American Institution, 1790-1880. By Anne M. Boylan. Reviewed by Lee Chambers-Schiller. Book Review. *Gender & History* 2, No. 2 (Summer 1990):235-236

**Sundin, Julia**

New Active Birth: A Concise Guide to Natural Childbirth. Book Review. *Healthright* 9, No. 3 (May 1990):40

**Sundquist, Kendra**

Caring for Children with HIV and AIDS. *Healthright* 9, No. 2 (February 1990):35

Healthworkers and AIDS. *Healthright* 9, No. 2 (February 1990):10-12

Loss of the Uterus. *Healthright* 9, No. 4 (August 1990):29-33

**Sung, Betty Lee** (about). *See also* Watts, Patti (editor), "Free Advice."

**Sunglasses**

Beauty and Fashion Hotline: Eye Openers. *Family Circle* 103, No. 9 (June 26, 1990):45

**Sun Protection.** *See* Solar Radiation – Physiological Effect

**Sunscreens.** *See* Suntan Products

**Suntan Products.** *See also* Skin – Care and Hygiene; Sunburn

Beauty: And the Glo Goes On. *Mademoiselle* (September 1990):72

Beauty Word of Mouth. *Glamour* (July 1990):19-22

Cover-Ups. Laurie Tarkan. *Lear's* (June 1990):126-131

Screening the New Sunscreens. Lorraine Calvacca. *Working Woman* (May 1990):120-123

Sports Makeup Goes the Distance. *Lear's* (June 1990):30

5 Sunless Ways to a Golden Tan. *Glamour* (May 1990):284-285

**Superwoman Syndrome.** *See* Balancing Work and Family Life; Workaholics

**Supplementary Employment.** *See* Moonlighting

**Support Groups**

Facilitating Productive Bereavement of Widows: An Overview of the Efficacy of Widow's Support Groups. Cheryl H. Kinderknecht and Laree Hodges. *Journal of Women and Aging* 2, No. 4 (1990):39-54

**Support Systems.** *See also* Activists; African-American Families; Community; Letter Writers; National Black Women's Health Project

Back Talk: Corporate Sisters. C. R. Saltpaw. *Essence* 21, No. 3 (July 1990):114

Best Friends. Barbara Bartocci. *Good Housekeeping* 211, No. 4 (October 1990):144-145 +

Health News. Bibliography. *Essence* 21, No. 2 (June 1990):25

Jake: A Man's Opinion. *Glamour* (June 1990):136

The Philadelphia Experiment. Carol Saline. *Lear's* (March 1990):94-101

Sisters Helping Sisters. Marilyn Milloy. *Essence* 21, No. 6 (October 1990):83-84 +

In the Spirit: Breaking the Silence. Susan L. Taylor. *Essence* 21, No. 3 (July 1990):49

Testing Positive. Darien Taylor. *Healthsharing* 11, No. 2 (March 1990):9-13

Why Women Get Addicted to Food. Bibliography. Marie Dawson. *Ladies' Home Journal* 107, No. 9 (September 1990):132-136

**Surarith, Somporn**

Women's Struggle for Housing Rights in Thailand. *Canadian Women's Studies* 11, No. 2 (Fall 1990):15-16

**Surgical Procedures.** *See also* Hysterectomy; Transplants

Anesthesia: The Essence of It All. Claudia M. Caruana. *Lear's* (May 1990):53-54

Eyes Can See Clearly Now: Surgery for the Nearsighted. Cynthia Hacinli. *Mademoiselle* (June 1990):124

Surgery: Weighing the Options. Leigh Silverman. *Lear's* (June 1990):48-50

**Surra, Catherine A.**

Research and Theory on Mate Selection and Premarital Relationships in the 1980s. *Journal of Marriage and the Family* 52, No. 4 (November 1990):844-865

**Surrey, Janet L.**

Mother-Blaming and Clinical Theory. *Women and Therapy* 10, Nos. 1/2 (1990):83-87

**Surrogate Mothers.** *See also* Whitehead, Mary Beth

Between Strangers: Surrogate Mothers, Expectant Fathers, and Brave New Babies. By Lori Andrews. Reviewed by Mary Gibson. *Women and Health* 16, No. 2 (1990):134-137

Birth Power: The Case for Surrogacy. By Carmel Shalev. Reviewed by Leigh Anne Chavez. *NWSA Journal* 2, No. 4 (Autumn 1990):652-656

Embryo Research & Rambo Technology. *Spare Rib* No. 211 (April 1990):14-17

Evolving Issues in Surrogate Motherhood. Judith A. Erlen and Ian R. Holzman. *Health Care for Women International* 11, No. 3 (1990):319-329

Infertility Counselling: Should Surrogacy Be an Option? Sue Craig. *Healthright* 9, No. 2 (February 1990):25-29

Young Mother's Story: "How Could I Let Them Separate My Twins?" Patty Nowakowski. *Redbook* 175, No. 3 (July 1990):38-41

**Survival Strategies.** *See* Employees – Training

**Sussex, Lucy**

The Fortunes of Mary Fortune. Reviewed by Judith MacBean. *Australian Feminist Studies* No. 12 (Summer 1990):123-125

**Süssman, Rita** (joint editor). *See* Lissner, Anneliese

**Sustendal, Diane**

Eclectic Expertise. *Harper's Bazaar* (April 1990):202-203

Fe3te Accompli. *Harper's Bazaar* (August 1990):176

Italian Spice. *Harper's Bazaar* (July 1990):116

Riviera Retreat. *Harper's Bazaar* (May 1990):60-68

Scented Treasures. *Harper's Bazaar* (October 1990):101-120

That's Entertainment! *Harper's Bazaar* (January 1990):133+

Uncommon Scents. *Harper's Bazaar* (September 1990):315+

**Sutherland, Kiefer** (about). *See* Actors

**Suttee**

Multiple Mediations: Feminist Scholarship in the Age of Multinational Reception. Lata Mani. *Women & Language* 13, No. 1 (Fall 1990):56-58

**Suwannond, Anchana** (joint author). *See* Sexton, Sarah

**Svirsky, Gila**

How I Get Started in a Life of Crime. Short Story. *Sinister Wisdom* 40 (Spring 1990):48-60

**Swan, Phyllis** (about)

Carrying On: Isaia N.Y.C. Elsie B. Washington. *Essence* 21, No. 5 (September 1990):66-67

**Swan, William S.**

The Art of the Interview. *Working Woman* (May 1990):96-97

**Swanson, Janice M.** (joint author). *See* Ledbetter, Carol

**Swanson, Suzanne**

Believe Me. Poem. *Iris* 23 (Spring-Summer 1990):inside back cover

In the Dark. Poem. *Iris* 24 (Fall-Winter 1990):IBC

**SWAPO.** *See* Namibia – Politics and Government

**Swart, Betsy**

Innocent Casualties in the War on Drugs. *On the Issues* 17 (Winter 1990):27-28+

**Swartz, Mimi**

A Day in the Life of a Victoria's Secret. *Mademoiselle* (April 1990):238-239, 264

**Swartzlander, Susan**

Dublin Belles. Book Review. *Belles Lettres* 5, No. 3 (Spring 1990):5

Give Them Stones. Book Review. *Belles Lettres* 5, No. 3 (Spring 1990):5

Lurking Beyond the Parlour. *Belles Lettres* 5, No. 3 (Spring 1990):5

**Swayze, Patrick** (about)

What's Hot: Summer Stars. Kathryn Casey and Bonnie Siegler. *Ladies' Home Journal* 107, No. 8 (August 1990):52-60

**Sweaters**

Fall's New Sweaters. *McCall's* 118, No. 1 (October 1990):05-07

Finally Free. *Glamour* (September 1990):324-331

Knit Picks. *Harper's Bazaar* (August 1990):102-109

Sweater Perfect. *Glamour* (April 1990):290-295

Whisper Soft. *Redbook* 175, No. 6 (October 1990):106-111

**Sweden – Gender Roles**

Working Parents: Transformation in Gender Roles and Public Policies in Sweden. By Phyllis Moen. Reviewed by Marika Lindholm. *Journal of Marriage and the Family* 52, No. 2 (May 1990):564-565

**Sweden – History – Feminist Perspectives**

The Lund Project on Women's Autobiographies and Diaries in Sweden. Christina Sjöblad. *Gender & History* 2, No. 1 (Spring 1990):87-88

**Sweden – Housing**

Helping Each Other: A Swedish Perspective. Birgit Krantz. *Canadian Women's Studies* 11, No. 2 (Fall 1990):77-79

**Sweden – Media and Communications**

Swedish Scholar Suggests New Approach to Studying Women in TV News. *Media Report to Women* 18, No. 2 (March/April 1990):8

**Sweden – Status of Women**

Fighting for Feminist Interpretations of the Law. Eva Tiby. *Connexions* 34 (1990):10-11

Swedish Politics: Women's Subordination in a Gender-Neutral Context. Amy Elman. *off our backs* 20, No. 3 (March 1990):4+

**Sweeny, John J.** and Nussbaum, Karen

Solutions for the New Work Force: Policies for a New Social Contract. Reviewed by Steven Deutsch. *Women and Health* 16, Nos. 3/4 (1990):201-205

**Sweet, Holland**

Cut Rates. Bibliography. *Harper's Bazaar* (November 1990):34-40+

**Sweet, James** (joint author). *See* Bumpass, Larry

**Sweet, Rachel** (about)

Clown about Town. Patricia Bibby. *Harper's Bazaar* (February 1990):72

**Sweet Honey in the Rock**

All For Freedom. Reviewed by Joanne Stato. *off our backs* 20, No. 5 (May 1990):20-21

**Sweney, Kathryn** (joint editor). *See* Benson, Bjorn

**Swicegood, Gary** (joint author). *See* Rindfuss, Ronald R.

**Swid, Nan** (about)

View. Stephanie Mansfield. *Vogue* (June 1990):70-72, 82

**Swift, Carolyn** and Steen, Judith (editors)

Georgiana, Feminist Reformer of the West: The Journal of Georgiana Bruce Kirby. Reviewed by Lynn Wenzel. *New Directions for Women* 19, No. 2 (March/April 1990):15

**Swimming**

Checkpoints for the Crawl. Kim Carlisle. *Women's Sports and Fitness* 12, No. 3 (April 1990):22-23

Turning Back the Clock. Kim Carlisle. *Women's Sports and Fitness* 12, No. 4 (May-June 1990):22

Underwater Eye Openers. Chip Zempel. *Women's Sports and Fitness* 12, No. 7 (October 1990):22

**Swimming – Safety.** *See* Aquatic Sports – Safety Measures

**Swimwear.** *See* Clothing and Dress – Swimwear

**Swindells, Julia**

Hanging up on Mum or Questions of Everyday Life in the Writing of History. *Gender & History* 2, No. 1 (Spring 1990):68-78

**Swindlers and Swindling**

Don't Get Ripped Off – Get Smart. Debra Wishik Englander. *Redbook* 175, No. 1 (May 1990):60-64

Glamour Guide. Bibliography. *Glamour* (October 1990):89-98; (November 1990):87-90

Glamour Guide. *Glamour* (May 1990):99-105

Great Impostors. *Harper's Bazaar* (November 1990):55-58

**Swir, Anna**

Her Belly. Poem. *Spare Rib* No. 212 (May 1990):57

**Switzer, Ellen**

Can This Marriage Be Saved? "I Just Don't Respect Him Anymore." *Ladies' Home Journal* 107, No. 10 (October 1990):14-20

**Switzer, M'Liss** and Hale, Katherine

Called to Account. Reviewed by Sandra Butler. *AFFILIA* 5, No. 1 (Spring 1990):110-112

**Switzerland – Reproductive Technology**

Sperm Smorgasbord. *Connexions* 32 (1990):21

**Switzerland – Status of Women**

La conservatisme politique féminin en Suisse: Mythe ou réalité. By Thanh-Huyen Ballmer-Cao. Reviewed by Sylvie Arend. *Canadian Women's Studies* 11, No. 2 (Fall 1990):93

**Swyripa, Frances**

Feminists Despite Themselves: Women in Ukranian Community Life, 1884-1939. Book Review. *Resources for Feminist Research* 19, No. 1 (March 1990):13

**Sybylla, Roe**

Old Plans, New Specifications: A Political Reading of the Medical Discourse on Menopause. *Australian Feminist Studies* No. 12 (Summer 1990):95-107

The Psychology of the Female Body. Book Review. *Australian Feminist Studies* No. 11 (Autumn 1990):129-131

Second Opinion: The Politics of Women's Health in New Zealand. Book Review. *Australian Feminist Studies* No. 11 (Autumn 1990):129-131

Wet Nursing: A History from Antiquity to the Present. Book Review. *Australian Feminist Studies* No. 11 (Autumn 1990):129-131

The Woman in the Body: A Cultural Analysis of Reproduction. Book Review. *Australian Feminist Studies* No. 11 (Autumn 1990):129-131

**Sylbert, Anthea** (about)

Reel Stylishness. Leslie Bennetts. *Lear's* (July 1990):64-67+

**Sylvester, Edward J.**

The Boy Who Beat the Odds. *Ladies' Home Journal* 107, No. 1 (January 1990):94-95+

**Symbols**

Lady of the Beasts. Buffie Johnson. *Woman of Power* 16 (Spring 1990):68-71

Rhythm and the Frame Drum: Attributes of the Goddess. Layne Redmond. *Woman of Power* 15 (Fall-Winter 1990):20-23

"Thinking in Things": A Women's Symbol Language. Jennifer Weston. *Trivia* 16/17 (Fall 1990):84-98

**Symonds Family – Genealogy**

The Symonds and Stephen Families. *Tulsa Studies in Women's Literature* 9, No. 2 (Fall 1990):228

**Syphilis.** *See* Sexually Transmitted Diseases

**Szabo, Julia**

Stepping Up. *Harper's Bazaar* (February 1990):72

**Szekely, Eva**

Never too Thin. Reviewed by Patricia A. Connor-Greene. *Women and Health* 16, Nos. 3/4 (1990):211-221

**Szirom, Tricia**

Teaching Gender: Sex Education and Sexual Stereotypes. Reviewed by Ann Marie Wolpe. *Gender and Education* 2, No. 2 (1990):254-255

Teaching Gender: Sex Education and Sexual Stereotypes. Reviewed by Helen Lenskyj. *Resources for Feminist Research* 19, No. 1 (March 1990):34

# T

**Tabak, Ayelet**

Kitchen Poem. *Bridges* 1, No. 2 (Fall 1990): 50

**Taber, Sara Mansfield**

A History of Schooling and Family Life on Southern Argentine Sheep Ranches. *Journal of Family History* 15, No. 3 (July 1990):335-356

**Tager, Marcia**

Bodies at Sea. Book Review. *New Directions for Women* 19, No. 1 (January/February 1990):22

Cartographies. Book Review. *New Directions for Women* 19, No. 1 (January/February 1990):22

Daneshvar's Playhouse. Book Review. *New Directions for Women* 19, No. 1 (January/February 1990):22

Verging on the Pertinent. Book Review. *New Directions for Women* 19, No. 1 (January/February 1990):22

**Taggart, Sophie** (joint author). *See* McCloy, Marjorie

**Tagore, Rabindranath**

Rabindranath Tagore on Nationalism. *Manushi* 58 (May-June 1990):13

**Tait, Lilian**

Fountains Weren't Meant to Be Predictable. Poem. *Hecate* 16, Nos. 1-2 (1990):119

There Is Always One Who Is Different. Poem. *Hecate* 16, Nos. 1-2 (1990):119

**Tait, Vanessa**

Israel: Peace Movement. *Spare Rib* No. 209 (February 1990):44

**Taiwan – Status of Women**

Women and Family in Rural Taiwan. By Margery Wolf. Reviewed by Kalpana Bardhan. *Journal of Women's History* 2, No. 1 (Spring 1990):200-219

**Taking Liberties Collective**

Learning the Hard Way: Women's Oppression in Men's Education. Reviewed by Mary Hughes. *Gender and Education* 2, No. 3 (1990):370-371

**Tal, Kali**

Fighting Racism in Brazil. *New Directions for Women* 19, No. 6 (November-December 1990):12

**Talarico, Susette M.** *See* Cook, Beverly B.

**Talbot, Sylvia Ross** (about). *See* De Veaux, Alexis, Milloy, Marilyn, and Ross, Michael Erik

**Talk Shows.** *See also* Winfrey, Oprah

National Radio Talk Show Launched on Women and Business. *Media Report to Women* 18, No. 1 (January/February 1990):5

**Tallen, Bette S.**

Twelve Step Programs: A Lesbian Feminist Critique. *NWSA Journal* 2, No. 3 (Summer 1990):390-407

**Talley, André Leon**

Fall 1990: Design Inspiration. *Vogue* (July 1990):138-161

The Kings of Color: Mizrahi. *Vogue* (September 1990):532-535

Vogue Arts: Design. *Vogue* (December 1990):200-202

**Tallmer, Abby** (joint author). *See* Ellis, Kate

**Tallmountain, Mary**

Green March Moons. Reviewed by Mitzi Myers. *NWSA Journal* 2, No. 2 (Spring 1990):273-281

**Tally, Justine and others**

A Meeting of Minds and Cultures: Teaching Black Women's Literature in the Canary Islands. *Sage* 6, No. 1 (Summer 1989):63-65

**Tamang, A. K.** (joint author). *See* Khan, M. E.

**Tamils – Marriage Age**

Socio-Economic Characteristics Influencing Age at Marriage in a Tamil Nadu Village. N. Audiarayana and M. Senthilnayaki. *Journal of Family Welfare* 36, No. 1 (March 1990):48-55

**Tampons**

Red Alert: A Safe Tampon Guide. Leslie Granston. *Mademoiselle* (October 1990):122

Truth in Tampons. *Ms.* 1, No. 1 (July/August 1990):55

**Tan, Amy**

The Joy Luck Club. Reviewed by Yem Siu Fong. *Frontiers* 11, Nos. 2-3 (1990):122-123

**Tan, Dali**

Sexism in the Chinese Language. *NWSA Journal* 2, No. 4 (Autumn 1990):635-639

**Tancred, Peta**

Few Choices: Women, Work and Family. Book Review. *Resources for Feminist Research* 19, No. 1 (March 1990):15

**Tandberg, Gerilyn G.**

Sinning for Silk: Dress-for-Success Fashions of the New Orleans Storyville Prostitute. *Women's Studies International Forum* 13, No. 3 (1990):229-248

**Tandem Bicycling.** See Bicycling

**Tandy, Jessica** (about). See also Johnson, Lois Joy, "Great Faces"

Tandy. Leslie Bennetts. *Lear's* (April 1990):80-83 +

Two for the Road. Mark Matousek. *Harper's Bazaar* (January 1990):58

**Tangier (Morocco) – Description and Travel**

Tangier Dream. Bruce Weber. *Vogue* (January 1990):160-185

**Tannen, Deborah**

You Just Don't Understand: Women and Men in Conversation. Reviewed by Anita Taylor. *Women & Language* 13, No. 2 (Winter 1990):44

**Tannenbaum, Elliot**

Badminton Is No Picnic. *Women's Sports and Fitness* 12, No. 7 (October 1990):57-58

**Tanouye, Elyse T.**

Management: What Is Your Staff Afraid to Tell You? *Working Woman* (April 1990):35-38

**Tanski, Alexandra**

No Fumes, No Chemicals, No Pests. *McCall's* 118, No. 2 (November 1990):21

Vital Signs: Windows to Well-Being. *McCall's* 117, No. 12 (September 1990):76

**Tanz, Christine** (joint editor). See Philips, Susan

**Tàpies, Antoni** (about). See Spain – Culture and Society

**Tap Water.** See Drinking Water

**Tarducci, Monica** (about)

Interview with an Organizer: "We Must Coordinate for the Next Meeting." Interview. Carmen Gloria Dunnage. *Women in Action* 3 & 4 (1990):9-10

**Tardy, Evelyne** (joint author). See Gingras, Anne-Marie

**Tarkan, Laurie**

For Autumn Eyes '90. *Lear's* (August 1990):102-107

Autumn Forecast I: In the Buff. *Lear's* (August 1990):49

Autumn Forecast II: Le Rouge et le Noir. *Lear's* (August 1990):50

The Busy Life: Weekends with No Regrets. *Working Woman* (November 1990):150-154

At Center Stage. *Lear's* (April 1990):84-91

Cover-Ups. *Lear's* (June 1990):126-131

Makeover Your Home . . . for More Warmth & Style. *Redbook* 176, No. 1 (November 1990):96-101

Perfect Isle of Calm. *Lear's* (May 1990):82-89

The Return of Glamour. *Lear's* (September 1990):66

Skin: Research, Revelations, and Refinements. *Lear's* (January 1990):91-95

Style. *Lear's* (March 1990):102-109

**Tarnovskii, Ippolit Mikhailovich** (about)

Lesbian Vignettes: A Russian Triptych from the 1890s. Notes. Laura Engelstein. *Signs* 15, No. 4 (Summer 1990):813-831

**Tarr, Carrie**

Tatie Danielle. Film Review. *Spare Rib* 219 (December 1990-January 1991):28-29

**Tarrago, Isabel** (interview)

Questions of Collaboration: Interview with Jackie Huggins and Isabel Tarrago. Carole Ferrier. *Hecate* 16, Nos. 1-2 (1990):140-147

**Tasende-Grabowski, Mercedes**

A Rosario Castellanos Reader: An Anthology of Her Poetry, Short Fiction, Essays, and Drama. Book Review. *Frontiers* 11, No. 1 (1990):88-89

**Tasker, Lynn**

A New Dance Step. *Healthsharing* 11, No. 2 (March 1990):14-16

**Tate, Claudia**

Afro-American Women Writers, 1746-1933: An Anthology and Critical Guide. Book Review. *Tulsa Studies in Women's Literature* 9, No. 2 (Fall 1990):317-321

Critical Essays on Toni Morrison. Book Review. *Tulsa Studies in Women's Literature* 9, No. 2 (Fall 1990):317-321

Inspiriting Influences: Tradition, Revision, and Afro-American Women's Novels. Book Review. *Tulsa Studies in Women's Literature* 9, No. 2 (Fall 1990):317-321

**Taub, Nadine** (joint editor). See Cohen, Sherrill

**Tavormina, Patricia**

International Summit for Women: Many Dimensions of Lesbians and Power. *off our backs* 20, No. 8 (August/September 1990):24

**Tavormina, Patrizia**

Living as a Sicilian Dyke. *Sinister Wisdom* 41 (Summer-Fall 1990):75-78

## Teaching Methods

Aesthetic Questions. Ruth Bass and Marsha Cummins. *Heresies* 25 (1990):53-54

African America: Images, Ideas, and Realities. Eva Grudin. *Heresies* 25 (1990):54-56

The Immediate Classroom: Feminist Pedagogy and Peter Brook's *The Empty Space*. Catherine B. Burroughs. *Feminist Teacher* 5, No. 2 (Fall 1990):10-14

Teaching and Learning from the Heart. Estelle Disch and Becky Thompson. *NWSA Journal* 2, No. 1 (Winter 1990):68-78

Teaching the New Majority: Guidelines for Cross-Cultural Communication Between Students and Faculty. Mercilee M. Jenkins. *Feminist Teacher* 5, No. 1 (Spring 1990):8-14

Tell Them a Story. Maude M. Jennings, Mary Patterson Thornburg, and Gari L. Williams. *Feminist Teacher* 5, No. 2 (Fall 1990):15

Women, Art, and Cross-Cultural Issues. Lucy R. Lippard. *Heresies* 25 (1990):53

## Teachman, Jay D.

Socioeconomic Resources of Parents and Award of Child Support in the United States: Some Exploratory Models. *Journal of Marriage and the Family* 52, No. 3 (August 1990):689-699

## Teachman, Jay D., and Morgan, S. Philip

A Brief Response to DeMaris. *Journal of Marriage and the Family* 52, No. 1 (February 1990):277

## Teachman, Jay D. and Polonko, Karen

Negotiation Divorce Outcomes: Can We Identify Patterns in Divorce Settlements? *Journal of Marriage and the Family* 52, No. 1 (February 1990):129-139

**Teamer, John** (about). *See* National Association of Black and White Men Together

**Team Sports.** *See* Sports

**Tec, Nechama** (about). *See* Holocaust (1939-1945) – Survivors

**Technical Education.** *See also* Job Skills

A Game Plan for the Future. Pamela Kruger. *Working Woman* (January 1990):74-78

Office Tech: More Power to Them. *Working Woman* (October 1990):63-68

Tech Talk. *Working Woman* (June 1990):38-40

**Technology.** *See also* Communication; Computer Technology; Information Services

Pleasure, Power and Technology. By Sally Hacker. Reviewed by Annette Burfoot. *Resources for Feminist Research* 19, No. 1 (March 1990):29

Reconstructing Babylon: Essays on Women and Technology. H. Patricia Hynes. Reviewed by Jalna Hanmer. *Women's Studies International Forum* 13, No. 6 (1990):608-609

Reconstructing Babylon: Women and Technology. By H. Patricia Hynes. Reviewed by Pat Spallone. *Spare Rib* No. 210 (March 1990):35

The Smart Office: Can You Tech It? Roxanne Farmanfarmaian. *Working Woman* (April 1990):58-68

Teaching Technology from a Feminist Perspective: A Practical Guide. By Joan Rothschild. Reviewed by Joseph Regna. *Signs* 16, No. 1 (Autumn 1990):175-177

## Technology – Health Aspects

The Introduction of New Technology: Health Implications for Workers. Anne Statham and Ellen Bravo. *Women and Health* 16, No. 2 (1990):105-129

## Technology – Impact on Women

McCallmanack. *McCall's* 117, No. 10 (July 1990):43-52

Pleasure, Power and Technology: Some Tales of Gender, Engineering and the Cooperative Workplace. By Sally Hacker. Reviewed by Colleen Chesterman. *Australian Feminist Studies* No. 11 (Autumn 1990):123-126

Women, Work, and Technology: Transformations. Edited by Barbara Drygulski Wright. Reviewed by Dula J. Espinosa. *NWSA Journal* 2, No. 3 (Summer 1990):499-501

## Tecumseh (MI) – Women's Health

Health and other Characteristics of Employed Women and Homemakers in Tecumseh, 1959-1978: Demographic Characteristics, Smoking Habits, Alcohol Consumption, and Pregnancy Outcomes and Conditions. Kristie L. Ebi-Kryston and others. *Women and Health* 16, No. 2 (1990):5-21

Health and other Characteristics of Employed Women and Homemakers in Tecumseh, 1959-1978: Prevalence of Respiratory and Cardiovascular Symptoms and Illnesses, Mortality Rates and Physical and Physiological Measurements. Kristie L. Ebi-Kryston and others. *Women and Health* 16, No. 2 (1990):23-39

**Teenage Mutant Ninja Turtles.** *See* Comic Books, Strips, etc.

**Teer, Barbara Ann** (about). *See* De Veaux, Alexis, Milloy, Marilyn, and Ross, Michael Erik

## Teeth – Care and Hygiene

Ask the Dentist: Smart Helps to a Healthy Smile. Susan Alai. *Family Circle* 103, No. 16 (November 27, 1990):144

Beauty: Answers. *Essence* 21, No. 5 (September 1990):17

Beauty & Health Report. Stephanie Young. *Glamour* (August 1990):48

Dental Questions You Were Afraid to Ask. Tara Flanagan and Ann Ferrar. *Ladies' Home Journal* 107, No. 9 (September 1990):140-143

Health Dept. *Lear's* (November 1990):82

Health & Fitness. Stephanie Young. *Glamour* (September 1990):65-72

Is Your Dentist Up-to-Date? Linda J. Heller. *Redbook* 174, No. 5 (March 1990):20-26

Medical News. Dana Points and Carla Rohlfing. *Family Circle* 103, No. 15 (November 6, 1990):167

Medinews. Ann Ferrar. *Ladies' Home Journal* 107, No. 2 (February 1990):82

Vital Signs. *McCall's* 117, No. 8 (May 1990):38-40; 118, No. 1 (October 1990):46-48

**Tegmeyer, Diane**

Rocky Mountain High. *Harper's Bazaar* (February 1990):185+

**Telecommunications.** *See also* Teleconferencing

**Teleconferencing**

Office Technology: Five Successful Alternatives to In-Person Meetings. Christine Begole. *Working Woman* (October 1990):70-76

**Telephone**

The Long-Distance Lowdown. Jeffrey Cohen. *Savvy Woman* (February 1990):32-36

**Telephone—Emergency Reporting Systems**

Dial 911: Computers Shrink Emergency Response Times. Celia Slom. *McCall's* 117, No. 8 (May 1990):58

**Telephone Pornography.** *See* Sex Industry

**Telephone Privacy.** *See* Privacy Rights

**Television**

Gender Politics and MTV: Voicing the Difference. By Lisa A. Lewis. Reviewed by Jane Caputi. *The Women's Review of Books* 8, No. 3 (December 1990):27

Quality Television and Feminine Narcissism: The Shrew and the Covergirl. Hilary Radner. *Genders* 8 (Summer 1990):110-128

Sex, Lies, and Videohabits. John Leo. *McCall's* 117, No. 9 (June 1990):36

**Television—Cable Programming**

Patrick's Rainbow. Lynn Braz. *Executive Female* 13, No. 6 (November-December 1990):50+

**Television—Homosexual Programs**

Lesbians Hit Prime Time. *Spare Rib* 213 (June 1990):39-42

**Television Actors.** *See also* Curtin, Jane; Delany, Dana; Ford, Faith; Harris, Neil Patrick; Hubert, Janet; Light, Judith (about); Parker, Corey; Reed, Shanna

What's Hot on TV: At Ease with Gerald McRaney. Jim Calio. *Ladies' Home Journal* 107, No. 5 (May 1990):56-58

**Television Actors—Interviews.** *See also* Bertinelli, Valerie; Burke, Delta (about); Fabares, Shelley (about); Fawcett, Farrah (about); Lipton, Peggy; Principal, Victoria (about); Ruttan, Susan (about)

**Television Anchors.** *See* Television Journalists

**Television Broadcasting—Religious Aspects.** *See* Television in Religion

**Television Evangelists.** *See* Television in Religion

**Television for Children**

On Screen: The New Videos. Eric Burns. *Family Circle* 103, No. 16 (November 27, 1990):121

**Television for the Blind.** *See* Descriptive Video Services

**Television in Religion**

Tammy at Twilight. Cliff Jahr. *Ladies' Home Journal* 107, No. 7 (July 1990):88-96

**Television Journalists.** *See* Journalists

Bernard Shaw: Anchoring the World. Michelle Morris. *Essence* 21, No. 7 (November 1990):42

Deborah Norville: Southern Belle or Steel Magnolia? Charla Krupp. *Glamour* (November 1990):168-170

TV: Broadcast Schmooze. James Kaplan. *Mademoiselle* (June 1990):108

Waiting for Prime Time: The Women of Television News. By Marlene Sanders and Marcia Rock. Reviewed by Marguerite J. Moritz. *Frontiers* 11, Nos. 2-3 (1990):124

**Television Journalists—Networking**

Broadcast Networking. Jennet Conant. *Working Woman* (August 1990):58-61

**Television News.** *See* Television Journalists

**Television Producers and Directors.** *See also* Los Angeles—Television Producers and Directors

Darlene Hayes: Producer Plus. Bebe Moore Campbell. *Essence* 21, No. 5 (September 1990):50

Women Could Dominate News Director Positions Early in 21st Century. *Media Report to Women* 18, No. 2 (March/April 1990):2-3

**Television Programs.** *See also* Black Entertainment Television; Brown, Blair (about); Cosby, Bill; Family Life—Humor; Goldberg, Whoopi (about); Stapleton, Jean (about); Talk Shows

Ain't No Black in the Union Jack. *Spare Rib* No. 216 (September 1990):29-30

All That Junk. James Kaplan. *Mademoiselle* (November 1990):106

Baby M/Q.E.D. Pam Mason. *Spare Rib* No. 216 (September 1990):30

On the Bias: Seduction. Lynne Tempest. *AFFILIA* 5, No. 4 (Winter 1990):105-107

Can He Bake a Cherry Pie? Meredith Brody and Christine Logan Wright. *Mademoiselle* (September 1990):248-249+

A Capital Proposal. Sidney Blumenthal. *Lear's* (August 1990):86-89

Carol Burnett Comes Home. Eric Sherman. *Ladies' Home Journal* 107, No. 9 (September 1990):92-94

Dishing with the Designing Women. Jeff Rovin. *Ladies' Home Journal* 107, No. 10 (October 1990):60-71

Gabbing with the Golden Girls. Eric Sherman. *Ladies' Home Journal* 107, No. 2 (February 1990):44-48

Getting Lynched. *Harper's Bazaar* (October 1990):130

Innocent Until Proven Otherwise. Jennifer Houlton. *Mademoiselle* (June 1990):88

It Ain't Over Till It's Over. James Kaplan. *Mademoiselle* (September 1990):179

Jill. Stephen Farber. *Lear's* (September 1990):86-89

Kristy McNichol Finds a Full Life on Empty Nest. Mark Morrison. *Ladies' Home Journal* 107, No. 3 (March 1990):100

Peter Falk Reigns in Columbo's Trench Coat. Eric Sherman. *Ladies' Home Journal* 107, No. 3 (March 1990):98-100

Playing Doctor. James Kaplan. *Mademoiselle* (December 1990):96

Popular Narrative and Commercial Television. John Fiske. *Camera Obscura* , No. 23 (May 1990):132-147

Prime-Time Affairs. Yona Zeldis McDonough. *Harper's Bazaar* (August 1990):50

Prime Time Provocateurs. James Servin. *Harper's Bazaar* (March 1990):67-68

Retire Early! Miss Nothing! James Kaplan. *Mademoiselle* (October 1990):110

Sandy Duncan Perks Up "The Hogan Family." Leslie Jay. *Ladies' Home Journal* 107, No. 3 (March 1990):96-98

Slipping into Stardom. Brook Hersey. *Glamour* (October 1990):248-251

The "Space" Behind the Dialogue: The Gender-Coding of Space on *Cheers*. Notes. Charles Acland. *Women & Language* 13, No. 1 (Fall 1990):38-40

Television: Behind the Screens at TV's Funniest New Show. Bibliography. Jill Rachlin. *Ladies' Home Journal* 107, No. 6 (June 1990):54-59

Tracey Untamed. Bonnie Allen. *Ms.* 1, No. 1 (July/August 1990):76

Turned-On TV. Tracy Young. *Vogue* (September 1990):584-587

Up Front. *Ladies' Home Journal* 107, No. 11 (November 1990):127-132

Vogue Arts: Television. Cathleen Schine. *Vogue* (August 1990):222-224; (September 1990):434-436

Will Nancy Survive? Brook Hersey. *Glamour* (April 1990):192

Word On . . . *Glamour* (March 1990):189

Word On . . . Showbiz TV. Charla Krupp. *Glamour* (September 1990):216

Word On . . . Kinder, Gentler Male Bonding. Brook Hersey. *Glamour* (May 1990):206

Word On the Most Intriguing Boss on TV. Charla Krupp. *Glamour* (June 1990):186

Word On TV's Office Comedies. Brook Hersey. *Glamour* (June 1990):184

**Television Programs – Family Influence**

Cosby vs. The Simpsons: Is TV Programming Your Family? Ira Wolfman. *Family Circle* 103, No. 14 (October 16, 1990):79-85

**Television Programs – Stereotyping**

Cagney and Lacey Revisited. Beverley Alcock and Jocelyn Robson. *Feminist Review* No. 35 (Summer 1990):42-53

Can TV Switch Off Bigotry? Barbara Grizzuti Harrison. *Mademoiselle* (November 1990):110

Fall 1989 TV Season "Takes Two Steps Bac," Says NCWW/WOW. *Media Report to Women* 18, No. 1 (January/February 1990):4-5

Full Circle: Wheel of Misfortune? Chava Willig Levy. *Family Circle* 103, No. 14 (October 16, 1990):192

Lynching Women. Diana Hume George. *Ms.* 1, No. 3 (November/December 1990):58-60

Media Stereotyping: A Comparison of the Way Elderly Women and Men Are Portrayed on Prime-Time Television. JoEtta A. Vernon, J. Allen Williams, Jr., Terri Phillips, and Janet Wilson. *Journal of Women and Aging* 2, No. 4 (1990):55-68

T.V. Men: Wimps or What? Maria Stieglitz. *Lilith* 15, No. 3 (Summer 1990):28-29

TV Portrayal of the Childless Black Female: Superficial, Unskilled, Dependent. *Media Report to Women* 18, No. 2 (March/April 1990):4

TV Rape: Television's Communication of Cultural Attitudes toward Rape. Susan L. Brinson. *Women's Studies in Communication* 12, No. 2 (Fall 1989):23-36

**Television Programs for Children.** See also Duvall, Shelley (about)

Kids' TV: A Report Card. Ron Givens. *Ladies' Home Journal* 107, No. 10 (October 1990):72-74

**Telstar Video Entertainment**

All Hail Queen Latifah. Reviewed by Esther Bailey. *Spare Rib* 217 (October 1990):27

**Temperance Movement**

As Wise as Serpents: Five Women and an Organization that Changed British Columbia, 1883-1939. By Lyn Gough. Reviewed by Shelley Bosetti-Piché. *Resources for Feminist Research* 19, No. 1 (March 1990):4-5

**Tempest, Lynne**

On the Bias: Seduction. *AFFILIA* 5, No. 4 (Winter 1990):105-107

**Temporality**

Taking Our Time: Feminist Perspectives on Temporality. By Frieda Johles Forman. Reviewed by Susan-Judith Hoffman. *Atlantis* 15, No. 2 (Spring 1990):111-113

Taking Our Time: Feminist Perspectives on Temporality. Edited by Frieda J. Forman. Reviewed by Julia Creet. *Resources for Feminist Research* 19, No. 1 (March 1990):33

**Tench, Darby**

Poetics and Politics: The Defiant Muse. *Iris* 24 (Fall-Winter 1990):49-53

**Tenhaaf, Nell** (joint author). *See* Hughes, Lynn

**Tennessee State Museum**

A Woman for Lear's: Downhome. Jane Howard. *Lear's* (May 1990):136-139

**Tennis**

Back from Burnout. Martina Navratilova. *Glamour* (May 1990):212

Chris Evert: My Love Match with Andy. Alan Ebert. *Good Housekeeping* 211, No. 4 (October 1990):86-90

Queen of the Ball. Lloyd Gite. *Essence* 21, No. 3 (July 1990):51+

Tennis: Coach in a Box. Joel Drucker. *Women's Sports & Fitness* 12, No. 6 (September 1990):22

Zina's Zenith. Josh Young. *Women's Sports and Fitness* 12, No. 4 (May-June 1990):52-56

**Tennyson, Alfred Lord – Criticism and Interpretation**

Nation, Class, and Gender: Tennyson's *Maud* and War. Joseph Bristow. *Genders* 9 (Fall 1990):93-111

**Tension Headaches.** *See* Headaches

**Terborg-Penn, Rosalyn**

From Myth to History. *The Women's Review of Books* 8, No. 1 (October 1990):8-9

Slave Women in Caribbean Society, 1650-1838. Book Review. *The Women's Review of Books* 8, No. 1 (October 1990):8-9

**Terminal Illness.** *See also* Right to Die

Full Circle: One Last Wish. Betty Rollin. *Family Circle* 103, No. 15 (November 6, 1990):170

Personal Journal. *Ladies' Home Journal* 107, No. 5 (May 1990):126-130

Women Who Make a Difference. Elin Schoen Brockman and Dianne Hales. *Family Circle* 103, No. 8 (June 5, 1990):15-17

**Terrell, Mary Church** (about)

Two Outstanding Women in Social Welfare History: Mary Church Terrell and Ida B. Wells-Barnett. Wilma Peebles-Wilkins and E. Aracelis Francis. *AFFILIA* 5, No. 4 (Winter 1990):87-100

**Terrorism**

Collusion, Raids and the Cult of Fear. *Spare Rib* No. 209 (February 1990):18-20

Terror, or Will the Real Terrorists Please Stand Up. Reviewed by Marcel Farry. *Spare Rib* 218 (November 1990):23

**Terry, Elizabeth** (about)

A Woman for Lear's: Taking the Cake. Jane Howard. *Lear's* (February 1990):130-132

**Terry, Ellen** (about)

Ellen Terry: Player in Her Time. By Nina Auerbach. Reviewed by Robin Sheets. *Tulsa Studies in Women's Literature* 9, No. 1 (Spring 1990):163-165

**Terry, Fiona**

Keep Smiling Through: Women in the Second World War. Book Review. *Gender & History* 2, No. 3 (Autumn 1990):371-373

Votes for Women. Book Review. *Gender & History* 2, No. 3 (Autumn 1990):371-373

Women as Healers: A History of Women and Medicine. Book Review. *Gender & History* 2, No. 3 (Autumn 1990):371-373

Women in the First World War. Book Review. *Gender & History* 2, No. 3 (Autumn 1990):371-373

**Terry, Mary Sue** (about). *See also* Leadership

**Testaferri, Ada** (editor)

Donna: Women in Italian Culture. Reviewed by Santo L. Arico. *Canadian Women's Studies* 11, No. 2 (Fall 1990):91

**Tetreault, Mary Ann**

Arms and the Enlisted Woman. Book Review. *Women & Politics* 10, No. 4 (1990):137-138

**Texas**

Deep in the Heart. Elizabeth Hand. *Belles Lettres* 5, No. 4 (Summer 1990):42-43

**Texas – Mayors**

The Women Who Run Texas. Molly Ivins. *McCall's* 117, No. 11 (August 1990):98-101+

**Texas – Politics and Government.** *See also* Houston – Politics and Government

**Textbook Bias**

Hidden by the Invisible Hand: Neoclassical Economic Theory and the Textbook Treatment of Race and Gender. Susan F. Feiner and Bruce B.

Roberts. *Gender and Society* 4, No. 2 (June 1990):159-181

Public Relations Textbooks Offer Skewed Image of Women in PR. *Media Report to Women* 18, No. 1 (January/February 1990):6-7

Visual Images of American Society: Gender and Race in Introductory Sociology Textbooks. Myra Marx Ferree and Elaine J. Hall. *Gender and Society* 4, No. 4 (December 1990):500-533

Women and Minorities in Introductory Economics Textbooks: 1974 to 1984. Susan F. Feiner and Barbara A. Morgan. *Women's Studies Quarterly* 18, Nos. 3-4 (Fall-Winter 1990):46-67

**Textile Fabrics**

Down the Stretch. *Harper's Bazaar* (May 1990):104-109

Fashion Questions. *Glamour* (November 1990):186

Night Meets Day. *Glamour* (November 1990):206-213

Spring Currents. *Glamour* (March 1990):230-237

Truth in Fashion. *Glamour* (December 1990):177-178

**Textile Industry**

Spinners and Weavers of Auffay: Rural Industry and the Sexual Division of Labor in a French Village, 1750-1850. By Gay L. Gullickson. Reviewed by Judith DeGroat. *Gender and Society* 4, No. 2 (June 1990):272-274

Working Women, Gender, and Industrialization in Nineteenth-Century France: The Case of Lorraine Embroidery Manufacturing. Whitney Walton. *Journal of Women's History* 2, No. 2 (Fall 1990):42-65

**Textile Industry – Third World**

Woes of Tribal Garment Girls: Bangladesh. Rosaline Costa. *Women in Action* 1-2 (1990):20

**Thaddeus, Janice Farrar**

Legal Fiction. *The Women's Review of Books* 8, No. 1 (October 1990):25-26

Married Women's Separate Property in England, 1660-1833. Book Review. *The Women's Review of Books* 8, No. 1 (October 1990):25-26

**Thailand – Acquired Immune Deficiency Syndrome**

Imported AIDS. Sarah Sexton, Chantawipa Apisuk, and Anchana Suwannond. *Connexions* 33 (1990):16-18

NGOs Against AIDS. Sarah Sexton. *Connexions* 33 (1990):19

**Thailand – Housing**

Women's Struggle for Housing Rights in Thailand. Somporn Surarith. *Canadian Women's Studies* 11, No. 2 (Fall 1990):15-16

**Thailand – Prostitution**

Get That Condom on Your Loogboub. Debra Chasnoff. *Out/Look* No. 7 (Winter 1990):62-64

Green Cards in Thailand. *Women's World* , No. 24 (Winter 1990/91): 55

Thailand: Against Prostitute Registration. *Women's World* , No. 24 (Winter 1990/91): 39-40

Thailand: The Six-Year Struggle Against The Phuket Brothel on Fire. *Women's World* , No. 24 (Winter 1990/91): 12

**Thailand – Sino-Thai Women**

Sino-Thai Women in Bangkok: Social Change and Marriage Patterns. Jiemin Bao. *NWSA Journal* 2, No. 4 (Autumn 1990):699-700

**Thaler, Susan**

Vinnie's Angel. Short Story. *Good Housekeeping* 211, No. 6 (December 1990):62 +

**Thames, Beth**

Calm Down! *Working Mother* (December 1990):34-39

**Thanksgiving Day**

Holidays are about the Future More than the Past. Mary Catherine Bateson. *McCall's* 118, No. 2 (November 1990):35-37

**Thanksgiving Day – Cookery**

Eat Light: Have a Thin Thanksgiving. *Redbook* 176, No. 1 (November 1990):174

Giving Thanks. Jean Anderson. *Family Circle* 103, No. 16 (November 27, 1990):74-77

Nathalie Dupree Cooks Southern Thanksgiving Favorites. Nathalie Dupree. *Redbook* 176, No. 1 (November 1990):125-129 +

Thanksgiving Cookbook. Marianne Langan. *McCall's* 118, No. 2 (November 1990):123-128 +

A Thanksgiving to Remember. *Ladies' Home Journal* 107, No. 11 (November 1990):232-245

**Thatcher, Margaret** (about)

Not a Man to Match Her: The Marketing of a Prime Minister. By Wendy Webster. Reviewed by Hazel Smith. *Spare Rib* No. 215 (August 1990):28-29

**Thayer, Millie**

Report from Nicaragua. *Spare Rib* No. 210 (March 1990):12-14

**Theater.** See also Black Theater; Burlesque; Costume Design; Playwrights

FAT LIP Readers Theatre. Laura Bock. *Woman of Power* 17 (Summer 1990):32-33

Feminine Focus: The New Women Playwrights. Edited by Enoch Brater. Reviewed by Kendall. *The Women's Review of Books* 7, No. 4 (January 1990):15-16

Feminism and Theatre. By Sue-Ellen Case. Reviewed by Catherine Burroughs. *Tulsa Studies in Women's Literature* 9, No. 2 (Fall 1990):326-329

Feminism and Theatre. By Sue-Ellen Case. Reviewed by Chezia Thompson-Cager. *NWSA Journal* 2, No. 4 (Autumn 1990):650-651

Feminism and Theatre. By Sue-Ellen Case. Reviewed by Jill Dolan. *Signs* 15, No. 4 (Summer 1990):864-869

Interviews Transformed into Play for Street Theater. Judith Pasternak. *New Directions for Women* 19, No. 1 (January/February 1990):metrö+

Making a Spectacle: Feminist Essays on Contemporary Women's Theatre. By Lynda Hart. Reviewed by Catherine Burroughs. *Tulsa Studies in Women's Literature* 9, No. 2 (Fall 1990):326-329

Making A Spectacle: Feminist Essays on Contemporary Women's Theatre. Edited by Lynda Hart. Reviewed by Gail Leondar. *Women and Performance: A Journal of Feminist Theory* 5, No. 1, Issue #9 (1990): 192-193

Spiderwoman Theater. Carolann Barrett. *Woman of Power* 17 (Summer 1990):34-37

Women in American Theatre. Edited by Helen Krich Chinoy and Linda Walsh Jenkins. Reviewed by Jill Dolan. *Signs* 15, No. 4 (Summer 1990):864-869

### Theater, Community

Health on Stage. Rachel Epstein. *Healthsharing* 11, No. 2 (March 1990):22-26

### Theater – Homosexual Experience

The Boys in the Band Come Back. Wendell Ricketts. *Out/Look* No. 9 (Summer 1990):62-67

**Theater Companies.** See Monstrous Regiment

Film Makers on Hot Topics. Penny Perkins. *New Directions for Women* 19, No. 2 (March/April 1990):metrö

### Theater Reviews

Bondage. See Hines, David

Curl Up and Dye. See Pam, Susan

Egg Dances. See Lee, Rosemary

The Factory Girls. See McGuinness, Frank

A Few Good Men. See Sorkin, Aaron

Lulu. See Wedekind, Frank

Machinal. See Treadwell, Sophie

Meridien. See Artiste, Cindy

Miss Saigon. See Suh, Mary

Song for a Sanctuary. See Ahmad, Rukhsana

Theater: A Few Good Men. See Sorkin, Aaron

Through the Wire. See Rosenblum, Nina

Vogue Arts: Oh, Kay!. See Gershwin, George

Vogue Arts: Once On This Island. See Ahrens, Lynn and Flaherty, Stephen

### Theology

God's Fierce Whimsy – Christian Feminism and Theological Education. By The Mud Flower Collective. Reviewed by Joanne Stato. *off our backs* 20, No. 8 (August/September 1990):26-27+

### Theology, Feminist

After the Revolution in Poland Today, Women Still Sweep the Floors. Mary E. Hunt. *Lilith* 15, No. 2 (Spring 1990):20

Emptiness, Otherness, and Identity: A Feminist Perspective. Paula M. Cooey. *Journal of Feminist Studies in Religion* 6, No. 2 (Fall 1990):7-23

The Illegitimacy of Jesus: A Feminist Theological Interpretation of the Infancy Narratives. By Jane Schaberg. Reviewed by Deborah Ann Light. *Ms.* 1, No. 2 (September/October 1990):27

The Story of I: Luce Irigaray's Theoretical Masochism. Emily S. Apter. *NWSA Journal* 2, No. 2 (Spring 1990):186-198

Unearthing the Present. Fatima Mernissi. *Ms.* 1, No. 3 (November/December 1990):74-75

The Ways We Are: Saying Goodbye to Friends. Jane Litman. *Lilith* 15, No. 1 (Winter 1990):31

White Women's Christ and Black Women's Jesus: Feminist Christology and Womanist Response. By Jacquelyn Grant. Reviewed by Paula Giddings. *Essence* 21, No. 6 (October 1990):52

Womanist Interpretation of the New Testament: The Quest for Holistic and Inclusive Translation and Interpretation. Clarice J. Martin, Joanna Dewey, Peggy Hutaff, and Jane Schaberg. *Journal of Feminist Studies in Religion* 6, No. 2 (Fall 1990):41-85

**Théoret, France** (joint author). See Bersianik, Louky

### Thering, Sister Rose

When Will We Come to Understand the Jews as They Do Themselves? *Lilith* 15, No. 2 (Spring 1990):19

**Thermal Pest Eradication.** See Insect Pests – Control

### Thernstrom, Melanie

The Dead Girl. Reviewed by Anne Lamott. *Mademoiselle* (September 1990):170

### Theroux, Phyllis

Lifelines: Women and Writing. *Lear's* (May 1990):56-58

### Thibault, Gisele

The Language of Love and Guilt: Mother-Daughter Relationships from a Cross-cultural Perspective. Book Review. *Resources for Feminist Research* 19, No. 1 (March 1990):23-24

**Thielen-Wilson, Leslie** (joint author). *See* Wylie, Alison

**Thigpen, David**

Charles Dutton: From Jail to Yale. *Essence* 21, No. 4 (August 1990):46

Marguerite Ross Barnett: University President. *Essence* 21, No. 6 (October 1990):50

**Thinness.** *See also* Beauty Standards; Body Image; Eating Behavior

Never too Thin. By Eva Szekely. Reviewed by Patricia A. Connor-Greene. *Women and Health* 16, Nos. 3/4 (1990):211-221

**Third World – Criticism**

Words in Silence: An Exercise in Third World Feminist Criticism. Jid Lee. *Frontiers* 11, Nos. 2-3 (1990):66-71

**Third World – Development**

Each in Her Own Way: Five Women Leaders of the Developing World. By Marion Fennelly Levy. Reviewed by Valerie de Plessis. *Resources for Feminist Research* 19, No. 1 (March 1990):9

**Third World – Housing**

Third World Housing Development and Indigenous People in North America. Winona LaDuke. *Canadian Women's Studies* 11, No. 2 (Fall 1990):12-14

**Third World Women**

Charting the Journey: Writings by Black and Third World Women. Edited by Shabnam Grewal, Jackie Kay, Liliane Landor, Gail Lewis and Pratibha Parmar. Reviewed by Amita Handa. *Resources for Feminist Research* 19, No. 2 (June 1990):38

A Home Divided: Women and Income in the Third World. Edited by Daisy Dwyer and Judith Bruce. Reviewed by Eileen Berry. *Women's Studies International Forum* 13, No. 6 (1990):614-617

**Third World Women – Economics**

Gender, Race, and Political Empowerment: South African Canning Workers, 1940-1960. Iris Berger. *Gender and Society* 4, No. 3 (September 1990):398-420

Latin American Women in the World Capitalist Crisis. June Nash. *Gender and Society* 4, No. 3 (September 1990):338-353

**Third World Women – Feminism**

Multiple Mediations: Feminist Scholarship in the Age of Multinational Reception. Lata Mani. *Feminist Review* No. 35 (Summer 1990):24-41

Women, Power and Policy: Toward the Year 2000. Edited by Ellen Boneparth and Emily Stoper. Reviewed by Joan Hulse Thompson. *Women & Politics* 10, No. 3 (1990):133-134

**Third World Women – History**

Putting Herself into the Picture. Notes. Bibliography. Jyofsna Kapur. *Manushi* 56 (January-February 1990):28-37

Restoring Women to History: Teaching Packets for Integrating Women's History into Courses. By Iris Berger and others. Reviewed by Janet J. Ewald. *GH* 2, No. 3 (Autumn 1990):349-351

**Third World Women – Oral History**

Rigoberta's Narrative and the New Practice of Oral History. Claudia Salazar. *Women & Language* 13, No. 1 (Fall 1990):7-8

**Third World Women – Status**

Geography of Gender in the Third World. Edited by Janet H. Momsen and Janet Townsend. Reviewed by Fiona Mackenzie. *Resources for Feminist Research* 19, No. 1 (March 1990):18

From Structural Subordination to Empowerment: Women and Development in Third World Contexts. Edna Acosta-Belén and Christine E. Bose. *Gender and Society* 4, No. 3 (September 1990):299-320

Women and Environment in the Third World: Alliance for the Future. By Irene Dankelman and Joan Davidson. Reviewed by Linda Carty. *Resources for Feminist Research* 19, No. 1 (March 1990):40-41

**Thom, Mary**

Campaign '90 Tip Sheet. *Ms.* 1, No. 1 (July/August 1990):89

We Have Met the Enemy and They Are Us. *Ms.* 1, No. 1 (July/August 1990):79

**Thom, Mary** (editor)

Letters to *Ms.* 1972-1987. *Woman of Power* 17 (Summer 1990):56-58

**Thomas, Clara**

Dance on the Earth. Book Review. *Canadian Women's Studies* 11, No. 2 (Fall 1990):87-89

**Thomas, Darwin L** and Cornwall, Marie

Religion and Family in the 1980s: Discovery and Development. *Journal of Marriage and the Family* 52, No. 4 (November 1990):983-992

**Thomas, Dylan** (about). *See also* Love-Letters

**Thomas, Elean**

Sheroes and Heroes. Poem. *Spare Rib* No. 210 (March 1990):10

Winnie and Nelson Mandela: Rising Above the Hype. *Spare Rib* No. 212 (May 1990):36-39

**Thomas, G. Scott**

The Ten Best Small Cities for Women. *Savvy Woman* (September 1990):47-49

**Tice, Karen W.**

A Case Study of Battered Women's Shelters in Appalachia. *AFFILIA* 5, No. 3 (Fall 1990):83-100

**Tickner, Lisa**

The Spectacle of Women: Imagery of the Suffrage Campaign 1907-1914. Reviewed by Lynne Walker. *Woman's Art Journal* 11, No. 2 (Fall 1990-Winter 1991):48-50

**Tiegs, Cheryl** (about)

Role Model. Laura Fissinger. *Harper's Bazaar* (August 1990):110-115

**Tienanmen Square.** *See* China – Political Protest

**Tierney, Daniel**, Romito, Patrizia, and Messing, Karen

She Ate Not the Bread of Idleness: Exhaustion Is Related to Domestic and Salaried Working Conditions among 539 Québec Hospital Workers. *Women and Health* 16, No. 1 (1990):21-42

**Tierney, Helen** (about)

An Encyclopedic Undertaking. Linda Shult. *Feminist Collections* 11, No. 3 (Spring 1990):11-12

**Tierney, John**

Mind Health. *Vogue* (July 1990):114-119

**Tiersten, Irene**

Brink of Womanhood. *New Directions for Women* 19, No. 5 (September-October 1990):7

**Tikaram, Tanita**

The Sweet Keeper. Reviewed by Jennifer Mourin. *Spare Rib* No. 210 (March 1990):41

**Tilak, Lakshmibai** (about). *See* India – Status of Women

**Tilin, Andrew**

Fame, Fortune, and Frisbees. *Women's Sports and Fitness* 12, No. 7 (October 1990):14

Monster Mama. *Women's Sports and Fitness* 12, No. 7 (October 1990):16

**Tilly, Louise A.**

Men, Women, and Work: Class, Gender and Protest in the New England Shoe Industry, 1780-1910. Book Review. *Gender and Society* 4, No. 2 (June 1990):269-272

**Time Magazine – Gender Discrimination**

Women Pictures on Only 14% of *Time* Magazine Covers since 1923, Study Finds. *Media Report to Women* 18, No. 1 (January/February 1990):3-4

**Time Management.** *See also* Balancing Work and Family Life; Beauty, Personal; Cookery; Leisure Activities; Marriage – Counseling; Overachievement; Planning; Recreation; Stress – Coping Strategies; Stress Relaxation; Writing, Business Purposes

The American Mother: A Landmark Survey for the 1990s. Margery D. Rosen. *Ladies' Home Journal* 107, No. 5 (May 1990):132-136

From an Office to a Gentleman. *Mademoiselle* (October 1990):48

Beat-the-Clock Dinners. Jan Turner Hazard. *Ladies' Home Journal* 107, No. 9 (September 1990):186-188+

Best 15-Minute Skillet Dinners. *Redbook* 174, No. 6 (April 1990):116-119

The Busy Life: The Career, the Husband, the Kids and Everything. Margaret Shakespeare. *Working Woman* (December 1990):94-98

The Busy Life: Weekends with No Regrets. Laurie Tarkan. *Working Woman* (November 1990):150-154

Career Workshop: How to Work Faster, Smarter. *Working Woman* (April 1990):77

Chic Expertise. Holland Scott. *Harper's Bazaar* (October 1990):170-173+

Contemporary Living: 20 Minute Meals. Jonell Nash. *Essence* 20, No. 11 (March 1990):87-95+

Cooking in the Fast Lane. *Ladies' Home Journal* 107, No. 3 (March 1990):224-227

By the Dawn's Early Light. Bibliography. *Mademoiselle* (November 1990):60

Easy as 1-2-3. *Ladies' Home Journal* 107, No. 4 (April 1990):216; 107, No. 6 (June 1990):174

Executive Agenda. *Working Woman* (December 1990):53-54

Get Organized. Regina Baraban. *Working Woman* (January 1990):116-119

The Hair You Want. *Family Circle* 103, No. 13 (September 25, 1990):70-75

Help! Vicki Lansky. *Family Circle* 103, No. 16 (November 27, 1990):100

High Profile: Happiness Is a Warm Filofax. Jacqueline Wasser. *Mademoiselle* (September 1990):154+

How to *Really* Enjoy Your Kids. Pamela Redmond Satran. *Ladies' Home Journal* 107, No. 11 (November 1990):146-151

Instant Chic: Busy Moms' Timesaving Tips. *Ladies' Home Journal* 107, No. 9 (September 1990):34-38

Is This a Dead-End Assignment? Kent L. Straat. *Working Woman* (March 1990):84-85+

Living Beautifully: Give Your House a Holiday Glow. Alexandra Stoddard. *McCall's* 118, No. 2 (November 1990):168

Living Beautifully: Make Time to Do It Now! Alexandra Stoddard. *McCall's* 118, No. 1 (October 1990):164

Make Minutes Count! *Family Circle* 103, No. 15 (November 6, 1990):97-116

To Herland and Beyond: The Life and Work of Charlotte Perkins Gilman. Book Review. *Belles Lettres* 6, No. 1 (Fall 1990):40-42

The High Road. Book Review. *Belles Lettres* 5, No. 3 (Spring 1990):4

Jean Stafford: The Savage Heart. Book Review. *Belles Lettres* 6, No. 1 (Fall 1990):40-42

Mary Austin: Song of a Maverick. Book Review. *Belles Lettres* 6, No. 1 (Fall 1990):40-42

Sexual Craving and Emotional Obsession. *Belles Lettres* 5, No. 3 (Spring 1990):4

**Tlou, Sheila**

Not Either an Experimental Doll: The Separate Worlds of Three South African Women. Book Review. *Women's Studies International Forum* 13, No. 4 (1990):408

**Tobias, Cynthia** (joint author). *See* Ide, Bette A.

**Tobias, Marlene** (joint author). *See* Bergman, Miranda

**Tobias, Sheila**

The Biological Is Political. *The Women's Review of Books* 8, No. 2 (November 1990):15

The Politics of Women's Biology. Book Review. *The Women's Review of Books* 8, No. 2 (November 1990):15

**Tobin, Ann**

Lesbianism and the Labour Party: The GLC Experience. *Feminist Review* No. 34 (Spring 1990):56-66

**Todd, Alexandra Dundas**

Intimate Adversaries – Cultural Conflict between Doctors and Women Patients. Reviewed by Mary A. Jansen. *Psychology of Women Quarterly* 14, No. 3 (September 1990):437-439

Intimate Adversaries: Cultural Conflict Between Doctors and Women Patients. Reviewed by Robert Kalechofsky. *On the Issues* 17 (Winter 1990):33-34

**Todd, Janet**

Feminist Literary History. Reviewed by Jane Lilienfeld. *Women's Studies International Forum* 13, Nos. 1-2 (1990):165-166

The Sign of Angellica: Women, Writing, and Fiction, 1660-1800. Reviewed by Ann B. Shteir. *Canadian Women's Studies* 11, No. 2 (Fall 1990):91-92

The Sign of Angellica: Women Writing and Fiction 1660-1800. Reviewed by Elaine Hobby. *Gender & History* 2, No. 3 (Autumn 1990):359-363

**Todd, Janet** (joint editor). *See* Spender, Dale

**Todd, Judith**, Friedman, Ariella, and Kariuki, Priscilla Wanjiru

Women Growing Stronger with Age: The Effect of Status in the United States and Kenya. *Psychology of Women Quarterly* 14, No. 4 (December 1990):567-577

**Todhunter, Emily** (about)

Eclectic Expertise. Diane Sustendal. *Harper's Bazaar* (April 1990):202-203

**Toilet Training.** *See* Child Development

**Tomán, René de la Pedraja**

Women in Colombian Organizations, 1900-1940: A Study in Changing Gender Roles. *Journal of Women's History* 2, No. 1 (Spring 1990):98-119

**Tomaso, Carla** (joint author). *See* Martinac, Paula

**Tomaszewski, Evelyn**

The Battered Women's Movement in Action. *off our backs* 20, No. 10 (November 1990):1-3

**Tomes, Nancy J.**

In Sickness and in Health: The British Experience, 1650-1850. Book Review. *Gender & History* 2, No. 3 (Autumn 1990):368-369

**Tomkins, Calvin** (joint author). *See* Rosen, Randy

**Tomm, Winifred** and Hamilton, Gordon (editors)

Gender Bias in Scholarship: The Pervasive Prejudice. Reviewed by Marilyn Biggerstaff. *AFFILIA* 5, No. 1 (Spring 1990):121-123

**Tomm, Winnie** (editor)

The Effects of Feminist Approaches on Research Methodologies. Reviewed by Dorothy L. Steffens and Jane Robbins. *Feminist Collections* 11, No. 2 (Winter 1990):7-9

**Tompkins, Doug** (about). *See* Partnership

**Tompkins, Sally L.** (about)

A Bandage in One Hand and a Bible in the Other: The Story of Captain Sally L. Tompkins (CSA). Patricia Paquette. *Minerva* 8, No. 2 (Summer 1990):47-54

**Tompkins, Susie** (about). *See* Partnership

**Toner, Gerald R.**

Remember the Oranges. Short story. *Ladies' Home Journal* 107, No. 12 (December 1990):84-92

**Tong, Rosemarie**

Feminist Thought: A Comprehensive Introduction. Reviewed by Phyllis Eckhaus. *AFFILIA* 5, No. 3 (Fall 1990):121-122

**Tonga – Culture and History**

Kinship to Kinship: Gender Hierarchy and State Formation in the Tongan Islands. By Christine Ward Gailey. Reviewed by Mary K. Anglin. *Signs* 15, No. 3 (Spring 1990):642-645

**Tonga – Gender Roles**

Deceptive Dichotomies: Private/Public, and Nature/Culture: Gender Relations in Tonga in the Early Contact Period. Caroline Ralston. *Australian Feminist Studies* No. 12 (Summer 1990):65-82

**Tonti-Filippini, Nick**

Are Superovulants Necessary in IVF Procedures? *Healthright* 9, No. 3 (May 1990):10-13

**Tools**

The Joys of Tooling Around. Rita Robinson. *Lear's* (June 1990):54

**Tooth, Isla**

Reproductive Health: The Knowledge and Attitudes and Needs of Adolescents. Book Review. *Healthright* 9, No. 4 (August 1990):40-41

**Topolnicki, Denise M.**

Equal Pay for Equal Work? Guess Again. *Savvy Woman* (January 1990):31-32

When Big Brother Is Watching. *Savvy Woman* (February 1990):39-40

**Torf, Adrienne**

Two Roads to Solo Keyboard Work: Julie Homi and Adrienne Torf. Laura Post. *Hot Wire* 6, No. 2 (May 1990):28-30+

**Tornadoes.** *See* Natural Disasters

**Toronto (Canada) – Film Festivals**

Remembering History: Films by Women at the 1989 Toronto Film Festival. Rhona Berenstein. *Camera Obscura* No. 22 (January 1990):159-166

**Toronto (Canada) – Lesbian Feminism**

The House That Jill Built: Lesbian Feminist Organizing in Toronto, 1976-1980. Becki Ross. *Feminist Review* No. 35 (Summer 1990):75-91

**Torre, Elizabeth**

Drama as a Consciousness-Raising Strategy for the Self-Empowerment of Working Women. *AFFILIA* 5, No. 1 (Spring 1990):49-65

**Torres, Eden E.** (joint author). *See* Brodsky, Michelle

**Torres, Lourdes**

Breaking Boundaries: Latina Writings and Critical Readings. Book Review. *Women's Studies International Forum* 13, No. 5 (1990):519-520

**Torsney, Cheryl B.**

Constance Fenimore Woolson: The Grief of Artistry. Reviewed by Alice Hall Petry. *Tulsa Studies in Women's Literature* 9, No. 2 (Fall 1990):331-332

**Tortu, Christian** (about). *See* Florists

**Toscano, Siobhan**

A Blessing on Both Your Houses. *Savvy Woman* (September 1990):24-28

Sound Raves. *Savvy Woman* (October 1990):21

**Toth, Emily**

Developing Political Savvy – Many Misadventures Later. *Women's Studies Quarterly* 18, Nos. 3-4 (Fall-Winter 1990):147-151

Doing Literary Business: American Women Writers in the Nineteenth Century. Book Review. *The Women's Review of Books* 8, No. 3 (December 1990):15-16

Jean Stafford: The Savage Heart. Book Review. *The Women's Review of Books* 8, No. 3 (December 1990):15-16

Writers' Wrongs. *The Women's Review of Books* 8, No. 3 (December 1990):15-16

**Tóth, Eva**

The Creation of the World. Poem. *Feminist Review* No. 36 (Autumn 1990):93-94

Wanted. Poem. *Feminist Review* No. 36 (Autumn 1990):92

**Touby, Laurel**

Four Strategies for Salary Negotiation. *Working Woman* (January 1990):110-112

Office Tech: The Thinking Machines. *Working Woman* (November 1990):87-98

Say the Magic Words. *Working Woman* (November 1990):120+

**Touchton, Judith G.** (joint editor). *See* Pearson, Carol S.

**Tough, Paul**

Live from Times Square. *Savvy* (December-January 1991):16

**Touliatos, John,** Perlmutter, Barry F., and Straus, Murray A. (editors)

Handbook of Family Measurement Techniques. Reviewed by Mary Ellen Oliveri. *Journal of Marriage and the Family* 52, No. 3 (August 1990):799-800

**Tourette Syndrome**

Tourette Syndrome and Human Behavior. By David E. Comings. Book Review. *Adolescence* 25, No. 100 (Winter 1990):997

**Toussaint, Pamela**

State of the Art Electronics. Bibliography. *Essence* 21, No. 3 (July 1990):88-93

**Toussaint, Pamela** (joint author). *See* Cain, Joy Duckett

**tova**

Does It Hurt? Poem. *Bridges* 1, No. 2 (Fall 1990): 69-73

"Does It Hurt?" This Is Not An Explanation. Essay. *Bridges* 1, No. 2 (Fall 1990): 74-76

**Townsend, Alison**

Her Soul Beneath the Bone: Women's Poetry on Breast Cancer. Book Review. *The Women's Review of Books* 7, No. 8 (May 1990):16

A Long Way to Go. *The Women's Review of Books* 7, No. 4 (January 1990):12-13

Poetry out of Tragedy. *The Women's Review of Books* 7, No. 8 (May 1990):16

The Writing or the Sex? Or Why You Don't Have to Read Women's Writing to Know It's No Good. Book Review. *The Women's Review of Books* 7, No. 4 (January 1990):12-13

**Townsend, Janet** (joint editor). *See* Momsen, Janet H.

**Towson State University**

Towson State University Community College Curriculum Transformation Project. Elaine Hedges, Sara Coulter, Myrna Goldenberg, and Gail Forman. *Women's Studies Quarterly* 18, Nos. 1-2 (Spring-Summer 1990):122-125

**Toxic Shock Syndrome**

Red Alert: A Safe Tampon Guide. Leslie Granston. *Mademoiselle* (October 1990):122

Toxic Shock Syndrome. Alison Costello, *Spare Rib* No. 212 (May 1990):58

Truth in Tampons. *Ms.* 1, No. 1 (July/August 1990):55

**Toxic Wastes.** *See* Hazardous Wastes

**Toy Industry.** *See* Educational Toys

**Toyota Celica.** *See* Automobiles – Design and Construction

**Toyota Motor Company.** *See* Automobiles – Purchasing

**Toys.** *See also* Dolls

Boys and Dolls, Girls and Trucks. Julia Kagan. *McCall's* 118, No. 3 (December 1990):88

The Flip Side: Some Assembly Required. John Leo. *Family Circle* 103, No. 17 (December 18, 1990):43-47

**Trade American Card**

My Kingdom for a Horse. Paul Neimark. *Executive Female* 13, No. 4 (July-August 1990):32-34

**Traditional Birth Attendants.** *See* Midwifery

**Traditions.** *See also* Christmas Cookery; Family Reunions; Nostalgia

Family Ties & Celebrations. Liza Nelson. *McCall's* 118, No. 2 (November 1990):104-108

Family Traditions: The Power of Knowing Who You Are. Susan Brenna. *McCall's* 117, No. 7 (April 1990):76-82

Full Circle: God Bless Us Everyone! Anna Quindlen. *Family Circle* 103, No. 17 (December 18, 1990):208

Fun for All. *Redbook* 176, No. 2 (December 1990):100-101

The Gift of Memories. Jane Mattern Vachon. *Ladies' Home Journal* 107, No. 12 (December 1990):78-79

Giving Thanks. Jean Anderson. *Family Circle* 103, No. 16 (November 27, 1990):74-77

Holiday Love. *Harper's Bazaar* (December 1990):120-123+

One Magic Christmas. *Family Circle* 103, No. 17 (December 18, 1990):94-103

Repeat Performance. Carol Cooper. *Essence* 21, No. 1 (May 1990):144-148

Swedish Noel. *Harper's Bazaar* (December 1990):124-125+

Traditions: O Christmas Tree. Mary Ann Johanson. *McCall's* 118, No. 3 (December 1990):31

Weddings that Made Me Laugh & Cry. Judith Viorst. *Redbook* 175, No. 3 (July 1990):18-20

Wonderful Family Traditions. Ellen Byron. *Redbook* 176, No. 2 (December 1990):98-99+

**Traffic Accidents.** *See* School Buses – Accidents

**Trafficking in Women.** *See also* Prostitution

Asian Women Marry Japanese Farmers. *Women's World* , No. 24 (Winter 1990/91): 16-17

Coalition Against Trafficking in Women. Kathleen L. Barry and Dorchen Leidholdt. *Woman of Power* 18 (Fall 1990):46-49

Germany. *Women's World* , No. 24 (Winter 1990/91): 19-20

Netherlands. *Women's World* , No. 24 (Winter 1990/91): 21

Stop Trafficking. *Women's World* , No. 24 (Winter 1990/91): 17-18

Traffic in Women in Ghana. *Women's World* , No. 24 (Winter 1990/91): 20

United Kingdom: Filipina Fiancee and Her Baby Fight to Stay. *Women's World* , No. 24 (Winter 1990/91): 15-16

**Trager, Hannah**

Votes for Women. *Journal of Women's History* 2, No. 1 (Spring 1990):196-199

**Train Travel.** *See* Railroad Travel

**Transplants – Personal Narratives**

A Mother's Gift of Life. Marianne Jacobbi. *Good Housekeeping* 211, No. 1 (July 1990):105, 199-203

**Transportation**

Carpooling Incentives Aim at Americans Who Solo (Or: Baby, You Can Drive My Car). Celia Slom. *McCall's* 117, No. 8 (May 1990):63

**Transportation – Safety**

Moving Forward on Public Transit. *Women and Environments* 12, No. 1 (Fall 1989/Winter 1990): 10-11

**Transvestism**

Amazons and Military Maids: Women Who Dressed as Men in Pursuit of Life, Liberty and Happiness. By Julie Wheelwright. Reviewed by C. Kay Larson. *Minerva* 8, No. 2 (Summer 1990):74-78

Amazons and Military Maids: Women Who Dressed as Men in the Pursuit of Life, Liberty and the Pursuit of Happiness. By Julie Wheelwright. Reviewed by Rita Victoria Gomez Dearmond. *Gender & History* 2, No. 2 (Summer 1990):229-232

A Boy's Guide to Feeling Pretty. D-L Alvarez. *Out/Look* No. 8 (Spring 1990):19-20

The Cavalry Maid: The Memoirs of a Woman Soldier of 1812. By Nadezhda Durova. Reviewed by Rita Victoria Gomez Dearmond. *Gender & History* 2, No. 2 (Summer 1990):229-232

Fantastic Women: Sex, Gender and Transvestism. By Annie Woodhouse. Reviewed by Holly Devor. *Resources for Feminist Research* 19, No. 1 (March 1990):11

Fantastic Women: Sex, Gender and Transvestism. By Annie Woodhouse. Reviewed by Martha Vicinus. *The Women's Review of Books* 7, No. 9 (June 1990):26

The House that Brenda Built: A Transvestite Response to AIDS in Brazil. Michael Adams. *Out/Look* No. 8 (Spring 1990):22-26

The Tradition of Female Transvestism in Early Modern Europe. By Rudolf M. Dekker and Lotte C. van de Pol. Reviewed by Patricia Crawford. *Australian Feminist Studies* No. 12 (Summer 1990):131-132

The Tradition of Female Transvestism in Early Modern Europe. Rudolf M. Dekker and Lotte C. Van de Pol. Reviewed by Rita Victoria Gomez Dearmond. *Gender & History* 2, No. 2 (Summer 1990):229-232

Tranformations: Crossdressers and Those Who Love Them. By Mariette Pathy Allen. Reviewed by Margaret McCarthy. *New Directions for Women* 19, No. 4 (July-August 1990):20

**Trapani, Catherine**

Transition Goals for Adolescents with Learning Disabilities. Book Review. *Adolescence* 25, No. 99 (Fall 1990):755

**Trask, Haunani-Kay**

Ka'ahumanu, Molder of Change. Book Review. *NWSA Journal* 2, No. 1 (Winter 1990):127-129

**Trasko, Mary**

Heavenly Soles: Extraordinary Twentieth-Century Shoes. Reviewed by Holly Hall. *Belles Lettres* 5, No. 4 (Summer 1990):35+

**Trason, Ann** (about)

Running Circles Around the Boys. Bob Cooper. *Women's Sports and Fitness* 12, No. 3 (April 1990):62-65

**Travel.** *See also* Business Travel; Caribbean – Description and Travel; France – Travel; Honeymoons; Infants – Travel; Mexico – Travel; *particular countries or cities*; Railroad Travel; Scotland

Beaches I Have Known and Loved. Rosanne Keller. *Lear's* (July 1990):38-39

Beauty Care Hits the Road. Diane Clehane. *Lear's* (December 1990):53

Best Family Resorts for the Holidays. Stephen Birnbaum. *Good Housekeeping* 211, No. 6 (December 1990):40+

Driving. Tad Friend. *Vogue* (August 1990):258-260

Everywhere to Run. Bob Cooper. *Women's Sports & Fitness* 12, No. 6 (September 1990):33

Fairways to Heaven. Brian McCallen. *Harper's Bazaar* (March 1990):56-62

Family Dream Vacations. Betty Holcomb and Linda Hamilton Clinton. *Working Mother* (November 1990):46-51

Goodbye to the Open Road and All That. V. S. Pritchett. *Lear's* (July 1990):128+

The Grand Canyon. Stephen Birnbaum. *Good Housekeeping* 211, No. 5 (November 1990):150+

Great Getaways. *Ladies' Home Journal* 107, No. 6 (June 1990):112

Head for the Hills. Bibliography. Khephra Burns. *Essence* 21, No. 8 (December 1990):108-112

Ideas to Fall for Now. *Glamour* (November 1990):200-205

Inside Istanbul. Tad Friend. *Vogue* (October 1990):290+

It's a Great Relationship, But Can It Travel? Karen Heller and John Milward. *Mademoiselle* (March 1990):152-154, 238

Kyoto Encounter. Tad Friend. *Vogue* (January 1990):134-138

London, Paris, Rome: Dressing Native. Carol Schatz. *Mademoiselle* (September 1990):140

The Long Hot Winter. *Vogue* (November 1990):294-302

Mother Nature's Fall Spectacular. Bibliography. Stephen Birnbaum. *Good Housekeeping* 211, No. 4 (October 1990):106-108

One for the Road: The Very Secret Life of a Solo Traveler. Julia Claiborne Johnson. *Mademoiselle* (July 1990):116-117, 154-155

Pleasure Plus: The New Way to Travel. Gary Belsky. *Working Woman* (June 1990):44-46

Puce Becomes You . . . And Other Secrets of European Style. Judy Bachrach. *Savvy Woman* (November 1990):68-71+

On Riding the Edges. Ralph Blum. *Lear's* (March 1990):138-143

The Road Test: First-Trip-Together Jitters. Skip Hollandsworth. *Mademoiselle* (December 1990):74-76

A Sea Change: His Ship Came In. Peter Feibleman. *Lear's* (November 1990):70-72

Separate Vacations. Elizabeth Benedict. *Glamour* (July 1990):188+

Seven Black-Owned Island Guest Houses. Allyson Reid-Dove. *Essence* 20, No. 12 (April 1990):89-92

Sounds of Music. Bibliography. Diana Burgwyn. *Harper's Bazaar* (November 1990):74+

Summer Fashion Savvy: One Bag Vacation. *McCall's* 117, No. 10 (July 1990):69-74

Take the Kids Cruising. Sarah Hutter. *Working Mother* (December 1990):98-103

There's Room at the Inn. Dana Nadel. *Lear's* (December 1990):118-119

Tips on Trips. Caterina Muccia. *Family Circle* 103, No. 14 (October 16, 1990):174

Total Recoil: Babes at Sea. Peter Feibleman. *Lear's* (January 1990):27-29

Travel: Away with the Kids. Bibliography. *Essence* 21, No. 2 (June 1990):91-92

Travel: Best Fun, Best Buys for 1990. Bibliography. *Glamour* (January 1990):78-82

Travel. Bibliography. *Glamour* (October 1990):173-176

Travel: Checking Into Hotel Lust. Bibliography. Liz Logan. *Mademoiselle* (June 1990):68-72

Travel: Get-Smart Getaways. Bibliography. Anita Gates. *Essence* 21, No. 5 (September 1990):100-102

Travel: Hotels Made for Romance. Bibliography. *Glamour* (February 1990):114-117

Travel: Last Chance for Summer. Bibliography. Deborah Gaines. *Essence* 21, No. 4 (August 1990):97-98

Travel: Last Minute Summer. Richard Alleman. *Vogue* (July 1990):124-128

Travel: Medieval Magic. Francine Prose. *Savvy Woman* (July/August 1990):78-79

Travel: Scenes of Senegal. Sherley Anne Williams. *Essence* 20, No. 11 (March 1990):110-112

Travel: Spa Vacations. Dari Giles. *Essence* 20, No. 9 (January 1990):87-88+

Travel: The Best Country Inns for Fall Weekend Getaways. Bibliography. *Glamour* (September 1990):205-208

Travel: The Florida Fix. Rachel Urquhart and George Kalogerakis. *Vogue* (December 1990):220-226

Travel: The Great Train Robbery. Rachel Urquhart and others. *Vogue* (August 1990):246-256

Travel: The Inside Stuff. *Glamour* (April 1990):179-180

Travel: Trading Places. Bibliography. Marti Wilson. *Essence* 21, No. 3 (July 1990):94+

Travel: Vacations that Pay Off. Bibliography. *Glamour* (June 1990):171-180

Travel: Where to Chill Out. *Glamour* (July 1990):103-106

Travel Bazaar: Scene Stealers. Julie Moline. *Harper's Bazaar* (December 1990):90-96+

Travel News. Richard Alleman. *Vogue* (January 1990):140; (September 1990):476; (December 1990):228

25 Travel Tips. Elaine C. Ray. *Essence* 20, No. 12 (April 1990):96

Travel USA: Trips by Car. *Glamour* (April 1990):173-176

Women Travelers. Willie Mae Kneupper. *On the Issues* 15 (Summer 1990):24+

**Travel, Airline**

Getting the Most from Frequent-Flyer Programs. Joan Brightman. *Executive Female* 13, No. 5 (September-October 1990):24-25

**Travel – Exercise**

Air-Obics. Shelley Downing. *Women's Sports and Fitness* 12, No. 7 (October 1990):14

Good Sports: Take Your Workout on Vacation. Joanne Mattera. *Glamour* (September 1990):92

**Travel – Fashion**

Intense! *Mademoiselle* (December 1990):180-185

Traveling in Style. Debra Michals. *Harper's Bazaar* (July 1990):14-16

Tropical Coolers. *Harper's Bazaar* (November 1990):192-199

**Travel – Humor**

Now, Now, Voyager: A Traveler's Lament. Peter Feibleman. *Lear's* (June 1990):24-26

Total Recoil: Downstairs, Upstairs. Peter Feibleman. *Lear's* (February 1990):38-41

**Travel – Psychological Aspects**

Personal Journal. Bibliography. *Ladies' Home Journal* 107, No. 9 (September 1990):122-126

**Travel – Victorian Period**

Spinsters Abroad: Victorian Lady Explorers. By Dea Birkett. Reviewed by Sarah Graham-Brown. *Gender & History* 2, No. 3 (Autumn 1990):373-375

**Travel – Winter Season**

First Resorts. Marjorie McCloy. *Women's Sports and Fitness* 12, No. 7 (October 1990):47-51

**Travel Costs**

Finances of the Frequent Flyer. Maria Lenhart. *Executive Female* (May/June 1990):40-41

Secret of the Airlines. Edward Jay Epstein. *Lear's* (February 1990):26-30

Shopping Smart. Joan Hamburg. *Family Circle* 103, No. 9 (June 26, 1990):26-28

Trains: All Aboard for Romance. Bibliography. Carol Schatz. *Mademoiselle* (October 1990):76-78

Travel. Bibliography. *Glamour* (August 1990):143-152; (December 1990):143-146

Travel: How to Get $1,000 Worth of Vacation for $600. Bibliography. *Glamour* (May 1990):193-200

Travel: Paris: The European City You Can Afford. Bibliography. *Glamour* (March 1990):177-179

Travel: The Best of the Caribbean. Bibliography. *Glamour* (November 1990):153-154

A Wayfarer's Guide to the Dollar. Bibliography. Nancy Dunnan. *Lear's* (July 1990):26-27

Yes, You Can Afford to Go to Europe! Bibliography. Stephen Birnbaum. *Good Housekeeping* 211, No. 3 (September 1990):76-81

**Traveling Womens' Information Network.** *See* International Trade Policy

**Travis, Cheryl Brown**

Can Psychotherapists Hurt You? Book Review. *Psychology of Women Quarterly* 14, No. 1 (March 1990):148-149

**Treadwell, Sophie**

Machinal. Reviewed by Laura Flanders. *New Directions for Women* 19, No. 2 (March/April 1990):13

**Trebilcot, Joyce**

More Dyke Methods. *Hypatia* 5, No. 1 (Spring 1990):140-144

**Treishler, Paula A.** (joint author). *See* Dalsamo, Anne

**Trépanie4re, Diane** (interview)

Mèmoire, reconnaissance. Helge Dascher. *Canadian Women's Studies* 11, No. 1 (Spring 1990):75-77

**Trescott, Jacqueline** (joint author). *See* Gomez-Preston, Cheryl

**Trials (libel)**

Radio News Director to Collect $700,000 after Being Butt of Sex Jokes on Air. *Media Report to Women* 18, No. 2 (March/April 1990):3

**Triathalon**

Triathalon: A Training Schedule for Mortals. Mike Plant. *Women's Sports and Fitness* 12, No. 2 (March 1990):47-51

**Tribe, Laurence H.**

Abortion: The Clash of Absolutes. Reviewed by Diana Blackwell. *The Women's Review of Books* 7, No. 12 (September 1990):8-9

**Trimberger, E. Kay**

Best Friends and Marriage. Book Review. *The Women's Review of Books* 7, No. 5 (February 1990):10-11

With Friends Like These . . . *The Women's Review of Books* 7, No. 5 (February 1990):10-11

**Tripp, Kathleen**

Oakland Exposé: A Hunch Pays Off. *Ms.* 1, No. 3 (November/December 1990):90

**Trips.** *See* Travel

**Troemel-Ploetz, Senta**

Mileva Einstein-Maric: The Woman Who Did Einstein's Mathematics. *Women's Studies International Forum* 13, No. 5 (1990):415-432

**Troiano, Linda**

Good Health: Stomach Distress! *Redbook* 175, No. 4 (August 1990):32-34

**Tronto, Joan C.**

Women, Political Action, and Political Participation. Book Review. *NWSA Journal* 2, No. 3 (Summer 1990):492-495

Women and Power in American Politics. Book Review. *NWSA Journal* 2, No. 3 (Summer 1990):492-495

Women in the Judicial Process. Book Review. *NWSA Journal* 2, No. 3 (Summer 1990):492-495

Women's Movements: Organizing for Change. Book Review. *NWSA Journal* 2, No. 3 (Summer 1990):492-495

Women's Rights, Feminism, and Politics in the United States. Book Review. *NWSA Journal* 2, No. 3 (Summer 1990):492-495

**Trotter, Robbie**

Monkey Mountain Morning. Short Story. *Minerva* 8, No. 4 (Winter 1990):56-59

**Trotter, Sharland**

Knowing Herself: Women Tell Their Stories in Psychotherapy. Book Review. *The Women's Review of Books* 8, No. 3 (December 1990):20-21

Learning from Psychotherapy. *The Women's Review of Books* 8, No. 3 (December 1990):20-21

**Troubridge, Una** (about)

Cutting a Dash: The Dress of Radclyffe Hall and Una Troubridge. Katrina Rolley. *Feminist Review* No. 35 (Summer 1990):54-66

**Trouillot, Ertha Pascal** (about)

Madame la Présidente. Elizabeth Barad. *Ms.* 1, No. 1 (July/August 1990):13

**Trueba, Fernando**

The Mad Monkey. Reviewed by Sue Murphy. *Spare Rib* 219 (December 1990-January 1991):28

**Trump, Ivana** (about)

Donald and Ivana Trump: What Went Wrong? Cindy Adams. *Good Housekeeping* 210, No. 5 (May 1990):62-67

Ivana's Heartache. Glenn Plaskin. *Ladies' Home Journal* 107, No. 5 (May 1990):75-78+

**Trump, Ivana** (interview)

The Real Ivana. Vicki Woods. *Vogue* (May 1990):246-251, 324

**Trust (Psychology)**

Development or Restoration of Trust in Interpersonal Relationships during Adolescence and Beyond. Christina E. Mitchell. *Adolescence* 25, No. 100 (Winter 1990):847-854

How Could I Be So Blind? Roberta Grant. *Ladies' Home Journal* 107, No. 3 (March 1990):56-62

Just One Peek. Carol Lynn Mithers. *Glamour* (January 1990):160

**Trustram, Myna**

Women of the Regiment: Marriage and the Victorian Army. Reviewed by Dorothy O. Helly. *Women's Studies International Forum* 13, No. 4 (1990):405-407

**Trusts.** *See* Land Trusts

**Truth, Sojourner** (about)

Sojourner Truth in Life and Memory: Writing the Biography of an American Exotic. Nell Irvin Painter. *Gender & History* 2, No. 1 (Spring 1990):3-16

**Trzetrzelewska, Basia** (about). *See* Basia (about)

**Tsutakawa, Mayumi** (joint editor). *See* Lim, Shirley Goek-Lin

**Tu, Kuei-Shen** (joint author). *See* Gay, Janice Templeton

**Tuana, Nancy** (editor)

Feminism and Science. Reviewed by Vera Kolb. *Feminist Collections* 11, No. 4 (Summer 1990):4-8 '

**Tubectomy.** *See* Contraception – Tubal Sterilization

**Tuchman, Gaye** and Fortin, Nina E.

Edging Women Out: Victorian Novelists, Publishers, and Social Change. Reviewed by Gladys Engel Lang and Kurt Lang. *Gender and Society* 4, No. 4 (December 1990):556-558

Edging Women Out: Victorian Novelists, Publishers, and Social Change. Reviewed by Jane Nardin. *Gender and Society* 4, No. 4 (December 1990):558-561

**Tucker, Bonnie** (about). *See* Leadership, "Achieving Personal Best"

**Tucker, Heather**

Search for an Alternative. *Healthsharing* 11, No. 3 (June 1990):18-19

**Tucker, Herbert F.**

Abandoned Women and Poetic Tradition. Book Review. *Iris* 23 (Spring-Summer 1990):71-73

**Tucker, Judith**

Domestic Life in Palestine. Book Review. *Journal of Women's History* 2, No. 1 (Spring 1990):245-250

Letters from Egypt. Book Review. *Journal of Women's History* 2, No. 1 (Spring 1990):245-250

Traveling with the Ladies: Women's Travel Literature from the Nineteenth Century Middle East. *Journal of Women's History* 2, No. 1 (Spring 1990):245-250

**Tucker, M. Belinda** and Mitchell-Kernan, Claudia

New Trends in Black American Interracial Marriage: The Social Structural Context. *Journal of Marriage and the Family* 52, No. 1 (February 1990):209-218

**Tucker, M. Belinda** (joint author). *See* Taylor, Robert Joseph

**Tucker, Marcia** (joint author). *See* Rosen, Randy

**Tucker, Margaret** (joint author). *See* Lawrence, Jean

**Tucker, Sara W.**

Opportunities for Women: The Development of Professional Women's Medicine in Canton, China, 1879-1901. *Women's Studies International Forum* 13, No. 4 (1990):357-368

**Tucker, Susan**

Telling Memories Among Southern Women: Domestic Workers and Their Employers in the Segregated South. Reviewed by Shelley Crisp. *Belles Lettres* 5, No. 2 (Winter 1990):3

**Tuer, Dot**

Screens of Resistance: Feminism and Video Art. *Canadian Women's Studies* 11, No. 1 (Spring 1990):73-74

**Tufts, Heather**

Filmmakers Robin J. Hood and Penny Joy. *Canadian Women's Studies* 11, No. 1 (Spring 1990):94-96

**Tufts University**

100 Great Little Tips to Make Healthy Eating Easier. Stanley Gershoff and Catherine Whitney. *Redbook* 174, No. 6 (April 1990):120-133

**Tufts University School of Nutrition**

How Safe Is Our Food? Excerpt. *Ladies' Home Journal* 107, No. 6 (June 1990):168-173

**Tuggle, Denise**

People of Color at White Elitist Colleges. *Heresies* 25 (1990):62-65

**Tullar, Amber**

Life's High Spot. *Minerva* 8, No. 1 (Spring 1990):68-81

**Tully, Jo**

Women and National Liberation. *Spare Rib* 219 (December 1990-January 1991):48-51

**Tumors in Children**

The Baseball Kid Who Beat the Odds. Carolyn Tiner. *Redbook* 175, No. 4 (August 1990):36-38

**Tyagi, Amita** and Uberoi, Patricia

Adjustment Is the Key – Postmarital Romance in Indian Popular Fiction. *Manushi* 61 (November–December 1990):15-21

**Tyler, Edwina Lee**

Drum Drama. Reviewed by Jill Benderly. *On the Issues* 14 (1990):28

**Tynan, Kathleen** (about)

Lunch. Interview. Frances Lear. *Lear's* (January 1990):19-22

**Tyson, Cicely** (about). *See* De Veaux, Alexis, Milloy, Marilyn, and Ross, Michael Erik

**Tyzack, Margaret** (about). *See also* Great Britain – Culture

**Tzuriel, David** (joint author). *See* Bar-Joseph, Hanna

## U

**Ubell, Al** and Shulman, Label

How to De-Tox Your Water. *Family Circle* 103, No. 15 (November 6, 1990):33-36

Tools & Tips of the Trade. *Family Circle* 103, No. 13 (September 25, 1990):139

**Uberoi, Patricia** (joint author). *See* Tyagi, Amita

**Uchida, Yoshiko**

Picture Bride. Reviewed by Cathie Brettschneider. *Belles Lettres* 5, No. 3 (Spring 1990):20

**Udall, Sharyn R.**

Between Dream and Shadow: William Holman Hunt's Lady of Shalott. *Woman's Art Journal* 11, No. 1 (Spring-Summer 1990):34-38

**Uganda – Acquired Immune Deficiency Syndrome**

AIDS in Uganda as a Gender Issue. Mere Nakateregga Kisekka. *Women and Therapy* 10, No. 3 (1990):35-53

**Uganda – Sserulanda Spiritual Planetary Community**

Spiritual Journey. Beverly Weston and Bebe Moore Campbell. *Essence* 21, No. 6 (October 1990):94-96+

**Uhlenberg, Peter** (joint author). *See* Cooney, Teresa M.

**Ullman, Tracey** (about)

Tracey Untamed. Bonnie Allen. *Ms.* 1, No. 1 (July/August 1990):76

**Ullmann, Liv**

Viewpoint: We *Are* Good – Deep Down. *Glamour* (January 1990):70

**Ullmann, Liv** (about)

Women Who Make a Difference: Reaching Out to Refugees. Stephanie Abarbanel. *Family Circle* 103, No. 9 (June 26, 1990):15-20

**Ulrich, Laurel Thatcher**

A Midwife's Tale: The Life of Martha Ballard, Based on Her Diary, 1785-1812. Reviewed by Lynn Z. Bloom. *Belles Lettres* 6, No. 1 (Fall 1990):48-49

**Ultimo.** *See* Weinstein, Joan (about)

**Ultramarathons**

Running Circles Around the Boys. Bob Cooper. *Women's Sports and Fitness* 12, No. 3 (April 1990):62-65

**Underwood, Agnes**

Demise of Los Angeles Newspaper Prompts Reminiscences of Pioneer Woman Editor. *Media Report to Women* 18, No. 1 (January/February 1990):6

**Unemployment.** *See also* Employees, Dismissal of

Young Mother's Story: "We Count Our Blessings Every Day." Stephanie Sermuksnis. *Redbook* 176, No. 1 (November 1990):42-44

**Unfair Labor Practices.** *See* Pregnancy Discrimination

**Ungaro, Susan** and Evans, Linda Moran

Star Gazing. *Family Circle* 103, No. 7 (May 15, 1990):73-74

**Unger, Kay** (about)

Staying on Top. Sarah Stiansen. *Savvy Woman* (November 1990):54-55

**Unions.** *See* Labor Unions

**United Nations – Children**

World Summit for Children – Report from New York. Barbara Day. *Spare Rib* 218 (November 1990):46

**United Nations – Decade for Women, 1975-1985**

One World Women's Movement. By Chilla Bulbeck. Reviewed by Mamie E. Locke. *Women & Politics* 10, No. 4 (1990):135-136

Women in the World: 1975-1985, The Women's Decade. Edited by Lynne B. Iglitzin and Ruth Ross. Reviewed by Jane Bayes. *Women & Politics* 10, No. 3 (1990):125-127

**United Nations – Housing Rights**

Housing Language, Housing Reality? Pamela Sayne. *Canadian Women's Studies* 11, No. 2 (Fall 1990):6

**United Nations Committee on the Elimination of Discrimination Against Women (CEDAW)**

U.N. Appeals an International Crime Against Women. *Ms.* 1, No. 1 (July/August 1990):12-13

**United Nations Development Fund for Women (UNIFEM)**

Daughter of Warriors Aids World's Women. Charlotte Innes. *New Directions for Women* 19, No. 1 (January/February 1990):3

United Network for Organ Sharing. *See also* Organ Donors

**United States – Civil Service – History**

Ladies and Gentlemen of the Civil Service: Middle Class Workers in Victorian America. By Cindy Aron. Reviewed by Carole Elizabeth Adams. *Gender & History* 2, No. 3 (Autumn 1990):343-348

**United States – Economic Development**

Facing the Biggest Threat to the American Way of Life. Lester C. Thurow. *McCall's* 118, No. 3 (December 1990):61-62

**United States – Environmental Protection Agency.** *See also* Environmental Movement

**United States – Family Structure.** *See* Family Structure

**United States – History**

Born for Liberty: A History of Women in America. By Sara Evans. Reviewed by Jo Freeman. *New Directions for Women* 19, No. 2 (March/April 1990):20

Into One's Own: From Youth to Adulthood in the United States, 1920-1975. By John Modell. Reviewed by Jeylan T. Mortimer. *Journal of Marriage and the Family* 52, No. 2 (May 1990):561-562

Settlement Folk: Social Thought and the American Settlement Movement, 1885-1930. By Mina Carson. Reviewed by Gwendolyn Mink. *The Women's Review of Books* 7, No. 12 (September 1990):23-24

The Social Origins of Private Life: A History of American Families, 1600-1900. By Stephanie Coontz. Reviewed by Patricia Crawford. *Australian Feminist Studies* No. 12 (Summer 1990):131-132

The Sound of Our Own Voices: Women's Study Clubs, 1860-1910. By Theodora Penny Martin. Reviewed by Angela Howard Zophy. *Signs* 15, No. 2 (Winter 1990):410-411

**United States – History – Civil War (1861-1865)**

Anna Ella Carroll: Invisible Member of Lincoln's Cabinet. Benjamin L. Abramowitz. *Minerva* 8, No. 4 (Winter 1990):30-40

A Bandage in One Hand and a Bible in the Other: The Story of Captain Sally L. Tompkins (CSA). Patricia Paquette. *Minerva* 8, No. 2 (Summer 1990):47-54

Bonny Yank and Ginny Reb. C. Kay Larson. *Minerva* 8, No. 1 (Spring 1990):33-48

The Southern Side of "Glory": Mississippi African-American Women During the Civil War. Noralee Frankel. *Minerva* 8, No. 3 (Fall 1990):28-36

**United States – History – Civil War, 1861-1865**

Civil Wars: Women and the Crisis of Southern Nationalism. By George Rable. Reviewed by Jane E. Schultz. *The Women's Review of Books* 7, No. 8 (May 1990):23-24

**United States – History – Cross-Cultural Studies**

Unequal Sisters: A Multicultural Reader in U.S. Women's History. Edited by Ellen Carol DuBois and Vicki L. Ruiz. Reivewed by Beverly Guy-Sheftall. *Ms.* 1, No. 1 (July/August 1990):69

**United States – History – New Deal**

Discrimination Against Women in New Deal Work Programs. Nancy E. Rose. *AFFILIA* 5, No. 2 (Summer 1990):25-45

**United States – History – Revolution, 1775-1783.** *See also* United States Constitution – History

"I Have Don . . . Much to Carrey on the Warr": Women and the Shaping of Republican Ideology After the American Revolution. Linda K. Kerber. *Journal of Women's History* 1, No. 3 (Winter 1990):231-243

Women in the Age of the American Revolution. By Ronald Hoffman and Peter J. Albert. Reviewed by Elaine Forman Crane. *NWSA Journal* 2, No. 4 (Autumn 1990):661-664

**United States – Immigration**

The Christmas that Changed My Life. Katie Kelly. *McCall's* 118, No. 3 (December 1990):65-68+

**United States – International Relations – Great Britain**

Thick as Thieves: Britain and the US in the Gulf. Marcel Farry. *Spare Rib* No. 216 (September 1990):18-19

**United States – International Relations – Panama.** *See* Panama – Invasion

**United States – Labor Movement** . *See* Labor Unions; Working Class

**United States – Prostitution**

Incest and Juvenile Prostitution in the United States. *Women's World* , No. 24 (Winter 1990/91): 31

USA: Legalised Prostitution in Nevada. *Women's World* , No. 24 (Winter 1990/91): 40

**United States Air Force**

For God, Country and the Thrill of It. By Anne Noggle. Reviewed by Pat Pateman. *Minerva* 8, No. 2 (Summer 1990):73-74

Women Pilots in Combat: Attitudes of Male and Female Pilots. Patricia M. Shields, Landon Curry, and Janet Nichols. *Minerva* 8, No. 2 (Summer 1990):21-35

**United States Congress – Status of Women**

Washington Notes: "The Process Stinks." Miranda S. Spivack. *Ms.* 1, No. 2 (September/October 1990):91

**United States Constitution.** *See also* United States Supreme Court – Decisions

**United States Constitution – History**

The Columbian Patriot: Mercy Otis Warren and the Constitution. Larry M. Lane and Judith J. Lane. *Women & Politics* 10, No. 2 (1990):17-31

From Three-Fifths to Zero: Implications of the Constitution for African-American Women, 1787-1870. Mamie E. Locke. *Women & Politics* 10, No. 2 (1990):33-46

Women and the Constitution: A Bicentennial Perspective. Sandra Day O'Connor. *Women & Politics* 10, No. 2 (1990):5-16

**United States Constitution – 19th Amendment**

The Significance of the 19th Amendment: A New Look at Civil Rights, Social Welfare and Woman Suffrage in the Progressive Era. Eileen Lorenzi McDonagh. *Women & Politics* 10, No. 2 (1990):59-74

**United States Marine Corps**

The Spirit of Molly Marine. Erika S. Nau. *Minerva* 8, No. 4 (Winter 1990):23-29

**United States Military Academy**

Indomitable. By Ben Alvord Spiller. Reviewed by Lillian A. Pfluke and Abigail Herrly. *Minerva* 8, No. 1 (Spring 1990):83-86

**United States Supreme Court.** *See also* United States Constitution

Backtalk: The Supremes. Fred Siegel. *Lear's* (February 1990):126-127+

With Brennan Gone . . . Saving the Bill of Rights. Rhonda Copelon and Kathryn Kolbert. *Ms.* 1, No. 2 (September/October 1990):89

Justice Sandra Day O'Connor and the Supreme Court's Reaction to Its First Female Member. Karen O'Connor and Jeffrey A. Segal. *Women & Politics* 10, No. 2 (1990):95-104

Sex Discrimination and the Supreme Court: Implications for Women Faculty. Barbara A. Lee. *Women's Studies Quarterly* 18, Nos. 1-2 (Spring-Summer 1990):155-173

**United States Supreme Court – Civil Rights**

Working: What Have They Done for Us Lately? Linda Villarosa. *Essence* 21, No. 1 (May 1990):66-71

**United States Supreme Court – Decisions**

When Should Differences Make a Difference: A New Approach to the Constitutionality of Gender-Based Laws. Susan Gluck Mezey. *Women & Politics* 10, No. 2 (1990):105-119

**United States Supreme Court – Reproductive Rights**

Supreme Court: Double Trouble for Repro Rights? Miranda S. Spivack. *Ms.* 1, No. 3 (November/December 1990):89

**United States Surgeon General**

The Country Doctor. Leslie Phillips. *Savvy Woman* (July/August 1990):11-12

**Universities and Colleges.** *See also* Education, Single-Sex; Women's Colleges

Harassing the Harassers. Barbara Schulman. *The Women's Review of Books* 7, No. 5 (February 1990):27

Telling Our Stories: The Academy and Change. Judith L. Johnston. *Women's Studies Quarterly* 18, Nos. 3-4 (Fall-Winter 1990):119-126

**Universities and Colleges – Administration.** *See* College Presidents

**Universities and Colleges – Affirmative Action**

Educating the Majority: Women Challenge Tradition in Higher Education. Edited by Carol S. Pearson, Donna L. Shavlik, and Judith G. Touchton. Reviewed by Gloria Bowles. *NWSA Journal* 2, No. 2 (Spring 1990):288-290

**Universities and Colleges, Black – Administration**

The Association of Deans of Women and Advisers to Girls in Negro Schools, 1929-1954: A Brief Oral History. Hilda A. Davis and Patricia Bell-Scott. *Sage* 6, No. 1 (Summer 1989):40-44

**Universities and Colleges – Costs**

Education: Steps to Studying Smart. Bibliography. *Essence* 21, No. 6 (October 1990):36

The Opening of the American Mind. Bibliography. Nancy Dunnan. *Lear's* (November 1990):32-34

Parenting. *Essence* 20, No. 9 (January 1990):90

**Universities and Colleges – Curricula**

Changing Our Minds: Feminist Transformations of Knowledge. By Susan Hardy Aiken. Reviewed by Elizabeth Higginbotham. *NWSA Journal* 2, No. 1 (Winter 1990):105-111

Designing an Inclusive Curriculum: Bringing All Women into the Core. Elizabeth Higginbotham. *Women's Studies Quarterly* 18, Nos. 1-2 (Spring-Summer 1990):7-23

Integrating Issues of Gender, Race, and Ethnicity into Experimental Psychology and Other Social-Science Methodology Courses. Donna Crawley and Martha Ecker. *Women's Studies Quarterly* 18, Nos. 1-2 (Spring-Summer 1990):105-116

Notes on a Decade of Change. Susan R. Van Dyne. *NWSA Journal* 2, No. 2 (Spring 1990):245-253

Restructuring the Curriculum: Barriers and Bridges. Barbara Paige-Pointer and Gale Schroeder Auletta. *Women's Studies Quarterly* 18, Nos. 1-2 (Spring-Summer 1990):86-94

Teaching and Learning from the Heart. Estelle Disch and Becky Thompson. *NWSA Journal* 2, No. 1 (Winter 1990):68-78

Towson State University Community College Curriculum Transformation Project. Elaine Hedges, Sara Coulter, Myrna Goldenberg, and Gail Forman. *Women's Studies Quarterly* 18, Nos. 1-2 (Spring-Summer 1990):122-125

Transforming Introductory Anthropology: The American Anthropological Association Project on Gender and the Curriculum. Sandra Morgen and Mary Moran. *Women's Studies Quarterly* 18, Nos. 1-2 (Spring-Summer 1990):95-103

Transforming the Curriculum. Debra Humphreys. *NWSAction* 3, No. 4 (Winter 1990): 5-6

### Universities and Colleges – Faculty

Selective Rejection: How Students Perceive Women's Studies Teachers. Beth Hartung. *NWSA Journal* 2, No. 2 (Spring 1990):254-263

The Situation of Women Members in Scottish Universities: A Questionnaire Study. By Association of University Teachers (Scotland). Reviewed by Linda McKie. *Gender and Education* 2, No. 2 (1990):257-258

Women of Academe: Outsiders in the Sacred Grove. By Nadya Aisenberg and Mona Harrington. Reviewed by Joan C. Chrisler. *Feminist Teacher* 5, No. 2 (Fall 1990):37

Women of Academe: Outsiders in the Sacred Grove. By Nadya Aisenberg and Mona Harrington. Reviewed by Linda McKie. *Gender and Education* 2, No. 2 (1990):257-258

### Universities and Colleges – Financial Aid

Education: Financing Your College Dreams. Bibliography. *Essence* 20, No. 12 (April 1990):34

### Universities and Colleges – Graduate Degrees

Do You Need (or Want) a Master's Degree? Denise Harrison. *Glamour* (July 1990):76

### Universities and Colleges – History

Education Institutions or Extended Families? The Reconstruction of Gender in Women's Colleges in the Late Nineteenth and Early Twentieth Centuries. Elizabeth Edwards. *Gender and Education* 2, No. 1 (1990):17-35

### Universities and Colleges – Personal Narratives

Developing Political Savvy – Many Misadventures Later. Emily Toth. *Women's Studies Quarterly* 18, Nos. 3-4 (Fall-Winter 1990):147-151

Moving toward the Center. Libby Falk Jones. *Women's Studies Quarterly* 18, Nos. 3-4 (Fall-Winter 1990):128-134

Unaccompanied Ladies: Feminist, Italian, and in the Academy. Maurizia Boscagli. *Differences* 2, No. 3 (Fall 1990):122-135

### Universities and Colleges – Postgraduate Degrees

Your Brilliant Career: Back to Graduate School? Rebecca Sharp. *Mademoiselle* (October 1990):114

### Universities and Colleges – Racism

People of Color at White Elitist Colleges. Denise Tuggle. *Heresies* 25 (1990):62-65

### Universities and Colleges – Sexism

Changing the System: The Board of Trustees Caper. Ellen Messer-Davidow. *Women's Studies Quarterly* 18, Nos. 3-4 (Fall-Winter 1990):136-146

The Feminist Transformation of a University: A Case Study. Evelyn Torton Beck, Sandra C. Greer, Diana R. Jackson, and Betty Schmitz. *Women's Studies Quarterly* 18, Nos. 1-2 (Spring-Summer 1990):174-188

Investigation of Sexual Harassment Complaints. Helen Remick, Jan Salisbury, Donna Stringer, and Angela B. Ginorio. *Women's Studies Quarterly* 18, Nos. 1-2 (Spring-Summer 1990):207-220

The Minnesota Plan II: A Project to Improve the University Environment for Women Faculty, Administrators, and Academic Professional Staff. Janet D. Spector. *Women's Studies Quarterly* 18, Nos. 1-2 (Spring-Summer 1990):189-205

Power and Gender Issues in Academic Administration: A Study of Directors of BSW Programs. Karen V. Harper. *AFFILIA* 5, No. 1 (Spring 1990):81-93

Sex Discrimination and the Supreme Court: Implications for Women Faculty. Barbara A. Lee. *Women's Studies Quarterly* 18, Nos. 1-2 (Spring-Summer 1990):155-173

Sexual Harassment on Campus: Individual Differences in Attitudes and Beliefs. Natalie J. Malovich and Jayne E. Stake. *Psychology of Women Quarterly* 14, No. 1 (March 1990):63-81

### Universities and Colleges – Southern States

Maintaining the Spirit and Tone of Robust Manliness: The Battle Against Coeducation at Southern Colleges and Universities, 1890-1940. Amy Thompson McCandless. *NWSA Journal* 2, No. 2 (Spring 1990):199-216

### Universities and Colleges – Status of Women

Get Smart! A Woman's Guide to Equality on Campus. By Montana Katz and Veronica Vieland. Reviewed by M. Jane Ayer. *Feminist Collections* 11, No. 3 (Spring 1990):3-4

Get Smart! A Woman's Guide to Equality on the Campus. By Montana Katz and Veronica Vieland. Reviewed by Anne Flintoff. *Gender and Education* 2, No. 2 (1990):259

Women in Academe: Progress and Prospects. By Mariam K. Chamberlain. Reviewed by Therese L. Baker. *Gender and Society* 4, No. 2 (June 1990):277-281

Women of Academe: Outsiders in the Sacred Grove. By Nadya Aisenberg and Mona Harrington. Reviewed by Therese L. Baker. *Gender and Society* 4, No. 2 (June 1990):277-281

### Universities and Colleges – Violence

Responding to Violence on Campus. By Jan M. Sherill and Dorothy G. Siegel. Reviewed by Wendy

L. Ng. *NWSA Journal* 2, No. 4 (Autumn 1990):660-661

## University of Cincinnati

Changing the System: The Board of Trustees Caper. Ellen Messer-Davidow. *Women's Studies Quarterly* 18, Nos. 3-4 (Fall-Winter 1990):136-146

## University of Illinois – Sexual Assault

Media Exploit Pompon Squad. Paula Kamen. *New Directions for Women* 19, No. 3 (May/June 1990):16

## University of Maryland, College Park

The Feminist Transformation of a University: A Case Study. Evelyn Torton Beck, Sandra C. Greer, Diana R. Jackson, and Betty Schmitz. *Women's Studies Quarterly* 18, Nos. 1-2 (Spring-Summer 1990):174-188

## University of Minnesota

The Minnesota Plan II: A Project to Improve the University Environment for Women Faculty, Administrators, and Academic Professional Staff. Janet D. Spector. *Women's Studies Quarterly* 18, Nos. 1-2 (Spring-Summer 1990):189-205

## University of Minnesota – Center for Advanced Feminist Studies, Personal Narratives Group (editors)

Interpreting Women's Lives: Feminist Theory and Personal Narratives. Reviewed by Laura Weiss Zlogar. *Feminist Collections* 11, No. 3 (Spring 1990):7-8

## University of Montreal – Lepine Massacre

Canadian Massacre: It Was Political. Diana E. H. Russell and Jane Caputi. *New Directions for Women* 19, No. 2 (March/April 1990):17

## University of Wisconsin-Milwaukee – Center for Women's Studies

News for UW-Milwaukee. Jan Yoder. *Feminist Collections* 11, No. 2 (Winter 1990):19-20

**University Presidents.** *See* College Presidents

## Uno, Kathleen

Flowers in Salt: The Beginnings of Feminist Consciousness in Modern Japan. Book Review. *NWSA Journal* 2, No. 1 (Winter 1990):112-119

Reflections on the Way to the Gallows: Rebel Women in Prewar Japan. Book Review. *NWSA Journal* 2, No. 1 (Winter 1990):112-119

## Unwed Mothers – Cross-Cultural Studies

"Wake Up Little Susie": Single Pregnancy and Race in the Pre-*Roe v. Wade* Era. Rickie Solinger. *NWSA Journal* 2, No. 4 (Autumn 1990):682-683

## Upton, Lee

Generous Poetries. *Belles Lettres* 5, No. 3 (Spring 1990):24

Green the Witch-Hazel Wood. Book Review. *Belles Lettres* 5, No. 3 (Spring 1990):24-25

No Mercy. Reviewed by Enid Dame. *Belles Lettres* 5, No. 4 (Summer 1990):17

Perpetua. Book Review. *Belles Lettres* 5, No. 3 (Spring 1990):24-25

The Sourlands. Book Review. *Belles Lettres* 5, No. 3 (Spring 1990):24-25

Unfinished Painting. Book Review. *Belles Lettres* 5, No. 3 (Spring 1990):24-25

## Uptown String Quartet

Four to Jam. Judy Simmons. *Ms.* 1, No. 2 (September/October 1990):23

**Upward Mobility.** *See* Career Ladders

## Urban Areas – Cost of Living

Where to Live Like a Millionaire. Nathalie Kurylko. *Savvy Woman* (September 1990):52-53

## Urban Areas – Violence

Growing Up with Violence. Kathy Dobie. *Vogue* (December 1990):310-315 +

**Urban Living.** *See also* Community Life; Urban Areas – Cost of Living

Apartment Life, 1990. Katherine Ann Samon. *Mademoiselle* (April 1990):220-221, 256-259, 264

Talking Out of Town: Rotten to the Core. Tracy Young. *Vogue* (August 1990):382

A Taste for Southern Comfort. Moira Crone. *Savvy Woman* (September 1990):54-55 +

The Ten Best Small Cities for Women. G. Scott Thomas. *Savvy Woman* (September 1990):47-49

The Way I Want to Live. Barbara Flanagan. *Lear's* (October 1990):80-85

## Urban Poor – Employment

Work Pattern of Women and Its Impact on Health and Nutrition. M. E. Khan, A. K. Tamang, and Bella C. Patel. *Journal of Family Welfare* 36, No. 2 (June 1990):3-22

**Uribe, Victor M.** (joint author). *See* Masserman, Jules H.

## Urinary Tract Infections

The After-Sex Pill. Mary Jo Schnatter. *McCall's* 118, No. 3 (December 1990):26

Health & Fitness. Bibliography. Stephanie Young. *Glamour* (July 1990):31-39

## Urla, Jackie

Language, Gender, and Sex in Comparative Perspective. Book review. *Signs* 15, No. 2 (Winter 1990):412-414

## Urquhart, Rachel

Fitness. *Vogue* (August 1990):191-200

Toying with Art. *Vogue* (April 1990):382-388, 420

**Urquhart, Rachel** and Kalogerakis, George

Travel: The Florida Fix. *Vogue* (December 1990):220-226

**Urquhart, Rachel** and others

Travel: The Great Train Robbery. *Vogue* (August 1990):246-256

**Useche, Bernardo,** Villegas, Magdalena, and Alzate, Heli

Sexual Behavior of Colombian High School Students. *Adolescence* 25, No. 98 (Summer 1990):291-304

**Usherwood, Paul**

Elizabeth Thompson Butler: A Case of Tokenism. *Woman's Art Journal* 11, No. 2 (Fall 1990-Winter 1991):14-18

**Ussher, Jane M.**

The Psychology of the Female Body. Reviewed by Lorelei Cederstrom. *Resources for Feminist Research* 19, No. 1 (March 1990):30-31

The Psychology of the Female Body. Reviewed by Roe Sybylla. *Australian Feminist Studies* No. 11 (Autumn 1990):129-131

**Uszkurat, Carol Ann**

Short Story. *Spare Rib* No. 209 (February 1990):38-39

**Uterine Fibroids.** *See* Leiomyoma uteri

**Utne, Birgit Brock**

Feminist Perspectives on Peace and Education. Reviewed by Deborah Jordan. *Australian Feminist Studies* No. 11 (Autumn 1990):127-128

**Utopian Fiction.** *See* Science Fiction

# V

**Vacation Exchanges.** *See* Home Exchanging

**Vacation Homes.** *See* Second Homes

**Vacations.** *See also* Health Resorts, Watering Places, etc.; Honeymoons; *particular countries*; Single Women – Vacations; Travel

Dress for Recess. *Savvy Woman* (July/August 1990):70-77

Get Up and Go. Dinah B. Witchel. *Family Circle* 103, No. 3 (February 20, 1990):N.P.

Get Up and Go. Gay Nagle Myers. *Family Circle* 103, No. 4 (March 13, 1990):N.P.

Travel: Best Fun, Best Buys for 1990. Bibliography. *Glamour* (January 1990):78-82

Travel: Last Minute Summer. Richard Alleman. *Vogue* (July 1990):124-128

Travel: The Inside Stuff. *Glamour* (April 1990):179-180

**Vacchiano, Jennifer**

Trip to the City (from my point of view). Short Story. *Women's Studies Quarterly* 18, Nos. 3-4 (Fall-Winter 1990):165-167

**Vaccination, Infant**

Managerial Skills: A Need for Effective Vaccination Coverage. P. L. Joshi, M. Bhattacharya and B. Raj. *Journal of Family Welfare* 36, No. 2 (June 1990):43-49

Yukon Vaccination Update. Lorene Benoit. *Healthsharing* 11, No. 2 (March 1990):7

**Vachon, Jane Mattern**

The Gift of Memories. *Ladies' Home Journal* 107, No. 12 (December 1990):78-79

**Vaid, Sudesh** (joint editor). *See* Sangari, KumKum

**Vaid, Urvashi**

Out of the Closet and Into the Fray: Should Gay Politicians and Celebrities Be Forced to "Come Out"? *On the Issues* 16 (Fall 1990):24+

**Vaillant, Caroline O.** (joint author). *See* Vaillant, George E.

**Vaillant, George E.** and Vaillant, Caroline O.

Determinants and Consequences of Creativity in a Cohort of Gifted Women. *Psychology of Women Quarterly* 14, No. 4 (December 1990):607-616

**Valdez (Alaska) – Oil Spill**

White Silk and Black Tar: A Journal of the Alaska Oil Spill. By Page Spencer. Reviewed by Paula DiPerna. *The Women's Review of Books* 7, No. 12 (September 1990):19-20

**Valdez (Alaska) – Oil Spills**

Valdez: How One Family Weathered the Storm. Linden Gross. *Ladies' Home Journal* 107, No. 4 (April 1990):164+

**Valdivia, Angharad N.**

Women-Centered Media Communications within Nicaragua. *Women & Language* 13, No. 1 (Fall 1990):59-63

**Valdivieso, Mercedes**

Breakthrough. Reviewed by Barbara Benham. *Belles Lettres* 5, No. 2 (Winter 1990):18

**Valentine, Sarah** (joint editor). *See* Penelope, Julia

**Valle, Norma**

When Does a Law Work Too Well? *Connexions* 34 (1990):20-21

**Vallely, Bernadette**

The Dark Side of White. *Healthsharing* 11, No. 3 (June 1990):8

**Values**

Lend a Helping Hand. Benjamin Spock. *Redbook* 176, No. 2 (December 1990):30

Me! Me! Me! Me! Me! Jeanne Marie Laskas. *Glamour* (April 1990):296-297+

Raising Kids with Good Values: 10 Golden Rules. Beverly Feldman. *Redbook* 176, No. 1 (November 1990):116-120

Viewpoint: We *Are* Good–Deep Down. Liv Ullmann. *Glamour* (January 1990):70

Young Mother's Story: "But for the Grace of God." Deborah Schall and Lorene Hanley Duquin. *Redbook* 176, No. 2 (December 1990):74-80

**Valverde, Mariana**

Revelations: Essays on Striptease and Sexuality. Book Review. *Atlantis* 15, No. 2 (Spring 1990):115

**Vammen, Tinne**

Modern English Auto/Biography and Gender: Introduction. *Gender & History* 2, No. 1 (Spring 1990):17-21

**Van Bockern, Steve** (joint author). *See* Brendtro, Larry K.

**Vance, Danitra**

An Interpretation of Performance Art. *Woman of Power* 17 (Summer 1990):44-46

**Vance, Linda**

Ecological Revolutions: Nature, Gender and Science in New England. Book Review. *The Women's Review of Books* 7, No. 4 (January 1990):14-15

Healing the Wounds: The Promise of Ecofeminism. Book Review. *NWSA Journal* 2, No. 3 (Summer 1990):485-489

Learning from the Land. *The Women's Review of Books* 7, No. 4 (January 1990):14-15

Rape of the Wild: Man's Violence Against Animals and the Earth. Book Review. *NWSA Journal* 2, No. 3 (Summer 1990):485-489

The Recurring Silent Spring. Book Review. *NWSA Journal* 2, No. 3 (Summer 1990):485-489

Staying Alive: Women, Ecology and Development. Book Review. *NWSA Journal* 2, No. 3 (Summer 1990):485-489

**Vance, Sherra D.** (joint author). *See* Cooper, Carolyn S.

**Van de Pol, Lotte C.** (joint author). *See* Dekker, Rudolf M.

**Vanderpool, Nathalie Akin** (about)

Making the Grade. Jane Howard. *Lear's* (November 1990):150-154

**Van De Velde, Christine K.**

An Eastern Solution to the Western Waist. *Savvy Woman* (July/August 1990):30-35

**Vandross, Luther** (about)

Luther Here and Now. David Ritz. *Essence* 21, No. 7 (November 1990):66-68+

**Van Dyne, Susan R.**

Notes on a Decade of Change. *NWSA Journal* 2, No. 2 (Spring 1990):245-253

**Vaness, Carol** (about). *See also* New York (City) – Metropolitan Opera

**Van Falkenburg, Carole** and Dall, Christie (producers)

Wild Women Don't Have the Blues. Reviewed by Lynn Wenzel. *New Directions for Women* 19, No. 3 (May/June 1990):9

**Van Gelder, Lindsy**

The Importance of Being Eleven. *Ms.* 1, No. 1 (July/August 1990):77-79

**Van Gerven, Claudia**

Artemis-Callisto: She Is Not Afraid. Poem. *Frontiers* 11, Nos. 2-3 (1990):59-60

How to Write a Love Poem: Instructions for Dr. Williams. Poem. *Frontiers* 11, Nos. 2-3 (1990):62-64

She Has Taken Up Writing. Poem. *Frontiers* 11, Nos. 2-3 (1990):65

The Spirit String. Poem. *Frontiers* 11, Nos. 2-3 (1990):61

**Van Hook, Bailey**

"Milk White Angels of Art": Images of Women in Turn-of-the-Century America. *Woman's Art Journal* 11, No. 2 (Fall 1990-Winter 1991):23-29

**Vanita, Ruth**

Hero Hiralal. Film Review. *Manushi* 61 (November-December 1990):44

Pestonjee. Film Review. *Manushi* 60 (September-October 1990):44

The Special Marriage Act: Not Special Enough. *Manushi* 58 (May-June 1990):14-21

**Vanita, Ruth** (joint author). *See* Kishwar, Madhu

**Vanity.** *See* Narcissism

**Van Kirk, Carol**

Lesbian Ethics: Toward New Value. Book Review. *Hypatia* 5, No. 3 (Fall 1990):147-152

Sarah Lucia Hoagland's *Lesbian Ethics: Toward New Value* and Ablemindism. *Hypatia* 5, No. 3 (Fall 1990):147-152

**Van Lokeren, Ronnie** (about)

A Woman for Lear's: Devotions. Jane Howard. *Lear's* (December 1990):128-131

**Van Meter, Jonathan**

Images: Bottled Fantasy. *Vogue* (September 1990):342-344

Pretty Woman. *Vogue* (October 1990):347+

Tale of a Twisted Sister. *Harper's Bazaar* (February 1990):63

Talking Fashion. *Vogue* (September 1990):631-650

The Sexual Politics of Meat: A Feminist-Vegetarian Critical Theory. By Carol J. Adams. Reviewed by Bettyann Kevles. *The Women's Review of Books* 7, No. 8 (May 1990):11-12

**Veillette, Denise**

La fin du mariage? jeunes couples des annees' 80. Book Review. *Resources for Feminist Research* 19, No. 1 (March 1990):15-16

**Velasquez, Sylvia**

Tie Me Up! Tie Me Down! Film Review. *Spare Rib* No. 216 (September 1990):32

**Vellacott, Jo**

The Long Road to Greenham: Feminism and Anti-Militarism in Britain since 1820. Book Review. *Resources for Feminist Research* 19, No. 2 (June 1990):44

**Vendela** (about)

Model Homes. *Harper's Bazaar* (November 1990):158-163+

**Vengasayi, Dolly** and Matopodzi, Saliwe

Zimbabwe: Opposing Violence. *off our backs* 20, No. 7 (July 1990):9

**Venice – Inquisition – History**

Witchcraft and the Inquisition in Venice, 1550-1650. By Ruth Martin. Reviewed by Carol F. Karlsen. *Gender & History* 2, No. 3 (Autumn 1990):354-356

**Venice – Travel**

Venetian Holiday. *Vogue* (December 1990):248-263

**Veno, Aro**

Baccalà. Poem. *Sinister Wisdom* 41 (Summer-Fall 1990):120

**Venture Capitalists**. *See* Financial Occupations

**Verbal Abuse**

Back Talk: Eat Those Dirty Words! Julianne Malveaux. *Essence* 20, No. 11 (March 1990):146

**Verbal Communication**. *See also* Communication; Public Speaking

Say the Magic Words. Laurel Touby. *Working Woman* (November 1990):120+

**Verey, Rosemary**

The Scented Garden: Choosing, Growing and Using the Plants that Bring Fragrance to Your Life, Home and Table. Reviewed by D. S. Oliver. *The Women's Review of Books* 7, No. 6 (March 1990):21-22

**Verma, Gajendra K.** (editor)

Education for All: A Landmark in Pluralism. Reviewed by Gill Crozier. *Gender and Education* 2, No. 3 (1990):368-369

**Verma, J.** (joint author). *See* Sachar, R. K.

**Vermont – Christmas**

One Magic Christmas. *Family Circle* 103, No. 17 (December 18, 1990):94-103

**Vernon, JoEtta A.**, Williams, J. Allen, Jr., Phillips, Terri, and Wilson, Janet

Media Stereotyping: A Comparison of the Way Elderly Women and Men Are Portrayed on Prime-Time Television. *Journal of Women and Aging* 2, No. 4 (1990):55-68

**Verrill-Rhys, Leigh** (editor)

On My Life: Women's Writing from Wales. Reviewed by Penny Simpson. *Spare Rib* 213 (June 1990):29

**Versace, Gianni** (about). *See* Talley, André Leon

The Kings of Color: Versace. Julia Reed. *Vogue* (September 1990):542-545

**Verthuy, Mai3r**

Muse de la raison. Book Review. *Resources for Feminist Research* 19, No. 1 (March 1990):25

**Vertinsky, Patricia A.** (joint author). *See* O'Brien, Sandra J.

**Viazzo, Pier Paolo** and Albera, Dionigi

The Peasant Family in Northern Italy, 1750-1930: A Reassessment. *Journal of Family History* 15, No. 4 (October 1990):461-482

**Vicinus, Martha**

Fantastic Women: Sex, Gender and Transvestism. Book Review. *The Women's Review of Books* 7, No. 9 (June 1990):26

TV Guide. *The Women's Review of Books* 7, No. 9 (June 1990):26

**Victim, Woman as**

"Basic Victim Positions" and the Women in Margaret Atwood's *The Handmaid's Tale*. Michael Foley. *Atlantis* 15, No. 2 (Spring 1990):50-58

**Victimization Concept**

Diversifying Feminist Theory and Practice: Broadening the Concept of Victimization. Lynne Bravo Rosewater. *Women and Therapy* 9, No. 3 (1990):299-311

Oppression and Victimization; Choice and Responsibility. Susan Wendell. *Hypatia* 5, No. 3 (Fall 1990):15-46

**Victorian Silver Plate**. *See* Silver-Plated Ware, Victorian

**Video Cameras**

On Screen: Lights! Camera! Action! Eric Burns. *Family Circle* 103, No. 17 (December 18, 1990):152

**Video Display Terminals**. *See also* Electromagnetic Waves

How to Rid Your Company of VDT Health Hazards. Shirley Chan. *Working Woman* (March 1990):52

## Video Games

Full Circle: Vidiot Box. Tricia Tunstall. *Family Circle* 103, No. 16 (November 27, 1990):146

**Video Reviews**. *See also* Exercise Videos

Abortion Denied: Shattering Young Women's Lives. *Ms.* 1, No. 2 (September/October 1990):90

Big Night Out. *See* Greig, David

Dispatches: The AIDS Catch. *See* Shenton, Joan

A Feminist in the Video Store. *Ms.* 1, No. 2 (September/October 1990):24

Hush-a-Bye Baby. *See* Harkin, Margo

Positive Images: Portraits of Women with Disabilities. *See* Harrison, Julie

A State of Danger. *See* Bresheet, Haim

There's Something About a Convent Girl . .. *See* Bamboo Productions

Through the Wire. *See* Daedalus Productions

Wild Women Don't Have the Blues. *See* Van Falkenburg, Carole

Women HIV and AIDS: Speaking Out in the UK. *See* Hummingbird Films

## Videos

On Screen. Eric Burns. *Family Circle* 103, No. 3 (February 20, 1990):101+; 103, No. 17 (September 4, 1990):153-154

Video: The New Family Fix. Katherine Barrett and Richard Greene. *Ladies' Home Journal* 107, No. 2 (February 1990):118-120+

## Videos – Festivals

Women's Video Festival to Reach National Audience in April. *Media Report to Women* 18, No. 2 (March/April 1990):7

## Videos for Children

On Screen: The New Videos. Eric Burns. *Family Circle* 103, No. 16 (November 27, 1990):121

**Vieland, Veronica** (joint author). *See* Katz, Montana

## Vienne, Véronique

Is Your Office an Erogenous Zone? *Savvy* (December-January 1991):60-63

## Vietnam – Amerasian Children

The Christmas that Changed My Life. Katie Kelly. *McCall's* 118, No. 3 (December 1990):65-68+

## Vietnam – Women's Health

Dioxin Levels in Adipose Tissues of Hospitalized Women Living in the South of Vietnam in 1984-89. Nguyen Thi Ngoc Phuong, Bui Sy Hung, Arnold Schechter, and Dan Quoc Vu. *Women's Health* 16, No. 1 (1990):79-93

## Vietnamese Conflict, 1961-1975 – Films

Surname Viet Given Name Nam. Directed by Trinh T. Minh-ha. Reviewed by Marina Heung. *New Directions for Women* 19, No. 1 (January/February 1990):11

Virulent Machismo Rampant in Vietnam War Films. Cindy Fuchs. *New Directions for Women* 19, No. 1 (January/February 1990):10

## Vietnamese Conflict, 1961-1975 – Women's Experience

American Women Writers on Vietnam: Unheard Voices: A Selected Annotated Bibliography. By Deborah A. Butler. Review. *Feminist Collections* 11, No. 3 (Spring 1990):14

1964: Vietnam and Army Nursing. Dretha M. Emo, Sharon Hall, and Darlene Kern. *Minerva* 8, No. 1 (Spring 1990):49-67

Recovering from the War. By Patience Mason. Reviewed by Susanne Carter. *Minerva* 8, No. 3 (Fall 1990):73-77

Vietnam Wives. By Aphrodite Matsakis. By Aphrodite Matsakis. Reviewed by Susanne Carter. *Minerva* 8, No. 3 (Fall 1990):73-77

## Vigier, Rachel

Educating the Body. *Heresies* 25 (1990):78-79

## Vijayan, Aleyamma

Struggling with Hope: The Story of Women Fish Vendors of South Kerala. *Manushi* 61 (November-December 1990):9-11

## Villarosa, Linda

Horizons: New Age Rage. *Essence* 20, No. 9 (January 1990):25

Prevention: The Angry Heart. *Essence* 20, No. 12 (April 1990):26-28

Working: What Have They Done for Us Lately? *Essence* 21, No. 1 (May 1990):66-71

**Villegas, Magdalena** (joint author). *See* Useche, Bernardo

**Vincent, Gérard** (joint editor). *See* Prost, Antoine

## Violato, Claudio and Wiley, Arthur J.

Images of Adolescence in English Literature: The Middle Ages to the Modern Period. *Adolescence* 25, No. 98 (Summer 1990):253-264

**Violence Against Women**. *See also* Abused Wives; Crime Victims; Disabled, Violence Against; India – Violence Against Women; Latin American Women – Violence; Men – Psychology; Music – Rap; Pornography; Sex Crimes; Sexual Assault; South Africa – Violence Against Women

Basic Feminist Lessons: Man-hating. Carolyn Gammon. *off our backs* 20, No. 3 (March 1990):25

Battered Women Are Strong, Wise. Pat Gowens. *off our backs* 20, No. 1 (January 1990):15+

A Case Study of Battered Women's Shelters in Appalachia. Karen W. Tice. *AFFILIA* 5, No. 3 (Fall 1990):83-100

Central American Women: Battered in USA. Carol Anne Douglas. *off our backs* 20, No. 5 (May 1990):3+

The Centre of the Backlash – Montreal. Joan Baril. *off our backs* 20, No. 4 (April 1990):13-15

The City for Women: No Safe Place. Linda MacLeod. *Women and Environments* 12, No. 1 (Fall 1989/Winter 1990): 6-7

Clearinghouse on Femicide Set Up. Joyoti Grech. *Spare Rib* 219 (December 1990-January 1991):69

Discourses of Sexual Violation in Mythic Accounts and Dramatic Versions of "The Girl's Tragedy." Adele Scafuro. *Differences* 2, No. 1 (Spring 1990):126-159

Dowry Death. Steve Lerner and Mary Ellin Barrett. *Lear's* (May 1990):98-101+

Ending the Rape of Our Liberty. Bibliography. Christine Doudna. *McCall's* 117, No. 8 (May 1990):94-100

Enter Password: Recovery. By Elly Bulkin. Reviewed by Susanna Sturgis. *off our backs* 20, No. 7 (July 1990):12

The Female Fear. By Margaret T. Gordon and Stephanie Riger. Reviewed by Karen Merriam. *AFFILIA* 5, No. 3 (Fall 1990):114-115

"Femicide": Speaking the Unspeakable. Jane Caputi and Diana E. H. Russell. *Ms.* 1, No. 2 (September/October 1990):34-37

Feminist Perspectives on Wife Abuse. Edited by K. Yllö and M. Bograd. Reviewed by Lorraine M. Gutiérrez. *AFFILIA* 5, No. 1 (Spring 1990):119-120

Florida Killer Brings Both Fear and Organizing. Kathy Freeperson. *off our backs* 20, No. 9 (October 1990):2-3

Fourteen Women Killed in Montreal. Jacquie Monthorne. *off our backs* 20, No. 1 (January 1990):1+

Fraternities of Fear: Gang Rape, Male Bonding, and the Silencing of Women. Kathleen Hirsch. *Ms.* 1, No. 2 (September/October 1990):52-56

Frontiers of the Imagination: Women, History, and Nature. Irene Diamond and Lisa Kuppler. *Journal of Women's History* 1, No. 3 (Winter 1990):160-180

Gender and Society. Reviewed by Carol Anne Douglas. *off our backs* 20, No. 6 (June 1990):17

A Hidden Struggle: Black Women and Violence. Amina Mama. *Spare Rib* No. 209 (February 1990):8-11

The High Park Safety Audit. *Women and Environments* 12, No. 1 (Fall 1989/Winter 1990): 12

Killing Women: Response to Increased Gender Equality? Rosemary Gartner. *Women and Environments* 12, No. 1 (Fall 1989/Winter 1990): 14-16

Lesbian Violence, Lesbian Victims: How to Identify Battering in Relationships. Lee Evans and Shelley Bannister. *Lesbian Ethics* 4, No. 1 (Spring 1990): 52-65

Like Committing Crimes, and You? Burcu Oxdemir. *off our backs* 20, No. 3 (March 1990):24

"Madam, May I Have a Word with You?" Eira Patnaik. *Sage* 6, No. 1 (Summer 1989):66

A Matter of Life and Death: The Case of Karanjit Ahluwalia. *Spare Rib* No. 214 (July 1990):19-21

Men, Power and the Exploitation of Women. Jalna Hanmer. *Women's Studies International Forum* 13, No. 5 (1990):443-456

Men Who Are Joining the Fight Against Rape. Christina Ferrari. *McCall's* 118, No. 3 (December 1990):71-74+

METRAC: A Catalyst for Change. *Women and Environments* 12, No. 1 (Fall 1989/Winter 1990): 4-5

Montreal Gynocide. Joanne Stato. *off our backs* 20, No. 1 (January 1990):1

Montreal Massacre Mobilizes Women Across Canada. Karen Herland. *Healthsharing* 11, No. 2 (March 1990):5

Moving Forward on Public Transit. *Women and Environments* 12, No. 1 (Fall 1989/Winter 1990): 10-11

A New Way of Looking at Violence Against Women. Lisa Heinzerling. *Glamour* (October 1990):112

No Way Out. Bibliography. Samme Chittum, Mark Bauman, and Irene Nyborg-Andersen. *Ladies' Home Journal* 107, No. 4 (April 1990):126-134

One Woman's Journey: Getting Ready to Fight Back. Norah Fraser. *off our backs* 20, No. 3 (March 1990):25+

The Politics of Violence. Charlotte Bunch. *On the Issues* 16 (Fall 1990):25

Pornography and Social Policy: Three Feminist Approaches. Barbara G. Collins. *AFFILIA* 5, No. 4 (Winter 1990):8-26

Prevention: Fighting Chance. E. K. Daufin. *Essence* 20, No. 10 (February 1990):27-29

Readers Speak Out: "Get Tougher on Rapists." *Redbook* 175, No. 6 (October 1990):160

Response to Graffiti: Death Is Not the Answer. Carol Anne Douglas. *off our backs* 20, No. 6 (June 1990):16

Response to Graffiti: The Writing on the Wall. Angela Johnson. *off our backs* 20, No. 6 (June 1990):14-15

A Safe World for Us All. Barbara Cowan. *Women and Environments* 12, No. 1 (Fall 1989/Winter 1990): 9

Sex . . . Violence . . . Rite of Passage? Erika Munk. *Lear's* (November 1990):112-115+

Sharing Stories: Saving Lives. Judy Baker Fronefield. *Women's Studies Quarterly* 18, Nos. 3-4 (Fall-Winter 1990):168-170

Tell Us What You Think: Violent Crime on the Rise. *Glamour* (December 1990):136

The Toronto Safe City Committee. Carolyn Whitzman. *Women and Environments* 12, No. 1 (Fall 1989/Winter 1990): 13

12 Steps Down: The Road From Recovery. Shana R. Blessing. *off our backs* 20, No. 4 (April 1990):19

Up Front. *Ladies' Home Journal* 107, No. 9 (September 1990):147-152

Victim of Family Conspiracy: The Abduction of Farah. *Manushi* 56 (January-February 1990):11-13

Violence Against Women. Nadipha Ngcobo. *Women in Action* 1-2 (1990):25-26

Violence Against Women and the Ongoing Challenge to Racism. By Angela Y. Davis. Reviewed by Jacqueline E. Wade. *NWSA Journal* 2, No. 2 (Spring 1990):315-319

Violence Increases After Earthquake. Kore Archer. *off our backs* 20, No. 3 (March 1990):15

"We Are More Than Fourteen": Montreal Mass Femicide. Chris Domingo. *off our backs* 20, No. 2 (February 1990):10-11

When Love Turns Violent. Debra Lewis. *Glamour* (August 1990):234-235

"Why Should Women Be Engineers When Men Can't?" Mona Forrest. *off our backs* 20, No. 1 (January 1990):6

Women's Safety Audits Move Into the Streets of Metro Toronto. *Women and Environments* 12, No. 1 (Fall 1989/Winter 1990): 8-9

Women Taking Space. *Women and Environments* 12, No. 1 (Fall 1989/Winter 1990): 5

Young But Not Innocent. Beth Weinhouse. *Redbook* 174, No. 6 (April 1990):135-139

**Violence Against Women – African-Americans**
The Next Wave. Helen Zia. *Ms.* 1, No. 2 (September/October 1990):48

**Violence Against Women – Cultural Defense**
Culture: A Refuge for Murder. Barbara Findlen. *Ms.* 1, No. 2 (September/October 1990):47

**Violence Against Women – History**
The Helen Jewett Murder: Violence, Gender, and Sexual Licentiousness in Antebellum America. Patricia Cline Cohen. *NWSA Journal* 2, No. 3 (Summer 1990):374-389

**Violence Against Women – Law and Legislation**
Double Jeopardy, Double Courage. Mary Suh. *Ms.* 1, No. 2 (September/October 1990):46

Fighting Straight Hate. Helen Zia. *Ms.* 1, No. 2 (September/October 1990):47

On the Legislative Front. Katie Monagle. *Ms.* 1, No. 2 (September/October 1990):45

US: Women Excluded from Hate Crimes Bill. *Spare Rib* No. 216 (September 1990):47

**Violence Against Women – Personal Narratives**
A Day in the Life. Rita Jensen. *Ms.* 1, No. 2 (September/October 1990):38-41

Delusions of Safety. Marcia Ann Gillespie. *Ms.* 1, No. 2 (September/October 1990):49-51

**Violence Against Women – Resources**
Group Profiles. Caroline Marrs. *Women in Action* 1-2 (1990):26-30

**Violence in the Media**
Hooked on Hate? Kathi Maio. *Ms.* 1, No. 2 (September/October 1990):42-44

Lynching Women. Diana Hume George. *Ms.* 1, No. 3 (November/December 1990):58-60

Miller's Crossing. By Joel Coen and Ethan Coen. Reviewed by Ron Rosenbaum. *Mademoiselle* (October 1990):98-101

Violence at the Movies. Brook Hersey. *Glamour* (September 1990):218

**Violinists**
A Plucky Prodigy. Margy Rochlin. *Harper's Bazaar* (February 1990):58

**Viorst, Judith**
Brainy, Beautiful & Blond. *Redbook* 175, No. 6 (October 1990):122-126

Earrings! Poem. *McCall's* 117, No. 11 (August 1990):90-91

Honor Thy Marriage (and Anniversary). *Redbook* 175, No. 2 (June 1990):48-51

Marriage & Humor – a Perfect Union. *Redbook* 175, No. 5 (September 1990):72-74

Tales from the Delivery Room. *Redbook* 174, No. 6 (April 1990):58-62

Weddings that Made Me Laugh & Cry. *Redbook* 175, No. 3 (July 1990):18-20

What Kids Say (When They Think You're Not Listening). *Redbook* 174, No. 5 (March 1990):42-45

What Makes a Woman Charming? *Redbook* 176, No. 1 (November 1990):84-87

What's the Best Advice You Can Give New Moms? *Redbook* 175, No. 1 (May 1990):40-43

**Viramontes, Helena María** (joint editor). *See* Sobek, María Herrera

**Virginia Festival of American Film, 1989**

Politics, Perseverance, and Passion from Hollywood. Anne Bromley. *Iris* 23 (Spring-Summer 1990):56-57

**Virgin Islands (G.B.) – Politics and Government**

Interiors: Is Your Hair Still Political? Audre Lorde. *Essence* 21, No. 5 (September 1990):40+

**Virgin Mary**

Salve Regina: Salvaging the Queen. Patricia Monaghan. *Woman of Power* 15 (Fall-Winter 1990):46

**Visions of Morality Scale (VMS)**

In Search of an Everyday Morality: The Development of a Measure. Charles M. Shelton and Dan P. McAdams. *Adolescence* 25, No. 100 (Winter 1990):923-943

**Vital Statistics**

Update: News, Trends, and Vital Statistics About Women. *Executive Female* (March/April 1990):8-10; (May/June 1990):20

**Vitamins**

Nutrinews. Densie Webb. *Ladies' Home Journal* 107, No. 10 (October 1990):210-212

**Vitamin Therapy.** *See also* Immune System

Can't Sleep? Tired? Tense? Peter J. Hauri and Shirley Linde. *Redbook* 175, No. 1 (May 1990):156-163

Diet Q & A. *Mademoiselle* (February 1990):198

Nutrition Now: 7 Vitamins & Minerals Women Need Most. Mona Sue Boyd. *Redbook* 175, No. 4 (August 1990):124-130

**Vittadini, Adrienne** (about). *See* Fashion Designers

**Vivenza, Francesca**

Cultural Dislocation Syndrome. *Canadian Women's Studies* 11, No. 1 (Spring 1990):63-64

**Vivisection – Opposition.** *See* Animal Rights

**Voda, Ann**

Hot Flashes. *Healthsharing* 11, No. 4 (December 1990):13

**Vogel, Lise**

Debating Difference: Feminism, Pregnancy and the Workplace. *Feminist Studies* 16, No. 1 (Spring 1990):9-32

**Volk, Patricia**

The Flip Side. *Family Circle* 103, No. 11 (August 14, 1990):27+

**Vollmer, Judith**

Father's Magic Trick. Poem. *The Women's Review of Books* 8, No. 1 (October 1990):22

Lines of Pain. *The Women's Review of Books* 7, No. 6 (March 1990):12-13

The Nuclear Accident at SL 1, Idaho Falls, 1961. Poem. *The Women's Review of Books* 8, No. 1 (October 1990):22

Time's Power. Book Review. *The Women's Review of Books* 7, No. 6 (March 1990):12-13

Woman of the River. Book Review. *The Women's Review of Books* 7, No. 6 (March 1990):12-13

**Volunteer Work.** *See also* Activism; Disaster Relief; New York (City) – Gay Men's Health Crisis; Values

Cause Celeb. Bibliography. Elaine Dutka. *McCall's* 118, No. 2 (November 1990):70-72

Cause Celeb. Linden Gross. *McCall's* 118, No. 3 (December 1990):56-58

Christmas Stars. *Harper's Bazaar* (December 1990):173+

Community Service among College and University Students: Individual and Institutional Relationships. Robert C. Serow and Julia I. Dreyden. *Adolescence* 25, No. 99 (Fall 1990):553-566

Economies. Bibliography. Marion Asnes. *Lear's* (September 1990):42

Formal Activities for Elderly Women: Determinants of Participation in Voluntary and Senior Center Activities. Masako Ishii-Kuntz. *Journal of Women and Aging* 2, No. 1 (1990):79-97

Give Your Best. Bibliography. Janet Margolies. *Ladies' Home Journal* 107, No. 12 (December 1990):108-121

Goodfellas. *Harper's Bazaar* (December 1990):154-155

Invisible Careers: Women Civic Leaders from the Volunteer World. By Arlene Kaplan Daniels. Reviewed by Beth B. Hess. *Gender and Society* 4, No. 2 (June 1990):283-284

On the Job. Christine Donovan. *Family Circle* 103, No. 11 (August 14, 1990):55

Tsena-Rena. Bibliography. *Lilith* 15, No. 1 (Winter 1990):30; 15, No. 2 (Spring 1990):30-31; 15, No. 3 (Summer 1990):30-31; 15, No. 4 (Fall 1990):43

**Von Bülow, Claus** (about)

Capital Offense. Frederick Eberstadt. *Harper's Bazaar* (October 1990):220-221+

**Von Furstenberg, Diane** (about)

Beauty and Fashion Journal: Mother-Daughter Beauty Secrets. *Ladies' Home Journal* 107, No. 5 (May 1990):29

**Wages – Negotiation**

Everything's Negotiable. Anna Sobkowski. *Executive Female* (March/April 1990):38-40

Four Strategies for Salary Negotiation. Laurel Touby. *Working Woman* (January 1990):110-112

**Wages, Negotiation**

Job Strategies: Can You Ask for a Raise Right Now? Marilyn Moats Kennedy. *Glamour* (February 1990):85-86

**Wage Surveys**

Working Woman 11th Annual Salary Survey, 1990. Edited by Anne M. Russell. *Working Woman* (January 1990):105-112

**Wagner, Anneliese**

Requiem for Oma Berta. Poem. *Lilith* 15, No. 4 (Fall 1990):28

**Wagner, Jane**

The Search for Signs of Intelligent Life in the 21st Century. *Ms.* 1, No. 3 (November/December 1990):68-71

**Wagner, Marsha L.**

"Our Family Fled China." *Working Mother* 13, No. 7 (July 1990):32-39

**Wagner-Martin, Linda**

A Poetics of Women's Autobiography: Marginality and the Fictions of Self-Representation. Book Review. *Tulsa Studies in Women's Literature* 9, No. 1 (Spring 1990):139-142

The Private Self: Theory and Practice of Women's Autobiographical Writings. Book Review. *Tulsa Studies in Women's Literature* 9, No. 1 (Spring 1990):139-142

**Wainwright, Margo** (about)

Women Who Make a Difference. Linda Marsa. *Family Circle* 103, No. 15 (November 6, 1990):15-17

**Wait, Marianne**

The Short-Order Spa. *Ladies' Home Journal* 107, No. 9 (September 1990):128

**Wait, Marianne** (joint author). *See* Aborn, Shana; Rachlin, Jill

**Waite, Desmond J.**

Lost Tribal Rites: A Lament. *Out/Look* No. 9 (Summer 1990):72-73

**Waite, Ellen J.** (joint author). *See* Dickestein, Ruth

**Waitresses – Unions**

Rethinking Troubled Relations between Women and Unions: Craft Unionism and Female Activism. Dorothy Sue Cobble. *Feminist Studies* 16, No. 3 (Fall 1990):519-548

**Wakefield, Denis** (joint editor). *See* Richmond, Robyn

**Walby, Sylvia**

Enterprising Women: Ethnicity, Economy, and Gender Relations. Book Review. *Gender and Society* 4, No. 3 (September 1990):425-427

From Private to Public Patriarchy: The Periodisation of British History. *Women's Studies International Forum* 13, Nos. 1-2 (1990):91-104

**Wald, Lillian D.** (about)

Always a Sister: The Feminism of Lillian D. Wald. By Doris Groshen Daniels. Reviewed by Katherine A. Kendall. *AFFILIA* 5, No. 4 (Winter 1990):113-114

Lillian D. Wald: Progressive Activist. Edited by Clare Coss. Reviewed by Katherine A. Kendall. *AFFILIA* 5, No. 4 (Winter 1990):113-114

**Waldby, Cathy** (joint author). *See* Kippax, Susan

**Waldron, Ingrid** and Lye, Diane

Relationships between Teenage Smoking and Attitudes toward Women's Rights, Sex Roles, Marriage, Sex and Family. *Women and Health* 16, Nos. 3/4 (1990):23-46

**Wales – Artists.** *See* Kinsey, Chris

**Wales – Poets**

Exchanges: Poems by Women in Wales. Edited by Jude Brigley. Reviewed by Penny Simpson. *Spare Rib* No. 216 (September 1990):25

**Walfish, Steven,** Massey, Renelle, and Krone, Anton

MMPI Profiles of Adolescent Substance Abusers in Treatment. *Adolescence* 25, No. 99 (Fall 1990):567-572

**Walker, Alice**

Did This Happen to Your Mother? Did Your Sister Throw Up a Lot? Poem. *Spare Rib* 218 (November 1990):26

Even as I Hold You. Poem. *Essence* 21, No. 5 (September 1990):110

Malcolm. Poem. *Essence* 21, No. 1 (May 1990):205

Ndebele. Poem. *Ms.* 1, No. 3 (November/December 1990):45

**Walker, Alice – Criticism and Interpretation**

Walker's Critique of Religion in *The Color Purple.* Calvin Mercer. *Sage* 6, No. 1 (Summer 1989):24-26

**Walker, Alice** (about). *See* Artiste, Cindy; De Veaux, Alexis, Milloy, Marilyn, and Ross, Michael Erik

**Walker, Barbara G.**

Women's Rituals: A Sourcebook. Reviewed by D. S. Oliver. *The Women's Review of Books* 8, No. 2 (November 1990):23-24

**Walker, C. J.**

Black Women's Health. *New Directions for Women* 19, No. 6 (November-December 1990):20

**Wallace, Michele**

Women Rap Back. *Ms.* 1, No. 3 (November/December 1990):61

**Wallace, Pamela M.** and Gotlib, Ian H.

Marital Adjustment During the Transition to Parenthood: Stability and Predictors of Change. *Journal of Marriage and the Family* 52, No. 1 (February 1990):21-29

**Wallberg, Larry**

First Person Singular: Takeout Shakeout. *Savvy Woman* (November 1990):96+

Sperm Story. *Lear's* (September 1990):100-101

**Wallis, Diana** (about). *See also* Franklin, I. E., "200 Words"

**Walls, Robert** (joint author). *See* Beck, Cornelia

**Wallsgrove, Ruth**

I'm a Material Girl. *off our backs* 20, No. 1 (January 1990):16-17

Lipstick Etc. *off our backs* 20, No. 10 (November 1990):13

Working Collectively. *off our backs* 20, No. 2 (February 1990):20-21

**Wallston, Barbara Strudler** (about)

Barbara Strudler Wallston: Pioneer of Contemporary Feminist Psychology, 1943-1987. Nancy Felipe Russo. *Psychology of Women Quarterly* 14, No. 2 (June 1990):277-287

**Walowitz, Paula**

Anonymous in My Own Time. *Hot Wire* 6, No. 2 (May 1990):14-15+

Report from Albuquerque: Wiminfest '89. *Hot Wire* 6, No. 1 (January 1990):36-37

**Walsh, Barent W.** and Rosen, Paul M.

Self-Mutilation: Theory. Book Review. *Adolescence* 25, No. 97 (Spring 1990):251-252

**Walsh, Froma** (joint editor). *See* McGoldrick, Monica

**Walter, Karin** (joint editor). *See* Lissner, Anneliese

**Walter, Lynn**

The Embodiment of Ugliness and the Logic of Love: The Danish Redstocking Movement. *Feminist Review* No. 36 (Autumn 1990):103-126

**Walters, Barbara** (about). *See also* Television Journalists – Networking

Barbara Walters: Media Mover. Jeff Rovin. *Ladies' Home Journal* 107, No. 11 (November 1990):199+

**Walters, Marianne** and others

The Invisible Web: Gender Patterns in Family Relationships. Reviewed by Ellen B. Bogolub. *AFFILIA* 5, No. 3 (Fall 1990):116-118

**Walton, Anne**

Equity in Education. Book Review. *Gender and Education* 2, No. 3 (1990):371-372

**Walton, Chris Gorman** (joint author). *See* Beck, Cornelia

**Walton, Whitney**

Working Women, Gender, and Industrialization in Nineteenth-Century France: The Case of Lorraine Embroidery Manufacturing. *Journal of Women's History* 2, No. 2 (Fall 1990):42-65

**Walzer, Emily**

In Pursuit of Excellence. *Women's Sports and Fitness* 12, No. 4 (May-June 1990):45-49

Put Your Money Where Your Foot Is: A Guide to Buying Running Shoes. *Women's Sports & Fitness* 12, No. 6 (September 1990):36-39

Sports Support: The ABCs – and Double Ds – of Athletic Bras. *Women's Sports and Fitness* 12, No. 3 (April 1990):66-68

Sticking with It. *Women's Sports and Fitness* 12, No. 7 (October 1990):66

**Wang, Vera** (about)

Brides Made. Dodie Kazanjian. *Vogue* (December 1990):316-321

**War.** *See also* Military Combat

Women and Their Wartime Roles. Mary Ann Attebury. *Minerva* 8, No. 1 (Spring 1990):11-28

**War – Prisoners**

The Possibility of American Women Becoming Prisoners of War: A Challenge for Behavioral Scientists. Wayne E. Dillingham. *Minerva* 8, No. 4 (Winter 1990):17-22

**War and Literature**

Nation, Class, and Gender: Tennyson's *Maud* and War. Joseph Bristow. *Genders* 9 (Fall 1990):93-111

**Ward, Debra A.**

The Fall Face. *McCall's* 117, No. 12 (September 1990):80

A Flawless Face. *McCall's* 118, No. 1 (October 1990):26

A Perfect Ten. *McCall's* 117, No. 11 (August 1990):12

Perfume Options. *McCall's* 118, No. 3 (December 1990):24

**Ward, Evelyn**

Poll Tax Greetings from Scotland. *Spare Rib* 219 (December 1990-January 1991):64-65

**Ward, Geoffrey**

Movies. *Vogue* (January 1990):94-96

**Ward, Glenyse**

Wandering Girl. Reviewed by Kathy Willetts. *Hecate* 16, Nos. 1-2 (1990):167-170

**Ward, Kathryn**

Enterprising Women. Book Review. *Women's Studies International Forum* 13, No. 5 (1990):523-524

**Ward, Nancy** (about)

Grandmothers of a New World. Beth Brant. *Woman of Power* 16 (Spring 1990):40-47

**Warde, John**

Beat the Clock. *Family Circle* 103, No. 6 (April 24, 1990):114+

**Ware, Susan**

Homeward Bound: American Families in the Cold War Era. Book Review. *Signs* 16, No. 1 (Autumn 1990):173-175

Partner and I: Molly Dewson, Feminism, and New Deal Politics. Reviewed by June Purvis. *Women's Studies International Forum* 13, Nos. 1-2 (1990):160-161

The Sound of Wings: The Life of Amelia Earhart. Book Review. *The Women's Review of Books* 7, No. 4 (January 1990):7-8

Still Missing. *The Women's Review of Books* 7, No. 4 (January 1990):7-8

**Warhol, Andy** (about)

Holy Terror: Andy Warhol Close Up. By Bob Colacello. Reviewed by Graydon Carter. *Vogue* (September 1990):440-452

**Waring, Cynthia**

The Masseuse. *Woman of Power* 18 (Fall 1990):75

**Waring, Marilyn**

Sabotaging Their Statistics. *Ms.* 1, No. 1 (July/August 1990):82-83

**Warland, Betsy**

Cutting Re/marks. *Sinister Wisdom* 42 (Winter 1990-1991):94-112

**Warn, Emily**

The Word Between the World and God. Poem. *Bridges* 1, No. 1 (Spring 1990): 30

**Warner, Michael** (about). *See* National Association of Black and White Men Together

**Warner, Sylvia Townsend** (about)

Sylvia Townsend Warner: A Biography. By Claire Harman. Reviewed by Carolyn G. Heilbrun. *The Women's Review of Books* 7, No. 6 (March 1990):8-9

**Warner-Berley, Judith**

"Perfect" Bodies to Die for. Bibliography. *McCall's* 117, No. 8 (May 1990):64-65

**Warren, Carol A. B.**

Gender Issues in Field Research. Reviewed by Carol Lupton. *Gender and Education* 2, No. 2 (1990):251-252

Gender Issues in Field Research. Reviewed by Dorothy L. Steffens and Jane Robbins. *Feminist Collections* 11, No. 2 (Winter 1990):7-9

Gender Issues in Field Research. Reviewed by Marilyn Biggerstaff. *AFFILIA* 5, No. 1 (Spring 1990):121-123

Gender Issues in Field Research. Reviewed by Sarah H. Matthews. *Journal of Marriage and the Family* 52, No. 1 (February 1990):282

**Warren, Catharine E.**

Women and Education: A Canadian Perspective. Book Review. *Gender and Education* 2, No. 1 (1990):102-104

**Warren, Lesley Ann** (about)

Fire and Spice. Lori Berger. *Harper's Bazaar* (August 1990):138-139+

**Warren, Mercy Otis** (about)

The Columbian Patriot: Mercy Otis Warren and the Constitution. Larry M. Lane and Judith J. Lane. *Women & Politics* 10, No. 2 (1990):17-31

**Warren, Rosalind**

After You've Gone. Book Review. *The Women's Review of Books* 7, No. 8 (May 1990):8-9

Of Cats and Women. *The Women's Review of Books* 7, No. 8 (May 1990):8-9

Curiouser and Curiouser. *The Women's Review of Books* 7, No. 5 (February 1990):9

Friend of My Youth. Book Review. *The Women's Review of Books* 7, No. 8 (May 1990):8-9

Good for a Laugh and a Little Cry. *New Directions for Women* 19, No. 6 (November-December 1990):17

Limited Partnerships. *New Directions for Women* 19, No. 1 (January/February 1990):21

A Natural Curiosity. Book Review. *The Women's Review of Books* 7, No. 5 (February 1990):9

The One You Call Sister. Book Review. *New Directions for Women* 19, No. 4 (July-August 1990):19

Read With a Sister. *New Directions for Women* 19, No. 4 (July-August 1990):19

Secrets. Book Review. *New Directions for Women* 19, No. 6 (November-December 1990):17

Silverleaf's Choice: An Anthology of Lesbian Humor. Book Review. *New Directions for Women* 19, No. 6 (November-December 1990):17

Teaching Docs to Improve Gyn Exams. *New Directions for Women* 19, No. 3 (May/June 1990):12

Who Wears the Tux? The Original Great American Dyke Quiz. Book Review. *New Directions for Women* 19, No. 5 (September-October 1990):20

**Warriors in Literature**

"Sisters in Arms": The Warrior Construct in Writings by Contemporary U.S. Women of Color. Mary K. DeShazer. *NWSA Journal* 2, No. 3 (Summer 1990):349-373

**Wartik, Nancy**

State Elections: Women on the Verge. *Ms.* 1, No. 2 (September/October 1990):92

**Warwick, Dionne** (about). *See also* Music, Popular

**Washer, Louise**

Enterprise: The Business Plan That Gets the Loan. *Working Woman* (January 1990):37-47

Opening Day: We're in Business. *Working Woman* (May 1990):55-62

**Washington, D.C.**

A Trip Through the Women's Communities of Washington D.C. Nancy Seeger and Rena Yount. *Hot Wire* 6, No. 1 (January 1990):40-44+

A Walk Through Women's History. Elaine Moran. *Iris* 23 (Spring-Summer 1990):35

**Washington, D.C. – Fashion**

Glamorous Liaisons. *Mademoiselle* (October 1990):156-161

**Washington, D.C. – Lawyers**

School for Scandal. Margaret Carlson. *Mademoiselle* (October 1990):154+

**Washington, D.C. – National Gallery of Art**

Altar Ego: A Titian Renaissance at the National Gallery. Thomas Connors. *Harper's Bazaar* (November 1990):168-169

**Washington, Denzel** (about). *See* Demarchelier, Patrick, "Le Jazz Haute"

**Washington, Dinah** (about)

Dinah Washington: Long Live the Queen! Rosetta Reitz. *Hot Wire* 6, No. 3 (September 1990):34-36+

**Washington, Elsie B.**

Be Jeweled. *Essence* 21, No. 5 (September 1990):68-69

Carrying On: Isaia N.Y.C. *Essence* 21, No. 5 (September 1990):66-67

Don't We Style! *Essence* 21, No. 1 (May 1990):125-129

The Family. Book review. *Essence* 21, No. 4 (August 1990):50

Gimmie Some Skin! *Essence* 21, No. 6 (October 1990):72-79

Housemates: The New Choice. *Essence* 21, No. 2 (June 1990):84-86

Naturally Natalie. *Essence* 21, No. 6 (October 1990):14-17

New York City's First Lady. *Essence* 21, No. 5 (September 1990):96-98

Reggie Wells, Man of a Thousand Faces. *Essence* 21, No. 2 (June 1990):10

Undeniably Billy. *Essence* 20, No. 12 (April 1990):14-15

**Washington, Mary Helen**

Invented Lives: Narratives of Black Women 1860-1960. Reviewed by Ann Phoenix. *Gender and Education* 2, No. 2 (1990):252-254

**Washington Governor's Mansion.** *See also* Governors – United States – Mansions

**Wasser, Jacqueline**

Hair Apparent. *Mademoiselle* (November 1990):86-88

High Profile: Happiness Is a Warm Filofax. *Mademoiselle* (September 1990):154+

**Wasserspring, Lois**

A Dream Compels Us: Voices of Salvadoran Women. Book Review. *The Women's Review of Books* 7, No. 6 (March 1990):23-24

Transformed by Terror. *The Women's Review of Books* 7, No. 6 (March 1990):23-24

**Wasserstein, Wendy** (about)

The Wendy Chronicles. Kent Black. *Harper's Bazaar* (March 1990):154-162

**Waste, Disposal of.** *See also* Refuse and Refuse Disposal

This Is What You Thought: Disposable Diapers. *Glamour* (June 1990):167

**Watches.** *See* Clocks and Watches

**Water.** *See also* Drinking Water

**Water Cure Movement.** *See* Hydrotherapy

**Water Pollution.** *See also* Drinking Water, Bottled

How to De-Tox Your Water. Al Ubell and Label Shulman. *Family Circle* 103, No. 15 (November 6, 1990):33-36

**Waters, Alice** (about). *See also* Chefs

**Waters, Chris**

Consuming Desire: Sexual Science and the Emergence of a Culture of Abundance, 1871-1914. Book Review. *Gender & History* 2, No. 2 (Summer 1990):218-222

Dangerous Sexualities: Medico-Moral Politics in England Since 1830. Book Review. *Gender & History* 2, No. 2 (Summer 1990):218-222

The Regulation of Desire: Sexuality in Canada. Book Review. *Gender & History* 2, No. 2 (Summer 1990):218-222

**Waters, Elizabeth**

Russian Women's Studies: Essays on Sexism in Soviet Culture. Book Review. *Australian Feminist Studies* No. 11 (Autumn 1990):117-120

**Weakland, Rembert** (about)

Compassion Comes for the Archbishop. Paula Kamen. *Ms.* 1, No. 1 (July/August 1990):85-86

**Wealth**

The Charmed Life. *Harper's Bazaar* (April 1990):164-169

Money: Quick – How Much are You Worth? Julianne Malveaux. *Essence* 21, No. 6 (October 1990):38-41

10 Best Paid Women in America. Anne B. Fisher. *Savvy Woman* (July/August 1990):44-51

**Wealth Distribution**

Where to Live Like a Millionaire. Nathalie Kurylko. *Savvy Woman* (September 1990):52-53

**Wearable Art**

Works of Art to Wear. *Essence* 21, No. 6 (October 1990):22

**Weatherford, Claudine**

The Art of Queena Stovall: Images of Country Life. Reviewed by Elaine Hedges. *NWSA Journal* 2, No. 2 (Spring 1990):282-287

**Weatherill, Anne** (about). *See also* Casey, Kathryn, "Voices of the Decade"

**Weathers, Diane** (editor)

White Boys. *Essence* 20, No. 12 (April 1990):64-66+

**Weaves.** *See* Hair Styles

**Webb, Cathleen Crowell** (about)

The Greatest Story (N)ever Told: The Spectacle of Recantation. Helena Michie. *Genders* 9 (Fall 1990):19-34

**Webb, Densie**

Food Advisory. *Working Woman* (November 1990):157

Nutrinews. *Ladies' Home Journal* 107, No. 10 (October 1990):210-212

Supermarket Diet. *Redbook* 175, No. 1 (May 1990):100

**Webber, Storme**

A Tribute to Rosa Parks – Mother of the Civil Rights Movement. *Spare Rib* 219 (December 1990-January 1991):68

**Webber, Storme** (interview)

On Love, Poetry, & Ancient Sisters. *Spare Rib* No. 211 (April 1990):22-26

**Weber, Bruce**

Tangier Dream. *Vogue* (January 1990):160-185

**Weber, Bruce** (joint author). *See* Reed, Julia

**Weber, Gail**

A Season for Sex. *Healthsharing* 11, No. 4 (December 1990):18-22

**Weber, Suzanne**

Of Limos and Lonely Dinners. *Executive Female* (May/June 1990):38-39

Signed, Sealed, Delivered. *Executive Female* (March/April 1990):36-37

**Weber, Suzanne** and Pusateri, D. M.

Ambassador of Technology. *Executive Female* 13, No. 4 (July-August 1990):47-48

**Webster, Harriet**

The Best Infant Care. *Working Mother* 13, No. 7 (July 1990):68-70

The Trouble with Teasing. *Working Mother* 13, No. 1 (January 1990):62-69

**Webster, Wendy**

Not a Man to Match Her: The Marketing of a Prime Minister. Reviewed by Hazel Smith. *Spare Rib* No. 215 (August 1990):28-29

**Wedding Cakes.** *See* Cake Decorating

**Wedding Ceremonies.** *See also* Paris – Social Life and Customs; Remarriage

Travel: Getting Married in Paradise. Bibliography. Stephanie Stokes Oliver. *Essence* 20, No. 10 (February 1990):99-100

What a Beautiful Wedding! *Redbook* 175, No. 3 (July 1990):14-16

**Wedding Ceremonies – Humor**

Maid of Honor, Inc. Elizabeth Bales Frank. *Glamour* (July 1990):86

Weddings that Made Me Laugh & Cry. Judith Viorst. *Redbook* 175, No. 3 (July 1990):18-20

**Wedding Costume**

Brides Made. Dodie Kazanjian. *Vogue* (December 1990):316-321

**Weddings – Food**

Tray Chic. Patricia Beard. *Harper's Bazaar* (June 1990):138

**Weddings – Photography**

Two on the Aisle. *Harper's Bazaar* (June 1990):135+

**Wedekind, Frank**

Lulu. Reviewed by Sue Murphy. *Spare Rib* 217 (October 1990):31

**Weedon, Chris**

Feminist Practice and Poststructuralist Theory. Reviewed by Wendy Luttrell. *Signs* 15, No. 3 (Spring 1990):635-640

**Weems, Renita J.** (about). *See* Writers – Interviews, "Graceful Passages"

**Wee Papa Girls**

Wee Papa Girls Rap Against the Tax. *Spare Rib* No. 211 (April 1990):12-14

**Weidner, Gerdi** and Helmig, Linda

Cardiovascular Stress Reactivity and Mood during the Menstrual Cycle. *Women and Health* 16, Nos. 3/4 (1990):5-21

**Weigel, Sigrid**

Body and Image Space: Problems and Representability of a Female Dialectic of Enlightenment. *Australian Feminist Studies* No. 11 (Autumn 1990):1-15

**Weight**

Medical News. Dana Points and Carla Rohlfing. *Family Circle* 103, No. 13 (September 25, 1990):24

Weighing Your Risks. *Glamour* (September 1990):306-309

**Weight Control**

Making Peace with Food. By Susan Kano. Reviewed by Patricia A. Connor-Greene. *Women and Health* 16, Nos. 3/4 (1990):211-221

Perceived Barriers to Exercise and Weight Control Practices in Community Women. Cheryl A. Johnson, Sheila A. Corrigan, Patricia M. Dubbert, and Sandra E. Gramling. *Women and Health* 16, Nos. 3/4 (1990):177-191

**Weight Loss.** *See also* Celebrities – Weight Loss; Exercise; Obesity; Reducing Diets

Burn Calories without Exercising. Excerpt. Bryant Stamford and Porter Shimer. *Redbook* 174, No. 6 (April 1990):110-113

Contemporary Living: Your Best Body by Summer. *Essence* 20, No. 9 (January 1990):73-78

Diet News. C. Wayne Callaway and Catherine Whitney. *Redbook* 175, No. 1 (May 1990):20

Diet News: Secrets from a Diet Diary. Ellen Kunes. *Mademoiselle* (February 1990):196

Health & Fitness. Stephanie Young. *Glamour* (March 1990):57-65

The Healthy Family. Carla Rohlfing. *Family Circle* 103, No. 3 (February 20, 1990):37-39

Lose 16 lbs. by Summer. *Family Circle* 103, No. 6 (April 24, 1990):77-79+

Medical News. Dana Points and Carla Rohlfing. *Family Circle* 103, No. 17 (December 18, 1990):72

Redbook's New Wise Woman's Diet: "We Lost – and How!" *Redbook* 175, No. 4 (August 1990):105-110

Star Gazing. Ellen Sherman. *Family Circle* 103, No. 1 (January 9, 1990):33-34

Ten Pounds Off by Christmas. *Family Circle* 103, No. 15 (November 6, 1990):158-162

10 Steps to a Great Summer Body. *Glamour* (May 1990):280-283

Update. Your Best Body by Summer. *Essence* 20, No. 11 (March 1990):102; 20, No. 12 (April 1990):98+

The Weekend Diet. *Family Circle* 103, No. 1 (January 9, 1990):64-68

Weight, Sex and Marriage. By Richard B. Stuart and Barbara Jacobson. Reviewed by Patricia A. Connor-Greene. *Women and Health* 16, Nos. 3/4 (1990):211-221

Weight Watchers Exclusive: Get Your Body Ready for the Beach. Ellie Grossman. *Ladies' Home Journal* 107, No. 6 (June 1990):96-102

Your Best Body by Summer Update. *Essence* 20, No. 10 (February 1990):94

**Weight Training**

Muscle Tone. Randi Hutter. *Harper's Bazaar* (May 1990):140-143

The Perfect Repetition. Maggie Greenwood-Robinson. *Women's Sports and Fitness* 12, No. 3 (April 1990):30

Periodization: Training for the Peak. Maggie Greenwood-Robinson. *Women's Sports and Fitness* 12, No. 2 (March 1990):12

Ski Lifts. Suzanne Nottingham. *Women's Sports and Fitness* 12, No. 7 (October 1990):20-21

Strength in Numbers. Maggie Greenwood-Robinson. *Women's Sports and Fitness* 12, No. 4 (May-June 1990):30

Weight Training Back in Action. Marjorie McCloy and Sophie Taggart. *Women's Sports & Fitness* 12, No. 6 (September 1990):18

**Weil, Connie** (editor)

Lucha: The Struggles of Latin American Women. Reviewed by Anne Sisson Runyan. *Women's Studies International Forum* 13, No. 5 (1990):520-521

**Weil, Simone** (about)

Simone Weil: An Intellectual Biography. By Gabriella Fiori. Reviewed by Johanna Selles-Roney. *Resources for Feminist Research* 19, No. 2 (June 1990):46

**Weiler, Kathleen**

Women Teaching for Change: Gender, Class and Power. Reviewed by Sandra Acker. *Gender and Education* 2, No. 1 (1990):105-107

**Weinbaum, Batya**

A Burst of Light. Book Review. *NWSA Journal* 2, No. 2 (Spring 1990):323-328

The Chess Game. Poem. *Feminist Review* No. 36 (Autumn 1990):95

Dear Professor Vile. *Heresies* 25 (1990):36-37

Panhandling Papers. Book Review. *NWSA Journal* 2, No. 2 (Spring 1990):323-328

Wildfire: Igniting the She/Volution. Book Review. *NWSA Journal* 2, No. 2 (Spring 1990):323-328

**Weinberg, Sydney Stahl**

The World of Our Mothers: The Lives of Jewish Immigrant Women. Reviewed by Lynne H. Kleinman. *Gender and Society* 4, No. 1 (March 1990):101-103

The World of Our Mothers: The Lives of Jewish Immigrant Women. Reviewed by Sally M. Miller. *NWSA Journal* 2, No. 2 (Spring 1990):301-303

**Weiner, Gaby**

Ethical Practice in an Unjust World: Educational Evaluation and Social Justice. *Gender and Education* 2, No. 2 (1990):231-238

**Weiner, Jonathan**

Fire and Rain. *Lear's* (April 1990):74-79+

**Weiner, Lori**

Copyrighting Music. *Hot Wire* 6, No. 2 (May 1990):15

**Weiner, Lynn**

The Eighth Berkshire Conference on the History of Women: A Report. *Journal of Women's History* 2, No. 2 (Fall 1990):174-176

**Weiner-Davis, Michele** (joint author). *See* O'Hanlon, William Hudson

**Weinhouse, Beth**

A Deadly Skin Cancer on the Rise. *Redbook* 175, No. 2 (June 1990):20-24

The Heir & the Spare. *Redbook* 175, No. 5 (September 1990):38-42

Kim Alexis – First-Rate Mom and Beauty. *Redbook* 175, No. 1 (May 1990):12-14

The Significant Other. *Savvy Woman* (October 1990):13-14

Young But Not Innocent. *Redbook* 174, No. 6 (April 1990):135-139

**Weinhouse, Beth** and Burgower, Barbara

Better Beginnings: The LHJ Guide to Pregnancy. *Ladies' Home Journal* 107, No. 8 (August 1990):35-42

**Weinstein, Joan** (about)

Perfect Isle of Calm. Laurie Tarkan. *Lear's* (May 1990):82-89

**Weinstein, Marion**

Take My Broom – Please! Early Steps Along the Path of A Stand-Up Priestess. *Woman of Power* 17 (Summer 1990):48-49

**Weinstein, Soledad** (joint author). *See* Charnes, Ximena

**Weinstock, Sylvia** (about)

Cake Master. Jennet Conant. *Harper's Bazaar* (June 1990):140

**Weisberg, Ruth**

June Wayne's Quantum Aesthetics. *Woman's Art Journal* 11, No. 1 (Spring-Summer 1990):4-8

**Weise, Beth Reba**

Feminism in Scandinavia. *off our backs* 20, No. 3 (March 1990):5-7

**Weisgarber, J.** and Osborne, J. W.

The Experience of Menarche. *Atlantis* 15, No. 2 (Spring 1990):27-39

**Weisinger, Hendrie**

How Should You Criticize Your Boss? Carefully. *Working Woman* (February 1990):90-91+

**Weisman, Mary-Lou**

Viewpoint: Being Smart the Woman's Way. *Glamour* (December 1990):138-140

**Weiss, Dorothy Glasser**

Cycles of Desire. *Glamour* (May 1990):278-279+

Don't Settle – Sizzle! *Redbook* 175, No. 1 (May 1990):120-121+

**Weiss, Jill**

Poem. *Women and Environments* 12, No. 2 (Spring 1990): 15

**Weiss, Penny** and Harper, Anne

Rousseau's Political Defense of the Sex-roled Family. *Hypatia* 5, No. 3 (Fall 1990):90-109

**Weissinger, Maurice** (joint author). *See* Hersey, Brook

**Weissman, Judith**

Half Savage and Hardy and Free: Women and Rural Radicalism in the Nineteenth-Century Novel. Reviewed by Susan Hardy Aiken. *Signs* 16, No. 1 (Autumn 1990):188-192

**Weisstein, Naomi**

Chicago '60s: Ecstasy as Our Guide. *Ms.* 1, No. 2 (September/October 1990):65-67

Daring to Be Bad. Book Review. *Ms.* 1, No. 3 (November/December 1990):54-55

**Weitz, Don** (joint editor). *See* Burstow, Bonnie

**Weitzman, Lenore J.**

The Divorce Revolution: The Unexpected Social and Economics Consequences for Women and Children in America. Reviewed by Barbara Risman. *Gender and Society* 4, No. 1 (March 1990):105-108

**Wekerle, Gerda R.**

Women and Housing: A Research Agenda. *Canadian Women's Studies* 11, No. 2 (Fall 1990):66-67

**Welch, Raquel** (about). *See* Johnson, Lois Joy, "Great Faces"

**Weldon, Fay**

The Cloning of Joanna May. Reviewed by Ann E. Kottner. *The Women's Review of Books* 7, Nos. 10-11 (July 1990):40-41

The Leader of the Band. Reviewed by Regina Barreca. *Belles Lettres* 5, No. 2 (Winter 1990):14

Sacred Cows. Reviewed by Clara Connolly. *Feminist Review* No. 35 (Summer 1990):113-117

Subject to Diary. Short story. *Lear's* (April 1990):112-115+

**Weldon, Fay** (about)

The Life & Loves of Fay Weldon. Eden Ross Lipson. *Lear's* (January 1990):112-115

**Welfare Mothers Voice** (newspaper)

Against the Odds: Welfare Mothers Publish Newspaper. Pat Redmond. *New Directions for Women* 19, No. 1 (January/February 1990):8

**Welfare Programs**

Biting the Hand that Feeds Them: Organizing Women on Welfare at the Grass Roots Level. By Jacqueline Pope. Reviewed by Margaret Nielsen. *AFFILIA* 5, No. 4 (Winter 1990):115

**Welfare State – Norway**

State Feminism: Norwegian Women and the Welfare State. Eugenie A. Lucas. *Feminist Issues* 10, No. 2 (Fall 1990):43-53

**Welker, Karen G.** (joint author). *See* Steitz, Jean A.

**Weller, Peter** (about). *See also* Actors

**Weller, Sheila** (joint author). *See* Aponovich, James

**Wellikoff, Alan**

Cars: 10 Expert Auto-Body Tips. *Essence* 20, No. 11 (March 1990):100

**Wells, Patricia** (about)

Food Notes. *Vogue* (January 1990):126

**Wells, Reggie** (about)

Reggie Wells, Man of a Thousand Faces. Elsie B. Washington. *Essence* 21, No. 2 (June 1990):10

**Wells-Barnett, Ida B.** (about)

Two Outstanding Women in Social Welfare History: Mary Church Terrell and Ida B. Wells-Barnett. Wilma Peebles-Wilkins and E. Aracelis Francis. *AFFILIA* 5, No. 4 (Winter 1990):87-100

**Wels, Barbara**

She JUST Can't Talk. Short Story. *Hecate* 16, Nos. 1-2 (1990):148-150

**Welsing, Frances Cress** (about). *See* De Veaux, Alexis, Milloy, Marilyn, and Ross, Michael Erik

**Welty, Ellen**

Boyfriends and Gifts: Present Tense. *Mademoiselle* (December 1990):116

Couples: 10 Reasons to Pair Off. *Mademoiselle* (September 1990):242-247

How Early to Bed? The New Sexual Timetables. *Mademoiselle* (June 1990):172-173+

Money & Friends: If She's Broke, Don't Fix It. *Mademoiselle* (January 1990):60

No Cleavage Required! Getting to the Soul of Sex Appeal. *Mademoiselle* (April 1990):198-201, 263

Scruples: Dish and Tell: Wy Do We Talk About Our Friends? *Mademoiselle* (February 1990):94

Scruples: He Cheated – Do You Rat on the Rat? *Mademoiselle* (June 1990):134

Scruples: I've Got a (Style) Secret. *Mademoiselle* (November 1990):124

Scruples: Make a Match, Play With Fire? *Mademoiselle* (September 1990):204

Scruples: Who's Sorry Later? *Mademoiselle* (October 1990):132

**Wendell, Susan**

Oppression and Victimization; Choice and Responsibility. *Hypatia* 5, No. 3 (Fall 1990):15-46

**Wendt, Ingrid**

Sing Soft, Sing Loud. Book Review. *Belles Lettres* 5, No. 3 (Spring 1990):25

**Wenger, Beth S.**

Radical Politics in a Reactionary Age: The Unmaking of Rosika Schwimmer, 1914-1930. *Journal of Women's History* 2, No. 2 (Fall 1990):66-99

**Wenkart, Henny** (editor)

Sarah's Daughters Sing: A Sampler of Poems by Jewish Women. Reviewed by Alicia Ostriker. *Lilith* 15, No. 3 (Summer 1990):6

**Wente, Carolyn** (about). *See* Family Owned Business

**Wenzel, Lynn**

Black Women Blaze Musical Trails. *New Directions for Women* 19, No. 1 (January/February 1990):9

Burning Questions. Book Review. *New Directions for Women* 19, No. 3 (May/June 1990):23

Closer to Home. Music review. *New Directions for Women* 19, No. 3 (May/June 1990):8

A Decade Later Burning Questions Remain Unanswered. *New Directions for Women* 19, No. 3 (May/June 1990):23

Familiar Faces. Music review. *New Directions for Women* 19, No. 3 (May/June 1990):8

Far from Home: Families of the Westward Journey. Book Review. *New Directions for Women* 19, No. 2 (March/April 1990):14

Fire in the Rain . . . Singer in the Storm: An Autobiography of Holly Near. Book Review. *New*

*Directions for Women* 19, No. 5 (September-October 1990):14

Georgiana, Feminist Reformer of the West: The Journal of Georgiana Bruce Kirby. Book Review. *New Directions for Women* 19, No. 2 (March/April 1990):15

The Harvey Girls, Women Who Opened the West. Book Review. *New Directions for Women* 19, No. 2 (March/April 1990):15

If You See a Dream. Music Review. *New Directions for Women* 19, No. 6 (November-December 1990):9

Jessie Benton Fremont. Book Review. *New Directions for Women* 19, No. 2 (March/April 1990):15

Klondike Women, True Tales of the 1897-98 Gold Rush. Book Review. *New Directions for Women* 19, No. 2 (March/April 1990):14

Libby, the Alaskan Diaries and Letters of Libby Beaman, 1879-1880. Book Review. *New Directions for Women* 19, No. 2 (March/April 1990):14

Litany of Change and Joy. *New Directions for Women* 19, No. 6 (November-December 1990):9

Love Will Find a Way. Music review. *New Directions for Women* 19, No. 3 (May/June 1990):8

No More Blues. Music Review. *New Directions for Women* 19, No. 5 (September-October 1990):6

Play Songs for Kids. *New Directions for Women* 19, No. 5 (September-October 1990):6

A Quilt of Words: Women's Diaries, Letters, and Original Accounts of Life in the Southwest, 1860-1960. Book Review. *New Directions for Women* 19, No. 2 (March/April 1990):15

Saffire: The Uppity Blues Women. Music review. *New Directions for Women* 19, No. 3 (May/June 1990):8

Shake It to the One That You Love the Best. Music Review. *New Directions for Women* 19, No. 5 (September-October 1990):6

She Got 40 Years for Bad Checks. *New Directions for Women* 19, No. 2 (March/April 1990):5

Speaking from Her Heart, Guts. *New Directions for Women* 19, No. 5 (September-October 1990):14

Wild Women Don't Have the Blues. Video review. *New Directions for Women* 19, No. 3 (May/June 1990):9

Women in Pacific Northwest History. Book Review. *New Directions for Women* 19, No. 2 (March/April 1990):14-15

Yes, Mendelssohn Was a Woman. *New Directions for Women* 19, No. 1 (January/February 1990):9

**Werden, Dyana**

Women's Languaging: An Image Word Conjunction. *Trivia* 16/17 (Fall 1990):40-49

**Wernick, Sarah**

The New Need for Neighborly Love. *Working Mother* 13, No. 9 (September 1990):50-53

**Wernick, Sarah** (joint author). *See* Fleming, Don; Shelov, Steven P.

**Werth, Margaret**

Engendering Imaginary Modernism: Henri Matisse's *Bonheur de vivre*. *Genders* 9 (Fall 1990):49-74

**Werthamer, Cynthia**

The Language of the Goddess. Book Review. *New Directions for Women* 19, No. 4 (July-August 1990):14

The Once and Future Goddess. Book Review. *New Directions for Women* 19, No. 4 (July-August 1990):14

Power Lies in the Stars and Ourselves. *New Directions for Women* 19, No. 4 (July-August 1990):8-9

Sacred Female Myths Reveal Goddess Culture. *New Directions for Women* 19, No. 4 (July-August 1990):14

**Wes**

Making a Difference. *Hot Wire* 6, No. 1 (January 1990):51+

**Wesley, Mary** (criticism)

Retrospective: Mary Wesley. Barbara Griffith Furst. *Belles Lettres* 5, No. 4 (Summer 1990):28-29

**Wesley, Valerie Wilson**

Parenting: Learning to Let Go. *Essence* 21, No. 1 (May 1990):188

Parenting: Taking Back Our Schools. *Essence* 20, No. 10 (February 1990):102+

**Wessel, David**

Not Another Ear Infection! *Working Mother* 13, No. 9 (September 1990):76-79

**West, Kathleene**

The Ante-Room. Book Review. *Belles Lettres* 5, No. 3 (Spring 1990):4

Exile of the Heart. *Belles Lettres* 5, No. 3 (Spring 1990):4

The Land of Spices. Book Review. *Belles Lettres* 5, No. 3 (Spring 1990):4

**Westheimer, Ruth K.**

"Talk to My Mom about Sex? No Way!" *Redbook* 175, No. 2 (June 1990):28-32

**West Indians.** *See also* Caribbean

Home Is Where My Heart Is. Elizabeth Nunez-Harrell. *Essence* 20, No. 12 (April 1990):36+

**West Indians – Festivals**

25 Years of Carnival. *Spare Rib* No. 216 (September 1990):14-17

West Indies. *See* Caribbean

**Westkott, Marcia C.**

On the New Psychology of Women: A Cautionary View. *Feminist Issues* 10, No. 2 (Fall 1990):3-18

**Weston, Beverly** and Campbell, Bebe Moore

Spiritual Journey. *Essence* 21, No. 6 (October 1990):94-96+

**Weston, Carol**

New Picturebooks: Redbook Picks 10 Winners. *Redbook* 176, No. 2 (December 1990):26-28

**Weston, Jennifer**

"Thinking in Things": A Women's Symbol Language. *Trivia* 16/17 (Fall 1990):84-98

**Westover, Belinda** (joint author). *See* Pennington, Shelley

**Westwood, Sallie** and Bhachu, Parminder (editors)

Enterprising Women: Ethnicity, Economy, and Gender Relations. Reviewed by Sylvia Walby. *Gender and Society* 4, No. 3 (September 1990):425-427

Enterprising Women. Reviewed by Kathryn Ward. *Women's Studies International Forum* 13, No. 5 (1990):523-524

**Wet Nursing**

Wet Nursing: A History from Antiquity to the Present. By Valerie Fildes. Reviewed by Judith S. Lewis. *Gender & History* 2, No. 2 (Summer 1990):232-234

Wet Nursing: A History from Antiquity to the Present. By Valerie Fildes. Reviewed by Roe Sybylla. *Australian Feminist Studies* No. 11 (Autumn 1990):129-131

**Wetterling, Patricia**

"Have You Seen My Son?" *Ladies' Home Journal* 107, No. 3 (March 1990):22-32

**Wettig, Patricia** (about)

Will Nancy Survive? Brook Hersey. *Glamour* (April 1990):192

**Wetzel, Janice Wood.** *See* Meyer, Carol and Young, Alma (editors), "On the Bias."

**Wetzler, Laura**

Smoke of the Battle. Song. *Bridges* 1, No. 1 (Spring 1990): 80-81

**Wetzsteon, Ross**

Lange Range. *Vogue* (February 1990):192-193, 200

**Wexler, Alice**

Emma Goldman in Exile: From the Russian Revolution to the Spanish Civil War. Reviewed by Eleanor Bader. *Lilith* 15, No. 1 (Winter 1990):7

**Whaley, Frank** (about)

Inside People. *Mademoiselle* (January 1990):48-50

**Wharton, Edith – Bibliographies**

Edith Wharton: An Annotated Secondary Bibliography. By Kristin O. Lauer and Margaret P. Murray. Review. *Feminist Collections* 11, No. 3 (Spring 1990):17

**Wharton, Edith – Criticism and Interpretation**

Edith Wharton's Mothers and Daughters. Susan Goodman. *Tulsa Studies in Women's Literature* 9, No. 1 (Spring 1990):127-131

**Wheatley, Elizabeth**

"Stylistic Ensembles" on a Different Pitch: A Comparative Analysis of Men's and Women's Rugby Songs. *Women & Language* 13, No. 1 (Fall 1990):21-26

**Wheatley, Pat**

A Subversive. Poem. *Canadian Women's Studies* 11, No. 1 (Spring 1990):64

**Wheeler, Caron**

UK Blak: Caron Wheeler Shares Her Thoughts With Spare Rib. *Spare Rib* 217 (October 1990):8-11

**Wheeler, Helen Rippier**

Getting Published in Women's Studies: An International, Interdisciplinary Professional Development Guide Mainly for Women. Reviewed by Linda Gardiner. *NWSA Journal* 2, No. 2 (Spring 1990):303-305

A Multidisciplinary Facts on Women's Aging Quiz to Enhance Awareness. *Journal of Women and Aging* 2, No. 4 (1990):91-107

**Wheeler, Karen**

Gimme Shelter: Toward Housing as a Right, Not a Commodity. *Canadian Women's Studies* 11, No. 2 (Fall 1990):63-66

**Wheelwright, Julie**

Amazons and Military Maids: Women Who Dressed as Men in Pursuit of Life, Liberty and Happiness. Reviewed by C. Kay Larson. *Minerva* 8, No. 2 (Summer 1990):74-78

Amazons and Military Maids: Women Who Dressed as Men in the Pursuit of Life, Liberty and the Pursuit of Happiness. Reviewed by Rita Victoria Gomez Dearmond. *Gender & History* 2, No. 2 (Summer 1990):229-232

**Wheelwright, Julie** (joint author). *See* Birkett, Dea

**Whelehan, Patricia** (editor)

Women and Health: Cross-Cultural Perspectives. Reviewed by Demetria Iazzetto. *NWSA Journal* 2, No. 4 (Autumn 1990):664-668

**Whitaker, Kerry**

The Thin Look. *Family Circle* 103, No. 10 (July 24, 1990):127-128

**Whitbeck, Les B.** (joint author). *See* Conger, Rand D.; Simons, Ronald L.

**White, Alexandra** (joint playwright). *See* Rosenblum, Nina

**White, Barbie** (about)

An Eastern Solution to the Western Waist. Christine K. Van De Velde. *Savvy Woman* (July/August 1990):30-35

**White, Betty** (about). *See also* Sherman, Eric, "Gabbing with the Golden Girls"

**White, Betty** (interview)

Conversation Fragments: Betty White. Frances Beer. *Canadian Women's Studies* 11, No. 1 (Spring 1990):93

**White, Claire Nicholas**

Fragments of Stained Glass. Reviewed Cecilia Konchar Farr. *Belles Lettres* 5, No. 2 (Winter 1990):9

**White, E. Frances**

Africa on My Mind: Gender, Counter Discourse and African-American Nationalism. *Journal of Women's History* 2, No. 1 (Spring 1990):73-97

**White, Edmund** (about)

An Interview with Edmund White. Interview. Adam Block. *Out/Look* No. 10 (Fall 1990):56-62

**White, Edmund** (joint author). *See* Kott, Jan

**White, Evelyn C.**

The Fibroid Epidemic. *Essence* 21, No. 8 (December 1990):22-24

Oakland: Power of the People. *Essence* 21, No. 1 (May 1990):160-164

**White, Evelyn C.** (editor)

The Black Women's Health Book. Reviewed by Beverly Guy-Sheftall. *Ms.* 1, No. 1 (July/August 1990):68-69

The Black Women's Health Book: Speaking for Ourselves. Reviewed by C. J. Walker. *New Directions for Women* 19, No. 6 (November-December 1990):20

The Black Women's Health Book: Speaking for Ourselves. Reviewed by Evelynn Hammonds. *The Women's Review of Books* 7, No. 9 (June 1990):1-4

The Black Women's Health Book: Speaking for Ourselves. Reviewed by M. Stephanie Ricks. *Belles Lettres* 5, No. 4 (Summer 1990):27-28

**White, George L., Jr.**, Murdock, Richard T., Richardson, Glenn E., Ellis, Gary D., and Schmidt, L. J.

Development of a Tool to Assess Suicide Risk Factors in Urban Adolescents. *Adolescence* 25, No. 99 (Fall 1990):655-666

**White, Karen Sethre**

Eggs, Savory-Style. *McCall's* 117, No. 12 (September 1990):150

Hamming It Up: Great Low-Calorie Dishes. *McCall's* 117, No. 11 (August 1990):120

**White, Katherine A.**

Precedent and Progress: The Impending Crisis of Fetal Rights. *Women & Language* 13, No. 1 (Fall 1990):47-49

**White, Kathleen, M.** (joint author). *See* Paul, Elizabeth L.

**White, Lisa Diane**

"Sisters in Session." *New Directions for Women* 19, No. 5 (September-October 1990):8

**White, Lynn K.**

Determinants of Divorce: A Review of Research in the Eighties. *Journal of Marriage and the Family* 52, No. 4 (November 1990):904-912

**White, Lynn K.** and Keith, Bruce

The Effect of Shift Work on the Quality and Stability of Marital Relations. *Journal of Marriage and the Family* 52, No. 2 (May 1990):453-462

**White, Mary A.**

Sarah. Short Story. *Sinister Wisdom* 40 (Spring 1990):40-47

**White, Michael C.**

Take Her Dancing. Short story. *Redbook* 175, No. 4 (August 1990):44-50

**White, Nancy E.** and Richter, Judith M.

Attitude Toward Menopause and the Impact of the Menopausal Event on Adult Women with Diabetes Mellitus. *Journal of Women and Aging* 2, No. 4 (1990):21-38

**White, Ryan** (about)

"I Don't Want My Son to Be Forgotten." Ann Marie Cunningham. *Ladies' Home Journal* 107, No. 8 (August 1990):102-103+

**White, Winifred Varia** (about). *See* Davis, Andrea R., "Power Players"

**White Collar Crime.** *See* Business Ethics; Crime – White Collar

**Whitehead, Mary Beth** (about)

Baby M/Q.E.D. Pam Mason. *Spare Rib* No. 216 (September 1990):30

Sacred Bond. Phyllis Chesler. *Spare Rib* No. 210 (March 1990):56-58

When Is a Mother Not a Mother? The Baby M Case. Sonia Jaffe Robbins. *Women & Language* 13, No. 1 (Fall 1990):41-46

**Whiteley, Elaine F.**

Every Mother's Nightmare. Bibliography. *Ladies' Home Journal* 107, No. 10 (October 1990):151-153+

**Whiten, Colette** (interview)

Conversation Fragments: Colette Whiten. Janice Andreae. *Canadian Women's Studies* 11, No. 1 (Spring 1990):91

**Whiteside, Reid** (joint author). *See* Corder, Billie F.

**Whitlock, Gillian** (editor)

Eight Voices of the Eighties. Reviewed by Susan Sheridan. *Australian Feminist Studies* No. 11 (Autumn 1990):133-135

**Whitman, Lee Miriam**

Four Poems in the Voice of Eve. Poem. *Bridges* 1, No. 1 (Spring 1990): 39-40

**Whitman, Sylvia**

Diary of a Marriage: Rediscovering the Real Ben. *McCall's* 117, No. 10 (July 1990):98-100+

Family Portrait:"There's Always Room for One More." *Ladies' Home Journal* 107, No. 3 (March 1990):126-131

**Whitmire, Kathryn J.** (about). *See* Houston – Politics and Government; Texas – Mayors

**Whitney, Catherine** (joint author). *See* Callaway, C. Wayne; Gershoff, Stanley

**Whittaker, Marion A.** (about). *See also* Lawyers

**Whitzman, Carolyn**

The Toronto Safe City Committee. *Women and Environments* 12, No. 1 (Fall 1989/Winter 1990): 13

**Wholesale Trade Industry**

Enterprise: They Can Get It for You Wholesale. David E. Gumpert. *Working Woman* (August 1990):33-36

**Whyte, Martin King** (joint author). *See* Xiaohe, Xu

**Wicks, Jerry W.** (joint author). *See* Groat, H. Theodore

**Widome, Mark** and Cassidy, Anne

Keeping Your Child Safe. *Good Housekeeping* 211, No. 3 (September 1990):148+

**Widow Burning.** *See* Suttee

**Widowhood**

A Comparison of Coping Strategies Used Effectively by Older Anglo and Mexican-American Widows: A Longitudinal Study. Bette A. Ide, Cynthia Tobias, Margarita Kay, Janice Monk, and Jill Guernsey de Zapien. *Health Care for Women International* 11, No. 3 (1990):237-249

Prime of Life. Barbara Gilder Quint. *Family Circle* 103, No. 11 (August 14, 1990):49+

On Their Own: Widows and Widowhood in the American Southwest, 1848-1939. Edited by Arlene Scadron. Reviewed by Manuel G. Gonzales. *Tulsa Studies in Women's Literature* 9, No. 1 (Spring 1990):152-156

On Their Own: Widows and Widowhood in the American Southwest, 1848-1939. Edited by Arlene

Scadron. Reviewed by Helena Z. Lopata. *Gender and Society* 4, No. 1 (March 1990):103-105

When a Widow Takes the Helm in a Male-Dominated Industry. Patti Watts. *Executive Female* 13, No. 4 (July-August 1990):18-21

**Wiedemann, Thomas**

Adults and Children in the Roman Empire. Reviewed by Janet Huskinson. *Gender & History* 2, No. 1 (Spring 1990):105-106

**Wiener, Joshua M.** (joint author). *See* Rivlin, Alice M.

**Wieringa, Saskia** (editor)

Women's Struggles and Strategies. Reviewed by Hester Eisenstein. *Resources for Feminist Research* 19, No. 1 (March 1990):43-44

**Wiessmann, Robin** (about). *See* Business – Ownership

**Wigs.** *See also* Hair Styles

Big Wigs. *Mademoiselle* (September 1990):268-271

Quick Changes. *Harper's Bazaar* (September 1990):308-311

Talking Fashion: Fake Out. *Vogue* (September 1990):656

**Wigutoff, Sharon** (joint author). *See* Bracken, Jeanne

**Wigwag Magazine**

No Place Like Home. *Harper's Bazaar* (February 1990):76

**Wilberforce, Octavia** (about)

Octavia Wilberforce. Edited by Pat Jalland. Reviewed by Moira Woods. *Women's Studies International Forum* 13, No. 5 (1990):524-525

Octavia Wilberforce, Pioneer Woman Doctor. By Pat Jalland. Reviewed by Angela V. John. *Gender & History* 2, No. 3 (Autumn 1990):375-377

**Wilbur, JoEllen** (joint author). *See* Dan, Alice J.

**Wilcox, Clyde**

Black Women and Feminism. *Women & Politics* 10, No. 3 (1990):65-84

**Wilcox, Helen** (joint editor). *See* Thompson, Ann

**Wilde, Oscar** (criticism)

Wilde, Barthes, and the Orgasmics of Truth. Kevin Kopelson. *Genders* 7 (Spring 1990):22-31

**Wilder, Laura Ingalls** (about)

Laura Ingalls Wilder and Rose Wilder Lane: The Politics of a Mother-Daughter Relationship. Notes. Anita Clair Fellman. *Signs* 15, No. 3 (Spring 1990):535-561

**Wildlife, Rehabilitation**

She Helps Them Return to the Wild. Carol Turkington. *Good Housekeeping* 210, No. 5 (May 1990):152-154

**Wildlife, Watching**

Pet Life. Michael W. Fox. *McCall's* 117, No. 10 (July 1990):111

**Wilds, Nancy G.**

Sexual Harassment in the Military. *Minerva* 8, No. 4 (Winter 1990):1-16

**Wiley, Arthur J.** (joint author). *See* Violato, Claudio

**Wilkens, Linda** (joint editor). *See* Ostenk, Annemiek

**Wilkinson, Peter**

The Meet Market. *Savvy Woman* (July/August 1990):52-55+

**Wilkinson, Shelagh** (joint author). *See* Luxton, Meg

**Willen, Diane**

Industry of Devotion: The Transformation of Women's Work in England, 1500-1660. Book Review. *Gender and Society* 4, No. 2 (June 1990):267-269

**Willens, Susan P.**

Lost in Translation: A Life in a New Languages. Book Review. *Belles Lettres* 5, No. 2 (Winter 1990):2

Sleeping Arrangements. Book Review. *Belles Lettres* 5, No. 2 (Winter 1990):7

**Willenz, Nicole** (about)

Ambassador of Technology. Suzanne Weber and D. M. Pusateri. *Executive Female* 13, No. 4 (July-August 1990):47-48

**Willetts, Kathy**

In Search of the Authentic Voice. *Hecate* 16, Nos. 1-2 (1990):167-170

Wandering Girl. Book Review. *Hecate* 16, Nos. 1-2 (1990):167-170

**Williams, Armstrong**

Back Talk: Friendship and Betrayal. *Essence* 20, No. 9 (January 1990):110

**Williams, Billy Dee** (about)

Undeniably Billy. Elsie B. Washington. *Essence* 20, No. 12 (April 1990):14-15

**Williams, Carol**

Operations in the Sphere of the Vulgar: The Work of Wilma Needham. *Canadian Women's Studies* 11, No. 1 (Spring 1990):56-59

**Williams, Carol** (about). *See* Alexander, Nanine

**Williams, Christine**

Gender Differences at Work: Women and Men in Nontraditional Occupations. Reviewed by Autumn Stanley. *NWSA Journal* 2, No. 4 (Autumn 1990):640-645

**Williams, Christine B.**

Women, Law and Politics: Recruitment Patterns in the Fifty States. *Women & Politics* 10, No. 3 (1990):103-123

**Williams, Claire**

Blue, White and Pink Collar Workers in Australia: Technicians, Bank Employees and Flight Attendants. Reviewed by Colleen Chesterman. *Australian Feminist Studies* No. 11 (Autumn 1990):123-126

**Williams, Claudette.** *See* Radio Broadcasting – Plays

Hallelujah Anyhow. *Spare Rib* 219 (December 1990-January 1991):8-12

**Williams, Cynda** (about). *See* Demarchelier, Patrick, "Le Jazz Haute."

**Williams, Daniel T.** (joint editor). *See* Kestenbaum, Clarice J.

**Williams, Gari L.** (joint author). *See* Jennings, Maude M.

**Williams, J. Allen, Jr.** (joint author). *See* Vernon, JoEtta A.

**Williams, Leslie A.** (about)

Style: Black & White in Color. *Essence* 20, No. 12 (April 1990):22

**Williams, Linda S.**

Motherhood, Ideology, and the Power to Technology: In Vitro Fertilization Use by Adoptive Mothers. *Women's Studies International Forum* 13, No. 6 (1990):543-552

**Williams, Lynna**

Personal Testimony. Short story. *Lear's* (January 1990):116-121

**Williams, Mary Alice** (about). *See also* Television Journalists – Networking

**Williams, Mavis**

Cheers for Mavis Williams. Elayne Clift. *New Directions for Women* 19, No. 3 (May/June 1990):3

**Williams, Megan**

AIDS and Sexual Assault. *Healthsharing* 11, No. 3 (June 1990):11

**Williams, Natalie**

Lesbian and Gay People of Colour Gather in London. *Spare Rib* 219 (December 1990-January 1991):66-67

**Williams, Robert** (joint author). *See* Stockmyer, John

**Williams, Sherley Anne**

The Lessons of This Decade. Poem. *Essence* 21, No. 5 (September 1990):112

Travel: Scenes of Senegal. *Essence* 20, No. 11 (March 1990):110-112

**Williams, Sherley Anne – Criticism and Interpretation**

"I Made the Ink": (Literary) Production and Reproduction in *Dessa Rose* and *Beloved*. Anne E. Goldman. *Feminist Studies* 16, No. 2 (Summer 1990):313-330

**Williams, Terry** (about)

Terry Williams Takes Drugs Seriously. Paula Giddings. *Essence* 20, No. 10 (February 1990):42

**Williams, Walter L.**

Women and Work in the Third World: Indonesian Women's Oral Histories. *Journal of Women's History* 2, No. 1 (Spring 1990):183-195

**Williams, Wendy** (about). *See also* Athletes, "The Competitive Edge"

**Willis, Julia**

Who Wears the Tux? The Original Great American Dyke Quiz. Reviewed by Rosalind Warren. *New Directions for Women* 19, No. 5 (September-October 1990):20

**Wills**

The Last Taboo. Andrea Gross. *Ladies' Home Journal* 107, No. 4 (April 1990):144-148

**Wilmer, Val**

Mama Said There'd Be Days Like This–My Life in the Jazz World. Reviewed by Robyn Archer. *Feminist Review* No. 35 (Summer 1990):123-124

**Wilms Montt, Teresa** (about)

Teresa Wilms Montt: A Forgotten Legend. Marjorie Agosin. *Women's Studies International Forum* 13, No. 3 (1990):195-199

**Wilson, Barbara**

The Dog Collar Murders. Reviewed by Linda Semple. *Feminist Review* No. 35 (Summer 1990):119-121

The Dog Collar Murders. Reviewed by Tracy Scott. *New Directions for Women* 19, No. 5 (September-October 1990):20

**Wilson, Barbara** (interview)

Barbara Wilson Talks About: Feminist Publishing, Crime and Punishment. June Thomas. *off our backs* 20, No. 1 (January 1990):10-11

**Wilson, Budge**

For Glynis Reaching the Age of 21. Poem. *Canadian Women's Studies* 11, No. 2 (Fall 1990):83

**Wilson, Cheryl F.**

Back Talk: Owning Our Share. *Essence* 20, No. 12 (April 1990):124

**Wilson, C.** (joint author). *See* Lester, David

**Wilson, Elizabeth**

Deviant Dress. *Feminist Review* No. 35 (Summer 1990):67-74

**Wilson, Gloria** (joint author). *See* Puskar, Kathryn R.

**Wilson, Iva** (about)

Just Tell Her She Can't. Celia Kuperszmid Lehrman. *Executive Female* (March/April 1990):41-43

**Wilson, Janet** (joint author). *See* Vernon, JoEtta A.

**Wilson, Judi**

Dispatches: The AIDS Catch. Video Review. *Spare Rib* No. 215 (August 1990):32-33

Women HIV and AIDS: Speaking Out in the UK. Video Review. *Spare Rib* 219 (December 1990-January 1991):34-35

**Wilson, Lauren** (joint author). *See* Brodsky, Michelle

**Wilson, Marti**

Travel: Trading Places. Bibliography. *Essence* 21, No. 3 (July 1990):94+

**Wilson, Nancy** (about). *See* Musicians, Popular, "Repeat Performance"

**Wilson, Robley, Jr.**

A Sweet Memory. Short story. *Redbook* 174, No. 5 (March 1990):172-174

**Wilson, Stephan M.** and Medora, Nilufer P.

Gender Comparisons of College Students' Attitudes toward Sexual Behavior. *Adolescence* 25, No. 99 (Fall 1990):615-627

**Wilson, Susan Kaye** (joint author). *See* Jaffee, Peter G.

**Wilson-Ford, Vanessa**

Poverty Among Black Elderly Women. *Journal of Women and Aging* 2, No. 4 (1990):5-20

**Wilson Phillips** (about)

Word On . . . Willson Phillips. Charla Krupp. *Glamour* (May 1990):204

**Wilt, Judith**

Burning Down the House. *The Women's Review of Books* 7, No. 9 (June 1990):20

The Contested Castle: Gothic Novels and the Subversion of Domestic Ideology. Book Review. *The Women's Review of Books* 7, No. 9 (June 1990):20

**Winbush, Angela** (about)

Angela Winbush Takes Care of Business. Carol Cooper. *Essence* 20, No. 10 (February 1990):39

**Winchell, Walter** (about)

Walter Winchell. Liz Smith. *Lear's* (June 1990):74-75+

**Winchester Three**

Winchester 3 Freed. *Spare Rib* No. 212 (May 1990):45

**Windinwood, Rebecca Wells**

Women's Bodies: Sacred Essence in Physical Form. *Woman of Power* 18 (Fall 1990):54-56

**Wine and Winemaking**

Bottled Blossoms. Lynn Fredericks. *Harper's Bazaar* (March 1990):239

Thirst for Knowledge. Lynn Fredericks. *Harper's Bazaar* (July 1990):114+

**Wineapple, Brenda**

Gene3t: A Biography of Janet Flanner. Reviewed by Scarlet Cheng. *Belles Lettres* 5, No. 3 (Spring 1990):8

**Wineberg, Howard**

Childbearing after Remarriage. *Journal of Marriage and the Family* 52, No. 1 (February 1990):31-38

**Winegarten, Ruthe**

Black Texas Women: Literary Self-Portraits. *Woman of Power* 16 (Spring 1990):29-31

**Winer, Laurie**

Seventh Heaven. Book Review. *Vogue* (August 1990):232-234

**Winfield, Marlene**

Shielding Women from the Truth: The Story of the Dalkon Shield. *Spare Rib* No. 216 (September 1990):58

**Winfrey, Oprah** (about)

Oprah's Wonder Year. Eric Sherman. *Ladies' Home Journal* 107, No. 5 (May 1990):157-159+

**Wings, Mary**

Mars Bar. Short story. *Out/Look* No. 9 (Summer 1990):32-35

**Winkfield, Trevor** (about). *See* Perl, Jed, "Vogue Arts: Charmed Lives."

**Winkler, John J.**

Phallos Politikos: Representing the Body Politic in Athens. *Differences* 2, No. 1 (Spring 1990):29-45

**Winninghoff, Ellie**

Entrepreneurial Edge: Grow, Baby, Grow! *Working Woman* (September 1990):101-104

**Winschel, Diane Perron** (about). *See* Casey, Kathryn, "Voices of the Decade"

**Winsom** (interview)

Conversation Fragments: Winsom. Janice Andreae. *Canadian Women's Studies* 11, No. 1 (Spring 1990):90

**Winter—Accidents**

"I Slipped on the Ice." Irene Nyborg-Andersen. *Ladies' Home Journal* 107, No. 1 (January 1990):52-56

**Winter, Metta**

School's Almost Out! What'll You Do With The Kids? *Working Mother* 13, No. 5 (May 1990):28-32

**Winter, Ruth**

Health Watch. *Family Circle* 103, No. 12 (September 4, 1990):51-54

**Winter Resorts.** *See* Ski Resorts

**Winterson, Jeanette**

Oranges are Not the Only Fruit. Television Play. Reviewed by Cherry Smyth. *Spare Rib* No. 209 (February 1990):34

Sexing the Cherry. Reviewed by Charlotte Innes. *New Directions for Women* 19, No. 5 (September-October 1990):17

Sexing the Cherry. Reviewed by Rosellen Brown. *The Women's Review of Books* 7, No. 12 (September 1990):9-10

**Winterson, Jeanette** (interview)

Belles Lettres Interview. Suzanne Scott and Lynne M. Constantine. *Belles Lettres* 5, No. 4 (Summer 1990):24-26

Unnatural Passions. *Spare Rib* No. 209 (February 1990):26-29

**Winter Sports.** *See also* Ski Resorts

Fitness: Wilderness Sports. Bibliography. Grace Lichtenstein. *Vogue* (January 1990):80-83

Good Sports: Hot Tips for Working Out in the Cold. Joanne Mattera. *Glamour* (February 1990):58

**Wintour, Anna**

AIDS 1990. *Vogue* (November 1990):366

**Wirka, Jeanne** (about). *See* D'Amico, Marie and Jubak, Jim

**Wisconsin—State Historical Society**

Historical Society Women's Collections to Be Published. Harry Miller. *Feminist Collections* 11, No. 2 (Winter 1990):13-14

State Historical Society of Wisconsin Welcomes Suffragist's Papers. Cindy Knight. *Feminist Collections* 12, No. 1 (Fall 1990):18-20

**Wisconsin Woman Suffrage Association.** *See* James, Ada Lois (about)

**Wise, Debra**

The Quest for the Perfect Winter Coat. *Glamour* (October 1990):214

Shopping Smart: What's New in Off-Price? Bibliography. *Glamour* (September 1990):272

**Wiseman, Richard** (joint author). *See* Jackson, Katherine

**Wiseman, Richard L.** (joint author). *See* Sanders, Judith A.

**Wishik, Debra**

Don't Be a Victim of Future Shock. *Savvy Woman* (January 1990):23-24

**Wisniewski, Shirley A.** and Gaier, Eugene L.

Causal Attributions for Losing as Perceived by Adolescents. *Adolescence* 25, No. 97 (Spring 1990):239-247

## Women's Movement – History

Andrea Dworkin: From a War Zone. Elizabeth Braeman and Carol Cox. *off our backs* 20, No. 1 (January 1990):8-9+

Chicago '60s: Ecstasy as Our Guide. Naomi Weisstein. *Ms.* 1, No. 2 (September/October 1990):65-67

Daring to Be Bad: Radical Feminism in American 1967-1975. By Alice Echols. Reviewed by Carol Anne Douglas. *off our backs* 20, No. 4 (April 1990):16-17

A Decade Later Burning Questions Remain Unanswered. Lynn Wenzel. *New Directions for Women* 19, No. 3 (May/June 1990):23

Evolution of the Feminist Movement in Japan. Machiko Matsui. *NWSA Journal* 2, No. 3 (Summer 1990):435-449

Letters From a War Zone. By Andrea Dworkin. Reviewed by Carol Anne Douglas. *off our backs* 20, No. 1 (January 1990):18-20

Letters from a War Zone: Writings 1976-87. By Andrea Dworkin. Reviewed by Alice Echols. *The Women's Review of Books* 7, No. 4 (January 1990):5-6

Letters from a War Zone: Writings 1976-1989. By Andrea Dworkin. Reviewed by Lisa Maher. *Women's Rights Law Reporter* 12, No. 3 (Fall 1990): 209-216

What Is *off our backs*? Jennie Ruby. *off our backs* 20, No. 2 (February 1990):1-3

## Women's Movement – Racism

The Politics of Difference. Hazel V. Carby. *Ms.* 1, No. 2 (September/October 1990):84-85

Young Women Fight Movement Racism. Rebecca Davis. *New Directions for Women* 19, No. 1 (January/February 1990):5

## Women's Museum

The Women's Museum in Denmark. Merete Ipsen and Jette Sandahl. *Journal of Women's History* 2, No. 2 (Fall 1990):168-170

## Women's Music Union. *See* Music Union Productions

## Women's Project, Inc.

Past and Promise: Lives of New Jersey Women. Reviewed by Phyllis Ehrenfeld. *New Directions for Women* 19, No. 5 (September-October 1990):20

## Women's Research and Employment Initiatives Program

New Brooms, Restructuring and Training Issues for Women in the Service Sector. Reviewed by Cora Vellekoop Baldock. *Australian Feminist Studies* No. 12 (Summer 1990):43-49

## Women's Shelters

Brent Women's Refuge Face Eviction. *Spare Rib* 217 (October 1990):45

A Case Study of Battered Women's Shelters in Appalachia. Karen W. Tice. *AFFILIA* 5, No. 3 (Fall 1990):83-100

Despite Quake Damage, Women's Building Essential Haven. Linda Roman. *New Directions for Women* 19, No. 1 (January/February 1990):6

Woman to Woman: Dealing with Domestic Violence. *Spare Rib* No. 216 (September 1990):8-13

Women's Refuge Faces Funding Cuts. Marie de Santis. *Spare Rib* 217 (October 1990):45

## Women's Sports Foundation

Teamwork. Kathryn Reith. *Women's Sports and Fitness* 12, No. 4 (May-June 1990):78

## Women's Studies

Abstracts. *Resources for Feminist Research* 19, No. 2 (June 1990):50-77

The Broadening Impact of Women's Studies. *NWSAction* 3, No. 4 (Winter 1990): 4-8

Canto, Locura y Poesia. Olivia Castellano. *The Women's Review of Books* 7, No. 5 (February 1990):18-20

Changing Our Minds: Feminist Transformations of Knowledge. Edited by Susan Hardy Aiken, Karen Anderson, Myra Dinnerstein, Judy Nolte Lensink and Patricia MacCorquodale. Reviewed by Margot I. Duley. *Signs* 15, No. 3 (Spring 1990):648-650

Conference Call. Barbara Christian, Ann DuCille, Sharon Marcus, Elaine Marks, Nancy K. Miller, and others. *Differences* 2, No. 3 (Fall 1990):52-108

At the Crossroads of Culture. Peggy Pascoe. *The Women's Review of Books* 7, No. 5 (February 1990):22-23

Feminist Theory in Practice and Process. Edited by Micheline R. Malson and others. Reviewed by Joan M. Fayer. *Women & Language* 13, No. 2 (Winter 1990):42

Ford Foundation Funds Curriculum Integration Project Mainstreaming Minority Women's Studies. Leslie I. Hill. *NWSAction* 3, No. 4 (Winter 1990): 6-7

The Ford Foundation Program on Mainstreaming Minority Women's Studies. Leslie I. Hill. *Women's Studies Quarterly* 18, Nos. 1-2 (Spring-Summer 1990):24-38

Male Students in Women's Studies. Tricia Lootens. *off our backs* 20, No. 8 (August/September 1990):20+

Nonfeminist and Feminist Students at Risk: The Use of Case Study Analysis While Transforming the Postsecondary Curriculum. Joan Poliner Shapiro. *Women's Studies International Forum* 13, No. 6 (1990):553-564

The Permanent Revolution. Sandra Harding. *The Women's Review of Books* 7, No. 5 (February 1990):17

Reconstructing the Academy: Women's Education and Women's Studies. Edited by E. Minnich, J. O'Barr, and R. Rosenfeld. Reviewed by Sara Delamont. *Gender and Education* 2, No. 2 (1990):245-246

Second Chance, Second Self? Judy Giles. *Gender and Education* 2, No. 3 (1990):357-361

Teaching Women's Studies: The Repersonalization of Our Politics. Chris Ruggiero. *Women's Studies International Forum* 13, No. 5 (1990):469-475

Teaching Women's Studies from an International Perspective. Anne Betteridge and Janice Monk. *Women's Studies Quarterly* 18, Nos. 1-2 (Spring-Summer 1990):78-85

"White Women, Racism and Anti-Racism": A Women's Studies Course Exploring Racism and Privilege. Ruth Frankenberg. *Women's Studies Quarterly* 18, Nos. 1-2 (Spring-Summer 1990):145-153

A Woman's Place Is Everyplace . . . Emily Toth. *The Women's Review of Books* 7, No. 5 (February 1990):28

Women's Studies: Science, Violence and Responsibility. Maria Mies. *Women's Studies International Forum* 13, No. 5 (1990):433-441

**Women's Studies – Bibliographies.** *See also* Suffrage Movement

Books Currently Received. *Feminist Collections* 11, No. 4 (Summer 1990):22-24

Books Recently Received. *Feminist Collections* 11, No. 2 (Winter 1990):30-32; 12, No. 1 (Fall 1990):38-39

Historical Society Women's Collections to Be Published. Harry Miller. *Feminist Collections* 11, No. 2 (Winter 1990):13-14

On the Lookout. *AFFILIA* 5, No. 2 (Summer 1990):97-99

On the Lookout. Edited by L. Diane Bernard and Miriam Dinerman. *AFFILIA* 5, No. 1 (Spring 1990):94-96

New Reference Works in Women's Studies. *Feminist Collections* 11, No. 2 (Winter 1990):20-25; 12, No. 1 (Fall 1990):25-33

Periodical Notes. *Feminist Collections* 11, No. 2 (Winter 1990):26-29; 11, No. 4 (Summer 1990):19-21; 12, No. 1 (Fall 1990):33-36

Publications of Interest. Bibliography. *Signs* 15, No. 2 (Winter 1990):429-432; 15, No. 3 (Spring 1990):662-665; 15, No. 4 (Summer 1990):884-886

Reading Lists on Women's Studies in Economics. Barbara R. Bergmann. *Women's Studies Quarterly* 18, Nos. 3-4 (Fall-Winter 1990):75-86

United States and International Notes. Bibliography. *Signs* 15, No. 2 (Winter 1990):429-430

Women of Color and the Core Curriculum: Tools for Transforming the Liberal Arts, Part 3. Susan E. Searing. *Feminist Collections* 11, No. 4 (Summer 1990):11-16

Women's Issues: An Annotated Bibliography. By Laura Stempel Mumford. Review. *Feminist Collections* 11, No. 3 (Spring 1990):17

**Women's Studies – Conferences**

Women's Studies in Europe: Conference Report. Tobe Levin and Jo Myers-Dickinson. *NWSA Journal* 2, No. 1 (Winter 1990):101-104

**Women's Studies – Publishing Opportunities**

Getting Published in Women's Studies: An International, Interdisciplinary Professional Development Guide Mainly for Women. By Helen Rippier Wheeler. Reviewed by Linda Gardiner. *NWSA Journal* 2, No. 2 (Spring 1990):303-305

**Women's Studies – Resources**

An Encyclopedic Undertaking. Linda Shult. *Feminist Collections* 11, No. 3 (Spring 1990):11-12

Center for Research on Women, Memphis State University. *NWSAction* 3, No. 4 (Winter 1990): 11-12

Electronic Records at the National Archives: Resources for Women's Studies. Margaret O. Adams. *NWSA Journal* 2, No. 2 (Spring 1990):269-272

New Reference Works in Women's Studies. *Feminist Collections* 11, No. 3 (Spring 1990):14-21

**Women's Studies – Study and Teaching**

Against Gendrification: Agendas for Feminist Scholarship and Teaching in Women's Studies. Susan Fraiman. *Iris* 23 (Spring-Summer 1990):5-9

Selective Rejection: How Students Perceive Women's Studies Teachers. Beth Hartung. *NWSA Journal* 2, No. 2 (Spring 1990):254-263

Small Group Pedagogy: Consciousness Raising in Conservative Times. Estelle B. Freedman. *NWSA Journal* 2, No. 4 (Autumn 1990):603-623

**Women's Studies – Conferences**

Women's Studies in Europe: Conference Reports, Part II. Angelika Koster-Lossack and Tobe Levin. *NWSA Journal* 2, No. 2 (Spring 1990):264-268

**Women's Studies Curricula**

Feminist Cultural Studies: Questions for the 1990s. Anne Balsamo and Paula A. Treichler. *Women & Language* 13, No. 1 (Fall 1990):3-6

News for UW-Milwaukee. Jan Yoder. *Feminist Collections* 11, No. 2 (Winter 1990):19-20

Nussbaum. Reviewed by Steven Deutsch. *Women and Health* 16, Nos. 3/4 (1990):201-205

**Work Space.** *See* Office Layout; Orderliness; Personal Space

**World Congress of Applied Linguistics – Conference Report**

Report from Ninth World Congress of Applied Linguistics. *Women & Language* 13, No. 2 (Winter 1990):33-34

**World War I, 1914-1918**

Not So Quiet. By Helen Zenna Smith. Reviewed by Bonnie Kime Scott. *Tulsa Studies in Women's Literature* 9, No. 2 (Fall 1990):339-342

We That Were Young. By Irene Rathbone. Reviewed by Boannie Kime Scott. *Tulsa Studies in Women's Literature* 9, No. 2 (Fall 1990):339-342

**World War I, 1914-1918 – Women's Roles**

Women in the First World War. By Gill Thomas. Reviewed by Fiona Terry. *Gender & History* 2, No. 3 (Autumn 1990):371-373

**World War II, 1939-1945**

War as Women Saw It. Mary Anne Schofield. *Belles Lettres* 5, No. 4 (Summer 1990):38-39

Widows of Hiroshima: The Life Stories of Nineteen Peasant Wives. Edited by Mikio Kanda. Reviewed by Takayo Mukai. *Belles Lettres* 6, No. 1 (Fall 1990):25

**World War II, 1939-1945 – Personal Narratives**

Life's High Spot. Amber Tullar. *Minerva* 8, No. 1 (Spring 1990):68-81

Miss You: The World War II Letters of Barbara Wooddall Taylor and Charles E. Taylor. Edited by Judy Barrett Litoff and David C. Smith. Reviewed by Mary Anne Schofield. *Belles Lettres* 5, No. 4 (Summer 1990):39

My War: WWII – As Experienced by One Woman Soldier. By Catherine (Bell) Chrisman. Reviewed by Eleanor Stoddard. *Minerva* 8, No. 4 (Winter 1990):48-53

One Woman's War: Letters from the Women's Army Corps, 1944-1946. By Anne Bosanko Green. Reviewed by Eleanor Stoddard. *Minerva* 8, No. 4 (Winter 1990):48-53

**World War II, 1939-1945 – Reservists**

Female Naval Reservists During World War II: A Historiographical Essay. Regina T. Akers. *Minerva* 8, No. 2 (Summer 1990):55-61

**World War II, 1939-1945 – Women's Roles**

Keep Smiling Through: Women in the Second World War. By Caroline Lang. Reviewed by Fiona Terry. *Gender & History* 2, No. 3 (Autumn 1990):371-373

**Worobow, Alyson L.** (joint author). *See* Heilbrun, Alfred B. (Jr.)

**Worsnop, Judith**

A Reevaluation of "The Problem of Surplus Women" in 19th-Century England: The Case of the 1851 Census. *Women's Studies International Forum* 13, Nos. 1-2 (1990):21-31

**Wortman, Camille B.** (joint author). *See* Tiedje, Linda Beth

**Wounds and Injuries**

"I Slipped on the Ice." Irene Nyborg-Andersen. *Ladies' Home Journal* 107, No. 1 (January 1990):52-56

**Wray, Lynnette**

AIDS and Other Sexually Transmitted Diseases. Book Review. *Healthright* 9, No. 3 (May 1990):38

Family Planning Handbook for Doctors. Book Review. *Healthright* 9, No. 2 (February 1990):38

**Wren, Jenny**

Guide to Women Book Publishers in the United States for 1988/89. Review. *Feminist Collections* 11, No. 3 (Spring 1990):19

**Wright, Barbara Drygulski** (editor)

Women, Work, and Technology: Transformations. Reviewed by Dula J. Espinosa. *NWSA Journal* 2, No. 3 (Summer 1990):499-501

**Wright, Christine Logan**

Anything Goes: Reclaiming the Songs of Cole Porter. *Mademoiselle* (November 1990):94

Need to Know. *Mademoiselle* (June 1990):86

One Nation Under a Groove. *Mademoiselle* (December 1990):95

**Wright, Christine Logan** (joint author). *See* Brody, Meredith

**Wright, Cynthia**

Uneven Developments: The Ideological Work of Gender in Mid-Victorian England. Book Review. *Resources for Feminist Research* 19, No. 1 (March 1990):35-36

**Wright, Cynthia A.**

Sexism in the Military: Reality Echoed in Haldeman's *Forever War* and Herbert's *God Emperor of Dune*. *Minerva* 8, No. 3 (Fall 1990):16-27

**Wright, Holly** (about)

Exposing Darkness to Light: Holly Wright's Vanity Images. Joseph Foley. *Iris* 23 (Spring-Summer 1990):21-24

**Wright, Joseph** (about)

Vogue Arts: Art. Douglas Blau. *Vogue* (September 1990):424-428

A Woman for Lear's: One for the Books. Jane Howard. *Lear's* (June 1990):132-135

Writers as Activists. Amber Hollibaugh. *Out/Look* No. 10 (Fall 1990):69-72

**Writing.** See also Children – Writings

The Women Writers' Handbook. Edited by Robson, Georgeson, and Beck. Reviewed by Margaretta Jolly. *Spare Rib* No. 215 (August 1990):28-29

Writing in the Feminine: Feminism and Experimental Writing in Quebec. By Karen Gould. Reviewed by Alice Parker. *The Women's Review of Books* 8, No. 3 (December 1990):28-29

The Writing Life. By Annie Dillard. Reviewed by Suzanne Berne. *Belles Lettres* 5, No. 3 (Spring 1990):6

The Writing or the Sex? Or, Why You Don't Have to Read Women's Writing to Know It's No Good. By Dale Spender. Reviewed by Dorothy Zaborszky. *Resources for Feminist Research* 19, No. 1 (March 1990):46-47

The Writing or the Sex? Or Why You Don't Have to Read Women's Writing to Know It's No Good. By Dale Spender. Reviewed by Alison Townsend. *The Women's Review of Books* 7, No. 4 (January 1990):12-13

The Writing or the Sex? or Why You Don't Have to Read Women's Writing to Know It's no Good. By Dale Spender. Reviewed by Anne Innis Dagg. *Atlantis* 15, No. 2 (Spring 1990):95-96

**Writing – Business Purposes**

Business Writing – Without Blood, Sweat and Tears. Judith Yellen and Barrett J. Mandel. *Working Woman* (June 1990):64-67 +

**Writing Workshops**

Lifelines: Women and Writing. Phyllis Theroux. *Lear's* (May 1990):56-58

Surviving Homelessness. Linda King. *Spare Rib* No. 209 (February 1990):38-41

**Written Communication.** See Speechwriting

**Wuest, Judith**

Trying It on for Size: Mutual Support in Role Transition for Pregnant Teens and Student Nurses. *Health Care for Women International* 11, No. 4 (1990):383-392

**Wulfhorst, Ellen**

Outsmarting Wall Street. *Savvy Woman* (November 1990):58

Surviving the Cut. *Savvy Woman* (September 1990):33-37

**Wurman, Richard Saul**

The Healthy Family. *Family Circle* 103, No. 1 (January 9, 1990):17-18 +

**Wurtzel, Elizabeth**

Tangled Up in Blues. *Mademoiselle* (April 1990):228-229, 260-261

**Wyatt, Gail Elizabeth,** Notgrass, Cindy M., and Newcomb, Michael

Internal and External Mediators of Women's Rape Experiences. *Psychology of Women Quarterly* 14, No. 2 (June 1990):153-176

**Wyatt, Monica** (about)

The Foxy Producer. Betty Goodwin. *Mademoiselle* (October 1990):155 +

**Wylie, Alison,** Okruhlik, Kathleen, Morton, Sandra, and Thielen-Wilson, Leslie

Philosophical Feminism: A Bibliographic Guide to Critiques of Science. *Resources for Feminist Research* 19, No. 2 (June 1990):2-36

**Wynder, Ernst L.** (about)

Lunch. Interview. Frances Lear. *Lear's* (August 1990):15-16

**Wynette, Tammy** (about). See Music – Country and Western

**Wyoming Governor's Mansion.** See Governors – United States – Mansions

**Wyse, Lois**

Precious. Short story. *Redbook* 175, No. 2 (June 1990):42-44

The Way We Are. *Good Housekeeping* 211, No. 3 (September 1990):314, 211, No. 4 (October 1990):264

**Wyse, Sharon**

Battered Women Fill Prisons. *New Directions for Women* 19, No. 2 (March/April 1990):4 +

Children of Battered Women. Book Review. *On the Issues* 17 (Winter 1990):34-35

# X

**Xiaohe, Xu** and Whyte, Martin King

Love Matches and Arranged Marriages: A Chinese Replication. *Journal of Marriage and the Family* 52, No. 3 (August 1990):709-722

# Y

**Yadav, R. J.** (joint author). See Singh, Padam

**Yaeger, Patricia** and Kowaleski-Wallace, Beth

Refiguring the Father: New Feminist Readings of Patriarchy. Reviewed by Miriam M. Johnson. *NWSA Journal* 2, No. 4 (Autumn 1990):656-658

**Yaffé, Maurice** and Fenwick, Elizabeth

If You Want Love to Last, Choose Smart. Excerpt. *Essence* 21, No. 5 (September 1990):85

**Yamada, Mitsuye**

My Genetic Goddesses. *Woman of Power* 15 (Fall-Winter 1990):25-27

**Yamaguchi, Natsuko**

Japan: "Rapeman" Comics. *Ms.* 1, No. 3 (November/December 1990):13

**Yamanaka, Keiko**

With Silk Wings: Asian American Women at Work. Film review. *NWSA Journal* 2, No. 1 (Winter 1990):120-124

**Yami, Hsila**

Women and the Democracy Movement in Nepal. *Manushi* 60 (September-October 1990):29-33

**Yanay, Niza** and Birns, Beverly

Autonomy as Emotion: The Phenomenology of Independence in Academic Women. *Women's Studies International Forum* 13, No. 3 (1990):249-260

**Yancey, Antronette** (about)

Bicoastal Career. Mary Alice Kellogg. *Harper's Bazaar* (October 1990):176-177 +

**Yang, Anand A.**

The Compassionate Memsahibs: Welfare Activities of British Women in India, 1900-1947. Book Review. *Women's Studies International Forum* 13, No. 4 (1990):407-408

White Women in Fiji, 1835-1930: The Ruin of Empire? Book Review. *Women's Studies International Forum* 13, No. 4 (1990):407-408

Women of the Raj. Book Review. *Women's Studies International Forum* 13, No. 4 (1990):407-408

**Yang, Linda**

The Small Garden: A Green and Flourishing Refuge. *McCall's* 117, No. 8 (May 1990):121-124

**Yarbrough, Jeff**

Bright Face, Big Future. *Harper's Bazaar* (February 1990):54

**Yard, Molly** (about)

Then and Now: From Epiphany to Excess. Margaret Carlson. *Lear's* (February 1990):72-77

**Yasmeen, Gisele**

Mutual Aid and Social Networks: A Feminist-Inspired Housing Co-op in Montreal. *Canadian Women's Studies* 11, No. 2 (Fall 1990):25-28

**Yayori, Matsui**

Women's Asia. Reviewed by Yukiko Hanawa. *The Women's Review of Books* 8, No. 2 (November 1990):25-26

**Yeager, Ann Lowrey**

Songs of Lost Children. Poem. *AFFILIA* 5, No. 4 (Winter 1990):119

**Yeatman, Anna**

Bureaucrats, Technocrats, Femocrats: Essays on the Contemporary Australian State. Reviewed by Lois Bryson. *Australian Feminist Studies* No. 12 (Summer 1990):133-136

**Yellen, Judith** and Mandel, Barrett J.

Business Writing – Without Blood, Sweat and Tears. *Working Woman* (June 1990):64-67 +

**Yezierska, Anzia**

Hungry Hearts and Other Stories. Reviewed by Laura Hapke. *Belles Lettres* 6, No. 1 (Fall 1990):54

**Yglesias, Helen**

Between the Hills and the Sea. Book Review. *The Women's Review of Books* 7, Nos. 10-11 (July 1990):16-17

Chronicle of the Class Wars. *The Women's Review of Books* 7, Nos. 10-11 (July 1990):16-17

**Yllö, Kersti** and Bograd, Michele (editors)

Feminist Perspectives on Wife Abuse. Reviewed by Freda L. Paltiel. *Women and Health* 16, Nos. 3/4 (1990):196-201

Feminist Perspectives on Wife Abuse. Reviewed by Lorraine M. Gutiérrez. *AFFILIA* 5, No. 1 (Spring 1990):119-120

Feminist Perspectives on Wife Abuse. Reviewed by Marcia Bedard. *NWSA Journal* 2, No. 3 (Summer 1990):464-475

**Yoder, Jan**

News for UW-Milwaukee. *Feminist Collections* 11, No. 2 (Winter 1990):19-20

**Yoder, Linda** (joint author). *See* Adams, Gail

**Yoga**

Mind Over Body. Judith Ripp. *Lear's* (January 1990):100-103

Yoga. Asar Ha-Pi. *Essence* 20, No. 11 (March 1990):66-67

**Yoga – Therapeutic Use**. *See also* Stress – Coping Strategies

Fast-Track Yoga. *Mademoiselle* (November 1990):168-171

**Yonover, Geri J.**

Fighting Fire with Fire: Civil RICO and Anti-Abortion Activists. *Women's Rights Law Reporter* 12, No. 3 (Fall 1990): 153-175

**Yoruba – Religion**

Using Your "Mind Sight." Iyanla Vanzant. *Essence* 21, No. 5 (September 1990):36

**Yost, Barbara Ann** (about)

In Memoriam: Barbara Ann (Holcroft) Yost. Kirk Yost. *Minerva* 8, No. 2 (Summer 1990):67-71

**Yost, Kirk**

In Memoriam: Barbara Ann (Holcroft) Yost. *Minerva* 8, No. 2 (Summer 1990):67-71

**Yost, Paddy**

A Survival Handbook for Moms. *Good Housekeeping* 211, No. 3 (September 1990):130 +

**Young, Alma.** *See* Meyer, Carol and Young, Alma (editors), "On the Bias."

**Young, Alma** (joint editor). *See* Meyer, Carol

**Young, Billie Jean**

Interiors: Mama's Legacy. *Essence* 21, No. 8 (December 1990):28

**Young, Billie Jean** (about). *See* De Veaux, Alexis, Milloy, Marilyn, and Ross, Michael Erik

**Young, Iris**

A Guide in the Labyrinth. *The Women's Review of Books* 7, No. 8 (May 1990):26

Sexual Subversions: Three French Feminists. Book Review. *The Women's Review of Books* 7, No. 8 (May 1990):26

**Young, Josh**

Zina's Zenith. *Women's Sports and Fitness* 12, No. 4 (May-June 1990):52-56

**Young, Lélia**

Aimer ou La Centaure. Poem. *Canadian Women's Studies* 11, No. 1 (Spring 1990):89

Jour. Poem. *Canadian Women's Studies* 11, No. 1 (Spring 1990):89

Sans titre. Poem. *Canadian Women's Studies* 11, No. 1 (Spring 1990):89

**Young, Marilyn B.** (joint editor). *See* Kruks, Sonia

**Young, Roger Arliner** (about)

Roger Arliner Young. Kenneth Manning. *Sage* 6, No. 2 (Fall 1989):3-7

**Young, Stephanie**

Beauty & Health Report. *Glamour* (July 1990):28; (August 1990):48

Beauty & Health Report: Holiday Sleep Survival Guide. *Glamour* (December 1990):48

The Bottom Line on Beautiful Skin. *Glamour* (November 1990):54

The Contact Lens Wearer's Guide to Cosmetics. *Glamour* (October 1990):48

Health and Fitness. Bibliography. *Glamour* (January 1990):26-29

Health & Fitness. Bibliography. *Glamour* (May 1990):63-74; (July 1990):31-39; (November 1990):59-66

Health & Fitness. *Glamour* (February 1990):43-44; (March 1990):57-65; (April 1990):69-74; (June 1990):47-48+; (August 1990):55-56+; (September 1990):65-72; (October 1990):55-56+; (December 1990):55-56+

PMS Update. Bibliography. *Glamour* (April 1990):94-98

Your Pregnancy. Bibliography. *Glamour* (May 1990):80

Your Pregnancy. *Glamour* (February 1990):55; (March 1990):74; (April 1990):86; (July 1990):40; (August 1990):64; (September 1990):100; (October 1990):74; (November 1990):78; (December 1990):80

**Young, Tracy**

Guessing Your Age. *Vogue* (July 1990):224

Talking Out of Town: Rotten to the Core. *Vogue* (August 1990):382

Talking Out of Turn: Frock Around the Clock. *Vogue* (September 1990):658

Turned-On TV. *Vogue* (September 1990):584-587

**Young Adult Literature**

Baby-Sitting Nights, Preteen Days. Kathleen Brady. *McCall's* 118, No. 2 (November 1990):57-58

**Youngblood, Julia**

Silent Shards. Poem. *Out/Look* No. 8 (Spring 1990):40

**Youngblood, Julia** (about). *See* Art – Exhibitions, "Racism"

**Youngs, George A. (Jr.),** Rathge, Richard, Mullis, Ron, and Mullis, Ann

Adolescent Stress and Self-Esteem. *Adolescence* 25, No. 98 (Summer 1990):333-341

**Yount, Rena** (joint author). *See* Seeger, Nancy

**Youth.** *See also* Adolescents

**Youth – Employment**

High School Student Employment in Social Context: Adolescents' Perceptions of the Role of Part-Time Work. David L. Green. *Adolescence* 25, No. 98 (Summer 1990):425-434

**Youth Ministry**

The Youth Ministry Resource Book. Edited by Eugene C. Roehlkepartain. Book Review. *Adolescence* 25, No. 100 (Winter 1990):1000

**Yu, Lucy C.,** Yu, Yanju, and Mansfield, Phyllis Kernoff

Gender and Changes in Support of Parents in China: Implications of the One-Child Policy. *Gender and Society* 4, No. 1 (March 1990):83-89

**Yu, Yanju** (joint author). *See* Yu, Lucy C.

**Yugoslavia**

Yugoslavian Women Pull Together. Jill Benderly. *New Directions for Women* 19, No. 5 (September-October 1990):3

**Yugoslavia – Religious Traditions**

Woman Cantor Breaks Tradition in Yugoslavia. Helen Leneman. *Lilith* 15, No. 2 (Spring 1990):28

**Yugoslavia – Violence Against Women**

Where Wives Are Never Battered . . . Sanja Milojevic. *Connexions* 34 (1990):6

**Yung, Judy**

Baotown. Book Review. *Belles Lettres* 6, No. 1 (Fall 1990):30-31

Heavy Wings. Book Review. *Belles Lettres* 6, No. 1 (Fall 1990):30-31

Urban and Rural China. *Belles Lettres* 6, No. 1 (Fall 1990):30-31

**Yuval-Davis, Nira** and Anthias, Floya (editors)

Woman-Nation-State. Reviewed by Ann Rossiter. *Feminist Review* No. 36 (Autumn 1990):131-134

# Z

**Zaborszky, Dorothy**

The Writing or the Sex? Or, Why You Don't Have to Read Women's Writing to Know It's No Good. Book Review. *Resources for Feminist Research* 19, No. 1 (March 1990):46-47

**Zacchino, Narda** (about)

Lunch. Interview. Frances Lear. *Lear's* (September 1990):19-20

**Zafris, Nancy**

The People I Know. Reviewed by Catherine Francis. *Belles Lettres* 5, No. 4 (Summer 1990):40+

**Zahave, Irene** (editor)

Through Other Eyes: Animal Stories by Women. Reviewed by Kore Archer. *New Directions for Women* 19, No. 1 (January/February 1990):19

**Zahn, Paula** (about). *See* Television Journalists – Networking

**Zahno, Kamila**

Feminist Fables. Book Review. *Spare Rib* 213 (June 1990):29

**Zaire – Colonization**

Domesticity and Colonialism in Belgian Africa: Usumbura's *Foyer Social*, 1946-1960. Notes. Nancy Rose Hunt. *Signs* 15, No. 3 (Spring 1990):447-474

**Zaki, Hoda M.**

Alien to Femininity: Speculative Fiction and Feminist Theory. Book Review. *Women's Studies International Forum* 13, No. 3 (1990):277-279

Holy Haoles. *The Women's Review of Books* 7, No. 9 (June 1990):19-20

Paths of Duty: American Missionary Women in Nineteenth-Century Hawaii. Book Review. *The Women's Review of Books* 7, No. 9 (June 1990):19-20

Worlds Within Women: Myth and Mythmaking in Fantastic Literature by Women. Book Review. *Women's Studies International Forum* 13, No. 3 (1990):277-279

**Zall, Milton**

Getting a Jump on Taxes. *Executive Female* 13, No. 1 (January-February 1990):14-16

**Zambia – Status of Women**

Body Politics: Sexuality, Gender, and Domestic Service in Zambia. Karen Tranberg Hansen. *Journal of Women's History* 2, No. 1 (Spring 1990):120-142

Zambia Association for Research and Development. *Women's World* 23 (April 1990):39

**Zamora, Daisy**

Death's Makeup. Poem. *The Women's Review of Books* 7, Nos. 10-11 (July 1990):21

**Zamora, Daisy** (interview)

When Art Meets Politics: Three Worlds, Three Stories. Margaret Randall. *The Women's Review of Books* 7, Nos. 10-11 (July 1990):21-22

**Zamora, Martha**

Frida Kahlo: The Brush of Anguish. Reviewed by Joan Philpott. *Ms.* 1, No. 2 (September/October 1990):27-28

**Zandy, Janet**

Dreaming in Color. Book Review. *Belles Lettres* 6, No. 1 (Fall 1990):58

Of Kitchens and Save Marts. *Belles Lettres* 6, No. 1 (Fall 1990):58

The Wreath Ribbon Quilt. Book Review. *Belles Lettres* 6, No. 1 (Fall 1990):58

**Zandy, Janet** (editor)

Calling Homes: Working-Class Women's Writings. Reviewed by Valerie Miner. *The Women's Review of Books* 7, No. 12 (September 1990):1-4

**Zarnow, Teryl**

Father Knows Best??? Mom Knows Better. *Redbook* 175, No. 2 (June 1990):112-113+

**Zaslow, Jeff** (about)

Mr. Manners. Stephen Rae. *Harper's Bazaar* (February 1990):76

**Zavella, Patricia**

Women's Work and Chicano Families: Cannery Workers of the Santa Clara Valley. Reviewed by Sandra Morgen. *Feminist Studies* 16, No. 1 (Spring 1990):53-67

**Zeff, Eleanor E.**

Women and Politics: An International Perspective. Book Review. *Women & Politics* 10, No. 3 (1990):135-136

**Zeidenstein, Sondra** (joint editor). *See* Abdullah, Tahrunnesa

**Zeidner, Lisa**

An Unmarried Man. Short story. *Mademoiselle* (November 1990):126-131

Limited Partnerships. Reviewed by Rosalind A. Warren. *New Directions for Women* 19, No. 1 (January/February 1990):21

**Zempel, Chip**

Underwater Eye Openers. *Women's Sports and Fitness* 12, No. 7 (October 1990):22

**Zenner, Boyd**

Reproductive Slights: What's Happened to Contraceptive Research? *Iris* 24 (Fall-Winter 1990):20-24

**Zettell, Susan**

Masks. Poem. *Atlantis* 15, No. 2 (Spring 1990):93

**Zia, Helen**

Fighting Straight Hate. *Ms.* 1, No. 2 (September/October 1990):47

Midwives: Talking about a Revolution. *Ms.* 1, No. 3 (November/December 1990):91

The Next Wave. *Ms.* 1, No. 2 (September/October 1990):48

Red Ivy, Green Earth Mother. Book Review. *Ms.* 1, No. 3 (November/December 1990):56

**Ziefert, Marjorie** (joint author). *See* Brown, Kaaren Strauch

**Ziegenmeyer, Nancy** (about)

The Woman Who Had to Speak Out. Marianne Jacobbi. *Good Housekeeping* 211, No. 2 (August 1990):82-89

**Ziety, Ann**

The Man Tells Her. Poem. *Spare Rib* No. 209 (February 1990):39

**Zimbabwe**

Zimbabwe: Opposing Violence. Dolly Vangasayi and Saliwe Matopodzi. *off our backs* 20, No. 7 (July 1990):9

**Zimbabwe – Acquired Immune Deficiency Syndrome**

An Uphill Battle. Helen Jackson. *Connexions* 33 (1990):4

Let's Fight it Together. *Connexions* 33 (1990):5

**Zimbabwe – Agriculture**

Working to Feed a Nation: Three Farmers in Zimbabwe Reflect on the Challenges They Face. *Women in Action* 1-2 (1990):9-10

**Zimbabwe – Marriage**

Appreciation or Oppression? *Connexions* 34 (1990):27

Perceptions on Communication and Sexuality in Marriage in Zimbabwe. Marvellous M. Mhloyi. *Women and Therapy* 10, No. 3 (1990):61-73

**Zimbabwe – Suicide**

Teenage Suicide in Zimbabwe. David Lester and C. Wilson. *Adolescence* 25, No. 100 (Winter 1990):807-809

**Zimmer, Lynn E.**

Women Guarding Men. Reviewed by Nancy Jurik. *Gender and Society* 4, No. 1 (March 1990):115-117

**Zimmerman, Bonnie**

The Safe Sea of Women: Lesbian Fiction 1969-1989. Reviewed by Jan Clausen. *The Women's Review of Books* 8, No. 2 (November 1990):7-8

**Zimmerman, D. Patrick**

Notes on the History of Adolescent Inpatient and Residential Treatment. *Adolescence* 25, No. 97 (Spring 1990):9-38

**Zimmermann, Patricia R.**

*Demon Lover Diary*: Deconstructing Sex, Class, and Cultural Power in Documentary. *Genders* 8 (Summer 1990):91-109

**Zingo, Martha T.** (joint author). *See* Arenal, Electa

**Zinn, Maxine Baca**

Family, Feminism, and Race in America. *Gender and Society* 4, No. 1 (March 1990):68-82

**Zinsser, Judith P.** (joint author). *See* Anderson, Bonnie S.

**Zipser, Arthur** and Zipser, Pearl

Fire and Grace: The Life of Rose Pastor Stokes. Reviewed by Annelise Orleck. *The Women's Review of Books* 7, No. 9 (June 1990):25-26

**Zipser, Pearl** (joint author). *See* Zipser, Arthur

**Zipter, Yvonne**

Finding the Hot Wire. Poem. *Hot Wire* 6, No. 3 (September 1990):7

Minnie Bruce Pratt Wins Lamont Prize. *Hot Wire* 6, No. 1 (January 1990):431

**Zita, Jacquelyn N.**

Flight to Objectivity: Essays on Cartesianism and Culture. Book review. *Signs* 15, No. 3 (Spring 1990):645-648

Lesbian Angels and Other Matters. *Hypatia* 5, No. 1 (Spring 1990):133-139

**Zlogar, Laura Weiss**

Interpreting Women's Lives: Feminist Theory and Personal Narratives. Book Review. *Feminist Collections* 11, No. 3 (Spring 1990):7-8

**Zoli Management Incorporated**

Where There's a Will, There's a Way. Joan Delaney. *Executive Female* (March/April 1990):70-71

**Zonana, Joyce**

Elizabeth Barrett Browning, Woman and Artist. Book Review. *Tulsa Studies in Women's Literature* 9, No. 1 (Spring 1990):160-163

**Zopf, Paul E., Jr.**

American Women in Poverty. Reviewed by Emily Stoper. *Women & Politics* 10, No. 4 (1990):140-141

**Zophy, Angela Howard**

The Sound of Our Own Voices: Women's Study Clubs, 1860-1910. Book review. *Signs* 15, No. 2 (Winter 1990):410-411

**Zophy, Angela Howard** and Kavenik, Frances (editors)

Handbook of American Women's History. Review. *Feminist Collections* 11, No. 3 (Spring 1990):20

**Zschoche, Sue**

Wash and Be Healed: The Water-Cure Movement and Women's Health. Book review. *Signs* 15, No. 2 (Winter 1990):414-416

**Zucca** (about). *See* Carter, Charla, "European Designers to Watch."

**Zucker, Jerry**

Ghost. Reviewed by Linda King. *Spare Rib* 217 (October 1990):28

**Zukerman, Eugenia** (about)

Music: Three in Concert. Diane Palacios. *Ms.* 1, No. 1 (July/August 1990):72-73

**Zulu, Itibari M.**

Deliverance. Poem. *Essence* 21, No. 4 (August 1990):120

**Zumwalt, Nancy**

Alcestis. Poem. *Feminist Review* No. 35 (Summer 1990):111-112

**Zussman, Shirley**

Sex & Health. *Glamour* (January 1990):163; (February 1990):219; (March 1990):298; (April 1990):318; (May 1990):320; (June 1990):276; (July 1990):195; (August 1990):250; (September 1990):86; (November 1990):272; (December 1990):246

**Zweig, Ellen**

The Lady and the Camel. Performance Piece. *Women and Performance: A Journal of Feminist Theory* 5, No. 1, Issue #9 (1990): 28-52

**Zwi, Rose**

Another Year in Africa. Reviewed by Barbara Berman. *Belles Lettres* 5, No. 3 (Spring 1990):13

**Zwilich, Ellen Taaffe** (about). *See also* Composers

**Zwozdesky, Joan**

Hypoglycemia. *Healthsharing* 11, No. 1 (December 1989):27-28

**Zydeco Music**

The Bayou Beat. Mimi Read. *Harper's Bazaar* (January 1990):136+